Transfer Pricing Rules, Compliance and Controversy

Third Edition

Marc M. Levey
Steven C. Wrappe

.CCH
a Wolters Kluwer business

Editorial Staff

Editor . . . . Kristina Kulle, J.D., LL.M.

Production . . . . Diana Roozeboom

Index . . . . Lynn Brown

This publication is designed to provide accurate and authoritative information in regard to the subject matter covered. It is sold with the understanding that the publisher is not engaged in rendering legal, accounting, or other professional service, and that the authors are not offering such advice in this publication. If legal advice or other expert assistance is required, the services of a competent professional person should be sought.

ISBN 978-0-8080-2166-7

No claim is made to original government works; however, within this Product or Publication, the following are subject to CCH's copyright: (1) the gathering, compilation, and arrangement of such government materials; (2) the magnetic translation and digital conversion of data, if applicable; (3) the historical, statutory and other notes and references; and (4) the commentary and other materials.

Printed in the United States of America

SUSTAINABLE FORESTRY INITIATIVE — Certified Chain of Custody — Promoting Sustainable Forest Management — www.sfiprogram.org

Preface

Nearly a decade has passed since publication of the first edition of this book. In that time, the statutory language of Section 482 has not changed at all; however, the transfer pricing practice in this country, and many others, has changed substantially. Currently, the United States is holding Congressional hearings on transfer pricing issues and restructuring of the Internal Revenue Service to enhance the focus on transfer pricing issues.

This edition has been revised and updated to capture the recent substantive changes to the regulations and the impact of a growing inventory of tax controversies around the world. In one important aspect this edition has not changed; it continues to present the technical transfer pricing concepts in a straightforward manner.

After forty years, the U.S. transfer pricing regulations for intercompany services have been substantially overhauled, creating tension between U.S. requirements and those of other countries regarding the allocation of headquarters costs and stock based compensation. New, more restrictive temporary regulations with respect to cost sharing arrangements have recently been issued, even while the old rules continue to be contested in the courts. Interpretation No. 48 of the Financial Accounting Standards Board Statement No. 109 (FIN 48), has encouraged greater corporate control of transfer pricing issues by requiring more detailed disclosure of uncertain tax positions.

In response to perceived inappropriate transfer pricing practices, especially with respect to transfers of intangibles, the Internal Revenue Service has really increased its transfer pricing enforcement efforts. The transfer pricing enforcement efforts of other countries have grown rapidly over the last decade. The current transfer pricing enforcement environment has greatly increased taxpayer reliance on the Mutual Agreement Procedure and Advance Pricing Agreements to resolve transfer pricing disputes. In expectation of higher numbers of sustained transfer pricing adjustments, this edition adds a chapter that explains the implementation and other tax and non-tax implications of transfer pricing adjustments.

This third edition benefits greatly from the authors' ongoing involvement in client transfer pricing issues and use of previous editions as a text for transfer pricing courses in the Graduate Tax Programs at the Georgetown University Law Center and New York University School of Law. Increased client questions surrounding transfer pricing adjustments prompted the new chapter that analyzes correlative and conforming adjustments, as well as customs and state tax implications of such adjustments. Student questions and comments have prompted an expansion of the early chapters on fundamental transfer pricing concepts and incorporation into the text of relevant examples from the regulations under Section 482.

This book reflects the diverse transfer pricing experience of the authors and their colleagues. Other individuals deserve mention in the development of this book, as their assistance has been tremendous. We want to thank Damon Pike and Colleen Warner for substantial contributions to Chapters 15 and 16, respectively; Carlos Mallo, Daniel Morris, Diana Organista, Loren Ponds, and Scott Scheule for their research and editing contributions.

We hope that this work provides meaningful assistance to you.

Marc M. Levey

Steven C. Wrappe

August 2010

About the Authors

Marc M. Levey, partner with the New York office of Baker & McKenzie, LLP, is a nationally recognized expert in international taxation, particularly in structuring and defending transfer pricing strategies. He has been repeatedly acknowledged by *Euromoney* magazine as one of the "World's Leading Tax Advisors" and included in its "Best of the Best" global tax experts; and by the *International Tax Review* as "one of the World's Leading Transfer Pricing Advisors." Mr. Levey is the author and editor of WG&L's treatises, *U.S. Taxation of Foreign-Controlled Businesses* and *International Transfer Pricing*, and is a frequent speaker and author for various forums. His practice focuses on transfer pricing and cross-border transactions, tax controversies and litigation, and general corporate, international and partnership taxation.

Mr. Levey has significant experience in structuring foreign investment in the United States; structuring intercompany pricing policies and programs both in the United States and in numerous foreign jurisdictions; establishing foreign operations for U.S. multinational companies, including the use of holding companies, contract manufacturing, and commissionaire arrangements; structuring international joint ventures, cross-border acquisitions and dispositions, foreign tax credit planning and subpart F income planning. Mr. Levey was the past chair of the firm's Global Transfer Pricing Steering Committee, and now serves on its transfer pricing management committee.

Steven C. Wrappe is a principal in Ernst & Young LLP's Washington, DC Transfer Pricing practice. He has 20 years of specialization in all aspects of transfer pricing across all industries, including: automotive, electronics, pharmaceutical, food products, spirits, chemicals, aerospace and energy. Mr. Wrappe's experience in transfer pricing controversy includes: examination, appeals, ADR solutions, advance pricing agreements (APA), mutual agreement procedures (MAP), and Customs agreements. His combined APA/MAP experience is well in excess of 100 cases.

Mr. Wrappe has served as Chair of the Transfer Pricing Committee of the American Bar Association's Tax Section. He is an Adjunct Professor (Transfer Pricing) at Georgetown University Law Center and New York University School of Law and has been published extensively on transfer pricing topics. Mr. Wrappe speaks globally on transfer pricing, with recent speaking engagements to Tax Executives Institute, Organisation for Economic Co-operation and Development, World Customs Organization, United Nations, NYU Institute, and the American Bar Association. Mr. Wrappe is routinely recognized by *Euromoney* magazine as "one of the World's Leading Transfer Pricing Advisors." He serves on the Board of Advisors of the NYU School of Law—Tax Program and BNA Tax Management (Transfer Pricing).

Table of Contents

Chapter 17: Adjustments to Taxable Income: Federal Tax, Customs and State Tax Implications

Practice Tools

Chapter 1

Introduction

¶ 101 What is Transfer Pricing?

The term "transfer pricing" refers to the pricing of transactions between related entities for goods, services, intangible property transfers, rents, and loans. The transfer price determines the division of total profit between the related entities. As market forces do not necessarily control transaction prices within a related group, the United States and numerous other countries have enacted transfer pricing rules and increased enforcement efforts to prevent the use of improper transfer prices to shift profits out of their taxing jurisdictions. Transfer pricing rules are complex and non-uniform, typically resulting in compliance and enforcement difficulties on a global basis.

¶ 110 The Origins of Transfer Pricing

The concept of transfer pricing was not originally established as a tax concept; instead, transfer pricing was created as a managerial accounting concept. The origins of transfer pricing can be traced back to the end of the nineteenth century, when some companies developed into multi-segment businesses. Managers were faced with the need to price intercompany transactions to better reflect the profitability of each segment and maximize the overall profitability of the firm.[1] Transfer pricing was therefore born as a management accounting tool to help administer the far flung operations of large organizations. Consistent with this understanding,

---

[1] *See* Robert G. Eccles, "The Transfer Pricing Problem, A Theory for Practice," p.16, Lexington Books (March 1986).

transfer pricing is defined as "the amount charged by one segment of an organization for a product or service that it supplies to another segment of the same organization."[2]

With the rise of multinational corporations, the tax law needed a mechanism to "clearly reflect income"[3] attributable to controlled entities under different national jurisdictions to prevent tax avoidance and double taxation. To this end, tax authorities have adopted the transfer pricing concept to ensure that taxpayers are taxable on the true taxable income in each tax jurisdiction. Consequently, transfer pricing is a normatively neutral concept, not to be identified per se with either tax avoidance or tax shelters. Indeed, paragraph 3 of the Preface of the 1979 OECD Report on Transfer Pricing and Multinational Enterprises specifically states: "the consideration of transfer pricing problems should not be confused with the consideration of problems of tax fraud or tax avoidance, even though transfer pricing policies may be used for such purposes."[4]

¶ 115 Why is Transfer Pricing Important?

Transfer pricing affects numerous points in a multinational enterprise's ("MNE's") financial statements. Table 1 below illustrates the impact of intercompany transfer pricing on financial statements.

Table 1 — Intercompany Transactions in Financial Statements

Income Statement

Revenues
- Sales of tangible property: raw materials, finished goods
- Services fees: technical, payroll, legal, tax, insurance, training, marketing and sales, R&D, management
- Rents: lease of tangible and real property
- Royalties for intangible property: licenses of patents, trademarks, and know-how

Cost of sales
- Purchases of tangible property: raw materials, work-in-progress, finished goods
- Services fees: payments for assembly or manufacturing services

---

[2] *See* Charles T. Horngren and Gary L. Sundem "Introduction to Management Accounting," p.336, ninth edition. Prentice Hall International Inc. as cited in "History, State of the Art, Perspectives," United Nations Secretariat (September 2001).

[3] Reg. § 1.482-1(a)(1).

[4] Paragraph 3 of the Preface of the 1979 OECD Report on Transfer Pricing, as cited in "History, State of the Art, Perspectives," United Nations Secretariat (September 2001).

Gross profit

Sales, general and administrative expenses

- Services fees: HQ allocations (management, accounting, legal, tax, insurance, HR), marketing and sales, R&D,
- Allocation of headquarters costs
- Rental payments: tangible and real property
- Royalties for intangible property: trademarks,

Other

- Interest income and expense on intercompany lending

Net profit before tax

Taxation

After tax profit

Balance sheet

Current assets/liabilities

- Intercompany accounts payables and receivables
- Short term lending, borrowing

Intangible assets

- Use of brands, trademarks, patents, goodwill

Long term liabilities

- Intercompany borrowing
- External borrowing using parent company guarantees

Absent transfer pricing rules, MNEs would be allowed to use transfer pricing to shift large amounts of income from one tax jurisdiction to another. The following table demonstrates how that benefit could be achieved through the reduction of the overall effective tax rate (ETR) if profits are shifted from a high-tax jurisdiction to a low-tax jurisdiction.

Table 2 — Potential Benefit of Transfer Pricing on Global Effective Tax Rate (ETR)

	Parent (Country A)	*Subsidiary (Country B)*	*Consolidated*
Total profit reported on tax return	700	300	1,000
Tax rate	40%	10%	
Tax liability before change to transfer price	280	30	310
Global ETR			31%
ETR Effect of Transfer Pricing Change			
Total profit after using transfer pricing to shift 400 of income	300	700	1,000
Tax rate	40%	10%	
Tax liability after 400 transfer pricing change	120	70	190
Global ETR			19%

The potential for MNEs to use transfer pricing to shift income to low-tax jurisdictions was the subject of a recent Joint Tax Committee on Taxation Report[5] and a House Ways and Means Committee Hearing.[6] Although no conclusions were reached in either, legislators continue to be concerned about the potential for tax revenue loss through tax planning that involves transfer pricing issues.

As part of a continuing effort to strengthen international tax compliance, the IRS realigned its Large and Mid-Size Business (LMSB) division to create the Large Business and International (LB&I) division.[7] A major goal of this change is centralizing and enhancing the IRS's focus on transfer pricing.[8]

---

[5] "Present Law and Background Related to Possible Income Shifting and Transfer Pricing," Joint Committee on Taxation Report 37-10, July 20, 2010.

[6] "Ways and Means: Hearing on Transfer Pricing Issues," 111th Cong. (July 22, 2010).

[7] IRS Realigns and Renames Large Business Division, Enhances Focus on International Tax Administration. IR-2010-88, Aug. 4, 2010.

[8] *Id.*

¶115

Faced with the prospect of substantial revenue loss, the United States and most of its trading partners have increased their transfer pricing enforcement. If a taxpayer receives a transfer pricing adjustment in one country and does not obtain correlative relief in the other country, the taxpayer will suffer double taxation on the amount of the adjustment. The following table demonstrates the strong negative impact of double taxation on the MNE's effective tax rate.

Table 3 — Detrimental Impact of Double Taxation on Effective Tax Rate (ETR)

	Parent (Country A)	*Subsidiary (Country B)*	*Consolidated*
Total profit reported on tax return	300	700	1,000
Tax rate	40%	10%	
Tax liability before Country B transfer pricing adjustment	120	70	190
Global ETR			19%
Double Taxation Effect on ETR			
Total profit after 400 Country A adjustment	700	700	1,400
Tax rate	40%	10%	
Tax liability after Country A transfer pricing adjustment[a]	280	70	350
Global ETR[b]			35%

---

[a] Note: Does not include penalty and interest amounts.

[b] Assumes no correlative relief from Country B.

¶115

¶ 120 Overview of Code Sec. 482

The United States enacted Code Sec. 482 to prevent tax avoidance and clearly reflect income by and among related entities and place a controlled taxpayer on parity with an uncontrolled taxpayer. Section 482 accomplishes this by determining, according to the standard of an uncontrolled taxpayer, the true and arm's length taxable income from the property or business of the controlled taxpayer.

From the taxpayer standpoint, Code Sec. 482 is the single largest tax issue for all foreign-based MNEs and nearly the largest single tax issue for U.S. based MNEs.[9] The prospect of potential 20 or 40 percent penalties, possibility of double taxation, increased enforcement by the tax authorities, and significant documentation requirements ensure that transfer pricing issues continue to receive attention outside the tax department.[10] The magnitude and the growing impact of the transfer pricing rules in the U.S. and worldwide speaks for itself. As of 2009, nearly 40 countries have adopted transfer pricing rules or followed general arm's length standards under OECD (Organisation for Economic Co-operation and Development) Transfer Pricing Guidelines for Multinational Enterprises and Tax Administrations;[11] more than 45 countries have either specific or ordinary penalties applicable to transfer pricing adjustments; and more than 32 countries have introduced documentation requirements in support of transfer pricing methods applied by taxpayers.[12]

¶ 130 Statutory Language and Scope of Code Sec. 482

.01 Statutory Language

Code Sec. 482 of the Internal Revenue Code ("Code") authorizes the Internal Revenue Service ("IRS") to reallocate income, deductions or tax attributes among the members of a controlled group of entities to prevent tax evasion or to ensure the clear reflection of income. Code Sec. 482 reads as follows:

> In any case of two or more organizations, trades, or businesses (whether or not incorporated, whether or not organized in the United States, and whether or not affiliated) owned or controlled directly or indirectly by the same interests, the Secretary may distribute, apportion, or allocate gross income, deductions, credits, or allowances between or among such organizations, trades, or businesses, if he determines that such distribution, apportionment, or allocation is necessary

---

[9] Transfer pricing adjustments and assessed penalties involve large dollar amounts. In September 2006, the U.S. subsidiary of U.K. based pharmaceutical giant GlaxoSmithKline PLC (Glaxo UK) settled the largest tax case in the history of the United States Tax Court. The taxpayer agreed to $3.4 billion in tax deficiencies stemming from Code Sec. 482 adjustments from tax years 1989 through 2005. *See* "Glaxo Case Highlights Marketing Intangibles, Lack of U.S. Jurisprudence, Practitioners Say," 15 *Tax Mgmt. Transfer Pricing Rep.* 519 (Nov. 22, 2006).

[10] Recent initiatives of the Internal Revenue Service (IRS) and tax authorities in other countries reflect their increased emphasis on transfer pricing enforcement. On January 22, 2003, the Commissioner of the IRS Large and Mid-Size Business Division (LMSB) issued a compliance directive to IRS examiners instructing them to examine and enforce strict compliance with transfer pricing documentation requirements, and to assert transfer pricing penalties when appropriate. *See* Memorandum for LMSB Executives, Managers, and Agents, "Transfer Pricing Compliance Directive," Jan. 22, 2003, *available at http://www.irs.gov/pub/irs-utl/transfer_pricing_compliance_directive_03.pdf.*

[11] Transfer Pricing Guidelines for Multinational Enterprises and Tax Administrations, Report of the Organisation for Economic Co-operation and Development Committee on Fiscal Affairs (1995).

[12] See Ernst & Young, Transfer pricing global reference guide (2009), *available at http://www.ey.com/Publication/vwLUAssets/2009_Transfer_Pricing_Global_Reference_Guide/$FILE/2009_Transfer_pricing_ global_reference_guide.pdf* (last visited on August 3, 2009).

in order to prevent evasion of taxes or clearly to reflect the income of any of such organizations, trades, or businesses. In the case of any transfer (or license) of intangible property (within the meaning of Code Sec. 936(h)(3)(B)), the income with respect to such transfer or license shall be commensurate with the income attributable to the intangible

With the exception of the last sentence, the statutory language of Code Sec. 482 is unchanged since originally enacted in 1928.[13] The last sentence was added in the Tax Reform Act of 1986 to combat perceived abuses regarding the transfer of intangibles developed through research and development.[14]

.02 Control

According to the statutory language, Code Sec. 482 is only applicable when two or more organizations, trades or businesses are controlled by the same interests. The term "control" is not defined in the Code. The regulations under Code Sec. 482 provide the following definition of the term "controlled":

"Controlled" includes any kind of control, direct or indirect, whether legally enforceable or not, and however exercisable or exercised, including control resulting from the actions of two or more taxpayers acting in concert or with a common goal or purpose. It is the reality of the control that is decisive, not its form or the mode of its exercise. A presumption of control arises if income or deductions have been arbitrarily shifted.[15]

Caution: The definition of "control" for Code Sec. 482 purposes is broadly defined to include taxpayers acting in a common design and should not be confused with the Code Sec. 368(c) definition of control used for subchapter C purposes.[16]

IRS Guidance. When structuring transactions, taxpayers often consult IRS guidance, including IRS field service advice (FSAs). FSAs are addressed to IRS field officers and detail the IRS National Office's views on a particular transaction. Although FSAs are not authority that can be relied on by taxpayers, they could be helpful in identifying the types of issues that the IRS might raise.

The IRS applied Code Sec. 482 in a series of FSAs on the basis of contractual relationships entered into by completely unrelated third parties.[17] The IRS was particularly concerned that the income attributable to the sale/leaseback transactions was allocated to persons who were not subject to U.S. taxation and the related losses were allocated to U.S. taxpayers. Most practitioners found it troubling that none of the parties in those FSAs identified by the IRS as being "controlled by the same interests" would be treated as such under a traditional Code Sec. 482 transfer pricing analysis. There was no interrelated ownership, directorship, family control, or any other indicia of common control. Consequently, many practitioners viewed the IRS's use of Code Sec. 482 in this situation as somewhat suspect.[18]

---

[13] Sec. 45 of the Revenue Act of 1928, 45 Stat. 806.

[14] Tax Reform Act of 1986, Pub. L. No. 99-514, Sec. 1231(e)(1), 100 Stat. 2085, 2562-63 (1986).

[15] Reg. § 1.482-1(i)(4). Some commentators have noted the circularity of this last point. *See* John P. Warner, "Control, Causality, and Section 482," 8 *Tax Mgmt. Transfer Pricing Rep.* 289 (Jul. 28, 1999).

[16] *See Eli Lilly & Co.*, 88-2 USTC ¶ 9502, 84 TC 996, 1115 n. 50 (1985).

[17] *See*, e.g., FSA 199909005 (Nov. 17, 1998); FSA 199914018 (Jan. 5, 1999). *See also*, Notice 95-53, 1995-2 CB 334 and Notice 99-5, 1998-3 IRB 49.

[18] *See Phil Morrison, et al.*, "IRS Expands the Reach of Section 482," 8 *Tax Mgmt. Transfer Pricing Rep.* 105 (June 2, 1999).

In 2003, the IRS reversed its position to assert that an application of Code Sec. 482 to completely unrelated third parties on the basis of contractual relationships is not consistent with the policies underlying the statute. In Rev. Rul. 2003-96, the IRS stated that "the fact that parties that were unrelated up to, and including the time of, a transaction engage in that transaction in an attempt to arbitrarily shift income or deductions among themselves does not by itself evidence the type of control necessary to satisfy the 'acting in concert or with a common goal or purpose' requirement of Reg. § 1.482-1(i)(4)."[19] However, the previous IRS practice should not be overlooked in determining the existence of common control.

Court Cases. Neither Code Sec. 482 nor the regulations provide a "bright line" test for determining what constitutes control for transfer pricing purposes. Absent statutory and regulatory guidance, the IRS and taxpayers have sought to identify the indicia of control in court cases. The cases discussed below do not serve as a clear guide on this issue, but they do demonstrate the application of the regulations to specific facts.

Courts have recognized that the language of Code Sec. 482 is "broad and sweeping, and its application depends on a finding of either ownership or control, thus allowing for a broad interpretation of the Code Sec. 482 by the IRS."[20]

Direct and Indirect Ownership / Voting Control. The scope of control is not limited to stock ownership percentages relating to voting rights. The taxpayer does not need to own a majority interest in one or more businesses to control them. It is the reality of control that is determinative.[21] In addition to where a party owns a majority of the stock of a corporation, courts have found common control in situations involving 50/50 ownership of the stock of a corporation.[22] Control was even found where only 2-percent of a corporation's outstanding stock was owned by two individuals who, according to the court, "were in effective control of the business."[23]

W.L. Gore & Associates, Inc.[24] involved a U.S. taxpayer (W.L. Gore & Associates, Inc.) that—together with Junkosha Ltd. (Junkosha), a Japanese corporation—formed JGT, a 50/50 joint venture, incorporated in Japan. In addition to JGT stock, the U.S. taxpayer owned 30 percent of the stock of Junkosha. The taxpayer discovered a new technology and entered into an agreement with JGT granting a royalty-free license to the joint venture. The IRS had asserted a deficiency under Code Sec. 482. The taxpayer moved for summary judgment, arguing that no

---

[19] Rev. Rul. 2003-96, 2003-34 IRB 386; *see also* Notice 2003-55, 2003-34 IRB 395 (the Notice 2003-34 modified and superseded Notice 95-53 in response to *Andantech LLC*, 2003-1 USTC ¶ 50,530, 331 F.3d 972 (D.C. Cir. 2003), *aff'g* in part and *remanding* CCH Dec. 54,714(M), TC Memo. 2002-97; *Nicole Rose*, 2003-1 USTC ¶ 50,137, 320 F.3d 282 (2d Cir. 2002), *aff'g per curium* CCH Dec. 54,578, 117 TC 328 (2001).

[20] *Collins Electrical Co., Inc., a CA Corp.*, CCH Dec. 34,287, 67 TC 911, 918 (1977).

[21] Reg. § 1.482-1(i)(4); *see generally* Wayne M. Gazur, "The Forgotten Link: 'Control' in Section 482," 15 *J. Intl. Bus.* 1 (1994). *See also J.E. Hall, Sr.*, CCH Dec. 23,615, 32 TC 390, 410 (1959) (the court disregarded the question of the ownership, while holding that Hall completely controlled and dominated the corporation); *see also P.W. Ach*, CCH Dec. 26,743, 42 TC 114, 125 (1964) (the court held that "it is not record ownership, but actual control, which counts in the application of the statute.").

[22] *B. Forman Co.*, 72-1 USTC ¶ 9182, 453 F.2d 1144, 1155 (2d Cir.) *cert denied*, 407 US 934 (1972). *See also, W.L. Gore & Assoc., Inc.*, CCH Dec. 50,507(M), 69 TCM (CCH) 2037 (1995).

[23] *Charles Town, Inc.*, 372 F.2d 415, 420 (4th Cir. 1967), *aff'g* CCH Dec. 27,819(M), TC Memo. 1966-15.

[24] *W.L. Gore & Associates, Inc.*, CCH Dec. 50,507(M), TC Memo. 1995-96.

common control of the taxpayer and JGT existed. The IRS opposed the taxpayer's motion for summary judgment on the ground that a trial would reveal additional facts, which would support the three bases for her determination that the taxpayer controlled JGT, namely: (1) taxpayer's ownership of 50 percent of the stock of JGT and its ownership of 30 percent of Junkosha, which owned the other 50 percent of JGT; (2) taxpayer's managerial control of the use of new technology in Japan by JGT by virtue of the web of interlocking arrangements between petitioner, Junkosha, and JGT; and (3) the arbitrary shifting of income from taxpayer to JGT resulting from the royalty-free transfer of new technology from taxpayer to JGT pursuant to the agreement.

Noting that the question of control involves a factually intensive inquiry, the Tax Court denied the taxpayer's motion for summary judgment. The Court stated that it was not persuaded by the taxpayer that it should not take its 30-percent ownership of Junkosha into account because the attribution rules do not apply for purposes of Code Sec. 482. "The fact of the matter is that, for purposes of determining common control, indirect ownership is an element which can properly be considered even if the usual standards for attribution of ownership, such as those found in section 318, are not met."[25] Unfortunately, the court did not offer a methodology to compute indirect ownership for Code Sec. 482 purposes.

Acting in Concert. Each shareholder can individually still be considered to control the corporation if the shareholder and at least one other shareholder (two or more in total) act in concert with a common goal of shifting income or deductions from or to the corporation.[26] Thus, it is unimportant that each shareholder lacks actual or effective control of the corporation. Courts have inferred control from the actions of the parties.[27]

In *B. Forman Co.*,[28] the court held that two unrelated 50-percent corporate shareholders who exerted control over a corporation were both subject to Code Sec. 482 because they acted in concert to direct its actions, and they had a common goal of avoiding income tax on interest income. The court described the requisite control under Code Sec. 482 as one of "actual, practical control rather than any particular percentage of stock ownership." Here, B. Forman and McCurdy & Co. owned competing retail department stores. The two corporations had no common shareholders, directors, or officers. To revitalize business at their stores' locations, the two corporations formed a third corporation, Midtown, which would develop a shopping center linking the two stores. Each competitor owned fifty percent of the shares of the new shopping center corporation. Each of the two shareholders loaned money to the new corporation at interest rates considered inadequate by the IRS, which invoked Code Sec. 482 to impute interest income to the two shareholders. The court used "the realistic approach" and applied a common goal analysis in finding control. The court concluded that with respect to the two shareholders of

---

[25] *Id.*

[26] Reg. § 1.482-1(i)(4); *B. Forman Co., Inc., supra* note 22; *South Texas Rice Warehouse Co.*, 66-2 USTC ¶ 9619, 366 F.2d 890 (5th Cir. 1966), *aff'g* CCH Dec. 27,223, 43 TC 540 (1965), *cert. denied*, 386 US 1016 (1967).

[27] *Grenada Industries, Inc.*, CCH Dec. 18,468, 17 TC 231 (1951), *aff'd* 53-1 USTC ¶ 9271, 202 F.2d 873 (5th Cir. 1953), *cert. denied*, 346 US 819 (1953).

[28] *B. Forman Co., Inc.*, CCH Dec. 30,087, 54 TC 912, 921 (1970).

Midtown "their interests in the existence and career of Midtown and the interests of Midtown are identical."

In *First Security Bank of Utah*,[29] the Supreme Court recognized that the IRS's authority to apply Code Sec. 482 is premised on the complete dominion (power) of common owners or managers to determine the actual economic results of the transacting business organizations. There, a holding company, First Security Corp., controlled two banks, First Security Bank of Utah and First Security Bank of Idaho; First Security Co., a management company; E.D. Smith & Sons, an insurance agency; and beginning in 1954, First Security Life Insurance Co. ("Security Life"), a life insurance company. In 1954, the banks began referring their credit life insurance business to an independent insurance company that then reinsured the policies with Security Life. Security Life retained 85-percent of the premiums for assuming the risks under the policies, and forwarded the remainder to the independent insurance company that provided actuarial and accounting services. No sales commissions were paid to either the banks or the management company. The Code Sec. 482 adjustment followed. The Commissioner argued that a Code Sec. 482 allocation was appropriate because the banks would have been compensated for making the credit insurance available to their customers had the parties been dealing with each other at arm's length.

In applying the Code Sec. 482 regulations, the Court found that the holding company did not have the "complete power" to shift income among its subsidiaries required by the regulations, unless it acted in violation of the federal banking laws. The court stated that "the 'complete power' referred to in the regulations hardly includes the power to force a subsidiary to violate the law."[30]

Management Control. In *Charles Town, Inc.*,[31] two brothers owned all of the stock of Fairmount Steel Corporation ("Fairmount"), which had significant net operating loss carryovers. The brothers formed a new corporation, Charles Town, Inc. ("Charles Town"), to acquire a West Virginia race track. A first cousin, and business associate, received 98-percent of the stock in Charles Town, while each brother received one percent. The brothers became the president and secretary-treasurer and directors of Charles Town, while the cousin was a vice-president and director. Fairmount agreed to advance funds to Charles Town to conduct racing at the track that Charles Town had leased from the owner. Charles Town operated the race track, retaining ten percent of the net profits, and paying the balance to Fairmount.

The court held that the brothers were in control of the "business" of Charles Town. The small stock ownership position of the brothers in Charles Town was supplemented by a provision in the management agreement that a majority of the officers would make all decisions for the corporation so long as Charles Town was indebted to Fairmount. This voting agreement gave the brothers practical control of Charles Town, and only 2-percent interest in Charles Town did not prevent the court from finding that control.

---

[29] *First Security Bank of Utah, N. A., et al.*, 72-1 USTC ¶ 9292A, 405 US 394, 404 (1972).

[30] *Id.* at 495.

[31] *Charles Town, Inc.*, 67-1 USTC ¶ 9243, 372 F.2d 415, 420 (4th Cir. 1967).

¶ 130.02

Common Goals and the Same Interests. In *South Texas Rice Warehouse Co.*,[32] the members of four families held identical shareholdings in two corporations. Those shareholders formed a new partnership to engage in the rice drying business, excluding two brothers who together owned 35-percent of each of the corporations. The taxpayers argued that the corporations and the partnership were not under the control of the same interests because the partners owned only 65-percent of each corporation, and the transaction in question, a lease, required the affirmative vote of shareholders holding at least 80-percent of the voting power of the corporations.

The Tax Court found that control was exercised. Although the excluded two brothers owned no interests in the partnership, the two corporations, which provided rice for processing by the partnership, and the partnership were an interdependent business operation that required the cooperation of all parties. The identities of the particular shareholders might have changed, but the overall control of the family enterprise did not change. The court held that the existence of common control was shown not only by the relationship of father and child with respect to the stockholders who permitted their family interest in the partnership to be taken over by their children, but also by the fact that the entire operations of the partnership were dependent on the overall family interests in various business entities.

Further, in *Brittingham*,[33] the Tax Court concluded that different persons acting with a common goal or purpose for artificially shifting income can constitute "the same interests" for purposes of the statute. There, two brothers each owned 37-percent of the stock of a U.S. ceramic tile distribution company, while one of the brothers owned all of the stock of a tile manufacturing company in Mexico which sold its products to the U.S. distributor. The IRS determined that the two companies were under common control and attempted to reallocate income from the Mexican company to the U.S. company.

In holding against the IRS, the Tax Court stated that different persons with a common goal or purpose for artificially shifting income can constitute the "same interest" for purposes of Code Sec. 482. Thus, it is not necessary that the same person or persons own or control each controlled business before Code Sec. 482 can apply, but there must be a common design for the shifting of income for different individuals to constitute the "same interest." The court reasoned that the brother who only had an interest in the U.S. company would not agree to shift income to a company in which he had no ownership because shifting of income would not be in his best economic interest. Further, the court stated: "to believe that Robert [one of the brothers] would be a part of a plan to divert $1.5 million from a corporation in which he and his children owned a 37-percent interest to a corporation in which his immediate family had no interest strains all credulity."

[32] *South Texas Rice Warehouse Co.*, CCH Dec. 27,223, 43 TC 540 (1965).

[33] *R.M. Brittingham, et al.*, CCH Dec. 33,856, 66 TC 373, 397-398 (1976), *aff'd per curiam*, 79-2 USTC ¶ 9499, 598 F.2d 1375 (5th Cir. 1979).

¶130.02

A similar holding was reached by the Tax Court in *Bransford*.[34] Here, a corporation sold real property to another company, the majority of which was owned by the owners of the selling company and an unrelated individual who owned 16.66-percent of the stock. The real property was sold by the purchasing company at a substantial gain. The IRS asserted that the companies were under common control and attempted to reallocate the purchase price to the selling company. The Tax Court reasoned that it was against the minority shareholder's self-interest to participate in a plan to shift $1.8 million from a company in which he had a minority interest to a company in which he had no ownership interest. Further, the court found that the minority shareholder, who also was the president of the company, would not expose himself to a shareholder suit for breach of fiduciary duty in protecting their interests.

Timing Issue. Determination of when control existed can be important to find whether certain transactions are controlled transactions within the meaning of Code Sec. 482. In *DHL Corp.*,[35] the Tax Court held control to exist prior to the transaction.[36]

.03 No "Intent" Requirement

Code Sec. 482 grants authority to the IRS to make an allocation when it is necessary to prevent evasion of taxes or clearly to reflect the income. Therefore, Code Sec. 482 applies to all transactions between commonly controlled or related entities, regardless of the taxpayers' intent.[37] The IRS's authority extends to any case in which the taxable income of a controlled taxpayer is other than it would have been had the taxpayer in the conduct of its affairs been an uncontrolled taxpayer dealing at arm's length with another uncontrolled taxpayer.[38] For example, in *Ruddick Corp.*,[39] the United States Court of Claims held that proof of a valid business purpose or of good faith will not defeat Code Sec. 482 allocation.

> *Comment:* Officially, the statute is a one way street. Code Sec. 482 grants no right to a controlled party to apply the provisions at will. Further, the statute does not grant any right to compel the IRS to apply these provisions.

The regulations provide taxpayers with two opportunities to affirmatively apply Code Sec. 482. First, taxpayers may report arm's length results on a timely filed return that are different than the results reported on their books.[40] Second, taxpayers can claim setoff treatment with respect to favorable non-arm's length transactions between the controlled taxpayers that occurred in the same taxable year for which the IRS proposes a transfer pricing adjustment.[41]

---

[34] *J.S. Bransford and H.D. Bransford, et al.*, CCH Dec. 34,641(M), TC Memo. 1977-314.

[35] *DHL Corp.*, CCH Dec. 53,015(M), TC Memo. 1998-461, *aff'd* in part and *rev'd* in part, 2002-1 USTC ¶ 50,354, 285 F.3d 1210 (9th Cir. 2002).

[36] *DHL Corp.*, CCH Dec. 53,015(M), TC Memo. 1998-461. For the discussion of timing issue *see also* Wayne M. Gazur, "The Forgotten Link: 'Control' in Section 482," 15 *J. Intl. Bus.* 1 (1994).

[37] Reg. § 1.482-1(f)(1)(i).

[38] Reg. § 1.482-1(a). *See also Eli Lilly & Co.*, 88-2 USTC ¶ 9502, 84 TC 996 (1985); *G.D. Searle & Co.*, CCH Dec.

43,685, 88 TC 252 (1987) (in both cases, the Tax Court upheld a portion of the IRS's allocation based on the clear reflection of income standard).

[39] *Ruddick Corp.*, 81-1 USTC ¶ 9221, 643 F.2d 747 (Ct. Cl. 1981). *See also Eli Lilly & Co.*, 67-1 USTC ¶ 9248, 372 F.2d 990, 998-999 (Ct. Cl. 1967) where a valid business purpose was not dispositive of Section 482.

[40] Reg. § 1.482-1(a)(3).

[41] Reg. § 1.482-1(g)(4). A potential opportunity for taxpayers to affirmatively apply Code Sec. 482 is contained in the procedures for the APA Program. *See* Rev. Proc. 2006-9, IRB 2006-2, 278. Advance Pricing Agreements

No untimely or amended returns are permitted to decrease taxable income based on adjustments to controlled transactions.[42] Although no express authority exists in the regulations for amended returns that increase taxable income, most practitioners believe that the IRS will accept the increased taxable income. Revenue Procedure ("Rev. Proc.") 99-32 provides additional guidance, explaining that if an adjustment results in an increase to U.S. taxable income, the taxpayer may report the adjustment "at any time," that is, on either an original or an amended return.[43] However, if the adjustment results in a decrease in U.S. taxable income, the adjustment may only be reported on the original (timely filed) return.[44] In the context of an advance pricing agreement (APA) (*see* Chapter 13 for discussion of APAs), taxpayers are allowed to make an upward adjustment within the APA term.[45]

¶ 140 Burden of Proof

The IRS's deficiency determinations under Code Sec. 482 are presumptively correct.[46] Courts have at times referred to this as a "heavy" burden of proof on taxpayers.[47] Accordingly, the taxpayer bears the burden of proving that the IRS's determinations under Code Sec. 482 are incorrect.[48] It is not sufficient for the taxpayer to rebut the presumption of correctness of IRS determinations, but rather the taxpayer must show that the IRS acted in an arbitrary and unreasonable manner. If the taxpayer successfully rebuts the Commissioner's presumption,[49] the burden of production shifts to the government. However, the taxpayer must still carry the ultimate burden of proof or persuasion.[50]

A taxpayer may satisfy its burden in one of two ways:[51]

* Establish that its prices were arm's length under Code Sec. 482 and the regulations;[52] or

---

(Footnote Continued)

(APAs) allow taxpayers and the IRS to avoid future transfer pricing disputes by entering into a prospective agreement, generally covering at least five tax years, regarding the taxpayer's transfer prices. Under certain circumstances, APAs could be applied to resolve transfer pricing issues for prior taxable years (rollback). Rev. Proc. 2006-9 provides clarification that rollback is not available in the case of unilateral APA requests if the rollback would decrease taxable income on a return filed for a taxable year not covered by the APA (Rev. Proc. 2006-9, §2.12). For the APA discussion, *see* Chapter 13.

[42] Reg. §1.482-1(g)(3).

[43] Rev. Proc. 99-32, 1999-2 C.B. 296, Section 2.

[44] *Id.*

[45] See 11.02 of Rev. Proc. 2006-9.

[46] *Welch v. Helvering*, 3 USTC ¶ 1164, 290 US 111, 115 (1933); *Eli Lilly & Co.*, 88-1 USTC ¶ 9502, CCH Dec. 42,113, 84 TC 996, 1131 (1985).

[47] *See, e.g., J. Procacci*, CCH Dec. 46,451, 94 TC 397, 414 (1990). Because the burden of proof is a litigation concept, it is not discussed in the Code Sec. 482 or regulations thereunder.

Generally, taxpayers are faced with the burden of proof when arguing their cases in courts (as discussed in more detail in Chapter 12, taxpayers in the U.S. have opportunities to argue their cases before the Tax Court, federal court of claims and district courts). The burden of

proof consists of the duty to bring forward evidence (the burden of production) and of the risk of nonpersuasion (the burden of persuasion). *See P. Anastasato*, 86-2 USTC ¶ 9529, 794 F.2d 884, 887 (3d Cir. 1986).

[48] *Welch v. Helvering*, 3 USTC ¶ 1164, 290 US 111, 115 (1933); *Eli Lilly & Co.*, 88-1 USTC ¶9502, CCH Dec. 42,113, 84 TC 996, 1131 (1985). *See also*, United States Tax Court Rule 142(a).

[49] In *J.W. Stout*, 60-1 USTC ¶ 9185, 273 F.2d 345 (4th Cir. 1959), the Fourth Circuit stated: "The presumption of correctness is procedural. It transfers to the taxpayer the burden of going forward with evidence, but it disappears in a proceeding to review the assessment when substantial evidence contrary to the Commissioner's finding is introduced."

[50] *Danville Plywood Corp.*, 90-1 USTC ¶ 50,161, 899 F.2d 3 (Fed. Cir. 1990), *aff'g*, 89-1 USTC ¶9248, 16 Cls. Ct. 584, 593-94 (1989). The courts recognized that the burden of proof signifies the burden of persuasion, and it remains with the taxpayer and never shifts to the government throughout the whole proceeding. It is the burden of production that can be shifted.

[51] To clarify, the burden of proving here goes beyond of just rebutting the presumption of correctness of IRS deficiency determinations.

[52] *Asiatic Petroleum Co.*, CCH Dec. 8868, 31 BTA 1152, 1157 (1935) *aff'd* 35-2 USTC ¶ 9547, 79 F. 2d 234 (2d Cir.

- Establish that the IRS's determinations were arbitrary, capricious, or unreasonable.[53]

In short, the IRS's deficiency determination will be sustained by a court absent a showing by the taxpayer that the IRS abused its discretion.[54] Whether the IRS has abused its discretion is a question of fact.[55] To make its determination, the court's task is to review the result of the allocation, and not necessarily the methodology used to reach its result.[56] Again, taxpayers must show that the IRS's allocations are arbitrary, unreasonable, and capricious before taxpayers can show their view of ascertaining an arm's length result. This standard by definition has released the government of meeting a reasonable standard in pursuing an assessment. However, in some cases, where the IRS attempts to establish that common control exists due to arbitrary shifting of income, the IRS has a burden of proving that arbitrary shifting of income took place.[57]

In *DHL Corp.*,[58] the taxpayer challenged the IRS's presumption of correctness. The taxpayer argued that it should be held to a lesser standard of showing, by a preponderance of the evidence, that its prices were arm's length because the IRS took a different position in its notice of deficiency than it advanced at trial. However, the court rejected the taxpayer's argument because the court found that the difference in the IRS's position was attributable to the taxpayer's refusal to share information with the IRS during the audit. To rule otherwise, the court said, would encourage taxpayers to withhold information from the IRS and then criticize it for not having it.[59]

¶ 150   Categories of Section 482 Transactions

The regulations provide for categories of transfer pricing transactions:

- Transfer of tangible property;[60]
- Use of tangible property;[61]
- Transfer, license and use of intangible property;[62]
- Cost-sharing arrangements;[63]

(Footnote Continued)

1935); *Seagate Technology, Inc.*, CCH Dec. 49,657, 102 TC 149 (1994).

[53] *Sundstrand Corp.*, CCH Dec. 47,172, 96 TC 226, 353 (1991); *Westreco Inc.*, 64 TCM (CCH) 849 (1992); *Ach*, 66-1 USTC ¶ 9340, 42 TC 114 (1964) *aff'd*, 358 F.2d 342 (6th Cir. 1966).

[54] *Bausch & Lomb, Inc.*, CCH Dec. 45,547, 92 TC 525, 582 (1989), *aff'd* 91-1 USTC ¶ 50,244, 933 F.2d 1084 (2d Cir. 1991). *See generally* Francis M. Allegra, "Section 482: Mapping the Contours of the Abuse of Discretion Standard of Judicial Review," 13 *Va. Tax Rev.* No. 3, 423 (1994).

[55] *Sundstrand, supra* note 53, CCH Dec. 47,172, at 353–354.

[56] Reg. § 1.482-1(f)(2)(v); *Bausch & Lomb, supra* note 54, CCH Dec. 45,547 at 582.

[57] Proof of shifting of income between two corporations establishes presumption of common control, but when government seeks to show applicability of Code Sec. 482 by this method, it has the burden of proving of shifting of income; although allocation of Code Sec. 482 is presumptively correct and it is insufficient for taxpayer to merely show that its determination of arm's length price is wrong, in order to arrive at that position, government must show that there was common control of corporation so that Code Sec. 482 applies. *Dallas Ceramic Co.*, 79-2 USTC ¶ 9500, 598 F.2d 1382 (1979).

[58] *DHL Corp.*, CCH Dec. 53,015(M), TC Memo 1998-461, *aff'd in part* and *rev'd in part*, 285 F.3d 1210 (9th Cir 2002).

[59] *See* Levey, Cunningham, Emmer & Grech "DHL, Tax Court Road Map for Transfer Pricing Audits," 10 *J. of Int'l Tax'n* 12 (June, 1999).

[60] Reg. §§ 1.482-3 through 1.482-6.

[61] Reg. § 1.482-2(c).

[62] Reg. § 1.482-3 through § 1.482-6.

[63] Reg. § 1.482-7.

- Performance of services;[64]
- Global dealing services (proposed regulations); and
- Use of funds (loans).[65]

All transactions between controlled taxpayers fall within one or more of the above categories, depending on its characterization. Even non-traditional transactions can be characterized according to the above categories.[66]

¶ 160 Historical Background to U.S. Transfer Pricing Law

.01 In General [67]

The concept contained in Code Sec. 482 dates back to the Regulation 41, Articles 77 and 78, of the War Revenue Act of 1917, which granted the Commissioner the authority to require related corporations to file consolidated returns "whenever necessary to more equitably determine the invested capital or taxable income."[68] In 1921, Congress enacted legislation permitting the government to require consolidated accounting of groups of related corporations "for the purpose of making an accurate distribution or apportionment of gains, profits, income, deductions, or capital between or among such related trades or business."[69]

The statutory predecessor to Code Sec. 482 was enacted by Congress in 1928, granting broad authority to the Commissioner of the IRS to allocate gross income, deductions and credits and other items between and among controlled taxpayers in order to prevent the evasion of taxes or to clearly reflect income. The purpose in 1928, as is today, is to determine a controlled parties' taxable income.[70] Shortly thereafter, in 1934, regulations applying the arm's length standard as a method of reallocation under the predecessor to Code Sec. 482 were issued.[71] For nearly thirty-five years, until 1968, there were no significant changes made to the U.S. transfer pricing rules.

Revenue Act of 1962. In 1962, the House of Representatives proposed a formulary approach similar to that used for multistate income apportionment in the U.S. The proposal was intended to address the problem of transfers of business activities by U.S. companies to their subsidiaries in low-tax jurisdictions. The Ways and Means Committee Report stated that the pricing of goods between U.S. corporations and foreign subsidiaries had tended "to understate the taxable income of the domestic corporation subject to U.S. tax and to overstate the income of the foreign subsidiary," and that existing rules forced Treasury into impracticable attempts to

---

[64] Reg. § 1.482-2(b) and Reg. § 1.482-9.

[65] Reg. § 1.482-2(a).

[66] *See,* e.g., Steven C. Wrappe and Kerwin Chung, "Teaching New Dogs Old Tricks: Transfer Pricing for E-Commerce," 9 *Tax Mgmt. Transfer Pricing Rep.* 897 (April 4, 2001).

[67] *See* Michael C. Durst, Robert E. Culbertson, "Clearing Away the Sand: Retrospective Methods and Prospective Documentation in Transfer Pricing Today," 57 *Tax L. Rev.* 37 (Fall 2003) for a comprehensive historical analysis of transfer pricing rules and the arm's length standard; *see also* Reuven S. Avi-Yonah, "The Rise

and Fall of Arm's-Length: A Study in the Evolution of U.S. International Taxation", 15 *Va. Tax Rev.* 89 (1995).

[68] T.D. 2694, 20 Treas. Dec. Int. Rev. 294, 321 (1918). *See also* War Revenue Act of 1917, ch. 63, 40 Stat. 300 (1917); Reuven S. Avi-Yonah, "The Rise and Fall of Arm's-Length: A Study in the Evolution of U.S. International Taxation", 15 *Va. Tax Rev.* 89, 96 (1995).

[69] Revenue Act of 1921, Pub. L. No. 67-98, ch. 136, 240(d), 42 Stat. 227, 260.

[70] Section 45 of the Revenue Act of 1928, Pub. L. No. 70-562, ch. 852, 45, 45 Stat. 791, 806; Reg. 74, art. 355, § 45 (1929).

[71] Reg. 86, art. 45 (1935).

enforce the arm's length standard by reference to an intractable volume of transactional pricing information.[72] If the House proposal had been adopted, the Treasury could have prescribed formulas for apportioning income from transactions in tangible property among affiliates, based generally on the location of assets, compensation received, and marketing and advertising expenses, when no comparable uncontrolled prices were available.[73] The House proposal was not enacted. The proposal was nevertheless important as the Treasury was invited to re-examine its existing regulations with a particular focus on "guidelines and formulas for the allocation of income and deductions."[74]

.02 The 1968 Regulations

In response to the Congress' invitation to re-examine the then-existing transfer pricing regulatory framework, in 1968, the IRS promulgated comprehensive regulations that restated that the arm's length standard is the basic guiding principle of all transfer pricing analyses and described specific pricing methods to test the arm's length nature of transfer prices.[75]

.03 The 1986 Amendments to Code Sec. 482

The federal tax treatment of intercompany transactions remained unchanged until the Tax Reform Act of 1986 (TRA of 1986) amended Code Sec. 482 by adding the final sentence to the statute as it reads today (the "commensurate-with-income" standard). Congress concluded that U.S. taxpayers were transferring high-profit-potential intangibles to related entities located in low-tax foreign jurisdictions or possessions corporations at an early stage in the intangible's development, for a low royalty, and taking the position that the low royalty was justified because comparable transactions were not ascertainable or available.[76] Congress therefore amended Code Sec. 482 to require that payments made in exchange for the transfer of intangibles must be commensurate with the income attributable to that intangible.

The commensurate-with-income standard applies to outright transfers of intangibles as well as to licenses or other similar arrangements involving the cross-border movement of intangibles between related parties.[77] The commensurate-with-income standard requires that the transfer price not only be tested against the income generation potential of the intangible at the time of initial transfer, but also requires that royalties or other forms of payment for the intangible be periodically adjusted to reflect significant changes in the income generated by such intangibles.[78]

The 1986 amendments to Code Sec. 482 provided little guidance on how to comply with the commensurate-with-income standard. Congress, aware of its lack of guidance, authorized the IRS and Treasury to conduct a comprehensive study of intercompany pricing rules and regulations.

---

[72] H.R. Rep. No. 87-1447, at 28 (1962), reprinted in 1962-3 CB 405, 432.
[73] Id.
[74] H.R. Rep. No. 87-2508, at 18-19 (1962), reprinted in 1962-3 CB 1129, 1146.

[75] Reg. §§ 1.482-1, 1.482-2; TC 6952, 1968-1 CB 218, 33, Fed. Reg. 5849 (April 16, 1968).
[76] Staff of Joint Comm. on Tax'n, General Explanation of the Tax Reform Act of 1986, at pp. 1013-1014 (1986).
[77] Reg. § 1.482-4(a).
[78] Reg. § 1.482-4(f)(2).

.04 The 1988 White Paper

Following their Congressional mandate, the IRS and Treasury released a "Study of Intercompany Pricing" on October 18, 1988 ("White Paper"), which principally addressed the need to clarify the existing regulations for intangibles, the balancing of the commensurate-with-income standard with the arm's length principle, and the need for greater taxpayer documentation at early stages of the audit.[79] In particular, the White Paper discussed several methods used to determine the proper charge for the transfer of intangibles under the commensurate-with-income standard.[80]

The White Paper proposed two basic methods by which a transfer price could meet the commensurate-with-income standard. Under the first method, taxpayers would look at comparable transactions. To the extent that comparable transactions were available, the results under a comparable transaction analysis were considered more reliable than any realized under the other methods discussed. Two types of comparables could be used: exact comparables or inexact comparables. Exact comparables were transactions in which the identical intangible that was transferred to a related party was also transferred between the taxpayer and an unrelated party. Inexact comparables, on the other hand, were transactions in which the intangible transferred to a related party was similar, but not identical, to the intangible transferred between the taxpayer and an unrelated party. If the intangibles and the material contract terms and economic relationships were similar, the transaction could be used as an inexact comparable.

The second method discussed in the White Paper was the basic arm's length return method ("BALRM").[81] The BALRM method could be used by itself or in conjunction with a profit split approach. Under the BALRM method, each relevant business line would be broken down into its measurable functions, risks, and assets, then economic rates of return for each business line would be calculated by reference to industry average rates of returns on such functions, risks, and assets. An income amount attributable to each business line would then be determined. To the extent that the income paid in the transaction exceeded that aggregate income amounts attributed, the residual income would be deemed to be allocated to the other party in the transaction. A profit split analysis was added to the BALRM method where both parties to the transaction bore significant economic risks and used significant proprietary intangibles. Called the "BALRM-Plus," the method split the residual income of each party based on the relative value of each party's intangibles.

---

[79] Notice 88-123, 1988-2 CB 458.

[80] *See* Fuller, "The IRS Section 482 White Paper," 41 *Tax Notes* No. 7 655 (1988); Levey et al., "Transfer Pricing Intangibles After the Section 482 White Paper," 71 *J. of Tax'n* 38 (July 1989); Bischell, "White Paper Analysis:

Ballroom Dancing with an Intangible," 41 *Tax Notes* No. 10, 1097 (1988).

[81] *See generally* Stoffregen et al., "The BALRM Approach to Transfer Pricing: One Step Forward, Two Steps Back," 42 *Tax Notes* No. 10, 1257 (1989).

.05 The 1992 Proposed Regulations

The IRS issued proposed regulations under Code Sec. 482 on January 30, 1992.[82] The most significant change proposed was the introduction of three new pricing methods for transfers of intangible property: the matching transaction method ("MTM"), the comparable adjustable transaction method ("CATM"), and the comparable profit method ("CPM"), which employed the comparable profit interval ("CPI").[83]

The MTM and the CATM were based on the concepts of exact and inexact comparable transactions, respectively.[84] The CPM was an income-based method under which the operating income resulting from a controlled transaction was compared with the operating income of comparable uncontrolled taxpayers.[85] The consideration charged in the controlled transaction would be considered arm's length if the taxpayer's operating income fell within a range of results derived from the uncontrolled taxpayers over a three-year period. The proposed regulations also required that the result derived from the CATM be verified by the CPI. In addition, the 1992 regulations implemented the commensurate-with-income standard by providing that these methods could be applied to adjust the consideration charged in the year of examination (i.e., periodic adjustments) unless one of three narrow exceptions applied.[86]

Other changes made by the proposed regulations included: modification of the rules for transfers of tangible property, principally by providing for the use of the CPI for tangible property transfers; requiring that the results derived from the resale price or cost-plus methods be verified by application of the CPI; introducing new cost sharing regulations and a limited comparable profit split method; and relaxing the fixed priority of methods set forth in the 1968 regulations.[87]

.06 The 1993 Temporary and Proposed Regulations

In response to taxpayers' comments to the 1992 proposed regulations, the IRS issued revised temporary and proposed regulations on January 21, 1993 (the 1993 regulations).[88] With the exception of the provisions on cost sharing, the 1993 regulations superseded the 1992 proposed regulations and added some new provisions. The 1993 regulations also modified other provisions of the 1968 regulations that had not been affected by the 1992 proposed regulations and adopted a regulatory structure different from that set forth under the 1968 regulations.[89]

---

[82] 1992-1 CB 1164, 57 Fed. Reg. 3571 (January 30, 1992).

[83] *See generally*, George N. Carlson et al., "The Proposed New Transfer Pricing Rules: New Wine in an Old Bottle," 54 *Tax Notes* 691 (1992); Levey et al., "Practical Problems Remain Under 482 Prop. Regs.-Part I," 3 *J. of Int'l Tax'n* 325 (March/April, 1992); Levey et al., "Practical Problems Remain Under 482 Prop. Regs.-Part II," 3 *J. of Int'l Tax'n* 5 (May/June 1992).

[84] Prop. Reg. § 1.482-2(d)(3); Prop. Reg. § 1.482-2(d)(4).

[85] Prop. Reg. § 1.482-2(d)(5).

[86] Prop. Reg. § 1.482-2(d)(6).

[87] Prop. Reg. § 1.482-2(e); Prop. Reg. § 1.482-2(f); Prop. Reg. § 1.482-2(g).

[88] T.D. 8470, 58 Fed. Reg. 5263 (January 21, 1993).

[89] *See generally*, Dolan, "Revised Transfer Pricing Regulations," 22 *Tax Mgt. Int'l Jnl.* No. 4, 159 (1993); Fuller and Aud, "The New Temporary and Proposed Section 482 Regulations: A Wolf in Sheep's Clothing" 58 *Tax Notes* No. 11, 1517 (1993); Levey et al., "New 482 Regs Still Favor the Comparable Price Method," 4 *J. of Int'l Tax'n* 202 (May 1993).

¶160.05

General Rules. The first part of the 1993 regulations set forth general rules for application of the Code Sec. 482 arm's length standard.[90] Most importantly, these rules provided extensive guidance in determining whether an uncontrolled transaction was sufficiently comparable to serve as a basis for application of a pricing method.[91] Determining comparability under these rules generally required consideration of the parties' functions, risks, contractual terms, economic conditions, and products. Detailed guidance was provided as to how these factors were to be assessed. The relative importance of any of these factors varied depending on the method applied.

The temporary regulations also adopted a "best method" rule to be used in determining which method provides the most accurate measure of an arm's length result in a given case.[92] The "best method" rule was based on a flexible approach whereby the determination of which method was most accurate depended on the facts and circumstances of the particular case. Factors to be considered in this determination included the completeness and accuracy of available data, the degree of comparability between the controlled and uncontrolled transactions, and the extent of adjustments required to apply a method. The "best method" rule further provided that when two methods provided inconsistent results and did not otherwise indicate which of the two analyses should be preferred, an additional factor to be considered was whether a third method provided a result that was consistent with the result of either of the first two methods.

The temporary regulations also introduced the concept of a range of arm's length results.[93] Here, two or more valid applications of any single method created a range of acceptable results within which the taxpayer's result was considered to satisfy the arm's length standard. No allocation was to be made if the taxpayer's result fell within the range. Results falling outside the range were subject to adjustment to any point within the range, but generally to the midpoint (the median if an interquartile range is used).

The 1993 regulations included proposed regulations to deal with foreign legal restrictions.[94] In general, this rule provided that a foreign legal restriction preventing or limiting payment of an arm's length amount would be respected for purposes of determining an arm's length consideration only if there was evidence of a comparable uncontrolled transaction in which unrelated parties agreed to enter a similar transaction subject to the restriction. In other cases, the foreign legal restriction would be disregarded in determining an arm's length amount, but the taxpayer was permitted to elect a deferred method of accounting to defer recognition of additional income until such time as the restriction was lifted, subject to the consistent deferral of related expenses.

Lastly, the temporary regulations set forth special rules addressing market penetration strategies, different geographic markets, "location savings," aggregation of transactions, analysis of contractual terms, multiple year analyses, collateral

[90] Temp. Reg. § 1.482-1T.
[91] Temp. Reg. § 1.482-1T(c).
[92] Temp. Reg. § 1.482-1T(b)(2)(iii)(A).
[93] Temp. Reg. § 1.482-1T(d)(2)(i).
[94] Prop. Reg. § 1.482-1T(f)(2).

adjustments, coordination with Code Sec. 936, and the consideration of alternative transaction structures.[95]

Transfers of Tangible Property. The 1993 regulations further revised the rules relating to transfers of tangible property.[96] Five principal methods were provided for transfers of tangible property:

- The comparable uncontrolled price ("CUP") method;
- The resale price method ("RPM");
- The cost-plus method;
- The comparable profit method ("CPM"); and
- When authorized by the regulations, profit split.

The CUP method was retained from the 1968 regulations and was modified to apply only if minor differences existed between the controlled and uncontrolled transactions.[97] Because the CUP method was likely to achieve the highest degree of comparability of any method potentially applicable to a transfer of tangible property, the 1993 regulations stated that the CUP method generally provides the most reliable measure of an arm's length result when it can be applied. The rules under the cost-plus method and RPM were not substantially changed from their predecessors in the 1968 regulations.[98] The temporary regulations also provided that if none of the enumerated methods could be applied, other (unspecified) methods may be used.[99] To employ an unspecified method, taxpayers were required to disclose the use of such method on the tax return and prepare contemporaneous documentation explaining why the method provides the most accurate measure of an arm's length result. Finally, the temporary regulation provided rules coordinating the application of the tangible and intangible rules where embedded intangibles existed.[100]

Transfers of Intangible Property. For transfers of intangible property, the temporary regulations combined the MTM and CATM from the 1992 regulations into a single method known as the comparable uncontrolled transaction ("CUT") method.[101] Unlike the CATM of the 1992 proposed regulations, the results of the CUT method were not subject to mandatory check by the CPI. The mandatory CPI check, however, was replaced by requiring that the intangibles transferred in the controlled and uncontrolled transactions have substantially the same profit potential.[102] In addition, to apply the CUT method, the property transferred must be from the same class of intangible property and relate to the same class of products or services.[103] Reliable adjustments were permitted to account for the effect of any differences.[104]

Rules were also provided for identifying the owner of an intangible for purposes of Code Sec. 482 (i.e., the developer-assistor rule).[105] These rules generally track rules provided in prior regulations, under which the owner normally is

---

[95] Temp. Reg. §§ 1.482-1T(c)(4); -1T(d)(3); -1T(f)(3).
[96] Temp. Reg. § 1.482-3T.
[97] Temp. Reg. § 1.482-3T(b).
[98] Temp. Reg. § 1.482-3T(c); Temp. Reg. § 1.482-3T(d).
[99] Temp. Reg. § 1.482-3T(e)(2).
[100] Temp. Reg. § 1.482-3T(f).

[101] Temp. Reg. § 1.482-4T(c).
[102] Temp. Reg. § 1.482-4T(c)(2).
[103] Temp. Reg. § 1.482-4T(c)(2).
[104] Temp. Reg. § 1.482-4T(c)(2).
[105] Temp. Reg. § 1.482-4T(e)(3).

considered to be the controlled taxpayer that bears the greatest share of the risk of developing the intangible. The party that bears the greatest risk of development generally is determined by identifying costs of development.[106] Under this rule, the owner for purposes of income allocation under Code Sec. 482 would not necessarily be the legal owner.

The temporary regulations also broadened the exceptions from periodic adjustments under the commensurate-with-income standard that were contained in the 1992 regulations.[107]

Comparable Profits Method ("CPM"). The temporary regulations also included the CPM, which could be applied to transfers of tangible and intangible property.[108] In response to taxpayer comments to the 1992 proposed regulations, the CPM no longer served as a mandatory check on the results provided by other methods. The temporary regulations also provided that the CPM ordinarily was inappropriate if the tested party owned "valuable non-routine intangible" property.[109] This limitation was added because the CPM could be expected to understate the income attributable to property due to the difficulty of locating uncontrolled taxpayers that possessed comparable intangible property. The 1993 regulations, however, made no attempt to define the term "valuable non-routine intangible."

The CPM generally was to be applied to the taxpayer with the simplest and most easily compared operations (the tested party).[110] In identifying potential comparables, the regulations provided that the standard of comparability was not as strict as other methods.[111] Some diversity in terms of the functions and products was permitted, although the degree of comparability affected the reliability of the results in relation to the results of other methods under the best method rule.[112] The regulations also described a number of adjustments, including adjustments to achieve accounting consistency, that were to be made (when possible) to the results of the uncontrolled comparables to enhance comparability.[113]

As under the 1992 proposed regulations, a result satisfied the arm's length standard under the CPM if it fell within a range of results, based on a single profit level indicator ("PLI") derived from uncontrolled comparables.[114] PLIs included the rate of return on capital employed (i.e., rate of return on assets) and financial ratios, such as operating profit to gross sales and gross profit to operating expenses.[115]

Profit Split Proposed Regulations. The 1993 regulations also contained a set of proposed regulations providing for and explaining profit split methodologies.[116] Three methods were described:

- The residual allocation rule;
- The capital employed allocation rule; and
- The comparable profit split.

---

[106] Temp. Reg. § 1.482-4T(e)(3).
[107] Temp. Reg. § 1.482-4T(e)(2)(ii).
[108] Temp. Reg. § 1.482-5T.
[109] Temp. Reg. § 1.482-5T(a).
[110] Temp. Reg. § 1.482-5T(b).
[111] Temp. Reg. § 1.482-5T(c)(1).

[112] Temp. Reg. § 1.482-5T(c)(1).
[113] Temp. Reg. § 1.482-5T(c)(2).
[114] Temp. Reg. § 1.482-5T(d).
[115] Temp. Reg. § 1.482-5T(e).
[116] Prop. Reg. § 1.486-6 (1993).

The basic objective of the profit split methods was to estimate an arm's length return by comparing the relative economic contributions that two parties make to the success of an activity (i.e., the relevant business activity) and dividing the returns from the relevant business activity between them on the basis of the value of such contributions.[117] The residual allocation rule here was similar to the BALRM with profit split described in the White Paper.[118]

The capital employed allocation rule would be applied only if all the controlled taxpayers participating in the relevant business activity assumed an approximately equal level of risk for their capital employed.[119] This method divided the combined operating profit from the relevant business activity by allocating an equal return to each controlled taxpayer's capital employed. Capital employed could be measured by either book or fair market value, provided all assets were valued on the same basis.

The comparable profit split rule was similar to the profit split rule set forth in the 1992 proposed regulations.[120] It essentially was applied only if it was possible to locate two unrelated parties that were each comparable to one of the controlled taxpayers and that deal with one another in a comparable manner. If two such unrelated parties could be located, the combined operating profit from the relevant business activity was divided among the controlled taxpayers in the same percentage as it was divided among the unrelated parties.

There were also a number of substantive and procedural restrictions on the use of the profit split method.[121] These restrictions were imposed because the profit split method relied either wholly or in part on internal data rather than on data derived from uncontrolled taxpayers, and it was therefore likely that other methods would provide a more reliable measure of an arm's length result under the best method rule. These substantive limitations restricted the application of the profit split method to situations in which both controlled taxpayers own valuable non-routine intangible property, the intangibles contributed significantly to the combined operating profit derived from the relevant business activity, and there were significant transactions between the controlled taxpayers. The most important administrative requirement was that the taxpayer was required to make a binding election to apply the profit split method, which could be revoked only with the consent of the Commissioner.[122] In addition, the taxpayer also was required to document the combined profit or loss attributable to the relevant business activity to the satisfaction of the District Director and explain in such documentation why the profit split method provided the best method for determining an arm's length result.[123] Further, prior to electing the profit split method, the taxpayer was required to execute a pricing agreement setting forth the method chosen, and the method had to be applied consistently from year to year.[124]

---

[117] Prop. Reg. § 1.482-6(a).
[118] Prop. Reg. § 1.482-6(c)(2).
[119] Prop. Reg. § 1.482-6(c)(3).
[120] Prop. Reg. § 1.482-6(c)(4).

[121] Prop. Reg. § 1.482-6(b).
[122] Prop. Reg. § 1.482-6(d)(1).
[123] Prop. Reg. § 1.482-6(d)(2).
[124] Prop. Reg. § 1.482-6(d)(2).

The District Director also was given the discretion to apply a profit split method if all of the substantive, but not procedural, requirements were satisfied.[125]

.07 The 1994 Final Regulations

On July 1, 1994, the IRS released final Code Sec. 482 regulations.[126] The preamble to the regulations indicates that they were written to "clarify and refine those provisions of the 1993 regulations that required improvement without fundamentally altering the basic policies reflected in the 1993 regulations (e.g., the best method rule was modified to provide that taxpayers were to use the 'most reliable' method instead of the 'most accurate' method)."[127] The 1994 regulations will be described in detail in the forthcoming chapters. Nevertheless, several observations can be made from a historical perspective.

First, unlike the IRS's earlier regulations, the significantly longer and more detailed 1994 final regulations are woven together with a single common thread: contemporaneous documentation. This contemporaneous documentation requirement to avoid penalties is consistent with the recommendations contained in the White Paper. To prevent the imposition of penalties, taxpayers must contemporaneously create and maintain detailed records of their transfer pricing transactions. The contemporaneous documentation required by the final regulations enables the IRS to conduct audits of controlled party transactions with unprecedented detail.

Second, although the preamble to the final regulations states that the final regulations "are generally consistent" with prior regulations in both format and substance, the final regulations introduce significantly greater judgment, flexibility, and subjectivity to the regulatory scheme. Taxpayers that conduct thorough pre-transaction analysis and compile appropriate types of documentation may benefit under the final regulations through their control of their own facts and methods. Ill-prepared taxpayers, however, who do not update their recordkeeping systems or engage in pre-transaction analysis, could be exposing their operations to prolonged and contentious audits and harsh penalties (ranging between 20 percent and 40 percent).[128]

Absent, however, from the final regulations was guidance about intercompany services and certain aspects of intangible property transfers, i.e., cost sharing arrangements.

.08 2003 Final Cost Sharing Regulations—Stock Options in Cost Sharing Agreements

The IRS has long argued that stock based compensation costs should be shared under a qualified cost sharing arrangement, and on August 25, 2003 the IRS issued final rules under Section 1.482-7[129] that require companies to share employee stock option costs with affiliates, even though most commentators objected to the

---

[125] Prop. Reg. § 1.482-6(f).

[126] T.D. 8552, 59 Fed. Reg. 34971 (July 8, 1994).

[127] *See generally* Dolan, "Final Transfer Pricing Regulations," 23 *Tax Mgt. Int'l Jnl.* No. 9, 423 (1994); Levey & Grauer, "Final 482 Regs. Aim at More Flexibility But Retain IRS Audit Focus," 5 *J. of Int'l Tax'n* 456 (October 1994); Magee et al., "If at First You Don't Succeed: The New Transfer Pricing Regulations," 62 *Tax Notes* No. 7, 899 (1994).

[128] Code Secs. 6662(e) and 6662(h).

[129] T.D. 9088, 68 Fed. Reg. 51171, 8/26/03.

proposed regulations in their entirety. The IRS designated at least two cases for litigation on the stock options question, *Seagate Technology Inc.*, TC, No. 15086-98, and *Xilinx Inc.*, No. 4142-01. The IRS conceded the issue in *Seagate* in 2001. The IRS lost the *Xilinx* case in the Tax Court in 2005, but the Ninth Circuit overturned that decision in favor of the IRS in 2009 (*Xilinx*, Ninth Circuit, Nos. 06-74246 and 06-74269).[130] On January 2010, the Ninth Circuit withdrew, without explanation or comment, its 2009 opinion and dissent in *Xilinx*. Ultimately, the Ninth Circuit followed its dissenting opinion and upheld the Tax Court decision.[131]

.09 2003 Proposed Regulations—Services

After 35 years of existence without update, the transfer pricing regulations for services, originally promulgated in 1968, finally drew the attention of the Treasury. On September 5, 2003, the IRS released Proposed Regulations Relating to Treatment of Services Under Section 482, Allocation of Income and Deductions From Intangibles.[132] These regulations would introduce a new transfer pricing regime for controlled services transactions under Code Sec. 482. The proposed regulations would generally replace current Reg. § 1.482-2(b) with a new set of controlled services transactions rules under Prop. Reg. § 1.482-9. The proposed regulations also would revise the rules under current Reg. § § 1.482-4(f)(3) and -1(d)(3) regarding the ownership and development of intangibles, focusing on the treatment of activities that contribute to the value of an intangible owned by a related taxpayer (the so-called "cheese examples").

The 2003 proposed regulations contained four main areas of change: (i) adoption of regulatory consistency with the other transfer pricing regulations; (ii) a substantially revised "benefit test"; (iii) a replacement regime for cost-only allocations (the simplified cost based method, or "SCBM"); and (iv) addressing overlaps between services and intangibles.[133]

.10 2005 Proposed Cost Sharing Regulations

In 2005, just two years after the previous cost sharing regulations were finalized, the IRS and Treasury proposed new cost sharing regulations which adopted fundamental changes aimed at combating perceived taxpayer abuses under the existing regulations.[134] The 2005 proposed cost sharing regulations are based upon the "investor model." The preamble states that, under this model, each controlled participant to the cost sharing arrangement may be viewed as making an aggregate investment to "cost contributions" (allocation of ongoing intangible development costs) and "external contributions" (formerly referred to as "buy-in") to achieve an anticipated return appropriate to the risks and the exportation of the resulting tangibles.

---

[130] *See* Alan Summers, Nicholas Ronan, and Simon Weber, "The Ninth Circuit's Opinion in Xilinx: Implications for the Arm's Length Standard," 18 *Tax Mgmt. Transfer Pricing Rep.* 543 (Sept. 24, 2009).

[131] *Xilinx*, No. 06-74246 (2010).

[132] REG-146893-02; REG-115037-00, *see Tax Notes*, Sept. 15, 2003, p. 1383; Doc 2003-20158, 2003 TNT 178-21.

[133] *See* Steven C. Wrappe and Brian P. Trauman, "The New Services Regulations: Are We There Yet?" *Tax Management Memorandum* 48 9 155-170 Bureau of National Affairs, Inc., (April 30, 2007).

[134] REG-144615-02.

The investor model frames the guidance for valuing the external contributions that, at arm's length, parties would not invest in the arrangement unless the total anticipated return is more than, or equal to, the total anticipated return it would have received through an alternative investment realistically available to it.

These proposed regulations employ the so-called the "investor model" to fundamentally re-write the cost-sharing regulations, including at least 20 new defined terms and four new transfer pricing methodologies. These regulations may have received numerous, consistently negative comments.[135]

.11 2006 Temporary and Proposed Services Regulations

In 2006, the IRS and Treasury published services regulations in temporary and proposed form, effective for tax years beginning after December 31, 2006.[136] The most significant difference from the 2003 proposed services regulations is the replacement of the SCBM with the services cost method ("SCM"). The SCM and the new shared services arrangements ("SSAs") allow taxpayers to elect to allocate costs among controlled parties without a mark-up. The changes to the benefit test, application of the general rules of Reg. § 1.482-1, and portions of the intangible regulations from the 2003 proposed are generally retained without substantial change.

The 2006 regulations require taxpayers to determine the arm's length amount charged in a controlled services transaction under a best method analysis, such that one of six specified methods, or an unspecified method, will be applied. The new entrant, the SCM, evaluates whether the price for certain services is arm's length by reference to the Total Services Costs with no markup. The SCM applies in some circumstances, based upon satisfying certain conditions, to specific services that the Treasury and IRS will identify annually in Revenue Procedures and to other "low-margin" services. The SCM, similar to the former SCBM, is intended to reduce compliance and administrative burdens for routine and lower-margin services. However, it may require substantial record-keeping and contemporaneous documentation efforts.

The 2006 regulations include three changes regarding the overlap between services and intangibles transactions: (i) ownership of the intangible (concept of legal ownership); (ii) compensation for contributors to non-owned intangibles (parties are entitled to an arm's length compensation); and (iii) services transactions that effect the transfer of intangibles (whether to evaluate such a transaction as a single transaction or as two separate transactions).[137]

Concurrent with its issuance of the 2006 temporary regulations, the IRS published Announcement 2006-05 with a proposed revenue procedure detailing the

[135] *See* John Wills and Lonnie Brist, "The Economic Flaw in the Investor Model," 15 *Tax Mgmt. Transfer Pricing Rep.* 402 (Sept. 27, 2006); "Cost Sharing: IRS Hears Concerns About Investor Model Technical Aspects of Cost Sharing Proposal," 14 *Tax Mgmt. Transfer Pricing Rep.* 671 (Dec. 21, 2005); Molly Moses, "Proposed Cost Sharing Rules Adopt 'Investor Model,' Practitioners See

Proposal as Attempt to Enlarge Buy-Ins," 14 *Tax Mgmt. Transfer Pricing Rep.* 331 (Aug. 31, 2005).

[136] REG–146893-02, REG–115037-00, and REG–138603-03 (T.D. 9278).

[137] For a more detailed analysis, *see* Steven C. Wrappe and Brian P. Trauman, "The New Services Regulations: Are We There Yet?" *Tax Management Memorandum* 48 9 155-170 Bureau of National Affairs, Inc., (April 30, 2007).

¶160.11

48 types of functions that would qualify as "specified covered services", eligible for cost-only treatment.[138]

On December 21, 2006, the IRS moved back the effective date of the temporary regulations by one year (with the exception of the business judgment rule).[139] Rev. Proc. 2007-13, which accompanied Notice 2007-5, expanded the list of services eligible for cost only allocation from 48 to 101 services.[140]

.12 2008 Temporary Cost-Sharing Regulations

On December 31, 2008, the IRS and Treasury released temporary cost-sharing arrangement ("CSA") regulations with an effective date of January 5, 2009.[141] These regulations revise the proposed regulations issued in 2005 and replace the existing CSA regulations from 1995.

These temporary regulations retain many of the concepts introduced in the 2005 proposed regulations, but contain significant modifications and clarifications, particularly with respect to guidance on the evaluation of the arm's length results of cost-sharing transactions ("CSTs") and platform contribution transactions ("PCTs").[142]

While the temporary regulations retain the investor model as a core concept of the CSA rules,[143] they nevertheless do introduce some additional flexibility in how that model is to be interpreted under the 'best realistic alternative' test, making it less onerous than it was in the CSA Coordinated Issue Paper, released in 2007.[144]

The new regulations also allow for a greatly expanded definition of the contributions that give rise to a buy-in requirement (now called a PCT payment), through, among other means, elimination of the link to the intangible property list of 936(h).[145] In addition, they state that an assembled R&D workforce constitutes a contribution to a CSA requiring compensation above and beyond the mere reimbursement of the associated personnel costs.[146]

The temporary regulations reaffirm that the commensurate-with-income provision is consistent with the arm's length standard and further refine when periodic adjustments are necessary in CSAs. The temporary regulations mechanically mirror the mechanism provided in the 2005 proposed regulations, but narrow the trigger to make periodic adjustments.[147]

---

[138] 2006-34 IRB 321 (August 21, 2006).

[139] Notice 2007-5, 2007-3 IRB 269, 12/20/06.

[140] Rev. Proc. 2007-13, 2007-3 IRB 295, 12/20/06.

[141] T.D. 9441, 74 Fed. Reg. 340.

[142] The preamble of the temporary cost-sharing regulations specifically states that: "The temporary regulations clarify that these principles [e.g. the realistic alternatives principle]were intended to provide supplementary guidance on the application of the best method rule to determine which method, or application of a method, provides the most reliable measure of an arm's length result in the CSA context. In other words, the principles provide best method considerations to aid the competitive evaluation

of methods or applications, and are not themselves methods or trumping rules."

[143] Temp. Reg. § 1-482-7T(g)(2)(ii).

[144] LMSB-04-090762.

[145] The preamble to the temporary cost-sharing regulations states that: "The temporary regulations, like the 2005 proposed regulations, do not limit platform contributions that must be compensated in PCTs to the transfer of intangibles defined in section 936(h)(3)(B)."

[146] See, e.g., Temp. Reg. § 1.482-7T(g)(2)(vii)(B) Example 1.

[147] See preamble to temporary cost-sharing regulations, section E, Periodic Adjustments. Also Temp. Reg. § 1.482-7T(i)(6).

¶160.12

The temporary regulations provide a more favorable grandfathering provision than did the 2005 proposed regulations by eliminating termination triggers. Generally, pre-existing qualified CSAs will continue to be treated as CSAs under the existing (1995) regulations provided that the intercompany contract is amended to conform to the new administrative requirements and the activities of controlled participants substantially comply with the temporary regulations.[148]

In addition, other features of the new regulations include:

- Greater flexibility and scope in the types and provisions of arrangements that may qualify as CSAs;[149]

- Elimination of the restriction to use only Territory to divide interests in the CSA—division of interests may be by reference to Field of Use,[150] Territory[151] or other reliable and non-overlapping measure,[152] but new restrictions (as compared with current regulations) have been added on what will qualify;

- Elimination of the terms "external contribution," "preliminary or contemporaneous transaction" and "reference transaction" in favor of a new term, "platform contribution transactions";[153]

- Expanded discussion on the determination of the appropriate Discount Rate;[154]

- Clarification of how arm's length ranges are to be calculated when there are multiple variable input parameters (as opposed to the simple case of a set of comparables, each with its own PLI value).[155]

.13 2009 Final Services Regulations

On July 31, 2009, the IRS and Treasury Department issued final regulations under Code Sec. 482 on taxable income in connection with a controlled services transaction.[156] The final regulations replaced Temp. Reg. § 1.482-9T (temporary regulations). The final regulations implement the temporary regulations with relatively few modifications.[157]

The adopted changes make certain clarifications and improvements without fundamentally altering the policies reflected in the temporary regulations. The final regulations also clarify the temporary regulations by providing more guidance in the following areas:

1. The requirements for the Services Cost Method ("SCM") have been reorganized to clarify that potential SCM services must meet all of the following conditions conjunctively: (i) the service must be a covered service; (ii) the service cannot be an excluded activity; (iii) the service cannot be precluded from constituting a covered service by reason of the

---

[148] Temp. Reg. § 1.482-7T(m)(1).

[149] *See* preamble to the temporary cost-sharing regulations, section B, Flexibility and Scope of CSA Coverage.

[150] Temp. Reg. § 1.482-7T(b)(4)(iii).

[151] Temp. Reg. § 1.482-7T(b)(4)(ii).

[152] Temp. Reg. § 1.482-7T(b)(4)(iv).

[153] *See* Temp. Reg. § 1.482-7T(c).

[154] *See* Temp. Reg. § 1.482-7T(c).

[155] Temp. Reg. § 1.482-7T(g)(2)(ix)(B).

[156] T.D. 9456, 7-31-2009.

[157] Molly Moses, "IRS Finalizes Intercompany Services Rules With Few Changes From Temporary Version," 146 DTR G-5 (August 3, 2009).

business judgment rule; and (iv) adequate books and records must be maintained.[158]

2. The application of the SCM is confirmed as a prerogative of the taxpayer if applied in accordance with the regulations.[159]

3. The business judgment rule is determined by reference to a trade or business of the controlled group versus the prior, more ambiguous reference in the temporary regulations to the "renderer, the recipient, or both." The business judgment rule requires a reasonable conclusion by the taxpayer. Whether the taxpayer's conclusion is reasonable may be subject to examination by the IRS in the course of an audit. The IRS reiterates that the final regulations incorporate a high threshold for application of the business judgment rule to exclude services otherwise eligible for SCM.[160]

The final regulations are effective on July 31, 2009, and apply to tax years ending after July 31, 2009. Taxpayers may elect to apply the regulations to any tax year beginning after September 10, 2003.[161]

¶ 170 Related Code Sections

.01 Code Secs. 6038A and 6038C Reporting and Disclosure Rules

The Omnibus Budget Reconciliation Act of 1989 (OBRA 1989) expanded the IRS's ability to conduct transfer pricing examinations.[162] These reporting requirements, contained in Code Sec. 6038A, apply to corporations that are owned by 25 percent foreign shareholders. Each corporation is required to maintain certain records as deemed appropriate by the IRS to enable its personnel to determine the correct treatment of transfer pricing transactions by the corporation. Under OBRA 1989, Congress increased the penalties for failure to comply with Code Sec. 6038A from $100 to $10,000 for each thirty-day period of noncompliance. There are exceptions to the penalties if a taxpayer can establish that noncompliance was due to reasonable care. Code Sec. 6038C was added to the Code under OBRA 1989 to assure that the rules under 6038A would apply to certain branch operations of foreign corporations that were previously outside the reach of Code Sec. 6038A.

.02 The Code Sec. 1059A

Congress was concerned that the transfer price reported for tax purposes could substantially exceed the transfer price reported for customs purposes, allowing related parties to avoid federal tax or customs duties. In response to this concern, Congress added Code Sec. 1059A in 1986. The coordination provisions apply to any property imported into the United States in a transaction, directly or indirectly, between related persons within the meaning of Code Sec. 482. Costs taken into account in computing the basis or inventory cost of the property by the purchaser, and are taken into account in computing the customs value of such property cannot, in computing basis or inventory cost, be greater than costs taken

---

[158] Preamble, Treatment of Services Under Section 482, 74 Fed. Reg. 38830 (August 4, 2009).

[159] Preamble, Treatment of Services Under Section 482, 74 Fed. Reg. 38832 (August 4, 2009).

[160] Preamble, Treatment of Services Under Section 482, 74 Fed. Reg. 38832 (August 4, 2009).

[161] Reg. § 1.482-9(n).

[162] H.R. Rep. No. 386, 101st Cong., 2d Sess. 594 (1989).

into account in computing the customs value. The strict statutory language prevents an importer from claiming a higher tax basis for imported merchandise than the customs value.

Code Sec. 1059A does not limit the authority of the IRS to increase or decrease the claimed basis or inventory cost under Code Sec. 482.[163] The coordination rule applies to merchandise subject to any customs duty or is subject to a free rate of duty[164] and further, the coordination rule does not apply to imported property not subject to customs duty based on value, including property subject.

.03 The Code Sec. 6662(e) Penalty Rules

A significant aspect of most transfer pricing issues includes penalty consideration. The enforcement in the transfer pricing area requires maintenance by the taxpayer of contemporaneous documentation for transactions subject to Code Sec. 482. Failure to meet this requirement could lead to significant penalties, which could substantially exceed the overall tax exposure of the taxpayer. Taxpayers with presence in various jurisdictions shall comply with the respective transfer pricing rules and documentation requirements in those jurisdictions.

Although the final Code Sec. 482 regulations provide guidance on how to evaluate whether the results of intercompany transactions are determined at arm's length, the major incentive for taxpayers to apply these guidelines rests with the documentation they are required to provide to the IRS to avoid penalties imposed under Code Secs. 6662(e) and (h). Code Sec. 6662(e) imposes a penalty of 20 percent of the tax imposed on a transfer pricing deficiency if the transfer prices are 50 percent or less, or 200 percent or more, of the arm's length price or if the net transfer pricing adjustment exceeds the lesser of $5 million or 10 percent of gross receipts. Code Sec. 6662(h) increases the penalty to 40 percent if transfer prices are 25 percent or less, or 400 percent or more, of the arm's length price or if the net transfer price adjustment exceeds the lesser of $20 million or 20 percent of gross receipts.

The penalty regulations require contemporaneous documentation and certain forms of pre-transaction functional analysis prior to the filing of a tax return. The documentation must show that the taxpayer reasonably concluded that the transfer pricing methodology chosen and its application provide the most reliable measure of an arm's length result under the best method rule. Consequently, to avoid the imposition of penalties under Code Sec. 6662, taxpayers must be able to explain how they selected their pricing method and the reasons for their rejection of other possible methods.[165]

.04 The Code Sec. 982 Evidentiary Rules

Code Sec. 982 is an evidentiary provision, rather than a penalty or documentation requirement. It provides that if a taxpayer fails to comply with a formal IRS document request (i.e., an IDR) for foreign-based documentation within 90 days of the mailing of such request, then any U.S. civil court adjudicating the tax treatment

---

[163] Reg. § 1.1059A-1(c)(7).
[164] Reg. § 1.1059A-1(c)(1).

[165] Reg. § 1.6662-6(d); *see also* Reg. § 1.6664-4T(f) ("Transactions between persons described in section 482 and net section 482 transfer price adjustments").

of an item that was the subject of the document request shall prohibit the introduction of foreign-based documentation that was the subject of the request.[166] "Foreign based documentation" is defined as any documentation that is located outside of the United States that may be relevant or material to the tax treatment of the examined item.[167] A reasonable cause exception is provided for in the statute; however, the existence of a foreign law that would impose a civil or criminal penalty for disclosing the requested information is not considered to be reasonable cause.[168]

The following chart shows the global proliferation of transfer pricing rules:

[166] Code Sec. 982(a).
[167] Code Sec. 982(d)(1).
[168] Code Sec. 982(b).

¶170.04

Major world economies with effective* documentation rules

1994-1997	1998-2000	2001-2002	2003-2004	2005-2009
US	US	US	US	US
Australia	Australia	Australia	Australia	Australia
France	France	France	France	France
Mexico	Mexico	Mexico	Mexico	Mexico
Brazil	Brazil	Brazil	Brazil	Brazil
	Canada	Canada	Canada	Canada
	South Korea	South Korea	South Korea	South Korea
	United Kingdom	United Kingdom	United Kingdom	United Kingdom
	Denmark	Denmark	Denmark	Denmark
	Venezuela	Venezuela	Venezuela	Venezuela
	South Africa	South Africa	South Africa	South Africa
	Germany	Germany	Germany	Germany
	Belgium	Belgium	Belgium	Belgium
		Japan	Japan	Japan
		Poland	Poland	Poland
		Kazakhstan	Kazakhstan	Kazakhstan
		India	India	India
		Portugal	Portugal	Portugal
		Argentina	Argentina	Argentina
		Colombia	Colombia	Colombia
		Netherlands	Netherlands	Netherlands
		Thailand	Thailand	Thailand
			Malaysia	Malaysia
			Indonesia	Indonesia
			Norway	Norway
			New Zealand	New Zealand
			Peru	Peru
			Spain	Spain
			Taiwan	Taiwan
			Hungary	Hungary
			Lithuania	Lithuania
				Ecuador
				Vietnam
				Singapore
				Sweden
				Israel
				Finland
				Estonia
				Romania
				Turkey
				Greece
				Slovak Republic
				China
				Uruguay
				Austria
				Italy

* Effective indicates that either the country has specific legislation or regulations requiring transfer pricing documentation or other guidance strongly suggests transfer pricing documentation should be in place.

¶170.04

¶ 180 The Global Approach to Transfer Pricing

Following U.S. efforts to improve transfer pricing compliance beginning in the early 1990s, other countries began to address transfer pricing issues. Concerns regarding revenue loss encouraged other countries to adopt transfer pricing rules including penalties and documentation requirements. Over 40 countries have now enacted their own documentation rules, including Argentina, Australia, Brazil, Canada, China, Colombia, France, Germany, Hungary, India, Korea, Malaysia, Mexico, Netherlands, New Zealand, the United Kingdom, and Venezuela. These countries also impose penalties on transfer pricing adjustments, which can significantly increase taxpayers' liability.[169]

Many countries, including Australia, Canada, China, Denmark, India, and United Kingdom have recently increased or announced that they would soon increase focus in the area of transfer pricing.[170]

For a number of years, the European Union Joint Transfer Pricing Forum ("EU JTPF") has been developing different approaches to taxpayers' compliance with the transfer pricing rules and regulations. In October 2005, the European Commission adopted the Code of Conduct for Transfer Pricing Documentation recommending to the EU member states to use European Transfer Pricing Documentation concept. The idea is to standardize the transfer pricing documentation and decrease compliance time and cost for both the taxpayer and the EU member countries' governments. While the Code of Conduct is not binding on the EU Member States and their tax administrations, and it can take considerable time for the EU Member States to agree to the concept and actually incorporate it in domestic legislation, the trend to standardize transfer pricing documentation requirements among 25 member countries clearly shows that transfer pricing has became a global area for both the governments and taxpayers.

The idea of a single transfer pricing documentation that would satisfy documentation requirements of several countries where the taxpayer has related entities is not new. It was attempted before EU JTPF by Pacific Association of Tax Administrations ("PATA"), an association of United States, Australia, Japan and Canada. Although in practice the PATA project is not working, the idea itself is still alive and there is more coordination between the tax authorities of the respective countries in the transfer pricing area.

In recent years, governments have been involved in information exchange programs on the basis of the exchange of information article found in bilateral tax treaties (Article 26, Exchange of Information and Administrative Assistance, U.S. Model Income Tax Convention). In 2004, the tax agencies of four countries—

---

[169] *See* Ernst & Young, Transfer pricing global reference guide (2009), *available at http://www.ey.com/Publication/vwLUAssets/2009_Transfer_Pricing_Global_Reference_Guide/$FILE/2009_Transfer_pricing_global_reference_guide.pdf* (last visited on August 3, 2009).

[170] *See*, e.g., "ATO to Boost Audits, Records Reviews that Target Small, Medium-Sized Companies," 14 *Tax*

Mgmt. Transfer Pricing Rep. 408 (Sept. 14, 2005); Guo Shui Han [2005] 239 (Circular 239 (issued by the State Administration of Taxation (SAT) of China on March 29, 2005; "Parliament Passes Bill Creating Penalties, Information and Documentation Requirements (Denmark)," 14 *Tax Mgmt. Transfer Pricing Rep.* 52 (May 25, 2005)); Ackerman et al., "US Government Continues to Increase Focus on Transfer Pricing," *Practical U.S. /International Tax Strategies*, Volume 13, Number 7 (April 15, 2009).

Australia, Canada, the United States and the United Kingdom—agreed to the formation of the Joint International Tax Shelter Information Center ("JITSIC") to "supplement the ongoing work of tax administrations in identifying and curbing abusive tax avoidance transactions, arrangements, and schemes."[171]

In 2009, the objectives of JITSIC were expanded to include collaboration on transfer pricing compliance.[172]

The OECD (Organisation for Economic Co-Operation and Development) has also been very active recently analyzing complex transfer pricing issues[173] and creating consensus among its members on how to address these issues. The most significant and most recent examples are the public discussion draft on business restructurings issued in 2008[174] and the proposed revision of chapters I to III of the transfer pricing guidelines issued in 2009.[175]

The result of the above global enforcement environment makes transfer pricing one of the primary areas for multinational enterprises with taxpayers designating more and more time and resources to adequately address transfer pricing planning, compliance, and audits by tax authorities. The tax authorities more often are engaged in transfer pricing related discussions with their counterparts in foreign jurisdictions.

One example of this growing coordination between governments is the application of advance pricing agreements ("APAs"). As of the end of 2009, there were 352 cases in inventory in the U.S., of which 282 involved bilateral APAs.[176] In addition, the IRS is expected to coordinate simultaneous exams with foreign countries.[177]

As a consequence of increased government enforcement, taxpayers are no longer able to ignore transfer pricing—it is generally not a case of whether their transfer pricing will be examined, but rather when it will be examined.

The United Nations ("UN") has also been engaged in transfer pricing discussions and developing of a manual of transfer pricing guidance, mostly from the perspective of developing nations. The UN published in 1980 the "United Nations Model Double Taxation Convention between Developed and Developing Countries," (revised in 2001) which has become the nucleus of the UN thinking on the matter.[178]

---

[171] "Joint International Tax Shelter Information Centre, Memorandum of Understanding," available at: *http://www.irs.gov/pub/irs-utl/jitsic-finalmou.pdf* (last visited on August 6, 2009).

[172] "Tax Enforcement Increased Information Sharing Among Tax Authorities Presenting New Challenges for Multinational Companies," *Daily Tax Report* (Feb. 18, 2009).

[173] *See* Chapter 14 for a detailed discussion of the OECD transfer pricing guidelines.

[174] "Transfer Pricing Aspects of Business Restructuring: Discussion Draft for Public Comment 19 September 2008 to 19 February 2009," OECD (Sept. 19, 2008). The OECD approved the 2010 revision of the Transfer Pricing Guidelines on July 22, 2010. The revision also introduces a new chapter on business restructuring, Chapter IX. *See http://www.oecd.org.*

[175] "Proposed Revision of Chapters I-III of the Transfer Pricing Guidelines 9 September 2009 to 9 January 2010," OECD (Sept. 9, 2009). The OECD approved the 2010 revision of the Transfer Pricing Guidelines on July 22, 2010. *See http://www.oecd.org.*

[176] Announcement 2010-21, 2010-15 IRB, Table 1 (4/12/10).

[177] Korb Says and Jeremiah Coder, "IRS Looking at Joint International Exams," 2008 *Tax Notes Today* 134-1 (July 11, 2008); Molly Moses, Tamu N. Wright, Kevin Bell, and Rita McWilliams, "Heightened Scrutiny Continues Worldwide in 2010; U.S. Official Says Simultaneous Audits 'On the Doorstep'," 18 *Tax Mgmt. Transfer Pricing Rep.* 943 (January 14, 2010).

[178] "United Nations Model Double Taxation Convention between Developed and Developing Countries," Department of Economic & Social Affairs, United Nations, New York, 2001.

¶ 190 Formulary Apportionment System of Transfer Pricing

Tax practitioners have long seen the U.S. corporate tax system as overly complicated and inefficient. There is also a perpetual perception that multinational corporations avoid paying their "fair share" of taxes by reducing their U.S. income through ingenious mechanisms, such as inaccurate transfer pricing. Accordingly, there has been vocal support from certain academics in recent years for the adoption of a formulary apportionment system of transfer pricing to replace the almost worldwide-recognized arm's length standard.[179]

Formulary apportionment was inspired by the U.S. state tax system, which allocates income among states based on relatively simple formulas usually based on property, payroll and sales. Under the proposed formulary apportionment system, the corporate worldwide net income before taxes would be calculated and apportioned between different countries based on a pre-established formula, for example, the share of worldwide sales to third parties.[180]

Supporters of the formulary apportionment system stress that its adoption would bring the following benefits:[181]

- Simplification and reduced cost of compliance

- Reduction of incentives to transfer income abroad

Many transfer pricing experts, however, disagree with these arguments and believe that the formulary apportionment systems "do not provide a satisfactory response to the problems stemming from the arm's-length principle that they are supposed to resolve—namely, ease of compliance and fairness."[182]

The replacement of the arm's length standard and the adoption of the formulary apportionment system could entail serious consequences for taxpayers and the tax administration. A list of objections to the adoption of an apportionment system includes:[183]

- It would signify a break with a long standing understanding of transfer pricing based on the adoption of the arm's length standard, which is at the core of most countries' transfer pricing legislation.

- Multinational corporations might adapt their practices accordingly, reducing the supposedly increased revenue for the U.S.

- Adopting a pre-established formula to allocate income (not based on facts and circumstances) could be considered arbitrary.

---

[179] *See, e.g.,* Kimberly A. Clausing and Reuven S. Avi-Yonah, "Reforming Corporate Taxation in a Global Economy: A Proposal to Adopt Formulary Apportionment," The Hamilton Project, The Brookings Institution (June 2007); Michael C. Durst, "A Statutory Proposal for Transfer Pricing Reform," 2007 TNT 113-47 (Jun. 12, 2007) and "It's Not Just Academic: The OECD Should Reevaluate Transfer Pricing Laws," 2010 *WTD* 11-14.

[180] Clausing and Avi-Yonah, 2007.

[181] *See, e.g.,* Joann M. Weiner, "Practical Aspects of Implementing Formulary Apportionment in the European Union," 8 *Fla. Tax Rev.*; Kimberly A. Clausing and Reuven S. Avi-Yonah, "Reforming Corporate Taxation in a Global Economy: A Proposal to Adopt Formulary Apportionment," p.12, The Hamilton Project.

[182] "OECD Officials Defend Arm's-Length Standard, Reject Formulary Approaches," *Tax Management Transfer Pricing*, (September 24, 2009).

[183] Clausing and Avi-Yonah, 2007 and Julie Roin, "Can the Income Tax be Saved? The Promise and Pitfalls of Adopting Worldwide Formulary Apportionment," 61 *Tax L. Rev.* 169 (New York University), Spring 2008.

- Existing or future intellectual property will impact future sales and therefore, is not related to current sales in any meaningful way (as mentioned before, current sales have been suggested as the basis for formulary apportionment). This means that the country that performs the R&D is not necessarily going to benefit from its profitability.[184]

¶ 192 Financial Accounting and Transfer Pricing

.01 FIN 48

On July 13, 2006, the Financial Accounting Standard Board released the final version of FASB Interpretation No. 48, Accounting for Uncertainty in Income Taxes—an Interpretation of FASB Statement No. 109 (FIN 48). FIN 48 explains how companies should deal with uncertain tax positions from an accounting reporting perspective. This includes a discussion on how to determine the minimum recognition threshold a tax position is required to meet before being recognized in the financial statement.

All tax positions (including those related to transfer pricing) are evaluated using a two-step process. The first step is recognition (or non-recognition) of a tax position: "an enterprise shall initially recognize the financial statement effects of a tax position when it is more likely than not, based on the technical merits, that the position [will] be sustained upon examination."[185] The second step, applied only if the position has been recognized, is measurement of the tax benefit. "A tax position that meets the more-likely-than not recognition threshold shall initially and subsequently be measured as the largest amount of tax benefit that is greater than 50 percent likely of being realized upon ultimate settlement with a taxing authority that has full knowledge of all relevant information."[186]

Given the increased IRS scrutiny of certain transfer pricing transactions (e.g., IP migrations, cost-sharing arrangements, etc.), transfer pricing has become increasingly relevant for FIN 48 purposes. From a transfer pricing perspective, FIN 48 raises a number of technical issues that need to be addressed by taxpayers and tax practitioners, such as the determination of the unit of account[187] that constitutes an individual tax position (e.g., aggregation or disaggregation of transactions, etc.), issues related to economic substance or business purpose which could affect recognition, etc.

.02 Sarbanes-Oxley Act of 2002

On July 25, 2002, Congress passed the "Sarbanes-Oxley Act of 2002" ("SOX"). Section 404 of SOX states that "[i]ssuers must (1) state the responsibility of management for establishing and maintaining an adequate internal control structure and procedures for financial reporting, and (2) contain an assessment as of the end of the most recent fiscal year of the effectiveness of the internal control

---

[184] A similar concern is discussed in "OECD Officials Defend Arm's-Length Standard, Reject Formulary Approaches," Tax Management Transfer Pricing, (September 24, 2009).

[185] Excerpt from FIN 48.

[186] Id.

[187] Paul A. DiSangro and John T. Hildy, "The Intersection Between FIN 48 and Transfer Pricing," *Global Tax Briefing*, Vol. 9, Issue No. 4 (June 20, 2007).

structure procedures of the issuer for financial reporting. The auditor must attest to and report on, management's assertion."[188]

Contrary to FIN 48, the emphasis of SOX 404 is on establishing and maintaining adequate internal controls. A lack of control could be suggested if, e.g., a transfer pricing study determines that the company should charge a certain price for a controlled transaction but the company charges a different amount. While such a situation would be undesirable under SOX 404, from a transfer pricing perspective, if, despite the (erroneous) study, the price charged turned out to be arm's length, there would be no consequences under FIN 48. The taxpayer would, however, probably need to be able to demonstrate that the transfer pricing study was wrong.[189]

---

[188] Sarbanes-Oxley Act of 2002, Pub. L. No. 107-204, 116 Stat. 745 (codified as amended in scattered sections of 15 U.S.C.).

[189] For a similar example and a more in depth explanation, see "Large Multinationals Taking Steps to Ensure Pricing Meets Requirements of Sarbanes-Oxley Act, Practitioners Say," 13 *Tax Mgmt. Transfer Pricing Rep.* 1091 (March 16, 2005).

Chapter 2

General Principles of Code Sec. 482

¶201 Overview—Structure of the Regulations under Code Sec. 482

This chapter discusses the general principles to be followed to determine and analyze intercompany transfer prices. It is essential to fully understand these principles in planning and defending the taxpayer's transfer pricing policies.

The regulations under Code Sec. 482 serve as a roadmap to taxpayers and the government in applying section 482 to various categories of transactions. The regulations start with an explanation of general concepts and principles governing transfer pricing (such as arm's length standard) and continue with specific rules and methods designed to address practical considerations when applying these rules to specific transactions.

Reg. §1.482-1 outlines general principles and guidelines to be followed under Code Sec. 482. Reg. §1.482-2 provides rules for the determination of taxable income of controlled taxpayers in specific situations, including controlled transactions involving loans or advances, services (for taxable years beginning before December 31, 2006), and leases of property. Regs. §§1.482-3 through 1.482-6 prescribe the rules for controlled transactions involving the transfer of tangible and intangible property. Temporary Reg. §1.482-7T sets forth the cost sharing provisions. Reg. §1.482-8 provides examples illustrating the application of the best method rule. Reg. §1.482-9 addresses rules to govern intercompany services for tax years beginning after December 31, 2006.

The regulations contain numerous examples to enhance the understanding of complex transfer pricing rules. Although the regulations do not provide answers to all questions, they should be the first stop for both the taxpayers and the IRS in the application of Code Sec. 482. To facilitate the reader's familiarity with the regulations and to increase comfort in applying the regulations' principles to actual transactions, this book incorporates a number of the examples from the regulations into the text.

Although the regulations have a logical structure, they do not list all methods in the most easily understood sequence. The following chart summarizes available transfer pricing methods (TPMs) contained in the current regulations:[1]

[1] The chart shows only those categories of transactions for which the regulations provide for a developed "inventory" of TPMs. The regulations do not list a set of TPMs for loans, leases, and cost sharing arrangements.

AVAILABLE TRANSFER PRICING METHOD (TPM) PER TYPE OF TRANSACTION*

Transfer of Tangible Property		Transfer of Intangible Property		Services	
CUP (Comparable Uncontrolled Price Method)[a]		CUT (Comparable Uncontrolled Transaction Method)[b]		CUSP (Comparable Uncontrolled Services Price Method)[c]	
RPM (Resale Price Method)[d]		x		GSM (Gross Services Margin Method)[e]	
Cost Plus (Cost Plus Method)[f]		x		CSPM (Cost of Services Plus Method)[g]	
CPM (Comparable Profits Method)[h] TNMM (Transactional Net Margin Method)[i]		CPM/TNMM Commensurate with income rules[j]		CPM	
PSM (Profit Split Method)[k]		PSM[l]		PSM[m]	
CPS (Comparable Profit Split Method)[n]	RPS (Residual Profit Split Method)[o]	CPS	RPS	CPS	RPS
x		x		SCM (Services Cost Method)[p]	
Unspecified Methods[q]		Unspecified Methods[r]		x	

*We have omitted alternative methods under the temporary cost-sharing rules, Reg. §1.482-7T.

---

[a] Reg. §1.482-3(b).
[b] Reg. §1.482-4(c).
[c] Reg. §1.482-9(c).
[d] Reg. §1.482-3(c).
[e] Reg. §1.482-9(d).
[f] Reg. §1.482-3(d).
[g] Reg. §1.482-9(e).
[h] Reg. §1.482-5.
[i] Paragraph 3.26 of Transfer Pricing Guidelines for Multinational Enterprises and Tax Administrations, Report of the Organisation for Economic Co-operation and Development Committee on Fiscal Affairs (1995).
[j] Reg. §1.482-4(a), (f)(2).
[k] Reg. §1.482-6.
[l] Reg. §1.482-6.
[m] Reg. §1.482-9(g).
[n] Reg. §1.482-6(c)(2).
[o] Reg. §1.482-6(c)(3).
[p] Reg. §1.482-9(b).
[q] Reg. §1.482-3(e).
[r] Reg. §1.482-4(d).

¶201

The governing principle under Code Sec. 482 is the globally-accepted arm's length standard. The arm's length standard is met if controlled taxpayers realize from their controlled transactions the results that would have been realized if uncontrolled taxpayers had engaged in the same transactions under the same circumstances.[2]

The "best method" rule provides that an arm's length result must be determined under the method that provides the "most reliable measure" of an arm's length result. No preset priority exists among specified and unspecified methods provided in the regulations. Instead, the applicability and reliability of each method must be evaluated using two factors: comparability and quality of data and assumptions.

Comparability is a guiding concept for evaluating relevant uncontrolled transactions. The regulations provide extensive guidance in determining the comparability of an uncontrolled transaction. Comparability must be assessed by comparing the functions performed and risks assumed by both controlled and uncontrolled taxpayers, contractual terms of controlled and uncontrolled transactions, economic conditions under which controlled and uncontrolled transactions are consummated, and property and services involved. The relative importance of any of these factors varies depending on the pricing method applied. Special consideration should be given to situations when the taxpayer engages in a market share strategy or a significant difference in geographical markets exists.

The arm's length range is the range of prices or profitability that are constructed from the results of the comparable uncontrolled transactions. If a material difference exists between the controlled transaction and the comparable uncontrolled transactions that cannot reliably be adjusted, the reliability of arm's length range must be enhanced by using statistical techniques such as the interquartile range. Aggregated and/or multiple-year data can also be used to form the range in certain occasions. However, an adjustment is still made on a single year basis, when the taxpayer's profits are outside the arm's length range over the multiple-year period. That is, the taxpayer's profits in each year under examination would generally be adjusted to the midpoint of the range for that year (to the median if using the comparable profits method).[3]

¶ 210 The Arm's Length Standard

Although the "arm's length standard" is not included in the text of Code Sec. 482, it has been included in the Treasury regulations since 1935, and has been the basis for the development of all transfer pricing regulations since that time. The arm's length standard requires that controlled taxpayers realize the same results from their controlled transactions as would have been realized if uncontrolled taxpayers had engaged in the same transactions under the same circumstances.[4] The arm's length standard is, in some measure, a fiction, in that it attempts to

---

[2] Reg. § 1.482-1(b)(1); *See also* paragraph 1.7 of Transfer Pricing Guidelines for Multinational Enterprises and Tax Administrations, Report of the Organisation for Economic Co-operation and Development Committee on Fiscal Affairs (1995).

[3] Reg. § 1.482-1(e)(3).

[4] Reg. § 1.482-1(b)(1).

measure the value of a transaction "as if" the parties had dealt with each other in an unrelated third party transaction. The arm's length standard also ignores certain efficiencies and economies of scale from operating related businesses that would not exist if the parties were not related.[5]

The arm's length standard first appeared in the 1935 regulations under section 45, predecessor of Code Sec. 482.[6] In 1934, the League of Nations report suggested that the tax authorities "should seek to approximate the results that would have obtained if the entities had been unrelated and had been dealing with one another at arm's length."[7] The report specifically rejected a model of "fractional" or "formulary" apportionment (also known as a "unitary" method), a different standard that is contrasted with the arm's length standard.[8]

The current Code Sec. 482 regulations modified the explanation of the arm's length standard, suggesting that a reliable arm's length result can be determined by "reference to the results of comparable transactions." By contrast, under the 1993 temporary regulations, the arm's length standard was satisfied only if the results of a controlled transaction were consistent with the results of a comparable transaction between uncontrolled taxpayers.[9] The consistency requirement was considered too rigid. This difference in approach is significant and has implications throughout the regulations because it recognizes that:

1. In most cases identical transactions between unrelated parties will not be available; and

2. It is appropriate to consider uncontrolled transactions that are comparable rather than identical.

One example of the application of the arm's length standard can be found in the description of the CUP method, which provides that, subject to the best method rule, an "inexact" comparable may be productively used and relied on. This

---

[5] *See* Higinbotham & Levey, "When Arm's Length Isn't Really Arm's Length: Problems in Application at the Arm's Length Standard," (1998) Vol. 7, no. 6 *Tax Management Transfer Pricing Report* 243-52.

[6] Art. 45-1(c) of Reg. 86 (1935) (Revenue Act of 1934).

[7] For a historical perspective of arm's length standard and unitary method, *see* Stanley I. Langbein, "The Unitary Method and the Myth of Arm's Length," 30 *Tax Notes* 625, 631-638 (Feb. 17, 1986); Reuven S. Avi-Yonah, "The Rise and Fall of Arm's Length: A Study in the Evolution of U.S. International Taxation," 15 *Va. Tax Rev.* 89 (1995); Brian D. Lepard, "Is the United States Obligated to Drive on the Right? A Multidisciplinary Inquiry into the Normative Authority of Contemporary International Law Using the Arm's Length Standard as a Case Study," 10 *Duke J. Comp. & Int'l L.* 43 (1999); John Turro, "The Battle Over Arm's Length and Formulary Apportionment," 65 *Tax Notes* 1595 (Dec. 26, 1994); Benjamin F. Miller, "None Are so Blind as Those Who Will Not See," 66 *Tax Notes* 1023 (Feb. 13, 1995); Michael C. Durst & Robert E. Culbertson, "Clearing Away the Sand: Retrospective Methods and Prospective Documentation in Transfer Pricing Today," 57 *Tax L. Rev.* 37 (2003).

[8] For more discussion on the formulary apportionment and arm's length method, *see*, e.g., William J. Wilkins &

Kenneth W. Gideon, "Memorandum To Congress: You Wouldn't Like Worldwide Formula Apportionment," 94 TNT 238-46 (Dec. 5, 1994) (as the title suggests, the authors argue against adopting a worldwide formulary apportionment); *see also* "Dorgan Tells Treasury To Reject OECD Draft On Transfer Pricing," 94 TNT 192-50 (Sep. 16, 1994) (the text of the letter by Sen. Byron L. Dorgan, D-N.D. to the Secretary of Treasury). For an academic proposal to implement the formulary apportionment system, *see*, e.g., Kimberly A. Clausing and Reuven S. Avi-Yonah, "Reforming Corporate Taxation in a Global Economy: A Proposal to Adopt Formulary Apportionment," The Hamilton Project, The Brookings Institution (June 2007); Michael C. Durst, "A Statutory Proposal for Transfer Pricing Reform," 2007 TNT 113-47 (Jun. 12, 2007) and "It's Not Just Academic: The OECD Should Reevaluate Transfer Pricing Laws," 2010 *WTD* 11-14. For a critique of the Brookings Institution's Hamilton Project from an academic perspective, *see*, e.g., Julie Roin, "Can the Income Tax Be Saved? The Promise and Pitfalls of Adopting Worldwide Formulary Apportionment," 61 *Tax L. Rev.* 169, New York University (Spring 2008). Chapter 1 also discusses formulary apportionment and some of its implications for transfer pricing.

[9] Temp. Reg. § 1.482-1T(b)(1) (1993).

relaxation and redefinition of the arm's length standard should also create more balance with multinational corporations that must apply the standards of Code Sec. 482 in the United States, yet rely on the standards set forth by the OECD in other countries.[10]

¶ 220 The Best Method Rule

.01 Description

Transfer prices must be determined in conformance with the best method rule. The best method is the transfer pricing methodology ("TPM") that, under the facts and circumstances, provides "the most reliable measure" of an arm's length result.[11] No strict priority of methods exists and no method will be considered inherently more reliable than others.[12] The best method rule provides not only that more than one method may be appropriate, but that a method may be applied in more than one way. The predecessor to the current best method rule used the terminology "most accurate measure."[13] Practically speaking, this difference in language provides more flexibility—for both taxpayers and the IRS. It also recognizes that the choice of method will often turn on the reliability of the data. Treasury Reg. § 1.482-8 contains nine examples illustrating the application of a best method analysis. Below is an example demonstrating the determination process and under what circumstances the residual profit split method would be preferred to other methods.

Reg § 1.482-8, Ex.8

> (i) USC is a U.S. company that develops, manufactures and sells communications equipment. EC is the European subsidiary of USC. EC is an established company that carries out extensive research and development activities and develops, manufactures and sells communications equipment in Europe. There are extensive transactions between USC and EC. USC licenses valuable technology it has developed to EC for use in the European market but EC also licenses valuable technology it has developed to USC. Each company uses components manufactured by the other in some of its products and purchases products from the other for resale in its own market.

> (ii) Detailed accounting information is available for both USC and EC and adjustments can be made to achieve a high degree of consistency in accounting practices between them. Relatively reliable allocations of costs, income and assets can be made between the business activities that are related to the controlled transactions and those that are not. Relevant marketing and research and development expenditures can be identified and reasonable estimates of the useful life of the related intangibles are available so that the capitalized value of the intangible development expenses of USC and EC can be calculated. In this case there is no reason to believe that the relative value of these capitalized expenses is substantially different from the relative value of the intangible property of USC and EC. Furthermore, comparables are identified that could be

---

[10] *See*, e.g., "Organisation for Economic Co-operation and Development Committee on Fiscal Affairs Report," Transfer Pricing Guidelines for Multinational Enterprises and Tax Administrators, Discussion Draft of Part 1: Principles and Methods, released July 8, 1994, *see* 129 *Daily Tax Report* G-1 (July 8, 1994) and "Proposed Revision of Chapters I-III of the Transfer Pricing Guidelines 9 September 2009 to 9 January 2010," OECD (Sept. 9, 2009).

The OECD approved the 2010 revision of the Transfer Pricing Guidelines on July 22, 2010. The revision also introduces a new chapter on business restructuring, Chapter IX. *See http://www.oecd.org.*

[11] Reg. § 1.482-1(c).

[12] Reg. § 1.482-1(c)(1).

[13] Temp. Reg. § 1.482-1T(b)(2)(iii) (1993).

used to estimate a market return for the routine contributions of USC and EC. based on these facts, the residual profit split could provide a reliable measure of an arm's length result.

(iii) There are no uncontrolled transactions involving property that is sufficiently comparable to much of the tangible and intangible property transferred between USC and EC to permit use of the comparable uncontrolled price method or the comparable uncontrolled transaction method. Uncontrolled companies are identified in Europe and the United States that perform somewhat similar activities to USC and EC; however, the activities of none of these companies are as complex as those of USC and EC and they do not use similar levels of highly valuable intangible property that they have developed themselves. Under these circumstances, the uncontrolled companies may be useful in determining a market return for the routine contributions of USC and EC, but that return would not reflect the value of the intangible property employed by USC and EC. Thus, none of the uncontrolled companies is sufficiently similar so that reliable results would be obtained using the resale price, cost plus, or comparable profits methods. Moreover, no uncontrolled companies can be identified that engaged in sufficiently similar activities and transactions with each other to employ the comparable profit split method.

(iv) Given the difficulties in applying the other methods, the reliability of the internal data on USC and EC, and the fact that acceptable comparables are available for deriving a market' return for the routine contributions of USC and EC, the residual profit split method is likely to provide the most reliable measure of an arm's length result in this case.[14]

.02 Application

To determine which TPM satisfies the best method rule, the taxpayer must consider comparability and quality of the data and assumptions.[15] The relative reliability of a method based on the results of transactions between unrelated parties depends on the degree of comparability between the controlled transaction or taxpayers and the uncontrolled comparables, taking into account the comparability factors[16] and after making adjustments for differences.[17]

In evaluating the comparability of uncontrolled transactions, taxpayers must consider the following factors:

1. Functions of the parties;

2. Contractual terms;

3. Assignment of risks;

4. Economic conditions; and

5. Property provided and services rendered by either party.

As the degree of comparability increases, the number and extent of potential differences that could render the analysis inaccurate is reduced. If adjustments are made to increase the degree of comparability, the number, magnitude, and reliability of those adjustments will affect the reliability of the results of the analysis. Therefore, the analysis under the comparable uncontrolled price method will

---

[14] Reg. § 1.482-8, Ex. 8.
[15] Reg. § 1.482-1(c)(2).

[16] Reg. § 1.482-1(d)(3) (factors for determining comparability).
[17] Reg. § 1.482-1(d)(2) (standard of comparability).

generally be more reliable than analyses obtained under other methods if the analysis is based on closely comparable uncontrolled transactions, because such an analysis can be expected to achieve a higher degree of comparability and be susceptible to fewer differences than analyses under other methods. An analysis will be relatively less reliable, however, as the uncontrolled transactions become less comparable to the controlled transaction.

To ascertain the quality of the data and assumptions utilized, the following factors must be considered:

1. Completeness and accuracy of the data (an analysis will be relatively more reliable as the completeness and accuracy of the data increases);

2. Reliability of the assumptions (all methods rely on certain assumptions, and the reliability of the results derived from a method depends on the soundness of such assumptions); and

3. Sensitivity of the results to deficiencies in the data and assumptions employed (deficiencies in the data used or assumptions made may have a greater effect on some methods than others).

Where no method clearly stands out as the best method, consistency in results of a number of methods may support the use of a particular method.[18] In such instances, the arm's length range is determined by the use of more than one method.[19] Accordingly, it may be beneficial for taxpayers to simulate their overall performance and particular transactions under a number of the prescribed methods to establish the appropriate transfer price, especially if there is a desire to maintain continuity with the method used in the foreign jurisdiction.[20]

.03 Limitations

The best method rule has its limitations, however. The increased flexibility and exercise of judgment under the rule could lead to an increased number of disputes with the IRS over issues such as:

1. What is the best method;

2. Which data is most accurate;

3. What results are most reliable;

4. What adjustments are material;

5. What level of adjustments are required to obviate the use of interquartiles; and

6. How objective are the judgments exercised by taxpayers.

Accordingly, taxpayers should carefully document the basis for their selection of a pricing method, to avoid such potential disputes and to defend their position against the IRS.

---

[18] Reg. § 1.482-1(c)(2)(iii).

[19] Reg. § 1.482-1(c)(2)(iii); Reg. § 1.482-1(e)(2)(i).

[20] *See* Levey & Borraccia, "Draft Amendments to Canadian Transfer Pricing Rules Tighten Taxpayer's Compliance Burden," 8 *J. of Int'l Tax'n* 498 (Nov. 1997).

¶ 230 Comparability

.01 In General

The regulations provide that an arm's length result is evaluated by comparing the results of the controlled transactions to the result of an uncontrolled transaction under similar circumstances. Comparability exists if transactions and circumstances are "sufficiently similar that it provides a reliable measure of an arm's length result."[21] Any material differences should be adjusted to preserve or enhance the reliability of the results.

.02 "Inexact Comparables"

The regulations allow the use of "inexact" comparables under all methods.[22] This increases the potential applicability of the CUP, resale price or cost plus methods because, although exactly comparable third-party transactions are rare, inexact comparables, which can be properly adjusted, are widely available.

.03 Adjustments

If material differences exist between the controlled transactions, adjustments must be made if the adjustment would improve the reliability of the results.[23] If adjustments for material differences cannot be made, the uncontrolled transaction may still be used but the reliability of the analysis will be reduced. When adjustments to account for material differences between controlled and comparable transactions cannot reliably be made, the reliability of the arm's length range constructed by the results of these inexact comparables must be enhanced by using statistical techniques such as the interquartile range.[24]

The following example illustrates a situation when an adjustment is required to account for differences in volume:

Reg. § 1.482-1(d)(3)(iii)(C), Ex.2

> (i) FS manufactures product XX and sells that product to its parent corporation, P. FS also sells product XX to uncontrolled taxpayers at a price of $100 per unit. Except for the volume of each transaction, the sales to P and to uncontrolled taxpayers take place under substantially the same economic conditions and contractual terms. In uncontrolled transactions, FS offers a 2% discount for quantities of 20 per order, and a 5% discount for quantities of 100 per order. If P purchases product XX in quantities of 60 per order, in the absence of other reliable information, it may reasonably be concluded that the arm's length price to P would be $100, less a discount of 3.5%.

> (ii) If P purchases product XX in quantities of 1,000 per order, a reliable estimate of appropriate volume discount must be based on proper economic or statistical analysis, not necessarily a linear extrapolation from the 2% and 5% catalog discounts applicable to sales of 20 and 100 units, respectively.[25]

---

[21] Reg. § 1.482-1(d)(2).
[22] *Id.*
[23] *Id.*

[24] Reg. § 1.482-1(e)(2)(iii)(C).
[25] Reg. § 1.482-1(d)(3)(iii)(C), Ex. 2.

.04 Factors

All facts and circumstances that could affect prices or profits in arm's length dealings are taken into account when evaluating comparability.[26] Consistent with the renewed emphasis on arm's length transactional analysis, the regulations recognize that the relative importance of any factor taken into account to evaluate comparability of transactions will depend on the pricing method being applied.[27] For instance, when the resale price method, the cost plus method, or the CPM is used, functional comparability is most important factor, and product comparability is a lesser priority than under the CUP.[28]

Comparability Factors used in Functional Analysis	
Transactional Transfer Pricing Methods	**Profit-based Transfer Pricing Methods**
• Product features	• Functions performed
• Nature of performed services	• Assets employed
• Geographic market differences	• Geographic market differences
• Risks assumed	• Risks assumed
• Business strategy	• Accounting methods
	• Business experience
	• Business strategy
	• Management efficiency

The general factors to be considered in evaluating comparability include:

Functional Analysis. Functional analysis is the most critical aspect of any transfer pricing determination. It is the engine that drives the project. It determines the set of comparable companies and may lead to necessary adjustments to bring a taxpayer's transfer pricing in line with economic and empirical data and distinguish the taxpayer's specific business from the stereotype often offered by IRS agents on audit. Functional analysis is not a method, but rather an approach to obtaining the most detailed understanding of the functions performed, risks incurred, assets owned, and intangibles used by the respective parties to the intercompany transaction.[29]

A functional analysis generally involves an evaluation of the functions of the parties, the capital invested, labor and economic risk incurred, and assets used, that give rise to profits of the taxpayer. In short, it tells the story of how a company earns its profit. In a transfer pricing audit, the IRS would evaluate the functions

[26] Reg. § 1.482-1(d)(1).
[27] Id.
[28] See, e.g., Reg. § 1.482-3(b)(2)(ii)(A); Reg. § 1.482-3(c)(3)(ii); Reg. § 1.482-3(d)(3)(ii); Reg. § 1.482-5(c)(2).
[29] Reg. § 1.482-1(d)(3)(i).

¶230.04

performed by each member of the corporate group to determine, among other things, the following:

- The nature of work or services performed;
- The precise nature of any economically significant functions;
- The identities of the economic risks assumed and the individual, department, or division that assumed each risk;
- The economic value of each function performed by each party;
- The identity of each intangible employed; and
- The identity of the developer of each intangible and the royalty paid for its use.

The effectiveness of the functional analysis depends on understanding the economic significance of the functions performed by each party. Proper understanding may require the advice of an outside economist or industry specialist, and a liaison with the taxpayer to access key people in the taxpayer's operations, in coordination with a competent tax practitioner.

The following functions need to be accounted for to determine the comparability of two transactions:

- Research and development;
- Product design and engineering;
- Manufacturing, production and process engineering;
- Product fabrication, extraction and assembly;
- Purchasing and materials management;
- Marketing and distribution functions including management, warranty administration and advertising;
- Transportation and warehousing;
- Managerial, legal, accounting, finance, credit and collection, training, and personnel management service.

In practice, the functional and risk analyses will require the cooperation of individuals outside of the corporate tax department, such as financial, marketing, operations, and technical personnel. A comprehensive transfer pricing study frequently involves interviews with individuals throughout an organization, as well as site tours and product demonstrations.

Contractual Terms. The specific terms of a contract between related parties to a transaction must be compared with contractual terms between unrelated parties for transactions involving substantially similar products.[30] Contractual comparability will generally be satisfied if the taxpayer relies on an internal comparable transaction (i.e., a transaction between the taxpayer and an unrelated party), rather than an external transaction (i.e., a transaction between two unrelated parties), largely because the information derived from public sources, generally Form 10-K filings, often does not contain sufficient detail about contractual relationships.

---

[30] Reg. § 1.482-1(d)(3)(ii).

If a comparable internal transaction exists, the contractual terms that must be reviewed include:

- Form of consideration paid;
- Sales or purchase volume;
- Scope and terms of warranty;
- Rights to updates, revisions modifications;
- Duration of license, contract, and termination or re-negotiation rights;
- Collateral transactions or ongoing business relationships between buyer and seller;
- Extension of credit and payment terms.

Taxpayers should be able to create a number of basic assumptions of the relevant contractual terms of their own agreements that are consistent with the economic substance or actual conduct of the taxpayer. The District Director may impute contractual terms that are consistent with the economic substance of the underlying transaction in the absence of such terms or when such terms are inconsistent with the economic substance.

The contractual terms, including the consequent allocation of risks agreed to in writing before the transactions are entered into, will be respected if such terms are consistent with the economic substance of the underlying transactions. In evaluating economic substance, greatest weight will be given to the actual conduct of the parties, and the respective legal rights of the parties.[31] If the contractual terms are inconsistent with the economic substance of the underlying transaction, the District Director may disregard such terms and impute terms that are consistent with the economic substance of the transaction.

Absent a written agreement, the District Director may impute a contractual agreement between the controlled taxpayers consistent with the economic substance of the transaction. In determining the economic substance of the transaction, greatest weight will be given to the actual conduct of the parties and their respective legal rights.[32] For example, if, without a written agreement, a controlled taxpayer operates at full capacity and regularly sells all of its output to another member of its controlled group, the District Director may impute a purchasing contract from the course of conduct of the controlled taxpayers, and determine that the producer bears little risk that the buyer will fail to purchase its full output. Further, if an established industry convention or usage of trade assigns a risk or resolves an issue, that convention or usage will be followed if the conduct of the taxpayers is consistent with it.[33] For example, unless otherwise agreed, payment generally is due at the time and place at which the buyer is to receive goods.[34] The below example provides for a situation when contractual terms are imputed from economic substance of underlying transactions.

---

[31] *See*, e.g., Reg. § 1.482-4(f)(3) (Ownership of intangible property).
[32] *Id.*

[33] *See* UCC 1-303.
[34] *See* UCC 2-310(a).

¶230.04

Reg. § 1.482-1 (d) (3) (ii) (C), Ex.3

(i) FP, a foreign producer of wristwatches, is the registered holder of the YY trademark in the United States and in other countries worldwide. In year 1, FP enters the United States market by selling YY wristwatches to its newly organized United States subsidiary, USSub, for distribution in the United States market. USSub pays FP a fixed price per wristwatch. USSub and FP undertake, without separate compensation, marketing activities to establish the YY trademark in the United States market. Unrelated foreign producers of trademarked wristwatches and their authorized United States distributors respectively undertake similar marketing activities in independent arrangements involving distribution of trademarked wristwatches in the United States market. In years 1 through 6, USSub markets and sells YY wristwatches in the United States. Further, in years 1 through 6, USSub undertakes incremental marketing activities in addition to the activities similar to those observed in the independent distribution transactions in the United States market. FP does not directly or indirectly compensate USSub for performing these incremental activities during years 1 through 6. Assume that, aside from these incremental activities, and after any adjustments are made to improve the reliability of the comparison, the price paid per wristwatch by the independent, authorized distributors of wristwatches would provide the most reliable measure of the arm's length price paid per YY wristwatch by USSub.

(ii) By year 7, the wristwatches with the YY trademark generate a premium return in the United States market, as compared to wristwatches marketed by the independent distributors. In year 7, substantially all the premium return from the YY trademark in the United States market is attributed to FP, for example through an increase in the price paid per watch by USSub, or by some other means.

(iii) In determining whether an allocation of income is appropriate in year 7, the Commissioner may consider the economic substance of the arrangements between USSub and FP, and the parties' course of conduct throughout their relationship. Based on this analysis, the Commissioner determines that it is unlikely that, *ex ante*, an uncontrolled taxpayer operating at arm's length would engage in the incremental marketing activities to develop or enhance intangible property owned by another party unless it received contemporaneous compensation or otherwise had a reasonable anticipation of receiving a future benefit from those activities. In this case, USSub's undertaking the incremental marketing activities in years 1 through 6 is a course of conduct that is inconsistent with the parties' attribution to FP in year 7 of substantially all the premium return from the enhanced YY trademark in the United States market. Therefore, the Commissioner may impute one or more agreements between USSub and FP, consistent with the economic substance of their course of conduct, which would afford USSub an appropriate portion of the premium return from the YY trademark wristwatches. For example, the Commissioner may impute a separate services agreement that affords USSub contingent-payment compensation for its incremental marketing activities in years 1 through 6, which benefited FP by contributing to the value of the trademark owned by FP. In the alternative, the Commissioner may impute a long-term, exclusive agreement to exploit the YY trademark in the United States that allows USSub to benefit from the incremental marketing activities it performed. As another alternative, the Commissioner may require FP to compensate USSub for terminating USSub's imputed long-term, exclusive agreement to exploit the YY trademark in the United States, an agreement that USSub made more valuable at its own expense and risk. The taxpayer may present additional facts that could indicate which of these or other alternative agreements best reflects the economic substance of the underlying

¶230.04

transactions, consistent with the parties' course of conduct in the particular case.[35]

Risk Analysis. The identification of risks assumed and adjustments to the transfer price to reflect risk differentials is also an important component of a comparability analysis. The underlying theory concerning risk is that entities with higher levels of risk should generally earn higher rates of return. Thus, the balance between risk and reward reflects a fundamental concept of transfer pricing analysis.

Risks commonly considered include, but are not limited to:

- Market risks, including fluctuations in cost, demand, pricing, and inventory levels;

- Risks associated with the success or failure of research and development activities;

- Financial risks, including fluctuations in foreign currency rates of exchange and interest rates;

- Credit and collection risks;

- Product liability risks; and

- General business risks related to the ownership of property, plant, and equipment.

Although the regulations do not detail methods for adjustments to account for specific risks, they place a heavy burden on the taxpayer to identify risks and provide a method to adjust the transfer price for these risks based on facts and circumstances.[36]

The assessment of risk begins with the identification of specific risks borne by each related party. Risks are typically categorized as demand related (e.g., market risk, inventory risk, price volatility of competing products), supply related (e.g., presence of technological change, volatility of costs, potential market exit or entry), or transactional (e.g., foreign exchange risks). Once the risks have been identified and ascribed to each of the related parties, the taxpayer should analyze the relative impact of each risk category on profitability. The taxpayer then should assess possible quantitative risk adjustments (e.g., hedging costs to mitigate foreign exchange risk) where profit split, comparable profits, or certain transactional pricing methods are employed.

To address risk, the regulations specify that the IRS may evaluate the allocation of risk based on the substance rather than the form of the risk borne by the controlled taxpayers. The regulations provide that the following facts are relevant in considering the economic substance of the transaction:

1. Whether the pattern of the taxpayer's conduct is consistent with the intended allocation of risk between controlled taxpayers;

2. Whether the controlled taxpayer's capacity to absorb large losses attributable to the risk is proportionate to the risk; and

---

[35] Reg. § 1.482-1(d)(3)(ii)(C), Ex. 3.

[36] Reg. § 1.482-1(d)(3)(iii).

¶230.04

3. Whether the controlled taxpayer exercises control over the business activities that directly influence the amount of income or loss to be realized.[37]

Reg. § 1.482-1(d)(3)(iii)(C), Ex. 1

FD, the wholly-owned foreign distributor of USM, a U.S. manufacturer, buys widgets from USM under a written contract. Widgets are a generic electronic appliance. Under the terms of the contract, FD must buy and take title to 20,000 widgets for each of the five years of the contract at a price of $ 10 per widget. The widgets will be sold under FD's label, and FD must finance any marketing strategies to promote sales in the foreign market. There are no rebate or buy back provisions. FD has adequate financial capacity to fund its obligations under the contract under any circumstances that could reasonably be expected to arise. In Years 1, 2 and 3, FD sold only 10,000 widgets at a price of $ 11 per unit. In Year 4, FD sold its entire inventory of widgets at a price of $ 25 per unit. Since the contractual terms allocating market risk were agreed to before the outcome of such risk was known or reasonably knowable, FD had the financial capacity to bear the market risk that it would be unable to sell all of the widgets it purchased currently, and its conduct was consistent over time, FD will be deemed to bear the risk.[38]

Reg. § 1.482-1(d)(3)(iii)(C), Ex. 2

The facts are the same as in Example 1, except that in Year 1 FD had only $100,000 in total capital, including loans. In subsequent years USM makes no additional contributions to the capital of FD, and FD is unable to obtain any capital through loans from an unrelated party. Nonetheless, USM continues to sell 20,000 widgets annually to FD under the terms of the contract, and USM extends credit to FD to enable it to finance the purchase. FD does not have the financial capacity in Years 1, 2 and 3 to finance the purchase of the widgets given that it could not sell most of the widgets it purchased during those years. Thus, notwithstanding the terms of the contract, USM and not FD assumed the market risk that a substantial portion of the widgets could not be sold, since in that event FD would not be able to pay USM for all of the widgets it purchased.[39]

Economic Conditions. A fourth significant factor is the economic conditions under which the controlled transactions are consummated.[40] Transactions occurring in two different markets may be comparable depending on the specific economic conditions of the two marketplaces.[41] Economists are often called on to analyze the markets to determine the level of comparability or the range of adjustments necessary to attain a reasonable level of comparability.

Potentially significant economic conditions include:

- The similarity of geographic markets;
- The relative size of each market, and the extent of the overall economic development in each market;
- The level of the market (e.g., wholesale, retail, etc.);
- The relevant market shares for the products, properties, or services transferred or provided;
- The location-specific costs of the factors of production and distribution;

---

[37] Reg. § 1.482-1(d)(3)(iii)(B).
[38] Reg. § 1.482-1(d)(3)(iii)(C), Ex. 1.
[39] Reg. § 1.482-1(d)(3)(iii)(C), Ex. 2.

[40] Reg. § 1.482-1(d)(3)(iv).
[41] Reg. § 1.482-1(d)(4)(ii).

- The extent of competition in each market with regard to the property or services under review;

- The economic condition of the particular industry, including whether the market is in contraction or expansion; and

- The alternatives realistically available to the buyer and seller.

Market Alternatives. Alternatives available to each of the controlled parties must be evaluated as part of the comparability assessment. Whichever party to the controlled transaction enjoys credible alternatives to the transaction under review (i.e., the choice to use other unrelated entities or to by-pass the related party by selling directly to the end-user), or has the least to lose by not participating in the transaction, should enjoy the bargaining advantage and a larger share of the profits.

The regulations also emphasize the presence or absence of competition in assessing market comparability because the degree of both price-based and non-price-based competition can significantly affect profits.[42] For example, providing greater service without a corresponding increase in price may be necessary in some markets to meet competition and gain market share. Greater competition within a market, generally reduces the level of profitability. Competition can be measured by examining industry concentration (i.e., the percentage of industry sales controlled by four of the eight largest suppliers), the presence of product differentiation, and entry barriers. Markets with few suppliers and high entry barriers are monopolistic, with incumbent firms enjoying higher-than-normal rates of return.

Although not mentioned in the regulations, the market characteristics of buyers, in addition to suppliers, should also be evaluated. If buyers are few, but large, then buyers may enjoy strong bargaining leverage, which would seemingly cause a reduction in the supplier's margins. When both buyers and sellers are monopolistic, however, the outcome is less certain.

The regulations' standard of comparability does not discuss a company's size. Size may be particularly important in applying comparable company pricing methods because it can be an important determinant of profitability among companies that otherwise may be comparable. For example, in industries characterized as possessing relatively high levels of operating leverage (i.e., a high degree of fixed costs relative to the total cost structure), the presence of scale economies often becomes a very important criterion of profitability. Thus, in certain industries, when sufficient volume is achieved to cover fixed costs, profit is earned more rapidly, as variable costs are relatively low. Also, economic theory suggests that smaller companies are more prone to profit declines in times of recession. In addition to firm size, other economic variables, such as industry sales growth, can be important.

---

[42] Reg. § 1.482-1(d)(3)(iv); Reg. § 1.482-1(d)(4)(i).

¶230.04

Comment: Documenting and affirmatively presenting comparability factors to the IRS can make the difference between success or failure in sustaining a transfer pricing policy at arm's length. The IRS is unlikely to have direct access to these critical factors, and absent documentation, may be unwilling to accept them as anything but hindsight argument.

Property and Services. The nature of the property and services must be also compared.[43] If technical services or special warranty considerations are provided for one transaction, but not the one to which the taxpayer is making a comparison, adjustments must be made for those services. Similarly, if property is being provided to assist with the production process, the value of that property, or its rental value, must be taken into account in analyzing the appropriate profit margin or cost-plus factor for the transaction. Most significant is whether intangibles are embedded in tangible property (or services) whereby the comparability of the embedded intangibles may be evaluated by analyzing the factors set forth under the rules for transfers of intangibles.[44]

.05 Adjustments

Once comparability has been initially analyzed, adjustments must be considered to account for differences between controlled and uncontrolled transactions.[45] Any adjustments must be reasonable in manner, have an ascertainable effect on the transaction under review, and be based on commercial practice, economic principles, or statistical analyses. Risk adjustments must meet the following criteria in order to be accepted by the IRS:

1. The adjustment for the risk is documented ("executed") before the results of the risk assumptions are known;

2. The taxpayer's conduct is consistent with its documentation; and

3. The adjustment is consistent for a reasonable period of time.

---

[43] Reg. § 1.482-1 (d) (3) (v).

[44] Reg. § 1.482-1 (d) (3) (v); *See also* Reg. § 1.482-4 (c) (2) (iii) (B) (1).

[45] Reg. § 1.482-1 (d) (2).

Common Section 482 Adjustments

- LIFO and FIFO inventory valuation adjustment
- Adjustment for amortization of intangibles
- Pension adjustment
- Working capital adjustments (e.g., accounts receivable, accounts payable, and inventory)
- Adjustments for different levels of resources employed
- Currency risk adjustments
- Business risk adjustments

.06 Special Circumstances: Market Penetration Strategies

The regulations provide guidelines on what types of market penetration strategies will be accepted by the IRS.[46] The regulations provide that increased marketing expenses on the setting of low prices in connection with a market penetration strategy may, for a limited (undefined) time, be considered at arm's length, provided that the strategy is reasonable, has economic substance, and is documented before the strategy is implemented.[47] Taxpayers executing a market penetration strategy should collect and retain whatever market and empirical data exist to support their strategy, including market proposals, budgets, or feasibility studies prepared internally or by outside consultants or analysts.

The regulations, however, limit the application of the market penetration strategy rule to when the taxpayer is entering a new market or is seeking to establish market share. The market share strategy rule may not be used when the taxpayer is seeking to maintain competitive levels.[48] The rationale for this limitation is briefly described in the preamble, which notes that if the taxpayer's competitors are also adjusting their prices to meet competition, the lower levels of profitability will be seen in the comparable company data. As a result, the regulations seem to limit the marketing strategy adjustment to a one-time adjustment at the initial stages of the business.

To take advantage of the market penetration strategy rule, a taxpayer's strategy must be comparable to the strategy that a similar company would pursue within the industry. That is, a controlled taxpayer must establish "that an uncontrolled taxpayer engaged in a comparable strategy under comparable circumstances for a comparable period of time."[49] This requirement can be satisfied by identifying an uncontrolled taxpayer in a different industry engaging in a market share strategy under comparable circumstances.[50] Although this requirement seems possible on its face, its practicalities are difficult at best because companies

---

[46] Reg. § 1.482-1(d)(4)(i).

[47] Reg. § 1.482-1(d)(4)(i).

[48] Reg. § 1.482-1(d)(4)(i). *See also* the preamble to the regulations under Code Sec. 482.

[49] Reg. § 1.482-1(d)(4)(i).

[50] The preamble to the regulations under Code Sec. 482 discussing Reg. § 1.482-(d)(4)(i).

¶230.06

are generally not privy to their competitors' market strategies and pricing. This further seems to place company-specific management and business strategies on an industry average level—a concept that taxpayers have variously criticized.

In addition, the controlled taxpayer must provide documentation that substantiates that:

1. The costs incurred to implement the market share strategy are borne by the controlled taxpayer that would obtain the future profits that result from the strategy;

2. There is a reasonable likelihood that the strategy will result in future profits that reflect an appropriate return in relation to the costs incurred to implement it;

3. The market share strategy is pursued only for a period of time that is reasonable, taking into consideration the industry and product in question; and

4. The market share strategy, the related costs and expected returns, and any agreement between the controlled taxpayers to share the related costs, were established before the strategy was implemented.[51]

.07 Special Circumstances: Different Geographic Markets

Uncontrolled comparables ordinarily should be derived from the geographic market in which the controlled taxpayer operates, because there may be significant differences in economic conditions in different markets. If information from the same market is not available, an uncontrolled comparable derived from a different geographic market may be considered if adjustments are made to account for differences between the two markets. If information permitting adjustments for these differences is not available, then information derived from uncontrolled comparables in the most similar market for which reliable data is available may be used, but the extent of these differences may affect the reliability of the method for purposes of the best method rule. For this purpose, a geographic market is any geographic area in which the economic conditions for the relevant product or service are substantially the same, and may include multiple countries, depending on the economic conditions.[52]

Reg. § 1.482-1(d)(4)(ii)(B)

> Manuco, a wholly-owned foreign subsidiary of P, a U.S. corporation, manufactures products in Country Z for sale to P. No uncontrolled transactions are located that would provide a reliable measure of the arm's length result under the comparable uncontrolled price method. The district director considers applying the cost plus method or the comparable profits method. Information on uncontrolled taxpayers performing comparable functions under comparable circumstances in the same geographic market is not available. Therefore, adjusted data from uncontrolled manufacturers in other markets may be considered in order to apply the cost plus method. In this case, comparable uncontrolled manufacturers are found in the United States. Accordingly, data from the comparable U.S. uncontrolled manufacturers, as adjusted to account for differences between the United States and Country Z's geographic market, is used to

---

[51] Reg. § 1.482-1(d)(4)(i).   [52] Reg. § 1.482-1(d)(4)(ii)(A).

test the arm's length price paid by P to Manuco. However, the use of such data may affect the reliability of the results for purposes of the best method rule. *See* Reg. § 1.482-1(c).[53]

.08 Special Circumstances: Location Savings

Location savings are the savings or other economic benefits generated by locating certain manufacturing or other functions in an offshore jurisdiction. This is generally an issue for U.S. multinationals manufacturing outside the United States. However, it also can be an issue for a U.S. affiliate of a foreign multinational that purchases products from such an offshore manufacturer directly, or through its foreign parent. The regulations provide that adjustments should be made to account for significant differences in costs attributable to the geographic markets.[54]

To prove that location savings should be recognized and a share of any location savings should be allocated to an offshore manufacturer, the taxpayer must show that the offshore manufacturer is in a position to bargain for that location savings. This requires that the offshore facility be shown to have some unique intangibles or other qualities that make it difficult to substitute another competing company at that location as an equally attractive substitute. In this case, the offshore facility is then in a position to bargain for a share of any location savings. Analysis of the facility's bargaining position can employ various economic tools, including certain game theory models used to analyze joint ventures and other arm's length transactions.

The regulations provide that the allocation of location savings must be consistent with the competitive positions of buyers and sellers in the market place. That is, if a U.S. company engages a controlled contract manufacturer to produce widgets in an offshore low-tax jurisdiction, location savings resulting from that arrangement do not necessarily accrue to the contract manufacturer. If other similarly qualified contract manufacturers compete in the same market, this competition might suppress the profitability of the controlled manufacturer and support a greater allocation of location savings to the U.S. company.[55] Consider the following example:

Reg. § 1.482-1(d)(4)(ii)(D), Ex.

Couture, a U.S. apparel design corporation, contracts with Sewco, its wholly owned Country Y subsidiary, to manufacture its clothes. Costs of operating in Country Y are significantly lower than the operating costs in the United States. Although clothes with the Couture label sell for a premium price, the actual production of the clothes does not require significant specialized knowledge that could not be acquired by actual or potential competitors to Sewco at reasonable cost. Thus, Sewco's functions could be performed by several actual or potential competitors to Sewco in geographic markets that are similar to Country Y. Thus, the fact that production is less costly in Country Y will not, in and of itself, justify additional profits derived from lower operating costs in Country Y inuring to Sewco, because the competitive positions of the other actual or potential producers in similar geographic markets capable of performing the same functions at

---

[53] Reg. § 1.482-1(d)(4)(ii)(B).
[54] Reg. § 1.482-1(d)(4)(ii)(C).

[55] Reg. § 1.482-1(d)(4)(ii)(C).

the same low costs indicate that at arm's length such profits would not be retained by Sewco.[56]

.09 Internal versus External Comparables

Transfer pricing practitioners often distinguish between internal and external comparables. The former term refers to transactions between one of the parties to the controlled transaction and an unrelated party. The latter term refers to transactions between two unrelated parties. Internal comparables usually have higher comparability with the transaction under consideration, e.g., it is likely that the product sold to the related party (the transaction under consideration) is the same or presents very similar characteristics to the product sold to a third party. Another reason why internal comparables are considered to increase comparability has to do with availability of information. It will obviously prove easier to access information regarding a comparable that the taxpayer has been a party to than to find information from a completely unrelated party. This information can prove useful to identify differences and develop adjustments to address those differences.

.10 Transactions Ordinarily Not Accepted as Comparable

The regulations specify certain transactions that generally will not be accepted by the IRS. Transactions ordinarily will not constitute reliable measures of an arm's length result if:

1. They are not made in the ordinary course of business; or

2. One of the principal purposes of the uncontrolled transaction was to establish an arm's length result with respect to the controlled transaction.

The examples below illustrate application of the above rules.

Reg. § 1.482-1(d)(4)(iii)(B), Ex. 1

Not in the ordinary course of business. USP, a United States manufacturer of computer software, sells its products to FSub, its foreign distributor in country X. Compco, a United States competitor of USP, also sells its products in X through unrelated distributors. However, in the year under review, Compco is forced into bankruptcy, and Compco liquidates its inventory by selling all of its products to unrelated distributors in X for a liquidation price. Because the sale of its entire inventory was not a sale in the ordinary course of business, Compco's sale cannot be used as an uncontrolled comparable to determine USP's arm's length result from its controlled transaction.[57]

Reg. § 1.482-1(d)(4)(iii)(B), Ex. 2

Principal purpose of establishing an arm's length result. USP, a United States manufacturer of farm machinery, sells its products to FSub, its wholly-owned distributor in Country Y. USP, operating at nearly full capacity, sells 95% of its inventory to FSub. To make use of its excess capacity, and also to establish a comparable uncontrolled price for its transfer price to FSub, USP increases its production to full capacity. USP sells its excess inventory to Compco, an unrelated foreign distributor in Country X. Country X has approximately the same economic conditions as that of Country Y. Because one of the principal purposes of selling to Compco was to establish an arm's length price for its controlled transactions with FSub, USP's sale to Compco cannot be used as an

---

[56] Reg. § 1.482-1(d)(4)(ii)(D).   [57] Reg. § 1.482-1(d)(4)(iii)(B), Ex. 1.

uncontrolled comparable to determine USP's arm's length result from its controlled transaction.[58]

The regulations provide that isolated internal comparables will not necessarily control the comparability standard for assessing an arm's length transfer price.[59] The IRS's need to state this presumption is questionable given the use of the best method rule. One regulatory example appears to be a direct attack on the result in the often-cited *U.S. Steel Corp.*,[60] where the Second Circuit relied on internal transactions with unrelated parties that made up less than five percent of U.S. Steel's sales to form the basis for comparability. It can be assumed that isolated transactions will be reviewed closely and will be presumed to be non-arm's length.

¶ 240 Arm's Length Range

.01 Arm's Length Range and Interquartile Range

The regulations recognize the concept of arm's length range, acknowledging that there could be more than one arm's length price that achieves the same level of comparability with the same qualitative level of data and assumptions. The Arm's Length Range establishes the parameters for adjustments that may be proposed by the IRS.[61] The selection of the comparable companies that comprise the range and adjustments to improve comparability may be the subject of controversy with the IRS.

The Arm's Length Range is to be derived from "two or more uncontrolled transactions of similar comparability and reliability."[62] Uncontrolled comparables must be sufficiently similar to the controlled transaction to provide a reliable measure of arm's length result. If material differences exist between the controlled and uncontrolled transaction, adjustments must be made to the results of the uncontrolled transactions if the effect of such differences can be ascertained with sufficient accuracy to improve the reliability of the results. The Arm's Length Range will only be derived from the uncontrolled comparables that have a similar level of comparability and reliability. Comparables with significantly lower comparability and reliability will not be used.

There are two ways in which the Arm's Length Range may be constructed: the full range of results ("full range") and the interquartile range of results ("interquartile range"). The full range is the collection of all results of uncontrolled comparables that meet the following conditions:

1. The information on the transaction and comparables is sufficiently detailed so that all material differences between them can be identified;

2. The material differences identified have a definite and reasonably ascertainable impact on price or profit; and

3. Adjustments are made to eliminate the effects of such material differences.[63]

[58] Reg. § 1.482-1(d)(4)(iii)(B), Ex. 2.

[59] Reg. § 1.482-1(d)(3)(ii)(C), Ex. 1.

[60] *U.S. Steel Corp.*, 80-1 USTC ¶ 9307, 617 F.2d 942 (2d Cir. 1980), *rev'g* CCH Dec. 34,400(M), TCM 1977-140.

[61] Reg. § 1.482-1(e).

[62] Reg. § 1.482-1(e)(2)(i).

[63] Reg. § 1.482-1(e)(2)(iii)(A).

Reg. § 1.482-1(e)(5), Ex. 1

Selection of comparables. (i) To evaluate the arm's length result of a controlled transaction between USSub, the United States taxpayer under review, and FP, its foreign parent, the district director considers applying the resale price method. The district director identifies ten potential uncontrolled transactions. The distributors in all ten uncontrolled transactions purchase and resell similar products and perform similar functions to those of USSub.

(ii) Data with respect to three of the uncontrolled transactions is very limited, and although some material differences can be identified and adjusted for, the level of comparability of these three uncontrolled comparables is significantly lower than that of the other seven. Further, of those seven, adjustments for the identified material differences can be reliably made for only four of the uncontrolled transactions. Therefore, pursuant to Reg. § 1.482-1(e)(2)(ii) only these four uncontrolled comparables may be used to establish an arm's length range.[64]

Reg. § 1.482-1(e)(5), Ex. 2

Arm's length range consists of all the results. (i) The facts are the same as in Example 1. Applying the resale price method to the four uncontrolled comparables, and making adjustments to the uncontrolled comparables pursuant to § 1.482-1(d)(2), the district director derives the following results:

Comparable	Result (price, $)
1	44.00
2	45.00
3	45.00
4	45.50

(ii) The district director determines that data regarding the four uncontrolled transactions is sufficiently complete and accurate so that it is likely that all material differences between the controlled and uncontrolled transactions have been identified, such differences have a definite and reasonably ascertainable effect, and appropriate adjustments were made for such differences. Accordingly, if the resale price method is determined to be the best method pursuant to Reg. § 1.482-1(c), the arm's length range for the controlled transaction will consist of the results of all of the uncontrolled comparables, pursuant to paragraph (e)(2)(iii)(A) of this section. Thus, the arm's length range in this case would be the range from $ 44 to $ 45.50.[65]

The interquartile range is used in the likely event that the conditions for the full range cannot be satisfied. Here, the reliability of the analysis must be increased by adjusting the range through the use of a statistical method, which is normally the interquartile range (the middle 50 percent). The interquartile range is the range for the 25th to 75th percentile of results from the uncontrolled comparables. The 25th percentile is the lowest result derived from an uncontrolled comparable such that 25 percent of the results are at or below the value of that result. If exactly 25 percent of the results are at or below a result, then the 25th percentile is equal to the average of that result and the next higher result. The 75th percentile is derived in a similar fashion. Other reliable statistical methods may be used as well.[66]

---

[64] Reg. § 1.482-1(e)(5), Ex. 1.
[65] Reg. § 1.482-1(e)(5), Ex. 2.

[66] Reg. § 1.482-1(e)(2)(iii)(B); Reg. § 1.482-1(e)(2)(iii)(C).

¶240.01

Reg. § 1.482-1(e)(5), Ex. 3

Arm's length range limited to interquartile range. (i) The facts are the same as in Example 2, except in this case there are some product and functional differences between the four uncontrolled comparables and USSub. However, the data is insufficiently complete to determine the effect of the differences. Applying the resale price method to the four uncontrolled comparables, and making adjustments to the uncontrolled comparables pursuant to § 1.482-1(d)(2), the district director derives the following results:

Comparable	Uncontrolled Result (price, $)
1	42.00
2	44.00
3	45.00
4	47.50

(ii) It cannot be established in this case that all material differences are likely to have been identified and reliable adjustments made for those differences. Accordingly, if the resale price method is determined to be the best method pursuant to § 1.482-1(c), the arm's length range for the controlled transaction must be established pursuant to paragraph (e)(2)(iii)(B) of this section. In this case, the district director uses the interquartile range to determine the arm's length range, which is the range from $ 43 to $ 46.25. If USSub's price falls outside this range, the district director may make an allocation. In this case that allocation would be to the median of the results, or $ 44.50.[67]

Where a taxpayer's results for a controlled transaction fall outside the Arm's Length Range, the IRS may make allocations that adjust the controlled taxpayer's result to any point within the Arm's Length Range. When the interquartile range is used to determine the Arm's Length Range, the IRS's adjustment ordinarily will be the median of all results. When the Arm's Length Range was calculated under another statistical method, the adjustment normally will be the arithmetic mean of all results. The IRS is not obliged to use the Arm's Length Range; it still can make Code Sec. 482 allocation using a single CUP. However, the taxpayer can avoid allocation if it subsequently demonstrates that the results claimed on its income tax returns are within the Arm's Length Range.[68]

Reg. § 1.482-1(e)(5), Ex. 4

Arm's length range limited to interquartile range. (i) To evaluate the arm's length result of controlled transactions between USP, a United States manufacturing company, and FSub, its foreign subsidiary, the district director considers applying the comparable profits method. The district director identifies 50 uncontrolled taxpayers within the same industry that potentially could be used to apply the method.

(ii) Further review indicates that only 20 of the uncontrolled manufacturers engage in activities requiring similar capital investments and technical know-how. Data with respect to five of the uncontrolled manufacturers is very limited, and although some material differences can be identified and adjusted for, the level of comparability of these five uncontrolled comparables is significantly lower than that of the other 15. In addition, for those five uncontrolled comparables it is not possible to accurately allocate costs between the business

---

[67] Reg. § 1.482-1(e)(5). Ex. 3.   [68] Reg. § 1.482-1(e)(3); Reg. § 1.482-1(e)(4).

¶240.01

activity associated with the relevant transactions and other business activities. Therefore, pursuant to §1.482-1(e)(2)(ii) only the other fifteen uncontrolled comparables may be used to establish an arm's length range.

(iii) Although the data for the fifteen remaining uncontrolled comparables is relatively complete and accurate, there is a significant possibility that some material differences may remain. The district director has determined, for example, that it is likely that there are material differences in the level of technical expertise or in management efficiency. Accordingly, if the comparable profits method is determined to be the best method pursuant to Reg. §1.482-1(c), the arm's length range for the controlled transaction may be established only pursuant to paragraph (e)(2)(iii)(B) of this section.[69]

¶ 250 Determination of True Taxable Income

.01 The Aggregation Rule

The regulations provide that the combined effect of more than one transaction may be considered if these transactions as a whole are so interrelated that consideration of the multiple transactions as a whole, rather than in segmented parts, leads to the most reliable means of determining an arm's length range.[70] Typically, aggregation involves related products, such as those that fall within a marketed portfolio of products or are segmented into distinct product lines.[71] The aggregation rule can also alleviate the compliance burdens for taxpayers with multiple products, although care must be exercised when selecting the products for aggregation or the product line. The aggregation rule similarly applies for services, for example, where services for marketing and distributing a product or products cannot be separated reasonably from the sales transactions.[72]

Reg. § 1.482-1(f)(2)(i)(B), Ex. 1

P enters into a license agreement with S1, its subsidiary, that permits S1 to use a proprietary manufacturing process and to sell the output from this process throughout a specified region. S1 uses the manufacturing process and sells its output to S2, another subsidiary of P, which in turn resells the output to uncontrolled parties in the specified region. In evaluating the arm's length character of the royalty paid by S1 to P, it may be appropriate to consider the arm's length character of the transfer prices charged by S1 to S2 and the aggregate profits earned by S1 and S2 from the use of the manufacturing process and the sale to uncontrolled parties of the products produced by S1.[73]

.02 Substance Over Form

The regulations contain somewhat contradictory rules on when the form of transactions between controlled entities will be respected. The regulations state that the IRS will respect the form that controlled taxpayers select, provided that it has economic substance.[74] The regulations, however, further provide that the IRS "may consider alternatives available to the taxpayer in determining whether the terms of the controlled transaction would be acceptable to an uncontrolled taxpayer faced with the same alternatives and operating under comparable circumstances."[75]

---

[69] Reg. §1.482-1(e)(5), Ex. 4.
[70] Reg. §1.482-1(e)(5).
[71] Reg. §1.482-1(f)(2)(i).
[72] Reg. §1.482-1(f)(2)(i).

[73] Reg. §1.482-1(f)(2)(i)(B), Ex. 1.
[74] Reg. §1.482-1(f)(2)(ii)(A).
[75] Reg. §1.482-1(f)(2)(ii).

This suggests that the IRS may adjust a transfer price to reflect the income a taxpayer might have earned had an available alternative been chosen. The IRS presented this concept in *Bausch & Lomb, Inc.*,[76] where it was argued that Bausch & Lomb could have manufactured its soft contact lens at significantly less cost than the transfer price it paid its Irish affiliate. This argument was rejected by the Tax Court on the basis that, among other things, the IRS had no right to substitute its judgment for the business judgment of the taxpayer.

A similar conclusion can be drawn regarding rules governing contracts between controlled taxpayers. Although the regulations provide that contractual arrangements will be respected if they have economic substance and are consistent with the parties' actual conduct, the IRS still may disregard the contract or infer the existence of an agreement based on the taxpayer's actual conduct.[77] The regulations generally provide for situations in which an agreement may be inferred involving a U.S. company that regularly purchases substantially all the output of its foreign manufacturing subsidiary, and implies the facts of both *Bausch & Lomb*, and *Sundstrand*, in which the IRS argued that the taxpayers' foreign manufacturing subsidiaries should be treated as contract manufacturers that bear no market risk and earn minimal operating returns for their seemingly riskless function.[78] In both cases, the contract-manufacturer argument was rejected by the Tax Court because, among other things, no agreement existed that required the U.S. parent to purchase the output of the subsidiary.[79]

Reg. § 1.482-1(f)(2)(ii)(B), Ex.

> P and S are controlled taxpayers. P enters into a license agreement with S that permits S to use a proprietary process for manufacturing product X. Using its sales and marketing employees, S sells product X to related and unrelated customers outside the United States. If the license agreement between P and S has economic substance, the district director ordinarily will not restructure the taxpayer's transaction to treat P as if it had elected to exploit directly the manufacturing process. However, the fact that P could have manufactured product X may be taken into account under Reg. § 1.482-4(d) in determining the arm's length consideration for the controlled transaction. For an example of such an analysis, see Example in Reg. § 1.482-4(d)(2).[80]

.03 Multiple-Year Data

Data from multiple years may be relevant for purposes of certain enumerated provisions, including the analysis of risk, market share strategy, periodic adjustments, and the comparable profit method. The regulations provide that results from other years may be examined to determine if the same economic conditions that caused the taxpayer's results had a comparable effect on the uncontrolled taxpayers' results.[81] For example, in determining whether a loss from controlled transactions is within an arm's length range, it may be relevant to consider data from other taxable years. Multiple-year averages may provide a more accurate reflection of a

---

[76] Reg. § 1.482-1(f)(2)(ii).

[77] CCH Dec. 45,547, 92 TC 525 (1989).

[78] Reg. § 1.482-1(f)(2)(ii); *See also* Reg. § 1.482-1(d)(3)(ii)(B).

[79] *Bausch & Lomb, Inc.*, 91-1 USTC ¶ 50,244, 933 F2d 1084, *aff'g* CCH Dec. 45,547, 92 TC 525 (1989); *Sundstrand Corp.*, CCH Dec. 47,172, 96 TC 226, 353 (1991).

[80] Reg. § 1.482-1(f)(2)(ii)(B).

[81] Reg. § 1.482-1(f)(2)(iii)(C).

taxpayer's transfer pricing practices over a period than an analysis based on a single year. The use of multiple-year averages also will reduce the effect of short-term variations. The focus of the evaluation is the result achieved, rather than the method employed in reaching that result.

The IRS is supposed to use multiple-year data only to determine if an adjustment is warranted, but not to determine the size of the adjustment. When the taxpayer's profits are outside the range of profits for the comparable over the multiple-year period, the taxpayer's profits in each year under examination would be adjusted to the midpoint of the range for that year.[82]

¶ 260 Collateral Adjustments

.01 General

Once the Code Sec. 482 allocation is made (whether it is IRS-initiated adjustment or a taxpayer-initiated adjustment),[83] collateral adjustments are necessary in order to avoid distortion in the taxpayer's and its related party accounts (correlative and conforming adjustments). Absent a special treatment, adjustments under Code Sec. 482 may result in adverse consequences to the taxpayer. For example, an allocation of income under Code Sec. 482 from a foreign parent corporation to its domestic subsidiary corporation could entail a deemed distribution from the domestic subsidiary to its foreign parent in an amount equal to the primary allocation in the year for which the allocation is made. The deemed distribution would be treated as dividend income to the foreign parent to the extent of the earnings and profits of the domestic subsidiary, as recomputed after taking into account the primary allocation. Under Code Sec. 881, the foreign parent would be subject to a 30-percent tax liability (as reduced by any applicable income tax treaty), and under Code Sec. 1442, the domestic subsidiary would be a withholding agent required to withhold the tax.[84] Pursuant to the regulations under Code Sec. 482, the IRS prescribed procedures[85] to allow the United States taxpayer to repatriate the cash attributable to a primary allocation via an account without the Federal income tax consequences of the conforming adjustments that would otherwise result from the primary allocation.[86]

The regulations provide that collateral adjustments may include correlative allocations, conforming adjustments, and setoffs.[87] The chart below summarizes various adjustments and their application sequence. Chapter 17 discusses these adjustments in greater detail.

---

[82] Reg. § 1.482-1(f)(2)(iii)(D).

[83] The regulations use the term "allocation" when referring to primary allocations under Code Sec. 482 (whether initiated by the IRS or taxpayers), and the term "adjustment" when referring to collateral adjustments, in general, and to conforming adjustments, in particular. The regulations use interchangeably the terms "correlative allocation" and "correlative adjustment." In practice, IRS and taxpayer initiated allocations are referred to as IRS-initiated or taxpayer-initiated "primary adjustments." The terms in this book are generally used consistently with the language of the regulations.

[84] *See* Rev. Rul. 82-80, 1982-1 CB 89; Reg. § 1.1441-2(e)(2). The example is incorporated from Rev. Proc. 99-32, 1999-2 CB 296.

[85] Rev. Proc. 99-32, 1999-2 CB 296.

[86] Reg. § 1.482-1(g)(3).

[87] Reg. § 1.482-1(g)(1).

Step 1: Original Transaction

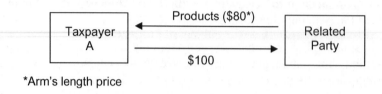

*Arm's length price

Step 2: Primary and Correlative Allocations

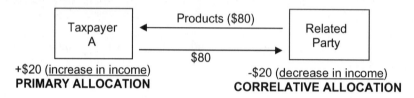

+$20 (increase in income)
PRIMARY ALLOCATION

-$20 (decrease in income)
CORRELATIVE ALLOCATION

Step 3: Conforming Adjustments

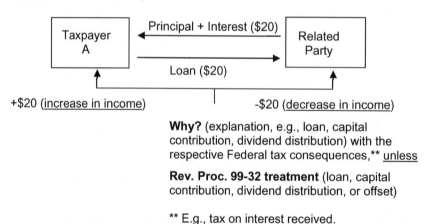

+$20 (increase in income)   -$20 (decrease in income)

Why? (explanation, e.g., loan, capital contribution, dividend distribution) with the respective Federal tax consequences,** unless

Rev. Proc. 99-32 treatment (loan, capital contribution, dividend distribution, or offset)

** E.g., tax on interest received.

.02 Correlative Allocation

When the District Director makes an allocation under Code. Sec. 482 (primary allocation), appropriate correlative allocations are also made with respect to any other member of the group affected by the allocation. Thus, if the District Director makes an allocation of income, the District Director will not only increase the income of one member of the group, but correspondingly decrease the income of the other member. In addition, where appropriate, the District Director may make such further correlative allocations as may be required by the initial correlative allocation.

¶260.02

The District Director will furnish to the taxpayer for which the primary allocation is made a written statement of the amount and nature of the correlative allocation. The correlative allocation must be reflected in the documentation of the other member of the group that is maintained for U.S. tax purposes, without regard to whether it affects the U.S. income tax liability of the other member for any open year. In some circumstances the allocation will have an immediate U.S. tax effect, by changing the taxable income computation of the other member (or the taxable income computation of a shareholder of the other member, for example, under the provisions of subpart F of the Internal Revenue Code). Alternatively, the correlative allocation may not be reflected on any U.S. tax return until a later year, for example when a dividend is paid.

A primary allocation is not considered to have been made (and therefore, correlative allocations are not required to be made) until the date of a final determination, which includes:

1. Assessment of tax following execution by the taxpayer of a Form 870 (Waiver of Restrictions on Assessment and Collection of Deficiency in Tax and Acceptance of Overassessment) with respect to such allocation;

2. Acceptance of a Form 870-AD (Offer of Waiver of Restriction on Assessment and Collection of Deficiency in Tax and Acceptance of Overassessment);

3. Payment of the deficiency;

4. Stipulation in the Tax Court of the United States; or

5. Final determination of tax liability by offer-in-compromise, closing agreement, or final resolution (determined under the principles of Code Sec. 7481) of a judicial proceeding.[88]

The following examples illustrate the application of above rules. X and Y are members of the same group of controlled taxpayers and each regularly computes its income on a calendar year basis.

Reg. § 1.482-1(g)(2)(iv), Ex. 1

(i) In 1996, Y, a U.S. corporation, rents a building owned by X, also a U.S. corporation. In 1998 the district director determines that Y did not pay an arm's length rental charge. The district director proposes to increase X's income to reflect an arm's length rental charge. X consents to the assessment reflecting such adjustment by executing Form 870, a Waiver of Restrictions on Assessment and Collection of Deficiency in Tax and Acceptance of Overassessment. The assessment of the tax with respect to the adjustment is made in 1998. Thus, the primary allocation, as defined in paragraph (g)(2)(i) of this section, is considered to have been made in 1998.

(ii) The adjustment made to X's income under section 482 requires a correlative allocation with respect to Y's income. The district director notifies X in writing of the amount and nature of the adjustment made with respect to Y. Y had net operating losses in 1993, 1994, 1995, 1996, and 1997. Although a correlative adjustment will not have an effect on Y's U.S. income tax liability for 1996, an adjustment increasing Y's net operating loss for 1996 will be made for purposes

---

[88] Reg. § 1.482-1(g).

of determining Y's U.S. income tax liability for 1998 or a later taxable year to which the increased net operating loss may be carried.[89]

Reg. § 1.482-1(g)(2)(iv), Ex. 2

(i) In 1995, X, a U.S. construction company, provided engineering services to Y, a U.S. corporation, in the construction of Y's factory. In 1997, the district director determines that the fees paid by Y to X for its services were not arm's length and proposes to make an adjustment to the income of X. X consents to an assessment reflecting such adjustment by executing Form 870. An assessment of the tax with respect to such adjustment is made in 1997. The district director notifies X in writing of the amount and nature of the adjustment to be made with respect to Y.

(ii) The fees paid by Y for X's engineering services properly constitute a capital expenditure. Y does not place the factory into service until 1998. Therefore, a correlative adjustment increasing Y's basis in the factory does not affect Y's U.S. income tax liability for 1997. However, the correlative adjustment must be made in the books and records maintained by Y for its U.S. income tax purposes and such adjustment will be taken into account in computing Y's allowable depreciation or gain or loss on a subsequent disposition of the factory.[90]

Reg. § 1.482-1(g)(2)(iv), Ex. 3

In 1995, X, a U.S. corporation, makes a loan to Y, its foreign subsidiary not engaged in a U.S. trade or business. In 1997, the district director, upon determining that the interest charged on the loan was not arm's length, proposes to adjust X's income to reflect an arm's length interest rate. X consents to an assessment reflecting such allocation by executing Form 870, and an assessment of the tax with respect to the section 482 allocation is made in 1997. The district director notifies X in writing of the amount and nature of the correlative allocation to be made with respect to Y. Although the correlative adjustment does not have an effect on Y's U.S. income tax liability, the adjustment must be reflected in the documentation of Y that is maintained for U.S. tax purposes. Thus, the adjustment must be reflected in the determination of the amount of Y's earnings and profits for 1995 and subsequent years, and the adjustment must be made to the extent it has an effect on any person's U.S. income tax liability for any taxable year.[91]

.03 Conforming Adjustments[92]

Appropriate adjustments must be made to conform a taxpayer's accounts to reflect allocations made under section 482.[93] These adjustments may include the treatment of an allocated amount as a dividend or a capital contribution (as appropriate), or, in appropriate cases, repayment of the allocated amount without further income tax consequences.

Under the regulations, a taxpayer whose taxable income has been adjusted pursuant to Code Sec. 482 must make certain adjustments ("collateral" adjustments, as discussed above) to reconcile their accounts to reflect the initial adjustment. However, these collateral adjustments may result in adverse tax consequences to the taxpayer. For example,

---

[89] Reg. § 1.482-1(g)(2)(iv), Ex. 1.

[90] Reg. § 1.482-1(g)(2)(iv), Ex. 2.

[91] Reg. § 1.482-1(g)(2)(iv), Ex. 3.

[92] See Chapter 9 for a more detailed discussion.

[93] In practice, the conforming adjustments are generally referred to as "secondary adjustments." *See, e.g.,* Rev. Proc. 99-32, 1999-1 CB 296.

an allocation of income under § 482 from a foreign parent corporation to its domestic subsidiary corporation would entail a deemed distribution from the domestic subsidiary to its foreign parent in an amount equal to the primary adjustment in the year for which the allocation is made. This deemed distribution would be treated as dividend income to the foreign parent to the extent of the earnings and profits of the domestic subsidiary, as recomputed after taking into account the primary adjustment. Under section 881 of the Code, the foreign parent would be subject to a 30 percent tax liability (as reduced by any applicable income tax treaty), and under section 1442 of the Code, the domestic subsidiary would be a withholding agent required to withhold the tax.[94]

The intent behind the IRS's issuance of Rev. Proc. 99-32 was to provide a means by which taxpayers could avoid or mitigate these collateral tax consequences. If a taxpayer requests, and is granted, treatment under Rev. Proc. 99-32, that taxpayer will be "allowed to repatriate the cash attributable to a primary adjustment via an account without the Federal income tax consequences of the collateral adjustments that might otherwise result from the primary adjustment."[95]

Rev. Proc. 99-32 allows the taxpayer to establish an interest-bearing account receivable from, or payable to, the related person in an amount equal to the primary adjustment for each of the years in which an allocation is made.[96] The amount shall be deemed to have been created as of the last day of the taxable year for which the primary adjustment is made. That amount shall bear interest, at an arm's length rate, and be expressed (both as to principal and interest) in the functional currency of a qualified business unit through which the controlled transaction was carried out—if that qualified business unit maintains United States residency—and the amount shall be paid within the 90-day period required in section 5 of the Revenue Procedure, or treated as prepaid by offset prior to that time (as provided in section 4.02).[97]

The following example from the regulations depicts a situation where the taxpayer elects Rev. Proc. 99-32 treatment.

Reg. § 1.482-1(g)(3)(ii), Ex.

(i) USD, a United States corporation, buys Product from its foreign parent, FP. In reviewing USD's income tax return, the district director determines that the arm's length price would have increased USD's taxable income by $ 5 million. The district director accordingly adjusts USD's income to reflect its true taxable income.

(ii) To conform its cash accounts to reflect the section 482 allocation made by the district director, USD applies for relief under Rev. Proc. 99-32 to treat the $ 5 million adjustment as an account receivable from FP, due as of the last day of the year of the transaction, with interest accruing therefrom.[98]

See expanded discussion in Chapter 17 and ¶ 20,120 in Practice Tools for Alternatives available under Rev. Proc. 99-32.[99]

---

[94] Rev. Proc. 99-32, 1999-1 CB 298, *citing* Code Secs. 881 and 1442.

[95] Rev. Proc. 99-32, 1999-1 CB 298.

[96] Rev. Proc. 99-32, 1999-1 CB 299.

[97] Rev. Proc. 99-32, 1999-1 CB 299.

[98] Reg. § 1.482-1(g)(3)(i).

[99] Rev. Proc. 99-32, 1999-2 CB 296.

.04 Setoffs

If an allocation is made under Code Sec. 482 with respect to a transaction between controlled taxpayers, the taxpayers may be allowed to claim setoff, provided certain requirements are met. If the effect of the setoff is to change the characterization or source of the income or deductions, or otherwise distort taxable income, in such a manner as to affect the U.S. tax liability of any member, adjustments will be made to reflect the correct amount of each category of income or deductions. For purposes of this setoff provision, the term arm's length refers to the amount defined in paragraph (b) (Arm's length standard) of this section, without regard to the rules in *§ 1.482-2* under which certain charges are deemed to be equal to arm's length.

The setoff can be available to a taxpayer only if the taxpayer:

1. Establishes that the transaction that is the basis of the setoff was not at arm's length and the amount of the appropriate arm's length charge;

2. Documents, pursuant to paragraph (g)(2) of this section, all correlative adjustments resulting from the proposed setoff; and

3. Notifies the District Director of the basis of any claimed setoff within 30 days after the earlier of the date of a letter by which the District Director transmits an examination report notifying the taxpayer of proposed adjustments or the date of the issuance of the notice of deficiency.

Reg. § 1.482-1(g)(4)(iii), Ex. 1

P, a U.S. corporation, renders construction services to S, its foreign subsidiary in Country Y, in connection with the construction of S's factory. An arm's length charge for such services determined under § 1.482-9 would be $100,000. During the same taxable year P makes available to S the use of a machine to be used in the construction of the factory, and the arm's length rental value of the machine is $25,000. P bills S $125,000 for the services, but does not charge S for the use of the machine. No allocation will be made with respect to the undercharge for the machine if P notifies the district director of the basis of the claimed setoff within 30 days after the date of the letter from the district director transmitting the examination report notifying P of the proposed adjustment, establishes that the excess amount charged for services was equal to an arm's length charge for the use of the machine and that the taxable income and income tax liabilities of P are not distorted, and documents the correlative allocations resulting from the proposed setoff.[100]

Reg. § 1.482-1(g)(4)(iii), Ex. 2

The facts are the same as in Example 1, except that, if P had reported $25,000 as rental income and $25,000 less as service income, it would have been subject to the tax on personal holding companies. Allocations will be made to reflect the correct amounts of rental income and service income.[101]

---

[100] Reg. § 1.482-1(g)(4)(iii), Ex. 1.   [101] Reg. § 1.482-1(g)(4)(iii), Ex. 2.

¶260.04

¶ 270 Transfer Pricing and Non-Recognition Provisions

.01 In General

The regulations explicitly provide that the non-recognition provisions of the Code may not bar a Code Sec. 482 allocation. *Reg. § 1.482-1(f)(1)(iii)(A)* provides that:

If necessary to prevent the avoidance of taxes or to clearly reflect income, the District Director may make an allocation under Code Sec. 482 for transactions that otherwise qualify for non-recognition of gain or loss under applicable provisions of the Internal Revenue Code (such as Code Secs. 351 or 1031).

This regulation also includes an example whose facts roughly approximate the facts in *National Securities Corp.*[102]

In addition to the non-recognition provisions of Code Secs. 351 and 1031, Code Sec. 482 has been applied in the contexts of Code Secs. 311 (pre- *General Utilities* repeal) and 368. Although most commentators agree with proposition that Code Sec. 482 can override other non-recognition provisions of the Code, at least one commentator has forcefully argued otherwise.[103]

In general, the cases in which the courts failed to apply Code Sec. 482 to non-recognition transactions fall into three distinct categories:

1. Cases in which property was transferred in a non-recognition transaction and subsequently disposed of by the transferee, and in which the primary purpose of the transfer was to achieve tax consequences on the disposition of the property by the transferee that were more favorable than the tax consequences of a disposition by the transferor;

2. Cases in which the non-recognition transfer of property resulted in an artificial separation of income from the expenses of earning the income; and

3. Cases in which high profit intangibles were transferred in a non-recognition transaction to offshore affiliates in low tax jurisdictions.

In none of the categories of cases have the courts failed to apply Code Sec. 482 to require the recognition of gain or loss by disregarding a non-recognition transaction itself. Rather, the courts have applied Code Sec. 482 to allocate to the transferor gain or loss subsequently realized by the transferee, or to allocate to the transferee expenses incurred by the transferor prior to the non-recognition transaction.

---

[102] *National Securities Corp.*, 43-2 USTC ¶ 9560, 137 F.2d 600 (3rd Cir. 1943), *cert. denied*, 320 US 794 (1943).

[103] *See* Townsend, "Reconciling Section 482 and the Nonrecognition Provisions," 50 *Tax Law* 701 (1997). *See generally* Berger, et al., "Section 482 and the Nonrecognition Provisions: An Analysis of the Boundary Lines," 26 *Tax Law* 523 (1973); Barrett & Rafferty, "Section 482 and Nonrecognition Transfers," 89 *TNI* 49-50 (1989); Melvin S. Adess, "The Role of Section 482 in Nonrecognition Transactions: the Outer Edge of its Applications," 57 *Taxes* 946 (1979); Jenks, "Section 482 and the Non-Recognition Provisions: the Transfer of Intangible Assets," 32 *Tax Law* 775 (1980).

.02 Property Transfers Made Prior to Sale by Transferee

Several courts have applied Code Sec. 482 to allocate income or deductions to the transferor from the transferee following a non-recognition transaction where the original transfer was made primarily for tax avoidance purposes and in anticipation of subsequent dispositions of the property by the transferee. These cases involved both upstream and downstream transfers. In these cases, the application of Code Sec. 482 was consistent with the judicially created "sham" transaction, "assignment of income," and *Court Holding Company* doctrines.[104]

Downstream Transfers. The leading case in this area is *National Securities Corp.*[105] In *National Securities*, a parent corporation, an insurance company, transferred to its wholly-owned, non-consolidated subsidiary 1,000 shares of stock of an unrelated company (Standard) that it held for seven years as an investment. At the time of the transfer, the stock had an adjusted basis of approximately $140,000 and a fair market value of approximately $8,500 (Standard had previously declared bankruptcy). This transfer, which occurred one month after the parent corporation sold an additional 2,500 shares of Standard in the market at a substantial loss, was treated as Code Sec. 351 non-recognition transfer. Ten months later, but still in the same taxable year, the subsidiary sold the shares for approximately $7,000 and reported the entire loss ($133,000) on its tax return.

The IRS challenged that subsidiary's loss on the stock as reported on its tax return, and at trial argued that in order to clearly reflect the income of the subsidiary, the subsidiary should only be entitled to the loss attributable to the period that it held the stock ($8,500 - $7,000 = $1,500). The IRS allocated the remainder of the loss ($131,500) to the parent. The parent argued that the stock was transferred for the purpose of ridding itself of an investment which it was unwise for an insurance company to retain. The Tax Court sustained the IRS's allocation and its decision was affirmed by the Third Circuit. In doing so, the court stated:

> [The predecessor to Code Sec. 482] is directed to the correction of particular situations in which the strict application of other provisions of the [Code] will result in a distortion of the income of affiliated organizations. In every case in which the section is applied its application will necessarily result in an apparent conflict with the literal requirements of some other provision of the [Code]. If this were not so [the predecessor to Code Sec. 482] would be wholly superfluous.[106]

Although the *National Securities* court based its ruling on the clear reflection of income prong of Code Sec. 482, later cases have viewed *National Securities* as a tax avoidance case because there was no business purpose for the transaction.[107]

---

[104] *Court Holding Co.*, 45-1 USTC ¶ 9215, 324 US 331 (1945).

[105] *National Securities Corp.*, 43-2 USTC ¶ 9560, 137 F.2d 600 (3rd Cir. 1943), *cert. denied*, 320 US 794 (1943).

[106] *Id.* at 602.

[107] *See* e.g., *Eli Lilly & Co.*, 88-2 USTC ¶ 9502, CCH Dec. 42,113, 84 TC 996, 1119 (1985).

¶270.02

Upstream Transfers. In *Northwestern National Bank of Minneapolis*,[108] the parent corporation, a bank, owned all of the stock of a subsidiary corporation, which in turn, owned all of the stock of a real estate holding company. The subsidiary corporation's basis in the stock of the real estate holding company was $100,000. When the real estate holding company announced its intention to sell one of its properties, the value of its stock rose to $800,000. The subsidiary corporation then decided to distribute the stock of the real estate holding company to its parent (this transaction occurred prior to *General Utilities* repeal), which would then contribute the stock to a charity. The parent corporation then claimed the charitable deduction on its tax return and derived a greater tax benefit than would have been derived had the subsidiary contributed the stock. On audit, the IRS disallowed the charitable contribution deduction claimed by the bank and allocated the deduction to the subsidiary. This allocation was upheld by the District Court. In affirming the lower court's opinion, the 8th Circuit Court of Appeals stated:

> The purpose behind the dividend distribution was to obtain a tax advantage not available in an arm's length transaction. The transaction was made possible solely on the basis of the [parent corporation's] relationship with and control of [subsidiary corporation], and the end result was a distortion of the respective net incomes of both parent and subsidiary corporations.[109]

.03 No Disposition of Transferred Property: Code Sec. 482 Not Applicable

The courts have consistently refused to apply Code Sec. 482 where there is no subsequent disposition of the transferred property.

Bank of America. In *Bank of America*,[110] the IRS sought to apply Code Sec. 482 to a bargain sale by a domestic corporation of its foreign branches to its domestic parent corporation, requiring the domestic corporation to include in income the difference between the fair market value of the branch assets and the amount the parent corporation paid for such assets. The parent company assumed the liabilities of the foreign branches and paid an additional amount of cash to its domestic subsidiary in consideration for the transfer of the assets of the various branches. Because the aggregate of the liabilities assumed and the cash paid by the parent company equaled the subsidiary's basis in the branch assets, the subsidiary reported no gain from the sale. The court agreed with the taxpayer that Code Sec. 311 applied to the bargain sale in question. The court correctly observed that Code Sec. 311 itself sets forth the circumstances in which a shareholder's assumption of liabilities in connection with a corporate distribution of property will cause the distributing corporation to recognize gain.

---

[108] *Northwestern National Bank of Minneapolis*, 77-2 USTC ¶ 9479, 556 F.2d 889 (8th Cir. 1977).

[109] *Id. See also, Southern Bancorporation*, CCH Dec. 34,322, 67 TC 1022 (1977) (sustaining a Code Sec. 482 allocation of income from a parent corporation to its subsidiary when the subsidiary contributed appreciated securities to its parent in anticipation of their sale in order to avoid ordinary income treatment under Code Sec. 582 of the 1954 Code); *Roger M. Dolese*, 87-1 USTC ¶ 9175,

811 F.2d 543 (10th Cir. 1987) (sustaining a Code Sec. 482 allocation based on disproportionate distributions from a partnership to its partners made such that each partner could maximize their tax benefits); *General Electric Co.*, 83-2 USTC ¶ 9532, 3 Cl. Ct. 289 (1983) (sustaining a Code Sec. 482 allocation based on a transfer upon liquidation of loss property by a Code Sec. 931 subsidiary).

[110] *Bank of America*, 79-1 USTC ¶ 9170 (N.D. Cal. 1978).

The court also recognized that there was a permissible shifting of income and a deferral of recognition of that income from the unrealized appreciation of the branch assets. It stated the following:

> [T]his deferral and shifting of tax liability from a corporation to its shareholder is the essence of the non-recognition provisions of section 311, which represents a Congressional policy decision that such a transfer would not be an appropriate occasion to impose tax liability on the distributing corporation . . . . Nor is there any distortion of income produced by this transfer which is not sanctioned by section 311. The income from the branches goes to the [parent] instead of to [the subsidiary] but that is because the income producing capital assets were transferred. The transaction has not run afoul of any of the judicially recognized exceptions to the non-recognition sections. There has been no anticipatory assignment of income, no attempt to transform ordinary income into capital gain, no violation of the tax benefit rule and no sham distribution of corporate property to a shareholder who immediately sells it to a third party. In taking advantage of the tax benefits afforded to a distributing corporation by section 311, the plaintiff has violated neither the letter nor the spirit of the tax laws.[111]

Huber Homes, Inc. In *Huber Homes, Inc.*,[112] a parent corporation that built and sold single-family houses, transferred several houses that it was unable to sell to its subsidiary at cost, and the subsidiary then rented them to families as part of its real estate rental business. The IRS attempted to allocate the difference between the fair market value and cost of the houses at the time of transfer to the parent. The Tax Court rejected the IRS's allocation on the grounds that to do so would result in the creation of income because the houses were not sold. It is significant to note that in this case the subsidiary did not immediately sell the property, but instead used the property in a bona fide rental business. It is also noteworthy that the IRS did not attempt to allocate the subsidiary's rental income to the parent.

.04 Artificial Separation of Income and Expenses: Clear Reflection of Income

Code Sec. 482 has been used to reallocate income and expenses in transactions between related parties which resulted in an excessive mismatching of income and expense. These cases make it clear that a Code Sec. 482 allocation can be made to clearly reflect income even though the transaction had a valid business purpose.

In *Central Cuba Sugar*,[113] the taxpayer, a U.S. corporation that had incurred expenses in growing a sugar crop, transferred all of its assets including the unharvested crop to a Cuban subsidiary corporation. Subsequently, the taxpayer distributed the stock of its subsidiary to its shareholders in liquidation. On its final tax return, the taxpayer reported substantial expenses related to growing the crop, generating a net operating loss, and requested a refund. The former subsidiary corporation then sold the crop and reported the income. The IRS denied the refund claim and allocated the growing expenses incurred by the taxpayer to its former

---

[111] *Id.* at 86,252–86,253.

[112] *Huber Homes, Inc.*, CCH Dec. 30,602, 55 TC 598 (1971).

[113] *Central Cuba Sugar Co.*, 52-2 USTC ¶ 9390, 198 F.2d 214 (2d Cir. 1952), *cert. denied*, 344 US 874.

subsidiary on the ground that such allocation was needed to clearly reflect income. The Second Circuit reversed the Tax Court's ruling and held in favor of the IRS.[114]

Code Sec. 482 has also been applied in the context of incorporations of professional service businesses.[115]

.05 Transfer of Intangibles

In Rev. Proc. 63-10, 1963-1 CB 490, the IRS directed revenue agents to impute royalties on intangibles owned by the U.S. parent corporations, but used by its Puerto Rican affiliate, and it made ownership of the intangibles the touchstone of whether royalties would be imputed. As a consequence, there was an incentive to transfer legal title of patents and manufacturing know-how to the Puerto Rican subsidiaries to avoid the imputation of royalties. Generally, these transfers were accomplished tax-free under Code Sec. 351 or as a contribution to capital. As discussed below, the IRS sought to attack these transactions under the authority of Code Sec. 482, but with only limited success.

Eli Lilly & Co. In *Eli Lilly & Co.*,[116] the taxpayer ("EL") transferred to a created a Puerto Rican subsidiary ("PR") and transferred to it patents and manufacturing intangibles related to the Darvon family of drugs. EL obtained a private letter ruling holding that this transaction qualified for non-recognition treatment under Code Sec. 351. PR then began manufacturing the drugs with some technical assistance provided by EL. PR sold the drugs to EL, which then distributed the drugs worldwide. In its notice of deficiency, the IRS disregarded PR's ownership of the intangibles and imputed a royalty agreement that treated EL as owning the intangibles and PR as a contract manufacturer. EL argued that Code Sec. 482 could only be applied in situations similar to the two lines of cases described above. The Tax Court agreed that the instant situation did not match either of the two lines of cases and rejected the IRS's argument that the ownership of the intangibles should be disregarded for transfer pricing purposes. However, the Tax Court went on to sustain a portion of the IRS's allocation on the basis that EL did not receive an arm's length amount of compensation (in the form of lower prices for the drugs) for the transfer of the intangibles and for other assistance rendered to PR.

On appeal, the Seventh Circuit rejected the portion of the allocation related to original transfer of the intangibles, but sustained the portion of the allocation based on the provision of other assistance by EL to PR.

G.D. Searle & Co. In *G.D. Searle & Co.*,[117] the facts were essentially the same as in *Eli Lilly*, with the exception that the Puerto Rican subsidiary distributed the manufactured drugs. The Tax Court, as in *Eli Lilly*, rejected the IRS's argument that Code Sec. 482 could be used to disregard the Code Sec. 351 transaction. However,

[114] *See also, F.L. Rooney*, 62-2 USTC ¶ 9598, 305 F.2d 681(9th Cir. 1962) (same); *P.J. Lynch*, 51-2 USTC ¶ 9507, 192 F.2d 718 (9th Cir. 1951), *cert. denied*, 343 US 934 (1952) (same).

[115] *See* Rev. Rul. 80-198 1980-2 CB 113; *Daniel F. Keller*, CCH Dec. 38,401, 77 TC 1014 (1981); *Silvano Achiro*, CCH Dec. 38,351, 77 TC 881(1981); *Frederick H. Fogle-song*, CCH Dec. 38,423, 77 TC 1102 (1981), *on remand*

from 80-1 USTC ¶ 9399, 621 F.2d 865 (7th Cir. 1980); and 78 TC No. 42 (1982).

[116] *Eli Lilly & Co.*, CCH Dec. 42,113, 84 TC 996 (1985), *aff'd in part and rev'd in part*, 88-2 USTC ¶ 9502, 856 F.2d 855 (7th Cir. 1988).

[117] *G.D. Searle & Co.*, CCH Dec. 43,685, 88 TC 252 (1987).

as in *Eli Lilly*, the court went on to sustain a portion of the IRS's allocation on the basis that the parent did not receive an arm's length compensation for the transfer in the form of an ongoing, profitable technical services relationship. *Searle* was settled before its appeal was heard by the Seventh Circuit. Nevertheless, the Seventh Circuit's decision in *Eli Lilly* implied that much of its analysis could have been applied to *Searle*.[118]

¶ 280 Blocked Income

.01 In General

Taxpayers faced with blocked income can avail themselves of two types of relief. First, the courts have historically ruled that the IRS is prohibited from making a Code Sec. 482 allocation when a legal restriction prevents a taxpayer from receiving or paying the arm's length amounts that an uncontrolled taxpayer would have received or paid without the restriction. Second, the regulations under Code Sec. 482 allow a taxpayer to elect a deferred income method of accounting if a foreign legal restriction prevents the payment or receipt of part or all of the arm's length amount.

When a U.S. corporation transfers goods or services to a related party, the related party may be unable to pay an arm's length amount of consideration for these goods or services because (i) the payments are prohibited by foreign law in form (e.g., a prohibition against the payment of royalties) or amount (e.g., limits on the amounts to be paid), or (ii) conversion of the foreign currency into U.S. dollars is prohibited. As a consequence, a taxpayer will likely be subject to double taxation if a Code Sec. 482 allocation is made, but the corresponding repatriation is prohibited or otherwise restricted under foreign law. As discussed below, two types of relief are available in these situations.

.02 The Blocked Income Doctrine

As developed by the courts, the blocked income doctrine precludes the IRS from allocating income from one related taxpayer to another under Code Sec. 482 if the receipt of such income by the taxpayer to which the IRS allocated the income is illegal under U.S. or foreign law.

First Security Bank of Utah. The blocked income doctrine was first articulated in *First Security Bank of Utah*.[119] In *First Security Bank*, the taxpayers, two related banks, assisted their customers in purchasing credit life insurance policies by performing limited originating and processing functions. The insurance policies were underwritten by an unrelated insurance company, which, in turn, reinsured the policies through an insurance company that was related to the banks. Under this arrangement, the unrelated insurance company kept 15 percent of the premiums in return for performing actuarial and accounting services and the related insurance company kept 85 percent of the premiums. The banks kept no part of the premiums because they were advised by counsel that a federal statute prohibited

---

[118] *See also Merck & Co., Inc.*, 91-2 USTC ¶ 50,456, 24 Cl. Ct. 73 (1991).

[119] *First Security Bank of Utah, N.A., et al.*, 72-1 USTC ¶ 9292A, 405 US 394 (1972).

the banks from conducting the business of an insurance agency or receiving income resulting from their customers' purchase of credit life insurance.

These transactions attracted IRS scrutiny because less tax was due, on a consolidated basis, under the taxpayer's structure than would be due if the related banks were allowed to retain a portion of the insurance premiums. This was because the related insurance company was subject to a lower effective tax rate than the banks. Consequently, the IRS, under the authority of Code Sec. 482, reallocated 40 percent of the insurance premiums received by the related insurance company to the two related banks as compensation for originating and processing services.

The Supreme Court rejected the IRS's allocation and held that the IRS's exercise of its authority under Code Sec. 482 was not warranted because the taxpayer lacked the ability to shift income from the banks to the related insurance company. Instead, the shifting of income was due to federal banking law restrictions. The Court stated, in part:

> [Code Sec. 482], as applied to the facts of this case, contemplates that . . . the controlling interest must have "complete power" to shift income among its subsidiaries. It is only where this power exists, and has been exercised in such a way that the "true taxable income" of a subsidiary has been understated, that the [IRS]is authorized to reallocate under Code Sec. 482. But [the common parent corporation] had no such power unless it acted in violation of federal banking laws. The "complete" power referred to in the regulations hardly includes the power to force [the banks] to violate the law.[120]

The holding of *First Security Bank* was followed in *Salyersville National Bank*[121] The facts in *Salyersville National Bank* were very similar to the facts in *First Security Bank*. However, in *Salyeresville National Bank*, the bank *could* have applied to be licensed as an insurance agent under state law, and therefore legally receive the income that the IRS sought to allocate to it. Nevertheless, the court held that the fact that the bank may have had the power to enable it to receive the income legally does not require it to actually exercise such power.[122]

Procter & Gamble Co. Following the Supreme Court's decision in *First Security Bank*, the IRS attempted to limit the scope of the decision to factual situations where the legal restriction in question arose under U.S. law.[123] These efforts were first reviewed by the courts in *Procter & Gamble Co.*[124]

In *Procter & Gamble* the Sixth Circuit Court of Appeals affirmed the Tax Court's rejection of the IRS's reallocation of income under Code Sec. 482 where foreign law prohibited the expatriation of royalties. The Procter & Gamble Company ("P&G"), a domestic corporation engaged in the business of manufacturing and marketing consumer and industrial products, operated its worldwide business both directly and indirectly through domestic and foreign subsidiaries and affili-

---

[120] *Id.* at 404-5.

[121] *Salyersville National Bank*, 80-1 USTC ¶ 9190, 613 F.2d 650 (6th Cir. 1980); 77-2 USTC ¶ 9711.

[122] *See also, Bank of Winnfield & Trust Co.*, 82-1 USTC ¶ 9292, 540 F. Supp. 219 (W.D. LA).

[123] *See e.g.*, Rev. Rul. 82-45, 1982-1 CB 89; Technical Advice Memorandum 7923003 (Feb. 22, 1979); Technical Advice Memorandum 8001017 (Sep. 28, 1979); Technical Advice Memorandum 8117012 (Dec. 31, 1980).

[124] *Procter & Gamble Co.*, 92-1 USTC ¶ 50,209, 961 F.2d 1255 (6th Cir. 1992).

ates. When P&G decided to organize a Spanish subsidiary ("España"), it was advised by Spanish counsel that it must submit an application letter to the Spanish government requesting authorization to organize a 100 percent owned entity in Spain. For business reasons, P&G decided to hold España through a wholly owned Swiss subsidiary ("Swiss A.G."). The Spanish government approved the application, however, the letter of approval expressly provided that España could not pay any amounts for royalties or technical assistance to Swiss A.G. or directly to P&G.

The IRS determined that an allocation of income pursuant to Code Sec. 482 from España to Swiss A.G. was necessary to clearly reflect income. The allocation was in the form of a deemed royalty equal to two percent of España's sales. In setting aside the IRS's allocation, the Tax Court followed *First Security* in ruling that Code Sec. 482 did not apply where legal restrictions, and not the actions of the controlling interest, distort income among the controlled group. The distortion of income was the result of P&G's actions involving its valid business purpose and its compliance with Spanish law.

The Tax Court's opinion in *Procter & Gamble* was affirmed on appeal to the Sixth Circuit. The Sixth Circuit rejected the IRS's argument that P&G could have reported the royalty income on a deferred basis and then pays the tax due once the foreign legal restriction was lifted. The court reasoned that the regulation was not applicable because it concerned only temporary restrictions and that P&G had no reason to believe that the restriction would be lifted.

Exxon Corp. In *Exxon Corp.*,[125] the Tax Court held that Saudi Arabia's price restrictions on oil prevented the IRS from reallocating profits under Code Sec. 482. In doing so, the Tax Court refused to adopt the IRS's position on the "Aramco advantage" earned by four of the largest U.S. multinational petroleum companies as a result of Saudi crude oil pricing policies from mid-1979 through late 1981. The holding also represents a firm rejection of the IRS's attempts to tailor the Supreme Court's opinion in *First Security* in a manner that minimizes the effect of foreign law of U.S. income recognition.

Aramco operated the Saudi Arabian oil concession during and prior to the years at issue. Its stock was owned by Exxon, Texaco, Mobil, and Chevron, or their predecessor corporations. Aramco was responsible for extracting Saudi crude oil and delivering it to export purchasers, including the four Aramco corporate share-holders. During these years, Aramco functioned as a service provider in return for stated fees. The transfer pricing issues arose because of crude oil resale price restrictions imposed by the Saudi government on the four participating oil companies in an attempt to moderate prices in the wake of OPEC actions to increase them worldwide.

In response to the requests of the U.S. government and the Aramco sharehold-ers, the Saudi government agreed in 1979 to mitigate the effect of the crisis by (i) increasing 1979 production above previously announced levels; (ii) maintaining 1978 price levels for crude production up to a stated limit; and (iii) imposing

---

[125] *Exxon Corp.*, CCH Dec. 49,496(M), 66 TCM (CCH) 1707.

¶280.02

specific resale price restrictions on companies that purchased Saudi crude oil, including the trading company subsidiaries of the Aramco shareholders. The restrictions applied only to sales of crude oil to refining companies and had no effect on prices for refined petroleum products, which rose during the years in question in response to perceived shortages. The Saudi 1979 pricing actions enabled the Aramco shareholders to obtain Saudi oil at prices below the market for comparable crude from other countries. This market discount was the "Aramco advantage." Because the Aramco shareholders' trading company subsidiaries were organized in the U.S. and their primary customers were foreign refining subsidiaries, the Saudi resale price restrictions had the effect of shifting profits from the U.S. to the foreign countries in which the refining subsidiaries were organized.

The IRS responded with allocations under Code Sec. 482, which were intended to shift the asserted Aramco advantage profits to the U.S. trading companies. The taxpayers countered that the Saudi price restrictions effectively prevented the U.S. trading companies from earning the profits reallocated in the deficiency notices. The Tax Court agreed with the taxpayers and its decision was affirmed by the Fifth Circuit Court of Appeals.[126]

Notwithstanding the IRS's continuing focus on limiting the application of *First Security*, *Exxon* is notable primarily for its analysis of whether a foreign legal restriction actually existed. The Tax Court's inquiry in this regard was broken into four separate questions: whether the restriction (i) is authorized by the requisite authority; (ii) is applied consistently; (iii) is mandatory; and (iv) was effective during the relevant period. Although no authority was cited by the court for this specific formulation of the issue, it was clearly intended to articulate the elements of a law that are common to most jurisdictions.[127]

.03 Relief Under the Code Sec. 482 Regulations

The regulations provide that the District Director will take into account the effect of a foreign legal restriction to the extent that such restrictions affect the results of transactions at arm's length.[128] A foreign legal restriction is taken into account only to the extent that it is shown that the restriction affected an uncontrolled taxpayer under comparable circumstances for a comparable period.[129] If the effect on uncontrolled taxpayers cannot be shown, the taxpayer may elect to treat the blocked income under the deferred income method of accounting method (described below). If the taxpayer is unable to show that the restriction affected an uncontrolled taxpayer under comparable circumstances for a comparable period, or fails to make an election to use the deferred income method of accounting, the taxpayer must report the blocked income currently.

Requirement for Electing the Deferred Income Method of Accounting. If a foreign legal restriction prevents the payment or receipt of all or part of an arm's length amount, the restricted amount may be treated as deferrable if: (i) the

---

[126] *Texaco, Inc.*, 96-2 USTC ¶ 50,556, 98 F.3d 825 (5th Cir. 1996), *aff'g sub nom, Exxon Corp.*, CCH Dec. 49,496(M), 66 TCM 1707.

[127] *See* Levey & Graver, "482 Allocation Barred in ARAMCO Advantage Cases," 5 *J. of Int'l Tax'n* 205 (May 1994).

[128] Reg. § 1.482-1(h)(2).

[129] *Id.*

taxpayer shows that the payment of receipt of the arm's length amount was prevented because of an applicable foreign legal restriction (see discussion below); and (ii) the taxpayer elects to use the deferred income method of accounting by attaching a written statement to a timely U.S. income tax return (or an amended return) filed before the IRS contacts any member of the controlled group concerning an examination of the return in which the restriction has an impact.[130] The election statement must identify the affected transactions, the parties to the transactions, and the applicable foreign legal restrictions.[131]

> *Comment:* This procedure is similar to the IRS's stated position with respect to the reporting of blocked income under Code Sec. 446.[132]

Applicable Foreign Legal Restrictions. An applicable foreign legal restriction is one that meets the following requirements:

1. The restrictions are publicly promulgated, generally applicable to all similarly situated persons (both controlled and uncontrolled), and are not imposed as part of a commercial transaction between the taxpayer and the foreign government;

2. The taxpayer (or the controlled party to which the restriction applies) has exhausted all practical remedies prescribed by local law or practice for obtaining a waiver of such restrictions;

3. The restrictions expressly prevent the payment or receipt, in any form, of part or all of the arm's length amount that would otherwise be required under Code Sec. 482; and

4. The related parties subject to the restriction did not engage in any arrangement with controlled or uncontrolled parties that had the effect of circumventing the restriction, and have not otherwise violated the restriction in any material respect.[133]

Deferred Income Method of Accounting. If a taxpayer makes an election attributable to an applicable foreign legal restriction, the portion of the payment or receipt which is prevented because of applicable foreign legal restrictions will be treated as deferrable until the restriction preventing that payment or receipt is removed.[134] The deductions and credits attributable to the deferred income must also be deferred in the event of an election under the provisions of Reg. § 1.461-1(a)(4).[135]

When Blocked Income Ceases to be Deferrable. The regulations do not specify the circumstances under which blocked income ceases to be "deferrable income." However, by reference to Rev. Rul. 74-351 (procedures for blocked income under Code Sec. 446), it would appear that blocked income ceases to be deferrable when:

---

[130] Reg. § 1.482-1(h)(2)(iii).
[131] Reg. § 1.482-1(h)(2)(iii)(B).
[132] *See* Rev. Rul. 74-351, 1974-2 CB 144.

[133] Reg. § 1.482-1(h)(2)(ii).
[134] Reg. § 1.482-1(h)(2)(iv).
[135] Reg. § 1.482-1(h)(2)(iv).

¶280.03

1. The foreign country allows payment of the income previously allocated under Code Sec. 482;

2. Payment of the allocated income is actually received by the taxpayer, notwithstanding the continuing existence of a legal prohibition against payment of that income;

3. The taxpayer's rights to the future receipt of the income are transferred; or

4. The stock of the foreign subsidiary becomes worthless. In such case, the taxpayer will presumably be entitled to a step-up on the basis of its investment in the foreign subsidiary corresponding to the blocked income never received.

Under Rev. Rul. 74-351, the investment of blocked income within the foreign country does *not* cause the blocked income to cease being deferrable income. Instead, the property purchased is said to have a "deferred income basis" which will be included in the taxpayer's income when the income would have ceased being "deferrable income."

Recharacterization of Dividends as Repatriation of Blocked Income. In Technical Advice Memorandum 9736003 (May 27, 1997), the IRS allowed a taxpayer to report blocked royalty income on a current basis and recharacterize a portion of the dividends that it received from its foreign subsidiary (from which the income was blocked) as the repatriation of blocked royalties. This recharacterization of a dividend into a royalty was made under the authority of Rev. Proc. 65-17 (superseded by Rev. Proc. 99-32), which generally allows taxpayers to repatriate cash on a tax free basis following an IRS adjustment. The IRS's ruling was further based on the reasoning that the taxpayer's reporting of the blocked royalty income for the years at issue was consistent with the treatment of IRS-initiated adjustments in prior years, and because there was no indicia tax avoidance.[136]

> *Comment:* In *Procter & Gamble*, the IRS argued that the royalty income was not truly blocked under Spanish law because the taxpayer could have entered into a transaction similar to that described in this FSA. The Sixth Circuit rejected this assertion because it would require the taxpayer to violate Spanish law.[137]

.04 Comment on the IRS Regulations

Following the promulgation of the Code Sec. 482 blocked income regulations, several commentators have suggested that the regulations would not survive judicial scrutiny because they overstep the IRS's authority under the statute.[138] The criticisms of the regulations can be summarized as follows:

1. *Lack of Statutory Authority:* Commentators have questioned whether the IRS has the authority to issue Code Sec. 482 regulations covering blocked

---

[136] *But see* FSA 1999797 (Jul. 2, 1993) (advising that a dividend should not be recharacterized as the payment of blocked income partly because to do so would prevent Code Sec. 902 deemed paid foreign tax credits from being available).

[137] *Procter & Gamble*, 92-1 USTC ¶ 50,209 at 1259.

[138] *See* Davlin, "Note: The Uncertainty of Foreign Blocked Income: Trying to Reconcile the 1994 482 Regulations with Proctor & Gamble," 5 *Duke J. Comp. & Int'l L.* 117 (1994); Levey & Clancy, "IRS Seeks to Reverse Procter & Gamble with Proposed 482 Regulations," *Journal of Int'l Tax* p. 137 (March 1993).

income when the Supreme Court in *First Security* held that Code Sec. 482 could not be applied in the blocked income situation.

2. *Payment Assumptions:* Commentators have also questioned whether blocked income regulation's assumption that the foreign legal restriction is only temporary and will eventually be lifted comports with reality. Further, this assumption is an apparent effort by the IRS to overrule the Sixth Circuit's opinion in *Procter & Gamble.*

Chapter 3

Methods for Transfers of Tangible Property

¶ 301 Overview

.01 In General

The most common situation in which Code Sec. 482 is applied is the sale of tangible property between related entities. For transfers of tangible property, the regulations provide the following six methods for determining the arm's length charge:[1]

- Comparable Uncontrolled Price ("CUP") method;
- Resale price method ("RPM");
- Cost-plus method;
- Comparable Profit Method ("CPM");
- Profit split method; and
- Other unspecified methods.

---

[1] Reg. § 1.482-3(a).

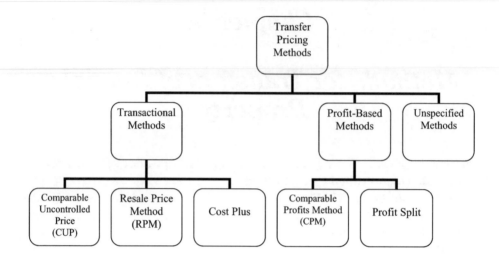

Transfer Pricing Method	Location in Regulations	Most Common Use	Comparability Considerations	Adjustments to Improve Comparability	Comment
I. TRANSACTIONAL TPMs					
CUP (Comparable Uncontrolled Price) (compares controlled price to CUP)	Reg. § 1.482-3(b)		Similar products Similar economic conditions Similar contractual terms (similarity of products generally has greatest effect on comparability under this method)	Product quality Contractual terms Market level Geographic market Transaction date Associated intangible property Currency risks Realistic alternatives of buyer and seller	Most direct and reliable measure (where information exists) Internal CUP generally has greater comparability than external CUP
RPM (Resale Price Method) (subtract appropriate gross profit from the resale price in controlled transaction)	Reg. § 1.482-3(c)	Purchase and resale of tangible property in which the reseller has not added substantial value to the tangible goods by physically altering them before the sale	Similar functions performed Similar risks Similar contractual terms Similar product category Significant differences in the value of distributed goods due to the value of a trademark Other (e.g., cost structures, business experience, management efficiency)	Inventory levels, turnover rates, and corresponding risks Operating expenses Contractual terms Sales, marketing, advertising programs and services Market level Currency risks Consistency in accounting practices	Generally, packaging, repackaging, labeling, or minor assembly do not constitute physical alteration
Cost Plus (Cost Plus Method) (compares gross profit markup in controlled transaction with uncontrolled transaction)	Reg. § 1.482-3(d)	Manufacture, assembly, or other production of goods sold to related parties	Similar functions performed Similar risks Similar contractual terms Similar product category Significant differences in the value of distributed goods due to the value of a trademark Other (e.g., cost structures, business experience, management efficiency)	Complexity of manufacturing or assembly Manufacturing, production, and process engineering Procurement, purchasing, and inventory control activities Testing functions Selling, general, and administrative expenses Currency risks Contractual terms Consistency in accounting practices	Not dependent on close physical similarity of products

¶301.01

Transfer Pricing Method	Most Common Use	Comparability Considerations	Adjustments to Improve Comparability
**II. TRANSACTIONAL TPMs**			
CPM (Comparable Profits Method) **TNMM** (Transactional Net Margin Method) (compares profitability of controlled transactions with profitability of similar uncontrolled transactions) [Reg. §1.482-5] **Comment:** Most widely used method. Compares operating profits earned on controlled transactions to the operating profit of uncontrolled comparables (entities of transactions). Evaluates the least complex entity (generally, controlled entity with no valuable intangibles) **(PLIs)** (Profit level indicators) • rate of return on capital employed; • financial ratios (ratio of operating profit to sales, ratio of gross profit to operating expenses); • other profit level indicators.	Manufacturers, Distributors, Service Providers	Resources employed; Risks; Functions performed; Other (e.g., cost structures, business experience, management efficiency)	Operating assets; Degree of consistency in accounting practices
PSM (Profit Split Method): **CPS** (Comparable Profit Split) CPS is derived from combined operating profit of uncontrolled taxpayers with similar transactions. Under this method, each uncontrolled taxpayer's percentage of the combined operating profit or loss is used to allocate the combined operating profit or loss of the relevant business activities. **Comment:** Seldom encountered in practice		Resources employed; Risks; Functions performed; Other (e.g., cost structures, business experience, management efficiency); Contractual terms	Results of uncontrolled comparables
PSM (Profit Split Method): **RPS** (Residual Profit Split) RPS involves a two-step process: • allocation of income to routine contributions; **PLIs** are used to measure profitability [Reg. §1.482-6; Reg. §1.482-6(c)(2)] • allocation of residual profit. [Reg. §1.482-6; Reg. §1.482-6(c)(3)] **Comment:** Most often used when each related entity owns significant valuable intangibles	Manufacturers, Distributors, Service Providers	Market benchmarks of profitability (when allocating income to routine contributions—step one); Functions performed; Risks, Resources employed; Product similarity; Accounting consistency	
Unspecified Methods [Reg. §1.482-3(e)]	—	—	—

¶301.01

.02 Preference for Internal Comparables

When employing transactional methods, the transfer pricing regulations indicate a clear preference for an "internal" comparable transaction (i.e., a comparable transaction between one of the controlled parties and an unrelated party) over an "external" comparable transaction (i.e., a transaction between unrelated parties that does not involve one of the controlled parties). This preference shows up in various locations in the regulations[2] and has been recognized in court cases and articles.[3]

The reason for this preference is twofold. First, comparable transactions involving one of the controlled parties can expect to have closer comparability of goods or services than transactions involving two unrelated parties. Second, by virtue of being one of the parties to the comparable transaction, the controlled parties have superior information with which to identify and adjust for differences between the controlled transaction and the comparable transaction.

¶ 310 Comparable Uncontrolled Price Method

.01 In General

The CUP method evaluates whether the amount charged in a controlled transaction is arm's length by reference to the amount charged in a comparable uncontrolled transaction.[4] Provided that the comparability requirement is satisfied, the results derived from applying the CUP method generally will be the most direct and reliable measure of an arm's length price.[5]

> **Example:** U.S. Parent Co. ("USP") manufactures widgets and distributes the widgets through both related and unrelated parties. On January 31st, USP sells 10,000 widgets for $5/widget to Unrelated Distributor ("UD"), a Canadian company that sells widgets in Canada. On January 31st, USP also sells 10,000 widgets to Related Distributor ("RD"), a Canadian company that also sells widgets in Canada. Other things being equal, the $5/unit price charged by USP to UD would be the arm's length price of the widgets sold by USP to RD.

.02 Comparability and Reliability

A CUP may be derived based on an internal or an external comparable.[6] In practice, of course, no two sales are exactly alike. Exact comparables, likely drawn from internal transactions with unrelated parties, tend to be the most reliable source for these types of comparable transactions. Nevertheless, the regulations provide that sufficient comparability exists if similar products are sold under circumstances that are substantially the same, and any differences in the products

---

[2] E.g., Reg. § 1.482-3(c)(3)(ii)(A). "If possible, appropriate gross profit margins should be derived from comparable uncontrolled purchases and resales of the reseller involved in the controlled sale, because similar characteristics are more likely to be found among different resales of property made by the same reseller than among sales made by other resellers." *See also* Reg. § 1.482-3(b)(2)(ii)(A) and § 1.482-3(d)(3)(ii)(A).

[3] Ackerman, Robert and Elizabeth Chorvat, "Tax Council Institute Symposium: The Future of International

Transfer Pricing: Practical and Policy Opportunities: Article: Modern Financial Theory and Transfer Pricing," 10 *Geo. Mason L. Rev.* 637 (Summer 2002). "The Tax Court has held that reasonable internal comparables, even when adjustments are required to achieve reliability, should be utilized in preference to a less precise method."

[4] Reg. § 1.482-3(b)(1).

[5] Reg. § 1.482-3(b)(2)(ii)(A).

[6] Reg. § 1.482-3(b)(1); Reg. § 1.482-1(i)(8).

or circumstances either have no effect on prices or have differences that can be measured and eliminated with a reasonable number of adjustments.[7]

Similarity of products generally has the greatest effect on comparability under the CUP method.[8]

.03 Adjustments

A proposed CUP may be adjusted for many factors, including:

- Quality of the product;
- Contractual terms (e.g., warranty terms, sales volume, credit terms, or delivery terms);
- Level of the market (i.e., wholesale v. resale);
- Geographic market;
- Date of the transaction;
- Intangible property associated with the sale;
- Foreign currency risks; and
- Purchaser or buyer alternatives.[9]

However, if there are material product differences for which reliable adjustments cannot be made, the CUP method will not satisfy the best method rule.[10]

The regulations under Code Sec. 482 which describe CUP transactions, provide some examples that demonstrate the IRS view of acceptable and unacceptable comparables.[11]

Reg. § 1.482-3(b)(4), Ex. 1

Comparable Sales of Same Product. USM, a U.S. manufacturer, sells the same product to both controlled and uncontrolled distributors. The circumstances surrounding the controlled and uncontrolled transactions are substantially the same, except that the controlled sales price is a delivered price and the uncontrolled sales are made f.o.b. USM's factory. Differences in the contractual terms of transportation and insurance generally have a definite and reasonably ascertainable effect on price, and adjustments are made to the results of the uncontrolled transaction to account for such differences. No other material difference has been identified between the controlled and uncontrolled transactions. Because USM sells in both the controlled and uncontrolled transactions, it is likely that all material differences between the two transactions have been identified. In addition, because the comparable uncontrolled price method is applied to an uncontrolled comparable with no product differences, and there are only minor contractual differences that have a definite and reasonably ascertainable effect on price, the results of this application of the comparable uncontrolled price

[7] Reg. § 1.482-3(b)(2)(ii)(A); *Compaq Computer Corp.*, CCH Dec. 53,443(M), 78 TCM 20, TC Memo 1999-220 (July 20, 1999) (taxpayer used a CUP analysis to show that the transfer prices paid for printed circuit assemblies ("PCAs") from its wholly-owned Singapore subsidiary were consistent with the arm's length prices). *See also, PPG Industries, inc.*, CCH Dec. 30,683, 55 TC 928 (1970), where the Tax Court found that an adjustment could be made to reflect the difference in price of uncut glass (controlled transaction) v. cut glass (uncontrolled transaction).

[8] *Id. But see Seagate Technology, Inc.*, CCH Dec. 49,657, 102 TC 149, 186-188 (1994), where the Tax Court rejected a proposed CUP involving the sale of identical goods because the circumstances of the sale were not sufficiently comparable.

[9] Reg. § 1.482-3(b)(2)(ii)(B).

[10] Reg. § 1.482-3(b)(2)(iii). *See, e.g., Sundstrand Corp.*, CCH Dec. 47,172, 96 TC 226 (1991).

[11] Reg. § 1.482-3(b)(3).

method will provide the most direct and reliable measure of an arm's length result. See Reg. § 1.482-3(b)(2)(ii)(A).[12]

Reg. § 1.482-3(b)(4), Ex. 2

Effect of Trademark. The facts are the same as in *Example 1*, except that USM affixes its valuable trademark to the property sold in the controlled transactions, but does not affix its trademark to the property sold in the uncontrolled transactions. Under the facts of this case, the effect on price of the trademark is material and cannot be reliably estimated. Because there are material product differences for which reliable adjustments cannot be made, the comparable uncontrolled price method is unlikely to provide a reliable measure of the arm's length result. See Reg. § 1.482-3(b)(2)(ii)(A).[13]

Reg. § 1.482-3(b)(4), Ex. 3

Minor Product Differences. The facts are the same as in *Example 1*, except that USM, which manufactures business machines, makes minor modifications to the physical properties of the machines to satisfy specific requirements of a customer in controlled sales, but does not make these modifications in uncontrolled sales. If the minor physical differences in the product have a material affect on prices, adjustments to account for these differences must be made to the results of the uncontrolled transactions according to the provisions of § 1.482-1(d)(2), and such adjusted results may be used as a measure of the arm's length result.[14]

Reg. § 1.482-3(b)(4), Ex. 4

Effect of Geographic Differences. FM, a foreign specialty radio manufacturer, sells its radios to a controlled U.S. distributor, AM, that serves the West Coast of the United States. FM sells its radios to uncontrolled distributors to serve other regions in the United States. The product in the controlled and uncontrolled transactions is the same, and all other circumstances surrounding the controlled and uncontrolled transactions are substantially the same, other than the geographic differences. If the geographic differences are unlikely to have a material effect on price, or they have definite and reasonably ascertainable effects for which adjustments are made, then the adjusted results of the uncontrolled sales may be used under the comparable uncontrolled price method to establish an arm's length range pursuant to § 1.482-1(e)(2)(iii)(A). If the effects of the geographic differences would be material but cannot be reliably ascertained, then the reliability of the results will be diminished. However, the comparable uncontrolled price method may still provide the most reliable measure of an arm's length result, pursuant to the best method rule of § 1.482-1(c), and, if so, an arm's length range may be established pursuant to § 1.482-1(e)(2)(iii)(B).[15]

.04 Indirect Evidence of CUP

The CUP method may also be applied based on data from public exchanges or quotation media.[16] This data will be typically used to price intercompany transactions involving commodity products (e.g., oil, minerals, *etc.*). In order to use such data, the following requirements must be met:

- Data is widely and routinely used in the ordinary course of business in the industry to negotiate prices for uncontrolled sales;

---

[12] Reg. § 1.482-3(b)(4), Ex. 1.

[13] Reg. § 1.482-3(b)(4), Ex. 2.

[14] Reg. § 1.482-3(b)(4), Ex. 3.

[15] Reg. § 1.482-3(b)(4), Ex. 4.

[16] Reg. § 1.482-3(b)(5).

- Data is used to set prices in the controlled transaction in the same way that it is used by uncontrolled taxpayers in the industry; and

- Amount charged in the controlled transaction is adjusted to reflect differences in product quality and quantity, contractual terms, transportation costs, market conditions, risks borne, and other factors that affect the price that would be agreed to by uncontrolled taxpayers.

However, the regulations warn that the use of data from public exchanges or quotation media may not be appropriate under extraordinary market conditions (e.g., times of war).[17]

Reg. § 1.482-3(b)(5), Ex. 1

Use of Quotation Medium. (i) On June 1, USOil, a United States corporation, enters into a contract to purchase crude oil from its foreign subsidiary, FS, in Country Z. USOil and FS agree to base their sales price on the average of the prices published for that crude in a quotation medium in the five days before August 1, the date set for delivery. USOil and FS agree to adjust the price for the particular circumstances of their transactions, including the quantity of the crude sold, contractual terms, transportation costs, risks borne, and other factors that affect the price.

(ii) The quotation medium used by USOil and FS is widely and routinely used in the ordinary course of business in the industry to establish prices for uncontrolled sales. Because USOil and FS use the data to set their sales price in the same way that unrelated parties use the data from the quotation medium to set their sales prices, and appropriate adjustments were made to account for differences, the price derived from the quotation medium used by USOil and FS to set their transfer prices will be considered evidence of a comparable uncontrolled price.[18]

Reg. § 1.482-3(b)(5), Ex. 2

Extraordinary Market Conditions. The facts are the same as in Example 1, except that before USOil and FS enter into their contract, war breaks out in Countries X and Y, major oil producing countries, causing significant instability in world petroleum markets. As a result, given the significant instability in the price of oil, the prices listed on the quotation medium may not reflect a reliable measure of an arm's length result. See § 1.482-3(b)(5)(ii).[19]

.05 Cases Applying the CUP

U.S. Steel Corp. *U.S. Steel Corp.*[20] involved the transfer prices for shipping services. Nevertheless, the courts have adopted its analysis in reviewing cases involving tangible property.[21]

In *U.S. Steel*, the Court of Appeals held that no portion of the shipping rates charged by a foreign transportation subsidiary to its domestic parent company was allocable to the parent where the rates charged were equal to those charged to unrelated U.S. importers. Under the facts of this case, U.S. Steel ("USS") estab-

---

[17] Reg. § 1.482-3(b)(5)(ii).
[18] Reg. § 1.482-3(b)(5)(iii), Ex. 1.
[19] Reg. § 1.482-3(b)(5)(iii), Ex. 2.

[20] *U.S. Steel Corp.*, 80-1 USTC ¶ 9307, 617 F.2d 942 (2d Cir. 1980), *rev'ing* CCH Dec. 34,400(M), 36 TCM (CCH) 586, TC Memo. 1977-140 (1977).

[21] *See, e.g., Bausch & Lomb, Inc.*, CCH Dec. 45,547, 92 TC 525 (1989), *aff'd* 91-1 USTC ¶ 50,244, 933 F.2d 1084 (2d Cir. 1991).

lished a wholly-owned shipping subsidiary ("ShipSub") in Liberia to engage in business from a base in the Bahamas. ShipSub chartered ships from independent shipping companies to transport iron ore from Venezuela to the United States. Although most of its revenue from the shipments was from USS, ShipSub also derived a small portion of its revenues (about 5 percent of its total) from unrelated foreign and domestic corporations. ShipSub charged the same price to its U.S. independent importers as it did to USS.

The court held that the intercompany prices at issue were equal to those charged for similar services in independent transactions, thus rejecting the IRS's adjustment under Code Sec. 482. The independent transactions of ShipSub with unrelated domestic corporations were found sufficient to establish an arm's length charge even though they constituted such a small percentage of gross sales and were not all at the same prices charged to affiliates.

Congress expressed frustration with *U.S. Steel* because of its use of seemingly isolated transactions as reliable comparables. The General Explanation of the Tax Reform Act of 1986 cites *U.S. Steel* as an example of a court decision that overemphasized the use of comparables in establishing transfer prices, particularly when significant differences existed in the volume of unrelated and related transactions, as well as differences in risks involved and other factors.[22]

Eli Lilly & Co. The Tax Court addressed the issue of comparability in *Eli Lilly & Co.*[23] Eli Lilly manufactures and distributes pharmaceutical products. Prior to the transactions at issue, all of Eli Lilly's manufacturing facilities were located in Indiana. In 1966, after developing and patenting a prescription drug called Darvon, Eli Lilly transferred the patents and related know-how to newly created and wholly-owned Puerto Rican manufacturing subsidiary ("Lilly PR") in a Code Sec. 351 transaction. From 1971-1973, Lilly PR manufactured and sold Darvon to Eli Lilly, which distributed the drug in the U.S. marketplace. The transfer prices for 1971-1973 tax years were established pursuant to a complex pricing formula agreed to by Eli Lilly and the IRS following the audit of Eli Lilly's 1966-1968 tax years. This pricing formula divided the combined profit as a basis for establishing a price for Lilly PR's Darvon sales to Eli Lilly.

In reviewing Eli Lilly's transfer pricing, the Tax Court applied a profit split analysis for the 1971-1972 tax years because the Darvon patent precluded unrelated parties from entering into comparable transactions for the same drug. The Darvon patent expired in late-1972, and generic equivalents for Darvon became available in the marketplace. Accordingly, the Tax Court found that the sales of the generic Darvon equivalent could support the application of the CUP method in determining an arm's length transfer price for 1973.[24] However, because there were many differences between sales of the generic Darvon equivalents by unrelated parties and sales of Darvon by the Lilly PR, the court made several adjustments to

[22] Staff of Joint Comm. on Taxation, 99th Cong., 2d Sess., General Explanations of the Tax Reform Act of 1986, pp. 1014-15.

[23] *Eli Lilly & Co.*, CCH Dec. 42,113, 84 TC 996 (1985), *aff'd in part and rev'd in part*, 88-2 USTC ¶ 9502, 856 F.2d 855 (7th Cir. 1988).

[24] *Id.* at 1168-1169.

¶310.05

determine an arm's length price for intercompany Darvon sales. The court considered several factors in adjusting the prices, including:

- Provision of raw materials to the manufacturer by the purchaser;
- Differences in credit terms;
- Provision of samples;
- Quality differences between Darvon and the generic equivalents; and
- Ownership of intangibles.

> **Comment:** Several transfer pricing cases were based on transactions involving "possessions corporations." Under Code Sec. 936, qualifying possessions corporations doing business in Puerto Rico were eligible for an effective 100 percent tax credit on their U.S. tax income liability. Qualifying corporations were eligible to receive generous tax benefits under Puerto Rico law. These tax benefits attracted many U.S. corporations to incorporate manufacturing subsidiaries in Puerto Rico, including the subsidiary at issue in *Eli Lilly*. However, the amount of the Code Sec. 936 tax benefit was substantially reduced in 1993.[25]

Bausch & Lomb, Inc. The comparability issue was also addressed by the Tax Court in *Bausch & Lomb, Inc.*[26] Beginning in 1966, Bausch & Lomb ("B&L"), a contact lenses manufacturer, acquired and further developed certain patent rights and manufacturing know-how to produce soft contact lenses. In 1980, B&L formed an Irish subsidiary ("B&L Ireland") to increase its manufacturing capacity and to decentralize its worldwide manufacturing facilities to prevent the risk of interruption by natural or man-made disasters. B&L licensed its manufacturing know-how to B&L Ireland, which manufactured the soft contact lenses and sold a substantial portion of its output to B&L for distribution in the United States.

B&L Ireland charged B&L a transfer price of $7.50 per lens. The IRS made an adjustment for B&L's 1979-1981 tax years based on a transfer price of between $2.25 and $3.00 per lens. In defending its transfer prices, B&L produced evidence showing that similarly situated distributors in the contact lens industry generally received a mark-up of approximately 25-40 percent on the resale of soft contact lenses. Because B&L's mark-up on the resale of lenses purchased from the Irish Subsidiary was about 50 percent, B&L argued that the $7.50 sales price was arm's length. After finding that soft-contact lenses are fungible products, the Tax Court applied the CUP method and ruled in favor of B&L, subject to an adjustment for duty and freight charges. In doing so, the Tax Court rejected the IRS's arguments that (i) the third-party sales relied on by B&L were not functionally similar to its transactions; (ii) these sales were at different market levels and volumes; (iii) the distributors relied on by B&L as a source of comparable sales performed only a distribution function; and (iv) B&L could have produced the same lenses for significantly less than the $7.50 per lens paid to the Irish affiliate.

---

[25] *See* Omnibus Budget Reconciliation Act of 1993, P.L. 103-66, § 13227(a)(1)-(2).

[26] *Bausch & Lomb, Inc.*, CCH Dec. 45,547, 92 TC 525 (1989), *aff'd.* 91-1 USTC ¶ 50,244, 933 F.2d 1084 (2d Cir. 1991).

National Semiconductor Corp. The Tax Court again addressed comparability in *National Semiconductor Corp.*[27] National Semiconductor ("NS") manufactured and sold semiconductor dies to several Asian subsidiaries ("AsiaSubs"). The AsiaSubs, in turn, purchased additional parts from unrelated parties and assembled/packaged the dies and parts into integrated circuits and other devices. The completed integrated circuits and other devices were sold to NS, NS affiliates, and other unrelated parties.

For financial and tax reporting purposes, NS treated the transfer of semiconductor dies to the AsiaSubs as outbound sales and the transfer of integrated circuits and other assembled devices from the AsiaSubs to NS as inbound sales. For the tax years at issue, NS reported only $11.8 million of income for the semiconductor dies sold to the AsiaSubs, whereas the AsiaSubs reported income of $182.8 million during that same period. In its notice of deficiency, the IRS reallocated $122.2 million from the AsiaSubs to NS on the theory that the AsiaSub's profits should be limited to that of contract manufacturers.

In defending its transfer prices, NS, relied in part on a "price-to-price" analysis prepared by its expert witness. This "price-to-price" analysis, which compared prices charged by the AsiaSubs with prices charged by unrelated assembler/packagers, was essentially a CPM analysis with certain adjustments. The Tax Court ultimately rejected this analysis as unreliable because it incorporated numerous adjustments (e.g., materials shipping costs) and arbitrary extrapolation when direct price comparisons were not available.

> **Comment:** *National Semiconductor* is one of the first cases in which the court actually worked with the parties' expert reports in conjunction with the taxpayer's actual pricing data to derive a reasonable transfer price instead of invoking the *Cohan*[28] rule and creating its own version of a transfer price from some abstract data or other empirical information. This approach represents a departure from prior cases such as *Sundstrand Corp.*[29] and *Bausch & Lomb Inc.*[30] where the court exhibited impatience and frustration with the parties and their expert reports and sought to reconstruct a transfer price based on its own independent analysis.

Compaq Computer Corp. In *Compaq Computer Corp.*[31] the Tax Court concluded that the transfer prices paid by Compaq for printed circuit assemblies (PCAs) from its wholly-owned Singapore subsidiary, Compaq Asia, were consistent with the arm's length prices. The IRS had determined deficiencies in the amount of $124.5 million for TYE November 30, 1991 and $90.4 million for TYE November 30, 1992. Prior to trial, the deficiencies were reduced to $42.4 million for TYE November 30, 1991 and $33.5 million (with a $547,000 Code Sec. 6662(a) penalty) for TYE November 30, 1992. In rejecting the IRS' deficiencies in their entirety, the Tax

---

[27] *National Semiconductor Corp.*, CCH Dec. 49,824(M), 67 TCM (CCH) 2849 (1994).

[28] *G.M. Cohan*, 2 USTC ¶ 489, 39 F.2d 54 (2d Cir. 1930).

[29] *Sundstrand Corp.*, CCH Dec. 47,172, 96 TC 226, 354 (1991).

[30] *Bausch & Lomb Inc.*, CCH Dec. 45,547, 92 TC 525 (1989), *aff'd*, 91-1 USTC ¶ 50,244, 933 F.2d 1034 (2d Cir. 1991).

[31] *Compaq Computer Corp.*, CCH Dec. 53,443, 78 TCM 20; TC Memo 1999-220.

¶310.05

Court was persuaded by Compaq's CUP analysis. Several of the CUP issues addressed by the Tax Court are discussed below.

Comparability of Turnkey and Consignment Transactions. The Tax Court concluded that the intercompany transactions, which were priced on a turnkey basis, were sufficiently comparable to Compaq's unrelated transactions, which were priced on a consignment basis, to support the use of the CUP method once Compaq made certain adjustments. Although the prices paid in the intercompany transactions were lower than those paid in the unrelated party transactions, the Tax Court was satisfied that Compaq's CUP analysis of the differences in the transactions supported the differences in prices. Compaq's analysis showed that adjustments were appropriate for the following transactional differences: payment terms, advance purchase costs, setup and cancellation charges, freight, duties, and defect costs.

No Volume Discount. The IRS argued that Compaq should have been granted a volume discount by Compaq Asia. Compaq successfully rebutted this argument by producing testimony showing that, in the case of the CUP transactions, volume had no effect on price because the unrelated parties gave Compaq their best prices in light of Compaq's market position and the overall level of potential business. In the court's words "Compaq was big enough and bought enough PCAs that it was able to demand the best prices regardless of volume."

Prices v. Profit. The IRS argued that under a CPM analysis, Compaq Asia, would have a much lower profit margin. The Tax Court compared this argument to a similar argument that was rejected in *Bausch & Lomb, Inc.*[32] In doing so, the court concluded that, as in *B&L*, when the CUP method is properly used to determine arm's length prices, a large profit margin earned by the seller does not affect the analysis. Note that this conclusion is consistent with Reg. § 1.482-3(b)(2)(ii)(A) (stating that the CUP method generally satisfies the best method rule only if the adjustments required are for minor differences).

¶ 320 Resale Price Method ("RPM")

.01 In General

The resale price method ("RPM") evaluates whether the amount charged in a controlled transaction is arm's length by reference to the gross profit margin realized in comparable uncontrolled transactions.[33] The RPM measures the value of functions performed and is intended primarily to determine an arm's length price for transfers to sales subsidiaries, which in turn sell or distribute the product to unrelated customers without physically altering the goods before resale.[34] In applying the RPM, packaging, repackaging, labeling, or minor assembly does not constitute impermissible physical alteration.[35] However, the use of the RPM is generally not appropriate where a controlled taxpayer uses its intangible property to add substantial value to the tangible goods.[36]

---

[32] *Bausch & Lomb, Inc.*, 91-1 USTC ¶ 50,244, 933 F.2d 1034 (2d Cir. 1991); CCH Dec. 45,547, 92 TC 525 (1989).

[33] Reg. § 1.482-3(c)(1).

[34] Reg. § 1.482-3(c)(1).

[35] Reg. § 1.482-3(c)(1).

[36] Reg. § 1.482-3(c)(1).

Mechanically, an arm's length price is determined under the RPM by subtracting the "appropriate gross profit" from the "applicable resale price" of the particular item of property involved.[37] The applicable resale price is equal to either the resale price of the particular item or the price at which sales of the same item are made to uncontrolled parties.[38] The appropriate gross profit is computed by multiplying the applicable resale price by the gross profit margin (expressed as a percentage of total revenue derived from sales) earned in comparable uncontrolled transactions.[39]

More particularly, the RPM establishes an arm's length price for the sale between a supplier and a related reseller (i.e., distributor, wholesaler, or retailer) by applying the gross margin achieved in a comparable transaction, but not necessarily involving exactly similar products, to the resale price of the affiliated reseller. The gross margin compensates resellers for their operating expenses and provides a return on the associated investment of capital and assumption of risk. The arm's length prices are therefore set to achieve the same gross margin percentage as that achieved by an independent reseller, which is assumed to have priced its product to achieve a gross margin just sufficient to cover operating expenses plus a competitive return on capital. Notwithstanding, the operating profit results will likely determine if the appropriate gross profit margin is at arm's length.

.02 Comparability and Reliability

Like the CUP method, application of the RPM requires a sufficient level of comparability between the controlled and uncontrolled transactions.[40] Unlike the CUP method, close physical similarity of the property involved in the controlled and uncontrolled transactions is not ordinarily necessary to establish the comparability of the distributor's gross profit margin (although the products should be of the same general type).[41] However, if there are physical differences in the products, it is necessary to show that those differences do not adversely affect the comparability of other factors considered important for comparability under the RPM. These factors include: the similarity of functions, risks borne, contractual terms, the presence of intangibles, cost structures, business experience, and management efficiency. The regulations list other specific factors that may be particularly relevant under the RPM[42]:

- Inventory levels and turnover rates, and corresponding risks, including any price protection programs offered by the manufacturer;

- Contractual terms (e.g., scope and terms of warranties provided, sales or purchase volume, credit and transport terms);

- Sales, marketing, advertising programs, and services (including promotional programs, rebates, and coop advertising);

- The level of the market (e.g., wholesale, retail, etc.); and

- Foreign-currency risk.

---

[37] Reg. § 1.482-3(c)(2)(i).
[38] Reg. § 1.482-3(c)(2)(ii).
[39] Reg. § 1.482-3(c)(2)(iii).

[40] Reg. § 1.482-3(c)(3).
[41] Reg. § 1.482-3(c)(3)(ii)(B).
[42] Reg. § 1.482-3(c)(3)(ii)(C).

Consistency in accounting practices between the controlled transaction and the uncontrolled comparables that materially affect the gross profit margin will also affect the reliability of the RPM.

The regulations under Code Sec. 482, which defines the RPM, provides some guidance as to the IRS's view of acceptable and unacceptable uses of this method. Some examples include:

Reg. § 1.482-3(c)(4), Ex. 1

> A controlled taxpayer sells property to another member of its controlled group that resells the property in uncontrolled sales. There are no changes in the beginning and ending inventory for the year under review. Information regarding an uncontrolled comparable is sufficiently complete to conclude that it is likely that all material differences between the controlled and uncontrolled transactions have been identified and adjusted for. If the applicable resale price of the property involved in the controlled sale is $100 and the appropriate gross profit margin is 20%, then an arm's length result of the controlled sale is a price of $80 ($100 minus (20% × $100)).[43]

Reg. § 1.482-3(c)(4), Ex. 2

> (i) S, a U.S. corporation, is the exclusive distributor for FP, its foreign parent. There are no changes in the beginning and ending inventory for the year under review. S's total reported cost of goods sold is $800, consisting of $600 for property purchased from FP and $200 of other costs of goods sold incurred to unrelated parties. S's applicable resale price and reported gross profit are as follows:

Applicable resale price	$1000
Cost of goods sold	
Cost of purchases from FP	600
Costs incurred to unrelated parties	200
Reported gross profit	$200

> (ii) The district director determines that the appropriate gross profit margin is 25%. Therefore, S's appropriate gross profit is $250 (i.e., 25% of the applicable resale price of $1000). Because S is incurring costs of sales to unrelated parties, an arm's length price for property purchased from FP must be determined under a two-step process. First, the appropriate gross profit ($250) is subtracted from the applicable resale price ($1000). The resulting amount ($750) is then reduced by the costs of sales incurred to unrelated parties ($200). Therefore, an arm's length price for S's cost of sales of FP's product in this case equals $550 (i.e., $750 minus $200).[44]

Reg. § 1.482-3(c)(4), Ex. 3

> FP, a foreign manufacturer, sells Product to USSub, its U.S. subsidiary, which in turn sells Product to its domestic affiliate Sister. Sister sells Product to unrelated buyers. In this case, the applicable resale price is the price at which Sister sells Product in uncontrolled transactions. The determination of the appropriate gross profit margin for the sale from FP to USSub will take into account the

---

[43] Reg. § 1.482-3(c)(4), Ex. 1.　　　　[44] Reg. § 1.482-3(c)(4), Ex. 2.

functions performed by USSub and Sister, as well as other relevant factors described in Reg. § 1.482-1(d)(3).[45]

Reg. § 1.482-3(c)(4), Ex. 4

USSub, a U.S. corporation, is the exclusive distributor of widgets for its foreign parent. To determine whether the gross profit margin of 25% earned by USSub is an arm's length result, the district director considers applying the resale price method. There are several uncontrolled distributors that perform similar functions under similar circumstances in uncontrolled transactions. However, the uncontrolled distributors treat certain costs such as discounts and insurance as cost of goods sold, while USSub treats such costs as operating expenses. In such cases, accounting reclassifications, pursuant to § 1.482-3(c)(3)(iii)(B), must be made to ensure consistent treatment of such material items. Inability to make such accounting reclassifications will decrease the reliability of the results of the uncontrolled transactions.[46]

Reg. § 1.482-3(c)(4), Ex. 5

(i) USP, a U.S. corporation, manufactures Product X, an unbranded widget, and sells it to FSub, its wholly owned foreign subsidiary. FSub acts as a distributor of Product X in country M, and sells it to uncontrolled parties in that country. Uncontrolled distributors A, B, C, D and E distribute competing products of approximately similar value in country M. All such products are unbranded.

(ii) Relatively complete data is available regarding the functions performed and risks borne by the uncontrolled distributors and the contractual terms under which they operate in the uncontrolled transactions. In addition, data is available to ensure accounting consistency between all of the uncontrolled distributors and FSub. Because the available data is sufficiently complete and accurate to conclude that it is likely that all material differences between the controlled and uncontrolled transactions have been identified, such difference have a definite and reasonably ascertainable effect, and reliable adjustments are made to account for such differences, the results of each of the uncontrolled distributors may be used to establish an arm's length range pursuant to § 1.482-1(e)(2)(iii)(A).[47]

Reg. § 1.482-3(c)(4), Ex. 6

The facts are the same as *Example 5*, except that sufficient data is not available to determine whether any of the uncontrolled distributors provide warranties or to determine the payment terms of the contracts. Because differences in these contractual terms could materially affect price or profits, the inability to determine whether these differences exist between the controlled and uncontrolled transactions diminishes the reliability of the results of the uncontrolled comparables. However, the reliability of the results may be enhanced by the application of a statistical method when establishing an arm's length range pursuant to § 1.482-1(e)(2)(iii)(B).[48]

Reg. § 1.482-3(c)(4), Ex. 7

The facts are the same as in *Example 5*, except that Product X is branded with a valuable trademark that is owned by P. A, B, and C distribute unbranded competing products, while D and E distribute products branded with other trademarks. D and E do not own any rights in the trademarks under which their products are sold. The value of the products that A, B, and C sold are not similar to the value of the products sold by S. The value of products sold by D and E,

---

[45] Reg. § 1.482-3(c)(4), Ex. 3.
[46] Reg. § 1.482-3(c)(4), Ex. 4.
[47] Reg. § 1.482-3(c)(4), Ex. 5.
[48] Reg. § 1.482-3(c)(4), Ex. 6.

however, is similar to that of Product X. Although close product similarity is not as important for a reliable application of the resale price method as for the comparable uncontrolled price method, significant differences in the value of the products involved in the controlled and uncontrolled transactions may affect the reliability of the results. In addition, because in this case it is difficult to determine the effect the trademark will have on price or profits, reliable adjustments for the differences cannot be made. Because D and E have a higher level of comparability than A, B, and C with respect to S, pursuant to Reg. § 1.482-1(e)(2)(ii), only D and E may be included in an arm's length range.[49]

To give due consideration to all these factors usually requires both a detailed functional analysis and careful consideration of the underlying economics. As with the CUP method, the most easily supportable application of the RPM can be developed using internal comparables.[50] That is, in many cases a reseller may purchase products from third parties under conditions and contractual arrangements that are similar to those of the reseller's transactions with the related supplier. In general, if the reseller sells those products to the same customer mix under the same general contractual terms and with the same associated distribution functions (e.g., marketing, warranty, and after-sale service), then the margins on the product purchased from the uncontrolled supplier can be an appropriate benchmark for setting prices on the products purchased from the related party (with, of course, any adjustments for quantifiable differences).[51]

In some cases, the taxpayer or an IRS agent may assert that the RPM can be applied using the total gross margin of a company with comparable functions operating in comparable markets as those of the taxpayer.[52]

> **Comment:** The examples in the regulations applying the RPM address common issues, such as warranty and advertising expenses, to show where adjustments may be necessary to ensure comparability. However, the regulations do not address common audit issues of whether such expenses are the manufacturer's or the distributor's, or the taxpayer's actual practice or business rationale regarding such expenses. Moreover, nuances of the marketplace, which can have a significant impact on a taxpayer, are often overlooked. This may cause the IRS to make mechanical and arbitrary adjustments without consideration of the taxpayer's facts and circumstances.

.03 Cases Applying the RPM

E.I. Dupont de Nemours & Co. One of the most prominent and frequently discussed cases involving the RPM is *E.I. Dupont de Nemours & Co.*,[53] where Dupont incorporated a Swiss subsidiary ("DISA") to serve as a distributor for its products in Europe. The transfer price was structured to allow DISA to earn 75 percent of the total profits involved, although DISA actually realized only 26 percent of the gross profits. There was also direct documentary evidence, in the form of

---

[49] Reg. § 1.482-3(c)(4), Ex. 7.

[50] Reg. § 1.482-3(c)(3)(ii)(C).

[51] Reg. § 1.482-3(c)(3)(ii)(B). *See, e.g., Perkin Elmer Corp.*, CCH Dec. 49,268(M), 66 TCM (CCH) 634, TC Memo 1993-414 (1993) (Tax Court concluded that the prices charged to the taxpayer by its Puerto Rican affiliate were at arm's length because the taxpayer's resale mar-

gin fell just outside a range of resale margins established by its purchase and resale of instruments manufactured by third parties).

[52] Reg. § 1.482-3(c)(3)(ii)(A).

[53] *E.I. Dupont de Nemours & Co.*, 79-2 USTC ¶ 9633, 608 F.2d 445, (Ct. Cl., 1979), *cert. denied*, 100 S. Ct. 1648, 445 U.S. 962 (1980).

several internal memoranda, that Dupont intended to shift a disproportionate level of profit to DISA for purposes of its foreign tax credit planning.

Relying solely on the RPM, Dupont challenged the IRS's proposed adjustment, asserting that similar companies with similar products experienced average mark-ups of 19.5 percent to 38 percent, which compared favorably with Dupont's 26 percent markup. The court rejected this approach because it failed to establish, at a minimum level, some similarity of the products, functions, and economic and geographic market conditions by and among DISA and the sample companies.

Sundstrand Corp. The RPM was later addressed by the Tax Court in *Sundstrand Corp.*[54] Sundstrand and its subsidiaries manufactured and sold numerous products, including the constant speed drive ("CSD"), an extremely complex avionics device used to drive an airplane engine's generator at a constant speed regardless of the speed of the engine. In 1974, Sundstrand decided to expand operations at SunPac, its wholly owned foreign subsidiary in Singapore, to include the production of CSDs. Pursuant to a license agreement entered into in July 1975, Sundstrand convey to SunPac the following rights:

- Exclusive right to use its industrial property rights for the manufacture of certain CSD spare parts in Singapore;
- Nonexclusive right to sell the spare parts anywhere in the world;
- Nonexclusive right for SunPac or its customers to use the parts anywhere in the world;
- Right for SunPac to subcontract in Singapore to third parties the partial manufacture of the spare parts; and
- Authorization for SunPac's use of Sundstrand's trademarks, which Sundstrand normally used in the sale of similar products.

Sundstrand also agreed to furnish copies of the existing industrial property rights that it used in the manufacture of the products and give SunPac reasonable technical assistance for the start-up of SunPac's manufacture of the spare parts. For further rights and assistance, SunPac agreed to pay Sundstrand a royalty of 2 percent of the net selling price of each spare part manufactured and sold by SunPac. Sundstrand purchased all of SunPac's output through 1978 at Sundstrand's catalogue price less a 15 percent discount pursuant to a distributor agreement that Sundstrand and SunPac entered into in 1976.

The Tax Court applied the RPM to address Sundstrand's transfer price based on the catalogue price less a 15 percent discount. In holding that the 15 percent discount was not determined at arm's length, the court reconstructed a 20 percent discount by relying on certain sales and/or distribution agreements between Sundstrand and certain unrelated parties and on certain representations made by Sundstrand to the U.S. Customs and IRS. The court believed that Sundstrand's catalogue prices for spare parts revealed an appropriate starting point for establishing an arm's length price for SunPac's parts. However, Sundstrand's history of

---

[54] *Sundstrand Corp.*, CCH Dec. 47,172, 96 TC 226 (1991).

¶320.03

granting discounts for its distribution agreements was varied, ranging from 5 percent to 20 percent. The court recognized that because Sundstrand would have to resell the SunPac parts at catalogue price to its own customers, it was reasonable to demand a discount. In arriving at the 20 percent discount rates, the court principally looked to Sundstrand's representations to the U.S. Customs and IRS where the common discount for similar parts for other discounters appeared to be 20 percent. This discount was also equal to the discount Sundstrand had previously granted to an unrelated third party.

Perkin-Elmer Corp. The Tax Court also addressed the *RPM in Perkin-Elmer Corp.*[55] Perkin-Elmer ("PE"), a U.S. analytical instruments manufacturer established a possessions corporation in Puerto Rico ("PEPR") to manufacture and sell certain low-end analytical instruments, accessories, and hollow cathode lamps ("HCLs"). The parties entered into a license agreement, which provided for a 3 percent royalty on all finished goods manufactured and sold by PEPR, and a distribution agreement under which PE purchased from PEPR finished products at a 30 percent discount.

For PE's distribution of finished products, PE relied on several sets of unrelated party transactions to establish under the RPM a gross profit margin. Most prominent in these unrelated transactions was PE's purchase and resale of instruments manufactured by *Spectra-Physics, Inc.* ("SPI"). There, the average gross margin was 34.1 percent. By contrast, the IRS proposed different resale margins for PEPR's instruments, accessories, and HCLs for purposes of the RPM. Interestingly, the IRS dropped its contract manufacturing argument as argued on audit and argued a transactional method to establish its view of an arm's length price. For PEPR's instruments, the IRS relied on PE's purchase and resale of SPI's instruments as well as others. For accessories, the IRS relied on PE's overall resale margin of 57.6 percent on the purchase and resale of numerous third-party accessories. For HCLs, the IRS relied on PE's 57.2 percent resale margin on the purchase and resale of deuterium lamps manufactured by Sylvania.

The court applied the RPM to determine PEPR's finished products transfer price, concluding that the instruments, accessories, and HCLs "were fundamentally different functionally, with the potential for different and predictable influences on their respective resale margins." More particularly, the court found that PEPR's instrument prices were arm's length because PE's resale margins fell just outside a range established by PE's purchase and resale of third-party instruments. In establishing this range, the court made adjustments for inventory and credit differences. Also, the court determined that the resale margin for PEPR's accessories should be 40 percent based on a subset of the IRS's uncontrolled resale transactions of accessories that excluded certain products not comparable to PEPR's accessories. Finally, the court followed a 40 percent resale price margin for the sales of HCLs based on evidence presented at trial that established the margin on resales of HCL prior to a manufacturing license.

---

[55] *Perkin-Elmer Corp.*, CCH Dec. 49,268(M), 66 TCM (CCH) 634, TC Memo 1993-414 (1993).

¶ 330 Cost-Plus Method

.01 In General

The cost-plus method determines an arm's length charge by comparing the gross profit markup realized in controlled and uncontrolled transactions.[56] The cost-plus method is ordinarily used in cases involving the manufacture, assembly, or other production of goods sold to related parties.[57] Like the RPM, the cost-plus method can be based on mark-ups earned for products that are not identical but share significant similarities.[58]

.02 Comparability and Reliability

In determining the arm's length benchmark, adjustments must be made for material differences between the uncontrolled and controlled transactions where it can be determined that such differences have a definite and reasonably ascertainable effect on the margins. As with the RPM, the cost-plus method must make adjustments for differences in operating expenses associated with functions performed and risk assumed. Specific factors that generally must be considered include:

- Complexity of manufacturing or assembly;
- Manufacturing, production, and process engineering;
- Procurement, purchasing, and inventory-control activities;
- Testing functions;
- Selling, general, and administrative expenses;
- Foreign-currency risks; and
- Contractual terms (e.g., scope and terms of warranties provided, sales or purchase volume, credit and transport terms).[59]

Consideration of these factors requires both functional and economic analyses. The cost-plus method can be based on internal comparables, that is, selected transactions involving sales from the taxpayer's manufacturing entity to an unrelated party, or external comparables, such as selected transactions between two unrelated parties or the average mark-up on all transactions earned by a comparable manufacturer on sales to unrelated parties.[60] As under the RPM, a cost-plus method based on the average mark-ups of all transactions earned by an independent manufacturer requires a demonstration that the functions performed and economic circumstances involved with the different kinds of transactions performed by the comparable are similar to those of the taxpayer.[61]

The cost-plus method is typically used to determine an arm's length price for components or unfinished goods that will be subject to substantial additional manufacturing, processing, or assembly prior to distribution. Cases in which the manufacturer merely performs this service for a related party and all risk of loss

---

[56] Reg. § 1.482-3(d)(1).
[57] Reg. § 1.482-3(d)(1).
[58] Reg. § 1.482-3(d)(3)(B).

[59] Reg. § 1.482-3(d)(3)(ii)(C).
[60] Reg. § 1.482-3(d)(3)(ii)(A).
[61] Reg. § 1.482-3(d)(3)(ii)(B).

from the manufacturing and subsequent distribution falls on the related party have been generally referred to as "contract-manufacturer method" cases.[62]

The cost-plus method, under a contract manufacturing theory, is the most common method used by the IRS in auditing non-U.S. manufacturing affiliates. Typically, the IRS allows a return only on direct and indirect costs of production. This approach has been rejected by the courts in both *Eli Lilly* and *Bausch & Lomb*, and the IRS refrained from arguing this theory in *Perkin-Elmer*. Notwithstanding, this issue continues to surface on audit.

The cost-plus method allows a manufacturer to recover its production costs plus an "appropriate gross profit percentage" on sales or transfers to related parties. The first step in determining an arm's length transfer price here is to calculate the manufacturer's production costs. The regulations do not require any particular method of accounting for production costs, nor do they provide a list of the types of costs that must be included or excluded.[63] Instead, the regulations focus on consistency.[64] Consistency in accounting for product costs is essential under the cost-plus method because the regulations provide that, whenever possible, the manufacturer's gross profit percentage for unrelated sales is to be used in determining the second component of the arm's length price for related sales.[65]

The importance of the consistency requirement can best be shown by the following example. Assume D, a U.S. corporation, manufactures widgets for sale abroad. Some of these widgets will be sold to unrelated purchasers, and others will be sold to F, D's wholly owned foreign sales subsidiary. F will then sell the widgets purchased from D to unrelated purchasers. Assume further that D would like to minimize its income on the related party sales and maximize F's income, and that the cost-plus method of determining an arm's length price is appropriate. D can sell a widget to an unrelated purchaser for $100. D's direct production costs for the widget are $60; indirect production costs are $20. D's gross profit percentage, expressed as a percent of cost, using the full costing method, is 25 percent ([$100 – $80] ÷ $80). D wants the lowest possible price on sales to F. Without the consistency rule, D could take the gross profit percentage of 25 percent and apply it to its direct production costs only, resulting in a $75 sales price to F and a $15 gross profit to D. Because of the consistency rule, however, D must apply the 25 percent gross profit percentage to direct and indirect costs. The result is a sales price to F of $100 ($60 + $20 = $80, $80 × 1.25 = $100), and a gross profit to D of $40 ($100 sales price - $60 direct costs). The consistency rule requires D to recognize an additional $25 of gross profit on the sale.

The second step in determining an arm's length price under the cost-plus method is to calculate the appropriate gross profit percentage. This is equal to the gross profit percentage, expressed as a percentage of cost, earned by the manufacturer or another party in the uncontrolled sale of property that is most similar to the controlled sale in question.[66] The regulations identify several basic factors that

---

[62] *See* generally the IRS's positions in *Bausch & Lomb Inc., supra* note 30, CCH Dec. 45,547 at 582; *Sundstrand Corporation, supra* note 54, CCH Dec. 47,172 at 353–354.

[63] Reg. § 1.482-3(d)(3)(iii)(B).

[64] Reg. § 1.482-3(d)(3)(iii)(B).

[65] Reg. § 1.482-3(d)(3)(iii)(B).

[66] Reg. § 1.482-3(d)(3).

should be considered in determining which of the uncontrolled sales is most similar: functions, risks, contractual terms, economic conditions, and property or services.[67]

Some examples regarding the application of the cost-plus method include:

Reg. § 1.482-3(d)(4), Ex. 1

> (i) USP, a domestic manufacturer of computer components, sells its products to FS, its foreign distributor. UT1, UT2, and UT3 are domestic computer component manufacturers that sell to uncontrolled foreign purchasers.

> (ii) Relatively complete data is available regarding the functions performed and risks borne by UT1, UT2, and UT3, and the contractual terms in the uncontrolled transactions. In addition, data is available to ensure accounting consistency between all of the uncontrolled manufacturers and USP. Because the available data is sufficiently complete to conclude that it is likely that all material differences between the controlled and uncontrolled transactions have been identified, the effect of the differences are definite and reasonably ascertainable, and reliable adjustments are made to account for the differences, an arm's length range can be established pursuant to § 1.482-1(e)(2)(iii)(A).[68]

Reg. § 1.482-3(d)(4), Ex. 2

> The facts are the same as in Example 1, except that USP accounts for supervisory, general, and administrative costs as operating expenses, which are not allocated to its sales to FS. The gross profit markups of UT1, UT2, and UT3, however, reflect supervisory, general, and administrative expenses because they are accounted for as costs of goods sold. Accordingly, the gross profit markups of UT1, UT2, and UT3 must be adjusted as provided in paragraph (d)(3)(iii)(B) of this section to provide accounting consistency. If data is not sufficient to determine whether such accounting differences exist between the controlled and uncontrolled transactions, the reliability of the results will be decreased.[69]

Reg. § 1.482-3(d)(4), Ex. 3

> The facts are the same as in Example 1, except that under its contract with FS, USP uses materials consigned by FS. UT1, UT2, and UT3, on the other hand, purchase their own materials, and their gross profit markups are determined by including the costs of materials. The fact that USP does not carry an inventory risk by purchasing its own materials while the uncontrolled producers carry inventory is a significant difference that may require an adjustment if the difference has a material effect on the gross profit markups of the uncontrolled producers. Inability to reasonably ascertain the effect of the difference on the gross profit markups will affect the reliability of the results of UT1, UT2, and UT3.[70]

.03 Cases

E.K. Edwards. In *E.K. Edwards*,[71] the IRS had relied on the CUP method to allocate to a partnership income from the sale of equipment to a commonly controlled corporation. The allocation was based on the determination that, under the CUP method, the proper arm's length price for such equipment was the manufacturer's list price. The taxpayer persuaded the Tax Court that sales by

---

[67] Reg. § 1.482-3(d)(3); Reg. § 1.482-1(d)(3).

[68] Reg. § 1.482-3(d)(4), Ex. 1.

[69] Reg. § 1.482-3(d)(4), Ex. 2.

[70] Reg. § 1.482-3(d)(4), Ex. 3.

[71] *E.K. Edwards*, CCH Dec. 34,098, 67 TC 224 (1976), *acq.* 1977-2 CB 1.

equipment dealers could not support the IRS's allocation because such dealers rarely, if ever, received the full list price for the type of equipment sold by the partnership to the controlled corporation. Because there were no other comparable uncontrolled sales and the corporation did not resell the equipment (the RPM method), the Tax Court held the arm's length price was to be determined using the cost-plus method. The proper gross profit percentage for the sale by the partnership to the controlled corporation was derived from single sale of equipment by the partnership to an unrelated party during the period at issue.

Eli Lilly & Co. The cost-plus method was also considered in *Eli Lilly & Co.*[72] for the 1971 and 1972 taxable years in issue in that case. Because the Darvon patents were still in existence in 1971 and 1972, the CUP method was inapplicable. Further, Eli Lilly's experts were precluded from using the RPM because their opinion on the appropriate arm's length price was based solely on evidence of Eli Lilly's internal transactions. The applicable resale price on which the RPM is based is defined as the price at which the property is sold in an uncontrolled sale.[73] Through its economic experts, the IRS argued that the cost-plus method should be applied under a formula that would allow Eli Lilly's Puerto Rican affiliate to recover manufacturing costs and location savings plus a manufacturing profit. Because the IRS did not allow the Puerto Rican affiliate any return on the manufacturing intangibles, the Tax Court rejected this method.

¶ 340 Comparable Profit Method

.01 In General

The CPM evaluates whether the amount charged in a controlled transaction is arm's length based on profit level indicators ("PLIs") derived from uncontrolled taxpayers that engage in similar business activities under similar circumstances.[74] Under the CPM, an arm's length result is determined by calculating what a taxpayer's operating profit would have been on related party transactions if its PLI were equal to that of an uncontrolled comparable and then comparing that result to the interquartile range calculated based on the results of the comparable companies.[75] In calculating the taxpayer's operating profit, the selected PLI should be applied solely to the taxpayer's financial data that is related to the controlled transactions.[76]

> **Example:** USCo, a U.S. subsidiary of ForCo, conducts contract manufacturing on behalf of unrelated companies and distribution functions on behalf of related companies. In determining whether the transfer prices for its distribution function satisfy the arm's length standard, the USCo decides that an adjusted Berry Ratio (gross profit divided by operating expense) is the proper PLI. To properly apply the PLI, USCo must first segregate its operating expenses attributable to its contract manufacturing functions and then apply the PLI to its operating expenses attributable to its distribution functions.

---

[72] *Eli Lilly & Co., supra* note 23.
[73] Reg. § 1.482-3(c)(2)(ii).
[74] Reg. § 1.482-5(a).
[75] Reg. § 1.482-5(b)(1).
[76] Reg. § 1.482-5(b)(1).

Comment: The CPM has been widely accepted by the IRS and has been variously employed by taxpayers in documenting their transfer pricing policies. This is largely due to the general ease in using this method and its cost savings potential. Notwithstanding, the CPM does not enjoy a universal acceptability in countries whose transfer pricing laws are based on the OECD guidelines. There, the Transactional Net Margin Method, although quite similar in application, is the preferred method.[77]

.02 Tested Party

Because the CPM is a profits based method, taxpayers must select which of the two related parties that engaged in the controlled transaction will be the party whose profits will be tested for meeting the requirements of the arm's length standard. The regulations provide that the tested party should be the party whose operating profit attributable to the controlled transactions can be verified using the most reliable data and requiring the fewest and most reliable adjustments, and for which reliable comparables data can be located.[78] In most cases, the tested party will be the party with the least complex functions and that owns little or no intangible assets or other unique property (e.g., distributors, contract manufacturers, service companies, etc.). Care and practicality must be observed in this selection process.

.03 Comparability

In selecting comparable companies from which a PLI will be determined, the standards of comparability allow for product diversity and even some functional diversity.[79] Relevant comparability factors include the size and scope of operations, lines of business, product and service markets involved, asset composition, and the age in the business product cycle.[80] The level of comparability achieved will determine the reliability of the range of results derived from the related comparable companies.[81] In the attempt to enhance the level of comparability, empirical adjustments should be applied where there will be a definite and reasonably ascertainable effect. The regulations also indicate that adjustments for differences in functions and risks should be evaluated.[82] The emphasis on comparability, particularly related to market differences for such variables as competition and bargaining power, will influence the choice of comparable. Thus, application of functional analysis needs to be broadened to cover more dimensions of those business factors that affect profitability.[83]

.04 Profit-Level Indicators

Once adjustments have been made, an appropriate PLI must be selected.[84] The regulations indicate that one PLI for the arm's length range should be chosen.[85] The choice among alternative PLIs should be based on the nature of the activities

---

[77] The OECD approved the 2010 revision of the Transfer Pricing Guidelines on July 22, 2010. *See http://www.oecd.org.*

[78] Reg. § 1.482-5(b)(2)(i).

[79] Reg. § 1.482-5(c)(2)(ii).

[80] Reg. § 1.482-5(c)(2)(i).

[81] Reg. § 1.482-5(c)(2)(i).

[82] Reg. § 1.482-5(c)(2)(iv).

[83] Reg. § 1.482-5(c)(2)(iii).

[84] Reg. § 1.482-5(b)(4).

[85] Reg. § 1.482-5(b)(3).

under review, and on data availability.[86] The following PLI alternatives are identified in the regulations:

- *Return on capital employed*, such as the ratio of operating income to operating assets (presumably interest-bearing debt plus equity, to be consistent with the use of operating income rather than profit before tax, which is after interest expense);

- Financial ratios such as the ratio of *operating profit to sales* (i.e., the operating margin) or the ratio of *gross profit to operating expenses* (i.e., the Berry Ratio).[87]

Return on Capital Employed. The return on capital ROCE employed focuses on productivity of assets used in the generation of business income. The formula is the:

$$\text{Return on Operating Income} = \frac{\text{Capital Employed}}{\text{Operating Assets}}$$

The measure of capital employed is based on the book value of capital, not the market value. The regulations do not preclude market value application as an alternative profit level indicator.

There are some obvious limitations to the use of this PLI. First, ROCE is best applied in a situation where significant amounts of capital are used in the enterprise. Labor productivity is not considered a major factor in the fixing of the transfer price. It follows, then, for comparability, the relative importance of capital as a contribution to income should be relatively comparable to the tested party. Second, the ages of the assets of controlled and uncontrolled parties are relevant. For example, a potential comparable using older assets may have depreciated significantly, thereby distorting the profitability of these assets. Third, it is necessary to insure that there is no distortion in the capital intensity of the operations (for example, whether the facilities are leased or owned by the controlled or uncontrolled parties, leasing could have the tendency to artificially inflate the return on capital employed).

Operating Profit Margin. Historically, much emphasis has been placed on the operating profit margin:

$$\text{Operating Profit Margin} = \frac{\text{Operating Profits}}{\text{Net Sales}}$$

Accounting adjustments are often crucial, especially because companies may differ in classification of costs as of operating expenses.

The operating profit margin can be affected by the number of functions performed by the tested party and selected comparables. It would be expected that a party would undertake additional functions only if that party were rewarded with

---

[86] Reg. § 1.482-5(b)(4).   [87] Reg. § 1.482-5(b)(4).

additional profits. Otherwise, it would eventually eliminate unprofitable operations. *Reg. § 1.482-5(c)(2)(ii)* takes a contrary viewpoint, noting that "because differences in functions performed often are reflected in operating expenses, taxpayers performing different functions may have very different gross profit margins but earn similar levels of operating profit." This profit level indicator might mask under certain conditions the functions performed by the tested party. For example, a controlled distributor may earn the same operating margin as the selected comparables while performing fewer functions as measured by the ratio of operating expenses to sales. This weakness may encourage the use of the third profit level indicator below.

Berry Ratio. The third PLI, commonly known as the Berry Ratio (named for well-known economist Charles Berry), was used in an IRC Code Sec. 482 court case (*E.I. Dupont De Nemours and Company*). This PLI was used to demonstrate the return that an uncontrolled chemical distributor earned in the performance of its storage and distribution functions. The profit level indicator is:

$$\text{Berry Ratio} = \frac{\text{Gross Income}}{\text{Operating Expense}}$$

The use of the Berry ratio was necessitated by the limitations of the Resale Price Method. In the Dupont case, the Berry Ratio was constructed to explain that the gross margins earned by unrelated distributors were the result of the market's valuation of their performed functions. In this way, profits and performances of services are tied to each other more closely.

The Berry Ratio can be used in a service-oriented industry such as distribution, advertising, marketing and engineering. One limitation is that the tested party and the uncontrolled parties should be performing a similar mix of functions. In the absence of the congruence of such activities, the resulting analysis may not identify the appropriate arm's length return. This concern would be more important if the market considered one function more valuable than another.

.05 Selection of PLI

The ROCE tends to be more reliable than the other two listed PLIs in the presence of functional differences between the tested party and the comparable companies (such differences being commonplace when the CPM is being contemplated). The reason is that the ROCE tends to be more resilient to differences in operating expenses to sales ratios, thus allowing a larger number of comparables. By the same token, the larger the difference in operating expenses and sales ratios, the less reliable the Operating Profit Margin and Berry Ratio PLIs become.

Of course, there are ways to counteract this. One can become restrictive with comparables selected: exclusion of comparables with different operating expenses to sales ratios will rehabilitate the Operating Profit Margin and Berry Ratio. However, given that quite often the pool of comparables is already small, further reduction may be impractical. Thus, as a practical matter, the ROCE will tend to be the best method.[88]

.06 Calculating the Arm's Length Range

The final step is to apply the best PLI to the comparable company operating profits to simulate an arm's length range. The arm's length range is generally determined by calculating the interquartile range from the comparable company operating profits. The interquartile range is the range from the 25th to the 75th percentile of the results derived from the uncontrolled comparables.[89] This range should be usable provided at least four potentially comparable parties can be identified. Given the broad CPM comparability standards, this may not be a difficult identification exercise, and few companies will be able to resort to other methods. Effectively, the use of one PLI to construct the range may nonetheless force taxpayers (at least for planning purposes) to simulate multiple ranges on a number of PLIs and then set, as the target range, that area where the simulated ranges overlap.

> **Comment:** The formula for calculating the interquartile range that is contained in the regulations is different from the formula used by many popular software spreadsheet programs such as Microsoft Excel or Lotus 1-2-3. The practical difference being that the 25th and 75th percentiles calculated pursuant to the regulations will be slightly lower (25th percentile) and higher (75th percentile) than would calculated by using a spreadsheet. Therefore, taxpayers are advised to manually calculate the arm's length range based on the formula contained in the regulations.[90]

If the tested party's results are outside of the arm's length range, as determined by calculating the interquartile range based on the comparable companies, the IRS may adjust the tested party's results so that they fall within the range.[91] Typically, the adjustment is made to the median (50th percentile) of the interquartile range.[92]

The regulation under Code Sec. 482 provide various examples illustrating the acceptable and unacceptable uses of the CPM. Some examples include:

Reg. § 1.482-5(e), Ex. 1

> *Transfer of tangible property resulting in no adjustment.* (i) FP is a publicly traded foreign corporation with a U.S. subsidiary, USSub, that is under audit for its 1996 taxable year. FP manufactures a consumer product for worldwide distribution. USSub imports the assembled product and distributes it within the United States at the wholesale level under the FP name.

> (ii) FP does not allow uncontrolled taxpayers to distribute the product. Similar products are produced by other companies but none of them is sold to uncontrolled taxpayers or to uncontrolled distributors.

> (iii) Based on all the facts and circumstances, the district director determines that the comparable profits method will provide the most reliable measure of an arm's length result. USSub is selected as the tested party because it engages in

---

[88] Clark, Richard A., "Choosing a Reliable Profit Level Indicator," 5 *Tax Mgmt. Trans. Pricing Rep.* 807 (April 9, 1997).
[89] Reg. § 1.482-1(e)(2)(iii)(C).
[90] *See* Reg. § 1.482-1(e)(2)(iii)(C).
[91] Reg. § 1.482-1(e)(3).
[92] Reg. § 1.482-1(e)(3).

activities that are less complex than those undertaken by FP. There is data from a number of independent operators of wholesale distribution businesses. These potential comparables are further narrowed to select companies in the same industry segment that perform similar functions and bear similar risks to USSub. An analysis of the information available on these taxpayers shows that the ratio of operating profit to sales is the most appropriate profit level indicator, and this ratio is relatively stable where at least three years are included in the average. For the taxable years 1994 through 1996, USSub shows the following results:

	1994	1995	1996	Average
Sales	500,000	560,000	500,000	520,000
Cost of Goods Sold	393,000	412,400	400,000	401,800
Operating Expenses	80,000	110,000	104,600	98,200
Operating Profit	27,000	37,600	(4,600)	20,000

(iv) After adjustments have been made to account for identified material differences between USSub and the uncontrolled distributors, the average ratio of operating profit to sales is calculated for each of the uncontrolled distributors. Applying each ratio to USSub would lead to the following comparable operating profit (COP) for USSub:

Uncontrolled Distributor	OP/S	USSub COP
A	1.7%	$8,840
B	3.1%	16,120
C	3.8%	19,760
D	4.5%	23,400
E	4.7%	24,440
F	4.8%	24,960
G	4.9%	25,480
H	6.7%	34,840
I	9.9%	51,480
J	10.5%	54,600

(v) The data is not sufficiently complete to conclude that it is likely that all material differences between USSub and the uncontrolled distributors have been identified. Therefore, an arm's length range can be established only pursuant to Reg. § 1.482-1(e)(2)(iii)(B). The district director measures the arm's length range by the interquartile range of results, which consists of the results ranging from $19,760 to $34,840. Although USSub's operating income for 1996 shows a loss of $4,600, the district director determines that no allocation should be made, because USSub's average reported operating profit of $20,000 is within this range.[93]

Reg. § 1.482-5(e), Ex. 2

Transfer of tangible property resulting in adjustment. (i) The facts are the same as in Example 1 except the USSub reported the following income and expenses:

---

[93] Reg. § 1.482-5(e), Ex. 1.

¶340.06

	1994	1995	1996	Average
Sales	500,000	560,000	500,000	520,000
Cost of Goods Sold	370,000	460,400	400,000	410,000
Operating Expenses	110,000	110,000	110,000	110,000
Operating Profit	20,000	(10,000)	(10,000)	0

(ii) The interquartile range of comparable operating profits remains the same as derived in *Example 1*: $19,760 to $34,840. USSub's average operating profit for the years 1994 through 1996 ($0) falls outside this range. Therefore, the district director determines that an allocation may be appropriate.

(iii) To determine the amount, if any, of the allocation, the district director compares USSub's reported operating profit for 1996 to comparable operating profits derived from the uncontrolled distributors' results for 1996. The ratio of operating profit to sales in 1996 is calculated for each of the uncontrolled comparables and applied to USSub's 1996 sales to derive the following results:

Uncontrolled Distributor	OP/S	USSub COP
C	0.5%	$2,500
D	1.5%	7,500
E	2.0%	10,000
A	1.6%	13,000
F	2.8%	14,000
B	2.9%	14,500
J	2.0%	15,000
I	4.4%	22,000
G	6.9%	34,500
H	7.4%	37,000

(iv) Based on these results, the median of the comparable operating profits for 1996 is $14,250. Therefore, USSub's income for 1996 is increased by $24,250, the difference between USSub's reported operating profit for 1996 and the median of the comparable operating profits for 1996.[94]

Reg. § 1.482-5(e), Ex. 3

Multiple year analysis. (i) The facts are the same as in *Example 2*. In addition the district director examines the taxpayer's results for the 1997 taxable year. As in *Example 2*, the district director increases USSub's income for the 1996 taxable year by $24,250. The results for the 1997 taxable year, together with the 1995 and 1996 taxable years, are as follows:

	1995	1996	1997	Average
Sales	560,000	500,000	530,000	530,000
Cost of Goods Sold	460,000	400,000	430,000	430,000
Operating Expenses	110,000	110,000	110,000	110,000
Operating Profit	(10,000)	(10,000)	(10,000)	(10,000)

---

[94] Reg. § 1.482-5(e), Ex. 2.

(ii) The interquartile range of comparable operating profits, based on average results from the uncontrolled comparables and average sales for USSub for the years 1995 through 1997, ranges from $15,500 to $30,000. In determining whether an allocation for the 1997 taxable year may be made, the district director compares USSub's average reported operating profit for the years 1995 through 1997 to the interquartile range of average comparable operating profits over this period. USSub's average reported operating profit is determined without regard to the adjustment made with respect to the 1996 taxable year. See 1.482-1(f)(2)(iii)(D). Therefore, USSub's average reported operating profit for the years 1995 through 1997 is ($10,000). Because this amount of income falls outside the interquartile range, the district director determines that an allocation may be appropriate.

(iii) To determine the amount, if any, of the allocation for the 1997 taxable year, the district director compares USSub's reported operating profit for 1997 to the median of the comparable operating profits derived from the uncontrolled distributor's results for 1997. The median of the comparable operating profits derived from the uncontrolled comparables results for the 1997 taxable year is $12,000, the difference between the median of the comparable operating profits for the 1997 taxable year and USSub's reported operating profit of ($10,000) for the 1997 taxable year.[95]

¶ 350   The Profit Split Method

.01 In General

The profit split method compares the allocation of the combined operating profit or loss attributable to controlled transactions to the relative value of each controlled taxpayer's contribution to that combined operating profit or loss.[96] The allocation should correspond to the division of profit or loss in an uncontrolled transaction, where each party performs functions similar to those of the controlled taxpayers.[97] The profit allocated to any particular member of a controlled group is not necessarily limited to the total operating profit of the group from the relevant business activity. Thus, in a given year, one member of the group may earn a profit while another member incurs a loss.

.02 The Comparable Profit Split Method

The comparable profit split method generally divides the total operating income of the buyer (licensee) and the seller (licensor) in the controlled transaction in a manner that is consistent with the way comparable unrelated parties divide their operating income in similar transactions.[98] Therefore, data on comparable transactions and resulting profit splits between unrelated parties must be employed, if available. That data must address two independent parties, each having risks, functions, and intangibles substantially comparable to those of the controlled parties.[99] The use of the comparable profit split method will be limited because it will typically be difficult to find comparable companies engaged in transactions that are similar to those of both the buyer and seller and data delineating how the independent parties shared the combined profits from a comparable transaction

---

[95] Reg. § 1.482-5(e), Ex. 3.

[96] Reg. § 1.482-6(a). *See also Eli Lilly & Co.*, CCH Dec. 42,113, 84 TC 996, 1147 (1985), *aff'd in part, rev'd in part* 88-2 USTC ¶ 9502, 856 F.2d 855 (7th Cir. 1988).

[97] Reg. § 1.482-6(b).

[98] Reg. § 1.482-6(c)(2)(i).

[99] Reg. § 1.482-6(c)(2)(ii).

rarely exists. Finding a comparable transaction is made more difficult because the regulations provide that comparability depends on the degree of similarity not only of the functions and risks, but also of the contractual terms.[100] The regulations further provide that the comparable profit split method "may not be used if the combined operating profits . . . of the uncontrolled comparable varies significantly from that earned by the controlled taxpayers."[101] Because these constraints on data and comparability make it difficult to apply the comparable profit split method, most profit split analyses are applied using the residual profit split method.

> *Comment:* In practice, the comparable profit split method is rarely used due to lack of information of controlled transactions.

.03 The Residual Profit Split Method

The residual profit split method operates in a two-step process. The first step assigns an arm's length return to the routine activities of the buyer and the seller in the controlled transaction.[102] This allocation is performed by first granting the buyer and seller an arm's length return for functions they perform that contribute to profits.[103] These functions include manufacturing, distributing, marketing, the performance of services, and the exploitation of routine intangibles. The functional return often employs a CPM. The second step involves allocating the residual profit between the buyer and seller based on the relative value of their nonroutine contributions to the business activity, with said value being measured in a "manner that most reliably reflects" the contribution.[104] In many cases, these nonroutine contributions will be some sort of intangible; in fact, the motivation behind the expansion of the language from the previous "intangible property" to the current "nonroutine contribution" was to ensure that imbedded intangibles would fall within the language's ambit.

There is no set method by which to split the residual profit, but the regulations prefer that this profit split use some market benchmark, which would yield insight on the value of an intangible.[105] The regulations, however, provide no guidance as to what constitutes a market benchmark, although the comparability standards within the regulations guide the parameters of the benchmark. Alternatively, the regulations suggest that relative value may be measured by the capitalized cost of developing the intangibles and all enhancements or the amount of actual expenditures in recent years for such intangible development or enhancement.[106]

---

[100] Reg. § 1.482-6(c)(2)(ii)(B)(1).

[101] Reg. § 1.482-6(c)(2)(ii)(B)(1).

[102] Reg. § 1.482-6(c)(3)(i)(A).

[103] Reg. § 1.482-6(c)(3)(i)(A).

[104] Reg. § 1.482-6(c)(3)(i)(B).

[105] Reg. § 1.482-6(c)(3)(ii)(B). The regulations also offer additional suggestions for measuring the value of a nonroutine intangible contribution, including, apart from external benchmarks: (1) estimation by the capitalized cost of developing the intangible property and all related improvements and updates, less an appropriate amount of amortization based on the useful life of each intangible property; and (2) in cases where the intangible development expenditures of the parties are relatively constant over time and the useful life of the intangible is approximately the same, the amount of actual expenditures in recent years. Reg. § 1.482-6(c)(3)(i)(B)(2).

[106] Reg. § 1.482-6(c)(3)(ii)(B).

¶350.03

Reg. § 1.482-6(c) illustrates the Residual Profit Split-Method as follows:

Reg. § 1.482-6(c) (3) (iii)

Application of Residual Profit Split. (i) XYZ is a U.S. corporation that develops, manufactures and markets a line of products for police use in the United States. XYZ's research unit developed a bulletproof material for use in protective clothing and headgear (Nulon). XYZ obtains patent protection for the chemical formula for Nulon. Since its introduction in the U.S., Nulon has captured a substantial share of the U.S. market for bulletproof material.

(ii) XYZ licensed its European subsidiary, XYZ-Europe, to manufacture and market Nulon in Europe. XYZ-Europe is a well-established company that manufactures and markets XYZ products in Europe. XYZ-Europe has a research unit that adapts XYZ products for the defense market, as well as a well-developed marketing network that employs brand names that it developed.

(iii) XYZ-Europe's research unit alters Nulon to adapt it to military specifications and develops a high-intensity marketing campaign directed at the defense industry in several European countries. Beginning with the 1995 taxable year, XYZ-Europe manufactures and sells Nulon in Europe through its marketing network under one of its brand names.

(iv) For the 1995 taxable year, XYZ has no direct expenses associated with the license of Nulon to XYZ-Europe and incurs no expenses related to the marketing of Nulon in Europe. For the 1995 taxable year, XYZ-Europe's Nulon sales and pre-royalty expenses are $500 million and $300 million, respectively, resulting in net pre-royalty profit of $200 million related to the Nulon business. The operating assets employed in XYZ-Europe's Nulon business are $200 million. Given the facts and circumstances, the district director determines under the best method rule that a residual profit split will provide the most reliable measure of an arm's length result. Based on an examination of a sample of European companies performing functions similar to those of XYZ-Europe, the district director determines that an average market return on XYZ-Europe's operating assets in the Nulon business is 10 percent, resulting in a market return of $20 million (10% x $200 million) for XYZ-Europe's Nulon business, and a residual profit of $180 million.

(v) Since the first state of the residual profit split allocated profits to XYZ-Europe's contributions other than those attributable to highly valuable intangible property, it is assumed that the residual profit of $180 million is attributable to the valuable intangibles related to Nulon, i.e., the European brand name for Nulon and the Nulon formula (including XYZ-Europe's modifications). To estimate the relative values of these intangibles, the district director compares the ratios of the capitalized value of expenditures as of 1995 on Nulon-related research and development and marketing over the 1995 sales related to such expenditures.

(vi) Because XYZ's protective product research and development expenses support the worldwide protective product sales of the XYZ group, it is necessary to allocate such expenses among the worldwide business activities to which they relate. The district director determines that it is reasonable to allocate the value of these expenses based on worldwide protective product sales. Using information on the average useful life of its investments in protective product research and development, the district director capitalizes and amortizes XYZ's protective product research and development expenses. This analysis indicates that the capitalized research and development expenditures have a value of $0.20 per dollar of global protective product sales in 1995.

¶350.03

(vii) XYZ-Europe's expenditures on Nulon research and development and marketing support only its sales in Europe. Using information on the average useful life of XYZ-Europe's investments in marketing and research and development, the district director capitalizes and amortizes XYZ-Europe's expenditures and determines that they have a value in 1995 of $0.40 per dollar of XYZ-Europe's Nulon sales.

(viii) Thus, XYZ and XYZ-Europe's together contributed $0.60 in capitalized intangible development expenses for each dollar of XYZ-Europe's protective product sales for 1995, of which XYZ contributed one-third (or $0.20 per dollar of sales). Accordingly, the district director determines that an arm's length royalty for the Nulon license for the 1995 taxable year is $60 million, i.e., one-third of XYZ-Europe's $180 million in residual Nulon profit.[107]

¶ 360 Unspecified Methods

In addition to the methods previously discussed, the regulations provide that other unspecified methods may be used to evaluate transfer prices.[108] As with the specified methods, any unspecified method must satisfy the best method rule.[109] One unspecified method provided in the regulations is a "bona fide" offer from a third party that is used to establish the floor of an arm's length range of prices.[110]

This method is illustrated in the regulations by the following example:

Reg. § 1.482-3(e)(2), Ex.

Amcan, a U.S. company, produces unique vessels for storing and transporting toxic waste, toxicans, at its U.S. production facility. Amcan agrees by contract to supply its Canadian subsidiary, Cancan, with 4000 toxicans per year to serve the Canadian market for toxicans. Prior to entering into the contract with Cancan, Amcan had received a bona fide offer from an independent Canadian waste disposal company, Cando, to serve as the Canadian distributor for toxicans and to purchase a similar number of toxicans at a price of $5,000 each. If the circumstances and terms of the Cancan supply contract are sufficiently similar to those of the Cando offer, or sufficiently reliable adjustments can be made for differences between them, then the Cando offer price of $5,000 may provide reliable information indicating that an arm's length consideration under the Cancan contract will not be less than $5,000 per toxican.[111]

---

[107] Reg. § 1.482-6(c)(3)(D)(iii).
[108] Reg. § 1.482-3(e)(1).
[109] Reg. § 1.482-3(e)(1).

[110] Reg. § 1.482-3(e)(2).
[111] Reg. § 1.482-3(e)(2).

Chapter 4

Methods for Transfers of Intangible Property

¶ 401 Overview

Transfer pricing for intangible property has been a primary source of disputes over the past 30 years. The 1988 White Paper reported that 50 percent of the reported Code Sec. 482 cases involved adjustments related to intangible property.[1] The principal reason for these disputes was the lack of comparable transactions from which to test the transfer of intangibles in question.[2] It was this concern over the proper transfer price for intangibles that prompted Congress to enact the commensurate-with-income standard in 1986.[3]

The Code Sec. 482 regulations describe four methods for testing the consideration paid for the transfer of intangible property:

- Comparable uncontrolled transaction ("CUT") method;

- Comparable profits method ("CPM");

- Profit split method; and

- Unspecified methods.

---

[1] *See* White Paper, Notice 88-123, 1988-2 CB 458, 166 n. 52.

[2] *See* White Paper, Notice 88-123, 1988-2 CB 458, 166 n. 52.

[3] *See* ¶ 450.

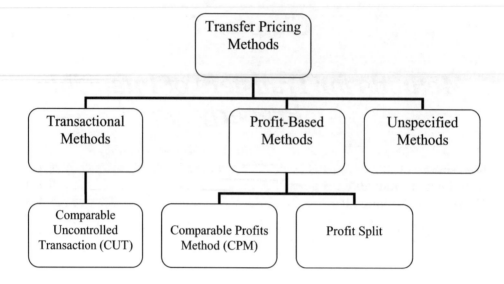

Transfer Pricing Method	Location in Regulations	Most Common Use	Comparability Considerations	Adjustments to Improve Comparability	Comment
I. TRANSACTIONAL TPMS					
CUT (Comparable Uncontrolled Transaction) (compares controlled transaction to CUT)	Reg. § 1.482-4(c)		Similar transactions/uniqueness Similar economic conditions Similar profit potential Similar industry/market Similar contractual terms/duration/upfront payments (similarity of products generally has greatest effect on comparability under this method) Use of updates	Product quality Contractual terms Market level Geographic market Transaction date Capital investment Currency risks Realistic alternatives of buyer and seller Start-up expenses Profit potential/RORs	Most direct and reliable measure (where information exists) Internal CUP generally has greater comparability than external CUP

Transfer Pricing Method	Location in Regulations	Most Common Use	Comparability Considerations	Adjustments to Improve Comparability	Comment
II. PROFIT BASED TPMS					
CPM (Comparable Profits Method) **TNMM** (Transactional Net Margin Method) (compares profitability of controlled transactions with profitability of similar uncontrolled transactions)	Reg. § 1.482-5	Relief of royalty	Resources employed Risks Functions performed Other (e.g., cost structures, business experience, management efficiency)	Operating assets Degree of consistency in accounting practices	Most widely used method Compares profits earned on controlled transactions to the operation profit of uncontrolled comparables (entities or transactions) Evaluates the least complex entity (generally, controlled entity with no valuable intangibles)
PLIs (Profit level indicators) - rate of return on capital employed; - financial ratios (ratio of operating profit to sales, ratio of gross profit to operating expenses); - other profit level indicators.	Reg §1.482-5(b) 4				
PSM (Profit Split Method) — **CPS** (Comparable Profit Split) CPS is derived from combined operating profit of uncontrolled taxpayers with similar transactions. Under this method, each uncontrolled taxpayer's percentage of the combined operating profit or loss is used to allocate the combined operating profit or loss of the relevant business activities. **PLIs** are used to measure profitability (Reg. § 1.482-6)	Reg. § 1.482-6(c)(2)	Unique intangibles on both sales of a transac-tion	Resources employed Risks Functions performed Other (e.g., cost structures, business experience, management efficiency) Contractual terms	Results of uncontrolled comparables	Seldom encountered in practice
PSM (Profit Split Method) — **RPS** (Residual Profit Split) PRS involves a two-step process: • allocation of income to routine contributions; • allocation of residual profit.	Reg. § 1.482-6(c)(3)	Manufacturers, Distributors, Service Providers	Market benchmarks of profitability (when allocating income to routine contributions – step one) Functions performed Risks Resources employed Product similarity Accounting consistency		Most often used when each related entity owns significant valuable intangibles
Unspecified Methods	Reg. § 1.482-3(e)	---	---	---	---

Each of these methods must be applied in accordance with the general transfer pricing rules, including the best method rule, comparability analysis and, the arm's length range. Regardless of the TPM chosen, the consideration paid for the use of intangible property for a term longer than one year will be subject to a periodic review and adjustment process, except in certain limited circumstances. For this and other reasons, a qualified cost sharing arrangement is a very attractive alternative where intangible property is to be jointly developed and exploited.

¶ 410 Definition of Intangible Property

The regulations define an "intangible" as an asset that "has substantial value independent of the services of any individual" and that "derives its value not from its physical attributes but from its intellectual content or other intangible properties."[4] Common examples of intangibles include:

- Patents, inventions, formulae, processes, designs, patterns, or know-how;

- Copyrights and literary, musical, or artistic compositions;

- Trademarks, trade names, or brand names;

- Franchises, licenses, or contracts;

- Methods, programs, systems, procedures, campaigns, surveys, studies, forecasts, estimates, customer lists, or technical data; and

- Other similar items.

In most instances, it will be evident that an intangible does in fact exist. However, because the definition contained in the regulations is very broad, there have been instances where the taxpayer and the IRS have disputed the existence of an intangible. In *Merck & Co.*,[5] the IRS unsuccessfully argued that a multinational taxpayer's organizational structure constituted an intangible, and that making the benefits of such structure available to a subsidiary required remuneration in the form of a royalty under Code Sec. 482. On the other hand, in *Hospital Corp. of America*,[6] the IRS successfully argued that a parent corporation's hospital management experience constituted an intangible, and making such experience available to a newly formed subsidiary, was entitled to a royalty.

> **Comment:** Transfer pricing case law and commentary often make a distinction between marketing intangibles (e.g., trademarks and brand-names) and manufacturing intangibles (e.g., patents and know-how).[7] However, as a practical matter, such distinction is of little significance as both types of intangibles are subject to the same transfer pricing rules with respect to their transfer. The only instance where such a distinction does have significance is in the area of cost sharing, where commentators have suggested that a marketing intangible cannot be the subject of a cost sharing agreement.[8]

---

[4] Reg. § 1.482-4(b).

[5] *Merck & Co., Inc.*, 91-2 USTC ¶ 50,456, 24 ClsCt 73 (1991).

[6] *Hospital Corp. of America*, CCH Dec. 40,476, 81 TC 520 (1985), nonacq. in part, 1987-1 CB 1.

[7] *See Eli Lilly & Co.*, 88-1 USTC ¶ 9502, 856 F.2d 855 (1988).

[8] *See* ¶ 460.

¶ 420 Ownership of Intangibles

.01 In General

Determining the ownership of the intangible is important because the owner is entitled to compensation for any transfer or license of the intangible. The regulations provide guidelines for determining the ownership of an intangible in two situations: (1) when the intangible is legally protected, and (2) when it is not.[9]

Intangibles that are Legally Protected. If the intangible is legally protected (i.e., it has been registered with the U.S. Patent and Trademark office), the legal owner will be treated as the owner for Code Sec. 482 purposes.[10] Legal ownership may be transferred by operation of law or contract.[11] The IRS may also impute an agreement by controlled parties to transfer legal ownership of the intangibles if their conduct indicates the existence of such agreement.[12]

Intangibles that are Not Legally Protected. If the intangible is not legally protected, the developer of the intangible will be treated as the owner for Code Sec. 482 purposes.[13] The developer is ordinarily the taxpayer that bore the largest portion of the direct and indirect costs of developing the intangible, including the uncompensated provision of property or services that contributed to its development.[14] As this rule implies, only one taxpayer will be treated as the developer. Other controlled parties involved in the development of the intangible will be treated as assistors. This issue was brought to the forefront in *DHL Corp.* where the taxpayer agreed that DHL International, its foreign affiliate, incurred the expenses ($380 million over a 10 year period) of the development of the DHL trademark outside the U.S. This argument failed, however, because the taxpayer failed to meet its burden of establishing the precise amount of expense incurred and that those expense items were incurred to the development of the respective intangibles.

A taxpayer will not be treated as the developer if, before the success of the project is known, another taxpayer becomes obligated to reimburse the controlled taxpayer for its costs (e.g., a parent corporation agrees to pays for research conducted by its subsidiary).[15] If it cannot be determined which taxpayer bore the greatest share of the costs of development, the developer will be determined by reviewing all of the relevant facts and circumstances.[16]

.02 Multiple Ownership of Intangible Property

The regulations explicitly provide that the ownership of an intangible may be subdivided, with the owners of each subdivided interest treated as an owner of intangible property for Code Sec. 482 purposes.[17] For example, the worldwide right

---

[9] *See* for example the taxpayer's alternative agreement in *DHL Corp.*, CCH Dec. 53,015(M), TC Memo. 1998-461, *aff'd in part* and *rev'd in part*, 285 F.3d 1210 (9th Cir 2002). *See also* the comments in Levey, Cunningham, Emmer & Grech, "DHL, Tax Court Road Map for Transfer Pricing Audits," 10 *J. of Int'l Tax'n* 12 (June, 1999).

[10] Reg. § 1.482-4(f)(3)(ii)(A).

[11] Reg. § 1.482-4(f)(3)(ii)(A).

[12] Reg. § 1.482-4(f)(3)(ii)(A).

[13] Reg. § 1.482-4(f)(3)(ii)(B).

[14] Reg. § 1.482-4(f)(3)(ii)(B).

[15] Reg. § 1.482-4(f)(3)(ii)(B).

[16] Reg. § 1.482-4(f)(3)(ii)(B). *See also*, Higinbotham & Levey, "When Arm's Length Isn't Really Arm's Length: Problems in Application at the Arm's Length Standard," (1998) Vol. 7, no. 6 *Tax Management Transfer Pricing Report* 243-52.

[17] Reg. § 1.482-4(f)(3)(i).

to exploit a trademark may be subdivided into separate rights to exploit the same trademark in different geographic markets.[18]

.03 Compensation for Assisting in the Development of Intangible Property

If other controlled taxpayers assisted the owner in the development or enhancement of the intangible, such other taxpayers are generally entitled to arm's length compensation (the amount of which is determined using Code Sec. 482 principles) from the owner of the intangible.[19] Compensable assistance may take the form of loans, services, or the use of tangible or intangible property.[20] However, assistance in the form of expenditures of a routine nature that an unrelated party dealing at arm's length would be expected to incur in comparable circumstances are not compensable.[21] These rules, commonly referred to as the "developer-assistor" rules, were controversial, and continue to be a source of controversy between taxpayers and the IRS.

The regulations contain four examples, designed to illustrate these rules. The first example describes the situation where one controlled party loans equipment to second controlled party for use in developing an intangible.[22] This example concludes that the lending party is entitled to arm's length compensation under Code Sec. 482 principles.

The other three examples, commonly referred to as the "cheese examples," are based on the following fact pattern: FP, a foreign producer of cheese, markets its cheese worldwide except in the United States.[23] The cheese carries a trade name that is well known outside the United States, USSub, established to distribute the cheese in the United States.

In example two, USSub undertakes all marketing and advertising to develop the name in the United States. The example concludes that FP would not be required to reallocate to USSub any portion of the market development expenses if comparable uncontrolled U.S. distributors (comparable to USSub) would incur comparable marketing and advertising expenses to develop the brand of the cheese they respectively distribute. In other words, no reallocation is required because USSub would have had to incur such marketing expenses if it were unrelated to FP.[24]

In example three, USSub is factually found to have incurred significantly higher market development and marketing expenses than comparable independent cheese distributors in the United States. Consequently, FP must reimburse USSub for the fair market value of the services that USSub is considered to have performed for FP.[25]

---

[18] Reg. § 1.482-4(f)(3)(i). Compare the arguments made by the taxpayers in *DHL Corp.*, *supra* note 9. *See also* Levey, Cunningham, Emmer & Crech, "DHL, Tax Court Roadmap for Transfer Pricing Audits," *supra* note 9; and Gregory J. Ossi, "The Significance of Intangible Property in Transfer Pricing," *Tax Notes Int'l* 993, (Sept. 13, 1999).

[19] Reg. § 1.482-4(f)(3)(iii).

[20] Reg. § 1.482-4(f)(3)(iii).

[21] Reg. § 1.482-4(f)(3)(iii).

[22] Reg. § 1.482-4(f)(3)(iv) (example 1).

[23] *See*, for a detailed discussion, Levey, "Transfer Pricing for U.S. Distribution Companies," 8 *J. of Int'l Tax'n* 540 (December 1997); Higinbotham & Levey, "When Arm's Length Isn't Really Arm's Length," *supra* note 16.

[24] Reg. § 1.482-4(f)(3)(iv) (example 2).

[25] Reg. § 1.482-4(f)(3)(iv) (example 3).

Comment: Here, the IRS does not acknowledge that USSub could be investing in its *own* marketing intangible for which it would be seeking a return in future years. Of course, that would require USSub to forego current-year profits for long-term profits, if any. Indeed, consistent with the provisions of the final regulations, the IRS could ensure the recognition of this potential income by asserting that a developer-assistor relationship exists under these facts.

Finally, in example four, FP and USSub are parties to a long-term agreement granting USSub the exclusive right to distribute cheese in the United States under FP's trade name. Consequently, no reallocation is required.[26] The justification for this position is that, because the price of the cheese USSub purchases from FP is arm's length, USSub will derive all benefit from the resale of the cheese in the United States, including any enhanced value of the trade name. As such, the expenses incurred by USSub are not considered to be a service performed for the benefit of FP, but rather for the development of the marketing intangible surrounding the trade name.

These examples arguably unduly focus on marketing and advertising expenses as a benchmark with which to compare comparable entities rather than as a tool to determine who bore the costs and risks of development. Further, they establish another comparability standard for taxpayers that, in practice, has no reliable benchmark; that is, what would an unrelated party spend on these items of expenditure with presumably the remainder having been incurred on behalf of another related party. Reliance on these benchmarks for marketing and advertising expenses could present difficult issues for international businesses. That is, international businesses may be postured to have profit and loss statements that are nearly identical to those of their competition or the fictitious comparable companies identified on a database used to establish arm's length transfer prices where "real" comparable transactions did not exist or were not ascertainable. Further, this type of analysis appears to directly interfere with management's ability to determine the levels of advertising and promotion expenses incurred. There is also the looming potential that an IRS examiner could disallow these expenses because he or she felt that (i) another related party should bear such expenses, (ii) the expenses are deemed too high, or (iii) the expenses do not yield an arm's length result. Also, capitalizing a portion of these expenses as creating a "future benefit" for purposes of Code Sec. 197 is not out of the realm of possibility.

.04 Concept of Marketing Intangibles

The concept of "marketing intangibles" has become a vigorously debated issue within the transfer pricing community in the United States and other key countries. In the United States, the concept presently appears in "IRS" transfer pricing regulations and administration announcements, some Tax Court cases, and Advance Pricing Agreement proceedings, and has been prevalent in most, if not virtually all, applicable transfer pricing audits. More frequently, foreign tax authori-

---

[26] Reg. § 1.482-4(f)(3)(iv) (example 4).

ties to whom the IRS has raised U.S. marketing intangibles issues are raising the issue for controlled distributors in their own countries.[27]

While its precise meaning is rather unclear, and may vary by company and industry, the breadth of its grasp seems to have grown over the years as the concept has been variously applied. Generally, however, the term marketing intangibles can be meant to include brands, trademarks, the local market position of a company or its products and know-how that surrounds a trademark such as the knowledge of distribution channels and customer relationship. The IRS believes the investment in these intangibles is derived from, among other things, the company's levels of advertising, marketing and promotion expenditures ("AMP").

The concept initially gained prominence in the late 1980's and particularly in a docketed Tax Court case involving the sale of vacation destinations by a U.S. distributor on behalf of a prominent foreign travel and vacation entity. The transfer price for the destination package was not directly at issue, but the level of AMP incurred by the U.S. distribution entity for these sales was scrutinized. The IRS sought either to (1) disallow a portion of the AMP under the notion that it was incurred on behalf of the foreign trademark owner, or (2) establish a service fee for the marketing efforts performed by the U.S. distributor on behalf of the foreign trademark owner. While the case was settled by the parties prior to litigation, this case foreshadowed the issues of today.

Subsequently in 1994, the IRS issued final transfer pricing regulations under Code Sec. 482 wherein it addressed the juxtaposition between the foreign owner of a trademark and the economic costs incurred by its U.S. affiliate to promote and exploit that item of intangible property in its territory as discussed in Section .03 above.

¶ 430 Transfer of Intangible Property

The Code Sec. 482 regulations governing intangible property are invoked when the owner of the rights to exploit the intangible property transfers these rights to a controlled party.[28] Although the current regulations do not define the term "transfer," the 1968 regulations specified that a transfer of intangible property occurs when it is "sold, assigned, loaned, or otherwise made available in any manner."[29] There are certain transactions, however, that while related to intangible property transfers, are nevertheless not covered by the intangibles regulations.

.01 Embedded Intangibles

Under the Code Sec. 482 regulations, the transfer of tangible property with an embedded intangible (e.g., brand-name goods) is not treated as a separate transfer of intangible property if the controlled purchaser does not acquire any rights to exploit the intangible other than relating to the resale of the tangible property

---

[27] Derived from Marc M. Levey, Monique van Herksen, Stephan Schnorberger, Stephen Breckenridge, Kazuo Taguchi and James Dougherty, "The Quest for Marketing Intangibles," 23 *Intertax* 2 (2005). *See also* Marc M.Levey, Pam Church, Monique van Herksen, Alexander Odle and Frank Gasparo, "Marketing Intangibles Require Close Legal and Tax Scrutiny," *European Business Review* (November/December 2007).

[28] Reg. § 1.482-4 (f) (3) (i).

[29] Reg. § 1.482-2A(d) (1) (i).

under normal commercial practices.[30] However, for purposes of determining the transfer price of the tangible property, the presence of the intangible must be considered to determine comparability.[31] Nevertheless, if the terms of the transfer of tangible property allow the purchaser to exploit the embedded intangible, the regulations provide that the arm's length price for the transfer of the embedded intangible may have to be determined separately from the arm's length price for the tangible property.[32]

.02 Services Rendered

The regulations provide that if services are provided in connection with the transfer of intangible property, then the arm's length price shall be determined under the rules for transfers of intangible property, and not the rules governing the provision of services.[33] Here, services are deemed to be rendered in connection with the transfer of intangible property if they are ancillary and subsidiary to the transfer of the property or to the commencement of effective use of the property by the transferee.[34] Whether services are rendered in connection with the transfer of intangible property is a question of fact.[35] The regulations give the following examples of services rendered in connection with the transfer of property:

- Demonstrating and explaining the use of property;
- Assisting in the effective starting up of the property transferred; or
- Performing under a guarantee related to such effective starting-up.

However, services performed after the effective starting-up of the property transferred (e.g., supervision of general manufacturing) could give rise to a separate allocation under the services rules.[36]

.03 Contract Research and Development

As will be discussed below, if a related party renders assistance in developing intangible property to the owner of the intangible property, then an allocation under the services rules would be appropriate.[37]

The *DHL* Tax Court case decided in 2002 become the next significant step in the evolution of the marketing intangible concept. This case addressed the IRS' attempt to impute a trademark royalty for the use of the DHL tradename by DHL's foreign affiliates. At issue was the taxpayer's assertion that a royalty should not be imputed from these foreign affiliates because they bore the economic investment for the development of the DHL trademark. While marketing intangibles surrounding the DHL tradename were not directly discussed, the *DHL* Tax Court case stood for the proposition that for items of intangible property, the party who bore the

---

[30] Reg. § 1.482-4(e); Reg. § 1.482-3(f). *See also* Rev. Rul. 75-254, 1975-1 CB 243.

[31] Reg. § 1.482-4(e); Reg. § 1.482-3(f). *See also* Rev. Rul. 75-254, 1975-1 CB 243.

[32] Reg. § 1.482-4(e); Reg. § 1.482-3(f). *See also* Rev. Rul. 75-254, 1975-1 CB 243.

[33] Reg. § 1.482-2(b)(8).

[34] Reg. § 1.482-2(b)(8).

[35] Reg. § 1.482-2(b)(8).

[36] Reg. § 1.482-2(b)(8).

[37] Reg. § 1.482-4(f)(3)(iii). *See e.g., Ciba-Geigy Corp.,* CCH Dec. 42,271, 85 TC 172 (1985) (holding that a U.S. subsidiary of a Swiss parent must be compensated for services performed in connection with the development of herbicides); *Westreco,* CCH Dec. 48,527(M), 64 TCM (CCH) 849 (1992) (determining the arm's length compensation for a U.S. subsidiary performing R&D activities on behalf of its Swiss parent corporation).

economic burdens of the investment should bear the economic rewards. The aggregate levels of AMP, as well as certain other expenses that were incurred by the DHL foreign affiliates, were considered for purposes of this economic invest-ment, although there was no real analysis of the accounting codes that made up the AMP nor what component of the underlying costs were directed to trademark development or surrounding intangibles. While the Tax Court found in favor of the IRS and assessed penalties against the taxpayer, in 2002 the Appellate Court reversed the finding holding that, under then applicable section 482 regulations, the DHL foreign affiliates made the economic investment for the development of the DHL trademark and were considered the owners of those intangibles for tax purposes and entitled to its economic return.

It was the dictum in the underlying Tax Court case, however, that bore real importance for purposes of the marketing intangible concept. Here, the Trial Judge espoused his "bright-line" test which notes that, while every licensee or distributor is expected to expend a certain amount of cost to exploit the items of intangible property to which it is provided, it is when the investment crosses the "bright line" of routine expenditures into the realm of non-routine that, economic ownership, likely in the form of a marketing intangible, is created. Unfortunately, the Trial Judge did not embellish on this test to provide practical guidelines to this theory because he essentially held that the taxpayer failed to meet its burden of proof. Stated otherwise, he was concerned that DHL did not expressly identify those costs that were actually incurred in the development of the DHL tradename and whether those costs were truly earmarked for such development.

The marketing intangible issue is most recently being considered in the *Glaxo* case in the U.S. Tax Court where the IRS has asserted a tax deficiency in amounts approximating $2.7 billion. The underpinning to the IRS claim is that Glaxo's U.S. affiliate is the economic owner of the U.S. marketing intangible through its invest-ment in a marketing strategy conceived and directed by Glaxo U.S. executives, that this investment arguably resulted in a fully integrated business, which lead to the success of its products in the U.S. market. Accordingly, the IRS asserted that the U.S. affiliate was entitled to operating income commensurate with its investments. While this case was the subject of a taxpayer favorable settlement, it does give credence to the IRS position on marketing intangibles and does not preclude the IRS from raising the issue in arguably better fact patterns.

It is the theories described above that continue to be raised in most tax audits and are presently under consideration by the U.S. Tax Court in current pending cases. Numerous unanswered questions remain, for example, such as how to define the company's marketing intangibles, how does one determine where the level of AMP transcends from routine to non-routine expenditures, what qualifies for these considerations, (e.g. registration costs, legal costs), and is an analysis of each underlying accounting code required to segregate routine from non-routine expen-ditures. One further practical problem is that not every taxpayer accounts for its AMP in the same accounting codes.

While there may be merit in the *DHL* "bright line" test, from a practical point of view, it is so industry and company specific, that it may be impossible to

¶430.03

consistently apply in most cases. Similar companies within the same industry may have vastly different approaches to their marketing philosophies, product launches, and/or product dependence or interdependence. This could create very different levels of AMP and different "bright lines." This may even occur within the same companies and for similar product categories. These expenditures can also be impacted by the product's position in other countries, the timing of product launches, and the competitors and their products, each of which impacts the "bright line" benchmarking.

The OECD added another twist to the international career of the concept of marketing intangibles when it included a discussion of their impact on the allocation of profits to either headquarter or permanent establishment. The re-drafted part I of the OECD Report on the Attribution of Profits to Permanent Establishment does not help to clarify the concept of marketing intangibles when it establishes that they include, *inter alia*, the name and logo of a company and a brand. Intentionally or unintentionally, the draft lends a hand to the inventive fiscal quest for marketing intangibles by sympathizing with the decentralized allocation of "global" marketing intangibles as key entrepreneurial risk taking functions, in particular day to day risk management, are hypothesized to be "dispersed within the enterprise". It should not be forgotten that the OECD draft is designed to be an analogous application of the OECD Transfer Pricing Guidelines to permanent establishment/headquarter cases.[38] Thus, by reverse analogy much the same principles may be applied to company to company transactions. Even more, the draft speculates that key entrepreneurial risk taking functions are unlikely to be dispersed within the enterprise but are concentrated either at the permanent establishment or at the headquarter where marketing intangibles are specific to a permanent establishment's host country. Such ideas may well be taken by tax administrators as an invitation to identify something specific about an international marketing intangible and to establish some key entrepreneurial risk taking functions in the distribution country.

Europe. European tax authorities have observed the marketing intangibles debate that was taking place in the United States. Not surprisingly, the German Government has been delighted to seize the opportunity offered to it by the judicial development of the concept of business opportunity developed in case law before the turn of the last millennium. Significant clarifications on the concept of business opportunity have been achieved since the early days of the concept. Today, it is understood that a business opportunity is an asset. Consequently, if there is no asset there can be no business opportunity. As a result, failed AMP investments cannot lead to an asset nor to a business opportunity. At the same time, important questions remain open such as when to attribute a business opportunity to a specific group entity among several, or how to value and establish a business opportunity. The spending of resources, for instance money, is a widely recognized—though not unambiguous—criterion for the allocation of a business opportu-

---

[38] The OECD approved the 2010 revision of the Transfer Pricing Guidelines on July 22, 2010. *See http://www.oecd.org.*

nity to an (distributor) entity. This is the link with the rather indiscriminate identification of (alleged) marketing intangibles that is so tempting to tax administrators.

The look back to an early landmark Federal Tax Court decision of 17-2-1993, on excessive startup distribution losses reveals a taxation concept competing with the allocation of marketing intangibles to a distributor. In the 1993 Aquavit decision, the center of the controversy were AMP expenses incurred by the German distributor in the hope of opening up and penetrating the German market for the foreign produced branded spirits. Rather than attributing a deemed marketing intangible and a corresponding return to the distributor the court disallowed the excessive AMP expenses and instructed the tax office to tax them as dividends in disguise. Systematically, and in practical cases financially it makes a difference whether excessive AMP expenses are taxed as hidden profit distributions or whether such expenses are capitalized as investment an adequate return being allocated on top of it.

Both the (justified or unjustified) deeming and allocation of a marketing intangible and the disallowance of excessive AMP expenses are based on a more general principle of arm's length taxation, namely the postulate that each entity ought to earn a return "commensurate" with the functions exercised, risks taken and the assets actually held by the entity.

The Dutch and French tax authorities are also raising the issue. While the concept initially surfaced in corporate restructurings, it has lately become an issue under audit as to whether the distributors have been sufficiently awarded for their development of the market. It is becoming predictable that upon restructurings, that tax authorities first raise the issue that the margin allocated to foreign activities are too high, and to pre-empt that discussion, might fail to yield the desired result of retaining revenue. The next determination is that marketing intangibles or goodwill are being transferred to the foreign country. As marketing intangibles are an economic, nearly synthetic, concept defined by nothing more than marketing investments and business savvy, which de facto are characteristics that are included in the generic distributor function (if not required to be successful in any case), this development is likely to be countered in litigation by the civil law concept of legal ownership of legally recognized intangibles at some point. While marketing intangibles are not defined and basically subject to a "you know it when you see it" test, the legal proposition is that a distributor that is particularly good at what it does (e.g. a super-distributor), needs to be rewarded with a margin that is comparable to that of (other) super-distributors who incur similar investments related to their functionality. In any case, the marketing effort and resulting marketing intangibles should not result in base erosion at the expense of the legal owner of the relevant intangibles.

In audit cases, the French tax authorities have been keen to protect their tax base by pointing at the legal protection granted to trademarks and patents and they might demand a return to the legal ownership for that term even where all AMP was incurred by the foreign distributors. Taxpayers are, therefore, caught between these tax authorities defending their tax bases. Taxpayers are bound to suffer

¶430.03

double taxation over this issue, and the competent authority procedure is one that is ill-equipped to address this issue, as it is factual and reasonable people can agree to disagree on what rises to the level of a marketing intangible, and what value ought to be allocated to the deemed intangible.

Transfer pricing, although a legal concept, is driven by economics and proportionality between functions performed, risks incurred and earnings made. The boundaries of this proportionality are provided by comparables, largely from public databases. As the European countries all largely adhere to a continental system of recording, where costs are classified by type of expenses (i.e., COGS, OPEX) rather than by stage of production, reliable data of profit margins are lacking and comparables need to be reviewed from an operating profit level and ratios need to be consulted, such as the Berry Ratio or ratios of operating expenses to gross receipts or gross profit margins, to derive a sense of comparability. However, as most European tax authorities doggedly adhere to a preference for the traditional transaction methods (i.e. Comparable Uncontrolled Price, Cost Plus or Resale Price Methods), absent the application of such a method there is little authority or defense against adjustments by tax authorities.

The discussion and issue are likely to peak soon as the European Court of Justice has been chipping away at the domestic tax bases by breaking down domestic tax rules that discriminate against foreign taxpayers. Because European tax authorities are seeking a last anchor to base their access to revenue on, transfer pricing, intangibles and marketing intangibles, seem to be ideal for that purpose. One way to attempt to minimize exposure on the marketing intangibles front is to carefully define and allocate ownership of client lists, responsibilities for follow up with clients and potential after sales activities, marketing and merchandizing responsibilities and in particular responsibilities for AMP spelled out in clear language contractual arrangements between related parties. This requires more than mere contract drafting, however, and de facto adherence to contract requirements becomes as important as functional and risk allocations. So far, the judiciary generally appears to be quite formalistic, and not in favor of creative economic theories that would merit allocation of income other than where it legally/contractually belongs, if the facts support that allocation and functionality. Therefore, contractual arrangements, documentation and a conservative economic analysis cannot be left out in defense against overindulgent tax authorities creatively construing a marketing intangibles theory to attract (additional) income.

Asia Pacific. In Japan, there exists no judicial precedents or regulations of tax authorities for this marketing intangibles issue, nor are there the same vigorous debates on the issue as in the United States. However, an officer responsible for international taxation at the National Tax Agency ("NTA"), (Director, International Taxation) delivered a lecture on the present situations and problems of international taxation at a meeting held in June, 2004 and referred to intangibles in general, and marketing intangibles specifically. This is presumably the only instant where the tax authorities have expressed their views on this issue. Some of the views are set forth below, wherein the Director stated:

¶430.03

> In Japan, it is generally thought that an intangible, irrespective of whoever has legal rights thereto, belongs to not the registered owner thereof but to the party who has developed or enhanced the value of the intangible. This is an important point.

The Director here quoted paragraph 6.38 of the Organisation for Economic Co-operation and Development ("OECD") Transfer Pricing Guidelines on Marketing Intangibles, which provides in relevant part:

> In general, in arm's length dealings the ability of a party that is not the legal owner of a marketing intangible to obtain the future benefits of marketing activities that increase the value of that intangible will depend principally on the substance of the rights of that party. For example, a distributor may have the ability to obtain benefits from its investments in developing the value of a trademark from its turnover and market share where it has a long-term contract of sole distribution rights for the trademarked product.

In the Instructions of the Commissioner dated June 1, 2001 (the "Guidelines of Administrative Processes for Transfer Pricing"), the NTA, declared, "The Agency shall exert its efforts to properly administer examinations of transfer pricing or audits for APAs by reference to the OECD Transfer Pricing Guidelines whenever necessary," and clarifies that it will make the OECD Guidelines a base for its administration. The OECD Guidelines may also work as a guideline for the treatment of marketing intangibles. Further, the Director refers to the draft U.S. Reg. § 1.482-4(f)(4), and comments that "The United States has placed emphasis on the status of legal owners, but we have an impression that the attitudes of Japan and the United States are getting closer." Hence, the Director believes that the arm's length consideration for a contribution by one controlled taxpayer that develops or enhances the value, or may be reasonably anticipated to develop or enhance the value, of an intangible owned by another controlled taxpayer shall be determined under the applicable rules Code Sec. 482.

Lastly, the Director stated that, "On the premise that an intangible belongs to the party who has developed or enhanced the value of the intangible, it must be determined who is the party who has developed or enhanced the value of the intangible." It can be considered that this party is the one who has made a decision to develop or enhance the value of the intangible, managed risks thereof, provided services therefor and bore the costs thereof. "Hence, even if a parent company, for the purpose of unifying the management of all manufacturing patents and trade-marks of its group companies unilaterally, holds the entire legal rights thereof, . . . if the brand value is enhanced through marketing activities by a subsidiary, we consider that for taxation purposes, the interest in the intangibles in connection with the manufacture and sale thereof shall belong to the subsidiary and the benefits corresponding to the economic value of the intangibles belong to the subsidiary."

These passages clearly imply that while there is no direct Japanese jurisprudence on this subject, the thinking of the NTA and the IRS regarding marketing intangibles fairly parallels each other and this issue may likely result in similar audit issues in Japan, as in the United States.

¶430.03

Australia's reaction to the "marketing intangibles" issue is also not well-developed, at least in so far as the public gaze is concerned. Although the OECD's work in this area has apparently been limited, the Australian Tax Office ("ATO"), however, is actively considering a number of applicable scenarios in which the concept may be applied.

Accordingly, while there is no "official" ATO position on how, if at all, it would treat "marketing intangibles," this may change in the near future by the possible release by the ATO of its views on this seemingly "difficult area."

Some limited scenarios that we understand may possibly be under examination are:

Where a related party distributor acting in Australia is reimbursed as to 100% of all of its marketing expenses on behalf of the foreign parent and also receives a marketing service fee based upon a percentage of its marketing expenses, the distributor is regarded as an agent being reimbursed for its promotional expenditure by the owner of the marketing intangible. The distributor is only entitled to compensation appropriate to its sales solicitation activities and would not be entitled to share in any return attributable to the increase in value of the marketing intangible.

Where the Australian taxpayer obtains no rights to use the trade name other than in marketing and distributing a branded product, it is anticipated that the ATO would, in general, not expect the Australian taxpayer to be charged a royalty in addition to the transfer price of the product. Where the marketing expenses, compared to arm's length comparables is "normal," its is likely that the ATO would not propose an adjustment to the distributor because the distributor would be receiving an arm's length return. On that basis the ATO would presumably accept that any increase in the value of the branded product would remain with the ownership of the parent company. This scenario is comparable to the facts under the DHL case where the marketing spend does not exceed the "bright line" test.

Where a distributor incurs marketing expenditure above and beyond what independent enterprises are assessed to do and has no right of recovery or reimbursement from the foreign parent so that the profits are lower than what unrelated parties would accept, it will be considered to have assumed a significantly greater and higher risk than the arm's length party. The expectation of the ATO in this case is likely to be that the distributor would obtain an additional return from the trade mark owner, possibly through a reduction in the transfer price or a reduction in any royalty rate. Here, of course, the marketing expenses would be considered in excess of the "bright line" test.

In latter circumstance, it is anticipated that the ATO could propose to increase the taxable income of the distributor by applying, in substitute for the taxpayer's transfer pricing methodology, a residual profit split methodology where it would attribute a basic return for the functions, assets and risks of each of the parent and Australian subsidiary and split the residual profit on the basis of the value of the intangible assets relevantly owned by the parent and the subsidiary. Presumably, the subsidiary's intangible assets will constitute the contractual rights it has from

¶430.03

the long-term distribution agreement which would need to have been valued at the time of entry into the original Agreement. The ATO is thought unlikely to accept (presumably in retrospect) a reimbursement by the foreign principal of the Australian subsidiary's marketing expenses because it would not be consistent with the legal arrangements between the parties.

It is thought that the ATO generally accepts that a distributor would enter into a short-term non-renewable royalty free distribution agreement, but only where the distributor stands to make a "reward" commensurate with the level of risk it is assuming. On that basis apparently, the ATO is of the view that independent marketing/distributors who have non-renewable short-term distribution agreements which provide no compensation on termination do not invest large sums on the development of marketing and distribution infrastructure, and that the short-term nature of the distribution agreement will not allow the marketer/distributor to benefit from the marketing distribution spend it incurs at its own risk and that the spend benefits the foreign parent/principal. Accordingly, it appears the ATO could seek to adjust taxable income of the marketing/distributor, presumably, by decreasing the transfer price to the extent of some form of fee for the marketing services actually undertaken. The ATO would also likely seek to preclude the marketer/distributor from sharing in any increase in the value of the trademark.

It is thought that the ATO also accepts that a current long-term distribution arrangement may be renegotiated before expiration without compensation, so that the basis of the new transfer price is automatically indexed for the CPI and a percentage of the previous transfer price provided that the distributor "stood to obtain an adequate net return" and/or there was "adequate compensation" to the distributor. Assuming that the distributor has not passed on to its arms-length customers the increasing price so that its original profit margin was retained, the ATO is likely to propose an adjustment to the distributor's taxable income by reducing the transfer price.

Further, it is thought that the ATO accepts that arm's length parties could renegotiate long-term contracts before expiration where the future agreement provides for the extension of the range of products subject of the agreement and the payment of a royalty based on selling prices, subject to the distributor receiving an adequate return on an after-royalty basis and that the marketing spend is not significantly disproportionate to the amount that a third party would spend. The ATO believes, consistent with paragraph 1.42 of the OECD Transfer Pricing Guidelines that where separate transactions which are so closely linked or continuous cannot be evaluated on a separate basis, they should be evaluated on an aggregate basis. Accordingly, the ATO might expect the transfer price to be reduced to ensure a comparable return to the distributor or it possibly could deny a deduction for the royalty.

The ATO's possible response to these scenarios may not set out how it would quantify the adjustments it was proposing nor how it would distinguish between routine or non-routine marketing spend. In the ordinary course of the self assessment tax system, any amounts of marketing spend would not be immediately

¶430.03

apparent to the ATO and would be expected to have been paid to arm's length providers in the first instant.

The ATO has not further indicated if it would determine, in the limited circumstances, an increase in the value of the intangible property. It is also unclear if the ATO is looking to attack or bifurcate the royalty payments from the transfer prices.

Most recently, China has indicated a growing interest in the marketing intangibles issue as they follow the global trends in transfer pricing.[39] The outgrowth of this announcement is that the State Tax Administration ("SAT") may likely seek more income from the supply chain allocated to Chinese affiliates of foreign companies (called Wholly Owned Foreign Enterprises or "WOFEs") for expanding market share in China through AMP expenditures. Concomitantly, the SAT may challenge royalty rates to foreign affiliates where brand recognition of its products are being developed locally in China by the WOFE. Particularly vulnerable in China are companies who have been unknown to the Chinese market, but are currently launching product into the marketplace.

The SAT is seeking input globally about how to address marketing intangibles, among other things. Most prominently, they may be following the lead of the U.S. IRS and the ATO in this area. Not only is the SAT addressing the technical tax issues surrounding marketing intangibles, but how to properly document the transaction. And, with the elimination of many tax holidays and incentives in a drive for an increased share of the supply chain profit, these issues are at the forefront, particularly as multinational companies restructure their Chinese WOFE.

Indirect taxes in China may also be largely impacted by the role of marketing intangibles. For example, a royalty is subject to a 10 percent withholding tax and a 5 percent business tax. Because the royalty may be part of the cost base of the Chinese affiliate for either tax or customs, there may exist some double counting of the tax base.

Economic Benchmarking Challenges. These disparities in approach, as well as the difficulties with the issue itself, make economic benchmarking extraordinarily difficult. First, one must actually review the precise accounting codes for what comprises the AMP. Factually, this by itself may establish the company's routine versus the non-routine expenditures; however, there are difficulties in both characterization and timing, such as for product launches. The amount of these expenditures may cross certain thresholds, or ratios set by either the IRS, taxpayer, or industry analysts, yet may be factually considered routine given the specific product, market, and timing of the launch. Even if this is all accomplished, economic benchmarking still remains a challenge.

What makes this economic benchmarking challenging is that there is no real database that addresses pure marketing intangibles. One can consider various rates of return on the cost of the investment, but that is not entirely reflective of a market

---

[39] "SAT Studying Marketing, Licensing Intangibles, Practitioners Say," 16 No. 6 *BNA Transfer Pricing Report* 175 (July 11, 2007).

value for intangible property. One can also extrapolate certain knowledge by reviewing the relationship of gross receipts to operating expenses to establish ratios to be applied to the taxpayer, but that analysis may be imprecise because operating expenses of all types are usually aggregated. Public companies are not required to disclose their AMP, and even for those who do, there is no way to determine the percentage of these expenses devoted to intangible property enhancement.

The idea that there are clear industry standards that establish what a distributor should spend on AMP can be problematic. The financial statements of companies within an industry may classify and define AMP expenses differently. One company may define spending as advertising while another company defines similar spending as media or distribution. Other items, such as market studies or promotional brochures may be classified under completely different accounting codes.

Contributing to the difficulty is the uncertain definition of what exactly constitutes marketing intangibles. In addition to trademarks and trade names, marketing intangibles can be company specific but may include customer lists and knowledge of distribution channels. Customers are not 'intangible' but, on the other hand, are certainly not, *stricto sensu*, under the control, or ownership of, the company. Yet, it is undeniable that customers (and more in general, all customer relationships) are a key value driver and one of the main indicators of growth potentials. Transfer pricing practitioners very often engage in discussions, for example, with the tax authorities over the value to be attributed to the 'customer list' in the context of business reorganizations and supply chain restructuring processes. It is not clear precisely where in the financial statements expenditures related to the development of these items may be reflected.

The lack of transparency and consistency in reporting practices for AMP spending makes it difficult to identify true benchmark levels of normal advertising expenses. There are a number of databases that are commonly used to conduct comparables analysis and benchmarking of financial data within industries, including Compustat, Disclosure, Moody's, Worldscope, Global Vantage, and Amadeus, among others. Although the database providers may attempt to standardize data across companies, they are faced with the same challenges regarding transparency and consistency as practitioners when reviewing company documents.

In compiling the financial data of the companies, the database providers also make certain decisions regarding classification and organization that may not easily align themselves with the needs of the practitioner analyzing AMP expenditures. For example, the Compustat database defines Advertising Expense as follows: "This item represents the cost of advertising media (radio, television, newspapers, periodicals) and promotional expenses. This item excludes selling and marketing expenses." It seems clear that there could be expenditures that relate to the creation of marketing intangibles that are not being captured by this line item. However, the category of Selling, General, and Administrative Expense is defined, as one would expect, far more broadly and includes 27 separate items, such as salaries and related costs, R&D, engineering, legal expenses, marketing, and

¶430.03

others in addition to advertising. Using this item as a proxy would surely overstate the investments in marketing intangibles.

Further, most contemporary databases that address trademark royalties (e.g. RoyaltySource and RoyaltyStat) contain information on license agreements between unrelated parties, but do not provide sufficient elements to segregate the remuneration paid for the intangible property (e.g. trademark) from the one paid, for instance, for ancillary services. Economic or financial modeling can be done to sometimes give rationale results, but for unique trademarks the challenge increases dramatically to estimate an arm's length price.

The level and nature of AMP spending can be also impacted by a variety of business factors, including management policies, market share, characteristics of the market, and the timing of product launches. The annual reports and SEC documents of public companies, as well as the database providers, generally do not provide the necessary level of detail that would be required to reconcile these management considerations and classification differences.

An additional challenge to an analysis of marketing intangibles is that AMP spending generally has spillover effects to or from other products or product lines. Also, the effects of AMP spending are distributed over time and so the accounting practice of expensing such AMP investments in the current period can create distortions in determining economic profits. This dynamic is most evident when dealing with issues such as a product launch, where there may be a sharp increase in spending prior to the launch of a product or product line, followed by subsequent decreases to more stable spending levels. It might be appropriate to segregate out the spending related to the product launch, or at least ensure that the data being considered covers a sufficient time period such that the lifecycle dynamics can be properly addressed. This requires estimations of the useful life of AMP spending.

In analyzing marketing intangibles for transfer pricing purposes one should consider, among others, the following questions:

- Will certain costs and expenditures result in an economically valuable asset?
- What is the expected use of the asset by the entity?
- What is the expected useful life?
- Are there any legal or regulatory restrictions?
- What are the effects of obsolescence or other external economic factors?
- What is the level of maintenance expenditures?

It is also important to consider the nature of the relationship between the related party manufacturer and the local distributor. Even assuming that it is possible to estimate a normal level of AMP spending for a particular industry, and that the distributor in question spends at a greater rate than this routine level, a critical factor is whether the intercompany arrangements are such that the distributor is assuming risks consist with an entrepreneurial role. If the intercompany arrangements are such that the distributor is effectively guaranteed a routine profit level regardless of the level of its marketing expenditure, then the question of whether these expenditures are above a normal level is not relevant because any

¶430.03

resulting profits would be attributable to the manufacturer that is assuming the entrepreneurial risk.

¶ 440 Transfer Pricing Methods for Intangibles

.01 Comparable Uncontrolled Transaction ("CUT") Method

The CUT method evaluates whether the amount charged for a controlled transfer of intangible property was arm's length by reference to the amount charged in a comparable uncontrolled transaction.[40] The CUT method is essentially the analog of the CUP method that is applicable to transfers of tangible property.

The CUT method generally provides the most direct and reliable measure of an arm's length result if the same intangible is transferred in the controlled and uncontrolled transactions, or there are only minor differences between the uncontrolled and controlled transactions that have a definite and reasonably ascertainable effect on the price, and appropriate adjustments are made for these differences.[41] The CUT method may also provide the most reliable measure of an arm's length result in other cases in which the method may best be described as the "inexact CUT" method. Comparable intangibles transferred under comparable rather than the same circumstances may be used.[42]

The CUT method depends on similarity in terms of contractual arrangements and economic conditions. It cannot be applied unless the intangible property involved in the controlled and uncontrolled transactions is comparable, meaning that the intangible must be used in connection with similar products or processes within the same general industry or market.[43] To evaluate the comparability of the controlled and uncontrolled transactions, the regulations identify several factors that should be considered.[44] They are:

- Terms of the transfer;
- Stage of development of the intangible;
- Rights to updates and enhancements;
- Uniqueness of the property;
- Duration of the license;
- Any economic and product liability risks;
- Existence of any collateral or ongoing business relationships; and
- Any services provided by the transferor or transferee.

> **Comment:** In practice, it is difficult to find a reliable CUT. This is primarily due to the lack of public information and the inherent uniqueness of intangible property.

.02 Comparable Profit Method

The CPM evaluates whether the amount charged in a controlled transaction is arm's length based on objective measures of profitability (PLIs) derived from

---

[40] Reg. § 1.482-4(c)(1).
[41] Reg. § 1.482-4(c)(2)(ii).
[42] Reg. § 1.482-4(c)(2)(ii).

[43] Reg. § 1.482-4(c)(2)(iii).
[44] Reg. § 1.482-4(c)(2)(iii)(B)(2).

uncontrolled taxpayers that engage in similar business activities under similar circumstances.[45] Under the CPM, an arm's length result is determined by calculating what taxpayer's operating profit would have been on related party transactions if its PLI were equal to that of an uncontrolled comparable and then comparing that result to the interquartile range calculated based on the results of the comparable companies.[46] To calculate the taxpayer's operating profit, the selected PLI should be applied solely to the taxpayer's financial data that is related to the controlled transactions.[47]

The CPM is more fully described in the chapter discussing transfers of tangible property.

.03 Profit Split Method

The profit split method compares the allocation of the combined operating profit or loss attributable to controlled transactions to the relative value of each controlled taxpayer's contribution to that combined operating profit or loss.[48] The allocation should correspond to the division of profit or loss in an uncontrolled transaction, where each party performs functions similar to those of the controlled taxpayers.[49] The profit allocated to any particular member of a controlled group is not necessarily limited to the total operating profit of the group from the relevant business activity. Thus, in a given year, one member of the group may earn a profit while another member incurs a loss. There are two types of profit split analyses: the comparable profit split method and the residual profit split method. The profit split method is more fully described in the chapter discussing transfers of tangible property.

¶ 450 The Commensurate-with-Income Standard and Periodic Adjustments

.01 Background

Congress amended Code Sec. 482 in 1986 to require that payments to a related party with respect to a licensed or transferred intangible be "commensurate with the income" attributable to the intangible.[50] This amendment was based on a Congressional finding that there is a strong incentive for taxpayers to transfer intangibles to related foreign corporations or possessions corporations in a low tax jurisdiction and that judicial interpretations of existing law did not require that the transferor receive an arm's length amount of compensation therefor.[51] This was particularly true for intangibles that had high future profit potential but no comparables at the time of transfer from which to currently determine an arm's length price.[52] These findings were repeated in the IRS and Treasury's "A Study of

---

[45] Reg. § 1.482-5(a).
[46] Reg. § 1.482-5(b)(1).
[47] Reg. § 1.482-5(b)(1).
[48] Reg. § 1.482-6(a).
[49] Reg. § 1.482-6(b).

[50] Tax Reform Act of 1986, P.L. 99-514, § 1231(e)(1).
[51] H.R. Rep. No. 426, 99th Cong., 1st Sess. pp. 423-425 (1985).
[52] H.R. Rep. No. 426, 99th Cong., 1st Sess. pp. 423-425 (1985).

Intercompany Transfer Pricing Under Section 482 of the Code," Notice 88-123, 1988-2 CB 458. (the "White Paper").[53]

> **Example:** *Assume R&D Corp.*, a U.S. corporation (a 35 percent taxpayer), develops and patents a drug that may cure a particular medical condition. While the future success of the drug is speculative, *R&D Corp.* transfers the patent to a Puerto Rico subsidiary (a zero percent taxpayer) for a one percent net royalty. A one percent royalty was selected because the success of the drug was speculative and no comparables were available from which to value the transfer. The subsidiary then exploits the drug to its full market potential. As a result, the *R&D Corp.* group eliminated U.S. tax on 99 percent of the profits attributable to the drug.

Prior to the 1986 amendment to Code Sec. 482, the strategy in the above example may likely have worked under the authority of *R.T. French*.[54] In *R.T. French*, the Tax Court held generally that if an arrangement provided for reasonable arm's length charges at its inception, the IRS could not reallocate profits based solely on hindsight.[55]

To counter this strategy, Congress added the commensurate-with-income standard to Code Sec. 482. In doing so, Congress specifically required that the actual profit experience realized from the exploitation of the intangible be considered in determining an arm's length compensation for the transfer of such intangible and that the amount of compensation be adjusted over time to reflect changes in the income attributable to that intangible.[56]

.02 Periodic Adjustments

The commensurate-with-income standard, as interpreted by the regulations, states that if intangible property is transferred for a period in excess of one year, the consideration charged is subject to an annual adjustment to assure that it is commensurate with the income attributable to the intangible property.[57] Because the income attributable to the use of intangible property can vary from year to year, the amount of the royalty can similarly vary.

Periodic adjustments are not required, however, when the royalty payment is based on a comparable third-party intangible property transfer of the same intangible under similar circumstances provided the amount paid in the first year is at arm's length.[58] For intangible property transfers of so-called "inexact" comparables, a series of requirements must be met to avoid the periodic adjustment.[59] These requirements include the following:

- A written agreement covering the period of the license must exist;
- No change must have occurred in the roles of the licensor and licensee since the agreement was executed;

[53] *See* generally, Mogle, "Intercompany Transfer Pricing for Intangible Property," BNA Tax Management Transfer Pricing—Special Report, Vol. 6, No. 2 (1997).

[54] *R.T. French Co.*, CCH Dec. 32,119, 60 TC 836 (1973).

[55] *R.T. French Co.*, CCH Dec. 32,119, 60 TC 836 (1973) at 854. *But see Nestle Co.*, CCH Dec. 25,919(M), 22 TCM

46 (CCH) (1963) (upholding the parties' post-transfer modification of transfer prices).

[56] H.R. Rep. No. 426, at 425.

[57] Reg. § 1.482-4(f)(2).

[58] Reg. § 1.482-4(f)(2)(ii)(A).

[59] Reg. § 1.482-4(f)(2)(ii)(B).

- The total profits earned from the exploitation of the intangible property in the relevant year and in all past years must lie between 80 percent and 120 percent of the profits projected at initiation of the agreement.[60] Stated otherwise, this means that a fluctuation in profitability in the current year may not trigger a periodic adjustment if the total fluctuation since the date of the agreements falls, in the aggregate, between 80 percent and 120 percent of the initially projected profits.

Periodic adjustments are also not required under two additional scenarios, notwithstanding the method used to determine the royalties. One scenario arises if an extraordinary event prevents a taxpayer from satisfying the above-described 80 percent to 120 percent test.[61] The other is that no periodic adjustments will be made in any subsequent year if no adjustment has occurred under these sales for each of five consecutive years, commencing with the first year of the agreement.[62]

Regulatory examples at Reg. § 1.482-4(f)(2)(iii) provide the following examples:

Reg. § 1.482-4(f)(2)(iii), Ex. 1

(i) USdrug, a U.S. pharmaceutical company, has developed a new drug, Nosplit, that is useful in treating migraine headaches and produces no significant side effects. A number of other drugs for treating migraine headaches are already on the market, but Nosplit can be expected rapidly to dominate the worldwide market for such treatments and to command a premium price since all other treatments produce side effects. Thus, USdrug projects that extraordinary profits will be derived from Nosplit in the U.S. and European markets.

(ii) USdrug licenses its newly established European subsidiary, Eurodrug, the rights to produce and market Nosplit for the European market for 5 years. In setting the royalty rate for this license, USdrug makes projections of the annual sales revenue and the annual profits to be derived from the exploitation of Nosplit by Eurodrug. Based on the projections, a royalty rate of 3.9% is established for the term of the license.

(iii) In Year 1, USdrug evaluates the royalty rate it received from Eurodrug. Given the high profit potential of Nosplit, USdrug is unable to locate any uncontrolled transactions dealing with licenses of comparable intangible property. USdrug therefore determines that the comparable uncontrolled transaction method will not provide a reliable measure of an arm's length royalty. However, applying the comparable profits method to Eurodrug, USdrug determines that a royalty rate of 3.9% will result in Eurodrug earning an arm's length return for its manufacturing and marketing functions.

(iv) In Year 5, the U.S. income tax return for USdrug is examined, and the district director must determine whether the royalty rate between USdrug and Eurodrug is commensurate with the income attributable to Nosplit. In making this determination, the district director considers whether any of the exceptions in § 1.482-4(f)(2)(ii) are applicable. In particular, the district director compares the profit projections attributable to Nosplit made by USdrug against the actual profits realized by Eurodrug. The projected and actual profits are as follows:

---

[60] Reg. § 1.482-4(f)(2)(ii)(B); Reg. § 1.482-4(f)(2)(ii)(C).

[61] Reg. § 1.482-4(f)(2)(ii)(D).
[62] Reg. § 1.482-4(f)(2)(ii)(E).

	Profit Projections	Actual Profits
Year 1	200	250
Year 2	250	300
Year 3	500	600
Year 4	350	200
Year 5	100	100
Total	1400	1450

(v) The total profits earned through Year 5 were not less than 80% nor more than 120% of the profits that were projected when the license was entered into. If the district director determines that the other requirements of Reg. § 1.482-4(f)(2)(ii)(C) were met, no adjustment will be made to the royalty rate between USdrug and Eurodrug for the license of Nosplit.

Reg. § 1.482-4(f)(2)(iii), Ex. 2

(i) The facts are the same as in Example 1, except that Eurodrug's actual profits earned were much higher than the projected profits, as follows:

	Profit Projections	Actual Profits
Year 1	200	250
Year 2	250	500
Year 3	500	800
Year 4	350	700
Year 5	100	600
Total	1400	2850

(ii) In examining USdrug's tax return for Year 5, the district director considers the actual profits realized by Eurodrug in Year 5, and all past years. Accordingly, although Years 1 through 4 may be closed under the statute of limitations, for purposes of determining whether an adjustment should be made with respect to the royalty rate in Year 5 with respect to Nosplit, the district director aggregates the actual profits from those years with the profits of Year 5. However, the district director will make an adjustment, if any, only with respect to Year 5.

Reg. § 1.482-4(f)(2)(iii), Ex. 3

(i) FP, a foreign corporation, licenses to USS, its U.S. subsidiary, a new air-filtering process that permits manufacturing plants to meet new environmental standards. The license runs for a 10-year period, and the profit derived from the new process is projected to be $15 million per year, for an aggregate profit of $150 million.

(ii) The royalty rate for the license is based on a comparable uncontrolled transaction involving a comparable intangible under comparable circumstances. The requirements of paragraphs (f)(2)(ii)(B)(1) through (5) of this section have been met. Specifically, FP and USS have entered into a written agreement that provides for a royalty in each year of the license, the royalty rate is considered arm's length for the first taxable year in which a substantial royalty was required to be paid, the license limited the use of the process to a specified field, consistent with industry practice, and there are no substantial changes in the functions performed by USS after the license was entered into.

(iii) In examining Year 4 of the license, the district director determines that the aggregate actual profits earned by USS through Year 4 are $30 million, less than 80% of the projected profits of $60 million. However, USS establishes to the satisfaction of the district director that the aggregate actual profits from the process are less than 80% of the projected profits in Year 3 because an earthquake severely damaged USS's manufacturing plant. Because the difference between the projected profits and actual profits was due to an extraordinary event that was beyond the control of USS, the could not reasonably have been anticipated at the time the license was entered into, the requirement under § 1.482-4(f)(2)(ii)(D) has been met, and no adjustment under this section is made.

¶ 460 Cost Sharing Arrangements

.01 In General

In adding the commensurate-with-income standard to Code Sec. 482, Congress explicitly stated that it did not intend to preclude the use of bona fide research and development cost sharing arrangements as an appropriate method of allocating income attributable to intangibles among related parties.[63] The primary tax benefit from entering into a cost sharing arrangement is that all participants to such arrangement will be considered the owner of their respective interest in the intangibles created, thereby precluding the application of the general transfer pricing rules relating to the transfer of intangible property. Consequently, cost sharing is viewed as a practical alternative to cross-border licensing.[64]

In enacting the commensurate-with-income standard, Congress set forth three guidelines intended to address specific concerns about the operation of cost sharing arrangements under pre-1986 law.[65] The first guideline addressed the issue of cherry picking high profit intangibles for inclusion in cost sharing arrangements. To prevent this type of abuse, Congress stated that participants are expected to bear their respective portion of all research and development costs, on unsuccessful as well as successful products within an appropriate product area, and that the costs of research and development at all relevant development stages would be included. Secondly, Congress stated that the allocation of research and development cost sharing arrangements generally should be proportionate to profit as determined before deduction for research and development. Lastly, Congress stated that if one participant contributes funds toward research and development at a significantly earlier point in time than the other participant, or is otherwise effectively putting its funds at risk to a greater extent than the other, it is expected that an appropriate return would be required to such party to reflect its investment.

> **Comment:** These guidelines were discussed in the White Paper, which relied on them to make suggestions as to provisions that should be required in bona fide cost sharing arrangements.[66] Some of the more controversial of these

---

[63] H.R. Rep. No. 841, 99th Cong. 2d Sess., p II-638.

[64] *See* generally, Dodge and Shapiro, "Planning Opportunities Under the Final U.S. Cost Sharing Regulations," 5 *Int'l Transfer Pricing J.* No. 2, 86 (1998).

[65] *Id. See* generally White Paper, 1988-2 CB 495.

[66] White Paper, 1988-2 CB at 495-499.

provisions included: (1) that the product areas covered by cost sharing arrangements should be within three digit SIC codes, (2) that participants should be assigned exclusive geographic rights to the developed intangibles, and (3) that marketing intangibles should not be the subject of cost sharing arrangements. These suggested provisions were omitted from the final cost sharing regulations as being too restrictive.

.02 Qualified Cost Sharing Arrangement

Regulations providing rules for qualified cost sharing arrangements were issued in 1995. A qualified cost sharing arrangement is a written agreement under which the participants agree to share the costs of developing intangible property proportionately to their relative shares of reasonable benefits from the individual exploitation of their assigned interests in the intangibles.[67] This arrangement is not treated as a partnership for U.S. federal income tax purposes, and is not a foreign corporation or non-resident individual treated as engaged in a U.S. trade or business solely due to its participation in a cost sharing arrangement.[68] Once the participants have entered into a qualifying cost sharing arrangement, the IRS is precluded from making Code Sec. 482 adjustments except to the extent necessary to make each participant's share of intangible development costs equal to its share or reasonably anticipated benefits.[69]

The requirements for a qualified cost sharing arrangement are as follows:

- It includes at least two participants;
- It provides a method to calculate each controlled participant's share of the intangible development costs based on factors that can reasonably be expected to reflect that participant's share of anticipated benefits;
- It provides for adjustment to each controlled participant's share of intangible development costs to account for changes in economic conditions, the business operations and practices of the participants, and the ongoing research and development of the intangibles under the arrangement;
- It is recorded in a document that is contemporaneous with the formation or any revision of the arrangement that includes:
  a. A list of the participants and any other member of the controlled group that will benefit from the use of the intangibles developed under the arrangement;
  b. The information described in (1)-(3) above;
  c. A description of the scope of the research and development to be undertaken, including a description of the intangible or class of intangibles intended to be developed;
  d. A description of each participant's interest in any covered intangibles (i.e., intangibles developed as a result of research and development undertaken under the cost sharing arrangement);

---

[67] Reg. § 1.482-7(a)(1).
[68] Reg. § 1.482-7(a)(1).
[69] Reg. § 1.482-7(a)(2).

¶460.02

    e. It sets forth the duration of the arrangement; and

    f. Sets forth the conditions under which the arrangement may be modified or terminated and the consequences of such modification or termination.[70]

The IRS may also recharacterize any arrangement that in substance constitutes a cost sharing arrangement notwithstanding a failure to comply with all of the above requirements.[71]

.03 Participants

A participant is a controlled taxpayer that: (1) reasonably anticipates that it will derive benefits from the use of covered intangibles (either from direct use of the intangible or through licensing the intangible); (2) substantially complies with certain enumerated accounting requirements; and (3) substantially complies with enumerated administrative requirements.[72] For this purpose, all members of a consolidated group (as defined by Code Sec. 1504) that join in the filing of a consolidated return shall be treated as one taxpayer.[73]

> **Comment:** The participation requirement described above reflects a fundamental change from the requirement as first promulgated. Originally, only a controlled taxpayer that used or reasonably expected to use the covered intangible in the active conduct of its trade or business could qualify as a participant.[74] For this purpose, a taxpayer was considered to actively conduct a trade or business only if it carried out substantial managerial an operational activities itself, or supervised the conduct of these activities by another.[75] This requirement was dropped following a substantial amount of criticism by taxpayers who rightly pointed out that there are sound business reasons for transferring intangibles to entities that do not conduct an active trade or business, as defined in the regulations.

If a controlled taxpayer that is not a participant renders assistance to the research and development undertaken pursuant to a qualified cost sharing arrangement, such taxpayer must be compensated under the rules applicable to controlled parties who provide assistance to the owner of an intangible described in Reg. § 1.482-4(f)(3)(iii).[76]

.04 Intangible Development Costs

For purposes of the cost sharing regulations, the term "costs related to the intangible development area" is equal to:

    1. Operating Expenses (all expenses not included in cost of goods sold except for interest expense, foreign income taxes, domestic income taxes, and any other expenses not related to the operation of the relevant business activity—ordinarily includes expenses associated with advertising, promotion, sales, marketing, warehousing and distribution, adminis-

---

[70] Reg. § 1.482-7(b).
[71] Reg. § 1.482-7(a).
[72] Reg. § 1.482-7(c)(1).
[73] Reg. § 1.482-7(c)(3).

[74] *See* Former Reg. § 1.482-7(c)(1) (1995).
[75] *See* Former Reg. § 1.482-7(c)(2)(ii) (1995).
[76] Reg. § 1.482-7(c)(2)(i).

tration, and a reasonable allowance for depreciation and amortization); plus

2. Charges for the use of tangible property made available to the cost sharing arrangement to the extent not included in operating expense; less

3. Depreciation and amortization expense.[77]

If a particular cost contributes to the cost sharing arrangement and other areas or other business activities, the cost must be allocated on a reasonable basis (i.e., the cost must be allocated based on the relative benefits to the cost sharing arrangement and the other area).[78] Costs that do not contribute to the cost sharing arrangement are not taken into account.[79]

A participant's costs of developing intangibles equals:

1. All costs related to the intangible development area incurred by the participant; plus

2. All cost sharing payments that it makes to other controlled and uncontrolled participants; less

3. All cost sharing payments that it receives from other controlled and uncontrolled participants.

Similarly, a participant's share of costs of developing intangibles is equal to its costs of developing intangibles divided by the intangible development costs of all controlled participants.[80]

.05 Reasonably Anticipated Benefits

A participant's reasonably anticipated benefits is equal to the aggregate benefits that it reasonably anticipates that it will derive from the covered intangibles.[81] For this purpose, benefits are the additional income generated or costs saved by the use of the covered intangibles.[82] A participant's share reasonably anticipated benefits is equal to its reasonably anticipated benefits divided by the reasonably anticipated benefits of all controlled participants.[83]

A participant's share of reasonably anticipated benefits must be determined using the most reliable estimates of benefits (this rule incorporates the best method rule under Reg. §1.482-1(c)).[84] The reliability of an estimate of benefits principally depends on two factors: (1) the reliability of the basis for measuring benefits used and (2) the reliability of the projections used to estimate benefits.[85]

Reliability of Measured of Benefits. To estimate a controlled participant's share of benefits, the measurement must be consistent for all participants.[86] Anticipated benefits can be measured directly or indirectly, provided that they are measured using the most reliable basis.[87] Benefits are measured directly by reference to estimated additional income to be generated or costs to be saved.[88] Benefits may be

[77] Reg. § 1.482-7(d)(1); Reg. § 1.482-5(d)(3).
[78] Reg. § 1.482-7(d)(1).
[79] Reg. § 1.482-7(d)(1).
[80] Reg. § 1.482-7(f)(2)(i).
[81] Reg. § 1.482-7(e)(2).
[82] Reg. § 1.482-7(e)(1).
[83] Reg. § 1.482-7(f)(3)(i).
[84] Reg. § 1.482-7(f)(3)(i).
[85] Reg. § 1.482-7(f)(3)(i).
[86] Reg. § 1.482-7(f)(3)(ii).
[87] Reg. § 1.482-7(f)(3)(ii).
[88] Reg. § 1.482-7(f)(3)(ii).

measured indirectly on the basis of (1) units used, produced, or sold; (2) sales; (3) operating profit; or (4) other reliable bases.[89]

Reliability of Projections. Projections include a determination of the time period between the inception of the cost sharing arrangement and the receipt of benefits, a projection of the time over which benefits will be received, and a projection of the benefits anticmpated for each year in which the intangibles will yield benefits.[90] Significant divergences between the projected and actual benefits may deem the projections unreliable and result in an adjustment by the District Director.[91] The regulations provide safe harbors where projections will not be considered unreliable if the divergence for every controlled participant is not more than 20 percent of the participant's projected benefit share or the divergence is attributable to extraordinary events that were not foreseeable or within the control of the participants.[92] For purposes of the 20 percent safe harbor, all controlled participants that are not U.S. persons are treated as a single controlled participant.[93]

.06 Cost Allocations

As discussed previously, each controlled participant's share of the intangible development costs must be calculated based on factors that can reasonably be expected to reflect that participant's share of anticipated benefits. Adjustments must be made to the extent that a participant's actual costs exceed its share of costs.

.07 Buy-In and Buy-Out Payments

Buy-In and Buy-Out Valuations—The Problems. If a controlled participant to a cost sharing agreement makes intangible assets available to the other participants for purposes of the cost sharing agreement, an arm's length "buy-in" payment must be made to the owner for the use of the intangible assets.[94] These intangible assets generally comprise either: (1) pre-existing intangibles; or (2) unfinished "work-in-process" R&D for intangible projects. Certain economic phenomena and/or events, however, may not qualify as intangible assets or property. This does not imply that these phenomena have no ascertainable effect on value, but merely that they may not be considered by themselves intangible assets for tax and legal purposes. The descriptive economic phenomena that may not qualify as identifiable intangible assets, but can be considered value or competitive factors and influences include (a) market share; (b) high profitability; (c) lack of regulation; (d) a regulated or protected market position; (e) monopoly position or barriers to entry; (f) market potential; (g) breadth of appeal; (h) mystique; (i) heritage or longevity; (j) competitive edge; (k) life-cycle status; (l) uniqueness; (m) discount prices; (n) liquidity or illiquidity; and (o) ownership control. However, the existence of many of these subtle characteristics may indicate the existence of valuable non-routine intangible assets or comprise a part of an overall marketing intangible.[95]

Various FSAs in the context of cost sharing agreements highlight the difficult problems that arise with intangible assets and the determination whether the

[89] Reg. § 1.482-7(f)(3)(iii).
[90] Reg. § 1.482-7(f)(3)(iv)(A).
[91] Reg. § 1.482-7(f)(3)(iv)(B).
[92] Reg. § 1.482-7(f)(3)(iv)(B).

[93] Reg. § 1.482-7(f)(3)(iv)(B).
[94] Reg. § 1.482-7(g).
[95] *See* Robert F. Reilly and Robert P. Schweihs, *Valuing Intangible Asset* (McGraw-Hill, 1999, 7).

parties must make a buy-in payment, the amount to be paid, and the form of the payment. IRS officials have publicly commented on perceived abuses of the buy-in process and undervaluing of existing intangibles used in cost sharing agreements.[96] These abuses seem to arise where either cost sharing arrangements are estab- lished in low tax jurisdictions[97] or the cost contributions to the arrangement are inconsistent with the benefits and results of the arrangement.

Determining the amount of the buy-in (or buy-out) payment involves difficult factual and valuation issues. These issues touch upon some of the most complex theoretical arguments and empirical research in economics, statistics, behavioral psychology, finance and game theory, and can pit the efficient market and random walk proponents[98] against those that argue that capital markets function with imperfect information that can lead inefficient and non-arm's length outcomes. Further, markets are not always efficient in the short-term and markets do not always follow a random walk. This imperfect information can influence decision making mechanisms that create short-term bubbles of opportunity for short-term profit maximizing opportunities.[99] These short-term anomalies in long-term market values can, under certain circumstances, lead to inappropriate valuations. These valuations can directly effect the buy-in or buy-out mechanism contained in cost- sharing agreements. Normal valuation challenges arise when the buy-in payment is made for pre-existing intangible assets, although identifying the appropriate valua- tion model components, business synergies, and useful lives of these apparent pre- existing intangible assets can be problematic. These intangibles can include (a) marketing-related intangible assets (e.g., trademarks, trade names, brand names, logos), (b) technology-related intangible assets (e.g., process patents, patent appli- cations, technical documentation, such as laboratory notebooks, technical know- how, work-in-process research and development), (c) artistic-related intangible assets (e.g., literary works and copyrights, musical compositions, copyrights, maps, engravings), (d) data processing-related assets (e.g., proprietary computer software, software copyrights, automated databases, integrated circuit masks and masters), (e) engineering-related intangible assets (e.g., industrial design, product patents, trade secrets, engineering drawings and schematics, blue prints, proprie- tary documentation), (f) customer-related intangible assets (e.g., customer lists,

---

[96] *See* articles cited in footnote 2; Morgan, "Buy-in Payments and Market Valuations," *Tax Mgmt. Transfer Pricing Rep.* 449 (September 15, 1999).

[97] *See*, e.g., "Economist Says E-Commerce Firms Using Cost Sharing to Cut Uncertainty," 9 Tax Mgmt. Transfer Pricing Rep. 70 (May 31, 2000).

[98] *See* John H. Kagel and Alvin E. Roth, *The Handbook of Experimental Economics* (Princeton University Press, 1995, 446-447). Informational efficiency of capital markets is a central theme in modern finance. Empirical observa- tions about the statistical properties of prices were made by Bachelier (1900), Kendall (1953), Roberts (1959), Al- exander (1961), Cootner (1964), Fama (1965), and others. Samuelson (1965) applied the no-arbitrage condition to prove that properly anticipated prices must behave like a random walk. The logic of arbitrage suggests that when the informed traders move to take advantage of their information, the price will move by an amount and in the

direction that eliminates this advantage. Neutral observ- ers of such a market would observe an association be- tween the unanticipated information obtained by the informed traders and the consequent movement of mar- ket prices. Information is not wasted; in equilibrium, price summarizes and reveals all relevant information in possession of all the traders (see Hayek 1945; Grossman 1976). The idea that prices in stock markets promptly and unbiasedly (though not precisely) adjust to reflect infor- mation came to be called the efficient market theory (*see* Fuma 1970). Price data gathered from stock and com- modity exchanges provided the initial impetus for devel- opment of the random walk theory and made it possible for researchers to test this statistical theory.

[99] *See* John H. Kagel and Alvin E. Roth, *The Handbook of Experimental Economics*(Princeton University Press, 1995). Shyam Sunder, *Experimental Asset Markets: A Sur- vey*, 445-500. Please note that much of this discussion is based on the research contained in this chapter.

¶460.07

customer contacts, customer relationships, open purchase orders), (g) contract-related intangible assets (e.g., favorable supplier contracts, license agreements, franchise agreements, noncompete agreements), (h) human capital-related intangible assets (e.g., a trained and assembled workforce, employment agreements, union contracts), (i) location-related intangible assets (e.g., leasehold interests, mineral exploitation rights, easement, air rights, water rights), (j) and goodwill-related intangible assets (e.g., institutional goodwill, professional practice goodwill, personal goodwill of a professional, celebrity goodwill, general business going-concern value).[100] These same issues arise when unwinding or terminating a cost sharing agreement and a "buy-out" of the intangibles is required. For simplicity's sake, this paragraph primarily focuses on the buy-in payments, although the issues for buy-out payments are often the same (except as noted below).

The real difficulties arise, however, when the intangible asset involves unfinished "work in process" R&D. There are three primary valuation models that are often used separately, and at times together, to face a specific valuation challenge. They are (a) Discounted Cash Flow ("DCF") Models, (b) Relative Valuation Models, and (c) Option Pricing Models. Under the DCF models, either cash flows-to-equity can be discounted at the cost of equity to determine a value of equity or cash flows to the company can be discounted at the cost of capital to arrive at the value of the company. These models can be further categorized on the basis of assumptions about the business growth into stable-growth, two-stage, and three-stage models.[101] The measurement of earnings and cash flows may also be adjusted to match the special characteristics of the company or transaction being valued. For the use of multiples, the price can be expressed in terms of a number of company-specific variables such as, earnings, cash flows, book value, and sales. The multiples themselves can be calculated by using comparable companies in the same business or from cross-sectional regressions that use the broader universe or from fundamental analysis.[102]

Under the DCF models, the value of a business generally is the future expected cash flow discounted at a rate that reflects the riskiness of the cash flow. Under the Relative Valuation Model (sometimes called the "accounting approach"), the importance of earnings of the business entity is stressed. Value is simply earnings times some multiple (e.g., the price-earnings or "P/E" ratio, price-to-book value or P/Book value ratio and the price to sales ratio or P/Sales). Simply put, this model states that only the current year's earnings is relevant. A more sophisticated approach to this model might discount the future stream of earnings at some acceptable rate.[103] The third approach uses an Option-Pricing Model which estimates the value of assets that have option-like characteristics. Generally, options are derivative securities that derive their value from underlying assets. An option provides the holder with the right to buy or sell a specified quantity of an underlying asset at a fixed price at or before the expiration date of the option. The

---

[100] *See* Robert F. Reilly and Robert P. Schweihs, *Valuing Intangible Assets* (McGraw-Hill, 1999, 19).

[101] *See* Aswath Damodaran, *Security Analysis for Investment and Corporate Finance* (*John Wiley & Sons, Inc.*, 1994, 366-375)

[102] *Id.*

[103] *See* Tom Copeland, Tim Koller, Jack Murrin, *Valuation: Measuring and Managing the Value of Companies* (*John Wiley & Sons, Inc.*, 2nd Ed., 1995, 70-71).

value of an option is determined by six variables: (a) the current value of the underlying asset, (b) the variance in this value, (c) the strike price, (d) the life of option, (e) the riskless interest rate, and (f) the expected dividends on the asset. Because, it is a right and not an obligation, the holder can choose not to exercise the right and allow the option to expire.[104]

These traditional valuation models, while typically viewed as the best and most appropriate starting points for estimating value, may be highly speculative and problematic in the context of the buy-in payment for work-in-process intangible assets simply because there may be little or no reliable cash flows or historical sales or profits on which to base projections and calculations. Using any of these models in isolation or without corroborative evidence to value a particular asset or potential asset, may therefore lead to erroneous or misleading valuations by not fully recognizing the synergies that may occur when entities combine. Using other traditional valuation models, such as P/E, market value-to-book value or any other earnings multipliers, may also not be possible or practical due to the dearth of necessary data[105] or suitable comparable companies available on which to base a calculation, or benchmark.

Another area of valuation analysis that has been considered applies to the area of mergers and acquisitions. Here, the bidding company must decide on a fair market value for the target company before making a bid, and the target company must determine a reasonable value for itself before deciding to accept or reject the offer. There are special factors that must be considered in a takeover or merger valuation. First, the effects of synergy on the combined value of the two companies have to be evaluated before a decision is made on the bid. Second, the effects on value of changing management and restructuring the target company will be considered in arriving at a fair price.[106] Mergers and acquisitions have often been blamed on undervaluation to management self-interest.

A favorite reason for an acquisition is the creation of a single business out of what was previously two independent businesses will create greater value for the equity owners. This occurrence is called "synergy." Synergy refers to the potential additional value gained from combining two businesses or companies, either from operational or financial sources. Stated otherwise, a whole is greater than the sum of the parts. In the context of takeovers, either operational or financial synergy, arguably, accrues to the combined firm in a merger. Because the bidding company and the target company are both contributors to the creation of this synergy, the sharing of the benefits or synergy among the two companies will depend in large part on whether the bidding company's contribution to the creation of the synergy is unique or easily replaced. If easily replaced, the bulk of the synergy benefits will

---

[104] *See* Aswath Damodaran, *supra* note 101, at 339.

[105] *See* Marc M. Levey, Jonathan E. Lubick, and Robert T. Bossart, "Defining Quality Data in a Transfer Pricing Analysis," *The Journal of International Taxation* 1996.

[106] It should be pointed out that that there are many economists that stress the importance of the efficient market theory. These economists argue that the market price at any one time represents the best estimate of the true value of the firm and that any attempt to exploit perceived market inefficiencies will cost more than it will make in excess profits. They assume that markets aggregate information quickly and accurately, that marginal investors promptly exploit any inefficiencies, and that any inefficiencies in the market are caused by friction, such as transactions costs, and cannot be arbitraged away. This assumption should not always be either considered a general rule or even always correct.

accrue to the target company; if unique, the sharing of the benefits will be much more equitable.[107]

There are several empirical studies that examine whether synergy exists and how much it may be worth. If synergy is perceived to exist in a takeover, the value of the combined company or business should be greater than the sum of the values of the bidding and target firms operating independently. Studies of stock returns around merger announcements generally conclude that the value of the combined operations increase in most takeovers and that increase may be significant.[108]

Another added complexity in determining a buy-in valuation for R&D related intangibles is the treatment of stock option values that are part of some management compensation plans.[109] The cost of these stock options, it is argued by the IRS, must be included in a company's R&D cost pool and then must be correctly allocated among the cost sharing arrangement's participants as part of the buy-in calculation. The result of this pooling is the shifting of some expense related to the R&D function and risk from the parent company to its foreign subsidiary, thereby increasing the tax deductions for the foreign subsidiary. This may or may not be a positive outcome for the taxpayer.

Suggested Parameters for Buy-In and Buy-Out Payments. Parameters for establishing the value of buy-in payments have been variously suggested.[110] For example, for companies with a history of R&D projects, the floor for the project value of work-in-process component of an R&D project may be determined by using the company's historic expected rate of returns for corporate investments, its anticipated cost of capital, or some accounting method of depreciation allowance for in-process R&D that is written off for book purposes.[111] By contrast, the ceiling may be the present value of the expected income stream to be derived from the intangible asset being developed. This ceiling may be derived from the income flows of comparable intangibles, business projections, or even the fair market value (or in some cases, market capitalization) of the entire business unit appropriately discounted or adjusted for market characteristics, assets not contributed, and business unit synergies. Where the business unit is either publicly traded[112] or the subject of a recent acquisition, the business unit value might be somewhat determinable, subject to various adjustments, such as reduction for any incremental value brought to the acquired unit by the purchaser.[113]

These guidelines may prove helpful in some cases, but certainly not all and especially for work-in-process R&D. Implicit in these guidelines is that the value of

---

[107] *See* Aswath Damodaran, *supra* note 101 at 294-295.

[108] *See* Aswath Damodaran, *supra* note 101 at 301.

[109] The IRS's treatment of stock option values is detailed in a IRS advice memorandum FSA 200003010. According to the IRS, a U.S. corporation attempting to establish a qualified CSA with a foreign subsidiary must include the value of stock options in its research and development cost pool to obtain an advance pricing agreement ("APA"). *See also* Levey and Garofalo, "The IRS Takes a Hard Line Cost Sharing Agreements", 11 *Journal of Internal Taxation* (September, 2000).

[110] *See* L. Dicker, "Stock Options Can Have Great Impact on Cost Sharing Pool, IRS Official Says," 9 *Tax Mgmt. Transfer Pricing Rep,* 96 (BNA) (June 14, 2000); Finan, "Reliably Determining a Buy-In Payment Under Code Sec. 482," *Journal of Global Transfer Pricing,* 17-18 (CCH) (February 1999).

[111] *See* Morgan, *supra* note 96, comments of L. Dicker, *supra* note 110; note that some companies may have expected rates of return specifically for R&D or other intangible development.

[112] The volatility of small cap and start-up stocks may make the use of stock market values problematic also.

[113] *See* John Wills, "Valuing Technology: Buy-In Payments for Acquisitions," *Journal of Global Transfer Pricing,* 29-32 (CCH) (Feb. 1999).

the work-in-process R&D exceeds cost. This may not be correct. The ultimate question to be asked is what an unrelated would third party pay for the knowledge gained through this work-in-process R&D. It cannot be assumed that an unrelated buyer will pay a price to the seller to assure a return based on its cost of capital. In fact, this profit benchmark or target will likely never come into the negotiation process between unrelated parties. Buyers must look for a return on their own investment and are not typically concerned with the sunk costs of the seller. Sellers may look to recoup their costs but will always be guided by the marketplace especially if they can get a return greater than cost.

Also likely to occur will be an analysis and/or negotiation to determine whether the final completion funding is more valuable than the initial seed money. While the answer here may be virtually impossible to ascertain without some significant conjecture based on the specific facts and circumstances involved, the question may therefore be framed as: who gets the benefit of the bargain or who bears the investment risk Stated otherwise, is the money brought into the project to bring it to a conclusion more valuable (or at a premium) as contrasted to the initial seed money If the answer to this question is yes, then the presumption contained in the above parameters, that the value of the work-in-process R&D should exceed its costs, may fail. Some economists believe that the initial investor in a speculative venture assumes the greatest risk and should get a higher return.[114] In practice, however, this is not always so. For example, assume company X has expended $750,000 to develop a new pharma product and has depleted its budgeted funds prior to completion of the project. Company X approaches company Y and offers it a 25 percent interest in the project for $250,000 completion funds. Company Y advises company X that it is very interested in participating in the project but desires a 40 percent interest in return for its premium funding. Company Y believes that its completion funding is more valuable to the project because it is this funding that takes the project to commercialization. Company X retorts that company Y's offered interest of 25 percent is more than generous because company Y would not have this investment opportunity if it were not for company X's entrepreneurial efforts and risk. In fact, Company X suggests that it should only have offered Company Y a 15 percent interest for this investment. Determining the value within this example to establish a buy-in amount for purposes of the cost sharing arrangement will be difficult.[115] This exercise, of course, can be highly speculative and subjective and the range of buy-in payment values using the above parameters can be quite wide. The facts and circumstances are indeed the most controlling factors. The variance in views in how to approach this valuation, however, can lead to many tax controversies and potential penalty issues where the IRS and the taxpayer widely differ.

Several possible methods have been suggested for valuing a work-in-process buy-in payment. The traditional Comparable Uncontrolled Transaction ("CUT")

---

[114] *See* Finan, *supra* note 110, at 16 and fn. 28; Morgan, *supra* note 96, at text after fn. 9.

[115] This example assumes a finite pharma project where all the costs are contained under a project code.

This example can get even more complicated if the buy-in payment were for marketing intangibles where there may not be a project code and, further, where certain historic costs had only an annual or temporary value or were replicated, enhanced, or replaced annually.

may exist, although experience tells us that there is a dearth of intangible asset CUT's in general, let alone for work-in-process which has no discernable market or commercial value. The Comparable Profits Method ("CPM") may work in certain situations, although generally not with potential "super" royalty type intangibles. The CPM's reliance on residual values also gives concern, given the wide fluctuations in rate of return data and imprecise comparables. These fluctuations can cause substantial year to year variances in the valuation process. And, of course, when all else fails, a profit split approach can be negotiated although this tends to create more long-term problems than the short-term solution that is attained.

A DCF method may be employed, despite its speculative nature. Issues with identifying assets, timing, and specific cash flow projections may also distort the results. Hence, this analysis is likely only useful as a corroborative measure.[116] One of the limitations of DCF method is its failure to adequately consider assets that do not produce cash flows currently and are not expected to produce cash flows in the near future, but are valuable nevertheless because of their potential to produce value for the company. A company with valuable product patents that are unutilized currently, but could produce significant cash flows in the future may, therefore, be undervalued using traditional valuation techniques. The option-pricing method approach to value these product patents may provide insight into the value that they add to the company.[117] Although many commentators recognize the problems in this methodology, the IRS may still use this or a similar market capitalization[118] approach in the absence of an alternative or because it yields a favorable tax result.

A market capitalization approach generally uses the price of a company's stock as the starting place for valuation of the company's intangible assets subject to the buy-in payment.[119] The Market Capitalization Method requires estimation of values for all of a company's intangible assets. This is a difficult and subjective process,[120] requiring a determination of the precise identity of each intangibles asset, and then separately valuing them. Instead of simply estimating the value of the intangible asset being used in the cost sharing agreement, numerous valuations must be performed (which can also be costly.)

Many taxpayers oppose the use of the IRS' market capitalization method because they dispute the fundamental assumption that a company's total value always equals its market capitalization.[121] Although the market capitalization method would at first glance appear to represent the true value of a company using all available information and based on the functioning of efficient markets, some

---

[116] *See* Finan, *supra* note 110, at 19; Wills, *supra* note 113, at 31.

[117] *See* Aswath Damodaran, *supra* note 101, at 360.

[118] *See* R.J. Shook and Robert L. Shook, *The Wall Street Dictionary* (New York Institute of Finance, 1990.) Typically, market capitalization is defined as the market price of the equity multiplied by the quantity of shares outstanding.

[119] *See* David W. Pearce, *The MIT Dictionary of Modern Economics*, 4th ed. 1992, 53. The total amount and structure of the share capital of a company. All companies must have owners who own the ordinary shares of equi-

ties. A company with only one class of share is said to have a straight capitalization. Many companies have several different types of capital issued and are then said to have a differentiated or structured capitalization. The total market value of a company's issued share capital is termed its market capitalization. The term capitalization also refers to the act of converting net retained profits or reserves into issued share capital.

[120] *See* legislative history for Code Sec. 197. Congress enacted Code Sec. 197 because of the huge number of controversies based upon the allocation of value to various taxpayer intangibles.

[121] *See* Wills, *supra* note 113, at 30-31.

would argue that it does not adequately address the process by which these values are created and equity prices are determined. The market capitalization method adopted by the IRS would seem to fail to adequately address why companies engage in mergers and acquisitions. Further, a pure reliance on a single "silver bullet" valuation method would seem to ignore short-term market anomalies such as, the formation of speculative market bubbles, the stability of markets, the impact of insider trading, and of alternative regulatory policies and trading institutions. As has been mentioned earlier, the price paid by an acquirer may include values for synergies, changes in business plan or other matters not reflective of the underlying asset value or stock price that is the subject of the "buy-in" payment. Stock value may fluctuate over time for many reasons unconnected with underlying asset value.

Thus, under a market capitalization model, intangible assets tend to be frequently overvalued or misvalued.[122] This is especially true if the market valuation is derived from an acquisition where the synergies of an acquisition increase value of the stock to address the premiums paid, say, for the results of the combination of the assets expected to be realized. Similarly, for intangible assets that are not fully developed, these taxpayers question whether work-in-process component may be valued without also allocating some value to "work to be performed", which obviously does not yet exist as an asset.[123]

This method can also lead to the assumption that the current work-in-process R&D equal the differential between total market capitalization and the book value of tangible assets. Further, the market capitalization method does not assist in determining the profit allocation among the intangible assets being valued which is the necessary element in assessing a buy-in or buy-out payment. market capitalization method valuation can actually blur past, present and future expectations of profit and, more specifically, the attribution of that profit which would therefore seem to short-circuit the intent of a bona-fide cost sharing arrangements, namely, the intent to share and distribute future profit based on cost contribution.

Further, a simple market capitalization model can sometimes fail to appropriately account for short term stock variability not based on fundamentals, and can cloud other short term anomalies that effect market capitalization or equity prices. Recently, there has been empirical research in the field of experimental economics dealing with modeling and testing decision making in environments of uncertainty. Some empiricists believe that in a world of uncertainty, expectations about the fundamentals replace fundamentals. Mutual dependence of current prices and current expectations about the future can yield to certain types of "bubble theories." First, deviation of asset price from its intrinsic value can be compounded over time in rational expectation equilibrium to form a bubble. When individuals have specific decision parameters and markets are incomplete, it cannot be guaranteed that asset prices will not create such a bubble. Second, "sunspot" equilibrium arises

---

[122] *Id.* at 29-30.
[123] *Id.* at 31-32. Note that the market capitalization method (if properly used) is generally consistent with the "residual method" used to allocate values to corporate assets after an asset acquisition or Code Sec. 338 acquisition. *See* Code Sec. 1060 and the regulations under Code Sec. 338.

when agents form certain arbitrary beliefs that alter the fundamentals of the economy in such a way that such beliefs become self-fulfilling.[124] Formal models can either rely on a consistency condition such as rational expectations or use Bayesian[125] revision[126] with some ad hoc prior and likelihood function, or use some ad hoc adaptive process.[127]

The P/E ratio approach, another possible method, assumes the company will be worth some multiple of its future earnings in the continuing period. This is obvious. The difficulty arises however, in trying to estimate an appropriate P/E ratio.

One-trap some analysts often fall into in acquisition situations is the circular reasoning that the P/E ratio for the continuing value equals the P/E ratio paid for the acquisition. Simply put, if one pays 15 times earnings, should he be able to sell the business for 15 times earnings. In most cases, the reason a company is willing to pay a given P/E for an acquisition is that the business management believes it can take actions or has the synergy to greatly improve earnings. Accordingly, the effective P/E it is paying on the improved level of earnings will be much less than 15. Once the improvements or synergies are in place and earnings are higher, buyers will not be willing to pay the same P/E unless they can make additional improvements in synergies.[128]

The market-to-book ratio approach assumes the company will be worth some multiple of its book value, often the same as its current multiple or the multiple of comparable companies. This approach is conceptually similar to the P/E approach and therefore faces the similar problems and issues. In addition, to the complexity of deriving an appropriate multiple, the book value itself is distorted by inflation and key accounting assumptions.[129]

FSA 200023014. In FSA 200023014 (dated February 29, 2000) the IRS suggests that the market capitalization method may be appropriate for the valuation of a buy-in. A footnote in the FSA notes that the market capitalization method will be more useful where the buy-in involves an acquisition of the intangible to be used rather than a short-term license, likely for the reasons noted above. With today's high historical price-to-earnings and market value-to-book multiples, some IRS examin-

---

[124] For a complete discussion of these arguments and underlying theory, see John H. Kagel and Alvin E. Roth, *supra* note 98; Shyam Sunder, *supra* note 99, at 468-474.

[125] *See* David W. Pearce, 1992, *supra* note 119, at 35. Bayesian techniques are methods of statistical analysis (including estimation and statistical inference) in which prior information is formally combined with simple data to produce estimates, or test hypotheses. The techniques provide a way of including subjective impressions and/or theoretical elements in quantitative analyses.

[126] *See* Richard Schmalensee and Robert D. Willig, *Handbook of Industrial Organization*, vol. 1, North-Holland, 1992, Chapter 5: Noncooperative Game Theory for Industrial Organization: An Introduction and Overview, by Drew Fudenberg and Jean Tirole. For a complete discussion, please see sections on Bayesian games and Bayesian equilibrium and Using Bayesian equilibria to justify mixed strategy equilibria and Daynamic games of incomplete information.

[127] *See* Richard Schmalensee and Robert D. Willig, *supra* note 126; Shyam Sunder, *supra* note 99, at 482. According to the author, a great deal of efficient markets literature in finance has held that the absence of arbitrage opportunities in the market implies that the price of a given equity reflects all information available to the market participants. If the price of a given equity at any time does not reflect the information, it would be possible for traders to make money through riskless arbitrage until the no-arbitrage condition holds. Further, says the author, an important contribution of experimental work to finance has been a demonstration that the absence of arbitrage opportunities in a market does not imply informational efficiency.

[128] *See* Aswath Damodaran, *supra* note 101.

[129] Tom Copeland, Tim Koller, Jack Murrin, *supra* note 103, at 285-290. This section draws heavily from this chapter.

ers will be attracted to the market capitalization method (and resulting high asset values) despite the many problems with that approach. The FSA also notes that a profit-split analysis may be useful for cases where two or more parties contribute non-routine intangibles to the cost sharing arrangement, although some commentators reject this approach on several grounds.[130]

FSA 200023014 does spell out the obvious. That is, valuation of the buy-in payment, especially work-in-process, generates big problems and potentially large tax controversies. Accordingly, we can expect continuous controversy in this highly subjective area of tax planning where large monetary transactions may come into play, notwithstanding that the taxpayers entering into these arrangements are most seeking simplicity in their inter-company transactions. This will be particularly true in cases where hindsight has determined that the non-routine intangibles generated more income and value than initially expected. Indeed, the IRS so stated when it announced it would review the correlation of the costs incurred to results produced.

A second issue addressed by FSA 200023014 is the form of payment for the buy-in. A party to a cost sharing agreement can make a buy-in payment in a lump sum, by installments, or a royalty payment.[131] The FSA carefully notes that the IRS generally will not change the form of the buy-in payment, although the amount of the payment will be subject to adjustment. The taxpayer in FSA 200023014 determined on a two year, declining percentage royalty for the buy-in. The FSA held that the royalty should last the life of the intangible, thus changing the form of payment. The FSA specifically concludes that "a buy-in payment in the form of an actual royalty should be evaluated as the amount of a royalty for the taxable year in a stream of commensurate-with-income royalties extending over the useful life of the transferred intangibles." Nothing in the regulations or elsewhere supports the apparent FSA position that buy-in royalties must go on for the life of the intangible. In fact, experience suggests that many taxpayers dealing at arm's length will put a time limit on royalties that is shorter than the life of the intangible. However, FSA 200023014 makes clear that on audit the IRS may attempt to increase the length of a royalty payment stream.

Buy-In Requirements of FSA 20001018. Another controversial FSA deals with buy-ins, illustrating again how important proper form is for a cost sharing agreement. In FSA 200001018 (dated January 7, 2000), the taxpayer P entered into a cost sharing agreement with foreign subsidiary FS, in which FS paid its share of P's costs for updating technology B. FS and P use technology B in manufacturing the Special Product.

P later entered into an agreement to acquire TechCorp, an unrelated research company that owns and is updating technology A. TechCorp licensed technology A to manufacturers of components. P and FS use technology B and the technology A component in the Special Product. Technology A components are also used for products other than the Special Product. P feared that TechCorp was moving away

---

[130] Finan, *supra* note 110, at 19-20.   [131] Reg. § 1.482-7(g)(7).

¶460.07

from continuing to develop technology A, which is a key part of the Special Product.

The FSA actually dealt with the prior cost-sharing regulations, but the IRS essentially applied the same rules as in the current regulations. In the FSA, the primary question was whether FS must make a buy-in payment to P for technology A (and continuing payments to the extent additional research was done for technology A).

An unrelated third party separately developed Technology A. Third parties used technology A for their products. P used technology A for products other than the Special Product. Seemingly, P and FS should not be required to share costs with respect to technology A if they do not elect to do so.

However, the IRS found that the terms of the cost sharing agreement itself required incorporation of any newly acquired technologies into the cost sharing agreement. Therefore, FS had to contribute to the acquisition of technology A (the buy-in) and to any work done to improve or update technology A (additional cost-sharing payments).

In some cases, it may be desirable to have additional technologies incorporated into an existing cost sharing agreement. In others, it may be more beneficial to have certain technologies outside the cost sharing agreement and therefore subject to the normal arm's length transfer pricing rules. P and FS probably could have preserved their ability to choose between the cost sharing agreement and standard transfer pricing rules by starting with a narrow cost sharing agreement, and amending it as needed to add new technologies. This procedure would allow P and FS a choice as to whether to share the costs of technology A. In contrast, the broad cost sharing agreement set out in the FSA resulted in required cost sharing and a buy-in for technology A. Thus, the drafting of the cost sharing agreement can alter the choices available to the parties.

The IRS also took an aggressive position as to the statute of limitations in FSA 20001018. The IRS originally examined the year in which the taxpayer P acquired TechCorp without making any buy-in adjustment. The IRS only picked up the issue in the subsequent audit, after the statute of limitations for the buy-in year expired. The FSA states that the subsidiary must make buy-in payments over five years, including three years still open under the statute of limitations. The FSA position thus allows the IRS multiple audit chances to catch the missing buy-in transaction.

P and FS never contracted for a buy-in payment for technology A. Therefore, the IRS could not be bound to the taxpayer's form for the buy-in. However, contrast this case with FSA 200023014, discussed above, in which the IRS unilaterally extended the royalty period originally set forth in the cost sharing agreement. The power of the IRS to extend the period for a buy-in royalty, coupled with a willingness to examine buy-in amounts in prior cycles, allows international agents to examine in hindsight buy-in payments made in prior years. This power also would prevent taxpayers from having any certainty as to the correctness of buy-ins made in prior years.

¶460.07

Same Differences With Buy-Out Valuations. While methods and approaches to value buy-in payments and, particularly, buy-ins of work-in-process intangibles, are generally similar to buy-out payments, same differences do exist. One obvious difference on a termination or winding down of a cost sharing arrangement is that the synergies that may have existed throughout the combination of joint efforts of the parties (or the comparable benchmarks) may not exist or may be significantly diminished. This fact may be most significant when considering the comparable benchmarks as those companies and/or transactions may be going in a different direction than the performance of the intangibles assets under review. Further, the value of the work-in-process R&D may be significantly discounted. (or even worthless) without the joint efforts of the parties. At least, a willing third party buyer would unlikely consider the parties' cost of capital as a flow for buying out of the deal.

Not to be underscored is the impact of facts and circumstances. Implied, if not expressed above, the facts and circumstances (and sometimes euphoria) of going into a transactions are not the same as those involved in the termination or winding down of the arrangement. And, it must be remembered that the facts control the outcome, the benchmarks, and any corresponding adjustments, premiums, or discount factors of the valuation. For example, the buy-out payment may be a result of failed expectations. Thus, the price of the buy-in going into the arrangement will not be the same as that exiting the deal if any semblance of the market controls.

Impact of *Veritas* Case. The Tax Court issued a strong message regarding cost sharing buy-ins in *Veritas Software Corp.*[132] U.S.-based Veritas, which was acquired by Symantec Corp. in July 2005, entered into the cost sharing arrangement with Veritas Ireland in November 1999. The arrangement consisted of a research and development agreement and a technology license agreement. Under the agreements, Veritas U.S. transferred preexisting intangible property to Veritas Ireland, which, in turn, made a $166 million buy-in payment to its U.S. parent in consideration for the preexisting intangible property.

Veritas U.S. reported the $166 million payment on its 200 U.S. income tax return—which was later amended to $118 million based on Veritas Ireland's updated sales figures and forecasts. The company used the comparable uncontrolled transaction method to calculate the payment.

The IRS examined Veritas U.S.'s 2000-2001 returns and, in March 2006, issued the company a deficiency notice that used an income method to determine a $2.5 million buy-in payment. Under those calculations, the IRS allocated $2.5 billion in income to Veritas U.S. and determined deficiencies of $704 million and $54 million for 2000 and 2001, respectively. It also imposed Section 6662 penalties of $281 million and $22 million for 2000 and 2001.

The IRS reduced the allocation from $2.5 billion to $1.675 billion in an amendment to its answer to the company's petition filed in March 2008. The amendment also claimed that the requisite buy-in payment must consider factors

---

[132] *Veritas Software Corp. & Subsidiaries*, CCH Dec. 58,016, 133 TC No. 14 (December 10, 2009).

¶460.07

such as that the deal bought access to Veritas U.S.'s research and development and marketing teams, as well as access to the company's distribution channels and customer lists.

In *Veritas,* Tax Court Judge Maurice Foley analyzed the IRS's revised position on the buy-in payment valuation in the case, which was based on the report of IRS expert witness John Hatch of Transfer Pricing Associates. In an opinion highly critical of the IRS's handling of the case, he found that Hatch's valuation was based on the theory that the collective effect of the technology licensing and research and development agreement is to be likened to a sale of Veritas' U.S. businesses. The court found that the IRS's assertion of the "akin to a sale" theory and its erroneous assumption that the preexisting intangibles have a perpetual life "are an unsuccessful attempt to justify (the IRS's) determination."

Judge Foley also found that the IRS's allocation for the buy-in payment:

- Took into account intangibles that either were not actually transferred or were of insignificant value; the result being that the aggregate increased the overall value beyond that of each individual asset;

- Improperly took into account intangibles developed subsequent to the R&D agreement;

- Employed the wrong useful life, discount rate, and growth rate; and

- Changed its valuation of the buy-in with no explanation.

Judge Foley's opinion also found that Reg. § 1.482-7(g)(2) requires only that taxpayers make a buy-in payment for preexisting, and not subsequently developed, intangibles.

Practitioners suggest that this opinion makes current temporary cost sharing regulations and their "investor model" approach more difficult to sustain in a legal challenge, particularly since the IRS's own expert, John Hatch, contradicted relevant provisions in the IRS's Coordinated Issue Paper[133] on this subject[134] and further that Judge Foley took a much narrower view of the statutory definition of "intangible" under Code Secs. 482 and 936(h)(3)(B).

.08 Character of Payments

Payments made under a qualified cost sharing arrangement are considered costs of developing intangibles of the payor and reimbursements of the same type of costs of developing intangibles of the payee.[135] Characterizations of these payments under foreign law will not impact this treatment even if foreign law does not recognize cost-sharing arrangements.[136]

---

[133] IRS Large and Mid Size Business Division, LMSB-04-0907-62, Coordinated Issue Paper—Section 482 CSA Buy-in adjustments (2007).

[134] *See* "Practitioners Say Veritas Opinion Weakens Principles Behind New § 482 Regs," Vol. 18. No. 15 BNA Transfer Pricing Report, December 17, 2009. For a more detailed analysis *see* Oates & O'Brien, "Tax Court Rejects IRS CIP on cost sharing Buy-ins in *Veritas,*" *International Tax Journal* (2010).

[135] Reg. § 1.482-7(h)(1).

[136] Reg. § 1.482-7(h)(1).

.09 Recordkeeping and Reporting Requirements

The controlled participants in a cost sharing arrangement must use a consistent method of accounting to measure costs and benefits, and must translate foreign currencies on a consistent basis.[137] In addition, a controlled participant to a cost sharing arrangement must maintain documentation showing that the requirements of the regulations have been complied with.[138] This is done principally by maintaining documents showing the following:

1. The total amount of costs incurred pursuant to the arrangement;

2. The costs borne by each controlled participant;

3. A description of the method used to determine each controlled participant's share of the intangible development costs, including the projections used to estimate benefits, and an explanation of why that method was selected;

4. The accounting method used to determine the costs and benefits of the intangible development (including the method used to translate foreign currencies), and, to the extent that the method materially differs from U.S. generally accepted accounting principles, an explanation of such material differences; and

5. Prior research, if any, undertaken in the intangible development area, any tangible or intangible property made available for use in the arrangement, by each controlled participant, and any information used to establish the value of pre-existing and covered intangibles.

A controlled participant is also required to disclose on its U.S. income tax return that it is a participant to a qualified cost sharing arrangement and to list the other controlled participant in the arrangement.[139] A controlled participant who does not file a U.S. income tax return must ensure that the same is disclosed in any Form 5471 or Form 5472 (see the Practice Tool at ¶ 20,050) filed by any other controlled participant who files a U.S. income tax return.[140]

> **Comment:** The above described documentation requirements override the transfer pricing documentation principal documents requirements described in Reg. § 1.6662(e)-6(d)(2)(iii)(B).[141]

.10 Proposed Cost Sharing Regulations of 2005

On August 29, 2005, the IRS issued proposed regulations under Code Sec. 482 for research and development ("R&D") cost sharing arrangements ("CSAs"). The proposed regulations constitute a radical departure from the current regulations and, if finalized in their current form, would substantially reduce the attractiveness of CSAs to taxpayers in the future.

The proposed regulations are based on a new fundamental concept called the "investor model." Under the IRS's investor model, the participants in a CSA are

---

[137] Reg. § 1.482-7(i).
[138] Reg. § 1.482-7(j)(2).
[139] Reg. § 1.482-7(j)(3).

[140] Reg. § 1.482-7(j)(3).
[141] *See* Reg. § 1.482-7(j)(2)(ii).

considered to make cost contributions (buy-in payments and shares of ongoing R&D costs) and external contributions (providing existing intangible property and other advantages) to the CSA to achieve an anticipated return on those contributions appropriate to the risk of the CSA and the exploitation of the intangibles resulting from the CSA. The IRS asserts that valuations of these contributions are "not appropriate if an investor would not undertake to invest in the arrangement because its total anticipated return is less than the return that it could have achieved through an alternative investment that is realistically available to it." The investor model contemplates determining the compensation that a party making external contributions to a CSA would require to allow an investor to join the arrangement, and the compensation that an investor not making external contributions would pay for the opportunity to invest in the arrangement. These valuations are to be made based on the forecasted revenues and costs of the CSA at the outset of the CSA (the *ex ante* expectations of the parties).

Under the investor model, a party making cost contributions, but no external contributions generally is limited to a financial return equal to its cost of capital and receives no share of the residual profits attributable to the intangible property resulting from the arrangement. The residual profits are allocated to the parties making non-routine external contributions. It is questionable whether, at arm's length, an entrepreneurial risk-taker would agree to bear the full risk of unsuccessful intangible development efforts, but accept a severely circumscribed upper limit on its permitted return. On the heels of the recent Tax Court decision in *Xilinx*, discussed in section .11 hereafter, where the arm's length standard was carefully delineated in the context of the commensurate-with-income standard, it is questionable how the investor model comports with the still vibrant arm's length standard. In application, it appears that the investor model disregards the actual allocation of risk implicit in CSAs as we have known them and characterizes the arrangement as a mere financing transaction. Interestingly, the proposed regulations assume that (1) comparable CSAs do not exist, and (2) that a hypothetical third party would not have allowed the potential extraordinary profit to get away, by allowing another party to take on the risk and concomitant reward. Hence, the CSA participant would be entitled to a return based on a discount rate, weighed, average cost of capital approach, with the transfer entitled to the residual return.

If the actual results of a CSA differ substantially from the forecasted results, the proposed regulations permit the IRS, but not the taxpayer, to make periodic adjustments to the compensation received by the parties making external contributions. The proposed regulations allow the IRS to make periodic adjustments using the residual profit split method. Under that method, a party making no external contributions generally will be limited to a financial return and, if the actual results exceed the forecasted results, will not participate in the unanticipated profits of the CSA. The proposed regulations, by prohibiting periodic adjustments by taxpayers, create a "heads I win, tails you lose" situation for the IRS. This one-way street for periodic adjustments is highly questionable.

The proposed regulations characterize a party's commitment of an assembled expert research team to a CSA as an external contribution and require the other parties to the CSA to compensate the contributing party for that contribution. Thus, the party actually performing the R&D services under the CSA may be required to earn a profit return for these services and not simply a reimbursement of its costs and may be required to share in the residual profits from the exploitation of the cost shared intangibles.

The proposed regulations would require all CSA parties to divide the interests in the cost shared intangibles among them on a territorial basis and each party to receive exclusive and perpetual rights to the profits from the cost shared intangibles from sales of products for use in its territory. Thus, the IRS has assumed an endless life for these items of intangible property. Further, parties would no longer be allowed to share non-exclusive worldwide rights to the cost shared intangibles.

The proposed regulations also adopt IRS litigating positions in pending controversies under the existing cost sharing regulations. In particular, the proposed regulations establish three new methods for valuing external contributions to CSAs—the income method, the acquisition price method and the market capitalization method—and substantially modify the residual profit split method. Although taxpayers generally are allowed to choose the form of consideration (lump sum, fixed installments or contingent payments, such as royalties) for external contributions, the form of consideration for an external contribution from an acquisition from an uncontrolled party after the start of the CSA must take the same form as the consideration paid for the acquisition to the uncontrolled party. In most cases, this rule will require lump sum payments for external contributions from post formation acquisitions. The proposed regulations also provide that the right to exploit an existing intangible without further development (e.g., the right to make or sell existing products) does not constitute an external contribution to a CSA and that the consideration paid for that right does not compensate the owner of the existing intangible for the right to use the intangible in the development of new products (e.g., future generations of the existing products).

The proposed regulations are to be effective on the date finalized and contain transition rules for CSAs established prior to the effective date of the new regulations. Although prior CSAs are grandfathered to some extent, they will be subject to the new regulations for cost contributions and external contributions made after the effective date. Moreover, under certain circumstances (e.g., periodic adjustments attributable to external contributions made after the effective date), grandfathered CSAs may lose their grandfathered status and become fully subject to the new regulations, including for external contributions made before the effective date.

.11 Xilinx Tax Court Decision

Xilinx, Inc. On March 22, 2010, the Ninth Circuit Court of Appeals issued its new opinion in the government's appeal of the *Xilinx* Tax Court decision.[142] The Ninth

---

[142] *Xilinx, Inc.*, 2010-1 USTC ¶ 50,302, Nos. 06-74246, 06-74269, 2010 U.S. App LEXIS 5795 (9th Cir. Mar. 22, 2010).

¶ 460.11

Circuit published its new opinion less than three months after withdrawing its previous decision on January 13, 2010. While the withdrawn May 27, 2009 opinion had reversed the Tax Court, the March 22, 2010 opinion affirms the Tax Court judgment. The IRS has stated it will not seek Supreme Court review of this decision.

The Ninth Circuit, with the majority opinion now written by Judge Fisher who dissented in the withdrawn opinion, affirmed the Tax Court's decision that stock option expenses need not be included in the pool of costs to be shared in a cost sharing agreement because unrelated parties operating at arm's length would not share such costs. The term "stock options" includes incentive stock options, non-statutory stock options, as well as purchase rights issued pursuant to an employee stock purchase plan.

Xilinx entered into a Technology Cost and Risk Sharing Agreement ("CSA") with Xilinx Ireland ("XI"), a second-tier wholly owned foreign subsidiary of Xilinx. Under the CSA, Xilinx and XI were required to share direct costs, indirect costs, and acquired intellectual property rights costs. The CSA did not specifically address whether employee stock options were costs includible in the cost share pool. Xilinx and XI also had a separate agreement, pursuant to which XI paid Xilinx an amount equal to the market price of Xilinx stock on the exercise date minus the exercise price (the "spread") each time that an XI employee exercised a Xilinx stock option.

In determining the allocation of costs pursuant to the CSA for tax years 1997, 1998, and 1999, Xilinx did not include any amount related to the employee stock options. In the Tax Court opinion,[143] Judge Foley concluded that "(the express language in section 1.482-1(a)(1) . . . establishes that the arm's-length standard applies to section 1.482-7 . . . for purposes of determining appropriate cost allocations." The Tax Court also found that because unrelated parties do not share the spread or the grant date value of stock options, the government's "imposition of such a requirement is inconsistent with section 1.482-1," and as such, the Commissioner's allocations of the spread of Xilinx's stock options exercised in 1997 and 1998 were arbitrary and capricious.

On appeal by the government, the first Ninth Circuit majority opinion, which is now withdrawn, reversed the Tax Court opinion. The withdrawn majority opinion had asserted that Reg. § 1.482-7(d) governed cost sharing arrangements and required cost sharing participants to include *all* costs in the cost sharing pool, naming this the "all costs requirement." The withdrawn majority opinion relied on the canon of statutory construction that a more specific regulation must be respected when it is contradicted by a more general statute. Concluding that the arm's length standard in the regulations under Reg. § § 1.482-1(a)(1) and (b)(1) and the all costs regulation under Reg. § 1.482-7(d)(1) were irreconcilably in conflict, the former majority opinion ruled that Reg. § 1.482-7(d)(1) controlled over the arm's length standard in Reg. § 1.482-1. The IRS acquiesced to the result of the Ninth Circuit's decision for years before the 2003 amendments to the section 482 regulations, even though it believes that the decision is erroneous. The IRS stated that the signifi-

---

[143] *Xilinx*, CCH Dec. 56,129, 125 TC 37, 62 (2005).

cance of the opinion is mooted by the 2003 amendments to the 482 regulations, effective for years after *Xilinx*, which provide that a CSA produces an arm's length result only if each controlled participant bears its allocable share of employee stock option costs.[144]

¶ 470 Special Rules for Transfer of Intangibles to a Foreign Corporation

Special rules are applied to a U.S. person's transfer of intangible property (except foreign goodwill or going concern value) to a foreign corporation in a Code Sec. 351 transfer to a controlled corporation or Code Sec. 361 tax-free reorganization.[145] Under the provisions, that person is treated as having (1) sold the intangible in exchange for annual payments contingent on the productivity or use of the property, and (2) receiving amounts which reasonably reflects the amounts that would have been received annually over the useful life of the intangible (or twenty years, which ever is shorter), or upon its subsequent disposition.[146] The transferor is then required to report as ordinary income, over the useful life of the property, an arm's length royalty determined under the provisions of Code Sec. 482 and regulations thereunder.[147] In addition, the foreign transferee is required to reduce its earnings and profits by the same amount.[148] A U.S. person who has a Code Sec. 367(d) transfer may elect to the transfer as a sale if the transfer meets certain conditions provided in Temp. Reg. § § 1.367(d)-1T(g)(2); -1T(b); -1T(c); and -1T(g). Special rules are also provided for situations where the stock of the foreign transferee or the intangible itself are subsequently transferred.[149]

The Taxpayer Relief Act of 1997 (P.L. 105-34) provided an amendment to Code Sec. 367(d) and repealed the requirement to treat the deemed royalty income as U.S.-source income. Accordingly, effective August 5, 1997, the deemed royalty income will be considered as foreign-source to the extent that an actual payment made by the foreign corporation under a license or sale agreement with the transferor would be treated as foreign-source income.[150] This change eliminates one of the disadvantages of contributing intangible property to a foreign corporation, as opposed to structuring the transaction as an actual royalty agreement. However, the biggest concern, which is the deductibility of deemed payments in a foreign country, remains.

---

[144] AOD-126401-10, I.R.B. No. 2010-33 (August 16, 2010).

[145] Code Sec. 367(d); Reg. § 1.367(d)-1T(b).

[146] Code Sec. 367(d)(2); Reg. § 1.367(d)-1T(c)(3).

[147] Code Sec. 367(d)(2)(C).

[148] Code Sec. 367(d)(2)(B).

[149] *See* Temp. Reg. § 1.367(d)-1T(c); Temp. Reg. § 1.367(d)-1T(d); and Temp. Reg. § 1.367(d)-1T(e).

[150] Code Sec. 367(d)(2)(C), as added by P.L. 105-34.

Code Sec. 482 Intangible Property Cases

Case	Description of the Intangibles	Issue and Holding
Bausch & Lomb Inc., 91-1 USTC ¶ 50,244, 933 F.2d 1084 (1991); CCH Dec. 45,547, 92 TC 525 (1989)	A non-exclusive license to manufacture soft contact lenses using B&L's spin cast technology	Royalty rate—TC increased the rate from 5% to 20%, calculating an appropriate level of ROI from discount cash flow analysis
Ciba-Geigy Corp., CCH Dec. 42,271, 85 TC 172 (1985)	Exclusive license to manufacture, formulate, and sell certain herbicides in the US	Royalty rate—The court held the IRS's assessment is an abuse of discretion
DHL Corp., CCH Dec. 53,015(M), TC Memo 1998-461.	DHL trademark	Ownership—DHL US; the foreign affiliate's registration or various activities do not create ownership. Value—Derived from entity value over net assets, with marketability discount. Royalty rate—rate used in a third party contract
Eli Lilly & Co., 88-1 USTC ¶ 9502, 856 F.2d 855 (1988)	Two propoxyphene patents along with proprietary information on manufacturing processes for production of prescription drug Darvon	§ 351 transfer—valid Royalty stream after transfer—unnecessary
R.T. French Co., CCH Dec. 32,119, 60 TC 836 (1973)	License to manufacture and sell in the U.S. instant mashed potatoes produced with the use of patent, know-how and other technical information	Royalty charge—arm's length, observing the contractual relationship and surrounding facts
Hospital Corp. of America, CCH Dec. 40,476, 81 TC 520 (1983)	Hospital management contract	Characterized the contract as intangible as well as service. Allocated 75 of taxable income of the transferee to the transferor

Case	Description of the Intangibles	Issue and Holding
Medieval Attractions N.V., CCH Dec. 51,592(M), 72 TCM(CCH) 924 (1996)	Franchise restaurant and entertainment services: "Medieval Times concept"	Royalty payments from U.S. co. to foreign affiliates were denied because the intangible was developed by U.S. co.
Merck & Co., Inc., 91-2 USTC ¶ 50,456, 24 Cl. Ct. 73 (1991)	R&D and market program for an antihypertensive drug	Royalty charge—the court found the IRS's assessment was arbitrary, capricious, or unreasonable
Nestle Holdings, Inc., 98-2 USTC ¶ 50,606, 152 F.3d. 83(1998); CCH Dec. 50,892(M), 70 TCM (CCH) 682, TC Memo. 1995-441 (1995)	Trademarks, trade names, patents and technology owed by Carnation, a U.S. Co. Nestle acquired	Value—The 2nd Circuit remanded TC's determination of the valuation with royalty-free-method
Perkin-Elmer Corp., CCH Dec. 49,268(M), 66 TCM (CCH) 634 (1993)	Exclusive right to manufacture in Puerto Rico and a nonexclusive right to use and sell worldwide certain instruments and accessories	Royalty rate—rates used in a third party licenses
Stephen D. Podd, CCH Dec. 52,765(M), 75 TCM (CCH) 2575 (1998)	Patent for a headliner (an intermodel container liner system)	Royalty rate—constructed from the rates used in uncontrolled licensing agreements of similar patents
Seagate Technology, Inc., CCH Dec. 49,657(M), 102 TC 149 (1994)	Manufacturing technology and know-how for hard disk drives	Royalty rate—constructed from the rates used in the licensing agreements of the same or similar intangibles to third parties
G.D. Searle & Co., CCH Dec. 43,685(M), 88 TC 252 (1987)	Patents, related technical data, copyright and trademarks; or their license for various pharmaceutical products	§ 351 transfer—valid Subsequent royalty or service charge—granted

Case	Description of the Intangibles	Issue and Holding
Sundstrand Corp, CCH Dec. 47,172(M), 96 TC, 226 (1991)	Technical license for manufacturing intangible of parts for constant speed drives (aircraft engine parts)	Royalty rate—constructed from the rates used in the licensing agreements of the same or similar intangibles to third parties

¶ 480 Temporary Regulations for Services Impact Intangibles

The Temporary Regulations, like the Proposed Regulations, address three critical areas at the intersection of the rules relating to intercompany services and intangibles, respectively: (a) should entitlement to compensation for contributions to the value of intangibles depend upon ownership and, if so, how should such ownership be determined? (b) should non-owners of intangibles that nevertheless contribute to the value of such intangibles be entitled to compensation and, if so, on what basis? And (c) where services transactions involve a transfer of intangibles, what rules should apply to determine the arm's length consideration? Each of these areas is discussed briefly below.

.01 Intangibles Ownership

The Proposed Regulations contained a new framework for determining, when related parties collaborate in the development of intangible property, the owner of the intangible and the compensation payable by the owner to related parties assisting in the development project.[151] The proposed rules were intended to replace the "developer-assister" rules in the 1994 final regulations.[152] The Temporary Regulations retain virtually all of the substantive provisions of the Proposed Regulations in this connection.

---

[151] Prop. Reg. § 1.482-4(f)(3)(i).

[152] Reg. § 1.482-4(f)(3)(ii)(B) (1994) (developer-assister rule). The 1968 Regulations attributed intangible ownership for tax purposes based on the economics of the intangible's development: The "developer" of the intangible was entitled to the benefits of ownership without deference to legal title, while an "assister" was entitled to compensation for its assistance in developing the intangible. To determine which party was the developer and assister, respectively, the 1968 Regulations focused on who bore the economic costs and risks of development, the location of the development activities, the capabilities of the potential developer to conduct the activity independently, and the degree of control exercised by each entity. Reg. § 1.482-2A(d)(1)(ii)(C). The 1994 Regulations changed the starting point to the legal owner of the right to exploit an intangible, although they recognize a party's right to an economic return for its role in developing the intangible, notwithstanding legal ownership being elsewhere. In fact, the Regulations and "cheese" examples contemplated multiple owners in a license relationship where the licensee contributed to development and enhanced the value of the licensed intangibles in the granted territory. Reg. § 1.482-4(f)(3)(iv) (1994) ("cheese" examples). The "cheese" examples commonly involve a U.S. distributor of foreign cheese products. The trademark is well-known outside the U.S. but not within the U.S. In the first "cheese" example, the U.S. distributor incurs advertising, marketing and promotional expenses comparable to those of a similar arm's length distributor. The example holds that no allocation is appropriate. In the second "cheese" example, the U.S. distributor incurs more marketing expense than an arm's length distributor and the example holds that an allocation must be made to the distributor for the value of the marketing services provided—i.e., to receive a return for the marketing intangible it paid for and developed. In the final "cheese" example, the U.S. distributor has a long-term, exclusive distribution agreement and incurs more marketing expense than an arm's length distributor. The example holds that the distributor should be treated as both the legal owner and economic owner of the marketing intangibles.

The current intangibles regulations, as finalized in 1994, provide that if intangible property is "legally protected" (e.g., patents, trademarks, copyrights, trade secrets), the legal owner of a right to exploit the intangible is considered the owner of that right for purposes of section 482.[153] Legal ownership may be acquired by operation of law or by contract. Thus, if a legal owner of an intangible licenses part of his rights to another person, the licensee is considered the owner of the licensed rights, and the licensor is considered the owner of the retained rights. If intangible property is not legally protected (e.g., customer lists), the developer of the intangible is considered the owner. The developer is determined based on all the facts and circumstances, but ordinarily is the related party that bore the largest portion of the costs and risks of developing the intangible. Related parties providing assistance to the developer are entitled to arm's length compensation for their assistance. However, related parties are not entitled to compensation for routine expenditures that an unrelated party would be expected to incur under similar circumstances (e.g., routine marketing expenses ordinarily incurred by an unrelated distributor).

The Temporary Regulations continue the approach of the 1994 final regulations with regard to legally protected intangibles. The legal owner of such an intangible is considered the owner for purposes of section 482.[154] The Temporary Regulations, however, take a different approach from the 1994 final regulations with regard to intangibles that are not legally protected. The sole factor in determining ownership of an intangible that is not legally protected is the practical "control" that each party has over the intangible.[155]

The IRS received extensive comments for the provisions of the Proposed Regulations regarding ownership of intangibles. After considering those comments, it decided to retain the legal ownership approach. The Preamble to the Temporary Regulations states that the legal owner of the intangible is the party that possesses legal title to the intangible under the relevant intangible property law (e.g., the U.S. patent laws) or the contractual arrangements among the parties (e.g., license agreements).[156] The IRS declined to open the door in the Regulations to a full-scale application of substantive intellectual property law in the relevant jurisdiction(s) on the ground that such an analysis would be burdensome and ultimately of little relevance. The purpose of substantive intellectual property law is to resolve competing claims to intangibles by unrelated parties, whereas the issue under section 482 is which of several related parties is the owner of an intangible.[157]

The Preamble to the 2006 temporary regulations confirms the importance of taxpayers' use of intercompany agreements to establish ownership of intangibles. Such intercompany agreements will be respected as establishing legal ownership of intangibles as long as they have economic substance.

---

[153] Reg. § 1.482-4(f)(3).
[154] Temp. Reg. § 1.482-4T(f)(3)(i)(A).
[155] Id.
[156] 71 Fed. Reg. 44476. The important proviso under the legal ownership standard adopted by the Temporary

Regulations is that such legal ownership not be "inconsistent with the economic substance of the underlying transactions." Temp. Reg. § 1.482-4T(f)(3)(i)(A).
[157] Id.

.02 Non-Owner Contributions to the Value of Intangibles

The 2006 temporary regulations provide that related parties that develop or enhance the value of intangible property owned by another related party are entitled to arm's length compensation for their contributions.[158] If the consideration for such a contribution is embedded in the price for a transaction that involves the intangible (e.g., the sales price for goods or royalties payable under a license), then ordinarily no separate consideration is made for the contribution. Instead, the contribution is taken into account in determining comparability of uncontrolled transactions and the arm's length consideration for the underlying transaction (such as the sale of goods or the license of intangibles).[159]

Commentators objected to several examples of the Proposed Regulations that indicated that if it were not possible to identify uncontrolled transactions with a similar range of interrelated elements (e.g., a license under which the licensee contributes to the development of the licensed intangible), it may be appropriate to apply a residual profit split analysis to determine the value of the contribution to the development of the intangible. In the Preamble to the Temporary Regulations, the IRS indicates that it did not intend to imply that the residual profit split method was the preferred method in such cases. Accordingly, the references to the residual profit split method have been deleted from the examples in the regulations and replaced with a general reference to the best method rule.

The Preamble notes that taxpayers can reduce the risks associated with contributions to the value of embedded intangibles by providing in their intercompany agreements for the separate compensation for such contributions based on reimbursement of costs plus a profit element. These agreements will be respected as long as they have economic substance.[160]

.03 Coordination of the Rules Applicable to "Bundled" Services and Intangibles

The Temporary Regulations continue to provide general "coordination" rules for services transactions that include other types of transactions and vice versa.[161] In general, whether these "bundled" or "integrated" transactions are evaluated separately under the services regulations or the intangibles regulations depends upon which approach provides the most reliable measure of an arm's length result.[162] The Temporary Regulations provide that "ordinarily" the bundled transaction may be evaluated under the services regulations rather than separately, provided that each component is adequately taken into account for comparability purposes.[163] This "most reliable measure" rule governs whether bundled transactions are evaluated separately or together in the case of services-tangibles transfers.[164]

This intangibles exception to the general applicability of the Temporary Regulations to bundled transactions reflects the continued presence (albeit to a reduced

---

[158] Temp. Reg. § 1.482-4T(f)(4). *Id.*
[159] *Id.*
[160] 71 Fed. Reg. 44477.
[161] Temp. Reg. § 1.482-9T(m).

[162] Temp. Reg. § 1.482-9T(m)(1).
[163] *Id.*
[164] Temp. Reg. § 1.482-9(m)(5), Examples 1, 2 and 3.

extent as compared with the Proposed Regulations) of the anti-abuse concern of the Treasury-IRS drafters that services transactions may constitute a potentially significant conduit for hidden, tax-free outbound transfers of valuable intangibles. It is certainly appropriate to insist, as the Temporary Regulations, like the Proposed Regulations, do explicitly, on proper characterization of services and other transactions consistent with their economic substance. However, the intangibles exception in Temp. Reg. §1. 482-9T(m)(2) seems an unnecessarily broad remedy for a problem that could be adequately addressed with a more narrowly drawn anti-abuse rule (or arguably is already adequately addressed by the recurrent economic substance caveats and provisos spread throughout the regulations). The exception in effect denies aggregation to many nonabusive services transactions that happen to include a material intangibles element, even if the intangibles are not "transferred" in the transaction (as distinguished from merely being "embedded").

¶ 490 Significant IRS Transfer Pricing Guidance

.01 Cost Sharing

FSA 200009022 (November 30, 1999). The IRS determined that the failure to attach the statement required by Reg. §1.482-7(j)(3) to a cost sharing participant's return disqualifies that participant from the cost sharing arrangement. For companies that have filed returns without the requisite statement for tax years beginning after January 1, 1996, there are two ways to cure that failure: (1) send a letter to the service center where the original 1120 is filed, or (2) file an 1120X for the U.S. Corp. and attach to it all the required statements for all the cost sharing participants associated with that return.[165]

FSA 200023014 (February 29, 2000). The IRS reviewed the application of the residual profit split method to determine a cost sharing buy-in payment under the pre-1996 temporary cost sharing regulations. The IRS challenged the arm's length nature of the buy-in payment based on a net present value analysis.

FSA 200003010 (October 18, 1999). The IRS concluded that stock options are an includable cost for cost sharing agreement purposes. This conclusion was made under the previous version of the cost sharing regulations found in Reg. §1.482-2A(d)(4). The IRS concluded that in the absence of any regulations for valuing stock options, any reasonable method may be used, so long as it is used consistently. Two valuation methods described by the IRS as reasonable are the Black-Scholes model and valuation upon exercise or disqualifying disposition.

FSA 200001018 (October 6, 1999). The IRS discusses the application of the cost sharing agreement (CSA) buy-in rules.

.02 Intangibles

FSA 200019026 (February 11, 2000). The IRS denied a deduction for the payment of royalties by a U.S. holding company and its U.S. subsidiaries to its foreign parent for the use of a trademark that it helped to develop. The taxpayer incurred significant marketing and promotional expenses related to a new trade-

---

[165] *See also* FSA 200009022.

mark, as well as its pre-existing trademarks, which were not reimbursed by its foreign parent. The IRS determined that the taxpayer was the owner/developer of the trademark, and even if it transferred its ownership interest in the trademark to its foreign parent, any (arm's length) royalty owing to the Forco by the subsidiaries would effectively be offset, in whole or in part, by an arm's length consideration owing by the parent to the subsidiaries in respect of that transfer under Code Sec. 482.

.03 Reinsurance

FSA 200027008 (July 7, 2000). The IRS determined that Code Sec. 482 can be applied to allocate insurance premium income arising from a reinsurance transaction. The IRS noted that the facts of this case were similar to those addressed by the Tax Court in *United Parcel Service of America, Inc.,*[166] and *Wright.*[167] In both cases, the Tax Court disregarded the reinsurance transactions under assignment of income and economic substance principles. However, the instant transaction contained significant economic substance so prevent the IRS from arguing that the transaction lacked economic substance. Nevertheless, the IRS determined that the reinsurance transaction was subject to allocation under Code Sec. 482.[168]

.04 Enforcement and Penalties

Chief Council Advice Memorandum 2000037048 (July 28, 2000). The IRS discussed the application of the Code Sec. 6662 transfer pricing penalties under several fact patterns including the imposition of both transfer pricing and non-transfer pricing penalties, and the effect of net operating losses.

FSA 200021011 (February 15, 2000). The IRS applied Code Sec. 482 to reallocate income within a consolidated group of corporations. Citing *Reg. § 1.482-1(f)(1)(iv)* and *Likens-Foster Honolulu Corp.,*[169] the IRS stated that if a controlled taxpayer is a party to a consolidated return, the true consolidated taxable income of the affiliated group and the true separate taxable income of the consolidated taxpayer must be determined consistently with the consolidated returns regulations.

FSA 200003001 (August 31, 1999) and FSA 200003009 (October 18, 1999). The IRS addressed whether a taxpayer that received loans from its foreign affiliates could later disavow the form of the transactions. The taxpayers had attempted to recharacterize loans from the affiliated entities as equity. The IRS noted that the Tax Court adopted the "strong proof" rule described in *Sonnleitner,*[170] for debt/equity issues, which provides that a taxpayer may not disavow the form of its transaction unless it presents strong proof that the form of the transaction does not reflect the actual intentions of the parties.

---

[166] *United Parcel Service of America, Inc.,* CCH Dec. 53,497(M), 78 TCM 262; TC Memo 1992-268.

[167] *W.T. Wright,* CCH Dec. 49,174(M), 66 TCM 214; TC Memo 1993-328.

[168] *Citing Local Corp.,* CCH Dec. 28,593, 48 TC 773 (1967), *aff'd,* 69-1 USTC ¶ 9246, 407 F.2d 629 (7th Cir. 1969), *cert. denied,* 396 US 956 (1969), *overruled in part*

other grounds, First Sec. Bank, 72-1 USTC ¶ 9292A, 405 US 394 (1972).

[169] *Likins-Foster Honolulu Corp.,* 69-2 USTC ¶ 9672, 417 F.2d 285 (10th Cir. 1969) *cert denied* 397 US 987 (1970).

[170] *A.M. Sonnleitner,* 79-2 USTC ¶ 9464, 598 F.2d 464 (5th Cir. 1979).

FSA 200031025 (April 28, 2000). The IRS determined that, for the purpose of Code Sec. 482, a potential decrease in taxable income disclosed on Form 8275 should be considered reported on a timely filed, original return. The IRS also determined that on an untimely or amended return, the taxpayer is prohibited by Code Sec. 482 from setting off the results of controlled transactions with one CFC against the results of controlled transactions with another CFC.

Chapter 5

Intercompany Services

¶ 501 Overview

This chapter addresses the issues surrounding intercompany services. Historically, the rules applicable to services had been the subject of significantly less commentary than the rules covering intercompany transfers of tangible or intangible property. The IRS and Treasury issued proposed services regulations on September 10, 2003 ("2003 proposed services regulations"),[1] temporary and proposed regulations on July 31, 2006 ("2006 temporary services regulations"),[2] and final regulations on July 31, 2009 ("2009 final services regulations").[3] Before the iterations published in 2003-2009, the transfer pricing regulations for controlled services had not been updated since originally promulgated in 1968 ("1968 services regulations").

This chapter focuses on the 2009 final regulations, which have an effective date of July 31, 2009. For prior tax years, the 2006 temporary services regulations, as modified by Notice 2007-5,[4] apply to intercompany services transactions for tax years beginning after December 31, 2006 (retroactive application to tax years beginning after September 10, 2003 at taxpayer's election). The effective date of the 2006 temporary services regulations, as pertains to identification of controlled services eligible to be priced at cost is moved back to taxable years beginning after December 31, 2007, except for the "business judgment" rule of Temp. Reg. § 1.482-9T(b)(2).[5] This chapter also discusses the rules applicable prior to 2007.

---

[1] REG-146893-02, REG-115037-00, 68 Fed. Reg. 53448 (Sep. 10, 2003).

[2] Fed. Reg. 44465-44519 (Aug. 4, 2006). The temporary regulations were given a delayed effective date and also issued as proposed regulations (71 Fed. Reg. 44247-44250 (Aug. 4, 2006).

[3] 74 Fed. Reg. 38830-38876 (Aug. 4, 2009).

[4] Notice 2007-5, IRB 2007-3, 269, 12/20/2006.

[5] *Id.* At 3.01.

The 2009 final services regulations are largely the same as the 2006 temporary services regulations, the latter of which incorporated many of the concepts advanced in the 2003 proposed services regulations. Unless specifically changed by the 2006 temporary services regulations, the intentions expressed in the preamble of the 2003 proposed services regulations are still indicative of the thinking of the drafters of the 2006 temporary services regulations, and thus, is also pertinent to interpretation of the 2009 final services regulations, which have not significantly changed from the proposed and temporary form issued in 2006.[6]

¶ 510 Background

Cross-border services have become an increasingly large and important segment of the U.S. and global economies. In particular, cross-border services transactions make up an increasingly significant segment of cross-border transactions among members of controlled groups. In 2003, the Treasury and the IRS believed new guidance on intercompany services transactions was necessary to reflect the major economic and legal developments that had taken place in the 35-year period since the issuance of the 1968 regulations.

The guidance on intercompany services provides generally that the arm's length amount charged in a controlled services transaction must be determined under one of the transfer pricing methods provided in the 2009 final services regulations. This guidance regarding transfer pricing methods is generally consistent in structure and approach to the current regulatory guidance regarding the transfer pricing methods applicable to transfers of tangible or intangible property. In addition, the regulations finalize the services cost method ("SCM") that was originally introduced in the 2006 proposed services regulations, and which may be used to price at cost only the low-margin controlled services transactions that meet certain quantitative and qualitative conditions and requirements. The SCM replaces the cost only safe harbor from the 1968 services regulations, which historically many taxpayers relied on when performing their transfer pricing analyses for intercompany services.

Also consistent with the rules governing transfers of tangible and intangible property, the 2009 final services regulations provide guidance concerning selection and application of the appropriate method by explicitly incorporating the general rules in § 1.482-1 (including the best method rule of § 1.482-1(c), the comparability analysis of § 1.482-1(d), and the arm's length range of § 1.482-1(e) of the existing regulations).

¶ 520 Intercompany Services—In General

The 2009 final services regulations adopt a very broad definition of what constitutes a service. Reg. § 1.482-9(l)(1) provides generally that a controlled services transaction includes any activity by one member of a group of controlled

---

[6] *See* David D. Stewart, *U.S. Issues Final Services Regs.*, 55 *Tax Notes Int'l* 418 (Aug. 10, 2009) (noting that most of the changes appearing in the final regulations were announced prior to their publication, and highlighting the clarification of when the Services Cost Method applies and clarifications to the business judgment rule as the largest differences between the 2006 and 2009 versions). The final services regulations also have one modification to ensure consistency with the cost-sharing regulations, noting at § 1.482-9(g)(1) that the residual profit split method is inapplicable where only one party makes significant, non-routine contributions.

taxpayers that results in a benefit to one or more other members of the controlled group. Activity is defined broadly to include "the performance of functions, assumptions of risks, or use by a renderer of tangible or intangible property or other resources, capabilities, or knowledge, such as knowledge of and ability to take advantage of particularly advantageous situations or circumstances. An activity also includes making available to the recipient any property or other resources of the renderer."[7]

The broad definition of an activity intentionally blurs the distinction between services and transfers of tangible or intangible property, rentals, or loans to minimize the importance of characterization. This is consistent with the overall approach of the 2009 final services regulations, which seek to produce consistent transfer pricing analyses for economically similar transactions, regardless of the characterization or structure of the transactions. In place of clear rules of characterization, the 2009 final services regulations rely on the coordination rules, which focus on the characterization and transfer pricing methods that will provide the most reliable measure of an arm's length result.[8]

¶ 530 The Benefit Test

.01 In General

The 2009 final services regulations provide specific rules for determining whether an activity results in a benefit to a related party. The 2009 final services regulations replace the benefit test contained in Reg. § 1.482-2(b)(2) of the 1968 service regulations with new provisions that effectively and significantly shift the focus from renderer to recipient. Specifically, an activity is considered to provide a benefit to the recipient if the activity directly results in a reasonably identifiable increment of economic or commercial value that enhances the recipient's commercial position, or that may be reasonably anticipated to do so.[9] Thus, the 2009 final services regulations generally provide that an activity will be considered to confer a benefit if an uncontrolled taxpayer in circumstances comparable to those of the recipient would be willing to pay an uncontrolled party to perform the same or similar activity, or would be willing to perform for itself the same or similar activity.[10]

According to the preamble to the 2003 proposed services regulations, which initiated this change, focus on the recipient is intended to conform to international standards and move toward greater consistency with the OECD Transfer Pricing Guidelines.[11] Consistent with this theme, the 2009 final services regulations provide that an activity is not considered to provide a benefit if the probable benefit is so indirect or remote that the *recipient* would not be willing to pay or perform such an activity itself.[12]

---

[7] Reg. § 1.482-9(l)(2).

[8] See Reg. § 1.482-9(m).

[9] Reg. § 1.482-9(l)(3)(i).

[10] Id.

[11] *Transfer Pricing Guidelines for Multinational Enterprises and Tax Administrations* (July 1995). The OECD approved the 2010 revision of the Transfer Pricing Guidelines on July 22, 2010. See http://www.oecd.org.

[12] Reg. § 1.482-9(l)(3)(ii).

.02 General Benefit

The 2009 final services regulations and the examples set forth under Reg. § 1.482-9(l)(5) do not adopt the so-called "general benefit" approach, under which certain activities in a corporate group are presumed to generate a benefit to the controlled group as a whole. According to the preamble to the 2003 proposed services regulations, the IRS and Treasury believe that the general benefit concept is inconsistent with the arm's length standard.[13] According to statements in the preamble to the 2003 proposed services regulations, and applied in the 2009 final services regulations, the IRS and Treasury intended to restrict the charge out of some types of headquarters activities, where the activity is allocated among all members of the group based on an overall allocation method, on the theory that the activities provide a general benefit to the group as a whole. The preamble states, however, that in certain cases the allocation or sharing among group members of expenses or charges relating to corporate headquarters-level activities or other centralized services may be consistent with the rules of the 2003 proposed services regulations. The correct test to apply is whether one or more controlled parties receive an identifiable benefit.

In response to comments received regarding the rejection of the general benefit test, the 2009 final services regulations authorize the use of shared services arrangements for the allocation of centralized services.[14] Below are two examples from Reg. § 1.482-9(l)(5) demonstrating under what circumstances a benefit is considered to be obtained.

Reg. § 1.482-9(l)(5), Ex. 2

Indirect or remote benefit. Based on recommendations contained in a study performed by its internal staff, Company X implements certain changes in its management structure and the compensation of managers of divisions located in the United States. No changes were recommended or considered for Company Y in Country B. The internal study and the resultant changes in its management may increase the competitiveness and overall efficiency of Company X. Any benefits to Company Y as a result of the study are, however, indirect or remote. Consequently, Company Y is not considered to obtain a benefit from the study.[15]

Reg. § 1.482-9(l)(5), Ex. 3

Indirect or remote benefit. Based on recommendations contained in a study performed by its internal staff, Company X decides to make changes to the management structure and management compensation of its subsidiaries, in order to increase their profitability. As a result of the recommendations in the study, Company X implements substantial changes in the management structure and management compensation scheme of Company Y. The study and the changes implemented as a result of the recommendations are anticipated to increase the profitability of Company X and its subsidiaries. The increased management efficiency of Company Y that results from these changes is considered to be a specific and identifiable benefit, rather than remote or speculative.[16]

---

[13] *See* Wrappe, Steven C. & Brian P. Trauman, "The New Services Regulations: Are we there yet?", 48 *Tax Mgmt Memorandum* 9, at 9 (April 30, 2007) (discussing Treasury and the IRS's reasoning behind narrowing both the benefit test and the definition of shareholder activities when drafting the precursors to the 2009 final services regulations in 2003 and 2006) (hereinafter *The New Services Regulations*).

[14] Preamble to 2006 temporary services regulations at T.D. 9278.

[15] Reg. § 1.482-9(l)(5), Ex. 2.

[16] Reg. § 1.482-9(l)(5), Ex. 3.

¶530.02

.03 Stewardship/Shareholder Expenses

Under the benefit test in the 1968 services regulations, no allocation could be made for services that merely duplicate a service the related party performed independently for itself. Such services were generally considered to constitute "stewardship," or "duplicative" activities. However, the 1968 services regulations did not contain detailed guidance on what activities constitute "stewardship" or "duplicative" activities.

The 2009 final services regulations provide more detailed guidance in this respect. First, the 2009 final services regulations specifically distinguish between duplicative activities and shareholder activities. If an activity performed by a controlled taxpayer duplicates an activity that is performed, or that reasonably may be anticipated to be performed, by another controlled taxpayer on or for its own account, the activity is not considered to provide a benefit to the recipient, unless the duplicative activity itself provides an additional benefit to the recipient.[17]

Under the guidance for shareholder activities, an activity is not considered to provide a benefit to a related party if the "sole effect" of that activity is to protect the renderer's capital investment in the recipient or other members of the controlled group, or if the activity primarily relates to compliance by the renderer with reporting, legal, or regulatory requirements applicable specifically to the renderer.[18] Generally, this requirement brings shareholder activities more in line with steward-ship expenses, which include the "expenses of an activity the sole effect of which is either to protect the corporation's capital investment or to facilitate compliance."[19]

The *sole effect* language conveys an absolute rule, such that if *any* benefit is conferred, remuneration is required. Thus, the potential for an activity to be considered a stewardship expense is greatly reduced. Moreover, even assuming the sole effect is not satisfied; i.e., another effect is realized through carrying out the activity, the benefit cannot be indirect or remote. If the benefit is indirect or remote, then allocation is improper.[20]

The 2009 final services regulations include a number of examples that illustrate the IRS's intention to narrowly limit the type of services that will be considered shareholder expenses. For example, some review or oversight activities that might be treated as duplicative under the 1968 services regulations are treated as chargeable in the examples, because the review provided some incremental benefit to the recipient. This is illustrated by the following example:

Reg. § 1.482-9(l) (5), Ex. 6

> *Duplicative activities.* Company X's in-house legal staff has specialized expertise in several areas, including intellectual property law. The intellectual property legal staff specializes in technology licensing, patents, copyrights, and negotiating and drafting intellectual property agreements. Company Y is involved in negotiations with an unrelated party to enter into a complex joint venture that

---

[17] Reg. § 1.482-9(l) (3) (iii).
[18] Reg. § 1.482-9(l) (3) (iv).
[19] Reg. § 1.861-8(e) (4).

[20] *See* Ernst & Young, *International Tax Alert: Treasury, IRS publish Section 482 services regulations, available at http://www.ey.com/Publication/vwLUAssets/Treasury,_IRS_publish_Section_482_services_regulations/$ FILE/2009US_CM1536.pdf* (Aug. 5, 2009).

includes multiple licenses and cross-licenses of patents and copyrights. Company Y retains outside counsel that specializes in intellectual property law to review the transaction documents. Company Y does not have in-house counsel of its own to review intellectual property transaction documents. Outside counsel advises that the terms for the proposed transaction are advantageous to Company Y and that the contracts are valid and fully enforceable. Company X's intellectual property legal staff possess valuable knowledge of Company Y's patents and technological achievements. They are capable of identifying particular scientific attributes protected under patent that stengthen Company Y's negotiating position, and of discovering flaws in the patents offered by the unrelated party. To reduce risk associated with the transaction, Company X's intellectual property legal staff reviews the transaction documents before Company Y executes the contracts. Company X's intellectual property legal staff also separately evaluates the patents and copyrights with respect to the licensing arrangements and concurs in the opinion provided by outside counsel. The activities performed by Company X substantially duplicate the legal services obtained by Company Y, but they also reduce risk associated with the transaction in a way that confers an additional benefit on Company Y.[21]

The tone of the 2009 final services regulations and above examples suggests that the IRS takes a fairly restrictive view of what qualifies as a nonchargeable stewardship or duplicative activity, and believes that many of the headquarters activities typically provided by corporate personnel should be subject to an arm's length intercompany charge. The impact is that many more of the headquarters costs will be charged out from U.S.-based multinationals to their foreign affiliates, likely raising vociferous objection from the foreign affiliates and their taxing authorities.[22]

.04 Passive Association

The 2009 final services regulations provide that a member of a controlled group that obtains a benefit solely on account of its status as a member of the group is generally not considered to receive a benefit.[23]

Reg. § 1.482-9(l)(5), Ex. 15

Passive association/benefit. Company X is the parent corporation of a large controlled group that has been in operation in the information-technology sector for ten years. Company Y is a small corporation that was recently acquired by the Company X controlled group from local Country B owners. Several months after the acquisition of Company Y, Company Y obtained a contract to redesign and assemble the information-technology networks and systems of a large financial institution in Country B. The project was significantly larger and more complex than any other project undertaken to date by Company Y. Company Y did not use Company X's marketing intangibles to solicit the contract, and Company X had no involvement in the solicitation, negotiation, or anticipated execution of the contract. For purposes of this section, Company Y is not considered to obtain a benefit from Company X or any other member of the controlled group because the ability of Company Y to obtain the contract, or to obtain the contract on more favorable terms than would have been possible prior to its acquisition by the Company X controlled group, was due to Company Y's

---

[21] Reg. § 1.482-9(l)(5), Ex. 6.

[22] *See The New Services Regulations* at 11-12 (noting that should foreign affiliates raise any objections, the shift in focus to the recipient's willingness to pay will likely bolster the affiliates' arguments against service cost allocations).

[23] Reg. § 1.482-9(l)(3)(v).

status as a member of the Company X controlled group and not to any specific activity by Company X or any other member of the controlled group.Reg. § 1.482-9(l)(5), Ex. 15.

This example concludes that the subsidiary did not receive a benefit from the parent or other related party, because its ability to obtain the contract was due to its status as a member of the group and not to any specific activity of the parent or other related party.

This concept could extend to a relatively common situation where, for example, a subsidiary of a multinational group receives large discounts on its purchases from external parties due largely to its parent's relationship with the supplier. To the extent the parent company does not undertake any specific activity to obtain this purchasing benefit for each individual affiliate, it is foreseeable that no benefit will arise to the subsidiaries under the proposed regulations.

The concept of passive association is consistent with Paragraph 7.13 of the OECD Guidelines.

¶ 540 Transfer Pricing Methods

The 2009 final services regulations provide generally that the arm's length amount charged in a controlled services transaction must be determined under one of the transfer pricing methods provided in the regulations. The 2009 final services regulations specify six transfer pricing methods. Three of the methods are transactional methods, two are profit-based, and one is a cost-based method that would replace the only cost safe harbor from the 1968 services regulations. The six methods are:

1. The comparable uncontrolled services price method;
2. The gross services margin method;
3. The cost of services plus method;
4. The comparable profits method;
5. The services cost method ("SCM"); and
6. The profit split method.[24]

---

[24] Reg. § 1.482-9(a).

Transfer Pricing Method	Location in Regulations	Comparability Considerations	Adjustments to Improve Comparability	Comment
Service TPMs				
CUSP (Comparable Uncontrolled Services Price) (controlled price to CUSP)	Temp. Reg. § 1.482-9T(c)	Services rendered Intangible used Contractual terms	Quality of services Intangibles used Geographic market Risks borne Duration of services Collateral transactions	(Most direct and reliable method (where information exists)) (Internal CUSP has greater comparability)
GSS (Gross Services Margin) (gross profit of uncontrolled provider)	Temp. Reg. § 1.482-9T(d)	Services rendered Intangible used Contractual terms Risks borne	Contractual terms Intangible Risks borne	Commission agent may be comparable
CSP (Cost of Services Plus) (gross profit of uncontrolled provider)	Temp. Reg. § 1.482-9T(e)	Functions (similar types of service) Risks Intangibles Contractual terms	Complexity of services Duration Contractual terms Economic circumstances Risks borne Accounting differences	(Controlled service provider renders same or similar service to uncontrolled) (Not used in a contingent payment context)
CPM (Comparable Profits Method) Profit Level Indicators	Temp. Reg. § 1.482-9T(f)	Consistency in accounting	Consistency in accounting	Less reliance on accounting consistency than CSS
PS (Profit Split) Comparable in Residual	Temp. Reg. § 1.482-9T(g)	Functions performed Risks assumed Resources employed	Functions performed Risks assumed Resources employed	Generally both controlled parties must make valuable contributions to the joint endeavor
SCM (Services Cost Method)	Temp. Reg. § 1.482-9T(b)	Cost only allowed if: • specified covered service *or* • low-margin covered service *and* • not excluded transaction • passes business judgment test	N/A	Cost
Unspecified Methods	Temp. Reg. § 1.482-9T(h)			

In addition, the 2009 final services regulations provide that unspecified methods may also be used in appropriate circumstances.[25]

All of the methods, with the exception of the SCM, are closely analogous to the methods set forth in the existing regulations for transfers of tangible property[26] and transfers of intangible property,[27] adapted to account for particular circumstances surrounding services transactions. The 2009 final services regulations require that each method be applied consistently with generally applicable transfer pricing concepts such as the arm's length range, the best method rule, and comparability analysis. In addition, the description of each of the methods includes comparability factors that may be of particular importance for that method.

[25] Discussed under Reg. § 1.482-9(h).
[26] Reg. § 1.482-3.
[27] Reg. § 1.482-4.

¶540

.01 Comparable Uncontrolled Services Price Method

The comparable uncontrolled services price ("CUSP") method[28] is analogous to the comparable uncontrolled price method applicable to transfers of tangible property.[29] The 2009 final services regulations emphasize that "[t]he results derived from applying the [CUSP] method generally will be the most direct and reliable measure of an arm's length price . . . if an uncontrolled transaction has no differences from the controlled transaction that would affect the price, or if there are only minor differences that have a definite and ascertainable effect on price and for which appropriate adjustments are made."[30] The 2009 final services regulations also provide that the most important factors in determining comparability under this method are similarity in the nature of the services and valuable intangibles used, if any, in providing the services. They also provide several examples[31] that illustrate the application of the CUSP method to cases in which the comparable uncontrolled transactions are internal or external. These examples underscore a strong preference for the use of internal comparables.

Finally, the 2009 final services regulations provide that the price of a comparable uncontrolled services transaction may be derived based on indirect measures of the price charged in comparable uncontrolled services transactions, but only if certain requirements are met.[32]

.02 Gross Services Margin Method

The gross services margin ("GSM") method[33] evaluates the arm's length price charged in a controlled services transaction by reference to the gross services profit margin realized in uncontrolled transactions that involve similar services. As is the case for the resale price method provided for transfers of tangible property,[34] the charge under the GSM method is calculated based on the gross profit margin realized in comparable uncontrolled transactions.[35]

This method may be used, for example, when a controlled taxpayer renders services (agent services) to another member of the controlled group regarding a transaction between that other member and an uncontrolled taxpayer. Under this method, the price charged to the other member is the appropriate gross services profit[36] of the controlled taxpayer that performed the agent services. This method may also be used in cases in which a controlled taxpayer contracts to provide services to an uncontrolled taxpayer (intermediary role) and another member of the controlled group actually performs the services. Under the GSM method, the price charged to the controlled intermediary is determined by subtracting from the

---

[28] Reg. § 1.482-9(c).
[29] Reg. § 1.482-3(b).
[30] Reg. § 1.482-9(c)(1).
[31] Reg. § 1.482-9(c)(4).
[32] Reg. § 1.482-9(c)(5).
[33] Reg. § 1.482-9(d).
[34] Reg. § 1.482-3(c).

[35] Defined as a "transaction between a member of the controlled group and an uncontrolled taxpayer as to which the controlled taxpayer performs agent services or an intermediary function." *See* Reg. § 1.482-9(d)(2)(ii).
[36] Computed by multiplying the applicable uncontrolled price by the gross services profit margin earned in comparable uncontrolled services transactions. *See* Reg. § 1.482-9(d)(2)(iv).

applicable uncontrolled price[37] the appropriate gross services profit of the intermediary controlled taxpayer.

In determining comparability under the GSM method, the 2009 final services regulations incorporate the general comparability factors of the existing regulations.[38] In addition, the regulations require that adjustments be made to the gross services profit margin if there are material differences between the controlled and uncontrolled transactions that would affect the gross services profit margin.[39]

The 2006 proposed regulations emphasize that if the functions performed by a controlled taxpayer are similar to those performed by an uncontrolled taxpayer, the gross profit margin earned by the uncontrolled taxpayer may be used as a comparable gross services profit margin, regardless of the structure of the uncontrolled services transaction. For example, if a controlled taxpayer that performs an agent service or intermediary function is comparable to a distributor that takes title to goods and resells them (i.e., a buy-sell distributor), the gross profit margin earned by the uncontrolled distributor on sales, stated as a percentage of the uncontrolled price for the goods, may be used as the comparable gross services profit margin.[40]

.03 Cost of Services Plus Method

The cost of services plus ("CSP") method evaluates whether the amount charged in a controlled services transaction is arm's length by reference to the gross services profit mark-up realized in comparable uncontrolled services transactions.[41] The 2009 final services regulations provide that, while this method is most reliably applied when the renderer in the controlled services transaction provides the same or similar services to both controlled and uncontrolled parties, this method is not appropriate when the controlled services transaction involves a contingent payment arrangement.[42]

The CSP method is similar to the cost plus method applicable to transfers of tangible property.[43] The 2009 final services regulations, however, incorporate certain necessary modifications, because the costs of providing services are presented differently for financial accounting purposes than costs of goods sold. For example, the 2009 final services regulations refer to the costs to be taken into account in evaluating controlled services transactions as "comparable transactional costs."[44] The 2009 final services regulations add that generally accepted accounting principles or, when income tax data for comparable transactions are available, income tax accounting rules may provide a useful starting point in determining the comparable transactional costs.[45]

---

[37] Defined as the price paid or received by the uncontrolled party in the relevant uncontrolled transaction. *See* Reg. § 1.482-9(d)(2)(iii).

[38] Reg. § 1.482-1(d).

[39] Reg. § 1.482-9(d)(3)(ii)(C).

[40] Reg. § 1.482-9(c)(3)(ii)(D).

[41] Reg. § 1.482-9(e)(1).

[42] *Id.*

[43] Reg. § 1.482-3(d).

[44] Defined as "the costs of providing the services under review that are taken into account as the basis for deter-

mining the gross services profit mark-up in comparable uncontrolled transactions. Depending on the facts and circumstances, such costs typically include all compensation attributable to employees directly involved in the performance of such services, materials, and supplies consumed or made available in rendering such services, and may include as well other costs of rendering the services." *See* Reg. § 1.482-9(e)(2)(iii). Comparable transaction costs may not necessarily equal "total service costs" as defined in Reg. § 1.482-9(j).

[45] Reg. § 1.482-9(e)(2)(iii).

In applying the CSP method, the 2009 final services regulations incorporate the general comparability factors of the existing regulations.[46] In addition, the 2009 final services regulations caution that the application of this method may produce unreliable results if, for example, a significant amount of the controlled taxpayer's comparable transactional costs consists of costs incurred in a tax accounting period other than the period under review, or if there are significant differences in the value of the services rendered, due, for example, to the use of valuable intangible property.[47]

.04 Comparable Profits Method

The 2009 final services regulations specify that the comparable profits method ("CPM"),[48] including the general guidance in the existing regulations,[49] is also applicable to controlled services transactions.[50] The 2009 final services regulations state that consistency in accounting practices between the relevant business activity of the tested party and the uncontrolled service providers is particularly important in determining the reliability of the results under this method, but less so than in applying the CSP method.[51]

The 2009 final services regulations add a new profit level indicator[52]—the ratio of operating profit to total services costs[53] —to the list of profit level indicators specified in the existing regulations.[54] The preamble to the 2003 proposed services regulations cautions that the application of the "rate of return on capital employed" profit level indicator of the existing regulations may produce unreliable results because the reliability of this profit level indicator decreases as operating assets play a lesser role in generating operating profits for both the tested party and the uncontrolled comparable.

.05 Profit Split Method

The 2009 final services regulations provide guidance regarding the application of the comparable profit split and the residual profit split methods to controlled services transactions.[55] In particular, the proposed regulations provide that a profit

---

[46] Reg. § 1.482-1(d).

[47] Reg. § 1.482-9(e)(3)(ii)(B).

[48] The comparable profits method evaluates whether the amount charged in a controlled transaction is arm's length based on analysis of objective measures of profitability (profit level indicators) derived from financial information regarding uncontrolled taxpayers that engage in similar activities under similar circumstances.

[49] Reg. § 1.482-5.

[50] Reg. § 1.482-9(f).

[51] Reg. § 1.482-9(f)(2)(iii).

[52] Reg. § 1.482-9(f)(2)(ii).

[53] Total services costs include all costs, based on analysis of the facts and circumstances, that can be directly identified with the act of rendering the services, and all other costs reasonably allocable to the services. See Reg. § 1.482-9(j).

[54] Stock option costs are to be considered in applying the new profit level indicator. Id. See also Xilinx, CCH Dec. 56,129, 125 TC 37, 2009-1 USTC ¶ 50,405, 567 F.3d 482 (9th Cir. 2009) (holding that stock options costs are

to be included in "costs" to be shared under the provisions of Reg. § 1.482-7A (cost sharing agreements)). The Xilinx opinion and dissent were withdrawn by the Ninth Circuit in a one sentence opinion issued in early 2010. See Xilinx, 2010-1 USTC ¶ 50,302, 592 F.2d 1017 (9th Cir. 2010).

The temporary cost sharing regulations, issued in 2009, explicitly include stock option costs as costs to be shared under CSAs. For a more in-depth discussion of cost-sharing agreements, see Chapter 4, infra. See also Summers, et al, "The Ninth Circuit's Opinion in Xilinx v. Comm'r. Implications for the Arm's Length Standard," 18 Tax Mgmt Transfer Pricing Rep. 543 (Sep. 24, 2009). But see Zollo & Cope, Lingering Issues, at 10 (noting that in a cost sharing analysis, the issue of stock options as costs arises because the taxpayer must determine how much of the deduction for costs incurred for joint benefit of the CSA participants must be retained in the U.S., such that the appropriate balance between the arm's length standard and the commensurate-with-income standard is struck).

[55] Generally, the profit split method evaluates whether the allocation of the combined operating profit or loss

split method may be appropriate when the controlled services transaction involves a combination of non-routine contributions by multiple controlled taxpayers.[56]

To accommodate the application of the profit split method to controlled services transactions, the 2009 final services regulations finalize earlier amendments[57] to the 1968 services regulations[58] applicable to the profit split method, which change the criterion for dividing residual profits. The 1986 services regulations provide for a division of residual profit "based upon relative value of each taxpayer's contributions of intangible property." The 2009 final services regulations divide residual profit "based upon the relative value of each taxpayer's nonroutine contributions,"[59] which may include contributions of intangible property.

.06 Services Cost Method

The 2009 final services regulations retain one of the most important new features of the 2006 temporary services regulations, which was the introduction of the SCM ("SCM")[60] as a replacement for the cost only safe harbor that existed under the 1968 services regulations.[61]

To qualify to use the SCM, a service must be considered a "covered service."[62] A covered service is one that meets the business judgment rule,[63] meets the adequate books and records requirement,[64] is not on the list of excluded services,[65] and is either a service that the IRS has included on the list of approved specified covered services[66] or qualifies as a low margin covered service.[67] The 2009 final services regulations include the coordination provision with the penalty regulations—also originally introduced in the 2006 temporary services regulations.[68]

Business Judgment Rule. For a service to qualify for the SCM, the service must not contribute significantly to the fundamental risks of business success or failure.[69] A taxpayer must reasonably conclude using its business judgment that the service does not contribute significantly to key competitive advantages, core capabilities, or fundamental risks of success or failure in one or more trades or businesses of the controlled group. Reasonableness will be determined using a facts and circumstances test. Appropriately, the preamble to the 2006 temporary services regulations stated that "in all but unusual cases, the taxpayer's business judgment will be respected."[70] When the SCM is applied, the focus on examination will be verification of total services costs and the allocation of those costs.[71]

(Footnote Continued)

attributable to one or more controlled transactions is arm's length by reference to the relative value of each controlled taxpayer's contributions to the combined operating profit or loss. *See* Reg. § 1.482-9(g).

[56] Reg. § 1.482-9(g)(1) (explicitly prohibiting usage of RPSM where only one taxpayer makes nonroutine contributions).

[57] *See* Reg. § 1.482-6(c)(3)(i)(B).

[58] Reg. § 1.482-6.

[59] Defined under Reg. § 1.482-6(c)(3)(i)(B) as contributions by controlled taxpayers that are "not routine;" i.e., cannot be accounted for by reference to market returns.

[60] Reg. § 1.482-9(b).

[61] Reg. § 1.482-2(b).

[62] Reg. § 1.482-9(b)(2)(i).

[63] Reg. § 1.482-9(b)(2).

[64] Reg. § 1.482-9(b)(3)(iii).

[65] Reg. § 1.482-9(b)(3)(iv).

[66] Reg. § 1.482-9(b)(3)(i).

[67] Reg. § 1.482-9(b)(3)(ii).

[68] Reg. § 1.6662-6(d)(2)(ii)(B), (iii)(B)(4).

[69] Reg. § 1.482-9(b)(2).

[70] Preamble to the 2006 temporary services regulations.

[71] *Id.*

¶540.06

Books and Records. Adequate books and records must contain sufficient detail to allow the IRS to verify total services costs, the nature of the services rendered, the identification of the renderer and the recipient of the services, and the allocation and apportionment of costs.[72] Additionally, a taxpayer must have a statement evidencing the intent to apply the SCM.[73] Apparently, the statement merely needs to be included within the documentation maintained. The 2006 temporary services regulations dropped the requirement contained in the 2003 proposed services regulations for the a similar cost-based method that a written contract must be "in place throughout the time when costs with respect to the controlled services are incurred by the renderer," and that requirement is omitted from the 2009 final services regulations as well.[74]

The 2009 final services regulations retain the amendments to the regulations under Code Sec. 6662, which include a section on the SCM.[75] Under this provision, a taxpayer must reasonably conclude that the SCM applies and reasonably allocate and apportion costs in accordance with Reg. § 1.482-9(k) in order to meet the specified method requirement and avoid the imposition of penalties. It appears, therefore, that maintaining adequate books and records in order to apply the SCM method along with the required statement of intent to apply the SCM is likely to substantially satisfy nearly all of the required documentation items under the penalty regulations.[76]

Excluded Transactions. The 2009 final services regulations list certain categories of services which, in whole or in part, are not covered services and therefore do not qualify for the SCM.[77] The list is the same as the list of excluded transactions for the SCM under the 2006 temporary services regulations and includes: manufacturing; production; extraction, exploration or processing of natural resources; construction; reselling, distribution, acting as a sales or purchasing agent, or acting under a commission or similar arrangement; research, development, or experimentation; engineering or scientific; financial transactions, including guarantees; and insurance or reinsurance.[78] The stated rationale for excluding these services is that Treasury and the IRS believe that these transactions are "high-margin" transactions.[79] Since the 2009 final services regulations define "low-margin" as 7-percent markup (or less).

The 2003 proposed services regulations had taxpayers speculating whether the exclusion of guarantees from the simplified cost-based method ("SCBM") meant that the Treasury Department and the IRS considered financial guarantees to be a service, which would then qualify under the safe harbor in Reg. § 1.482-2(b). Citing cases involving the source of guarantee fees, the Treasury Department and the IRS state in the preamble that financial guarantees do not constitute services for

[72] Reg. § 1.482-9(b)(6).
[73] Id.
[74] Prop. Reg. § 1.482-9(f)(3)(ii) (2003).
[75] Reg. § 1.6662-6(d)(2)(ii)(B), (iii)(B)(4).
[76] Reg. § 1.6662-6(d)(2)(iii)(B)(3) requires that transfer pricing documentation for penalty purposes include any

documentation explicitly required by the section 482 regulations.
[77] Reg. § 1.482-9(b)(4).
[78] Id.
[79] Preamble to the 2006 temporary regulations (citing *Centel Communications, Inc.*, 90-2 USTC ¶ 50,603, 920 F.2d 1335 (7th Cir. 1990); *Bank of America*, 82-1 USTC ¶ 9415, 680 F.2d 142 (Ct. Cl. 1980)).

sourcing purposes.[80] Apparently, they were less certain for transfer pricing purposes, stating that "no inference is intended by this exclusion [from the SCM] that financial transactions (including guarantees) would otherwise be considered the provision of services for transfer pricing purposes."[81] Because the Treasury Department and the IRS did not believe that financial guarantees should be covered by a cost safe harbor (which would mean that there would be a uniform no-charge rule for financial guarantees), financial guarantees are excluded from the SCM.[82] Additionally, they promised future transfer pricing guidance on financial guarantees at the same time the long-awaited global dealing regulations are issued.

Specified Covered Services. The list of specified covered services will include those types of services that the IRS specifies in a Rev. Proc. 2007-13, which was released on December 21, 2006, concurrent with the January 1, 2007 effective date of the 2006 temporary services regulations. This revenue procedure remained in effect as of the date the temporary services regulations became final: July 31, 2009.

Rev. Proc. 2007-13 identifies 101 specified covered services in the meaning of Reg. § 1.482-9(b)(3)(i). The covered services are enumerated in the Practice Tools at ¶ 20,030.

Low-Margin Covered Services. Low-margin covered services are those services that command arm's length markups on total services costs of 7 percent or less.[83] The arm's length markup is determined using general Code Sec. 482 principles and the arm's length markup is based on the median comparable markup on total services costs.[84]

It is not clear under these regulations whether the median used is the median based on a single year or multiple year analysis. If the arm's length markup is determined directly using the comparable profits method ("CPM"),[85] the general rule is that a three-year analysis is performed in determining the interquartile range.[86]

Another unanswered issue is whether the comparable analysis of low margin covered services has to be updated each year to meet documentation requirements in order to avoid transfer pricing penalties. For example, if for 2007 a taxpayer obtains a comparable study providing that the median arm's length markup was 2 percent, making the service at issue a low-margin covered service, then the service qualifies for use of the SCM. The frequency with which updates to that study must be made is an open question. While this is not a new issue specific to the SCM, the stated objectives of the SCM—reduced complexity and administrative burden for low margin services—would be furthered if a taxpayer could reasonably rely on a prior year's study without having to reconfirm that the arm's length markup does not exceed 7 percent on an annual basis.

---

[80] Preamble to the 2006 temporary services regulations.

[81] *Id.*

[82] *Id.*

[83] Reg. § 1.482-9(b)(3)(ii).

[84] *Id.*

[85] The median arm's length markup can be determined using a method other the CPM. For example, the comparable uncontrolled services price method, and then converted to an arm's length markup on total services costs. *See* Prop. Reg. § 1.482-9(b)(6), Ex. 17 (2003).

[86] Reg. § 1.482-5(b)(4).

.07 Shared Services Arrangements

The 2009 final services regulations explicitly permit taxpayers to use shared service arrangements to allocate certain costs within a controlled group.[87] These costs, however, are limited to certain services which meet requirements for use of the SCM under Reg. § 1.482-9(b)(1). The purpose of these provisions seemingly was to bring these rules into conformity with the guidelines of the OECD for cost contribution arrangements.[88]

The requirements for a shared service arrangement include: (1) two or more participants, (2) all controlled participants that reasonably anticipate a benefit from one or more of the covered services, and (3) the arrangement must be structured so that each covered service confers a benefit on at least one participant in the arrangement.[89] Services may be aggregated if the aggregation is reasonable and reflects the magnitude of the benefits each participant reasonably anticipates.[90]

The 2009 final services regulations set out numerous examples to assist with these basic rules regarding shared services arrangements.[91] In large part, these examples define the new SCM and illustrate certain types of services that would be considered appropriate for shared service arrangements, and give examples of various cost allocation keys that may be considered in order to achieve a measure of reasonably anticipated benefits. There is nothing unusual or controversial about these examples. At a minimum, these examples make clear that the facts and circumstances of the controlled taxpayer will control. Examples of cost allocation keys include order volume, headcount, and transaction volume.

.08 Unspecified Methods

Finally, the 2009 final services regulations provide that, in addition to the six specified methods, an unspecified method may be used to determine an arm's length charge if such a method will provide the most reliable measure of an arm's length result under the best method rule.[92] The 2006 temporary services regulations emphasize that under the arm's length standard "an unspecified method should provide information on the prices or profits that the controlled taxpayer might have realized by choosing a realistic alternative to the controlled transaction . . . ."[93]

.09 Definition of Cost

Under the 1968 services regulations, when the arm's length charge for controlled services is determined with reference to costs incurred for those services, "costs" is defined to include all direct operating costs and an allocable portion of all indirect operating costs (other than cost of goods sold) related to the services.[94] The 2009 final services regulations use a term—total services costs. The term "total services costs" is used to determine the arm's length charge under two of the six specified methods: (1) in the comparable profits method, which uses the ratio of

---

[87] Reg. § 1.482-9(b)(7).
[88] OECD Guidelines, Chapter VIII, Cost Contribution Arrangements (1995).
[89] Reg. § 1.482-9(b)(7)(ii)(A).
[90] Reg. § 1.482-9(b)(7)(iii)(B).

[91] Reg. § 1.482-9(b)(8).
[92] Reg. § 1.482-9(h).
[93] Id.
[94] Reg. § 1.482-2(b)(4).

operating profits to total services costs as the profit level indicator, and (2) in the SCM. It is also used in the cost of services plus method in cases in which an analysis of the ratio of operating profits to total services costs is necessary.

The 2009 final services regulations define total services costs[95] as the cost of rendering those services for which total services costs are being determined, including all costs in cash or in kind (including stock-based compensation) that, based on an analysis of the facts and circumstances, are directly identified with the act of rendering the services, as well as all other costs reasonably allocable to the services, except for interest expense, foreign income taxes,[96] or domestic income taxes. The 2009 final regulations add that for purposes of determining total services costs, generally accepted accounting principles or income tax accounting rules may provide a useful starting point, but caution that neither will be conclusive.[97]

With respect to the inclusion of stock-based compensation in the total services costs definition, real questions arise as to the proper method for valuation, which again raises the specter of increased likelihood of controversy with the taxing authorities. At the heart of the matter is whether the valuation methodology should be that employed for tax purposes (under Code Sec. 83) or for book purposes (pursuant to the Financial Accounting Standards Board's SFAS No. 123r, valuation model).[98]

.10 Allocation of Costs

The 1968 services regulations provide that costs may be allocated and apportioned to a services transaction under a method of allocation and apportionment that is reasonable and in keeping with sound accounting practices.[99] While the 2009 final services regulations[100] retain this flexible approach, they also provide that consideration should be given to all bases and factors, including, for example, total services costs, total costs for a relevant activity, assets, sales, compensation, space utilized, and time spent.

The 2009 final services regulations also provide that consideration should be given to taxpayers' general practices to apportion costs for other purposes, such as for use by management, creditors, minority shareholders, customers, and potential investors. The 2009 final services regulations caution, however, that the IRS is not necessarily bound by the taxpayer's use of such general practices. The regulations

---

[95] *See* Reg. § 1.482-9(j).

[96] As defined in Reg. § 1.901-2(a).

[97] Reg. § 1.482-9(j).

[98] *See* Camillo, *et al.*, *The Temporary Services Regulations: A substantive review,* 10 *Global Tax Briefing* 4, at 4 (CCH Aug. 15, 2008) (noting that even if the FASB approach is chosen, it still remains to be decided how much of the value should be included in the cost pool); *see also* Wilcox, Shari & E. Miller Williams, *Confronting the Temporary Services Regulations in an Internal Revenue Service Examination,* 10 *Global Tax Briefing* 4, at 7 (CCH Aug. 15, 2008) (anticipating increased scrutiny of the taxpayer's records and documentation from the IRS as to

how stock-based compensation is accounted for in the cost pool and an uptick in the number of proposed adjustments). *But see* Thomas M. Zollo & Charles Cope, *The Services Regulations Go Final, But an Issue Lingers* (Sep. 14, 2009), *available at http://us.kpmg.com/microsite/taxnewsflash/2009/Sep/Services_Regs.pdf* [hereinafter *Lingering Issues*] (identifying the Service's failure to take a definitive stance on how to treat stock options when calculating "total services costs," and distinguishing the treatment of stock options as costs for services purposes from the treatment of stock options as costs in the context of cost sharing).

[99] Reg. §§ 1.482-2(b)(3) through (6).

[100] Reg. § 1.482-9(k).

specify that "in no event will an allocation of costs based on a generalized or non-specific benefit be appropriate."[101]

The principles of these paragraphs are illustrated by the following example:

Reg. § 1.482-9(k)(3), Ex. 2

(i) Company A is a consumer products company located in the United States. Companies B and C are wholly owned subsidiaries of Company A and are located in Countries B and C, respectively. Company A and its subsidiaries manufacture products for sale in their respective markets. Company A hires a consultant who has expertise regarding a manufacturing process used by Company A and its subsidiary, Company B. Company C, the Country C subsidiary, uses a different manufacturing process, and accordingly will not receive any benefit from the outside consultant hired by Company A. In allocating and apportioning the cost of hiring the outside consultant (100), Company A determines that sales constitute the most appropriate allocation key.

Company A and its subsidiaries have the following sales:

Company	A	B	C	Total
Sales	400	100	200	700

Because Company C does not obtain any benefit from the consultant, none of the costs are allocated to it. Rather, the costs of 100 are allocated and apportioned ratably to Company A and Company B as the entities that obtain a benefit from the campaign, based on the total sales of those entities (500). An appropriate allocation of the costs of the consultant is as follows:

Company	A	B	Total
Allocation	400/500	100/500	
Amount	80	20	100

¶ 560 Special Rules

.01 Contingent-Payment Service Arrangements

The 2009 final services regulations contain guidance regarding contingent payment service contracts. A contingent payment service contract is a contract in which the service provider agrees to accept payment for its services in whole or in part contingent on the occurrence of one or more specified events, such as the commercialization of a product. The 2009 final services regulations require that the arrangement must be set forth in a written contract entered into prior to the start of the activity, that the contract must state it is contingent on the happening of a future benefit, and that the contract must provide for payment on a basis that reflects the recipient's benefit from the services rendered and the risks borne by the renderer.[102] The examples suggest that payment could take the form of a royalty.

Reg. § 1.482-9(i)(5), Ex. 1

(i) Company X is a member of a controlled group that has operated in the pharmaceutical sector for many years. In Year 1, Company X enters into a written services agreement with Company Y, another member of the controlled group, whereby Company X will perform certain research and development

---

[101] *Id.*   [102] Reg. § 1.482-9(i)(2)(i)(A)-(B).

activities for Company Y. The parties enter into the agreement before Company X undertakes any of the research and development activities covered by the agreement. At the time the agreement is entered into, the possibility that any new products will be developed is highly uncertain and the possible market or markets for any products that may be developed are not known and cannot be estimated with any reliability. Under the agreement, Company Y will own any patent or other rights that result from the activities of Company X under the agreement and Company Y will make payments to Company X only if such activities result in commercial sales of one or more derivative products. In that event, Company Y will pay Company X, for a specified period, x% of Company Y's gross sales of each of such products. Payments are required with respect to each jurisdiction in which Company Y has sales of such a derivative product, beginning with the first year in which the sale of a product occurs in the jurisdiction and continuing for six additional years with respect to sales of that product in that jurisdiction.

(ii) As a result of research and development activities performed by Company X for Company Y in Years 1 through 4, a compound is developed that may be more effective than existing medications in the treatment of certain conditions. Company Y registers the patent rights with respect to the compound in several jurisdictions in Year 4. In Year 6, Company Y begins commercial sales of the product in Jurisdiction A and, in that year, Company Y makes the payment to Company X that is required under the agreement. Sales of the product continue in Jurisdiction A in Years 7 through 9 and Company Y makes the payments to Company X in Years 7 through 9 that are required under the agreement.

(iii) The years under examination are Years 6 though 9. In evaluating whether the contingent payment terms will be recognized, the Commissioner considers whether the conditions of § 1.482-9(i)(2) are met and whether the specified contingency and basis of payment are consistent with the economic substance of the controlled services transaction and with the conduct of the controlled parties. The Commissioner determines that the contingent-payment arrangement is reflected in the written agreement between Company X and Company Y; that commercial sales of products developed under the arrangement represent future benefits for Company Y directly related to the controlled services transaction; and that the basis for the payment provided for in the event such sales occur reflects the recipient's benefit and the renderer's risk. Consistent with § 1.482-1(d)(3)(ii)(B) and (iii)(B), the Commissioner determines that the parties' conduct over the term of the agreement has been consistent with their contractual allocation of risk; that Company X has the financial capacity to bear the risk that its research and development services may be unsuccessful and that it may not receive compensation for such services; and that Company X exercises managerial and operational control over the research and development, such that it is reasonable for Company X to assume the risk of those activities. Based on all these facts, the Commissioner determines that the terms of the contingent-payment arrangement are consistent with economic substance.

(iv) In determining whether the amount charged under the contingent-payment arrangement in each of Years 6 through 9 is arm's length, the Commissioner evaluates under § 1.482-9 and other applicable rules under § 482 the compensation paid in each year for the research and development services. This analysis takes into account that under the contingent-payment terms Company X bears the risk that it might not receive payment for its services in the event that those services do not result in marketable products and the risk that the magnitude of its payment depends on the magnitude of product sales, if any. The Commissioner also considers the alternatives reasonably available to the parties in connection with the controlled services transaction. One such alternative, in view of Company X's willingness and ability to bear the risk and expenses of research and development activities, would be for Company X to undertake such activities on its own behalf and to license the rights to products successfully developed as a result of such activities. Accordingly, in evaluating whether the compensation of x% of gross sales that is paid to Company X during the first four years of commercial sales of derivative products is at arm's length, the Commissioner may consider the royalties (or other consideration) charged for intangible property that are comparable to those incorporated in the derivative products and that resulted from Company X's research and development activities under the contingent-payment arrangement.[103]

The proposed contingent payment rules appear on their face to be permissive and to illustrate, consistent with general transfer pricing principles, that taxpayers are entitled to allocate risk by contract as long as the allocation is consistent with economic substance. However, the 2009 final services regulations provide the IRS with authority to impute a contingent payment arrangement.[104] For example, if a distributor provides "incremental marketing" activities without charge for the benefit of the trademark owner in years one, two, and three, the IRS may not be able to make an adjustment to the distributor's income for those years if the statute of limitations has run. However, under the contingent payment rules, the IRS may be entitled to impute a contingent payment contract. An imputed contingent payment contract would permit the IRS to make an adjustment to the distributor's income in the current year to ensure the distributor receives the arm's length value of the services it provided to the trademark holder in the earlier years, notwithstanding the expiration of the statute of limitations on the earlier years.

Reg. § 1.482-1(d)(3)(ii)(C), Ex. 3

Contractual terms imputed from economic substance. (i) FP, a foreign producer of wristwatches, is the registered holder of the YY trademark in the United States and in other countries worldwide. In Year 1, FP enters the U.S. market by selling YY wristwatches to its newly organized U.S. subsidiary, USSub, for distribution in the United States market. USSub pays FP a fixed price per wristwatch. USSub and FP undertake, without separate compensation, marketing activities to establish the YY trademark in the U.S. market. Unrelated foreign producers of trademarked wristwatches and their U.S. distributors respectively undertake similar marketing activities in independent arrangements involving distribution of trademarked wristwatches in the U.S. market. In Years 1 through 6, USSub markets and sells YY wristwatches in the United States. Further, in Years 1 through 6, USSub undertakes incremental marketing activities in addition to the activities similar to those observed in the independent distribution transactions in the U.S. market. FP does not directly or indirectly compensate USSub for performing these incremental activities during Years 1 through 6. Assume that, aside from these incremental activities, and after any adjustments are made to improve the reliability of the comparison, the price paid per wristwatch by the independent, authorized distributors for wristwatches would provide the most reliable measure of the arm's length price paid per YY wristwatch by USSub.

(ii) By Year 7, the wristwatches with the YY trademark generate a premium return in the U.S. market, as compared to wristwatches marketed by the independent distributors. In Year 7, substantially all the premium return from the YY trademark in the U.S. market is attributed to FP, for example through an increase in the price paid per watch by USSub, or by some other means.

---

[103] Reg. § 1.482-9(i)(5), Ex. 1.   [104] Reg. § 1.482-1(d)(3)(iii)(B).

(iii) In determining whether an allocation of income is appropriate in Year 7, the Commissioner may consider the economic substance of the arrangements between USSub and FP, and the parties' course of conduct throughout their relationship. Based on this analysis, the Commissioner determines that it is unlikely that, *ex ante,* an uncontrolled taxpayer operating at arm's length would engage in the incremental marketing activities to develop or enhance an intangible owned by another party unless it received contemporaneous compensation or otherwise had a reasonable anticipation of receiving a future benefit from those activities. In this case, USSub's undertaking the incremental marketing activities in Years 1 through 6 is a course of conduct that is inconsistent with the parties' attribution to FP in Year 7 of substantially all the premium return from the enhanced YY trademark in the United States market. Therefore, the Commissioner may impute one or more agreements between USSub and FP, consistent with the economic substance of their course of conduct, which would afford USSub an appropriate portion of the premium return from the YY trademark wristwatches. For example, the Commissioner may impute a separate services agreement that affords USSub contingent-payment compensation for its incremental marketing activities in Years 1 through 6, which benefited FP by contributing to the value of the trademark owned by FP. In the alternative, the Commissioner may impute a long-term exclusive U.S. distribution agreement to exploit the YY trademark that allows USSub to benefit from the incremental marketing activities it performed. As another alternative, the Commissioner may require FP to compensate USSub for terminating USSub's imputed long-term exclusive agreement to exploit the YY trademark in the United States, an agreement that USSub made more valuable at its own expense and risk. The taxpayer may present additional facts that could indicate which of these or other alternative agreements best reflects the economic substance of the underlying transactions, consistent with the parties' course of conduct in the particular case.[105]

.02 Coordination with Transfer Pricing Rules for Other Transactions

General Rule. The 2009 final services regulations contain guidance for evaluating service transactions that include elements comprising a different type of transaction, such as a tangible or an intangible property transfer, loan or rental, that is covered by a separate set of rules in the transfer pricing regulations. For example, a transaction structured as a service transaction may involve the transfer of tangible property by the service provider (such as spare parts provided under a maintenance services contract). Similarly, a transaction structured as another type of transaction may include service elements.

In providing guidance regarding these types of transactions, the IRS is trying to achieve consistent transfer pricing results for economically similar transactions, regardless of how they are structured or characterized.

As a general rule, the 2009 final services regulations provide that the determination of whether to evaluate such an integrated transaction as a single transaction, or whether to evaluate one or more elements separately, depends on which approach will provide the most reliable measure of an arm's length result.[106] The 2009 final services regulations contemplate that, ordinarily, the different elements need not be analyzed separately, provided the single-transaction approach can

---

[105] Reg. § 1.482-1(d)(3)(ii)(C), Ex. 3.   [106] Reg. § 1.482-9(m)(1).

¶560.02

adequately account for each component of the transaction in assessing comparability and determining the arm's length result.[107]

The general rule for evaluating integrated transactions under the 2009 final services regulations is consistent with the generally applicable aggregation concept of Reg. § 1.482-1(f)(2)(i)(A). Under this concept, multiple interrelated transactions are evaluated in the aggregate when an aggregate approach is the most reliable means to determine the arm's length result. Moreover, the general rule is consistent with guidance in the 1968 services regulations indicating that no separate allocation for services is required when the services are ancillary and subsidiary to the transfer of intangible property.[108]

Services Transactions that Effect a Transfer of Intangible Property. In addition to the general rule for integrated transactions, the 2009 final services regulations incorporate a special rule for services transactions that constitute or result in the transfer, in whole or in part, of an intangible. Under this special rule, if the element relating to the transfer of the intangible is material, the arm's length result for the intangibles element of the services transaction must be determined or corroborated by an analysis under the transfer pricing rules for transfers of intangible property. This rule is illustrated by the following example:

Reg. § 1.482-9(m)(5), Ex. 4

> (i) Company X, a U.S. corporation, and Company Y, a foreign corporation, are members of a controlled group. Both companies perform research and development activities relating to integrated circuits. In addition, Company Y manufactures integrated circuits. In years 1 through 3, Company X engages in substantial research and development activities, gains significant know-how regarding the development of a particular high-temperature resistant integrated circuit, and memorializes that research in a written report. In years 1 through 3, Company X generates overall net operating losses as a result of the expenditures associated with this research and development effort. At the beginning of year 4, Company X enters into a technical assistance agreement with Company Y. As part of this agreement, the researchers from Company X responsible for this project meet with the researchers from Company Y and provide them with a copy of the written report. Three months later, the researchers from Company Y apply for a patent for a high-temperature resistant integrated circuit based in large part upon the know-how obtained from the researchers from Company X.[109]

¶ 570 Regulations for Taxable Years Beginning Prior to 1/1/2007

.01 Overview

For intercompany service transactions for taxable years prior to January 1, 2007, the guidance contained within Section 1.482-2(b) of the 1968 regulations controls. There is significantly less commentary for service transactions prior to the taxable year 2007.

---

[107] *Id.*

[108] Reg. § 1.482-2(b)(8).

[109] Reg. § 1.482-9(m)(5), Ex. 4.

The 1968 services regulations require that where one member of a group of controlled entities performs marketing, managerial, administrative, technical, or other services for the benefit of, or on behalf of another member of the group, the service renderer must generally be compensated. If the renderer is not compensated, or is compensated at other than arm's length, the IRS may make an allocation to reflect arm's length compensation for those services.[110]

.02 The Benefit Test

The initial inquiry in a transfer pricing analysis of intercompany services focuses on issue of benefit. The regulations adopt a benefit test whereby the IRS may make allocations to reflect arm's length charges for services performed by a member of a group of controlled entities, if the services were performed for the joint benefit of the group or for the sole benefit of another member of the group. The allocation must correspond to the relative benefits intended to be conferred through performance of the services, based on the facts known at the time. No allocation is to be made, however, to the extent that the probable benefits are "so remote or indirect" that unrelated parties would not charge for the services.[111] Conversely, the IRS may make an allocation if, at the time the services are performed, the services related to the carrying on of an activity by another member of the group or were intended to benefit another member, either in that member's overall operations or as part of its day-to-day activities.[112] Any allocation must correspond to the relative benefits intended to be conferred, based on the facts known at the time of performance, even if the benefits are not realized.[113] Compare Reg. § 1.482-2(b)(2)(i) Examples 2 and 3:

Reg. § 1.482-2(b)(2)(i), Ex. 2

X operates an international airline, and Y owns and operates hotels in several cities which are serviced by X. X, in conjunction with its advertising of the airline, often pictures Y's hotels and mentions Y's name. Although such advertising was primarily intended to benefit X's airline operations, it was reasonable to anticipate that there would be substantial benefits to Y resulting from patronage by travelers who responded to X's advertising. Since an unrelated hotel operator would have been charged for such advertising, the district director may make an appropriate allocation to reflect an arm's length charge consistent with the relative benefits intended.[114]

Reg. § 1.482-2(b)(2)(i), Ex. 3

Assume the same facts as in Example 2 except that X's advertising neither mentions nor pictures Y's hotels. Although it is reasonable to anticipate that increased air travel attributable to X's advertising will result in some benefit to Y due to increased patronage by air travelers, the district director will not make an allocation with respect to such advertising since the probable benefit to Y was so indirect and remote that an unrelated hotel operator would not have been charged for such advertising.[115]

---

[110] Reg. § 1.482-2(b)(1).
[111] Reg. § 1.482-2(b)(2)(i).
[112] *Id.*

[113] *Id.*
[114] Reg. § 1.482-2(b)(2)(i), Ex. 2.
[115] Reg. § 1.482-2(b)(2)(i), Ex. 3.

This benefit test was illustrated in *Hospital Corporation of America*.[116] Hospital Corporation of America (HCA) was a hospital management company that conducted most of its business in the United States. When HCA was approached to manage a hospital in Saudi Arabia, the corporation decided to form a foreign subsidiary to handle the negotiations and actual performance of the management contract. The IRS asserted that the foreign subsidiary was a sham and assigned 100 percent of the subsidiary's income to HCA. The Tax Court found that the foreign subsidiary was a separate and viable legal entity and not a sham for tax purposes, but agreed that Code Sec. 482 was applicable because HCA's skills in hospital management were an integral part of the contract negotiated with the Saudi government. Because the most important factor contributing to the subsidiary's success was the expertise and experience of HCA, the Tax Court allocated 75 percent of the subsidiary's profits to HCA. It is interesting to note that the Tax Court made its determination in this case despite "little quantitative evidence in this record upon which it could determine what a reasonable allocation of profits would be."[117]

Under the benefit test, no allocation may be made for services that merely duplicate a service the related party has performed independently for itself.[118] The most notable type of qualifying duplicative services are "stewardship" services. Although only defined in Reg. §1.861-8 under Code Sec. 861, the courts have interpreted stewardship expenses to include services performed for the renderer's own benefit as an investor in the related corporation.[119] Reg. §1.861-8 views the expenses resulting from stewardship functions as incurred by the parent as a result of, or incident to, the ownership of the related corporation and thus, allocates such expenses to dividends received or to be received from the related corporation.

The 1968 services regulations do not actually use the term "stewardship" and the only discussion in the regulations of stewardship-type activities relates to "duplicative" activities which are activities already performed by, or able to be performed by, the related entity.[120] To distinguish between supportive and stewardship services, the regulations provide that taxpayers must consider the related entity's ability to independently perform the activity (i.e., in terms of qualification and availability of personnel).[121]

Without specific guidance on what constitutes stewardship activities, taxpayers generally relied on a 1988 technical advice memorandum, TAM 8806002 and the *Young & Rubicam* case.[122]

In TAM 8806002, to make the determination of which expenses constitute stewardship expenses and which constitute operating expenses of the subsidiaries, the IRS divided the services at issue into four classes, and then applied a "proximate and direct" standard. The classes were:

[116] CCH Dec. 40,476, 81 TC 520 (1983).

[117] *See Hospital Corporation America*, CCH Dec. 40,476, 81 TC *supra* at 596.

[118] Reg. §1.482-2(b)(2)(ii).

[119] *Eli Lilly & Co.*, CCH Dec. 42,113, 84 TC 996, 1154-1155 (1985), *aff'd in part* and *rev'd in part*, 88-2 USTC ¶9502, 856 F.2d 855 (7th Cir. 1987).

[120] Reg. §1.482-2(b)(2)(ii).

[121] *Id.*

[122] *See, e.g., Young & Rubicam, Inc.*, 69-1 USTC ¶9404, 410 F.2d 1233 (Ct. Cls. 1969).

Class I.	Expenses for the direct benefit of one or more of the subsidiary corporations, even though the parent corporation may receive an indirect benefit from some of these expenditures.
Class II.	Stewardship expenses allocable to the parent, such as expenses in connection with the U.S. tax return, information report filings with the IRS and Securities and Exchange Commission, periodic review of the subsidiary, and financing the parent's ownership in the subsidiary.
Class III.	Expenses for the operating members of the group as a whole, allocated on a facts-and-circumstances test by an end-result analysis.
Class IV.	Expenses of the parent that are not properly included as stewardship expenses, such as expenses for investigation of new business activities using employees of existing entities that would not participate in the business opportunity if it came to fruition.

Expenses that clearly fall within a specific class may be easily allocated between the parent and affiliate. The "proximate and direct" test is applied to those expenses that are difficult to classify because both the parent and affiliate receive benefits in varying degrees from the same expenditures.

In *Young & Rubicam,*[123] the Court of Claims considered the deductibility by a U.S. parent corporation of salaries paid to its own employees for periods of time when they were detailed to foreign subsidiary corporations. The Court of Claims distinguished between expenses that were concerned with the day-to-day operations of the subsidiary corporations and those that were in the nature of supervisory controls. The court held that the corporation could not claim as its own expense compensation paid for activities that were concerned with the day-to-day operations of the subsidiary corporations business, because any benefit the corporation obtained could not be considered "proximate and direct" to its own business. Expenses that were in the nature of supervisory controls were allowed as deductible.

.03 Determining the Amount of the Arm's Length Service Charge

Once it has been determined that an intercompany allocation for services is required, it is necessary to determine the amount of an arm's length charge. For this purpose, the 1968 services regulations distinguish between services that are an integral part of either entity's business and those that are not.

The 1968 services regulations allow taxpayers to charge the cost of services rendered for the benefit of related parties, provided such services are not "integral" to the business operations of either the service renderer or the recipient. The 1968 services regulations include the following four tests for determining whether a particular service is considered to be "integral" to an entity's business:

- The renderer or the recipient of the service is engaged in the trade or business of rendering or providing similar services to unrelated parties.[124]

---

[123] *Id.*

[124] Reg. § 1.482-2(b)(7)(i).

- The renderer provides services to one or more related parties as one of its principal activities.[125] Except for services which constitute a manufacturing, production, extraction, or construction activity, it is presumed that the renderer does not provide services to related parties as one of its principal activities if the cost of services provided to related parties during the taxable year does not exceed 25 percent of the total costs or deductions of the renderer for the taxable year. For the purposes of this calculation, the cost of services rendered to related parties includes all costs and deductions directly or indirectly related to the rendition of such services as well as the cost of services that constitute a manufacturing, production, extraction or construction activity. The total costs or deductions of the renderer does not include the amount reflected in the cost of goods sold. If the renderer fails the 25 percent test, or the 25 percent does not apply (in the case of manufacturing, production, extraction or construction activities) the determination is based on the facts and circumstances. The time devoted to the rendering of the services, its relative cost, the regularity with which the services are rendered, the amount of capital investment, the risk of loss involved, and whether the services are in the nature of supporting services or independent of the renderer's other activities will be considered.[126]

- The renderer is "peculiarly capable" of rendering the services, and such services are a principal element in the operations of the recipient.[127] For example, when the renderer makes use of a particularly advantageous situation or circumstance, such as an influential relationship with customers or use of its intangible property. The renderer is not considered peculiarly capable, however, unless the value of the services is substantially in excess of the costs or deductions of the renderer attributable to the services.[128]

- The recipient has received the benefit of a substantial amount of services from one or more related parties during its taxable year.[129] Generally, if the costs or deductions of the renderer that are directly or indirectly related to the services exceed an amount equal to 25 percent of the total costs or deductions of the recipient for the taxable year, a substantial amount of services are considered to have been received. For purposes of this calculation, the total costs or deductions of the recipient include the renderers' costs or deductions directly or indirectly related to the rendition of such services, and does not include the service fees paid or accrued by the recipient for such services or the material cost reflected in the cost of goods sold of the recipient.[130]

If the services provided satisfy any of these four tests, they are considered integral, and the related intercompany charge must include a profit element. For services other than those considered to be integral, an arm's length charge is deemed to be equal to the costs or deductions incurred for such services, unless

---

[125] Reg. § 1.482-2(b)(7)(ii).
[126] Id.
[127] Reg. § 1.482-2(b)(7)(iii).
[128] Id.
[129] Reg. § 1.482-2(b)(7)(iv).
[130] Id.

the taxpayer establishes a more appropriate charge.[131] In practice, this means that the taxpayer may elect whether to charge these services out at cost or at cost plus an appropriate profit mark-up.

Reg. § 1.482-2(b)(7)(v) contains 16 examples which demonstrate the application of the "integral" test. Examples 4 and 10 are provided below:

Reg. § 1.482-2(b)(7)(v), Ex. 4

> Z is a domestic corporation and has several foreign subsidiaries. Z and X, a domestic subsidiary of Z, have exercised the privilege granted under section 1501 to file a consolidated return and, therefore, constitute a *consolidated group* within the meaning of paragraph (b)(7)(ii)(C) of this section. Pursuant to paragraph (b)(7)(ii)(C) of this section, the taxpayer treats X and Z as the renderer. The sole function of X is to provide accounting, billing, communication, and travel services to the foreign subsidiaries of Z. Z also provides some other services for the benefit of its foreign subsidiaries. The total costs or deductions of X and Z related to the services rendered for the benefit of the foreign subsidiaries is $ 750,000. Of that amount, $ 710,000 represents the costs of X, which are X's total operating costs. The total costs or deductions of X and Z for the taxable year with respect to their operations (exclusive of amounts properly reflected in the cost of goods sold of X and Z) is $ 6,500,000. Since the total costs or deductions related to the services rendered to the foreign subsidiaries ($ 750,000) is less than 25 percent of the total costs or deductions of X and Z (exclusive of amounts properly reflected in the costs of goods sold of X or Z) in the aggregate ($ 6,500,000 * 25% = $ 1,625,000), the services rendered by X and Z to the foreign subsidiaries will not be considered one of the principal activities of X and Z within the meaning of paragraph (b)(7)(ii) of this section.[132]

Reg. § 1.482-2(b)(7)(v), Ex. 10

> X and Y are members of the same group of controlled entities. X is a finance company engaged in financing automobile loans. In connection with such loans it requires the borrower to have life insurance in the amount of the loan. Although X's borrowers are not required to take out life insurance from any particular insurance company, at the same time that the loan agreement is being finalized, X's employees suggest that the borrower take out life insurance from Y, which is an agency for life insurance companies. Since there would be a delay in the processing of the loan if some other company were selected by the borrower, almost all of X's borrowers take out life insurance through Y. Because of this utilization of its influential relationship with its borrowers, X is peculiarly capable of rendering selling services to Y and, since a substantial amount of Y's business is derived from X's borrowers, such selling services are a principal element in the operation of Y's insurance business. In addition, the value of the services is substantially in excess of the costs incurred by X. Thus, the selling services rendered by X to Y are an integral part of the business activity of a member of the controlled group as described in paragraph (b)(7)(iii) of this section.[133]

A taxpayer seeking the benefit of the cost only safe harbor need only satisfy itself of the reasonableness of the method for allocating and apportioning total services costs to the controlled service and ensure that such services are not "integral" to the business operations of either the service provider or the recipient (as determined using the three objective and one subjective tests described above).

---

[131] Reg. § 1.482-2(b)(3).

[132] Reg. § 1.482-2(b)(7)(v), Ex. 4.

[133] Reg. § 1.482-2(b)(7)(v), Ex. 10.

¶570.03

Other than the cost only safe harbor provisions of Reg. § 1.482-2(b)(7), the historical services provisions do not describe specified methods to determine an arm's length charge.

.04 Costs or Deductions

Whether the services are considered integral or non-integral, an intercompany charge must at least be sufficient to cover the provider's costs. Therefore, one must determine costs that must be reimbursed, generally taking into account both direct and indirect costs for the purpose. Direct costs are those identified specifically with a particular service. These would include compensation and travel expenses of employees engaged in performing the services, the costs of materials and supplies consumed in rendering the services and other costs, such as those for overseas cables.[134] Indirect costs are those that are not specifically identified with a particular activity or service, but that relate to the direct costs. Expenses such as utilities, occupancy, supervisory and clerical compensation, and other overhead burdens of the department incurring the direct costs are examples of includable indirect costs. Indirect costs also generally include an appropriate share of the expenses of supporting departments and other allocable general and administrative expenses.[135]

The regulations provide that certain costs may not be taken into account. They include interest expense on indebtedness not incurred specifically for the benefit of another member of the group, expenses associated with the issuance of stock and maintenance of shareholder relations, and expenses of compliance with regulations or policies imposed on the renderer by its government that are not directly related to the service in question.[136]

.05 Allocation and Apportionment

To determine total costs included in an arm's length charge, it is necessary to allocate and apportion indirect costs to a particular service. It may also be necessary to allocate and apportion the total costs (direct and indirect) of a particular service among group members when that service is undertaken for the joint benefit of two or more members of the group. The regulations provide that, although the use of one or more bases may be appropriate in establishing the method of allocation and apportionment, consideration should be given to all bases and factors, including, for example, total expenses, asset size, sales, manufacturing expenses, payroll, space utilized, and time spent.[137]

When one member of a controlled group has allocated and apportioned costs in an attempt to reflect an arm's length charge for services, the method used will generally not be challenged by the IRS provided such member employs generally accepted accounting principles and the method is consistently applied.[138] Indirect costs, such as the costs incurred by supporting departments, may be apportioned to other departments on the basis of reasonable overall estimates or reflected in the other departments' costs by applying departmental overhead rates. In either case,

---

[134] Reg. § 1.482-2(b)(4)(ii).
[135] Reg. § 1.482-2(b)(4)(iii).
[136] Reg. § 1.482-2(b)(5).

[137] Reg. § 1.482-2(b)(6)(ii).
[138] Reg. § 1.482-2(b)(6)(i).

the allocation and apportionment of costs must be made on the basis of the full cost as opposed to the incremental cost.[139]

¶ 580 Proposed Global Dealing Regulations

.01 General Principles of Proposed Regulations

On March 2, 1998, the U.S. Treasury released the long-awaited proposed regulations on global dealing.[140] The trading nations of the world that regularly deal in cross-border financial products have struggled with allocation methods to apportion gains and losses among the appropriate taxing jurisdictions. The Organisation for Economic Co-operation and Development issued a discussion draft on this topic in 1997. While the Treasury has issued general apportionment regulations in the past, it has not heretofore issued regulations that deal specifically with the allocation of gains and losses on cross-border dealing of financial instruments.

Scope of Application. The proposed global dealing regulations are the first transfer pricing regulations to deal specifically with the global trading of financial instruments. The lack of transfer pricing regulatory guidelines for global trading has led many financial institutions to enter into advance pricing agreements ("APAs") with the IRS. In 1994, the IRS published Notice 94-40, which described the IRS's experience with global dealing transactions in the APA process. The typical global trading APA involved a profit-split method based on a three-factor formula. Notice 94-40 was intended to provide guidance only in those situations in which the global dealing operations were conducted in a functionally fully integrated manner. The proposed regulations are broader and intended to apply to global dealing operations, whether or not the operations are functionally fully integrated. Accordingly, the potential scope of the regulations is broad and may have an impact on banks, brokerage firms, and various types of financial institutions.

Prop. Reg. § 1.482-8(a)(2) defines "global dealing operation," "participant," "regular dealer in securities," and other terms that apply for purposes of these regulations. A "global dealing operation" consists of the execution of customer transactions (including marketing, sales, pricing, and risk management activities) in a particular financial product or line of financial products, in multiple tax jurisdictions and/or through multiple participants. However, the global dealing operation need not be conducted around the world or on a 24-hour basis. Instead, to be considered a global dealing operation under the proposed regulations, the operation need only perform one of the enumerated functions in more than one tax jurisdiction.

The taking of proprietary positions, other than in a dealer capacity, and traditional lending activities are excluded from the definition of a global dealing operation. Thus, a hedge fund that does not have customers is not covered by these regulations. Only transactions that are entered into in a dealer capacity are covered.

---

[139] Reg. § 1.482-2(b)(6)(ii).

[140] *See* Breindel, *et al.*, "U.S. Treasury Proposed Global Dealing Regulations," 16 *Tax Notes International* 837

(March 16, 1998); Chip and Beattie, "Proposed IRS Global Dealing Regulations Warrant Prompt Attention from Multinational Banks, Securities Firms," 6 *Tax Management Transfer Pricing Report* 893 (April 8, 1998).

A "participant" is defined as a controlled taxpayer that is either (i) a regular dealer in securities or (ii) a member of a group of controlled taxpayers that includes a regular dealer in securities. The non-dealer member must conduct one or more activities "related to the activities" of that dealer. Related activities include marketing, sales, pricing, risk management activities, and possibly brokering. Related activities do not include credit analysis, accounting services, back office services, or the provision of a guarantee of one or more transactions entered into by a regular dealer in securities or other participants. The current regulations under Code Sec. 482 would apply to routine functions in that situation.

A "security" is defined as a security in the meaning of Code Sec. 472(c)(2) or foreign currency. A Code Sec. 472(c)(2) security encompasses any option, forward contract, or other similar derivative financial instruments in interest rate, currency or security and a hedge position with respect to a security as well as a security in a traditional sense, such as stock, bonds and partnership interest. Commodity transactions are excluded from the definition.

Segregating Transactions. Another potentially significant issue that arises in the proposed regulations is related to the segregation of transactions. The preamble to the proposed regulations states that it may be necessary to segregate each dealing activity and determine on a transaction-by-transaction basis within each dealing activity which method provides the most reliable measure of an arm's length price. An example given is one in which transactions in notional principal contracts require a different method than foreign exchange trading activity. In fact, the preamble states that the best method rule may even require that different methods be used to determine whether different controlled transactions are priced at arm's length *even within the same product line.* The provisions on segregation appear to apply to both the transactional methods and the profit-split methods. Further, non-dealing activities must be segregated from dealing activities, and priced according to current regulations.[141]

Comparability Analysis. Because of the special nature of a global trading operation, the proposed regulations provide factors for determining comparability in lieu of or addition to the factors provided in Reg. § 1.482-1(d)(3).[142] These factors generally focus on specific features of product subject to dealing, including level of market, pricing and brokering practices, market risks such as volatility and liquidity, counter-parties' credit risks, etc.

Arm's Length Range. Reg. § 1.482-1(e)(1) of the current regulations applies in determining arm's length range for purposes of global dealing operations. The preamble to the proposed regulations states that the specific nature of financial products such as high volatility and thin profit margins earned by participants should be considered among other facts and circumstances in determining the reliability of the arm's length range. It further states that close proximity in time between a controlled transaction and an uncontrolled transaction may be a more relevant factor in a global dealing operation than in other types of transactions.

---

[141] *See* Prop. Reg. § 1.482-8(a)(2)(i).   [142] Prop. Reg. § 1.482-8(a)(3).

.02 The Transfer Pricing Methods

The proposed regulations contain new specified transfer pricing methods for global dealing operations that replace the current specified methods in Reg. § 1.482-3 through Reg. § 1.482-6. The proposed regulations specify four methods that can be used to allocate dealing income. Three of the four methods are transaction-based; the fourth is profit-based. The transactional methods include the comparable uncontrolled financial transaction ("CUFT") method, the gross margin method, and the gross markup method. Within the profit-based method are two separate methods: the total profit-split and the residual profit-split. These methods are described in greater detail below.

The proposed regulations will apply to taxable years beginning after final regulations are published, although a retroactive election of the final regulations may be possible. In the past, for those transactions for which Notice 94-40 did not apply, many financial service companies employed the CPM from the current relations under Code Sec. 482. The proposed regulations exclude the CPM as a specified method for a global dealing operation. In many cases, the CPM was much easier to apply than some of the new specified methods in the proposed regulations. In the preamble to the proposed regulations, the IRS has expressed its view that the reliable application of a CPM to a global dealing operations is unlikely because the use of unique intangibles, such as trader know-how and a different level of risk taking by participants, make reliable adjustments extremely difficult.

The regulations recognize that capital or risk-taking in a multiple legal entity controlled group is an element in global trading for which compensation must be provided, although they provide limited guidance as to how this function should be rewarded. When the capital or risk-taking function is provided by a non-dealer participant (for example, in the form of a guarantee), the related compensation is not governed by the global dealing regulations because this activity is not among the related activities that give rise to participant status. Hence, the current transfer pricing regulations would apply. When the dealer itself assumes the global dealing risk, compensation for this function is within the global dealing transfer pricing regulations. The general view expressed in the regulations is that capital is a routine function. Accordingly, in the examples related to the residual profit-split method, capital is compensated as a routine function in the first step of the residual profit-split. The residual profits are then split among the marketing and trading entities. Once capital is compensated under Code Sec. 482, the sourcing and effectively connected income rules apply. These are discussed in detail below.

Transactional Methods. Three transactional methods are proposed: the comparable uncontrolled financial transaction method, the gross margin method, and the gross markup method. As with the transactional methods in the current regulations, the reliability of these methods depends on the comparability of the financial transactions being compared, or the ability to adjust for differences.

Comparable Uncontrolled Financial Transaction Method. The comparable uncontrolled financial transaction ("CUFT") method is similar to the CUP method for tangible property and the CUT method for intangible property in the current regulations. The CUFT method evaluates whether the amount charged in a con-

¶580.02

trolled financial transaction is arm's length by reference to the amount charged in a comparable uncontrolled transaction.[143]

When the CUFT method is based on indirect evidence, participants must establish data from a public exchange or quotation media contemporaneously to the time of the transaction.[144] The fact that taxpayers are permitted to use indirect evidence provides additional options to the taxpayers beyond typical comparable transactions, which often tend to be difficult to find. Although not discussed in the proposed regulations, one possible shortcoming of this type of indirect evidence from public exchanges is that this information would tend to be available only in those situations in which market prices and bid-offer spreads are readily available in the market, such as for liquid securities that are relatively heavily traded, and when the parties are performing functions that primarily involve the buying and selling of securities. Hence, this type of indirect evidence would be less reliable in situations in which the securities or financial products are not heavily traded or when the functions and/or risks go beyond simply buying and selling securities.

Indirect evidence for a CUFT may also be provided based on internal pricing models.[145] If a company prices all transactions with its related party using the same pricing models that the company used to price transactions with third parties, and if the pricing models utilize data that could be derived from public exchanges, such as interest rates and volatilities, then this internal pricing model can be used as the basis for a CUFT. Although the proposed regulations do not give much detail on this type of indirect evidence, the limited guidance provided suggests that this may be quite promising for the more sophisticated financial taxpayers that have in-house pricing models and that tend to be market-makers. As with the data from a public exchange or quotation media, this gives taxpayers important additional options beyond typical comparable transactions. If a taxpayer uses this evidence, it will be necessary for the model to become part of the taxpayer documentation, which must be provided to the IRS upon request.

Gross Margin and Gross Markup Methods. Two other transactional methods in the proposed regulations on the global dealing are the gross margin method and the gross markup method, each quite similar in application to the other transactional methods in the current regulations for tangible property, namely, the resale price method and the cost-plus method, respectively. The gross margin and gross markup methods typically will apply when a taxpayer performs only a routine marketing or sales function as part of a global dealing operation.

The gross margin method may be used to establish an arm's length price for a transaction in which a participant resells a financial product to an unrelated party that the participant purchased from a related party. An arm's length price is determined by subtracting the appropriate gross profit from the applicable resale price for the financial product involved in the controlled transaction under review. The applicable resale price is equal to either the price at which the financial product involved is sold in an uncontrolled sale (internal comparable) or the price at which

---

[143] Prop. Reg. § 1.482-8(b).
[144] Prop. Reg. § 1.482-8(b)(3).
[145] *See* Prop. Reg. § 1.482-8(b)(5), Ex. 4.

contemporaneous resales of the same product are made (external comparable). The appropriate gross profit margin should generally be derived from comparable uncontrolled purchases and resales of the reseller involved in the controlled sale because similar characteristics are more likely to be found among different resales of financial products made by the same reseller than among sales made by other resellers. The appropriate gross profit is then computed by multiplying the applicable resale price by the gross profit margin earned in comparable uncontrolled transactions. The gross profit earned by a participant must adequately compensate for the resale functions performed and any risks assumed, including the investment of capital.[146] A participant may take title to a security and may become a party to a derivative transaction. This method can therefore also apply to an agency transaction.

The gross markup method may be used to establish an arm's length price for a transaction in which a participant purchases a financial product from an unrelated party that the participant sells to a related party. This method is different than the gross margin method because in the gross margin method the participant buys from a related party and resells to an unrelated party. The gross markup method measures an arm's length price by adding the appropriate gross profit to the participant's cost or anticipated cost of purchasing, holding, or structuring the financial product involved in the controlled transaction under review.

The appropriate gross profit is computed by multiplying the participant's cost or anticipated cost of purchasing, holding, or structuring a transaction by the gross profit markup earned in comparable uncontrolled transactions. The gross markup earned by a participant must adequately compensate for the selling functions performed and any risks assumed, including the investment of capital.[147] As in the gross margin method, a participant may take title to a security and may become a party to a derivative transaction. Again, this method can apply to an agency transaction.

As with the CUFT method, a participant may establish a gross margin or gross markup by comparing the bid and offer prices on a public exchange or quotation media. These quoted prices must be contemporaneous to the controlled transaction. This provides an additional option to the taxpayer beyond a typical external comparable transaction, which tends to be difficult to find.

One major difference in applying the CUFT method compared to the gross margin and gross markup methods is that, although close product similarity will improve the reliability of all three transactional methods, the reliability of the gross margin and gross markup methods is less dependent on product similarity than the CUFT method. Both the gross margin method and the gross markup method are more reliable when applied to situations in which a participant does not substantially contribute to the development of products or in tailoring the product to the unique requirements of a customer, such as when the participant is acting simply as a broker.

---

[146] Prop. Reg. § 1.482-8(c).   [147] Prop. Reg. § 1.482-8(d).

¶580.02

Profit-Based Methods. An important profit-based method in the proposed regulations is the profit-split method. Operating profit or loss from a global dealing operation is split based on the relative value of each participant's contribution to that combined operating profit or loss.[148] These relative values must reflect the functions performed, risks assumed, and resources employed by each participant. In some cases, a multifactor formula may be the most reliable measure of the relative value of contributions to profitability.

There is no further guidance in Notice 94-40 or in the proposed regulations as to what types of multifactor formulas may be most appropriate under the profit-split method. The regulations state it should not be assumed that the profits or losses should be shared equally among the participants. In fact, an example is provided whereby one participant may earn a profit while another participant incurs a loss, provided the arrangement is comparable to an arrangement to which two uncontrolled parties would agree. This provision is similar to the existing transfer pricing regulations for the transfer of tangible property whereby a distributor can earn profits even if the worldwide operation is experiencing losses.

Total Profit-Split Method. The total profit-split method is one of two profit-split methods specified in the regulations. This method involves a one-step process in which no distinction is made between routine and non-routine contributions. This method will tend to apply to situations in which the global dealing operation is highly integrated so that all routine and non-routine dealer functions are performed by each participant in each location.

The total profit-split method, in theory, is based on the allocation of profits by comparable uncontrolled taxpayers. Thus, the method should be based on external market benchmarks whereby unrelated parties have comparable arrangements and allocate profits in the same manner. However, even if these comparable uncontrolled transactions do not exist, the proposed regulations indicate that a taxpayer may still be able to demonstrate that the profit-split employed reflects the relative contribution of the participants by relying on other objective factors.

To determine the relative contributions, the regulations discuss various factors related to comparability standards, risk, contractual terms, and economic conditions. The only specific guidance given in the proposed regulations is in the preamble, which indicates that if a method does not rely on external market benchmarks, the reliability of the method is increased to the extent that the allocation has economic significance for non-tax purposes, such as satisfying regulatory standards and reporting or determining bonuses paid to management or traders.

In addition, an example is given whereby an allocation of profits can be based on trader compensation if the taxpayer can demonstrate that the compensation is based on the value added by the individual traders.[149]

---

[148] Prop. Reg. § 1.482-8(e)(1).

[149] Prop. Reg. § 1.482-8(e)(8), Ex. 1.

¶580.02

Residual Profit-Split Method. The other profit-based method specified in the proposed regulations is the residual profit-split method. This method involves a two-step process.

In the first step, routine functions are compensated with a market return based on the best transfer pricing method applicable to that transaction. Examples of routine contributions given in the regulations include transactions processing and credit analysis. In addition, the proposed regulations claim that a participant that guarantees obligations of or provides credit support to a related party in a global dealing operation is regarded as making a routine contribution.

After compensating the routine functions, the remaining operating profit, or residual profit, is allocated among the participants based on their respective non-routine contributions to profitability. The proposed regulations state that non-routine contributions are contributions so integral to the global dealing operation that it is impossible to segregate them and find a separate market return for the contribution.

Examples given in the regulations of non-routine contributions include pricing and risk management of financial products, product development, information technology, and marketing if the marketer substantially participates in developing a product or in tailoring the product to the unique requirements of a customer.[150]

The proposed regulations require that the first step of the residual profit-split rely on external market benchmarks. In the second step of the residual profit-split, however, it may not be possible to rely as heavily on external market benchmarks. The absence of these benchmarks in the second step does not preclude the use of the residual profit-split method if the allocation of the residual profit in the second step considers the relative contribution of each participant. This is similar to the residual profit-split specified in the existing transfer pricing regulations.

Although the CPM is not one of the specified methods under the proposed regulations, it may still be necessary to employ the CPM in the first step of the residual profit-split approach, in which routine contributions are compensated. The preamble indicates that routine functions should be compensated with a market return based on the best transfer pricing method applicable to that transaction. Although not stated in the proposed regulations, it is likely that there will be situations in which the CPM is the best transfer pricing method applicable to many routine transactions.[151]

Unspecified Methods. The proposed regulations also provide an option to use an unspecified method if it is determined to be the best method. Although neither the regulations nor the preamble state it, there may be situations when the CPM could be used as the unspecified method.

---

[150] Prop. Reg. § 1.482-8(e)(6).   [151] *See* Breindel, *supra* 140.

¶580.02

Chapter 6

Intercompany Loans and Leases

¶ 601 Intercompany Loans

.01 Overview

If one member of a controlled group makes a loan or advance directly or indirectly to, or otherwise becomes a creditor of, another member of that group, the Service is authorized to make allocations to reflect an arm's length rate of interest for the use of such loan or advance.[1] In reviewing intercompany indebtedness under Code Sec. 482, taxpayers should ask the following questions:

- Is the indebtedness subject to Code Sec. 482?

- When does interest begin to accrue?

- What is an arm's length interest rate?

- What are the withholding implications?

- What are the "interest stripping" implications?

.02 Indebtedness Subject to Code Sec. 482

In a review of intercompany indebtedness under Code Sec. 482, the first issue that must be addressed is whether the indebtedness in question is one to which Code Sec. 482 applies at all. Code Sec. 482 only applies to bona fide indebtedness between members of a controlled group.[2] Examples of such indebtedness include:

1. Loans or advances of money or other consideration (whether or not evidenced in writing); and

2. Indebtedness arising in the ordinary course of business from sales, leases, the rendition of services, or any other similar extension of credit (i.e., trade receivables).

Indebtedness that is not bona fide (e.g., contributions to capital or leases of property), however, is not subject to Code Sec. 482.[3] For Code Sec. 482 purposes, payments with respect to non bona fide indebtedness are treated according to their substance.[4]

---

[1] Reg. § 1.482-2(a)(1)(i).
[2] Reg. § 1.482-2(a)(1)(ii)(A).
[3] Reg. § 1.482-2(a)(ii)(B).
[4] *Id.*

.03 Accrual of Interest

Subject to several exceptions, interest on bona fide intercompany indebtedness begins to accrue on the day after the indebtedness arises and ends on the day the indebtedness is paid, canceled, offset, or is otherwise satisfied.[5]

The regulations contain several exceptions for receivables incurred in the ordinary course of business from sales, services, etc., and that are not evidenced in a document that requires the payment of interest (i.e., "trade receivables").[6] For purposes of these exceptions, a trade receivable is deemed to arise at the time that economic performance occurs (as defined by Code Sec. 461(h)).[7]

General Trade Receivables. For general trade receivables, interest does not begin to accrue until the first day of the third calendar month following the month in which the trade receivable arises.[8] For example, if a general trade receivable arises on January 10th, interest will not begin to accrue until April 1st.

Business Conducted Outside of the United States. If the debtor actively conducts a trade or business outside the United States, and that trade or business gives rise to the trade receivable, interest begins to accrue on the first day of the fourth calendar month following the month in which the indebtedness arose.[9] For example, if the trade receivable arises on January 10th, interest will not begin to accrue until May 1st.

Industry Practice Exception. The period before interest begins to accrue on trade receivables can be extended to match the interest-free period common for similar transactions among unrelated parties in the creditor's industry.[10]

Property Purchased for Resale Abroad. If the trade receivable arises from the sale of property that will be resold to unrelated persons in a particular foreign country, the related parties may defer the accrual of interest for a number of days equal to the reseller's average collection period (for sales of the same property within the same product group sold to unrelated persons in the ordinary course of business in the same foreign country), plus 10 days.[11] However, this period of non-accrual may not exceed 183 days.[12]

.04 Arm's Length Interest Rate

An arm's length interest rate is the rate that was charged, or would have been charged, at the time the indebtedness arose in independent transactions with or between unrelated parties under similar circumstances.[13] The determination of an arm's length interest rate is made by considering all relevant factors, including the amount and duration of the loan, the security provided by the borrower, the borrower's credit rating, and the prevailing interest rate for comparable loans between unrelated parties.[14]

---

[5] Reg. § 1.482-2(a)(1)(iii)(A).
[6] Reg. § 1.482-2(a)(1)(iii)(A).
[7] Reg. § 1.482-2(a)(1)(iii)(A).
[8] Reg. § 1.482-2(a)(1)(iii)(B).
[9] Reg. § 1.482-2(a)(1)(iii)(C).

[10] Reg. § 1.482-2(a)(1)(iii)(D).
[11] Reg. § 1.482-2(a)(1)(iii)(E)(1).
[12] Reg. § 1.482-2(a)(1)(iii)(E)(2).
[13] Reg. § 1.482-2(a)(2)(i).
[14] Reg. § 1.482-2(a)(2)(i).

If the loan represents the proceeds of a loan obtained by the related party lender at the situs of the related party borrower, the arm's length rate of interest shall equal the rate of interest actually paid by the related party lender, increased by an amount that reflects the costs incurred by the lender in borrowing such amounts and making such loans.[15] However, if the related parties can establish a more appropriate interest rate under the standards of Code Sec. 482, then such rate may be used.[16]

The regulations contain provisions specifying safe harbor interest rates for intercompany indebtedness incurred after May 8, 1986.[17] The rate of interest actually charged will meet the safe harbor requirements if the rate is between 100 percent and 130 percent of the applicable federal rate (AFR).[18] In the case of a sale-leaseback transaction described in Code Sec. 1274(e), the lower limit is 110 percent of the AFR, compounded semiannually.[19] If no interest is charged, or if interest is charged at a rate lower than the lower limit (100 percent of the AFR), then such lower limit, compounded semiannually, will be considered to be an arm's length rate.[20] If the rate actually charged is higher than the upper limit (130 percent of the AFR), then such upper limit, compounded semiannually, will be considered an arm's length rate, unless the parties can establish a more appropriate rate.[21]

There are two important exceptions to the safe harbor interest rates. First, the safe harbor rules do not apply if the lender is regularly engaged in the business of making loans to unrelated parties.[22] Second, the safe harbor rules do not apply to loans when their principal or interest is expressed in a foreign currency.[23] In either instance, the arm's length rate of interest shall be determined under the general rule contained in Reg. § 1.482-2(a)(2)(i).

.05 Coordination with Other Code Provisions

Code Sec. 482 can apply even where other Code provisions would also be applicable.[24] In these circumstances, the order in which the different Code provisions will be applied is as follows:

1. The substance of the transaction is determined based on all of the relevant facts and circumstances.

2. The non-Code Sec. 482 Code provision is applied to determine whether any amount other than stated interest is to be treated as interest, and if so, the amount according to the provisions of such other Code provision.

3. Code Sec. 482 and the regulations pertaining to loans and advances are applied to determine whether the interest rate charged (as adjusted by any other Code provision) is equal to an arm's length amount of interest.

4. Other Code Sec. 482 provisions may be applied to reflect an arm's length transaction based on the principal amount of the loan or advance and the

---

[15] Reg. § 1.482-2(a)(2)(ii).
[16] Reg. § 1.482-2(a)(2)(ii).
[17] Reg. § 1.482-2(a)(2)(iii)(A).
[18] Reg. § 1.482-2(a)(2)(iii)(B)(1).
[19] Reg. § 1.482-2(a)(2)(iii)(B)(3).

[20] Reg. § 1.482-2(a)(2)(iii)(B)(2).
[21] Reg. § 1.482-2(a)(2)(iii)(B)(3).
[22] Reg. § 1.482-2(a)(2)(iii)(D).
[23] Reg. § 1.482-2(a)(2)(iii)(E).
[24] Reg. § 1.482-2(a)(3).

arm's length rate of interest previously determined (e.g., restating the sales price of tangible property in a deferred sales transaction).

.06 Withholding on Imputed Code Sec. 482 Interest Charges

Code Secs. 1441 and 1442 impose a 30 percent withholding requirement on payments of fixed or determinable annual or periodic income (e.g., interest and royalties) to foreign entities. Liability for the withholding tax attaches at the time when such income is "paid." Because of this payment prerequisite, taxpayers and commentators have long argued that an allocation under Code Sec. 482 does not give rise to a withholding liability.[25]

Recently issued withholding regulations (effective January 1, 2001) take the opposite position. These regulations state that a payment is made to the extent that income subject to withholding is allocated under Code Sec. 482.[26] The regulation further provides that payment is considered to be made regardless of whether cash or property is actually transferred.[27] For the purpose of determining liability for withholding, the regulations provide that payment is deemed to occur on the last day of the taxable year in which the transactions giving rise to the withholding obligation take place.[28] Although these regulations are not effective until January 1, 2001, the IRS has been litigating cases on the basis of withholding on Code Sec. 482 allocations for some time. The primary issue in these cases was whether an actual payment, not a deemed payment stemming from a Code Sec. 482 adjustment, is required to trigger the withholding obligations.[29]

.07 Code Sec. 163(j) Earnings Stripping Rules

Taxpayers must also consider the impact of the Code Sec. 163(j) earnings stripping rules on their related party loans. Although a complete discussion of Code Sec. 163(j) is beyond the scope of this book, the salient provisions are summarized below:

Code Sec. 163(j) limits the deductibility of interest paid or accrued by U.S. and certain foreign corporations to related persons in situations where all or a portion of that interest is exempt from U.S. taxation (these rules also limit the deductibility of certain interest associated with a debt that is guaranteed by a foreign related party). Where interest is paid to a foreign related party that qualifies for tax treaty relief from all or a portion of the U.S. withholding tax otherwise payable, all or a portion of the interest will be considered exempt from U.S. taxes for purposes of Code Sec. 163(j). For purposes of these rules, all members of the same affiliated group of corporations (as defined by Code Sec. 1504(a)) are treated as one taxpayer, regardless of whether a consolidated return is filed.

If the above requirements are satisfied, Code Sec. 163(j) causes interest to be disqualified and not currently deductible to the extent that (1) the debtor corporation's debt to equity ratio exceeds 1.5:1 and (2) the debtor's net interest expense

---

[25] *See* generally, Stark and Bailiff, "Do Section 482 Allocations to Foreign Entities Trigger a Withholding Obligation?" 82 *J. Tax'n* 178 (March 1995).

[26] Reg. § 1.1441-2(e)(2).

[27] Reg. § 1.1441-2(e)(2).

[28] Reg. § 1.1441-2(e)(2).

[29] *See Central de Gas de Chihuahua, S.A.*, CCH Dec. 49,763, 102 TC 515 (1994) (concerning imputed rental charges).

exceeds 50 percent of (i) its adjusted taxable income, plus (ii) its excess limitation carry-forward. If interest is not deductible under Code Sec. 163(j) for the current year, the interest may be carried forward and deducted in a subsequent year, to the extent that Code Sec. 163(j) does not prevent a deduction of such interest in the subsequent year.

¶ 610 Leasing Tangible Property

.01 In General

Frequently one member of a controlled group owns real property or equipment that it leases to another member of the controlled group. As with other types of intercompany transactions, if possession, use, or occupancy of tangible property owned or leased by one member of a group of controlled entities is transferred by lease or other arrangement to another member of that group, and if the transfer is made without an intercompany charge, or at a charge that is not arm's length, the IRS is authorized to make an allocation under Code Sec. 482 to reflect an arm's length charge.[30]

.02 The Regulations

The regulations provide that an arm's length rental charge is determined by reference to independent transactions with or between unrelated parties under similar circumstances. The period and location of use, the owner's investment in the property or rent paid for the property, expenses of maintaining the property, the type of property involved, its condition, and all other relevant facts are to be considered. In other words, an arm's length charge is the amount of rent that was charged or would have been charged for the use of the same or similar property, during the time it was in use, in independent transactions with or between unrelated parties.[31] The regulations further provide that when possession, use, or occupancy of only a portion of such property is transferred, the determination of the arm's length charge and the allocation shall be made with reference to the portion transferred.[32]

For subleases, if neither of the related entities is regularly engaged in the trade or business of renting property of the same general type, the arm's length rental charge generally will be an amount equal to all the deductions claimed by the original lessee that are attributable to the property (or subleased portions of the property) for the period the property is used by the sublessee. Such deductions include rent paid or accrued as well as other direct and indirect expenses, such as maintenance, repairs, utilities, and management fees. Under the regulations, however, the taxpayer is given the opportunity to establish a more appropriate rental charge.[33]

.03 Cases

Under relevant case law, where the parties to a rental agreement are related, closer attention is given to that agreement.[34] In addition, if related parties occupy

---

[30] Reg. § 1.482-2(c)(1).
[31] Reg. § 1.482-2(c)(2)(i).
[32] Reg. § 1.482-2(c)(1).

[33] Reg. § 1.482-2(c)(2)(iii).
[34] See, e.g., Safeway Steel Scaffolds Co., 79-1 USTC ¶ 9253, 590 F.2d 1360 (5th Cir. 1979).

the same space, the lessee must be able to supply evidence as to the amount of space occupied, whether the lessees shares the space equally, and whether the lessees paid any other amounts as rental for the space occupied by them.[35]

It should also be noted that if a sublessee corporation and lessee corporation are related, excess rent paid by the sublessee to the lessee over the lessee's annual obligation under the lease may not be deductible. For example, in *Bluefeld Caterer, Inc.*,[36] Corporation 1 ("C1"), a loss corporation, subleased a building to related Corporation 2 ("C2"). The rent paid by C2 to C1 was greater than the rent paid by C1 to the owner of the building. The apparent reason for this arrangement was to allow C1 to use its NOL carryover while generating a current deduction in C2. The Tax Court in *Bluefeld* held that the rental agreement between C1 and C2 was not at arm's length and allocated back to C2 the excess of rent paid by C2 to C1 over the rent paid by C1 to the owner.

Central De Gas De Chihuahua. The allocation of leases and/or rental income was also addressed in *Central De Gas De Chihuahua*.[37] There, Central De Gas De Chihuahua ("the taxpayer"), a Mexican corporation, rented a fleet of tractor-trailers to a related Mexican corporation, Hidro Gass de Juarez, S.A., for which Hidro did not pay rent. The taxpayer rented equipment that was used to transport liquefied petroleum gas from the United States to the Mexican border, where it was sold to a Mexican government-operated oil company for distribution in Mexico. Central De Gas De Chihuahua and Hidro Gas de Juarez were under common control within the meaning of Code Sec. 482. Therefore, the IRS, acting under Code Sec. 482, allocated to the taxpayer the amount of $2,320,800 as fair rental value of the equipment for 1990 and determined that the taxpayer was liable for the 30 percent tax imposed by Code Sec. 881 on that amount. Code Sec. 881(a) imposes a tax of 30 percent of the amount received from sources within the United States by a foreign corporation as rents.[38]

The taxpayer argued that, for Code Sec. 881(a) to apply, there must be an actual payment of the income item and that the allocation of rent to the taxpayer from Hidro under Code Sec. 482 does not satisfy that requirement. The IRS countered with the assertion that the allocation of rent to the taxpayer under Code Sec. 482 provides sufficient grounds for imposing the 30 percent tax under that section. The Tax Court agreed with the IRS and ruled in its favor.

Central De Gas De Chihuahua represents an important victory for the IRS, allowing it to expand the reach of Code Sec. 482 beyond allocation of income, deductions, and credits, to impute the flow of cash from rental income and thereby trigger a liability for withholding tax under Code Sec. 881.

---

[35] *See*, e.g., *R.M. Cooper*, CCH Dec. 32,448, 61 TC 599 (1974), in which the Tax Court denied a deduction for rent expense, at least in part because the taxpayer did not provide such information.

[36] *Bluefeld Caterer, Inc.*, CCH Dec. 29,504(M), 28 TCM 315, TC Memo. 1969-56 (1969).

[37] *Central de Gas de Chihuahua, S.A.*, CCH Dec. 49,763, 102 TC 515; 102 TC No. 19 (1994) (Slip. Op.).

[38] *See* Levey & Graver, "Chihuahua: Tax Court Accepts IRS Withholding on Deemed Payments," 4 *J. of Int'l Tax'n* 148 (April 1995).

¶610.03

.04 Notice 95-53

In Notice 95-53 the IRS announced its intention to use its authority under Code Sec. 482 to reallocate income, deductions, credits and allowances between related parties engaging in "lease stripping transactions." The IRS was concerned that taxpayers were entering into leasing transactions that shift (1) income to tax-exempt taxpayers or taxpayers with available NOLs and (2) depreciation and other deductions related to the leased property to taxpayers with positive tax liabilities. The IRS believes the claimed tax treatment separates income from related deductions.

Examples of lease stripping transactions provided by the IRS in Notice 95-53 include "transferred basis transactions," where a tax exempt transferor sells or assigns a lease receivable (i.e., the right to receive future lease payments) to a third party in connection with a subsequent transfer of the leased property in a carryover basis transaction (e.g., Code Sec. 351) to another third party. Other stripping transaction include sales by a partnership of a "lease receivable" to a third party followed by a transfer of the leased property in a transaction where basis is not reduced to a tax-exempt partner who was allocated the income resulting from the lease receivables sale. The IRS stated that the parties in lease stripping transactions should be characterized as under common control for purposes of Code Sec. 482 because they are acting in concert to arbitrarily shift income or deductions.

Notice 95-53 also states that, depending on the facts, the IRS may determine that one or more of the following authorities are also applicable to a lease stripping transaction: (1) Code Sec. 269, Code Sec. 382, Code Sec. 446(b), Code Sec. 701 or Code Sec. 704; (2) authorities recharacterizing assignments or accelerations of future income as financings; (3) assignment of income principles; (4) business purpose doctrine or (5) substance over form doctrines. Finally, Notice 95-53 states that the IRS intends to address certain lease stripping transaction by using its authority under Code Sec. 7701(l) to promulgate regulations recharacterizing multi-party financing transactions as transactions directly between two or more parties. The anticipated Treasury Regulations will apply for stripping transactions where any "significant element" was entered into after October 12, 1995.

The IRS has released two Field Service Advice memorandums ("FSAs") in which it challenged the proposed tax consequences of separate lease stripping transactions involving the sale and leaseback of equipment.[39] Although the IRS's challenge of these transactions and their anticipated tax consequences was not unexpected, what was unexpected was its reliance on the Code Sec. 482 transfer pricing rules. In both instances, the IRS maintained that Code Sec. 482 could be applied because otherwise unrelated parties were "controlled by the same interests," as evidenced by their acting in concert pursuant to a common design to improperly shift income and deductions through their contractual relationships. Taken to its logical conclusion, the IRS's Code Sec. 482 analysis could be used to

---

[39] FSA 199909005 (Nov. 17, 1998); FSA 199914018 (Jan. 5, 1999).

challenge any transaction in which the parties have bargained for a particular tax advantage.

The transactions challenged by the IRS in the FSAs were complex lease stripping transactions. The anticipated tax consequences of the transactions particularly troubled the IRS because the income attributable to sale/leaseback transactions was allocated to persons who were not subject to U.S. taxation and the related deductions and losses were allocated to U.S. taxpayers. In both FSAs, the IRS applied Code Sec. 482 to alternatively disregard portions of the overall transaction or to reallocate income and deductions such that the resulting economic benefits were not the benefits bargained for by the parties.

What is particularly disturbing about these FSAs is that none of the parties identified by the IRS as being "controlled by the same interests" would be treated as such under a traditional Code Sec. 482 transfer pricing analysis. There was no interrelated ownership, directorship, family control, or any other indicia of common control. The IRS applied Code Sec. 482 solely on the basis of a contractual relationship entered into by unrelated third parties. The IRS claimed authority for doing so under Notice 95-53, 1995-2 CB 334, in which the IRS warned taxpayers that it would challenge lease stripping transactions under Code Sec. 482. However, Notice 95-53 does not give any indication that the IRS would apply Code Sec. 482 in the situation described in the FSAs, where the basis for finding common control among otherwise unrelated parties was the execution of a contract. Furthermore, in neither the FSA nor Notice 95-53 did the IRS cite any case in which a court upheld the application of Code Sec. 482 solely on the basis of a contractual relationship.

Chapter 7

Penalties

¶ 701 Overview

For the past forty-five years, Congress has expressed concern over the ability of multinational enterprises ("MNEs") to shift income out of the U.S., thereby reducing the amount of U.S. Federal income tax paid, by manipulating transfer prices.[1] In 1999, IRS Publication 3218 estimated that the average annual Code Sec. 482 tax gap (i.e., the loss of tax revenues resulting from non-compliance with Code Sec. 482) amounts to $2.8 billion.[2]

The IRS maintained that a principal obstacle to the administration and enforcement of Code Sec. 482 has been taxpayers' failure to comply with the arm's length standard and document their compliance on a contemporaneous basis.[3] As a consequence, the IRS and taxpayers have engaged in lengthy transfer pricing litigation in which the parties adopted extreme positions. In response, Congress and the IRS implemented a five-part strategy to improve the administration of Code Sec. 482. The five parts were:

- Finalize the substantive regulations under Code Sec. 482;

- Enact a penalty and contemporaneous documentation regime;

- Build a worldwide consensus behind the arm's length principle;

- Promote the APA program; and

- Coordinate of IRS technical and litigation support for litigation involving cross-border transactions.

The second part of this strategy, the penalty and contemporaneous documentation regime, is the subject of this chapter and chapter 10.

---

[1] This concern was strongly expressed in the Omnibus Consolidated and Emergency Supplemental Appropriations Bill Act, Pub. L. 105-277, when Congress directed the Treasury Department to prepare a report on the application and administration of Code Sec. 482.

[2] IRS Pub. 3218, April 21, 1999, pp. 2-3.

[3] IRS Pub. 3218, April 21, 1999, p. iii.

It is important to note that IRS imposition of the § 6662(e) and (h) penalties has increased drastically. The IRS's transfer pricing penalty oversight committee approved 54 of 55 penalty years submitted to it for its fiscal year ended September 30, 2006. This was significantly more than previous years, as detailed below.

The penalty review board approved:

- All 27 of 30 tax years submitted in fiscal 2005;
- 32 of 33 tax years submitted in fiscal 2004;
- All 34 tax years submitted in fiscal 2003;
- All 15 tax years submitted in fiscal 2002;
- All 10 tax years submitted in fiscal 2001;
- All 30 tax years submitted in fiscal 2000; and
- At least 32 of the 44 tax years submitted in 1999 and prior years.[4]

From 2007 to 2009, the IRS assessed penalties in roughly 20% to 40% of the cases in which transfer pricing adjustments were issued. Further, the IRS predicted that incidence of penalties would continue to increase at least through 2011, due to the more taxpayers being examined as a result of internal efforts to boost electronic review, as well as hiring efforts to augment the number of international examiners working on transfer pricing cases.[5]

¶ 710 History of Code Sec. 482 Enforcement

.01 *Historical Enforcement Problems*

IRS Publication 3218 identified several factors that have historically hindered the effective enforcement of Code Sec. 482. These factors include:

- Taxpayers typically did not take the arm's length standard into account in setting their prices or in reporting their taxable income from intercompany transactions. Instead, transfer pricing was only considered once that taxpayer was being examined. As a consequence, taxpayers had incentive to take positions to support extreme results.

- The 1968 regulations contained an hierarchy of TPMs that often led to disputes when either the taxpayer or the IRS asserted that a lower-hierarchy TPM should be applied.

- IRS examiners faced taxpayer delays in collecting records and information located outside the United States. As a consequence, IRS examiners were forced to close transfer pricing examinations without adjustments, or to make adjustments based on limited data.

- Transfer pricing disputes often became contentious and protracted due to the IRS's lack of facts and because of polar positions taken by the parties in litigation.

---

[4] "Penalties: Transfer Pricing Penalties Approved Doubled From 2005 to 2006, Ng Says," 15 *Tax Mgt Transfer Pricing Report*, 522 (Nov. 22, 2006).

[5] *See* Ernst & Young 2009 Global Transfer Pricing Survey, United States, *available at http://www.eoy-award.com/GL/en/Services/Tax/2009-Global-Transfer-Pricing-survey—United-States-of-America.*

.02 IRS Plan to Improve Enforcement

In response to the above-described factors, the IRS in 1992 adopted a five-part strategy to improve administration and enforcement of Code Sec. 482:

- The IRS finalized its substantive transfer pricing regulations in 1994.

- The IRS persuaded Congress to enact a contemporaneous documentation requirement in Code Sec. 6662(e) in 1993. This requirement was supplemented by regulations that were finalized in 1996.

- The U.S. built a worldwide consensus on the appropriateness of the arm's length standard for transfer pricing. This consensus is reflected in the OECD's *Transfer Pricing Guidelines for Multinational Enterprises*, which was issued in 1995 and updated in 1999 and 2009.[6]

- The IRS has successfully promoted the use of its APA program to resolve transfer pricing disputes on a proactive basis.

- The IRS developed procedures to coordinate technical and litigation support for litigation involving cross-border transactions.

¶ 720 U.S. Transfer Pricing Penalties

There are two types of penalties that can generally be assessed in the transfer pricing context: (1) valuation misstatement penalties and (2) reporting penalties. In addition to these penalties, general civil and criminal tax penalties and interest charges may be assessed.

.01 Valuation Misstatement Penalties

Code Sec. 6662(e) and (h) sets forth penalties of 20 and 40 percent for certain increases in U.S. income tax attributable to Code Sec. 482 adjustments. These penalties may be assessed on both a transactional and a net adjustment basis. The primary objective of the transfer pricing penalty was to improve taxpayer compliance with the arm's length standard by strongly encouraging taxpayers to make reasonable efforts to determine and document arm's length prices.

20 Percent Substantial Valuation Misstatement Penalty. A 20 percent penalty may be assessed by the IRS under Code Sec. 6662(a) for a substantial valuation misstatement. In the transfer pricing context, Code Sec. 6662(e) defines a substantial valuation misstatement as any one of the following: (1) the price for any property or services (or for the use of any property) claimed on a return in connection with any transaction between taxpayers controlled by the same interests that is 200 percent or more, or 50 percent or less, of the correct arm's length amount; or (2) the net Code Sec. 482 transfer price adjustment for the taxable year exceeds the lesser of $5 million or 10% of the taxpayer's gross receipts. However, no penalty will be imposed unless the substantial valuation misstatement exceeds $5,000 in the case of individuals or $10,000 in the case of a corporation other than an S corporation or a personal holding company.[7]

---

[6] The OECD approved the 2010 revision of the Transfer Pricing Guidelines on July 22, 2010. *See http://www.oecd.org.*

[7] Code Sec. 6662(e)(2).

40 Percent Gross Valuation Misstatement Penalty. A 40 percent penalty may be assessed by the IRS under Code Sec. 6662(h) for a gross valuation misstatement. A gross valuation misstatement is any one of the following: (1) the price for any property or services (or for the use of any property) claimed on a return in connection with any transaction between taxpayers controlled by the same interests when it is 400 percent or more, or 25 percent or less, of the correct arm's length amount; or (2) the net Code Sec. 482 transfer price adjustment for the taxable year exceeds the lesser of $20 million or 20 percent of the taxpayer's gross receipts.

	Transactional	*Net Adjustment*
Substantial Valuation *(20% penalty)*	Price or value is 200% or more (50% or less) than the correct amount	Net adjustment exceeds the lesser of $5 million or 10% of gross receipts
Gross Valuation *(40% penalty)*	Price or value is 400% or more (25% or less) than the correct amount	Net adjustment exceeds the lesser of $20 million or 20% of gross receipts

.02 Application of the Valuation Misstatement Penalty

Whether a valuation misstatement has been made is determined based on the results of controlled transactions reported on the taxpayer's tax return.[8] If the taxpayer is a member of a consolidated group, the determination is made based on the consolidated tax return.[9] If the taxpayer files an amended tax return, the results reported therein will be used only if the taxpayer filed the amended return before it was contacted by the IRS about the original return.[10]

> *Example:* Taxpayer files its Year 1 income tax return on September 15th of Year 2 showing taxable income from intercompany transactions of $500,000. On March 1st of Year 3, Taxpayer files an amended tax return for Year 1 in which it increases its taxable income from intercompany transactions to $700,000. On December 1st of Year 3, the IRS commences a transfer pricing examination of the Taxpayer for Year 1, in which the IRS determines that the correct amount of taxable income from intercompany transactions is $800,000. Under these facts, the application of the substantial valuation misstatement penalty will be made based on the amount claimed on the Taxpayer's amended tax return ($700,000) and not the return as originally filed ($500,000).

.03 Setoff Allocation Rule

If the taxpayer meets the requirements of Reg. §1.6662-6(d) (amounts excluded from adjustments) with respect to some, but not all, of the allocations made under Code Sec. 482, then for the purpose of determining the net Code Sec. 482

---

[8] Reg. § 1.6662-6(a)(2).
[9] Reg. § 1.6662-6(a)(2).
[10] Reg. § 1.6662-6(a)(2).

adjustment, setoffs under § 1.482-1(g)(4) must be applied ratably against all such allocations.

Reg. § 1.6662-6(c)(4), Ex.

(i) The Internal Revenue Service makes the following section 482 adjustments for the taxable year:

(1) Attributable to an increase in gross income because of an increase in royalty payments	$9,000,000
(2) Attributable to an increase in sales proceeds due to a decrease in the profit margin of a related buyer	6,000,000
(3) Because of a setoff under § 1.482-1(g)(4)	(5,000,000)
Total section 482 adjustments	10,000,000

(ii) The taxpayer meets the requirements of paragraph (d) with respect to adjustment number one, but not with respect to adjustment number two. The five million dollar setoff will be allocated ratably against the nine million dollar adjustment ($9,000,000/$15,000,000 × $5,000,000 = $3,000,000) and the six million dollar adjustment ($6,000,000/$15,000,000 × $5,000,000 = $2,000,000). Accordingly, in determining the net section 482 adjustment, the nine million dollar adjustment is reduced to six million dollars ($9,000,000 – $3,000,000) and the six million dollar adjustment is reduced to four million dollars ($6,000,000 – $2,000,000). Therefore, the net section 482 adjustment equals four million dollars.

.04 Reasonable Cause Exception

The transactional penalty will not be imposed on any portion of an underpayment with respect to which the requirements of § 1.6664-4 are met. In applying the provisions of § 1.6664-4 in a case in which the taxpayer has relied on professional analysis in determining its transfer pricing, whether the professional is an employee of, or related to, the taxpayer is not determinative in evaluating whether the taxpayer reasonably relied in good faith on advice. A taxpayer that meets the requirements of paragraph (d) of this section with respect to an allocation under Code Sec. 482 will be treated as having established that there was reasonable cause and good faith with respect to that item for purposes of § 1.6664-4. If a substantial or gross valuation misstatement under the transactional penalty also constitutes (or is part of) a substantial or gross valuation misstatement under the net adjustment penalty, then the rules of paragraph (d) of § 1.6662-6 (and not the rules of § 1.6664-4) will be applied to determine whether the adjustment is excluded from calculation of the net section 482 adjustment.

A taxpayer will be treated as having a reasonable cause under Code Sec. 6664(c) for any portion of an underpayment attributable to a net Code Sec. 482 adjustment, only if the taxpayer meets the requirements of Reg. § 1.6662-6(d) with respect to that portion.

Reg. § 1.6662-6(c)(7), Ex. 1.

(i) The Internal Revenue Service makes the following section 482 adjustments for the taxable year:

(1) Attributable to an increase in gross income because of an increase in royalty payments	$2,000,000
(2) Attributable to an increase in sales proceeds due to proceeds proceeds due to a decrease in the profit margin of a related buyer	$2,500,000
(3) Attributable to a decrease in the cost of goods sold because of a decrease in the cost plus mark-up of a related seller	$2,000,000
Total section 482 adjustments	$6,500,000

(ii) None of the adjustments are excluded under paragraph (d) of this section. The net section 482 adjustment ($6.5 million) is greater than five million dollars. Therefore, there is a substantial valuation misstatement.[11]

Reg. § 1.6662-6(c)(7), Ex. 3.

(i) The Internal Revenue Service makes the following section 482 adjustments to the income of an affiliated group that files a consolidated return for the taxable year:

(1) Attributable to Member A	$1,500,000
(2) Attributable to Member B	$1,000,000
(3) Attributable to Member C	$2,000,000
Total section 482 adjustments	$4,500,000

(ii) Members A, B, and C have gross receipts of 20 million dollars, 12 million dollars, and 11 million dollars, respectively. Thus, the total gross receipts are 43 million dollars. None of the adjustments are excluded under paragraph (d) of this section. The net section 482 adjustment ($4.5 million) is greater than the lesser of five million dollars or ten percent of gross receipts ($43 million × 10% = $4.3 million). Therefore, there is a substantial valuation misstatement.[12]

.05 Exclusions from Adjustments for Calculation of "Transfer Pricing Adjustment"

The regulations provide defenses against the net adjustment penalty by establishing exceptions to the net Code Sec. 482 transfer pricing adjustment definition. A net Code Sec. 482 transfer price adjustment is defined as the net increase in taxable income for the taxable year (without regard to any carrybacks or carry forwards) resulting from adjustments under Code Sec. 482.[13] However, certain adjustments are excluded in determining whether the numerical threshold has been satisfied.[14] These exclusions are applied in lieu of the reasonable cause and good faith defenses applicable to most civil tax penalties.[15] In addition, if the taxpayer meets the requirements for exclusion with respect to only a portion of the Code Sec. 482 adjustment, then any setoff that would otherwise be allowed must be applied ratably to both the excluded and unexcluded portions of the adjustment.[16] The defenses

---

[11] Reg. § 1.6662-6(c)(7), Ex. 1.
[12] Reg. § 1.6662-6(c)(7), Ex. 3.
[13] Code Sec. 6662(e)(3)(A).

[14] Code Sec. 6662(e)(3)(B).
[15] Reg. § 1.6662-6(c)(6).
[16] Reg. § 1.6662-6(c)(4).

against the transactional penalties are the same as those for the net adjustment penalty.[17] These exclusions are described below:

Specified Method Exclusion. Under the specified method exclusion, adjustments are excluded from the net Code Sec. 482 adjustment calculation if the taxpayer satisfies the specified method requirement and the documentation requirement.[18] To satisfy the specified method requirement, the taxpayer must use one of the transfer pricing methods enumerated in the regulations under Code Sec. 482 in a reasonable manner.[19] The use of a specified method is reasonable only if the taxpayer concludes that it provides the "most reliable measure of an arm's length result under the principles of the best method rule."[20] The taxpayer must make a reasonable effort to evaluate the potential applicability of the other specified methods, but need not conclude that the selected method provides a more reliable method than any unspecified method.[21] Whether the taxpayer's use of a particular method was reasonable is determined from all facts and circumstances.[22] The regulations set forth factors relevant to this determination:

1. Experience and knowledge of the taxpayer;

2. Extent to which the taxpayer obtained accurate data and analyzed it in a reasonable manner. The taxpayer must make a reasonably thorough search for data necessary to determine which method should be selected and how it should be applied. The expense of additional efforts to locate new data may be weighed against the likelihood of finding additional data that would improve the reliability of the results and the amount by which the taxpayer's income would change;[23]

3. Extent to which the taxpayer used the most current reliable data available before the end of the tax year in question. The taxpayer must maintain as a principal document relevant data obtained after the end of the year but before the return is filed;

4. Extent to which the taxpayer followed relevant requirements in the regulations under Code Sec. 482 with respect to application of the methods;

5. Extent to which the taxpayer reasonably relied on a study or other analysis prepared by a qualified professional;

6. If the taxpayer used more than one uncontrolled comparable, whether the taxpayer arbitrarily selected a result that corresponds to an extreme point in the range;

7. Extent to which the taxpayer relied on a TPM developed and applied under an APA for a prior year, provided that the facts and circumstances have not materially changed; and

8. Size of the net transfer pricing adjustment in relation to the size of the controlled transaction out of which the adjustment arose.[24]

---

17 Reg. § 1.6662-6(b)(3).
18 Reg. § 1.6662-6(d)(2).
19 Code Sec. 6662(e)(3)(B)(i)(I).
20 Reg. § 1.6662-6(d)(2)(ii).
21 Reg. § 1.6662-6(d)(2)(ii).
22 Reg. § 1.6662-6(d)(2)(ii).
23 Reg. § 1.6662-6(d)(2)(ii)(B).
24 Reg. § 1.6662-6(d)(2)(ii).

The regulations make it clear that in the appropriate circumstances the cost of performing additional searches for relevant data can justify a decision not to perform such searches.[25] Cost becomes relatively less persuasive, however, as the dollar amount of the transactions increase, thereby leaving the taxpayer open on examination to the IRS substituting its judgment of whether the cost of additional searches would have been justified for the taxpayer's judgment.

Unspecified Method Exclusion. If the transaction is one for which there are specified methods, but an unspecified method was nevertheless applied, the taxpayer must reasonably conclude, given the available data: (1) that none of the specified methods was likely to provide a reliable measure of an arm's length result; and (2) that it applied an unspecified method in a way that would likely provide a reliable measure of an arm's length result.[26] This latter conclusion will be considered reasonable if the taxpayer made a reasonable effort to evaluate the potential applicability of the specified methods in a manner consistent with the principles of the best method rule.[27] If the transaction is one for which there are no specified methods, the taxpayer will be considered to meet the requirements of the regulation if it selected and applied the unspecified method reasonably.[28] This standard will be satisfied if the taxpayer reasonably concludes that the unspecified method provides the most reliable measure of an arm's length result.[29]

Documentation Requirement. The documentation requirement is met if the taxpayer maintains sufficient documentation to demonstrate that the taxpayer concluded the method applied provided the most reliable measure of an arm's length result under the best method rule.[30] Taxpayer must also provide the documentation to the IRS within 30 days of request.[31]

The documentation is divided into principal documents and background documents—both are described in Chapter 10.

Defenses—Foreign to Foreign Transactions. In calculating the amount of any net Code Sec. 482 adjustment, any allocations attributable to transactions between solely foreign corporations are excluded unless the treatment of such transactions affects the determination of either corporation's U.S. source income, or income that is effectively connected with the conduct of a U.S. trade or business.[32]

.06 Carryovers and Carrybacks

If a valuation misstatement for a taxable year gives rise to a loss, deduction or credit that is carried to another year, the transactional penalty and the net adjustment penalty will be imposed on any resulting tax underpayment in that other tax year.[33] In determining whether there is a substantial or gross valuation misstatement for a taxable year, no amount carried from another year is included.[34]

---

25 Reg. § 1.6662-6(d)(2)(ii)(B).
26 Reg. § 1.6662-6(d)(3)(ii)(B).
27 Reg. § 1.6662-6(d)(3)(ii)(B).
28 Reg. § 1.6662-6(d)(3)(ii)(C).
29 Reg. § 1.6662-6(d)(3)(ii)(C).
30 Reg. § 1.6662-6(d)(2)(iii)(A).
31 *Id.*
32 Reg. § 1.6662-6(d)(4).
33 Reg. § 1.6662-6(f)(2).
34 *Id.*

Reg. § 1.6662-6(e), Ex.

The Internal Revenue Service makes a section 482 adjustment of six million dollars in taxable year 1, no portion of which is excluded under paragraph (d) of this section. The taxpayer's income tax return for year 1 reported a loss of three million dollars, which was carried to taxpayer's year 2 income tax return and used to reduce income taxes otherwise due with respect to year 2. A determination is made that the six million dollar allocation constitutes a substantial valuation misstatement, and a penalty is imposed on the underpayment of tax in year 1 attributable to the substantial valuation misstatement and on the underpayment of tax in year 2 attributable to the disallowance of the net operating loss in year 2. For purposes of determining whether there is a substantial or gross valuation misstatement for year 2, the three million dollar reduction of the net operating loss will not be added to any section 482 adjustments made with respect to year 2.[35]

.07 Coordination between Transactional Penalty and Net Adjustment Penalty

If the net Code Sec. 482 adjustment exceeds 20 million dollars or 20 percent of gross receipts, the entire amount of the adjustment is subject to the net adjusted penalty at 40 percent.[36] No portion of the adjustment is subject to the 20 percent rate.[37]

Reg. § 1.6662-6(f)(3), Ex. 3

(i) Applying section 482, the Internal Revenue Service makes the following transfer pricing adjustments for the taxable year:

(1) Attributable to an adjustment that is 400 percent or more of the correct section 482 arm's length result	$ 6,000,000
(2) Not a 200 or 400 percent adjustment	$15,000,000
Total	$21,000,000

(ii) None of the adjustments are excluded under paragraph (d) (Amounts excluded from net section 482 adjustments) in determining the twenty million dollar or 20% of gross receipts test under section 6662(h). The net section 482 adjustment (21 million dollars) is greater than twenty million dollars and thus constitutes a gross valuation misstatement. Accordingly, the total adjustment is subject to the net adjustment penalty equal to 40 percent of the underpayment of tax attributable to the 21 million dollar gross valuation misstatement. The six million dollar adjustment will not be separately included for purposes of any additional penalty under section 6662.[38]

.08 Transfer Pricing Penalty Oversight Committee

In 1996, the IRS established a transfer pricing oversight committee charged with ensuring the uniform application of the Code Sec. 6662(e) reasonableness and documentation standards on a uniform basis.[39] To that end, this committee reviews all cases in which the IRS district office is considering asserting a transfer pricing penalty. The committee also collects data relating to cases in which the statutory penalty thresholds were satisfied, but no penalty was recommended. The commit-

---

[35] Reg. § 1.6662-6(e), Ex.
[36] Reg. § 1.6662-6(f)(2).
[37] *Id.*

[38] Reg. § 1.6662-6(f)(3), Ex. 3.
[39] Announcement 96-16, 1996-13 IRB 22.

tee is composed of IRS representatives from Assistant Commissioner International, Examinations, Appeals, and Associate Chief Counsel (International). The committee, however, is not a forum in which a taxpayer can appeal a preliminary recommendation that a penalty be assessed.[40]

As mentioned above, the numbers of tax years for which transfer pricing penalties are submitted and approved increased drastically in the fiscal year ended September 30, 2006.

.09 DHL Corp.

DHL Corp.[41] is the first transfer pricing case in which the Tax Court upheld the IRS's imposition of the 40 percent substantial valuation misstatement penalty under Code Sec. 6662(h) as well as the 20 percent penalty under Code Sec. 6662(b). The primary dispute concerned the ownership of the DHL trademark and the amount of royalties payable for the use thereof. DHL unsuccessfully argued that DHLI owned the rights to use the DHL trademarks outside of the United States because DHLI had legally registered the trademarks. The Tax Court, based on DHL internal documents, concluded that DHL owned the trademarks. Nonetheless, the Tax Court held that doubt concerning ownership of the trademarks would affect what a third party would pay. The Tax Court ultimately held that the value of the trademarks was $100 million.

Arguing against the imposition of penalties, DHL asserted that it had reasonably relied on a contemporaneous appraisal. After reviewing the circumstances surrounding that appraisal, the Court concluded that DHL could not reasonably rely on the appraisal to avoid the penalties.

The IRS asserted substantial valuation misstatement and gross valuation misstatements penalties on the proposed adjustments regarding the valuation of the trademarks and the related royalties. DHL asserted that it reasonably relied on an appraisal prepared at the time it entered the agreement with the foreign shareholders. After reviewing the circumstances surrounding that appraisal, the court concluded that the appraiser was prepared to meet the value set by DHL; therefore, DHL could not reasonably rely on the appraisal to avoid penalties. DHL has stated its intention to appeal the Tax Court's decision.

¶ 730 Reporting Penalties—Code Sec. 6038A

Code Sec. 6038A imposes a reporting obligation on certain foreign-owned domestic corporations. In general, each corporation subject to the reporting obligation (a "reporting corporation") must file a separate annual information return on Form 5472 for each related party with which it has had any reportable transaction (discussed below) during the year.[42] Form 5472 must be filed with the taxpayer's tax return.[43] (See Form 5472 at ¶ 20,050.)

---

[40] Announcement 96-16, 1996-13 IRB 22.

[41] *DHL Corp.*, CCH Dec. 53,015(M), 76 TCM (CCH) 1122 (1998).

[42] Reg. § 1.6038A-2(a)(1).

[43] Reg. § 1.6038A-2(d).

.01 Reporting Corporations

General Definition. Code Sec. 6038A(a) defines a "reporting corporation" as a domestic corporation that is 25 percent foreign-owned. The definition of reporting corporation also includes a foreign corporation that is 25 percent foreign-owned and that is engaged in a U.S. trade or business.[44]

A corporation is 25 percent foreign-owned if at least 25 percent of its stock (by vote or value) is owned (directly or indirectly) by one foreign person at any time during the taxable year.[45] For this purpose, a foreign person is anyone who is not described by Code Sec. 7701(a)(3) (defining a U.S. person), except that any individual who is a citizen of a U.S. possession, but is not otherwise a U.S. resident or citizen, is not treated as a U.S. person.[46] In addition, in determining whether a domestic corporation is 25 percent foreign-owned, the constructive stock ownership rules of Code Sec. 318 are applied with certain modifications, the most notable of which is that the ownership threshold for attributing stock ownership from a corporation is reduced from 50 percent to 10 percent.[47]

Exceptions. There are two complete exceptions and two partial exceptions to the Code Sec. 6038A reporting requirements. A complete exception is granted to foreign corporations: (i) with no U.S. permanent establishment under an applicable income tax treaty; and (ii) whose gross income is exempt from U.S. tax under Code Sec. 883 (qualified shipping income).[48]

Partial exceptions are granted to corporations that: (i) have less than $10 million in U.S. gross receipts for the taxable year; and (ii) have related party transactions that are not more than $5 million and less than 10 percent of its U.S. gross income.[49]

.02 Required Disclosure

Taxpayer Information. A reporting corporation must report the following information on Form 5472:[50]

- Taxpayer identifying information (name address and EIN);
- List each country in which the taxpayer files an income tax return as a resident of that country;
- Country of organization and incorporation;
- Total assets;
- Places where it conducts business; and
- Principal business activity.

In addition, the taxpayer must report the information concerning all of its direct and indirect 25 percent shareholders:[51]

---

[44] Code Sec. 6038C; Reg. § 1.6038A-1(c)(1).
[45] Code Sec. 6038A(c)(1); Reg. § 1.6038A-1(c)(3).
[46] Code Sec. 6038A(c)(3); Reg. § 1.6038A-1(f).
[47] Code Sec. 6038A(c)(5).

[48] Reg. § 1.6038A-1(c)(5)(i); Reg. § 1.6038A-1(c)(5)(ii).
[49] Reg. § 1.6038A-1(h); Reg. § 1.6038A-1(i).
[50] *See* Reg. § 1.6038A-2(b)(i).
[51] *See* Reg. § 1.6038A-2(b)(ii).

- Taxpayer identifying information (name address and EIN);
- Each country in which it files an income tax return as a resident of that country;
- The places where it conducts business; and
- The countries of organization, citizenship or incorporation.

Lastly, the taxpayer must disclose the number of Forms 5472 filed for the taxable year and the aggregate value in U.S. dollars of gross payments made with respect to all foreign related party transactions reported on all Forms 5472.[52]

Related Party Information and Reportable Transactions. If the taxpayer had a reportable transaction (defined below) with a related party, then it must disclose the following information about each such related party:[53]

- Taxpayer identifying information (name address and EIN);
- Each country in which it files an income tax return as a resident of that country;
- Nature of the related party's business and its principal place of business; and
- Relationship of the related party to the taxpayer.

Reportable transactions are those transactions described in Reg. § 1.6038A-2(b)(3) (foreign related party transactions for which only monetary consideration is paid or received) and -2(b)(4) (foreign related party transactions involving non-monetary consideration or less than full consideration). For foreign related party transactions for which only monetary consideration is paid or received, the taxpayer must disclose the total amount of such transactions and the amount attributable to the specified types of transactions (reasonable estimates— those within 25 percent of the actual amount—are permitted).[54] The specific categories of transactions that must be reported are expansive and include almost every type of transaction that could have an impact on the calculation of the taxpayer's taxable income.

For foreign related party transactions involving non-monetary consideration or less than full consideration, then the taxpayer must provide a detailed description of the transactions and a reasonable estimate (within 25 percent of the actual amount) of the market value of the transaction.[55]

Additional Information Regarding Imported Goods. If the taxpayer imports goods from a related party, then the taxpayer must disclose whether the costs taken into account in determining the basis of such goods is higher than the costs taken into account for Customs valuation purposes.[56] If so, then the taxpayer must also disclose whether adequate records documenting the difference are available for review.[57]

---

[52] Reg. § 1.6038A-2(b)(iii). *See* Rev. Proc. 91-55, 1991-2 CB 784.

[53] *See* Reg. § 1.6038A-2(b)(2).

[54] Reg. § 1.6038A-2(b)(3); Reg. § 1.6038A-2(b)(6).

[55] Reg. § 1.6038A-2(b)(4); Reg. § 1.6038A-2(b)(6).

[56] *See* Code Sec. 6038A Reg. § 1.6038A-2(b)(5)(i).

[57] Reg. § 1.6038A-2(b)(5)(ii).

¶730.02

Exceptions. There are several full and partial exceptions to the reporting requirements, including exceptions if there are no reportable transactions, the reportable transactions are solely with a domestic reporting corporation, transactions with corporations that are subject to reporting under Code Sec. 6038A, and transactions with foreign sales corporations.[58]

.03 Record Maintenance

Code Sec. 6038A works in conjunction with Code Sec. 6001 with respect to record maintenance. In general, a reporting corporation must keep permanent books and records that are sufficient to establish the correctness of its tax return.[59] In addition, the reporting corporation must maintain records that include cost data from which an income statement can be prepared for products or services transferred between the reporting corporation and its foreign related parties.[60] This includes the records of any foreign related party that may be relevant (based on the facts and circumstances).[61] Documents can be maintained by the reporting corporation, a foreign related party, or by a third party.[62] If the documents are in a foreign language, they must be translated when the documents are requested by the IRS.[63]

The regulations provide a safe harbor for record maintenance under Code Sec. 6038A.[64] The safe harbor merely includes an exhaustive list of documents that may be relevant under different facts and circumstances.[65] It is not a checklist of records that a reporting corporation must maintain or of records that should be requested by the IRS.[66] The reporting corporation need only maintain those enumerated records that may be relevant to its business or industry and to the correct tax treatment of its transactions with foreign related persons.[67]

Specific Records. The regulations contain an exhaustive list of documents that may be relevant under different facts and circumstances. In general, these documents need not be created solely for purposes of meeting the safe harbor.[68] However, there are two categories of documents that must be prepared regardless of whether they are prepared for business purposes: (1) basic accounting records that document the U.S. tax effects of the transactions, and (2) records from which an income statement can be prepared for products or services transferred between the reporting corporation and its foreign related parties.[69]

The categories of documents are as follows:[70]

- Original entry books and transaction records;
- Profit and loss statements;
- Pricing documents;
- Foreign and third-party filings;

---

[58] Reg. § 1.6038A-2(f).
[59] Reg. § 1.6038A-3(a)(1).
[60] Reg. § 1.6038A-3(a)(1).
[61] Reg. § 1.6038A-3(a)(1).
[62] Reg. § 1.6038A-3(b)(2).
[63] Reg. § 1.6038A-3(b)(3).
[64] Reg. § 1.6038A-3(a)(2).

[65] Reg. § 1.6038A-3(a)(2).
[66] Reg. § 1.6038A-3(a)(2).
[67] Reg. § 1.6038A-3(a)(2).
[68] Reg. § 1.6038A-3(c)(1).
[69] Reg. § 1.6038A-3(c)(1).
[70] *See* Reg. § 1.6038A-3(c)(2).

- Ownership and capital structure records; and

- Records of loans, services, and other non-sales transactions.

Taxpayers may enter into agreements with the IRS District Director regarding the documents that must be maintained, how the records are to be maintained, the period of retention, and by whom the records must be maintained.[71]

Special Rules and Exceptions. Foreign governments are exempt from the record maintenance obligation.[72] In addition, special rules are provided for conduit financing arrangements.[73]

.04 Authorization of Agent

The IRS may request the reporting corporation to act as the agent of a foreign related party for limited information disclosure purposes.[74] This agency relationship is established solely for complying with Code Sec. 7602 (examination of books and witnesses), Code Sec. 7603 (service of summons), and Code Sec. 7604 (enforcement of summons).[75] The agency relationship will not be considered in determining whether the foreign related party is engaged in a U.S. trade or business.[76]

.05 Penalty for Failure to Disclose

Reporting corporations failing to comply with the Code Sec. 6038A information reporting requirements are subject to a $10,000 penalty with respect to each year for which the failure occurs.[77] However, failure to comply may be excused by a showing of reasonable cause.[78]

.06 Non-Compliance with Summons or Failure to Obtain Authorization of Agent

If the reporting corporation fails to obtain an authorization of agent upon request by the IRS, or fails to respond to an IRS summons, then the IRS is given broad power to determine the arm's length amount attributable to transactions with foreign related parties.[79] Specifically, the IRS may: (1) determine the amount of any deduction allowed for any amount paid or incurred by the reporting corporation to the related party, or (2) determine the cost to the reporting corporation of any property acquired from the related party.[80] This determination is made at the District Director's sole discretion based on his or her own knowledge or information that he or she may choose to obtain.[81] The District Director is required to consider materials submitted by the reporting corporation or by a foreign related party.[82] However, the District Director may, in his or her sole discretion, disregard any information that is deemed to be insufficiently probative of the relevant facts.[83]

---

[71] Reg. § 1.6038A-3(e). *See* Rev. Proc. 91-38, 1991-2 CB 692.

[72] Reg. § 1.6038A-3(b)(4).

[73] Reg. § 1.6038A-3(b)(5); Reg. § 1.881-4.

[74] Code Sec. 6038A(e)(1); Reg. § 1.6038A-5(b).

[75] Code Sec. 6038A(e)(1); Reg. § 1.6038A-5(b).

[76] Reg. § 1.6038A-5(a).

[77] Code Sec. 6038A(d); Reg. § 1.6038A-4(a)(1).

[78] Reg. § 1.6038A-4(b).

[79] Code Sec. 6038A(e)(3); Reg. § 1.6038A-5(a); Reg. § 1.6038A-6(a).

[80] Reg. § 1.6038A-7(a).

[81] Reg. § 1.6038A-7(b).

[82] Reg. § 1.6038A-7(b).

[83] Reg. § 1.6038A-7(b).

¶730.04

ASAT, Inc. ASAT, Inc.,[84] illustrates what can happen to a taxpayer for failing to comply with Code Sec. 6038A. In *ASAT*, the Tax Court upheld the IRS's actions following a U.S. taxpayer's failure to obtain an authorization of agent from its foreign parent. During the tax year at issue, FYE April 30, 1991, ASAT, Inc. ("ASAT") was a wholly-owned U.S. subsidiary of ASAT, Ltd., a Hong Kong corporation. In July 1992, Worltek International, Ltd. ("Worltek"), an unrelated U.S. corporation, acquired 95 percent of ASAT's stock.

After the acquisition by Worltek was completed, the IRS initiated an examination of ASAT for tax years prior to the acquisition. On examination, the IRS requested that ASAT obtain the authorization of agent from ASAT, Ltd. under Code Sec. 6038A(e)(1) and requested other information about ASAT, Ltd. through IDRs and a summons. ASAT failed to substantially comply with the request for authorization of agent, as well as the summons. Consequently, under the authority of Code Sec. 6038A(e)(3), the IRS issued a proposed adjustment based on information in its possession.

At trial, ASAT argued that it was legally impossible to compel ASAT, Ltd. to provide the requested information and authorization of agent because it was acquired by Worltek before the examination was initiated. Therefore, ASAT argued it was not subject to Code Sec. 6038A with respect to ASAT, Ltd. The Tax Court rejected ASAT's argument, based on a plain reading of the statute that subjected ASAT to Code Sec. 6038A with respect to ASAT, Ltd. if they had related party transactions during the year in which the IRS request was made. Consequently, the Tax Court sustained the IRS notice of deficiency and the assessment of the 20 percent negligence penalty for failing to comply with Code Sec. 6038A.

.07 Extension of the Statute of Limitations

The statute of limitations is also extended for three years after the date on which the IRS receives the information required under Code Sec. 6038A, as well as Code Secs. 6038, 6038B, 6046, 6046A, or 6048.[85]

¶ 740 Code Sec. 982

Code Sec. 982 is an evidentiary provision, rather than a penalty or documentation requirement. It provides that if a taxpayer fails to comply with a formal IRS document request (i.e., an IDR) for foreign-based documentation within 90 days of the mailing of such request, then any U.S. civil court adjudicating the tax treatment of an item that was the subject of the document request shall prohibit the introduction of foreign-based documentation that was the subject of the request.[86] "Foreign based documentation" is defined as any documentation that is located outside of the United States that may be relevant or material to the tax treatment of the examined item.[87] A reasonable cause exception is provided for in the statute; however, the existence of a foreign law that would impose a civil or criminal penalty for disclosing the requested information is not considered to be reasonable cause.[88]

---

[84] *ASAT, Inc.*, CCH Dec. 51,966, 108 TC 147 (1997).

[85] Code Sec. 6501(c)(8).

[86] Code Sec. 982(a).

[87] Code Sec. 982(d)(1).

[88] Code Sec. 982(b).

¶ 750 Other Penalties of General Application

In addition to the substantial understatement penalties described in Code Sec. 6662(e) and (h) and the reporting penalty described in Code Sec. 6038A, all general civil and criminal tax penalties can apply in the context of a transfer pricing matter. These penalties include:

- Failure to file penalty;
- Failure to pay penalty;
- Failure to pay estimated tax penalty; and
- Preparer penalties.

¶ 760 OECD Transfer Pricing Penalties

The OECD Transfer Pricing Guidelines state that the appropriate use of tax penalties may play a role in addressing transfer pricing compliance.[89] Although the OECD Guidelines do not contain any recommended penalties, they do emphasize that penalties should be fair and not unduly onerous.[90] It is particularly useful to note that the OECD Guidelines explicitly recognize that transfer pricing penalties can have the effect of encouraging non-compliance (in the form of non-arm's length prices) in low penalty jurisdictions in order to avoid harsh penalties in other jurisdictions.[91] In this respect, the OECD Guidelines make the following observations about transfer pricing penalties:

- The imposition of sizable "no fault" penalties based on the mere existence of an understatement of a certain amount would be unduly harsh if it is attributable to a good faith error rather than negligence or a tax avoidance intent; and
- It is unfair to impose sizable penalties on taxpayers that made a reasonable effort in good faith to set their transfer prices in accordance with the arm's length principle.

---

[89] Organisation for Economic Co-operation and Development, Transfer Pricing Guidelines for Multinational Enterprises and Tax Administrations, Par. 4.25.

[90] *Id.*
[91] *Id.* at Par. 4.26.

¶750

Chapter 8

The Code Sec. 1059A Limitation

¶ 801 Overview

Congress added Code Sec. 1059A to the Code by the Tax Reform Act of 1986 to prevent related party importers from improperly avoiding U.S. income tax or customs duties by reporting a higher transfer price for income tax purposes than the price reported for customs purposes. By doing so, related party importers were able to reduce their income tax (because they reported higher cost of goods sold) and keep their customs duties low (because they reported a low customs value).[1] Code Sec. 1059A prevents this perceived abuse by requiring that the value of imported property reported for income tax purposes be no higher than the value reported for Customs duty purposes. However, as described below, this general rule is subject to several significant exceptions.[2]

¶ 810 Background—U.S. Import Requirements

All goods imported into the United States must "clear" customs and are subject to a customs duty unless specifically exempted from duty by statute. The process of "clearing" customs involves several phases—entry, inspection, appraisal, classification, and liquidation. These and other U.S. import requirements are enforced by the U.S. Customs and Border Protection Service ("Customs").

Customs duties are payable during the "entry" phase of the customs clearance process, and, for the most part, are assessed on an *ad valorem* basis (i.e., a percentage of the value of the imported goods). The importer is required to use reasonable care in valuing imported goods and providing any other information necessary for Customs to properly assess duties. The value of imported goods is determined under the methods prescribed by statute (discussed below at ¶ 830.). The rates of duty are published in the *Harmonized Tariff Schedule of the United States*, which is published by the International Trade Commission. The tariff schedule lists several rates of duty for each type of product: (1) "general" rates for

---

[1] S. Rep. No. 313, 99th Cong., 2d Sess., pp. 418-419. *See* e.g., *R.M. Brittingham*, CCH Dec. 33,856, 66 TC 373 (1976), *aff'd* 79-2 USTC ¶ 9499, 598 F.2d 1375 (5th Cir. 1979).

[2] *See* generally, Cole, "Customs Issues Arising Out of Transfer Pricing Compliance," 97 TNI 230-18 (1997).

imports from most-favored nations, (2) "special" rates for special trade programs, and (3) "column 2" rates for imports not subject to either "general" or "special" rates.

¶ 820　Statute and Application

.01　Statute

Code Sec. 1059A provides that:

> (a) IN GENERAL. If any property is imported into the United States in a transaction (directly or indirectly) between related persons (within the meaning of Code Sec. 482), the amount of any costs—
>
> > (1) which are taken into account in computing the basis or inventory cost of such property by the purchaser, and
> >
> > (2) which are also taken into account in computing the customs value of such property,
>
> shall not, for purposes of computing such basis or inventory cost for purposes of this chapter, be greater than the amount of such costs taken into account in computing such customs value.
>
> (b) CUSTOMS VALUE; IMPORT. For purposes of this section—
>
> > (1) CUSTOMS VALUE. The term "customs value" means the value taken into account for purposes of determining the amount of any customs duties or any other duties which may be imposed on the importation of any property.
> >
> > (2) IMPORT. Except as provided in regulations, the term "import" means the entering, or withdrawal from warehouse, for consumption.

.02　Exceptions to Code Sec. 1059A

If imported property is not subject to any customs duty or is subject to a free rate of duty, the value of such property is not subject to Code Sec. 1059A.[3] For example, the following transactions are not subject to Code Sec. 1059A:

- American goods that are returned and that are not subject to duty;
- Imports on which no duty is imposed that are valued by Customs solely for statistical purposes;
- Property subject to a zero rate of duty;
- Property not subject to Customs duty based on value (e.g., property subject to duty based on volume or on a per unit basis); and
- Property subject only to the user fee under 19 USC 58(c), or the harbor maintenance tax under 26 USC 4461, or only to both.

.03　Coordination with Code Sec. 482

Code Sec. 1059A does not limit the authority of the IRS to increase or decrease the claimed basis or inventory cost under Code Sec. 482 or any other appropriate provision of law.[4] In addition, Code Sec. 1059A does not allow a taxpayer to adjust upward its cost basis or inventory cost under Code Sec. 482 because such cost is less than the Customs value with respect to the same

---

[3] *Id.*

[4] Reg. § 1.1059A-1(c)(7).

property.[5] This last rule is an extension of the rule prohibiting taxpayers from affirmatively invoking Code Sec. 482 other than on a timely filed tax return.[6]

¶ 830 Determining Customs Value

.01 In General

Code Sec. 1059A provides a ceiling (i.e., customs value) and not a floor for valuing property imported from related parties for income tax purposes.[7] For this purpose, the term "customs value" is defined as the value required to be taken into account for purposes of determining the amount of any customs duties or any other duties which may be imposed on the importation of any property.[8]

United States Customs law is enforced by U.S. Customs and Border Protection Service. Although Customs and the IRS used to be sister agencies within the Department of Treasury, their respective jurisdictions are inherently in conflict with respect to valuing imported goods. The IRS, in its enforcement of Code Sec. 482, makes adjustments when the stated value of imported property is too high (thus improperly shifting income out of the United States). Customs, in its collection of Customs duties, makes adjustments when the stated value of imported property is too low. This conflict can cause U.S. taxpayers/importers to be whipsawed.

.02 Valuation Methods

The goal of Customs valuation is to determine the of goods at the time that they are ready to be shipped from the exporting country. Unlike the Code Sec. 482 pricing regulations, the Customs valuation rules are ranked in order of priority of use. There are five Customs valuations methodologies prescribed by statute.[9] In theory, each of the valuations methodologies should arrive at the same value. The five valuation methodologies are:

1. Transaction value;

2. Transaction value of identical or similar property;

3. Deductive value;

4. Computed value;

5. Other Valuation Methods.

Although these methods are different than the methods prescribed by the regulations of Code Sec. 482, both sets of methods have as their goal the determination of an arm's length value. Furthermore, Customs and the IRS have recently begun efforts to reconcile their pricing methods so as to ease the administrative burden on importers.[10]

---

[5] *Id.*

[6] *See* Reg. § 1.482-1(a)(3).

[7] *See* Staff of the Joint Committee of Taxation, General Explanation of the Tax Reform Act of 1986, 100th Cong., 1st Sess., p. 1062.

[8] Reg. § 1.1059A-1(c)(1).

[9] 19 USC 1401a.

[10] *See* generally Wrappe and Pike, "Reconciliation and Reconsideration of Customs Value," 11 *Customs Record* No. 524, p. 19 (1998); Meyer and Outman, "Treasury's Tag Team: The IRS and Customs Join To Combat Inconsistent Import Valuations in Related-Party Transactions," 25 *Tax Management International Journal* 231 (Apr. 12, 1996).

Transaction Value. Transaction value is the preferred method for valuing imported goods under the statute.[11] The transaction value of imported goods is the price actually paid or payable when sold for export to the United States, plus the following amounts:

1. Packing costs incurred by the buyer;

2. Selling commissions incurred by the buyer;

3. The value of any assist (apportioned as appropriate);

4. Any royalty or license fee (whether paid directly or indirectly); and

5. The proceeds of any subsequent resale, disposal, or use of the goods that accrue to the seller (directly or indirectly).[12]

Such amounts are included only to the extent that they are not otherwise included in the price actually paid or payable, and are based on sufficient information.

The statutory definition of "assist" includes:

1. Materials, components, parts, and similar items incorporated in the imported goods;

2. Tools, dies, molds, and similar items used in the production of imported goods;

3. Merchandise consumed in the production of the imported goods; and

4. Subject to certain exceptions, engineering, development, artwork, design work, and plans and sketches that are other than in the United States and are necessary for the production of imported goods.[13]

The above are included as assists only to the extent that they are supplied directly or indirectly, and free of charge or at reduced cost, by the buyer.[14]

The transaction value of imported goods is equal to its appraised value, but only if:[15]

1. There are no restrictions on the disposition or use of the goods by the buyer other than restrictions that are (i) required by law, (ii) limit the geographical area in which goods may be resold, or (iii) do not substantially affect the value of the goods;

2. The sale of, or the price actually paid or payable for, the goods is not subject to any condition or consideration for which a value cannot be determined;

3. No part of the proceeds of any subsequent resale, disposal, or use of the goods by the buyer will accrue, directly or indirectly, to the seller, unless an appropriate adjustment is made; and

4. The buyer and seller are not related, unless (i) the facts and circumstances indicates that the relationship did not influence the price paid or payable, or (ii) if the value of the imported goods closely approximates the transac-

---

[11] 19 USC 1401a(a)(1).
[12] *Id.*
[13] 19 USC 1401a(h)(1)(A).

[14] 19 USC 1401a(b)(2).
[15] *Id.*

¶830.02

tion value of identical or similar merchandise sold to unrelated buyers in the United States or the deductive value (see below) for identical or similar merchandise.

Moreover, the following amounts, if separately stated, are not included in transaction value:[16]

1. Any reasonable cost for: (i) the construction, erection, assembly, or maintenance of, or technical assistance provided with respect to the goods after it has been imported, or (ii) the transportation of the goods after importation; and

2. Customs Duties and Other Federal Taxes.

Transaction Value of Identical or Similar Property. If the transaction value, as described above, cannot be applied, the value of imported goods can be determined by valuing the transaction value of identical or similar property.[17]

Deductive Value. Deductive value is determined by taking the resale price of the imported goods and deducting the following amounts: commissions, transportation and insurance costs, customs duties and other federal taxes, and the value of any processing done in the United States.[18]

Computed Value. Computed value is determined by adding the following amounts: (i) the cost of materials and fabrication or other processing; (ii) an amount of profit and general expenses of the same class of goods; (iii) any assists; and (iv) packing costs.[19]

Other Valuation Methods. If none of the above methods can be successfully applied to determine the value of imported goods, such methods may be reasonably adjusted to determine value.[20]

.03 Adjustments to Customs Value

In enacting Code Sec. 1059A, Congress intended that the IRS issue regulations that allowed for adjustments to Customs value attributable to freight charges, items of American content returned, and sales commissions where Customs pricing rules may differ from appropriate tax valuation rules.[21] The regulations provide that, to the extent not otherwise included in Customs value, taxpayers may increase the Customs value of imported property for:[22]

1. Freight charges;

2. Insurance charges;

3. The construction, erection, assembly, or technical assistance provided with respect to, the property after its importation into the United States; and

4. Any other amounts which are not taken into account in determining the customs value, which are not properly includable in customs value, and

---

[16] 19 USC 1401a(b)(3).
[17] 19 USC 1401a(c).
[18] 19 USC 1401a(d).
[19] 19 USC 1401a(e).

[20] 19 USC 1401a(f).
[21] H.R. Rep. No. 841, 99th Cong., 2d Sess. p. II-656.
[22] Reg. § 1.1059A-1(c)(2).

which are appropriately included in the cost basis or inventory cost for income tax purposes.[23]

However, to the extent that the Customs value is adjusted under one of the above provisions, the amount of the adjustment must be offset or reduced by amounts that reduce the cost basis of inventory and that are not taken into account in determining Customs value (e.g., rebates or other reductions in the price actually incurred).[24] The regulations provide for further adjustments for imported property that has dutiable and nondutiable portions.[25]

For more discussion of the Customs valuation issue, see Chapter 15.

¶ 850 Special Circumstances

.01 First Sale Rule for Customs Valuation

In *Nissho Iwai American Corp.*,[26] the court upheld a special valuation rule applicable when a foreign manufacturer sells goods to a foreign distributor, who, in turn, sells the goods to a U.S. importer. The *Nissho Iwai* court held that the amount paid by the foreign distributor to the foreign manufacturer (as opposed to the price paid by the U.S. importer to the foreign distributor) was the appropriate amount to be reported for Customs duty purposes. In order to use this lesser amount, two requirements must be satisfied: (1) the U.S. importer must show that the sale from the foreign manufacturer to the foreign middleman was arm's length, and (2) that the goods were clearly destined for the United States when sold to the distributor.[27]

In IRS Letter Ruling 9515011 (Jan. 10, 1995), the IRS held that the Code Sec. 1059A limitation was equal to the amount paid by the U.S. importer to the related foreign distributor, and not the amount paid by the foreign distributor to the foreign manufacturer. This ruling is significant in that it allowed the taxpayer to report a lower value for Customs duty purposes than it reported for income tax purposes. However, IRS Letter Ruling 9515011 also provided that the Service is not precluded from making an adjustment under Code Sec. 482 if the purchase price paid by the U.S. importer to the related foreign distributor exceeds an arm's length price. This ruling was extended to the situation where the foreign distributor is related to the foreign manufacturer as well.[28]

IRS Letter Ruling 9515011 is also significant because it partially superseded IRS Letter Ruling 9406026, issued to the same taxpayer on this issue, but which stated that the Code Sec. 1059A limitation applies only when there has been an underpayment of customs duty. The new ruling clarifies that Code Sec. 1059A is not restricted to underpayment situations.

.02 Payment of Related Party's Expenses

In IRS Letter Ruling 9301002 (July 10, 1992), the IRS held that certain overhead and administrative costs that were paid directly by the U.S. importer for the

---

[23] *See* Reg. § 1.471-11 and Code Sec. 263A.

[24] Reg. § 1.1059A-1(c)(3).

[25] Reg. § 1.1059A-1(c)(4); Reg. § 1.1059A-1(c)(5); *See also* FSA 200026015.

[26] *Nissho Iwai American Corp.*, 982 F.2d 505 (Fed. Cir. 1992).

[27] *See also E.C. McAfee Co.*, 842 F.2d 314 (Fed. Cir. 1988).

[28] *See* IRS Letter Ruling 9543048.

benefit of its foreign affiliate were includable in its cost basis for income tax purposes, even though those amounts were not reported for Customs duty purposes. However, the IRS cautioned that the U.S. importer's income tax basis could be adjusted under Code Sec. 482 if the costs incurred were not arm's length or incurred in the ordinary course of the importer's trade or business.

Chapter 9

Overall Strategy for Compliance and Controversy

¶ 901 Overview

To compete in the global economy, multinational companies must constantly pursue business opportunities in new geographic locations and new business structures. Depending on the industry, a company might attempt to reduce costs by pursuing low-cost labor in developing countries, transfer the ownership of intangibles to a country known to protect intellectual property, or seek to penetrate closed consumer markets by establishment of a local distribution or manufacturing facility. The success of these global business models increases both the number and aggregate value of cross-border transactions between related entities.

Multinational companies continue to adopt complex global business structures to facilitate operational efficiency. Global product line management allows multinational corporations to evaluate the profitability of a product line based on global revenue and expenses, irrespective of the geographic location of the legal entity. Specialized legal entities and elections allow taxpayers to elect either entity or pass-through tax treatment. Each of these business developments contribute to the complexity of transfer pricing determinations and the difficulty of documenting those determinations.

In the current economic climate, corporations can be expected to engage in a number of business activities that impact their transfer pricing. The United States and other governments recognize the opportunity for multinational companies to use transfer pricing to shift income to avoid taxation;[1] therefore, the governments have strengthened their transfer pricing laws and increased enforcement to protect tax revenues from taxpayer manipulation.[2] These transfer pricing enforcement efforts by the United States and other governments, place multinational companies at considerable risk for transfer pricing disputes and double taxation. In response to an increased number of transfer pricing disputes, the United States and its trading partners have instituted a number of procedural changes to reduce both the incidence of double taxation as well as the burden of seeking relief from double taxation.

This chapter will present an overview perspective for managing transfer pricing disputes. Chapters 10 through 13 will present a comprehensive discussion how taxpayers can document transfer pricing determinations to avoid disputes, how to manage a transfer pricing examination, post-examination procedural alternatives to resolve transfer pricing disputes, and advance pricing agreements ("APAs") to avoid transfer pricing disputes.

¶ 905 Global Changes to Transfer Pricing Enforcement

The United States was the first country to modernize and enforce transfer pricing laws. The inability to obtain taxpayer information has historically been the main obstacle to the IRS' enforcement of its transfer pricing rules.[3] Two other impediments have been inadequate resources[4] and the inherent subjectivity in the application of the transfer pricing regulations.[5] In the late 1980's, the U.S. government moved to reverse the unsatisfactory IRS transfer pricing enforcement record with statutory, regulatory and administrative changes, including increased penalties and contemporaneous documentation requirements.

Taxpayers are increasingly subjected to two general types of disclosure requirements: (1) the identification of related-party transactions in the taxpayer's tax return, and (2) preparation and retention of detailed documentation that substantiates the taxpayer's transfer pricing determinations. This increase in transfer pricing

---

[1] See "Restructuring: Practitioners Say Tax Authorities' Attacks On Restructurings May Lack Legal Support," 17 *Tax Mgmt. Trans. Pricing Rep.* 326 (August 28, 2008). *See also,* "Tax Policy: Finance Leaders Say GAO Report Highlights Possible Rate Manipulation By Multinationals," 17 *Tax Mgmt. Trans. Pricing Rep.* 326 (September 11, 2008). *See also,* "Audits: More Than Half Of 850 MNCs Surveyed Faced Transfer Pricing Audits Since 2003," 16 *Tax Mgmt. Trans. Pricing Rep.* 667 (January 17, 2008).

[2] "Transfer Pricing Competent Authority to Add Fourth Group, Expand Tax Shelter Task Force, Shott Says" 59 *Daily Tax Rep.* G-6 (Mar. 31, 2009) (detailing efforts at increased transfer pricing enforcement through the hiring of 700 additional international examiners and the creation of the Transfer Pricing Council). *See also* "Losses, Restructurings Triggering Transfer Pricing Audits, Fueling Disputes, E&Y Survey Of Tax Authorities Finds," 18 *Tax Mgmt. Transfer Pricing Rep.* 551 (Oct. 8, 2009). *See also* "Enforcement: LMSB Will Undertake Mul-

tiyear Expansion Of Staff For International Issues, Shott Says," 17 *Tax Mgmt. Trans. Pricing Rep.* 590, (December 4, 2008).

[3] A Study of Intercompany Pricing Under Code Sec. 482 of the Code, Notice 88-123, Chapter 3, 1988-2 CB 458, 461 ("White Paper").

[4] The [Oversight] Subcommittee found that the Federal government's efforts to enforce our tax laws were inadequate and largely unsuccessful. The IRS was simply 'outgunned and outmanned.' Tax Underpayments by U.S. Subsidiaries of Foreign Companies: Hearings Before Subcomm. on Oversight of the House Comm. on Ways and Means, 102nd Cong., 2nd Sess.(1992) (Statement of the Honorable J. J. Pickle, Chairman of Subcomm. on Oversight).

[5] Mogle, "Intercompany Transfer Pricing in the 1990s: Trading Old Lamps for New Ones," 69 *Taxes* 961, 986 (1991).

information has made it easier for tax authorities to examine taxpayers' transfer pricing decisions. Foreign tax authorities have generally responded to the IRS efforts by modernizing their own transfer pricing laws and increasing enforcement. Thus, there has been a similar increase in the disclosure requirements imposed by foreign tax authorities. Many foreign jurisdictions have enacted laws requiring taxpayers to report details of their related party transactions on their tax return and have enacted tax penalties.[6]

As a result of the increased global transfer pricing enforcement, multinational corporations face much greater exposure to double tax than just a few years ago. Although each country's transfer pricing rules purport to adhere to the universally approved arm's length standard, application of that standard has always been the subject of local interpretation. Consequently, transfer prices established in one country might not be acceptable in the other country because of differences in preferred methodology or application.

¶ 910 Documentation Strategies

The taxpayer's first opportunity to prevent transfer pricing disputes is through the initial planning and documentation of the related party transactions. Planning for transfer pricing generally involves reviewing the terms and conditions of the transactions, analyzing the functions and risks of the parties to the transactions, and identifying comparable transactions or companies that can be used to determine an arm's length price or range. The taxpayer should consider collateral effects on other transactions, including transactions with related parties directly linked with the proposed transaction and similar transactions where the taxpayer or related party undertake similar functions and risks.

As a practical matter, tax personnel are seldom consulted prior to the occurrence of transactions and must instead document related party transactions that have already occurred. After identifying the most appropriate transfer pricing methods and quantifying the potential transfer pricing exposure, the taxpayer has sufficient information to develop an overall transfer pricing strategy. The primary issues are (1) whether to prepare documentation, and (2) planning for the potential for transfer pricing disputes. The taxpayer should consider the cost of a transfer pricing examination and whether the lack of a thoroughly-documented transfer pricing policy might result in a difficult IRS examination.

Any documentation strategy will need to take into account the documentation requirements of the other involved countries. The taxpayer will need to consider deadlines for completion, choice of transfer pricing method and the likelihood that the IRS or the foreign tax authority will ultimately obtain copies of documentation prepared for the other jurisdiction. Given the cross-border nature of transfer pricing issues, the taxpayer will need to consider the likelihood that an examination in either country will raise issues that can only be resolved through the competent authority process.

---

[6] Ernst & Young, 2009 Global Transfer Pricing Survey, *available at*: *http://www.ey.com/Publication/vwLUAssets/ 2009_Global_transfer_pricing_survey /$FILE/Ernst%* *20&%20Young%202009%20Global%20transfer%20pric- ing%20survey.pdf.*

The manner in which the taxpayer presents its transfer pricing analysis can be as important as the underlying substantive content. For example, U.S. transfer pricing regulations make it clear that the IRS will evaluate the taxpayer's transfer price based on results rather than the method used to determine the price.[7] On the other hand, tax examiners in foreign countries often focus their examination on the taxpayer's method used to set prices. Therefore, the taxpayer may benefit from presenting the taxpayer's results under several methods, depending on the degree of acceptability in each country.

¶ 915 Taxpayer Reaction—Overall Substantive/Procedural Strategy

Increased global enforcement of transfer pricing forces taxpayers to devote more time and resources to the development and execution of global transfer pricing policies. Taxpayers should develop an overall transfer pricing strategy to determine, document, and defend their transfer pricing decisions. This overall transfer pricing strategy should be developed at the earliest practical stage and should include both substantive analysis and procedural alternatives. The transfer pricing strategy should be globally consistent. Further, the strategy should be flexible enough to incorporate any new information received throughout the examination and post-examination administrative processes.

.01 Examination Strategies

The examination stage will focus on the taxpayer's substantive development of its transfer pricing issues. The IRS will review the taxpayer's documentation, request additional factual and financial information, and interview taxpayer personnel. The IRS will attempt to understand the taxpayer's business, functions and risks, and intercompany transactions. Ultimately, the IRS will develop a position with respect to the taxpayer's transfer pricing determinations and may propose an adjustment to the taxpayer's income. Some limited opportunity for settlement negotiations is available at the end of the examination.

Taxpayers would be well-advised to be prepared, cooperative and proactive throughout the examination process. Transfer pricing involves multiple factual determinations and the subjective application of transfer pricing rules. Taxpayers should not wait for the IRS economists and examiners to formulate their positions before engaging in a discussion of the issues; instead, taxpayers should avail themselves of every opportunity to explain the taxpayer's industry, structure and transactions and every step of transfer pricing analysis. This proactive approach is calculated to avoid the misinterpretation of taxpayer facts and transfer pricing analysis.

During the examination process, the taxpayers should pay attention to the IRS examiner's responses to taxpayer's positions and representations. These reactions by the IRS may be important indicators of which substantive arguments will be persuasive and which procedural alternatives hold the most promise for subsequent negotiations.

---

[7] Reg. § 1.482-1(f)(2)(v).

¶915

.02 Procedural Alternatives

Toward the end of the examination, the IRS team's position regarding the taxpayer's facts and transfer pricing analysis will become somewhat fixed. When that happens, the taxpayer should shift its emphasis to its procedural strategy. A taxpayer's facts, the IRS examination team's reaction to those facts, and the IRS positions and proposed adjustments in the economist's report will dictate the best procedural strategy to move the dispute to the most favorable forum.

The taxpayer's most important procedural decision is the choice between unilateral and bilateral procedural alternatives. A preliminary decision on this point should be made very early in the dispute process and re-evaluated throughout the process. Should the taxpayer choose a unilateral approach, the taxpayer is unlikely to receive full correlative relief in the other involved country or countries. The bilateral approach is more likely to produce full relief from double taxation, but generally takes longer and may be more expensive than a unilateral approach. Thus, taxpayers must balance the likelihood of a full IRS concession and the taxpayer's willingness to accept a certain level of double taxation against the additional time and expense of a bilateral approach.

Taxpayers have a growing assortment of post-examination procedures available to resolve transfer pricing disputes. Once the unilateral/bilateral decision has been made, the remaining procedural decisions revolve around moving the dispute to the procedural forum with the decision-maker and standard for decision most likely to resolve the dispute.

Nearly all unilateral strategies, and some bilateral strategies, involve the IRS' administrative appeals process. In addition to providing a different IRS decision-maker with a fresh perspective, the Appeals standard for decision incorporates the "hazards of litigation" into its evaluation of the IRS settlement positions. If the taxpayer and the IRS cannot agree in Appeals, the taxpayer must choose between litigation (Tax Court or other Federal Court) and the IRS alternative dispute resolution ("ADR") alternatives (mediation and arbitration).

All bilateral strategies involve competent authority negotiations. Taxpayers can request competent authority assistance as early as the end of the examination, as late as after litigation is decided, and any point in between. Bilateral APAs also involve competent authority negotiations, albeit on a prospective basis. A number of these procedures can sometimes be combined to achieve the most effective resolution.

¶915.02

Transfer Pricing Dispute Procedural Flow Chart

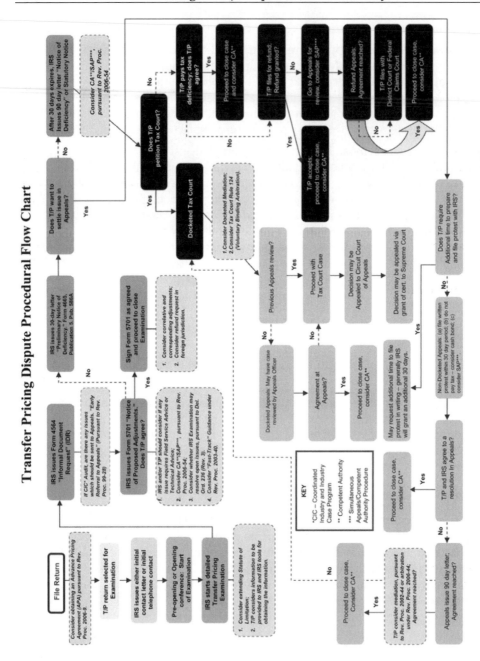

¶ 920 The Taxpayer's Biggest Decision: *Unilateral v. Bilateral Procedural Alternatives*

If the taxpayer is unable to resolve its transfer pricing issues with the IRS by the end of the examination process, the taxpayer must be prepared to pursue its remaining procedural alternatives. These alternatives will be discussed in detail in this chapter. These procedures will be categorized into "unilateral" procedures (involving taxpayer resolution with the IRS) and "bilateral" procedures (involving the IRS and the fiscal authority of other involved countries) and discussed briefly to illustrate the opportunity for settlement. Most of these procedures can be categorized as seeking a favorable forum for negotiation or enabling taxpayers to extend an agreement achieved in one tax year to resolve the same issues in other tax years.

The taxpayer's major decision is whether the taxpayer wishes to pursue a unilateral resolution with the IRS or a bilateral resolution with both the IRS and the other involved country. Although the taxpayer can decide between unilateral or bilateral resolution at various points in the administrative review process, and the decision can sometimes be reversed, it is generally most desirable for the taxpayer to commit early to a unilateral or bilateral approach, as the arguments may differ substantially between the two approaches.

The substantive standard for a unilateral approach is Code Sec. 482 and the regulations; the substantive standard for a bilateral approach is the OECD guidelines. The taxpayer should apply the information learned through the examination process about the IRS positions on factual and legal points to choose the procedure or procedures most likely to produce a favorable outcome.

¶ 925 Summary of Unilateral Procedural Alternatives—U.S. Only

.01 Different Forums for Resolution

Unilateral Advance Pricing Agreement. A prospective agreement between the taxpayer and the IRS concerning the taxpayer's facts, the appropriate TPM, and an arm's length range of results with regard to specific intercompany transactions.[8]

Early Referral to Appeals. The Early Referral Procedure ("Early Referral") allows taxpayers to request the transfer of one or more developed, unagreed issues from Examination to Appeals while the remaining issues continue to be developed in Examination.[9]

Appeals. The IRS administrative appeals process ("Appeals"), available since 1925, employs face-to-face settlement conferences between taxpayers and independent Appeals Officers to resolve tax disputes after the examination.[10]

Mediation. Mediation is the process of using an objective, neutral third party to assist the taxpayer and IRS Appeals to negotiate to settlement.[11]

---

[8] Rev. Proc. 2006-9, IRB 278; Rev. Proc. 2008-31, IRB 1133.

[9] Rev. Proc. 99-28, Rev. Proc. 99-29.

[10] Reg. § 601.106 et seq.

[11] Rev. Proc. 2009-44, IRB 462.

Fast-Track Mediation. Fast-Track mediation is a process whereby traditional mediation procedures are employed between the taxpayer and Examination before Examination closes the case.[12]

Non-Docketed Arbitration. Arbitration is a dispute resolution process, available for non-docketed disputes under Rev. Proc. 2006-44,[13] whereby the taxpayer and the IRS submit their dispute to a neutral person agreed to by both parties for binding resolution. Unlike in mediation, the neutral third party is the decision-maker.

Docketed Arbitration. Taxpayers whose dispute is docketed with the Tax Court may request voluntary binding arbitration pursuant to Tax Court Rule 124.

Litigation. If the taxpayer and the IRS are unable to resolve the dispute through the administrative process, the taxpayer may choose between the Tax Court and the U.S. District Court or the U.S. Court of Federal Claims. The decision on any of these counts may be appealed to the U.S. Court of Appeals, and, if necessary, to the U.S. Supreme Court.[14]

Tax Court. The Tax Court is available to taxpayers on a deficiency basis, meaning the taxpayer has not yet paid the disputed amount of tax and seeks a declaratory judgment on the issues between the parties.

Other Federal Courts. The U.S. District Court or the U.S. Court of Federal Claims are only available to taxpayers that have already paid the tax in full and are suing for refund.

.02 Extending the Resolution

Accelerated Issue Resolution ("AIR"). Allows Coordinated Issue Case ("CIC")[15] taxpayers that achieve resolution of issues in tax years under examination to extend that resolution to the same issue in all open tax years.[16]

Del. Ord. 236 (Rev. 3). Extends limited authority to Examination personnel to settle issues consistent with an Appeals settlement of the same issue in prior or subsequent tax years.[17]

¶ 930 Summary of Bilateral Procedural Alternatives—U.S. and Treaty Partners

.01 Competent Authority Assistance

Where the application of the tax rules of U.S. and a treaty partner country would produce double taxation, a taxpayer may request competent authority assistance to eliminate the double tax under the mutual agreement procedure article of the tax treaty.[18]

---

[12] Rev. Proc. 2003-40, IRB 1044; Rev. Proc. 2003-41, IRB 1047.

[13] Rev. Proc. 2006-44, IRB 800; Announcement 2008-111.

[14] Code Sec. 7482 and 28 USC §§ 1294, 1295.

[15] "An Appeals Coordinated Issue is an issue or category of case of Service-wide impact or importance that requires Appeals' coordination to ensure uniformity and consistency nationwide. This is achieved through coordi-

nation of efforts between appeals officers and designated ACI coordinators." Appeals Coordinated Issues, *available at: http://www.irs.gov/individuals/aritcle/0,,id=108652,00.html.*

[16] Rev. Proc. 94-67, 1994-2 CB 800.

[17] Del. Ord. 236 (Rev. 3); IRM 1.2.43.35(2).

[18] United States Model Income Tax Convention, Art. 25; *See also* Rev. Proc. 2006-54, 2006-2 CB 1035.

.02 Simultaneous Appeals/Competent Authority Consideration ("SAP")

Coordinates simultaneous involvement of Appeals and competent authority consideration to expedite case resolution.[19]

.03 Accelerated Competent Authority

Taxpayers requesting competent authority assistance with respect to an issue raised by the IRS may also request that the competent authority attempt to resolve the issue for the subsequent taxable years for which returns have been filed.[20]

.04 Bilateral Advance Pricing Agreement

A prospective agreement between the taxpayer, the IRS, and the tax authority of the other involved country (U.S. treaty partner) concerning the taxpayer's facts, the appropriate TPM, and an arm's length range of results with regard to specific intercompany transactions.[21]

¶ 935 Reasons to Favor Unilateral Resolution

.01 No Treaty Partner

A taxpayer may have several reasons to seek unilateral resolution with the IRS and forego the possibility of simultaneous relief with the relevant foreign tax authority. Of course, unilateral resolution with the IRS will be the sole alternative if the transaction involves a non-treaty country.

> **Comment:** There is no authority for the U.S. competent authority to provide relief from U.S. tax or provide assistance due to taxation arising under the tax laws of a foreign country or the United States unless such authority is granted by treaty.[22] The United States currently is a party to over 60 income tax treaties.

.02 Cost/Benefits

Some taxpayers may choose unilateral resolution over bilateral resolution, risking a certain level of double tax, based on a cost/benefit analysis that the additional cost of bilateral negotiations might exceed the benefit of eliminating double tax. First, if the amount in issue is not large enough to justify the incremental cost of bilateral negotiations, taxpayers will choose unilateral resolution. Second, taxpayers are unlikely to seek bilateral resolution if the United States is the only tax jurisdiction likely to impose a transfer pricing adjustment. In that case, the benefit of a bilateral agreement would not justify the additional cost of three-party negotiations. However, recent increases in the transfer pricing enforcement efforts by other countries have greatly reduced the likelihood that the United States would be the only country likely to impose a transfer pricing adjustment.

---

[19] Rev. Proc. 2006-54, at § 8.01.
[20] *Id.* at § 7.06.
[21] Rev. Proc. 2006-9 IRB 278.

[22] Rev. Proc. 2006-54, § § 2.01 and 2.02; *see also* Internal Revenue Service, *The Tax Gap and International Taxpayers*, Feb. 2008, *available at http://www.irs.gov/businesses/article/0,,id=180215,00.htm.*

.03 Time

Bilateral resolution of transfer pricing issues also takes considerably longer than unilateral resolution. For example, bilateral APAs take nearly twice as long to resolve as unilateral APAs.[23] Competent authority resolution takes an average of approximately 2 years in addition to unilateral discussions.[24] Some taxpayers would rather resolve their transfer pricing issues quickly and turn their attention to other matters than to spend the additional time needed to achieve bilateral resolution.

.04 Other Tax Issues

In addition, the taxpayer may decide to seek a unilateral resolution either (1) to preclude the costs of a bilateral effort, or (2) to avoid drawing attention to itself in the other taxing jurisdiction. The taxpayer may be unwilling to disclose information regarding its U.S. operations to the foreign tax authorities. For example, the laws of a foreign jurisdiction may require that a corporation receive certain government approvals to operate outside of its home country, which the taxpayer may have failed to obtain before establishing its U.S. operations. Further, the taxpayer may limit itself to unilateral resolution with the IRS because it believes that, during the competent authority process, it may draw attention to other issues with tax exposure.

¶ 940 Reasons to Favor Bilateral Resolution

.01 Exposure to Material Double Tax

The primary reason to seek a bilateral resolution with the IRS and a foreign tax authority is to avoid the double taxation exposure arising from any U.S. or foreign-initiated adjustment. By invoking the competent authority process, the tax authorities of both treaty countries will attempt to reach a settlement that eliminates double taxation through the mutual attribution of income, deductions, credits or allowances between related taxpayers. The timing of the competent authority request is important because an administrative or judicial determination will limit the relief sought by the U.S. competent authority to a correlative adjustment from the treaty partner.

> **Comment:** If a taxpayer either executes a closing agreement with the District (whether or not contingent upon competent authority relief) with respect to a potential competent authority issue or reaches a settlement on the issue with Appeals or Counsel pursuant to a closing agreement or other written agreement, the U.S. competent authority will endeavor only to obtain a correlative adjustment from the treaty country and will not undertake any actions that would otherwise change such agreements.[25]

Thus, when the taxpayer is dealing with an adjustment involving a treaty partner, proceeding directly to the competent authority process provides the U.S. competent authority greater latitude to resolve double taxation issues.

---

[23] 2009 Announcement and Report Concerning Advance Pricing Agreements, Announcement 2009-28, 2009-15 IRB 760, March 2009, *available at http://www.irs.gov/pub/irs-drop/a-09-28.pdf.*

[24] "Transfer Pricing Inventory of U.S. Double-Tax Cases Highest on Record; Foreign Adjustments Exceed U.S.," 240 *Daily Tax Rep.* I-1 (Dec. 15, 2008).

[25] Rev. Proc. 2006-54, at § 7.05.

.02 Tax Credit Issues

Another reason to favor a bilateral resolution is that the use of competent authority procedures may protect the taxpayer's foreign tax credits from disallowance. When the U.S. entity is the direct or indirect parent of the related foreign entity, the IRS may treat the foreign taxes paid by the foreign related entity on the income reallocated to the U.S. entity as a voluntary payment, rather than a creditable foreign tax.[26] To be a creditable tax, the levy must be a compulsory payment paid to a foreign country pursuant to its authority to levy taxes.[27] The levy will not be considered a compulsory payment unless the taxpayer exhausts all effective and practical remedies to reduce the taxpayer's liability for the foreign tax.[28] Failure to seek competent authority assistance may constitute a failure to exhaust all effective and practical remedies.

Further, because the IRS may require a reduction of the related foreign entity's E&P and subpart F income upon the reallocation, there may be a reduction in the type of income that attracts indirect foreign tax credits.[29] If the IRS proposes an adjustment increasing the income of the U.S. entity, the taxpayer can use the competent authority process to have the U.S. competent authority seek a reduction in the related entity's taxable income, reducing the foreign taxes paid by the foreign entity, and approving any remaining foreign taxes as creditable for foreign tax credit purposes.[30]

.03 Special Industries

Finally, a bilateral resolution should be considered when the transfer pricing issues involve certain industries, including pharmaceuticals, oil, grain, data processing, heavy construction, and electronics. These industries are part of the industry-wide exchange of information that allows the IRS and the tax authorities of U.S. treaty partners to share their cumulative experience regarding a particular industry.[31] These industry-wide exchanges of information may reveal the need for an examination of tax issues and, in certain circumstances, may result in the simultaneous examination of specific taxpayers. Thus, the taxpayer should anticipate that, in these industries, the foreign tax authority may become involved in the transactions at issue.

¶ 945 Statute of Limitations Issues

Generally, the IRS must assess an income tax deficiency within three years of the later of the due date of the taxpayer's return or date the taxpayer files its income tax return.[32] The Internal Revenue Code deems a return filed on the later of its due date or the date actually filed.[33] The Internal Revenue Code places no restrictions on the time within which assessments may be made for periods for which the taxpayer did not file a return.[34] Several events will extend this period,

---

[26] *Id.* at § 2.04,11.

[27] Reg. § 1.901-2(a)(2)(i).

[28] Reg. § 1.901-2(e)(5)(i).

[29] *See generally* Code Secs. 902 and 960.

[30] Rev. Proc. 2006-54, at § 2.04 and § 11.

[31] *See* IRS Publication 3218 (Apr. 1999) at Ch. 5, Sec. IV.B., *available at http://www.irs.gov/pub/irs-pdf/p3218.pdf.*

[32] Code Sec. 6501(a).

[33] Code Sec. 6501(b).

[34] Code Sec. 6501(c)(3).

including the IRS issuing a notice of deficiency (90-day letter) and the taxpayer entering into an agreement with the IRS to extend the period.

The IRS completes very few CIC examinations, and completes virtually none of its transfer pricing examinations, within this three year period. This occurs for two reasons. First, CIC examination cycles generally involve multiple years. As a result, several years usually pass between the filing of the return for the examination cycle's initial year and the initiation of the examination. Second, transfer pricing examinations require extensive information gathering and expert analysis. Planning the examination, gathering information, analyzing that information, and preparing the necessary reports frequently takes more than two years. Because of the time required for a transfer pricing examination, the IRS will generally seek an extension of the assessment statute of limitations.

Agreements to extend the statute of limitation can be for a fixed period or open ended, restricted or unrestricted.[35] The IRS uses Form 872, "Consent to Extend the Time to Assess Tax," for fixed period extension agreements. The IRS uses Form 872-A, "Special Consent to Extend Time to Assess Tax," for open-ended agreements. In addition, the IRS uses Form 872-O, "Special Consent to Extend Time to Assess Tax Attributable to Partnership Items," for post-TEFRA unified partnership examinations, and Form 872-R, "Special Consent to extend the Time to Assess Tax Attributable to Items of an S Corporation," for post-TEFRA unified S corporation examinations. Open-ended agreements terminate when the IRS issues a notice of deficiency or when the taxpayer or the IRS sends the other party a notice terminating the extension agreement, generally a Form 872-T.[36] The IRS enters into restricted consent agreements when the taxpayer agrees to extend the statute of limitations only for specific identified issues.[37] Restricted consents can be for a fixed or open-ended period of time.

Generally, an officer with authority to sign tax returns may sign the extension agreement on behalf of a corporation.[38] For affiliated corporations filing a consolidated return, the common parent has the authority to extend the statute as the agent for the group.[39]

A taxpayer considering entering into an agreement to extend the statute of limitations must balance several factors. A refusal to extend the statute will increase the pressure on the examination team to complete the examination. While this may appear to limit the examination team's ability to gather information or strengthen its case, the pressure may also encourage the examination team to issue summonses and a designated summons. A designated summons tolls the period for assessment during the period the IRS seeks judicial enforcement of the summons, and for a period thereafter. The IRS may seek enforcement of the summons even after it issues a notice of deficiency.[40] A refusal to give the IRS more time to

---

[35] IRM 25 Chapter 6 at § 22.

[36] Rev. Proc. 79-22, 1979-1 CB 563.

[37] *See* Rev. Proc. 68-31, 1968-2 CB 917, as modified by Rev. Proc. 77-6, 1977-1 CB 539 (detailing the circumstances under which the IRS will enter into a restricted consent).

[38] Rev. Rul. 83-41, 1983-1 CB 349, as amplified and clarified by Rev. Rul. 84-165, 1984-2 CB 305.

[39] Reg. § 1.1502-77(a).

[40] *See M.K. Ash*, CCH Dec. 47,221, 96 TC 459 (1991).

complete its examination could also push the IRS to issue a deficiency notice that could include an artificially large adjustment amount.[41] The taxpayer will then have reduced its options for contesting the adjustment.

Although a hastily drafted transfer pricing notice of deficiency can limit a taxpayer's procedural options, it also may provide benefits to taxpayers considering litigation. In transfer pricing litigation, as in most tax litigation, the taxpayer bears the general burden of proof, the burden of establishing the arm's length amount of the prices at issue. However, due to the discretion granted the IRS by Code Sec. 482, transfer pricing cases impose an additional threshold burden on the taxpayer. Specifically, the taxpayer bears the burden of proving that the IRS abused its discretion in making an arbitrary, capricious, and unreasonable adjustment. The issue of whether the IRS abused its discretion represents a threshold question that must be resolved by the court before it can directly address the pricing issues. If the IRS abandons the theories used in the notice of deficiency at trial, the court may find that the taxpayer has met its threshold burden of establishing that the notice of deficiency set forth an arbitrary, capricious, or unreasonable allocation. However, the extensive oversight involved in CIC examinations makes the return of a transfer pricing case to the examination team unlikely for practical reasons.

Once the IRS has issued a statutory deficiency notice, the taxpayer can only obtain Appeals consideration by filing a Tax Court petition.[42] Furthermore, when Appeals is considering a docketed case involving a transfer pricing issue, the Deputy Associate Chief Counsel (International) has the authority (after consulting with Appeals officials and Regional Counsel) to determine that the transfer pricing issue should not be considered by Appeals and to send the issue back to the Tax Court.[43] The taxpayer could still litigate the adjustment in a District Court or the Court of Federal Claims, but could not get the benefit of Appeals consideration prior to the litigation. This course of action also restricts the ability of competent authority to obtain complete double tax relief.[44]

Under certain circumstances, the taxpayer may want to force the examination team into concluding the examination and move the case to Appeals. For example, the IRS examination team may fail to follow its timetable, or consuming an inordinate amount of the taxpayer's time and resources, without identifying any bona fide issues or building a case that justifies their examination. This may happen if the examination extends over a number of years during which key team members change a number of times. By refusing to enter into an agreement to extend the statute, the taxpayer may force the examination team to issue a premature notice of proposed adjustment (30-day letter). The taxpayer could then file its protest and offer to enter into an agreement to extend the statute with the Appeals office, preserving its Appeals and competent authority opportunities. After the Appeals office receives the case and the statute extension, however, it might

---

[41] See IRS Pub. No. 1035, Extending the Tax Assessment Period (Rev. June 2007), *available at http://www.irs.gov/pub/irs-pdf/p1035.pdf.*

[42] See Rev. Proc. 87-24, 1987-1 CB 720 at §2.01; IRM 8.1.1.3.

[43] Rev. Proc. 87-24, at §2.08.

[44] See Rev. Proc. 2006-54, at §7.05.

conclude that the case requires greater factual development and return the case to the IRS examination team.[45]

In transfer pricing cases, taxpayers generally seek collateral adjustments through the competent authority process. Therefore, taxpayers must give consideration to the statute of limitations of the other countries involved in the transactions. The United States attempts to include procedures in its income tax treaties permitting transfer pricing collateral adjustments where the domestic law limitations periods has expired.[46] The United States is not always successful in this effort, however, and many U.S. income tax treaties impose time limits on the period within which claims for collateral adjustments must be presented to the tax authorities of the other treaty country.

As explained by the above discussion, the decision of whether and for how long to extend the statute of limitations is an important strategic decision faced in nearly every transfer pricing examination. Taxpayers need to consider both the domestic and the foreign implications of the decision in order to avoid unexpected and unfavorable results.

¶ 950 Privilege Against Disclosure

.01 Attorney-Client Privilege

General. If the taxpayer believes it has substantial exposure to a transfer pricing adjustment or anticipates that the matter will result in litigation with the IRS, the taxpayer should consider conducting the transfer pricing analysis under the oversight of internal or external legal counsel to obtain protection under the attorney-client privilege or the work-product doctrine. The attorney-client privilege protects communications between the client and the attorney or the attorney's agents. The principles of the attorney-client privilege have been stated as follows:

1. Where legal advice of any kind is sought;
2. From a legal advisor in his capacity as such;
3. The communications relating to that purpose;
4. Made in confidence;
5. By the client;
6. Are at his instance permanently protected;
7. From disclosure by himself or by the legal advisor;
8. Except the protection be waived.[47]

The attorney-client privilege encompasses legal advice by the attorney in response to the client's communication.[48] The attorney work product doctrine

---

[45] IRM 8.20.

[46] *See* United States Model Income Tax Convention of September 20, 1996, Article 25(2).

[47] *Rockwell International*, 90-1 USTC ¶ 50,151, 897 F.2d 1255, 1264 (3d Cir. 1990) (quoting *The El Paso Co.*, 82-2

USTC ¶ 9534, 682 F.2d 530, 538 at n.9 (5th Cir. (1982)) (quoting 8 J. Wigmore Evidence §2292 at 554 (J. McNaughton rev. 1961)).

[48] *See J. Bell*, 95-1 USTC ¶ 50,006 (N.D. Cal. 1994).

protects materials prepared for trial or in anticipation of litigation by an attorney or his/her agent or representative.[49]

Protecting the Privilege. If the taxpayer reasonably anticipates litigation and its attorneys conduct the transfer pricing analysis to advise and assist the taxpayer with regard to the anticipated litigation, the disclosure to the IRS of the results of the transfer pricing exposure analysis and related advice concerning strategy may be precluded.[50] However, the taxpayer's underlying transfer pricing information, such as facts and contracts, and documentation intended to be provided to the IRS for purposes of the transfer pricing penalty rules in Code Sec. 6662(e)(3) are not privileged and must be disclosed to the IRS. In addition, to the extent the documents serve management or business purposes, or mixed (litigation and business) purposes, neither privilege will apply.[51]

.02 The Practitioner-Client Privilege

In 1998, Congress extended the attorney-client privilege and attorney work product privileges to include similar communications and activities performed by non-attorneys, such as tax accountants, and other professionals authorized to practice before the IRS in non-criminal tax matters. This privilege does not mirror the attorney client privilege and attorney work product privilege and, in numerous instances, may be more restrictive.[52]

¶ 955 Documentation of Agreement

Taxpayers must carefully document their transfer pricing resolutions to avoid certain traps. Different types of documentation may be used, each with its own benefits and detriments. The two basic settlement forms are Closing Agreements and Waivers of Restriction on Assessment and Collection.

.01 Waivers of Restriction on Assessment and Collection

The most common form for documenting the settlement of a transfer pricing case is the Waiver of Restriction on Assessment and Collection, either a Form 870 or a Form 870-AD.[53] By executing either of these forms, the taxpayer waives the restrictions on the assessment and collection of the deficiency and, if the case has not been considered by Appeals, the taxpayer's right to avail itself of the Appeals procedures. In addition, the taxpayer waives its right to petition the Tax Court for a redetermination of its deficiency. The taxpayer may limit the issues covered by the Form 870 or Form 870-AD and thereby reserve the ability to have Appeals or the Tax Court consider the other issues.

The biggest difference between the Form 870 and the Form 870-AD lies in the taxpayer's ability to re-open or challenge the terms of the settlement. The Form 870 only provides that the IRS will not open the settled issues, whereas the Form 870-AD provides that neither the IRS nor the taxpayer will reopen the settled

---

[49] Fed. R. Civ P. 26(b)(3); *J. Bell*, 95-1 USTC ¶ 50,006 (N.D. Cal. 1994).

[50] *See J. Bell*, 95-1 USTC ¶ 50,006 (N.D. Cal. 1994).

[51] *The El Paso Co.*, 82-2 USTC ¶ 9534, 682 F.2d 530, 542-3 (5th Cir. 1982) (concluding that the documents that included legal analyses were not prepared in anticipation of litigation, but for purposes of determining the financial impact of potential litigation).

[52] *See* Internal Revenue Service Restructuring and Reform Act of 1977 (H.R. 2676), § 341 (as approved by the Ways and Means Committee, October 22, 1997.

[53] Code Sec. 6213(d); IRM 8811.

issues. Therefore, a taxpayer may file a refund claim after executing a Form 870, but not after executing a Form 870-AD. There exists a split of authority over the finality of a Form 870-AD. Some courts apply an estoppel theory to prevent taxpayers from reopening issues resolved by way of a Form 870-AD.[54] Some courts have held, however, that only agreements meeting the requirements of Code Sec. 7121, a requirement not met by Form 870-AD, operate as a final settlement of issues, absent material misrepresentations by the taxpayer.[55] The IRS will not re-open cases closed by either a Form 870 or 870-AD absent:

- Fraud, malfeasance, collusion, concealment, or misrepresentation of material fact;
- The existence of substantial error in the settlement or closing, based on established IRS positions existing during the audit; or
- Circumstances indicating that failure to re-open would be a serious administrative omission.

Because Forms 870 do not constitute closing agreements within the meaning of Code Sec. 7121, they do not limit the relief available from competent authority.[56] However, the IRS takes the position that Appeals settlements reflected on Forms 870-AD constitute "other written agreements," and consequently competent authority will only seek correlative adjustments from foreign competent authorities if the taxpayer has executed a Form 870-AD.

.02 Closing Agreements

Code Sec. 7121 provides the authority for the IRS to enter into formal closing agreements. Formal closing agreements conclusively settle the issues encompassed by the agreement absent fraud, malfeasance, or misrepresentation of material fact.[57] In transfer pricing cases, U.S. competent authority will only seek correlative adjustments from the treaty partner when the IRS and taxpayer enter into a closing agreement relating to the transfer pricing issues.[58]

.03 When to Discuss Form of Agreement

The timing of the discussion regarding the form of the closing agreement depends on the taxpayer's overall strategy for resolving the case. Large case examination teams understand the taxpayer's options regarding Appeals and competent authority. If the taxpayer can tolerate a limited amount of double taxation, the examination team may resolve the case for a lesser amount than it would otherwise if the taxpayer agrees to enter into a formal closing agreement. However, if the examination team or Appeals believes the taxpayer will proceed to competent authority, they will have less incentive to reduce the adjustment in the belief that a higher assessment will be to the advantage of competent authority during its negotiations. Therefore, the size of the adjustment, the availability of competent authority assistance, and the taxpayer's ultimate strategy all contribute to the taxpayer's decision of when and how to discuss the closing documentation.

---

[54] *See* e.g., *M.R. Flynn*, 86-1 USTC ¶ 9285, 786 F.2d 586 (3d Cir. 1986); *A.L. Stair*, 75-1 USTC ¶ 9463, 516 F.2d 560 (2d Cir. 1975).

[55] *See W. Whitney*, 87-2 USTC ¶ 9503, 826 F.2d 896 (9th Cir. 1987).

[56] Rev. Proc. 2006-54, at § 7.05.

[57] *See* Code Sec. 7121(b) (explaining the finality associated with the signing of closing agreements, absent circumstances of fraud, malfeasance, or misrepresentation of a material fact).

[58] Rev. Proc. 2006-54, at § 7.05.

Chapter 10

Preparing Transfer Pricing Documentation

¶ 1001 Overview

A number of U.S. treaty partners have voiced concerns that the emphasis placed by the United States on transfer pricing enforcement (particularly penalties), coupled with relatively low U.S. corporate tax rates encouraged taxpayers to shift income to the United States.[1] In response, these countries have taken action to protect their revenue bases and discourage the shifting of income to the United States or any other country. Over the past few years, most of the major trading partners have either added transfer pricing rules to their tax laws or substantially modified their existing rules to be consistent with the revised OECD guidelines. These countries include: Australia, Brazil, Canada, China, Denmark, France, Germany, Hong Kong, India, Japan, Korea, Mexico, New Zealand, and the United Kingdom. These countries and others have increased their enforcement efforts and many are considering enacting penalties and record keeping requirements.

¶ 1010 U.S. Documentation Requirements

The IRS's inability to obtain taxpayer information has historically been the main obstacle to its effective enforcement of U.S. transfer pricing laws.[2] When taxpayers have delayed or resisted IRS information requests, the IRS has been unable to develop a supportable and sustainable case. Two other impairments to IRS enforcement efforts have been inadequate resources and the inherent subjectiv-

---

[1] *See* generally, OECD Guidelines ¶ 4.26 ("[A] penalty system in one jurisdiction may give taxpayers an incentive to overstate taxable income in that jurisdiction").

[2] *See*, A Study of Intercompany Pricing Under Section 482 of the Code, Notice 88-123, Chapter 3, 1988-2 CB 458, 461 (hereinafter referred to as the "White Paper").

ity in the application of the transfer pricing regulations. More recently, the U.S. government has made a concerted effort to reverse the unsatisfactory IRS enforcement record with statutory, regulatory and administrative changes. The combined impact of these changes has greatly enhanced the IRS ability to enforce U.S. transfer pricing laws.

.01 Reporting of Related Party Transactions

In 1989 and 1990, Congress amended Code Sec. 6038A and added Code Sec. 6038C to require disclosure of certain related party transactions and the maintenance of accessible books and records. Pursuant to these sections, (1) foreign corporations related to U.S. taxpayers, and (2) certain foreign-owned U.S. corporations and foreign corporations engaged in a U.S. trade or business through a branch must disclose information with respect to certain related party transactions on an annual basis. These disclosures are made on IRS Forms 5471 and 5472. (See ¶ 20,050 for the forms.)

.02 Contemporaneous Documentation Requirements

As stated above, the creation and maintenance of contemporaneous transfer pricing documentation is a prerequisite to avoiding penalties. Contemporaneous means prepared on or before the filing of the relevant federal tax return. There are two categories of documentation that a taxpayer must maintain—principal documents and background documents. The principal documents must include:

1. an overview of the taxpayer's business, including an analysis of the economic and legal factors affecting pricing;

2. a description of the taxpayer's organizational structure covering all related parties engaged in transactions potentially relevant under Code Sec. 482;

3. any documentation specifically required by the regulations under Code Sec. 482 (e.g., documents related to a qualified cost sharing arrangement);

4. a description of the method selected and an explanation of why that method was selected;

5. a description of the alternative methods that were considered and an explanation of why they were not selected;

6. a description of controlled transactions and any internal data used to analyze those transactions;

7. a description of the comparables that were used, how comparability was evaluated, and what adjustments (if any) were made;

8. an explanation of the economic analysis and projections relied upon in developing the method;

9. a description or summary of any relevant data obtained after the end of the tax year and before filing a tax return; and

10. a general index of the principal and background documents and a description of the record keeping system used for cataloguing and accessing those documents.

The last two items on the list need to be provided within 30 days of a request, but do not have to be prepared at the time the return is filed.[3]

The background documents, which support the assumptions, conclusions, and positions contained in the principal documents, may include the documents required under the Code Sec. 6038A regulations, such as original entry books and records and profit and loss statements, or other documents not specifically listed in either set of regulations, which the IRS determines are necessary to establish that the taxpayer's method was selected and applied in a way that provides the most reliable measure of an arm's length result.[4] Background documents need not be provided to the IRS unless they are specifically requested, and the 30-day period for producing the documents can be extended.[5]

¶ 1020 OECD Documentation Requirements

.01 OECD

In July, 1995, the OECD published transfer pricing guidelines (the "Guidelines") that focus on the application of the arm's length principle to evaluate the transfer pricing of multinational corporations ("MNCs"). Guidance in Chapter V of the Guidelines was provided to assist taxpayers in identifying documentation that would be most helpful in showing that their controlled transactions satisfy the arm's length principle.[6] Under the guidelines, the following types of information should be made available through documentation, although it is neither a minimum compliance list nor an exclusive list of information that tax administrators may be entitled to request:

1. Information about the associated enterprises involved in the controlled transactions, the transactions at issue, the functions performed, and information derived from independent enterprises engaged in similar transactions or businesses.

2. Information regarding the nature and terms of the controlled transactions, economic conditions and property involved in the transactions, how the product or service that is the subject of the controlled transaction in question flows among the associated enterprises, and changes in trading conditions or renegotiations of existing arrangements;

3. Description of the circumstances of any known transactions between the taxpayer and an unrelated party that are similar to the transaction with a foreign associated enterprise and any information that might bear upon whether independent enterprises dealing at arm's length under comparable circumstances would have entered into a similarly structured transaction;

4. Outline of the business, structure of the organization, and ownership linkages within the MNC group;

[3] Reg. § 1.6662-6(d)(2)(iii)(A).

[4] Reg. § 1.6662-6(d)(2)(iii)(C).

[5] Reg. § 1.6662-6(d)(2)(iii)(C).

[6] Levey and Shapiro, "OECD Transfer Pricing Avoids Overpapering the Best Method," 6 *J. Int'l Tax* 52 (Feb. 1995); Levey and Shapiro, "OECD Transfer Pricing Draft Targets Excessive Documentation," 6 *J. Int'l Tax'n* 244 (June 1995); Levey and Shapiro, "OECD Transfer Pricing Rules Stress Dispute Resolution Methods," 6 *J. Int'l Tax'n* 301 (July 1995).

    5. Information about the amount of sales and operating results from the last few years preceding the transaction;

    6. Information on pricing, including business strategies and special circumstances at issue.

Among the countries that do not have specific documentation provisions, but follow the OECD Guidelines, are Belgium, the Czech Republic, Italy, Singapore, Spain and Sweden.

¶ 1030 Pacific Association of Tax Administrators

.01 Pacific Association of Tax Administrators

On March 13, 2003, PATA released its "Transfer Pricing Documentation Package," (the "PATA Documentation Package") which provides for a harmonized transfer pricing documentation procedure among PATA member states, namely, Australia, Canada, Japan, and the United States. Compliance with the PATA Documentation Package, which is voluntary, requires that taxpayers prepare one set of documentation that will meet the transfer pricing documentation requirements of all the PATA members. Taxpayers that choose to use the PATA documentation package to avoid the imposition of PATA member transfer pricing penalties must satisfy three operative principles. MNCs must: (1) make reasonable efforts to establish arm's length transfer prices; (2) maintain contemporaneous documentation of their efforts to comply with the arm's length principle; and (3) produce, in a timely manner, that documentation upon request by a PATA member tax administrator.

This PATA Documentation Package seeks to respond to the potential difficulties that MNCs face in complying with the laws and administrative requirements of multiple tax jurisdictions. By providing taxpayers with the option of applying this uniform documentation package, the PATA members intend to help taxpayers efficiently prepare and maintain useful transfer pricing documentation, and timely produce such documentation upon request to PATA member tax administrations while precluding any related transfer pricing penalties. This documentation package is intended to be consistent with the general principles outlined in Chapter V of the OECD Guidelines, although the package has drawn criticism for the significant level of detail required, which is perceived to be greater than that required by any particular member country.

The documentation required by PATA is, by contrast to some countries, quite extensive and arguably greater than that required by the participating member countries. Among other things, the following information and documentation is necessary to comply with the PATA documentation requirements:

    1. Description of the nature of the business/industry and market conditions, including an identification of the participants in the related party dealings and their relationship;

    2. Description of taxpayer's worldwide organizational structure (including an organization chart) covering all associated enterprises engaged in transac-

tions potentially relevant to determining an arm's length price for the documented transactions;

3. Outline of the business including a relevant recent history of the taxpayer, the industries operated in, the general economic and legal issues affecting the business and industry, and the taxpayer's business lines;

4. Analysis of the economic and legal factors that affect the pricing of taxpayer's property and services;

5. Description of intangible property potentially relevant to the pricing of the taxpayer's property or services in the controlled transactions;

6. Information as to the functions performed, assets employed and risks assumed relevant to the transactions

7. Description of the controlled transactions that identifies the participants, the property or services to which the transaction relates and any intangible rights or property attached thereto, the scope, timing, frequency of, type, and value of the controlled transactions (including all relevant related party dealings in relevant geographic markets), as well as the currency of the transactions, and the terms and conditions of the transactions and their relationship to the terms and conditions of each other transaction entered into between the participants;

8. Copies of all relevant inter-company agreements;

9. Relevant information regarding business strategies and special circumstances at issue, for example, set-off transactions, market share strategies, distribution channel selection and management strategies that influenced the determination of transfer prices;

10. Information concerning cost contribution agreements to which the taxpayer is a party;

11. If the taxpayer pursues a market share strategy, documentation demonstrating that appropriate analysis was done prior to implementing the strategy, that the strategy is pursued only for a reasonable period, and that the costs borne by each associated enterprise are proportionate to projected benefits to such enterprise

12. Description of the comparables including, for tangible property, its physical features, quality, availability; for services, the nature and extent of the services; and for intangible property, the form of the transaction, the type of intangible, the rights to use the intangible that are assigned, and the anticipated benefits from its use;

13. For the taxpayer and the comparable firms, identify the factors considered when evaluating comparability, including the characteristics of the property or service transferred, the functions performed (and the significance of those functions in terms of their frequency, nature and value to the respective parties), the assets employed (taking into consideration their age, market value, location, etc.), the risks assumed (including risks such as market risk, financial risk, and credit risk), the terms and conditions of

¶1030.01

the contract, the business strategies pursued, the economic circumstances (for example, the geographic location, market size, competitive environment, availability of substitute goods and services, levels of supply and demand, nature and extent of government regulations, and costs of production, etc.), and any other special circumstances;

14. Information about criteria used in the selection of comparables including database screens and economic considerations;

15. Information about adjustments made to the comparables, aggregation analysis (grouping of transactions for comparability), the supporting Transfer Pricing Methodology or methodologies used, if any;

16. Information and documentation about the selected TPM, the data and methods considered and the analysis performed to determine the transfer pricing, and an explanation of why alternate methods considered were not selected;

17. Documentation of assumptions and judgments made in the course of determining an arm's length outcome; and

18. Information about updates made to prior year documentation relied upon in the current year to reflect adjustments for any material changes in the relevant facts and circumstances.

Despite the benefits available to taxpayers that attempt to satisfy documentation requirements in multiple PATA jurisdictions by preparing "PATA-compliant" documentation, practitioners have identified several problems with this procedure.[7] While the PATA guidelines state that the required documentation should not impose higher documentation requirements than those set forth in any PATA member's local laws, this is not necessarily the case. Additionally, while the PATA Documentation Package provides a uniform system for creating documentation, it leaves the question of whether taxpayers have used "reasonable efforts" to prepare documentation subject to determination by local tax authorities under their respective local laws. Finally, while the PATA Documentation Package requires substantial information about a MNC's comparable transactions to support the arm's length nature of the its transfer pricing, it contains no guidance as to the nature of the comparable transactions, whether local comparables must be used, or whether some form of blended comparable is required.[8]

¶ 1040 Preparing and Relying on Transfer Pricing Documentation

.01 Overview

As previously discussed, the amount of any IRS transfer pricing adjustment that relates to transactions that are included within the transfer pricing documentation requirement of Reg. § 1.6662-6(d)(2), will not be included in the calculation of

---

[7] *See* Tropin, "PATA Documentation Package Seen Offering Little Help with Compliance Burden, Penalty Insurance," 12 *Tax Management Transfer Pricing Report* 1 (May 2003).

[8] *See* Lebovitz, van Herksen, Kirschenbaum and Nijhof, "Achieving Transfer Pricing Com-PATA-bility," 14 *J. Int'l Tax'n*, Vol. 14, Part 9, pp. 14-19 (September 2003).

whether the 20 percent or 40 percent understatement penalties will apply. This section discusses the preparation of transfer pricing documentation pursuant to the U.S. rules. Following sections will discuss OECD and foreign documentation requirements as well as methods for satisfying multiple jurisdictions with the same set of transfer pricing documentation. This section is not intended to be an exacting "how-to" guide because there is no set standard for the preparation of documentation. Instead, it will give a rather detailed outline of the U.S. documentation process. However, before discussing the U.S. transfer pricing documentation process in greater detail, it is important to keep the following points in mind.

Subjectivity. The process of determining arm's length transfer prices and transfer pricing documentation is inherently subjective. Therefore, except for the case of an exact CUP or CUT, the arm's length transfer price will be found in a range of prices.

Disclosure. Although transfer pricing documentation can be viewed as being prepared in anticipation of an audit or litigation, it is not subject to the attorney-client, accountant-client, or any similar evidentiary privileges. In fact, transfer pricing documentation *must* be turned over to the IRS within 30 days of a request in order to comply with the regulations. Therefore, transfer pricing documentation should be prepared with the intent to demonstrate the taxpayer's compliance with the Code Sec. 482 arm's length standard, and not in a manner that critically examines the weaknesses of the taxpayer's transfer pricing practices.

.02 Factors Considered in Determining Compliance

To avoid the imposition of penalties, the taxpayer, through the preparation of transfer pricing documentation, must be able to reasonably conclude that, given the available data, its selection of the method for determining transfer prices and the application of such method satisfies the best method rule.[9] This requires the taxpayer to make a reasonable effort to evaluate the potential applicability of other TPMs.[10] However, the taxpayer need not make an exhaustive analysis or detailed application of each method. Instead, after a reasonably thorough search for data, the taxpayer should consider which TPM would satisfy the best method rule given that data.[11] However, the regulations recognize that the nature of the available data may allow for only the cursory consideration of alternative TPMs (e.g., the availability of CUPs may eliminate the need to make a detailed CPM analysis). In addition, the taxpayer is not required to analyze whether an unspecified TPM would satisfy the best method rule.[12] Whether the taxpayer's conclusion was reasonable is determined after considering all facts and circumstances. Several factors to be considered include the following:

Taxpayer Experience. The taxpayer's experience and knowledge of transfer pricing is relevant in determining how thorough and precise its transfer pricing analysis must be.[13] For this purpose, transfer pricing experience and knowledge will be determined on a controlled-group basis.[14] Consequently, a relatively minor

---

[9] Reg. § 1.6662-6(d)(2)(ii).
[10] Reg. § 1.6662-6(d)(2)(ii).
[11] Reg. § 1.6662-6(d)(2)(ii).

[12] Reg. § 1.6662-6(d)(2)(ii).
[13] Reg. § 1.6662-6(d)(2)(ii)(A).
[14] Reg. § 1.6662-6(d)(2)(ii)(A).

subsidiary in a substantial multinational group would not likely be able to claim to have little or no transfer pricing experience.

> **Comment:** The inference made by this regulation that the transfer pricing knowledge of the significant members of a multinational group is imputed to the less significant members of the same group, while being theoretically true and necessary on a regulatory basis, is not necessarily true in practice. The collective experience of the authors indicates that it is not uncommon to find a tax director of a relatively minor (sales less than $100 million) subsidiary of a multinational group with little or no transfer pricing experience.

Availability of Data. A taxpayer must conduct a reasonably thorough search for the data necessary to determine which TPM satisfies the best method rule and how that method should be applied.[15] In making this search, the taxpayer may weigh the expense of additional search efforts against: (i) the likelihood that they will find additional data that will improve the reliability of the results, and (ii) the amount by which any new data would change the taxpayer's taxable income.[16] In addition, the preamble to the final regulations indicates that as the amount of taxable income potentially at stake declines (either because of low dollar amounts of the controlled transactions or because of low variability in expected results), the need to search for additional data decreases.

Taxpayers must prepare their transfer pricing documentation using only the data available before the end of the taxable year.[17] This rule represents a change from the proposed and temporary regulations, which required the use of the most current data available prior to the filing of the tax return. This requirement was criticized by taxpayers and commentators as being unduly burdensome because taxpayers would be required to continuously update their transfer pricing analysis if they acquire additional data before their return was filed. Although the final regulations have eliminated the requirement of the proposed and temporary regulations, they do require the taxpayer to include that data as a principal document in its documentation report if the taxpayer acquires additional relevant data before the time that the tax return is due.[18]

Compliance with Other Code Sec. 482 Requirements. Another factor considered is the extent to which the taxpayer complied with the requirements in the substantive regulations under Code Sec. 482 regarding the application of the TPMs (e.g., whether the taxpayer made adjustments to the comparables to increase accuracy).[19]

Reliance on Professionals and Prior Analyses. In preparing their transfer pricing documentation, taxpayers may reasonably rely on a study or other analysis prepared by a qualified professional such as an accountant, economist, or attorney.[20] It does not matter whether the professional is an employee or is otherwise related to the taxpayer so long as the analysis is objective, thorough, and well-

---

[15] Reg. § 1.6662-6(d)(2)(ii)(B).
[16] Reg. § 1.6662-6(d)(2)(ii)(B).
[17] Reg. § 1.6662-6(d)(2)(ii)(B).
[18] Reg. § 1.6662-6(d)(2)(ii)(B).
[19] Reg. § 1.6662-6(d)(2)(ii)(C).
[20] Reg. § 1.6662-6(d)(2)(ii)(D).

¶1040.02

reasoned.[21] Reliance on a professional is reasonable only if the taxpayer discloses all relevant information regarding the controlled transactions at issue.

> *Comment:* Failure to satisfy this requirement led to the imposition of transfer pricing penalties in the *DHL* case.

The regulation also allows the taxpayer to reasonably rely on a study prepared for a prior year if the relevant facts and circumstances have not changed or if the study has been appropriately modified to reflect any change in facts or circumstances.[22]

> *Comment:* Although this regulation contemplates the use of a transfer pricing study for more than one tax year, thus lowering compliance costs, there are instances where a taxpayer would want to obtain a new study. For instance, the cost of a new study may be more than offset by lower required profitability if the taxpayer operates in an industry experiencing losses. In addition, if the other party to the controlled transaction is in need of cash, conducting a new study *may* allow for lower profitability for the taxpayer, and thus higher profitability (and more cash) for the other party.

Selection of Comparables. Another factor to consider is whether the taxpayer arbitrarily selected its comparables with the intention of arriving at a low arm's length range.[23]

Prior Approved TPMs. Another factor to consider is whether the TPM applied by the taxpayer was specifically approved by the IRS in a prior APA or examination for a prior year.[24] In such a case, the taxpayer must also demonstrate that it applied the TPM in a manner that is reasonable and consistent with its previously approved application.[25] In addition, the taxpayer must show that the facts and circumstances surrounding the previous application of the TPM have not materially changed, or if they have, that appropriate adjustments have been made.[26]

Relative Size of the Adjustment. The last of the specified factors is a consideration of the size of the net transfer pricing adjustment relative to the size of the controlled transaction from which the adjustment originated.[27]

¶ 1050 The Transfer Pricing Report

The principal transfer pricing documents specified in Reg. § 1.6662-6(d)(2)(iii)(B) are usually included within a report prepared by a qualified transfer pricing professional. This report typically contains a narrative description of the controlled taxpayers and the controlled transactions followed by an economic analysis that supports the use of the selected TPM as the best method for evaluating the transfer prices. (See the Practice Tools at ¶ 20,060 and ¶ 20,070 for a Model Transfer Pricing Documentation Outline and Process Steps in Transfer Pricing Documentation, respectively.)

---

[21] Reg. § 1.6662-6(d)(2)(ii)(D).
[22] Reg. § 1.6662-6(d)(2)(ii)(D).
[23] Reg. § 1.6662-6(d)(2)(ii)(e).
[24] Reg. § 1.6662-6(d)(2)(ii)(F).

[25] Reg. § 1.6662-6(d)(2)(ii)(F).
[26] Reg. § 1.6662-6(d)(2)(ii)(F).
[27] Reg. § 1.6662-6(d)(2)(ii)(G).

.01 Description of the Taxpayer and Covered Transactions

Taxpayer Description. The report should begin with an introduction of the taxpayer and its related parties. This introduction should include an organizational chart and describe the structure of the worldwide group, the roles of each entity within the group, and the industries in which the entities compete. Ideally, the report should provide the following information with respect to each of the relevant entities:

- Legal name and employer identification number;
- Legal status (corporation, partnership, branch, joint venture, disregarded entity, etc.);
- Country of incorporation and tax residence;
- Ownership structure and percentages of ownership;
- Type of business conducted (e.g., manufacturing, distribution, retail, R&D, etc.);
- The nature of products or services provided;
- Description of customers (e.g., retail v. wholesale, geographic locations); and
- Description of suppliers.

    Comment: This information can usually be found in the taxpayer's annual report, other SEC filings, internet site, marketing materials, and through the corporate secretary's office.

This introduction should also provide a fairly detailed description of the taxpayer's industry. In doing so, the following information should be provided:

- Type of industry (e.g., automotive, pharmaceutical, consumer goods, etc.);
- Competition within the industry (e.g., number and type of competitors, market shares, barriers to entry, whether the good or service is considered a commodity);
- External factors affecting the industry (e.g., technological advances, foreign exchange, global economies, domestic or foreign legal restrictions, etc.)

    Comment: This information can usually be found in the taxpayer's annual report, other SEC filings, Internet site, marketing materials, and trade publications.

Covered Transactions. Following a description of the taxpayer, its industry, and its business, the report should identify and describe the controlled transactions that will be the subject of transfer pricing documentation.

    Comment: It would also be appropriate at this point to identify and catalog all controlled transactions between the taxpayer and related entities, whether or not consideration is paid. While not all controlled transactions must be the subject of the report (e.g., small transactions), cataloging all controlled transactions is useful in identifying transactions that would otherwise be overlooked. In addition, it should be kept in mind that not all controlled

¶1050.01

transactions are readily recognizable. Examples of such transactions that are sometimes overlooked include: the provision of technical assistance or administrative services; the use of tradenames or designs, know-how, customer lists, or distribution networks; or loans in the form of intercompany receivables.

Each transaction that will be covered by the report should be described in detail, with particular emphasis on the following information:

- Type of transaction (e.g., tangible goods, services, intangibles, loans, etc.);
- Copies of any contracts concerning the covered transactions;
- The amount of consideration received and how the amount was determined;
- Any costs incurred by the taxpayer in obtaining the goods that were sold or in providing the services; and
- Reasonable alternatives available to the taxpayer (i.e., unrelated suppliers).

.02 Functional and Risk Analysis

The purpose of the functional analysis is to determine how each related party adds value to the covered transaction, which, in turn, is used to assess the comparability of prospective uncontrolled transactions or entities. The theory behind the functional analysis is that each function or risk has an impact on the transaction's pricing or profitability. This analysis requires a review of the functions performed, assets (tangible or intangible) and skills used, and risks assumed by each related party.

> *Comment:* In practice, a functional analysis is really an exercise in transfer pricing issue spotting. The information for the functional analysis is usually obtained through databases, contract reviews, annual reports, taxpayer interviews, site-visits, and library and internet research. However, as with any issue-spotting exercise, facts must be established based on economic substance, and not merely by reviewing documents.

Some of the specific functions that must be identified and reviewed include:

- Type of activity performed (i.e., manufacturing v. distribution);
- Whether R&D activities are performed;
- Whether intangibles are used;
- Whether quality control activities are performed;
- Advertising and marketing;
- Ordering and distribution;
- Invoicing and collection;
- Inventory management;
- Warranty activities; and
- Human resources.

Some of the risks that must be identified and reviewed include:

- R&D failure risk;
- Inventory risk;
- Product defect risk;
- Credit risk;
- Foreign exchange risk; and
- Product liability risk.

   Comment: Acquiring this information requires a thorough review of the taxpayer's financial information, including annual reports, securities filings, and corporate minutes. In addition, questionnaires are often sent to relevant departments to collect information on their activities, and key personnel are interviewed.

.03 Identification of Comparable Transactions and Comparable Unrelated Entities

   The next step of a transfer pricing study is the selection of comparable transactions or comparable uncontrolled entities.

Comparable Transactions. The taxpayer's transactions with unrelated entities, if any, are reviewed to determine whether the CUP or CUT methods can be applied. In addition, the regulations allow for transactions between unrelated third parties to be used in a CUP or CUT analysis (this data is usually found in market or industry reports). In order to successfully apply the CUP or CUT method, the uncontrolled transactions must be sufficiently similar to the controlled transactions to provide a reliable measure of an arm's length result. Several factors to consider in evaluating comparable transactions include:

- Availability of competitor pricing information;
- The presence or absence of trademarks or tradenames;
- Level of the market (e.g., wholesale v. resale)
- Contract terms;
- Quantity and volume discounts;
- Geographic markets;
- Exchange rate risks;
- Whether available pricing information concerns transactions between unrelated parties; and
- Whether adjustments can be made to eliminate the pricing differences resulting from differences in the transactions.

   The regulations allow a reasonable number of adjustments to the uncontrolled transaction to account for material differences between the controlled and uncontrolled transactions, if such differences have a definite and reasonably ascertainable effect on prices or profits. Recognizing the relative impossibility of obtaining exact

¶1050.03

comparables, the Tax Court created the "sufficiently similar" standard for determining whether an uncontrolled transaction is comparable to a controlled transaction.[28]

> **Comment:** The "inexact CUP" analysis has recently been applied by the Tax Court in a variety of contexts.[29]

Comparable Companies. While comparable transactions may exist between two entities unrelated to the tested party, reliable data and information about such transactions is exceedingly difficult to obtain. If adequate comparable transaction data cannot be found, whether from internal or external sources, it is necessary to conduct additional searches for companies with functional comparability. These searches are typically done using commercially available corporate information databases, such as Moody's, Standard and Poors, or Compustat, and are based on SIC codes.

The functional and risk analysis is used to develop and apply screening criteria to publicly available databases to identify potential comparable companies. Factors to be considered include whether the potential comparable company:

- Engages in similar business activities (e.g., distribution, manufacturing, etc.);

- Operates in the same geographic location;

- Operates in the same level of the market (e.g., wholesale v. retail);

- Underwent a major disruption to the normal course of business;

- Had significant related party transactions that could not be segregated;

- Assumes similar risks (e.g., warranty, credit, foreign exchange);

- Uses similar assets (e.g., intangibles, asset intensity); and

- Lacked sufficient data.

.04 Analysis of Comparables

Once the comparable companies are selected, their financial statements are reviewed and adjustments made to increase their reliability.

Segmentation of Financial Statements. The financial data of each comparable should be reviewed in order to separate out data that is not relevant to the transfer pricing analysis, such as:

- Sales to/from different geographic markets;

- Transactions with related parties; and

- Balance sheet assets dedicated to different operations (e.g., separating manufacturing assets from distribution assets).

---

[28] *See Bausch & Lomb, Inc.*, CCH Dec. 45,547, 92 TC 525 (1989), *aff'd*, 91-1 USTC ¶ 50,244, 933 F.2d 1084 (2d Cir. 1991).

[29] *See GAC Produce Co.*, CCH Dec. 53,349(M), 77 TCM 1890, TC Memo 1999-134 (marketing services);

Compaq Computer Corp., CCH Dec. 53,443, 78 TCM 20, TC Memo 1999-220 (computer circuit boards); *H Group Holding, Inc.*, CCH Dec. 53,575(M), 78 TCM 533, TC Memo 1999-334 (hotel group trade name).

Accounting Adjustments. The taxpayer and comparable companies' financial data may also need to be adjusted to eliminate the impact of different accounting practices. Examples of these adjustments include:

- Differences in income and expense recognition or classification;
- Characterization and depreciation of fixed assets;
- Characterization and amortization of intangible assets;
- GAAP differences;
- Restructuring charges;
- Characterization of leases; and
- Foreign exchange gains and losses.

Diagnostic Adjustments. Diagnostic ratios are also calculated to help determine whether a potential company is sufficiently comparable to the taxpayer. Some of these ratios include:

- Days inventory, payables, and receivables;
- Ratio of intangible assets to tangible assets;
- Ratio of current depreciation to accumulated depreciation; and
- Ratio of assets to sales.

Selecting the TPM. The next stage of a transfer pricing study is the selection and application of a TPM. The regulations require taxpayers to select a method that provides "the most reliable measure" of an arm's length result.[30] The regulations provide for the following TPMs:

- Comparable Uncontrolled Price Method ("CUP")—Reg. § 1.482-3(b);
- Resale Price Method "(RPM")—Reg. § 1.482-3(c);
- Cost Plus Method ("CP")—Reg. § 1.482-3(d);
- Comparable Profits Method ("CPM")—Reg. § 1.482-5; and
- Profit Split Method—Reg. § 1.482-6.

The selection of the most reliable TPM will ultimately depend on:

- the degree of comparability between the controlled and uncontrolled transactions;
- the quality of the data and assumptions used in the analysis;
- the completeness and accuracy of the data;
- the soundness of the assumptions relied upon;
- the sensitivity of results to deficiencies in data and assumptions; and,
- where two methods produce inconsistent results, the confirmation of the chosen results by comparison with a third method.

Although a detailed discussion of the TPMs is beyond the scope of this chapter (see chapters 3 and 4), a brief discussion of each TPM, and their strengths and weaknesses follows.[31]

---

[30] Reg. § 1.482-1(c)(1).   [31] *See* Chapter 3.

¶1050.04

CUP. The CUP method is based on a direct observation of the prices charged in the market. However, because of the lack of publicly available data concerning external CUPs (i.e., comparable transactions between two unrelated parties), internal CUPs (i.e., comparable transactions between the taxpayer and an unrelated party) are often used. Nevertheless, if data is available to support the use of the CUP with appropriate adjustments, if necessary, then the use of the CUP method will almost always satisfy the best method rule.[32]

The CUP method is often difficult to apply in practice, however. Most of the problems encountered in trying to apply the CUP method involve finding transactions that are sufficiently comparable to the related party transaction being tested. These problems include:

- Differences in product quality;
- Differences in the level of the market;
- Differences in geographic markets;
- Limited publicly available information; and
- Differences in contractual terms;

RPM. The RPM, which is based on a comparison of gross margins, is typically applied to distribution companies. Application of the method, however, requires the use of comparable companies that have similar risks and that only have routine intangibles. Furthermore, adjustments must be made for functional differences such as:

- Advertising;
- Warranty;
- Product liability;
- Inventories;
- Scale of operations;
- Contract terms;
- Additional services performed; and
- Credit terms.

Cost Plus. The Cost Plus method is typically used for routine manufacturing (e.g., contract manufacturing) and service operations (e.g., contract R&D). The Cost Plus method is less often used for distributors, but a limited function distributor may be treated economically as a mere service provider (e.g., freight forwarders). In applying the Cost Plus method, the comparable companies must have similar characteristics regarding the following:

- Functions, risks, and routine intangibles;
- Production processes;
- Cost structure; and
- Accounting consistency.

---

[32] Reg. § 1.482-3(b)(2)(ii)(A).

CPM. The CPM, which in practice is the preferred TPM in the United States, tests the taxpayer's operating income as a proxy for testing transfer prices. As such, it is most useful when the other TPMs cannot be applied because of a lack of adequate data. The use of the CPM is dependent on functional comparability and not product comparability. Although CPM is not officially recognized by several of the United States' major trading partners (because of its departure from transactional methods), variations of the CPM have been applied to their satisfaction.

Profit Split. The profit split method allocates shares of the groups' total profits based on the relative value of each party's contribution. The value of contributions are determined by applying a functional analysis. The profit split method is usually used in very complex intercompany relationships when one of the following conditions is satisfied:

- No other TPM can be successfully applied;

- Vertically integrated companies have achieved profitability substantially in excess of non-integrated firms; or

- Unique intangibles are embedded in the transfer price.

Transactional v. Profits-Based Methods. As a practical matter, taxpayers are unlikely to have access to reliable data on external comparable transactions, assuming they exist. Therefore, the use of transactional methods will depend on the existence of internal comparable transactions. Experience has shown that internal comparable transactions rarely exist, and when they do, they often require significant adjustments to account for differing markets, terms, and risks. In addition, small differences in the pricing of potential internal transactional comparables can lead to significant differences in profits, making such methods overly sensitive to deficiencies in data or necessary adjustments.

Deficiencies in transactional methods frequently lead to the use of a profit-based method such as a profits based resale price method or the CPM. Due to the difficulties in using transactional methods and the IRS' experience with CPM, both taxpayers and the IRS generally rely on the CPM as the method of choice. Although nearly all countries other than the U.S. explicitly reject the CPM approach, a number of cases developed pursuant to a CPM approach have been resolved through the APA process. Taxpayers generally demonstrate the results under the primary TPM employed by each involved country to facilitate competent authority discussions.

Selection of Profits-Based Profit-Level Indicators ("PLIs"). If a profits-based CPM is used, then an appropriate PLI must be selected. Although the regulations only specify three PLIs, return on capital ("ROC"), operating margin, and the Berry Ratio, other PLIs, such as gross margins, have been applied. Nevertheless, these three PLIs, or variations thereof, are the ones most used in practice.

¶1050.04

Comment: When a taxpayer is under audit, the choice of PLI can often make the difference between a substantial adjustment with penalties and no adjustment.[33]

Each PLI has its own strengths and weaknesses. For instance, the use of the ROC as a PLI can be based on the economic theory that similar firms operating in a competitive environment will earn similar returns on their capital. In addition, the ROC PLI is often more reliable than the Berry Ratio or Operating Margin when there are functional differences between the taxpayer and the comparable companies. However, its use is hampered by its reliance on balance sheet information, which may not properly reflect the true amount of capital employed. Similarly, operating margin, and berry ratio PLIs are sensitive to different levels of operating expense to sales ratios.

.05 Applying the TPM to the Facts

If the CPM is selected as the best method, then the interquartile range is calculated and compared to the taxpayer's results. If the taxpayer's results are below the interquartile range, then a compensating adjustment will likely be necessary.

¶ 1060 Satisfying Multiple Jurisdictions

.01 Background

During the 1980s and 1990s, the United States spent considerable effort to modernize its transfer pricing laws and enhance the IRS's ability to enforce those laws. These changes were both substantive (enacting the commensurate-with-income standard and finalizing the regulations under Code Sec. 482) and procedural (enactment of penalties and documentation requirements). These changes are now allowing the IRS to better enforce Code Sec. 482 and the arm's length standard, thus making the costs of non-compliance prohibitive. Because transfer pricing can be a zero-sum game, any income shifted to the United States must ultimately reduce the amount of income subject to tax in other tax jurisdictions. Other countries, concerned that U.S. statutory and regulatory changes encourage taxpayers to shift income to the United States, are implementing similar legislation, enforcement, and penalty approaches. Consequently, taxpayers must be prepared to defend their transfer pricing practices on a global basis.

.02 Transfer Pricing Penalties and Documentation Goes Global

Like the United States, many foreign countries are relying upon the combination of transfer pricing penalties and documentation requirements to encourage taxpayers to comply with transfer pricing laws and to cooperate with transfer pricing examinations. These countries include almost all of the United States's major trading partners, including: Australia, Belgium, Canada, China, France, Germany, Korea, Mexico, the Netherlands, and the United Kingdom. This global emphasis on transfer pricing has forced taxpayers to manage transfer pricing exposure on a global basis. Consequently, documentation should be prepared to

---

[33] *See* Richard A. Clark, "Choosing a Reliable Profit Level Indicator," 5 *Tax Management Transfer Pricing Re-* port No. 25 (1997) for a discussion of applying the various PLIs.

defend transfer pricing to the local tax authorities while simultaneously facilitating global compromise with other tax authorities; the ultimate goal being to avoid lengthy/expensive controversies and double taxation.

.03 Strategies for Multiple Jurisdictions

Factual Development. The first step in preparing transfer pricing documentation that satisfies multiple jurisdictions is to conduct a thorough analysis of the relevant facts. This would include function (e.g., manufacturer v. distributor, full-service distributor v. stripped distributor) and risk (e.g., entrepreneurial service provider v. contract service provider) analysis of each of the related parties, as well as an examination of the contractual provisions and economic conditions under which each entity operates. It is critical that this analysis be accurate and consistently presented, as any inaccuracies or differences in presentation will be the source of a considerable amount of controversy with the local tax authorities.

Reconciling Economic Analysis. Although many countries have enacted or are currently considering similar transfer pricing methodologies, most have explicitly rejected the CPM approach favored by the United States. Even if most of the major trading partners agreed on acceptable methods, the risk remains that examiners in the various countries would nonetheless interpret and apply those methods inconsistently. These differences (both substantive and administrative) place taxpayers at a higher risk of double taxation.

To satisfy the inconsistent TPM positions of multiple countries, taxpayers must reach a consistent result by making adjustments to the TPMs favored by the involved countries. Many taxpayers are able to reach this result by making appropriate economic adjustments to the applicable transfer pricing methodologies to make them more acceptable to foreign tax authorities. This has resulted in the creation of "hybrid TPMs" that can be accepted by multiple tax jurisdictions.

For instance, a U.S. documentation report that relies on the CPM application of the operating margin PLI as the best method can be reconciled with a Japanese documentation report relying on the resale price method by backing out SG&A expenses. Similarly, the CPM method preferred by U.S. taxpayers can be reconciled with foreign rules requiring the use of transactional methods by aggregating economically similar transactions.

Other taxpayers may be unable, or may find it difficult, to adjust the application of competing TPMs to achieve a consistent result. These taxpayers may ultimately need to seek competent authority assistance to avoid double taxation.

.04 Competent Authority

Despite a taxpayer's efforts to prepare global transfer pricing documentation, it could still be exposed to double taxation if one country proposes adjustments that are not accepted by the other countries. In situations where the application of United States and foreign tax laws would result in the taxpayer being subject to double taxation, a taxpayer may invoke a tax treaty's competent authority (mutual assistance) procedure to request relief from double taxation. Through the competent authority process, the U.S. and foreign government will negotiate a settlement to prevent double taxation. A settlement can take the form of one country withdrawing its adjustment, the other country making a correlative adjustment, or a combination of the two. The competent authority process is described more fully in Chapter 18. Although competent authority successfully resolves nearly all double taxation cases, taxpayers may find the competent authority process unsatisfactory due to the time required for resolution and the limited taxpayer involvement in the process.

.05 Advance Pricing Agreements

An alternative to preparing documentation that satisfies multiple jurisdictions is to negotiate either a bilateral or multilateral APA. An APA is a binding, written contract between the taxpayer, the IRS, and a foreign tax authority. In an APA, the parties agree on the TPM for determining the arm's length price for certain covered transactions and the proper application of such method to the taxpayer's particular facts and circumstances. Once an APA is finalized and executed by the parties, the IRS and the foreign tax authority will regard the results of applying the TPM as satisfying the arm's length standard provided the taxpayer complies with its terms. Although the approaches discussed in this section would likely be applied in negotiating the APA to the satisfaction of each of the parties, such negotiation will cover multiple future years and facilitate future settlements of potential transfer pricing disputes. The APA process is described in detail in Chapter 13.

For more on preparing transfer pricing documentation, see the Practice Tools at ¶ 20,070.

¶ 1070 Considerations and Issues Global Documentation

.01 Background

With the substantial efforts of the above countries and globally related organizations to establish precise documentation requirements, there is no question in today's environment that an MNC must design a consistent, cogent, and economically benchmarked global transfer pricing policy. An MNC's transfer pricing position is enhanced measurably with such documentation. Moreover, the increased focus in recent years on the role of transfer prices in a tax efficient structure means that an increasing number of MNCs have developed, on a global or regional basis, comprehensive transfer pricing systems. MNCs therefore increasingly have in their possession policies, strategic analyses, and documents that address transfer pricing in the context of either tax planning, management and/or commercial objectives. The question is first whether MNCs should present these policies, analyses, or documents (hereinafter sometimes referred to as "global documentation"), in either present or redacted form, to a tax authority as compliance documentation, assuming that global documentation is even feasible, and second, whether it is more prudent to produce regional or local documentation to meet specific jurisdictions' documentation requirements.[34]

---

[34] Derived from "Levey and Balaban," Global Transfer Pricing Documentation; "Many Considerations," 12 *BNA* *Transfer Pricing Report* No. 17 Special Report, January 21, 2004.

While each MNC must be considered separately based on its unique circumstances, it is possible that certain portions of this global documentation can, and maybe should, be presented in its global format for local compliance documentation. For example, the global documentation may present a general description and analysis of the MNC's distribution operations. If, for example, the TPM is the Resale Price Method, and an appropriate gross profit margin (or even targeted range of operating profit margin) is constructed for similarly situated distribution operations in relatively similar markets, this may become an efficient compliance vehicle to fulfill some of the requirements for compliance documentation in those countries with such distribution operations.

Of course, challenges will arise in explaining regional market differences and trends, differing levels of operating expenses, and converging of the various databases (e.g., Compustat, Amadeus, Disclosure, etc.) that may be required in each country or region. Here, however, the key consideration in assessing the applicability of global to local needs for compliance documentation lies in functionally similar distribution operations with similar risk and market profiles and reasonably measurable and consistent economic benchmarks.

Global management and services arrangements may be another area where global documentation can be applied for local documentation purposes. While each country may have somewhat different legal and practical approaches to these rules, most countries, and particularly OECD members, will generally seek to determine both the benefit of the service to the renderer and recipient and the rationale of the allocation system. Here, a global approach (likely extracted from the global planning document) could be useful and persuasive when locally applied. An example here may be where a financial institution establishes global service arrangements for settlement and possibly certain sales/marketing services that may be supporting a centrally managed portfolio or "book."

A global approach to supporting certain royalty charges may also be useful in local documentation, largely because there is usually symmetry between the benefits to the licensor and licensee. Further, elements of consistency can be persuasive in establishing the reasonableness of a royalty rate globally or regionally. In addition, some royalties involve routine intangibles that are not by their nature controversial or are couched within ranges of industry standards. Nevertheless, royalties must be analyzed carefully because different jurisdictions may have alternative views on issues such as

- how trademark/trade income royalties may be charged (if at all),
- the characterization of network or bundled intangible property charges,
- internal or statutory restrictions or predilections on royalty rates,[35] or
- how to identify the legal or economic owners/developers of the intangible assets, which happened in the recent *DHL* case.[36] Royalties can also be a

---

[35] *See,* e.g., Levey, Oster, and Greco "Section 482 Regs. and Italian Transfer Pricing Rules are Often at Odds," 4 *J. Int'l Tax'n* 456 (Oct. 1993) (describing Italy's statutory presumptions regarding royalty rates).

[36] *DHL Corporation,* 2002-1 USTC ¶ 50,354, 285 F.3d 1210; *aff'g in part, rev'g in part* CCH Dec. 53,015(M), 76 TCM 1122, TC Memo 1998-461. *See* Levey, Shapiro, Cunningham, Lemein, Garofalo, "DHL: Ninth Circuit Sheds Very Little Light on Bright-Line Test," 13 *J.Int'l Tax'n* 10

hotbed for audit controversies, not only because of the above issues, but also due to the highly subjective nature of their valuation and the dearth of public data in this area, especially for nonroutine intangibles. And, of course, if the licensor happens to be in a low tax jurisdiction, the degree of sensitivity and skepticism increases, as has been seen in the IRS's approach to cost sharing arrangements with such jurisdictions.

While a global documentation package may be more cost effective than a series of local compliance documentation packages, a significant tax audit can erase all of these anticipated cost savings. Hence, taxpayers should consider the following issues when contemplating global documentation versos regional or local documentation.

.02 Different Markets

Markets for products vary worldwide. They may vary from country-to-country or region-to-region. Apart from consumer preferences, similar products may produce very different economic results based on competitive factors in different markets. For example, a product that has strong presence in the United States may be a middle market product in Europe (or vice versa) and have on a scattered presence or be a residual market in the Asia/Pacific region. Further, the MNC's product mix in these regions may have a significant overall impact on profit margins. These market differences may also greatly impact the level of operating expenses of these distributors in their respective regions. At first blush, and based solely on these factual assumptions, it would appear that a global documentation study might not benefit all those distributors nor would it be prudent or even relevant to disclose the global or regional financial results to each local tax authority. It may, however, be possible to construct regional distribution documentation or make regional or country adjustments to the global model to adjust for these differences, assuming the variances are not significant or are economically quantifiable.

.03 Product Mixes

The product mix of an MNC, as mentioned above, can vary considerably from market-to-market, and each market's reception to that product can vary significantly depending on such factors as market level competition, operating expense support, and price restrictions. To illustrate, assume an MNC has four product lines with the following market characteristics:

- Product A—global, high volume, low margin product, mass-produced for OEMs with low operating expenses to promote.

- Product B—global, medium to high volume, median margin potential product subject to strong competition from other MNCs and requiring varying levels of operating expenses to promote.

(Footnote Continued)

(Oct. 2002); Levey, Cunningham, Emmer, Grech, "DHL: A Tax Court Road Map for Handling Transfer Pricing Audits," 10 *J.Int'l Tax'n* 12 (June 1999).

- Product C—highly specialized product, short obsolescence period, high margin product, subject to constant technological changes within markets, modest competition from other MNCs.

- Product D—global product but subject to varying and sometimes significant local price controls.

Depending on the product mix and sales volumes, significant variations may exist for each distributor's operating margin and comparable firm benchmarks as can be seen from the variations of Products A through D. For example, for the products listed above, such as Products A and B, not only should the economic results of these product sales vary significantly, but the comparability benchmarks and economic adjustments for each could be quite different. For Product C there may no (or few) comparable firms due to the products highly specialized nature and modest level of competition. For Product D, the comparability analysis may only lie with firms subject to the same local restrictions. Of course, each of these product groups may simply command a separate comparability analysis and in some cases an analysis that is derived from other industry segments.

This benchmarking can even vary substantially depending on the TPM selected, such as an aggregated comparable profits method ("CPM") versus a segmented transactional net margin method ("TNMM"), as discussed more fully below. Indeed, Products A through D can provide different results under a series of TNMM analyses, which could also vary considerably from an aggregated CPM. Further, the TNMM may vary from market-to-market. These considerations also do not contemplate market penetration or new product launch factors, or varying market cost differences that may be evident through the level of advertising, marketing and promotional expenditures of each firm. Therefore, global documentation may be helpful to some of an MNC's distributors and have a negative impact on others, but in total may produce inconsistent and unmanageable results for future years' compliance.

Quite possibly, regional or local documentation studies may be more appropriate, assuming regional market similarity, unless the global documentation is segmented to establish targeted ranges of profit for each product, subject where possible to proper economic adjustments.

.04 Differences in Record Review

While local documentation requirements may appear similar, as illustrated in the different countries' documentation requirements listed above, the practices and interpretations of these requirements, the importance placed on different types of documentation, the availability of benchmarking data, and the tax authorities' levels of sophistication may vary considerably from jurisdiction-to-jurisdiction. Newcomers in the transfer pricing arena, such as Malaysia and China, will not likely have the experience and staffing capability found in more seasoned jurisdictions such as Australia, Canada and the United States. Even Germany, while not inexperienced in transfer pricing issues, may find new and unusual nuances in dealing with its new documentation rules and burdens. Accordingly, a complex functional and economic analysis prepared for some countries may fall on deaf ears in other countries, where a more simple pragmatic approach would be more appropriate and appreciated. These differences can also be important in addressing a tax authority during an audit, as they may take offense to disregarding their preferred approach in lieu of one required by another tax authority, even if the latter is deemed more technically proficient. Also, the same tax authorities may feel "talked down to" by, or skeptical of, the detailed and sophisticated economic analysis, which never breeds good taxpayer-tax authority relations.

There are also countries where local company data is sparse and the use of comparable firms from elsewhere may lead the tax authorities to use secret comparables or customs data. This is currently commonplace in Canada, Japan, Australia, Korea, China, Mexico and many South American countries. In fact, in Canada, where the official position is that secret comparables will be used in isolated cases, practitioners have suggested that " . . . in many instances secret comparables drive the audit and the ultimate assessing position on files" notwithstanding that there is no actual disclosure of these comparables.[37] In practice, it has been suggested that audit adjustments are typically supported by some empirical evidence in order to back into the conclusions drawn from the secret comparables. It is also unlikely that these tax authorities will accept the notion that the MNC was trying to achieve cost savings or cost efficiencies in its global documentation process, but will rather focus on that fact that the MNC has not paid attention to its local or cultural requirements and concerns.

These issues must be carefully considered. Strong relationships, open communication and mutual trust with the local tax authorities are as important as, if not more than, the documentation study. Regionalization of the documentation rather than globalization may address these specific local concerns better. Or, simply separate country studies may be required even if largely and selectively borrowed from the global study.

Similarly, some countries prefer local comparables. Canada, the Netherlands and France are examples. Typically, Revenue Canada will not accept U.S. comparables without, at a minimum, some showing that (i) there are no available Canadian comparable firms, and (ii) there has been some attempt to adjust or "Canadianize" the data to the Canadian market. Additionally, if a pan-European data search produces numerous potential comparable firms, but within that set of comparable firms are a few French and Dutch firms, it is likely that the initial reviews of these respective taxing authorities will focus on their local firms' results before considering the results of the entire sample, if at all.

.05 Differing Views of Transfer Pricing Methods

While tax authorities may have different interpretations and practices regarding documentation rules, they also may have differing views of the TPMs and the required and underlying economic data.

---

[37] Oatway, "Secret Comparables Alive and Well in Canada," 4 *Tax Planning International Transfer Pricing* 7 (July 2003).

The most pronounced difference in TPMs is between the U.S. rules and the OECD Guidelines regarding the Comparable Profits Method ("CPM") and the Transactional Net Margin Method ("TNMM"), respectively. The above analysis is one illustration of these difficulties. Equally important is the OECD's apparently strong preference for the use of transactional methods such as the Resale Price Method ("RPM"). These differences are most evident in the economic data used to support these TPMs and the comparability standards for each method.

For example, in the United States, the CPM is the most frequently employed TPM largely due to the relative abundance of public data and the relative simplicity of the CPM. Because the CPM can transcend numerous product lines for a diversified MNC (and be calculated net of royalty and other intercompany charges), the standards of comparability many vary from those used in a more "segmented" TNMM search. Further, because the databases for U.S. public companies tend to be more detailed, more precise economic modeling through more fact-based economic adjustments is more prevalent and attainable.

The same operation in Europe (and likely Asia), for example, may be required to use either a TNMM or RPM analysis, but clearly not a CPM. Here, the analysis under the TNMM, through its product or divisional segmentation, as noted above, should establish different comparability standards and, because of the dearth of detail and/or inconsistency in the publicly available financial statements in the local European databases, the same level of economic adjustments cannot be effectively assured as with the CPM. Further, under a RPM, a gross margin analysis may be more preferable and reliable to a tax authority instead of the TNMM's operating margin approach. The latter is especially true if there are few local comparable firms that are more comparable to the tested party, as noted above, instead of the typically vast array of comparables that are less than comparable, but are employed to create a general range of operating margins.

Therefore, even if the targeted range of operating margins are consistent in a global documentation study, failure to pay attention to the taxing authorities' different preferences in TPMs and their specific nuances will make the use of a global documentation study questionable. Again, regional documentation may be a better alternative in addressing these issues and precluding the disclosure to other jurisdictions of the global data, and sometimes the documentation must be country-specific.

.06 Disclosure of Information

Holding companies, or the like, established in a low tax jurisdictions are often found in MNCs' supply chains. While established for solid tax and commercial reasons, these low tax jurisdictions attract undue attention and are often at the heart of tax controversies where a taxing authority is seeking to reallocate that low tax jurisdiction entity's income to its jurisdiction. Critical points to consider are that each tax authority has its own sensitivity to these types of arrangements, and particularly if the low tax entity is located in a non-tax treaty jurisdiction. These considerations must be weighted heavily in providing global documentation especially if the low tax jurisdiction has no real or direct bearing on the economic benchmarking of the tested party. In this instance, giving too much information can only create untoward issues, especially if, in a tax treaty context, information is shared among other taxing authorities.

.07 Excessive or Gratuitous Facts

The premise here is that the facts used to describe the growth and profit potential of an MNC globally may bear no real relevance on the specific tested legal entity. In fact, it may create entirely the wrong impression and in a worse case scenario act as an admission against interest. For example, assume an MNC has enjoyed steady global growth in its business and reasonable market share for its products, but that this success has been largely in the North American and Asian markets. However, presently it is entering the European market and requires significant investment for its various markets to gain market penetration. Further, assume the European market has more intensive cost requirements, is far more competitive for the MNC's products than the other regions and is also a price-controlled market. Here, the strong market and financial performance of the North American or Asian regions, or that regions market elasticity, when used, or the general description of the MNC can only confuse the market and risk profiles for establishing acceptable firms and benchmarks for Europe. In short, this data is largely irrelevant to the European market and gratuitous and likely would be either confusing to, or used affirmatively by a tax authority in assessing a tax deficiency against the MNC.

Often global studies derive their information about an MNC from the MNC's Annual Report, product brochures, website and other marketing data. Generally, this information, while interesting, is overly optimistic and marketing oriented and should be used carefully to the extent it is relevant to the transfer pricing policy. At the very least, it may not clearly reflect the MNC's supply chain and success drivers, nor profit potential in a given market. More importantly, because it is not geared to any transfer pricing model, its use in total or without context is highly questionable and its use in part must be clearly explained and focused to the intended transfer pricing policy.

Aside from disclosure of low tax jurisdiction documentation to other tax jurisdictions, it may not be prudent to provide any tax jurisdiction with the globally targeted ranges of profits for the global business. This data may cause certain tax authorities to engage in profit allocations based solely on perceptions of global profit splits of the MNC instead of focusing solely on the specific local entity's markets and benchmarks. This could indeed change the playing field in a tax controversy, especially to the disadvantage of the MNC.

¶ 1080 FIN 48 Adds to the Complexity in Transfer Pricing Compliance

FIN 48 has marked one of the most significant changes to accounting for income taxes in the last 20 years. These changes required companies to re-evaluate their tax liability calculations and disclosures for uncertain tax positions under the standard of "more likely than not" to be sustained under audit. Further, the assessment of the standard must be based on, among other things, probability of settlement with the tax authorities. The allocation of income across jurisdictions caused by transfer pricing is central to the scope of FIN 48.

The transfer pricing documentation is only one factor to be considered in assessing whether intercompany pricing would be upheld under a tax audit. While the transfer pricing documentation is geared to protect companies from penalties, there is no assurance that this documentation will protect companies from tax adjustments. The assessment standard for transfer pricing documentation is one of "reasonableness" which falls short of the "more likely than not" standard. Accordingly, for FIN 48 purposes, auditors now require a more detailed review of several items related to each intercompany transaction including the quality of available documentation, intercompany agreements, invoices, overall profitability, and whether the charges fall within the targeted arm's length range. Sometimes even the selected comparable transactions and/or companies and the resulting arm's length range is scrutinized.

The sources of information that can influence transfer pricing positions are numerous and can fluctuate over time. One obvious source is audit activity. Transfer pricing audits that have been settled indeed have a direct impact on any uncertain tax positions for FIN 48 purposes. Communications with tax authorities regarding transfer pricing such as informational document requests, notices of proposed adjustments, and even verbal conversations that convey some view or attitude about the potential transfer pricing exposures are also relevant. Closed statutes of limitations could impact that analysis. More obvious sources are proposed regulations or tax announcements or memorandum as well as decided tax cases.

Companies have struggled with these onerous requirements dedicating significant internal and external resources to developing policies specially designed for retrieving information for, and monitoring, the designated uncertain tax positions related to transfer pricing. This, of course, also involves monitoring sources of information that can influence these positions, including but limited to, specific industry and regulatory trends as well as identifying new units of account resulting from the growth of the business or transactions that may be affected by new tax trends and announcements, such as the IRS recently issued regulations for service transactions.

Many questions remain regarding the tangential issues surrounding FIN 48. One critical issue is whether the FIN 48 work papers as well as notes and memoranda reflecting counsel's views on the same are protected by the attorney-client privilege or the work protect doctrine from disclosure to the IRS on audit. Indeed, FIN 48 is too new to have any meaningful jurisprudence on this issue, however, the District Court for the District of Rhode Island in its opinion on *Textron*,[38] sheds some light on how the courts may consider the issue. Here, the court held that tax accrual work papers were privileged (under both the attorney client privilege and Section 7525 Federal tax practitioner privilege) and, most

---

[38] *Textron Inc.*, 2007-2 USTC ¶ 50,605, 507 FSupp2d 138 (D.R.I. August 29, 2007).

significantly, the work papers were prepared *because of* the potential of litigation and therefore met the requirement to be protected under work product doctrine. The court then went further and held that the taxpayer waived the respective privileges by providing the work papers to its financial auditor. The court also held that this disclosure did not negate the work product protection, however, because the role and confidentiality protections applicable to the financial auditor did not make it any more likely that the IRS would lay its hands on the materials as a result of a disclosure.

Taxpayers are most concerned that this evaluative type roadmap work papers remain confidential and are not discoverable by any tax authority. Not only does it provide a roadmap to the taxpayer's vision of its tax exposure, it may preclude a realistic analysis of an uncertain tax position. This issue for resolution is of the specific work papers at issue are prepared for the "primary purpose" of or "because of" the prospect or likelihood of controversy with the tax authorities. In *Textron*, the court commented that the company had a reasonable anticipation of litigation because "seven of Textron's right persons audit cycles included unagreed" issues that were forwarded to IRS Appeals and three of those issues were in fact litigated. Would the result have been different if the company regularly settled the same or similar issues at examination, or even Appeals? Or, what if the company had no such contentious audit history, but believed that the tax authorities would target certain issues or simply had not previously focused on issues that were likely to be debated or contentious? And, furthermore, what if the tax authorities simply just want a roadmap to specific transactions?

While IRS has maintained a mild practice of "policy of restraint" in asking for tax accrual work papers, FIN 48 work papers can be a different animal and quite damning. Likely, IRS will argue both a "substantial need" for these papers, seeking to show some type of malice aforethought when it reported the transaction on its tax return, and that the analysis did not give rise to, or was "because of," a reasonable anticipation of litigation. This gets even more complicated if certain items among many in the workpapers were not analyzed by counsel. The U.S. Justice Department filed a notice of appeal on this decision on October 22, 2007, and IRS Chief Counsel Don Korb vowed to continue to challenge cases in this area in order to sort out how the rules apply here.

A component of FIN 48 that may distinguish itself from work product protection for accrual work papers is that a FIN 48 analysis assumes that this tax authority will have full knowledge of all the relevant information and will audit the issue. These assumptions do not exist in the context of either the "primary purpose" or "because of" tests for work product production. Accordingly, the FIN 48 analysis is required for an item where there may be no reasonable potential of controversy. That being said, if discoverable, the FIN 48 analysis may be argued to provoke the controversy and thus necessitates the work product protection. Until clarified, this fact may be sufficient reason to anticipate a controversy.

The spectrum of FIN 48 compliance and its attending issues is uncomfortable and provocative. Where do we go from here. It's anybody's guess!

¶1080

¶ 1090 Conclusion

Global documentation is indeed a goal worth pursuing but it must be done with caution and care and should not be confused with the documentation that may be employed for planning or other management purposes. Critical attention should be given to the points described above to avoid unnecessary tax audit controversies. Of particular importance will be the determination of whether it is more prudent to consider regional or local documentation notwithstanding that all documentation must be centralized and controlled for factual consistency and quantative analysis. One message should be clear, however. That is, global documentation is not a "product" that can be generically produced. It is specific to each MNC in all material respects and especially geared to its particular transfer pricing policy and the nuances of the local or regional tax authority or authorities. This is easy to understand when it is considered that the documentation package serves to meet regulatory requirements in a specific country for a specific legal entity and in the end serves to support the arm's length nature of the income allocation to that specific entity.

Chapter 11

Examination

¶ 1101 IRS Pre-Examination Preparation

.01 Selection for Examination

The IRS has the authority to examine a taxpayer's books and records to determine its correct income tax liability.[1] In exercising this authority in the context of Code Sec. 482, adjustments are not limited to cases of fraudulent transactions, sham transactions, or tax avoidance devices. Instead, the IRS's authority to allocate income, deductions, credits, and allowances between controlled taxpayers extends to all cases where a taxpayer's taxable income from related party transactions fails to reflect dealings at arm's length.[2]

.02 IRS Planning

The Planning Process. Planning for a Large and Middle Size Business ("LMSB") examination is the most important activity performed by a team manager.[3] The team manager performs a risk analysis, establishing a priority of issues based on the potential adjustments for a particular issue and the resources necessary to examine that issue.[4] Due to the potential for substantial adjustments associated with transfer pricing issues, significant cross-border related party transactions usually receive high priority.

The IRS has released revised guidelines to examiners for developing transfer pricing cases as part of its LMSB International Program Audit Guidelines (hereinafter referred to as the "TP Audit Guidelines").[5] The TP Audit Guidelines contain a list of documents and other information resources that the IRS case manager should review prior to the examination.[6]

---

[1] Code Sec. 7602(a); Reg. § 301.7602-1(a).
[2] Reg. § 1.482-1(f)(1).
[3] IRM 4.46.3.1.3.
[4] IRM 4.46.3.2.2.
[5] IRM 4.61.3.
[6] IRM 4.61.3.4.1.

The Examination Plan. The formal examination plan contains three parts: the Taxpayer Information Section (Examination Arrangements); the Service Management Information Section (Examination Programs); and the Examination Procedures Section (Examination Assignments).[7]

Taxpayer Information Section. The Taxpayer Information Section consists of the agreements with the taxpayer regarding the location of the examination, scheduling of IRS examination team members, space and equipment to be provided by the taxpayer, records to be provided by the taxpayer, analyses to be prepared by the taxpayer, and the lines of communication between the taxpayer and the IRS examination team.[8]

The Service Management Information Section. The Service Management Information Section includes a description of the taxpayer's organizational structure, business activities, major product lines, and accounting and internal control systems. This section also includes administrative matters such as instructions for the routing of requests for information to and from the taxpayer and procedures for raising issues during the examination. More importantly, however, this section will identify any areas subject to intensive examination, special examination techniques to be used, documentation desired for specific issues, and the priority of issues to be examined.[9]

If the IRS intends to examine the taxpayer's transfer pricing practices, it will usually seek the early disclosure of the taxpayer's transfer pricing documentation prepared for purposes of the transfer pricing penalty provisions under Code Sec. 6662. The taxpayer is required to provide within 30 days of an IRS request certain principal and background documentation that the taxpayer reached reasonable conclusions on its transfer pricing.[10]

Examination Procedure Section. The Examination Procedures Section sets forth the assignments of the various IRS team members (with any special instructions), the commencement date and completion date for each assignment, the sequence of the examination, the depth of the examination for each issue, and the examination priorities.[11] It also allows IRS team members to identify anticipated examination procedures and techniques.

Taxpayer Involvement. The IRS recognizes the need for taxpayer involvement at the planning stage. In fact, the IRS case manager is encouraged to seek an understanding with the taxpayer regarding priorities, resources and time frames.[12] To avoid surprises late in the examination, the case manager should discuss expected examination issues with the taxpayer throughout the planning process.[13] The case manager should also discuss the use and role of specialists, the role of IRS attorneys, efforts to keep the examination process current, potential problems associated with examining proprietary information, trade secrets, and other sensitive information, and potential penalties.[14] The case manager is encouraged to reach

---

[7] IRM 4.46.3.5.2.

[8] IRM 4.46.3.5.2.1.A.

[9] IRM 4.46.3.5.2.1.B.

[10] Code Sec. 6662(e)(3)(B)((i)(III); Reg. § 1.6662-6(d)(2)(iii)(A); IRM 4.46.3.3.3.3.J.

[11] IRM 4.46.3.5.2.(1)(C).

[12] IRM 4.46.3.3.1.1.

[13] IRM 4.46.3.3.1.4.

[14] IRM 4.46.3.3.1.3.

an understanding with the taxpayer regarding procedures for resolving questions on the content of the information document request ("IDR") and time periods for responding to IDRs, coordinating the examination of off-site facilities and records, and establishing the need for examiners to advise the taxpayer of potential new issues.[15] Finally, the case manager should discuss appropriate methods to resolve issues at the lowest possible level, through the use of requests for technical advice, identification of issues appropriate for case manager settlement authority, and APAs.[16]

The IRS examination planning process is the taxpayer's first opportunity to avoid or reduce transfer pricing disputes. It is far easier to persuade the exam team of the appropriateness of the taxpayer's TPM prior to the examination rather than attempt to change the view of the examination team after they have expended significant resources in an examination. Therefore, taxpayers should seize this opportunity to proactively explain its transfer pricing policies and results to the IRS examination team.

After the pre-examination conference, the case manager should prepare the formal examination plan.[17] The IRS routinely provides a copy of Part One of the case plan, the taxpayer information section.[18] When requested, the IRS will generally provide the taxpayer with Parts Two (Service Management Information Section) and Three (Examination Procedure Section).

A properly prepared examination plan provides a description of the areas to be examined, the scope of the examination, and a description of the resources to be applied by the IRS. This information will assist the taxpayer in planning and coordinating its activities regarding the examination. Case managers shall discuss and coordinate all changes of the examination plan with the taxpayer.[19] Whenever the taxpayer suspects that there has been a change to the examination plan, such as raising new issues or the changes in the IRS personnel assigned to the examination, the taxpayer should contact the case manager for an explanation and a copy of any changes to the plan.

.03 IRS Examination Approach

Examination Guidelines. The IRS provided guidance to examiners for developing transfer pricing cases as part of its International Program Audit Guidelines (hereinafter the "TP Audit Guidelines"). At the outset, the TP Audit Guidelines warn examiners to exercise care and good judgment when recommending transfer pricing adjustments.[20] Examiners are not to make *de minimis* adjustments, rather, they are instructed to pay close attention to situations where there have been substantial deviations from the arm's length standard, resulting in significant shifting of income.[21] Further, examiners are instructed to obtain economic assistance whenever a function and risk analysis is to be performed.[22]

---

[15] IRM 4.46.3.3.1.6.
[16] IRM 4.46.3.3.1.8.
[17] IRM 4.46.3.5.1.
[18] Field Exam Handbook, § 615(2), § § 632(1)(a), 634(1)(a), IRM 4.46.3.5.2.3.4.

[19] IRM 4.46.3.5.2.3.4.
[20] IRM 4.61.3.1.2.
[21] *Id.*
[22] IRM 4.61.3.3.

Examination Procedures. The TP Audit Guidelines contain step-by-step procedures for conducting a transfer pricing examination.[23] In the inbound context, the steps are generally as follows:

Pre-examination Techniques. The goal of the pre-examination step is for the examiner to determine whether a potential Code Sec. 482 issue exists. To do so, the examiner is instructed to review the taxpayer's history, including its permanent file, prior examination reports, and prior Appeals reports. The examiner often in coordination with assistance from IRS economists, then reviews the return under examination (Forms 1120 and 5472) and calculates key financial ratios for the taxpayer. The calculated ratios are compared to published financial ratios for the same industry to determine if there are significant differences that may indicate that transfer pricing issues are likely to exist.

Gaining an Understanding of Operations. In this step, the examiner is instructed to review documents that describe the taxpayer's operations. The TP Audit Guidelines include a lengthy list of documents to be reviewed, including: the foreign parent's annual reports and financial statements, SEC filings, newspapers and periodical search, organizational charts, other governmental reports, board of director minutes, corporate policy and procedure manuals, and product catalogs, faxes and e-mails.

Reviewing Financial Statements. The examiner is then instructed to review the taxpayer's most recent financial statements, preferably segmented, and determine whether the scope of the examination should be limited to particular product lines. This is done by comparing key financial ratios for the separate product lines to published ratios for the same industry.

The examiner is instructed to obtain copies of the following documents: the taxpayer's internal pricing policy, transfer pricing documentation, and all intercompany agreements. The examiner then conducts a detailed function and risk analysis by reviewing documents, interviewing employees of the taxpayer, and conducting a site-visit to the taxpayer's premises.

Once the function and risk analysis is conducted, the examiner is instructed to determine the arm's length result of the intercompany transactions by: (1) searching for internal and external comparables; (2) conducting a function and risk analysis for the comparables; (3) adjusting the comparables for differences with the taxpayer; (4) determining an arm's length range from the comparables; and (5) determining whether an adjustment should be made.

.04 Special Rules for Coordinated Industry Cases ("CIC")

While the IRS may initiate a transfer pricing examination on any return reflecting related party transactions, these examinations frequently arise in the Coordinated Industry Case ("CIC") Exam. The CIC allows the IRS to coordinate the examination of large, corporate taxpayers as one unit and centralize responsibility

---

[23] IRM 4.61.3.4.

¶1101.04

in one district.[24] The IRS selects taxpayers for inclusion in the CEP based on a point formula based upon the following factors:[25]

- Gross assets of the entity and all effectively controlled domestic and foreign entities;
- Gross receipts of the entity and all effectively controlled domestic and foreign entities;
- Number of operating entities;
- Number of separate industries involved;
- Total foreign assets;
- Total related transactions; and
- Foreign taxes paid.[26]

The IRS may include a case not meeting this point criteria in the CIC if it believes that the case has sufficient complexity to warrant inclusion and the case would benefit from a team examination approach.[27]

Once a case becomes designated as CIC, the IRS assigns a team manager to organize, control and direct the examination.[28]

If the team manager determines that an examination is appropriate, the IRS assembles an examination team composed of a team manager, a team coordinator, relevant specialists such as international examiners, computer examination specialists, engineer revenue agents, commodity and financial products agents, and other agents and non-specialist agents. The use of an economist by the examination team is mandatory in most transfer pricing cases.[29] The team manager surveys the return, reviews the taxpayer's planning file and discusses the case with the prior team manager and team coordinator, and meets with the examination team to discuss the scope of the examination. The team manager identifies the areas to be included in the examination plan.[30]

Taxpayer involvement in the CIC examination planning process is encouraged. Early involvement of the taxpayer in the planning process and the requirement that the IRS work to maintain an effective working relationship provides the taxpayer with an opportunity to influence the characterization and development of transfer pricing issues.

The team manager in a CIC examination has access to resources not generally available outside the CIC, including: the case planning file from the prior examination cycle, economists, engineering specialists, the international examiners, the industry specialists, the International Field Assistance Specialization Program ("IFASP"), the Special Counsels (International) in the Office of Assistant Chief Counsel (International) for field service and litigation, and outside consultants. Attorneys from District Counsel's offices are frequently assigned to assist CIC

---

[24] IRM 4.46.2.4.1.

[25] IRM 4.46.2.5.

[26] *See* IRM Exhibit 4.46.2-2 (assigning point values to each of the criteria for inclusion in the program).

[27] IRM 4.46.2.5.5.

[28] IRM 4.46.2.3.

[29] IRM 4.61.3.3.

[30] IRM 4.46.2.2.2.

teams. The team manager can also consult with attorneys from the various Associate Offices within the Chief Counsel's office, and request formal Technical Advice and Field Service advice from the various Associate Chief Counsel Offices in the National Office.

The Planning File. The IRS maintains a planning file for each CIC examination that is updated and passed to the next examination team. The planning file contains significant information about the taxpayer as well as information concerning issues raised in previous examination cycles.[31]

When preparing for a CIC transfer pricing examination, taxpayers should keep in mind the detailed background information available to the IRS examination team. Further, the taxpayer should initiate early discussions to modify examination techniques from the prior cycle that were inefficient or detrimental to resolution of the transfer pricing issues.

¶ 1110   Taxpayer Pre-Examination Preparation

.01 *Recognizing Differences Between Transfer Pricing and Other Tax Issues*

Statutory and Administrative Differences. Each country's transfer pricing laws are generally premised on the arm's length either standard advanced by the OECD, according to local interpretation, or under specific local law (i.e., Germany, Australia, Mexico, Canada). Consequently, transfer prices that are established by adherence to a particular TPM in one jurisdiction might not be accepted in another. Even if the methodology were the same in all jurisdictions, the inherent subjectivity and local practices involved in applying the transfer pricing methodologies allows for a difference in transfer pricing results.

Size of Potential Adjustments and Penalties. The scrutiny surrounding the settlement of very large proposed adjustments can have a chilling effect on the negotiations. According to one observer, " . . . a large adjustment assumes a life of its own and, regardless of the merits, it becomes difficult for anyone at subsequent stages to take responsibility for 'giving up' a substantial proposed deficiency."[32]

Transfer pricing adjustments are almost always the largest component of the IRS proposed adjustments for a taxpayer. For CEP taxpayers during the 1992-1993 audit cycle, the average proposed transfer pricing adjustment was $3.1 million.[33] For the 1994-1995 audit cycle, the average proposed transfer pricing adjustment was $3.8 million.[34] In one recent case in the U.S. Tax Court, the proposed adjustment for all years was approximately $16 billion.[35]

Procedural Options. In the current enforcement environment, procedural decisions are often as important as the underlying substantive development of a transfer pricing issue. The IRS has recently developed or expanded the number of techniques to resolve difficult tax disputes; some were specifically developed for

---

[31] IRM 4.46.2.8.

[32] Thomas C. Durham "International Tax Controversy Resolution: Techniques and Developments," speech at J.L. Kellogg School of Management, Northwestern University 31 (Feb. 10, 1993) (transcript available in J.L. Kellogg School of Management Library).

[33] Pub. 3218, Appendix B.

[34] Pub. 3218, Appendix B.

[35] *GlaxoSmithKline Holdings (America), Inc.*, U.S. Tax Court Docket No. 5750-04.

transfer pricing. ADR techniques available for transfer pricing issues include the following:

1. Early Referral to Appeals;

2. Fast Track Mediation;

3. Accelerated Issue Resolution ("AIR");

4. Simultaneous Appeals/Competent Authority Procedure ("SAP");

5. Mediation; and

6. Non-docketed Arbitration.

.02 Developing a Preliminary Substantive/Procedural Strategy

Overview. As explained above, transfer pricing is a complex issue with great potential for differing interpretations of both facts and law and significant procedural latitude regarding the forum for resolution of any dispute. Given the importance of the transfer pricing issue and the factual and legal variables, taxpayers would be well advised to expend time and effort to prepare a substantive and procedural strategy for dealing with any transfer pricing dispute.

First, the taxpayer should assemble an examination team composed of persons qualified to analyze, discuss and resolve issues. These may include, but not be limited to, a tax practitioner, accounting and systems assistance, economic valuation expert, industry expert and a tax litigator (if the tax practitioner has no actual tax litigation expertise). Next, the taxpayer should critically review its transactions, transfer pricing practices, and documentation and evaluate its exposure to adjustments and penalties for prior years and the impact on future years. Finally, the taxpayer should develop a defense strategy that incorporates substantive arguments and procedural alternatives and considers all applicable legal privileges.

Assemble Transfer Pricing Team. The taxpayer should assemble a transfer pricing team of individuals with an understanding of and familiarity with the taxpayer's global operations, the taxpayer's transfer pricing strategy and the location and content of detailed background documents. Ideally, the team will consist of outside advisors and economic industry specialists, as well as knowledgeable taxpayer employees who can coordinate the flow of taxpayer data.

The team leader, usually the taxpayer's director of tax or an outside representative, will be the primary point of contact with all IRS personnel. The team leader should be responsible for all responses to Informal Document Requests ("IDRs") the IRS, and should be the primary spokesperson during interviews, site tours, and negotiations concerning facts or issues. The team leader should identify other individuals within the company who might provide information concerning manufacturing, sales, marketing, and R&D.

Assembling the team before the examination begins will minimize the risk of inadvertent, gratuitous disclosures, which could lead to an unfavorable result. Consideration should be given to how and when the IRS will view the involvement of outside consultants and experts. Some IRS field service personnel may view such involvement as an indication that the taxpayer has transfer pricing problems.

¶1110.02

Therefore, taxpayers must develop a plan concerning when and how to disclose the involvement of outside consultants and experts.

Evaluate Exposure in Prior Tax Years. Risk assessment is intended to determine the taxpayer's exposure to transfer pricing adjustments and the imposition of tax penalties. If the taxpayer has thoroughly planned and documented its transfer pricing strategy on a current basis, the exposure analysis may consist of verifying that the taxpayer executed its transactions as planned and that appropriate documentation was developed and maintained.

Review Internal Information. A risk assessment of a prior taxable year requires the identification of issues and development of support for the taxpayer's existing pricing practices. The taxpayer and its advisors should examine the same books and records that the IRS is expected to review in preparation for the examination: schedule M, corporate minutes, internal control documents and training materials, internal management reports, accounting manuals, account analyses and comparative analyses of balance sheet and profit and loss accounts for areas of potential non-compliance. An objective review of such items often sheds light on issues the IRS may raise during the course of the examination, including but not limited to transition issues.

> **Comment:** If a previous transfer pricing examination resulted in a substantial proposed adjustment, the taxpayer should expect the IRS to revisit the same issue in the current cycle, regardless of whether or not the adjustment was sustained. A review of the previous examination, including transfer pricing questions or issues that the IRS raised but did not examine in full, will provide the taxpayer and its advisors with likely areas of IRS inquiry.

The taxpayer should identify all related party transactions. Form 5471 (Information Return of U.S. Person With Respect to Certain Foreign Corporations) and Form 5472 (Information Return of a 25% Foreign-Owned U.S. Corporation or a Foreign Corporation Engaged in a U.S. Trade or Business) filed with the taxpayer's U.S. federal income tax return are good starting points. However, it may be necessary to undertake a broader survey to ensure that all transactions are identified and to confirm their volume or value. If the company has a transfer pricing policy, the taxpayer should next determine whether the policy has been followed for the identified transactions. If not, it is important to determine the transfer pricing practices being used for all of the company's transactions with related parties involving financing, services, or the transfer or use of tangible or intangible property. For this purpose, the taxpayer team might have to contact the relevant officers and employees, such as financial officers and the heads of marketing, research and development, operations and manufacturing for various related parties.

Transactions with related entities in low-tax jurisdictions or jurisdictions with tax holidays will draw particular IRS scrutiny and should be reviewed closely. The taxpayer should also calculate and analyze the financial ratios used by the IRS to determine whether to pursue a transfer pricing examination. This analysis will often provide clues to particular subsidiaries, product lines or transactions that the IRS may investigate or the overall level of interest the IRS may have in the taxpayer's transfer pricing activities.

A taxpayer must provide its principal and background documentation prepared for purposes of the transfer pricing penalty rules within 30 days of an IRS request.[36] Because this request is likely to be made early in the examination, the taxpayer's transfer pricing team should review the taxpayer's documentation to be certain that the team is prepared to defend its transfer pricing determinations on that basis, beginning with the principal and background documents the taxpayer compiled for purposes of the Code Sec. 6664(c)(1) reasonable cause exception to the Code Sec. 6662(e) transfer pricing penalties. The description of the transactions and the functions and risks of related parties should be compared with the transactions as actually conducted. The documentation should also be evaluated in light of developments since the date the documentation was compiled that might affect the taxpayer's interpretation of the regulations under Code Secs. 482 or 6662(e) and (h).

Controversial Issues. Before the examination begins, the taxpayer should determine whether it has any issues that will be controversial and difficult to resolve with the examination team (e.g., valuable intangibles, marketing or beneficially owned intangibles, cost sharing, or U.S. operations with persistent losses). A taxpayer with controversial transfer pricing issues should focus on a procedural strategy to move the case to the most favorable forum for resolution of the transfer pricing issue.

If the taxpayer believes the IRS examination team will be unwilling to narrow or resolve the issue, the taxpayer's examination strategy should include if and when to seek National Office involvement in the examination and when and how to move the case or the issues to the next level. In this regard, the taxpayer will have to consider whether to file the standard Appeals protest, invoke the early referral procedures or seek simultaneous consideration by Appeals and Competent Authority under the Simultaneous Appeals Procedure (SAP).

In the last several years, as the U.S. treaty partners have become more aggressive in their transfer pricing rules, taxpayers face an increasing number of issues that cannot easily be resolved with the IRS because of the transfer pricing rules or practices of these other jurisdictions. If the taxpayer expects relief from double taxation resulting from a transfer pricing adjustment to ultimately come through the mutual agreement procedure, its IRS examination defense may have to strike a delicate balance.[37] That is, while defending its prices to the IRS the taxpayer must also be mindful of the transfer pricing methods or analyses that are most likely to persuade the U.S. and the foreign tax jurisdiction to reach a compromise that avoids double taxation. This will require the taxpayer to consider the foreign tax implications in preparing its documentation and responding to IDRs.

If a transfer pricing adjustment exceeds the penalty thresholds, the IRS can impose penalties if the taxpayer does not provide the requested documents within 30 days. The District Director has discretion to extend the period for providing

---

[36] Code Sec. 6662(e)(3)(B)((i)(III); Reg. § 1.6662-6(d)(iii)(C).

[37] *See* Rev. Proc. 2006-54, 2006-2 CB 1035.

background documents, but no extension of time is provided for principal documents.[38] Although the District Director has discretionary authority to excuse a minor or inadvertent failure to provide required documents, taxpayers cannot rely on such relief for additional time to remedy incomplete documentation.[39]

If possible, the taxpayer should seek to establish that its pricing was appropriate using information in existence at the time the tax return was filed. The regulations require that principal and background documents be "in existence when the return is filed," but this requirement does not extend to the general index of relevant documents.[40] While any analyses created after the return was filed will not be considered timely, many existing documents may nonetheless serve as principal and background documents.

During the search for contemporaneous information, the taxpayer team should search for information concerning comparable transactions that might be relevant to the taxpayer's related party transactions. If these transactions are not present, it will be difficult to satisfy the principal documentation requirement using comparable companies with information in existence at the time the return was filed. The taxpayer's team may need to supplement the documentation existing when the return was filed with additional analysis supporting the taxpayer's transfer pricing determinations. This supplemental material will not, however, satisfy the requirement for contemporaneous documentation and should not be represented as being in existence when the return was filed. The international agent could, nonetheless, treat this information as relevant supplemental information, possibly allowing the taxpayer to avoid a transfer pricing adjustment.

If the taxpayer team determines that the taxpayer's transfer pricing is not defensible, they should search for setoffs to reduce or eliminate any underpayment arising from any transfer pricing adjustments.[41] The regulatory rules for setoffs are specific and should involve transactions between the same related parties.[42] Those rules should not be confused with self adjustments. If setoffs would not eliminate the potential exposure, the taxpayer's team should consider filing an amended return before the IRS first contacts the taxpayer regarding the examination of that tax year to bring its transfer pricing into a defensible range.

> *Comment:* Many transfer pricing statutes preclude taxpayers from filing amended returns that: (1) reduce the amount of previously reported income, or (2) revise the amount of reported income (either upward or downward). Consequently, a taxpayer may be subject to double taxation if it files an amended tax return containing transfer pricing adjustments.

Adequate Documentation. If the taxpayer has appropriately employed a TPM and achieved defensible financial results, the taxpayer should attempt to demonstrate the appropriateness of these results early in the examination. The taxpayer should use plain language to explain its operations, the related party transactions, the basis for the TPM, and the contemporaneous documentation supporting both

---

[38] *See* Code Sec. 6662(e) and (h).
[39] Reg. § 1.6662-6(d)(2)(iii)(A).
[40] Reg. § 1.6662-6(d)(2)(iii)(A).

[41] Reg. § 1.482-1(g)(4), Reg. § 1.6662-6(c)(4).
[42] *Id.*

¶1110.02

the methodology and results. The taxpayer should demonstrate the strength of its analysis and the results to the IRS examination team before the team has invested significant resources in the transfer pricing examination. Early presentation of a strong case may allow the taxpayer to conclude the IRS review of its transfer pricing at the examination level.

Poor Documentation. If the taxpayer's application of TPM achieved defensible results, but the taxpayer failed to maintain appropriate documentation, the tax-payer's team should focus on developing the necessary documentation to establish the appropriateness of its methodology and results. The taxpayer needs to commu-nicate to the IRS that the lack of contemporaneous documentation does not necessarily mean that the results are inappropriate. Although the IRS examination team will subject subsequently-developed documentation to greater scrutiny, a well-presented and thorough analysis supporting the taxpayer's results may still allow the IRS examination team to agree with the taxpayer before expending significant resources.

In the pre-examination transfer pricing self-review, the taxpayer's team may conclude that the taxpayer has no documentation, contemporaneous or otherwise, to support its financial results. The taxpayer should investigate whether setoffs might cure the exposure and consider filing an amended return reporting more defensible results before the IRS begins the examination. However, if the taxpayer files an amended return to revise its transfer pricing, the IRS is likely to focus on transfer pricing early in the examination. The taxpayer should complete documen-tation supporting the amended results before the IRS begins the exam and prepare to defend that position.

Evaluate Impact on Future Years. Whatever strategy the taxpayer employs, the taxpayer must consider the impact of that strategy on future years. If the taxpayer's related party transactions in those years are similar, the acceptance or rejection of its transfer pricing method by the IRS examination team are likely to influence the IRS in any examination of future years.

> *Comment:* If a U.S. distributor were to insist on IRS acceptance of start up losses on the penetration of the U.S. market, the IRS would be likely to insist on superior profits in the future to reflect the return on investment and the development of a marketing intangible by the U.S. distributor.

If returns for those years have been filed, the regulations prohibit the filing of amended returns invoking Code Sec. 482 to decrease taxable income.[43] If, however, the taxpayer determines that its transfer pricing method, or its application of the method, resulted in an underreporting of income, consideration should be given to amending the returns to minimize the taxpayer's penalty exposure.[44] If returns have not been filed, the taxpayer can report its transfer prices determined under an appropriate method, regardless of the transfer prices reflected in the taxpayer's books and records, and prepare contemporaneous documentation. For the current

---

[43] Reg. § 1.482-1(a)(3). *But see Pikeville Coal Co.*, 97-1 USTC ¶ 50,257 (Fed. Cl. 1997) (holding that where the United States asserts a Code Sec. 482 adjustment in the taxpayer's favor, the taxpayer may introduce evidence establishing that a greater adjustment is appropriate).

[44] *See* Reg. §§ 1.6662-6(a)(2) *and* 1.6664-2(c)(3).

¶1110.02

and future years, the taxpayer should have ample opportunity to modify and document its related party transactions to reflect the appropriate tax consequences.

Develop Substantive Transfer Pricing Arguments. Following an initial review of available information, the taxpayer and its advisors should determine what additional analysis might be beneficial (e.g., a transfer pricing study to quantify exposure and support a defensible transfer pricing method). This analysis will provide the foundation for a transfer pricing procedural strategy (e.g., whether to defend transfer prices in examination, request competent authority assistance, or apply for an APA). These tax exposure analyses done in contemplation of a tax controversy are usually done under the attorney client work product doctrine.

Following the evaluation by the taxpayer's transfer pricing team of exposure in prior years and the impact on future years, the taxpayer should develop a substantive transfer pricing strategy. In this stage, the taxpayer should consider additional tax or economic analysis to bolster any weaknesses uncovered in the evaluation stage. For example, taxpayers may want to undertake a review of transfer pricing cases to further refine and discuss similarities between the taxpayer's fact pattern and those in favorable transfer pricing cases. The taxpayer may also want to further refine the economic adjustments in the documentation or to perform analysis to demonstrate convergence of results under the different methods. Finally, the taxpayer's team should anticipate possible IRS arguments and develop a comprehensive strategy to effectively rebut the substantive arguments raised by the IRS and affirmatively raise arguments to persuade the IRS to agree with the taxpayer's position.

Develop Preliminary Procedural Alternatives. Because transfer pricing involves complex factual determinations and subjective application of the regulations, the opportunity plainly exists for disputes between the IRS and taxpayers. A defense strategy based on substantive arguments alone is insufficient. Taxpayers should develop a procedural component to the overall defense strategy to achieve the most favorable resolution of the transfer pricing dispute.

The main purpose of the procedural strategy is to seek out the most favorable forum for settlement. The IRS examination team has a different motivation than Appeals, APA or competent authority staff. The substantive rules that govern the case are different for the competent authority staff (OECD guidelines) than for Examination, Appeals, and counsel (U.S. regulations). Further, the interpretation of facts and taxpayer substantive arguments may differ significantly between different IRS personnel. A well-planned procedural strategy will allow the taxpayer to move the dispute to the most favorable forum for resolution.

The preliminary procedural strategy should incorporate all information known prior to the examination (e.g., taxpayer facts, taxpayer substantive arguments) yet be flexible enough to incorporate subsequent information (e.g., new facts, IRS examination reaction to facts, IRS arguments).

The preliminary procedural strategy should tentatively commit to a decision to seek either unilateral or bilateral alternatives, as this choice has a significant impact on the substantive arguments (e.g., difference in controlling law—U.S. regulations

¶1110.02

for unilateral, OECD guidelines for bilateral). A more detailed procedural strategy can be developed throughout the examination process.

¶ 1120 Pre-Examination Conference

An IRS case manager is instructed to seek taxpayer involvement in examination planning through pre-examination conferences.[45] These conferences provide the taxpayer an understanding of the IRS's examination interests and plans. They also provide the IRS with an impression of the taxpayer's examination concerns and the level of the taxpayer's cooperation.

The IRS carefully plans its strategy for these conferences and the taxpayer should do the same. The taxpayer should be prepared to engage the examination team in discussions regarding the issues to be examined, the use and roles of specialists on the examination team, the pace of the examination, the protection of confidential information, and the sharing of information necessary to conclude the examination. The taxpayer can obtain an understanding of the scope of the transfer pricing examination and the extent of the IRS's interest in particular issues.

.01 Taxpayer Goals

The taxpayer should first understand the IRS's goals for the conference before setting its own strategy. The IRS generally intends to reach an agreement with the taxpayer on the following points:

- Lines of communication between the IRS and the taxpayer;
- Use of taxpayer resources such as office space, hours, equipment, etc.;[46]
- Procedures for providing the IRS with returns of related parties;[47]
- Procedures for the taxpayer to present documentation of items that may reduce its tax liability;[48]
- Periods for submitting and responding to IDRs;[49] and
- Procedures and timing of the examination of off-site records and facilities.[50]

In addition, the IRS examination team should be willing to discuss:

- Areas it intends to examine;
- Team's use of experts and their role;
- Advisory role of counsel; and
- Need for the IRS to timely advise the taxpayer of potential new areas of examination.[51]

While the taxpayer's specific objectives for the meeting will depend on the facts and circumstances, most taxpayers will have certain common goals. These goals include:

---

[45] IRM 4.46.3.5.5.
[46] IRM 4.46.3.3.1.6.
[47] IRM 4.46.3.3.1.7.
[48] *Id.*
[49] IRM 4.46.3.3.1.6.
[50] *Id.*
[51] IRM 4.46.3.3.1.6.

¶1120.01

- Understanding the areas the examination team intends to examine;

- Defining and focusing the records and information to be sought by the IRS examination team;

- Establishing lines of communication between the IRS and the taxpayer to insure an accurate and timely flow of information;

- Avoiding last-minute surprises in the IRS Form 5701, Notice of Proposed Adjustments; and

- Developing an examination timetable that can fit within its staffing and business planning cycles.

.02 Preliminary Strategies for Resolution

Before the initial meeting with the IRS at the Pre-Examination Conference, the taxpayer should identify issues that it hopes to resolve with the IRS examination team. Even before the IRS formally commences its examination, the taxpayer's examination team should start planning preliminary strategies for narrowing or resolving anticipated transfer pricing issues.

The taxpayer's strategy will depend on its level of preparation for the examination and the nature of the anticipated transfer pricing issues. Strategies available to a taxpayer that maintains a well-documented, defensible transfer pricing policy will probably not be available to taxpayers with incomplete documentation or significant exposure. While a unique strategy must be developed for each case, some broad, practical guidelines exist.

¶ 1130 Overview of the Examination Process

A transfer pricing examination goes through a number of stages, beginning with information gathering and ending with the issuance of the revenue agent's report ("RAR") and the notice of proposed adjustment. During the examination process, the taxpayer must maintain interaction with the examination team beyond responding to IRS demands for information and documents. The taxpayer should speak with the IRS examination team regularly about the theories and issues being developed. If the taxpayer is successful in giving the IRS a thorough understanding of its business and the economic analysis that supports its application of the transfer pricing rules, the taxpayer should get appropriate case development with little conflict and avoid or minimize adjustments unrelated to the taxpayer's facts and circumstances.

Despite the taxpayer's best efforts, the IRS examination team will sometimes apply the regulations under Code Sec. 482 in a manner that the taxpayer's team believes is inappropriate. The taxpayer's response to this situation will depend largely on the taxpayer's expectations regarding the ability to satisfactorily resolve the case at the examination level. If the taxpayer believes it can make substantial progress at the examination level, one approach would be to acknowledge the problem and convene a meeting including the case manager for the sole purpose of exchanging views—not to negotiate or resolve—on the technical or economic issues. If this is not successful in breaking the impasse, such a meeting will at least be useful to later demonstrate to Appeals that every effort was made to develop and resolve the case with the examination team.

A taxpayer with a strong, well-documented case might encourage the international examiner to consult with a Chief Counsel (International). This approach should be used with caution if the taxpayer has any transfer pricing exposure, because the Special Counsel (International) may offer the international examiner an effective alternative support or identify new issues. If a narrow legal issue is an obstacle to resolution of the case and the taxpayer's legal position is particularly strong, the taxpayer may ask the IRS examination team to seek a Technical Advice Memorandum ("TAM") from the National Office or a Field Service Advisory ("FSA") from District Counsel.

If, after information gathering and the development of the IRS position, the taxpayer has little expectation of narrowing or resolving the case at the examination level, numerous procedural alternatives exist to seek a more favorable forum for resolution.

¶ 1140 The Examination Begins—Gathering of Information

Transfer pricing examinations often involve substantial volumes of information and may take years to conclude. The TP Audit Guidelines state that a transfer pricing examination requires the international examiner to understand: (1) the U.S. taxpayer's operations; (2) the operations of foreign affiliates; (3) the relationship between the U.S. taxpayer and its foreign affiliates; (4) the role that each entity plays in carrying out the activities of a controlled group; and (5) the U.S. taxpayer's intangibles.[52]

The IRS has several tools for gathering information, including IDRs, interviews of taxpayer's employees, requests to related and unrelated third parties, formal document requests, designated summonses, and treaty exchange of information procedures. These tools provide the IRS with the ability to gather significant amounts of information regarding the taxpayer's industry and transactions. Examinations proceed in the following order: the IRS requests and receives information, analyzes it, revises its plan, and issues follow-up requests.

.01 Taxpayer Interaction

The information gathering portion of a transfer pricing examination should not involve a series of short answers to IRS questions. The taxpayer should not stop at answering the IRS examination questions, but should offer to explain its favorable documentation and pricing determinations to the IRS examination team. An initial examination meeting provides the opportunity to explain the taxpayer's industry and marketplace, organization structure, and intercompany transactions, as well as the choice of methodology, criteria for comparables, and adjustments to support its transfer price determinations. Consistent with pre-examination planning, the taxpayer interaction with the IRS should be cooperative, professional and interactive. Taxpayers should anticipate and address IRS concerns with contemporaneous documentation supplemented by open-ended discussions of the relevant issues.

---

[52] IRM 4.61.3.4.2.

If the IRS inquiries stray significantly from the examination plan, taxpayers should respectfully request a meeting to discuss the propriety of the departure from the agreed upon plan and the taxpayer's willingness to comply. Taxpayers should be advised that leniency should be shown for the development of legitimate issues to avoid the development of an adversarial environment.

Whenever information requests create a significant burden, taxpayers should discuss the request and attempt to uncover the underlying concern. Substitute data can sometimes be found or developed to address the IRS concerns with less effort by the taxpayer. The taxpayer should behave in a professional, respectful manner in order to avoid an adversarial environment in the development of subjective transfer pricing topics.

.02 Information Sought

The TP Audit Guidelines contain a comprehensive list of documents that international examiners should review as part of the transfer pricing examination.[53] The stated purpose of reviewing the listed documents is to gain an understanding of the taxpayer's business operations, its intangibles, and its industry. Two items are singled out for special attention by the international examiner: the taxpayer's financial statements and its transfer pricing documentation.[54] For the transfer pricing documentation, the TP Audit Guidelines provide that it should be requested at the onset of the transfer pricing examination, and if the documentation provided is not adequate, to use other means (e.g., a summons) to get the requested information, or to consider imposing the Code Sec. 6662 penalty.

.03 IRS Tools

Code Secs. 6038A and 6038C Documentation. Code Secs. 6038A and 6038C provide additional sources of information to the IRS examination team by requiring twenty-five percent foreign-owned domestic corporations and foreign corporations engaged in a trade or business within the United States to maintain records of transactions with related parties.[55] These Code sections apply to domestic corporations for whom foreign persons own at least 25 percent of the voting power of all classes of stock or at least 25 percent of the value of all classes of stock.[56] These provisions require taxpayers to maintain records sufficient to prepare profit and loss statements for products or services transferred between the taxpayer and its foreign related parties. The IRS instructs its international examiners to seek this information through IDRs and summonses, as necessary, and to seek penalties if dissatisfied with the taxpayer's responses.[57]

The taxpayer need not directly maintain all of the necessary records if other entities maintain the records outside the United States.[58] If the books and records are in the control of a foreign parent, the taxpayer must provide the records to the IRS within 60 days of the IRS's IDR.[59] A failure to maintain and provide the records exposes the taxpayer to substantial penalties.[60] Further, if a 25 percent or greater

[53] IRM 4.61.3.4.2.
[54] IRM 4.61.3.4.3, IRM 4.61.3.4.4.
[55] Reg. § 1.6038A-2(b).
[56] Code Sec. 6038A(c)(1). Reg. § 1.6038A-3(a)(1).
[57] IRM 4.46.4.4.2, IRM 4.46.5.
[58] Reg. § 1.6038A-3(b)(2).
[59] Reg. § 1.6038A-3(f).
[60] Code Secs. 6038A(d) and 6038C(c).

foreign shareholder owns the U.S. subsidiary, the IRS can ask the subsidiary to obtain an authorization of agent from the foreign parent or other related party that engaged in transactions with the U.S. taxpayer.[61] The IRS can then request the information from the foreign entity through its agent.[62]

IDRs. IDRs, issued on Form 4564, are the IRS' primary information-gathering tool.[63] Taxpayers can expect IDRs regarding the documentation specified in the transfer pricing penalty regulations, other information relating to the taxpayer's transfer pricing practices, follow-up information, and interviews with taxpayer personnel. Each IDR presents an opportunity for the taxpayer to affirmatively present the taxpayer's viewpoint on the transfer pricing issues in question.

IDRs should be specific, clear and concise. The taxpayer should carefully adhere to its agreement with the case manager concerning procedures for clarifying any ambiguity in the language of the IDRs or notifying the IRS concerning any difficulty or delays in obtaining records required to satisfy the request. The IRS encourages discussions with the taxpayer regarding the information needed and records available.[64] Although the taxpayer is generally expected to respond to IDRs within 30 days (60 days for records located outside the United States), most examiners allow a reasonable extension of time to respond to IDRs.

> **Comment:** The taxpayer should meet agreed upon deadlines for IDR responses or contact the IRS for an extension of time to respond, as any unexplained delay could cause unnecessary friction with the IRS examination team.

The IRS is generally discouraged from issuing IDRs that require the taxpayer to prepare or create original documents. However, as a practical matter, it may not be advisable to provide "raw data" to the IRS without accompanying summary and analysis. Taxpayers should provide information in a clear and understandable manner with appropriate explanations to reduce the risk of misinterpretation. All information should be provided to the IRS in written form, and the taxpayer's team leader should maintain a log of IDRs received and responses provided.

Initial Requests for Transfer Pricing Documentation. One of the first actions of an international examiner conducting a transfer pricing examination will be to obtain the contemporaneous documentation compiled by the taxpayer for purposes of complying with the provisions of Reg. § 1.6662-6(d).[65] The taxpayer must provide the IRS with the documentation within thirty days of the request to avoid the Code Sec. 6662(e) and (h) transfer pricing penalties.[66] This documentation represents the taxpayer's first opportunity to persuade the IRS that its transfer pricing is appropriate. If incomplete or inarticulate, the documentation may provide the IRS with a road map for its transfer pricing audit. The taxpayer must quickly decide whether to provide this information or to rely on other analyses to demonstrate the reasonableness of its transfer pricing practices. Although the District Director may excuse minor or inadvertent failures to provide in a timely manner this documentation if

---

[61] Code Sec. 6038A(e)(1); Reg. § 1.6038A-5(b).

[62] Code Sec. 6038A(e)(1).

[63] Code Sec. 6038A(e)(1).

[64] Code Sec. 6038A(e)(1).

[65] IRM 61.3.4.4, IRM Exhibit 4.46.4-1.

[66] Reg. § 1.6662-6(d)(2)(iii).

the taxpayer establishes that it acted in good faith in attempting to comply and promptly remedies any failure, taxpayers should not expose themselves to the discretion of the District Director.[67]

To meet the reasonable cause and good faith requirements of Code Sec. 6662 for either a specified or unspecified methodology, the taxpayer must maintain and provide the IRS with sufficient documentation to demonstrate that the taxpayer reasonably concluded that the TPM, and its application, provided the most reliable measure of an arm's length result, given the available data.[68] The regulations refer to two categories of documentation: principal documents and background documents. If the taxpayer uses an unspecified method, additional documentation is required. Principal and background documents have been described in detail in Chapter 10 and a Model Transfer pricing report can be found at ¶ 20,060.

Supplemental IDRs. IDRs are not limited to the taxpayer's contemporaneous documentation, and taxpayers should be prepared to receive IDRs requesting some of the following documents:

- An overview of the taxpayer's business with an analysis of the factors, legal and economic, affecting the pricing;
- Market share strategy documentation;
- Balance sheet and profit and loss statements, with a breakdown of major income and expense items as well as profit and loss statements for the taxpayer's major product lines;
- Internal audit and management reports, including budget reports;
- All intercompany pricing policies; and
- Copies of all agreements between the taxpayer and its foreign affiliates, including all distribution agreements, warranty and service agreements, advertising and marketing agreements, as well as trade name and trademark agreements.

U.S.-based multinational companies should be prepared to receive IDRs for some of the following documents:

- Profit and loss statements for all controlled foreign corporations ("CFCs");
- Audited financial statements of the CFCs;
- Documents relating to the formation of each CFC including applicable Board of Directors' minutes, all reports, studies, and analyses provided to the Board of Directors when considering the creation of the CFC as well as all Board documents authorizing the creation of the CFC;
- Copies of applications for tax exemption and/or assistance (financial, training or other) submitted by the taxpayer and/or each CFC to the CFC's host country, along with the responses of the host country;
- Copies of blueprints or plans for each CFC's facility showing footage and allocations by functional activity;

---

[67] Reg. § 1.6662-6(d)(2)(iii).   [68] Reg. § 1.6662-6(d)(2)(iii).

¶1140.03

- Each CFC's organizational charts reflecting departmental relationships and identifying department managers by name, title, and nationality;
- Information on the products manufactured by each CFC including catalogs, brochures, price lists, bills of materials, standard cost sheets, and competitor's products;
- Copies of technology transfer or sharing agreements and the royalties paid pursuant to those agreements;
- Copies of research and development sharing agreements between each CFC and all affiliated entities and with any unrelated parties;
- Copies of all trade name and trademark agreements;
- Copies of intercompany pricing policies regarding the purchase of raw materials and work-in-process goods; and
- Copies of all distribution agreements with related and unrelated parties.[69]

Transactions involving intangible property present some of the most challenging problems in a transfer pricing analysis. The international examiner will probably request copies of the taxpayer's license agreements as well as any correspondence concerning modifications to the agreements. If a license fee or royalty is based on production, rather than sales, the IRS will probably request production figures. In addition, the international examiner can be expected to ask about the existence of unrelated third party agreements involving the same or similar intangible property.

The IRS frequently issues IDRs for transfer pricing analyses prepared by or on behalf of a taxpayer for management or risk assessment purposes, which were not relied upon by the taxpayer in establishing its pricing practices or reporting positions. Responses to these requests must be carefully considered to determine whether any privileges apply. To the extent the reports were prepared for management in the ordinary course of business or tax return purposes, privileges are unlikely to apply.[70]

Requests for Interviews. In addition to the review of taxpayer documents, transfer pricing examinations generally involve interviews of the taxpayer's officers and employees. The identity of those to be interviewed, the scope of the interview, and site of the interview are usually the subject of negotiation between the taxpayer and the international examiner. International examiners can be expected to focus interview questions on the taxpayer's history and operations, including:

- Marketing of the products prior to the organization of distribution subsidiaries;
- Functions performed by each entity;
- Risks inherent in the industry and how the taxpayer allocates them between related entities;
- Financial history of the related entities;

---

[69] IRM Exhibit 4.61.3-2 at 2(j)(4).

[70] *See J. Bell*, 95-1 USTC ¶ 50,006 (N.D. Cal. 1994); *M. Adlman*, 95-2 USTC ¶ 50,579, 68 F.3d 1495, 1501 (2d Cir. 1995).

- Taxpayer's products and markets;
- Taxpayer's competitors;
- Taxpayer's customers;
- Current and future outlook for the products or services involved; and,
- Importance of manufacturing versus marketing intangibles.[71]

If the taxpayer refuses to provide access to the requested individuals, the IRS can issue a summons requiring officers and employees to appear.

> *Comment:* Information provided in the interviews should be accurate and consistent. As with any tax dispute, discrepancies or differences in the way different people present the same information can lead the international examiner to erroneous conclusions or encourage inquiries into ultimately irrelevant issues.

The taxpayer's team leader should be aware of the timing and purpose for all interviews, and a representative from the taxpayer's team should attend interviews to take notes of the questions and responses. Formal transcriptions or tape recordings of the interviews are only done with mutual consent, but rarely do occur. Taxpayer's should generally reject such requests. A member of the taxpayer's team should brief all potential interviewees prior to the interview to explain the purpose of the interview, the scope of IRS questions, and the importance of providing accurate responses. Interviewees should be advised to inform the IRS when they are unable to respond because a question is outside their area of expertise, responsibility, or direct knowledge. Further, interviewees should not respond quickly to questions that could be answered more accurately with reference to specific data or analyses. For example, an employee should refer to data concerning manufacturing output and sales trends rather than provide a personal impression concerning the efficiency of a production unit or the benefits of an advertising campaign.

> *Comment:* It is common for employees in various parts of the taxpayer's operations to overstate the importance of their contribution to the overall operations. The only way to counter this overstatement is to provide additional financial information or additional interviews to clear up any false impression.

Responding to Requests for Information and Interviews. Responses to the first round of IDRs or interviews will generally generate additional IDRs with follow-up questions. The taxpayer should attempt to provide the IRS with the information requested by the IDRs without inadvertently raising new issues. Also, the taxpayer should take advantage of agreements made in the examination planning phase to focus IDRs, follow-up IDRs, and interviews on relevant and available information.

Failure to provide the IRS with the information requested in IDRs or to make employees available for interviews will cause the IRS to employ more formal tools for gathering information. The IRS is authorized to summons a taxpayer's officers, employees, persons having possession of its books and records, or "any other

---

[71] IRM Exhibit 4.61.3-2 at 1.e.

¶1140.03

person the Secretary may deem proper" to provide the requested information.[72] Absent privileges against the disclosure of information, the issue is not whether the information will be disclosed, but only when and how. A cooperative working relationship with the examination team is generally the best way to reduce the scope of the IRS's requests for information.

The taxpayer should maintain regular contact with the examiner to discuss potential requests even before the IRS issues the IDRs. Through this open discussion the taxpayer can identify the objectives behind the factual inquiry and satisfy the IRS with readily available information. For example, if the international examiner is preparing to request product line profit and loss statements (which do not exist) to determine whether intercompany transactions bear a higher than appropriate level of overhead allocation, the examiner may be satisfied with a schedule that demonstrates that the net profit margins on related party transactions is higher than that of unrelated party transactions. Similarly, the taxpayer can make certain that the IRS team interviews the persons with the appropriate knowledge and authority.

As a general rule, taxpayers should respond to all IDRs, even requests for detailed financial information, in an open-ended fashion, adding a narrative explanation to assist the IRS in reaching the appropriate conclusions. Also, graphs, tables and charts are extremely helpful to develop the appropriate context in which to understand the requested information. This open-ended approach also gives the taxpayer the opportunity to provide additional relevant information that complements the requested information, such as multi-year trends or industry norms. For example, when responding to an IDR requesting a single year of information with respect to a single product line, it may be appropriate to include information regarding that product in prior years and explain how sales in that product line are integrally related to sales in other product lines.

The need to respond in an open-ended fashion is particularly important for IDRs concerning comparable taxpayers and transactions. For example, the IRS may request information regarding the price charged by a related manufacturer for the sale of products to unrelated parties. Even though the IRS has not asked, the taxpayer should not fail to point out that the products sold to the unrelated party do not carry the brand that forms a valuable part of the related party transactions.

Taxpayers will often be required to respond to an overly broad IDR. In this situation, the taxpayer should either request the IRS to narrow its request or indicate how it interpreted the question and respond fully to what the taxpayer believes is the question. In any event, the taxpayer should respond in a timely manner and demonstrate that a further line of inquiry would not produce the desired results. If the IRS wishes to pursue the issue, such responses should assist them in framing a more specific follow-up question. Overly narrow IDRs can also be challenging. The taxpayer should carefully review such questions to determine all implications before responding.

---

[72] Code Sec. 7602(a)(2).

The resolution of a transfer pricing dispute is achieved by agreement on a number of ambiguous issues. By working with the IRS examination team to focus the inquiry on relevant information and providing the information in a way that demonstrates the reasonableness and accuracy of the taxpayer's transfer pricing practices, the taxpayer greatly increases its chances of resolving transfer pricing issues at the examination level.

Code Sec. 7602 Summons. The IRS may issue a summons to any taxpayer subject to a U.S. court's jurisdiction, requiring the production of books, papers, records or other information relating to matters affecting the taxpayer's tax liability. The IRS also has the authority to summons any officer or employee of the taxpayer, or any person who has possession, custody or care of the relevant materials to produce the information requested by the IRS and also to give testimony that may be relevant to the tax return.[73] The type of summons is called a Subpoena Duces Tecum. The physical location of the documents outside the United States generally is irrelevant from a U.S. perspective, provided the taxpayer has possession or control over them.[74] Because courts impose a presumption that corporations have control over their books and records, a corporation must produce clear proof of any asserted lack of possession and control.[75] The issuance of a summons requires District Counsel involvement, but the IRS will generally cooperate internally to issue a summons when deemed necessary.

If the taxpayer is having difficulty responding to one or more IDRs despite repeated requests, the taxpayer should maintain communication with the case manager to avoid receiving a summons. If the taxpayer does not respond or provides an incomplete response, the case manager will generally issue a pre-summons letter requesting the taxpayer's cooperation and warning that a summons will be issued if the requested information is not provided.[76] At this point District Counsel will become involved, which may alter the working relationship between the taxpayer and the IRS examination team. If the taxpayer fails to respond satisfactorily within the stipulated time frame, an administrative summons will be issued on Form 2039 requesting the information.[77] Although the taxpayer (or other person summoned) can resist enforcement of the summons by rebutting the IRS allegations or presenting an affirmative defense, taxpayers seldom prevail in a summons enforcement action.[78]

Third Party Requests. Information from third parties, unrelated or related, is an additional source of potentially relevant information for the IRS. Special procedural rules apply to the IRS's ability to gather this information and the taxpayer's obligation to obtain it for the IRS.

Information Obtained From Foreign Related Parties. By its very nature, a transfer pricing determination often requires an examination of information held by

---

[73] Code Sec. 7602(a)(1) and Code Sec. 7602(a)(2).

[74] *In re Grand Jury Subpoenas Duces Tecum Addressed to Canadian International Paper Co.*, 72 F. Supp. 1013 (S.D.N.Y. 1947); *Marc Rich & Co.*, 707 F.2d 663 (2d Cir.), *cert. denied*, 463 US 1215 (1983).

[75] *First National City Bank of New York*, 59-2 USTC ¶ 9755, 361 U.S. 948 (1960).

[76] IRM 4.46.4.4.

[77] IRM 4.46.4.4.

[78] *J. McCarthy*, 75-1 USTC ¶ 9402, 514 F.2d 368, 372-3 (3d Cir. 1975).

¶1140.03

foreign related parties. The IRS initially seeks this information by issuing IDRs to the taxpayer.[79] If the taxpayer fails to provide the information and the information is held by a foreign subsidiary, the IRS may seek to obtain the information by serving a summons on the taxpayer.[80]

To strengthen the IRS's ability to obtain information from foreign related entities, Congress enacted Code Sec. 6038A(e), which allows the IRS to request a taxpayer to obtain authority from a foreign related entity to act as an agent of the entity for purposes of the summons procedures of Code Secs. 7602, 7603, and 7604.[81] If a taxpayer fails to obtain the authorization, Code Sec. 6038A(e)(3) permits the IRS to determine the amount of a deduction for any amount paid or incurred by the taxpayer to the related foreign corporation, or the cost of any property acquired, based solely on the information available to it.[82] Code Sec. 6038A(e) applies regardless of whether the foreign related party is a parent, subsidiary, or sibling to the taxpayer.[83]

Unrelated Third Party Information. Occasionally, the IRS examination team will seek information from unrelated parties that engaged in transactions with the taxpayer, an entity related to the taxpayer or unrelated third parties in a similar business that have entered into comparable transactions.[84] For unrelated parties that have engaged in transactions with the taxpayer or an entity related to the taxpayer, the IRS examination team will initially seek this information through IDRs addressed to the taxpayer. For unrelated entities having no business transactions with the taxpayer, the IRS will first contact the unrelated entity's tax director by telephone, with a written follow-up letter.[85] The IRS contends that it has the power in either case to issue third party summonses for this information.[86]

The acquisition and use of unrelated third party information by the IRS examination team, whether provided voluntarily or pursuant to summons, raises serious concerns for the taxpayer: (1) whether the information will be made available to the taxpayer; and (2) whether the taxpayer will be able to investigate behind the information to determine the strength of comparability and reliability of data. The use of "hidden" data represents a significant handicap that the taxpayer may not be able to remedy unless it litigates the case and can employ the discovery tools available in litigation.[87] The taxpayer may be able to obtain this information during the examination if the IRS obtains the third party's consent to the disclosure and the taxpayer enters into an agreement not to make any further disclosures of the information. As a practical matter, it is important to note that the U.S. competent authority will neither use nor accept undisclosed third party information in its negotiations with the competent authorities of other countries.

> **Comment:** Because the IRS must disclose the third party information during trial preparation or if the IRS intends to use that information in

---

[79] IRM 4.46.4.4.

[80] Code Sec. 7602.

[81] Code Sec. 6038A(e).

[82] Code Sec. 6038A(e)(3).

[83] Code Sec. 6038A(e)(1) and (c)(2).

[84] IRM 4.61.4.3.1.

[85] IRM 4.61.4.10.

[86] Code Sec. 7602(a)(2); *see also Donruss Co.*, 67-2 USTC ¶ 9736 (3d Cir. 1967).

[87] *See* Tax Court Petition in Pentax Corporation, No. 3915-94, 94 *Tax Notes International* 179-13.

competent authority proceedings, the IRS is much less likely to use that information to develop a case.

Comment: As a result of all of the inherent difficulties associated with using information obtained from unrelated third parties, the IRS generally relies on public sources rather than exercising its third party summons power.

Code Sec. 982—Formal Document Requests. Formal document requests under Code Sec. 982 are another tool available to the IRS to obtain foreign-based documentation, or at least prevent taxpayer use of such information.[88] Foreign based documentation is any documentation that may be relevant or material to the tax treatment of an examined item and that is outside the United States.[89] When the examination team fails to receive a satisfactory response to an IDR for information that is in the control of a foreign subsidiary or other foreign member of a domestic taxpayer's group, it may issue the taxpayer a formal document request.[90] The formal document request specifies:

- Time and place for the production of the documents;
- Reasons any documentation previously provided was insufficient;
- Description of the documents sought; and
- Consequences of not providing the documents.[91]

The examination team must mail the formal document request to the taxpayer's last known address by registered or certified mail.[92] The taxpayer may then attempt to quash the request in a proceeding similar to that used to quash a subpoena or summons.[93] If the taxpayer fails to have the request quashed and fails to provide the information within 90 days after the IRS mails the request, the taxpayer may be precluded from introducing any foreign-based documentation covered by the request into evidence in any subsequent proceeding in which the tax treatment of the examined item is at issue.[94] The 90 day period for providing the documents may be extended by the IRS or a court with jurisdiction over a proceeding to quash the formal document request.[95]

Designated Summonses. In CEP audits, the IRS has the ability to suspend the statute of limitations on assessments by issuing, and seeking judicial enforcement of, a "designated summons," and any other summons issued within 30 days after the issuance of the "designated summons" that relates to the same return as the designated summons.[96] Code Sec. 6503(j) suspends the statute of limitations on assessment for the period necessary to resolve the enforcement proceedings relating to these summonses.[97]

Office of International Programs. In transfer pricing examinations, taxpayers should expect the examination team to use the services of the Office of Assistant Commissioner (International). Through the Office of International Programs in the

---

[88] Code Sec. 982; IRM Exhibit 4.6.1.4-1.
[89] Code Sec. 982(d)(1).
[90] Code Sec. 982(c). *See* IRM Exhibit 4.61.4-1.
[91] Code Sec. 982(c)(1)(A)–(D).
[92] Code Sec. 982(c)(1).

[93] Code Sec. 982(c)(2).
[94] Code Sec. 982(a).
[95] Code Sec. 982(d)(3).
[96] Code Sec. 6503(j).
[97] Code Sec. 6503(j).

¶1140.03

Office of Assistant Commissioner (International) the examination team has several sources of foreign information, including Revenue Service Representatives, Specific Requests for Information made to foreign competent authorities ("Specific Requests"), exchanges made through the Simultaneous Examination Program ("Simultaneous Examination"), and Spontaneous Exchanges.

Tax Attaches. The Office of International Programs in the Office of Assistant Commissioner (International) maintains Tax Attaches in various foreign locations. The examination team, with the approval of a Chief, may request that the Tax Attaches obtain the following types of information:

- Public records;
- Information provided voluntarily by third party witnesses and record keepers; and
- Any other information the Tax Attaches may secure through legal sources.[98]

The examination team makes the request directly to the RSR and the RSR responds directly to the examination team.

Specific Requests. The United States maintains tax treaties and Tax Information Exchange Agreements ("TIEAs") with many countries, which provide for the exchange of information for use in tax examinations. The methods for acquiring foreign information under the treaties and TIEAs in transfer pricing examinations include Specific Requests, Simultaneous Examinations, and Spontaneous Exchanges.[99]

Specific Requests start with a request from the examination team, approved by a Branch Chief, which is sent to the International Operations Division of the Office of Assistant Commissioner (International). This generates a letter from the United States competent authority to the competent authority of the country where the information is located, requesting the information.[100] Under the treaties and TIEAs, the competent authority of the other country attempts to obtain the information and provides it to the U.S. competent authority, who forwards it to the examination team.[101] The IRS may or may not notify the taxpayer that it made a Specific Request or that the competent authority issued a Specific Request to a foreign country. In addition, nothing requires the IRS to notify the taxpayer of any responses from the foreign country.

Simultaneous Exchange under the Simultaneous Examination Program. The Simultaneous Examination Program provides a mechanism for information sharing between the United States and another country that is a treaty or TIEA partner during the separate and independent examinations of a taxpayer or related taxpayers by the respective taxing authorities.[102] The Simultaneous Examination procedure provides for meetings between representatives of the United States and the foreign country to discuss audit plans, issues to be developed, and information

---

[98] IRM 35.4.5.2.2.
[99] IRM 35.4.5.2.4.
[100] *Id.*

[101] *Id.; see also* 2006 U.S. Model Income Tax Treaty Article 26, Exchange of Information and Administrative Assistance, and 1984 U.S. Draft Tax Information Exchange Agreement, Article 4, Exchange of Information.
[102] IRM 4.60.1.3.

necessary and appropriate for a Specific Exchange request for each of their respective examinations.[103] The IRS should inform taxpayers that they are the subject of a Simultaneous Examination, but there is no mechanism for the taxpayer to obtain the information exchanged between the countries during the course of the simultaneous examination.[104]

Spontaneous Exchange. Spontaneous Exchanges occur when the IRS or foreign tax authority obtains information during the course of its examination of the taxpayer suggesting noncompliance with the tax laws of the treaty or TIEA partner.[105] In the United States, when the examination team obtains such information, it forwards it to the U.S. competent authority who sends it on to the foreign competent authority.

Taxpayer Knowledge. Taxpayers that suspect that a request was made or information was exchanged for them can file a Freedom of Information Request for the request, the foreign country's response, or any other information exchanged. However, the IRS is likely to assert various privileges against providing this information, especially the cover letter from the U.S. competent authority to the foreign competent authority and the response from the foreign competent authority. The IRS generally refuses to disclose information relating to a taxpayer obtained from a foreign competent authority arguing that treaty secrecy provisions, Code Sec. 6103(e)(7) impairment of tax administration considerations, and/or the state secret privilege preclude its disclosure.[106] However, the taxpayer should be able to obtain, at a minimum, the request sent from the examination team to the U.S. competent authority.

Priority of Procedures. The IRS starts its information gathering activities in the examination in a cooperative manner through IDRs and follow-up requests. The IRS may seek information and interviews not only from the taxpayer and other related U.S. entities, but also from and regarding foreign related entities. If the taxpayer responses do not satisfy the IRS, the IRS will issue summonses. For foreign-based documentation, the IRS will issue formal document requests to obtain the information. If taxpayer efforts do not satisfy the IRS, the agency can apply Code Sec. 982 to preclude the introduction of relevant evidence at trial.

If a foreign shareholder owns 25 percent or more of a U.S. subsidiary, the IRS will ask the taxpayer under Code Sec. 6038A(e) to obtain authorization for the taxpayer to act as the foreign entity's agent for purposes of the Code's summons procedures. If agency authorization is not received, the IRS is authorized under Code Sec. 6038A(e) to make an adjustment based on the information available to it.

Information requests generally fall into two broad categories: IDRs and other, more severe information-gathering tools. Once the IRS moves beyond IDRs to summonses, the transfer pricing examination is likely to be conducted in a less cooperative atmosphere and the taxpayer is likely to find its opportunities to anticipate and influence the IRS's strategy greatly restricted.

[103] *Id.*
[104] *Id.*
[105] *Id.*
[106] IRM 4.60.1.2.2.

¶1140.03

Due to the negative impact of a summons on the overall tone of the examination, the taxpayer should not proceed to a summons lightly. The taxpayer should not allow a summons situation to arise from preventable misunderstandings. An open exchange of objectives and concerns may enable the parties to develop a compromise that provides the case manager with sufficient information without seriously compromising the taxpayer's issues.

¶ 1150 Narrowing the Issues—Development of IRS Positions

.01 The IRS Transfer Pricing Analysis

During its pre-examination planning, the IRS examination team reviews information concerning the taxpayer's business and compares the taxpayer's key financial ratios to broad benchmarks to determine where to focus information gathering and analysis. During the analysis, the IRS examination team reviews the taxpayer's response to IDRs and other materials to understand its business operations. They also carry out a function and risk analysis to understand the role of the taxpayer and affiliates in the related party transactions and investigate the economic conditions surrounding the transactions. The IRS examination team compares the taxpayer's results to comparable transactions or companies to determine whether the taxpayer's transfer pricing achieves an arm's length result. The process should parallel the analysis conducted by the taxpayer in preparing its transfer pricing documentation.

Understanding the Taxpayer's Business. Before evaluating the arm's length nature of the taxpayer's transaction, the IRS examination team will want to gain an understanding of the taxpayer's operations. The IRS examination team is instructed to issue IDRs early in the examination to understand the roles carried out by the U.S. entity and its foreign affiliates. In addition to information typically requested in early IDRs, they will seek answers to questions along the lines of the following:

- Are the affiliates manufacturing the same or similar products or components as the taxpayer with the same technology?

- How is on-going technology transferred within the group? Is there a cost sharing arrangement?

- Which group members perform R&D and how are new developments shared within the group?

- Do distribution affiliates use marketing intangibles (such as advertising plans or materials)? If so, which entity in the group develops them?[107]

The IRS will review product line financial statements for multiple years to detect unusual fluctuations or deviations from industry norms that may not result from business cycles or product life cycles. Internal audit reports will be reviewed to understand the functions of various affiliates and how they are integrated in the overall group.[108]

---

[107] IRM 4.61.3.4.2.

[108] IRM 4.61.3.4.3.4.

The IRS examines closely the taxpayer's transfer pricing documentation to understand the contractual terms of the related party transactions, how prices are established, and the functions and risk of members within the group.[109]

Function and Risk Analysis. The IRS examination team first attempts to understand the functions and risks of the taxpayer and its affiliates before attempting to determine whether particular transactions or companies are comparable to the taxpayer. The examiner attempts to identify the functions that are most important in creating value in the taxpayer's related party transactions. Depending on the content of the taxpayer's documentation, the examiner uses information obtained in IDRs and interviews to trace the flow of transactions through the company. The IRM instructs the examiner to seek information outside the tax department. Key personnel may be interviewed to determine who performed significant functions, whether any valuable intangibles were involved, and reasons for the transactional structure.[110]

The international examiner will attempt to determine the effect of intangible property on the transactions. As more and more foreign-based multinationals increase their manufacturing in the United States, international examiners routinely focus on the intangibles typically found in inbound manufacturing operations. They may inquire about the cost, age and source of machinery, and also whether the machinery is specialized or custom-designed. If custom designed, they will inquire into who designed it and whether any related services were provided. An IRS engineer may be assigned to determine the uniqueness or effectiveness of the machine. Similar analyses may also be carried out for offshore manufacturing subsidiaries of U.S.-based multinationals.

The international examiner will also search for intangibles when analyzing distribution subsidiaries. The international examiner will collect basic information such as the compensation of sales staff, the capital required to support warehouses, the amount of bad debts, levels of advertising, market and promotional spending, and any commission rates paid to unrelated parties before the subsidiary was established. The international examiner may also look into whether any sophisticated, technical assistance may have been required to support the sales staff and whether any affiliate selling in the same geographic area may have developed a distributor network or customer base before the subsidiary was created. The examination team will compare the level of the selling and marketing activities to that of other distributors to determine if the taxpayer undertook extraordinary or non routine activities in its selling and marketing activities. If so, the examination team may look to see whether those activities created a valuable marketing intangible worthy of a significant return to the distribution entity.

Because higher risk justifies a higher return, the international examiner will determine which companies within the group bear market risk, financial risk, product liability and general business risks and whether they receive an appropriate benefit. The international examiner will also compare the contracts or unwritten

---

[109] IRM 4.61.3.4.4.3.   [110] IRM 4.61.3.5.1.6.

¶1150.01

policies with the actual conduct of the taxpayer's transactions.[111] The IRS also investigates whether the taxpayer has artificially manipulated risks, i.e., whether the risk-bearing entity has the financial capacity to fund losses that the party assuming the risk might reasonably be expected to incur.[112]

> **Comment:** The taxpayer is responsible for giving the IRS examination team an understanding of the risks assumed by the taxpayer and its affiliates. IRS personnel without industry experience may require assistance to distinguish risk manipulation from normal and reasonable business practices. If a distributor contributes to certain R&D projects or bears product liability risk, the taxpayer should be prepared to demonstrate that the subsidiary was properly rewarded for the risks it bears. If the taxpayer does not clearly assign risks in writing before transactions are initiated, the taxpayer should be prepared to explain their policies to the IRS.

The international examiner analyzes the economic conditions regarding the taxpayer's transactions to later identify comparable transactions and companies. The taxpayer should participate in this area of the examination to insure that the IRS does not identify inappropriate comparables. If the IRS examination team bases its expectations on inappropriate comparables, such as companies operating at a different level of the market (e.g., retail rather than wholesale) or in an expanding rather than a contracting industry, it is considerably more difficult to resolve the transfer pricing issues on satisfactory terms.

After performing the function and risk analysis, the IRS examination team begins the "best method" analysis and seeks to quantify potential adjustments. The taxpayer's influence on the outcome of the examination is greater during the function and risk analysis than it will be later, when the IRS is calculating potential adjustments. To prevent the IRS from misinterpretation of the taxpayer's situation, the taxpayer should pay attention to the specific facts that might cause the IRS to misunderstand its operations. To be most effective, the taxpayer should also have a clear understanding and explanation regarding the types of inappropriate "comparable" transactions or companies the IRS economist is likely to encounter in the early stages of the IRS analysis.

Tangible Property Transactions. Based on an understanding gained from the function and risks analysis, the IRS identifies comparable transactions and companies and determines what it believes to be the best method for determining the transfer prices for the taxpayer's related party tangible property transactions. The IRM specifically advises the examination team not to select a transfer pricing method before gathering the relevant facts.[113] The taxpayer can often determine the methodology the IRS is considering by the questions being asked by the IRS examination team. For example, if the economist asks detailed questions about products rather than functions, it may indicate that the IRS examination team favors the application of a transaction-based method.

---

[111] Reg. § 1.482-1(d)(3)(ii)(B); IRM 4.61.3.5.4.
[112] IRM 4.61.3.5.3.

[113] IRM 4.61.3.7.

Comment: At this point in the examination the taxpayer should already have thoroughly considered each of the methodologies and PLIs. This preparation can be useful in keeping the IRS examiner on track. For example, it can often be time-consuming to properly analyze a potentially comparable transaction. The taxpayer may obviate the need for the IRS to invest time in a difficult, and ultimately unfavorable analysis by pointing out with some specificity the number of imprecise adjustments that might be required by the transaction-based analysis.

To identify and quantify any tangible property issues, the IRS investigates a number of items including:

- Whether products have been "bundled" (e.g., software combined with hardware);
- The global allocation of overall profit in the group;
- Whether parts are assembled into component products as well as end products;
- Volume/price discounts in the industry;
- Supplementary items such as warranties, service, etc.; and
- Foreign exchange rates; and
- The existence of any associated services to the sale of tangible property.

The IRS analysis generally is sensitive to the aggregation of product lines. The taxpayer should give the IRS sufficient information to reach appropriate conclusions when combining its various product lines.

The taxpayer should discuss possible sources of comparable companies and any necessary adjustments with the international examiner and economist. The IRS examination team may have expectations from previous cases concerning potential comparable companies. If the taxpayer has conducted a reasonably thorough search, a brief discussion may prevent the IRS examination team from setting itself an unrealistic "target" by testing the taxpayer's results against a prior set of inappropriate (e.g., functionally dissimilar) comparables.

Intangible Property Transactions. The review of intangible property transactions can be an extremely important if not critical aspect of the IRS examination.[114] Because the economic return from intangibles can be substantial, taxpayers should track the direction of the IRS analysis. If the IRS examination team were to misconceive the benefit contributed by an intangible, the differential between the IRS and the taxpayer positions may be too large to resolve the case without the investment of significant additional time and resources.

These issues can also make it difficult for the taxpayer to achieve a timely resolution of the case at competent authority. Many foreign tax authorities are not receptive to an IRS analysis that attempts to either create items of intangible property or establish a return for an intangible by applying a profit-based analysis, such as comparable profit method, with comparables that are only broadly compa-

---

[114] IRM 4.61.3.4.6.

¶1150.01

rable.[115] The international examiner frequently seeks assistance from IRS economists and engineers when analyzing intangibles and occasionally engages outside experts.[116] The IRS examination team seeks to identify situations in which parent companies have made "clusters" of intangibles available to affiliates. This could occur, for example, if the affiliates are supported in their manufacturing, marketing, financial or other business activities by a series of similar intangible properties. These can be far more difficult to analyze than a one-time transfer of an intangible.

.02 Economist's Report

The IRS economist's report is the main component of the examination team's transfer pricing case. However, high case loads and scarce resources interfere with the work of IRS economists. As previously discussed, the taxpayer should take every opportunity to explain the taxpayer and its industry to the IRS economists, including the way the industry normally allocates functions and risks and the unique factors affecting pricing in the industry. The taxpayers providing such assistance may help prevent the economist from applying inappropriate theories or using inaccurate data.

The examination team will often provide the taxpayer with a copy of the economist's report for comment before issuing the notice of proposed adjustments. Ideally, taxpayers should provide not just comments, but data and information backing up the comments, to the examination team so that the IRS economist, the international examiner and the case manager all have an opportunity to reevaluate the report before taking a final position in the audit. Of course, the manner in which the audit is proceeding determines if this is prudent, or if it is better to await the next level of administrative review.

When the economist completes the report, the international examiner generally accepts the report and presents its conclusions in the report as those of the examination team.[117] Therefore, if the report contains flaws in economic theory, industry analysis, or factual understanding of the taxpayer's activities, the taxpayer should consider discussing these flaws with the international examiner before the international examiner's acceptance of the report.

.03 Technical Advice Memorandums and Field Service Advice

During the course of the examination, the IRS examination team may seek technical assistance and advice from IRS attorneys in the National Office. The advice can take the form of formal Technical Advice Memorandums ("TAMs") or Technical Expedited Advice Memorandums ("TEAMs").[118] Although taxpayers may ask the IRS examination team to request a TAM or TEAM, such requests are not automatically granted.

TAMs and TEAMs allow the IRS examination team to receive the input of the Chief Counsel's office on the interpretation and proper application of the law, including treaties, regulations, and cases, to a specific set of facts. The procedure for obtaining a TAM or TEAM provides for taxpayer involvement in developing the

[115] Reg. § 1.482-5(c)(2)(ii).
[116] IRM 4.61.3.4.6.7.
[117] IRM 4.2.3.4.
[118] See IRM 33.2.2; Rev. Proc. 2006-2, IRB 2006-1, 89.

facts submitted with the request. Unlike the FSA process, the procedure for obtaining a TAM provides for taxpayer involvement in developing the facts submitted with the request. In addition, the TAM and TEAM processes allow the taxpayer to provide a statement setting forth its application of the law to the facts.[119]

> **Comment:** The IRS examination team usually follows the findings set forth in a TAM.[120] Therefore, if the taxpayer strongly believes that the examination team has incorrectly interpreted legal principles or incorrectly applied the legal principles to an agreed-upon factual situation, the taxpayer should consider requesting a TAM. However, because the resolution of transfer pricing issues generally rests on the development and analysis of complex factual situations, rather than the correct interpretation of narrow technical issues, the TAM process is usually of limited use in the transfer pricing setting.

.04 IRS Attorney Role

For a taxpayer undergoing a transfer pricing examination, an understanding of counsel's involvement is important to accurately assess the IRS's strategy. As discussed, District Counsel is involved in the wording of summonses.[121] The IRS also assigns District Counsel attorneys to CIC audits to help develop audit strategies, develop issues and provide advice as to the type of information necessary to defend a proposed Code Sec. 482 adjustment in court.[122] The case manager can also request advice from District Counsel or Regional Counsel on legal issues.[123] However, the request by the IRS examination team for informal advice from IRS counsel can raise a question whether counsel is taking a more active role than merely advising the case manager.

> **Comment:** In a Tax Court case involving an IRS attorney who was involved both in a trial of certain years and an examination of the same issue in other years, the Court ordered the attorney's involvement to be limited to either the trial or the examination function.[124] Subsequently, however, the Tax Court has gone out of its way to limit the application of that ruling to the particular facts of that case.[125] This suggests that IRS attorneys have fairly wide latitude to be involved with litigation as well as examinations of subsequent years for the same taxpayer.

.05 Draft Proposed Adjustments

Once the IRS examination team has developed the transfer pricing issues sufficiently to determine the appropriateness of an adjustment, it presents its findings to the taxpayer.[126] If the examination team determines that the taxpayer's pricing falls outside of the interquartile range, it can make an adjustment to any point within the arm's length (interquartile) range. However, normally the adjustment will be made to the median or mean of all the results.[127]

---

[119] *See* Rev. Proc. 2006-2.
[120] *See Id.* at 314.
[121] IRM 4.61.3.9.
[122] *Id.*
[123] *Id.*

[124] *See Westreco Inc.*, CCH Dec. 46,882(M), 60 TCM 824 (1990).
[125] *Ash*, CCH Dec. 47,221, 96 TC 459 (1991).
[126] IRM 4.61.3.8.
[127] IRM 4.61.3.8; Reg. § 1.482-1(e)(3).

The taxpayer should review the IRS's basis for the contemplated adjustment, including its determination of the facts and applicable law, its arguments, the taxpayer's arguments, and the IRS conclusion. The draft examination report provides the taxpayer with the opportunity to address any factual, economic, or legal errors or insufficiencies in the IRS's materials as well as any inaccuracies in the presentation of the taxpayer's arguments and positions.

After the taxpayer thoroughly reviews the examination report it must decide whether and how to address the issues raised therein. This decision involves several steps. First, the taxpayer should distinguish between the issues that have a possibility of being resolved at the examination level and those that likely will have to go to competent authority (e.g., issues involving intangibles or losses, or extremely large adjustments).

For those issues that the taxpayer feels might be resolved at examination, the taxpayer should consider preparing a thorough response identifying factual, legal, and economic errors in the examination team's work, which might convince the IRS to reduce its proposed adjustment. The taxpayer should remember, however, that the IRS would have to invest additional time and effort to make substantial revisions to the report. Also, if the taxpayer has other issues in the case that will require competent authority involvement, both sides may have little incentive to devote additional, and possibly unproductive, time reevaluating the case at the examination level.

Even absent the competent authority aspect, there can be some strategic disadvantages to preparing a detailed rebuttal to the examination report, in that the IRS might go back and correct the deficiencies in its work, strengthening its case. In such a situation, the taxpayer's advantage may lay in not responding, but subsequently addressing the government's weaknesses in a formal Appeals protest after the IRS issues the 30-day letter. The taxpayer must balance this strategy against the benefit of demonstrating to Appeals that the taxpayer presented its position in time for the examination team to address its arguments. By demonstrating to Appeals that the taxpayer presented the arguments to the examination team, the taxpayer may reduce any tendency or need of the Appeals Officer either to send the case back for further development or to further consult with the IRS examination team regarding the taxpayer's arguments.

The examination report provides the taxpayer with two additional opportunities to consider: raising setoffs, seeking an early Appeals referral or Fast Track Mediation. The final transfer pricing regulations require the IRS to allow a setoff of the proposed transfer pricing adjustment for any other non-arm's length transactions, which the taxpayer identifies between the same controlled taxpayers for the same taxable year.[128] Taxpayers must meet certain requirements for the IRS to take the setoffs into account, including advising the IRS of the potential setoff within 30 days after the earlier of the IRS issuing the examination report or the notice of deficiency.[129] If a taxpayer knows of potential setoffs, they can be raised at this time,

---

[128] Reg. § 1.482-1(g)(4).   [129] Reg. § 1.482-1(g)(4).

or the taxpayer can wait until receiving Form 5701, "Notice of Proposed Adjustment."

The taxpayer should also identify correlative allocations that the IRS must make to modify the income of the foreign related party to correspond with the transfer pricing adjustment to the taxpayer. When the IRS makes an adjustment increasing the income of a U.S. parent, the corresponding adjustment would decrease the U.S. income of the foreign taxpayer.[130] Opportunities for relief under Rev. Proc. 99-32[131] should also be identified. If the IRS increases a U.S. parent/taxpayer's taxable income, the U.S. taxpayer may still be able to repatriate the funds without being subject to withholding taxes that would otherwise apply to dividend payments.

.06 Formal Notification of Proposed Adjustment

After completing the transfer pricing examination, the IRS provides the taxpayer with an explanation of its proposed adjustments by providing the taxpayer with a Form 5701, "Notice of Proposed Adjustment" for each issue. In transfer pricing cases, the IRS issues a Form 5701 for each category or type of transaction for which it proposes an adjustment. The Form 5701 identifies the amount of the transfer pricing adjustment and the accompanying Form 886-A provides an explanation of how the IRS arrived at the adjustment. Frequently, the IRS will include the reports of any industry experts and economists involved in the examination. If these reports are not included, the taxpayer should request copies of relevant reports so that it can fully understand the IRS position. The Form 5701 and accompanying Form 886-A generally will serve as the revenue agent's report on the transfer pricing issues. (See the Practice Tool at ¶ 20,090 for an example of Forms 5701 and 886-A.)

Upon receiving the Form 5701 with the explanatory Form 886-A, the taxpayer has several options. These options include agreeing to the adjustments or attempting to meet and discuss the case with the examination team one last time before issuance of the 30-day letter. In non-CIC audits, there have been instances where the Form 5701 was issued when the taxpayer was expecting further examination or a draft proposed adjustment. In such cases, the taxpayer should confirm the case manager's view concerning the status of the case and suggest a schedule for developing and resolving the case.

In a CIC audit, the time pressures on the examination team to complete the audit can create a significant impediment to any changes in the examination team's positions following the issuance of the Form 5701. However, if the attached reports contain clear errors of fact or in the application of the transfer pricing regulations, the taxpayer should consider meeting one last time with the IRS examination team to discuss the case.

From the issuance of Form 5701, the taxpayer has 30 days to notify the IRS of any setoffs for other non-arm's length transactions between the same controlled

---

[130] Reg. § 1.482-1(g)(2).   [131] 1999-2 CB 296.

taxpayers for the same taxable year.[132] Taxpayers must meet certain requirements for the IRS to take the setoffs into account, including advising the IRS of the potential setoff within 30 days after the earlier of the IRS issuing the examination report or the notice of deficiency. To the extent a taxpayer knows of potential setoffs, they must now be raised. If the taxpayer has not already planned for possible correlative allocations or conforming adjustments resulting from the proposed assessment, they should do so at this time.

.07 Revenue Agent's Report and the 30-Day Letter

If the taxpayer and the IRS fail to resolve all issues raised in the Forms 5701, the IRS will issue a Revenue Agent's Report (RAR) explaining the proposed adjustments. The RAR generally includes Form 4549-B, "Income Tax Examination Changes—Adjustments to Income" and Form 886-A, "Explanation of Items," explaining the adjustments, and the reports of the international examiner and any economists and industry experts who worked on the examination. If the proposed adjustments raise the possibility of double taxation, the team manager must inform the taxpayer of its right to seek relief under the mutual agreement provisions of the applicable income tax treaty.[133]

The IRS separately issues a 30-day letter notifying the taxpayer of the adjustment if such is not provided with the RAR. A waiver form and a copy of the examination report are attached to the 30-day letter. The waiver form generally is a Form 870, Waiver of Restrictions on Assessment and Collection of Deficiency in Tax and Acceptance of Overassessment, or a Form 870-AD, Offer to Waive Restrictions on Assessment and Collection of Tax Deficiency and to Accept Overassessment. By executing either form, the taxpayer consents to the immediate assessment and collection of the tax reflected on the form. In addition, the taxpayer forfeits the ability to file a petition with the Tax Court unless the IRS assesses deficiencies in excess of those set forth on the waiver. Under the Form 870, the taxpayer retains the right to file a claim for refund for any taxes paid pursuant to the waiver and to file suit for a refund in either a Federal District Court or the Court of Federal Claims. The instructions to the Form 870-AD indicate that it acts as an agreement by the taxpayer not to file or pursue a claim for refund or credit for the years covered by the form, implying that the form will have the same effect as a closing agreement. While a Form 870-AD does not rise to the level of a closing agreement under Code Sec. 7121, the IRS has successfully raised estoppel arguments against suits for refunds for years covered by a Form 870-AD.[134]

.08 The 90-Day Letter

Within 60 days of a taxpayer's failure to protest the 30-day letter, or failure to pay any deficiency set forth in the 30-day letter, the IRS will issue a notice of deficiency (90-day letter). Under Code Sec. 6212 a taxpayer has 90 days from the date of the notice of deficiency to file a petition with the United States Tax Court to

---

[132] Reg. § 1.482-1(g)(4)(ii)(C).

[133] IRM 4.60.2.

[134] See Elbo Coals, Inc., 85-2 USTC ¶ 9454, 763 F.2d 818 (6th Cir. 1985), aff'g, 84-1 USTC ¶ 9524 (D. Ky. 1984);

A.L. Stair, 75-1 USTC ¶ 9463, 516 F.2d 560 (2d. Cir. 1975), affirming an unreported District Court decision. But, see M.R. Davilman, 95-1 USTC ¶ 50,292 (W.D. Okla. 1995).

contest the IRS's determination of an income tax deficiency, 150 days if the notice is addressed to a person outside the United States.[135] Neither the Tax Court nor the IRS has the authority to extend this period.[136]

While the taxpayer has the ability to request Appeals consideration during this 90 day period, as a practical matter in transfer pricing cases, this period will be used to prepare the Tax Court petition, or to pay the deficiency and commence preparation of a refund claim in anticipation of District Court or Court of Federal Claims litigation.

¶ 1160 Settlement Opportunities Near the End of the Examination Process

.01 Re-Evaluation of Preliminary Substantive/Procedural Strategy

Throughout the examination process, the taxpayer team should continue to re-evaluate its preliminary substantive/procedural strategy in light of new information: new facts, IRS arguments, IRS concessions, and IRS positions. As the taxpayer reacts to IRS questions and IDRs, new substantive arguments may come to light that may, in turn, change the desirability of the preliminary procedural strategy. Taxpayers must remain flexible enough to adapt to changes in understanding regarding factual and legal arguments and seek the best procedural strategy under the revised circumstances.

> *Example:* A taxpayer expected to pursue a unilateral Appeals settlement without recourse to competent authority because of the weakness of the international examiner's initial arguments. Subsequently, the IRS examination team raised a new, stronger argument. The increased likelihood of a sustainable IRS-initiated adjustment could greatly increase the likelihood of double tax and the need for a bilateral settlement, thus changing the taxpayer team's approach to substantive arguments in the examination.

.02 Settlement Opportunities with Examination Team

Proper transfer pricing planning and documentation and active involvement in the examination process may permit the taxpayer to achieve settlement with the IRS examination team. A properly planned related party transaction supported by credible documentation of both the choice and application of the pricing methods creates a strong base upon which to build a transfer pricing examination defense. Further, early and active taxpayer involvement in the examination process will assist the IRS in understanding the taxpayer's transactions and the pricing methods applicable to those transactions. Anticipating the IRS' requests for information will enable the taxpayer and its advisors to offer the IRS suggestions on readily-available information and analyses, minimizing the risk that significant time must be devoted to defusing inappropriate proposed adjustments.

The taxpayer should be actively involved in all levels of the examination process. Because the IRS may not begin to appreciate the full implications of any

---

[135] Code Sec. 6231(a).

[136] *See,* e.g., *Kahle,* CCH Dec. 43,871, 88 TC 1063 (1987); *Shipley,* 78-1 USTC ¶ 9211, 572 F.2d 212 (9th Cir. 1977).

issues identified until the end of the audit, when the issues are fully developed, the taxpayer may not be able to conclude whether they can settle at the examination level until this time. Thus, if the taxpayer fails to maintain open communications with the IRS examination team, an opportunity to settle may be lost.

Active taxpayer involvement is important even if the taxpayer is unable to settle with the examination team. For example, if the taxpayer knows it will be invoking the competent authority process to ultimately avoid double taxation, the taxpayer can benefit by developing the case during the examination process in a manner that will make the competent authority process more efficient. This may not only avoid a slow or partial settlement at competent authority, but may influence the taxpayer's strategic options (e.g., APA) for the future. Also, by working closely with the examination team, the taxpayer can develop the case and seek an early referral of the issue to Appeals where litigation hazards may be considered.

.03 Delegation Order 236

Del. Ord. 236 (Rev. 3)[137] gives case managers limited authority to settle issues where Appeals has reached a settlement on the merits in another tax period for CIC taxpayers. This eliminates the need for CIC taxpayers to protest an issue to obtain the same result reached with Appeals in prior or subsequent tax years, resulting in considerable resource savings for both taxpayers and the IRS.[138] Del. Ord. 236 (Rev. 3) can also be used in conjunction with settlements reached in Appeals through Early Referral and Nondocketed Mediation.

.04 Early Referral to Appeals

Taxpayers may request the transfer of developed, but unagreed, issues from Examination to Appeals while the examination team completes the development of the remaining issues ("Early Referral").[139] The principal benefit of Early Referral is the ability to produce an expected resolution of a difficult issue while the rest of the case continues through examination. Issues that are unlikely to be resolved at examination (i.e., those requiring a litigation hazards review) are moved to Appeals while the rest of the case continues through examination. The simultaneous development of issues in Examination and Appeals should expedite resolution of the case.

---

[137] 1996-21 IRB 7. Del Ord. 236 is expected to be, but has not yet been, revised as Del. Ord. 4-24. In a December 4, 2009, LMSB memorandum, an Industry Director advised that examiners and team managers may not use Del. Order 236 to resolve issues surrounding whether stock-based compensation costs are costs to be shared under a qualified cost sharing arrangement for any open year. The memorandum is available at *http://www.irs.gov/businesses/article/0,,id=216802,00.html*. Del. Ord. 236 (rev. 3) is still valid in all other respects.

[138] The following factors must be present in the tax year under Examination:

- Facts in the tax year under examination must be substantially similar, including the relative amounts at issue, to those in the settled period;

- Underlying issue must have been settled by Appeals on the merits independently of other issues;

- Legal authority regarding the issue must be unchanged;

- Appeals settlement must have been reached with the same taxpayer or another taxpayer directly involved in the transaction; and

- Proposed settlement and any related closing agreement must be approved by an Examination branch chief prior to finalization. Del. Ord. 236 (Rev. 3), § 2.

[139] Rev. Proc. 99-28, 1999-2 CB 109.

¶1160.04

Further, early referral does not trigger "hot" interest under Code Sec. 6621(c).[140] Although Examination issues a notice of proposed adjustment, Form 5701, on the Early Referral issue, Form 5701 is not a 30-day letter. Therefore, "hot" interest does not accrue until the IRS issues a 30-day letter at the examination's conclusion. The avoidance of hot interest can be a significant benefit to a taxpayer with a large transfer pricing issue in dispute.[141]

Early Referral is considered appropriate when: (1) the issue, if resolved, can reasonably be expected to result in a quicker resolution of the entire case; (2) both the taxpayer and District Director agree that the issue should be referred early; (3) the issue is fully developed; and (4) the issue is part of a case where the remaining issues are not expected to be completed before Appeals could resolve the early referral issue.[142] A request for early referral must be submitted by the taxpayer in writing to the case manager (the case manager may also suggest that the taxpayer make such a request).[143] A taxpayer may withdraw any one or more Early Referral issues from the Appeals process at any time before reaching an agreement with Appeals. Upon doing so, the issues are treated subsequently as if the taxpayer did not reach an agreement with Appeals.[144]

However, from a practical standpoint, Early Referral procedure may be difficult to apply because the extensive factual and expert development required to resolve a transfer pricing issue makes it one of the last issues fully developed by the examination team, leaving little time to seek Early Referral. Nonetheless, the Early Referral procedures could be useful if the taxpayer has a discrete transfer pricing issue or an isolated transfer pricing issue for a division or product line that is not integrated with other transfer pricing issues in the company. This might occur, for example, if the IRS has questioned the transfer pricing in one of the taxpayer's distribution divisions but already has resolved its concerns with respect to manufacturing, research and development and other distribution activities.

Normal Appeals procedures are used in Early Referral, which includes face-to-face settlement conferences.[145] If the taxpayer and the IRS reaches an agreement, the parties will enter into a specific matters closing agreement (Form 906).[146] If the taxpayer and the IRS fail to reach an agreement, the taxpayer may request mediation of the issue if it meets the requirements for mediation contained in Announcement 98-99.[147] If mediation is not requested, or the issue is not eligible for

---

[140] Code Sec. 6621(c)(3) provides for a 2% increase in the underpayment rate for large corporate underpayments.

[141] If Examination issues a preliminary notice of deficiency ("30-day letter") with respect to any issue that is not accepted for Early Referral, all unagreed issues, including any Early Referral issues that have not yet been settled by Appeals, will be combined in the 30-day letter. Rev. Proc. 99-28, § 2.17. Likewise, if no issues in the case remain unagreed except for the Early Referral issues that are pending in Appeals, a 30-day letter will be issued solely with respect to the Early Referral issues. The 30-day letter will constitute the first letter of proposed deficiency for purposes of the increased underpayment rate for large corporate underpayments under Code Sec. 6621(c). If no issues in the case remain unagreed except

for an Early Referral issue that could not be settled by Appeals and has been returned to Examination, no 30-day letter will be issued. Rather, a statutory notice of deficiency ("90-day letter") will be issued, which will start the period for the increased underpayment rate for large corporate underpayments under Code Sec. 6621(c). *Id.*

[142] Rev. Proc. 99-28, 1999-2 CB 109, § 2.02.

[143] *Id.* at § 2.04.

[144] *Id.* at § 2.19.

[145] *Id.* at § 2.14.

[146] *Id.* at § 2.15. If the agreement results in a refund requiring Joint Committee approval, the IRS will not sign the agreement until it obtains that approval.

[147] *Id.* at § 2.16.

¶1160.04

mediation, Appeals will return the case to the Examination division with a memorandum regarding the referred issues.[148] Appeals will not reconsider an unagreed early referral issue if the entire case is later protested to Appeals, unless there has been a substantial change in the circumstances regarding the early referral issue.[149]

Before invoking the procedure, however, the taxpayer should assess whether it expects final and full resolution of the case at Appeals. Early Referral is not available for issues for which the taxpayer has requested or intends to request competent authority assistance.[150] An Appeals settlement restricts U.S. competent authority to seeking correlative relief from treaty partners, exposing the taxpayer to double taxation if the treaty partner doesn't agree to make a correlative adjustment.[151] In such cases, the Simultaneous Appeals Procedure ("SAP"), discussed below, may be a more appropriate alternative.

To ensure that Appeals all continue to seek to resolve tax disputes objectively and fairly, the IRS recently issued Rev. Proc. 2000-43[152] which attempts to ensure this role by, among other things, limiting ex parte communications between Appeals and the rest of the IRS. Of particular interest are Q&A Nos. 5 and 11. Q&A 5 limits communications with the IRS to procedural matters. No comments on the merits of the case or the accuracy of the facts are allowed without the presences of either the taxpayer or its counsel. Q&A 11 provides that Appeals may discuss the case with the IRS' National Office and Field Office attorneys in non-docketed cases, provided that those attorneys have not previously advised Examination on this matter. The ex parte rules do not affect, however, cases docketed in Tax Court and sent to Appeals. The key point to Rev. Proc. 2000-43 is to assure that the independence of the Appeals Officer is not compromised.

---

[148] *Id.* at § 2.16.

[149] *Id.* at § 2.16.

[150] If a taxpayer enters into a settlement with Appeals (including an Appeals settlement through the Early Referral process), and then requests competent authority assistance, the U.S. competent authority will endeavor only to obtain a correlative adjustment with the treaty country and will not take any actions that would otherwise amend the settlement. Instead, taxpayers are encouraged to request SAP. *See* Rev. Proc. 2006-54, 2006-2 CB 1035, at § 7.05.

[151] *Id.*

[152] 2000-2 CB 404.

Chapter 12

Post-Examination Procedural Alternatives

¶ 1201 Unilateral and Bilateral Alternatives

Should the taxpayer and the IRS be unable to resolve a transfer pricing dispute at the Examination level, numerous procedural alternatives remain. The most important procedural decision will be whether to pursue the unilateral procedures (involving only the taxpayer and the IRS) or the bilateral procedures (involving the IRS and the competent authority of a U.S. treaty partner). This decision can be altered at a subsequent point in time, but the initial choice of unilateral or bilateral approach emphasizes different substantive issues. This chapter will review the workings of the various unilateral and bilateral procedural alternatives. Next, it will discuss the situations which might favor the use of any particular procedure. Finally, it will describe how several of the procedures could be combined to resolve a transfer pricing issue.

¶ 1210 Post-Examination Unilateral Procedures

.01 Appeals

Overview. The predecessor to the National Office of Appeals was established in 1925 to conduct individual negotiations with taxpayers or their representatives to seek a mutually satisfactory settlement of tax disputes. Since 1925, Appeals has successfully settled a majority of tax disputes facing the IRS.

The mission of the National Office of Appeals is: "to resolve tax controversies, without litigation, on a basis which is fair and impartial to both the Government and the taxpayer and in a manner which will enhance voluntary compliance and public confidence in the integrity and efficiency of the Service."[1] Appeals is the last administrative option the IRS and taxpayer can pursue to resolve their tax dispute without litigation. The success of Appeals rests on its ability to remain independent

---

[1] IRM 8.1.1.1(1).

of other IRS functions to reach a resolution that is fair for both the Government and the taxpayer.

Procedures. If the taxpayer decides go to Appeals, it must prepare a protest letter and submit it to the examination team in response to the 30-day letter. Taxpayers generally have 30 days, plus an automatic extension of 60 days, to prepare and submit the protest.

The protest must include the following:

- Taxpayer's name and address;
- A statement that the taxpayer desires to appeal the examination findings to the Appeals Office;
- Date, identifying symbols from the 30-day letter and the findings with which the taxpayer disagrees;
- Tax period(s) involved;
- An itemized schedule of the changes the taxpayer challenges, including the Code Sec. 482 adjustments;
- A statement of facts supporting the taxpayer's position;
- Taxpayer's analysis of the law; and
- A perjury statement.

In addition, the taxpayer's representative must file an appropriate power of attorney.[2]

> *Comment:* The typical transfer pricing dispute is considerably more factually complex than other tax disputes, requiring subjective interpretation of those factual issues by IRS personnel. Because the protest letter serves as the taxpayer's first presentation to the Appeals Officer, the taxpayer should present its arguments, and itself, in the best possible light. The taxpayer should prepare a thorough, convincing, and even-handed protest that demonstrates to the Appeals Officer that the taxpayer considered all points raised by the examination team, giving credit to the position of the IRS when appropriate, but that in good faith the taxpayer believes that the position of the IRS is erroneous. Negative comments regarding the actions of the examination team serve no purpose.

The taxpayer files its protest with the examination team. The examination team reviews the protest and prepares comments in response to the taxpayer arguments. The examination team may also have the economists or other industry experts prepare comments and supplementary reports. The examination team then forwards the case files, the protest, the examination team's comments, and any supplementary reports to Appeals. In rare circumstances, the District may have the examination team conduct a further examination based on matters raised in the protest. Due to the resources already incurred, and time expended by this point, however, further consideration of the case by Examination is unlikely.

---

[2] 26 CFR Reg. §601.106(f)(5); IRM 8.2.1.2.

¶1210.01

A thorough protest lets the examination team comment on any information the taxpayer plans to provide to Appeals, thereby minimizing the need for Appeals to seek further input from the examination team, and minimizing the likelihood that the examination team will stay involved in the case. Generally the IRS examination team will provide the taxpayer with a copy of its Note, and any supplemental reports of its economists and industry experts. If the taxpayer does not receive a copy of the Note and any supplemental reports, the taxpayer should request them from Appeals or seek them with a request under the Freedom of Information Act.

Once Appeals assumes jurisdiction over the case, it is assigned to one or more Appeals officers.[3] Transfer pricing cases are assigned to International Specialists or Team Chiefs within Appeals who have experience in large complex cases. The Appeals officer may hold one or more pre-conferences with members of the examination team to discuss the case. Taxpayers should be aware of Act Section 1001(a)(4) of the IRS Restructuring and Reform Act of 1998 ("RRA '98") that states, "[The plan shall] ensure an independent appeals function within the Internal Revenue Service, including prohibition in the plan of *ex parte* communications between appeals officers and other Internal Revenue Service employees to the extent that such communications appear to compromise the independence of the appeals officers." In response to the *ex parte* communication provision of RRA '98, the Internal Revenue Service issued IRS Notice 99-50, 1999-40 IRB 444, which states that a pre-conference meeting with the Examination team would appear to compromise the independence of Appeals Officers.[4] Therefore, pre-conference meetings should not be held unless the taxpayer/representative is given the opportunity to participate.[5]

Taxpayers should keep in mind that Appeals Officers do not apply the evidentiary standards that would apply in a courtroom setting.

> ***Comment:*** While Appeals conducts conferences in an informal manner, "to promote frank discussion and mutual understanding," factual statements by the taxpayer or its representatives constitute admissions, admissible in a later trial if the taxpayer fails to reach a settlement. Therefore, if employees or officers of the taxpayer attend Appeals conferences, they should be cautioned about the potential use by the IRS of their statements.

To make the best use of the Appeals process, taxpayers should understand the settlement practices of the Appeals Office. This in turn requires an understanding of the standards applied by Appeals in settling cases, the types of settlements Appeals enters into, its ability to resolve penalty issues, and the limits on its settlement authority.

The distinguishing factor between the settlement authority of exam and the settlement authority of Appeals lies in the respective standards each must use in performing its function. The IRS exam function may resolve issues on an all or nothing basis based on an application of the IRS's interpretation of the law to the facts as determined by the examination team. In contrast, Appeals seeks to obtain a

---

[3] IRM 8.2.1.5.
[4] Rev. Proc. 2000-43, 2000-2 CB 404.
[5] *Id.*

"fair and impartial resolution," a resolution that reflects the probable result in the event of litigation, or that reflects the relative strengths of positions where uncertainty would exist in the event of litigation.[6] Under this settlement authority, referred to as the *"hazards of litigation"* settlement standard, Appeals Officers may settle cases conceding issues, in whole or in part, to reflect the Appeals Officer's belief of how a court would resolve the issue or the risks of the IRS not prevailing on an issue.

This *hazards of litigation* standard frequently results in the Appeals function deriving a different view of the facts than the examination function. Examination teams frequently demand a high level of proof of facts favorable to the taxpayer, and are skeptical about information provided by the taxpayer. Appeals, on the other hand, examines the case by looking at the information provided by the taxpayer and the examination team from the perspective of an impartial third party. In doing so, Appeals tries to resolve factual questions based on a weighing of the materials presented to it.

Appeals will enter into two types of settlements, mutual concession settlements and split-issue settlements. Mutual concession settlements involve situations where both the government's and the taxpayer's positions have substantial strength and both parties have justification for not conceding in full. In this type of settlement, the parties attempt to reach a settlement that reflects the result a court could reach.[7] Due to the factual nature of transfer pricing cases, mutual concession settlements are quite common and can involve concessions about the size and make-up of comparables, or taxpayers, or the formula for adjustment for functional differences.

In a split-issue settlement, the parties resolve a single issue on a compromise basis where a court would resolve it on an all or nothing basis. In other words, the parties reach a resolution that a court would be unable to obtain. Split-issue settlements reflect the parties' agreement as to the relative strengths of their positions.[8] For example, the IRS proposed adjustment might allege, contrary to the taxpayer's position, that an intangible was owned by the U.S. entity and should receive a large royalty. The taxpayer might agree to the ownership issue, and in return the IRS might agree to a smaller royalty.

In addition to mutual concession and split issue settlements, the Taxpayer and Appeals may engage in the "trading" of issues. In cases of "trading," the *hazards of litigation* must clearly support the conclusion that the relative values of the traded issues are equal.[9] Trading of issues, which is quite common in transfer pricing cases, might involve elements of both mutual concession and split issue settlement. For example, the IRS proposed adjustment might allege "control" under Code Sec. 482, U.S. ownership of certain intangibles, and the 28 comparables for a CPM. The taxpayer might agree to the control issue, deny the ownership of intangibles and agree to the CPM with 14 comparables and a cost of capital adjustment.

---

[6] IRM 8.6.4.1, 26 CFR § 601.106.

[7] IRM 8.6.4.1.1; IRS Policy Statement P-8-47 (4/6/87).

[8] IRM 8.6.4.1.2; IRS Policy Statement P-8-48 (12/23/60).

[9] IRM 8.6.4.1.2(5); IRS Policy Statement P-8-48 (12/23/60).

¶1210.01

Despite its wide latitude and mandate, Appeals does not have unlimited authority to settle transfer pricing cases. In addition, the requirements of the Competent Authority process place limits on the propriety of settling a transfer pricing case at Appeals.

Many taxpayers are concerned that the Appeals Officer might raise a "new" issue in the course of discussions. This would be highly unlikely. Policy Statement P-8-49 provides that a new issues should not be raised unless the ground is "substantial" and the potential effect on tax liability is "material."[10]

Issues and Cases Appeals May Decline to Settle. Appeals' ability to settle is limited in certain situations by IRS policy. These situations include Appeals Coordinated Issues, certain controlled issues, cases designated for litigation, issues under the Industry Specialization program, and issues for which the National Office has issued Technical Advice for the particular taxpayer.

Appeals Coordinated Issues ("ACI") are those issues or cases with service-wide impact or importance that have been identified as requiring coordination.[11] The Appeals Director of the Office of Large Case Programs assigns a coordinator for each ACI, who prepares the Appeals settlement position (for legal issues) or settlement guidelines (for factual issues) for the ACI. An Appeals settlement of an ACI issue generally requires the review and approval of the Technical Guidance coordinator for that issue.[12] The current list of Appeals Coordinated Issues includes two issues directly relevant to transfer pricing cases: Code Sec. 6662(e)(1)(B) and (h) penalties; and research credit gross receipts from intra-group transactions.[13]

The IRS may, in certain situations, determine that an issue should be litigated rather than settled. The issue is usually one that is significant in nature, in an area where the IRS would like to establish judicial precedent, or has determined that it would like to conserve resources and forego administrative appeals procedures. Designation is not limited to international or CIC issues. However, given the factual nature of many transfer pricing cases the IRS does not generally designate a transfer pricing case. Specific procedures apply for cases non-docketed cases under jurisdiction of the District Director, non-docketed cases under jurisdiction of Appeals, and docketed cases under jurisdiction of Appeals or Counsel.[14]

In cases where the National Office has issued technical advice favorable to the taxpayer, Appeals must settle the case on a basis consistent with the technical advice. However, where the National Office has issued technical advice adverse to the taxpayer, Appeals may nonetheless settle the case under its usual standards.[15]

Potential Competent Authority Cases. The likelihood of negotiations between the U.S. and foreign Competent Authorities necessitates special consideration by Appeals in transfer pricing cases. First, an Appeals settlement of a transfer pricing case will limit the U.S. Competent Authority to seeking correlative adjustments

---

[10] IRM 8.6.1.6.2(6).

[11] IRM 8.7.3.2.2; *see also* IRS Website, *www.irs.gov/ individuals/article/0,,id=128327.html.*

[12] IRM 8.1.3.9.

[13] *See* *http://www.irs.gov/pub/irs_utl/ tg_issues_index.pdf.*

[14] IRM 8.4.1 et seq.

[15] Rev. Proc. 2003-2, 2003-1 IRB 76, §22.01(2); 26 C.F.R. Reg. §601.106(f)(9)(viii).

from the foreign Competent Authority.[16] This limitation places the taxpayer at risk of double taxation.

Second, to protect the interests of the U.S. in the Competent Authority negotiations, the IRS has issued the following guidelines to Appeals Officers:

1. do not attempt to hinder or prohibit taxpayers as part of a settlement from seeking Competent Authority consideration, and do not make settlement concessions based on taxpayers' offers to waive their rights to Competent Authority consideration;

2. scrutinize the issue to determine whether the facts and case documentation are sufficiently developed so Appeals can consider the merits of the adjustment. All cases not sufficiently developed are to be returned to Compliance; and

3. to serve the overall best interest of the U.S. Treasury, Appeals should avoid lump-sum and traded-issue settlement involving potential Competent Authority issues. Sacrificing part or all of an international tax adjustment in order to obtain an agreement on a domestic issue may result in uneven treatment between the U.S. and "treaty" taxpayers. On a case-by-case basis, Appeals case processing and settlement objectives may appear better served by employing traded-issue or lump-sum settlements; however, the overall result (when combining all potential Competent Authority issues resolved in Appeals) may render unjust financial benefits not intended by the tax treaties to treaty partner countries. Therefore, Appeals does not settle a potential Competent Authority issue, except on its merits.[17]

After the Appeals Officer has reviewed the applicable resources available, a meeting (or series of meetings) will convene to discuss the merits of the case. Opportunities for settlement will be pursued through interactions with the Appeals Officer in the Appeals conferences. The protocol of an Appeal's conference is informal. There are no formal evidentiary procedures or established ordering of issues. Open communication and cooperative interaction with the Appeals Officer is encouraged. Thus, negative or personal comments are inappropriate for such proceedings.

Taxpayers should carefully document their transfer pricing resolutions. There are two basic settlement forms: (1) a Closing Agreement and (2) a Waiver of Restriction on Assessment and Collection ("Waiver").

A closing agreement is the only statutorily authorized method for entering into an agreement that is binding on both the IRS and the taxpayer.[18] It is considered a "final and conclusive" resolution of the matter, only subject to attack upon a showing of fraud, malfeasance, or misrepresentation of material fact.[19] Because of the finality of a closing agreement, the IRS encourages the use of a Waiver in the settlement of an Appeals office case.[20]

---

[16] Rev. Proc. 2006-54, 2006-2 CB 1035, at § 7.05.

[17] IRM 8.7.3.7.2.

[18] Code Sec. 7121.

[19] Code Sec. 7121(b).

[20] IRM 8.8.1.1.5.

¶1210.01

Accordingly, the Waiver (i.e., either a Form 870 or a Form 870-AD) is the most common form for documenting the settlement of a transfer pricing case. By executing a Waiver, the taxpayer waives the restrictions on the assessment and collection of the deficiency and, if the case has not been considered by Appeals, the taxpayer's right to avail itself of the Appeals procedures. In addition, the taxpayer waives its right to petition the Tax Court for a re-determination of its deficiency. The taxpayer may limit the issues covered by the Form 870 or Form 870-AD and thereby reserve the ability to have Appeals or the Tax Court consider the other issues.

With respect to transfer pricing controversies, the primary difference between the two settlement forms is the effect on subsequent competent authority relief available to the taxpayer. As indicated above, in transfer pricing cases, U.S. competent authority will only seek correlative adjustments from the treaty partner when the IRS and taxpayer enter into a closing agreement relating to the transfer pricing issues.[21] Because Form 870 does not constitute a closing agreement within the meaning of Code Sec. 7121, it does not limit relief available in subsequent competent authority procedures.[22] The IRS has taken the position, however, that a Form 870-AD constitutes "other written agreements," and consequently, U.S. competent authority will only seek correlative adjustments from foreign competent authorities in such cases.

The form of the settlement agreement will depend on the taxpayer's overall strategy for resolving the case. If the taxpayer can tolerate a limited amount of double taxation, the IRS may resolve the case for a lesser amount than it would otherwise if the taxpayer agrees to enter into a formal closing agreement. However, if the IRS or Appeals believes the taxpayer will proceed to competent authority, it will have less incentive to reduce the adjustment in the belief that a higher assessment will be to the advantage of competent authority during its negotiations. Therefore, the size of the adjustment, the availability of competent authority assistance, and the taxpayer's ultimate strategy all contribute to the taxpayer's decision regarding the closing documentation.

.02 Mediation of Non-docketed Cases

Mediation is a form of assisted negotiation whereby a neutral third party, the mediator, facilitates the negotiation efforts between the parties. The mediator holds meetings, defines issues, defuses emotions, and suggests possible ways to resolve a dispute. The mediator has no authority to impose a decision on the parties; rather, the mediator helps the parties define the issues and works to promote settlement negotiations.

Outside of the tax arena, mediation is a popular dispute resolution vehicle. Mediation is particularly valuable as a dispute resolution mechanism when the parties to the dispute have a continuing relationship. The following benefits are associated with mediation:

---

[21] Rev. Proc. 2006-54, at § 7.05.   [22] Id.

- It may provide an opportunity to deal with underlying issues in the dispute;

- It builds among disputants a sense of accepting and owning their eventual settlement;

- It has a tendency to mitigate tensions and build understanding and trust among disputants, thereby avoiding the bitterness that may follow adjudication;

- It may provide a basis by which parties negotiate their own dispute settlements in the future; and

- It is usually less expensive than other processes.

Availability of Mediation. Post Appeals Mediation is controlled by Rev. Proc. 2009-44.[23] Generally, the program is available for cases with a limited number of legal and factual issues remaining. Either the taxpayer or Appeals may request mediation, but only after good-faith Appeals negotiations prove unsuccessful, and mediation will only be available after all other issues are resolved, but for the issue going forward to mediation.[24] Further, the mediation process does not create any special settlement authority for Appeals—it is still subject to the same procedural rules that are applicable in the standard Appeals process.[25] The IRS considers mediation to be appropriate for:

1. Legal issues;

2. Factual issues;

3. Compliance Coordinated Issues or Appeals Coordinated Issues, but only if the taxpayer has taken the opportunity to discuss the CCI or ACI with the Appeals CCI or ACI coordinate during regular Appeals settlement discussions;

4. Early referral issues when an agreement is not reached (provided other mediation requirements are met under Rev. Proc. 99-28, section 2.16);

5. Issues for which competent authority assistance has not yet been filed;[26]

6. Unsuccessful attempts to enter into a Section 7121 closing agreement; and

7. Offers in compromise and other cases as designated in Ann. 2008-111.[27]

Conversely, cases that are, *inter alia*, designated for litigation, docketed in any court, or include "whipsaw" issues are not appropriate for mediation.[28]

Either the taxpayer or Appeals may request mediation, but only after consultation with each other.[29] If Appeals approves the request, the Appeals Team Manager will so inform the taxpayer and the Team Case Leader or Appeals officer, and the parties will then enter into a written agreement setting forth the terms of the mediation.[30]

---

[23] 2009-40 IRB 462.

[24] *Id.* at § 4.01.

[25] *Id.* at § 4.02.

[26] If a taxpayer requests Competent Authority assistance after reaching a settlement with Appeals and enters into a closing agreement, even through mediation, Competent Authority will only seek a correlative adjustment from the treaty partner. *Id.* at § 4.03(5).

[27] *Id.* at § 4.03.

[28] *Id.* at § 4.04.

[29] *Id.* at § 5.01.

[30] *Id.* at § § 5.03, 6.01.

Parties to the Mediation. The taxpayer and Appeals are the central parties to the mediation, and each party must have at least one decision-maker present at the mediation.[31] The participants to the negotiations may include the taxpayer's representative and others with the necessary authority to resolve the case, including its chief financial officer.

Agreement to Mediate. The first step of the mediation process between a taxpayer and the IRS involves the joint preparation of the mediation agreement, which should be as concise as possible. In this agreement, the parties should set forth:

- Issue(s) the parties have agreed to mediate;
- An initial list of witnesses, attorneys, representatives, and observers for each party;
- A location and date for the mediation; and
- A prohibition on *ex parte* communications between the mediator and the parties.[32]

The activity of working together to prepare the mediation agreement may assist the parties in developing a conciliatory working attitude that can carry over into the actual mediation negotiations.

.03 Selecting the Mediator

After the mediation agreement has been prepared, the taxpayer and the IRS must select a mediator(s). The mediator will be an Appeals employee trained as a mediator. Appeals will pay all expenses associated with the use of an Appeals mediator. The taxpayer and Appeals will select the mediator from a list of trained employees who will generally be located in the same Appeals office or geographic location as the taxpayer, but not a member of the original Appeals team. Additionally, and at its own expense, the taxpayer has the option of selecting a co-mediator who is not employed by the IRS.[33]

Taxpayers and the IRS consider the following criteria when selecting a mediator: completion of mediation training, previous mediation experience, and substantive knowledge of relevant tax law or industry practices.[34]

The Mediation Process. Each party should conduct its own pre-mediation planning. This planning should include an evaluation of the discussion summaries, an identification of its interest and options, and an identification of the interests and options of the other party. This exercise should also include an evaluation of each party's alternatives if they fail to reach a settlement.

When offering guidance on the mediation process, Rev. Proc. 2009-44 notes that the first step is for both of the parties to prepare a discussion summary of the issues for consideration by the mediator. The discussion summary will contain the party's arguments in favor of its position, and should be submitted to the mediator and the other party at least two weeks before mediation is scheduled to occur.[35]

---

[31] *Id.* at § 6.02.

[32] *Id.* at Ex. 2 (providing a model mediation agreement).

[33] *Id.* at § 7.01.

[34] *Id.*

[35] *Id.* at § 8.01.

Two important features of the mediation are confidentiality and the prohibition of the *ex parte* contacts. On the issue of confidentiality, all information concerning the dispute resolution process may not be disclosed by any party, participant, observer, or mediator, except as provided by statute (as in Section 6013).[36]

With regard to *ex parte* communications, the prohibition only applies to unsolicited contacts from one of the parties outside the mediation session. The prohibition is designed to ensure that the mediator does not receive information of evidence of which the other party is unaware, and to which the other party is unable to respond or offer a rebuttal. The prohibition does not, however, prevent the mediator from contacting a party, or a party from answering a question or request posed by the mediator.[37]

Any party may withdraw from the mediation proceedings at any time prior to reaching a settlement by notifying the other party and the mediator in writing.[38]

At the end of the mediation, the mediator prepares a brief report, subject to the confidentiality requirements, and submits a copy to each party.[39] If the parties reach an agreement, the IRS asks the taxpayer to execute a closing agreement. If the mediation fails, the parties may request arbitration, provided the issue meets the requirements for arbitration. If arbitration is not suitable or not approved, Appeals will not reconsider the issue, and will instead issue a statutory notice of deficiency.[40]

Fast-Track Guidance. Fast-track guidance is a process whereby traditional mediation procedures are employed between the taxpayer and Examination Division before closing the case.[41] The process is designed to resolve factual issues, such as transfer pricing, with a swift turnaround and can take place at a case manager's closing conference or before issuance of an unagreed report. In fast track guidance, an Appeals Officer acts as a neutral, third-party mediator to facilitate negotiations between the taxpayer and the case manager of Examination.

Fast track guidance is voluntary and non-binding. Therefore, the taxpayer and case manager retain the decision-making authority to accept or reject the mediator's recommendation. Each party must enter into a written agreement to mediate in good faith and the agreement is subject to the same criteria as traditional mediation. Taxpayers retain the option to request an administrative review by Appeals if a resolution cannot be reached through fast-track guidance. In this situation, taxpayers can elect to have their case reviewed by the same mediating Appeals Officer or a different Appeals Officer once it has been transferred.

.04 Arbitration of Non-Docketed Cases

The IRS has a voluntary binding arbitration program for factual issues in docketed cases (Tax Court Rule 124). In response to RRA '98, requiring the IRS to implement arbitration procedures for non-docketed cases, the IRS began a pilot

---

[36] *Id.* at § § 8.02, 10.01.
[37] *Id.* at § 8.03.
[38] *Id.* at § 8.04.

[39] *Id.* at § 9.01, Ex. 5.
[40] *Id.* at § 9.02.
[41] Rev. Proc. 2003-40, 2003-1 CB 1044.

¶1210.04

program on January 18, 2000 to conduct a two-year test of non-docketed arbitration.[42]

Non-docketed arbitration is only available for factual issues under dispute after the taxpayer and Appeals have first made attempts to negotiate a settlement. Arbitration is an optional process whereby the taxpayer and Assistant Regional Director of Appeals-Large Case ("ARDA-LC") formally agree that the parties will be bound to the findings made by the arbitrator with respect to the issues to be resolved.[43]

A factual issue is eligible for arbitration if it is susceptible to being resolved solely upon a finding of fact and does not require the Arbitrator to make any interpretation of law, regulation, ruling or other legal authority.[44] Transfer pricing issues often meet this definitional requirement for arbitration. Taxpayers should consider arbitration as a viable alternative to litigation. Arbitration, however, is not available for an issue for which the taxpayer has filed, or will file, a request for competent authority assistance.[45] Thus, arbitration may not be a viable option where bilateral consideration is necessary.

Arbitration Procedures. A taxpayer submits a written request to the appropriate Appeals Team Manager who has responsibility for the case to initiate arbitration proceedings.[46] The Appeals Team Manager prepares a written recommendation for action on the request that is forwarded, with the request, to the Chief, Appeals— Office of Tax Policy and Procedure. The Chief will reach a determination within 30 days of receipt the request by the Appeals Team Manager.[47] The Appeals Team Manager will schedule an administrative conference for approved requests to discuss the process.[48] Denied requests are not afforded formal appeals procedures, however the taxpayer may request a conference with the Appeals Team Manager to discuss the case.[49]

Arbitration Agreement. The taxpayer and Office of Appeals enter into a written arbitration agreement, which is negotiated at the administrative conference, or series of conferences.[50] At a minimum, the agreement must contain the following:

1. Issues that the parties have agreed to arbitrate;

2. Assignment to an arbitrator the prescribed task of finding facts;

3. Description, with precision, of the answer sought; e.g., specific dollar amounts, ranges of dollar values, a "yes" or "no" finding, etc . . . ;

4. Description and limit of the kind of information the arbitrator may consider, e.g., the parties' agreement as to any legal guidance the arbitrator must rely upon in coming to a decision;

5. Initial list of witnesses, attorneys, representatives, and observers for each party;

---

[42] IRS Announcement 2000-4, 2000-1 CB 317 (superseded by Rev. Proc. 2006-44).

[43] Rev. Proc. 2006-44, 2006-2 CB 800, at § 5.01.

[44] *Id*. at Ex. 1, Model Arbitration Agreement.

[45] *Id*. at § 3.04(6).

[46] *Id*. at § § 4.01 and 4.02.

[47] *Id*. at § 4.03.

[48] *Id*. at § 4.03(1).

[49] *Id*. at § 4.03(2)

[50] *Id*. at § 5.01.

¶1210.04

6. Provision that the time and place for any hearing will be determined by mutual agreement, and;

7. Prohibition of *ex parte* communications between the arbitrator and the parties.[51]

Selection of Arbitrators. Under Rev. Proc. 2006-44, non-IRS and Appeals personnel may serve as arbitrators.[52] An administrator is assigned to the case and either party must communicate with the arbitrator through the administrator unless both parties are present.[53] An administrator may be either a non-IRS employee or from the Chief, Appeals, Office of Tax Policy and Procedure.[54]

Binding Procedure. Arbitration is completely confidential, including all information and communication conveyed during the process.[55] A final report on the findings of fact will be issued by the arbitrator. Established Appeals procedures apply to close the case once a decision by the arbitrator has been reached.[56] While the process is binding for the specific case presented to the arbitrator, the findings are not binding for taxable years not covered by the arbitration agreement.[57]

The most distinct difference between arbitration and mediation is that arbitration is a binding process between the IRS and taxpayer. In arbitration the decision-making authority shifts from the taxpayer and the IRS to the arbitrator. Arbitration may be an attractive alternative to litigation when the taxpayer does not want certain information inherent in the case to be disclosed as part of a public record, because the arbitration process and findings are confidential. Also, the taxpayer and IRS in arbitration may specify the limited scope of information that can be made available to the arbitrator on which to base the decision, while the Tax Court utilizes all sources available to make a determination. Additionally, arbitration may be a less costly alternative to litigation.

.05 Mediation of Docketed Cases

The parties to Docketed Mediation are the taxpayer and District Counsel, but other parties from each side may participate. The taxpayer and District Counsel should jointly select a mediator. If the parties reach an agreement on all or some of the issues through the mediation process, District Counsel will draft a stipulation of settled issues for sub-mission to the Tax Court. If the parties are not able to reach an agreement on an issue being mediated, the parties prepare for trial as normal.

The Tax Court Rules contain no specific provisions for mediation, but support for mediation may be inferred from Tax Court Rule 124(b)(5)—*Other Methods of Resolution:* "Nothing contained in this Rule shall be construed to exclude use by the parties of other forms of voluntary disposition of cases, *including* mediation" (emphasis added). Finally, the Chief Counsel's office has acknowledged the potential benefits of providing for mediation of docketed Tax Court cases.[58]

---

[51] *Id.* at § 5.01(1)-(7).
[52] *Id.* at § 6.02.
[53] *Id.* at § 4.03(1).
[54] *Id.* at § 6.02.
[55] *Id.* at § 7.03.
[56] *Id.* at § 8.02.
[57] *Id.* at § 9.06.
[58] *See* IRM 35.5.5.4(3) ("The use of mediation, in appropriate cases, can result in a more efficient use of judicial and Internal Revenue Service resources and assist in reducing the Tax Court's inventory.")

The Chief Counsel's office has established mediation procedures substantially mirroring those set forth in Announcement 95-86. Mediation may not be used to delay trial and trial preparation; nevertheless, the prospect of mediation offers the parties an opportunity for reasoned and supervised negotiations that otherwise become overly charged during the trial preparation process. The mediation provisions for cases docketed in the Tax Court are not limited to CIC taxpayers.

Although no Tax Court Rule specifically provides for mediation in docketed cases, support could be inferred under the court's general authority.[59] The Tax Court consistently has encouraged parties to settle valuation disputes, especially transfer pricing issues, outside of litigation. Mediation should be utilized when other standard settlement procedures, such as Appeals consideration, have failed and it is cost effective and otherwise appropriate.[60]

.08 Arbitration of Docketed Cases

Rule 124 of the Tax Court Rules of Practice and Procedure provides for voluntary binding arbitration of cases docketed before the Tax Court. After the parties file a motion and meet the requirements of Rule 124, the Chief Judge assigns a judge to supervise the arbitration and appoints the arbitrator. The motion filed under Rule 124 must have an attached stipulation, signed by the parties and containing the following points:

- Statement of issues to be resolved by the arbitrator;
- Agreement of the parties to be bound by the findings of the arbitrator;
- Identity of the arbitrator or procedure for selection;
- Resources available to the arbitrator to use in reaching a decision;
- Allocation of costs between parties;
- Prohibition against *ex parte* communication with the arbitrator; and
- Other matters deemed appropriate.

The arbitrator then carries out the mandate of the appointing order and reports a decision to the parties. If neither party raises a valid objection the judge adopts the arbitrator's report as the decision of the court. Rule 124, Tax Court Rules of Practice and Procedure.

Rule 124 is intended to present a number of benefits to a taxpayer and the IRS regarding factual disputes, particularly valuation cases. Nearly all cases that have invoked Rule 124 have involved single arbitrators and placed no restrictions on the ability of the arbitrator to decide the outcome.[61] In these cases the taxpayer and the IRS could hope to achieve:

- Swift resolution;
- Substantively expert decision-maker;

---

[59] Hamblen, Jr., "The Changing Tide of Tax Court Litigation: Large Case Management", 14 *Va. Tax Rev.*, No. 1, 1, 9 (Summer 1994); *BNA Daily Tax Rep.* No. 219, 11/12/92, at p. G-9.

[60] *W.L. Gore*, CCH Dec. 50,507(M), 69 TCM 2037 (1995).

[61] Carlton Smith, "Innovative Settlement Techniques Can Reduce Litigation Costs", *J. Tax'n*, Fall 1993, pg. 76, 79.

- Confidentiality; and
- Cheaper resolution.

The *Apple* arbitration case was the first transfer pricing case to employ the Rule 124 arbitration.[62] In that case, the parties used the flexible nature of Rule 124 to structure an arbitration procedure quite different from the previous Rule 124 arbitration procedures. The parties submitted their dispute to a three-judge panel consisting of a business professor, a retired Federal judge, and an economist, all with transfer pricing experience.[63] In addition, the parties stipulated to "baseball-type" arbitration, thus requiring the panel to choose either the taxpayer's or the IRS's proposed number. The parties engaged in discovery and presented their case to the panel as if presenting a full blown case to a judge. The panel found for the IRS. It does not appear that any taxpayers have seriously considered arbitration after the *Apple* case.

> **Comment:** The *Apple* arbitration, crafted to achieve the unique goals of the parties involved, failed to achieve the goals normally sought through Rule 124 arbitration. Due to the extensive discovery and presentation, Rule 124 resulted in no financial savings to the parties as would otherwise be expected in arbitration. Furthermore, the use of "baseball" type arbitration caused the parties to incur the expenses in a "win or lose" effort. Had the *Apple* arbitration presented the panel with abbreviated, condensed cases, similar to other Rule 124 cases and permitted the panel to use its judgment of the proper pricing, a lower cost may have been achieved.

Because a case must be in docketed Tax Court status before the Rule 124 election of binding arbitration, this approach does not present the opportunity to coordinate with the other procedures. In contrast to nondocketed mediation, no coordination with Early Referral or Del. Ord. 236 (Rev. 3) is possible. Therefore, the value of arbitration rests solely in its potential to achieve satisfactory resolution of the issue for the tax years in question.

.07 Delegation Order 236 (Rev. 3)

Del. Ord. 236 (Rev. 3) extends limited authority to Examination personnel to settle issues in a manner consistent with an Appeals settlement in prior or subsequent tax years for certain Coordinated Examination Program ("CEP") taxpayers.[64] This change eliminates the need for CEP taxpayers to protest an issue in order to obtain the same result reached with Appeals in prior or subsequent tax years, resulting in considerable resource savings for both taxpayers and the IRS. The following factors must be present in the tax year under Examination:

1. The facts surrounding a transaction or taxable event in the tax period under examination are substantially the same as the facts in the settled period;
2. The legal authority relating to such issue must have remained unchanged;

---

[62] *Apple Computer Co.*, Docket No. 2178-90 (1993).

[63] "Panel Sides With IRS on All Years in Apple Computer Arbitration, Judge Says," 2 *Tax Mgmt. Transfer Pricing Rep.* 266 (1993).

[64] Del. Ord. 236 (Rev. 3), IRM 1.2.43.37(3).

3. The underlying issue must have been settled by Appeals independently of other issues (e.g., no trading of issues) in the settled tax period; and

4. The issue must have been settled in Appeals with respect to the same taxpayer (including consolidated and unconsolidated subsidiaries) or another taxpayer who was directly involved in the transaction or taxable event in the settled period.[65]

This procedure appears particularly well suited to resolve recurring factual disputes, like transfer pricing. Del. Ord. 236 (Rev. 3) allows Examination case managers to accept settlement offers with respect to issues where a settlement on the merits Appeals has reached in another tax period with respect to CEP taxpayers. Del. Ord. 236 (Rev. 3) can also be used in conjunction with settlements reached in Appeals through Early Referral and Non-docketed Mediation.

.08 Litigation

Available Alternatives. In seeking judicial review, three forums are available to the taxpayer in litigating the controversy: the U.S. District Court, the U.S. Court of Federal Claims or the U.S. Tax Court. The taxpayer has the option of paying the deficiency and subsequently seeking a refund by bringing an action in either federal district court or in the Court of Federal Claims (the "refund" method). Alternatively, the taxpayer can contest the notice of deficiency without paying the tax and file a petition in Tax Court (the "deficiency" method). In selecting a forum several factors should be considered.

Considerations in Selecting a Judicial Forum. The primary determination in selecting a judicial forum is whether the taxpayer wants to pursue the refund method or the deficiency method. Under the refund method, the taxpayer pays the tax in full and seeks a refund of the erroneously assessed tax in federal district court or the Court of Federal Claims. Under the deficiency method, a taxpayer does not pay the tax, but rather, files a petition in the U.S. Tax Court for a re-determination of the amount of the deficiency. In selecting between these two methods, relevant factors include the taxpayer's ability to pay the tax, its cash flow needs, and the interest and penalties that will be assessed on any deficiency.

Another factor to consider is the relevant discovery rules, and the ability for the government to obtain additional materials during the litigation process. In district court and the Court of Federal Claims, the discovery procedures are fairly liberal, allowing inquiry into and document production of any matter which could reasonably lead to the discovery of admissible evidence.[66] In contrast, the Tax Court, with its separate discovery procedures, is more limited. Although certain discovery techniques are available in Tax Court, "the Court expects the parties to attempt to attain the objectives of discovery through informal consultation or communication before utilizing the discovery procedures" as provided in the Tax Court rules.[67] This factor impacts both parties, as the taxpayer is equally limited in obtaining materials from the IRS.

---

[65] IRM 1.2.43.37(5).
[66] Fed. R. Civ. P. 26(b)(1); U.S. Cl. Ct. Rule 26(b)(1).
[67] TC Rule 70(a).

Further, the complexity of the case and the need for an experienced jurist, or, perhaps, a sympathetic jury, will be factor. In Tax Court, the judges are experienced tax specialists who preside exclusively over tax cases. In contrast, district and claims court judges preside over various types of cases and generally are not tax specialists. The level of experience also extends to the attorneys representing the government. In Tax Court, the government is represented by attorneys from the IRS Regional Counsel or District Counsel office, one of which is likely to have Code Sec. 482 experience. In district and the Court of Federal Claims, the government is represented by attorneys from the Tax Division of the Department of Justice, who, although may have tried tax cases, are unlikely to have Code Sec. 482 experience. The district court is the only court of the three that allows a jury trial.

¶ 1220 Post-Examination Bilateral Procedures

.01 The Competent Authority Process

Currently, all U.S. bilateral tax treaties include a Mutual Agreement Procedure ("MAP") article that allows the taxpayer to request assistance when the actions of the United States, the treaty country, or both result in taxation that is contrary to the treaty.[68] The MAP article authorizes the treaty partners to use "best efforts" to mitigate double taxation. The MAP is commonly referred to as "competent authority" negotiations (hereinafter, the MAP will be referred to as the competent authority process).

The competent authority process is a remedy to avoid the denial of treaty benefits and avoid double tax (the majority of the focus). The competent authority procedure is also a major tool to resolve disputes involving re-allocation of income or deductions under transfer pricing laws, particularly for taxpayers who want correlative relief. The competent authorities evaluate the merits of the proposed adjustment and, through a negotiated process, reach a mutual agreement with the foreign competent authority regarding the proper amount of the adjustment.

The competent authority process is designed to grant full relief from double taxation. Correlative relief is granted for the entire amount of the agreed-on adjustment. If the competent authorities agree on an amount less than the adjustment originally proposed, the U.S. competent authority will usually withdraw any amount of the proposed adjustment in excess of the negotiated agreement. As a result, the procedures can resolve a domestic dispute without prior recourse to traditional channels.[69]

Issues Addressed by Competent Authority. In general, the competent authority process is available whenever the actions of the United States, the treaty country, or both result in taxation that is contrary to the treaty issues taken to competent authority include:

---

[68] Article 25 of U.S. Model Tax Treaty.
[69] *See* Marc Levey, Steven C. Wrappe and Kerwin Chung, "The Future of Transfer Pricing: All Roads Lead to Competent Authority," 27 *Taxation Management Int'l. J.* 379 (August 7, 1998).

¶1220.01

- Transfer pricing and APAs;

- Creditability of foreign taxes (foreign taxes are not creditable if the foreign country is a treaty country that could have made a correlative adjustment);[70]

- Permanent establishment issues (the Service will not issue private letter rulings on this issue);[71]

- Sourcing of income;

- Allocation of deductions;

- Limitation on benefits; and

- Residency issues.

In the United States, more than half of the cases referred to competent authority involve transfer pricing (including APAs).

Requesting Competent Authority Assistance. Rev. Proc. 2006-54 is the current authority governing the competent authority process.[72] A request for competent authority assistance may be filed at any time after an action occurs that would give rise to a claim for competent authority assistance.[73] In a case involving a U.S.-initiated adjustment of tax or income resulting from a tax examination, a request for competent authority assistance may be submitted after the amount of the proposed adjustment is communicated in writing to the taxpayer.[74] In the case of a foreign-initiated adjustment, a request may be submitted as soon as the taxpayer believes such filing is warranted based on the actions of the country proposing the adjustment.[75] There are also procedures relating to competent authority requests concerning residence and treaty limitation of benefits issues.[76]

A request for competent authority assistance must be in the form of a letter addressed to the Assistant Commissioner (International) which must be dated and signed by a person having the authority to sign the taxpayer's federal tax returns.[77] The request for competent authority assistance should include the following information:

- Reference to the specific treaty and the provisions therein pursuant to which the request is made;

- Names, address, U.S. taxpayer identification number and foreign taxpayer identification number (if any) of the taxpayer and, if applicable, all related persons involved in the matter:

- If applicable, a description of the control and business relationships between the taxpayer and any relevant related person for the years in issue, including any changes in such relationship to the date of filing the request;

- Brief description of the issues for which competent authority assistance is requested, including a brief description of the relevant transactions, activi-

---

[70] *See* Reg. § 1.901-2(e)(5)(i), Rev. Rul. 92-75, 1992-2 CB 197 (cited in Rev. Proc. 2006-54, 2006-2 CB 1035).

[71] *See* Rev. Proc. 2010-7, 2010-1 IRB 231.

[72] Rev. Proc. 2006-54, 2006-2 CB 1035.

[73] *Id.* at § 4.01.

[74] *Id.*

[75] *Id.*

[76] *Id.* at § § 4.07; 4.08.

[77] *Id.* at § 4.04.

ties or other circumstances involved in the issues raised and the bias for the adjustment, if any;

- Years and amounts involved with respect to the issues in both U.S. dollars and foreign currency;

- If applicable, the district office which has made or is proposing to make the adjustment;

- Explanation of the nature of the relief sought or the action requested in the United States or in the treaty country with respect to the issues raised, including a statement as to whether the taxpayer wishes to avail itself of the relief provided under Rev. Proc. 99-32.

- Statement whether the period of limitations for the years for which relief is sought has expired in the United States or in the treaty country;

- To the extent known by the taxpayer, a statement of relevant foreign judicial or public administrative proceedings that do not involve the taxpayer or related persons but involve the same issue for which competent authority assistance is requested;

- Statement whether the request for competent authority assistance involves issues that are currently, or were previously, considered as part of an APA proceeding in the United States or in a similar proceeding in the foreign country;

- If applicable, powers of attorney with respect to the taxpayer;

- Statement whether the taxpayer is requesting the Simultaneous Appeals procedure;

- Amended return, if required under section 9.02 of Rev. Proc. 2006-54;

- On a separate document, a statement that the taxpayer consents to the disclosure to the competent authority of the treaty country (with the name of the treaty country specifically stated) and the competent authority's staff of any or all of the items of information set forth or enclosed in the request for U.S. competent authority assistance within the limits contained in the tax treaty under which the taxpayer is seeking relief;

- Perjury statement; and

- Any other information required or requested under Rev. Proc. 2006-54, as applicable. For example, section 7.06 requires the provision of certain information in the case of a request for the accelerated competent authority procedure, and section 10 requires provision of certain information in the case of a request for Rev. Proc. 99-32 treatment. Requests for supplemental information may include items such as detailed financial information, comparability analysis, or other material relevant to a transfer pricing analysis.

Steps in the Competent Authority Process. The steps of the competent authority process are as follows:

¶1220.01

1. The Service or the treaty partner proposes a re-allocation of income;

2. Taxpayer sends a letter to the Tax Treaty Division of the Assistant Commissioner (International), requesting competent authority assistance. This request should include, among other things, references to the specific treaty, any business relationships with controlled entities in the other country, a summary of the transactions involved, and a brief description of the relief sought or action requested;

3. Tax Treaty Division accepts the request;

4. Case is assigned to a competent authority analyst;

5. Examination Division prepares a Competent Authority Process report;

6. Competent authority analyst in the Tax Treaty Division prepares a position paper with the assistance of the taxpayer and the examination division;

7. Competent authorities exchange position papers;

8. There may be quarterly, semi-annual, or annual competent authority meetings;

9. Competent authorities negotiate to agreement; and

10. Taxpayer must agree to any resolution negotiated between the two competent authorities. A closing agreement may be required.

Successes and Criticisms of the Competent Authority Process. The competent authority process is very successful in eliminating double tax. The most recent statistics show that the competent authority is able to obtain full relief from double taxation approximately 95 percent of the time.[78]

> **Comment:** As more countries become aggressive with their enforcement of their respective transfer pricing laws, this rate of success is likely to decrease.

Despite the historic success of the competent authority process, it has not been immune from criticism. For years, taxpayers have criticized the competent authority process for delays. In response to this criticism, the IRS hired additional staff, began conducting more conferences with major treaty partners, and scheduling more face-to-face meetings. These efforts appear to have been successful, and the processing time for a case decreased.

Another criticism of the competent authority process is that taxpayers are excluded from the negotiation process. The IRS is unlikely to change its actions in response to this criticism. The competent authority process is a government-to-government program where the governments must engage in sensitive negotiations to achieve resolution to avoid double taxation. According to the IRS commen-

---

[78] *See* EY Tax Alert, "IRS Issues Competent Authority Statistics Report," Jan. 21, 2010, *available at http://www.ey.com/Publication/vwLUAssets/ITA_IRS_issues_Competent_Authority/$File/ITA-IRS%20issues%20competent%20athority%20statistics%20report.pdf* (reporting an average full relief rate of roughly 95 percent for 2004 through 2009). Full relief includes cases where correlative relief is granted, or where the adjust- ment is withdrawn by one of the taxing authorities. The alert goes on to note that the percentage of cases where an adjustment was withdrawn increases sharply, from 32.8 percent in 2008, to 60.8 percent in 2009. Not surprisingly, there was a corresponding decline in the number of cases solved with correlative adjustments, from 56.5 percent in 2008, to 34.8 percent in 2009. *Id.*

tators, the presence of taxpayers at negotiations might undermine the competent authorities' ability to act independently and reach an agreement. However, the U.S. competent authority is generally more open than the competent authority of other countries. Taxpayers can often obtain regular progress reports regarding the status of their case and the respective positions of the competent authority.

Using Competent Authority to Prevent Controversies Regarding Compensating Adjustments. Compensating adjustments are pricing adjustments made by a taxpayer in filing its original tax return. These adjustments are made after the close of the books for the tax year and represent a book/tax difference in income. Under Reg. § 1.482-1(a)(3), taxpayers may make compensating adjustments after completing a transaction (or after the close of the tax year) to adjust the price to an arm's length price. Unfortunately, the OECD transfer pricing guidelines and the transfer pricing laws of several major treaty partners (e.g., Belgium, Canada, France, Germany, and Japan) do not allow compensating adjustments on the grounds that tax returns should reflect actual transactions.

Further, some taxpayers fear they will not be able to obtain competent authority assistance in a foreign country because the foreign country will not recognize a taxpayer-initiated adjustment. For instance, Japan has taken the position that a compensating adjustment that has the effect of increasing the income of a U.S. subsidiary of a Japanese multinational should be treated as a nondeductible corporate contribution to capital. In addition, Japan has taken the position that the denial of the deduction is a purely Japanese domestic issue that is not subject to the competent authority process.

The Service has recognized this problem and is discussing it with several treaty partners. Occasionally, the Service has stated that it would regard potential double taxation as a matter proper for immediate competent authority consideration. The Service has further stated that the competent authority process would be available to taxpayers that anticipate double taxation when a taxpayer initiates a compensating adjustment in the U.S. that cannot be reflected in the foreign country on a self-help basis.

Arbitration Between Competent Authorities. Despite the historic success of the U.S. competent authority in eliminating double taxation, a mechanism is needed to address the situation where the two competent authorities are unable to reach an agreement. One possible solution for this dilemma is arbitration. The protocols to the United States' treaties with Canada,[79] Germany, Belgium, France, and Switzerland each contain a binding arbitration requirement for all competent authority

---

[79] *See* 17 *Tax Mgmt. Transfer Pricing Rep.* 815 (March 5, 2009) (relaying Phil Fortier's views that the mechanics of arbitration under the U.S.–Canada treaty would be worked out "fairly soon," with the caveat that the agreement to the procedures under the treaty comes not from Canadian competent authority or international tax groups, but from the Legislative Policy Division). As of March 2010, arbitration procedures still have not been articulated.

cases unresolved after two years.[80] All employ the "baseball" or "last best offer" form of arbitration.[81]

There is also an arbitration process for transfer pricing disputes between two countries within the European Union. The European Union Arbitration Convention on transfer pricing was signed on July 23, 1990 and became effective on January 1, 1995. It guarantees the elimination of double taxation by requiring the competent authorities to submit to arbitration if they are unable to resolve a case of double taxation.

Under the convention, the respective competent authorities are first required to attempt to resolve instances of double taxation through the competent authority procedures of their tax treaties. If the competent authorities are unable to reach agreement on how to eliminate double taxation within two years, the competent authorities are required to submit the matter to an arbitration committee, which has six months to render advice on resolving double taxation.

The arbitration committee consists of two members from each of the respective countries, as well as five independent experts. During the arbitration procedure, the taxpayer and the respective tax authorities will have an opportunity to submit relevant information or documentation. The taxpayer also has the right to appear before the committee and be heard. The committee decides which advice to give by majority vote. Within six months following the advice of the arbitration committee, the respective competent authorities must reach a settlement that eliminates double taxation. Although the settlement does not have to follow the advice of the arbitration committee, it must be in accord with the arm's length principle.

As of December 31, 2008, there were between 196 and 201 cases pending under the Convention, with the majority having been presented for resolution during 2007 and 2008.[82] The largest concentration of the pending cases were between Germany and France, Germany and the U.K., and the U.K. and France.[83] Faced with evidence of arbitration's increasing popularity, some commenters may be forced to revisit their opinion that the greatest benefit of binding arbitration is its ability to strongly encourage the tax authorities of the involved countries to seriously re-evaluate their negotiating position prior to losing settlement authority over the case.

---

[80] "Senate Committee Urged to Ratify Treaty, Protocol with Mandatory Arbitration Terms," 16 *Tax Mgt Transfer Pricing Report* 212 (July 26, 2007).

The United States–Mexico double taxation treaty provides an early example of an arbitration clause. In this incarnation, arbitration is not mandatory, but it is binding. In cases where the competent authorities are unable to agree, the taxpayer must agree in writing that it will be bound by the arbitration board's decision before the case can be submitted. Ratified in 1992, this arbitration clause is still in force. *See* United States–Mexico 1992 Income Tax Convention and Final Protocol (Sep. 18, 1992), Treaty Doc. 103-31.

[81] This approach requires the arbitrators to choose between the last offers submitted by the parties without compromise.

[82] *See* European Union Joint Transfer Pricing Forum, *Draft Table on the number of pending cases under the Arbitration Convention,* (doc JTPF/009/REV2/BACK/2009), *available at http://ec.europa.eu/taxation_customs/resources/documents/taxation/company_tax/ transfer_pricing/forum/JTPF/2009/JTPF_009_REV2_BACK_2009_en.pdf* (explaining that the range of pending cases is due to the fact that a case may be considered as closed in one member state, but not in another).

[83] *See id.*; *see also* "France, Germany EU Competent Authority Inventories Increase, U.K. Cases Decrease," 18 *Transfer Pricing Report* 1101 (Feb. 25, 2010).

An updated Arbitration Convention was ratified by the then-members of the European Union on November 1, 2004 (with retroactive effective date to January 1, 2000). The new convention clarified time restrictions and functions in the arbitration phase, how to submit a case, and taxpayer protections.[84] Subsequent enlargements in 2004 and 2008 extended the Convention's applicability to new member states of the European Union.[85]

On December 30, 2009, the Council of the European Union issued a Code of Conduct to the Convention. This Code of Conduct was designed to clarify certain issues with the Convention that were identified through the work of the Joint Transfer Pricing Forum and the Commission itself. The issues largely surrounded the Convention's scope (e.g., whether issues such as thin capitalization were to be covered), as well as technical aspects (e.g., when the two-year period commences). The drafters of the Code of Conduct strongly emphasized that the document was to be used in determining whether and how the Convention would apply, but that no member state's rights or obligations under the Convention were altered.[86]

.02 Simultaneous Appeals/Competent Authority Consideration ("SAP")

Background. Before the issuance of Rev. Proc. 96-13, the IRS required taxpayers to pursue resolution of double taxation issues with Appeals before seeking competent authority assistance. This resulted in an increase in the time required to settle cases through the Appeals/competent authority process. In addition, competent authority negotiations following Appeals settlements are made more difficult if the U.S. competent authority is defending a *hazards of litigation* settlement that is not supported by actual facts or a TPM.[87]

Goal of SAP. Rev. Proc. 96-13 changed this process by providing a mechanism for the simultaneous involvement of competent authority and Appeals in resolving the double tax matter under the SAP.[88] The goal of this procedure is to expedite the resolution of issues by enabling Appeals to participate actively in the competent authority process. Combining Appeals consideration with the development of the U.S. competent authority negotiating position under SAP generally provides for a stronger U.S. competent authority negotiating position.

Availability of SAP. Under section 8 of Rev. Proc. 2006-54, taxpayers may seek SAP consideration of an issue. This provides Appeals involvement consistent with the development and negotiation of the competent authority review and negotiations. Also, simultaneous application of the Appeals and competent authority functions should reduce the time required to resolve the disputes. In addition, the

---

[84] "Eleven EU Members Ratify Revised Arbitration Convention Report," 15 *Transfer Pricing Report* 301 (Aug. 16, 2006).

[85] *See* Transfer Pricing and the Arbitration Convention—Extension of its scope to acceding Member States, *available at http://ec.europa.eu/taxation_customs/taxation/company_tax/transfer_pricing/arbitration_convention/index_en.htm* (noting that the Convention was extending to the Czech Republic, Estonia, Cyprus, Latvia, Lithuania, Hungary, Malta, Poland, Slovenia, the Slovak Republic, Bulgaria, and Romania,

and that the Convention is generally applicable amongst all EU member states).

[86] *See* European Council of Ministers, Revised Code of Conduct for Arbitration Convention (doc. 2009/C322/01), Dec. 30, 2009, *reprinted in* 18 *Transfer Pricing Report* 967 (Jan. 14, 2010); *see also* "EU Clarifies Arbitration Convention Covers Thin Capitalization, Triangulation," 18 *Transfer Pricing Report* 959 (Jan. 14, 2010).

[87] *See* Christine Halphen and Ron Bordeaux, "International Issue Resolution Through the Competent Authority Process," 94 *TNT* 152-156 (Aug. 4, 1994).

[88] Rev. Proc. 96-13, 1996-1 CB 616, at §8.

combined involvement of Appeals and the taxpayer in the development of the competent authority case are intended to improve the settlement discussions with the treaty partner.

Time for Requesting SAP. Taxpayers may request simultaneous consideration when initially filing for competent authority assistance. Thus, the taxpayer can request SAP: (1) after the examination team has proposed an adjustment but before filing a protest; (2) when it files its protest, by seeking competent authority assistance on the transfer pricing issue while Appeals considers the rest of the case; and (3) after Appeal stakes the case but before settlement of the transfer pricing issue.[89]

Taxpayers may seek the application of SAP even after competent authority has accepted the case for consideration. However, the IRS encourages taxpayers to make their requests before the competent authority presents the U.S. position paper to the foreign competent authority. The IRS denies requests made after that time, unless the U.S. competent authority finds that the application of the SAP will assist in an early resolution of the issue or is otherwise in the best interest of the IRS.[90]

Rev. Proc. 2006-54 permits competent authority to accept cases for consideration for tax periods pending in court or designated for litigation with the consent of the Chief Counsel.[91] Taxpayers can request SAP for those cases in which Chief Counsel has granted consent for competent authority consideration, but the Chief Counsel's office must again give its consent.[92]

Form of SAP Request. Taxpayers request SAP either in their initial competent authority assistance request, or later as a separate letter to the U.S. competent authority.[93] The taxpayer should indicate in the request whether the taxpayer ever presented the issue to Appeals for the period in competent authority or any prior periods.[94] If Appeals considered the issue for prior periods, the taxpayer must provide copies of the relevant portions of its earlier protest and an explanation of the Appeals outcome. An example of a Request for Competent Authority Assistance and an example of a Request for SAP are included in the Working Papers.

Role of Appeals Under SAP. Once competent authority accepts an issue for SAP, it obtains jurisdiction over that issue. Nevertheless, the Appeals Officer attempts to develop a tentative resolution that can form the basis of the U.S. negotiating position presented to the foreign competent authority. In doing so, the Appeals Officer applies traditional Appeals methods and principles. In addition, the Appeals Officer works with the U.S. competent authority to insure that the tentative resolution of the issues, as well as the principles and facts underlying the resolution, meet the requirements of the case the U.S. competent authority intends to present to the foreign competent authority. Accordingly, any settlement between the taxpayer and Appeals remains tentative, binding on neither the IRS nor the taxpayer. Rather, the

---

[89] Rev. Proc. 2006-54 , 2006-2 CB 1035, at §§ 8.02(a)(1) & (2).
[90] *Id.* at § 8.02(a)(3).
[91] *Id.* at § 7.03.
[92] *Id.* at § 8.03.
[93] *Id.* at § 8.04.
[94] *Id.* at § 8.04.

settlement generally will represent the position used in the U.S. competent author-ity negotiating position paper.[95] If the competent authorities fail to reach an agree-ment or the taxpayer does not accept their agreement, the taxpayer may refer the issue back to Appeals for further consideration.[96]

Role of Competent Authority Under SAP. The role of competent authority is the same under SAP as it is in other cases; that is, competent authority is responsible for developing the U.S. position paper and for conducting the mutual agreement negotiations.[97] The U.S. competent authority may meet with the taxpayer to discuss the issues. In addition, U.S. competent authority may request that the Appeals representative participate in the negotiations with the foreign competent authority. However, competent authority retains jurisdiction over the issue during this process.

Denial or Termination of SAP. The taxpayer may withdraw its SAP request at any time. In addition, the IRS may deny SAP when it determines that SAP would be prejudicial to competent authority procedures or to the Appeals administrative process. Such a situation would include taxpayers who received Appeals considera-tion but failed to resolve the issue, who then seek SAP as a "second bite at the apple." Taxpayers may request a conference to discuss the denial or termination of SAP.[98]

Experience with SAP. Not all taxpayer experience with SAP has been favorable. At least one commentator concludes that SAP is not a "simultaneous" process, but instead remains a two-step process whereby Appeals develops the case without consulting competent authority and then transmits a summary of the case to competent authority for use in development of the U.S. negotiating position.[99]

> *Comment:* All users of the SAP do not share this unfavorable impression. As a relatively new procedure, SAP can be flexible, and the taxpayer needs to work with the IRS personnel to ensure appropriate development of the case. To that end, a taxpayer should take advantage of the pre-filing conference option to establish the roles and expectations of the Appeals and competent authority personnel assigned to a particular SAP.[100] On occasions where this has been done, taxpayers have achieved satisfactory results.

.03 Accelerated Competent Authority

The Service has sought to use the competent authority procedure to resolve issues before disputes arise. This is accomplished by rolling forward the competent authority resolution to later years, and may be appropriate when the facts remain substantially unchanged. A taxpayer may request competent authority assistance regarding a transfer pricing adjustment, and further request that the competent authorities resolve the allocation issue for all filed years, even though these years have not been examined.[101] However, the application for accelerated competent

---

[95] *Id.* at § 8.05(1).
[96] *Id.* at § 8.07.
[97] *Id.* at § 8.05(2).
[98] *Id.* at § 8.06.

[99] Berger, "The Simultaneous Appeals-Competent Au-thority Procedure: The Holy Roman Empire of U.S. Inter-national Tax Administration." 38 *Tax Mgmt. Memo* 135 (May 12, 1997).
[100] Rev. Proc. 2006-54, at § 4.09.
[101] *Id.* at § 7.06.

authority assistance may require the prior consent of Chief Counsel in situations where the tax years and issues involved may be subject to litigation.[102]

Form of Request. A request for accelerated competent authority assistance may be made at the same time of filing an original request for competent authority assistance or any time thereafter.[103] However, a request for accelerated competent authority assistance should be made before the matter is resolved and taxpayers are encouraged to request it as soon as practicable.[104] The request must contain a statement that the taxpayer agrees that: (1) the inspection of books of account or records under the accelerated competent authority procedure will not preclude or impede (under Code Sec. 7605(b) or any administrative provision adopted by the Service) a later examination of a return or inspection of books of account or records for any taxable period covered in the accelerated competent authority assistance request and (2) the Service need not comply with any applicable procedural restrictions (for example, providing notice under Code Sec. 7605(b)) before beginning such examination or inspection.[105] In addition, if the taxpayer is a CIC taxpayer, the taxpayer must furnish all relevant information requested by the District Director.[106]

The Process. The U.S. competent authority will contact the appropriate District to consult whether the issue should be resolved for subsequent tax years.[107] If the District consents, the U.S. competent authority will present the request to the foreign competent authority.[108] Assuming that the competent authorities agree, based on an inspection of the books, the taxpayer may obtain an agreement for all filed years, even though the Service has not conducted a traditional examination.

.04 Bilateral APAs

The bilateral APAs are discussed in great detail in Chapter 13.

¶ 1230 Choosing Among Unilateral Alternatives

All cases must proceed through Examination before considering other procedural alternatives. After that, procedural decisions will be driven by differences in cost, decision-maker, and the standard for decisions.

Appeals is generally the lowest cost alternative. Appeals officers are more generalist by training than international examiners and are motivated to achieve settlement. The Appeals *"hazards of litigation"* standard is more favorable to taxpayers than the Examination standard.

Mediation and arbitration are only available after good faith negotiations at Appeals, so the cost of these procedures is incremental. Both mediation and arbitration introduce a third party neutral, but the role of the neutral differs between the two procedures. In mediation, the taxpayer and the IRS remain the decision-makers and the neutral merely facilitates negotiations. In arbitration, the

[102] *Id.*
[103] *Id.*
[104] *Id.*
[105] *Id.*
[106] *Id.*
[107] *Id.*
[108] *Id.*

neutral actually becomes the decision-maker; the taxpayer and the IRS become advocates for their positions.

Taxpayers can seek litigation of the transfer pricing issue in Tax Court at any time after receipt of the 90-Day letter or can pursue litigation for refund upon payment and refusal of refund. The cost of either litigation approach for a transfer pricing issue is considerably more expensive than any of the other alternatives. The decision-maker will be a Tax Court or other federal judge and the standard for decision will be "more likely than not."

Transfer pricing examinations are time consuming and expensive. The IRS has a variety of tools to obtain information from and about the taxpayer. The IRS's use of some or all of these tools requires the taxpayer to expend significant time and money providing the IRS with great quantities of information, only some of which will ultimately be relevant to the taxpayer's transfer pricing issues.

Rather than beginning with a wide-ranging factual examination followed by the aggressive pursuit of the largest possible adjustment, the Advance Pricing Agreement (APA) process begins with the taxpayer describing its relevant operations and a proposed TPM. The taxpayer and the IRS agree on a TPM, comparable companies, and adjustments. By focusing on the relevant facts and an appropriate methodology, the APA process minimizes the information that must be analyzed by both the taxpayer and the IRS. The negotiations focus on the determination of an appropriate TPM and range of arm's length results, rather than on a desired tax result. This cooperative approach results in significant cost savings to both taxpayers and the IRS.

The APA process also takes less time to complete than a transfer pricing examination. An examination can last three to four years, with complex examinations continuing for longer periods. If the dispute leads to litigation, the matter may take over fifteen years to reach resolution. For example, in one case, the court decision resolving a taxpayer's transfer pricing issues for its 1975 through 1980 tax years the resolution of a taxpayer's was not filed until September, 1993, 17 years after the taxpayer filed its returns for the 1975 year.[109] In contrast, the IRS has set a goal of concluding unilateral APAs within twelve months, and agreeing on the U.S. competent authority negotiating position for bilateral APAs within nine months.

Also, an APA eliminates the need to annually update the comparability data used in the taxpayer's transfer pricing penalty documentation. An APA generally may eliminate the need for comparable updates. In some cases, particularly those involving taxpayers in volatile industries, both the IRS and taxpayers are interested in a mechanism whereby the comparables are "freshened" during the term of the APA. The APA generally sets a range of results for the entire term of the APA, usually five years. The taxpayer need only compare its results to the range of results required by the APA.

---

[109] *Perkin-Elmer Corporation*, CCH Dec. 49,268(M), TC Memo 1993-414.

Unless the IRS totally concedes its position, the taxpayer must also keep in mind the opportunity to seek competent authority assistance, if necessary, following the unilateral procedure.

> If a taxpayer either executes a closing agreement with the District (whether or not contingent upon competent authority relief) with respect to a potential competent authority issue or reaches a settlement on the issue with Appeals or Counsel pursuant to a closing agreement or other written agreement, the U.S. competent authority *will endeavor only* to obtain a correlative adjustment from the treaty country and will not undertake any actions that would otherwise change such agreements (emphasis added).[110]

For a unilateral APA, the U.S. competent authority is more accommodating:

> The restrictions imposed under § 7.05 of Rev. Proc. 2006-54 with respect to the discretion of the U.S. competent authority to negotiate correlative relief will not apply to a unilateral APA.[111]

Therefore, only examination settlements without a closing agreement and unilateral APAs offer the option of unrestricted competent authority assistance.

The receipt of the 30-day letter presents the taxpayer with several options. The taxpayer can go to Appeals by filing a protest letter or wait for the IRS to issue the 90-day letter. Upon receipt of the 90-day letter, the taxpayer can file a Tax Court petition or pay the tax and file a refund claim and, if the claim is denied, file a refund suit in the appropriate Federal District Court or the Court of Federal Claims. Taxpayers now have additional procedural options for administrative resolution of transfer pricing issues.

The decision whether to continue the administrative process at Appeals or go directly to a judicial forum requires the consideration of several factors. These factors include:

- Existence of favorable or unfavorable precedent in the likely judicial forums;
- Possibility of Appeals raising new issues or new bases for the adjustments;
- Ability to seek judicial resolution if negotiations with Appeals fail;
- Cost and time of engaging Appeals in negotiations versus the likelihood of settlement;
- "Hot interest" provisions of Code Sec. 6621(c);
- Public nature of litigation; and
- Discovery tools available to the IRS in litigation.

Comment: If the adjustment arises from transactions involving the U.S. and a treaty partner, in addition to deciding between Appeals and litigation, the taxpayer must consider the impact of any settlement on its ability to seek competent authority relief from potential double taxation. Both administrative and judicial determinations limit the ability of the U.S. competent authority to obtain a correlative adjustment from the treaty partner. If a taxpayer either executes a closing agreement with the District (whether or not contingent upon competent authority relief) with respect to a potential competent author-

---

[110] Rev. Proc. 2006-54, § 7.05.   [111] *Id.* at § 7.

ity issue or reaches a settlement on the issue with Appeals or Counsel pursuant to a closing agreement or other written agreement, the U.S. competent authority will endeavor only to obtain a correlative adjustment from the treaty country and will not undertake any actions that would otherwise change such agreements.[112] Thus, when dealing with an adjustment involving a treaty partner, proceeding directly to the competent authority process provides the U.S. competent authority greater latitude to resolve double taxation issues.

.01 Appeals v. Litigation

Impact of Judicial Precedent. Appeals seeks to resolve tax controversies "on a basis which is fair and impartial to both the Government and the taxpayer and in a manner that will enhance voluntary compliance and public confidence in the integrity and efficiency of the Service."[113] This "fair and impartial" resolution should reflect the probable result of litigating the matter.[114] While the Appeals Officer must take relevant judicial precedent into consideration, the taxpayer must weigh its view of such precedent against how it believes an Appeals officer will view such precedent when deciding Appeals consideration or litigation.

Potential for New Issues. Appeals has the authority to raise new issues if the grounds for such action are "substantial" and the potential effect upon the tax liability is "material."[115] "Substantial" means strong and possessing real merit.[116] "Material" means having real importance and great consequence.[117] Because of this high standard, the Appeals Officer does not often raise new issues. Of greater concern is the possibility that Appeals will assign a poorly developed transfer pricing case to an experienced Appeals Officer who will develop a stronger basis for the transfer pricing adjustment. However, experience has shown that this, too, rarely occurs. It is more likely that an Appeals Officer will return a poorly developed case to Examination for further development of specific issues.

Costs of Continuing to Appeal. The taxpayer should consider the costs associated with Appeals. As indicated above, pursuing Appeals does not foreclose the taxpayer's ability to litigate the matter if negotiations with Appeals fail. Thus, taxpayers should weigh the cost of preparing the protest letter and meeting with Appeals against the likelihood of reaching a settlement. If litigation appears likely, the taxpayer may not want to expend additional resources on Appeals. Further, the taxpayer may wish not to disclose its arguments and its analyses of the IRS's weaknesses before trial.

Hot Interest. The taxpayer also must consider the "hot interest" provisions of Code Sec. 6621(c). Code Sec. 6621(c) provides for an increased rate of interest (an additional two percentage points) on certain deficiencies and accrued interest of subchapter C corporations outstanding as of January 1, 1991. Generally, interest at the increased rate commences 30 days after the earlier of the date the IRS issues the 30-day letter or the 90-day letter.[118] Given the large dollar amounts in issue for

---

[112] *Id.* at § 7.05.

[113] IRM 1.1.7.1.

[114] IRM 5.19.8.4.12.

[115] 26 CFR Reg. § 601.106(d)(1). *See also* IRM 8.6.1.6.

[116] IRM 8.6.1.6.2.

[117] *Id.*

[118] *See* Dennis I. Meyer, *et al.*, "Transfer Pricing: Judicial Strategy and Outcomes," *BNA Portfolio* 888, for a more thorough discussion of the "Hot Interest" issue.

¶1230.01

transfer pricing disputes and the long periods required for resolution, the substantial interest cost associated with transfer pricing disputes is an important factor in taxpayer consideration of procedural options.

Exposure of Confidential Information in Litigation. Generally, matters occurring before courts in the U.S. constitute matters of public record. Transfer pricing cases frequently require the disclosure of financial and other information that taxpayers prefer not to disclose to competitors. Taxpayers can seek protective orders for their sensitive information in the judicial proceedings, however, the IRS frequently opposes motions for protective orders. Motions for protective orders require that courts balance the interests of the taxpayers with the interest of the public in disclosure. Absent general common law protections for that information, courts may be reluctant to issue a protective order. In addition, taxpayers must exercise care in attempting to protect this information, for their efforts may convince the court of the extraordinary value of this intangible property, contrary to the assertions the taxpayer makes in its substantive case. These public disclosure issues may encourage taxpayers to favor administrative resolution over judicial resolution.

IRS Discovery Tools in Litigation. Once in court, the IRS may use various discovery devices unavailable to the examination team and can raise new issues by way of an amended answer. Aggressive counsel for the IRS may use the discovery process to further develop the case and raise new issues.

> *Comment:* Appeals Officers, while able to issue administrative summonses under Code Sec. 7602, generally limit their evaluation of the case to the facts presented by the examination team and the taxpayer. Further Appeals inquiry is generally limited to resolving inconsistencies and filling in gaps in information.

.02 Appeals v. Other Unilateral Settlement Opportunities

Other unilateral settlement opportunities such as non-docketed mediation and non-docketed arbitration require that the parties make a good faith attempt to negotiate a settlement before the procedures can be requested. Therefore, taxpayers do not have an either/or opportunity to pursue Appeals or non-docketed mediation or arbitration.

One of the benefits of Appeals over litigation is that Appeals offers additional ADR procedures in the event traditional Appeals negotiations break down. For example, if the taxpayer is faced with an assigned Appeals Officer who is perceived to be unreasonable in his or her analysis of the case, mediation is an economical alternative to litigation whereby the taxpayer can request that the case be mediated by a *different* Appeals Officer. Conversely, if the taxpayer and Appeals Officer disagree about the merits of the case in good faith, both parties have an opportunity to request that a third-party arbitrate the matter to reach a settlement.

The ADR procedures come with some costs. Mediation and/or arbitration extend the process of negotiation. Thus, taxpayers incur additional professional fees and opportunity costs to participate in a process that is not guaranteed to produce a resolution acceptable to the taxpayer. Additional professional fees may

be incurred while the IRS and taxpayer adjust to changing administrative procedures over time to implement the ADR techniques. Finally, taxpayers may view the
binding nature of arbitration as a cost that is too high relative to the benefits gained
from the procedure.

¶ 1240 Choosing Between Bilateral Alternatives

.01 Bilateral APA v. Competent Authority

The competent authority process discussed above, provides the taxpayer with
a limited opportunity to present its views to the competent authorities. In contrast, a
bilateral APA allows taxpayers to actively participate in the development of the U.S.
competent authority negotiating position. Even though the taxpayer is not present
during the actual negotiations between the U.S. and foreign competent authorities,
taxpayers remain in contact with both for purposes of assisting in the factual
development of the case and providing the taxpayer's viewpoint regarding the
methods and adjustments discussed.

The bilateral negotiation of APAs often takes less time than the competent
authority resolution of double tax cases. APA cases may be scheduled for negotiation without adherence to the schedule for double tax cases. Second, the APA
request includes nearly all information necessary to negotiate the case to its
bilateral conclusion. Taxpayer involvement in the APA process eliminates factual
questions and misunderstandings that may complicate the competent authority
negotiations. Finally, the prospective nature of the APA case means that neither
country will be required to give up revenue already received from the taxpayer,
except where the taxpayer requests rollback of the APA approach. Application of
the TPM developed in an APA to prior tax years not covered by the APA—
"rollback"—is an effective means of addressing unresolved transfer pricing issues.
IRS policy dictates that, whenever feasible, the TPM used in the APA should also
be used to resolve transfer pricing issues for prior taxable years.[119] The IRS deems
rollback appropriate where the business and economic conditions for the rollback
years are consistent with those of the APA years. Rollback contemplates application
of the TPM, comparable selection criteria, and financial adjustments to the rollback
years, not the application of the arm's length range developed in the APA. The
taxpayer may request a rollback in its APA request at any time before completion of
APA negotiations. Even without a taxpayer request for rollback, the IRS may
determine that the approach agreed to in an APA should be applied to prior
years.[120]

By seeking rollback with a bilateral or multilateral APA, the taxpayer can
resolve its open transfer pricing issues with all countries involved in a transaction.
The IRS will consider a taxpayer rollback request of a bilateral or multilateral APA
to years under examination, as a request for accelerated competent authority
assistance.[121] The IRS will treat a rollback request of a bilateral or multilateral APA
to years before Appeals as a request for SAP consideration.[122] In either circumstance, the taxpayer resolves all of its transfer pricing issues in one forum on an

---

[119] Rev. Proc. 2006-9, § 2.12.

[120] *Id.* at § 8.01.

[121] *Id.* at § 8.03.

[122] *Id.* at § 8.04.

accelerated basis. Not all treaty partners of the U.S. share the IRS enthusiasm for the rollback of APA methodologies; however, taxpayers have generally been able to obtain rollback for open years as long as no significant economic differences exist between the APA years and the prior years.

> *Comment:* As a practical matter, rollback is more difficult to achieve when one of the treaty partners would be required to provide a tax refund.

The prospect of rolling back an APA-developed TPM to resolve prior tax years often provides significant cost savings. Taxpayers can resolve all open tax years as well as five prospective tax years in a single negotiation.

> *Example:* XYZ Corporation's transfer pricing determinations are being examined for tax years 2000-2002 and tax years 2003-2005 are filed but not yet examined. ABC could potentially negotiate an APA to cover tax years 2006-2010 and rollback the approach to resolve all the other open years, both those under examination and those not yet under examination. A number of APAs have resolved 8 or more tax years through rollback.

.02 SAP v. Competent Authority

Where a taxpayer intends to seek competent authority assistance because the transfer pricing issue has merit and the *hazards of litigation* present the possibility of a substantial adjustment, the taxpayer should consider the SAP procedures. This also permits the linking of different audit cycles. Appeals may have jurisdiction over some years, while later years are subject to a bilateral or multilateral APA request involving competent authority. By requesting SAP, competent authority and Appeals can resolve the years together. Taxpayers can even request SAP to join intervening years under examination's jurisdiction by filing a SAP request as soon as the examination team proposes the adjustment but before filing a protest. By placing the years in Appeals and examination with years currently before competent authority and seeking an APA for future years, taxpayers can wrap up all of their transfer pricing issues in one coordinated negotiation.

¶ 1250 Coordination of Dispute Resolution Procedures

By coordinating these various approaches, taxpayers can minimize the costs and impose the results of resolving their transfer pricing disputes.

The APA program offers taxpayers the opportunity to resolve transfer pricing issues before the initiation of an audit, to apply a consensus-building approach to resolving such questions, and to apply the APA resolution to prior tax periods that may be in Examination or awaiting examination. In addition, when combined with proactive transaction planning, a taxpayer can plan its transfer pricing policies and practices with an eye toward obtaining an APA, and resolve transfer pricing issues prospectively. The use of bilateral and multilateral APAs offers taxpayers the opportunity to obtain cross-border certainty for many of its related party transactions.

For CIC taxpayers, Del. Ord. 236 (rev. 3) offers a mechanism for the Examination Case Manager to accept settlement offers consistent with Appeals settlements of the taxpayer's prior transfer pricing audits. This applies whether the Appeals settlement arose through the normal Appeals processes or through Early Referral or mediation.

AIR permits the extension of an examination resolution of an issue to subsequent unexamined, but filed, returns. Taxpayers can consider this for recurring transfer pricing issues; however, an APA may be preferable due to its consensus building approach, greater flexibility, and involvement of skilled IRS team leaders in the APA program office.

Issues incapable of resolution other than on a litigation hazards basis, or challenges to the validity of an established IRS position, may be appropriate for the Early Referral Program. If the IRS examination team can fully develop a transfer pricing issue, the taxpayer should consider requesting Early Referral. Early Referral offers few benefits when the taxpayer intends to seek competent authority assistance, except when the taxpayer hopes to combine years under audit with prior years already before competent authority. In addition, where a taxpayer believes that competent authority offers no benefit because the proposed adjustments lack any merit or the transaction involves non-treaty partner countries, pushing the development of the transfer pricing issues and seeking Early Referral may be appropriate.

The number of procedural alternatives to resolve transfer pricing and other tax disputes has increased dramatically in recent years. Most of these procedures can be categorized as providing one of two benefits: (1) moving the dispute to a more favorable forum, or (2) applying the resolution to additional tax years. Further, these procedures are not mutually exclusive. By coordinating these various approaches, taxpayers can minimize the costs of resolving their transfer pricing issues.

.01 APA: Linkage to Other Years and Procedures

The APA process can easily be combined with other procedures to resolve transfer pricing issues in the past years under the jurisdiction of Examination, Appeals and Counsel.[123] Further, IRS APA team members already possess jurisdiction for the taxpayer's other tax years.[124] Therefore, the APA process provides a vehicle to initiate resolution of transfer pricing issues for all prior tax years.

A bilateral APA presents the taxpayer with the opportunity to resolve transfer pricing issues with the United States and treaty partners for the prospective years covered by the APA and all open tax years. First, the prospective years will be developed through the APA process and transferred to the U.S. competent authority analyst for bilateral negotiations.[125] Filed but unexamined years can be resolved through the accelerated competent authority process.[126] Prior year transfer pricing issues under Appeals jurisdiction can be moved to competent authority by SAP.[127] Transfer pricing issues under jurisdiction of Examination can be segregated from other issues by the Early Referral procedure, and then transferred to the competent

---

[123] It is the Service's position that, whenever feasible, the TPM should be used for resolving such issues for prior years, with appropriate adjustment for differences in facts, economic circumstances, and applicable legal rules. Rev. Proc. 2006-9, § 2.12.

[124] Rev. Proc. 2006-9, § 8.

[125] *Id.*

[126] *Id.* at § 8.03.

[127] *Id.*

authority by SAP.[128] In this manner, transfer pricing issues in all prior and prospective years can be consolidated in the hands of the U.S. competent authority, who is then able to obtain resolution for all open tax years and the enumerated prospective years.

Rollback of TPM is not limited to bilateral APAs. The IRS is also committed to rollback of the TPM produced in the APA process for unilateral APAs.[129] In unilateral APAs, the prospective years are resolved with the IRS APA Team. Prior filed but not examined years remain under the jurisdiction of Examination, as do tax years currently under examination. Prior examined tax years with unagreed issues could be under the jurisdiction of either Appeals or Counsel. In this situation, the taxpayer could resolve prospective years with an APA, and "rollback" could be accomplished for all other years with closing agreements.

.02 Early Referral: Moving the Issue to Appeals

Taxpayers that are under examination and who can identify issues that are incapable of resolution at that level because of a Service position or *hazards of litigation*, can use Early Referral to accelerate the Appeals review of that issue. Interested taxpayers should make a written request to the CIC case manager with a copy to the Assistant Regional Director of Appeals. The approval process by both Appeals and the District should be accomplished within 45 days.

Because the Form 5701 containing the proposed adjustment may not be completed by Examination before submission of the Early Referral request, the request is not required to be as complete as an Appeals protest. Upon subsequent receipt of the Form 5701, the taxpayer's response to the proposed adjustment will serve the same purpose as an Appeals protest. This may also be the case where the IRS issues Form 5701 in draft form.

Compliance Coordinated Issues (CCI) can be referred to Appeals for resolution under the Early Referral procedures.[130] This can be important for taxpayers considering whether to use Examination or Appeals as the forum for resolving the issue. Examination may use an Appeals CCI guideline to resolve an issue in Examination's jurisdiction.[131] However, taxpayers who prefer an Appeals application of the CCI guideline should use Early Referral.

Transfer pricing issues are often not fully developed until the end of the examination process, and therefore in many cases there might not be sufficient time to seek Early Referral on those issues. Taxpayers may prefer not to "isolate" the transfer pricing issue by using Early Referral, preferring instead to use the transfer pricing issue to help resolve the entire case. Further, Early Referral is not available for issues for which the taxpayer has requested or intends to request

[128] Early Referral may be especially important when the taxpayer is negotiating an APA and there are unagreed, non-transfer pricing issues under Examination jurisdiction. If a 30-day letter is issued by Examination, it will include not only the unagreed domestic issues but also the transfer pricing issues, notwithstanding that there are ongoing APA negotiations. In this situation, the taxpayer should explore with Examination whether an

Early Referral request for the domestic issues could be submitted to Appeals, when it appears that the domestic issues will be unagreed.

[129] Rev. Proc. 2006-9, § 2.12.

[130] CCIs and ACIs are available at *www.irs.gov/pub/irs_utl/tg_issues_index.pdf; see also,* IRM 8.7.3.2.

[131] *See* Del. Ord. 247.

competent authority assistance.[132] If a taxpayer enters into a settlement with Appeals (including an Appeals settlement through the Early Referral process), and then requests competent authority assistance, the U.S. competent authority will endeavor only to obtain a correlative adjustment with the treaty country and will not take any actions that would otherwise amend the settlement.[133] Instead, taxpayers are encouraged to request SAP.[134]

As a planning matter, competent authority assistance may not be needed for transfer pricing adjustments that the taxpayer believes do not have merit. These types of transfer pricing issues lend themselves to settlement in Appeals. Taxpayers should identify this type of transfer pricing issue early in the examination process and consider using Early Referral to transfer the issue to Appeals for resolution.

.03 Delegation Order 236 (Rev. 3): Extending Appeals Settlements

Del. Ord. 236 (Rev. 3) allows Examination case managers to accept settlement offers with respect to issues where a settlement on the merits has been effected by Appeals in another tax period with respect to Coordinated Exam Program taxpayers. Del. Ord. 236 (Rev. 3) settlement authority also can be used in conjunction with settlements reached in Appeals through Early Referral and mediation.[135]

.04 SAP: Moving Issue to Competent Authority

For those transfer pricing issues that have merit, where the *hazards of litigation* are such that a large percentage of the adjustment may be sustained, the taxpayer should consider other dispute resolution options such as the SAP process. It appears that many taxpayers use the SAP process to combine several cycles of tax years with transfer pricing issues for resolution.[136] Since the resolution of an APA often is done in conjunction with a foreign competent authority, if there are prior years in Appeals jurisdiction, taxpayers can link their resolution of the prior years in Appeals with the APA by requesting the SAP. The SAP can also be used effectively when the taxpayer has intervening years under Examination jurisdiction.

SAP is available when Examination has proposed an adjustment regarding an issue which the taxpayer wishes to submit to competent authority, when the taxpayer files a protest letter and decides to seek competent authority relief regarding one issue while others remain with Appeals, or when, while the case is in Appeals the taxpayer decides to request competent authority assistance.[137]

The SAP encourages taxpayers to request competent authority assistance while the case is under Examination jurisdiction. This represents a change from the prior competent authority Rev. Proc. 91-23, which encouraged taxpayers to seek Appeals review before requesting competent authority assistance. The resulting Appeals settlements often made negotiations difficult with foreign competent authorities. Now, using the SAP, a taxpayer can obtain Appeals and competent

---

[132] Rev. Proc. 99-28, 1999-2 CB 109, at § 2.03(5).
[133] Rev. Proc. 2006-54, § 7.05.
[134] *Id.* at § 8.

[135] *Id.* at § 8.
[136] *Id.*
[137] *Id.* at § 8.02.

authority involvement while the case remains under Examination jurisdiction without issuance of a 30-day letter.[138]

SAP can also be accessed when the taxpayer is under Appeals jurisdiction. It may become evident at the first taxpayer conference with Appeals, or later, that it would be beneficial to transfer the issue to competent authority for resolution. This can be done using the SAP instead of waiting until the entire case is resolved by Appeals or there is a 90-day letter.[139]

Taxpayers should consider resolving the prospective APA years and the prior years under Appeals jurisdiction at the same time by requesting SAP for the prior years and linking the competent authority resolution of both prior and prospective years. Pre-filing conferences similar to the APA process are encouraged.[140] If the competent authority resolution of an SAP is rejected, the taxpayer can automatically return to Appeals.[141] In this event, the ACM prepared during the SAP would be applied by Appeals and the taxpayer to resolve the issue.

.05 Mediation and Arbitration: Alternatives to Litigation

Mediation, whether docketed or nondocketed, is generally considered only after good faith negotiations in the Appeals process have failed to produce resolution. Thus, discussion about mediation does not have to wait until the end of the Appeals process. Mediation can also be used in conjunction with Early Referral. If a taxpayer has an Early Referral issue in Appeals, and after settlement discussions it appears that the parties are at an impasse, mediation may be available as a part of the resolution of the Early Referral issue by Appeals.

Mediation is somewhat limited in coordination with other IRS ADR procedures. Mediation cannot be used if the issue is a coordinated issue under CCI or an ACI (CCI and ACI issues can go to Appeals under Early Referral). Mediation also generally is not used to resolve a competent authority issue. For the same reasons that apply in an Early Referral context, if mediation results in a settlement in Appeals, and competent authority assistance is later requested, the Assistant Commissioner (International) will seek only to obtain a correlative adjustment and will not take any actions that would otherwise amend the mediation settlement.[142] For those transfer pricing cases involving nontreaty countries, mediation may be an effective technique to resolve these issues without litigation.[143]

---

[138] *Id.* at § 5.02. Also "hot interest" is triggered under Code Sec. 6621(c). This is the same result when Early Referral is requested before a 30-day letter is issued.

[139] *Id.* at § 8.05.

[140] Representatives from Appeals National Office, Assistant Commissioner (International), and the Appeals region meet with the taxpayer to discuss SAP and whether it is appropriate for the taxpayer's case. When a taxpayer schedules an APA conference and there are also prior years involved in an SAP, efforts are made to schedule conferences on the same day. Usually, the APA conference takes place in Washington, D.C. and a morning session is scheduled for the taxpayer, Chief Counsel, Exam and Appeals representatives. The SAP conference for the taxpayer, competent authority and Appeals repre-

sentatives would follow the APA conference. In this way, the taxpayer can assemble all the necessary experts for meetings with the appropriate IRS personnel in a one-day session.

[141] Rev. Proc. 2006-54, § 8.07.

[142] For this reason, the Simultaneous Appeals/Competent Authority process described above may be more appropriate as a dispute resolution technique.

[143] *See* Comments of Elliot R. Fox, ed., 6 *J. Int'l Tax'n*, (Jan. 1995): "The success of the mediation program remains to be tested, but one can only imagine that it will reduce the inevitable hostility between taxpayers and the IRS in intercompany pricing cases. Even if mediation resolves only a small percentage of these cases, it will be well worth the effort put forth by the IRS."

If mediation was used in conjunction with an Early Referral request, and the issue was not resolved, a change in circumstances may occur. If mediation takes place at the end of the Appeals process and the parties cannot reach agreement, a change of circumstances is not likely to occur before the taxpayer is issued a 90-day letter. This result places emphasis on the fact that mediation is the last chance for the parties to resolve the issue in nondocketed status.[144]

If resolution is achieved through nondocketed mediation, the resulting settlement could then be used pursuant to Del. Ord. 236 (Rev. 3) to resolve other tax years. Thus, taxpayers can achieve a more efficient resolution for subsequent years through mediation.

Because a case must be in docketed in Tax Court prior to invoking the Rule 124 election of binding arbitration, this approach does not present the same opportunity to coordinate with other ADR procedures as some of the other new ADR procedures. In contrast to nondocketed mediation, no coordination with Early Referral or Del. Ord. 236 (Rev. 3) is possible. Therefore, the value of arbitration rests solely in its ability to achieve satisfactory resolution of the issue for the tax years in question.

---

[144] Form 906, Specific Matters Closing Agreement, is used.

¶1250.05

Chapter 13

Advance Pricing Agreements

¶ 1301 Introduction

Multinational enterprises ("MNEs") engaged in significant cross-border intercompany transactions are increasingly confronted with inconsistent home- and local-country transfer pricing rules and interpretations. Although there are several multinational groups working toward the goal of greater harmonization of global transfer pricing rules, the fruits of such efforts are still subject to inconsistent interpretation and enforcement at the local country level.[1] Consequently, MNEs need an approach that enables them to operate in a complicated and globally inconsistent transfer pricing enforcement environment.

Since 1991, the IRS Advance Pricing Agreement ("APA") Program has offered a common sense forum to address difficult transfer pricing issues.[2]

As of December 31, 2009, the IRS APA Program had completed 904 APAs since inception and has 352 APAs pending.[3] The IRS completed 63 APAs during the year ended December 31, 2009, consisting of 21 unilateral (with IRS only) and 42 multilateral (with both IRS and tax authority of U.S. treaty partner) agreements.[4] As of the end of 2009, at least 35 countries have adopted APA programs or similar procedures to obtain prospective confirmation of a taxpayer's transfer prices. These countries include most of the United States' major trading partners.

¶ 1310 APAs and APA Programs

.01 APAs Generally

The IRS increased its transfer pricing enforcement efforts in the late 1980s. In anticipation of a corresponding increase in transfer pricing disputes with taxpayers, the IRS developed the APA Program and issued its first revenue procedure to

---

[1] "Report on European Transfer Pricing—Related Penalty Regimes," 14 *Tax Management Transfer Pricing Report* 744 (Jan. 18, 2006); "EU Transfer Pricing Forum Report on Documentation," 14 *Tax Management Transfer Pricing Report* 558 (Nov. 9, 2005).

[2] Rev. Proc. 91-22, 1991-1 CB 526. The current IRS procedures for negotiating an APA are found in Rev. Proc. 2006-9, 2006-2 IRB 278.

[3] Announcement 2010-21, 2010-15 IRB, Table 1 (4/12/2010).

[4] *Id.*

govern the process in 1991.[5] APAs are prospective legal contracts between taxpayers and tax authorities that specify an arm's length range of results for specified intercompany transactions (the "covered transactions") between commonly controlled entities operating in different countries. The APA Program allows the taxpayer and the IRS to avoid future transfer pricing disputes by entering into a prospective agreement, generally covering at least five tax years, regarding the taxpayer's transfer prices. The agreement specifies the covered transactions, transfer pricing method ("TPM"), APA term, operational and compliance provisions, appropriate adjustments, critical assumptions regarding future events, required APA records, and annual compliance reporting responsibility.[6]

In 2006, the IRS published Rev. Proc. 2006-9 to update the process and incorporate a number of procedural innovations developed through sixteen years of experience.[7]

.02 Bilateral v. Unilateral APAs

Taxpayers may enter into APAs with more than one tax authority under the Mutual Agreement Procedure ("MAP") of most income tax treaties. Such APAs are referred to as "bilateral" or "multilateral," as opposed to "unilateral" APAs that involve agreements between only the IRS and the taxpayer. When a bilateral APA is available to be negotiated via the MAP process, the taxpayer must show sufficient justification for seeking a unilateral APA.[8] Although a unilateral APA with the United States may provide protection from U.S.-initiated adjustments and penalties, it provides no protection from foreign-initiated adjustments. The bilateral approach creates efficiency by involving both the U.S. and foreign tax authorities in the negotiation from the outset. According to the IRS, bilateral APA requests outnumber unilateral APA requests by at least a 2-to-1 margin.

.03 APA Rollbacks

APAs are intended to provide prospective resolution of transfer pricing issues. However, application of the TPM developed in an APA to open tax years not included in the APA term (rollback) may be an effective means of addressing unresolved transfer pricing issues. The IRS view is that the TPM agreed to in the APA should be applied to resolve transfer pricing issues for prior taxable years whenever feasible based on consideration of the facts, law and available records.[9] This policy does not apply to unilateral APAs in which a rollback decreases U.S. taxable income for a return filed in a taxable year not covered by the APA.[10]

Rollback is considered appropriate when the business and economic conditions for the rollback years are consistent with those of the APA years. Rollback contemplates application of the TPM, comparable selection criteria, and financial adjustments to the rollback years, not the application of the arm's length range

---

[5] Rev. Proc. 91-22.

[6] Rev. Proc. 2006-9, § 2.04.

[7] Rev. Proc. 2006-9. Additional information regarding the IRS APA process *available at http://www.irs.gov/businesses/corporations/article/0,,id=96277,00.html.*

[8] *Id.* § 2.08. Sufficient justification can include a balancing of the additional costs to negotiate a bilateral APA

versus the potential exposure for adjustment in the other country. It is for this reason that most small business taxpayer ("SBT") APAs are unilateral even though a bilateral APA is available.

[9] *Id.*, § 2.12.

[10] *Id.*

developed for the prospective period in the APA. The taxpayer may request a rollback in its APA request at any time prior to execution of the APA.[11] Taxpayers should be aware that the IRS might on its own initiative determine that the approach agreed to in an APA should be applied to prior years.[12]

For the year ended December 31, 2009, 35 percent of the APAs negotiated by the IRS included rollback periods ranging from one to more than five years.[13] Since most APAs have a prospective five year term, the addition of a rollback term could allow a taxpayer to cover eight or more years of transfer pricing issues in a single negotiation process.[14]

.04 The IRS APA Program

The APA Program is part of the Office of the Associate Chief Counsel (International) and is overseen on policy matters by the APA Policy Board.[15] The APA Director supervises and has overall responsibility for the APA Program and reports to the Associate Chief Counsel (International).[16] The APA Policy Board establishes policy on matters of substantial general importance pertaining to the APA Program and consists of the Associate Chief Counsel (International), the APA Director, the Director, International (Large and Mid-Size Business (LMSB) Operating Division), Treasury's International Tax Counsel, and other senior officials.[17]

In 2001, the IRS APA Program instituted an extensive training program to assist with its expansion efforts. The training materials are referred to as the Internal Revenue Service APA Program New Hire Training Manual (the Training Manual is not frequently updated).[18]

¶ 1320 Benefits Sought by Taxpayers

Taxpayers approach the APA process with a variety of goals. Some of the more common taxpayer goals include:

.01 Certainty

For most taxpayers, obtaining certainty regarding their transfer prices is the most important benefit sought via the APA process. This certainty extends to approval of the TPM, the arm's length range, protection against Code Sec. 482 adjustments and Code Sec. 6662 penalties, relief from double taxation and more accurate estimation of financial reserves attributable to potential transfer pricing adjustments. Assuming the taxpayer complies with terms and conditions of the APA, the IRS will regard the results of the taxpayer's TPM as satisfying the arm's length standard.[19] Further, any examination of transactions covered by the APA is limited to establishing the taxpayer's compliance with the APA.[20]

---

[11] *Id.*, § 8.02.

[12] *Id.* § 7.03.

[13] Announcement 2010-21, Table 29.

[14] *Id.*

[15] Rev. Proc. 2006-9, § 2.06.

[16] *Id.*

[17] *Id.*, § 2.09.

[18] The training materials have previously been released publicly. 10 *Tax Management Transfer Pricing Report (BNA)*, No. 15, Special Report No. 37, (Nov. 28, 2001). The APA Program updates the training materials on the IRS website, *www.irs.gov. See also,* "Seven APA Officials Discuss Program's Work in Financial Products, Cost Sharing, Other Areas," 16 *Transfer Pricing Report*, 80 (May 30, 2007).

[19] Rev. Proc 2006-9, § 10.02.

[20] *Id.* § 11.03.

An APA also addresses a taxpayer's uncertainty regarding transfer pricing recordkeeping.[21] Without an APA, a taxpayer may feel compelled to prepare annual documentation that analyzes all possible TPMs to establish that its methodology complies with the best method rule. After the taxpayer and the IRS negotiate an APA, the taxpayer may realize immediate recordkeeping reductions because it is only required to create documentation sufficient to support compliance with the APA.[22]

Another area of uncertainty that can be addressed through the APA process is the taxpayer's exposure to inconsistent and evolving interpretation and enforcement of transfer pricing rules in other countries and the attendant risk of double taxation.[23] The potential cost of uncertainty regarding a TPM has risen dramatically in recent years as many countries, including the United States, have stepped up their local transfer pricing enforcement efforts. These risks can only be eliminated prospectively by negotiating a bilateral APA. Therefore, it is not surprising that in 2009 over 80 percent of pending APAs were for bilateral agreements.[24]

.02 Make Changes or Fix Transfer Pricing Mistakes

Taxpayers sometimes negotiate APAs because they would like to implement changes in their transfer pricing policies (e.g., converting buy-sell distributors to marketing service providers) or fix prior mistakes (e.g., begin to charge royalties when no royalties were previously charged) in a controlled environment to limit U.S. and foreign audit exposure. In addition, if the taxpayer can demonstrate that a simplified TPM produces results similar to those produced under a more complex TPM, the IRS and foreign tax authorities will generally agree to the simplified TPM.

.03 Specific Tax Result

Some taxpayers want to achieve a specific tax result. This goal may be driven by a non-tax goal (e.g., repatriate profits to the parent corporation, geographic need for capital), an interest in moving all appropriate income to a low tax jurisdiction, or to utilize expiring net operating losses or to avoid a valuation allowance on net operating losses. Although governments may resist specific tax results as a goal of the taxpayer, such results are possible if the taxpayer can clearly demonstrate entitlement to the desired result.

.04 Taxpayer Involvement in Negotiations

All U.S. income tax treaties contain a Mutual Agreement Procedure (MAP) provision that encourages negotiations between the competent authorities to resolve disputes arising under the treaty, including transfer pricing disputes.[25] Taxpayers facing a U.S. or foreign-initiated transfer pricing adjustment may seek competent authority assistance to eliminate double taxation.[26] The competent au-

---

[21] Code Secs. 6038A and 6038C created recordkeeping exposure for taxpayers who are more than 25 percent foreign owned and for foreign corporations engaged in a trade or business within the United States, respectively. Code Sec. 6001 requires every person liable for tax to file tax returns and keep sufficient support for the positions taken therein.

[22] Rev. Proc. 2006-9, § 11.03.

[23] *Id.*, § 2.08.

[24] Announcement 2010-21, Table 1.

[25] U.S. Model Income Tax Convention of November 15, 2006, Art. 25.

[26] A taxpayer can seek competent authority assistance through several procedural paths. *See* Rev. Proc. 2006-54, 2006-49 IRB 1035.

thority process, a government-to-government negotiation intended to eliminate double taxation, provides the taxpayer with only a limited opportunity to present its views to the competent authorities once an adjustment has been proposed. In particular, the actual competent authority negotiations are conducted without the presence of the taxpayer or its representatives. In contrast, a bilateral APA allows taxpayers to actively participate in the development of the U.S. competent authority negotiating position. Even though the taxpayer is not present during the actual negotiations between the U.S. and foreign competent authorities, taxpayers remain in contact with both for purposes of assisting in the factual development of the case and providing the taxpayer's viewpoint regarding the TPMs and adjustments discussed.[27]

.05 Time and Cost Savings

Transfer pricing examinations are often time-consuming and expensive. Transfer pricing disputes involve complex factual and economic issues requiring subjective judgment. The confrontational approach often employed in an examination combined with poor communication can produce an impasse between the IRS and the taxpayer.

In a transfer pricing examination, the IRS will request extensive information about the taxpayer and the related parties involved in transactions with the taxpayer. The IRS's information requests often require the taxpayer to expend significant time and money providing great quantities of information, only some of which will ultimately be relevant to transfer pricing issues.

The APA process generally takes substantially less time to complete than a transfer pricing examination. An examination can easily last three to four years, with complex examinations continuing for longer periods. Following an unagreed examination, the taxpayer has a number of administrative and judicial alternatives, each of which could take years to conclude. In contrast, the IRS has set a goal of concluding unilateral APAs, and agreeing on the U.S. competent authority negotiating position for bilateral APAs within twelve months.[28] However, at this point the goal is more an aspiration than practical; in 2009, the median time to complete a unilateral APA was 18 months and the median time to complete a competent authority position paper was 18 months.[29]

.06 No Need to Update Comparables

An additional benefit of an APA is the elimination of the need to annually update the comparable company information used in preparing the taxpayer's transfer pricing documentation. Taxpayers without an APA are required to create contemporaneous documentation on an annual basis to support their transfer prices to avoid penalty exposure.[30] In doing so, taxpayers often rely on the comparable companies used in prior year documentation.[31] However, the taxpayer must update

---

[27] Rev. Proc. 2006-9, § 7.

[28] Rev. Proc. 2006-9, § 6.01.

[29] Announcement 2010-21, Tables 2 and 5.

[30] Reg. §§ 1.6662-6(b)(3); 1.6662-6(c)(6). The likelihood that the IRS will request the taxpayer's documentation has been increased dramatically by the LMSB Transfer Pricing Compliance Initiative.

[31] Reg. § 1.6662-6(d)(2)(ii)(D).

¶1320.06

the financial data of the comparable companies and perform all of the adjustments made in the initial report and compare the results to the taxpayer's results for the year.

An APA eliminates the need to update the comparables data. The APA generally sets a range of results for the entire term of the APA. The taxpayer need only compare its results to the range of results specified in the APA.[32]

.07 Rollback

In some cases, the prospect of the rollback of a TPM developed in an APA to resolve prior tax years provides the greatest incentive for seeking an APA. Rollback to resolve tax years under examination provides a cost-effective way to resolve an ongoing transfer pricing dispute. Taxpayers can resolve all open tax years as well as five prospective tax years in a single negotiation.[33] The term of the rollback is usually one to three years with several instances in which the rollback term has been five years or longer.[34] Consequently, the time and cost savings of eliminating transfer pricing controversy for a substantial number of years in one set of negotiations is a compelling reason to negotiate an APA.[35]

.08 Financial Accounting Goals

Since the enactment of the Sarbanes-Oxley Corporate Fraud and Accountability Act of 2002,[36] taxpayers have a new reason to request APA. Section 404 of the Sarbanes-Oxley Act requires a company to establish that it had controls in place to ensure accurate financial reporting.[37] Due to the subjective standards of transfer pricing and the large amounts at stake, some taxpayers have pursued APAs to ensure financial accounting certainty.[38]

More recently, FASB Interpretation No. 48 (FIN 48), *Accounting for Uncertainty in Income Taxes* (an interpretation of FASB Statement No. 109) (released in June 2006) requires a more detailed evaluation of their tax positions to determine the reportable amounts. FIN 48 applies to fiscal years beginning after December 15, 2006. Practitioners expect that FIN 48 will also encourage MNES to seek APAs to eliminate financial uncertainty.[39]

¶ 1330 The APA Negotiation Process

.01 General

Revenue Procedure 2006-9 sets forth the procedures the taxpayer must follow to negotiate an APA. In this process, taxpayers and the IRS reach prospective agreement regarding transfer pricing issues through negotiation. The negotiating

---

[32] Rev. Proc. 2006-9, § 10.02.

[33] Filing an APA request does not suspend any examination or other enforcement proceedings. *Id.*, § 2.13. As a practical matter, the IRS APA team will coordinate its efforts with the examination to avoid duplicative information requests, enhance efficiency, and reduce taxpayer compliance burdens.

[34] Announcement 2010-21, Table 29.

[35] 20 percent of the APAs negotiated in 2006 involved rollback. *Id.*

[36] P.L. 107-204.

[37] *Id.*

[38] "Large Multinationals Taking Steps to Ensure Pricing Process Meets Requirements of Sarbanes-Oxley Act, Practitioners Say," 13 *Tax Management Transfer Pricing Report* 1091 (March 16, 2005).

[39] "Practitioners Debate Impact of new M-3 FASB Guidance on Transfer Pricing Audits," 15 *Tax Management Transfer Pricing Report* 333 (September 13, 2006).

approach employed in the APA process differs greatly from the adversarial approach often employed in the examination process. The APA process employs cooperative and principled negotiations between the taxpayer and the IRS.[40] The IRS and taxpayer APA teams are expected to take reasonable positions consistent with objective standards. The taxpayer APA team must be open to and respond to the IRS APA team's concerns and viewpoints. Ultimately, the APA approach is more efficient than the adversarial approach due to more effective sharing of information.

The taxpayer's side of the APA process can be organized into phases:

- APA strategy and transfer pricing analysis;
- Prefiling Conference (PFC);
- Formal APA request;
- Evaluation and negotiation of the APA; and
- Administration and renewal.

As the APA proceeds, the interaction evolves from a general discussion of the taxpayer's industry and business to the specific transactions, through negotiations regarding the appropriate pricing approach and selection of comparable companies to drafting and administering the agreement.

.02 APA Strategy and Transfer Pricing Analysis

The Taxpayer's APA Team. The APA process involves a series of negotiations between experts from different disciplines: legal, accounting, and economics. The taxpayer's APA team usually includes both in-house personnel and outside representatives, depending on the capabilities and availability of in-house personnel. To establish credibility for the taxpayer's position and avoid confusion regarding the taxpayer's position on various points, it is important to clearly establish specific responsibility and authority within the taxpayer's APA team.

Lead Negotiator. The lead negotiator is the general spokesperson and coordinator for the taxpayer's APA team. The lead negotiator delegates responsibility for specific issues to other members of the taxpayer's APA team, but bears overall responsibility for the taxpayer's negotiating position and procedural decisions.

Tax Lead. The tax lead is responsible for the substantive correctness of the taxpayer's positions. The lead negotiator may also function as the tax lead, depending upon the complexity of the issues and the lead negotiator's familiarity with the taxpayer's operations.

Economic Lead. The economic lead is responsible for developing and defending the functional and risk analysis, the selection of the TPM, the selection of the comparables, and the adjustments to the comparables. Ideally, the economic lead will possess the communication skills necessary to explain complicated economic issues to non-economists.

Factual Lead. The factual lead is responsible for educating the IRS APA team regarding the taxpayer's industry, organization, and transactions. The factual lead

---

[40] Rev. Proc. 2006-9, § 2.01.

also obtains the internal information necessary to respond to subsequent factual inquiries made by the government APA team. The factual lead is often an in-house tax professional who is familiar with the transfer pricing decisions and the business reasons supporting those decisions.

Taxpayer Goals. As discussed above, taxpayers can enter the APA process with several goals. To best achieve those goals, the goals must be identified and prioritized. A clear understanding and ranking of goals will allow more effective preparation for the APA process.

Transfer Pricing Analysis. The transfer pricing analysis performed for an APA generally requires the same effort and level of detail and precision as is required to produce transfer pricing documentation. In fact, should the taxpayer and the IRS fail to conclude an APA, the transfer pricing analysis can, with minor adjustments, be used as a part of the taxpayer's documentation package.

.03 Prefiling Conference

General. A taxpayer is allowed to request a pre-filing conference ("PFC") before formally requesting an APA to explore informally the suitability of an APA and the level of information that will be required by the IRS in considering the request.[41] A taxpayer, or their representative, may contact the APA Program Office to schedule a PFC at the following offices:

Washington, DC
Voice: (202) 435-5220
Fax: (202) 435-5238

California
Voice: (949) 360-3486
Voice: (949) 360-3446

The taxpayer or its representative should be prepared to propose three alternative dates and should allow two weeks before the first proposed date.[42] PFCs can last from one to several hours, depending on the complexity of the case.

The PFC will be attended by an IRS APA program team leader, an economist, a competent authority analyst, and, a representative from the IRS Service Operating Division with jurisdiction over the taxpayer's return (i.e., a member from the IRS's local examination team). In appropriate circumstances, representatives from Appeals and Division Counsel may also attend.

Discussions at the PFC generally center on the taxpayer's business operations, past transfer pricing practices, and anticipated problems with the APA process. At the PFC, the taxpayer or its representative generally presents a proposed TPM and proposed parameters for the agreement, including the term of the APA, the parties to the APA, the transactions and businesses to be covered, and supporting documents. Taxpayers should take advantage of the PFC to determine what specific information, documentation, and analyses, in addition to that specified in the revenue procedure, should be included in their formal APA request.

---

[41] *Id.*, § 3.01.

[42] *Id.*, § 3.03.

If the TPM itself is expected to be the subject of considerable negotiation, the taxpayer may wish to present its preferred methodology at a PFC to receive the IRS reaction to the method before completing its analysis of other potentially applicable methods. Thus, a taxpayer can initiate the formal APA process with a proposed TPM without the expense of defensively analyzing all other methods.

Pre-File Submission. Before the PFC, the taxpayer is required to provide APA officials with a written document listing the persons expected to attend, and outlining the issues to be discussed.[43] The pre-file submission is usually the IRS APA team's first contact with the taxpayer, so the taxpayer should treat the pre-file submission as an opportunity to make a favorable first impression. The pre-file submission should be written in a non-adversarial fashion and explain the taxpayer's industry, corporate organization, transactions, and covered transactions (in practice many pre-file submissions take the form of a detailed PowerPoint presentation). It should also set out the proposed TPM (and historic TPM, if different), the term of the proposed APA, the terms and conditions of its comparable search, and proposed adjustments. Finally, it should indicate whether the taxpayer requests a bilateral or unilateral APA and whether the taxpayer wishes to request rollback of the agreement to resolve prior tax years. Pre-file submissions less than twenty pages may be faxed; for documents longer than twenty pages, eight copies (or if anonymous, three copies) and one original should be delivered.[44]

Named v. Anonymous Basis. Some taxpayers may be hesitant to discuss a potential APA due to the concern that a failure to pursue an APA may trigger an examination. To accommodate such taxpayers, the IRS permits PFCs to be held with the taxpayer's representatives on an anonymous basis. If the taxpayer has been involved or is currently involved in a difficult transfer pricing examination, there may be some tactical advantage to pursuing the PFC anonymously. If the PFC is anonymous, no representative of the district examination office will attend.[45] Thus, the taxpayer can discuss the issues without the potential baggage of the earlier relationship with the examination team.

Taxpayer and Taxpayer Representative Role. In the PFC, the taxpayer or its representative is expected to provide an explanation of the relevant facts, covered transactions, and proposed TPM. Typically, taxpayers use the pre-file submission as an agenda for the PFC. The taxpayer explains the industry, the taxpayer's organization, functions and risks, the proposed covered transactions, proposed TPM (and the previous TPM, if different), comparable selection criteria, and proposed data adjustments. Based on this presentation, the taxpayer requests the IRS APA Program's response to the proposed APA and recordkeeping requirements and any concerns or questions.

Government Role. The IRS APA personnel read the pre-file submission before the PFC to develop a familiarity with the taxpayer's facts and the proposed APA. The taxpayer's presentation at the PFC further familiarizes the IRS APA team and allows them to ask general background questions. The IRS representatives can then

---

[43] *Id.*, § 3.06.
[44] *Id.*

[45] *Id.*, § 3.05.

specifically respond, based on IRS APA Program experience with similar cases, to the taxpayer's proposed APA regarding the acceptability of the TPM, comparable search criteria, data adjustments, recordkeeping requirements, competent authority issues, level of requisite additional information and any other concerns. Note however, that while the IRS's comments made during a PFC are often very specific, the IRS APA program will reserve its rights to change its views and positions based on its review of the taxpayer's complete APA request.

.04 Formal APA Request

Filing Deadline. If the PFC is successful, the taxpayer should have a good understanding of the IRS reaction to the proposed APA and the areas of concern to the APA Program. Armed with this information, the taxpayer can begin drafting its formal APA request. The taxpayer must file the APA request within the time prescribed by statute for filing its Federal income tax return for the first year of the proposed APA term.[46] If the taxpayer receives an extension to file its Federal income tax return, it must file its APA request no later than the actual filing date of the return. The APA will be considered filed on the date the required user fee is paid provided that a substantially complete APA request is filed with the APA Program within 120 days of the return due date (including extensions) for the first proposed APA year.[47] The APA Director will consider extending this deadline only in unusual circumstances. Furthermore, the Director may consider the request to have been filed on a date subsequent to its actual filing in the event the APA Program's evaluation of a request is delayed due to a lack of responsiveness or timeliness by the taxpayer.[48]

Filing Fees[49]

	User Fee Structure (in U.S. Dollars)
Regular APA Request	50,000
Renewal of APA Request (routine/non-routine)	35,000/50,000
Small Business (SBT) APA Request	22,500
Renewal of SBT APA (routine/non-routine) Request	22,500
Amending APA Request or a Completed APA	10,000

General Content of APA Request. Rev. Proc. 2006-9 specifies the required contents of an APA request. Each taxpayer that is a member of a consolidated group (defined in Reg. § 1.1502-1) must comply with the provisions of § 1.1502-77 (a parent is the sole agent for the affiliated group).[50] Original documents will not be returned; only copies should be submitted with the request.[51] The taxpayer must

[46] *Id.*, § 4.07(2).

[47] For example, a taxpayer's calendar year 2006 could be covered by filing the user fee before September 15, 2006 (or the date on which the 2006 return was actually filed, if an extension was granted) if a comprehensive APA request submitted within 120 days of the user fee.

[48] Rev. Proc. 2006-9, § 4.07(2).

[49] *Id.*, § 4.12.

[50] *Id.*, § 4.02(1).

[51] *Id.*, § 4.02(2).

submit copies of any documents relating to the proposed TPM.[52] All materials must be properly labeled, indexed, and referenced in the request. Any previous documents that the taxpayer wishes to associate with the request must be referenced. If any of the required documents are too voluminous, the taxpayer must describe such items and confirm that they will be made available upon request.[53] All documents submitted in a foreign language must be accompanied by an accurate English translation.[54] Any documents that are available in electronic form (particularly the APA request itself and spreadsheets for the economic model) should be submitted on diskette or on a CD-ROM.[55]

Specific Content. The information required to be included in the APA request are listed in the Practice Tool at ¶ 20,130.

Signatures. The taxpayers or the taxpayer's authorized representative must sign the APA request.[56]

Copies and Mailing. User fees must be sent to:

> Internal Revenue Service
> Attn: CC:PA:LPD:DRU
> P.O. Box 7604
> Ben Franklin Station
> Washington, D.C. 20044[57]

One original and eight copies of the APA request and any supplemental materials must be mailed or delivered to:

> Office of Associate Chief Counsel (International)
> Advance Pricing Agreement Program
> Attn: CC:INTL:APA;MA2-266
> 1111 Constitution Avenue, N.W.
> Washington, D.C. 20224[58]

The APA Program office is physically located at:

> 799 9th Street, N.W.
> Washington, D.C. 20001

.05 Evaluation and Negotiation

General. Upon the filing of a substantially complete APA request, the IRS will designate an APA Team Leader to oversee the APA team's processing of the request. If the taxpayer participated in a PFC before filing the APA request, the IRS will generally select the team leader who presided over the PFC.[59] Within 45 days after the selection of the APA Team Leader, the IRS APA team is expected to meet with the taxpayer and its representatives to discuss the taxpayer's facts, issues, and reach agreement on the scope and nature of the APA team's due diligence.[60] The parties discuss the IRS concerns and questions and agree on any additional

---

[52] *Id.*, § 4.02(3).
[53] *Id.*, § 4.02(4).
[54] *Id.*, § 4.02(5).
[55] *Id.*, § 4.02(6).
[56] *Id.*, § 4.10.

[57] *Id.*, § 4.11(1).
[58] *Id.*, § 4.11(2).
[59] *Id.*, § 6.03.
[60] *Id.*, § 6.07(1).

information to be provided. After the IRS APA team receives the additional information from the taxpayer it evaluates the information, focusing on determining the appropriate transfer pricing methodology and an acceptable range of results. The parties then attempt to reach an informal agreement on the taxpayer's request, followed by a formal agreement. The evaluation of the request will not constitute an examination or inspection of the taxpayer's books and records under Code Sec. 7605(b) or other provisions of the Code.[61]

As discussed previously, the IRS APA program schedules the evaluation and negotiation with the goal of completing a unilateral APA or completing the recommended U.S. negotiating position within 12 months from the date the full request was filed.[62]

IRS Team. The function of the APA Team is the following: (1) for a bilateral or multilateral APA, to develop, in consultation with the taxpayer and consistent with sound tax administration, a competent authority negotiating position that it can recommend for approval, and (2) for a unilateral APA, to make best efforts, consistent with sound tax administration, to develop an APA that the APA Program can recommend for approval by the Associate Chief Counsel (International).[63] The roles of the team members are as follows:

IRS APA Team Leader. The IRS APA Team Leader coordinates the IRS negotiating efforts and sets the tone of the negotiations. Team leaders are usually attorneys or accountants. Team leaders have extensive transfer pricing experience and have received training in interest-based negotiating methods. They work to coordinate the activities of the other IRS team members and to focus the negotiations on resolving the issues necessary to reach an agreement, applying the best method principles and a principled negotiation approach. Although the IRS APA team leader may negotiate the APA, authority to conclude or execute an APA resides with the APA Director.[64]

APA Branch Chief. The IRS APA Program has four branch chiefs who assist the APA Director in managing the APA caseload. The branch chiefs are charged with reviewing the cases within their respective branch to ensure that Section 482 is applied in a consistent manner. In addition, the branch chiefs monitor the scheduling of individual cases to ensure that cases are processed in a timely manner. Branch chiefs also assist in resolving any differences in opinion between the IRS team leader, economist and field representatives.

IRS APA Economist. The IRS APA economist is responsible for reviewing and critiquing the functional and risk analysis, the comparables selection and adjustments, and the TPM proposed by the taxpayer. The IRS APA economist frequently suggests modifications to the selection and adjustments of the taxpayer's proposed comparables. Occasionally, the economist will suggest changes in the TPM; however, this can generally be avoided if the PFC was both thorough and candid. Due

---

[61] *Id.*, § 6.06.
[62] *Id.*, § 6.01.
[63] *Id.*, § 6.05.

[64] In March 2001, the Associate Chief Counsel (International) delegated authority to the APA Director to execute APAs on behalf of the IRS. Internal Revenue Service—Office of Chief Counsel, Notice CC-2001-016, (Mar. 1, 2001).

¶1330.05

to heavy caseloads, some cases will include an IRS transfer pricing economist from other than the APA program.

IRS Field (Examination) Team. The IRS APA team generally includes an LMSB international examiner and LMSB field counsel from the IRS Operating Division that would otherwise conduct an examination of the taxpayer. If the taxpayer is currently undergoing a transfer pricing examination, the international examiner comes from the examination team conducting the transfer pricing examination. In addition, when the taxpayer is subject to a transfer pricing examination, the IRS field team may include the IRS examination Team Coordinator and others from the examination team with knowledge of the taxpayer, the taxpayer's operations, and its related party transactions. The IRS field team assists other IRS team members to obtain a thorough understanding of the taxpayer's operations and activities, functions, risks, and evaluate the impact of a rollback of the APA TPM on the years under examination. This group will be provided an opportunity to review and comment on the recommended U.S. competent authority negotiating position in the case of a bilateral or multilateral APA, and the proposed APA in the case of a unilateral APA.[65]

Competent Authority Analyst. When a taxpayer requests a bilateral APA, the IRS APA team includes a competent authority analyst. The competent authority analyst advises the IRS APA team and the taxpayer's APA team of positions likely to be acceptable to the foreign competent authority in the negotiations with the United States. The IRS and taxpayer's APA teams use this information to develop an initial negotiating position for the United States that has the greatest likelihood of success, taking into account the concerns of the foreign tax administration.

Issue/Industry Coordination Teams. The IRS APA Program has created formal Issue/Industry Coordination Teams to specialize in specific issues and industries. One of the primary goals of such teams is to improve consistency in negotiating cases. The teams are as follows:

- Autos and Auto Parts
- Pharmaceuticals and Medical Devices
- Cost Sharing
- Financial Products
- Semiconductors

APA Case Plan. The APA case plan was adopted by the APA Program to ensure that APA cases proceed in a timely fashion. The APA procedures require the taxpayer and the IRS APA teams to agree on a case plan during their initial post-filing meeting.[66] The case plan will be signed by both an APA manager and an authorized official of the taxpayer.[67] The case plan may identify issues raised by the APA Team's initial review of the APA request. Firm dates should be agreed upon for resolving all outstanding issues, and case milestones should be cited. Case milestones include: (a) submission of any necessary additional information by the

---

[65] Rev. Proc. 2006-9, § 6.05.
[66] *Id.*, § 6.07(2).
[67] *Id.*

taxpayer; (b) any planned site visits or interviews; (c) evaluation of the information by the Service; (d) meeting dates; and (e) presentation of the competent authority negotiating position or recommended agreement to the APA Director.[68] Generally, the case plan should reflect an agreement between the taxpayer and the IRS on the scope and nature of any additional information that will be required to resolve the identified issues.[69] This provides the taxpayer with the opportunity to negotiate with the IRS regarding the information to be provided, in many cases limiting such information to only that necessary to resolve the issue.

Failure to meet case deadlines will be addressed promptly. The APA Director will assist in remedying any difficulties to ensure a course of action to meet case milestones.[70]

For the taxpayer, failure to meet its obligations under the case plan can result in the Service treating the APA request as withdrawn.[71] Failure of the IRS team to meet its obligations may result in the involvement of IRS District and Regional supervisors.[72] As a practical matter, taxpayers seldom fail to meet the case deadlines and they appreciate the ability to encourage the IRS to reach closure on preliminary issues.

Working Groups. Issues that arise in APA negotiations generally fall into one of three broad categories: procedural, factual, or economic. Occasionally, the development of one or more issues within a category requires in-depth study by persons from both the IRS and taxpayer APA teams, but not necessarily all of the APA team members from both sides. In this situation, the involvement of all team members in the discussions can hinder, rather than assist, in the prompt resolution of the issue. To efficiently resolve such issues, APA teams often form "working groups" to deal with those issues. The working groups generally consist of specialists in a particular issue and the working groups have no authority to bind their respective team. Rather, if the working groups achieve tentative resolution of the issues, the tentative resolution will be presented to the full APA teams for approval.

Most commonly, economic working groups have been formed to focus on economic issues such as propriety of selection criteria for comparables and adjustments to the comparables. However, working groups have also been used to develop issues such as allocation of overhead expenses between different product lines or life of intangibles. The ability of working groups to segregate and achieve tentative resolution of preliminary issues without full involvement of the APA teams improves the efficiency of the APA process.

Critical Assumptions. The taxpayer requesting an APA must propose critical assumptions to support the APA. Critical assumptions are facts outside the control of the taxpayer or the IRS, the continued existence of which is material to the outcome of the TPM.[73] Critical assumptions might include, for example, a particular

---

[68] *Id.*

[69] *Id.*

[70] *Id.*, § 6.07(4).

[71] *Id.*

[72] Initially, taxpayers and practitioners objected to the Case Plan because a taxpayer failure to reach case mile-

stones was met with more severe consequences than an IRS failure to meet a case milestone. However, taxpayer criticisms have subsided because the consequences of a taxpayer failure were reduced. In fact, practitioners are generally pleased with the Case Plan.

[73] Rev. Proc. 2006-9, § 4.05.

mode of conducting business operations, a particular corporate or business structure, a range of expected business volume, or the relative value of foreign currencies. There is one critical assumption that is included in every APA:

> The business activities, functions performed, risks assumed, assets employed, and financial and tax accounting methods and classifications [and methods of estimation] of Taxpayer in relation to the Covered Transactions will remain materially the same as described or used in Taxpayer's APA Request. A mere change in business results will not be a material change.

While most taxpayers view critical assumptions as protecting the IRS, they can also protect the taxpayer in the event unforeseen events cause the taxpayer to report a lower profitability. For example, if the IRS was concerned that large currency fluctuations could impact the taxpayer's results and the taxpayer did not believe that large fluctuations would occur, the taxpayer could agree to a critical assumption that currency values remain within a particular range. On the other hand, a taxpayer concerned about the impact of anticipated new technology on existing products could request critical assumption that would allow the taxpayer to revise downward the profit expectations on transactions regarding products that are suddenly obsolete.

Although taxpayers are required to include proposed critical assumptions in their APA request, as a practical matter, most critical assumptions are drafted during the final APA negotiations when the parties, who may have differing factual expectations, are attempting to find agreement. Critical assumptions used in APAs executed in 2006 include, among others:

- Material changes to the business;
- Material changes to tax and/or financial accounting practices; and
- Assets will remain substantially the same.

Recent public statements by the APA Program staff indicate that the IRS is taking a formal legal approach to determine whether an APA should be amended or cancelled by reason of a critical assumption being triggered. This has caused taxpayers to carefully consider the critical assumptions included in the APA.

Competent Authority Negotiations. The IRS assigns a competent authority analyst to participate in the APA negotiations for all bilateral and multilateral APAs. Assuming the negotiations between the taxpayer APA team and the IRS APA team have been successful, the next stage of a bilateral APA consists of the competent authority negotiations. The involvement of a U.S. competent authority analyst throughout the APA process should ensure that the U.S. negotiating position takes into account positions maintained by the foreign tax authority. In addition, the IRS competent authority staff maintains contact with the foreign competent authority so that both the U.S. and foreign competent authorities will have developed a simultaneous understanding of the APA request, including the relevant facts and the proposed TPM. Finally, the taxpayer's foreign affiliate should keep the foreign competent authority advised of the U.S. APA negotiations and their progress, and forward to the taxpayer APA team the concerns of the foreign tax authority. If these coordination activities have gone well, the final competent authority negotiations should go smoothly and relatively quickly.

¶1330.05

Competent authority negotiations do not permit direct taxpayer involvement. However, the competent authority analysts generally both share a position paper and meet with the taxpayer to obtain information and listen to the taxpayer's position on issues. These meetings can be helpful to both the taxpayer and the competent authority analyst as the taxpayer remains involved in the process and the competent authority analyst has access to taxpayer information.

Final agreement to the negotiated APA will be sought among the taxpayer, the IRS, and the foreign competent authority. If a competent authority agreement is not acceptable to the taxpayer, the taxpayer may withdraw the APA request. When competent authorities are unable to reach agreement, the IRS will attempt to negotiate a unilateral APA with the taxpayer.[74]

Bilateral APA negotiations are not limited to the terms of the TPM. Additional issues include exchanges of information between tax authorities on issues such as subsequent modifications, cancellations, revocations or renewals of the APA, rollback of the TPM to resolve transfer pricing issues in prior years, evaluations of the annual reports, and examinations of the taxpayer's compliance with the terms and conditions of the APA. Bilateral APAs may require simultaneous filing of annual reports with the IRS and the foreign tax administration.[75]

Drafting the APA. The IRS has released a boilerplate draft APA which is used to draft APAs. The most recent boilerplate is included as an appendix to the most recent IRS APA annual report and is included herein at ¶ 20,140.[76]

.06 Administration and Renewal

The APA Annual Report. Once the APA has been finalized, certain administrative procedures must be followed, including the filing of an annual report that demonstrates: (1) the taxpayer's good faith compliance with the terms and conditions of the APA; (2) the calculation of any adjustments; and (3) compliance with any critical assumptions.[77] Taxpayers must submit an original and four copies of the annual report to the IRS APA office by the later of a) 90 days after the time prescribed by statute for filing its federal income tax return for the year covered by the report, or b) 90 days after the effective date of the APA.[78] A copy of the APA Annual Report Summary Form is attached at ¶ 20,140.[79] In addition, the taxpayer must maintain books and records sufficient to enable the IRS to examine the taxpayer's compliance with the APA. Although this is a significant undertaking, it is less effort than a documentation update.

Generally, the taxpayer will represent in the annual report that its activities have not materially changed from those described to the IRS during the APA negotiations and the critical assumptions continue to be met. The taxpayer will then apply the TPM to its results for the year in question and compare those results to the results required by the APA, make any necessary adjustments and reflect the computations and adjustments in a report provided to the IRS. The IRS APA office

---

[74] *Id.* § 7.02.
[75] *Id.* § 7.05.
[76] Announcement 2010-21.

[77] Rev. Proc. 2006-9, § 11.01.
[78] *Id.*, § 11.01(2).
[79] Announcement 2010-21, Appendix E.

¶1330.06

reviews the annual reports, contacting taxpayers if it in necessary to clarify or complete the information in the report.[80]

APA Primary Adjustments. If the taxpayer's results for a year covered by an APA do not come within the range called for in the APA, the APA will generally require the taxpayer to make an adjustment to move its results to a point within the agreed range of results.[81] Whereas the Section 482 regulations call for an adjustment to the median in the examination context, most APAs call for an adjustment to a point at the edge of the range.[82] The taxpayer should reflect the APA primary adjustment on its timely filed return for the period in question.[83] If the taxpayer is unable to make the adjustments on its original return for the period, the taxpayer must reflect the adjustments on an amended return filed within 120 days of entering into the APA.[84] APA primary adjustments are deemed to have been made on the last day of the tax year to which the adjustment applies.[85]

Taxpayers may also face "Secondary Adjustments" when normal or routine adjustments are made by the taxpayer or the IRS. These adjustments may arise, for example, from the correction of computational errors. Such subsequent compensating adjustments will be subject to generally applicable Code provisions relating to assessments, collection, and refunds of tax.[86]

Examination. An APA provides protection against an in-depth transfer pricing examination and corresponding transfer pricing examination. The existence of an APA does not prevent an examination per se, but the IRS may still require the taxpayer to establish:

- Compliance with the APA's terms and conditions;
- Validity and accuracy of the annual report's material representations;
- Correctness of the supporting data and computations used to apply the TPM;
- Satisfaction of the critical assumptions; and
- Consistent application of the TPM.[87]

The IRS will not reconsider the APA's TPM.[88] If the examination determines that any of these elements are not satisfied, the Service Operating Division must inform the APA Director. After consultations with the appropriate Service Operating Division personnel, the Associate Chief Counsel (International) must then determine whether to enforce, revise, cancel or revoke the APA.[89]

Any other audit adjustments not involving the interpretation of the TPM that affect the determination or computation of the operating results under the APA, can be made without affecting the validity of the APA.[90] If agreed by the taxpayer, the corresponding adjustment to the transfer pricing is made through an additional

---

[80] *Id.*, § 11.01(3).
[81] *Id.*, § 11.02.
[82] Announcement 2007-31, Table 27.
[83] Rev. Proc. 2006-9, § 11.02(1).
[84] *Id.*
[85] *Id.*, § 11.02(3).

[86] *Id.*, § 11.02(2).
[87] *Id.*, § 11.03(2).
[88] *Id.*, § 11.03(1).
[89] *Id.*, § 11.03(3).
[90] *Id.*, § 11.03(4).

compensating adjustment and treated as a subsequent compensating adjustment. Taxpayers have the right to challenge the proposed adjustments using normal administrative and judicial procedures.[91]

Recordkeeping. Generally, taxpayers are required to maintain books and records sufficient to establish the correctness of their returns. In the APA context, taxpayers must maintain records sufficient to demonstrate their compliance with the terms and conditions of the APA. As part of APA negotiations, the taxpayer and the IRS may agree to the documents that the taxpayer must maintain to demonstrate compliance. If requested during an examination, the taxpayer must produce the agreed-upon records within 30 days of the request as extended for good cause.

Revocation, Cancellation, or Revision of an APA. Fraud, malfeasance, or disregard on the part of the taxpayer involving material facts set forth in the APA request, submissions made during the APA negotiations, or in the annual report, or lack of good faith compliance with the terms or conditions of an APA can lead to IRS revocation of the APA.[92] The IRS can revoke the APA retroactively to the first day of the first tax year to which the APA applies.[93] Revocation of the APA exposes the taxpayer to a transfer pricing examination, adjustments and penalties for all open years, and the possibility of a limitation or loss of Rev. Proc. 99-32 relief. In addition, in egregious cases, the IRS may deny the taxpayer foreign tax credits under Rev. Rul. 80-231 and unilateral relief under Rev. Proc. 2006-54.[94]

The IRS may cancel, rather than revoke, the APA due to the taxpayer's misrepresentation, mistake as to a material fact, failure to state a material fact, failure to file a timely annual report, or lack of good faith compliance with the terms and conditions of the APA.[95] Generally, the cancellation will be effective as of the beginning of the year in which the misrepresentation, mistake, failure to state a material fact, or noncompliance occurs.[96] The IRS may waive cancellation if the taxpayer can establish good faith and reasonable cause, and agrees to make the adjustments required by the IRS to correct for the misrepresentation, mistake, failure to state a material fact, or noncompliance.[97]

Failure to meet a critical assumption, or changes in a law or treaty that supersedes and conflicts with the APA, may require a revision of the APA.[98] If the IRS and the taxpayer fail to reach an agreement on the revision, the IRS can cancel the APA. If the revision relates to a bilateral APA, the revised APA is submitted by the U.S. competent authority to the foreign competent authority for its agreement with the revisions.

.07 Renewal

A taxpayer may request a renewal by following the same procedures that apply to an initial APA request, updating information and highlighting significant changes. As long as the functions and risks between the parties remain similar to those in the initial APA, the renewal should be granted relatively quickly with little

---

[91] *Id.*

[92] *Id.*, § 11.06(1).

[93] *Id.*, § 11.06(6).

[94] *Id.*

[95] *Id.*, § 1.06(2).

[96] *Id.*, § 11.06(7).

[97] *Id.*, § 10.06(5).

[98] *Id.*, § 11.05.

debate or renegotiation. The user fee for a routine renewal is less than that for the original request. Taxpayers are encouraged to file their requests to renew an APA no later than nine months before the end of the term of the existing APA.[99]

In general, negotiating a renewal APA should take less time and fewer resources than negotiating the original APA. If the relevant intercompany transactions, functions, and risks remain the same as the original APA, negotiating a renewal should be limited to updating the economic analysis. However, the APA program has indicated that it would more closely scrutinize an APA renewal application if the taxpayer's results during the term of the original APA consistently fall at the bottom edge of the agreed upon arm's length range.[100]

¶ 1340 Small Business Taxpayer APAs

The Small Business Taxpayer ("SBT") APA Program uses streamlined procedures that are designed to allow eligible taxpayers to obtain the compliance certainty of an APA at a cost that is reasonable relative to the size and complexity of the transactions involved.[101] SBT APAs are generally unilateral, but can also be bilateral.

The SBT APA Program is generally available to taxpayers with gross income of $200 million or less, determined by aggregating the gross income of all of the organizations, trades, or businesses owned or controlled directly or indirectly by the same interests controlling the taxpayer (the "gross income test").[102] In addition, SBT procedures are available to small transaction APAs, if the transactions that are the subject of the APA (the "covered transactions") involve either: (1) tangible property and/or services with a total annual value not in excess of $50 million per year, or (2) payments for intangible property not exceeding $10 million per year (the "small transactions test").[103] Taxpayers engaging in intercompany transactions involving valuable intangible property will be considered on a case-by-case basis due to the complexity of valuing such intangibles.

A SBT taxpayer may request a PFC to determine as early as possible the best method for the proposed covered transactions. At least 60 days prior to the PFC, the taxpayer will need to submit a detailed description of the underlying facts and proposed TPM to the APA Program.[104] The SBT will then be advised of the APA Team's initial conclusions before the PFC so that it can address the issues before or at the conference.[105] The goal of the IRS APA Program is to finalize recommended negotiating positions for a bilateral APA or conclude a unilateral APA within six months of the date the SBT files its APA request.[106]

In addition, the APA Program:

- May reduce or eliminate specific items otherwise required for an APA submission;[107]

---

[99] *Id.*, § 12.01.

[100] *See generally* "Foley Reveals Thinking on Commissions, Averaging Versus Pooling, Other Areas," 10 *BNA Transfer Pricing Report* No. 2 (May 16, 2001).

[101] *See generally* Rev. Proc. 2006-9, at § 9.

[102] *Id.*, § 9.01.

[103] *Id.*

[104] *Id.*, § 9.02(2).

[105] *Id.*, § 9.02(3).

[106] *Id.*, § 9.02(4).

[107] *Id.*, § 9.03.

- Will endeavor to hold meetings with the SBT at a location convenient to the SBT, including holding teleconferences whenever possible;[108] and,
- Will assist the SBT in the selection and evaluation of comparables, including adjustments to comparables.[109]

For unilateral requests, a SBT should consult the APA Program's current Model APA when submitting a proposed draft APA.

The SBT APA Program has proven to be very successful in providing transfer pricing certainty to small and mid-size taxpayers. The IRS negotiated 5 SBT APAs in 2009.[110]

¶ 1350 Global APA Programs

APA Programs in Other Countries. The APA approach for resolving transfer pricing issues continues to gain greater global acceptance. Increases in APA caseloads and significant revisions and additions to APA programs occur daily, as nations are rapidly incorporating their negotiating experience into formalized procedures for obtaining APAs.[111] APAs are now available in the following countries: Australia, Belgium, Brazil, Canada, China, Colombia, Denmark, Finland, France, Germany, Hungary, Ireland, Israel, Japan, Korea, Mexico, Netherlands, New Zealand, Peru, Singapore, Spain, Sweden, Thailand, United Kingdom, and Venezuela.[112] Many of these countries have adopted APA models similar to that of the United States.[113] Summarized below are basic facts about the APA programs, and some of the latest APA developments, in the major treaty partners of the United States and other OECD countries.

.01 Australia

Australia has formal guidelines for taxpayers who wish to pursue either unilateral or bilateral APAs. The Australian program incorporates the benefits of one or several PFCs, and allows for anonymity in the process, up to a point, beyond which it becomes impractical to continue anonymously. Usually, APAs are negotiated to cover three to five years, and rollback, as in the United States, is an available and useful tool for resolving issues in prior years.

---

[108] *Id.*, § 9.04.

[109] *Id.*, § 9.05.

[110] Announcement 2010-21, Table 10.

[111] "Countries Report Growing Interest in APAs; Canada Restructures, Creates Two Divisions," 10 *Tax Management Transfer Pricing Report* 718 (Jan. 9, 2002). "Sweden: Swedish Parliament to Take Up Legislation for an APA Program," 18 *Tax Management Transfer Pricing Report* 601 (October 22, 2009). "India: India Advised to Make APA Program Bilateral to Stem Potential MAP Cases," 18 *Tax Management Transfer Pricing Report* 854 (December 17, 2009).

[112] Deloitte Touche Tohmatsu, *Strategy Matrix for Global Transfer Pricing: Comparison of Methods, Documentation, Penalties and Other Issues*, 2007. The *Strategy Matrix for Global Transfer Pricing* is not a complete survey of global APA programs.

[113] *See* e.g., "NTA Releases Japan's First APA Report, Says Requests, Completed Cases Growing," 12 *Tax Management Transfer Pricing Report* 521 (Oct. 15, 2003); Wrappe et al, "APA Procedures: U.S. vs. OECD," 39 *Tax Notes Int'l.*, 67 (July 4, 2005); Wrappe et al, "Side-by-Side Comparison of Advance Pricing Agreement Procedures: United States and Japan," 37 *Tax Notes Int'l* 401 (Jan. 31, 2005); Wrappe et al, "Advance Pricing Agreement Procedures: U.S. and Mexico," 38 *Tax Notes* 341 (April 25, 2005); Wrappe et al, "Side-by-Side Comparison of APA Procedures: United States and Canada," 36 *Tax Notes Int'l* 1043 (Dec. 20, 2004); Wrappe et al, "Side-By-Side Comparison of Advance Pricing Agreement Procedures for the U.S. and France," 37 *Tax Notes Int'l*, 1195 (March 28, 2005); Wrappe et al, "Side-By-Side Comparison Of Advance Pricing Agreement Procedures for the U.S. and the U.K.," 18 *Tax Notes Int'l* 845 (Aug. 29, 2005); Wrappe et al, "Side-by-Side Comparison of Advance Pricing Agreement Procedures: United States and China," 37 *Tax Notes Int'l* 809 (Feb. 28, 2005).

A report released by the Australian Taxation Office ("ATO") concluded that the transactional net margin method ("TNMM") is the most commonly used transfer pricing method in APAs. The TNMM is very similar to the U.S. comparable profits method, also the most common method in U.S. APAs.[114]

The ATO completed 29 APA cases for the year ending June 30, 2009.[115]

.02 Canada

Canada issued revised procedural guidelines for obtaining APAs in March 2001. The guidelines introduced structural as well as procedural changes to the already existing APA program, including case planning enhancements to expedite cases. Canadian taxpayers can pursue both unilateral and bilateral APAs. Informal pre-File meetings are available and can be conducted anonymously. Pre-File meetings should be held within 180 days of the end of the first taxation year to be covered by the APA. Generally, APAs are negotiated prospectively for terms of three to five years, although facts and circumstances may allow for lesser or greater periods of coverage. Rollback is available for non-statute-barred taxation years.

The Canada Revenue Agency accepted 32 APA requests in 2008-2009, completed 10 cases and the inventory reached a total of 84 cases at the end of March 2009.[116]

.03 China

China first began processing APAs in 1998, and it has completed approximately 130 unilateral APAs since then. On September 20, 2004, China's State Administration of Taxation ("SAT") released formal APA rules that may open the door for taxpayers to negotiate agreements for entities in different regions directly with the SAT.[117] The rules for the first time clearly delineate that it is the SAT's responsibility to ensure coordination among tax authorities if an APA involves companies in more than two provinces, more than one tax authority, or intercompany transactions of more than RMB 10 million (approximately US$1.25 million).

Under the formal APA rules, the APA process includes six major phases: pre-File, formal application, review and evaluation, negotiation and drafting of the APA, signing the APA, and administration. The formal rules extend the APA term to a maximum of five years (including the application year).

On October 26, 2009, the SAT signed the first bilateral APA with a European tax authority.[118]

---

[114] "Australian Advance Pricing Arrangement Program Developments in 2002-2003," 12 *Tax Management Transfer Pricing Report* 673 (Nov. 26, 2003).

[115] "Competent Authority: Competent Authority Inventories Growing, Despite More Completed Cases, Officials Say," 18 *Tax Management Transfer Pricing Report* 852 (December 17, 2009).

[116] "Canada: Canada's APA Inventory Climbs to 84, With 32 New Cases Received in 2008-2009," 18 *Tax Management Transfer Pricing Report* 1166 (March 25, 2010).

[117] Implementation Rules on Advance Pricing Agreements for Related-Party Transactions, released 9/20/04.

[118] "Advance Pricing Agreements: Danish Biotech Firm Novozymes First to Obtain European-Chinese APA," 18 *Tax Management Transfer Pricing Report* 654 (November 5, 2009).

.04 France

France has formal APA guidelines according to which taxpayers may pursue bilateral APAs. In practice, unilateral APAs are also available. While PFCs are available to taxpayers (and may be anonymous), the process is limited to special consideration cases.[119] APAs are generally negotiated for three to five years and rollback is currently not available.

France concluded its first bilateral agreement at the end of 2001.[120] The program has since overcome early problems and has reached "cruising speed," with 20 APAs in the negotiation stage as of May 2004.[121] Recent APA initiatives in France include introduction of unilateral APAs and establishing procedures designed to facilitate the APA process for small business taxpayers.[122]

.05 Japan

On June 1, 2001, Japan issued a directive providing updated guidelines for pursuing an APA. Unilateral and bilateral APAs are available to taxpayers in Japan, although the National Tax Administration ("NTA") prefers bilateral APAs. PFCs are available. In principle, APAs are for three years, although longer terms may also be negotiated. Rollback is available.

The NTA accepted 130 APA requests in 2008, processed 91 cases and the inventory reached a total of 261 cases.[123]

.06 Mexico

Under Mexico's formal APA guidelines, unilateral and bilateral APAs are permitted. Taxpayers are able to request PFCs. APA terms can be up to three years prospectively, and rollback is allowed for one year only.

In June 2002, Mexico's Tax Administration Service negotiated its first break-even maquiladora APA.[124] The achievement allows a maquiladora to report a break-even result, despite historically requiring a profit for the low-risk exposure maquiladoras.[125] The move, coupled with other efforts to expedite the APA process, such as eliminating a burdensome six-member board approval of each APA, clearly indicates Mexico's commitment to the success of the APA program, as well as to preserving the competitiveness of its maquiladora industry.[126] In 2004, Mexico had around 300 APA requests pending, signifying the continued success of the program.[127]

---

[119] Implementation Rules on Advance Pricing Agreements for Related-Party Transactions, released 9/20/04.

[120] "First French APA Concluded With Automaker, More APAs May Be Coming, Practitioner Says," 10 *Tax Management Transfer Pricing Report* 927 (Mar. 20, 2002).

[121] "French APA Program Seeing Boost in Completions, Requests, APA Head Says," 13 *Tax Management Transfer Pricing Report* 65 (May 26, 2004).

[122] *See* "France: Parliament Passes Annual Finance Bill Creating Unilateral APAs, Advance PE Rulings," 13 *Tax Management Transfer Pricing Report* 909 (Jan. 19, 2005).

[123] "Japan: NTA Says 90 Percent of MAP Cases Concern Transfer Pricing Disagreements," 18 *Tax Management Transfer Pricing Report* 652 (November 5, 2009).

[124] Ricardo Gonzalez Orta, et al., "Negotiating Mexico's First Break-Even Maquiladora APA," 11 *Tax Management Transfer Pricing Report* 265 (July 10, 2002).

[125] *Id.*

[126] "First 2002-03 Maquiladora APAs Issued; Most Accords For Electronics Sector Firms," 11 *Tax Management Transfer Pricing Report* 139 (May 29, 2002).

[127] "Mexico's Transfer Pricing Chief Says Resources Shifting to Audits," 12 *Tax Management Transfer Pricing Report* 1016 (Mar. 17, 2004).

¶1350.04

.07 Netherlands

Taxpayers may pursue unilateral, bilateral, or multilateral APAs in the Netherlands.[128] Pre-File meetings are available to reduce administrative burden.[129] APA terms are typically in the range of four to five years, although a longer term may be appropriate based on the facts and circumstances.[130] Normally, APAs will only be issued prospectively; however, taxpayers can request rollback if the facts and circumstances of the preceding fiscal years are similar to those of the years in the request.[131]

In December 2001, the Dutch Parliament enacted legislation formalizing the nation's APA program, and codifying transfer pricing legislation and documentation requirements.[132] The legislation established a separate APA program based in Rotterdam, and authorized the APA team to issue binding advice to the regional revenue offices where APA requests are submitted.[133]

.08 Other Global Developments

The Korean National Tax Service ("KNTS") introduced several structural changes designed to enhance the efficiency of its APA program and to encourage taxpayers to seek APAs.[134] In addition, the KNTS held a special seminar for the promotion of APAs, further emphasizing the success of its APA program.[135] Korean officials have also noted a recent shift in the KNTS toward preventing double taxation as opposed to protecting corporations' fiscal base.[136]

The first European multilateral APAs were completed in early 2004; one involved a European financial services corporation with operations in Belgium, France, and the Netherlands and the other involved the Airbus consortium and tax authorities in France, Germany, Spain, and the United Kingdom.[137]

---

[128] Decree No. DGB2004/1338M (8/11/04); Decree NO. IFZ2004/124M (8/11/04).

[129] Decree No. IFZ2004/124M (8/11/04), at Sec. 1.

[130] *Id.* at Sec. 4.

[131] *Id.* at Sec. 5.

[132] "Government Enacts Legislation Codifying APAs, Documentation, Arm's-Length Rules," 10 *Tax Management Transfer Pricing Report* 717 (Jan. 9, 2002).

[133] *Id.*

[134] "Agency Reorganizes to Strengthen Work on Transfer Pricing, Competent Authority, APAs," 10 *Tax Management Transfer Pricing Report* 806 (Feb. 6, 2002).

[135] *Id.*

[136] "Japanese, Korean Taxpayers Using APAs More to Resolve Double Tax Issues, Officials Say," 12 *Tax Management Transfer Pricing Report* 738 (Jan. 7, 2004).

[137] "First Two Multilateral European APAs Signed; Airbus, Financial Firm, Six Nations Involved," 12 *Tax Management Transfer Pricing Report* 1113 (Apr. 14, 2004).

¶1350.08

Chapter 14

The OECD Approach to Transfer Pricing

¶ 1401 Overview

The Organisation for Economic Co-operation and Development ("OECD") is a Paris-based international policy body composed of 30 member countries that provides governments with a forum in which to discuss, develop and perfect economic and social policy.[1] The aims of the OECD are to promote policies designed to:

1. Achieve the highest sustainable economic growth and employment and a rising standard of living in Member countries, while maintaining financial stability, and thus to contribute to the development of the world economy;

2. Contribute to sound economic expansion in Member as well as non-Member countries in the process of economic development; and

3. Contribute to the expansion of world trade on a multilateral, non-discriminatory basis in accordance with international obligations.

Because the OECD membership produces over two-thirds of the world's goods and services, its transfer pricing guidance carries considerable weight. In several instances, countries have enacted their transfer pricing legislation in whole or in part based on the OECD transfer pricing guidelines.

The OECD first issued its transfer pricing guidelines in 1979. In 1995 and again in 2009, the OECD substantially revised its Guidelines in *Transfer Pricing Guidelines for Multinational Enterprises and Tax Administrations*.[2] Additional mater-

---

[1] The OECD website is *www.oecd.org*.

[2] The OECD approved the 2010 revision of the Transfer Pricing Guidelines on July 22, 2010. *See http://www.oecd.org*.

ials are published periodically. The OECD's guidelines are based on the principles concerning taxation of multinational enterprises that are incorporated in the OECD Model Tax Convention.

> *Comment:* The OECD Guidelines are generally consistent with the U.S. transfer pricing regulations. Two areas in which the U.S. regulations and the OECD Guidelines appear to differ significantly, however, are the relationship between the CPM and the OECD's transactional net margin method ("TNMM") and the U.S. "commensurate-with-income" standard.

Other OECD guidance that should be reviewed in applying the Guidelines is the OECD Report *International Tax Avoidance and Evasion* (1987). In addition, in August 2007 the OECD published its *Report on the Attribution of Profits to Permanent Establishments (2007)*.

Further, the OECD acts as a forum for the debate of the most pressing current transfer pricing issues. Current items involve: comparability issues, improvements to the mutual agreement procedure, review of profit-based methods, stock option issues, business restructuring, and the interaction of transfer pricing and Customs valuation issues. The OECD has also addressed issues related to transfer pricing, notably the permanent establishments and business profits issues.

¶ 1410 The Arm's Length Principle

.01 General

Chapter I of the Guidelines reaffirms the OECD's commitment to the arm's length principle to establish pricing by and among related parties. The OECD's commitment to the arm's length standard was authoritatively expressed in its Model Tax Convention, Article 9, which provides:

> [When] conditions are made or imposed between . . . two [associated] enterprises in their commercial or financial relations which differ from those which would be made between independent enterprises, then any profits which would, but for those conditions, have accrued to one of the enterprises, but, by reason of those conditions, have not so accrued, may be included in the profits of that enterprise and taxed accordingly.

The OECD's embrace of the arm's length principle is based on its view that it is sound in theory and provides the closest approximation of the workings of the open market where goods and services are transferred between related companies. Further, while the arm's length principle may not always apply in a straightforward manner, it generally produces results that have been acceptable to tax administrations.

The Guidelines acknowledge that there are practical difficulties in applying the arm's length principle because a taxpayer may not be able to locate or gather information on transactions between independent enterprises that are sufficiently comparable to the controlled transactions. However, the Guidelines conclude that there is no legitimate or realistic alternative to the arm's length principle. The global formulary apportionment approach, sometimes mentioned as a possible alternative, is not acceptable in theory, implementation, or practice. (The global formulary apportionment approach is discussed in Chapter III of the Guidelines). The Guidelines also incorporate the following concepts:

1. A range of acceptable transfer pricing results;
2. Recognition of the actual transaction undertaken;
3. Evaluation of separate and combined transactions;
4. Use of multiple year data;
5. Losses;
6. Effect of government policies;
7. Intentional set-offs; and
8. Use of customs valuations.

The Guidelines' discussion of these factors is generally consistent with that of the Code Sec. 482 regulations.

.02 Factors Determining Comparability

The Guidelines provide guidance for applying the arm's length principle, including a detailed discussion of comparability.[3] Five factors are provided for determining comparability: characteristics of property or services; functional analysis; contractual terms; economic circumstances; and business strategies.

Characteristics of Property or Services. Differences in the specific characteristics of the property or services transferred, or the services rendered in connection with the transfer of property, often account for differences in their value in the open market. As under the Code Sec. 482 regulations, similarity in the characteristics of the property or services transferred will matter most when comparing prices of controlled and uncontrolled transactions under the traditional transactional methods and less when comparing profit margins under transactional profit methods.[4]

Functional Analysis. To determine whether controlled and uncontrolled transactions or entities are comparable, comparison of the functions of the parties is necessary. As under the Code Sec. 482 regulations, this comparison is based on a functional analysis which seeks to identify and compare the economically significant activities and responsibilities undertaken or to be undertaken by the uncontrolled and controlled companies.[5] In addition to identifying the principal functions performed by the party under examination, the Guidelines suggest considering the type of assets employed or to be employed, the risks assumed by the respective parties, as well as whether a purported allocation of risks is consistent with the economic substance of the transaction.[6]

Contractual Terms. An analysis of the contractual terms of a transaction is a part of the functional analysis.[7] In arm's length dealings, the contractual terms of a transaction generally define how the legal responsibilities, risks, and benefits are to be divided between the parties. In dealings between uncontrolled companies, the

---

[3] *Id.* Transfer Pricing Guidelines for Multinational Enterprises and Tax Administrations, 1.9 (OECD, 2001).
[4] *Id.*, 1.19.
[5] *Id.*, 1.20.
[6] *Id.*, 1.21-28.
[7] *Id.*, 1.28.

divergence of interests between the parties ensures that they will ordinarily seek to hold each other to the terms of the contract.

The same divergence of interests may not exist where related companies are involved, thus, the Guidelines state that it is important to examine whether the conduct of the parties conforms to the terms of the contract or the parties' conduct indicates that the contractual terms have not been followed. In these cases, further analysis is required to determine the true terms of the transaction and certain conduct may be attributed to the parties.[8]

Economic Circumstances. Achieving comparability requires that the markets in which the controlled and uncontrolled companies operate are comparable, and that differences do not have a material effect on price. The Guidelines states that it is essential to identify the relevant market or markets, taking account of available substitute goods or services.[9] This is akin to the bargaining theory in economics where market leaders generally obtain the benefit of the bargain and, thus, the better price. It is questionable, however, whether the Guidelines would require parties to delve into a detailed economic analysis of the relevant market or markets—as is currently the trend in U.S. transfer pricing cases under the Code Sec. 482 regulations.

Business Strategies. Although certain business strategies may be taken into account when determining the comparability of controlled and uncontrolled transactions and companies, certain issues and problems should be considered when evaluating a taxpayer's claim that it was following a business strategy that distinguishes it from potential comparables. The Guidelines observe that the timing of a determination that a taxpayer's claim of following a certain strategy was valid presents a problem if legal constraints prevent re-examinations of earlier tax years. This would be true in a market penetration strategy where current profits are reduced in anticipation of increased profits in the future.

For this reason, the Guidelines advise tax administrations to review such strategies with particular scrutiny. Factors to be considered include: (i) the conduct of the parties to determine if it is consistent with the business strategy; (ii) whether the nature of the relationship between the parties to the controlled transaction would be consistent with the taxpayer bearing the costs of the business strategy; (iii) whether the strategy in question could plausibly be expected to prove profitable within the foreseeable future, and (iv) whether a party operating at arm's length would have been prepared to sacrifice profitability for a similar period under such economic circumstances and competitive conditions.[10] For the most part, this position fairly tracks the same issue in the Code Sec. 482 regulations.[11]

.03 Arm's Length Range

The Guidelines acknowledge that while in some cases it is possible to apply the arm's length principle to arrive at a single reliable arm's length price or result; there will be occasions when the application of the most appropriate method

---

[8] *Id.*, 1.28-29.
[9] *Id.*, 1.30.
[10] *Id.*, 1.31-35.
[11] Reg. § 1.482-1(d)(4)(i).

produces a range of reliable prices or results.[12] If the relevant indicator of the related party transaction falls outside the arm's length range asserted by the tax administration, the Guidelines state that the taxpayer should have the opportunity to argue that the conditions of the transaction satisfy the arm's length principle, and that the range includes this result.

Consistent with the Code Sec. 482 regulations, the Guidelines state that if the taxpayer cannot show that the results of the related party transaction fall within the range, an adjustment should be made to any point within the arm's length range.[13] Unlike the regulations under Code Sec. 482 (providing for an adjustment to the median), however, the Guidelines adds that where it is possible, such adjustments should be made to the point within the range that best reflects the facts and circumstances of the related party transaction.

.04 Use of Transfer Pricing Methods

In contrast to the Code Sec. 482 regulations, the Guidelines' arm's length principle does not require either the tax examiner or the taxpayer to perform analyses under more than one method or prove that a particular method does not apply (i.e., there is no best method rule).[14] In difficult cases, where no one approach is conclusive, the Guidelines will allow for a flexible approach which would enable the evidence of various methods to be used in conjunction. This is a practical advancement compared to the regulations under Code Sec. 482 which require detailed analysis and compliance to establish the "best method" and often require extensive documentary evidence to prove that a particular method is not a best method.

The Guidelines acknowledge that it cannot provide specific rules that will cover every situation. As a general rule, taxpayers are instructed to attempt to reach a "reasonable accommodation keeping in mind the imprecision of the various methods and the preference for higher degrees of comparability . . . ."[15] Transactions that are not fully comparable may be useful and should not be dismissed because the indices of comparability are not fully met. Any method, in fact, will be permitted where its application is agreeable to the members of the multinational company group involved with the transaction and the tax administrations in the jurisdictions of all those members.[16]

This open attitude toward "inexact" comparables conveys a very different philosophical approach to comparability from that of the Code Sec. 482 regulations. The OECD philosophy still appears to couch transfer pricing on some market transaction benchmark with the belief that business people should be able to adjust for the differences in the compared transactions. This is very different than the IRS attitude, which is to proceed directly to the operating results of comparable companies from which they extrapolate a transfer price.

---

[12] *Id.*, 1.45.

[13] *Id.*, 1.48; Reg. § 1.482-1(e)(3).

[14] *Id.*, 1.69.

[15] *Id.*, 1.70.

[16] *Id.*

¶ 1420 Transfer Price for Tangible Property

.01 In General

Chapters II and III of the Guidelines set forth the methods to be used to establish an arm's length price. Chapter II provides three traditional transactional methods and Chapter III provides other methods or transactional profit methods, such as the profit split and transactional net margin methods. The Guidelines clearly state a preference for traditional transactional methods over transactional profit methods and provide a relaxed standard of comparability to expand the applicability of the traditional methods. However, the Guidelines acknowledge that there are situations in which the traditional transaction methods cannot be applied; thus, the necessity to address whether and under what conditions other methods may be used. This is particularly true where there is no data available or the available data is not of sufficient quality to rely solely or at all on the traditional transaction methods.[17]

.02 Traditional Transaction Methods

Comparable Uncontrolled Price Method. The CUP method compares the price for property or services transferred in a controlled transaction to the price charged for property or services in a comparable uncontrolled transaction. Differences between the two prices may indicate that the conditions of the commercial and financial relations are not arm's length.[18]

> *Comment:* This definition makes no reference to arm's length "results" as is now critical under the Code Sec. 482 regulations.[19] This distinction is significant because the 1968 Code Sec. 482 regulations referenced only transactional methods under its prescribed methods, and did not focus on results. Rather, the only criteria of importance under those regulations was the market benchmark. By contrast, the final Code Sec. 482 regulations use the transaction's results to justify the benchmark.

The Guidelines state that an uncontrolled transaction is comparable to a controlled transaction for purposes of the CUP method (and the other traditional transaction methods) if one of two conditions is met:

1. none of the differences between the transactions being compared or between the companies undertaking those transactions could materially affect the price in the open market; or

2. reasonably accurate adjustments can be made to eliminate the effect of such differences.[20]

Departing from the Code Sec. 482 regulations, the Guidelines' preference for the CUP method exists even where there are differences between the controlled and uncontrolled transactions or between the companies undertaking those transactions and it is difficult to make reasonably accurate adjustments to eliminate the effect on price. Here, the Guidelines state that the difficulties that arise in attempt-

---

[17] *Id.*, 2.49.
[18] *Id.*, 2.6.

[19] Reg. § 1.482-3(b)(2)(i).
[20] *Id.*, 2.7.

ing to make reasonably accurate adjustments should not, as a matter of routine, preclude the application of the CUP method. Rather, in those situations, practical considerations would dictate a more flexible approach to enable the CUP method to be used.[21]

Resale Price Method. The Guidelines advise that the resale price method ("RPM"), expressed as a percentage of gross sales, is most useful where it is applied to marketing operations. Here, the price at which a product purchased from a related company is resold to an uncontrolled company is reduced by an appropriate gross margin ("resale price margin"). The resale price margin represents the amount out of which the reseller would seek to cover its selling and other operating expenses and, in the light of the functions performed, make an appropriate profit. The remainder after subtracting the gross margin can be regarded as the arm's length price for the original transfer of property between the related companies.[22]

The Guidelines state that the arm's length resale price margin may be determined by reference to the resale price margin that the same reseller earns on items purchased and sold in comparable uncontrolled transactions or, by reference to the resale price margin that an unrelated company earns in comparable uncontrolled transactions.[23] The same approach used in the CUP method is used in the RPM to determine if an uncontrolled transaction is comparable to a controlled transaction for these purposes.[24] The Guidelines observe, however, that in making comparisons for the purposes of the RPM, fewer adjustments are normally needed to account for product difference than under the CUP method because minor product differences are less likely to have as material an effect on profit margins as they do on price.[25] This is consistent with the Code Sec. 482 regulations that require a lesser standard on product comparability and more emphasis on functional comparability for the RPM. Thus, where uncontrolled and controlled transactions are comparable in all characteristics other than the product itself, the RPM might produce a more reliable measure of arm's length conditions than the CUP method, unless reasonably accurate adjustments could be made to account for the product differences.

> *Comment:* Unlike the RPM under the Code Sec. 482 regulations, the Guidelines' RPM is a pure gross margin analysis. Further, given the more flexible comparability standards and the stronger focus on transaction-based analysis, it is less likely the RPM will start to parallel a CPM analysis.

Cost Plus Method. The Guidelines observe that the cost plus method is most useful where either semi-finished goods are sold between related parties; related parties have concluded joint facility agreements or long-term buy-and-supply arrangements; or the controlled transaction is the provision of services. Under the cost plus method, an appropriate gross margin ("cost plus mark-up") is added to the costs incurred by the supplier of property or services in a controlled transaction for property transferred or services provided to a related purchaser.[26]

---

[21] *Id.*, 2.9.
[22] *Id.*, 2.14.
[23] *Id.*, 2.15.
[24] *Id.*, 2.16.
[25] *Id.*
[26] *Id.*, 2.32.

The cost plus mark-up of the supplier in the controlled transaction should be established by reference to the cost plus mark-up that the same supplier earns in comparable uncontrolled transactions or by reference to the mark-up that would have been earned in comparable uncontrolled transactions.[27] To determine whether a transaction is comparable for the purposes of the cost plus method, the same principles apply as for the RPM. As under the RPM, fewer adjustments may be necessary to account for product differences under the cost plus method than the CUP method, and it may be appropriate to give more weight to other factors of comparability, some of which have a more significant effect on the cost plus mark-up than they do on price.

The Guidelines note that in applying the cost plus method, attention should also be given to apply a comparable mark-up to a comparable cost basis. As with the RPM, the cost plus method relies upon a comparison of the mark-ups achieved by the controlled supplier of goods or services and by one or more uncontrolled entities on their costs for comparable transactions. Therefore, the Guidelines provide that the differences between the controlled and uncontrolled transactions that have an effect on the size of the mark-up must be analyzed to determine what adjustments should be made to the uncontrolled transactions' respective mark-up.[28] For this purpose, it is particularly important to consider differences in the level and types of expenses, including operating and non-operating expenses, associated with functions performed and risks assumed by the parties or transactions being compared. Accounting consistency is another important aspect that should be considered. The cost that may be considered in applying the cost plus method should be limited to those of the supplier of goods or services. Since accounting practices regarding what is included in the costs could vary in countries and industries and no general rule can be set out to deal with all cases, the same accounting method should be used in controlled and uncontrolled transactions.[29]

.03 Profit Methods

In General. Two transactional profit methods are discussed: the profit split method and the transactional net margin method. The OECD has apparently added the word "transactional" to make it clear that the analysis under the profit methods should be conducted on particular controlled transactions, not on a company-wide basis. The Guidelines repeatedly stress that an analysis under transactional profit methods, especially transactional net margin methods, should be performed on a transactional basis.[30] This implies a significant difference from the U.S. Code Sec. 482 regulations where the analysis on a company-wide basis is widely adopted in practice, although the regulations require the isolation of the "most narrowly identifiable business activity."[31]

Profit Split Method. The profit split method seeks to divide profits that uncontrolled companies would expect to realize from engaging in controlled transactions. In application, this method identifies and splits profits based upon an economically

---

[27] *Id.*, 2.33.
[28] *Id.*, 2.37.
[29] *Id.*, 2.38-45.

[30] *Id.*, 1.42 and 3.42.
[31] Reg. § 1.482-5(b)(1).

valid basis that approximates the division of profits that would have been antici-pated and reflected in an agreement made at arm's length.

One strength of the profit split method is that it generally does not rely directly on closely comparable transactions and, it can therefore be used where transactions between uncontrolled companies cannot be identified. The profit split method offers flexibility by taking into account specific facts and circumstances of the related companies that are not present in uncontrolled companies, while still constituting an arm's length approach to the extent that it reflects what uncon-trolled companies reasonably would have done if faced with the same circum-stances. Another strength is that under the profit split method, neither party to the controlled transaction will likely be left with an extreme profit result, such as one entity recognizing income when the combined operations incur significant losses.[32]

The weaknesses of the profit split method are:

1. The external market data considered in valuing each companies' contribu-tion to the controlled transactions will be less closely connected to those transactions than is the case with the other available methods;

2. The profit split method is difficult to apply due to the challenge related companies and tax administrations may have in accessing information from foreign affiliates;

3. Independent enterprises do not ordinarily use the profit split method to determine their transfer pricing;

4. It may be difficult to measure combined revenue and costs for all partici-pating entities to the controlled transactions, which would require stating books and records on a common basis and making adjustments in account-ing practices and currencies; and

5. Allocation of costs may be difficult when the profit split method is applied to operating profit.[33]

There are a number of approaches for estimating the division of profits, based either on projected or actual profits, as may be appropriate, that unrelated compa-nies would have expected. Two approaches that are discussed in the Guidelines are the contribution analysis and the residual analysis.

Under a contribution analysis, the combined profits (the total profits from the controlled transactions under examination) are divided between the related compa-nies based upon the relative value for the functions performed by each of the related parties participating in the controlled transactions, supplemented as much as possible by external market data that indicate how uncontrolled companies would have divided profits in similar circumstances. Generally, the profit to be combined and divided under the contribution analysis is operating profit, because the use of operating profit will ensure that both income and expenses of the combined operations are attributed to a respective participant on a consistent basis. Occasionally, it may be appropriate to carry out a split of gross profits and then deduct the expenses incurred in, or attributable to, each relevant company. In the

---

[32] *Id.*, 3.6 and 3.7.   [33] *Id.*, 3.8 and 3.9.

latter case, care should be taken that gross profits and expenses credited/charged or allocated to each company are consistent with the functions and risks undertaken there.[34]

The residual analysis divides the combined profit from the controlled transactions under examination in two stages. In the first stage, each party is allocated sufficient profit to provide it with a basic return appropriate for the type of transactions in which it is engaged. Ordinarily this basic return would be determined by reference to the market returns achieved for similar types of transactions by uncontrolled companies. In the second stage, any residual profit (or loss) remaining after the first stage division would be allocated by and among the parties based on an analysis of the facts and circumstances that might indicate how this residual would have been divided between uncontrolled companies.[35]

The residual could derive from the application of other methods. For example, market data from traditional transactional methods could assist in the preliminary assessment of normal profits attributable to related parties where one manufactures a unique product using proprietary processes and then transfers the product to another related party for further processing and distribution.[36]

Other possible approaches suggested in the Guidelines are to split the combined split so that each of the related companies participating in the controlled transactions earns the same rate of return on the capital employed, and to determine the profit split based on the division of profits that actually results from comparable transactions among independent companies. The latter method appears to approximate the U.S. comparable profit split.[37] The Guidelines state that it does not seek to provide an exhaustive catalogue of ways in which the profit split method may be applied; rather it suggests that the applicability of alternative approaches be measured based on the circumstances of the case and the information available to identify the method that would approximate as closely as possible the split of profits that would have been realized had the parties been uncontrolled companies operating at arm's length.[38]

Transaction Net Margin Method. Like the U.S. CPM, the Guidelines' transactional net margin method ("TNMM") determines the level of profits that would have resulted from a controlled transaction if the results (i.e., net profit margin or operating profit) on those transactions, as indicated by various PLIs, were equal to the results realized by comparable uncontrolled companies. A functional analysis of the controlled and uncontrolled companies is required to determine whether they are comparable and what adjustments may be necessary to obtain reliable results.[39]

Comment: The OECD guideline's TNMM and the U.S. CPM, in theory, should reach the same or similar result. Application of the TNMM allows the transaction being tested to be aggregated with similar transactions in appropriate circumstances. Application of the CPM requires that the PLIs be applied to the tested party's financial data related only to the covered transactions.

---

[34] *Id.*, 3.16-17.
[35] *Id.*, 3.19.
[36] *Id.*, 3.20.

[37] Reg. § 1.482-6(c)(2).
[38] *Id.*, 3.23-25.
[39] *Id.*, 3.26.

¶1420.03

Therefore, the TNMM and the CPM should arrive at the same arm's length result from opposite ends of the transactions/profit spectrum. Nevertheless, debate continues over whether the CPM and the TNMM are truly consistent with one another.[40]

The TNMM has both strengths and weaknesses in terms of its ability to establish whether conditions in the financial and commercial relations of controlled companies are arm's length. One strength is that the TNMM uses net margins represented by PLIs (e.g., return on assets, operating income to sales and other satiable financial ratios) that are less affected by transactional differences than is the case with a transactional price method, as the CUP method. Net margins are also considered more tolerant to some functional differences between the controlled and uncontrolled transactions than the gross profit margins, as differences in the functions performed between enterprises are often reflected in variations in operating expenses.[41]

Another practical strength is that it is not necessary to determine how the functions and responsibilities are shared among the related companies or to state the books and records of all participants participating in a controlled transaction on a common basis to allocate indirect costs, because the analysis required by the TNMM usually focuses on the least complex participant in the transaction.[42]

A number of weaknesses of the TNMM are also pointed out in the Guidelines. First, a net margin can be influenced by some factors that either do not have an effect, or have a less substantial or direct effect, on price or gross margins, because of the potential for variations of operating expenses across enterprises. Another weakness relates to data availability, a real concern outside the U.S. Taxpayers may not have access to enough specific information on the profitability of uncontrolled companies to make a valid application of the TNMM at the time of the controlled transactions.[43]

The Guidelines suggest that the comparability of functions and economic circumstances between related and unrelated companies be carefully examined to ensure an appropriate application of the TNMM, and warn against its insensible application without adjustments to account for the relevant differences.[44]

¶ 1430 A Non-Arm's Length Approach: Global Formulary Apportionment

Global formulary apportionment has sometimes been suggested as an alternative to the arm's length principle. This method allocates the global profits of a multinational company ("MNC") group on a consolidated basis among the controlled companies in different countries on the basis of a predetermined formula.

---

[40] *See* Culbertson, "A Rose By Any Other Name: Smelling the Flowers at the OECD's (Last) Resort," 95 *Tax Notes Today* 180-39 (September 11, 1995); Michel Taly, "Comparison of CPM and TNMM Transfer Pricing Methods: A Point of View," 12 *Tax Notes International* 351 (January 29, 1996); Vishnevsky, "Competent Authorities Discuss APAs," 97 *Tax Notes Today* 211-21 (October 31, 1997) (debate among U.S., Canadian, Japanese and German tax officials).

[41] *Id.*, 3.27.

[42] *Id.*, 3.28.

[43] *Id.*, 3.29-30.

[44] *Id.*, 3.34-40.

Three essential components are identified to apply a global formulary apportionment method:

1. Determining the unit to be taxed (which branch or subsidiary of an MNC group should comprise the taxable entity);

2. Determining global profits; and

3. Establishing the formula to be used to allocate the global profits of the unit. This formula would most likely be based on a combination of costs, assets, payroll, and sales.[45]

Supporters of this method argue that it would provide greater administrative convenience and certainty for taxpayers while comporting with economic reality. Further arguments include that an MNC group must be considered on a consolidated basis to reflect the business realities of the relationships among the controlled companies in the group. In addition, it is argued, the global formulary apportionment approach reduces the costs of compliance for taxpayers because only one set of accounts would be needed for the entire group.[46]

The Guidelines are clear that the OECD Member countries do not accept these arguments and do not consider global formulary apportionment a realistic alternative to the arm's length principle.[47] The most significant concern is the difficulty of implementing a formulary system in a manner that both protects against double taxation and ensures single taxation. To achieve this would require substantial international coordination and consensus on the predetermined formula to be used and on the composition of the group in question. To reach an agreement on all of the factors used in the formula would be time consuming and extremely difficult and each country involved in the MNC group would have a strong incentive to devise a formula or use factors that would maximize that country's own revenue.[48]

Other significant concerns raised in the Guidelines are:

1. Predetermined formulae are arbitrary and disregard geographical differences, market conditions, the particular circumstances of the individual companies, and management's own allocation of resources, thus producing an allocation of profits that may bear no sound relationship to the specific facts surrounding the transaction;

2. Difficulties would arise on how to deal with exchange rate movements and how to measure the factors used in the formulae, i.e., sales, asset values, etc.;

3. Contrary to the assertions of its supporters, global formulary apportionment methods may present intolerable compliance costs and data requirements because information would be gathered about the entire MNC group and presented in each jurisdiction on the basis of the currency and the book and tax accounting rules of that particular jurisdiction;

---

[45] *Id.*, 3.59.
[46] *Id.*, 3.61-62.

[47] *Id.*, 3.63.
[48] *Id.*, 3.64-66.

4. A global formulary apportionment method would have the effect of taxing an MNC group on a consolidated basis and therefore abandons the separate entity approach. Consequently, it would raise questions about the relevance of imposing withholding taxes on cross-border payments between group members and would involve a rejection of a number of rules incorporated in bilateral tax treaties; and

5. Unless the global formulary apportionment approach includes every member of an MNC group, it must retain a separate entity rule for the interface between the related companies excluded from the arrangement and the rest of the MNC group.[49]

For these reasons, the Guidelines reiterate its support for the arm's length principle that has emerged over the years and agree that the theoretical alternative to the arm's length principle represented by global formulary apportionment should be rejected.

¶ 1440 Intangible Property

.01 In General

Chapter VI of the Guidelines discusses several considerations that should be given in establishing transfer pricing for transactions involving intangible property. The general guidance set forth in Chapters I, II and III for applying the arm's length principle applies equally to the determination of an appropriate transfer price between related companies for intangible property. These principles, however, may be difficult to apply to controlled transactions involving intangible property. This is generally because the intangible property may be unique and/or the relationship between the parties might be structured in a way that unrelated companies would not contemplate.

.02 Factors Determining Comparability

When applying the arm's length principle to related party transactions for intangible property, certain special factors affecting comparability must be considered, including:

1. The profits that would be expected from the use of intangible property (e.g., the profit potential);

2. Any limitations in the geographic areas in which the rights may be exercised;

3. Any restrictions that might apply on the exportation of goods;

4. The exclusive or nonexclusive character of the rights being transferred;

5. The capital investment, the start-up expenses, and the development work required in the market; and

6. The possibility of sub-licensing;

7. The licensee's distribution network; and

---

[49] *Id.*, 3.67-73.

    8. Whether the licensee has the right to participate in further developments of the property by the licensor.[50]

When the intangible being transferred between related parties is a patent, the comparability analysis should also consider:

1. The nature of the patent;

2. The degree and duration of protection afforded;

3. The length of the period under which patents are likely to maintain their economic value; and

4. The process of production for which the patent is used.[51]

.03 Methods

The Guidelines identify certain pricing methods to establish the arm's length charge for the transfer of intangibles. Similar to the comparable uncontrolled transaction method under the Code Sec. 482 regulations, the Guidelines provide that the CUP method may be used where the same owner has transferred comparable intangible property under similar circumstances to unrelated companies. In addition, the price charged in similar transactions between unrelated companies in the same industry is mentioned as useful, as well as the offers that an entity makes to unrelated parties.[52]

While the Guidelines make clear its preference for traditional transaction methods, the profit split method discussed in Chapter III has a distinct role for the transfer of intangibles. The Guidelines point out that where both parties to a controlled transaction contribute highly valuable intangible property or unique assets to the transaction, it is extremely difficult to apply the traditional transaction methods and the TNMM because uncontrolled transactions that involve similar valuable intangible or unique assets are difficult to be located. In such cases the profit split method may be the best method in both technical and practical senses.[53]

.04 Periodic Adjustments

The Guidelines acknowledge that there may be instances in which it is appropriate for the tax administration to adjust the price originally set years before.

> **Comment:** This is an important concession by the OECD because, in the past, they have been vehemently against any periodic adjustments. This step should also reduce the tension on competent authorities when confronted with correlative adjustments.

The Guidelines state that no adjustment should be made if comparable unrelated companies would have initially agreed to comparable fixed amounts for the sale of the intangible property (and would not have agreed to a subsequent modification of the terms of the agreement). If unrelated companies would have relied on a particular projection in determining the transfer price, the tax administration's examination should be limited to an inquiry of whether the projection was adequate

---

[50] *Id.*, 6.20.

[51] *Id.*, 6.21-22.

[52] *Id.*, 6.23.

[53] *Id.*, 6.26. (C).

considering all the developments that were reasonably available when it was made, without using hindsight.[54]

Accordingly, periodic adjustments are limited to those exceptional cases where the related entities have sold or licensed intangible property under fixed terms for multiple years under the situations in which comparable unrelated parties would have insisted on certain price adjustment clauses (such as a bonus payment) or could renegotiate the contract. The mere fact that the actual profit experience has differed is not enough to warrant an adjustment.[55]

¶ 1450 Intra-Group Services

.01 In General

Chapter VII of the Guidelines addresses issues arising where services have been provided by one member of a multinational group to other members of that group and how to establish arm's length pricing for those intra-group services.[56] The Guidelines identify two common issues for intra-group services: first, whether intra-group services have in fact been provided; second, whether an arm's length charge for those services has been charged.[57]

.02 Determining Whether Intra-group Services Have Been Performed

The first issue depends on whether a comparable unrelated party would have concluded that the activity has provided economic or commercial value to enhance the recipient's commercial position. This may be ascertained by considering whether an independent party in a comparable situation would have been willing to pay for the activity if performed by an independent company, or whether it would have performed the activity itself. If the activity is not one for which the independent party would have been willing to pay or perform itself, the Guidelines state that the activity ordinarily will not be considered as an intra-group service under the arm's length principle.[58]

Often an intra-group activity is performed for all group members even though some members do not require the service, such as a service by the parent company in its capacity as shareholder. Examples of "shareholder activities" include costs of activities to the juridical structure of the parent company itself, costs relating to reporting requirements of the parent company, and costs of raising funds. "Shareholder activities" would not justify a charge to the recipient companies because such activities would not be paid for by an independent third party.

> **Comment:** "Shareholder activities" should be distinguished from the broader term "stewardship activity" used in the 1979 Guidelines. Stewardship activities covered a range of activities by a shareholder that may include the provision of services to other group members, for example services that would be provided by a coordinating center, such as planning services for particular operations, emergency management and technical advice, or in some cases assistance in day-to-day management.

---

[54] *Id.*, 6.32.
[55] *Id.*, 6.34.
[56] *Id.*, 7.1.

[57] *Id.*, 7.5.
[58] *Id.*, 7.6.

Activities ordinarily will be considered intra-group services because independent companies would have been willing to pay for or perform the services themselves.[59] Similar to the position in the U.S. regulations, no allocation is made for an intra-group service that merely duplicates a service of another group member unless the duplication of service is only temporary.[60]

.03 Arm's Length Charge

Once it is determined that an intra-group service has been rendered, it is necessary to determine whether the amount charged is at arm's length. Here, the tax administrations must identify what arrangements, if any, have actually been provided to facilitate the charge. Certain intra-group services can be readily identified, such as where a direct charge method is used.[61]

While the direct charge method is of great convenience to tax administrations, this method might be difficult to apply in practice. The practice of charging for intra-group services is often to make arrangements that are either readily identified, but not based on a direct charge method; or not readily identifiable and either incorporated into the charge for other transfers, allocated among group members on some basis or, in some cases, not allocated among group members at all.[62] When determining the arm's length price for intra-group services, the perspective of both the service provider and the recipient must be considered. Relevant considerations include the value of the service to the recipient, the amount a comparable unrelated company would pay for that service in similar situations, and the cost of the service to the service provider. The method used should be determined under the guidelines set forth in Chapters I, II, and III. These guidelines often lead to the CUP or cost plus method for pricing services. The CUP method is used where there is a high degree of comparability between the intra-group service being provided and a similar service provided between unrelated companies. Otherwise, the cost plus method is more practical.[63]

¶ 1460 Cost Contribution Arrangements

Chapter VIII of the Guidelines addresses cost contribution arrangements.[64] A cost contribution arrangement is an agreement among businesses to share the costs and risks of developing, producing or obtaining assets, services, or rights and to determine the nature and extent of each participant's interest in those assets, services, or rights.[65] Accordingly, traditional transfer pricing questions do not normally exist because there is no transfer of property or services by or among the participating companies. Cost contribution arrangements typically include research and development agreements and the joint acquisition or provision of products, tangible property or services.[66] The OECD's concept of cost contribution arrange-

---

[59] *Id.*, 7.9 and 7.14.

[60] *Id.*, 7.11; Reg. § 1.482-2(b)(2)(ii).

[61] *Id.*, 7.20.

[62] *Id.*, 7.22.

[63] *Id.*, 7.29-31.

[64] *See generally*, Becker, "Commentary on Chapter VIII of the OECD Transfer Pricing Guidelines: Cost Contribution Arrangements," 5 *Int'l Transfer Pricing J.* 62 (March/April 1998).

[65] *Id.*, 8.3.

[66] *Id.*, 8.6-7.

ments is wider in scope than that of the U.S. cost sharing arrangements, which by definition can be applied only to costs of intangible development.[67]

Like the U.S. cost sharing regulations, the OECD Guidelines specifically state that a cost contribution arrangement does not necessarily imply the formation of a separate legal entity (partnership) or a permanent establishment of the participants.[68]

The primary issue surrounding cost contribution arrangements is whether the allocation of costs among the participants is consistent with the parties' interests in the arrangement and the results of the activity. It is here that the arm's length principle applies; that is, whether the allocation reflects the relative benefits inuring to the parties.[69] Under the arm's length principle, the allocation should be consistent with the allocation that would be undertaken by unrelated companies dealing with each other at arm's length in a similar joint arrangement.

To establish an arm's length cost sharing arrangement, it is necessary to calculate the amount of the overall cost incurred by the participants in carrying out the joint activity and then to choose the appropriate method of allocation consistent with the relative benefits and burdens of the arrangement. The Guidelines acknowledge that allocation may involve projections of the participants' shares of the benefits when a material part or all of the benefits from a cost contribution arrangement are expected to be realized in the future. In such cases, the Guidelines suggest that it may be appropriate for a cost contribution arrangement to provide for possible adjustments of proportionate shares of contributions on a prospective basis to reflect changes in relevant circumstances resulting in changes in shares of benefits. The Guidelines also suggest that the tax administration's examination be made on whether the projections made would have been considered acceptable by independent enterprises in comparable circumstances, taking into all the developments that were reasonably foreseeable by the participants, without hindsight.[70]

> **Comment:** The OECD Guidelines with respect to cost contribution arrangements acknowledge that they are a work in progress. In particular, the guidelines note that additional guidance is required for the valuation of contributions, the effect of public subsidies on the valuation of contributions, and buy-in and buy-out payments.

From a compliance perspective, it is important that the arrangement be readily verifiable. Ready verification exists if the arrangement is evidenced in a written contract concluded in advance of incurring the cost of the joint activities. If the arrangement is not in writing or it is argued that a de facto arrangement exists, the Guidelines observe that it will be difficult to determine that a cost contribution arrangement exists and properly allocates benefits and costs, although (and unlike the U.S. rules) the Guidelines does not require an actual written agreement for a cost contribution arrangement to be effective. In addition, it might even be difficult to determine that there was even an intention to establish a cost contribution arrangement. In a written cost contribution arrangement, the terms and conditions

---

[67] Reg. § 1.482-7(a)(1).
[68] 8.3.
[69] 8.8.
[70] *Id.*, 8.20.

should be precisely defined and the participants should be able to demonstrate that the terms of the agreement have been or will be carried out in practice.[71]

¶ 1470 Global Trading of Financial Instruments

In March 1998, the OECD published *The Taxation of Global Trading of Financial Instruments* (the "Global Trading Report"). The Global Trading Report is a revised and updated version of the February 1997 discussion draft, and primarily discusses the two issues that arise when global trading is conducted in more than one jurisdiction: a transfer pricing issue among related companies and an issue related to the attribution of income and expenses within a single legal entity. The Global Trading Report is still in the form of a discussion draft and does not provide the OECD's firm recommendations. The OECD intends to use the Global Trading Report as the basis for its work on developing a multinational consensus on how global trading activities should be taxed.

The Global Trading Report generally applies the Guidelines to the taxation of global trading. Accordingly, it adopts the arm's length principle and maintains its preference of traditional transaction methods over transactional profit methods. However, it acknowledges that, when trading function is fully integrated, it may be difficult to reliably apply traditional transaction methods, and a profit split may be the only available method.

As provided in the Guidelines, profit split can be applied to the global trading activities by employing a contribution analysis, a residual analysis or other types of analyses. The Global Trading Report provides that, whichever of these approaches are used, it is essential that the functions necessary to earn global trading profits or losses are included, valued and appropriately rewarded. Such functions most likely include "front office" functions (e.g., those of traders and marketers); and sometimes include "middle office" functions (e.g., those of system developers, economic forecasters and product engineers), depending on the extent of their relationship with the profitability of the whole operation. "Back office" functions (e.g., credit analysis, legal compliance and trade confirmation and processing) are more likely rewarded by means of traditional transaction methods.

The Global Trading Report suggests compensation as a factor to measure the relative value or the relative contribution of each function to the world-wide profit of the trading activity, although it acknowledges that difficult issues exist when the global trading operation incurs an overall loss or the geographical differences significantly affect compensation levels. The Global Trading Report also reserves its position as to how the relationship between risk management or assumption and the expected profits should be reflected in profit split.[72]

Finally, the Global Trading Report discusses various issues that may arise in applying the arm's length principle to global trading conducted in a branch form. The business community has expressed the necessity of special rules applicable to the global trading operation to cope with the potential problems in permanent establishment and income attribution areas. The Global Trading Report opposed to

---

[71] *Id.*, 8.40-43.   [72] *Id.*, III-3.

¶1470

establishing a different set of rules for global trading, generally because a PE issue is fact sensitive and the arm's length principle and other relevant provisions under the current OECD Model Tax Convention are capable of resolving the potential issue when applied carefully to each case; consequently there is little justification for such special rules for global trading.[73]

See the Practice Tool at ¶ 20,040 for a comparison of the transfer pricing laws of various countries.

---

[73] *Id.*, V.

Chapter 15

Customs Valuation Issues

¶ 1501 Overview[1]

As agencies of the U.S. Government, the IRS and U.S. Customs and Border Protection ("Customs" or "CBP") have a similar interest in correct transfer pricing determinations. Although both IRS and Customs seek an arm's length transfer price for transactions between related parties,[2] little effort has been made to coordinate tax and customs issues on sales of imported goods. The IRS asserts pricing adjustments against taxpayers when it believes that the transfer price into the U.S. is too high to prevent the improper shifting of income out of the U.S. Customs asserts adjustments against importers when it believes that the transfer price into the U.S. is too low to prevent an understatement of customs duties. This difference in approach makes it difficult for importers to construct a transfer price that satisfies each agency's rules.

---

[1] The authors would like to express their thanks to Damon V. Pike and Cylinda Parga of the Pike Law Firm, P.C. in Atlanta, Georgia for their assistance in the preparation of this chapter.

[2] It should be noted at the outset that Customs defines "related parties" very differently than the IRS. The Customs statute defines related parties to include: (a) members of the same family, including brothers and sisters (whether by whole or half blood), spouse, ancestors, and lineal descendants; (b) any officer or director or an organization and such organization; (c) an officer or director of an organization and an officer or director or another organization, if each individual is also an officer or director in the other organization; (d) partners; (e) employer and employee; (f) any person directly or indirectly owning, controlling, or holding with power to vote, 5 percent or more of the outstanding voting stock or shares of any organization and such organization; and (g) two or more persons directly or indirectly controlling, controlled by, or under common control with, any person. 19 USC § 1401a(g)(1).

In contrast, tax law in this area is less restrictive. The statute provides in pertinent part: "[i]n any case of two or more organizations, trades, or businesses (whether or not incorporated, whether or not organized in the United States, and whether or not affiliated) owned or controlled directly or indirectly by the same interests, the Secretary may distribute, apportion, or allocate gross income, deductions, credits, or allowances between or among such organizations, trades, or businesses, if he determines that such distribution, apportionment, or allocation is necessary in order to prevent evasion of taxes or clearly to reflect the income of any of such organizations, trades, or businesses." Reg. § 1.482-1(i) defines "controlled" taxpayers as having ". . . any kind of control, direct or indirect, whether legally enforceable or not, and however exercisable or exercised, including control resulting from the actions of two or more taxpayers acting in concert or with a common goal or purpose. It is the reality of the control that is decisive, not its form or the mode of its exercise. A presumption of control arises if income or deductions have been arbitrarily shifted."

¶ 1510 Customs Valuation Methodologies

Customs law prescribes a hierarchy of methodologies to determine the dutiable value of goods. The primary method is the transaction method. Alternative transaction valuations apply if transaction valuation is unavailable. The process continues with the transaction value of identical merchandise and similar merchandise, deductive value, computed value, and the "adjusted" or "fall-back" method.[3]

.01 Transaction Value

Transaction value is the principal methodology employed by importers when declaring a basis of appraisement to Customs. It is defined as "the price actually paid or payable for the merchandise when sold for exportation to the United States . . . ."[4] The statute also directs that transaction value shall be adjusted by adding amounts equal to:

- Packing costs borne by the buyer;
- Selling commission borne by the buyer;
- Value of any "assist," apportioned as necessary;
- Royalty or license fee that the buyer is required to pay, directly or indirectly, as a condition of sale with respect to the imported merchandise; and
- Proceeds of any subsequent resale, disposal, or use of the merchandise that accrue, directly or indirectly, to the seller.[5]

The following items constitute "assists:"

- Materials, components, parts, and similar items incorporated in the imported merchandise;
- Tools, dies, molds, and similar items used in the production of the imported merchandise;
- Merchandise consumed in the production of the imported merchandise; and
- Engineering, development, art work, design work, and plans and sketches that are undertaken elsewhere than in the United States and are necessary for the production of the imported merchandise.[6]

The customs valuation statute states that transaction value may not be used if the buyer and seller are related, unless the relationship did not influence the terms and conditions of sale, the price includes non-cash consideration that cannot be valued, or compensation is dependent in whole or in part upon the price realized upon the occurrence of a future event that cannot be quantified in a reasonable period of time.[7] Should importers choose to apply transaction value, it must be demonstrated that an examination of the "circumstances of the sale" of the imported merchandise indicates that the relationship between the buyer and the seller did not influence the price paid or payable.[8] Ironically, in spite of the language of

---

[3] 19 USC § 1401a(a).

[4] 19 USC § 1401a(b)(1).

[5] *Id.*

[6] 19 USC § 1401a(h)(1)(A). Incidental services performed overseas do not constitute assists if they are

undertaken by U.S. domiciliaries acting in their capacity as employees or agents of the buyer of the merchandise. 19 USC § 1401a(h)(1)(B)(iii).

[7] 19 USC § 1401a(b)(2)(A).

[8] 19 USC § 1401a(b)(2)(B).

the statute, the vast majority of all imports between related parties utilize transaction value based upon the representation that the relationship did not influence the terms and conditions of the sale.[9]

.02 Transaction Value of Identical or Similar Merchandise

Identical merchandise is "identical in all respects to, and produced in the same country and (except in the case of related-party transactions) by the same person as, the merchandise being appraised."[10] If there is no merchandise manufactured by the same person, or the buyer and seller of the goods being appraised are related, merchandise manufactured in the country of exportation by another person will be treated as identical.[11]

Similar merchandise is produced in the same country, by the same person as the merchandise under appraisement, and is generally commercially interchangeable with it, taking into account its quality, reputation, and the existence of a trademark. Similar merchandise manufactured by another manufacturer in the country of exportation may also be used.[12] Generally, sales of identical or similar merchandise must have been made at the same commercial level and quantity to serve as a basis of valuation. If there are no sales in the same quantity at the same level, the transaction value of other sales may be used, but the value is adjusted to reflect the differences in the circumstances of sale, provided such adjustments can be demonstrated with sufficient information.

.03 Deductive Value

Deductive value can be applied in three different ways, depending upon when and in what condition the imported merchandise is sold in the United States - in other words, it starts with the importer's (distributor's) price to the U.S. customer, and then works backwards to deduct out certain costs in arriving at a unit price upon which to calculate the declared value of the imported article.[13]

The three variations of deductive value are:

1. If the merchandise concerned is sold in the condition as imported at or about the date of importation of the merchandise being appraised, the price is the unit price at which the merchandise concerned is sold in the greatest aggregate quantity at or about such date;

2. If the merchandise concerned is sold in the condition as imported but *not* sold at or about the date of importation of the merchandise being appraised, the price is the unit price at which the merchandise concerned is sold in the greatest aggregate quantity *after* the date of importation being appraised but *before* the close of the 90th day after the date of such importation; or

3. If the merchandise concerned was not sold in the condition as imported and not sold before the close of the 90th day after the date of importation of

---

[9] *See* Pike, "Decision Time at Customs HQ: Harmonization of Customs Valuation and Transfer Pricing Rules," 1 *Customs and International Trade Bar Associate Quarterly Newsletter* 1 (Fall 2006).

[10] 19 CFR § 152.102(d).

[11] 19 USC § 1401a(h)(2).

[12] 19 USC § 1401a(h)(4).

[13] 19 USC § 1401a(d)(2)(A).

the merchandise being appraised, the price is the unit price at which the merchandise being appraised, after further processing, is sold in the greatest aggregate quantity before the 180th day after of such importation. The importer must affirmatively notify Customs if it chooses this option.[14]

Because of the administrative burden involved in applying deductive value and the artificial pricing calculations involved, it is generally disfavored by importers and Customs alike.

.04 Computed Value

Computed value is derived from the cost of producing the imported merchandise. Computed value is defined as the sum of the following:

- The cost or value of the materials and the fabrication and other processing of any kind employed in the production of the imported merchandise;

- An amount of profit and general expense equal to that usually reflected in sales of merchandise of the same class or kind of the imported merchandise that are made by producers in the country of exportation for export to the United States;

- Any "assist," if its value is not included under subparagraph (A) or (B); and

- The packing costs.[15]

This option may be chosen in lieu of deductive value, and must be reported to Customs on a periodic basis (usually semi-annually or annually) via the Reconciliation Program, *see infra*.

.05 Other Approaches

If the above methodologies cannot be applied, taxpayers may use one of those methods, "reasonably adjusted" to the extent necessary to arrive at a value. The requirement that identical or similar merchandise should be exported at or about the same time as the merchandise being appraised may be interpreted flexibly. For deductive value, the 90-day requirement may also be administered flexibly.[16]

¶ 1520 Differences in Customs and Tax Approach

Because customs and tax rules pursue fundamentally different theoretical goals, differences result in the customs and tax approach to the item to be taxed, the relevant time for determination, and the level of detailed determination.

Customs applies duty based upon the value of dutiable goods. Customs seeks to *attach the correct dutiable value on specific imported goods*. The relevant time for determination of whether a transfer price is correct for customs purposes is the date of entry of the item into the United States.[17] Customs imposes a duty at the goods classification level, including component parts, and requires a detailed

---

[14] *Id.* The deductive value method is broadly similar in approach to the resale price method for tax purposes.

[15] 19 USC § 1401a(c). The computed value method is broadly similar in approach to the Cost Plus method for transfer pricing purposes.

[16] 19 USC § 1401a(f).

[17] The valuation statute directs that "any rebate of, or other decrease in, the price actually paid or payable that is made or otherwise effected between the buyer and seller *after* the date of importation shall be disregarded in determining the transaction value . . ." (emphasis added). 19 USC § 1401a(b)(4)(B).

transaction-by-transaction approach with a determination at the goods classification level. Differences between customs and tax goals show up in the practical application of the relevant transfer pricing rules. The tax rules start with gross income and determine taxable income after appropriate deductions. These rules seek to properly allocate income between related parties to achieve the clear reflection of income and prevent the shifting of income between tax jurisdictions. The relevant time for determination of whether a transfer price is correct for tax purposes is the date on which the tax return is filed.[18] The IRS' goal of clear reflection of income does not require that the valuation be correct for each transaction, but only that the ultimate result of any underpayments and overpayments achieves an appropriate income result in the aggregate. This difference allows for aggregation of transactions and "offsetting adjustments" for tax purposes.[19]

¶ 1530 Customs Enforcement

Customs appraises goods at the port of entry. The appropriate Customs import specialist is empowered to determine the final appraisement of merchandise "by all reasonable ways and means," including the use of any statement of cost or costs of production in any invoice, affidavit, declaration, or other documents.[20]

After an appraised value has been determined, the amount of duty collected is based on the duty rate assigned to the product's tariff code as set forth in the Harmonized Tariff Schedule of the United States ("HTSUS"). The HTSUS contains thousands of tariff codes, each with its own product description and corresponding duty rate, as well as applicable preferential duty rates (such as under NAFTA). Duty rates are generally assessed on an *ad valorem* basis, i.e., as a percentage of the declared value, but can also be based on units of measure, or a combination of those methods.

These items (valuation and tariff classification), as well as the other information required to be reported to Customs, are transmitted to the government via the Entry Summary (Customs Form 7501). This key document serves as the "transactional tax return" and is the starting point for all recordkeeping and audit issues.

Under U.S. Customs laws, an importer is required to maintain records relating to import transactions for five years.[21] The regulations[22] broadly define the term "records" to include statements, declarations, books, papers, correspondence, documents, electronic data, and accounting books. These records are of the type normally kept in the ordinary course of business and that:

- Pertain to any importation of merchandise;
- Establish the right to make entry;
- Establish the correctness of any entry;
- Determine the liability of any person for duties and taxes due or which may be due to the U.S.;
- Determine the liability of any person for fines, penalties, and forfeitures; or

---

[18] Reg. § 1.482-1(a)(3).
[19] Reg. § 1.482-1(g)(4)(i).
[20] 19 USCA § 1500(a).

[21] 19 USCA § 1508.
[22] 19 CFR § 162.1a(a).

- Determine whether the person has complied with the laws and regulations administered by Customs.

In general, relevant records for transaction value include commercial or pro forma invoices, bills of lading/air waybills, packing lists, receiving records, certain production records, evidence of freight and insurance charges, and proof of payment.

In addition to separate recordkeeping penalties, civil (and, where fraud is involved, criminal) penalties can be assessed against any person who enters or attempts to enter merchandise into the United States by means of a "materially false" document or statement. The "section 592" penalties for noncompliance vary according to the level of culpability:

- **Negligent violations** can result in civil penalties in an amount not to exceed:

  —The lesser of the domestic value of the merchandise, or

  —**Two times** the loss of revenue (duties, taxes, and fees) or

  —If the violation did not affect the assessment of duties, 20% of the dutiable value of the merchandise.

- **Gross Negligent** violations can result in a civil penalty in an amount not to exceed:

  —The lesser of the domestic value of the merchandise or

  —**Four times** the loss of revenue (duties, taxes and fees), or

  —If the violation did not affect the assessment of duties, 40% of the dutiable value of the merchandise.

- **Fraudulent** violations can result in a penalty in an amount not to exceed the domestic value of the merchandise.[23]

Documents or statements that contain "material misstatements or omissions" are considered materially false. It should also be noted that these penalties can be assessed even if the government has not lost any revenue as a result of such material false documents or statements; in other words, even if an item is duty-free, the importer faces liability for materially false omissions or misstatements, and—as noted above—the potential penalties are far *greater* in instances when no revenue loss occurs.

Importers can protect themselves from these penalties by filing "Prior Disclosures" with Customs when, on their own initiative, they uncover misstatements and omissions and report them to Customs prior to being notified that a formal investigation has been launched.[24]

¶ 1540 Problems of Inconsistency

.01 Taxpayer Whipsaw

Early tax cases took little notice of the differences between the tax and customs approaches to transfer pricing. In *Ross Glove Co.*, the Tax Court found that

---

[23] 19 USCA § 1592; 19 CFR § 162.73.   [24] 19 CFR § 162.74.

the "methods adopted by Customs and [IRS] . . . are quite similar."[25] Markups used by Customs to compute the value of gloves purchased from a related party were considered adequate to determine the arm's length price under Code Sec. 482.

According to the court, the Customs markups were the "best available evidence as to the amounts that a seller would receive to cover overhead and product in an arm's length sale."[26] The court rejected the IRS's arguments that Customs valuations are basically unreliable and cannot form the basis for a determination of an arm's length price for tax purposes. In fact, the court used the Customs valuation to demonstrate the unreasonableness of the IRS position.[27]

In *Brittingham*,[28] the IRS attempted to use a Customs value to establish an arm's length price for tax purposes. In that case, the IRS determined that a U.S. importer paid more than an arm's length price[29] for ceramic tile imported from a related party in Mexico. The purchase price substantially exceeded the value reported for customs duty purposes. The Tax Court rejected the IRS argument, holding that the Customs value was based on an erroneous assumption that a competitor's product was similar. An arm's length price is the price an unrelated party charges another unrelated party for a product or service. The Customs determinations were not indicative of an arm's length price, even though the taxpayer had won a previous dispute with Customs on the same issues.[30]

Congress was concerned that the holding in *Brittingham* encouraged taxpayers to declare a low customs value and a higher tax value. Therefore, in 1986 Congress enacted Code Sec. 1059A, specifically to prevent this whipsaw.[31]

.02 Liquidation

Customs value generally becomes final 180 days following the date of "liquidation" of the imported goods.[32] Liquidation means the final "closing out" of all information reported to Customs on the Entry Summary (CF7501), which generally takes place on or about 314 days after the date of importation. If, for whatever reason, formal liquidation does not occur, customs entries are "deemed" liquidated as a matter of law within one year from the date of entry unless:

1. Customs extends liquidation to gather further information;
2. The importer requests an extension for good cause;
3. Customs has reason to withhold liquidation; or
4. Customs is ordered to do so by the courts or is required to do so by statute.[33]

---

[25] *Ross Glove Co.*, CCH Dec. 32,053, 60 TC 569, 604 (1973), *acq.*, 1974-1 CB 2.

[26] *Id.* at 605.

[27] *Id.* at 604.

[28] *R.M. Brittingham*, CCH Dec. 33,856, 66 TC 373 (1976), *aff'd*, 79-2 USTC ¶ 9499, 598 F.2d 1375 (5th Cir. 1979).

[29] International Taxation: Problems Persist in Determining Tax Effects of Intercompany Prices (GAO/GGD-92-89, June 15, 1992).

[30] *R.M. Brittingham*, CCH Dec. 33,856, 66 TC at 389.

[31] General Explanation of the Tax Reform Act of 1986 (Staff, Joint Committee on Taxation), 100th Cong., 1st Sess. 1061, 1062 (1987).

[32] "Liquidation" is the administrative action taken to finalize all information reported to Customs in connection with the importation and determination of the final duty and fees owed.

[33] 19 USC §§ 1504(a) and (b).

This timing can create an unfortunate whip-saw exposure for importers. Under the IRS's current audit cycle, it is highly likely that, unless an extension of liquidation occurs, a substantial portion of an importer's import entries will have been closed out for Customs purposes before completion of an IRS audit.

¶ 1550 Code Sec. 1059A

Congress was concerned that the transfer price reported for tax purposes could substantially exceed the transfer price reported for customs purposes, allowing related parties to avoid federal income tax. In response to this concern, Congress added Code Sec. 1059A in 1986.

The coordination provisions apply to any property imported into the United States in a transaction, directly or indirectly, between related persons within the meaning of Code Sec. 482. Code Sec. 1059A states that costs taken into account in computing a purchaser's basis or inventory cost of the property cannot be greater than costs taken into account in computing the customs value, if such costs also form the basis of appraisement for customs valuation purposes.

The strict statutory language prevents an importer from claiming a higher tax basis for imported merchandise than the customs value. Application of this statutory language is considerably more complicated.

The legislative history to Code Sec. 1059A stated that the Secretary of the Treasury would provide rules coordinating customs and tax valuation principles. The Treasury issued regulations under Code Sec. 1059A in 1989. These regulations apply the customs value basis limitation to all transactions between controlled taxpayers, but exclude imported items that are not subject to customs duties.[34] If an item or a portion of an item is not subject to customs duty, or is subject to a free rate of duty, that item or portion of the item is not subject to the provisions of the coordination provision.[35] The following examples are not subject to the coordination provision:

1. The portion of an item that is an "American good returned" (reported under heading 9802 of the HTSUS) and not subject to duty;[36]

2. Imports on which no duty is imposed that are valued by customs for statistical purposes only;

3. Items subject to a zero rate of duty;[37]

4. Items subject only to the user fee[38] or the harbor maintenance tax,[39] or only to both such levies.

The tax basis may differ from the customs value because of legitimate differences between customs and tax valuation rules. Regulations allow certain adjustments to the customs value, and the taxpayers may increase the customs value of imported property by:

---

[34] As defined in Reg. § 1.482-1(a).

[35] Reg. § 1.1059A-1(c)(1).

[36] Items 806.20 and 806.30. Tariff Schedules of the United States, 19 USCA § 1202.

[37] 19 USCA § 1202, General Headnote 3.

[38] 19 USCA § 58(c).

[39] Code Sec. 4461.

1. Freight charges;

2. Insurance charges;

3. The construction, erection, assembly, or technical assistance provided for property after its importation into the United States; and

4. Any other amounts which are not taken into account in determining the customs value, which are not properly included in customs value, and which are appropriately included in the cost basis or inventory cost for income tax purposes.

Code Sec. 1059A does not limit the authority of the IRS to increase or decrease the claimed basis or inventory cost under Code Sec. 482.[40] The coordination rule does not apply to goods that are not subject to any customs duty or are subject to a free rate of duty.[41] This exemption also applies to any *portion* of a good that may not be subject to any duty or subject to a free rate of duty.

¶ 1560 Joint Agency Efforts

Tax authorities from member countries have been able to minimize their differences with regard to transfer pricing and provide consensus guidelines for transfer pricing through commitment to the transfer pricing guidelines developed by the Organisation for Economic Co-operation and Development (OECD).[42] Although a certain amount of difference in application is inevitable, the commitment to the OECD guidelines represents a positive step toward harmonization.

The World Customs Organization ("WCO") has achieved a certain level of harmonization of customs treatment among contracting states, especially in the area of customs valuation. The WCO's Technical Committee on Customs Valuation ("TCCV") meets twice a year at the WCO Headquarters in Brussels, Belgium, and reviews issues of current global concern, which often result in the publication of formal Opinions and Case Studies, which can then be used and applied by the 176 member states' customs authorities in formulating local policies and rules.

.01 Mutual Assistance Agreement

Customs and the IRS established a Mutual Assistance Agreement in 1992 as to international compliance and importation issues. The purpose of the agreement was to develop a general framework in providing assistance and exchanging information and data between the respective agencies. The agreement has three objectives:

1. To achieve greater efficiency in the administration and enforcement of federal laws;

2. To promote certainty and objectivity in the administration of issues pertaining to complex international transactions; and

3. To promote an environment conducive to voluntary compliance.

---

[40] Reg. § 1.1059A-1(c)(7).

[41] Reg. § 1.1059A-1(c)(1).

[42] "Transfer Pricing Guidelines for Multinational Enterprises and Tax Administration," Report of the OECD Committee on Fiscal Affairs (July 1995). The OECD approved the 2010 revision of the Transfer Pricing Guidelines on July 22, 2010. *See http://www.oecd.org.*

The Mutual Assistance Agreement provides each agency with "the opportunity to seek assistance in the collection and exchange of information, as well as the ability to share knowledge, experiences, and techniques regarding areas of mutual interest." The Mutual Assistance Agreement recites that joint efforts may be beneficial as to functional activities, such as administration, compliance, enforcement, audit, and the regulatory process.

Both agencies are actively seeking methods to collect and track information pertaining to the import of products into the United States. It is expected that the availability of import data will assist both agencies in their enforcement and compliance efforts in the following areas:

1. Verification of quantities and amounts reported as purchases of foreign goods, particularly transactions involving related parties;

2. Identification of entities importing similar foreign produced goods;

3. Identification of pricing/valuation data on imported foreign products for specific periods; and

4. Determination of international pricing and valuation issues, particularly as to the application of the arm's length standard to related party transactions.[43]

Each agency agrees that it will make a "good faith effort" to provide information to the other agency and to be "as responsible as possible" to requests for information, giving consideration to the strict disclosure guidelines placed on each agency by statute. The Mutual Assistance Agreement provides the opportunity to develop interagency understanding of similarities and differences in transfer pricing approaches. Despite the conflicting goals of the two organizations regarding transfer prices, a sustained effort should be made by these two agencies to minimize the impact of those differences.

.02 Removal of IRS Disclosure Obstacle

Uncertainty existed before 1993 regarding the scope of restrictions on the IRS's ability to disclose taxpayer information to Customs.[44] The North American Free Trade Agreement Implementation Act caused a change in policies.[45] The Treasury Department (which then had jurisdiction over Customs; that responsibility now rests with the Department of Homeland Security) issued regulations delineating the procedure by which Customs may obtain access to tax return information in connection with a Customs audit of the taxpayer or related party. These regulations specifically prohibit the IRS disclosure of information disclosed in an APA or information that would violate a tax treaty or executive agreement.[46]

.03 Combined Customs/Transfer Pricing Enforcement

Some countries are establishing joint transfer pricing and customs examinations, either through formal integration of customs and tax offices or through less

---

[43] "Transfer Pricing Guidelines for Multinational Enterprises and Tax Administration," Report of the OECD Committee on Fiscal Affairs (July 1995). The OECD approved the 2010 revision of the Transfer Pricing Guidelines on July 22, 2010. *See http://www.oecd.org.*

[44] *See* Code Sec. 6103.

[45] Regs. § 1.6103(l)(14)-1T(d). Pub. L. No. 103-182, § 552.

[46] Reg. § 301.6103(1)(14)-1(d).

formal methods. Several countries that have integrated tax and customs administrations are Canada, Norway, Spain, Sweden, and the United Kingdom.

In 2005, the OECD published an updated model convention that allowed competent authorities to exchange tax information for other than tax purposes, opening the way for information exchanges between tax officials and customs officials if:

- Domestic law allows use of tax information for non-tax purposes; and

- There is a need for the information.

The Canada Revenue Agency ("CRA") and the Canada Border Services Agency ("CBSA") work together even though they are no longer part of one administration. The two agencies have written a formal memorandum of understanding on information- sharing that is awaiting final signature. Under the MOU, information released by the CRA to the CBSA may be used only to ensure compliance with Canada's Customs Act. In turn, the CBSA may give information to the CRA only to assist in determining whether arm's length results have been achieved. On confidentiality matters, if release of the information is prohibited under a bilateral or multilateral treaty, the MOU does not override the treaty.

Spain's tax and customs agencies have been sharing information for several years. Agreements between the two offices allow for the spontaneous exchange of relevant information, and customs officials will coordinate their audits with tax officials. Under provisions of a 2005 plan to combat tax and customs fraud, Spain conducts joint tax and customs audits if the taxpayer has assets of more than [Euros] € 100 million.

Sweden's customs and tax offices have been working more closely since a 2004 declaration of intent for closer cooperation.

Norway coordinates transfer pricing and customs enforcement through a joint working group that was established under a 1997 agreement.

Other countries have begun to coordinate transfer pricing and customs valuation guidance. Canada released an Information Circular addressing the overlap of Customs and Transfer Pricing in October 2006.[47] In 2009, Australian Customs and Border Protection ("Australian Customs" or "Customs") issued a Practice Statement ("PS2009/21") providing potential applicants with guidance about applying for an official transfer pricing Valuation Advice Ruling.[48] This policy document was noteworthy for several reasons. First, it acknowledges the following:

> In the context of this practice statement, transfer pricing is an agreement between related companies of multi-national enterprises to adjust original prices of goods sold by one related company to another with the purpose of maximising profit and minimising taxation liabilities. The adjustment may result in either an increase or a decrease in the price of the goods. From a Customs and Border Protection perspective this may mean that the Customs value of the imported

---

[47] Canada Information Circular on Transfer Pricing and Customs Valuation, No. IC06-1 (10/05/06).

[48] Australian Customs and Border Protection Service Practice Statement, No. PS2009/21 (July 13, 2009).

goods could possibly be adjusted after the importation of the goods, either up or down.[49]

Thus, Australian Customs has recognized that transfer pricing explicitly encompasses price adjustments as part of the *normal course of business*. In other words, "compensating adjustments" (as they are otherwise called) are recognized by the agency as something to be *expected* as part of a multinational enterprise's global transfer pricing policy, and not as an aberration or unusual occurrence. In essence, this definition of Customs' view of transfer pricing at the outset of the document seems to recognize that transaction values can be, and are, based on transfer prices when sales between related parties occur. It also stands in contrast to the view of some officials with U.S. Customs that adjustments somehow prevent the use of transaction value because there is no fixed "price actually paid or payable" at the time of import, and that alternative bases of appraisement (such as deductive or computed value) must somehow apply instead.

PS2009/21 is also notable because it reinforces the view among many practitioners that importers should obtain a binding ruling from the respective customs authority in order to have "business certainty" that transaction value is the appropriate basis of appraisement and that duty refunds (and payments) will be allowed/required as a result of any compensating adjustments. While the Practice Statement does not *require* importers in Australia to obtain a transfer pricing valuation advice, the thrust of the document makes it clear that a valuation advice is highly recommended so that *all* parties to the transaction (including Australian Customs) have transparency on the rules, processes, policies, and documentation requirements, and reach an outcome that has been analyzed and acted upon by the relevant valuation experts in Melbourne (the location of the Valuation Advice Unit).

However, PS2009/21 unequivocally states that the importer may be entitled to a refund of duty, but *only* "[w]here a VA [Valuation Advice] has been issued and an adjustment results in the customs value decreasing."[50] The Practice Statement essentially then *requires* the importer to obtain a VA (ruling) before any duty refunds can be issued.

In addition, PS2009/21 states that "[b]efore any adjustments can be made to the customs value, there must be an actual transfer of funds related to the transaction that flows in and out of Australia."[51] Compensating adjustments for transfer pricing purposes that are "merely notional adjustments" will not be accepted for customs purposes.[52] While the document does not further define what "notional adjustments" would consist of, it is clear that a "transfer of funds" does not mean actual cash payments from the buyer to the seller or vice-versa. Intercompany debits and credits would be acceptable forms of adjustments.

In 2007, Customs issued its own policy statement as an "Informed Compliance" publication on the interplay between transfer pricing and customs valuation, discussed *infra*. The agency is currently formulating a policy with respect to the

---

[49] PS2009/21, at 2.
[50] *Id.* at 7.

[51] *Id.* at 4.
[52] *Id.*

impact of post-importation transfer pricing adjustments on the use of transaction value, and whether transaction value even applies when such adjustments occur.[53]

¶ 1570 U.S. Customs Involvement in the APA Process

Customs' first involvement in the APA process came in 1998, when a U.S. wholesale distributor ("Importer") filed a Customs ruling request seeking to validate the declared Customs values using the transfer prices developed pursuant to a bilateral APA between the Internal Revenue Service and a foreign tax authority. During the APA negotiation process (and while the ruling request was pending at Customs), a representative of Customs participated at the request of the Importer. This involvement during the actual APA negotiations played a central role in Customs' analysis and made it easier for Customs to issue a favorable ruling in 2000.[54] Another ruling followed in 2003 involving substantially the same set of facts and circumstances for another Importer.[55] In December 2009, Customs issued a third ruling on the issue, once again ruling in favor of the Importer—despite the fact that in this case, Customs was not involved in the APA negotiating process.[56] As of January 2010, these are the only U.S. Customs HQ Rulings that have approved the importer's transfer prices as valid "transaction values" pursuant to an APA.

.01 Transaction Value—Circumstances of Sale Test

Prior to these three rulings, Customs had issued guidance in 1993 regarding the appraisement of transactions between related parties.[57] The existence of a related party relationship between buyer and seller does not give Customs the right to reject the transaction value. However, this relationship alerts Customs to inquire as to the circumstances surrounding the sale.

Customs has the right to inquire. However, an examination of the circumstances is not required in every case, but only in those cases in which Customs has doubts about the acceptability of the price. Customs is not required to communicate its doubts to the importer when seeking information on the circumstances surrounding the sale. Customs may not indicate whether the price has been influenced by the relationship between the buyer and the seller. Customs must communicate its grounds to the importer if it has grounds for maintaining that the transaction value is unacceptable because the relationship has influenced the price. Moreover, the importer must be given a reasonable opportunity to respond and is entitled to be advised in writing of the grounds for Customs' beliefs.

These guidelines harkened back to the statute, which states that transaction value may be acceptable in a related party context if the circumstances of the sale ("COS") of the imported merchandise indicate that the relationship did not influence the price actually paid or payable, or if the price of the imported merchandise approximates enumerated test values.[58] The implementing regulations state that the importer will be given an opportunity to supply such further detailed information as

---

[53] *See* Pike, *supra* note 9.

[54] HQ546979 (Aug. 30, 2000).

[55] HQ548233 (Nov. 11, 2003).

[56] HQ H029658 (Dec. 8, 2009).

[57] Customs Directive 4820-02 (Jan. 13, 1993).

[58] *See* 19 CFR § 152.103(j)(2)(iii) for more detail on the use of test values, which essentially allow the use of previously declared and accepted transaction values to act as surrogates for determining whether current transaction values are acceptable.

may be necessary to enable Customs to examine the COS.[59] Customs will consider pertinent details of the transaction, e.g., the manner in which the parties organize their commercial relations and the methodologies utilized to derive the price in question, to determine whether the relationship influenced the price actually paid or payable.[60] In making this determination, Customs will also seek evidence that the price has been settled in a manner consistent with the normal pricing practices of the industry in question, or with the manner in which the seller settles prices for sales to unrelated buyers.[61] Furthermore, if it is shown that the price is adequate to ensure recovery of all costs plus a profit that is equivalent to the seller's total profit realized over a representative period of time, in sales of merchandise of the same class or kind,[62] then Customs will accept that the relationship did not influence the price.[63] All of these COS tests seek to ensure that the transaction value is essentially an arm's length price—which is also the goal of the income tax regulations when examining transfer pricing under Code Sec. 482.

The three rulings noted above focused on the COS test in seeking to persuade Customs that the particular facts and circumstances presented met the rules for use of transaction value. In the 2000 ruling, Customs noted that merchandise imported into the United States is generally appraised in accordance with Code Sec. 402 of the Tariff Act of 1930[64] and that the preferred method of appraisement is "transaction value."[65] The agency further noted that transaction value (the "price actually paid or payable") between related parties is acceptable if the importer demonstrates that the circumstances of sale demonstrate that the declared values are arm's length.

In determining whether the COS test had been satisfied in the 2000 ruling, Customs found that "the information submitted during the APA negotiation process constituted valuable information in applying the COS test . . . ." Customs noted that the importer's invitation to participate in the APA process allowed it to review the selection of the tested party, how the comparable companies were selected, the determination of financial results related to the controlled transactions, the selection of the years for comparison, what accounting adjustments were made to the financial statements of the comparable companies and the tested party, the selection of the most reliable PLI, the capital adjustments and the use of the interquartile range. In deciding the 2003 ruling, Customs likewise found valuable the information submitted during the APA approval process, despite the fact that in that case Customs was not directly involved in the APA negotiations.

In both the 2000 and 2003 rulings, Customs referenced the tests contained in its regulations for determining that the relationship between the parties did not influence the price, noting in the 2000 ruling that Customs regulations require that

---

[59] 19 USC § 1401a(b)(2)(B).

[60] Interpretive Note 1 – 19 CFR § 152.103(l)(1).

[61] Interpretive Note 2 – 19 CFR § 152.103(l)(1).

[62] The regulations define "merchandise of the same class or kind" as including, but not limited to, identical merchandise and similar merchandise within a group or range of merchandise produced by a particular industry or industry sector. 19 CFR § 152.102(h).

[63] Interpretive Note 3 – 19 CFR § 152.103(l)(1).

[64] 19 USC § 1401a.

[65] Even though the regulations under Code Sec. 482 do not prioritize the transfer pricing methods, it should be noted that the comparable profit method has been used in 58 percent of the completed APAs.

¶1570.01

"the price is adequate to ensure recovery of all costs, plus a profit that is equivalent to the firm's overall profit realized over a representative period of time in sales of merchandise of the same class or kind."[66] In both rulings, Customs stated that the bilateral nature of the APA negotiations was persuasive in satisfying this requirement because it ensured that both the IRS and the foreign tax authority reviewed the pricing information—including profit margins—and negotiated a fair result for both taxing authorities.

Customs agreed with the importer's position that the information submitted in the APA request provided Customs with the necessary profit information to conclude that the COS test was met, and thus satisfied that the transaction value was the proper basis for valuing the imported goods. Specifically, in the 2000 ruling, Customs held that:

> [o]ur review of the information, including attending the APA prefiling conference and review of information submitted to the IRS . . . allows us to conclude that we have examined the relevant aspects of the transaction, including the way in which the importer and its related suppliers organize their commercial relations, as well as the way in which the price in question was arrived at between the parties. Based on this review, we hold that the [i]mporter has demonstrated that the price has not been influenced by the relationship for purposed of the COS test.

.02 Detailed Analysis of 2009 Ruling

The company at issue in the ruling was a U.S. corporation that functioned as the exclusive distributor of motor vehicles, parts, accessories, and service tools for its foreign-owned parent company. As part of a "Focused Assessment," the importer was asked to justify the arm's length nature of its vehicle and parts pricing to the audit team, which it explained and summarized in the ruling as follows:

> The sales process between these two entities begins with the U.S. buyer/importer preparing a pricing proposal for each vehicle model that it will import during the upcoming year. This pricing proposal analyzes the market segment for each model and includes information on competitor's vehicles, sales plans, and suggested vehicle trim levels. The pricing proposal also includes recommendations regarding dealer margins and the Manufacturer's Suggested Retail Price ("MSRP"). A similar proposal is also prepared by the foreign parent seller/manufacturer, and includes recommendations for an FOB amount for the vehicles, dealer costs, and MSRPs based on sales and profit goals. Once these proposals are created, the two parties negotiate an acceptable price that the buyer will pay for the imported vehicles. The U.S. buyer/importer then uses this negotiated price on purchase orders it sends to the foreign seller/manufacturer, who in turn issues an invoice for the ordered vehicles that transfers title and risk of loss at the port of embarkation.[67]

The U.S. buyer/importer had previously applied for a bilateral APA with both the U.S. Internal Revenue Service ("IRS") and the foreign tax authority of the parent company. An APA is a prospective agreement between a taxpayer and the national tax authorities, and it establishes the correct transfer pricing methodologies to be applied to transactions between related parties. Having an APA allows taxpayers to avoid audits and disputes, and validates that the covered transactions

---

[66] 19 CFR § 152.103(l).

[67] HQ H029658 (Dec. 8, 2009), at 2.

between the related parties subject to the APA, like those at issue in this case, are priced at "arm's length," or as if the parties were unrelated. When an APA is bilateral, as it was here, the agreement has been examined and ratified by the tax authorities of the two countries involved, i.e., that of the distributor and the manufacturer. The APA in this case was approved for a five-year term, and the transfer pricing method selected was the "comparable profits method" ("CPM").

Pursuant to the CPM, an arm's length price range of operating profits was selected by comparing the profitability of the "tested party" (in this case, the U.S. buyer/importer/taxpayer) to that of a set of unrelated companies selected and refined through a sophisticated economic analysis performed by the importer's outside accounting firm. The comparable companies finally selected for examination in this APA were 21 companies identified as performing similar functions and assuming similar risks as the U.S. buyer/importer. None of the 21 companies selected were automobile distributors or manufacturers because pricing data for sales from vehicle manufactures to unrelated distributors did not exist. Instead, the final comparable set of companies included those selling a variety of products, from heating equipment to tires to roofing materials. Using the CPM, the APA set forth an acceptable arm's length range of operating profits for transactions between the two companies, which range was ratified by both the IRS and the foreign tax authorities. As with all APAs, the agreement also provided for reporting formal "compensating adjustments" should the profits fall outside of the range for any given year covered by the APA Term.

Upon this factual background, the audit team (working with the local import specialist) was unable to make a determination of the appropriate appraisement basis. Thus, the importer's outside counsel prepared a request for Internal Advice for the Port Director to forward on to Customs HQ, posing the single issue for resolution: whether the prices paid between the related seller/manufacturer and the buyer/importer, established pursuant to the approved bilateral APA, were acceptable for the purposes of using the transaction value method of appraisement under the U.S. Customs regulations?

In answering this question, Customs first had to examine whether or not the transactions between the U.S. buyer and the foreign seller qualified as *"bona fide sales."* This determination was necessary because the Customs regulations only permit importers to value goods using transaction value when the transaction qualifies as a *"bona fide* sale." In examining whether or not a *bona fide* sale has occurred, Customs considers such factors as risk of loss, transfer of title, whether the goods were paid for, and whether the parties generally functioned as a buyer and a seller. In this case, Customs determined that a *bona fide* sale *did* occur, based in part on the preparation of the pricing proposals by both parties, the price negotiations between the parties, the fact that the importer set the dealer cost and MSRP, and the overall "structure" of the transactions, which included the issuance of purchase orders and invoices that transferred title and risk of loss to the buyer at the port of embarkation.

After determining that the transactions between the U.S. buyer/importer and foreign seller/manufacturer were *bona fide* sales, Customs focused on the other

¶1570.02

requirement for using transaction value—whether or not the price actually paid or payable by the buyer to the seller was influenced by the relationship between the parties. Customs made this determination by examining the circumstances of the sale for signs that the parties' relationship influenced the sales price of the vehicles.

In examining the circumstances of the sales at issue, Customs focused on three main areas: (1) whether the sales prices of the transactions were settled in a similar manner to the way the seller settled prices with unrelated parties or with the normal pricing practices of the industry; (2) whether the sales prices were adequate to ensure the recovery of all costs plus a profit equivalent to the company's overall profit realized over a representative period of time; and (3) whether there were any other factors that indicated that the relationship between the buyer and seller did not influence the sales prices.

Customs first examined whether the sales prices of the transactions were settled in a similar manner to the way the seller settled prices with unrelated parties or with the normal pricing practices of the industry. Although the manufacturer at issue had some independent distributors of its vehicles in other jurisdictions (especially in South America), Customs agreed that because of different volumes, consumer preferences, and government regulations in those countries, using those prices as surrogates to determine whether transaction value was acceptable would yield a meaningless comparison.[68]

The ruling then turned to a discussion of whether the sales prices were set in a manner consistent with the normal pricing practices of the automotive industry. Customs noted that the importer's ruling request included a paper prepared by Ernst & Young entitled "Pricing Practices in the Automotive Industry," which provided a comprehensive overview of how prices are set in the automotive industry. Customs acknowledged that this paper provided evidence (although not "entirely objective" evidence) describing the "market-driven" pricing of how the automotive industry sets it vehicle and parts pricing, and agreed that:

> vehicle pricing at all levels is based on the market driven MSRP. In other words, once a vehicle has been produced, pricing through the chain of manufacturing, assembly, marketing, and retail sale is based on actual retail prices paid by consumers, and not on some hypothetical and expected prices or costs used in the development stage.[69]

Although the ruling then declined to address the validity of the comparables selected and approved by both the IRS and the foreign taxing authority, Customs nonetheless found that the importer had submitted "some evidence that the price was settled in a manner consistent with the normal pricing practices of the industry."[70]

Customs next examined whether the declared import values were adequate to ensure the recovery of all costs plus a profit equivalent to the company's overall profit realized over a representative period of time in sales of merchandise of the same class or kind, as required by 19 C.F.R. § 152.102(i)(1)(iii) to demonstrate that

[68] HQ H029658, at 7.
[69] Id.
[70] Id. at 8.

the relationship between the parties did not influence the price paid for the merchandise. To support its claim that the sales prices were adequate, the importer relied on the approved bilateral APA, in which the IRS and the foreign tax authority had approved the importer's submitted range of profitability based upon comparisons made between the importer's profitability and the profitability of the 21 "comparable" companies. The importer asserted that the IRS's approval of its profitability range would ensure that the company recovered "all costs plus a profit" as required by the Customs regulations, and that this in turn supported the importer's claim that the sales prices it paid to its parent company for the vehicles were set at arm's length and could properly be used with the transaction value appraisal method.

While Customs acknowledged that the APA's comparison between the importer's profitability and that of other companies "may provide some evidence that the price is adequate to ensure recovery of all costs plus a profit,"[71] Customs found this kind of information to be "less valuable since the companies are not engaged in the sale of the same class or kind of merchandise."[72]

Customs also addressed the importer's argument that the *buyer's* overall profit over a representative period of time should be considered in determining whether the relationship between the seller/buyer influenced the price. Although the ruling noted that Customs has normally examined the *seller's* (manufacturer's) profit in addressing this part of the regulation, it also found that "the buyer's overall profit may be relevant," and that "the buyer's overall profit is one of the factors that may be considered to indicate that the relationship between the buyer and the seller did not influence the price."[73]

Finally, Customs focused its attention on whether any other factors indicated that the relationship between the parties did not influence the sales price. To begin this examination, Customs once again turned to the approved APA. Despite having expressed concerns about the aspect of comparing profits of "functionally equivalent" companies to those of an automotive importer for purposes of the "all costs plus a profit" examination, Customs stated that, overall, it found "that the information submitted to the IRS and the fact that there is a bilateral APA constitute valuable information in evaluating the circumstances of the sale."[74] Customs noted that the existence of an APA covering *all* of the buyer's imported products reduced the possibility of profit manipulation between the buyer and the seller. Customs also stated that while Customs did not participate in the APA pre-filing conference that was held between the importer and the tax authorities, the importer did give Customs access to all of the documents submitted to the IRS during the APA approval process via a waiver.[75] These documents provided Customs with additional support to substantiate the claims the U.S. importer made in its Customs ruling request.

---

[71] *Id.* at 9.
[72] *Id.* at 9.
[73] *Id.*

[74] *Id.*
[75] *Id.*

¶1570.02

Another factor showing that the parties' relationship did not influence the price, according to Customs, was the fact that a *foreign* tax authority approved the APA profit levels, indicating that the foreign seller also earned sufficient profit to cover its operating costs. Finally, Customs identified the rigorous price negotiations between the buyer and the seller that set an FOB price which allowed the importer's operating profit to fall within the profit range established by referencing the unrelated comparable companies as another factor indicating the relationship between the parties did not influence the sales price.[76]

.03 Product Line Analysis Not Required

In all three of the HQ rulings, Customs was careful to note that it normally requires more detailed information pertaining to the valuation of imported merchandise, i.e., pricing information on a more detailed product-by-product level. In the rulings, it did not require the Importer to provide Customs with a further breakdown of product line profitability for comparability since the APA covered all of the Importer's imported products.[77] However, Customs did state in the 2000 ruling that in any future verification, it expected the Importer to demonstrate that the profit earned by product line falls within the agreed upon range specified in the APA.[78]

.04 Adjustments Must Be Reported

The final conclusion of the 2000 ruling noted that if, pursuant to the APA, the importer was required to make compensating adjustments, those adjustments were required to be reported to Customs and any additional duties owed had to be tendered. The ruling was silent, however, with respect to whether *all* adjustments had to be reported, or just those resulting in additional duty owed because of an increase in the declared value, i.e., cost of goods sold—where compensating adjustments are typically booked when tangible property is involved.

.05 2003 Ruling Clarifies Adjustment Reporting

Another importer came forward seeking a Customs HQ ruling with facts and circumstances very similar to those in the 2000 ruling, and also received a favorable ruling approving the use of transaction values based upon transfer prices set pursuant to a bilateral APA. In this ruling, Customs clarified that all compensating adjustments, whether upward or downward, had to be reported to Customs and any additional duties owed had to be tendered. The ruling was silent with respect to the issue of potential refunds in duties due to downward adjustments where the importer's initially-reported value was overstated.[79]

---

[76] *Id.* at 10.

[77] The IRS does not require taxpayers to include all of their intercompany transactions in the APA negotiations.

[78] This "product line" issue is extremely relevant in the computation of duties because the duty rate for all imported merchandise, as noted above, is determined by the HTSUS classification—which is determined on a product-by-product basis.

[79] It is important to note that, while the cited rulings pertained to situations where Advance Pricing Agree-

ments were in effect, their directives have been widely understood to apply to ALL transfer pricing compensating adjustments, not just those applied in the context of an Advance Pricing Agreement. A transfer pricing adjustment is the same regardless of whether it is self-initiated as a result of an internal audit, a recommendation from its outside tax advisors or counsel, because it did not fall within the interquartile range specified in the APA, or whether the IRS initiates the adjustment after its own audit.

The 2009 ruling did not address the issue of future compensating adjustments made pursuant to the approved APA, or whether the Importer would be required to report such adjustments to Customs.

.06 Reconciliation Program

Under Customs' Reconciliation program, importers may flag entries for which certain information is not available at the time of entry. The importer may then review the flagged entries, after importation, to reconcile certain changes to entered information, such as value and report those changes to Customs within 21 months of the date of filing of the Entry Summary (CF7501). Importers have availed themselves of this program to obtain duty refunds for transfer pricing adjustments which result in lower declared values.[80]

.07 Post-Importation Rebates and Price Decreases

Whether the use of Reconciliation, Protests, and Post Summary Adjustments will continue to remain viable options for obtaining duty refunds due to compensating adjustments resulting in lower values depends on the outcome of Customs' internal policy debate on this issue, which as of this writing is still ongoing. Presumably, Customs will clarify its position via request for notice and comment, which will address the issue of whether these adjustments (both upward and downward) preclude the use of transaction value in the first instance, given that they call into question whether a true "sale for export" has occurred at the time of entry. Even if transaction value is allowable in these circumstances, the ultimate HQ ruling is also expected to address whether the statute's prohibition on recognizing "rebates" or other "decreases in price" after the date of importation disallows duty refunds for transfer pricing adjustments.

.08 Informed Compliance Publication ("ICP")[81]

Customs issues publications on a periodic basis addressing a wide variety of import-related topics, and posts these documents on its website (*www.cbp.gov*). These documents are known as "Informed Compliance," or "ICPs," and in April 2007, Customs issued "Determining the Acceptability of Transaction Value for Related Party Transactions." It remains the agency's most comprehensive attempt to delineate its current policy on the overlap between transfer pricing and customs valuation rules, and makes clear that transfer pricing documentation prepared for purposes of section 482 is, standing alone, insufficient to meet the requirements of 19 USC § 1401a(b). The publication is also noteworthy because it specifically references the relevance of APAs in reviewing its previous rulings, and placed the burden squarely on the importer for identifying specific information in the APA or transfer pricing study which may be relevant to the COS test.[82]

Although this ICP may eventually be revised and updated, in light of the 2009 HQ ruling, it currently summarizes a variety of information regarding the intersec-

---

[80] Importers have also filed Protests and Post Summary Adjustments to obtain these refunds when entries were not "flagged" for Reconciliation at the time of entry, but it is unclear as of this writing whether Customs will continue to allow these refunds.

[81] See ¶ 20,160.

[82] *See* ¶ 20,160 of the Practice Tools.

tion of valuation for income tax purposes and valuation for customs purposes. The ICP first summarizes the two ways that related parties can establish the validity of using transaction value for customs valuation—by using either the circumstances of sale test, or by using test values.[83] The ICP then examines how Customs should treat APAs and transfer pricing studies when evaluating related-party transactions under the circumstances of sale test. This examination begins with a brief summary of the requirements that U.S. *tax* laws place upon related-party transactions, as it is generally within this context that related parties will obtain an APA or a transfer pricing study. After this summarization, the ICP examines the key issue of what relevance, if any, these documents have to Customs valuation.

As previously mentioned, the ICP plainly states that an APA or transfer pricing study is *insufficient, in the absence of other evidence,* to establish the validity of transaction value for related-party transactions. Customs maintains this position due to the substantial differences between the legal requirements of U.S. tax laws versus U.S. customs laws, despite the fact that the primary concern of both respective agencies is ensuring that related-party transactions are conducted at arm's length. One difference highlighted by the ICP is that customs laws require importers to determine and report Customs values on an entry-by-entry, product-by-product basis. In contrast to this transaction-based approach, the tax code is concerned with aggregate values, and allows importers to aggregate the value of transactions and offsetting adjustments, in appropriate circumstances. The ICP also notes the differences in the methods used by the IRS and Customs to determine whether the transfer price is set at arm's length. Of particular concern to Customs, according to the ICP, is the fact that it is acceptable under the comparable profits method used by the IRS to compare the profitability of the company at issue with other companies that merely perform similar functions—e.g., that the compared companies are both contract manufacturers. This is in contrast to the requirements of the circumstances of sale test required by Customs, for which the company at issue must present data related to the sale of goods of the *same class or kind,* as well as showing that the price was settled in a manner consisted with the normal pricing practice of the *industry in question.* In light of these differences, Customs asserts that it is difficult to make direct comparisons between the values determined according to customs laws and the values determined according to tax laws.

Although the ICP states that an APA or transfer pricing study in isolation is insufficient to establish the validity of transaction value between related parties, it does acknowledge that the underlying facts and conclusions of these documents may contain information that is relevant to the application of the circumstances of sale test. The ICP goes on to state that Customs will determine how much weight to give the information contained within these documents based upon the particular circumstances in each case, as well as the specific transfer pricing methodology used. As an example, the ICP states that Customs will give "much more weight" to an APA that is based upon the comparable uncontrolled price method ("CUP") than

---

[83] For more information on the Circumstances of Sale Test, *see supra* ¶ 1570.01. For more information the use of test values, *see supra* n.54.

one that is based upon the comparable profits method. Other considerations that Customs may deem relevant include whether the transfer pricing study has been considered by the IRS, whether the APA is bilateral or unilateral, and whether the products covered by the study are comparable to the imported products at issue.

The ICP's bottom line regarding APAs and transfer pricing studies is that it is the importer's responsibility to identify relevant information within these documents and then *explain* the relevancy to Customs. The ICP warns that "[i]f the importer simply submits a copy of an APA or transfer pricing study without further explanation and documentation, the circumstances of sale claim will be rejected."[84]

.09 Conclusion

The relationship of customs valuation and transfer pricing is a complex and evolving area, but once which now appears to have garnered the full attention of Customs and other customs authorities around the world. With its HQ rulings and IC publication, U.S. Customs has finally, although perhaps only tacitly, acknowledged the primary role that transfer pricing plays in valuing imported merchandise. Other customs officials are also taking the lead on this vitally important issue for multinational companies, which seek only to achieve certainty with respect to both their transfer prices and their customs valuation—without the overly burdensome hurdle of preparing completely separate compliance documentation for two different sets of rules on a multi-jurisdictional basis. A "unified" approach to both tax and customs compliance, acceptable to both income tax and customs authorities, would be a far preferable outcome.

---

[84] Customs and Border Protection, "Informed Compliance Publication: Determining the Acceptability of Transaction Value for Related Party Transactions" (April 2007).

Chapter 16

State Transfer Pricing

¶ 1601 Overview[1]

Currently, 47 states plus the District of Columbia impose some sort of tax based on periodic business results.[2] While not all of the taxes are called corporate income or franchise taxes (and indeed, several of them reflect neither the GAAP definition nor the U.S. federal income tax definition of "net income"), the tax levy in each case is a function of a tax rate applied to a tax base.[3] The tax base, in turn, is determined by a formula based on gross business receipts with certain modifications. For purposes of this chapter, the tax base will be referred to as "taxable income."

Whether transfer pricing is relevant in these states depends on the filing methodology employed by the state. In general, states either require members of a unitary business group to file some form of combined or consolidated return ("combined reporting states") or on a separate company basis ("separate return states"). In combined reporting states, transfer pricing reports generally are not germane because intercompany transactions are eliminated, but on occasion may be beneficial (e.g., between two related but separate unitary groups in California).[4] In separate returns states, however, transfer pricing is more relevant and may play a key role in determining a taxpayer's tax liability.

In separate return states, the impact of related party transactions may be greater on state tax returns than on federal returns,[5] for two main reasons:

---

[1] The authors would like to express their thanks to Darrell Coppin, Rebecca Bertothy, Marc Speer, and Scott McShan of Ernst & Young LLP for their assistance in the preparation of this chapter.

[2] All states except Nevada, South Dakota and Wyoming.

[3] E.g., Washington Business and Occupation Tax, Ohio Commercial Activity Tax, New Hampshire Business Profits Tax, etc.

[4] States with mandatory combined or consolidated return filing requirements are: Alaska, Arizona, California, Colorado, Hawaii, Idaho, Illinois, Kansas, Maine, Massachusetts, Michigan, Minnesota, Montana, Nebraska, New Hampshire, New York State and City (only if significant intercompany transactions), North Dakota, Ohio (for CAT and only if consolidated filing is not elected) Oregon, Texas, Utah, Vermont, West Virginia, and Wisconsin. Note, other states may allow, or force, the use of combined/consolidated filing.

[5] Where the difference in effective tax rates between the U.S. and other countries, the impact of related party transactions often times is much greater than the impact on state rates.

1. Every cross-border transaction that originates, terminates or otherwise involves operations in the United States will impact the taxable income of one or more entities in the involved Federal consolidated group, however;

2. Domestic transactions between members of the group will generally not be considered when calculating the taxable income of the group.

Even though transfer pricing, as a concept, in separate return states has at least as large a role in determining state taxable incomes as it does in determining federal taxable income, as a discipline and as a point of controversy, it has not enjoyed the same high profile among state taxpayers and taxing authorities as it has at the federal level. Taxpayers have historically expended less energy to document transfer pricing policies at the state level, and states have provided little or no guidance about what is required.

Further, states have generally not focused audit efforts on transfer pricing, *per se*. And while transfer pricing has been a point of litigation in a handful of state tax cases (mainly out of New York), few cases have turned on the competency or timeliness of transfer pricing documentation. Other reasons for the relatively low profile of transfer pricing at the state level as compared to the federal level, include differences in tax systems, authority and available remedies. These differences will be discussed in subsequent sections, along with relevant, exemplary cases of tax litigation. This lack of attention to state transfer pricing, however, may be and, in fact, seems to be yielding to at least some attempt on the part of states to develop their approaches to transfer pricing and we will likewise address these developments and some possible reasons for them.

¶ 1610 Underlying Concepts

To understand the state approach to income allocation, and especially to dealing with perceived misallocations of income, several concepts must be explained.

.01 Taxable Income

In most states that levy a tax based on net income, the starting point for calculating state taxable income is Federal taxable income. For related affiliates that are members of a single Federal consolidated filing group, there is a single calculation of Federal taxable income for the group. The Federal taxable income for each corporation is calculated on a pro forma basis, as if it was going to file a separate Form 1120, and then in each state certain adjustments are made. On a *pro forma* basis, intercompany transactions are considered, and affect taxable income unless and until consolidations occur.

.02 Allocable Income

After determining each member's share of Federal taxable income, those members doing business in, and considered to be taxpayers in, multiple states must further allocate taxable income to the respective states in which they file. The term "allocable income" is used when describing the income of a multistate tax filer that is attributable to only one state. An example of allocable income is the gain on the sale of non-business real property.

.03 Apportionment

After determining an entity's share of Federal taxable income and allocating any portions of that share that are not attributable to interstate commerce, the remainder is divided among the various states in which the taxpayer does business. This is accomplished by applying a formulary *apportionment* methodology to the total remaining, or *apportionable* income.

States employ a variety of apportionment formulas, but all are based on some ratio of business attributes. Although many states use the Uniform Division of Income for Tax Purposes Act (UDITPA) three-factor apportionment formula consisting of equally-weighted payroll, property and sales factors,[6] many states use a modified three-factor apportionment formula that assigns more weight to the sales factor than the other two factors. Some of these states assign a double weight to the sales factor, i.e., 50 percent sales, 25 percent property, 25 percent payroll.[7] However, several states have adopted other variations in this formula.[8] Further, a recent trend has led to several states adopting a single sales-factor apportionment formula.

.04 Arm's Length Standard/Arm's Length Doctrine

As in the general body of transfer pricing knowledge, the *Arm's Length Standard* requires that transactions between related parties be consummated at prices and under terms that are as close as possible to those of transactions between unrelated parties.

.05 Distortion

Distortion simply means that income reflected on a taxpayer's state income tax return is distorted, or inaccurate, due to intercompany transactions included in the results. As we shall discuss below, until January 1, 2007, the New York State Tax Code provided that the presence of significant intercompany transactions creates a rebuttable presumption of distortion, with the burden of proof being on the taxpayer. As a point of definition, the presumption of distortion necessarily includes a presumption that transactions are not at arm's length.

.06 Economic Substance Doctrine

The economic substance doctrine is inclusive of the concept of *business purpose* and requires the application of a two-pronged test to a related party transaction:

1. the subjective intent of the taxpayer entering into the transaction—is there a motive (i.e., a profit motive) beyond that of saving federal taxes (a "non-tax business purpose"), and

2. the objective economic substance of the transaction; was there actually a substantive economic impact from the transaction (beyond the impact of reducing federal taxes).

---

[6] States that use an equally weighted three-factor apportionment formula include: Alabama, Delaware, District of Columbia, Hawaii, Kansas, Montana, New Mexico, North Dakota, and Rhode Island.

[7] Corporate income tax states that utilize a double-weighted sales factor apportionment formula include: Arizona, Arkansas, California, Florida, Idaho, Kentucky, Louisiana, Maryland, Massachusetts, New Hampshire, New

Jersey, North Carolina, Ohio, Pennsylvania, Tennessee, Vermont, Virginia, and West Virginia.

[8] States that have adopted or are phasing-in a single sales factor include: Colorado, Connecticut, Georgia, Illinois, Indiana, Iowa, Maine, Michigan, Minnesota, Nebraska, New York, New York City, Oregon, South Carolina, Texas, Utah, Washington (B&O tax purposes) and Wisconsin.

¶1610.06

It should be noted that the use of the connector "and" predated the actual codification of the economic substance doctrine. Prior to the enactment of Code Sec. 7701(o), the economic substance doctrine generally was considered to turn on *either* a non-tax business motive *or* actual substantive non-tax economic impact.

When states apply the economic substance doctrine, the term "state" is substituted for "federal," and transactions must be seen to have a non-state-tax business purpose and a non-state-tax economic effect. For instance, under Wisconsin law, a transaction will have economic substance, if all of the following are met: (1) the transaction changes the taxpayer's economic position in a meaningful way, apart from federal, state and foreign tax effects; and (2) there is a substantial nontax purpose for entering into the transaction and the transaction is a reasonable means of accomplishing the substantial nontax purpose (i.e., the transaction has substantial potential for profit, disregarding any tax effects). Transactions between members of a controlled group will be presumed to lack economic substance. Taxpayers can rebut the presumption by establishing by clear and convincing evidence that a transaction or series of transactions between the taxpayer and one or more members of the controlled group has economic substance.[9]

.07 Sham Transaction Doctrine

The sham transaction doctrine is to be viewed as a threshold issue that should be considered even before the application of the economic substance doctrine. The sham transaction doctrine refers to transactions that do not in fact occur as purported. An example of a sham transaction is a transaction in which certain income is attributed through accounting entries to one entity, while the transactions giving rise to the income are wholly attributable to another entity.

The sham transaction doctrine is essentially about the lack of economic activity, while the economic substance doctrine refers to a lack of economic result. However, many make little distinction between the two, and in fact the doctrines are often used interchangeably.

.08 Nexus

The first step in defining the taxable income of a particular taxpayer is determining "who is a taxpayer?" A threshold issue is the determination of "nexus."

For purposes of this chapter, we will simplify the definition of nexus to be: "The right of a state to require a taxpayer (however that is defined in each state) to file an income tax return and pay a tax measured by net income."[10]

Some states employ a "nexus combined" theory for determining which related entities are included in the consolidated state tax return. Under that concept, only those entities with nexus in the state are included as members of the group.

¶ 1620 Authority to Reallocate Income

Generally speaking, if the allocation of income between related parties has an impact on a state tax return, that state will have some statutory authority to

---

[9] Wis. Stat. §§ 71.10, 71.30, and 71.80.

[10] In February 4, 2010 testimony to the Congressional Subcommittee on Commercial and Administrative Law, Professor Walter Hellerstein stated: "In the state tax context, nexus generally means the connection that a state must have with a person, property, transaction, or activity in order for a state to exercise its taxing power constitutionally over such person, property, transaction, or activity."

reallocate income if it perceives a misallocation. The state's authority to reallocate may be found in various statutory provisions, including the following.

.01 Incorporation of Code Sec. 482

Code Sec. 482-1(a)(2) gives the IRS authority to make allocations among taxpayers:

> The district director may make allocations between or among the members of a controlled group if a controlled taxpayer has not reported its true taxable income. In such case, the district director may allocate income, deductions, credits, allowances, basis, or any other item or element affecting taxable income (referred to as allocations). The appropriate allocation may take the form of an increase or decrease in any relevant amount.

Many states incorporate the IRC, including section 482, by reference. While some states have interpreted this to mean they have the authority to make adjustments to intercompany pricing, others believe that the specific references to "the district director", "controlled group" and "controlled taxpayer" limits the application of Code Sec. 482 to federal taxpayers.[11]

.02 UDITPA Section 18

In 1959, the National Conference of Commissioners on Uniform State Laws approved a model statute for the allocation of income resulting from interstate operations, known as the Uniform Division of Income for Tax Purposes Act, or UDITPA. UDITPA set out formulae and standards for determining the respective state taxable incomes for companies doing business in multiple jurisdictions. However, UDITPA also recognized that the formulae and standards may need to be supplemented by further analysis in certain cases. In order for adoptees to retain the flexibility to deviate from the standard approach, a final section was added.

> Section 18: If the allocation and apportionment provisions of this Act do not fairly represent the extent of the taxpayer's business activity in this state, the taxpayer may petition for or the [tax administrator] may require, in respect to all or any part of the taxpayer's business activity, if reasonable:
> (a) separate accounting;
> (b) the exclusion of any one or more of the factors;
> (c) the inclusion of one or more additional factors which will fairly represent the taxpayer's business activity in this state; or
> (d) the employment of *any other method* to effectuate an equitable allocation and apportionment of the taxpayer's income. (emphasis added)

Subsequent to the adoption of UDITPA, the Multistate Tax Commission (MTC) approved allocation and apportionment regulations, to provide guidance with respect to when an alternative method of apportionment may be required or permitted.

The very general authority granted in paragraph (d) of Section 18 likely gives adopting states the authority to adjust the price of intercompany transactions, even where they do not incorporate Code Sec. 482 or do not believe Code Sec. 482

---

[11] States that have adopted 482-type provisions include: Alaska, Arizona, Arkansas, California, Colorado, Connecticut, District of Columbia, Florida, Georgia, Hawaii, Illinois, Indiana, Iowa, Kansas, Kentucky, Louisiana, Massachusetts, Minnesota, Mississippi, Montana, New Hampshire, New Jersey, New York, North Carolina, North Dakota, Oklahoma, Oregon, Tennessee, Texas, Utah, Virginia, and Wisconsin.

applies to transactions at the state level. Over 30 states adopted provisions similar to UDITPA Section 18 and MTC Article IV.18.[12]

.03 Other General Authority

Even without the other points of authority discussed in this section, most states have given their executives broad authority to make adjustments to "accurately reflect" a taxpayer's taxable income within the state. Generally, then, states have the authority to seek remedy when it appears that a transaction between related parties has been conducted at an other than arm's length price, resulting in excess deductions for the in-state taxpayer.

What is lacking, in most cases, are detailed directions for the application of transfer pricing principles, as provided in Treas. Reg. § § 1.482-2 through 1.482-9. This is true if the relied upon authority is the UDITPA Section 18 or a more general authority. Only New Jersey has promulgated regulations controlling the application of transfer pricing principles to specific taxpayer situations.[13]

¶ 1630 Income Allocation Issues and Approaches

.01 Need For Transfer Pricing Documentation

As noted, distortion is often presumed when a substantial number of intercompany transactions are transacted and, in such cases, it is the taxpayer's burden to rebut the assumption. As stated earlier, the presumption of distortion is inclusive of a presumption that the pricing of the underlying transactions, in whole or in part, are not at arm's length. In such cases, the common and logical approach is for the taxpayer to present evidence that the transactions *are* at arm's length.

While there is little regulatory or statutory guidance regarding the form of such evidence or the standards to apply, the approach most commonly taken is the application of Treas. Reg. § § 1.482-2 through 1.482-9.

Under these circumstances, and even though few states require such documentation, the prudent taxpayer documents his or her transfer pricing policies and methods. Documentation is likely to be the first line of argument in rebutting the presumption of distortion, and the first line of defense against other arguments regarding the arm's length nature of intercompany transactions. In New York, for instance, the fact that a Code Sec. 482 compliant transfer pricing study was prepared by the taxpayer shifts the burden of proof from the taxpayer to the state.

While the timely preparation of competent transfer pricing documentation is a prudent precaution, taxpayers must be aware of the limitations of the protection offered by such documentation. While states have penalty provisions that could be levied for failure to maintain adequate transfer pricing documentation (for instance, a "good faith" penalty or an inaccuracy or underreporting penalty), there currently are no penalties specifically enacted to that effect. Likewise, states are unlikely to rely on a single doctrine when mounting an attack. As we will see, rather than a

---

[12] States adopting UDITPA section 18, MTC Article IV.18, or other similar provisions include: Alabama, Alaska, Arizona, Arkansas, California, Colorado, District of Columbia, Florida, Georgia, Hawaii, Idaho, Illinois, Indiana, Kansas, Kentucky, Maine, Minnesota, Missouri, Montana, Nebraska, New Mexico, North Carolina, North Dakota, Ohio, Oregon, Pennsylvania, Rhode Island, South Carolina, Tennessee, Utah, Vermont, and Virginia.

[13] N.J. Admin. Code § 18:7-5.10.

threshold issue, the arm's length doctrine is often the final and conclusory issue argued.

.02 The States' Approach: Application of Doctrines

While the *arm's length doctrine* is available to many states and may, if properly applied, produce the desired result, states have other options available and have shown some preference for the broader brush approaches of applying the *sham transaction doctrine* and the *economic substance doctrine*. In any case, the goal of the audit is to increase the income subject to the state's tax.

A Hierarchy of Doctrines. Donald Korb (former Chief Counsel for the IRS) has advocated a hierarchical approach to applying the sham transaction doctrine and the economic substance doctrine. He called the sham transaction test a "threshold" issue to be considered first and to be followed by applying the economic substance doctrine. The reason for establishing this hierarchy is readily apparent: conservation of effort. It is easier to determine if economic activity actually took place than it is to determine if the activity resulted in a substantial change in economic conditions. If a transaction fails the first test, there is no need to proceed to the more difficult (and more costly) second test.

Likewise, state taxing authorities have pursued a hierarchy of doctrines in auditing intercompany transactions. As demonstrated by some of the cases analyzed below, the arm's length standard can be added to that hierarchy as the final and most difficult doctrine to argue.

.03 Arguing Multiple Theories

While the logical development and consideration of the three doctrines—Sham transaction, economic substance and arm's length—may be hierarchical in nature, states often argue them simultaneously as multiple theories in the same audit. In this context, we consider the *Syms* case out of Massachusetts.[14]

Syms, a New Jersey based "off-price" retailer, operated stores in the state of Massachusetts. Syms filed and paid the Massachusetts corporate excise tax (a tax measured by net business income). In 1986, based on the recommendations of an outside state tax consultant, Syms formed a subsidiary corporation, SYL, to which it contributed its intellectual property ("IP") which consisted of the Syms name, a trademarked logo and a copyrighted slogan. Thereafter, Syms paid SYL a royalty for the use of the contributed IP, equivalent to 4% of Syms' retail sales, pursuant to a licensing agreement with SYL.

After entering into the royalty agreement with SYL, Syms deducted from its Massachusetts excise tax return the amounts it paid to SYL, significantly lowering its Massachusetts tax liability. SYL was a Delaware corporation, with no operations in Massachusetts. SYL was not subject to the Massachusetts excise tax, and it also was exempt from the Delaware corporate income tax. Thus, the income received by SYL effectively escaped taxation.

In an audit of the tax years 1986 through 1991, the Massachusetts Commissioner of Revenue disallowed the deductions taken by Syms for the royalty expenses paid to SYL. Syms protested the audit and proceeded to an evidentiary

---

[14] *Syms Corp. v. Commissioner of Revenue*, 436 Mass. 505 (2002).

hearing before the Appellate Tax Board. The Board found that the Commissioner had property disallowed the expenses because:

(1) the transfer and leaseback of the marks was a sham and could be disregarded under the "sham transaction doctrine";

(2) the royalty payments were not deductible as ordinary and necessary business expenses where there was no valid business purpose justifying the expense and SYL added little or no value to the marks; and

(3) *M.G. L. c. 63, §39A*, permitted the commissioner to eliminate the royalty payments from the calculation of net income because they were made between affiliated corporations and were in excess of fair value.

All three of the doctrines we defined earlier (sham transaction, economic substance and arm's length) were pursued by the Commissioner and confirmed by the Board. It is worth noting that the definitions extended to the sham transaction doctrine by the Board vary somewhat from what has been previously discussed. In this case, the Board defined a "sham transaction" to mean a transaction that in fact occurred in an effort to exploit a feature of the tax laws, not a transaction that did not occur, or did not occur as reported.

In essence, the Board applied the sham transaction and business purpose doctrines together in these proceedings.

Syms appealed to the Supreme Judicial Court of Massachusetts, where the finding of the Board was upheld.

Interestingly, even though the arm's length nature of the transactions was disputed by the Commissioner, and the Board agreed, no evidence was presented on that point. In fact, though the Board found the intercompany transactions to be ". . . in excess of fair value . . ." it reasoned that the "circular" nature of the transaction made it ". . . irrelevant that the measure of royalty payments might have been equivalent to what would have been paid in an arm's-length transaction."

The results of the *Syms* case are to be contrasted with those of the *Sherwin-Williams* case.[15] These two cases were decided in the same year, both by the Massachusetts Supreme Judicial Court and both appear to have very similar facts and circumstances. The outcomes, however, were very different.

Sherwin-Williams is an Ohio-based manufacturer and seller of paint and related products. In 1990, Sherwin-Williams began to evaluate a plan for the management of valuable IP. In 1991, a wholly owned subsidiary was formed and valuable IP, including the name "Sherwin-Williams," various other trade names and trademarks and slogans were contributed to this new subsidiary, Sherwin-Williams Investment Management Company, Inc. ("SWIMC"). A similar transaction was separately transacted to create Dupli-Color Investment Management Company, Inc. ("DIMC"), which held the IP for the Dupli-Color line of business.

After contributing the IP, Sherwin-Williams paid a royalty to SWIMC, and deducted the royalty payments from its Massachusetts excise tax return, thereby reducing its Massachusetts excise tax expense. SWIMC, a Delaware corporation,

---

[15] *Sherwin William v. Massachusetts*, 438 Mass. 71 (2002).

¶1630.03

was not a Massachusetts taxpayer and, similar to SYL, was exempt from the Delaware corporate income tax.

To this point, the facts and circumstances of Sherwin-Williams (even the early history of the case) appear to be similar, if not identical, to those in *Syms*. The Commissioner disallowed the royalty expenses paid by Sherwin-Williams to SWIMC, arguing the same three theories:

> (1) the transfer and license back of the marks was a sham and could be disregarded under the "sham transaction doctrine";
>
> (2) the royalty payments were not deductible as ordinary and necessary business expenses when there was no valid business purpose justifying the expense; and
>
> (3) M.G. L. c. 63, § 39A, permitted the commissioner to adjust the taxable income of Sherwin-Williams by eliminating the royalty payments because they were not made at arm's length and distorted the actual income of Sherwin-Williams.

In this case, however, the outcome was significantly different. On every point, the Court disagreed with the Commissioner and the Board, holding that the transactions were not a sham and had a valid non-tax business purpose and economic substance. Much was made of the documented efforts on the part of management to explore, with outside counsel and other experts, the business and legal advantages of separately owning the IP.

With regard to the price paid by Sherwin-Williams to SWIMC for the license, the Commissioner argued that the transactions were not at arm's length because of the nature of the relationship between the entities; therefore, any payments made had to be in excess of "fair value." Interestingly, the Court agreed that the transactions were not "arm's length" (presumably because Sherwin-Williams controlled SWIMC and, as in *Syms*, the transactions were circular in nature), but agreed with Sherwin-Williams that fair value was established by the valuation study done by a third party consultant. The merits of the study were not argued, and indeed one of the Commissioner's experts testified: "If [the Sherwin-Williams's marks] were owned by an independent third party . . . a stranger . . . chances are that a very high royalty would be paid."

It should be noted that the Commissioner relied on his authority under Mass. G.L. c. 63, § 39A, which is a "fair value" test, rather than his presumed authority under Code Sec. 482 which requires the transactions be at arm's length. Perhaps if the Commissioner had made the arm's length argument, the circularity of the transaction would have resulted in a different verdict.

Since there was no argument or evidence presented regarding either the fair value or the arm's length nature of these transactions, one cannot say that this case was decided on the question of transfer pricing or economics, but one may infer that without the competent valuation and royalty study, the taxpayer would have failed to sustain its position. The transfer pricing documentation, such as it was, was a necessary but partial requirement to successfully sustaining the taxpayer's position.

.04 Alternative Remedies

At the federal level, the remedy most applied when intercompany transactions are found to be not at arm's length is an adjustment of the transfer price. In *Syms* and in *Sherwin-Williams*, the Commissioner sought to deny the entire deduction for the intercompany royalties paid, under authority granted by Mass. G. L. c. 63, § 39A. As made clear by the court in Sherwin-Williams, § 39A granted the authority to deny deductions " . . . only to the extent that such payments are in excess of fair value . . . " In essence, § 39A granted the commissioner the authority to adjust the price, and in these two cases the intended adjustment was 100 percent of the deduction.

While price adjustments are available to some state taxing authorities, many also have alternative remedies available. In the last twenty years, the most commonly applied alternative remedy is "forced combination", the use of which exceeds pricing adjustments in its incidence.

Forced combination occurs when a taxpayer is required to file a combined state tax return with a non-taxpayer, even though the default filing method in the state is separate company. The difference in result between a 100 percent price adjustment (as in *Syms*) and forced combination is that the tax attributes of the non-taxpayer may be combined with the attributes of the original taxpayer. These attributes include the entire taxable income of the non-taxpayer, as well as the apportionment factors. To the extent the non-taxpayer does business with third parties or affiliates other than the taxpayer, the taxpayer's apportionable taxable income is increased to a greater extent than if the transaction were merely adjusted, even if the adjustment is 100 percent.

Just as we discussed in the earlier cases, the application of the forced combination remedy may be made in cases where the key issue in controversy is the arm's length nature of intercompany transactions, but it is more likely that a state taxing authority will argue multiple theories, just as in *Syms* and *Sherwin-Williams*.

Unsurprisingly, a taxpayer's facts may attract the attention of more than one state. Ironically, the same facts may result in different results based on the doctrine applied by the state. Such was the case for Sherwin-Williams.

In 2004, two years after the Massachusetts decision, Sherwin-Williams argued the same facts before the New York Appellate Court.[16] At the time, New York State employed a separate company filing method. However, the statute in effect at the time provided that substantial intercorporate transactions created a rebuttable presumption of distortion.[17]

While the primary argument made by the New York Department of Taxation and Finance ("DTF") was that Sherwin-Williams had failed to rebut the presumption of distortion, the underlying reasoning was similar to the arguments by

---

[16] *Sherwin-Williams Co. v. New York Tax Appeals Tribunal*, 830 N.E.2d 320 (2005).

[17] See 20 NYCRR 6-2.3 [a] [b]. It should be noted that effective January 1, 2007, for purposes of New York State franchise tax on general business corporations and on insurance corporations, New York law requires related corporations file a combined report that covers any re-
lated corporations if there are substantial inter-corporate transactions among the related corporations, regardless of the transfer price for such inter-corporate transactions. This change eliminates the rebuttable presumption of combination due to intercompany transactions; however, the Commissioner still has the authority to seek to compel combination where the requisite intercompany transactions are lacking.

Massachusetts, save one: the DTF did not claim that the intercompany transactions were sham transactions. Rather, the DTF argue that the transactions were without a valid business purpose, lacked economic substance, and were not at arm's length. Since Massachusetts effectively combined the sham transaction and business purposes/economic substance arguments into a single argument, the rationale employed in this case *is* functionally equivalent to that argued by Massachusetts.

While the arm's length arguments were made by each side, the New York court focused almost entirely on the business purpose/economic substance arguments, merely noting the positions of the taxpayer and the DTF (and their outside experts). Ultimately, the Court found that the DTF had the authority to force combined Sherwin-Williams with SWIMC and DIMC because the transactions lacked economic substance and business purpose.

Both the direction of the arguments and the results of the cases discussed above provide a clear view of the hierarchy of doctrines noted earlier. In each case, the sham transaction and economic substance/business purpose doctrines were considered (albeit as a single analysis, rather than separately) before the arm's length nature of the transactions were considered. Where the case turned on the sham transaction/economic substance analysis, little attention or weight was given to the arm's length arguments.[18]

There are several reasons that explain why the arm's length doctrine is subordinated to the others: (1) states have considerably fewer resources at their disposal to consider the arm's length nature of transactions; (2) the arm's length determination may change over time; and (3) the arm's length standard does not lend itself to a single answer, but rather a range of considerations.

Even so, there are cases (primarily out of New York) wherein a taxpayer's transfer pricing documentation has been subjected to intense scrutiny.

In *Lowes Home Centers*,[19] the New York Department of Tax and Finance, Division of Taxation ("the Division") conducted an audit of Lowes Home Centers, Inc. ("LHC"). LHC owned and operated home improvement stores in the state of New York. During the audit, it was noted that LHC was paying royalties for the use of trade names and trademarks to a wholly owned subsidiary, LF Corporation ("LF"). As in the cases discussed earlier, LF was a Delaware corporation with no physical presence in any other state, having the ownership and management of intangible property as its only business activity.

In New York, the Commissioner is empowered to make adjustments of, among other things, "items of income or deduction in computing entire net income" in order to correct "distortions of income or assets."[20] Beginning in tax year 2007, New York requires combined reporting if there are substantial intercorporate transactions, but during the period under audit in this case, the default method for a New York corporate tax filing was separate company."

---

[18] *See also In the Matter of the Petition of Talbots, Inc.*, No. 820168 (N.Y. Tax App. Trib. Sept. 8, 2008) (Because there was substantial evidence to support the finding that the arrangement lacked economic substance and a valid business purpose, the Tribunal did not find it necessary to address whether the royalty rates reflected market rates).

[19] *Matter of Lowe's Home Centers, Inc.*, No. 818411 (N.Y. Div. Tax App. Sept. 30, 2004).

[20] 20 NYCRR § 18-1.3(a)(1).

However, pursuant to 20 NYCRR § 6-2.2, the commissioner could, in order to correct distortion, require combined reporting of two or more corporations where the existence of substantial intercorporate transactions created the rebuttable presumption of distortion, if two tests were met:

1. A stock ownership test, and

2. A unitary business test.

By the time the Lowes case was adjudicated, it was long established that the presumption of distortion could be rebutted by the proper application of the principles embodied in Code Sec. 482.[21] In *Silver King Broadcasting*, it was established that where the taxpayer has rebutted the presumption (through the application of Code Sec. 482), the burden to dispute the rebuttal was with the Division.[22]

In *Lowes*, the taxpayer did indeed commission several studies by third party service providers. The goal of the studies in each case was to determine the fair royalty rate that LF should be paid for use of the marks and names. The first study was a valuation, and the fair royalty rate was based on the fair market value of the asset. In subsequent studies, the methods focused on the arm's length standard, including use of the Comparable Uncontrolled Transaction Method ("CUT") and the Comparable Profits Method ("CPM").

The Division discounted the valuation study as being irrelevant to the arm's length principle. As for the § 482 studies, the Division found fault with each method employed. When analyzing the CUT method, the Division asserted that the study failed to compare the profit potentials of the intangibles involved in the unrelated transactions to those owned by Lowes.[23] The Division rejected the CPM analysis, in part, because the segmented financial information was unaudited.

The Division employed outside experts, including one who testified, in essence, that the intangible assets at issue had no value when not owned by the entity that used them.[24] He also testified to an expansive theory of intangible assets, asserting that LHC owned non-routine intangibles that not only contributed to the value of the trade names and trademarks but invalidated the analyses conducted under Code Sec. 482. The Division held that, considering the ownership of non-routine intangibles by both parties to the transaction, a Residual Profit Split method would have been more appropriate.

In addition to attacking the validity of the taxpayer's studies, the Division argued that the transaction was without economic substance, discounting testimony by executives from the taxpayer's parent company, Lowes Companies, Inc. ("LCI"). The Division cited the circular nature of the transaction, as well as the lack of real economic effect of the transaction on the parties.

The Division also engaged an expert witness in the areas of economics and transfer pricing.[25] The witness testified, in brief, that:

---

[21] *See Matter of USV Pharmaceutical Corporation*, DTA No. 801050, (NY Tax App. Trib. July 16, 1992); *Matter of Standard Manufacturing Co., Inc.*, DTA No. 801415 (NY Tax App. Trib. Feb. 6, 1992).

[22] *See Matter of Silver King Broadcasting of New Jersey, Inc.*, DTA No. 812589 (NY Tax App. Trib. May 9, 1996).

[23] *See* Code Sec. 482-4(c)(2)(iii)(B)(ii).

[24] *See* testimony of Dr. Alan Shapiro.

[25] *See* testimony of Dr. Ednaldo A. Silva, Ph.D.

¶1630.04

- By employing a number of pre-audit screens of financial ratios, he could identify problems with transfer pricing, and indeed he found the profit margin of LHC to be extremely low and that of LF to be extremely high;

- There was an unsupportable disparity between LF's revenue and expenses (and based on this finding alone distortion was present); and

- The financial screens employed in the process of selecting comparable companies were inappropriately designed, and resulted in the inclusion of companies that were too small to be comparable to LHC.

Like the first expert witness, the second expert witness concluded that the profit split method was the appropriate "best method" to be used in this case.

Of course, LHC employed its own outside experts to counter the testimony of the Division's experts. To counter assertions of other non-routine intangibles, an expert witness for Lowes testified that the assets in question were not protectable and could be copied at will.[26] While agreeing that earlier use of CUT was inappropriate, his testimony supported the use of the CPM.

In the end, the case was decided largely on two issues: (i) whether the non-routine intangibles existed and, therefore, neither method employed by the taxpayer was appropriate to determine an arm's length range, and (ii) whether there was business purpose and economic substance to the transaction.

Before discussing the outcome, it is useful to consider another New York case, *Matter of Hallmark Marketing*.[27]

Hallmark Marketing Corporation ("HMC") was a wholly-owned subsidiary of Hallmark Cards, Inc. ("HCI"). Pursuant to an agreement with HCI, HMC was the exclusive distributor of product designed and manufactured by HCI in the United States. HMC also manufactured and sold display fixtures used by unrelated retailers throughout the United States. HMC was a New York state taxpayer, filing a corporate franchise tax return annually. HCI was not a New York state taxpayer and filed no tax returns in New York.

Following an audit for the tax year 1999, the Division adjusted the income of HMC by combining HMC with HCI in a single tax return, and assessed additional taxes in excess of $1 million dollars (plus penalties and interest).

The transaction in question was the sale of product by HCI to HMC. In 1999, HMC engaged a third party service provider to perform a transfer pricing analysis, to determine whether the prices charged by HCI to HMC for the sale of product was at arm's length. The service provider concluded that the appropriate method for determining an arm's length range was the CPM, and the appropriate profit level indicator was the Berry Ratio.[28]

It should be noted that other intercompany transactions occurred regularly, namely a royalty license from HCI to HMC for the use of the Hallmark trade names and trademarks (in conjunction with sales activities), and the sale of HMC's trade accounts receivables to a related party, Hallmark Funding Corporation ("HFC"), at

---

[26] See testimony of William J. Coyle, Ph.D.

[27] *In the Matter of the Petition of Hallmark Marketing Corporation*, DTA No. 819956 (NY Tax App. Tribunal July 19, 2007).

[28] Both Profit Level Indicator and Berry Ratio are adequately discussed and defined in earlier chapters.

a discount. Neither of those transactions was at issue in the audit, and neither was considered in the transfer pricing analysis except that the discount "loss" on accounts receivables realized by HMC was taken into account in the Berry ratio analysis.

Once again, the Division engaged the same expert witnesses it used in the Lowe's case. One of the experts had an expansive view of non-routine intangibles.[29] Perhaps not surprisingly, this witness asserted that HMC, through its daily business activities, created and owned several non-routine intangibles and, therefore, the CPM method was inappropriate and the residual profit split method should have been selected as the "best method." As in *Lowes*, this witness argued that the financial screens did not produce truly comparable companies.

Also introduced into evidence was the testimony of a second expert witness.[30] Among the issues he had with the transfer pricing report prepared for HMC, this witness testified it was unreliable because of:

- the use of financial screens that inappropriately selected companies that were too small to be comparable to HMC; and
- the failure to consider non-routine intangibles created by HMC.

It should be noted that there were very different sets of facts and circumstances in these last two cases, but the Division asserted very similar arguments. The very similar findings of fact relating to the central issues are worth noting, as is the disparity in the outcomes of the two cases. The administrative law judge ("ALJ") held for the Division in *Lowes*, but for the taxpayer in *Hallmark*. This is all the more remarkable when considering that in *Lowes*, the ALJ agreed that the appropriate method would have been the residual profit split method, based on the presence of non-routine intangibles in LHC. In *Hallmark* that same argument was rejected, despite the fact the Division's witness cited many more, and more specific, examples of intangibles owned by HMC.

In *Lowes*, in addition to citing the failure to use the profit split method, the ALJ also said the transaction lacked business purpose apart from tax avoidance (even though most of the testimony concerned the arm's length nature of the transaction). While little was made of it in argument, it seems clear the circular nature of the transaction weighed heavily in that determination.

It is axiomatic that the differing results in these two cases occurred because of different facts and circumstances. Perhaps the most important difference in fact is the nature of the transactions considered: in one instance, the license of intangibles from a holding company to the entity that first created them (a circular transaction); and in the other instance, the purchase and resale of tangible personal property by an entity with significant business purpose from an entity with significant business purpose.

We must note here that none of the cases analyzed here inform the current state of the law. In both states discussed (Massachusetts and New York), the basic filing regime has changed from separate company filing to combined filing. Therefore, the impact of intercompany transactions on taxpayers in those states has been eliminated, or at least greatly reduced.

---

[29] See testimony of Dr. Shapiro.   [30] See testimony of Dr. Ednaldo A. Silva, Ph.D.

¶1630.04

The value of examining these cases is not in understanding the outcomes, because they are likely to be of only persuasive authority going forward. Rather, the value is in examining the approach the states have taken to examining intercompany transactions and the impact they have on taxable income.

Taxpayers managing intercompany transactions in their own corporate structures should remember the hierarchy of doctrines. Of paramount importance is the sham transaction doctrine, the "threshold question". All transactions undertaken should be fully consummated. Of nearly equal importance is economic substance and business purpose. Transactions that fail these tests may not be sustained. Finally, while it is absolutely necessary that transactions be conducted at arm's length and it is equally necessary that the arm's length nature be documented, the quality and competency of this documentation is moot if it is determined that the transactions at issue were shams that lacked economic substance and a valid business purpose.

¶ 1640 Recent Developments (and Potential Future Developments)

To close this chapter on state tax transfer pricing, very recent developments (and some potential future developments) are examined.

.01 Third Party Auditors

As demonstrated in the cases discussed earlier, adjustments proposed to correct transactions that are perceived to not be at arm's length have tended to be of the "all-or-nothing" variety. Recall that in *Sherwin-Williams* and in *Syms*, Massachusetts proposed 100 percent adjustments, in essence requiring the in state taxpayer to "add back" the transaction.

One likely reason for this all-or-nothing approach, which is not unique to Massachusetts, may be the lack of resources available to states to examine and revise transfer pricing reports. It largely has been beyond the capabilities of the states to propose more refined adjustments. However, in the last few years, some states have begun employing the services of third party consultants to conduct transfer pricing audits on state taxpayers. As of this writing, it is known that at least two states (Alabama and New Jersey) as well as the District of Columbia have proposed assessments based on transfer pricing adjustment audits performed by third parties. These audits are purportedly conducted using standards and methods set out in Code Sec. 482. None of these assessments has been litigated to date, and so the sustainability of these audits is yet to be proven. It is also unclear which if any other states will avail themselves of the services of the third parties. It is likely, however, that the firms providing these services are offering them to a wider market of state taxing authorities. Accordingly, this is a development worth tracking.

.02 APAs at the State Level

Long a staple of the transfer pricing environment at the federal level, Advance Pricing Agreements ("APAs") provide an opportunity for taxpayers to enter into agreements with taxing authorities regarding their transfer pricing methods. In the absence of substantive changes to the facts upon which the agreements are based, an APA typically is in effect for three to five years and is binding on both the taxpayer and the taxing authority. Many APAs are "bilateral" APAs, i.e., agreements between two different jurisdictions (such as the U.S. and Canada) that provide complete definition to the tax treatment of a cross border transaction.

While no states have established similar programs, there is evidence that some are at least considering doing so. A taxpayer's motivation for entering into an APA is certainty, often a more valued commodity than tax savings in the post-Sarbanes-Oxley world. The motivation for a taxing authority to enter into an APA program is efficiency and resource management. Negotiating a transfer pricing approach in a non-adversarial environment, and without the statute of limitation time constraints of an audit process, can allow a taxing authority to accomplish more with less.

The states (including their revenue agencies) are under budget pressures. It certainly seems logical that some would consider this approach to efficient management of resources.

¶ 1650 Summary

In summary, we would like to reiterate the central themes of this chapter:

1. While not universal, the power and authority to review and react to transfer pricing does exist in states;

2. While not a controlling issue in most cases, states have demonstrated that they are aware of and care about the arm's length nature of transactions (or the lack of it); and

3. While taxpayers cannot rely on competent transfer pricing documentation to protect the viability of their intercompany transactions, the lack of credible documentation could have detrimental results.

Chapter 17

Adjustments to Taxable Income: Federal Tax, Customs and State Tax Implications

¶ 1701 Introduction

Global transfer pricing controversy continues to escalate, due to increased governmental resources, new rules, and better access to information from fiscal authorities around the world. In the United States, for example, the Internal Revenue Service ("IRS") has announced a new pilot program under which a small number of transfer pricing cases of "high strategic importance" will be audited using the IRS's "best international examiners, technical advisers, and economists."[1] While the examination team will control the case—as in other audits—the IRS's transfer pricing team will be present as advisers. The program has engendered a positive response, already attracting volunteers among taxpayers.

The logical result of increased enforcement is an increased incidence of transfer pricing adjustments. Despite the development of additional dispute resolution alternatives, it is likely that the increasing number of transfer pricing examinations will produce a growing number of sustained transfer pricing adjustments. Taxpayers should be aware of the federal tax, customs, and state implications of a transfer pricing adjustment.

This chapter will first analyze the three types of transfer pricing adjustments: primary adjustments, correlative adjustments and conforming adjustments. Next, it will review the non-transfer pricing federal tax implications of a sustained adjustment. Finally, it will discuss the customs and state tax implications of a sustained adjustment. This combined approach to these topics demonstrates the interrelatedness of the decisions involved in a transfer pricing adjustment.

---

[1] Moses, Molly, "Competent Authority: IRS Will Extend Audit Time Where Needed in Transfer Pricing Practice, Danilack Says," 18 *Tax Mgmt. Trans. Pricing Rep.* 1214.

¶ 1710 Primary Adjustments

IRS authority to adjust the price of intercompany transactions to clearly reflect income (or prevent tax evasion) is provided in the statutory language of Code Sec. 482. Generally, when the IRS uncovers inappropriately priced intercompany transactions that cause the U.S. party to the transaction to report less taxable income, the IRS will propose a transfer pricing adjustment—the "primary" adjustment.

The following simplified example illustrates this primary adjustment and will be used to illustrate the two other resulting adjustments—the correlative and conforming adjustments.

Example: A US subsidiary ("USSub") sells cheese to its Canadian parent ("CP") for $75. After the IRS reviews USSub's transfer pricing documentation and performs its own analysis, it determines that the correct arm's length value should have been $100. Given that CP paid $75 for a good valued at $100, it received $25 of value in excess of the price paid to USSub. In this situation, in order to reflect the sale of the goods at the arm's length price (i.e., to clearly reflect income), the IRS adjusts USSub's income upwards by $25. This adjustment is referred to as the primary adjustment. See illustration below:

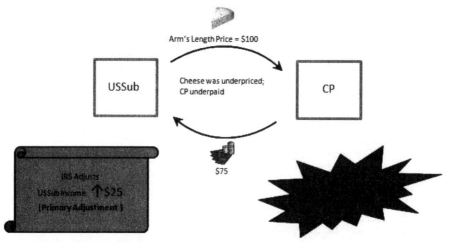

In limited circumstances, the taxpayer may initiate the primary adjustment if necessary to reflect an arm's length result. The transfer pricing regulations allow a taxpayer to report the results on intercompany transactions based upon pricing different from what was actually charged.[2] This primary adjustment is referred to as a self-initiated adjustment. Self-initiated adjustments may adjust U.S. taxable income up or down if reported on a timely filed return; if the self-initiated adjustment increases U.S. taxable income, the taxpayer may make it at any time.[3]

---

[2] Reg. § 1.482-1(a)(3).

[3] Rev. Proc. 99-32, 1999-2 CB 296, Section 2.

¶ 1720 Correlative Adjustments

One of the main taxpayer concerns stemming from a primary adjustment is the possibility of double taxation on the income that has been re-allocated or adjusted. Theoretically, when the IRS effects a primary adjustment to increase the income of one consolidated return member, it also makes a "correlative adjustment" whereby it decreases the income of the other member by the same amount. The correlative adjustment is intended to create a "mirror image" adjustment to the income of the party on the other side of the transaction in order to reflect the primary allocation/adjustment. Put another way, the purpose of collateral adjustments is to retroactively "correct" the transaction at issue, so that proper income tax and book results are reflected by the taxpayer.

The regulations under Code Sec. 482 address correlative adjustments with the following language:

> When the district director makes [a primary adjustment], appropriate correlative allocations will also be made with respect to any other member of the group affected by the allocation. Thus, if the district director makes an allocation of income, the district director will not only increase the income of one member of the group, but correspondingly decrease the income of the other member. In addition, where appropriate, the district director may make such further correlative allocations as may be required by the initial correlative allocation.[4]

The IRS is typically less concerned with making such adjustments in domestic cases because domestic related parties often file a consolidated return featuring internal offsets. However, when one of the related parties is located within another tax jurisdiction, a correlative adjustment can involve several steps and competent authority negotiations on the part of the taxing authorities.

In the above example, if the IRS finds that the arm's length price of the good sold by USSub to CP is $100 rather than $75, the IRS will propose increasing the taxable income of USSub by $25. The multi-national enterprise ("MNE") will be double taxed on the $25 that should have been allocated from CP to USSub—provided that the taxpayer agrees to such an increase by signing Form 870—unless CP's income is correspondingly decreased.[5] The purpose of the correlative adjustment is to avoid this result by creating a mirror image to the primary adjustment for the foreign affiliate (in this case CP) in an amount that correlates to the primary adjustment ($25). See illustration below:

---

[4] Reg. § 1.482-1(g)(2).

[5] One of many forms a final determination may take (see subsequent paragraph).

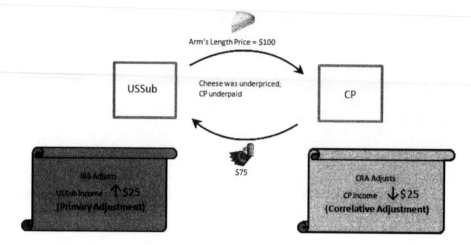

Accordingly, the correlative adjustment will resolve the double taxation issue and the consolidated income of the MNE should equal the same amount after the primary and correlative adjustments as it did before any such adjustment.

Because CP is outside of the U.S. tax jurisdiction, the MNE must seek Competent Authority assistance in order to convince the Canada Revenue Agency ("CRA") to reduce CP's income. The timing of a correlative adjustment is important. A correlative adjustment need not be made until the primary allocation is considered made, which occurs on one of the following five dates:[6]

- Date of assessment following the taxpayer's execution of a Form 870;
- Taxpayer's acceptance of a Form 870-AD;
- Taxpayer's payment of the tax deficiency attributable to the primary allocation;
- Tax Court stipulation or final determination by offer in compromise;
- Closing agreement or final resolution of a judicial proceeding.

¶ 1730 Conforming Adjustments

Conforming adjustments are made, following the primary and correlative adjustments, to reconcile the discrepancy between the taxpayer's cash accounts and the newly altered tax accounts in order to arrive at the appropriate federal income tax treatment of that shifting of income. In other words, the primary and correlative adjustments shift the income from one entity to another but only insofar as the tax liability is concerned. Continuing with the example in ¶ 1720, the cash accounts of CP and USSub still reflect that CP paid $100 to CP, thus raising the question: if only $75 was for cheese, what was the additional $25 for? Therefore, the excess value paid to by USSub to CP must be appropriately characterized from a federal tax perspective.

The regulations describe conforming adjustments with the following language:

> Appropriate adjustments must be made to conform a taxpayer's accounts to reflect allocations made under section 482. Such adjustments may include the

---

[6] Reg. § 1.482-1(g)(2)(ii).

treatment of an allocated amount as a dividend or a capital contribution (as appropriate), or, in appropriate cases, pursuant to such applicable revenue procedures as may be provided by the Commissioner (see § 601.601(d)(2) of this chapter), repayment of the allocated amount without further income tax consequences.[7]

While technically this step in the process is referred to as an adjustment, it could be seen as a recharacterization. The conforming adjustment addresses the correct characterization of the excess asset that resides with one of the related parties due to incorrect transfer pricing. This excess value must be correctly characterized in order to receive appropriate federal income tax treatment.

The recharacterization may take one of two forms: a deemed distribution/dividend, or a capital contribution. Under U.S. tax law, payment in excess of fair market value by a parent corporation to its subsidiary is considered a deemed capital contribution. However, payment in excess of fair market value by a subsidiary to a parent will be deemed a distribution or dividend.[8] There is a third variant of this kind in which a payment in excess of fair market value from a subsidiary to another subsidiary results in a constructive deemed distribution to the parent corporation followed by a capital contribution from the parent corporation to the other subsidiary. Thus a conforming adjustment may characterize income as a deemed distribution or a capital contribution depending on the direction of the allocation.

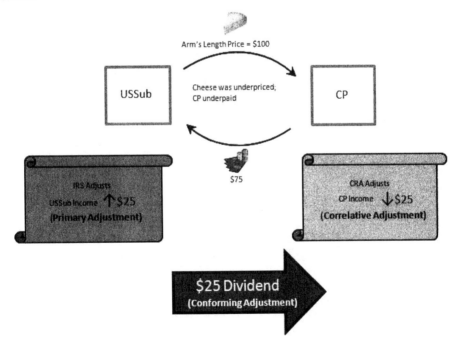

In the example, the primary adjustment increased USSub's income by $25, and the correlative adjustment decreased CP's income by $25. The tax accounts have

---

[7] Reg. § 1.482-1(g)(3).   [8] *Id.*

been adjusted and are balanced such that the MNE will not be double-taxed on the $25. However, the cash accounts reflect that the actual $25 still resides with CP. The conforming adjustment establishes that the $25 in excess of the arm's length price residing with CP is a deemed distribution/dividend from USSub to CP in the year for which the primary allocation is made.

An allocation of income under Code Sec. 482 from a foreign parent corporation to its domestic subsidiary corporation would generally entail a deemed distribution from the domestic subsidiary to its foreign parent in an amount equal to the primary adjustment in the year for which the allocation is made. This deemed distribution would be treated as dividend income to the foreign parent to the extent of the earnings and profits of the domestic subsidiary, as recomputed after taking into account the primary adjustment. Under applicable sections of the Code,[9] the foreign parent would be subject to a 30 percent tax liability (as reduced by any applicable income tax treaty), and the domestic subsidiary would be a withholding agent required to withhold the applicable amount of tax.

¶ 1740 Revenue Procedure 99-32

As demonstrated above, the taxpayer may suffer adverse income tax consequences if it relies solely on the regulations to implement conforming adjustments. Taking these circumstances into account, the IRS issued Rev. Proc. 99-32 to provide a means by which taxpayers could avoid or mitigate such potential detrimental collateral tax consequences.[10] If a taxpayer elects treatment under Rev. Proc. 99-32, such taxpayer will be "allowed to repatriate the cash attributable to a primary adjustment via an account without the federal income tax consequences of the collateral adjustments that might otherwise result from the primary adjustment."[11] Rather than dealing with the withholding obligation that might result from the recharacterization of the excess profits of a foreign parent as a dividend, the excess profit may be transformed into a loan and repaid without further income tax consequences.

.01 Eligibility

The election is not automatically available to all taxpayers. On its face, Rev. Proc. 99-32 applies only to corporations.[12] However, the IRS has, on occasion, been willing to apply the principles of Rev. Proc. 99-32 to partnerships.

An IRS-initiated adjustment of a U.S. taxpayer will be eligible for treatment under Rev. Proc. 99-32 provided that no penalty exists under Code Sec. 6662(e) or (h) with regard to the transfer pricing adjustment and no portion of the adjustment is due to taxpayer fraud. A taxpayer-initiated adjustment by a U.S. taxpayer will be eligible for treatment under Rev. Proc. 99-32 provided that the taxpayer is bound by the treatment provided by the revenue procedure and no portion of the adjustment is due to taxpayer fraud.[13]

---

[9] *See* Code Secs. 881 and 1442.

[10] In discussing the effects of collateral adjustments as referred to in the regulations cited, Rev. Proc. 99-32 refers exclusively to "secondary" adjustments and does not clarify the definition of the term. However, section 2 (Background and Scope) of the revenue procedure mentions that the purpose of such secondary adjustments is to conform the taxpayer's accounts to reflect the primary adjustment. As such, for purposes of this chapter, the term "collateral" adjustments will be used in the same manner as the term "secondary adjustment" is used in the revenue procedure.

[11] Rev. Proc. 99-32, Sec. 2.

[12] *See* Rev. Proc. 99-32, Sec. 2 (definition of "United States taxpayer").

[13] *See* Rev. Proc. 99-32, Sec. 3.

.02 Document Submission

Provided a taxpayer is eligible, there are a number of documents the taxpayer must submit in order to avail itself of the benefits of the Rev. Proc. 99-32 election.

In order to elect treatment under Rev. Proc. 99-32, taxpayers whose taxable income has been adjusted by the IRS must file a request in writing with the IRS before closing action is taken on the primary adjustment.[14] For purposes of the revenue procedure, "closing action" means any of the following:

- Taxpayer's execution and acceptance of a Form 870-AD (Offer of Waiver of Restrictions on Assessment);
- Taxpayer's execution of a closing agreement;
- Stipulation to the Code Sec. 482 allocation in Tax Court;
- Expiration of the statute of limitations on assessments; or
- Final determination of tax liability for the year to which the allocation relates by offer-in-compromise, execution of a closing agreement or court action.

Such a taxpayer's request, which must be signed by a person having the authority to sign the taxpayer's federal income tax returns, must include:

- Statement that the taxpayer desires the treatment provided by section 4 of Rev. Proc. 99-32;
- Designation of the years for which such treatment is requested;
- Description of the arrangements or transactions which gave rise to the primary adjustment; and
- Offer to enter into a closing agreement with the IRS that will memorialize the treatment afforded under Rev. Proc. 99-32.

Upon a determination by the IRS that the revenue procedure is applicable and an agreement on the amount of the primary adjustment, the IRS will enter into a closing agreement with the taxpayer.[15]

In order to elect treatment under Rev. Proc. 99-32, taxpayers making a self-initiated adjustment must file a statement with the tax return reporting the primary adjustment. The statement must include:

- Statement that the taxpayer desires the treatment provided by section 4 of Rev. Proc. 99-32;
- Designation of the years for which such treatment is requested;
- Acknowledgement that the taxpayer will be bound by its election of treatment under Rev. Proc. 99-32;
- Description of the arrangements or transactions that gave rise to the primary adjustment and the amount of the primary adjustments;
- Description of any correlative adjustments;
- Amount and currency of any indebtedness created by Rev. Proc. 99-32;
- Obligee(s) and obligor(s) with respect to such indebtedness;
- Amount (and timing) of any interest includible or deductible with respect to such indebtedness;

---

[14] Rev. Proc. 99-32, Sec. 5.01(1).   [15] Rev. Proc. 99-32, Sec. 5.01(2)-(4).

- Amount of any foreign tax credit claimed with respect to payment(s) on the indebtedness; and

- Manner and payment of the indebtedness.[16]

.03 Closing Agreement

Following an IRS-initiated adjustment, the IRS and a taxpayer desiring treatment under Rev. Proc. 99-32 will enter into a Closing Agreement memorializing such treatment. The Internal Revenue Manual provides two model closing agreements for use with Rev. Proc. 99-32.[17] Both presume that the U.S. corporation has entered into a transaction with a related foreign entity that has given rise to the need for a primary, correlative and conforming adjustment. One closing agreement presumes that the U.S. taxpayer is the parent and the foreign entity its subsidiary while the second presumes that the foreign entity is the parent and the U.S. taxpayer the subsidiary. Two examples of closing agreements are included at ¶ 20,150 in the Practice Tools.

Establishment and Satisfaction of Accounts Payable/Receivable. Once an election under Rev. Proc. 99-32 is effective following an IRS-initiated adjustment, the taxpayer must establish an interest-bearing debt that the revenue procedure refers to as an account receivable if payment is received from, or account payable if payment is to be made to, the related party (the account). A separate account is established for each year in which there is a primary adjustment with the amount of the account initially being equal to the amount of the primary adjustment for each year in which an allocation is made. Each account is deemed created as of the last day of the taxpayer's taxable year for which the primary adjustment is made.[18] The account must bear interest at an arm's length rate, computed in the manner provided in the regulations, from the day after the date the account is deemed to have been created to the date of payment.[19] The account must be satisfied within ninety (90) days after execution of the closing agreement with the IRS.[20] The interest so computed must be accrued to or deducted from taxable income for each taxable year during which the account is deemed outstanding. The account must be expressed, both as to principal and interest, in U.S. dollars if the residence of either or both qualified business units ("QBU") through which the controlled transaction was carried out is in the United States. Otherwise, if one of the participants was a domestic corporation, the functional currency will be the functional currency of the domestic corporation's QBU through which the transaction was carried out. If neither of the participants was a domestic corporation, then the functional currency will be the functional currency of the QBU of the obligee through which the transaction was carried out.[21]

To return to the example, under Rev. Proc. 99-32, the $25 conforming adjustment would be recharacterized as a $25 loan made by USSub to CP on the last day of the applicable tax year. The loan will be reflected on USSub's books as an accounts receivable, will bear interest at the appropriate rate, will be expressed in U.S. dollars, and will be satisfied within 90 days of the execution of the closing

---

[16] Rev. Proc. 99-32, Sec. 5.02.

[17] *See* I.R.M. 8.13.1, Exhibit 21 (Practice Tools, ¶ 20,150).

[18] Rev. Proc. 99-32, Sec 4.01.

[19] Reg. § 1.482-2(a)(2).

[20] Rev. Proc. 99-32, Sec 5.01(4)(e).

[21] Rev. Proc. 99-32, Sec. 4.01(3).

¶1740.03

agreement by the taxpayer and the IRS. Satisfaction may be by cash or by written debt obligation (payable at a fixed date and bearing interest at an arm's-length rate) or by an offsetting accounting entry against a pre-existing debt owed by the obligee of the account to the obligor.[22]

Although no closing agreement is necessary for a taxpayer-initiated adjustment, the statement filed by the taxpayer with its tax return, described above, essentially commits the taxpayer to a course of action approximating that required of a taxpayer following an IRS-initiated adjustment.

Satisfaction of the Accounts by Set-off. All or part of the interest and principal of an account may be treated as prepaid prior to the beginning of the 90-day period to the extent of an accounting entry offsetting a pre-existing debt owed by the obligee of the account to the obligor. In addition, an account can be offset if the obligee of the account is the parent, by a distribution or, if the obligor of the account is the parent, by a capital contribution during the taxable year for which the section 482 allocation is made. If the offset relates to an IRS-initiated adjustment, then the offsetting accounting entry must occur during the same taxable year as the closing agreement is entered into by the taxpayer and the IRS. The offset will be treated as a reduction in the amount of the account at its inception. Consequently, the pre-existing debt must exist as of such date. Similarly, the capital contribution or distribution must relate to such year.[23]

If the offset relates to a taxpayer-initiated adjustment, the offset may occur during the tax year during which the U.S. taxpayer files the return reporting the primary adjustment or during the taxable year for which the section 482 allocation is made. However, in the latter case, the offset is treated as made as of the beginning of the day after the date of the deemed establishment of the account and taxpayers cannot claim offset treatment on an untimely or amended return.[24]

Consequences of Satisfaction of the Accounts. Provided that the requirements stipulated in Rev. Proc. 99-32 are met and satisfaction of the account occurs within the period required, the payment will be free of the federal income tax consequences that would otherwise apply.

Payment on this account will be treated as a payment of the account for all federal income tax purposes, regardless of how such payment is characterized under foreign law. Moreover, a foreign tax credit will be allowed for any foreign withholding tax with respect to the repayment of the principal or interest of the account to the extent and subject to the limitations in Code Sec. 901.

¶ 1750 Deciding Whether to Elect 99-32

An election under Rev. Proc. 99-32 causes a recharacterization of the movement of cash (i.e., the conforming adjustment), which would otherwise be viewed as deemed dividends or deemed contributions to capital, as a loan between the two parties to the controlled transaction that was the subject of the primary adjustment. Under federal income tax rules, the treatment of a repayment of debt between related parties differs significantly from the treatment of dividends or contributions between the same parties. As such, it is important for taxpayers considering the

---

[22] Rev. Proc. 99-32, Sec. 4.01(4).
[23] Rev. Proc. 99-32, Sec. 4.02.
[24] Rev. Proc. 99-32, Sec. 4.02.

election to be cognizant of the potential federal income tax consequences of this recharacterization.

Although a comprehensive discussion of these implications is beyond the scope of this chapter, there are a number of issues that may arise. First, adjustments made pursuant to Rev. Proc. 99-32 could significantly affect a taxpayer's foreign tax credit profile. Specifically, recharacterizing a dividend as payment for goods or services may result in a reversal of foreign tax credits under Code Sec. 902. Additionally, decreasing or increasing a foreign subsidiary's earnings may alter income inclusions for the U.S. parent company under Subpart F or Code Sec. 956 rules, thereby impacting the taxpayer's foreign tax credits under Code Sec. 960. In fact, there is also the possibility that the account itself, mandated through application of the revenue procedure, could give rise to a Code Sec. 956 liability for the taxpayer, if such account is set up so that a U.S. company has, in effect, created an obligation to a foreign subsidiary. Finally, taxpayers who have repatriated earnings pursuant to Code Sec. 965 should be aware of the possibility of an IRS redetermination with respect to their Code Sec. 965 dividend amounts as a result of having elected treatment under the revenue procedure. In general, Code Sec. 965 provides that a corporation that is a U.S. shareholder of a controlled foreign corporation ("CFC") may elect, for one tax year, an 85 percent dividends received deduction ("DRD") for certain qualifying cash dividends received from such CFC.[25] To determine the allowable DRD amount, the statute requires that the deduction must be reduced by any increase in related-party indebtedness ("RPI"), on a dollar-for-dollar basis. Through a number of notices and industry directives regarding the treatment of Code Sec. 965 foreign earnings, the IRS has asserted that accounts receivables established pursuant to a Rev. Proc. 99-32 election will be treated as related party indebtedness under Code Sec. 965(b)(3).[26] While some have questioned the authority of the IRS to take this position, nonetheless, taxpayers should be aware that the directives instruct examiners to make the appropriate adjustments to and potentially recompute the Code Sec. 965 DRD where adjustments under Code Sec. 482 and an election under Rev. Proc. 99-32 were also present.

Rev. Proc. 99-32 reflects the IRS's policy of encouraging taxpayers to comply with the arm's length standard under Code Sec. 482. Election of the revenue procedure treatment allows taxpayers to properly conform their accounts to reflect primary adjustments without the corresponding federal tax consequences. However, while the revenue procedure mitigates federal tax consequences relating directly to the conforming adjustments, it does not eliminate or even address other concomitant tax consequences, as described above. Therefore, in determining whether or not to seek treatment under the revenue procedure, the full range of federal income tax consequences that result from making the election should be considered.

---

[25] Code Sec. 965(a).
[26] *See* Notice 2005-10, 2005-1 CB 474; Notice 2005-38, 2005-1 CB 1100; Notice 2005-64, 2005-2 CB 471; Industry Directive #1 on Section 965 Foreign Earnings Repatriation (October 2, 2007); Industry Directive #2 on Section 965 Foreign Earnings Repatriation, (April 21, 2008); Industry Directive #3 on Section 965 Foreign Earnings Repatriation (May 26, 2009).

¶ 1760 Customs Impact of Transfer Pricing Adjustments

As discussed in Chapter 15, the United States Bureau of Customs and Border Protection ("Customs") and the IRS share the same overall objective with regard to related-party transactions: to achieve arm's length pricing. However, the two agencies serve fundamentally different purposes. The IRS tax rules seek to properly allocate income between related parties necessary to prevent evasion of taxes and to clearly reflect the income of the parties. The Customs laws are intended to attach the correct dutiable value to specific imported goods. The conflicting agency concerns become apparent when discussing the Customs impact of transfer pricing adjustments. Where appropriate, the IRS is looking to increase taxable income in the U.S.; where appropriate, Customs is looking to increase the duties due.

An upward adjustment in a sale to a related party made to increase the profit of the seller, by decreasing the transfer price paid for products, has the corresponding result of decreasing potential duties of the buyer in that importing country. A downward adjustment made to decrease the profit of the seller by increasing the transfer price paid for products, has the corresponding result of increasing the potential duties of the buyer in that importing country.

The impact of a transfer pricing adjustment on Customs duties will depend on whether it is an upward or a downward adjustment and whether the adjustment is contemplated and self-initiated by the company or if it is mandated by the tax authorities. It also depends on whether the adjustment affects the price of imported products, as opposed to services or intangibles.

A transfer pricing adjustment arising in a U.S. IRS examination would usually result in an increase to the taxable income in the U.S., which would have the result of decreasing duties in the U.S. Under this scenario, it is often difficult to position the price adjustment as contemplated or agreed to prior to the importation of the merchandise into the U.S. As such, this type of transfer pricing adjustment is generally disregarded for transaction value purposes, is not reportable to Customs and creates no opportunity for refund.

The scenario that has the greatest impact on a U.S. importer is where a foreign tax authority, as part of a tax audit, determines that the taxable income of the foreign exporter must be increased through an upward price adjustment. The result for the U.S. importer will be an increase in the transfer price paid, resulting in increased duties owed to U.S. Customs. All transfer pricing adjustments that result in an increase of duties owed to Customs must be reported.

Customs authorities are only interested in transfer pricing adjustments that have an impact on the transaction value of the imported merchandise. Many audit-initiated transfer pricing adjustments are not well-defined in terms of what product, intangible and service transactions were or were not considered at arm's length. As Customs duty only applies to tangible products, and as duty rates vary by product category, an in-depth analysis may be required to properly allocate the adjustment to dutiable products. A determination by the tax authority that attributes an adjustment to payments for services and intangibles unrelated to the price of the imported goods, or to goods that are not dutiable, can avoid the Customs issues resulting from a foreign-initiated transfer price adjustment.

¶1760

U.S. importers should be aware of the Customs issues created by transfer pricing adjustments mandated by tax authorities, including the necessity to report certain changes in values to Customs and the possibility of paying additional duties plus interest.

¶ 1770 State Tax Consequences

Federal taxable income is the starting point used by most states to compute corporate income taxes; thus, any change in federal taxable income directly affects the state tax base.[27] In most cases, however, the federal adjustment is made without regard to the U.S. state and local tax implications.

When the IRS makes an adjustment, the adjustment is generally not allocated among affiliated domestic entities, as their income is consolidated on the federal tax return. For state income tax purposes, affiliated corporations, depending on the state, may be required or allowed to determine income by filing a combined or consolidated return (i.e., file as a group), or a separate return (i.e., each corporation in the group files its own return).[28] The failure to split the adjustment among the affiliates has little effect in states that require or allow combined or consolidated filing, but may result in the overpayment of U.S. state and local tax in separate return states.

The state and local implications of international tax adjustments vary depending on the nature of the adjustment and the domestic structure of the U.S. group. To illustrate the state tax impact of an IRS-initiated adjustment on a multistate filer, we will evaluate an IRS adjustment arising from an *inbound* transaction followed by a discussion of an adjustment from a foreign tax authority arising from an *outbound* transaction.

.01 Inbound Transactions

For an inbound transaction, consider a U.S. distributor that purchases tangible goods from a foreign related party. A typical U.S. structure might consist of a headquarters company with nexus in a single state that purchases tangible goods from related and unrelated parties and then sells those products to a related sales company with nexus in multiple states. The headquarters company typically owns the trade names and trademarks and performs strategic and management functions, while the sales company performs routine distribution functions. The income of the sales company is typically limited to a routine distribution return while the headquarters company earns the residual income.

An adjustment by the IRS to increase the overall margin earned by the U.S. entity on the purchase and resale of products from the foreign affiliate could be based upon an argument that the increased margin relates to the return for the

---

[27] State statutes, regulations or unpublished policy generally prescribe the time limitations for reporting federal adjustments. Although the time limitations vary among the states, it is the receipt of the RAR by the corporate taxpayer that is generally thought to trigger the resulting state and local income tax considerations.

[28] Currently, the following states require taxpayers to file separate returns and do not require taxpayers to file on a combined or consolidated basis: Alabama, Arkansas, Connecticut, Delaware, District of Columbia, Florida, Georgia, Indiana, Iowa, Louisiana, Maryland, Mississippi,

Missouri, New Jersey, New Mexico, Oklahoma, North Carolina, Pennsylvania, Rhode Island, South Carolina, Tennessee and Virginia. Since 2004, the following separate return states adopted mandatory combined or consolidated filing: Kentucky (effective 2005), Massachusetts (effective 2009), Michigan (effective 2008), New York (effective 2007 and only if there are significant intercompany transactions), Ohio (effective 2005 and only for Commercial Activity Tax purposes), Texas (effective 2008), Vermont (effective 2006), West Virginia (effective 2009) and Wisconsin (effective 2009).

sales function performed or that the U.S. company was insufficiently compensated for its locally developed marketing intangibles. The corresponding state and local impact of this adjustment depends on the structure of the domestic company.

If the taxpayer's U.S. operations were consolidated into one legal entity, its domestic tax exposure would increase based on the increase to the federal taxable income. If the taxpayer had multiple entities performing different functions with different intangible asset positions, the domestic tax impact must be further evaluated. For instance, where an IRS-initiated controversy results in a determination that the initial price paid for the tangible goods failed to recover the fair value of services rendered, or intangibles provided, U.S. state and local tax may be overpaid if the sales company's separate state tax effective rate is higher than that of the U.S. affiliate that actually provided the services or intangibles that supported the IRS adjustment. The conclusion as to whether this adjustment relates to an intangible asset utilized or a function performed would dictate which entity should earn the additional income.

In the example, the adjustment should be allocated to the headquarters company if it were concluded that it was a return for an intangible, leaving the income of the sales company unchanged. If, on the other hand, the increased income is based on a conclusion that the return to the routine distribution functions was understated, the adjustment would be allocated to the distribution company.

Allocation of the adjustment within the domestic supply chain may have significant domestic tax consequences. An adjustment to the headquarters company's income would, in general, be a more tax favorable adjustment than an adjustment to the sales company's income. The sales company, as the multistate filer, will usually have a higher effective state tax rate.

In situations such as this, it may be prudent to analyze the U.S. state and local tax implications and require federal income tax adjustments to be split among the affiliates that actually earned the incremental income.

.02 Outbound Transactions

In an example of an adjustment arising from an outbound transaction, consider a U.S. manufacturer selling to a foreign, related-party distributor. A typical structure for a U.S. manufacturer might consist of a headquarters company with nexus in a single state that houses the valuable intellectual property for the group and a contract manufacturer and sales company, which earn routine manufacturing and distribution returns, respectively. The headquarters entity in this example is responsible for the sales to the foreign entity.

If U.S. income is adjusted by a foreign tax authority on the grounds that the routine manufacturing return is overstated, the adjustment would most logically be applied to the contract manufacturer. On the other hand, if the adjustment reflects a conclusion that the return earned by the foreign related-party distributor was too low, this could be viewed as an additional cost of the headquarters company.

.03 Additional Issues

Allocating the additional income or expense to the appropriate domestic entity is an important element of determining the state and local impact of an adjustment

¶1770.03

to a company's federal taxable position. However, the implications of a foreign adjustment can extend beyond the simple allocation of the income and/or expense.

The fundamental characterization of the income or expense can be as important, if not more important, than the determination of the appropriate entity. Although characterization of expenses may not be relevant to the U.S. group and federal taxable position, it often is very significant for U.S. state and local purposes. For example, numerous states have adopted provisions that require the add-back of intangible costs and expenses paid to related parties.[29] The term "related parties" is generally defined broadly to include foreign affiliates. Currently, few states require expenses paid for services to be added back. Consequently, it is important to make sure expenses paid for services are not treated as "intangible costs or expenses." Although various exceptions to the add-back provisions exist, they may be difficult to fall within due to the subjective nature of the qualifying conditions.

---

[29] The following states provide that intercompany royalty and interest expense should be added back to federal taxable income in determining state taxable income: Alabama, Arkansas, Connecticut, District of Columbia, Georgia, Illinois, Indiana, Kentucky, Maryland, Massachusetts, Michigan, Mississippi, New Jersey, New York, Ohio, Rhode Island, Virginia, West Virginia and Wisconsin. North Carolina, South Carolina and Tennessee have unique rules.

¶1770.03

Practice Tools

¶ 20,001 Overview

The Practice Tools are aids to assist the transfer pricing specialist to develop transfer pricing strategies and defense decisions. Each Practice Tool begins with introductory comments which place the Practice Tools in the context of its usage. These Practice Tools include definitions, charts, sample documents and forms that can be expected to be used in a transfer pricing practice.

¶ 20,010 Glossary of Transfer Pricing Terms

Advance pricing agreement (APA)—An agreement negotiated between the MNE and one or more tax authorities about the taxpayer's facts, methodology, and arm's length range over a specified prospective period.

Arm's length principle—Seeks to determine the transfer prices and profits of members of a MNE group by reference to the prices and profits which would have applied in comparable transactions and comparable circumstances between independent companies.

Arm's length range—A range if figures acceptable for establishing whether the conditions of a controlled transaction are arm's length. The range may be derived from applying the same transfer pricing method to multiple comparable data or from applying different transfer pricing methods.

Arm's length result—A figure or range of figures for a subsidiary's profits which accords with the arm's length principle.

Associated enterprise—When one enterprise controls another, or both are under common control.

Berry Ratio (BR) BR equals:
$$\frac{\text{Gross profit}}{\text{Operating expenses}}$$

Best method—The IRS defines the "best method" as the one which provides the most reliable measure of an arm's length result.

Comparable analysis—A comparison of the margins, prices or profits of a controlled transaction with those of uncontrolled transactions.

Comparable profit split—A profit split method which splits profits between controlled entities on the same basis as profits would be split between independent companies in a similar situation.

Comparable profits method—Compares profitability at company rather than at transaction level. A variety of profitability measures may be used.

Comparable uncontrolled price method (CUP)—The method consists of a direct comparison of the price on a transaction in goods between two related parties with the price on a comparable transaction between independent companies.

Comparable uncontrolled transaction method (CUT)—The same as the CUP method but applies to transfers of services and intangible property rather than goods.

Compensating Adjustment—An adjustment in the tax return to produce an arm's length result if the financial statements reflect transactions which are not arm's length.

Competent Authorities—Officers working for the tax authority or ministry of finance in each country responsible for the resolution of claims for a corresponding adjustment under the mutual agreement procedure of a tax treaty.

¶20,010

Controlled transaction—A transaction which takes place between related parties.

Corresponding adjustment—A downward adjustment to the profits or a credit against the tax liability incurred in one country to reflect an upward transfer pricing adjustment in another country so as to avoid economic double taxation.

Cost plus method—The application of an appropriate margin to the cost of the production of goods or services.

Embedded intangibles—Intangible assets aggregated with tangible assets, e.g. where goods are sold under a brand name.

Functional analysis—An analysis of the functions performed (taking into account assets used and risks assumed) by associated enterprises in controlled transactions and by independent enterprises in comparable uncontrolled transactions.

Formulary apportionment—A means of allocating the total profits if a multinational group among its national subsidiaries according to some predetermined formula.

Interquartile range—For any set of profit results, the interquartile range is found by eliminating the upper and lower quartiles thus leaving only the central range of results.

IRS—The Internal Revenue Service.

Market penetration strategy—A strategy for entering a new market not previously exploited by the MNE. The MNE may wish to transfer goods into such a market at a low price to establish a base, or may be prepared to support a subsidiary through sustained losses.

MNE—Multinational enterprise.

Mutual agreement procedure—A means through which tax administrations consult to resolve disputes regarding the application of double. The procedure is described and authorized by Article 25 of the US Model Tax Convention.

Net cost-plus margin (NCPM) equals:
$$\frac{\text{Operating profit}}{\text{Cost of goods sold}}$$

OECD—The Organisation for Economic Co-operation and Development. Current members are Australia, Austria, Belgium, Canada, the Czech Republic, Denmark, Finland, France, Germany, Greece, Hungary, Iceland, Italy, Japan, Korea, Luxembourg, Mexico, the Netherlands, New Zealand, Norway, Poland, Portugal, Spain, Sweden, Switzerland, Turkey, the UK and the USA.

OECD guidelines—Guidelines reflecting international concerns on the application of the arm's length principle. The updated guidelines on transfer pricing were issued in 1995 with subsequent amendments and updates, and now form the basis for many countries' transfer pricing practice.

¶20,010

Primary adjustment—If a revenue authority feels that a company has declared its taxable profit incorrectly, it may impose a primary adjustment to change the profit to the correct figure. This will change the profits for tax purposes.

Profit level indicator (PLI)—A profit comparison, usually within the TNMM, e.g. net margin on sales.

Profit spilt methods (PSM)—These allocate operating profit or loss from controlled transactions in proportion to relative contributions made by each party in generating the combined profit or loss. There are two main types of profit splits, the comparable profit split and the residual profit split.

Resale price method (RPM)—Based on the gross margin which a distributor earns by buying goods and reselling them.

Residual profit split—A profit split method which uses a two-step process to (1) determine market returns for routine assets via another method, e.g. CPM, and (2) allocate or split any residual profits between non-routine, unique or intangible assets.

Return on assets (ROA) equals:
$$\frac{\text{Operating profit}}{\text{Operating assets}}$$

Return on operating assets (ROA)—A measure of profitability used in comparability analysis based on a company's return on the assets employed in the business.

Secondary adjustment—An adjustment that arises from imputation of interest or dividend treatment on a primary adjustment.

Set-off—A benefit provided by one associated enterprise that is rewarded to some extent by different benefits received from the other enterprise in return.

SIC code—Standard Industrial Classification code, assigned by government to different Industries for national accounting purposes.

Tested party—The unit of the MNE which is selected to have its transactions or profits compared with independent third parties.

Toll manufacturers—Manufacturers carrying out manufacturing to a strict order. Such manufacturers have no control over the design of the manufacturing process, and analogous to a 'toll gate' they are paid a rate based on throughput. In essence they provide a basic service of making their manufacturing capacity available.

Transactional methods—The comparable uncontrolled price method, the resale price method and the cost plus method.

Transactional net margin method (TNMM)—A method that compares the net profit margin made on a group of transactions of independent companies with the net profit margin of comparable transactions between related parties.

Transfer price—The price at which a company undertakes any transactions with associated enterprises. When a company transfers goods, Intangible property or services to a related company, the price charged is defined as a transfer price.

¶20,010

Uncontrolled transaction—An uncontrolled transaction is one which takes place between unrelated parties.

Unspecified method—A method not specified in the US transfer pricing regulations may be chosen over a specified method if it provides a more reliable measure of an arm's length result.

¶ 20,020 Applied Comparison of Transfer Pricing Methods

Appendix 2 — Transfer Pricing Methods: Formulas, Steps to Compute, and Examples

Introduction

This appendix explains the transfer pricing methods from a number of different perspectives and demonstrates the impact of the resulting company's financial statements. It begins by assuming the global enterprise is comprised of a manufacturing entity located in one taxing jurisdiction and an affiliated distributor located in another. First, the relevant formulas are provided and broken down into computation steps. Next, the transfer pricing methods are applied to a numerically consistent fact pattern for the global enterprise. Finally, the resulting transfer pricing determination is applied to the company's income statement to demonstrate the impact of a transfer pricing change.

General fact pattern. In all of the examples, the combined income of the related manufacturer and distributor remain the same. Although this may produce somewhat unrealistic results for some of the industries portrayed, the numerical consistency helps to demonstrate the impact of the different methods on the allocation of profits between the manufacturers and distributors.

With respect to each example, Table 1 shows the financial information available before the setting of the transfer price. On a related group basis, all of the following financial information is known: sales, cost of goods sold, gross profit, sales general and administrative expense, and net operating income. The transfer price will be the sales figure for the manufacturer and the cost of goods sold figure for the distributor. In each example, Table 2 demonstrates how the transfer price developed through the transfer pricing method impacts the income statement.

Comparable Uncontrolled Price Method

Formula

Price charged in internal or external comparable uncontrolled product sales.

Computation Steps

Step 1:	Determine	**Arm's length price**	(charged by tested party in internal or included party in external comparable uncontrolled product sales)
Step 2:	Minus/plus	**Adjustments**	(account for minor differences or differences that can be readily quantified)
Step 3:	Equals	**Transfer price**	

Example A-1: U.S. Manufacturer (MFTR) produces generic AM/FM radios and sells them to Controlled Foreign Distributor (D'OR), a wholly-owned subsidiary of MFTR with sales operations in France. Information is available also on the terms MFTR negotiates for the sale of the same type of radios to an unrelated party distributor, who has an existing distribution chain for radios in Germany. The economic conditions and demand for radios in Germany are approximately the same in France. Apart from country differences, the only other distinguishing fact between these two transactions is that in the German case, MFTR covers the cost of a warehouse for the radios, while in France D'OR pays for the warehouse. We are informed that the warehouse charges amount to $1000.

Additionally, the products were sold to D'OR under approximately the same contractual terms as those sold to the unrelated party, with the D'OR purchasing 130 radios at $100 apiece versus the unrelated party purchasing 200 radios at $105 apiece. The difference between the prices charged in France and Germany can be accounted for entirely by the cost of the warehouse in Germany. That is, MFTR charges D'OR and the unrelated party the same price per radio after recognizing its $5 cost per unit for the German warehouse. The $100 charged by MFTR to the unrelated party net of the warehouse cost is an example of a "comparable uncontrolled price."

Table 1

	Manufacturer		Distributor		Total
Sales	**13,000**		15,000		15,000
COGS	< 10,000 >		< ? >		< 10,000 >
Gross Profit	(%)	?	(%)	?	5,000
S, G & A	< 1,750 >		< 1,250 >		< 3,000 >
Net Operating Income	(%)	?	(%)	?	2,000

Table 2

	Manufacturer		Distributor		Total
Sales	**13,000**		15,000		15,000
COGS	< 10,000 >		< 13,000 >		< 10,000 >
Gross Profit	(%)	3,000	(%)	2,000	5,000
S. G & A	< 1,750 >		< 1,250 >		< 3,000 >
Net Operating Income	(%)	1,250	(%)	750	2,000

Resale Price Method

Formula

Gross Profit / Net Sales

Computation Steps

Step 1:	Determine	**Gross Sales**	(charged by tested party to unrelated parties)
Step 2:	Minus	**Gross margin**	(earned by the comparable uncontrolled resellers)
Step 3:	Minus/plus	**Adjustments**	(account for minor differences or differences that can be quantified)
Step 4:	Equals	**Transfer price**	

Example A-2: U.S. Manufacturer (MFTR) sells different versions of its circular saws to both controlled (D'OR) and uncontrolled foreign distributors. Generally, the high-end products are sold to its controlled distributors. As part of its efforts to offer a broad line of high-end products, D'OR also sells drills purchased from an unrelated manufacturer and generally realizes a 15% gross profit on these sales. The related and unrelated sales of circular saws and drills are substantially similar in terms of resale value, sales terms, sales volume, distribution functions and customers. The transaction does not qualify as a CUP due to unquantifiable differences in the quality nature of products sold to D'OR and uncontrolled parties. However, because the products and distribution activities are substantially similar for circular saws and drills, the RPM may be used to determine the arm's length price. Thus, D'OR's gross profit on its purchases of circular saws from MFTR should also equal 15%.

Table 1

	Manufacturer	Distributor	Total
Sales	?	15,000	15,000
COGS	< 10,000 >	< ? >	< 10,000 >
Gross Profit	(%) ?	**(15%)**	5,000
S, G & A	< 1,750 >	< 1,250 >	< 3,000 >
Net Operating Income	(%) ?	(%) ?	2,000

Table 2

	Manufacturer	Distributor	Total
Sales	12,750	15,000	15,000
COGS	< 10,000 >	< 12,750 >	< 10,000 >
Gross Profit	(%) 2,750	**(15 %)** 2,250	5,000
S, G & A	< 1,750 >	< 1,250 >	< 3,000 >
Net Operating Income	(%) 1,000	(%) 1,000	2,000

Cost Plus Method

Formula

Gross Income / COGS

Computation Steps

Step 1:	Determine	**Cost of goods sold**	(incurred by tested party)
Step 2:	Plus	**Mark-up on cost**	(gross margin earned by comparable uncontrolled manufacturers)
Step 3:	Minus/plus	**Adjustments**	(account for minor differences or differences that can be quantified)
Step 4:	Equals	**Transfer price**	

Example A-3: U.S. Manufacturer (MFTR) produces welding parts in the United States and sells them to a controlled foreign distributor (D'OR). MFTR sells to other U.S. distributors (unrelated to MFTR and D'OR) various types of machine tool parts.

The comparable transaction is closely similar to the sales to D'OR in terms of functions and risks and MFTR earns a gross margin of 30 percent on these sales. Although the products MFTR sells to the unrelated distributors differ in terms of purpose and use from those sold to D'OR, the detailed accounting information on the comparable transactions is identical to that for D'OR - both appear equally reliable and significant differences in contractual terms do not appear to exist. Thus, applying the Cost Plus Method, which compares the gross profit mark-up on costs MFTR earns on sales to D'OR to those sales to the unrelated distributor, is the most appropriate method to evaluate the transfer price as long as the data is reliable.

Table 1

	Manufacturer	Distributor	Total
Sales	?	15,000	15,000
COGS	< 10,000 >	< ? >	< 10,000 >
Gross Profit	(30%)	(%) ?	5,000
S, G & A	< 1,750 >	< 1,250 >	< 3,000 >
Net Operating Income	(%) ?	(%) ?	2,000

Table 2

	Manufacturer	Distributor	Total
Sales	13,000	15,000	15,000
COGS	< 10,000 >	< 13,000 >	< 10,000 >
Gross Profit	(30 %) 3,000	(%) 2,000	5,000
S, G & A	< 1,750 >	< 1,250 >	< 3,000 >
Net Operating Income	(%) 1,250	(%) 750	2,000

Comparable Profits Method

PLIs (Profit Level Indicators). The following formulas and examples describe the three specified PLI's.

Formulas

$$\text{Operating Margin} \quad \frac{\text{Operating Profit}}{\text{Net Sales}}$$

Computation Steps

Step 1	Determine	**Gross sales**	(charged to by tested party to unrelated parties)
Step 1	Minus	**Operating Margin**	(earned by comparable uncontrolled resellers)
Step 2	Minus/plus	**Adjustments**	(account for minor differences or differences that can be quantified)
Step 3	Equals	**Transfer price**	

Example A-4: Foreign Manufacturer (MFTR) produces refrigerators and sells them to a Controlled U.S. Distributor (D'OR). Five uncontrolled U.S. distributors of similar household appliances are identified but there are significant differences in the appliances sold such as the brand name and overall quality of the appliances. It is determined that reliable adjustments for product differences could not be made. Further analysis reveals that four of the uncontrolled distributors are substantially similar in terms of markets, marketing activities, inventory levels, warranties, currency risk and other functions and risks. Reliable adjustments can be made for differences in inventory levels and payment terms. However, accounting data does not exist to make adjustments for differences in accounting which are significant such as consistent reporting in costs of goods sold and operating expenses that can have a significant effect on gross margin.

The CPM is the best method because the four distributors are functionally very similar to D'OR and there exists data to make necessary adjustments. The CUP method is not the best method because reliable adjustments could not be made for significant differences in the products sold. The RPM is not the best method because the gross profit margins under the RPM are not as reliable as operating profit measures under CPM because gross profit margins cannot be adjusted for differences in accounting, and operating costs versus costs of goods sold.

The operating margin is the most commonly applied PLI when evaluating the transfer price charged to the related distributor.

¶20,020

Table 1

	Manufacturer	Distributor	Total
Sales	?	15,000	15,000
COGS	< 10,000 >	< ? >	< 10,000 >
Gross Profit	(%) ?	(%) ?	5,000
S, G & A	< 1,750 >	< 1,250 >	< 3,000 >
Net Operating Income	(%) ?	(3%)	2,000

Table 2

	Manufacturer	Distributor	Total
Sales	13,300	15,000	15,000
COGS	< 10,000 >	< 13,300 >	< 10,000 >
Gross Profit	(%) 3,300	(%) 1,700	5,000
S, G & A	< 1,750 >	< 1,250 >	< 3,000 >
Net Operating Income	(%) 1,550	(3%) 450	2,000

Example A-5: The facts are the same as the Cost Plus example, except that there are significant differences between the controlled and uncontrolled transactions in terms of the types of parts manufactured and the complexity of the manufacturing process. However, a set of 10 uncontrolled U.S. manufacturers have been identified as potential comparable companies. Close functional similarity exists between the controlled and uncontrolled transactions, including similarity between the compositions of operating expenses.

The interquartile range of Berry Ratios produced by the comparable set extends from 1.10 to 1.30 with a median of 1.25. Because information is not available to make reliable adjustments for differences between the transaction with D'OR and those with the unrelated distributors, the Comparable Profits Method will be more reliable than the Cost Plus Method. The similarity of composition of operating expenses increases the reliability of the Berry Ratio as the appropriate profit level indicatorions.

Table 1

	Manufacturer	Distributor	Total
Sales	?	15,000	15,000
COGS	< 10,000 >	< ? >	< 10,000 >
Gross Profit	**(1.25)**	(____%) ?	5,000
S, G & A	< 1,750 >	< 1,250 >	< 3,000 >
Net Operating Income	(____%) ?	(____%) ?	2,000

Table 2

	Manufacturer	Distributor	Total
Sales	12,100	15,000	15,000
COGS	< 10,000 >	< 12,100 >	< 10,000 >
Gross Profit	**(1.25)** 2,100	(____%) 2,900	5,000
S, G & A	< 1,750 >	< 1,250 >	< 3,000 >
Net Operating Income	(____%) 350	(____%) 1,650	2,000

¶20,020

Return on Operating Assets

Formula

$$\text{Return on Operating Assets} = \frac{\text{Operating Profit}}{\text{Operating Assets}}$$

Computation Steps

Step 1:	Determine	**Operating Assets**	(tested party)
Step 2:	Times	**ROA**	(earned by comparable unrelated parties)
Step 3:	Minus/plus	**Adjustments**	(account for minor differences that can be quantified)
Step 4:	Equals	**Transfer Price**	

Example A-6: The facts are the same as the Cost Plus example, except the industry requires a significant investment in plant and equipment. Due to comparability concerns regarding the importance of plant and equipment, a CPM approach is considered more reliable than the Cost Plus method. A group of similar uncontrolled manufacturers is chosen. The composition of the controlled tested party's operating assets is similar to that of the comparable companies. The return on operating assets is the most commonly applied PLI when considering the transfer price charged by a manufacturer. The interquartile range for the ratios of operating profit to operating assets for the set of comparable companies is 5 percent to 15 percent, with a median of 10%. MFTR has operating assets of $35,000.

Table 1

	Manufacturer	*Distributor*	*Total*
Sales	?	15,000	15,000
COGS	< 10,000 >	< ? >	< 10,000 >
Gross Profit	3,500	(___%) ?	5,000
S, G & A	< 1,750 >	< 1,250 >	< 3,000 >
Net Operating Income	(___%) ?	(___%) ?	2,000

Table 2

	Manufacturer	*Distributor*	*Total*
Sales	13,500	15,000	15,000
COGS	< 10,000 >	< 13,500 >	< 10,000 >
Gross Profit	3,500	1,500	5,000
S, G & A	< 1,750 >	< 1,250 >	< 3,000 >
Net Operating Income	1,750	250	2,000

¶20,020

Comparable Profit Split Method

Formulas

Combined Net Operating Profit / Sharing Percentage

Computation Steps

Step 1	Determine	**Combined net operating profit**	(combined operating profit of controlled taxpayers)
Step 2	Multiply/Times	**Each uncontrolled taxpayer's share**	(each uncontrolled taxpayer's share expressed as a percentage of their combined net operating profit/loss)
Step 3	Minus/plus	**Adjustments**	(accent for minor differences or differences that can be quantified)
Step 4	Equals	**Transfer Price**	

Example A-7: U.S. manufactures (MFTR) manufactures high-end video equipment and sells to a German subsidiary (D'OR) for distribution in Germany under D'OR's own brand name. MFTR also sells similar video equipment to an unrelated distributor (UND'OR) for distribution in Germany under UND'OR's own brand name.

MFTR and UND'OR have agreed to share the joint operating profit from sales of video equipment 67%/33%. Because the products, functions, risks and contractual arrangements are very similar, MFTR and D'OR also share joint operating profits 67%/33%.

Table 1

	Manufacturer	Distributor	Total
Sales	?	15,000	15,000
COGS	< 10,000 >	< ? >	< 10,000 >
Gross Profit	(%) ?	(%) ?	5,000
S, G & A	< 1,750 >	< 1,250 >	< 3,000 >
Net Operating Income	(67%) ?	(33%)	2,000

Table 2

	Manufacturer	Distributor	Total
Sales	13,083	15,000	15,000
COGS	< 10,000 >	< 13,083 >	< 10,000 >
Gross Profit	(%) 3,083	(%) 1,917	5,000
S, G & A	< 1,750 >	< 1,250 >	< 3,000 >
Net Operating Income	(67%) 1,333	(33%) 667	2,000

Residual Profit Split Method

Formulas

Manufacturing Intangibles

Return for manufacturing ± (Combined operating Profit –
Mfg Return – D'OR Return) ×

_____

Total Intangibles

Computation Steps

Step 1	Determine	A	**Combined net operating profit**	(controlled parties)
Step 2	Compute	B	**Mfg routine return**	(generally CPM is used)
Step 3	Compute	C	**D'OR routine return**	(generally CPM is used)
Step 4	Compute	D	**Residual profit (A-B-C)**	
Step 5	Compute	E	**Relative contribution percentages**	(usually based upon NPV computations)
Step 6	Multiply	F	**Residual profit X contribution percentage**	(D × E)
Step 7	Add		**Routine return + allocation of residual**	(B + F)
Step 8	Equals		**Transfer Price**	

Example A-8: U.S. Manufacturer (MFTR) and Controlled Foreign Distributor (CFC) develop, manufacture and market communications equipment. MFTR conducts R&D to adapt products to local market needs. Brand names and patents are developed by both companies. The Residual Profit Split method must be used to allocate the combined operating profit between the related entities.

This allocation is done in a two-step process. First, the combined operating income is reduced by a market return for routine manufacturing and distribution activities of MFTR and CFC, respectively. This requires a functional analysis and a comparison to uncontrolled entities engaged in similar activities. Second, the residual profit is divided between MFTR and the controlled entities based on the relative value of contributed intangibles.

A routine profit return for manufacturers similarly situated to MFTR is found to be a 5 percent ROA on operating assets of 200,000 (5% × 200,000 = 1,000). A routine return for distributors similarly situated to CFC is found to be a 2 percent operating margin to gross sales (2% × 15,000 = 300). Thus, combined, the routine profit attributable to MFTR and CFC's activities equals $1,300.

To apportion the remaining profit between MFTR and CFC, the relative value of contributions to the business activity is determined by computing the

¶20,020

capitalized cost of developing the global enterprise's intangibles for each party. These are found to be 50 percent by each of the controlled parties.

Based on the amounts in the tables below, the residual net operating income allocated to MFTR is $(2,000 - 1000 - 300) \times 50\% = 350$. Similarly, for CFC the residual income equals $(2000 - 1000 - 300) \times 50\% = 350$. Total operating income to MFTR equals 1000 of routine income plus 350 of residual profit. CFC's total income equals 300 plus 350, or 650.

Table 1

	Manufacturer	Distributor	Total
Sales	?	15,000	15,000
COGS	< 10,000 >	< ? >	< 10,000 >
Gross Profit	(%) ?	(%) ?	5,000
S, G & A	< 1,750 >	< 1,250 >	< 3,000 >
Net Operating Income	**1,000 + 350**	**300 + 350**	2,000

Table 2

	Manufacturer	Distributor	Total
Sales	13,100	15,000	15,000
COGS	< 10,000 >	< 13,100 >	< 10,000 >
Gross Profit	(%) 3,~~083~~100	(%) 1,900	5,000
S, G & A	< 1,750 >	< 1,250 >	< 3,000 >
Net Operating Income	**1,350**	**650**	2,000

¶ 20,030 Specified Covered Services under Rev. Proc. 2007-13

Payroll:

1. Compiling and posting employee time and other information needed to calculate periodic compensation to employees. Computing employees' time worked, production, and commissions. Computing and posting wages and deductions to appropriate accounting records. Preparing paychecks, travel reimbursement and expense reimbursement.

2. Preparing payroll tax forms (such as the preparation of Forms 940, 941 and W-2 in order to comply with U.S. requirements or similar requirements under another country's laws).

3. Administering garnishment and other wage withholding orders.

4. Other activities similar to those specified in paragraphs (1) through (3).

Premiums for Unemployment, Disability and Workers Compensation:

5. Processing employees' unemployment insurance premiums, disability premiums and workers compensation premiums.

6. Other activities similar to those specified in paragraph (5).

Accounts Receivable:

7. Compiling, analyzing and recording current credit data and other financial information regarding individuals or firms (including preparing reports with this information for use in decision-making).

8. Compiling and recording billing, accounting and other numerical data for billing purposes. Preparing billing invoices for services rendered or for delivery or shipment of goods.

9. Locating and notifying customer(s) of delinquent accounts by mail (either electronic or otherwise) or telephone to solicit payment. Receiving payment from customers and posting payment to customer accounts. If customer fails to respond, preparing statements to credit department, initiating repossession proceedings or service disconnection. Keeping records of collection activities and status of accounts.

10. Other activities similar to those specified in paragraphs (7) through (9).

Accounts Payable:

11. Compiling information and records to draw up purchase orders for procurement of materials and services.

12. Making payment to vendors and posting payment to status of accounts.

13. Other activities similar to those specified in paragraphs (11) and (12).

General Administrative:

14. Performing clerical and administrative functions such as drafting correspondence, scheduling appointments, and organizing and maintaining paper and electronic files.

¶20,030

15. Performing data entry through use of a keyboard or scanning device, including verifying data and preparing materials for printing.

16. Using a word processor/computer or typewriter to generate (without substantial modification) letters, reports, forms, or other material from another person's rough draft, corrected copy, or voice recording.

17. Performing duties relating to office management systems and procedures, such as answering telephones, bookkeeping, typing, word processing, office machine operation, and filing.

18. Operating any of the following office machines: photocopying, scanning and facsimile machines.

19. Providing interoffice service/document delivery, including mailroom services, document management, and graphics, video, and website preparation.

20. Other activities similar to those specified in paragraphs (14) through (19).

Corporate and Public Relations:

21. Planning and executing a public relations program or corporate communication policy, including the distribution of internal and external corporate communications, but not to include specific advertising and/or marketing of a product or service.

22. Other activities similar to those specified in paragraph (21).

Meeting Coordination and Travel Planning:

23. Coordinating activities of staff and convention personnel to make arrangements for group meetings and conventions.

24. Negotiating airline, rental car, and hotel contracts.

25. Assisting in travel arrangements, including providing a system for reservations and ticket purchases.

26. Managing motor pool and fleet.

27. Other activities similar to those specified in paragraphs (23) through (26).

Accounting and Auditing:

28. Gathering and reviewing information in accounting records for use in preparing financial statements.

29. Computing, classifying, and recording numerical data to maintain accurate and complete financial records, performing any combination of calculating, posting, and verifying duties to obtain primary financial data for use in maintaining accounting records, checking the accuracy of figures, calculations, and postings pertaining to business transactions recorded by other workers; and calculating investment performance and net asset values of investments.

30. Consolidating legal entity financial results per country for use in statutory financial statements and tax returns and consolidating worldwide results by business area for use in management accounting.

¶20,030

31. Developing a company-wide accounting manual that prescribes accounting policies and methods to be used and providing related advice.

32. Performing operational and financial internal audits.

33. Preparing government census and related forms required by a service recipient's home country.

34. Preparing reports required by escheat laws required by a service recipient's home country.

35. Completing import/export documentation and arranging for customs payment.

36. Overseeing audits by customs authorities.

37. Other activities similar to those specified in paragraphs (28) through (36).

Tax:

38. Processing tax payments according to prescribed laws and regulations.

39. Gathering information from accounting records and including that information in the preparation of income, property, sales/use, VAT, excise and other tax returns.

40. Overseeing audits conducted by tax authorities.

41. Providing tax advice to businesses to ensure compliance with tax laws, including access to electronic research and tax compliance software.

42. Reviewing local country tax provisions for purposes of inclusion in the consolidated world-wide provision and preparation of the world-wide tax provision.

43. Negotiating advance pricing agreements and other local incentives that benefit the consolidated organization.

44. Other activities similar to those specified in paragraphs (38) through (43).

Health, Safety, Environmental and Regulatory Affairs:

45. Developing company health, safety, and environment standards, monitoring compliance with such standards, and training affected personnel.

46. Gathering information and preparing documentation relating to eligibility for or compliance with laws and regulations governing contracts, licenses and permits.

47. Gathering information, verifying data and preparing documentation relating to compliance with laws and regulations governing financial and securities institutions and financial and real estate transactions. Examining and verifying correctness of, or establishing authenticity of records.

48. Providing security services (e.g., executive protection or global headquarters security).

49. Providing common health risk management systems development, clinical services, industrial hygiene, alcohol and drug testing services (laboratory analyses done by third parties), and advice to business management on health issues.

¶20,030

50. Providing guidance and support operations, integrity management support implementation, coaching, and conducting operations integrity management assessments, development and implementation of safety behavior based programs, and incident reporting and accident investigations.

51. Providing strategies, resources, and training for effective crisis preparedness and response.

52. Other activities similar to those specified in paragraphs (45) through (51).

Budgeting:

53. Compiling data for use by cost estimators in determining cost projections and in preparing budget estimates, including verifying information for completeness, accuracy, and conformance with internal procedures and regulations.

54. Compiling data to prepare budget and accounting reports for management.

55. Other activities similar to those specified in paragraphs (53) and (54).

Treasury Activities:

56. Establishing bank accounts and lock boxes for use by controlled parties, including overdraft facilities and lines of credit.

57. Providing staff and facilities to hedge currency exposures that arise from operations in the normal course of business. This paragraph does not apply to banks (including investment banks), insurance companies, investment companies, similar entities that provide financial services to the public, and investment funds (including hedge and private equity funds).

58. Coordinating investment activities in connection with short-term management of cash generated from operations in the normal course of business. This paragraph does not apply to related-party factoring activities, or to banks (including investment banks), insurance companies, investment companies, similar entities that provide financial services to the public, and investment funds (including hedge and private equity funds).

59. Other activities that are ancillary to the activities specified in paragraphs (56) through (58).

Statistical Assistance:

60. Compiling data for use in statistical studies.

61. Other activities similar to those specified in paragraph (60).

Staffing and Recruiting:

62. Providing staffing support that includes creating job announcements, determining eligibility, evaluating qualifications of candidates, conducting background checks on final candidates, verifying references, developing performance evaluation procedures and forms, and conducting exit interviews for departed employees.

63. Coordinating with temporary employment agencies, applicants, and management throughout the recruiting process.

¶20,030

64. Providing information to applicants regarding open positions, the application and recruiting process, and employment policies.

65. Providing administrative support that includes sourcing and processing resumes, arranging interview schedules for open positions, preparing offer letters, and entering new employee information into the human resource system.

66. Establishing and maintaining employee files relating to payroll, performance and other personnel issues.

67. Assisting with new employee orientations and paperwork.

68. Implementing recruiting plan and locating potential candidates by working with professional search firms, colleges, universities and professional associations. Organizing and attending job fairs and other recruitment events.

69. Developing recruiting and marketing materials and assisting in developing and maintaining content for recruiting website.

70. Analyzing recruiting data and review all job analysis, promotion and placement products.

71. Posting job opening advertisements in appropriate markets through publications, journals and other media.

72. Managing company-wide job postings and employee referral program.

73. Administering a compensation policy, including grading and determining salary ranges for positions.

74. Other activities similar to those specified in paragraphs (62) through (73).

Training and Employee Development:

75. Assisting in training of personnel including assessing development and training needs, creating and conducting internal development and training programs and communicating training opportunities to personnel.

76. Arranging for management training on employment law compliance, employer liability avoidance, interviewing, hiring, terminations, promotions, performance reviews, safety, and sexual harassment.

77. Developing and implementing plans regarding career-development and succession.

78. Developing and implementing a job evaluation process including procedures and forms.

79. Other activities similar to those specified in paragraphs (75) through (78).

Benefits:

80. Developing and implementing employee compensation and benefits including healthcare, life insurance, 401(k), pension, worker's compensation, unemployment, dental, profit sharing, employee incentive compensation, and employee assistance programs.

¶20,030

81. Providing benchmarking studies for compensation and other benefit programs.

82. Providing guidance and direction to employees regarding elections for benefits, applications for benefits and receipt of benefits (including providing assistance to employees in completing all necessary forms).

83. Arranging annual benefit enrollment meetings and employee benefit seminars.

84. Processing employee benefits inquiries and complaints, and reconciling billing issues.

85. Coordinating with hospitals, physicians, insurers, employees, and beneficiaries to facilitate proper and complete utilization of benefits for all employees.

86. Other activities similar to those specified in paragraphs (80) through (85).

Information and Technology (IT) Services:

87. Supporting company-wide computer systems including those used in connection with operations, accounting, manufacturing, customer service, human resources, payroll, and email.

88. Formulating guidelines with respect to the use of IT systems.

89. Maintaining and repairing IT systems.

90. Providing telecommunications facilities.

91. Providing technical assistance and training to users of computer systems and other information technology devices. Answering questions or resolving technical problems relating to computer systems and other information technology devices in person, via telephone or from remote location. Providing assistance concerning the use of computer hardware and software, including printing, installation, word processing, electronic mail, and operating systems, as well as disaster recovery back-up services.

92. Maintaining and testing existing computer databases (including implementing security measures to safeguard computer databases), but not to include analyzing user needs or developing hardware or software solutions (such as systems integration, website design, writing computer programs, modifying general applications software, or recommending the purchase of commercially available hardware or software).

93. Supporting an organization's existing local area network (LAN), wide area network (WAN), and Internet system or a segment of a network system, regular maintenance of network hardware and software, monitoring network to ensure network availability to all system users and performing necessary maintenance to support network availability, supervising other network support and client server specialists (including implementing network security measures), but not to include analyzing user needs or developing hardware or software solutions (such as systems integration, website design, writing computer programs, modifying general applications software, or recommending commercially available software).

¶20,030

94. Other activities similar to those specified in paragraphs (87) through (93).

Legal Services:

95. General legal services performed on behalf of the taxpayer by in-house legal counsel, including but not limited to, drafting, negotiating and review of contracts or agreements, legal documents, and opinions, representation and advocacy before courts, administrative agencies, arbitrators, legislatures, or other bodies, preparing advice in respect of structuring and reorganization, acquisition, and divestment transactions, and maintaining corporate books and records. Support and administrative functions associated with the above activities (legal research, secretarial, filing and document retrieval, etc.).

96. Other activities similar to those specified in paragraph (95).

Insurance Claims Management:

97. Securing insurance coverage for general, product, and worker's compensation liability, property loss, business interruption, and other business risks.

98. Coordinating with third party insurers, with respect to insurance policies, including preparing claims for submission to such third party insurers.

99. Other activities similar to those specified in paragraphs (97) and (98).

Purchasing:

100. Planning and executing procurement of services and material pursuant to company standard for support functions.

101. Other activities similar to those specified in paragraph (100).

¶ 20,040 Ernst & Young's 2010 Transfer Pricing Global Reference Guide

ARGENTINA

Taxing authority and tax law

Internal Revenue Service (Administración Federal de Ingresos Públicos — AFIP); Income Tax Law (ITL) and Regulations.

Relevant regulations and rulings

Currently in effect: AFIP-DGI (AFIP-Dirección General Impositiva) Regulation No. 1,122 (Published 31 October 2001, but applicable for fiscal years beginning on 31 December 1999) as amended by several regulations (No. 1,227/02; No. 1,296/02; No. 1,339/02; No. 1,590/03; No. 1,663/04; No. 1,670/04; No. 1,918/05; No. 1,958/05, No. 1,987/05 and External Note No. 1/08). Binding tax rulings for general application are not provided. Opinions from the tax authority are scarce and non-binding.

OECD guidelines treatment

Argentina is not an OECD member, and the OECD Transfer Pricing Guidelines are not referenced in Argentina's Tax Law and Regulations. However, the tax authority usually recognizes the OECD Transfer Pricing Guidelines in practice as long as they do not contradict the ITL and Regulations. A first-level court case dated 15 August 2007 was based on the provisions of the OECD Transfer Pricing Guidelines. Given this, from a practical point of view, the OECD restructuring paper is likely to affect the transfer pricing analyses of the Argentine companies.

Priorities/pricing methods

The tested party must be the local entity (i.e., the entity based in Argentina). The taxpayer selects the most appropriate method, but the AFIP may oppose the selection. The accepted methods for transactions with related parties and tax havens pursuant to the ITL are the Comparable Uncontrolled Price (CUP), Resale Price, Cost Plus, Profit Split and Transactional Net Margin Methods. The ITL does not prioritize methods. Regulation 1,122/01 states the best method rule. The use of an interquartile range is mandatory. Unless there is evidence to the contrary, the market price must be used for tangible goods transactions with both related and independent parties where there is an international price in a transparent market. In addition, for transactions involving grains, oleaginous products, other soil products, oil and gas and in general all goods with well-known prices in transparent markets and where the local company operates through international intermediaries who are not the final consignees of the goods, the applicable price is the prevailing price in the respective market on the day loading for shipment is finished, or the agreed-upon price if higher. This method may not apply, however, if the local exporter is able to prove the substance of the operations of the consignee abroad. The AFIP has the power to limit the application of this method or extend it to other transactions under certain circumstances. Export and import transactions with independent parties not located in tax havens are subject to information requirements if the annual amount of the transaction exceeds ARS 1,000,000 or the transactions are exports and imports of commodities. The requirements depend on different annual transaction amounts and, in some cases, may include calculations of profit margins.

Transfer pricing penalties

For unpaid taxes related to international transactions, the taxpayer is fined 100% to 400% of the unpaid tax. Penalties for fraud are two to ten times the unpaid taxes. Criminal tax law stipulates imprisonment for two to six years if the unpaid tax exceeds ARS 100,000 for each tax and fiscal year. If the unpaid tax exceeds ARS 1,000,000, the prison term will increase, ranging from three-and-a-half to nine years. For the late filing of tax returns containing international transactions involving the export/import of goods with independent parties, the taxpayer will be fined ARS 9,000. For the late filing of tax returns concerning other international transactions, the taxpayer will be fined ARS 20,000. For the application of penalties related to late filing or lack of filing, it is irrelevant whether the transactions were arm's length. For non-compliance with the formal duties of furnishing information requested by the AFIP, the taxpayer faces fines up to ARS 45,000. The same applies to a failure to keep vouchers and evidence of prices on available files and failure to file tax returns upon request. If tax returns are not filed after the third request, and the taxpayer has income amounting to more than ARS 10,000,000, the fine is increased from ARS 90,000 to ARS 450,000. Interest is applicable on unpaid tax balances (as from 1 July 2006, the rate is 2% on a monthly basis and 3% upon lawsuit filing).

Penalty relief

Concerning underpayment and fraud, if the non-recidivist taxpayer voluntarily amends the tax returns before receiving a special notice (or vista) from the AFIP, the penalty is reduced to one-third of the minimum fine. If the tax returns are amended within 15 days of receiving the notice, the penalty is reduced to two-thirds of the minimum fine. If the non-recidivist taxpayer accepts the adjustments assessed by AFIP and pays the amounts due, the penalties are set at the minimum amount. If the taxes due do not exceed ARS 1,000 and are paid voluntarily, or within 15 days from the special notice, then no penalty shall be applied.

Documentation requirements

Transfer pricing regulations require extensive contemporaneous documentation. Taxpayers are required to keep and eventually submit all the documents evidencing that prices, amounts received and profit margins have been established on an arm's length basis. Furthermore, taxpayers are required to keep an annual transfer pricing study for transactions, subject to transfer pricing methods, with related parties, deemed related parties and independent parties located at tax havens."

Documentation deadlines

The transfer pricing documentation must be ready for filing with the AFIP by the date the corresponding transfer pricing return filings are due. A special report, financial statements and certification must be filed with the tax authority by the end

¶20,040

of the eighth month after the end of the fiscal year. The annual transfer pricing return must also be filed by the end of the eighth month after the end of the fiscal year. The semi annual returns must be filed by the end of the fifth month after the end of the relevant six-month period. The annual return for export and import transactions with independent parties not located at tax havens must be filed by the end of the seventh month after the end of the fiscal year.

Statute of limitations on transfer pricing assessments

The general statute of limitations for federal tax matters is five years for registered taxpayers or for those who are exempt from registration and 10 years for unregistered taxpayers. These periods begin on 1 January of the year following the year in which the tax return is due. The transfer pricing documentation must be kept by the taxpayer and provided upon AFIP's request for up to five years after the period established by the statute of limitations.

Return disclosures/related-party disclosures

Taxpayers are required to file the following documentation with the AFIP: a special report including the key elements of the transfer pricing study, such as the methods used for the transfer pricing analysis and the conclusions made; audited financial statements for the fiscal year; an independent Certified Public Accountant's certification of certain contents of the special report; Annual Form 743 return; Form 742 return (for the first six-month period of each fiscal year); Semi-Annual Form 741 return for commodities exports and imports with independent parties not located at tax havens; and Annual Form 867 return for other exports and imports with independent parties not located in tax havens.

Audit risk/transfer pricing scrutiny

Transfer pricing audits are becoming more frequent and intensive, so that a medium risk may be assessed. It is likely that the Argentine tax authority will try to increase revenue and strictly enforce penalties with companies that are not complying with transfer pricing requirements.

APA opportunity

APAs are not specifically addressed.

AUSTRALIA

Taxing authority and tax law

Australian Taxation Office (ATO); Division 13 of Part III of Income Tax Assessment Act and relevant provisions of double tax treaties.

Relevant regulations and rulings

Taxation Ruling (TR) TR92/11: Loans, TR94/14: Application of Division 13, TR95/23: APAs, TR97/20: Methodologies, TR98/11: Documentation, TR98/16: Penalties, TR 1999/1: Services, TR2000/16: Relief from Double Taxation, TR2001/11: Permanent Establishments, TR2001/13: Interpretation of Australia's Double Tax Agreements, TR2002/2: Meaning of Arm's Length for the purposes of § 47A(7) Dividend Deeming Provisions, TR2002/5: Definition of Permanent Establishment, TR2003/1: Arm's Length Debt Test, TR 2004/1: Cost Contribution Arrangements, TR2005/11: Branch Funding for Multinational Banks and TR2007/1: Consequential Adjustments.

Tax Determinations (TD) TD2002/20: Film Production Companies and the Impact of the Tax Offset Scheme, TD2202/28: Foreign Bank Election to not Apply Part IIIB of the Income Tax Assessment Act (1936), TD2007/1: Market Value of Goodwill of an Entity that becomes a Member of a Consolidated Group. Draft Tax Determinations, TD2007/D20: Interaction of Division 13 and the Thin Capitalization Rules, TD2008/D3: Interaction of Division 13 and the Debt/Equity Rules.

ATO Booklets: *Concepts and Risk Assessment, Applying the Arm's Length Principle, Advance pricing arrangements, Documentation and Risk Assessment for Small to Medium Businesses, Dependent Agent Permanent Establishments, Marketing Intangibles, Business Restructuring - Discussion Paper on application of Australia's transfer pricing rules, and ATO Discussion Paper on Intra-group finance guarantees and loans - Application of Australia's transfer pricing and thin capitalization rules*

OECD guidelines treatment

The ATO accepts the principles of the OECD guidelines and indicates in the relevant ATO transfer pricing tax rulings where there are "differences in emphasis or extensions of OECD principles." The ATO will consider the use of all of the OECD-recognized transfer pricing methods and will also consider broader (or other) methods for particular facts and circumstances.

Priorities/pricing methods

The ATO seeks to adopt the "most appropriate" method. Methods outlined in ATO rulings include traditional transaction methods (CUP, Resale Price and Cost Plus) and profit methods (Profit Split and TNMM). Although traditional transaction methods (e.g., CUP) may be preferred by the ATO, the TNMM is accepted as an appropriate method by the ATO in circumstances where traditional transaction data is not available, comparable or reliable. A recent Administrative Appeals Tribunal decision has placed more emphasis on transaction methods and was critical of the particular application of the TNMM.

¶20,040

Transfer pricing penalties

If the Commissioner applies Division 13 and the relevant section of the International Tax Agreement Act, and it is determined that there is a transfer pricing adjustment resulting in a tax shortfall, a penalty of 25% applies, but is reduced to 10% where the taxpayer can demonstrate that it has a reasonably arguable position (RAP). Where the tax commissioner can demonstrate that the sole or dominant purpose is tax avoidance, a penalty rate of 50% applies, but is reduced to 25% where the taxpayer can demonstrate that they have a RAP.

The taxpayer may have a RAP "if it would be concluded in the circumstances, having regard to relevant authorities, that what is argued for is about as likely to be correct as incorrect or is more likely to be correct than incorrect."

Penalties could increase by a further 20% if the taxpayer "took steps to prevent or obstruct" the ATO from discovering the tax shortfall or if a penalty was imposed for a previous accounting period.

For 2004-05 and later income years, a Shortfall Interest Charge (SIC) will apply to any amount of tax shortfall from the day on which income tax under the first assessment for that income year was due and payable to the day on which the Commissioner gave notice of an assessment. SIC applies regardless of whether or not the taxpayer is liable for any shortfall penalty. The SIC rate is the base interest rate plus an uplift factor of three percentage points.

Penalty relief

Penalties will be reduced by 20% for voluntary disclosure after notification of an audit or by 80% for voluntary disclosure before notification of an audit. Where the taxpayer has contemporaneous documentation (i.e., prepared prior to or at the time of filing the company's annual tax return and Schedule 25A) to support a RAP the penalty may be reduced. Additionally, the Commissioner of Taxation has discretionary power to remit penalties where he considers it fair and reasonable to do so. A taxpayer with an APA will not incur penalties except in relation to non-arm's length dealings that are not covered by the APA or non-compliance with the terms and conditions of the APA.

Documentation requirements

The ATO has outlined a four-step process in TR98/11 to assist companies in satisfying contemporaneous documentation requirements. This process is not mandatory but is highly recommended. The documentation should record the transfer price setting process and, in particular, verify the outcome of those transactions against the arm's length standard. The documentation should include business, economic and industry analyses. In addition, taxpayers are expected to implement a review process to ensure that transactions and outcomes are reviewed at appropriate intervals and to ensure that the impact of material changes in the business are considered and documented. The documentation should be relevant to the Australian operations (i.e., country- and company-specific).

¶20,040

Documentation deadlines

Documentation should be contemporaneous with the relevant transactions. Documentation is generally only required to be submitted to the ATO following a specific notification, for example, during an ATO transfer pricing documentation review or audit.

Statute of limitations on transfer pricing assessments

There is generally no statute of limitations with respect to transfer pricing adjustments. The tax legislation specifically empowers the Commissioner of Taxation to make amendments to tax assessments in respect of any year for transfer pricing adjustments. Australia and Japan have recently signed a new double tax agreement which provides for a statute of limitations on transfer pricing adjustments. A tax authority must initiate an enquiry into an enterprise's profits within seven years from the end of the taxable year in which the profits at issue might have been expected to have accrued to the enterprise. However, the statute of limitations does not apply in the case of fraud, willful default or if the inability to initiate the enquiry results from the actions or inaction of the enterprise. The treaty is yet to receive ratification and as such is not yet in force.

Statute of limitations on transfer pricing assessments

The ATO requires a Schedule 25A to be filed with each tax return where the aggregate amount of transactions or dealings with international related parties was greater than $1 million. Information disclosed on the Schedule 25A includes (1) industry classification code(s), (2) countries with which the taxpayer has international related-party transactions, (3) international related-party transaction types and quantum, (4) the percentage of transactions covered by contemporaneous documentation that has been prepared in accordance with the four-step process, (5) transfer pricing methodologies selected and applied and (6) interests in foreign companies or foreign trusts.

The ATO is planning to introduce the International dealings schedule - financial services in 2010, which will be completed by all financial services entities meeting the following criteria: (1) foreign bank, (2) foreign bank branch, or (3) financial services provider with gross turnover of $250 million or more on their previous year's income tax return. The International dealings schedule will replace the Schedule 25A and thin capitalization schedule.

Audit risk/transfer pricing scrutiny

In determining whether an Australian taxpayer's transfer pricing should be reviewed or audited by the ATO, the ATO generally gives consideration to the size and nature of the related-party dealings, the quality of any transfer pricing documentation and whether or not the taxpayer's results appear to be commercially realistic. The ATO has developed a sophisticated risk engine which takes these factors, along with a number of other financial and industry data, into consideration in determining which taxpayers to review. Related-party transactions undertaken in connection with the following may receive particular attention by the ATO:

- Royalties
- Intangibles (both Australian and foreign-owned)
- Management services
- Financing arrangements, including interest-free loans, interest-bearing loans and guarantee fees
- Companies undergoing supply chain restructurings

The ATO also focuses on taxpayers whose overall operations do not achieve a commercially realistic result (e.g., incur losses or low returns in any particular year or over a range of years). Additionally, the ATO has been focusing on the arm's length nature of business restructures.

The ATO concentrates on a range of industries each year, including mining, energy and utilities, motor vehicles, pharmaceuticals, distributors, banking and insurance. The ATO continues to conduct transfer pricing reviews (documentation reviews) and transfer pricing audits. These reviews and audits target small and medium-sized enterprises as well as large enterprises.

The risk of transfer pricing audit in Australia would be assessed as medium/ high as the ATO continues to perform transfer pricing audits and make transfer pricing adjustments.

APA opportunity

The ATO actively promotes the use of APAs and has a well-established program for both unilateral and bilateral APAs. Circumstances that the ATO has indicated may be unsuitable for an APA include those where (1) timely agreement is unlikely to be reached with respect to the methodology, comparable data and overall arm's length outcome, (2) there is a lack of materiality in the dealings in the context of the business, (3) there is insufficient complexity to warrant the level of certainty that is provided by an APA or (4) obtaining a tax benefit in Australia or overseas was a principal element of the dealings.

AUSTRIA

Taxing authority and tax law

Ministry of Finance (MF). § 6(6) Income Tax Act, § 8(2) Corporate Income Tax Act, § 138 Federal Tax Code.

Relevant regulations and rulings

Income Tax Guidelines 6.13.3, 2511 -2513; Corporate Income Tax Guidelines 14.8.2, 1147; ministerial decrees AÖF Nr. 114/1996, 122/1997, 155/1998, 171/2000; and several published opinions regarding selected transfer pricing issues.

OECD guidelines treatment

Austria, as an OECD member country, has fully adopted the OECD Guidelines by publishing them in the form of several ministerial decrees. The OECD Transfer Pricing Guidelines may be considered internally binding upon the tax authorities. As they are not legally binding in Austria, Austrian tax courts and the taxpayer are not obliged to follow them. In practice, however, there is a strong reliance on the OECD Guidelines not only by the tax authorities but also by the tax courts and in Austrian literature. In addition to the OECD Guidelines the tax authorities generally follow OECD papers, such as the OECD Discussion Draft on Transfer Pricing Aspects of Business Restructurings, published on 19 September 2008. According to ministerial decree BMF 010221/0626-IV/4/2006, the tax authorities plan to enact national Transfer Pricing Guidelines based on the OECD Transfer Pricing Guidelines in the near future.

Priorities/pricing methods

Based on the OECD Transfer Pricing Guidelines, the MF accepts CUP, Resale Minus, Cost Plus, Profit Split and TNMM. However, it strongly prefers traditional transaction methods.

Transfer pricing penalties

If the income is increased because the arm's length criterion has not been met, non-deductible interest in the amount of 2% points above the base rate is levied on any prior year's corporate income tax payments. Lack of, or insufficient, transfer pricing documentation does not lead to specific penalties but increases the risk that the tax authorities will regard a transaction as non-compliant with the arm's length criterion and estimate a tax base adjustment.

Penalty relief

If the taxpayer provides formerly lacking or insufficient documentation to the tax authorities, the tax authorities are obliged to base their consideration upon such documentation. However, the interest will become due regardless of whether there is sufficient documentation or not.

Documentation requirements

In practice, transfer pricing documentation is required. However, there are no specific documentation rules. Austrian tax authorities promote the opinion that an obligation to prepare contemporaneous transfer pricing documentation can be

¶20,040

derived from the general regulations concerning bookkeeping for tax purposes. Following the OECD Transfer Pricing Guidelines or the annex to the code of conduct on transfer pricing documentation for associated enterprises in the European Union (EU) is therefore recommended.

Documentation deadlines

Documentation should be prepared contemporaneously. The documentation should be available upon request of the tax authorities within two to three weeks following the request.

Statute of limitations on transfer pricing assessments

The statute of limitations on a transfer pricing adjustment usually is six years after the end of the calendar year in which the relevant fiscal year ends. The term may be extended up to 10 years.

Return disclosures/related-party disclosures

No specific continuous disclosure is required in the annual tax return. In case of a tax audit, the auditors usually ask for a description of major related-party transactions as well as for disclosure of all contracts in place with related parties and transfer pricing studies available. In some cases, an extensive questionnaire is discussed.

Audit risk/transfer pricing scrutiny

Tax authorities regularly examine related-party transactions and transfer prices charged. There is a noticeable trend towards increased awareness of transfer pricing problems among tax auditors. Generally, the transfer pricing audit risk can be considered medium.

APA opportunity

Currently, there is no legal basis for APAs in Austria. The introduction of APAs is subject to discussion. It is possible to get a unilateral ruling for transfer pricing issues only.

BELGIUM

Taxing authority and tax law

The taxing authority responsible for transfer pricing in Belgium is the Belgian Administration of Direct Taxes, which is part of the Federal Public Service Finance. While transfer pricing issues can be raised in the course of an ordinary tax audit, a specific transfer pricing audit team has been created within the Belgian tax authority. This highly specialized team, which has nation-wide authority, operates autonomously and selects its audit targets, but also provides support to other field inspectors if requested.

While no specific transfer pricing legislation exists in Belgium, the arm's length principle was formally introduced into the Belgian tax law by the law of 21 June 2004, introducing Article 185, § 2 of the Belgian Income Tax Code (ITC) (entered into force on 19 July 2004). This article's content is equivalent to Article 9, § 1 and § 2 of the OECD Model Tax Convention.

In addition, the ITC contains various provisions which directly or indirectly relate to transfer pricing. These provisions can be found in articles 26, 49, 54, 55, 79, 207, 344 and 345 of the Belgian ITC. These articles deal with the notion of abnormal and gratuitous benefits (indirectly embodying the arm's length principle), the deductibility of expenses and avoidance of the shifting of profits.

The general provisions of the Belgian ITC, e.g., regarding penalties, late interest payments, etc., also apply in transfer pricing matters.

A general advance ruling (or APA) regime was introduced through the law of 24 December 2002 and became effective as of 1 January 2003.

New accounting rules, introduced through the Royal Decree of August 10, 2009, oblige companies to provide in their statutory annual accounts in Belgium certain additional information linked to transfer pricing in the notes/annexes of their annual accounts:

- Companies must provide information as regards the nature and business purpose of their relevant off-balance sheet arrangements, if underlying risks and benefits are considered material and when the disclosure is necessary to assess the financial position of the company correctly (e.g., intra-group guarantees, pledges, factoring liabilities, etc. and especially relations with special purpose entities transparent or not and offshore entities).

- Companies must disclose their material transactions with affiliated parties that can be considered as not at arm's length. Depending on the type of company a different scope of information is to be provided, ranging from a mere listing of such transactions to the mentioning of the amounts involved as well as all other information necessary to provide a correct view of the financial position of the company.

While this new rule is as such not included in the Belgian tax code, it creates a clear obligation for the relevant entities to review (and document) the arm's length nature of their intercompany transactions. Non-compliance may potentially result in, amongst other, director liability. In addition, any such information disclosed will

¶20,040

provide an excellent source of information for a tax inspector to initiate a (targeted) transfer pricing audit

Relevant regulations and rulings

The Belgian tax administration has issued various guidelines on transfer pricing:

- Administrative guidelines on the offensive aspects of transfer pricing, issued in 1999

- Administrative guidelines on the defensive aspects of transfer pricing, issued in 2000 and 2003

- Administrative guidelines providing the tax authority's view on the interpretation of article 185, §2 ITC, which introduced the arm's length principle into Belgian tax law, issued in July 2006

- Administrative guidelines regarding the formal creation of a transfer pricing audit team within the Belgian tax authorities, issued in July 2006

- Administrative guidelines on transfer pricing documentation, the transfer pricing code of conduct and transfer pricing audits, issued in November 2006

Rulings are provided on the basis of a general ruling practice (see APA opportunity). APAs are provided on an individual basis, taking into account the specifics of each case. The Belgian government has furthermore implemented a regime which provides, for tax purposes, a deduction on risk capital (i.e., qualifying equity), also known as a Notional Interest Deduction.

In addition, the Belgium government also introduced a special tax deduction for income derived from the use of patents. As a result of this deduction, income that is patent-related is subject to an effective Belgian tax rate of 6.8%, which is a very advantageous regime compared to the standard corporate income tax of 33.99% that is normally levied.

OECD guidelines treatment

The Belgian tax authority indicates several times in its administrative guidelines that taxpayers should generally follow the guidance mentioned in the OECD Transfer Pricing Guidelines.

Priorities/pricing methods

Although taxpayers are in principle free to choose any OECD transfer pricing method as long as the method chosen results in arm's length pricing for the transaction, conceptually, transaction-based methods are preferred over profit-based methods.

Taxpayers are not required to use more than one method, although they should be able to support their decision to apply a particular method.

Transfer pricing penalties

The general tax penalty framework applies to transfer pricing adjustments. These penalties vary from 10% up to (in very exceptional cases) 200% of the additional tax; the rate depends on the degree of intent to avoid tax or the degree of the company's gross negligence.

Furthermore, interest for late payments is due on additional tax assessments (including assessments resulting from a transfer pricing adjustment).

Penalty relief

Since additional tax assessments depend on the degree of intent to avoid taxes or on the company's gross negligence, penalties can be reduced or eliminated if the taxpayer can demonstrate its intent to establish transfer prices in accordance with the arm's length principle (e.g., through its documentation efforts).

Documentation requirements

No legislative guidance regarding the nature and content of proper transfer pricing documentation exists. However, the 1999 administrative guidelines state that documentation should demonstrate that the taxpayer's pricing complies with the arm's length principle to avoid an in-depth transfer pricing audit. These 1999 guidelines recommend that documentation includes, at a minimum:

- Activities of the group (including competitive position, level of market, economic circumstances, business strategies, etc.)

- Identification and characterization of intercompany transactions and contractual relationships among affiliates

- Functional analysis (including an overview of the functions, risks and intangibles)

- Transfer pricing methods used

- Economic analysis

The 2006 administrative guidelines on transfer pricing confirm Belgium's agreement with the principles outlined in the EU Code of Conduct. Therefore, the information expectation contained in this Code of Conduct should also be considered from a Belgian transfer pricing documentation perspective. These administrative guidelines also refer to the concept of a prudent business manager in order to encourage companies to ensure that transfer pricing documentation is available.

Although the burden of proof lies with the tax authorities, the taxpayer needs to provide information on its transfer pricing policies applied to allow the tax authorities to verify the company's tax position.

Documentation deadlines

Given the absence of any formal transfer pricing documentation requirements, there is no deadline for the preparation of transfer pricing documentation. However, since upon a tax audit, a taxpayer has a one-month period (which can be prolonged if valid reasons exist) to provide all information requested, including all information that allows verification of its taxable income - and therefore, the arm's length nature of the transfer prices - it is recommended that each transaction be documented at the time it is executed. Additionally, the 1999 guidelines provide that if the taxpayer can demonstrate upon a tax audit that it has made sufficient

¶20,040

efforts to prepare transfer pricing documentation, the tax inspector does not need to carry out an in-depth tax audit..

Statute of limitations on transfer pricing assessments

The general rules regarding the statute of limitations apply to transfer pricing assessments. Therefore, generally speaking, the tax authority is entitled to make additional assessments during a period of three years starting from the closing of the accounting year.

However, in the case of fraud, the tax authority has the right to adjust the income during a five-year period, provided that the taxpayer receives prior notice of serious indications of fraud. Some other, exceptional statutes of limitations also exist for specific situations.

Return disclosures/related-party disclosures

No specific disclosure requirements exist for filing the tax return.

Audit risk/transfer pricing scrutiny

The transfer pricing audit risk may be regarded as medium-high.

The Belgian tax authorities have demonstrated an increased interest in transfer pricing since the first circular letter on transfer pricing, introduced in 1999. Thereafter, the introduction of the arm's length principle in the Belgian legislation in 2004 and the organization of a special transfer pricing team in 2006 increased the focus on transfer pricing. This transfer pricing audit team is expected to be informed of every transfer pricing investigation performed by the local tax audit teams to ensure a consistent and experienced approach. The tax authorities have their own targets and perform multinational tax audits (e.g., in case of a restructuring).

The transfer pricing audit team is also involved in cross-border transfer pricing audits, which are held jointly with the tax authorities of Belgium's neighboring countries. In addition to this special team's increased audit activity, tax inspectors are also increasing their focus on transfer pricing during general tax audits.

The 2006 administrative guidelines contain a list of events that could trigger a high transfer pricing risk and lead to increased audit scrutiny:

- Structural losses
- Business reorganizations
- Migration of businesses
- The use of tax havens or low-tax rate countries
- Back-to-back operations
- Circular structures
- Invoices for services sent at the end of the year (i.e. management services)

The Belgian tax authorities indicated in their November 2006 circular that transfer pricing cases associated with business restructurings will be among the priorities in their audit efforts.

¶20,040

These developments are likely to result in an increased focus on transfer pricing, especially considering the evolution of the Belgian TP audit relationship with other tax authorities. Transfer pricing audits have become more aggressive. They are being approached from an economic perspective and are focused on such specific issues as business conversions and restructurings.

In our experience with the Belgian tax authorities, the recent developments will result in more focus on transfer pricing, especially considering the evolution that the Belgian TP audit cell is working closely together with other tax authorities.

APA opportunity

The 2003 corporate tax reform introduced a general ruling practice under Belgian tax law. Additional guidance in this respect is provided through various Royal Decrees.

As a result of the law of 21 June 2004, the Service for Advance Decisions became an autonomous department (led by a committee of four) as of 1 January 2005. More than 100 specialists in various domains of taxation, including transfer pricing, assist the committee. This service has increased flexibility in the ruling process and shortened the decision period (usually less than three months from the filing date for unilateral APAs). This committee is also able to rule prospectively on corresponding downward profit adjustments under Article 185, § 2, thus offering significant transfer pricing planning opportunities.

BRAZIL

Taxing authority and tax law

Brazilian Internal Revenue Service (IRS); Internal Revenue Code by Decreto 3000, 26 March 1999 (RIR99).

Relevant regulations and rulings

Coefficients to compensate exports for Brazilian currency appreciation:

- 2008 coefficient: 1.20 (Normative Instruction No. 898/08 and Ordinance No. 310/08)

- 2007 coefficient: 1.28 (Normative Instruction No. 801/07 and Ordinance No. 329/07)

- 2006 coefficient: 1.29 (Normative Instruction No. 703/06 and Ordinance No. 425/06)

- 2005 coefficient: 1.35 (Normative Instruction No. 602/05 and Ordinance No. 436/05)

Ordinance No. 222/08; provides guidance with respect to requests for changing statutory profit margins.

Normative Instruction No. 243, 11 November 2002; changed application of Resale Minus 60%, Law No. 9.959, 27 January 2000; introduced new method: Resale Minus 60% (applicable for raw materials).

Law No. 9.430, 27 December 1996; introduced transfer pricing rules in Brazil.

OECD guidelines treatment

Brazil's transfer pricing rules deviate significantly from international standards (including the OECD guidelines) in that there are no profitbased methods. Intercompany transactions need to be documented on a strict transactional basis, and fixed statutory profit margins (generally not arm's length) apply. No functional or industry analyses are required. Instead, the local subsidiary will have to document for each imported (or exported) product or service that it complies with at least one of Brazil's statutory transactional methodologies (CUP, Resale Minus or Cost Plus).

Priorities/pricing methods

As a first step in the transfer pricing documentation process, Brazilian companies have applied the Brazilian Resale Price less Profit Method (Método do Preço de Revenda menos Lucro or (PRL)) to document a company's transfer prices. Brazilian companies have started the documentation process with the PRL because the method relies entirely on import cost, local production cost and resale price information available internally, relieving the company of the burden of soliciting data from its foreign-related suppliers. In addition, since the PRL is the method favored by the Brazilian tax authority in the case of an audit, this approach provides a reliable estimate of Brazil's potential transfer pricing exposure.

¶20,040

Transfer pricing penalties

Since there are no special penalties for transfer pricing, general tax penalties are applicable. The amount of the penalty may be up to 20% of the omitted tax (or 0.33% per day) if the taxpayer pays the related taxes late but before an audit. Meanwhile, if the tax authority assesses the taxpayer as part of a transfer pricing audit, the applicable penalties may range from 75% to 225% of the omitted taxes.

Penalty relief

Not applicable.

Documentation requirements

Brazilian taxpayers are required to document their international intercompany transactions on an annual basis. The Brazilian annual tax declaration (DIPJ) contains five specific forms that require taxpayers to disclose detailed information regarding their main intercompany import and export transactions. As part of these contemporaneous documentation requirements, taxpayers need to disclose the total transaction values for the most traded products, services or rights, the names and locations of the related trading partners, the methodology used to test each transaction, the calculated benchmark price, the average annual transfer price and the amount of any resulting adjustment.

Given the detailed transactional focus of the Brazilian regulations and the absence of any basket approach, taxpayers are required to document their transfer prices on a product code by product code basis, service type by service type and right by right. In this context, product code refers to a company's internal product codes used for inventory management purposes and not the much broader fiscal nomenclature used for customs and indirect tax purposes.

Taxpayers are expected to have the calculations and documentation necessary to support the information filed as part of the annual tax declaration ready for potential inspection by the tax authority as of the declaration's filing date, i.e., usually the end of June of the ensuing calendar year.

Documentation deadline

The contemporaneous documentation required as part of the DIPJ usually has to be filed by the end of June of the following fiscal year. Taxpayers are expected to have the detailed calculations and documentation necessary to support the information filed as part of the DIPJ ready for potential inspection as of the declaration's filing date.

Statute of limitations on transfer pricing assessments

A general statute of limitations applies, which is five years from the first day of the following fiscal year.

Return disclosures/related-party disclosures

The transfer pricing adjustments must be effected in December and reflected in the annual income tax return (usually due June of next year), when the company

¶20,040

will also have to disclose the transfer pricing methods chosen and any related information.

Audit risk/transfer pricing scrutiny

In an effort to expedite audits in Brazil's data-intensive transfer pricing documentation environment, Brazilian audit teams have been equipped with new computers and specialized software applications, including internally developed systems capable of analyzing and auditing large volumes of accounting and transaction data.

The Brazilian tax authority expects the International Affairs Special Office (DEAIN) and the regional audit groups to continue to increase their numbers of specialized transfer pricing auditors. It is believed that the DEAIN and the regional transfer pricing auditors are becoming increasingly sophisticated in their audit approaches as they grow in number and experience.

There is a growing concern that many transfer pricing auditors, because of their particular training and tools, tend to rely on mechanical approaches to audits, while they ignore, or are unaware, of possible underlying business economics. While efforts are being made to increase auditors' knowledge of economics, it is expected that this approach to auditing will continue for the next few years.

APA opportunity

Not applicable.

CANADA

Taxing authority and tax law

Section 247 of the Income Tax Act (Canada) (ITA) received Royal Assent on 18 June 1998 and became generally applicable to taxation years that began after 1997. It constitutes Canada's transfer pricing legislation and deals with the determination of transfer pricing adjustments, the recharacterization of transactions, penalties, records/documents required to be made or obtained, contemporaneous documentation requirements and timing of provision to the Minister when requested, plus ministerial discretion regarding acceptance of downward adjustment requests.

The Canada Revenue Agency (CRA) is responsible for ensuring that taxpayers meet the requirements of the law.

Relevant regulations and rulings

The CRA does not set out its views and positions on transfer pricing issues by legal doctrine or in a detailed fashion or examples. The CRA prefers to outline its views in general principles.

It provides its administrative interpretations and guidance with respect to § 247 and its application through the release of Information Circulars (IC), Transfer Pricing Memoranda (TPM) and pronouncements at public conferences, symposia and conventions. ICs usually address major subjects from a general perspective, while TPMs typically provide supplementary detailed explanations and guidance on specific issues related to the major subject.

CRA's current key pronouncements on transfer pricing are:

- *IC87-2R, International Transfer Pricing, 27 September 1999*
- *IC94-4R, International Transfer Pricing: Advance Pricing Arrangements (APAs), 16 March 2001*
- *IC94-4R (Special Release), Advance Pricing Arrangements for Small Businesses, 18 March 2005*
- *IC71-17R5, Guidance on Competent Authority Assistance Under Canada's Tax Conventions, 1 January 2005*

The CRA issued TPM-12 on 12 December 2008, which provides formal guidance regarding the Accelerated Competent Authority Procedure (ACAP). Taxpayers may request assistance for subsequent assessed (but unaudited) taxation years on the same issues included in a Mutual Agreement Procedure (MAP) process. The main objective of the ACAP is to streamline certain steps in the MAP process, such as being able to simultaneously negotiate with the foreign competent authority for both MAP and ACAP years.

The CRA is a member of the Pacific Association of Tax Administrators (PATA). Relevant guidance is issued by PATA from time to time on topics of mutual interest, e.g., the PATA Transfer Pricing Documentation Package, released March 2003.

Additional information and guidance on transfer pricing related matters can be obtained from the CRA's website: www.cra-arc.gc.ca/tx/nnrsdnts/cmmn/trns/menu-eng.html

¶20,040

OECD guidelines treatment

While no mention is made of the OECD guidelines in § 247 of the ITA, the legislative provision is intended to reflect the arm's length principle as set out in the OECD guidelines. The CRA has also endeavored to harmonize its administrative guidance and approach to transfer pricing with the OECD guidelines. As noted in IC87-2R: "This circular sets out the Department's views on transfer pricing and also provides the Department's position with respect to the application of the OECD guidelines."

When dealing with transfer pricing issues domestically, reliance is placed on the relevant Canadian statutory provisions. CRA's related ICs and other administrative guidance are considered instructive but not definitive. Moreover, the OECD guidelines are not usually recognized as authoritative; however, courts and other dispute resolution channels (e.g., competent authority) may consider the international principles and standards established by the OECD in reaching a decision.

Priorities/pricing methods

The CRA accepts the transfer pricing methods recommended in the OECD guidelines when such methods are applied correctly and result in an arm's length price or allocation. These transfer pricing methods specified in IC 87-2 include

- CUP method
- Resale Price method
- Cost Plus method
- Profit Split method (residual/contribution)
- TNMM

However, the CRA considers the use of the Profit Split method as a method of last resort.

The CRA considers, notwithstanding that § 247 does not so stipulate, that there is a natural hierarchy in the application of the above-noted transfer pricing methods, with the CUP method providing the most reliable indication of an arm's length transfer price or allocation and the Profit Split method providing the least reliable indication of an arm's length result. The Tax Court of Canada, in the 2008 Glaxo case, has embraced the hierarchy of methods as outlined in the OECD Guidelines.

The CRA does not require or impose a "best method" rule. The CRA believes that the most appropriate method to be used in any situation will be that which provides the highest degree of comparability between transactions, following an analysis of the hierarchy of methods.

Transfer pricing penalties

Subsection 247(3) of the ITA causes a taxpayer to be liable for a penalty of 10% of the net upward transfer pricing adjustments made under subsection 247(2) of the ITA, if such adjustments exceed the lesser of 10% of the taxpayer's gross revenue for the year and CAD 5,000,000, and if the taxpayer has not made reasonable efforts to determine and use arm's length transfer prices.

¶20,040

A taxpayer will be deemed not to have made reasonable efforts to determine and use arm's length transfer prices or allocations unless the taxpayer has prepared or obtained records or documents that provide a description that is complete and accurate in all material respects of the items listed in subsection 247(4) of the ITA, and such documentation is in existence as of the tax filing due date. In the case of Canadian corporate entities, such documentation must exist six months after the year-end. For partnerships, the due date is five months after the year-end. Further, a taxpayer will be deemed not to have made reasonable efforts to determine and use arm's length transfer prices or allocations if the taxpayer does not provide the records or documents to the CRA within three months of the issuance of a written request to do so.

Transfer pricing related penalties are exacted without reference to the taxpayer's income or loss for the relevant reporting year and are not tax deductible.

Penalty relief

If a taxpayer is considered to have made reasonable efforts to determine and use arm's length transfer prices or allocations with respect to adjusted non-arm's length transactions, no penalty would be applicable to such adjustments.

As required by TPM-07, all proposed reassessments involving transfer pricing penalties are required to be referred to the Transfer Pricing Review Committee (TPRC) for review and recommendation for final action. The TPRC, after consideration of the facts and circumstances and representations by the relevant taxpayer, will conclude whether or not a transfer pricing penalty is justified.

No transfer pricing adjustments under subsection 247(2) of the ITA should arise regarding transactions covered by an APA as long as the APA remains in effect and the taxpayer complies with its terms and conditions.

When the CRA has reassessed a transfer pricing penalty and the Canadian competent authority and relevant foreign counterpart negotiate a change to the amount of the transfer pricing adjustment, the CRA will adjust the amount of the Canadian transfer pricing penalty accordingly. If the result of the change is that the adjustment no longer exceeds the penalty threshold, the penalty would be rescinded.

Documentation requirements

Subsection 247(4) of the ITA requires that a taxpayer must have records or documents, as a minimum, that provide a complete and accurate description, in all material respects, of the following items:

- The property or services to which the transaction relates
- The terms and conditions of the transaction and their relationship, if any, to the terms and conditions of each other transaction entered into between the persons or partnerships involved in the transaction
- The identity of the persons or partnerships involved in the transaction, and their relationship at the time the transaction was entered into

¶20,040

- The functions performed, the property used or contributed and the risks assumed by the persons or partnerships involved in the transaction

- The data and methods considered and the analysis performed to determine the transfer prices, the allocations of profits or losses, or contributions to costs for the transaction

- The assumptions, strategies and policies, if any, that influenced the determination of the transfer prices, the allocations of profits or losses, or contributions to costs for the transaction

In addition, although its views are not law, the CRA indicates in Information Circular 87-2R that it expects a taxpayer's documentation to include certain additional information (e.g., details of cost contribution arrangements, translations of foreign documents and other general guidance).

The CRA issued TPM 09 on 18 September 2006. The purpose of this memo was to define the meaning of "reasonable efforts" under § 247 of the Act. In practice, TPM 09 has not significantly enhanced clarity with respect to the reasonable efforts standard and, thereby, the potential application of transfer pricing penalties.

Documentation deadlines

Taxpayers must prepare or obtain records and documents that provide a description that is complete and accurate in all material respects of the items listed in subsection 247(4) of the ITA, and such documentation must be in existence as of the tax filing due date. In the case of Canadian corporate entities, such documentation must exist six months after the year-end. For partnerships, the due date is five months after the year-end.

Taxpayers must provide documentation to the CRA within three months of the issuance of a written request.

Statute of limitations on transfer pricing assessments

Under subsection 152(4) of the ITA, the Minister may not ordinarily reassess after the normal reassessment period as defined in subsection 152(3.1) of the ITA. For most multinational taxpayers, that period is four years beginning after the earlier of the day of mailing a notice of an original assessment for the year and the mailing of an original notification that no tax is payable for the year, unless the taxpayer has made misrepresentations, committed a fraud or filed a waiver, in which case the Minister may reassess a taxpayer at anytime. Where a Notice of Reassessment is issued at a later date, the first assessment notice is still viewed as the original assessment for the purposes of determining the normal reassessment period under subsection 152(3.1) of the ITA.

With respect to transactions involving non-arm's length dealings with non-residents, the reassessment period is extended an additional three years to seven years. This time period may be further extended when taxpayers provide CRA with a waiver, i.e., authorization by the taxpayer to the CRA to waive the normal reassessment period in respect of a taxation year, as defined in subsection 152(3.1) of the ITA, within which the Minister may assess, reassess or make additional

¶20,040

assessments under subsection 152(4) of the ITA. As of March 2009 a waiver may be provided by the taxpayer within the seven - year extended reassessment period. Previously, waivers were only allowed to be filed within the four - year normal reassessment period.

Return disclosures/related-party disclosures

Taxpayers are required to file a T106 information return annually, reporting the transactions they had with non-arm's length non-residents during the taxation year. The T106 is a separate information return but is usually filed together with the corporate tax return. Data from the T106 is entered into a CRA database and is used to screen taxpayers for international tax audits.

Audit risk/transfer pricing scrutiny

The CRA continues to receive additional funding for its audit of international activities and to focus its audit resources on the examination of international transactions, especially transfer pricing.

The risk of a transfer pricing audit in Canada is high. Canadian companies with cross-border dealings with related parties can expect a request from the CRA for their required transfer pricing documentation prior to or during the course of an audit. As noted in TPM-05, "Contemporaneous Documentation," effective October 2004, it is mandatory for field auditors to issue a formal written request to taxpayers for their transfer pricing documentation prior to commencement of the audit or when cross-border non-arm's length transactions with non-residents are identified during the course of an audit.

APA opportunity

The CRA launched its APA program in July 1993. As set out in its Information Circular 94-4R, it offers taxpayers the opportunity to pursue unilateral, bilateral or multilateral APAs. In addition, the CRA has made a small business APA program available to Canadian taxpayers under certain conditions. The CRA charges taxpayers only travel costs it incurs in the completion of an APA.

On 20 August 2008, the CRA issued TPM 11, which discussed the CRA policy with respect to rolling an APA back to prior years. The main limitation imposed by TPM 11 is that APAs may not be rolled back to years for which a request for contemporaneous documentation has been issued. Effectively, this means that APAs cannot be rolled back to taxation years under transfer pricing audit.

An updated version of IC94-4R is expected to be released soon.

CHINA

Taxing authority and tax law

State Administration of Taxation (SAT). People's Republic of China (PRC) Corporate Income Tax Law, Chapter 6, Articles 41 through 48 and PRC Corporate Income Tax Law Implementation Regulations, Articles 109 through 123.

Notice Containing Related Party Transaction Annual Reporting Forms (Guoshuifa (2008) No. 114) and Implementation Measures for Special Tax Adjustments (Guoshuifa (2009) No. 2).

Notice on the Tax Deductibility of Interest Expense Paid to Related Parties (Caishui (2008) No. 121), Notice on the Strengthening, the Monitoring and Investigation of Cross border Related Party Transactions [for Single Function Entities] (Guoshuihan (2009) No. 363), and Notice on Intensifying the Transfer Pricing Follow-up Administration (Guoshuihan (2009) No. 188.

In principle, the SAT recognizes the OECD guidelines and the relevant transfer pricing methods.

Priorities/pricing methods

The SAT accepts a reasonable method. The SAT will accept CUP, Resale Price and Cost Plus. Other methods, including the Profit Split, and the Transactional Net Margin Method (TNMM), are also considered. For the TNMM, the profit level indicators most often used are operating margin and total cost markup. Balance sheet profit level indicators such as return on assets or return on capital employed are rarely used.

Article 48 of the PRC Corporate Income Tax Law stipulates that interest will be applied to the under-reported tax resulting from special adjustments to tax payments, including transfer pricing adjustments. Article 122 of the PRC Corporate Income Tax Law Implementation Regulations references Article 48 and states that interest imposed on special tax adjustments is based on the base renminbi (RMB) lending rate published by the People's Bank of China plus an additional 5% interest charge.

Additionally, per Article 106 of Guoshuifa (2009) No. 2, taxpayers that refuse to provide contemporaneous documentation or those that refuse to file, file false information, and/or file incomplete related-party reporting forms are subject to monetary penalties pursuant to Article 70 of the PRC Tax Collection and Administration Law and Article 96 of the PRC Tax Collection and Administration Law Implementation Regulations, as well as Article 44 of the PRC Corporate Income Tax Law and Article 115 of PRC Corporate Income Tax Law Implementation Regulations.

Penalty relief

According to Article 122, the additional 5% interest can be avoided if contemporaneous documentation has been prepared in accordance with the relevant law and regulations and can be provided within 20 days of request.

¶20,040

Documentation requirements

The PRC Corporate Income Tax Law and the PRC Enterprise Income Tax Law Implementation Regulations imply that taxpayers are expected to maintain contemporaneous transfer pricing documentation. Articles 13 through 20 of Guoshuifa (2009) No. 2 formally introduces and clarifies China's contemporaneous transfer pricing documentation requirements.

Article 14 of Guoshuifa (2009) No. 2 specifies five primary components of China's contemporaneous documentation:

- Organization structure
- Information of business operations
- Information of related-party transactions
- Comparability analysis
- Selection and application of transfer pricing methods

Article 15 states that certain enterprises can be exempted from the preparation, maintenance, and provision of contemporaneous documentation:

- Those conducting RMB 200m or fewer in annual related-party purchase and sale transactions and RMB 40m or fewer in annual related-party "other" transactions (intangibles, services, and interest from financing transactions)
- Those with transactions covered by an advance pricing arrangement(APA)
- Those with a 50% or less share of foreign ownership that only conduct related-party transactions within China

Documentation deadlines

Article 16 of Guoshuifa (2009) No. 2 specifies that taxpayers should finish the preparation of contemporaneous documentation on or before 31 May of the following year and that all documentation should be submitted to tax authorities within 20 days of a request.

Statute of limitations on transfer pricing assessments

The statute of limitations for transfer pricing adjustments may vary; however, adjustments can be applied for a period of up to 10 years.

Article 20 of Guoshuifa (2009) No. 2 states that contemporaneous documentation should be maintained for a period of 10 years (starting from 1 June of the year following the transactions).

Return disclosures/related-party disclosures

Article 43 of the Corporate Income Tax Law and Guoshuifa (2008) No. 114 requires that taxpayers complete and submit nine comprehensive Related Party Transaction Annual Reporting Forms along with their annual tax filing. Per Article 16 of Guoshuifa (2009) No. 2, these forms must be submitted on or before 31 May following a fiscal year, including related-party transactions conducted during fiscal year 2008, i.e. Related Party Transaction Annual Reporting Forms for fiscal year 2008 are due on or before 31 May 2009.

¶20,040

Audit risk/transfer pricing scrutiny

The risk of transfer pricing issues being reviewed under audit is high.

In 2008, 174 new transfer pricing audits were initiated and 152 cases were closed. Taxable incomes were adjusted by an aggregate of RMB 15.5b during 2008 - a significant increase from the approximate RMB 9b adjusted in 2007 and 5.9b adjusted in 2006.

The SAT continues to focus on enterprises that have sustained losses in the past, especially those paying intercompany service charges or royalties. With the release of China's final implementation rules contained within Guoshuifa (2009) No. 2, we believe there will be an increase in transfer pricing audit activity in the coming years.

Within Guoshuihan (2009) No. 363, the SAT also reiterated its position that "single-function" entities should not be subjected to losses. Any such "single-function" entity that generates losses is required to prepare and submit contemporaneous documentation, regardless of its quantum of related party transactions.

APA opportunity

APAs are available in China. Guidance regarding the APA process and procedures is provided in Articles 46 through 63 of Guoshuifa (2009) No. 2.

The validity of an APA is generally between three and five years. Enterprises no longer need to have ten years of operating history before applying for an APA and the ban on enterprises with major tax evasion history has been lifted as well. Annual related-party transaction volumes must only be greater than or equal to RMB 40m, rather than the previously required RMB 100m. Applications for APAs involving more than one in-charge province can be submitted directly to the SAT in Beijing.

COLOMBIA

Taxing authority and tax law

Dirección de Impuestos y Aduanas Nacionales (DIAN). Law 788 enacted in 2002 and Law 863 enacted in December 2003 established the transfer pricing practice in the Tax Code; articles 260-1 to 260-10.

The definition of related parties is found in articles 450 and 452 of the Tax Code; articles 260, 261, 263 and 264 of the Commercial Code; and article 28 of Law 222 of 1995.

Relevant regulations and rulings

Regulatory Decree 4349 published in December 2004 provides the Transfer Pricing Guidelines applicable in Colombia, including the contents of the transfer pricing documentation and return, use of financial data and APA program.

OECD guidelines treatment

Although Colombia is not a member of the OECD, its guidelines are generally followed in the local regulations.

Priorities/pricing methods

The law establishes six methods: CUP, Resale Price, Cost Plus, Profit Split, Residual Profit Split and TNMM. The selection of the method should be based on the characteristics of the transaction under analysis. The selected method should be the one that better reflects the economic reality of the transaction, provides the best information and requires fewer adjustments. Local companies' information is available and should be used for benchmark analyses when applicable.

Transfer pricing penalties

In the case of partial noncompliance with transfer pricing documentation requirements, taxpayers bear penalties of 1% of the total value of transactions with foreign related parties during the relevant tax year or 0.5% of the taxpayer's net income or gross capital reported in the income tax return of the same tax year or in the last tax return filed. Penalties cannot exceed 28,000 UVT (Tax Value Unit)[1]. Additionally, when the taxpayer does not present the required documentation, the penalties are calculated in the same way as in partial noncompliance, and those penalties cannot exceed 39,000 UVT.

Regarding the transfer pricing return, penalties for late filing are calculated in the same manner as penalties for noncompliance with documentation requirements, but applied on a monthly basis and cannot exceed 39,000 UVT.

If a taxpayer fails to fulfill its obligation of declaring transfer pricing transactions and is unable to determine the value of the transactions with foreign related parties, the default fine is 10% of the taxpayer's net income or gross capital reported in the income tax return of the same tax year or in the last tax return filed. The penalties cannot exceed 39,000 UVT.

---

[1] 2009 UVT = COP 23.763.

¶20,040

Regarding transfer pricing adjustments, the tax authority penalizes taxpayers with an extra penalty of 160% of the unpaid tax.

Regarding transfer pricing documentation, penalties are reduced by 50% if the omission, mistake or inconsistency is corrected before penalty notification or reduced by 25% if corrected within two months after penalty notification.

With respect to the transfer pricing return, once the taxpayer becomes liable for penalties for not presenting the return form, such penalties can be reduced by 25% if the taxpayer presents the return before the new deadline.

Documentation requirements

Taxpayers must prepare supporting documentation proving each transaction with foreign related parties complies with the arm's length principle. The transfer pricing documentation includes organizational structure, business descriptions, functions, assets, risks, detailed information of intercompany transactions, among others.

Documentation is not required for transactions within the fiscal year that do not exceed 10.000 UVT.

Regulatory Decree 4349 outlines the information to be included in transfer pricing documentation.

Documentation deadlines

Documentation should be in existence by 30 June of the next fiscal year.

For fiscal year 2009, transfer pricing returns were submitted between 8 July and 22 July depending on the Taxpayers' Tax ID number.

Statute of limitations on transfer pricing assessments

The statute of limitations is five years. The tax authority can request and review transfer pricing documentation at any time during this period.

Return disclosures/related-party disclosures

As part of the transfer pricing return, taxpayers must disclose information on related parties such as country and Tax ID number. Other information disclosed on the transfer pricing return are the type of intercompany transaction, value, transfer pricing methodology applied, company assessed, price/margin obtained in the transaction and arm's length interquartile range.

Audit risk/transfer pricing scrutiny

In February 2006, the tax authority requested a transfer pricing study from almost all of the taxpayers who had filed the transfer pricing return for fiscal year 2004 (approximately 1,250 taxpayers).

After the review of the documentation, some corrections were requested. Until May 2006, approximately six taxpayers were under the tax authority's scrutiny for lack of proper 2004 documentation.

Additionally, the tax authority has requested clarifications from some taxpayers regarding whether they had intercompany transactions that were not declared.

¶20,040

The tax authority's interest and knowledge in transfer pricing matters has increased during the last years.

During 2007, approximately 350 taxpayers had requests for their transfer pricing documentation for fiscal year 2005 and 2006. In 2008, over 10 taxpayers were requested to deliver their transfer pricing studies for fiscal year 2007, mainly in coal and oil industries. In 2009, all taxpayers that submitted transfer pricing returns were requested to present documentation for fiscal years 2007 and 2008. All taxpayers that did not comply with the arm's length principle were subject to adjustment, which according to Article 2 of the Regulatory Decree 4349 of 2004 should be the median of the interquartile range. In this sense, audit risk has been medium.

APA opportunity

The tax reform enacted in 2003 established APA regulations. APAs may be granted for a four-year term and they can be renewed. For the time being, only unilateral APAs are available. No double taxation treaties are currently in force.

A treaty with Spain became effective during 2008, and a new treaty with Switzerland is expected to be approved during 2009.

CROATIA

Taxing authority and tax law

Ministry of Finance - Tax Authorities.

Transfer pricing rules in Croatia are stipulated by the Corporate Income Tax Act (the "CIT Act") and the Corporate Income Tax Bylaw (the "CIT Bylaw").

Relevant regulations and rulings

Article 13 of the CIT Act and Article 40 of the CIT Bylaw prescribe arm's length pricing as the basic principle to be followed, define the methods allowed and documentation required to support prices between related parties.

At present, neither the CIT Act nor the CIT Bylaw provides extensive guidance or instruction to taxpayers with regard to meeting the transfer pricing requirements.

OECD guidelines treatment

Although Croatia is not an OECD member country, the provisions of relevant Croatian tax legislation are generally based on the OECD Transfer Pricing Guidelines. Furthermore, the Ministry of Finance issued instructions for the tax officials performing transfer pricing audits. The instructions are also based on the OECD Transfer Pricing Guidelines.

Priorities/pricing methods

The Croatian CIT regulations do not provide detailed rules on how to arrive at the market price that should be applied in related party transactions. However, the CIT Act prescribes the methods that a taxpayer can use to determine the market price: Resale Minus, Comparable Uncontrolled Price ("CUP"), Cost Plus, Profit Split and Transactional Net Margin Method. The relevant legislation states that the CUP method has priority over the other methods.

Transfer pricing penalties

Fines up to HRK 200,000 (approximately EUR 28,000) for a company and up to HRK 20,000 (approximately EUR 2,800) for the responsible individual within the company, per offence, may be imposed in respect of any underestimation of the corporate income tax liability. Penalty interest would also be calculated from the date when the tax was due until the date when the tax is paid.

Penalty relief

There are no specific provisions concerning penalty relief.

Documentation requirements

According to the CIT Bylaw, a taxpayer should perform (and provide documentary evidence of) the following activities in the process of proving that market prices have been applied in transactions with any related parties:

¶20,040

- List of related parties and specification of transactions with them;
- Identification of the transfer pricing method applied (description of the method chosen for determining the transfer prices and a statement justifying the reasons for choosing the particular method);
- Comparable search - description of data, methods and analysis used for determination of transfer prices. Specification of assumptions and evaluations used in the process of determining transfer prices (in line with the principle of unbiased transactions), with reference to comparability, functional analysis and risk analysis;
- Documentation of all calculations based on the selected method (such documentation should enable a comparison with the prices applied by other comparable taxpayers);
- Update of the transfer pricing documentation to reflect adjustments made due to changes in relevant facts and circumstances;
- Prepare other documentation substantiating the analysis and determination of transfer prices.

The taxpayer must maintain readily available data and information concerning related parties and the business transaction conducted between them.

Documentation deadlines

There is no specific deadline for the preparation of the transfer pricing documentation prescribed by the legislation. The law requires the transfer pricing documentation to be available and to be provided to the Tax Authorities upon their request in a tax audit. The documentation should be available in Croatian.

Statute of limitations on transfer pricing assessments

The general statute of limitation for determination of tax liabilities and rights in a particular tax period expires at the end of the third year following the year in which a tax return should have been filed (e.g. as the 2009 corporate tax return has to be filed by 30 April 2010, 2009 becomes statute barred on 1 January 2014). However, the general statute of limitations may be prolonged and recommences after each intervention by the Tax Authority with respect to a tax return which has been filed. The absolute statute of limitations expires after 6 years. Therefore, 2009 becomes statute barred absolutely on 1 January 2017.

Return disclosures/related-party disclosures

No specific disclosures are required in the annual tax return.

Recently many taxpayers have received a simple request following the filing of their tax return asking what transfer pricing methodology they used.

Audit risk/transfer pricing scrutiny

In past few years the Tax Authorities have increased the frequency of transfer pricing audits. As they still have limited experience in transfer pricing, there are many disputes, as well as requirements for supporting explanations with respect to related party charges and additional documentation. However, there is a noticeable

¶20,040

trend towards increased awareness of transfer pricing problems among the Tax Authorities' officials.

The Tax Authorities are in particular focused on examining documentation related to service fees charged by related parties. Tax inspectors tend to challenge service costs based on the argument that the available documentation is insufficient to prove the benefit arising to the Croatian company from the respective services. They also challenge the appropriateness of the prices applied in such transactions.

Generally, the transfer pricing audit risk can be considered high.

APA opportunity

Currently there is no legal basis for APAs in Croatia.

Czech Republic

Taxing authority and tax law

Ministry of Finance. The Income Tax Act § 23(7) — arm's length principle and § 38nc — APA scope and procedures.

Relevant regulations and rulings

Directive D-258 discusses the application of international standards in the taxation of transactions between associated companies, i.e., transfer prices. D-258 confirms the applicability of the OECD Transfer Pricing Guidelines for both international and domestic transactions (with certain exceptions).

Directive D-292 outlines requirements concerning § 38nc of the Income Tax Act. D-292 comments on the principles of binding assessments, which correspond to the preliminary price agreement principles within the meaning of the OECD guidelines.

Directive D-293 outlines requirements on the expected scope of documentation of a transfer pricing method agreed between related persons. D-293 comments on the scope and nature of transfer pricing documentation in accordance with the European Union (EU) Transfer Pricing Documentation requirements created by the EU Joint Transfer Pricing Forum.

Directives D-258, 292 and 293 are not legally binding but are usually followed in practice by the Czech tax authority.

OECD guidelines treatment

Based on Directive D-293 (not legally binding), the OECD guidelines as well as the Code of Conduct on Transfer Pricing Documentation for Associated Enterprises in the EU are generally accepted in the Czech Republic. This directive also mentions that transfer pricing documentation prepared in accordance with the Code of Conduct "should be sufficient" for substantiating the method of calculation of the arm's length price.

Priorities/pricing methods

The Ministry of Finance follows the OECD Transfer Pricing Guidelines. Use of profit-based methods is possible where substantiated.

Transfer pricing penalties

There are no specific transfer pricing penalties. Generally, upon a successful challenge of transfer pricing prices by the tax authority, a penalty of 20% of the unpaid tax or 5% of the decreased tax loss may be applied. Thereafter, interest is assessed at 14% above the "repo rate" (or repurchase agreement rate) of the Czech National Bank (for five years at maximum).

Penalty relief

There is no specific relief or reduction of penalties for transfer pricing. It is at the discretion of the Ministry of Finance to decrease penalties; however, this is limited to specific situations.

¶20,040

Documentation requirements

There are no specific statutory requirements in place. It is crucial for the taxpayer to have supporting documentation in case the transactions are audited by the Czech tax authority, as the burden of proof remains with the taxpayer. The Czech tax authority has great discretion in deciding what level and nature of documentation is sufficient. During the tax audit, the authority may request any documentation that reasonably substantiates the actual character and substance of the transaction, its benefits for taxpayers, the appropriateness of the level of fees and the transfer pricing method selected. The analysis of a controlled transaction and the identification of comparables could be useful. Therefore, a high level of formal evidence may be necessary to support various aspects of the transaction. Deadlines for submitting the required documentation may be 15 or 30 days after the request is delivered to the taxpayer.

D-293 describes the documentation that is expected and may be required by the tax authority. Nevertheless, as the directive is not legally binding, there is no legal requirement to prepare documentation.

D-292 sets out documentation that should serve as the initial basis for filing the application for issuance of a binding assessment. The submitted documentation should contain information on the group, information on the company, information on the business relationship, information on other circumstances affecting the business relationship and information on the transfer pricing method.

Documentation deadlines

There is no specific deadline to prepare documentation, since no specific statutory documentation requirement exists.

In the event of a transfer pricing challenge, the taxpayer must file information before the statutory deadline for tax proceedings. This is generally within 15 days of the receipt of a request by the tax authority. This time limit may be extended at the discretion of the tax authority if a request is made by the taxpayer.

Statute of limitations on transfer pricing assessments

The general statute of limitations applies. The limit is three years from the end of the taxable period in which the tax liability arose. However, if the Czech tax authority undertakes an act directed at the assessment of tax, then the three-year time limit begins again. The limit will also be prolonged if the supplementary tax return for the respective period is filed or if a tax loss carry forward may be utilized in the particular period. Tax may not be assessed, however, later than 10 years or 17 years if tax losses were incurred (15 years in case of tax losses incurred in 2004 and onwards).

Return disclosures/related-party disclosures

Effective from 1 January 2001, the executives of a controlled entity are required to complete a memorandum with respect to relations and transactions with companies in the group. This does not apply if a controlling agreement is concluded. Note that this is based on commercial legislation rather than tax legislation, and the memorandum has no direct tax impact or tax aspects. Taxpayers must

¶20,040

provide documentation of transactions with related parties in the corporate income tax return.

Audit risk/transfer pricing scrutiny

The risk of transfer pricing issues being reviewed under an audit is medium. The Czech tax authority has adopted a global approach. Audit subjects are selected based on complex criteria and transfer pricing is only one aspect among many others. Intangibles, royalties and service fees are seen as the most likely transfer pricing audit issues. Although no specific country is targeted for transfer pricing audits, transactions with tax haven countries are closely scrutinized.

APA opportunity

APA regulations were established under § 38nc of the Income Tax Act, which became effective on 1 January 2006. Upon the tax entity's request, the tax administrator decides whether a taxpayer has chosen a transfer pricing method that would result in a transfer price determination on an arm's length basis. The binding assessment can only be issued for transactions effective in a particular tax period or that will be effective in the future. It is impossible to apply for a binding assessment of business relationships that have already affected the tax liability. D-292 details the procedure for issuing binding assessments and the necessary particulars for the application. Generally, the tax administrator should issue the decision within six months assuming all documentation and information are provided, but this deadline is not legally binding.

DENMARK

Taxing authority and tax law

Ministry of Taxation (MT). § 2 of the Tax Assessment Act; §§ 3B, 14(4) and 17(3) of the Tax Control Act; and §§ 26 and 27 of the Tax Administration Act.

Relevant regulations and rulings

Regulation number 42 of 24 January 2006 pertains to the documentation of the pricing of intercompany transactions and guidelines for preparation of written documentation. The Regulation sets forth the minimum requirements and guidelines for tax assessment and for disclosing information. The Regulation is referred to as the Executive Order on Transfer Pricing Documentation.

OECD guidelines treatment

The MT will, for the purpose of its assessment, apply the principles of the OECD Transfer Pricing Guidelines.

Priorities/pricing methods

The MT accepts CUP, Resale Price, Cost Plus, Profit Split and TNMM.

Transfer pricing penalties

Fines were introduced for income years commencing on or after 2 April 2006, if the transfer pricing documentation requirements are not observed either intentionally (deliberate omission) or due to gross negligence or if incorrect and misleading information on the exemption rule for small and medium-sized companies is given. The amount of penalty is twice the costs saved for not having prepared the transfer pricing documentation in the first place. The penalty may be reduced by 50% if the documentation required is produced subsequently. If, in addition, the income is increased because the arm's length criterion has not been satisfied, the minimum fine will be increased by an amount equal to 10% of the income increase.

In case of income adjustments, a 6.3% (5.8% for 2007, 5.3% for 2006, 5.4% for 2005, 5.7% for 2004 and 10% for 2003) non deductible surcharge on all adjustments of prior years' corporate taxes payable will be levied. Furthermore, a non-deductible interest of 0.6% (0.6% for income year 2007, 0.5% for the income years 2005-2006 and 0.6% for the income years 2003-2004) for each month since the due date for the corporate tax payable for the income year in question is applicable.

Penalty relief

If the taxpayer prepares the lacking or insufficient documentation and ensures that the documentation meets the requirements, the fine (except that which is related to the increase of taxable income) will be reduced to half of the original amount.

Documentation requirements

The documentation must be available upon request from the tax authority within 60 days' notice. The earliest such a request can be made is the date of filing for a company's tax return. The transfer pricing documentation requirements affect

¶20,040

both domestic and foreign intercompany transactions. In certain circumstances the transfer pricing documentation requirements are reduced for small and medium-sized companies (companies are classified according to thresholds measured at group level), as well as for entities subject to tonnage tax.

The documentation requirements were tightened as of 2006. According to the Executive Order on Transfer Pricing Documentation, the documentation should include:

- A description of the group, including the legal group structure, the history of the group, including a description of restructurings, operational structure and primary business activities, as well as a description of the industry in which it operates

- A description of the Danish entity, its intercompany transactions and the other entities involved (primary business activities and three years' key financials for all entities involved)

- A description of each intercompany transaction including (1) parties, types of products/services/assets transferred and the volumes involved, (2) an analysis of functions and risks undertaken and assets employed by the entities involved, (3) contractual terms, (4) economic conditions and (5) business strategies

- Comparability analysis by intercompany transaction, including (1) information about the transfer pricing policy and method applied, and how the transfer pricing principles are implemented in practice, e.g., whether year-end adjustments are made, and (2) an analysis of how the transfer prices satisfy the arm's length principle

- A list of any written intercompany agreements entered into by the Danish entity and a copy of any written agreements in place with foreign tax authorities regarding transfer prices

According to the tightened documentation requirements, a taxpayer must, within 60 to 90 days' notice, provide external comparable searches as part of the arm's length analysis upon request from the Danish tax authority.

Documentation deadlines

The deadline for preparing documentation is the same as the deadline for filing the tax return. Documentation must be provided upon request. Sixty days' notice is given.

Statute of limitation on transfer pricing assessments

The statute of limitations for a transfer pricing assessment is 1 May in the sixth year after the end of the calendar year following the income year.

Return disclosures/related-party disclosures

Form 05.021 (05.022 ——English version) discloses information on all controlled transactions and whether the company is qualified for reduced documentation requirements.

¶20,040

Audit risk/transfer pricing scrutiny

The risk of transfer pricing issues being reviewed under an audit is high. Six transfer pricing audit centers across Denmark are operated by the tax authorities with the single purpose of carrying out transfer pricing audits. Consequently, we see a strong focus on transfer pricing. Also, we see a tendency towards most normal tax audits being initiated with requests related to transfer pricing. Intensified cooperation between the Nordic tax authorities has led to a higher level of information sharing and a significant increase in the number of coordinated cross-Nordic audits.

APA opportunity

The Danish legislation provides for unilateral APAs only. There is no APA regime in place, but the MT has entered into a limited number of bilateral APAs. For instance, MT has entered into the first bilateral APA between China and a European country.

We expect this area will develop significantly within the next few years.

ECUADOR

Taxing authority and tax law

Internal Revenue Service (Servicio de Rentas Internas or SRI); Master Tax Code, Internal Tax Regime Organic Law (Ley Orgánica de Regimen Tributario Interno or LORTI) and its Regulation.

Relevant regulations and rulings

Article 56 of the Law for Reform and Tax Fairness (R.O. 242-3S, 29-XII-2007) defined related parties. Article 78 established the transfer pricing regime. Article 10.2 established the concept of sub-capitalization, which requires the amount of the external debt not be greater than 300% of the equity in order to consider interest payments abroad as deductible expenses. The SRI Resolution NAC-DGER2008-0464 established the transfer pricing exhibit and transfer pricing integral report content requirements. Resolution NAC-DGER 2005-0641 established the median calculation and arm's length standard. Resolution NAC-DGER2008-0182 established a list of tax havens or low tax rate jurisdictions as well as the contents and the mandatory filing of a transfer pricing study. The OECD Transfer Pricing Guidelines are applicable as an indices technique.

OECD guidelines treatment

The SRI considers the OECD guidelines as a technical reference for analyzing intercompany transactions.

Ecuador follows a hierarchy of transfer pricing methods. Local regulations establish that only the six methods established in the OECD Guidelines are applicable. The CPM and full profit split method are considered the last resort methods by the SRI.

Priorities/pricing methods

The SRI accepts the CUP, Resale, Cost Plus, Profit Split, Residual Profit Split, and TNMM. There is a best method rule and a hierarchy of methods. Indeed, the SRI has made the application of the CUP method mandatory. If the CUP method cannot be applied, the Resale or the Cost Plus methods must be implemented. If none of these methods can be executed due to the complexity of the transactions under analysis, the SRI accepts the other analyses frameworks mentioned above as valid ones, leaving the Transactional Net Margin Method as the method of last resort. The direct implication is that all method rejections must be thoughtfully documented.

There are specific CUP method applications. More specifically, for exports and imports of tangible goods between related and independent parties where there is an international price in transparent markets, the market price is used, unless there is evidence to the contrary. In addition, there is another application for companies that operate through international intermediaries, who are not the final consignees or producers of the goods. Such goods include all products with well-known prices in transparent markets. In these cases, the price to be applied is the price in those markets on the day the goods are loaded for shipment or the agreed-upon price if higher. This method may not apply if the local exporter or importer is able to prove

¶20,040

the substance of the operations of the consignee abroad and that this intermediary party has not more than 20% of its operations with related parties.

Transfer pricing penalties

Ecuador has a specific transfer pricing penalty regime. There are processes in place to ensure the consistent application of transfer pricing penalties in the jurisdiction.

Penalties up to USD 15,000 could be applied if deadlines are not met or where inaccuracies are detected. Interest could be applicable on unpaid adjustments as part of the income tax.

Penalty relief

No penalty relief regime has been provided.

Documentation requirements

The SRI requires a Transfer Pricing Annex report to be filed, detailing all transactions with foreign related parties, methods applied in analyzing each transaction and calculated adjustments for each transaction, using software provided by the tax administration.

This declaration must be filed by companies with accumulated transactions with related parties exceeding USD 3m in the reported fiscal year or companies with accumulated transactions with related parties between USD 1m and USD 3m in the reported fiscal year, which amount represents up to 50% of the total revenues.

Additionally, the Transfer Pricing Integral Report must be presented to the SRI by companies with accumulated transactions with related parties exceeding USD 5m in the reported fiscal year. This Report must substantiate the analyses made of all transactions reported in the Annex. Both documents must be filed up to two months after the income tax return deadline.

Nevertheless, the SRI may require, at any time, the Transfer Pricing Annex and/or the Integral Report even though the company does not reach the threshold, or in the case of intercompany transactions between domestic related companies.

Transfer Pricing Integral Report Requirements:

- Full functional analysis of the multinational group and the local party
- Risk analysis of the local company and assets detail
- Intercompany transactions detail and functional description
- Market analysis including global and local descriptions and a demand analysis for both levels
- Economic analysis including:
  - Detailed and quantified information for each type of operation held with foreign related parties
  - Detailed reasoning for acceptance or rejection of a method
  - Profit level indicator selection process
  - Comparable companies detail

¶20,040

- Applied adjustments explanation
- Reason for rejection of searched comparable companies
- Accepted comparable companies activities description and financial statements
- Analysis description and conclusion

Documentation deadlines

Adjustments and intercompany transaction figures must be included on an Income Tax Return form (due in April).

The Transfer Pricing Annex and Integral Report must be filed two months after filing the tax return. That is, from 10 June to 28 June depending on the ninth digit of the company Tax ID Number.

Statute of limitations on transfer pricing assessments

The statute of limitations is three years from the date of the income tax return filing and six years if overall tax compliance was not accomplished.

The obligation to prepare and present the Transfer Pricing Annex starts when related parties' transactions exceed USD 3m or when related parties' transactions between USD 1m and USD 3m represents up to 50% of the total revenues.

The Integral Report must be delivered in addition to the Annex only when those transactions exceed USD 5m.

Return disclosures/related-party disclosures

No specific related-party information, aside from the documentation required by transfer pricing regulations, is required. However, these regulations also require the following additional parties to be treated as related:

- Tax-haven located companies
- Parties buying or selling more than 50% of the products sold or bought by the local company
- Parties on which the local company has at least a threshold of 25% ownership

Audit risk/transfer pricing scrutiny

Recent audit activity included a specific focus on transfer pricing.

Nowadays there is one ongoing case in litigation and three pending cases undergoing domestic appeals (preceding court action). Tax havens are frequently involved in disputes.

The sale of tangible goods (representing 80% of the current case load) and intra-group services (approximately 20% of the current case load) are currently the focus of the Directorate of Taxes for transfer pricing review.

A transfer pricing audit is instigated by a central decision-making body. Various considerations are taken into account in determining which taxpayers to audit, including (ranked in order of importance):

¶20,040

- The outcome of a risk assessment by the SRI
- The nature of related-party transactions undertaken by the taxpayer
- The outcome of customs
- Previous tax audits of the taxpayer
- The profitability of the local taxpayer

A high risk of audits could be assessed for oil, agriculture and fishing industries and the activities related with them. Several auditor teams are acting simultaneously on about 40 relevant companies at a time.

APA opportunity

Ecuador has no formal APA program. The local law outlines the possibility of APA procedures and prescribes that regulations will be issued by the tax administration on the application process of APA. However, the relevant regulations have not been issued. Therefore, no taxpayers have started consultation for an APA.

Generally, the procedures require taxpayers to satisfy inquiries relating to the previous two taxable years from the tax administration, after which taxpayers may propose, through consultation with the tax administration, applicable prices for the APA Term. The APA Term includes the year preceding the APA application, the year of the APA application and the two tax years following the application and the SRI has two years to resolve the proposal.

EGYPT

Taxing authority and tax law

Egyptian Tax Authority, Income Tax Law No. 91 of 2005.

Relevant regulations and rulings

According to Article no. 30 of the income tax law "If the associate persons set conditions in their commercial or financial dealings different from the conditions taking place between non-associate persons, which are liable to reduce the tax base or transfer its burden from a taxable person to another tax-exempted or non-taxable person, the Administration may determine the taxable profit on basis of the neutral price."

The head of the Administration may conclude agreements with associate persons on one or more methods for determining the neutral price in the Administration's dealings.

OECD guidelines treatment

Pursuant to the executive regulations of the income tax law, in case none of the three methods referred to in the law are possible to apply, any one of the methods mentioned in the form of the OECD, or any other method suitable for the taxpayer may be followed.

Priorities/pricing methods

According to Article no. 39 of the executive regulations of the Income Tax Law, the fair market price prescribed in Article no. 30 of the law shall be determined according to the following methods:

- Comparative uncontrolled price method
- Cost plus method
- Re-sale price method

Note that according to Article no. 40 of the executive regulations the preferred method for determining the neutral price shall be the comparative uncontrolled price method. In case the data necessary for applying this method are unavailable, any of the two other methods prescribed in the previous article may apply.

Transfer pricing penalties

According to the income tax law, if the tax amount the taxpayers include in the tax return is less than the amount of the finally estimated tax, they shall be liable for a penalty based on the following:

- 5% of the tax payable on the non-included amount if such amount is between 10% and 20% of the legally payable tax;
- 15% of the tax payable on the non-included amount if such amount is between 20% and 50% of the legally payable tax;
- 80% of the tax payable on the non-included amount if such amount is more than 50% of the legally payable tax

¶20,040

Penalty relief

As of this date, the Tax Authority has not issued any instructions or guidelines regarding proper TP documentation.

Documentation requirements

As of this date, the Tax Authority has not issued any instructions or guidelines regarding proper TP documentation.

Documentation deadlines

As of this date, the Tax Authority has not issued any instructions or guidelines regarding proper TP documentation.

Statute of limitations on transfer pricing assessments

According to the income tax law the statute of limitations is five years.

Return disclosures/related-party disclosures

According to the corporate tax return format, the tax payer is obliged to declare the following:

- Name of the related party/parties along with the group structure
- The nature of the relationship
- Type of the related parties transactions, if any
- The value of the transactions
- The method used to determine the FMP and the reasons of selecting this method
- The country of origin for tangible and intangible goods
- The country of the supplier

Audit risk/transfer pricing scrutiny

No TP assessment has taken place as of this date. To the best of our knowledge the Tax Authority will demand that the taxpayer file a TP study starting in financial year 2009 along with the corporate tax return.

APA opportunity

The head of the Administration may conclude agreements with associate persons using one or more methods for determining the neutral price in the Administration's dealings.

ESTONIA

Taxing authority and tax law

The Tax and Customs Board. Current Estonian transfer pricing legislation is effective as of 1 January 2007. Transfer pricing issues are regulated by the Estonian Income Tax Act: Article 50 subsections 4 - 6, Article 53 subsection 4[6], and Article 14 subsection 7. The documentation requirements are stipulated in the Income Tax Act, Article 50 subsection 7.

Based on the amendments to the Income Tax Act, which are expected to come into effect as of 2010, the definition of related parties shall be broadened, thus expanding the list of persons that must conclude transactions at arm's length to persons that have common economic interest and operate towards a common goal - if one person has a prevalent influence over another person.

Therefore, the persons that, although formally not related based on the current Income Tax Act, but who, in spite of the formal unrelated status, undertake transactions that decrease the taxable income in Estonia, shall be considered from 2010 as related entities and should undertake transactions at arm's length.

Relevant regulations and rulings

The Ministry of Finance issued a transfer pricing regulation on 10 November 2006 (No. 53), which came into force on 1 January 2007. The regulation sets out in more detail the principles for determining arm's length prices, and it also establishes documentation requirements. There have been a few court rulings and an increasing number of tax proceedings on transfer pricing issues in Estonia.

OECD guidelines treatment

The Estonian tax authorities follow the OECD Transfer Pricing Guidelines. Nevertheless, the domestic legislation is the prevailing law.

Priorities/pricing methods

The Tax and Customs Board accepts the CUP, Resale Price, Cost Plus, Profit Split, Transactional Net Margin methods or, if necessary, any other suitable method. The methods are not hierarchical and are all treated as equal. However, if available, internal and Estonian domestic data is preferred for determining arm's length prices.

Transfer pricing penalties

If the required documentation or the relevant tax return is not submitted in time, the fine may be as high as EEK 50,000. In the case of intentional submission of wrong information in the tax return that results in less tax paid, a criminal penalty may be imposed and the fine may be as high as EEK 250 million. If tax is assessed, interest from the tax amount at the rate of 0.06% per day will be imposed retroactively as of the date when the tax was supposed to be paid.

Penalty relief

There is no penalty relief if a taxpayer has the necessary documentation, but the transfer pricing is determined to be non-arm's length and there is an income tax

¶20,040

adjustment. However, imposing a fine is probably more an exception than a rule. Interest for the delay of the tax fine payment is always enforced.

Documentation requirements

The documentation requirement is imposed in the following cases:

- Resident credit institution, financial institution, insurance agency and listed company
- If one party of the transaction is a resident of a low tax rate territory
- Resident legal person
    - who has more than 250 employees with related parties or
    - whose turnover, including related parties, in the previous financial year was at least EUR 50 million or
    - whose consolidated net assets were at least EUR 43 million
- Non-resident who has a permanent establishment in Estonia and
    - who has more than 250 employees with related parties or
    - whose turnover, including related parties, in the previous financial year was at least EUR 50 million or
    - whose consolidated net assets were at least EUR 43 million

Categories of documentation required:

- Company analysis
- Industry analysis
- Functional analysis
- Economic analysis

Documentation deadlines

There is no deadline for preparing transfer pricing documentation. However, taxpayers are obliged to submit the documentation within 60 days upon the request of the tax authority.

Statute of limitations on transfer pricing assessments

The statute of limitations period for making an assessment of tax is three years. In the event of intentional failure to pay or withhold an amount of tax, the limitation period for making an assessment of tax is six years. A limitation period starts from the due date of submission of the tax return, which was not submitted or which contained information that caused an amount of tax to be calculated incorrectly.

Return disclosures/related-party disclosures

An annual report including a description of transactions with related parties is required to be filed within six months from the end of the relevant financial year. If the taxpayer has the obligation to keep the necessary documentation, a respective analysis must have been carried out.

The documentation does not have to be filed with the tax return.

¶20,040

Audit risk/transfer pricing scrutiny

The taxpayers in Estonia run a high risk that transfer prices will be scrutinized during a tax audit. However, today the overall risk for Estonian taxpayers can be evaluated as medium.

APA opportunity

Currently, the Estonian tax laws do not provide any opportunity to conclude APAs.

FINLAND

Taxing authority and tax law

Ministry of Finance; Finnish Fiscal Assessment Act § 14 a-c, § 31, § 32, § 75 and § 89.

Relevant regulations and rulings

Finnish Fiscal Assessment Act § 14 a-c, § 31, § 32, § 75 and § 89, Government Proposal and Tax Administration's Guidelines of 19 October 2007.

OECD guidelines treatment

The Finnish regulations and tax practice in general follow the OECD Transfer Pricing Guidelines and the approaches presented in the OECD Discussion Draft on Business Restructurings.

Regarding the business restructurings, the Finnish Tax Administration's Guidelines state that the business restructurings should be examined as a whole from a transfer pricing perspective. However, the guidelines state that the specific circumstances and effects of the restructuring on the material functions of parties should be taken into account and the arm's length principle has to be utilized. Nevertheless, the guidelines are general in nature and do not specifically state how the tax authorities should consider individual cases.

There is no established case law on business restructurings in Finland. However, there have been some advance rulings relating mainly to the transfer and valuation of intangibles.

Priorities/pricing methods

Taxpayers may choose any OECD transfer pricing method as long as the chosen method results in an arm's length pricing for the intra-group transaction. In its selection of the method, a taxpayer should take into consideration the aspects regarding the application of methods stated in the OECD Transfer Pricing Guidelines.

Transfer pricing penalties

A tax penalty of up to EUR 25,000 can be imposed for a failure to comply with the transfer pricing documentation requirements, even if the pricing of intra-group transactions has been at arm's length. In addition, the possible adjustment of taxable income may result in a separate tax penalty of up to 30% of the adjusted amount of income as well as penalty interest.

Penalty relief

Penalties can be reduced or removed if the taxpayer presents supplementary transfer pricing documentation that supports the arm's length nature of the intra-group transactions. The determination of penalties will be made on a case-by-case basis.

¶20,040

Documentation requirements

Transfer pricing legislation came into effect on 1 January 2007. The provisions contained in the law apply to financial periods beginning on 1 January 2007 or later.

The transfer pricing documentation aims to prove that the prices used in cross-border intra-group transactions are acceptable from the perspective of the tax authority. According to the law, the documentation obligation applies to the following entities:

- Group companies if the group employs at least 250 employees, regardless of the amount of turnover or assets

- Group companies if the group employs less than 250 employees and if the company's turnover exceeds EUR 50m and their assets are worth more than EUR 43m

- The Finnish branches of a foreign company if the above conditions are met by this company

- Companies which are not small- and medium-size enterprises, as defined by criteria (related to, for example, a company's independence) contained in the European Commission's Recommendation on the definition of micro, small- and medium-sized enterprises (2003/361/EC).

When calculating the amount of employees, turnover or assets of an enterprise or a branch owned by a foreign company, information regarding the foreign owners is also taken into account, depending on the share of ownership.

Group companies are required to prove the arm's length nature of cross-border intra-group transactions by preparing transfer pricing documentation. According to the law, the documentation should contain the following information:

- A description of the business

- A description of associated enterprises

- Information on transactions between associated enterprises

- Functional analysis regarding transactions between associated enterprises

- A comparability analysis, including available information on comparables

- A description of the transfer pricing method and its application

Less extensive documentation is required if the total amount of transactions between two parties during a fiscal year does not exceed EUR 500,000.

Documentation deadlines

A taxpayer has to submit the transfer pricing documentation for a specific fiscal year within 60 days upon a request of the tax authorities, but not earlier than six months after the end of the financial period. The additional clarifications concerning the documentation have to be submitted within 90 days of a request by the tax authorities.

¶20,040

Statute of limitations on transfer pricing assessments

The time limit for the adjustment of income due to the failure to apply arm's length principles to the pricing of a transaction is five years from the beginning of the following year during which the taxation was finalized.

Return disclosures/related-party disclosures

Based on Paragraph 26.4 of the Taxation Procedure Act, if the other party of the transaction is a non-resident, and if the tax authorities cannot obtain adequate information on the transaction by using an appropriate international treaty, the taxpayer is responsible for presenting such information.

Audit risk/transfer pricing scrutiny

The tax authority is being very active and the risk for transfer pricing audit is high. All kinds of intra-group transactions have been under scrutiny in tax audits.

APA opportunity

Advance rulings are available in Finland. There is no legislation for APAs; however, the tax authorities have indicated their willingness to utilize them.

Taxing authority and tax law

Generally referred to as the French Tax Authorities (FTA), or Direction Générale des Finances Publiques (DGFiP), or Direction Générale des Impôts (DGI).

Main technical provisions. French Tax Code: Articles 57 and 238 A. French Procedural Tax Code: Articles L 13 B, L 80 B and L 188 A. Case law about application of the theory of Abnormal Act of Management.

Thin capitalization rules are also covered by articles 212 and 39-1 of the French Tax Code.

A new set of texts about TP documentation requirements could be adopted in December 2009 in the framework of the finance bill.

Relevant regulations and rulings

Administrative doctrine pertaining mainly to Articles 57 and 238A of the French Tax Code, and Articles L 13B and L80B of the French Procedural Tax Code.

OECD guidelines treatment

The French Tax Authorities consider the French transfer pricing regulations to be consistent with the OECD Guidelines.

There is no specific French transfer pricing related regulation pertaining to business restructuring, and the FTA did not comment so far on the recent draft released by the OECD. Experience in business restructuring shows that tax auditors often consider that a decrease in profit is an indicator that an intangible has de facto been transferred and should be taxed. In addition, specific care should also be paid to closure costs in light of the transfer pricing profile undertaken by the group entities at hand.

Priorities/pricing methods

The FTA accept the CUP, Resale Price, Cost Plus, Profit Split and TNMM; yet tax inspectors usually prefer transactional methods.

Transfer pricing penalties

A transfer pricing reassessment from the FTA triggers an adjustment of the taxable profit for Corporate Income Tax purposes. Except for a possible fine in the context of Article L 13 B (see below), there is no specific transfer pricing penalties today. As indicated above a new penalty regime could be adopted in December 2009.

- After a transfer pricing reassessment is made, the additional profit is usually analyzed as deemed dividends, therefore, a withholding tax on deemed distribution is usually required (when a double tax treaty applies, the withholding tax depends on the relevant tax treaty provisions; see often the Dividends or the Other Income clause).

¶20,040

- Late payment interests are applied in case of tax reassessments made on the ground of Article 57 of the French Tax Code. Since 1 January 2006, the ordinary late payment interest rate is 0.40% per month (i.e. 4.80% per year).

- Supplementary penalties are applicable if the taxpayer committed a willful offence (40%) or acted fraudulently (80%).

Specific transfer pricing penalties are also applicable in situations where the taxpayer failed to answer the tax authorities' request for documentation (on the ground of Article L 13 B of the French Tax Procedural Code). Failure to provide complete information may result in (i) a reassessment of the company's taxable profit based on information the tax authorities possess, and (ii) the application of EUR 10, 000 penalties for each year audited.

In addition, the adjustment may also result in a reassessment of other taxes and contributions such as the Business Tax and of Employee Profit Sharing.

Penalty relief

During a tax audit and before the tax authorities send the notice of reassessment, taxpayers, in the framework of a specific provision of the French Procedural Tax Code, are allowed to correct their errors or omissions in consideration of a reduced late payment interest rate (3.36% per year) that is equal to 70% of the ordinary late payment interest rate. In this respect, taxpayers must file a complementary tax return and pay the corresponding additional taxes at the same time.

Documentation requirements

French regime as of October 2009

The FTA may require information pertaining to transfer pricing in the course of an audit (based on Articles L 13 B and L 10 of the French Procedural Tax Code). The nature of this required information, and the short deadline under which a taxpayer may have to provide it, lead to a de facto documentation requirement. The following documents are usually expected:

- Business and organizational structure overview,

- Functional analysis, contracts, legal and management account information,

- Method selected and economic analysis (including as need be, identification of competitors and comparables, usually French when the tested party is French), and

- Description of the tax regime applied to the subsidiaries of the audited French company.

French draft documentation requirements to be published

A new regulation should be released within the framework of the Finance Act to be published end of December 2009. This TP documentation requirement would come into force for fiscal years starting as from 1 January 2010. It is mostly about legal documentation requirement inspired from the European Code of Conduct.

In case of absence of documentation or if the taxpayer fails to provide an exhaustive and comprehensive documentation within 30 days after a formal notice from the FTA, the latter would apply an additional penalty, in case of adjustment, equal to 5% of the amount reassessed with a minimum of EUR 10,000 per fiscal year under audit. An extra deadline to complete the documentation could however be granted by the FTA.

This draft documentation requirement should apply to companies meeting at least one of the three following criteria:

- companies with annual total sales (VAT excluded) or total assets (before depreciations/reserves) exceeding EUR 400 million, as well as (i) companies/organizations directly or indirectly holding at least 50% of shares/voting rights of firstly-mentioned companies, or (ii) companies/organizations directly or indirectly held at least 50% of shares/voting rights by firstly-mentioned companies; or

- companies taxable in France and included within the scope of the global tax consolidation group regime; or

- companies belonging to a French tax group where one of the members complies with one of the previously mentioned criteria.

The other companies (i.e. those that do not fulfill any of the three above listed criteria) would remain out of the scope of the new legal documentation requirement. However they would remain subject to the ordinary regime according to which the FTA may request general information in the course of a tax audit (Articles L 13 B and L 10).

The final text may be different from information available today.

Documentation deadlines

As mentioned above, there is no formal requirement yet to provide the FTA with contemporaneous documentation without a specific request.

However, in the case of a tax investigation, transfer pricing documentation requested by the FTA must be provided within a short time period. If a specific request is made by the FTA (on the ground of Article L 13 B of the French Procedural Tax Code), then the documentation must be submitted within 60 days, though it may be possible to obtain a 30-day extension in exceptional circumstances.

Statute of limitations on transfer pricing assessments

The statute of limitations for transfer pricing adjustments is the same as for all French corporate tax assessments: generally three years following the year for which the tax is due (it might be longer under certain circumstances e.g. Permanent Establishment qualification, losses).

In cases where a mutual agreement procedure to avoid double taxation (on the ground of a tax treaty or the European Arbitration Convention) is initiated further to a tax reassessment, tax collection can be suspended during the entire mutual agreement process and is postponed until the competent authorities reach an agreement (Article L 189 A of the French Procedural Tax Code).

¶20,040

Return disclosures/related-party disclosures

In the event of a specific request from the FTA at the time of an audit (on the ground of Article L 13 B of the French Procedural Tax Code), there is an obligation to disclose the nature of the relations involving the taxpayer with related parties (i.e., the links of dependence between the French audited entity and the related parties). This legal provision also states an obligation to disclose the activities of the related parties and to provide the authorities with TP comments.

Audit risk/transfer pricing scrutiny

The risk of transfer pricing issues being scrutinized during a tax audit is high. The number of tax audits in transfer pricing is considerably increasing, and the FTA are becoming more extensive and accurate in their queries since they now also use economic references in addition to legal grounds.

Transfer pricing issues that receive the greatest scrutiny are:

- Product sale prices (under or over estimated prices), especially but not only, in case of losses;
- Management fees;
- Agents and commissionaire operations (e.g., conversion of a distributor into an agent);
- Permanent establishment;
- Closure/conversion costs;
- Intangibles and economic ownership (including questions about royalties);
- Benchmarking exercises, and
- Business restructuring (transfer of intangibles, indemnity . . .).

There are rather few court decisions in France going into detailed TP issues. One of the main questions being about burden of proof, which is usually said to be lying on the tax auditors.

APA opportunity

Bilateral and, under certain circumstances, unilateral APAs, are available (Article L 80 B 7° of the French Procedural Tax Code). This section was provided by the Finance Amendment Act for 2004 and has come into force since 1 January 2005. It incorporates existing procedures as described by the French administrative guideline #4 A-8-99 dated 7 September 1999. A specific procedure also exists for certain activities (e.g. HQ profile).

On 28 November 2006, the FTA released a new administrative guideline (#4 A-13-06), adding a simplified APA procedure for small and medium enterprises, and presenting an online guide pertaining to transfer pricing methods.

The process requires that, in theory, the submission has to be performed at the latest 6 months before the beginning of the first fiscal year covered. It has also to be noted that there is no roll-back possibility.

Besides and following a tax reassessment, taxpayers can request the introduction of a mutual agreement procedure (on the ground of tax treaty or the European

Arbitration Convention) in order to avoid double taxation resulting from the reassessment. On 23 February 2006, the FTA published administrative guidelines (#14 F-1-06) specifying the scope and the conditions to be met for the introduction of such procedure.

GERMANY

Taxing authority and tax law

German taxes are administered either by the German Federal Central Tax Office (Bundeszentralamt für Steuern) or by German state tax authorities. German tax law is found in tax acts, executive order laws, double taxation treaties and supranational norms.

Relevant regulations and rulings

German tax law assesses intercompany transactions by following the arm's length principle (§ 1 Foreign Tax Act). Detailed transfer pricing regulations concerning the cross-border transfer of functions were incorporated into § 1 of the Foreign Tax Act since 1 January 2008. An Executive Order Law providing details on how the new transfer pricing provisions relate to business restructurings and function transfers is effective from 2008 onwards. In July 2009 Draft Administration Principles were released that include 72 pages of clarifications concerning the application of § 1 (3) of the Foreign Tax Act and the Executive Order Law on Transfer of Business Functions. The final administration principles are expected to be released in early 2010.

Other relevant provisions for transfer pricing issues in German tax law are § 8 (3) German Corporate Income Tax Act (hidden profit distribution), § 4 (1) German Income Tax Act with Directive R40 of the German Corporate Tax Directives (hidden capital injection), as well as §§ 90 (3), 162 (3), (4) German General Tax Code and the Executive Order Law to § 90 (3) German General Tax Code.

To help interpret the above outlined provisions, the German tax authority issued a circular on the *Principles Governing the Examination of Income Allocation between Multinational Enterprises* in 1983, known as the Administration Principles. The Administration Principles do not constitute binding law for taxpayers or the courts but are binding for the tax authority and, thus, serve as an indication to taxpayers as to how the tax authority will treat specific intercompany transactions between related parties. The purpose of the Administration Principles can be interpreted as to provide a directive concerning the tax audit treatment of transfer pricing cases and to ensure the uniform application of rules and methods by the tax authorities.

In addition to the Administration Principles, administration circulars concerning income allocation with regard to cross-border secondment, costs contribution arrangements, permanent establishments and procedures have been published since December 1999.

OECD guidelines treatment

The German tax authority considers its transfer pricing laws and regulations to be consistent with OECD guidelines. The OECD guidelines provide support for domestic use; however, German transfer pricing regulations and practices differ with regard to certain issues, e.g., reluctance to use transactional profit methods and documentation requirements for secondments.

¶20,040

Priorities/pricing methods

Under the arm's length principle, it is assumed that the taxpayers have acted in a manner comparable to unrelated parties. This assumes that all material information about the transaction (complete information about the counterparty) is available and that the parties acted as prudent and diligent business managers.

Under the new law (effective 1 January 2008), the application of the transfer pricing method is dependent on the availability and quality of third-party comparable data. Three different situations are distinguished: full comparability of the data, limited comparability of the data and non-availability of third-party comparable data.

When full comparability of third-party data exists, the new law stipulates the priority of the traditional transaction methods: CUP, Resale Price and Cost Plus. Any price within the full range of full comparable third-party data meets the arm's length principle.

If limited comparability of data is available, the taxpayer has to select an appropriate transfer pricing method to determine the transfer price. In case of limited comparability of data, only the interquartile range of the comparable data, considering the appropriate adjustments, can be applied.

If no comparable data is available, a "hypothetical arm's length price" determination applies. Accordingly, in compliance with the socalled prudent and diligent business manager principle, and based on the functional analysis and internal projections, the taxpayer has to establish an area of "hypothetical" arm's length prices. The area of negotiation is defined by the minimum price of a hypothetical seller and by the maximum price of a hypothetical purchaser. The taxpayer must prove the value with the highest probability within the area of negotiation, otherwise the mean value is assumed to be the arm's length transfer price for the transaction under review.

Transfer pricing penalties

If a taxpayer does not comply with its duty to document its transfer pricing to the extent outlined in § 90 (3) German General Tax Code, a refutable presumption applies according to which the income of the German company under review has been reduced by means of inappropriate transfer prices, which forms the basis of a transfer pricing adjustment by the tax authority.

Tax authorities may apply § 162 (3) of the German General Tax Code if the taxpayer submits no or only insufficient documentation or if exceptional transactions have not been recorded contemporaneously. In all three cases, the tax authority is authorized to estimate the income, provided that the taxpayer cannot rebut the presumption.

The legislation takes into consideration that an appropriate single transfer price does not exist and that comparable third-party prices may vary within price ranges. However, it explicitly entitles the tax authority to make use of the full price range estimating the income, in case of insufficient documentation, to the detriment of the taxpayer.

¶20,040

If the taxpayer fails to submit transfer pricing documentation or if the documentation is unusable or insufficient, or if the documentation for extraordinary business transactions is not prepared contemporaneously, a surcharge of 5%-10% on the income adjustment will be applied, with a minimum surcharge of EUR 5,000. For late filing, the taxpayer faces a penalty up to EUR 1m (minimum penalty of EUR 100 per day of delay). Penalties are imposed after the closing of a tax audit. The aforementioned penalties constitute non-tax deductible expenses.

Under the law effective 1 January 2008, in the event that the taxpayer's transfer price falls outside the full range (in case of full comparability of third-party data) or the interquartile range (in case of limited comparability of third-party data) of arm's length prices, the transfer price is adjusted to the median of the range.

Interest is assessed on tax payments (6% p.a., which is non-deductible for tax purposes).

There are also penalties for tax evasion.

Penalty relief

The taxpayer is required by law to present utilizable documentation to the tax authority. Accordingly, no penalty relief applies.

Documentation requirements

Section 90 of the German General Tax Code contains transfer pricing documentation requirements. For the documentation of transfer pricing issues, an Executive Order Law (effective 30 June 2003) prescribes general requirements and the documentation required in special circumstances. A circular (Administration Principles - Procedures) dated 12 April 2005 provides the tax authority's interpretation of the requirements set out in the General Tax Code and in the Executive Order Law.

General documentation requirements are:

- General information: shareholder relationships, organizational and operative group structure and operations

- Description of intercompany transactions: manner and extent of transactions, intercompany contracts and a list of important intangibles

- Functions and risks analysis: description of functions and risks the taxpayer bears within the intercompany transaction, contractual terms, business strategies and value chain

- Transfer pricing analysis: selection of the transfer pricing method, appropriateness of the method selected, calculation of the transfer price, list of comparables and documentation of adjustment calculations

Special documentation requirements:

The taxpayer has to document special circumstances which are used to substantiate the arm's length nature of the price determined, including: special business strategies, cost allocation agreements, overview of APAs and mutual agreement procedures, information on transfer price adjustments, causes for losses

¶20,040

from intercompany transactions, as well as countermeasures (if losses occur in more than three consecutive financial years).

Documentation deadlines

Contemporaneous documentation requirements exist only for exceptional business transactions. For extraordinary business transactions (e.g., legal restructuring within the group), the documentation must be contemporaneous, i.e., prepared within six months of the end of the business year in which the transaction has occurred. However, the preparation of contemporaneous documentation is strongly recommended for all cross-border transactions.

Documentation must be submitted within 60 days upon receipt of the tax authority's request. In the case of extraordinary business transactions (e.g., transfer of functions), documentation must be submitted within 30 days of the tax authority's request. In general, the request is made in the course of a tax audit.

Statute of limitations on transfer pricing assessments

There are no special time limit provisions applicable if intercompany transactions are involved. The general regime of the statute of limitations applies in accordance with the General Tax Code. Accordingly, each case has to undergo careful consideration to determine the specific statute of limitations. Most taxes are levied by way of assessment. Assessments can only be made within the statutorily prescribed assessment period, which is subject to the statute of limitations for assessments. The assessment period for taxes (§ 169 General Tax Code) is four years. For customs duties, it is shorter, and in case of grossly negligent evasion of taxes or tax fraud, it is much longer (10 years in the case of tax fraud). These periods commence at the end of the calendar year in which the tax liability arose. The assessment period, however, does not start prior to the end of the calendar year in which the taxpayer has submitted the tax return (but also does not start later than three years after the year the tax liability has arisen). There are a number of statutory exceptions to the statute of limitations for assessments, e.g., it should be kept in mind that the limitation period is interrupted when a tax audit begins.

Return disclosures/related-party disclosures

There are no specific disclosure requirements.

Audit risk/transfer pricing scrutiny

The risk of transfer pricing issues being scrutinized during a tax audit is high. Due to the documentation requirements, and in the light of the new stricter law effective 1 January 2008, it is expected that transfer pricing issues will attract significantly more attention in tax audits than in the past. It is expected that transactions qualifying as exceptional business transactions under the documentation provisions, such as the transfer of functions and risks, will particularly attract the tax auditors' attention.

APA opportunity

APAs are generally available. The German Ministry of Finance issued an APA circular on 5 October 2006 which defines the APA procedures and provides

¶20,040

guidance with regard to the negotiation of APAs. Additionally, the Annual Tax Act 2007 introduced fees for APAs. The administrative competence for APAs is centralized in the Federal Central Tax Office. The APA process typically takes from one and a half years to several years from application to conclusion. An agreement reached between two competent authorities will be made conditional in two regards: the taxpayer must consent to the intergovernmental agreement, and must waive its right to appeal against tax assessments to the extent they are in line with the contents of the APA.

GREECE

Taxing authority and tax law

Two separate sets of law and authorities regulate the Transfer Pricing Documentation requirements. The Ministry of Development has introduced Transfer Pricing Documentation Rules by Law 3728/18-12-2008 and the Ministerial Decision Á2- 8092 /31.12.2008, applicable for the fiscal years 2008 and onwards. Within the aforementioned legislative framework, the Ministry of Development is the auditing authority of the TP rules, while in case of identification of TP infringements the case is referred to the supervising tax authorities for the application of the relevant provisions of the tax legislation and the imposition of the relevant tax sanctions.

In addition, Transfer Pricing Documentation rules were recently introduced also by Ministry of Finance (L.3775/2009, applying for fiscal years 2010 and onwards). No Ministerial Decision has been issued yet to this end.

Relevant regulations and rulings

The aforementioned legislative framework confirms the applicability of the OECD Transfer Pricing Guidelines

OECD guidelines treatment

The Ministry of Development and the Ministry of Finance, the two Greek supervising authorities of intra-group transactions, recognize the OECD guidelines and consider their transfer pricing laws and decisions to be consistent with OECD guidelines. However, due to the limited time period since the Greek TP Law was approved by the Greek Parliament and applied in the Greek market, the tax audit treatment of transfer pricing cases cannot be ascertained, nor is it known whether the tax authorities will follow the uniform application of rules and methods.

Priorities/pricing methods

The Ministry of Development and the Ministry of Finance follow the OECD Transfer Pricing Guidelines. All three of the traditional transactional methods (CUP, Resale Price and Cost Plus) can be applied while the use of profit-based methods is possible where substantiated. In particular, other (non-traditional) transfer pricing methods such as the TNMM and the Transactional Profit Split Method can be used only in the cases where the use of the above traditional transfer pricing methods is considered ineffective, provided that a detailed justification is included in the documentation files.

Transfer pricing penalties

In accordance with the Ministry of Development TP Documentation Rules, a penalty equal to 10% of the value of the transactions for which no file has been submitted to the auditing authorities or for which the lists of intra-group transactions have not been submitted timely is imposed. Also the Ministry of Finance imposes a minor penalty of EUR 2.640 (with the possibility of reducing it to one third), in case the TP file is not submitted at all or with a delay. Either the case is initially examined by the Ministry of Development or the Ministry of Finance, if an infringement of the arm's length principle is assessed from the audit report, the

¶20,040

supervising tax authorities impose the relevant tax sanctions, i.e. any price differ-ence (over-or under-invoiced amount) is deemed to be an accrued profit for the respective enterprise and will be included in its actual profits and be taxed accord-ingly. Additionally, a penalty equal to 10% of the price difference assessed will be imposed, regardless of any other penalties applicable for inaccurate tax return filings. In addition, if the case is examined by the Ministry of Development, a fine of EUR 5000 as well as penal sanctions are triggered.

Penalty relief

The Ministry of Development provides that the decision of the Head of the Market Supervision Authority is given to the company under audit within 30 days of its issuance. The above decision may be challenged by means of recourse to the Ministry of Development within five working days of its receipt by the audited company. The Minister of Development should decide within 10 working days of the filing of the recourse. In case of rejection of the recourse by the Minister, the audited company is entitled to appeal against the negative decision by filing a recourse to the competent Administrative First Instance Court within 60 days of its formal notification of the company. The recourse to the Administrative Court is legally acceptable provided that 20% of the fines and penalties assessed to the company, is paid.

The Ministry of Finance provides that the penalty equal to 10% of the price difference assessed may be reduced to one third.

Documentation requirements

For the purposes of assessing the compliance of the liable companies with the arm's length principle, the following documentation files should be available upon request of the supervising authorities of either the Ministry of Development or the Ministry of Finance within 30 and 60 days, respectively, from the notification of such request.

With respect to groups of companies with a Greek parent company, the Master Documentation File should include the following information:

Group - related information:

- The organizational, legal and operational structure of the Group, including any permanent establishments and interests in partnerships, as well as general background information of the Group's industry and the financial data relating to it

- General description of the Group activity, the business strategy, including changes of the business strategy as compared to the previous financial year

- General description and implementation of the Intra-Group transfer pricing policy, if applicable.

- General presentation of transactions concluded between the Greek parent company and its affiliated companies (Greek or foreign), as well as of the transactions among the affiliated companies, if one of these is Greek, namely:

¶20,040

- Nature of transactions (e.g. sale of goods, provision of services, financial transactions, etc.)
- Invoices' flows
- Amounts of transaction flows

The description of the affiliated companies or of their permanent establishments that enter into the above transactions shall include the scope of their activities, the years of operations, the annual turnover, the number of employed personnel, etc.:

- General description of functions and risks undertaken by the affiliated companies, including the changes incurred to this end as compared to the previous year.

In addition, a general description of the tangible assets used by the Group for the purposes of carrying out the above functions.:

- The ownership of intangibles (patents, trademarks, brand names, know-how, etc.) and royalties paid or received.
- List of any Advance Pricing Agreements concluded by the Group companies with foreign tax authorities.

Company-related information:

- A detailed presentation of the transactions with associated companies for which the obligation documentation exists:
  - Nature of transactions (sale of goods, provision of services and financial transactions)
  - Invoice flows
  - Amounts of transaction flows
- Comparative analysis:
  - Characteristics of goods and services
  - Functional analysis (functions, risks, used fixed assets, etc.)
  - Contractual terms
  - Economic circumstances
  - Specific business strategies
- Description of the transfer pricing method implemented, among those specified in the OECD Transfer Pricing Guidelines as well as argumentation on the selection criteria thereof
- Relevant information on internal and/or external comparables, if available
- Description of other data or circumstances, which are deemed to be relevant

With respect to groups of companies with a foreign parent company as well as foreign companies operating with any type and legal form in Greece, the Greek Documentation File, should include the following information:

¶20,040

Group - related information:

- The organizational, legal and operational structure of the Group, including any permanent establishments and interests in partnerships, as well as general background information of the Group's industry and the financial data relating to it

- General description of the Group activity, the business strategy, including changes of the business strategy as compared to the previous financial year

- General description and implementation of the Intra-Group transfer pricing policy, if applicable

- General presentation of transactions concluded between the Greek parent company and its affiliated companies (Greek or foreign)

- General description of functions and risks undertaken by the affiliated companies, including the changes incurred to this end as compared to the previous year

- The ownership of intangibles of the Group (patents, trademarks, brand names, know-how, etc.) and royalties paid or received

- List of any Advance Pricing Agreements concluded by the Group companies with foreign tax authorities

Company-related information:

- A detailed presentation of the transactions with associated companies for which the obligation documentation exists:
  - Nature of transactions (sale of goods, provision of services, financial transactions)
  - Invoice flows
  - Amounts of transaction flows

- Comparative analysis:
  - Characteristics of goods and services
  - Functional analysis (functions, risks, used fixed assets, etc.)
  - Contractual terms
  - Economic circumstances
  - Specific business strategies

- Description of the affiliated companies or of their permanent establishments that enter into those transactions or agreements

- Description of the transfer pricing method implemented, among those specified in the OECD Transfer Pricing Guidelines as well as argumentation on the selection criteria thereof

- Relevant information on internal and/or external comparables, if available

- Description of other data or circumstances that are deemed to be relevant

¶20,040

Documentation deadlines

The liable companies should submit annually to the Ministry of Development, within 4 months and 15 days of their fiscal year-end, a list with the details of their intra-group transactions, such as, especially, the number and the value thereof.

The above - mentioned documentation files should be available upon request from the supervising authorities of the Ministry of Development and within 30 days from the notification of such request.

In the context of a tax audit performed by Ministry of Finance, the documentation data in accordance with the law of the Ministry of Finance should be available to the tax authorities within reasonable time of no less than two months.

Statute of limitations on transfer pricing assessments

Documentation files must be kept by the liable companies for a period equal to the prescription period of the State's right to impose tax (statute of limitations), as the latter is specified by the provisions of tax legislation.

Return disclosures/related-party disclosures

The liable companies disclose their intra-group transactions through the submission of a list to the Ministry of Development, annually. In particular, the said list should be filed within 4 months and 15 days from their fiscal year-end (as stated above in "Documentation deadlines").

Audit risk/transfer pricing scrutiny

Transfer pricing audits are expected to become more frequent and intensive. It is likely that the Greek tax authority will try to increase revenue through the imposition of penalties on companies that are not complying with transfer pricing requirements.

APA opportunity

Currently, the use of APAs is not permitted. It is expected that the introduction of APAs will be discussed in the near future. However, a unilateral APA procedure has been introduced that addresses intra-group service centers operating for the exclusive benefit of affiliates abroad. Under this proposal, after filing an application with the Greek tax authority, the entities may be taxed on a cost plus basis, using an agreed markup, for a period of up to five years.

HUNGARY

Taxing authority and tax law

The organization responsible for dealing with tax issues in Hungary is the Hungarian Tax and Financial Control Office (tax authority).

The following transfer pricing legislation is effective in Hungary:

- Section 4.23 (definition of related party for Corporate Income Tax (CIT) purposes) and § 18 (correction of prices applied between related parties) of Act LXXXI of 1996 on Corporate Income Tax and Dividend Tax (Act on CIT)

- Section 1.8 (definition of fair market price), § 23(4) (b) (reporting related party at the tax authority), § 132/A and 132/B (provisions on the Hungarian APA) and § 178.17 (definition of related party) of the Act XCII of 2003 on Tax Procedure (Act on Tax Procedure)

- Section 259.13 (definition of non-independent party for value-added tax (VAT) purposes) of the Act CXXVII of 2007 on Value Added Tax (Act on VAT)

- Section 3.69 (definition of independent party for Personal Income Tax (PIT) purposes) of the Act CXVII of 1995 on PIT

- Ministry of Finance Decree 18 of 2003 on the fulfillment of transfer pricing documentation obligations effective until 31 December 2009

- Ministry of Finance Decree 38 of 2006 on the administrative procedure for obtaining an APA

- Ministry of Finance Decree 22 of 2009 on the fulfillment of transfer pricing documentation obligations effective from 1 January 2010 and to be applied firstly for the tax liabilities of the year of 2010[1]

Relevant regulations and rulings

37/2004 Guideline issued by the Hungarian tax authority on fulfillment of the transfer pricing documentation requirement.

55/2006 Guideline issued by the Hungarian tax authority on the application of the Transactional Net Margin Method.

77/2007 Guideline issued by the Hungarian tax authority on the preparation of consolidated transfer pricing documentation.

139/2007 Guideline issued by the Hungarian tax authority on the application of transfer pricing methods in practice.

17/2008 and 48/2007 Guidelines issued by the Hungarian tax authority on the preparation of simplified transfer pricing documentation and default penalties.

OECD guidelines treatment

OECD Discussion Draft on Business Restructurings: Business restructuring issues have occurred more often in the past few years in Hungary. However, the

---

[1] containing the new provisions with regard to the EU Masterfile concept.

Hungarian tax authority does not have much experience in reviewing or challenging business restructurings from a transfer pricing perspective. Therefore, business restructuring issues have been dealt with on a case by case basis with the Hungarian tax authority so far.

Priorities/pricing methods

Hungarian legislation does not prioritize transfer pricing methods. As a general rule, the arm's length price should be determined by one of the traditional transaction methods described by the OECD, including CUP, Resale Price or Cost Plus methods. Any other method may be applied if the traditional methods are not applicable. If a non-traditional method is applied, the reasoning behind the use of the method must be provided by the taxpayer.

Transfer pricing penalties

A penalty of 50% of the unpaid tax may be imposed, as well as a late payment interest charge at double the prime rate of the National Bank of Hungary, in line with general rules. A default penalty up to HUF 2m (approximately EUR 7,000) may be levied for not fulfilling, or not properly fulfilling, the content and formal documentation requirements. The HUF 2m default penalty is applicable per documentation and per year under tax audit.

Penalty relief

Not applicable.

Documentation requirements

The Act on CIT states that companies which do not qualify as small companies (small companies are defined as employing less than 50 persons and having less than EUR 10m in total turnover on a consolidated basis) must document the methods they used to determine the fair market prices, as well as the facts and circumstances supporting them. The detailed documentation obligation must be applied for all agreements in effect and where there was a supply in the tax year. The details of the documentation obligation are regulated by the Ministry of Finance Decree 18 of 2003. Foreign entities (usually foreign taxpayers carrying out business activities through a Hungarian permanent establishment) are also subject to the documentation obligation. However, according to the relevant transfer pricing regulation, there is an option to prepare simplified documentation if the value of the transactions does not exceed HUF 50m.

The Hungarian transfer pricing documentation requirements are consistent with the OECD Transfer Pricing Guidelines. The following list outlines the compulsory elements of the Hungarian transfer pricing documentation:

- Name, registered seat (official location) and tax number (or company registration number and the name and seat of the registering authority) of the related party
- Content of the agreement with the related party, which includes:
  - Subject of the agreement
  - Signing date (amendment date) of the agreement

- Period during which the agreement is effective
- Characteristics of the service provided and/or goods sold (functional analysis)
- Method and terms of the fulfillment of the agreement
- Analysis of the market (industry analysis)
- The method applied for establishing the arm's length price
- Reasons for selecting the method applied
- Description of comparable services and goods transactions
- Factors affecting the arm's length price, margin or profit and the extent of any necessary adjustments
- The arm's length price or margin
- Information on pricing agreements and court procedures
- Preparation date of the documentation

According to the Ministry of Finance Decree 22 of 2009, a taxpayer can choose to prepare a separate or a joint documentation. The joint documentation consists of two parts: a common documentation containing a standard information on the members of the group within the EU (i.e. masterfile) and a specific documentation describing the agreements concluded between the Hungarian taxpayer and its related parties.

The common document has to be prepared with respect to the member states of the European Union also including the controlled transactions carried out between third country companies and EU group companies.

The obligatory elements of the common documentation are the following:

- General description of the business and the business strategy of the business enterprise including the changes compared to the previous year
- General description of the organization, legal and operational structure of the group (including an organization chart, list of the group members, and a description of the participation of the parent company in the operation of the subsidiaries)
- List of the related parties carrying out controlled transactions with group members within the EU
- General description of the controlled transactions (list of the significant controlled transactions, e.g. sale of tangible fixed assets, provision of services, development of intangible assets, provision of financial services including the values of these transactions)
- General description of the functions and risk and the changes in these compared to the previous year
- Information of the ownership of intangible assets and the royalties paid and received
- Description of the transfer pricing policy or transfer pricing system of the group

¶20,040

- Cost contribution agreements and APAs relating to the determination of the arm's length price and court decisions on the arm's length price
- Date of preparation and modification of the documentation

The specific document must include the following information:

- Name, registered seat (official location) and tax number (or company registration number and the name and seat of the registering authority) of the related party
- Description of the business enterprise and the strategy of the business enterprise including the changes compared to the previous year
- Subject of the agreement, description of the transactions, value of the transactions, signing date (amendment date) of the agreement, period during which the agreement is effective
- Comparable search (characteristics of the service provided and/or goods sold, functional analysis, contractual conditions, economic circumstances)
- Description of the comparable data
- Transfer pricing policy of the group
- Preparation date and modification date of the documentation

According to the new Ministry of Finance Decree, the documentation can also be prepared in foreign languages. However, at the Tax Authority's request, the taxpayer has to prepare Hungarian translation. This is also applicable for the year 2009.

Documentation deadlines

The transfer pricing documentation for contracts effective in a given tax year is required to be prepared by the deadline for filing the annual corporate income tax return (basically, within 150 days from the year-end).

Statute of limitations on transfer pricing assessments

The general rules are applicable. The statute of limitations lapses on the last day of the fifth calendar year calculated from the tax year in which taxes should have been declared, reported or paid in the absence of a tax return or reporting.

Return disclosures/related-party disclosures

Within 15 days of concluding its first contract with a related party, the taxpayer must report the name, registered seat and tax number of the contracting party to the tax authority.

In the CIT return, the tax base should be adjusted if the price used in the related-party transaction differs from the fair market price.

According to the Hungarian transfer pricing regulations, the taxpayer is not required to file the transfer pricing documentation with the tax authority; however, the taxpayer needs to present the documentation during a tax audit.

The Financial Statements of companies include certain compulsory disclosures on related-party transactions.

¶20,040

Audit risk/transfer pricing scrutiny

The risk of transfer pricing issues being scrutinized during a tax authority audit is steadily growing. Since the decree on the documentation obligation came into force, the tax authority checks the existence of the documentation. Based on our experience, the tax authority usually inspects whether the content and formal requirements are fulfilled in the documentation. From the beginning of 2007, the tax authority started to train transfer pricing specialists. The tax authority's knowledge of the application of transfer pricing methods is expected to increase during the tax audits.

Overall, the risk of a transfer pricing audit can be set at medium. The tax authority focuses on reviewing the transfer pricing documentation in the framework of almost every tax audit. As a result, significant default penalties are levied if the transfer pricing documentation is missing or incomplete. Recently, the tax authority has started to challenge the transfer prices applied in related-party transactions (not only in very obvious cases). We expect this to increase in the near future.

APA opportunity

As of 1 January 2007, a formal APA regime was introduced in Hungary. Unilateral, bilateral and multilateral APAs are available according to the new provision. APAs requested for future transactions can be used for three to five years and they can be extended for a further three years. The application fees for APAs range from HUF 0.5m (approximately EUR 1,900) to HUF 10m (approximately EUR 37,000) depending on the type of APA and the transaction value. The tax authority is responsible for the establishment of APAs and dealing with other transfer pricing-related issues.

INDIA

Taxing authority and tax law

Income Tax Department. Section 40A (2), §§ 92-92F, 144C, 271, 271AA, 271BA and 271G of the Income Tax Act, 1961.

Relevant regulations and rulings

Rule 10 to 10E of the Income Tax Rules, 1962.

OECD guidelines treatment

The Indian legislation is broadly based on the OECD guidelines. In conformity with the OECD guidelines, the legislation prescribes the same five methods to compute the arm's length price. Further, the revenue authorities generally recognize the OECD guidelines and refer to the same for guidance, to the extent they are not inconsistent with the domestic law.

Priorities/pricing methods

The Indian legislation prescribes the following methods: CUP, Resale Price, Cost Plus, Profit Split and Transactional Net Margin Method. The legislation also grants the power to the Central Board of Direct Taxes (CBDT) to prescribe any other method; however, no other method has been prescribed by the CBDT to date. No hierarchy of methods exists. The most appropriate method should be applied.

Transfer pricing penalties

For inadequate documentation, the taxpayer is fined 2% of the transaction value. For not furnishing sufficient information or documents requested by the tax officer, the taxpayer is fined 2% of the transaction value. If due diligence efforts to determine the arm's length price have not been made by the taxpayer, then 100% to 300% of incremental tax on transfer pricing adjustments may be levied by the tax officer. For not furnishing an Accountant's Certificate (Form 3CEB) along with the return of income, the taxpayer is fined USD 2,200 approx.

Penalty relief

Penalties may be avoided if the taxpayer can demonstrate that it exercised good faith and due diligence in determining the arm's length price. This is also demonstrated through proper documentation and timely submission of documentation to the revenue authority during assessment proceedings.

Documentation requirements

A detailed list of mandatory documents are listed in Rule 10D (1). The categories of documentation required are:

- Ownership structure
- Profile of the multinational group
- Business description
- The nature and terms (including prices) of international transactions
- Description of functions performed, risks assumed and assets employed

¶20,040

- Record of any financial estimates
- Record of uncontrolled transaction with third parties and a comparability evaluation
- Description of methods considered
- Reasons for rejection of alternative methods
- Details of transfer pricing adjustments
- Any other information or data relating to the associated enterprise which may be relevant for determination of the arm's length price

A list of additional optional documents is provided in Rule 10D (3). The taxpayer is required to obtain and furnish an Accountant's Certificate (Form 3CEB) regarding adequacy of documentation maintained.

Documentation deadlines

The information and documentation specified should, as far as possible, be contemporaneous and exist by the specified date of the filing of the income tax return, which is 30 September following the end of the financial year.

Although an Accountant's Report must be submitted along with the tax return, the taxpayer is not required to furnish the transfer pricing documentation with the Accountant's Report at the time of filing the tax return. Transfer pricing documentation must be submitted to the tax officer within 30 days of the notice during assessment proceedings.

Statute of limitations on transfer pricing assessments

Tax assessments (where a matter has been referred to the transfer pricing officer) are to be completed within three years and nine months of the end of the financial year (1 April to 31 March). However, if the revenue authority determines that income has escaped assessment, an assessment may be re-opened within seven years of the end of the financial year.

Return disclosures/related-party disclosures

Under § 92E, an Accountant's Report is required to be provided along with the tax return. The accountant certifies whether proper documentation is maintained by the taxpayer.

In accordance with Indian Accounting Standard 18, the company is required to disclose related-party transactions in its financial statements.

Audit risk/transfer pricing scrutiny

Internal guidelines have been issued by the revenue authority, pursuant to which companies with related-party transactions in excess of USD 3.75m are being scrutinized. In most cases, the revenue authority does not seem to have adopted a centralized or coordinated approach to audits, with officers in different locations taking divergent positions on similar taxpayer fact patterns. Substantial documentation is being requested in the course of audit proceedings. The information technology, business process outsourcing, banking and pharmaceutical sectors have received particular attention. The revenue authority has sought an updated analysis using data that may not be available to the taxpayer at the time of the preparation of contemporaneous documentation. Furthermore, officers have insisted on unbundling transactions in cases where the taxpayer has adopted an aggregate or combined approach to its transfer pricing documentation. During recent audits, the approach adopted by the taxpayer in the selection of comparable data has received considerable attention from the revenue authorities.

The government has recently introduced an alternate dispute resolution process wherein the taxpayer can approach a dispute resolution panel in case a transfer pricing adjustment is proposed by the tax officer. The panel should dispose off the matter within 9 months, which shall be binding on the tax officer. This process is expected to significantly expedite the first level of litigation process in India, which usually takes a much longer time.

APA opportunity

APAs are not available yet, but the Indian government has proposed to introduce the APA provisions in near future.

INDONESIA

Taxing authority and tax law

Indonesian Tax Authority. Article 18 of the Indonesian income tax law.

Relevant regulations and rulings

A new income tax law implemented on 1 January 2009 contains transfer pricing provisions in Article 18, but implementing regulations have not yet been issued. The only regulations issued to date (Director General of Tax Circular Letter No SE-04/PJ.7/1993) are old and predate the new income tax law. Indonesia's transfer pricing rules apply to both domestic and cross-border transactions between parties that have a special relationship. Domestic transfer pricing rules apply because there is no grouping of tax losses in Indonesia. There are discussions that new transfer pricing rules will be issued and may be issued before the end of 2009 or in the first half of 2010.

OECD guidelines treatment

Indonesia is not a member of the OECD, but generally favors its principles and methods.

Priorities/pricing methods

The CUP is favored. Other allowable methods include Cost Plus, Resale Price, Profit Split Method and TNMM.

Transfer pricing penalties

There is a penalty of 2% per month, up to a maximum of 48%, on any tax underpayment discovered during a transfer pricing audit.

Penalty relief

Not applicable.

Documentation requirements

There are no formal documentation requirements at this time. However, the tax authority would require the taxpayer to provide documentation to show that the price of the related party transactions is at arm's length. Contemporaneous documentation is not currently not required.

Documentation deadlines

Currently there has not yet been specific requirement for transfer pricing documentation, including transfer pricing documentation deadlines. Generally speaking, in a tax audit, any document requested by tax auditor must be provided within a month from the request.

Statute of limitations on transfer pricing assessments

Not applicable.

Return disclosures/related-party disclosures

Disclosure of related-party transactions in the tax return has been required since 1 January 2002. Domestic and international relatedparty transactions are required to be disclosed. The information that must be disclosed includes the type of transaction, the value of the transaction, the transfer price and the method used to determine the transfer price. However, for the annual income tax return for 2009, vthe disclosure requirements have increased and in addition to the to the information previously requested confirmation of the issues that have been considered by the taxpayer in relation to these related party transactions will also need to be disclosed.

Audit risk/transfer pricing scrutiny

There is no specialized investigation unit in the Indonesian tax authority and most transfer pricing queries arise during regular tax audits. The number of transfer pricing adjustments increased significantly since last year, especially in cases where Indonesian entities have suffered losses, or where the export prices to related entities differs from the local sales price. In the past, the Indonesian tax authority's efforts have traditionally concentrated on intangibles and services (e.g., management fees, royalties, service fees and interest), but recent experience shows an increasing interest in the transfer pricing of tangible goods.

In practice, taxpayers that exhibit the following characteristics are more at risk of being subject to a transfer pricing audit:

- A large number of related-party transactions
- Losses for more than two consecutive years
- An increase in gross revenue or receipts but no change in net profit
- Erratic profit and loss histories
- Associated parties in tax havens
- Lower net profit in comparison to the industry average or other similar enterprises.

APA opportunity

The income tax law of 2001 contains bilateral and unilateral APA mechanisms. The income tax law suggests that APAs are only for cross border transactions, but conflicting statements have been made by senior tax officials that APAs may also apply to domestic transactions.

¶20,040

ISRAEL

Taxing authority and tax law

Israeli Tax Authority (ITA). Income Tax Ordinance § 85A and Income Tax Regulations (Determination of Market Terms), 2006.

Relevant regulations and rulings

The ITA Income Tax Regulations (Determination of Market Terms) were drafted pursuant to § 85A of the Israeli Income Tax Ordinance. Final regulations were adopted in November 2006. The Israeli Transfer Pricing (ITP) Regulations apply to all international intercompany transactions. The Regulations apply to all transactions carried out subsequent to their validation on 29 November 2006. The ITP Regulations are based upon a combination of the OECD Transfer Pricing Guidelines and the US Transfer Pricing Regulations.

Taxpayers are required to comply with the proper timing for the submission of documentation (i.e., 60 days from official demand of a tax inspector), which shifts the burden of proof to the tax authority if the prices do not appear to be at arm's length.

As a transitional provision, for tax years 2007 to 2008, a transfer pricing study documented prior to the publication of the ITP Regulations will be accepted for a period of two years upon their publication provided that the documentation was conducted based on the OECD guidelines or guidelines published by its members (e.g., the US).

The ITP requires that, commencing with tax year 2007, Israeli annual tax returns include a form (Form 1385), specific to transfer pricing, that delineates the intercompany transactions, details of the other party and its residency, the price of the transactions and signatures on declarations that the international intercompany transaction is at arm's length.

OECD guidelines treatment

The ITA considers its transfer pricing laws and regulations to be wholly consistent with the OECD guidelines and the US Treasury Regulations under § 1.482. For domestic use, the OECD guidelines do not provide support and would not be directly relevant to the application of any pricing methods. However, an arm's length study documented prior to the publication of the ITA Regulations will be accepted for a period of two years as of the Regulations' publication provided that the documentation was conducted based on the OECD guidelines or guidelines published by its members.

Priorities/pricing methods

To determine whether an international transaction is at arm's length terms, the ITP Regulations require the taxpayer to apply one of the following methods in the following hierarchy:

- CUP or Comparable Uncontrolled Transaction (CUT)
- Comparable profitability

¶20,040

- Cost Plus or Resale Price method
- CPM or TNMM
- Profit Split Method
- Other methods

An international transaction is at arm's length if through the application of an approved method, the result falls within a defined interquartile range. As an exception, the entire range of values will apply when the transfer pricing method applicable is a CUP or CUT, and no adjustments were performed. If the international transaction is outside the range of comparable transactions, the median should be applied as the transaction's price.

Additionally, the ITP Regulations stipulate the use of several profit level indicators (PLIs) depending on the particular industry and environment. For example, when appropriate, the following PLIs may apply: A cost-plus mark-up may be applied to a company's direct costs

- A gross profit margin may be applied
- The operating profit or loss applicable for comparable transactions
- The profit or loss derived as a proportion of the firm's assets, liabilities or capital
- Other measures considered appropriate under the circumstances

Transfer pricing penalties

The ITA has not specified any penalties with regards to its transfer pricing regulations. However, general tax penalties applied by the ITA, with regards to a tax deficit, will also apply on transfer pricing adjustments.

Penalty relief

Not applicable.

Documentation requirements

A taxpayer is required to file a transfer pricing report with the Tax Assessing Officer, at the Tax Assessing Officer's request, within 60 days from the application date. Documentation is required to include the following data:

- Details of the taxpayer, including group structure, the parties to the international transaction, their residency and any special relations between the taxpayer and the other transaction parties
- The contractual terms, including specifications of the asset, the service granted, the price paid, the loan and credit terms and related guarantees
- The taxpayer's area of activity and any relevant developments
- The economic environment in which the taxpayer operates and the related risks
- Details of all transactions entered into by the taxpayer with a related party
- An economic analysis

¶20,040

The taxpayer is also required to attach additional documents that corroborate the data submitted, such as transaction contracts and any other contracts between the related parties and tax returns filed with foreign tax authorities.

Documentation deadlines

A taxpayer is required to file a transfer pricing report with the Tax Assessing Officer, at the Tax Assessing Officer's request, within 60 days of the application date.

Form 1385 should be attached to the annual tax return. The ITA has published a tax circular 3/2008 where they stressed their opinion that this form must be backed with a benchmark analysis. Under this interpretation the deadline equals the timetable of the tax return.

Statute of limitations on transfer pricing assessments

The Israeli Income Tax Ordinance has general rules for auditing a tax return. As such, the statute of limitations is usually three years (or four if the commissionaire extends the time period) beginning at the end of the fiscal year tax return was filed.

Return disclosures/related-party disclosures

Commencing with the fiscal year ending 2007, taxpayers must attach to the annual tax returns a specific transfer pricing form (Form 1385), in which the following should be disclosed:

- a short description of the intercompany transaction details of the other party and its residency
- the prices of the transactions
- signatures on declarations that the international transactions were at arm's length

Audit risk/transfer pricing scrutiny

Medium Risk: The risk of transfer pricing scrutiny during a tax audit has increased exponentially following the issuance of the ITP Regulations and Form 1385. Transfer pricing will now be monitored with greater regularity and with increased ITA experience. In order to cope with the changing transfer pricing climate in Israel, the ITA has established a new division to enforce and regulate the ITP Regulations.

APA opportunity

The Israeli Income Tax Ordinance's § 85A, which governs the ITP Regulations, stipulates in article 85A (d) the condition under which an APA may be conducted and delineates the scope of an APA. The process starts with a detailed application filed by the taxpayer that includes all the relevant details. Under the APA process, the ITP must respond within 120 days (though the time can be extended up to 180 days) otherwise the application will be approved automatically, and the intercompany policy will be deemed as providing reasonable arm's length prices.

ITALY

Taxing authority and tax law

Amministrazione Finanziaria (Administration of Finance and revenue authority). Tax law is embedded in the Presidential Decree n. 917 of 22 December 1986, where transfer pricing is regulated in Article 110 (7) and Article 9 (3)-(4).

Relevant regulations and rulings

Administration of Finance Circular Letter n. 32/9/2267 of 22 September 1980, and Circular Letter n. 42/12/1587 of 12 December 1981. Circular Letter n. 1 dated 20 October 1998, that outlines general methods for tax audits and includes transfer pricing in the framework of regular audits of multinational enterprises.

Decision of the Italian Supreme Court (Corte di Cassazione) n. 22023 of 13 October 2006 that held the burden of proof is on the tax authority for transfer pricing issues. According to the Supreme Court, and following the 1995 OECD guidelines, in the jurisdictions where the burden of proof is on the tax authority, the taxpayer is not obliged to give evidence that the transfer prices comply with the arm's length principle unless the tax authority has already proved (prima facie) that the taxpayer has not complied with the arm's length principle.

OECD guidelines treatment

The Italian transfer pricing rules are mainly provided by the tax law provisions (Article 110 (7) and Article 9 (3)-(4) of the Presidential Decree n. 917 of 22 December 1986), Administration of Finance Circular Letter n. 32/9/2267 of 22 September 1980 and Circular Letter n. 42/12/1587 of 12 December 1981.

The 1980 Circular Letter follows the 1979 OECD Transfer Pricing Guidelines and, although it was issued before the date of enforcement of Article 110 (7) mentioned above, its provisions are still fully applicable. On the other hand, the 1995-1999 OECD guidelines have not been converted yet into specific official Italian guidelines, but only translated by the Italian Ministry of Finance.

The Decision n. 22023 of the Italian Supreme Court makes a clear reference to the OECD guidelines stating that the burden of proof is on the tax authority.

Ernst & Young is not aware of any official interpretation of the Italian Tax Authorities on the OECD Discussion Draft on Business Restructurings. The only case law on cross-border business restructurings Ernst & Young is aware of is the Ruling n. 124 dated 7 November 2006 in which the Revenue Agency deemed as occurred a sort of transfer of business concern (not specified if going concern or single assets) abroad in the case of a British insurance company which, after having operated on the Italian market for a certain number of years through a permanent establishment, subsequently provided directly its services to the Italian customers, by appointment of a fiscal representative in Italy (free supply of services).

Priorities/pricing methods

Transactional-based methods, such as CUP, Resale Price and Cost Plus, are preferred over profits-based methods, such as Profit Split, Profit Comparison, Economic Sector Gross Margin and Invested Capital Profitability.

¶20,040

According to the Italian transfer pricing rules (particularly the 1980 Circular Letter), the profits-based methods could be used:

- When it is impossible to use the three basic methods
- When
  - Uncertainties arise in verifying the correct use of the three basic methods
  - It is necessary to separate the differential element between two transactions which are susceptible to comparison in order to use one of the three basic methods

Transfer pricing penalties

General penalties for underpayment apply (Legislative Decree n. 471 of 18 December 1997). In particular, in a case where the tax return has been filed, general administrative penalties apply in the amount equal to a minimum of 100% up to a maximum of 200% of the additional tax or the minor tax credit assessed by Italian tax authorities. This penalty applies when, with reference to the single taxes, (1) the taxable income declared is lower than the one assessed, (2) the taxes declared are lower than those due or (3) the tax credit declared is greater than the one due to the taxpayer. The same penalties apply where undue tax allowances or deductions from the taxable income have been declared in the tax return. Interests on taxes or additional taxes due also apply. The yearly interest rate is presently equal to 2.75% of the taxes due (Article 20 of Presidential Decree n. 602 of 29 September 1973). Because of the relatively high amount of potential tax revenue in a transfer pricing audit, tax officers often refer assessments to public prosecutors to explore possible criminal tax law ramifications, as permitted under Legislative Decree n. 74 of 10 March 2000. Some mitigation is provided by Art. 7 whereby taxpayers are supposed to disclose their transfer pricing policy in their financial statement.

Penalty relief

There is no provision concerning penalty relief.

Documentation requirements

There are no specific documentation requirements provided. However, it is highly recommended that one prepare transfer pricing documentation that adheres to the OECD Transfer Pricing Guidelines. All income and deduction items should be adequately substantiated. According to Article 32 of Presidential Decree n. 600 of 20 September 1973, Italian tax authorities may require taxpayers to produce or send deeds and documents (in the form of questionnaires) concerning the assessment to which they are subject. Taxpayers are required to comply with the tax authority's requests.

Italian substantive and procedural law does not contain specific rules on the relevance of the documentation. Taxpayers are only obligated to submit the compulsory accounting books and other documents specifically required by the tax authorities (a completely different approach must be followed under the Italian anti-tax-haven provisions where, legally, the burden of proof shifts to the taxpayer).

¶20,040

Documentation deadlines

There is no statutory deadline. However, the deadline cannot be less than 15 days from the notification of the tax authorities' documentation request, in accordance with Article 32 of Presidential Decree n. 600 of 29 September 1973. The tax authority retains discretion over extension requests.

Statute of limitations on transfer pricing assessments

There is no specific statute of limitations on an assessment for transfer pricing. The general statute of limitations period for tax purposes applies. Therefore, tax assessments must be notified to the taxpayer by 31 December of the fourth year following the year for which the tax return has been filed. If the tax return has been omitted or is treated as null and void, the assessable period for the relevant year is extended by one additional year. Furthermore, for companies that do not benefit from the 2002/2003 Italian Tax Amnesty, the assessable period is extended by two additional years.

Return disclosures/related-party disclosures

Italian companies must officially communicate (in documents, correspondence, register of companies) whether they are managed and controlled by another company and the name of the related company (Article 2497-bis of the Italian Civil Code). Financial statements should include essential data of the managing or controlling company's financial statement and relations with related parties (Articles 2424, 2427, 2428 and 2497-bis of the Italian Civil Code). The tax return should disclose transactions with tax havens concerning costs and expenses.

Audit risk/transfer pricing scrutiny

The risk of transfer pricing scrutiny during a tax audit is high. In fact, transfer pricing receives the greatest scrutiny. Italian tax authorities usually challenge the price of intercompany transactions that do not comply with the arm's length principle or that result in a mismatch between the characterization of entities and their remuneration. There appears to be a tendency toward challenging transfer pricing in combination with issues related to tax havens and permanent establishments (especially since the Italian Supreme Court's "Philip Morris" case decision in 2002: Ministry of Finance (Tax Office) v. Philip Morris (GmbH), Case 7682/05 of 25 May 2002).

In addition, there is generally greater tax audit activity and particular attention paid to major taxpayers, where the Italian tax authorities are devoting greater resources in intelligence and monitoring activities on multinationals (see also, Italian Tax-Police Command, Results of the first eleven months of the 2002 and future strategies, press release of 19 December 2002). According to Article 42 of the Financial Law of 2000 (n. 388 of 23 December 2000), beginning from 2002, taxpayers with a business volume or turnover not lower than about EUR 26m are expected to be systematically audited at least once every two years, while the taxpayers with a business volume not lower than EUR 5.2m will be audited at least once every four years. These audits may be complete and extensive or just focus on specific items.

¶20,040

This approach of the Italian tax authorities has also been confirmed by the Circular Letter n. 3/E of 29 January 2004 which stressed a special focus on tax havens, reorganizations, rulings and fiscal units. For these goals, the Italian tax authorities will increase the exchange of information with the foreign tax authorities.

Likewise, the Circular Letter n. 6/E issued by Central Revenue Agency on 25 January 2008 provides operating guidelines to tax authorities in relation to the prevention and combat of tax avoidance, and among the most delicate and crucial areas to be assessed, it mentions intercompany transactions and transfer prices according to the provisions of Art. 110 (7) of the Presidential Decree n. 917 of 22 December 1986.

Furthermore, Law Decree n. 185 issued on 29 November 2008 is introducing the category of "mega" taxpayers stating that "in relation to the corporate income tax and VAT returns of relevant size companies, the Central Revenue activate substantial controls by the year following the one of the filing," where "relevant size companies are the ones which achieve a (yearly) turnover not lower than EUR [300m]. Such threshold will be gradually lowered to EUR [100m] by 31 December 2011."

In addition to all the above, the Italian Supreme Court is developing a broad concept of "abuse of law," deemed to be inspired by the Italian Constitution Law, that is trying to introduce a general anti-avoidance principle potentially applicable to all the operations that appear to be carried out for tax reasons only, without real business purposes.

APA opportunity

The Italian government introduced a unilateral ruling system mainly relating to transfer pricing, dividends and royalties. The law has been enacted with the "Provvedimento del Direttore dell'agenzia delle entrate," dated 23 July 2004. This document provides a number of practical guidelines to apply and conduct the ruling program. Since Italy provides a variety of tax rulings, the interactions between the APA and the other tax rulings should be evaluated on a case-by-case.

¶20,040

JAPAN

Taxing authority and tax law

National Tax Agency (NTA). Special Taxation Measures Law (STML) Article 66-4 (Special Provisions for Taxation of Transactions with Foreign Related Persons) and Article 68-88 (Special Taxation Measures of Transactions between Consolidated Corporations and Foreign Related Persons).

Relevant regulations and rulings

STML-Enforcement Order 39-12, STML Enforcement Regulations Art. 22-10, STML-Circular 66-4-(1)-1 to 66-4-(8)-2, Commissioner's Directive on the Establishment of Instructions for the Administration of Transfer Pricing Matters (Administrative Guidelines), and Commissioner's Directive on the Establishment of Instructions for the Administration of Transfer Pricing Matters for Consolidated Corporations (Administrative Guidelines for Consolidated Corporations), Commissioner's Directive on Mutual Agreement Procedures.

OECD guidelines treatment

The NTA refers to the OECD guidelines for direction, and the Japanese transfer pricing Administrative Guidelines contain the following statement: "In light of the importance of a common understanding regarding transfer pricing by each country's tax authorities for the resolution of international double taxation that arises due to taxation pursuant to the transfer pricing tax system, appropriate administration shall be carried out by referring to the OECD Transfer Pricing Guidelines to the extent necessary in examinations and in reviews of requests for APA's" (Para. 1-2(3)). However, under audit tax examiners often point out that Japan is not bound by the OECD guidelines and that they will follow their interpretation of Japanese tax laws and regulations even where there may be a disagreement over whether their approach is consistent with the OECD guidelines. On the other hand, the most recent US-Japan tax treaty explanation refers extensively to the OECD guidelines and suggests greater harmonization in the future.

Priorities/pricing methods

In general, transaction-based methods are preferred over profit-based methods. The tax authorities require that the CUP, Resale Price, and Cost Plus methods be used whenever possible, only allowing the use of other methods (e.g., Profit Split and Transactional Net Margin Method) after the first three have been discounted. The TNMM is available for fiscal years starting on or after 1 April 2004. Note that there are some cases in which the Residual Profit Split Method, which is accepted by the Japanese tax authorities as one type of the Profit Split Method mentioned above, is applied.

Transfer pricing penalties

Transfer pricing assessments are subject to the same penalties that apply to general corporate tax assessments. There are two types of penalties: underpayment penalty tax and delinquency tax (interest). Underpayment penalty tax is computed

¶20,040

as either 10% of the additional assessed taxes (up to JPY 500,000) or 15% of the additional tax, depending on the amount of underpayment.

The delinquency tax (interest) rate begins from 4% per year plus the official discount rate and increases after a certain period to 14.6% per year.

There is no separate penalty for failure to prepare and maintain transfer pricing documentation.

Penalty relief

There are no specific provisions for reductions in underpayment penalties.

However, the 2007 tax reforms allowed for the provision of a grace period for the payment of assessed taxes - including penalty taxes - for taxpayers submitting an application for mutual agreement procedures. The taxpayer must submit a separate application to be entitled to the grace period, which is defined as the period starting on the initial payment due date of assessed taxes and ending on the day one month after the day following the day on which the "correction" based on the mutual agreement has been made (or the day on which a notification was issued that an agreement could not be reached). Any delinquency taxes accrued during the grace period will be exempted. However, under STML Article 66-4-2(2), where the tax authority grants a postponement of tax payment, the tax authority requires the taxpayer to provide security (i.e., collateral) equivalent to the amount of the tax payment. This new transfer pricing rule will be applicable for applications for a grace period made on or after 1 April 2007.

Documentation requirements

There are currently no statutory documentation requirements. The documentation that will be examined during a transfer pricing audit is disclosed in the Administrative Guidelines. Failure to provide such documentation in a timely manner upon request can trigger the tax examiner's authority to collect transactional data from comparable firms to use as "secret comparables" for the taxpayer. That is, the comparables are not disclosed to the taxpayer because the transactional data of the companies are confidential. Alternatively, an examiner can resort to "presumptive taxation", presuming an arm's length price with reference to profit ratios of other corporations in the industry which carry out similar activities.

Documentation deadlines

The taxpayer is required to provide the tax authority with documentation (i.e., information and records) relevant to the establishment of the arm's length price in a timely manner upon request. There is no exact deadline specified.

Statute of limitations on transfer pricing assessments

The statute of limitations on transfer pricing assessments is six years from the deadline for filing tax returns for a fiscal year (STML Article 66-4(16)).

A corporation must maintain corporate tax records for seven years from the fiscal year end (Corporation Tax Law Art. 126 and 150-2; Corporation Tax Law Enforcement Regulation, Article 59 and 67).

¶20,040

Return disclosures/related-party disclosures

The taxpayer must file Schedule 17-4 (previously Schedule 17-3), Detailed Statement Concerning Foreign Affiliated Persons and Related Party Transactions for fiscal years beginning on or after 1 April 2003. Schedule 17-4 requires that taxpayers disclose the transfer pricing methods applied in calculating the arm's length prices of the foreign related-party transactions. This requirement implies that taxpayers are expected to identify the appropriate transfer pricing methods for their related-party transactions and be able to demonstrate the appropriateness of those methods. Therefore, this rule can be interpreted as a de facto transfer pricing documentation requirement as taxpayers are expected to maintain documents in support of any tax return disclosure.

Effective 30 April 2008, Schedule 17-4 requires taxpayers to disclose the following three additional information items:

- The number of employees of the foreign related party
- The amount of retained earnings of the foreign related party for the preceding year
- Any APA agreed between the taxpayer and the foreign Competent Authority.

Audit risk/transfer pricing scrutiny

Audit risk is generally medium-high for large taxpayers with significant related-party transactions. The risk is increased for taxpayers who meet any of the following criteria:

- In industries targeted by the NTA
- With low profits or losses in Japan
- High profits in foreign affiliates as disclosed on Schedule 17-4 (relative to profits reported in Japan)
- With fluctuating profitability
- Who have significant transactions with tax havens
- In industries with high margins. The NTA is likely to seek to apply comparables, including secret comparables available only to the NTA.

APA opportunity

Unilateral and bilateral APAs are available, though the NTA prefers bilateral. APA guidelines are included in the Administrative Guidelines.

The NTA has recently shown a willingness to accept profit-based methods, such as the TNMM.

The NTA amended the filing deadline for APA applications on 22 October 2008. Previous guidance required that the APA application be filed by the tax return filing deadline of the first year to be covered by the APA. The new NTA guidance sets the APA filing deadline as the day preceding the first day of the first fiscal year to be covered by the proposed APA.

¶20,040

However, the new guidance does allow for a transition period. If the first covered year starts between 1 November 2008 and 1 November 2009, the transition rule applies. The transition rule indicates that the APA application is due eight months after the due date of the tax return for the last year before the covered period. In practice, this means the application is due eleven months after the first day of the covered period.

KAZAKHSTAN

Taxing authority and tax law

Tax and customs authorities are the authorized bodies to conduct control over transfer pricing. Tax authorities include Tax Committee of the Ministry of Finance of the Republic of Kazakhstan (TCMF) and territorial tax bodies. Customs authorities include Customs Control Committee of the Ministry of Finance (CCC), its territorial subdivisions, custom houses, customs points, checkpoints at the customs border of the Republic of Kazakhstan, specialized customs offices.

The following legal acts regulate transfer pricing:

* Law of the Republic of Kazakhstan No. 67-IV, On Transfer Pricing, of 5 July 2008 (Law).

* Code of the Republic of Kazakhstan on Taxes and Other Obligatory Payments to the Budget (Tax Code) No. 99-IV of 10 December 2008.

Relevant regulations and rulings

The following subordinate legal acts regulate transfer pricing:

* Instruction on control over transfer pricing in international business transactions (pending approval of the Ministry of Finance);

* Rules for conducting of transactions monitoring (No. 62 of 12 February 2009);

* Rules for concluding agreements on application of transfer pricing (No. 63 of 12 February 2009);

* Rules on the procedure for cooperation of the authorized bodies in conducting control over transfer pricing issues (No. 129 of 26 March 2009);

* List of goods (work, services) international business transactions with which are subject to transactions monitoring (No. 293 of 12 March 2009);

* List of officially recongnized sources of information on market prices (No. 292 of 12 March 2009).

OECD guidelines treatment

Although the currently effective transfer pricing law has some common features with the OECD Transfer Pricing Guidelines, the principal difference with the OECD Transfer Pricing guidelines is that the Kazakhstan transfer pricing legislation targets all international business transactions irrespective whether the parties related or not. The OECD guidelines are not binding for Kazakhstan.

Priorities/pricing methods

The law allows for five pricing methods in the following priority: Comparable Uncontrollable Price, Cost Plus, Resale Price, Profit Split and Net Margin.

Transfer pricing penalties

Special fines are envisaged for failure to comply with the documentation requirements established by the transfer pricing legislation, i.e. monitoring report-

¶20,040

ing and documentation supporting the transaction price. The maximum amount of fine is set at approximately USD 2,725.

The fine for understatement of tax payment resulting from transfer pricing adjustment is up to 50% of the additionally accrued tax amount. In addition, interest for delayed payment of additionally assessed tax resulting from transfer pricing adjustments is 2.5 times the National Bank refinancing rate.

Penalty relief

Not applicable.

Documentation requirements

Different requirements are established for two categories of transactions: (i) transactions with goods (works, services) that are subject to monitoring and (ii) all other transactions subject to transfer pricing control.

Participants involved in transactions subject to monitoring are obliged to prepare and submit transaction monitoring reports on annual basis ("Monitoring reports") that should include information on the applied prices, information on relationships of the parties, industries and market conditions, business strategy, transfer pricing methodology, functional and risks analysis, tangible and intangible assets, method, source of information used for determination of a market price and other information.

Transaction participants executing transactions of other goods that are subject to transfer pricing control should maintain documentation supporting the applied prices which is less detailed than the monitoring reports.

Documentation deadlines

Monitoring reports must be submitted to the tax authorities no later than 15 April of the year following a reporting year. The filing deadline can be extended up to the extension period granted for filing a corporate income tax declaration.

The documentation supporting the applied transaction prices must be submitted within 90 days from date of competent authorities' request.

Statute of limitations on transfer pricing assessments

There is no specific statute of limitations on transfer pricing assessments. The general statute of limitations period for the assessment of underpayments of tax, understatements of income or overstatements of expenses penalties is five years from the date of the relevant violation.

Return disclosures/related-party disclosures

No related-party disclosure is required currently on tax declarations, though both National Accounting Standards and International Financial Reporting Standards require such disclosures in financial statements.

Audit risk/transfer pricing scrutiny

Transfer pricing audits can take place once per year. The risk of transfer pricing issues being scrutinized during an audit is high. The export of goods from

¶20,040

Kazakhstan receives greater scrutiny. The review of the method, its use and the interpretation of information on market prices applied by the tax authority often result in transfer pricing adjustments that are contested by taxpayers in many cases.

APA opportunity

Transaction participants are allowed to conclude an agreement on application of transfer prices. The procedure for concluding such agreements is envisaged in the Rules for concluding agreements on application of transfer pricing (No. 63 of 12 February 2009) that determine the following:

- List of documents required for concluding the Agreement;
- Procedure for consideration the request by tax authorities;
- Duration of the Agreement (i.e. 3 years from the date of signing);
- Conditions for termination;
- Other.

The tax authorities reserve the right to unilaterally terminate an agreement in case a participant violates its conditions.

KENYA

Taxing authority and tax law

Kenya Revenue Authority (KRA)

Income Tax Act (Cap 470, Laws of Kenya) and the Income Tax (Transfer Pricing) Rules 2006 are the applicable regulations

Relevant regulations and rulings

Section 18(3) of the Income Tax Act provides: 'Where a non-resident person carries on business with a related resident person and the course of that business is so arranged that it produces to the resident person either no profits or less than the ordinary profits which might be expected to accrue from that business if there had been no such relationship, then the gains or profits of that resident person from that business shall be deemed to be the amount that might have been expected to accrue if the course of that business had been conducted by independent persons dealing at arm's length.'

(6) For the purposes of subsection (3), a person is related to another if

(a) either person participates directly or indirectly in the management, control or capital of the business of the other; or

(b) a third person participates directly or indirectly in the management, control or capital of the business or both.

The Transfer Pricing guidelines apply to:

- transactions between associated enterprises within a multinational company, where one enterprise is located in, and is subject to tax in Kenya, and the other is located outside Kenya;

- transactions between a permanent establishment and its head office or other related branches, in which case the permanent establishment shall be treated as a distinct and separate enterprise from its head office and related branches.

OECD guidelines treatment

The Income Tax (Transfer Pricing) rules provide for the application of the OECD methods in determining the arm's length pricing.

Priorities/pricing methods

Rule 4 of the aforesaid rules provides that a tax payer may choose to employ in determining the arm's length price from among the 6 methods as follows:

- Comparable Uncontrolled Price (CUP) method
- Resale price method
- Cost price method
- Profit split method
- Transactional net margin method
- Such other method as the commissioner for Domestic Taxes may prescribe

¶20,040

Transfer pricing penalties

There are no specific TP penalties. However, the Commissioner for Domestic Taxes can conduct an audit and make adjustments in the taxable profit and demand tax where applicable. Any tax due and unpaid tax in a transfer pricing arrangement is deemed to be additional tax for purposes of Section 94 and Section 95 of the Income Tax Act.

- Section 94 of the Income Tax Act provides that 'late payment interest of two per cent per month or part thereof shall be charged on the amount, including the penalty remaining unpaid for more than one month after the due date until the full amount is recovered'.

- Section 95. (1) provides that if, for a year of income, the difference between the amount of tax assessed on the total income of a person and the amount of the estimate of the tax chargeable contained in a provisional return of income made by that person in respect of that year is greater than ten per cent of that estimated tax, interest at the rate of two per cent per month shall be payable on the whole of the difference between the tax so assessed and the tax so estimated.

Penalty relief

There is no specific penalty relief for Transfer pricing arrangements.

Documentation requirements

The Commissioner for Domestic Taxes may, where necessary request a person to whom these rules apply for information, including books of accounts and other documents relating to transactions where the transfer pricing is applied. Such documents shall include information relating to:

(a) the selection of the transfer pricing method and the reasons for the selection;

(b) the application of the method, including the calculations made and price adjustment factors considered;

(c) the global organization structure of the enterprise;

(d) the details of the transaction under consideration;

(e) the assumptions, strategies and policies applied in selecting the method; and

(f) other background information as may be necessary regarding the transaction.

The books of accounts and other documents shall be prepared in, or be translated into, the English language, at the time the transfer price is arrived at.

Where a person avers the application of arm's length pricing, such person shall:

(a) develop an appropriate transfer pricing policy;

(b) determine the arm's length price as prescribed under the guidelines provided under these rules; and

¶20,040

(c) avail documentation to evidence their analysis upon request by the commissioner.

Documentation deadlines

The deadline for preparing documentation is the same as the deadline for filing the tax return.

Documentation must be provided upon request.

Statute of limitations on transfer pricing assessments

According to Section 56(3) of the Income Tax Act, the statute of limitations for TP assessments is seven years after the relevant year of income unless the Commissioner has reasonable cause to believe that fraud or gross or willful neglect has been committed in connection with, or in relation to, tax for a year of income.

Return disclosures/related-party disclosures

According to the corporate tax return format, the tax payer is obliged to declare the following:

- Name of the related party/parties outside Kenya
- The address of the related parties

Audit risk/transfer pricing scrutiny

The KRA has commenced TP audits.

KRA is still requesting for TP policies for scrutiny.

APA opportunity

There are no specific APA rules.

¶20,040

LATVIA

Taxing authority and tax law

The State Revenue Service. The arm's length principle is established in the Law on Corporate Income Tax. Article 12 of the Law on Corporate Income Tax of Latvia determines that the taxable income of the taxpayer may be increased if related-party transactions are not arm's length.

Relevant regulations and rulings

4 July 2006 Cabinet Regulations No. 556 set the transfer pricing methods applicable for determining arm's length prices in related-party transactions.

OECD guidelines treatment

Latvian transfer pricing legislative acts contain a reference to the OECD Guidelines on the application of the transfer pricing methods. The State Revenue Service also generally accepts the OECD Guidelines principles regarding transfer pricing documentation structure.

Priorities/pricing methods

Five methods are accepted - Comparable uncontrolled price method, Resale price method, Cost plus method, Profit split method and TNMM.

Transfer pricing penalties

There is no separate penalty for not having transfer pricing documentation. In case the prices applied in transactions between related parties are not at arm's length, the taxable income of the taxpayer may be increased and a penalty in the amount of 30 - 50% and a late penalty charge (annual rate of 18%) on additionally payable corporate income tax may be applied.

Penalty relief

There is no penalty relief; however, the existence of transfer pricing documentation generally reduces transfer pricing risks.

Documentation requirements

Latvian legislative acts do not provide specific requirements regarding preparation of transfer pricing documentation. However during tax audits taxpayer should be able to justify that prices applied in transactions between related parties are arm's length. Generally transfer pricing risks are lower if the documentation prepared is based on the OECD Guidelines.

Documentation deadlines

There is no specific deadline for the preparation of the transfer pricing documentation but the relevant documentation could be required during the State Revenue Service tax audit.

¶20,040

Statute of limitations on transfer pricing assessments

Generally the State Revenue Service has rights to make a tax assessment for three years from the payment date of respective tax. This general rule is applicable also to transfer pricing tax assessments.

Return disclosures/related-party disclosures

Related-party transactions must be disclosed in appendix 2 of the corporate income tax return. The taxpayer should disclose related parties involved in related-party transactions, type of transaction (e.g. purchase or sale of goods, services or fixed assets), volume of transactions and transfer pricing methods applied.

Audit risk/transfer pricing scrutiny

Taxpayers in Latvia run a medium risk that transfer prices will be scrutinized during a tax audit.

APA opportunity

There are no specific APA rules.

LITHUANIA

Taxing authority and tax law

Ministry of Finance of the Republic of Lithuania and the State Tax Inspectorate. The arm's length principle is established in the Corporate Income Tax of Lithuania and its implementation rules introduced in 2004.

Relevant regulations and rulings

Article 40 of the Law on the Corporate Income Tax of Lithuania. Order of the Minister of Finance No 1K- 123 as of 9 April 2004 on transfer pricing evaluation and documentation rules. Order of the Head of the State Tax Inspectorate No VA-27 as of 22 March 2005, on the associated party transaction disclosure in the annual corporate income tax return.

OECD guidelines treatment

The use of the OECD Transfer Pricing Guidelines for Multinational Enterprises and Tax Administrators is explicitly advocated in the regulations and rulings applicable in Lithuania. Other OECD papers, such as regarding business restructurings and profit allocation to permanent establishments, are not explicitly implemented in the Lithuanian legislation, however, in practice they are frequently referred to for practical guidance.

Priorities/pricing methods

Transaction-based methods are preferred over profit-based methods. Taxpayers are encouraged to use profit-based methods only if transaction-based methods are not sufficient. Taxpayers are not required to use more than one method; however, a combination of methods may be used in all cases providing support for the decision to apply any particular method.

Transfer pricing penalties

There are no specific transfer pricing penalties. General tax penalties applicable in the case of the taxable income adjustments by the tax authority are equal to 10% to 50% of the tax additionally calculated. In addition, the penalty interest will apply.

There are no special penalties related to the non-provision of the transfer pricing documentation at the request of the tax authorities.

Penalty relief

Not applicable.

Documentation requirements

The transfer pricing documentation requirements are binding for resident and non-resident legal entities registered as corporate income taxpayers in Lithuania, whose revenues in Lithuania in the year before the transactions were conducted exceeded EUR 2.9m.

¶20,040

In addition, transfer pricing documentation requirements are applicable to the credit institutions such as banks and entities providing financial services (e.g., insurance companies), irrespective of their revenue size.

The transfer pricing documentation has to contain:

- Details of the transactions
- Terms and conditions of the transactions
- Participants in the transactions, including their legal and organizational structure
- Functions performed, property used or contributed and the risks assumed by the parties
- Data and methods considered and the analyses performed to determine the transfer prices
- All relevant assumptions, strategies and policies that influenced the determination of the methods applied

In general, the OECD guidelines' principles are to be followed.

Documentation deadlines

There are no specific requirements or schedules for the preparation of transfer pricing documentation. Taxpayers must submit the transfer pricing documentation within 30 days of the corresponding notice by the tax authorities.

Statute of limitations on transfer pricing assessments

Transfer pricing assessments may occur during the five years before the year in which the assessment takes place.

Return disclosures/related-party disclosures

An associated party disclosure annex to the annual corporate income tax return has to be submitted within nine months after the end of each tax period, in case the associated-party transactions of the taxpayer exceed in annual value approximately EUR 87,000. In the annex, taxpayers are required to inform the tax authorities whether any prescribed transfer pricing methods have been used in the transactions disclosed.

Audit risk/transfer pricing scrutiny

Taxpayers in Lithuania run a high risk that transfer prices will be scrutinized during a tax audit.

APA opportunity

Currently, the Lithuanian tax laws do not provide for an opportunity to conclude APAs.

MALAYSIA

Taxing authority and tax law

Inland Revenue Board (IRB). General Anti-Avoidance Provision (§ 140 of the Malaysian Income Tax Act, 1967: Power to disregard certain transactions if not deemed arm's length), (§ 138C of the Malaysian Income Tax Act, 1967: Advance Pricing Arrangement), (§ 140A of the Malaysian Income Tax Act, 1967: Power to substitute the price and disallowance of interest on certain transactions) and Transactions by Non-Residents (§ 141 of the Malaysian Income Tax Act, 1967: Powers regarding certain transactions by non-residents).

The IRB released the Malaysian Transfer Pricing Guidelines on 2 July 2003 which specify documentation requirements.

OECD guidelines treatment

The Malaysian Transfer Pricing Guidelines are largely based on the governing standard for transfer pricing, which is the arm's length principle as established in the OECD guidelines. The IRB respects the general principles of the OECD guidelines.

Priorities/pricing methods

The IRB accepts CUP, Resale Price, Cost Plus, Profit Split and TNMM. However, the Malaysian Transfer Pricing Guidelines state that the traditional methods are preferred over the profit methods and advise that the profit methods should only be used when the traditional methods cannot be reliably applied or cannot be applied at all.

Transfer pricing penalties

There are no specific penalties for transfer pricing. However, the existing legislation and penalty structure under the Malaysian Income Tax Act, 1967, are applied. Penalties for transfer pricing adjustments can range from 100% to 300% of the undercharged tax. There are no transfer-pricing-specific documentation penalties.

Penalty relief

A reduction in penalties can be negotiated based on quality of contemporaneous transfer pricing documentation.

Documentation requirements

Contemporaneous documents pertaining to transfer pricing need not be submitted with the tax return form, but should be made available to the IRB upon request. All relevant documentation must be in, or translated into, Bahasa Malaysia (the national language) or English. There is no disclosure required on a tax return to indicate that transfer pricing documentation has been prepared.

The IRB has set out a list of information and documentation to be prepared for transfer pricing purposes. This list is neither intended to be exhaustive nor meant to apply to all types of businesses. Instead, taxpayers are advised to maintain

¶20,040

information and documentation that are applicable to their circumstances. The list includes:

- Company details
  - Ownership structure showing linkages between all entities within the Multinational Enterprise (MNE)
  - Company organization chart
  - Operational aspects of the business including details of functions performed
- Transaction details
  - A summary of transactions with other entities in the same MNE, indicating the name and address of each entity in the MNE with whom international transactions have been entered into, and the type of transactions, e.g., purchase of raw material or fixed assets, sale of finished goods, borrowing of money.
  - A summary of transactions similar to the above that are conducted with independent parties or information derived from independent enterprises engaged in similar transactions or businesses.
  - Economic conditions during the time of the transactions
  - Terms of the transactions, including where applicable contractual agreements with overseas associated parties with regard to technical assistance fees, management fees, marketing fees, recruitment fees or other services provided, royalties payable, purchase or rental of equipment or other assets, handling charges, loans, allocation of overhead expenses or any specific expenses (e.g., promotional or advertising) borne by the foreign entity or other forms of payment to overseas associates
  - Pricing policy over the past seven-year period
  - Breakdown of product manufacturing costs
  - Product price list
- Determination of arm's length price
  - The pricing method adopted, showing how the arm's length price is derived, and indicating why that method is chosen over other methods
  - Functional analysis taking into consideration all risks assumed and assets employed
  - If a comparability analysis results in a range of arm's length outcomes, then the furnishing of documents relating to all of the outcomes and the reasons for choosing that particular arm's length price from the range of outcomes must be given.

Documentation deadlines

There is no documentation deadline. However, documentation should be prepared contemporaneously. As tax returns are due for filing to the IRB within seven months of the close of a company's financial year-end, it is advisable that

¶20,040

transfer pricing documentation be prepared before the submission date of the return.

Statute of limitations on transfer pricing assessments

There is a six-year statute of limitations for tax adjustments, and documentation must be kept for seven years. There is no statute of limitations in instances of fraud, willful default or negligence.

Return disclosures/related-party disclosures

Disclosure of arm's length values is required in the tax return for the following transactions:

- Sales to related companies
- Purchases from related companies
- Other payments to related companies
- Lending to and borrowing from related companies
- Receipts from related companies

Audit risk/transfer pricing scrutiny

The risk of transfer pricing scrutiny during an audit is high. Tax audits are carried out under a self-assessment regime. Every company is expected to be subject to a desk or field audit at least once every five years. With the release of the Malaysian Transfer Pricing Guidelines, greater scrutiny on transfer pricing has been observed in these field audits. Ernst & Young's experience is that every multinational corporation that was audited over the last 12 months was scrutinized on its transfer pricing policy. Since the beginning of 2005, the number of transfer pricing audits and investigation activity by the IRB increased significantly. There is a specific transfer pricing unit in the IRB to handle all transfer pricing audits.

This scrutiny is expected to increase significantly with the introduction of § 140A of the Malaysian Income Tax Act, 1967: Power to substitute the price and disallowance of interest on certain transactions. This section effectively shifts the onus unto the taxpayer to prove arm's length pricing in acquisition or supply of property and services. Furthermore, this section also imposes thin capitalization rules, disallowing deductions for interest, finance charge and other consideration in respect of financial assistance between related persons.

APA opportunity

The introduction of § 138C in the Malaysian Income Tax Act, 1967 effectively formalizes the availability of unilateral and bilateral APAs in Malaysia. However, at this stage, formal guidelines on APAs are still in draft form, and the IRB has previously indicated that it will consider any terms and conditions which are the norm observed in the transfer pricing regimes in other jurisdictions. A specific transfer pricing unit in the IRB has been established to oversee the APA applications and negotiations.

¶20,040

MEXICO

Taxing authority and tax law

The Central Administration of Transfer Pricing Audits of the Mexican Tax Administration Service (SAT) is in charge of enforcing transfer pricing rules. This office is in charge of the transfer pricing audits and the APA Program. The main legal provisions dealing with transfer pricing are Articles 86-XII, XIII and XV, 215, 216, 216-BIS and 217 of the Mexican Income Tax Law (MITL), as well as Article 34-A of the Federal Fiscal Code (FFC). Article 216-BIS of the MITL provide special rules for maquiladoras.

Additionally, questionnaires related to the tax review by the registered external auditor (external CPA) as part of the Financial Audit Report are published as Miscellaneous Tax Resolutions in the Federal Register (*Diario Oficial de la Federación*). Four of such questionnaires relate to inter-company transactions and require a great deal of detail.

Relevant regulations and rulings

Tax regulations are issued by the Ministry of Finance and approved by Congress. The SAT publishes administrative rules on a regular basis, and few rules and regulations deal with transfer pricing issues.

OECD guidelines treatment

The OECD guidelines can be relied upon for interpretation of the rules as long as they do not contradict the MITL or International Tax Treaties.

Priorities/pricing methods

The transfer pricing methods in Mexico are the CUP, Resale Price, Cost Plus, Profit Split, Residual Profit Split and TNMM. Effective 2006, there is a best method rule and a hierarchy of methods. The CUP and other traditional transactional methods are preferred to profit-based methods. No alternative methods are acceptable.

Transfer pricing penalties

No specific penalties are applied when taxpayers do not maintain contemporaneous transfer pricing documentation. However, the SAT has taken the position, confirmed by a tax court case, that failure to comply with the documentation requirements results in non-deductibility of the corresponding payments to non-resident related parties. There are also penalties for failure or untimely filing of the transfer pricing information return. A penalty of USD 4,100 to USD 8,037 can be assessed if the information return on related-party transactions is not filed or is incomplete or incorrect.

If a transfer pricing adjustment is determined, and as a consequence unpaid contributions are established, a monetary sanction of 55% to 75% applies.

Also, if a transfer pricing adjustment reduces a net operating loss (NOL), the penalty ranges from 30% to 40% of the difference between the determined NOL and the NOL in the return. It is worth mentioning that both penalties described above will also need to be calculated based on surcharges and updates.

There are no penalties if self-correction of tax results is made before an audit and reduced penalties apply if self-correction is made during the audit but before the tax assessment. Waivers and abatements are possible under limited circumstances.

Penalty relief

According to Art76 of the Federal Fiscal Code, if the taxpayer prepares and maintains annual transfer pricing documentation, a penalty relief between 27.5% and 37.5% of the tax omitted applies.(50% of the corresponding penalty). Waivers and abatements are possible under limited circumstances such as financial hardship (during 2006). Penalties may be reduced after the audit has started by self-correction procedures.

Documentation requirements

Contemporaneous transfer pricing documentation related to cross-border intercompany transactions must be maintained. Documentation must include the name, address and tax residency of the non-resident related persons with whom transactions are carried out, as well as evidence of direct and indirect participation between related parties. It is necessary to include in the documentation information on the functions, activities, assets used and risks assumed by the taxpayer involved in each transaction. It is also necessary to include information and documentation on comparable transactions or companies by type of transaction. Domestic intercompany transactions are also required to be documented by demonstrating that an accepted pricing methodology is being applied.

Taxpayers are required to identify non-resident related-party transactions clearly on their accounting records. Documentation must be readily available by due date of the tax return. The Multiple Annual Tax Return includes an appendix for the disclosure of information related to intercompany transactions with non-resident related parties. Tax returns require the following information by type of transaction and by related party:

- Names, countries and tax identification numbers of affiliates
- Types of transactions and corresponding amounts
- Transfer pricing methods
- Gross or operating margins earned on each transaction (only applicable under certain types of transactions)

Documentation deadlines

A transfer pricing study must be in place at the time the company files its annual income tax return (by the end of March of the following year) and must be kept along with the company's accounting records for five years after the filing of the last tax return for each year.

The external auditor of each Mexican taxpayer is required to disclose the company's compliance with all tax obligations, including those related to transfer

¶20,040

pricing. This disclosure is made through the Financial Audit Report (*Dictamen Fiscal*) that must be filed by certain companies by 30 June every year.

In order to issue the Financial Audit Report, the auditor must verify, among other things, that the company's transfer pricing documentation is in place for the fiscal year under analysis and that it complies with the requirements stated in the MITL and complete extensive questionnaires, four of which deal with inter-company transactions, as follows:

- Attachment 5: Segmented Profit and Loss Statement (Not required for the Financial Audit Report for fiscal year 2008 but compulsory for fiscal year 2009)

- Attachment 34: Information regarding related party transactions: i) Tax ID; ii) Tax Name; iii) Country of residence; iv) Amount of the intercompany transaction; v) Transfer Pricing Methodology; vi) Profit Level Indicator; assessment regarding transfer pricing compliance (YES / NO). This information is required for all intercompany transactions, i.e., with foreign and local related parties per party and type of transaction. This questionnaire is intended to verify compliance with MITL not only to verify transfer pricing aspects per se but also deductibility transfer pricing requirements of all tax deductions.

- Attachment 34.1: Questionnaire on Related Party Transactions. This questionnaire includes the following sections: i) Advance Pricing Agreement (if applicable); ii) Transfer Pricing Documentation compliance and filing date of Informative Tax Return; iii) Cost of Sales Segmentation; iv) Related rules regarding Pro-rata charges; v) Information regarding financial derivative operations; and vi) Maquiladora rules compliance.

- Transfer Pricing Questionnaire related to the review conducted by the external auditor: More than 90 questions regarding dealing with all aspects related to cross-border and domestic intercompany transactions.

Additionally, an information return on related-party transactions must be filed electronically along with the annual income tax return. Transfer pricing documentation must be readily available as part of the accounting records by 31 March. The SAT has taken the position that failure to comply with the documentation requirements results in non-deductibility of payments to non-resident related parties.

Statute of limitations on transfer pricing assessments

The statute of limitations on assessment in Mexico is five years. The term is affected by amended returns with respect to items changed, and it is suspended by audit. The SAT has two years to complete a transfer pricing audit.

Return disclosures/related-party disclosures

Mexican taxpayers must submit a transfer pricing return to the SAT (Exhibit 9) which is due contemporaneously with the submission of the annual tax return. Information to be disclosed includes non-resident related-parties' tax address and tax identification number, transaction classifications, amounts, methods to be ap-

¶20,040

plied for analyses and profit or loss obtained. The information return must be filed by 31 March of each year.

Audit risk/transfer pricing scrutiny

High audit risk focusing on business restructuring (limited risk structures, migration of intangible property and centralization of functions and risks in favorable tax jurisdictions), highly leveraged structures, cost-sharing agreements, and pro-rata based management fees.

APA opportunity

Unilateral and bilateral APAs are available under Article 34-A of the Federal Fiscal Code and Mexico's tax treaties. Unilateral APAs can cover the fiscal year of the application, the three subsequent fiscal years and a one-year rollback.

¶20,040

NETHERLANDS

Taxing authority and tax law

Tax authority Articles 3.8 and 3.25 of the Dutch Income Tax Act 2001. Articles 8 and 8b of the Dutch Corporate Income Tax Act 1969. Effective 1 January 2002, Article 8b codifies the arm's length principle and introduces transfer pricing documentation requirements in the Netherlands that came into force.

Relevant regulations and rulings

Besides the articles in Dutch tax law as mentioned above, the Dutch Under-Minister of Finance issued several decrees in August 2004, which bring up to date existing decrees published in 2001, with adjustments and improvements in the rules for obtaining advance certainty. These 2004 decrees provide more clarity regarding how the fiscal rules within the APA/Advance Tax Ruling (ATR) practice should function. Furthermore, one decree clarifies how the Dutch tax authorities will treat certain issues regarding the application of the arm's length principle. The decrees provide the formal position of the Dutch tax authority, but do not legally bind the taxpayer.

The eight decrees published are:

- APA decree, IFZ2004/124M
- ATR decree, IFZ2004/125M
- Decree regarding financial service activities, IFZ2004/126M
- Questions and answers on the decree regarding service entities and grand-father regime ruling policy, IFZ2004/127M
- Decree on advance certainty and good faith versus treaty partners, DGB2004/1337M
- Decree on APAs, advance tax rulings (atrs), financial services entities, interposed holdings, contact point potential foreign investors, organization and competency rules, DGB2004/1338M
- Implementation decree regarding the Coordination Group Transfer Pricing, DGB2004/1339M
- Adjustments to the transfer pricing decree of 30 March 2001, application of the arm's length principle and the OECD guidelines, IFZ2004/680M

OECD guidelines treatment

The Dutch tax authority in general follows the OECD guidelines. Further guidance regarding the interpretation and application of the arm's length principle is provided by the Dutch transfer pricing decrees (as published by the Under-Minister of Finance in the decree of 30 March 2001, updated with the decree of 21 August 2004). According to these decrees, the OECD guidelines leave room for interpretation or require clarification on several issues. The goal of these decrees is to provide insight into the position of the Dutch tax authority regarding these issues. The transfer pricing decree of August 2004 is an excellent source for transfer pricing guidance. It provides specific guidance on intra-group services and shareholder activities, support services, contract research, cost contribution ar-

¶20,040

rangements, arm's length price determination when the value at the time of the transaction is uncertain and other topics. With respect to business restructuring no specific guidance has been issued to date but as already noted the Dutch tax authority in general follows the OECD guidance in this respect.

Priorities/pricing methods

There is no "best method" rule. Taxpayers are in principle free to choose any OECD transfer pricing method as long as the method chosen results in arm's length pricing for the transaction. Taxpayers are not obligated to test all the methods, though they must substantiate the method chosen. The Dutch tax authority prefers traditional transaction methods over transactional profit methods.

Transfer pricing penalties

The lack of transfer pricing documentation will shift the burden of proof regarding the arm's length nature of the transfer prices used to the taxpayer.

During the parliamentary discussions regarding the introduction of the arm's length principle and transfer pricing documentation requirements (i.e., Article 8b) into the Dutch Corporate Income Tax Act, a question was raised regarding the Dutch policy in connection with the levying of administrative penalties in case of a transfer price adjustment. The Dutch Under-Minister of Finance declared that in case of transfer price adjustments the levy of an administrative penalty under the circumstance of an incorrect income tax return should be limited to cases in which it is plausible that the agreed transfer price is not regarded as arm's length as a result of a pure intentional act. Therefore, an administrative penalty will not be imposed even in the case of gross negligence or conditional intentional act according to this policy announcement.

In case of a pure intentional act as set forth above, the tax may be increased with a maximum penalty of 100% of the (additional) tax due, plus interest.

Penalty relief

It is unlikely that there will be transfer pricing-related tax penalties if there is proper transfer pricing documentation available by the taxpayer and the documentation at hand adequately substantiates the arm's length nature of the intercompany transactions undertaken by the taxpayer.

Documentation requirements

Taxpayers are obliged to prepare documentation that describes how the transfer prices have been established and which must be included in the accounting records. Furthermore, the documentation needs to include sufficient information that would enable the Dutch tax authority to evaluate the arm's length nature of the transfer prices applied between associated enterprises. The parliamentary explanations to Article 8b do not describe an exhaustive list of information that should be documented.

¶20,040

The transfer pricing documentation could consist of the following elements:

- Information about the associated enterprises involved
- Information on the intercompany transactions between these associated enterprises
- A comparability analysis, describing the five comparability factors as set forth in Chapter I of the OECD guidelines
- A substantiation of the choice of the transfer pricing method applied
- A substantiation of the transfer price charged
- Other documents, such as management accounts, budgets and minutes of shareholder and board meetings

Documentation deadlines

Documentation is generally expected to be available at the time when the taxpayer enters into a transaction. This has been communicated by the Dutch Ministry of Finance. However, if the transfer pricing documentation is not available upon the request of the Dutch tax authority, taxpayers are granted a minimum time frame of four weeks to prepare the documentation. This period may be extended to a maximum of three months depending on the complexity of the intercompany transactions in which the taxpayer is engaged.

Statute of limitations on transfer pricing assessments

The statute of limitations on transfer pricing assessments is the same as the statute of limitations on tax assessments (as covered by the General Tax Act). The statute of limitations for making an assessment is three years from the end of the fiscal year. If the tax inspector has granted an extension for filing the tax return, the assessment period is extended with the period of extension. An additional assessment must be made within a period of five years, starting from the end of the fiscal year (this period will also be extended with the possible period of the filing extension). With respect to foreign-source income, the period for making an additional assessment is 12 years. For the tax authority to be able to impose such an additional assessment, there needs to be a new fact which the Dutch tax authority did not know or could reasonably not have known upon the moment of imposing the initial tax assessment (unless the taxpayer did not act in good faith).

Return disclosures/related-party disclosures

Dutch corporate income taxpayers are required to confirm in the corporate income tax return (by checking a separate box) whether they have been involved in related-party transactions during the fiscal year. The related-party transactions need to be specified in a separate appendix to the Dutch corporate income tax return.

Audit risk/transfer pricing scrutiny

The risk of transfer pricing issues being scrutinized during a tax authority audit is high and consequently the controversy risk is high as well. Transfer pricing is a key issue in any tax audit, and many companies are subject to separate transfer pricing audits. A functional analysis is incorporated into many of these audits and forms the basis of transfer pricing risk analyses of taxpayers. The tax authority has,

¶20,040

among others, shown interest in performing head office audits (which include intra-group services and other activities performed by the head office) and characterizations in terms of alignment of functions and risks. Next to head office activities intangibles transactions are being evaluated, as well as business reorganizations. The Dutch tax authority has also focused, as a natural result of the risk analyses, on transactions with entities located in low effective tax rate countries.

APA opportunity

Unilateral, bilateral and multilateral APAs with rollback features are available. The APA process currently operates well in the Netherlands, despite earlier criticism regarding the uncertainty of obtaining APAs for financial service entities (see below). Pre-filing meetings with taxpayers to discuss the case before a formal APA request is made, support for small taxpayer APAs and case management plans have been introduced and processing time has been reduced.

Financial services entities consist of both financing (mere receipt and payment of intercompany interest) and licensing (mere receipt and payment of intercompany royalties) companies. For license companies, the first APA under the new regime was granted by the Dutch tax authority in 2005. For finance companies, the APA process had been functioning successfully for a number of years already by 2005. A number of substantial improvements for Dutch financial services entities were introduced in 2005, which mainly relate to a reduction in the applicable transfer pricing documentation requirements.

Mutual agreement procedure

On 29 September 2008 a decree (IFZ2008/248M) describing the Mutual Agreement Procedure (MAP) process under bilateral treaties and the EU arbitration convention has been published. The decree aligns the MAP process in the Netherlands with the OECD Memorandum on Effective Mutual Agreement Procedures (MEMAP) making the route to obtaining avoidance of double taxation more accessible and transparent for taxpayers. Key features of the new Decree are: formal introduction of an Accelerated Competent Authority Procedure (ACAP); endorsement of arbitration to resolve MAP cases; targeting a reduction of MAP related expenses; introducing transparency into the process by providing regular feedback and updates to the taxpayer; encouraging use of Article 9(2) of the OECD Model Convention; commitment to tackle resolution of double taxation in cases "not provided for in the Convention" (Article 25(3) of the OECD Model Convention) in addition to the more traditional double taxation cases.

New Zealand

Taxing authority and tax law

The taxing authority in New Zealand is the Inland Revenue Department (IRD). Sections YD 5, GB 2 and GC 6 to GC 14 of the Income Tax Act 2007. New Zealand's double tax agreements are also relevant tax laws in New Zealand.

Relevant regulations and rulings

The final version of Transfer Pricing Guidelines issued in October 2000.

OECD guidelines treatment

The IRD fully endorses the positions set out in chapters one to eight of the OECD guidelines and proposes to follow those positions in administering New Zealand's transfer pricing rules. Consequently, New Zealand's guidelines should be read as supplementing the OECD guidelines, rather than superseding them. This applies for the domestic application of the New Zealand rules, as well as in relation to issues raised under New Zealand's double tax agreements. On business restructuring, IRD's approach seems to be largely in line with the recently published OECD paper. The IRD are cognisant of the fact that multinational enterprises undergo restructuring activities during the course of their existence and lifecycle. In addressing the restructuring issues, IRD will be seeking to ensure that there is a commercial case for effecting any restructure and that the economic substance aligns with the legal form of the arrangement. The IRD has released some high-level guidance in the form of the following ten questions that should be addressed by companies undertaking cross-border business restructures. These questions aim to help ascertain the commercial viability of the restructuring.

Priorities/pricing methods

The IRD accepts the most reliable method chosen from CUP, Resale Price, Cost Plus, Profit Split and CPM (TNMM).

Transfer pricing penalties

Penalties are imposed under § 141A-K of the Tax Administration Act 1994: 20% penalty for not taking reasonable care, 20% penalty for an unacceptable tax position, 40% penalty for gross carelessness, 100% penalty for an abusive tax position and 150% penalty for an evasive or similar act.

Penalty relief

Shortfall penalties may be reduced upon voluntary disclosure to the Commissioner of the details of the shortfall. If the disclosure occurs before notification of an investigation, the penalty may be reduced by 100% (only for lack of reasonable care or unacceptable tax position categories) or 75% for other shortfall penalties. If disclosure occurs after notification of an investigation, but before the investigation commences, the penalty may be reduced by 40%. Shortfall penalties may be reduced by a further 50% if a taxpayer has a past record of "good behavior."

¶20,040

Documentation requirements

There are no explicit requirements in New Zealand's transfer pricing legislation (§ GC 6 to GC 14 of the Income Tax Act 2007) for any particular category of information to be included in transfer pricing documentation. Section GC 13 requires taxpayers to select and apply an appropriate transfer pricing method for tax return purposes. The New Zealand Transfer Pricing Guidelines indicate that a taxpayer's main purpose in preparing and maintaining documentation should be to place the taxpayer in the position where they can readily demonstrate to the IRD that a transfer pricing method has been used to determine whether the taxpayer's transfer prices are consistent with the arm's length principle in light of the facts and circumstances.

Documentation deadlines

There is no express legislative requirement for a taxpayer to document its transfer pricing policies and practices in New Zealand. However, the New Zealand Transfer Pricing Guidelines indicate that taxpayers who prepare and maintain transfer pricing documentation are more likely to ensure the burden of proof (that prices are not arm's length) remains with the Commissioner.

Statute of limitations on transfer pricing assessments

The Commissioner's power to issue amended assessments is subject to a four-year time limit. A taxpayer has the ability to extend the applicable time bar by up to an additional six months by signing a waiver, which generally arises when a dispute is not resolved, and more time would allow completion of the dispute process by mutual agreement of both parties or where another case before the court is likely to resolve the issue in current dispute.

Return disclosures/related-party disclosures

A company's income tax return requires disclosure of:

- Payments to non-residents such as dividends, interest, management fees, "know-how" payments, royalties or contract payments made
- Whether the company is controlled or owned by non-residents
- Whether the company holds an interest in a controlled foreign company

Audit risk/transfer pricing scrutiny

The risk of transfer pricing scrutiny during a tax audit is high. Risk Assessment Review questionnaires relating to transfer pricing and thin capitalization are typically issued to companies during general income tax audits or risk reviews and as part of the IRD's specific transfer pricing review process. The IRD also uses questionnaires in respect of interest, guarantee fees and royalties. In addition, there is a separate transfer pricing questionnaire for branches.

APA opportunity

Section 91E of the Tax Administration Act 1994 allows a unilateral APA to be issued in the form of a binding ruling. Bilateral or multilateral APAs may be entered into pursuant to New Zealand's double tax agreements under the mutual agreement

¶20,040

procedure provisions. The IRD has not established any formal guidelines for APAs, as each case is considered to be different, depending on a taxpayer's specific facts and circumstances. The IRD has suggested pre-application conferences to make the APA application process less time consuming.

NORWAY

Taxing authority and tax law

The Norwegian Tax Authority (NTA) is the taxing authority. The arm's length principle is stated in § 13-1 of the General Taxation Act, and the transfer pricing filing and documentation requirements are stated in the Tax Administration Act § 4-12.

Relevant regulations and rulings

In June 2007, the Norwegian Parliament adopted new transfer pricing regulations. The requirements became effective as of January 2008. The requirements entail that all companies subject to the requirements are to submit a form with the tax return, outlining the extent of the company's transactions with related parties.

While there have not been legal documentation requirements as such previously, Norwegian taxpayers have for a long time been required to provide extensive information and documentation to the tax authorities on their request.

OECD guidelines treatment

The NTA has a long history of following the OECD Transfer Pricing Guidelines. The Norwegian regulations follow OECD principles, and documentation prepared in line with the OECD guidelines will generally meet the Norwegian requirements.

The Norwegian General Tax Act § 13-1 gives the OECD guidelines a strong and formal status under Norwegian tax law. However, OECD chap. IV (Administrative Approaches to Avoiding and Resolving Transfer Pricing Disputes) and chap. V (Documentation) are not included. The status of the OECD guidelines is limited to that of guidance, and they do not constitute binding rules.

We have also seen that the principles outlined in the OECD Discussion Draft on the Transfer Pricing Aspects of Business Restructurings are already being applied by the NTA. Recent tax audits and court cases have shown that although the discussion draft is not part of Norwegian legislation, the principles described in the draft are applied in practice.

Priorities/pricing methods

The OECD pricing methods are accepted by the NTA. The traditional transaction methods (CUP, RPM and Cost Plus) are generally preferred to the transactional profit methods (TNMM and Profit Split). There seems to be increasing support for the applicability of the profit methods under certain circumstances.

There is no specified priority under Norwegian tax law, but reference is often made to the OECD hierarchy. As stated by the Norwegian Supreme Court, the Norwegian General Tax Act § 13-1 allows for the use of several transfer pricing methods, including methods not described by the OECD guidelines, provided those methods will provide arm's length results.

¶20,040

Transfer pricing penalties

Transfer pricing penalties (surtax) is 30% of the tax adjustments, provided that the tax authorities conclude that incomplete or incorrect information has been provided by the tax payer. If complete and correct information has been provided, no penalty will be imposed. In case of gross negligence, a surtax of up to 60% may be levied. However, the normal surtax rate is 30%. Additionally, a non-deductible interest charge will apply per year.

Failure to comply with the filing requirement (described below) will carry the same penalties and risk as failure to complete the annual tax return. The same is applicable if the documentation is not submitted by the deadline.

Penalty relief

A 30% penalty is normal; however, the risk of a penalty being imposed may be reduced if proper documentation has been prepared.

Disclosure in the tax return may in principle relieve penalties, as the tax authorities will then have been informed and may further investigate the transfer pricing case. The application of penalties is, however, becoming increasingly common.

Documentation requirements

The Norwegian transfer pricing requirements consist of two specific parts: filing and documentation requirements.

The filing requirement is an attachment to the annual tax return (Form RF-1123), which includes a listing of all intercompany transactions. The form will serve as a basis for the NTA when targeting transfer pricing tax audits. The filing requirements are applicable for all transactions reported in the tax return.

In addition, covered taxpayers are obliged to prepare transfer pricing documentation that describes how the transfer prices have been established between associated enterprises. The documentation needs to include sufficient information that would enable the NTA to evaluate the arm's length nature of the transfer prices applied between associated enterprises. Both cross-border and domestic transactions are covered.

Documentation deadlines

The transfer pricing documentation must be submitted within 45 days after a request by the NTA. All documentation must be retained for 10 years.

Statute of limitations on transfer pricing assessments

The general statute of limitations for tax assessments in Norway states that issues regarding the tax return cannot be raised more than 10 years after the end of the income year. Transfer pricing documentation must therefore be retained and stored for at least 10 years.

The deadline is three years for changes of the tax return based on the tax authority's discretionary assessments, or the interpretation of the tax legislation, if the tax return filed is correct and complete.

¶20,040

The statute of limitations is two years if any tax adjustment is against the taxpayer, provided the taxpayer has not given incorrect or incomplete information to the tax authority.

Return disclosures/related-party disclosures

The filing requirement is an attachment to the annual tax return (Form RF-1123) that includes a statement of all intercompany transactions. The form serves as a basis for the NTA when targeting transfer pricing tax audits.

Audit risk/transfer pricing scrutiny

The risk of transfer pricing issues being reviewed during an audit is high. The tax authority has a strong focus on intercompany transactions and has established an in-house transfer pricing network where the major tax offices, including the Directorate of Taxes, are members. The introduction of the 2007 transfer pricing documentation and filing requirements exemplifies the increased transfer pricing focus. The NTA has launched a transfer pricing audit campaign against Tax Effective Supply Chain Management (TESCM) conversions, and the first cases have been brought to court. Situations especially targeted by the tax authority are limited risk distributors or commissionaires with low margins and those that have recently experienced reduction in margins.

In addition, the transfer pricing of intangible property and finance - related transfer pricing (loans etc.) is expected to be a focus area for the NTA going forward.

APA opportunity

APAs on transfer pricing assessments are currently unavailable. There is one exemption for the transfer pricing on the sale of gas under the Norwegian Petroleum Tax Act.

¶20,040

PERU

Taxing authority and tax law

Superintendencia Nacional de Administración Tributaria (SUNAT); Article 32, Item 4 and 32-A of the Peruvian Income Tax Law (PITL).

Relevant regulations and rulings

Transfer pricing regulations were in force as of 1 January 2001 (Article 32 of PITL). Subsequently, Legislative Decree 945 and Legislative Decree 953 introduced transfer pricing amendments into the PITL and tax code, which were in force as of fiscal year 2004. The regulations are detailed in Article 24 and Chapter XIX (Articles 108 to 119) of the Peruvian Income Tax Regulations.

The transfer pricing rules will be applicable solely when the valuation agreed by the parties determines an income tax lower than the one it would have been calculated if the market value would have been considered. To this effect, the Regulations consider that a lower income tax is also determined when: i) the deferral of income is detected, or ii) the calculation of higher tax losses than the ones that would have corresponded.

In addition, the transfer pricing rules apply both to cross-border and domestic transactions between related parties. Moreover, all transactions with tax haven residents are considered to be with related parties. Thus, they are subject to the transfer pricing regulations.

In the case of domestic transactions, they must be considered not only for income tax purposes but also for VAT and excise tax.

OECD guidelines treatment

The PITL refers to the OECD guidelines as a source of interpretation for transfer pricing analysis as long as they do not contradict the PITL.

Priorities/pricing methods

Peruvian law implicitly adopts a best-method rule. Under Peruvian legislation, the transfer pricing methods identified are CUP, Resale Price, Cost Plus, Profit Split, the Residual Profit Split and Transactional Net Margin Method.

Transfer pricing penalties

Non-compliance with the obligation to present a transfer pricing technical study, or documentation and information supporting the calculation of the prices agreed on in transactions with related parties, is penalized with a fine of 0.6% of the company's net income of the year before that under scrutiny. The penalty cannot be less than 10% of a Tax Unit, nor more than 25 Tax Units (one Tax Unit is equivalent to approximately USD 1,200).

Likewise, non-compliance with the obligation to file the transfer pricing return according to the dates established by SUNAT is subject to a fine of 0.6% of the company's net income of the year before that under scrutiny. The penalty cannot be less than 10% of a Tax Unit nor more than 25 Tax Units.

¶20,040

The adjustments to annual taxable income resulting from the tax authority's application of the transfer pricing provisions will be subject to additional penalties that may be up to 50% of the resulting tax deficiency (income misstatement penalties).

Penalty relief

The penalty reductions that a taxpayer can be subject to for not complying with the obligations of having a transfer pricing technical study or presenting the transfer pricing informative return are the following:

- 80% penalty reduction if the taxpayer rectifies the infraction and pays the corresponding fine within the time established by SUNA.

- 50% penalty reduction if the taxpayer rectifies the infraction but does not pay the corresponding fine within the time established by the SUNA.

- 100% penalty reduction if the taxpayer files the transfer pricing informative return after the due date but before it is detected and compelled to do so by SUNA.

Documentation requirements

Since 2006, taxpayers are compelled to keep a transfer pricing study if they fall within the scope of the transfer pricing rules contained in Article 32-A of the PITL and if they meet any of the following conditions:

- The company's income exceeds PEN 6m and the amount of its intercompany transactions exceeds PEN 1m.

- The company has been engaged in transactions from, to or through a low-tax jurisdiction.

Documentation deadlines

There is no deadline to present the transfer pricing study to the tax authority. Nevertheless, as provided in Resolution N° 167-2006-SUNAT, the tax authority can request a transfer pricing study from taxpayers once the fiscal year is closed.

According to the tax regulations published in 2009, the deadline for filing the transfer pricing return for the fiscal year 2008 to the tax authority was from 9 to 26 October 2009, depending on the last digit of the tax identification number of the company. It is expected that the deadlines to file transfer pricing returns in the future will be during similar dates.

Statute of limitations on transfer pricing assessments

According to Articles 87-7 and 43 of the Peruvian Tax Code, the statute of limitations on income tax assessments is four years after 1 January of the year that follows the year the annual income tax return is due (generally, 31 March) and six years for returns that were never filed.

Return disclosures/related-party disclosures

The main aspects to be disclosed in the transfer pricing information return are the amount of the transactions, the transfer pricing method selected, the related

¶20,040

party with whom the transactions were made and the amount of the adjustments, among others.

Audit risk/transfer pricing scrutiny

The risk of transfer pricing issues being reviewed under a tax audit is moderate. The Peruvian Tax Administration has not yet initiated any tax audits regarding transfer pricing issues. Nevertheless, transfer pricing technical studies are being requested by SUNAT during fiscal audits.

APA opportunity

APAs are available for cross-border transactions only.

POLAND

Taxing authority and tax law

Corporate Income Tax Act dated 15 February 1992 (CIT Act), Articles 9a, 11 and 19 § 4 (Journal of Laws No. 21, item 86) Personal Income Tax Act dated 26 July 1991 (PIT Act) Articles 25, 25a and 30d (Journal of Laws No. 80, item 350); Tax Ordinance Act dated 29 August 1997, Articles 20a-20r (Journal of Laws No. 137, item 926); Ministry of Finance Decree of 16 May 2005, on the countries and territories applying harmful tax competition rules (Journal of Laws No. 94, item 791); Ministry of Finance Decree of 10 September 2009, on the method and procedure for assessing taxpayers' income by estimating the prices in transactions conducted by these taxpayers, and on the method and procedure for eliminating double taxation of taxpayers in case of related parties' income adjustment (Journal of Laws No. 160, item 1268).

Relevant regulations and rulings

Article 11 of CIT Act and Article 25 of PIT Act introduce the arm's length principle, providing a definition of affiliation and criteria for the determination of the size of direct and indirect shares held in another entity. Documentation requirements can be found in Article 9a of the CIT Act and Article 25a of the PIT Act. Transfer pricing penalties are defined in Article 19 section 4 of the CIT Act and Article 30d of the PIT Act.

Article 9a of the CIT Act and Article 25a of the PIT Act provide detailed information on transactions which are subject to documentation requirements, including value limits and categories of such transactions.

According to Articles 9a of the CIT Act and 25a of the PIT Act, the documentation requirements also encompass transactions in which payment is made directly or indirectly to an entity in a territory or country considered to be a tax haven. The list of these territories and countries is presented in the Ministry of Finance Decree of 16 May 2005, on the countries and territories applying harmful tax competition rules. The Decree was issued separately for personal and corporate taxation purposes.

As of 1 January 2007, documentation requirements apply also to permanent establishments (based in Poland) of foreign companies.

The pricing methods recognized by the tax authority are described in the Ministry of Finance Decree of 10 September 2009. This Decree replaces the one dated October 1997 where the major changes concern redefinition of selected TP methods (more precise description) and introduction of the corresponding adjustment procedure (based on the OECD guidelines, Arbitration Convention and Code of Conduct for Arbitration Convention and the revised Polish corporate income tax act, i.e. as of 1 January 2009). Provisions of the Decree apply also to Polish permanent establishments of the foreign companies and foreign permanent establishments of the Polish taxpayers.

The APA regulations are specified in Articles 20a-20r of the Tax Ordinance Act. Introduction of APAs has brought with it special reporting requirements. According

¶20,040

to the Ministry of Finance Decree of 31 May 2006, taxpayers who have agreed to an APA must submit together with their annual CIT return a progress report on the implementation of the method stipulated in the APA decision. APA may also be concluded by permanent establishments of foreign companies in Poland as well as permanent establishments of Polish taxpayers, based abroad.

OECD guidelines treatment

The Polish transfer pricing regulations do not refer to the OECD guidelines directly. Reference to the OECD guidelines is made with respect to the topic of tax havens. According to Article 9a section 6 of the CIT Act (Article 25a section 6 of the PIT Act), the list of countries recognized as tax havens is issued with regard to settlements made by the OECD. At the same time, the transfer pricing methods presented in the Polish rules are based on the OECD approach. There are no specific rules regarding the business restructuring issues in the Polish transfer pricing law. The OECD business restructuring report should, however, be an indication for the Polish tax authorities when verifying the restructuring cases in Poland.

Priorities/pricing methods

Generally, the transfer pricing methods accepted by the tax authority are based on the OECD guidelines. These methods are: CUP, Resale Price, Cost Plus, Profit Split and TNMM. The transactional methods are preferred. When the transfer price is determined by the tax authority, the application of CUP method is verified in the first instance.

If a taxpayer has determined the arm's length value of a transaction by applying one of the three accepted transactional methods (CUP, Resale Price and Profit Split), and there is no doubt about the objectivity in choosing the method, the method is also binding on the tax authority.

Transfer pricing penalties

Taxpayers face a 50% penalty tax rate for income assessed by the tax authority (instead of the standard tax rates).

Penalty relief

The penalty rate can be reduced to the normal tax rate only if the taxpayer provides the required documentation in due time as specified by the tax authority (7 days on request).

Documentation requirements

Taxpayers carrying out transactions with related parties and permanent establishments of foreign companies functioning in Poland, as defined in the Polish CIT and PIT Acts, are obliged to prepare tax documentation. Requirements for such transactions apply where the total transaction amount in a tax year exceeds the following limits:

- EUR 100,000, if the transaction value does not exceed 20% of the share capital

¶20,040

- EUR 30,000, if the transaction refers to services or intangibles
- EUR 50,000, for other types of transaction between related entities

Taxpayers carrying out transactions in which payments are made directly or indirectly to an entity in a territory or country recognized as a tax haven are obliged to prepare tax documentation for such transactions when the total transaction amounts in a tax year exceed EUR 20,000.

As there is no required specific form for transfer pricing documentation, the CIT and PIT regulations instead determine the extent of the documentation. The statutory transfer pricing documentation should cover at least the following elements:

- Functions performed by the parties to the transaction (with the consideration of assets employed and risks borne)
- Expected transactional costs and the method and payment due dates
- Method and manner of calculating profits and the transaction value
- Business strategy, if it influenced the transaction value
- Other factors influencing the transaction value
- Expected benefits from intangible performances or services — this element applies only to the purchase of intangibles or services

These elements are mandatory, so if the documentation prepared does not meet one of these requirements, such documentation may be disregarded by the tax authority.

In addition, the statutory Polish transfer pricing documentation should be prepared and if requested, provided to the tax authorities in Polish.

Documentation deadlines

There is no deadline for preparing the transfer pricing documentation; however, taxpayers are obliged to submit the documentation within seven days of the tax authority's request.

Statute of limitations on transfer pricing assessments

There are no special time limit provisions applicable to intercompany transactions. The general regime of the statute of limitations applies in accordance with the Tax Ordinance Act. According to Article 70, § 1 of the Tax Ordinance Act, the assessment period for tax is five years from assessment to the end of the calendar year in which the tax fell due.

Return disclosures/related-party disclosures

Information about related-party transactions is one of the elements of the annual income tax return. The taxpayer is required to indicate in the return whether it was obliged to prepare transfer pricing documentation or not.

Taxpayers who have concluded APAs must enclose, with their annual tax returns, a special report on the implementation of the transaction method chosen. The form of this report is given in the Ministry of Finance Decree of 31 May 2006.

¶20,040

Definition of related parties

Polish regulations recognize related entities in the following situations:

- The domestic entity participates directly or indirectly in managing or controlling the foreign entity or has a share in its capital

- The foreign entity participates directly or indirectly in managing or controlling a domestic entity or has a share in its capital

- The same legal and natural persons participate directly or indirectly at the same time in managing or controlling a domestic entity and foreign entity or have shares in their capital

- The domestic entity participates directly or indirectly in the managing or controlling of another domestic entity or has a share in its capital

- The same legal and natural persons participate at the same time directly or indirectly in managing or controlling domestic entities or have shares in their capital

Capital relations exist if one of the entities or contracting parties holds in the capital of the other entity, directly or indirectly, at least a 5% share. Domestic entities are also considered related for tax purposes by virtue of family, property or employment relations between them or between their management, supervision or control personnel, or if the same person carries out management, supervision or control functions in both these entities.

If the parties to a transaction, due to their relationship, agree or impose terms and conditions which differ from those that would be agreed to by unrelated parties, and as a result of these terms and conditions a domestic entity does not report income from the transaction or reports income that is lower than would be expected if the connection did not exist, the tax authorities may assess additional income and determine the tax due on such income for the domestic entity.

The above rules also apply to the allocation of taxable profit to the permanent establishment of a foreign entity in Poland and to Polish taxpayers carrying out transactions with their permanent establishments abroad.

Domestic entities transacting with foreign related parties are allowed to adjust their income if the foreign tax authorities question the transactional prices as not meeting the arm's length principle and, consequently, additional income for the foreign entity is assessed and the tax due on such income is determined (the so-called "corresponding adjustment"). Prerequisites of making the adjustment must however be justified and accepted by the tax authorities.

Adjustments to the domestic entities' income will be allowed as long as the agreement on the avoidance of double taxation between Poland and the country (i.e. country of the domestic entity's related party) will provide for the opportunity to do so. An application regarding such adjustments should be filed within three years since receiving the decision on assessing the additional income of the contracting party.

In addition, regulations relating to income adjustment apply also to permanent establishment.

¶20,040

Analogous elimination of double taxation is not allowed by Polish regulations in case of domestic related transactions.

Audit risk/transfer pricing scrutiny

The number of transfer pricing audits has steadily increased and the risk is growing. The risk of scrutiny and a very detailed approach of the tax authorities during transfer pricing audit and consequently a tax assessment are high. While the acceptance of OECD guidelines and international practices has increased, the local approach tends to prevail during audits. Local benchmarks are preferred over pan-European ones. The pricing information from cross controls in the industry is used for benchmarking. Internal third-party transactions are used as a comparison for application of the CUP method, which is preferred by tax authorities. Moreover, Polish tax authorities have increased cooperation in the exchange of information with other countries.

The compliance regime is still rigorous in Poland. The court rulings focus mainly on legal rather than economic issues. The most frequently audited types of transactions are limited risk structures such as limited risk distributors or contract manufacturers, immaterial services (including cost-sharing arrangements) and loans.

APA opportunity

The APA regulations came into force on 1 January 2006. The APA procedures are described in Articles 20a-20r of the Tax Ordinance Act. An APA concluded for a particular transaction is binding on the tax authority with regard to the method selected by the taxpayer. APAs in Poland may apply to transactions that have not yet been executed or transactions that are in progress at the time the taxpayer submits an application for an APA. Under the Polish rules, three types of APAs are available:

- Unilateral Agreement: This type of APA is defined in the Tax Ordinance Act as an agreement on the method of setting transfer prices between:
  - Two domestic entities - those without foreign capital links
  - A domestic entity and its related foreign party
  - A domestic entity related to a foreign entity and another domestic entity related to the same foreign entity
- Bilateral Agreement: This is an agreement concerning cross-border transactions which can be given by the Polish Ministry of Finance upon the request of a domestic entity, but only after consultations and upon obtaining consent issued by the tax authority of the related foreign entity
- Multilateral Agreement: If the agreement concerns a transaction concluded by a domestic entity with foreign entities from more than one country, in order to conclude such an agreement, the consents of all foreign entities' tax authorities are required

There are no transaction value limits to be covered by the APAs. In order to submit an application for an APA, the taxpayer must pay a fee which is usually 1% of the transaction value. However, the Tax Ordinance Act sets the following fee limits:

¶20,040

- Unilateral APA — fee cannot be lower than PLN 5,000 and cannot exceed PLN 50,000
- Unilateral APA concerning a foreign entity — fee cannot be lower than PLN 20,000 and cannot exceed PLN 100,000
- Bilateral or multilateral APA — fee cannot be lower than PLN 50,000 and cannot exceed PLN 200,000

The mandatory elements of an APA application are:

- The suggested method for determining prices and an indication of the pricing method recognized by the tax authority
- A description of the manner of application of the suggested method, with an indication of the principles for price calculation, forecasts and analyses on which the calculation is based
- A description of the circumstances which may affect the prices
- The documents which may determine the transaction price (agreements, arrangements and other documents indicating the intentions of the parties to the transaction)

The suggested length of the APA arrangement

- A list of entities with whom the transaction will be concluded, including their agreement to submit to the tax authority all documents and provide necessary explanations with regard to the relevant transaction
- The application must be submitted in the Polish language

The Tax Ordinance Act precisely defines the terms under which the APA procedure is to be completed:

- The unilateral APA must be issued without unnecessary delay within six months of the start of the APA application procedure
- The bilateral APA must be issued without unnecessary delay within 12 months of the start of the APA application procedure
- The multilateral APA must be issued without unnecessary delay within 18 months of the start of the APA application procedure

The APA is issued by the Ministry of Finance in the form of an administrative decision and the general administrative procedure resulting from the Tax Ordinance Act applies to the APA. In consequence, the above time limits for the APA procedure may be extended if necessary.

The period for which the APA may be concluded must be no longer than five years. The APA may be extended for another five years if the criteria applied in concluding the APA have not changed or the entity applies for an extension of the APA not later than six months before it expires. The decision is valid from the date of its delivery to all parties (including the Polish and foreign - if applicable -tax authorities).

¶20,040

PORTUGAL

Taxing authority and tax law

Article 58 of the Corporate Income Tax Code tax authority.

Relevant regulations and rulings

Administrative Decree 1446-C/2001 of 21 December 2001.

OECD guidelines treatment

The Portuguese tax authority recognizes both the transactional and profit-based methods in the OECD Transfer Pricing Guidelines.

Theoretically, any method is acceptable provided that it can be justified and that the traditional transactional or profit-based methods are not applicable.

Priorities/pricing methods

The transfer pricing methods described in the Portuguese legislation are based on the OECD guidelines and, thus, do not introduce significant changes to the widely accepted methods recognized among transfer pricing administrators and practitioners. However, the Portuguese rules also state (paragraphs 1 and 2 of Article 4 of the transfer pricing Ministerial Order) that the most appropriate method should be applied to a controlled transaction or to a series of transactions in order to determine whether those transactions comply with the arm's length principle.

This principle reflects a best method rule. This means that a taxpayer is expected to use the method or methods most suitable to each case, thus explaining not only the reason why a certain method is considered as the most appropriate to test whether the controlled transactions comply with the transfer pricing rules, but also why other methods are rejected.

Transfer pricing penalties

Transfer pricing adjustments are subject to the general tax penalty regime and, thus, are subject to withholding, late payment and bad-faith penalty provisions. Penalties for non-compliance with mandatory contemporaneous documentation rules may reach EUR 100,000 per year and per company. A late payment interest penalty is also applicable for transfer pricing adjustments at the rate of 4% per year. Failure to comply with documentation requirements may result in the application of secret comparables.

Penalty relief

The general tax penalty regime applies.

Documentation requirements

The Portuguese transfer pricing rules require taxpayers with a turnover and other income in excess of EUR 3m in the prior year to prepare contemporaneous documentation in the Portuguese language, which should provide evidence of market parity regarding the terms and conditions agreed, accepted and practiced in the operations made with related parties, as well as the selection and utilization of

¶20,040

the best method. The regulations divide the documentation between relevant, supporting documentation and that which is applicable to cost contribution arrangements and intra-group services.

The transfer pricing documentation should include:

- Related-party status, according to the definition presented in Article 58 of the Corporate Income Tax Code (a company subject to a substantially favorable tax regime or included in the Portuguese offshore blacklist is considered to be a related party, independent of other related-party criteria)
- Characterization of the taxpayer's activity and that of the related parties with whom it engages in commercial transactions
- Identification of all intercompany transactions
- The volumes, terms and conditions of the transactions for the past three years
- The counter parties to the transactions
- A functional analysis for each relevant transaction
- Technical studies focusing on essential areas of business
- A description of the method used and demonstration of how the prices are calculated
- Information about Portuguese comparables (geographical comparability requirement)
- The legal entity organization structure
- A description of the activities
- All intercompany contractual agreements and unrelated-party agreements

Documentation deadlines

For companies adopting the calendar year for tax purposes, the documentation must be prepared by the last day of June of the year following the one which it concerns or six months after the corresponding tax year end for those not using the calendar year.

All Portuguese-based companies have a statutory obligation to keep available and in good order their tax documentation file for the relevant year for a 10-year period. It must be kept at the Portuguese establishment or premises and should be prepared by the last working day of the six-month period following the tax year end. However, the tax authorities may, and do, ask for documentation on transactions at any time after they take place.

Statute of limitations on transfer pricing assessments

Assessment is possible during the four years after the end of the assessment year. The transfer pricing documentation must be kept by the taxpayer for 10 years.

Return disclosures/related-party disclosures

The main disclosure requirements at this level are contained in annexes A, B, C and H (transfer pricing annexes) of the annual declaration. The deadline for

¶20,040

submission is the same as for the annual documentation. Taxpayers have to state in good faith in the annual declaration whether they have complied with the contemporaneous documentation requirements. Criminal ramifications may result in the case of misleading information.

Audit risk/transfer pricing scrutiny

Since January 2004, entities resident in blacklisted offshore countries or territories are deemed related parties for transfer pricing purposes. Additionally, in 2007, the Portuguese tax authority began making positive adjustments to taxpayers' taxable profits as a result of tax audits. These adjustments are based on a benchmark computed with the financial information of an internal database called MGIT.

In respect to the comparables analysis performed by the tax authority, the following issues are relevant:

- Entities with a recurrent loss situation are excluded from the comparables final sample
- Comparables identification is not disclosed in the final sample
- A transaction is considered arm's length only if within the computed interquartile range
- Only the median of the interquartile range of the benchmark is considered when the tax adjustments are made

More recently special emphasis is being put on the quality of comparables, namely on royalty CUP analysis. Head-office interest charged to branches is the most recent area of scrutiny and adjustments.

APA opportunity

An APA program was included in the Portuguese corporate income tax code in 2008. Taxpayers are now allowed to negotiate clearance for a period of three years regarding a transaction with transfer pricing implications.

ROMANIA

Taxing authority and tax law

Ministry of Finance — National Agency for Fiscal Administration (ANAF). Law 571/2003 regarding the Fiscal Code as subsequently completed and amended. Government Decision 44/2004 for the approval of the Norms for the application of Law 571/2003 regarding the Fiscal Code, as subsequently completed and amended.

Relevant regulations and rulings

ANAF Order 222 /2008 on the content of the transfer pricing documentation file and Rulings. Decision 529/2007 approving the procedure for the issuance of advance individual rulings and advance pricing agreements. Government Ordinance 92/2003 regarding the Fiscal Procedure Code, as subsequently completed and amended.

OECD guidelines treatment

The Romanian Fiscal Code and the related Norms provide that the Romanian tax authority should also take into consideration the OECD guidelines when analyzing the prices applied in related-party transactions. In addition, the legislation on transfer pricing documentation requirements also refers to the EU Code of Conduct on transfer pricing documentation (C176/1 of 28 July 2006).

Priorities/pricing methods

The transfer pricing methods provided by the OECD guidelines are accepted by the Romanian tax authority. The traditional methods (CUP, Resale Price Method and Cost Plus Method) are generally preferred to the transactional profit methods (TNMM and Profit Split). More specifically, when it is possible to apply, the CUP is the preferred traditional method for assessing the market value of related-party transactions.

Transfer pricing penalties

Failure to provide the authorities with transfer pricing documentation upon request and within the required term is sanctioned with a fine of approximately EUR 4,000.

Additionally, failure to present the transfer pricing documentation file or presentation of an incomplete file could trigger an estimation of the transfer prices by the tax authority. Such estimation would be performed by simply using the arithmetic average of prices for any three transactions identified as similar by the authority. The resulting adjustments would trigger a profits-tax liability of 16% (the standard profits tax rate) and late payment interest of around 36% p.a.

Penalty relief

No specific penalty relief provisions are currently in place under the Romanian transfer pricing legislation.

Documentation requirements

Even though the documentation requirements were introduced in the Romanian regulations from 2006, the specific content of the transfer pricing documentation file was formally detailed by Romanian tax authorities only in February 2008.

Such requirements provide that Romanian entities having transactions with non-resident related parties should make available upon the request of the tax authority, and within a required term, a file comprising the transfer pricing documentation for such transactions. Taxpayers that entered into APAs for related-party transactions are not required to prepare and submit a transfer pricing documentation file for the periods and transactions covered by such APAs.

The transfer pricing documentation file should comprise information regarding the taxpayer, the group and the related-party transactions (including an analysis of functions performed and risks assumed by the related parties), as well as information on the transfer pricing methods used for determining the value of related-party transactions and a set of relevant statistical comparables.

Documentation deadlines

The term for the provision of the transfer pricing documentation file is set by the tax authority depending on the complexity of transactions, and it can be for a period of up to three months from the date of tax authority's request (such term may be extended only once for a period equal to the initial period). The transfer pricing documentation may be requested by the tax authority during any tax audit (e.g., audits for VAT reimbursement requests), and there is no specific requirement to have the transfer pricing documentation submitted to the Romanian tax authority together with annual tax returns.

Separately, taxpayers that have an APA must submit annually to ANAF a report regarding observance of the APA terms and conditions. This report deadline is similar to that of the submission of annual financial statements, i.e., normally the end of May. Noncompliance leads to cancellation of the APA.

Statute of limitations on transfer pricing assessments

No specific statute of limitations rules are provided for transfer pricing assessments; however, general rules for statute of limitations are applicable, i.e., the Romanian tax authority may normally review tax-related matters retroactively for five years (or 10 years in the case of fiscal evasion or fraud).

Return disclosures/related-party disclosures

Generally, information on the related-party transactions undertaken by a Romanian entity is disclosed only upon the specific request of the Romanian tax authority. Also, for statutory accounting reporting purposes, Romanian companies are required to disclose the transactions undertaken with related parties.

Separately from the above, the Romanian legislation provides for the following general disclosure requirements:

- Disclosure of transactions performed by Romanian entities with non-resident companies for which the Romanian company has an obligation to withhold taxes

¶20,040

- Disclosure or registration of contracts concluded by Romanian entities with non-resident companies and individuals performing in Romanian construction works, assembly, supervisory activities, advisory and technical assistance activities and any other similar activities which may trigger Romanian permanent establishment exposure
- Disclosure of long-term financing contracted by a Romanian entity with non-resident companies or individuals

Audit risk/transfer pricing scrutiny

The risk of transfer pricing scrutiny by the Romanian tax authority during a tax audit is medium to high.

APA opportunity

Comprehensive APA procedures and requirements have been in effect in Romania since June 2007. An APA may be unilateral (involving only one tax administration) or bilateral or multilateral (involving two or more tax administrations).

By means of an APA, the ANAF will approve the specific transfer pricing method utilized by a multinational entity prior to the actual transaction. APAs are binding on the tax authority as long as their terms and conditions are observed by taxpayers.

The term for issuing an APA is 12 months for unilateral agreements and 18 months for bilateral or multilateral APAs. The fees payable to ANAF for issuance or amendment of an APA are:

- EUR 20,000/EUR 15,000 —in case of large taxpayers or for agreements on transactions with a consolidated value exceeding EUR 4m
- EUR 10,000/EUR 6,000 — in all other cases

As a general rule, APAs are issued for a period up to five years; however, this term may be extended in certain cases.

RUSSIA

Taxing authority and tax law

The Federal Tax Service of the Russian Federation. The Tax Code of the Russian Federation (the Tax Code).

Relevant regulations and rulings

Transfer pricing rules are stipulated primarily in Articles 20 and 40 of the Russian Tax Code. A number of clarifications from the tax authority and extensive court practice exist; however, these sources are of a non-binding nature.

OECD guidelines treatment

The taxing authority does not recognize the OECD guidelines. However, to a certain extent, the Russian Tax Code's provisions follow these guidelines, e.g., three transfer pricing methods are stipulated (CUP, Resale Minus and Cost Plus), though it is noted that the application of the Resale Minus and the Cost Plus methods differ from the approach set out in the OECD guidelines.

An updated TP draft law was released on 30 October 2009. If the amendments are introduced, the Russian transfer pricing rules will be brought much more in line with international practice, including explicit functional analysis requirements, transfer pricing documentation and reporting on transfer prices and policies when filing a tax return. However, certain differences will remain between the expected Russian rules and OECD practice. In relation to the treatment of restructuring the draft law does not introduce any new provisions.

The targeted introduction date of the new law is 1 January 2011.

Priorities/pricing methods

There are three methods mentioned in the Tax Code: CUP, Resale Minus and Cost Plus methods. In the Tax Code, the three methods are set out in a strict hierarchy. The Resale Minus method is used only if there is no information available about the prices used in identical or similar transactions by independent entities, and the Cost Plus method is applied only if both the CUP and the Resale Minus methods are inapplicable. The Resale Minus and Cost Plus methods are tested at the operating margin level, which in effect makes them similar to the OECD guidelines' TNMM method.

Transfer pricing penalties

There are no specific transfer pricing penalties. In case of a tax assessment as a result of a transfer pricing adjustment, the tax authority will charge the tax itself and interest, which is calculated as 1/300 of the refinancing rates of the Russian Central Bank for each day while the tax was underpaid. The current refinancing rate is 9.50%. The tax authority may also seek to charge a 20% penalty (40% in the case of a deliberate tax violation), and although the Tax Code does not provide the tax authority with the right to do so, it has been successful in imposing such penalties in a number of court cases.

¶20,040

Currently, transfer pricing documentation is not required. However, the above-mentioned expected amendments may stipulate the obligation to have such documentation for certain transactions (and corresponding fines for its absence are expected to be stipulated). These amendments may be brought into effect from 1 January 2011.

Penalty relief

Penalties are not imposed if the taxpayer voluntarily pays the tax before the tax authority indicates the tax underpayment.

As noted above, there are no specific transfer pricing penalties in the Tax Code and the court practice has been of conflicting nature in this area. In some cases, there were penalties imposed by the tax authority for transfer pricing violations, but these were cancelled by the court (generally, based on the grounds that transfer pricing rules are of an estimative nature rather than a precise tax calculation). At the same time, there are at least three court cases at the level of the Federal Arbitration Court where the court upheld both the transfer pricing adjustment and the penalty imposed by the tax authority.

Documentation requirements

There are no specific documentation requirements under the Russian transfer pricing rules.

Documentation deadlines

Not applicable.

Statute of limitations on transfer pricing assessments

The general rule is that the tax authority may audit three years proceeding the year when the audit is conducted. For example, if the tax audit is performed in 2009, in addition to 2009, the authority can audit 2006, 2007 and 2008. In a case where it is proved that a taxpayer acted in "bad faith," including where a taxpayer actively prevented the tax audit procedures, the statute of limitations could be expanded.

Return disclosures/related-party disclosures

There are no disclosure requirements at the present time. However, the expected amendments to the transfer pricing rules would require the disclosure of transactions with related parties and also other types of third-party transactions which would remain subject to TP control (e.g., transactions with parties located in low-tax jurisdictions and cross-border sale of oil, gas, minerals etc.).

Audit risk/transfer pricing scrutiny

If the proposed amendments to the Russian transfer pricing rules are introduced and as the authorities become more experienced at implementing legislation which conforms more closely to OECD guidelines, it is likely that the level and effectiveness of transfer pricing scrutiny will increase from its historically relatively low level. For example, as of 2008, based on the available data, the tax authority only succeeded in approximately 15% of the transfer pricing tax court cases.

¶20,040

However, although taxpayers win the majority of transfer pricing cases, the tax authority continues to increase the number of cases they take to court year by year, and in 2008, more than 750 court cases included references to the transfer pricing rules. Out of those cases, it is estimated that approximately 20% were primarily focused on transfer pricing issues.

APA opportunity

APAs are not allowed under the current legislation, but it is included in the draft law. The APA program would be available from 1 January 2012 and at the initial stage it might be available only for "major taxpayers". Both unilateral and bilateral APAs are expected to be available.

Taxing authority and tax law

Singapore does not have a specific transfer pricing legislation yet. Currently, general income tax provisions contained in § 53 (2A) and § 33 of the Income Tax Act cover transfer pricing. § 53 (2A) concerns related-party business dealings between a non-resident and a resident, and § 33 of the Income Tax Act is a general anti-avoidance provision. A draft tax bill currently contains a specific section regarding transfer pricing, however, this has not yet been finalized.

Relevant regulations and rulings

The Inland Revenue Authority of Singapore (IRAS) issued Transfer Pricing Guidelines on 23 February 2006 (Singapore Transfer Pricing Guidelines). Subsequent to the release of the Singapore Transfer Pricing Guidelines, the IRAS also published circulars/other guidelines on the following topics:

- Transfer pricing consultation process - relates to the IRAS' program to assess whether taxpayers are following the recommendations in the Singapore Transfer Pricing Guidelines (IRAS Circular - *Singapore Transfer Pricing Consultation,* published on 30 July 2008).

- Procedures for advance pricing agreements (APA Guidelines) - outlines timelines and format for information provided to the IRAS in connection with a taxpayer's request for an APA (IRAS Supplementary Circular - *Supplementary Administrative Guidance on Advance Pricing Arrangements,* published on 20 October 2008).

- Transfer pricing guidelines for related party loans and related party services (*Singapore Loans and Services Guidelines*) - further guidance on the application of the arm's length principle to related parties (IRAS Supplementary e-Tax Guide - *Transfer Pricing Guidelines for Related Party Loans and Related Party Services,* published on 23 February 2009).

OECD guidelines treatment

The Singapore Transfer Pricing Guidelines and circulars/other guidelines are generally consistent with the OECD guidelines. The principles and transfer pricing methods set out in the OECD guidelines are acceptable in Singapore.

However, there are certain differences between the OECD Transfer Pricing Guidelines and the *Singapore Loan and Services Guidelines.* Specifically, services provided by a Singapore taxpayer in a cost pooling arrangement should not be the "principal activity" of the taxpayer. Services are considered the principal activity of the Singapore service provider if the costs relating to the provision of the service exceed 15% of the Singapore service provider's total expenses in a financial year. Further, cost pooling should only be used for "routine" services as defined by the *Singapore Loans and Services Guidelines.*

Priorities/pricing methods

The IRAS does not have a specific preference for any of the five prescribed methods outlined in the OECD guidelines, with the exception of loan transactions where the IRAS indicates in the Singapore Loans and Services Guidelines that the comparable uncontrolled price method is the preferred method for substantiating the arm's length nature of interest charges. The transfer pricing method that produces the most reliable results should be selected and applied.

Transfer pricing penalties

There are no specific penalties regarding transfer pricing adjustments. Under general tax provisions relating to understatements of income, the penalty range is from 100% to 400% of the tax underpaid. In practice, where a transfer pricing adjustment is made, the general penalty rates are applicable and penalties will most likely be applied if the taxpayer has no or insufficient transfer pricing documentation.

Penalty relief

In general, tax penalties can be mitigated if there is reasonable cause for the understatement of income. Good-quality transfer pricing documentation is important in mitigating penalties.

Documentation requirements

Singapore tax law and the Singapore Transfer Pricing Guidelines do not explicitly impose a formal requirement to prepare transfer pricing documentation. The IRAS expects taxpayers to assess their transfer pricing risk and prepare transfer pricing documentation commensurate with that risk. At a minimum, Singapore taxpayers should perform and document a transfer pricing risk assessment regarding their relatedparty dealings. Based on the assessment, the taxpayer should determine whether more detailed transfer pricing documentation should be prepared.

A transfer pricing risk assessment should cover at least the following information:

- A description of the taxpayer's related-party transactions, including the amount of the transactions and their contractual terms
- A high-level functional analysis that describes the key contributors to the relevant transactions in terms of functions performed, assets developed, assets used and risks assumed
- An outline of the taxpayer's assessment of its tax risk

If a Singapore taxpayer has complex or large transactions, preparation of more detailed transfer pricing documentation may be necessary to substantiate compliance with the arm's length principle. More detailed transfer pricing documentation would usually include:

- Detailed factual information regarding the related-party transactions, including the functions performed, assets developed, assets used and risks assumed in relation to the transaction
- An analysis of the applicable industry in which the taxpayer operates
- Selection and application of one of the transfer pricing methods specified in the Singapore Transfer Pricing Guidelines

¶20,040

- An economic analysis that supports the use of the selected method using appropriate benchmarking data and analysis

Documentation deadlines

There is no deadline for the preparation of documentation. However, when a taxpayer believes that it has potential transfer pricing risk, then transfer pricing documentation should be prepared contemporaneously. There is also no submission requirement or deadline. However, documentation should be made available if requested by the IRAS.

Statute of limitations on transfer pricing assessments

The statute of limitations for transfer pricing adjustments is as follows:

- If the year of assessment is 2007 or a preceding year of assessment, the statute of limitations is six years from the end of the year of assessment to which the transfer pricing issue relates.

- If the year of assessment is 2008 or a subsequent year of assessment the statute of limitations is four years from the end of the year of assessment to which the transfer pricing issue relates.

Singapore corporate taxpayers are required to file tax returns by 30 November of the following year after the applicable financial year. For example, a Singapore corporate taxpayer that had a 31 December 2008 financial year end will be required to file its Singapore corporate tax return by 30 November 2009. The applicable year of assessment in this case is the 2009 year of assessment which corresponds to the financial year ended 31 December 2008.

Return disclosures/related-party disclosures

No specified disclosures are required on Form C, Singapore income tax return.

Audit risk/transfer pricing scrutiny

The purpose of the Singapore Transfer Pricing Guidelines is to create an awareness of transfer pricing issues. Given the IRAS' desire to create awareness about transfer pricing, it is likely that over time there will be an increase in the number of tax audits that involve transfer pricing.

In July 2008 the IRAS issued a circular on transfer pricing consultation. The transfer pricing consultation process is intended to assess the level of taxpayers' compliance with the Singapore Transfer Pricing Guidelines and to identify potential areas where the IRAS can further facilitate and advise taxpayers on appropriate transfer pricing practices. The initial phase of the consultation process involves the issuance of a questionnaire regarding certain transfer pricing matters. These questionnaires are (and have been) issued to various taxpayers. Based on the answers to the questionnaire the IRAS will assess whether a field visit to the taxpayer's business operations and review of the taxpayer's transfer pricing documentation are necessary. Further steps may involve specific guidance from the IRAS to the taxpayer regarding compliance with the arm's length principle.

The risk of a transfer pricing audit is currently medium.

¶20,040

APA opportunity

Unilateral, bilateral and multilateral APAs are available. However, for bilateral and multilateral APAs, there must be a double tax agreement between Singapore and the other involved country or countries. The Singapore Transfer Pricing Guidelines outline the procedures for applying for an APA. Further procedural guidance on the APA process has been provided in the IRAS circular *"Supplementary Administrative Guidance on Advance Pricing Arrangements"* issued in October 2008. The circular applies to APA requests made after 20 October 2008 and includes guidance on the following:

- Suggested timing for the overall APA process
- The circumstances where the IRAS may reject a taxpayer's APA request
- The nature of taxpayer resources and commitments that should be made when an APA is requested
- That "roll-backs" are limited to bilateral and multilateral APAs

SLOVAK REPUBLIC

Taxing authority and tax law

Slovak Tax Directorate, local tax authorities and Ministry of Finance.

Sections 2, 17 (5, 6, 7) and 18 of the Income Tax Act. Act on International Assistance and cooperation by tax administrators.

Relevant regulations and rulings

The Slovak transfer pricing rules laid down in the Income Tax Act generally conform to the OECD guidelines. The OECD Transfer Pricing Guidelines were published in the Slovak Financial Newsletter but are not legally binding. Nevertheless, the tax authority should follow them in practice.

The Slovak Income Tax Act has been amended with effect as of 1 January 2009. The amendment introduced an obligation of the taxpayer to prepare and keep transfer pricing documentation supporting the transfer pricing method used in transactions with foreign related parties. The required content of transfer pricing documentation is stipulated in Guidance No. MF/8288/2009-72 of the Slovak Ministry of Finance.

OECD guidelines treatment

The Slovak tax authorities usually follow the provisions of the OECD guidelines. The acceptable methods listed in the Income Tax Act correspond with the methods stipulated by the OECD guidelines.

Priorities/pricing methods

The Slovak Income Tax Act prefers the methods based on the comparison of prices over methods based on the comparison of profits, combined methods or other alternative methods. The method used must respect the arm's length principle. The general recommendations provided in the OECD guidelines should be followed.

Transfer pricing penalties

No penalties specific to transfer pricing exist. The penalty rate for unpaid (or understated) tax liability equals three times the basic interest rate of the European Central Bank (at the date of issue 3*1% = 3%). As of 1 January 2010, the penalty rate will be three times the basic interest rate of the European Central Bank or 10 % (whichever will be higher). This is not a per annum rate, but rather the penalty would be a multiple of this rate and the under-declared tax, irrespective of the time of tax underpayment. In addition, a penalty for the breach of non-monetary obligations (e.g., non-existing or insufficient supporting documentation) of an amount up to EUR 33,193.92 can be imposed. On assessing the penalty for the breach of non-monetary obligations, the tax authorities have to take into account all the circumstances that led to the breach of non monetary obligations (e.g. importance, duration and consequences of the breach).

¶20,040

Penalty relief

There are no specific reductions in penalties. Generally, a penalty is reduced by half if the taxpayer submits a supplementary income tax return where the tax base is adjusted upwards. Upon a successful challenge of transfer prices by the tax authority, no specific reduction in penalties is available.

Documentation requirements

The required content of transfer pricing documentation is stipulated in Guidance No. MF/8288/2009-72 of the Slovak Ministry of Finance. The intent of the Guidance is to conform with the EU Code of Conduct on transfer pricing documentation for associated enterprises in the European Union (No. 2006/C 176/01).

Transfer pricing documentation must be prepared for related-party transactions with an amount exceeding the level of materiality for accounting purposes (as defined by International Financial Reporting Standards). Documentation must be prepared separately for each transaction or homogenous group of transactions.

For taxpayers obliged to use International Financial Reporting Standards (banks, insurance companies, pension funds, companies exceeding a certain size), the Guidance prescribes the required contents of the transfer pricing documentation, which are generally in line with the Masterfile approach set out by the EU Code of Conduct on Transfer Pricing Documentation. The documentation will consist of global (masterfile) and local documentation. The masterfile will have to contain information with regard to the whole group of related parties (overview of the industry, business strategies and general overview of functions, risks and assets of the members of the group). The local documentation will contain information regarding the Slovak taxpayer. Moreover, the approach to transfer pricing, methods used, and description of transactions with related parties should be covered by the documentation. The local documentation should also include analysis of the comparability of the transactions.

For other taxpayers, the Guidance does not stipulate the contents of the documentation. However, the transfer pricing documentation must prove that prices applied in related-party transactions conform to the arm's length principle.

The language of the documentation should be Slovak, unless approved otherwise at the taxpayer's request. The Slovak authorities have unofficially stated that documentation presented in English, German or French should also be accepted.

It is not clear from the Guidance whether the documentation requirements will also apply for transactions performed or contracts concluded prior to 1 January 2009. However, the tax authorities already require taxpayers to have sufficient transfer pricing documentation prepared in the case of a tax audit. This stems from the provision of the Income Tax Act stipulating that the burden of proof rests with the taxpayer.

Documentation deadlines

If requested by the tax authorities, transfer pricing documentation must be submitted within 60 days of the request. The documentation does not have to be disclosed, unless requested by the tax authorities.

¶20,040

Statute of limitations on transfer pricing assessments

The statute of limitations in Slovakia in the case of applying a Double Tax Treaty is 10 years from the end of the year in which the respective tax return is filed.

Return disclosures/related-party disclosures

Transfer pricing documentation does not need to be enclosed with the tax return. The taxpayer should state (on a specific row of the tax return) the difference (if any) between the prices used in transactions with related parties and the prices at an arm's length level which decreased the tax base. The tax base must be at the same time increased by this difference.

The 2009 corporate income tax return includes a summary table where the amounts of various types of related party sales and purchases must be stated (regardless of whether there are differences from arm's length prices).

Audit risk/transfer pricing scrutiny

Overall, the likelihood that a company with significant related-party transactions will get a transfer pricing audit can be classified as medium.

The Slovak Tax Authorities have been historically relatively inactive in this area, with only few complex transfer pricing audits performed. However, following the amendment to the Income Tax Act, the Slovak Tax Authorities have recently intensified their activities in the area of transfer pricing and are increasingly focusing on the transfer pricing and related documentation when auditing companies that form part of a multinational group. Thus, we expect the level of risk to increase in the future.

APA opportunity

According to Section 18 (4) of the Slovak Income Tax Act, in cases of cross-border related party transactions, the taxpayer may request the tax authority to approve the selected transfer pricing method. If approved, the method should be applied for a maximum of five tax periods. The Income Tax Act, however, does not explicitly stipulate that the tax authority may approve the particular price or margin percentage used. Therefore the use of advance pricing agreements in Slovakia is rather limited.

SLOVENIA

Taxing authority and tax law

Tax Authority: Davèna uprava Republike Slovenije

Relevant legislation:

- Corporate Income Tax Act (Zakon o davku od dohodkov pravnih oseb)
- Regulation on Transfer Prices (Pravilnik o transfernih cenah)
- Regulation on the Acknowledged Interest Rate (Pravilnik o priznani obrestni meri)
- Tax Procedure Act (Zakon o davènem postopku)

Relevant regulations and rulings

Articles 16 and 17 of the Corporate Income Tax Act provide the definitions of related parties and general requirements they need to comply with. The latter are explained in more detail in the Regulation on Transfer Prices.

Article 18 of the Corporate Income Tax Act sets the basis for documentation requirements which are then elaborated in the Tax Procedure Act.

Article 19 of the Corporate Income Tax Act provides the general rules in relation to acknowledged interest rate on loans between related parties. The rules are defined in more detail in the Regulation on the Acknowledged Interest Rate. The acknowledged interest rate rules determine a safe harbor for loans between related parties.

OECD guidelines treatment

As the Slovenian transfer pricing regulations follow the principles of the OECD Transfer Pricing Guidelines, the Tax Authorities, where there is no guidance in Slovenian legislation, also consider them in their tax audits.

Priorities/pricing methods

All five standard methods are acceptable, however the CUP and in the next stage also resale price method and cost plus method are preferred. If none of the specifically identified methods are suitable for determining the arm's length price, the taxpayer is permitted to adopt a suitable combination of such specified methods.

Transfer pricing penalties

A company may be fined up to EUR 25,000 if the transfer pricing documentation is not submitted in the prescribed manner; additionally, the individual responsible for the preparation of the documentation on behalf of the company may also be fined up to EUR 4,000. In case of a tax adjustment, late payment interest and penalties for offences may be charged.

Penalty relief

If the tax authority is able to conclude that the taxable person has cooperated well during the tax audit, fines are usually not levied.

¶20,040

Documentation requirements

The Slovenian transfer pricing documentation requirements are based on the master file concept. Under this concept, as recommended by the European Community (EC) Council as well as the EU Joint Transfer Pricing Forum, the transfer pricing documentation should consist of a master file and a country-specific file. Disclosure of any related parties transaction amounts should be provided with the tax return when it is filed with the tax authorities.

The local legislation sets the following documentation requirements:

The Master File

The master file normally includes documentation common to the whole group. It may be prepared by the group's headquarters and should include a general description of the way business is conducted by the group companies. The file should include the following:

- a description of the taxable person,
- a description of the global organizational structure of the group,
- an explanation of the type of connections between the companies in the group,
- an explanation of the method used in the determination of transfer prices,
- a description of the business activities and business strategies, including any general economic and other factors, an assessment of the competitive environment, etc.

Country specific documentation

As in the Master file, the local documentation should describe the company's course of business but on a local level. The country-specific documentation should normally include:

- a description of transactions between affiliated persons,
- a functional analysis determining the main functions performed by the tax payer and outlining which adjustments may need to be made in relation to comparable situations,
- a description of any comparable search performed,
- a description of business strategies,
- a description of goods/services transferred/rendered,
- a description of the method applied for establishing the arm's length price,
- any other information that might be relevant from the transfer pricing perspective should also be included in the documentation.

Documentation deadlines

The documentation should be provided to the tax authorities upon their request, usually made in the course of a tax inspection. Wherever any such documentation proves impossible to submit immediately, a deadline extension of up to 90 days (depending on the extent and complexity of the information) may be

¶20,040

granted. If the master file is not kept in the Slovenian language, it must be translated, before submission, at the tax authority's request. An additional period of 60 days may also be granted for the translation of the Master file.

Statute of limitations on transfer pricing assessments

The statute of limitation on transfer pricing assessments is five years. The transfer pricing documentation must be archived for a period of 10 years.

Return disclosures/related-party disclosures

Related party transactions are reported in the scope of the annual corporate income tax return.

Audit risk/transfer pricing scrutiny

Medium risk

The tax authorities mainly initiate a transfer pricing audit where a Slovenian taxable person is part of a multinational group. Additional risk factors are the profitability of the local taxpayer, business restructurings, the nature and volume of related-party transactions, transfer pricing issues identified in previous tax audits, information available from media.

APA opportunity

The possibility of applying for APAs is not available.

SOUTH AFRICA

Taxing authority and tax law

Section 31 of the Income Tax Act 58 of 1962 (the Act) contains the main legislative provisions concerning transfer pricing. Section 31 authorizes the Commissioner of the South African Revenue Services (SARS) to adjust the consideration for goods or services to an arm's length price for the purposes of computing the South African taxable income of a person.

Relevant regulations and rulings

There are no specific regulations or rulings; however, guidance on the application of § 31 is contained in Practice Notes Number 2 (14 May 1996) and 7 (6 August 1999).

OECD guidelines treatment

Although South Africa is not a member of the OECD, the South African tax authority accepts the OECD guidelines and has largely based Practice Note 7 on these Guidelines. By the same token, the South African tax authority recognizes the five methods accepted by the OECD.

Priorities/pricing methods

The SARS accepts the methods prescribed by the OECD, i.e., CUP, RPM, Cost Plus, TNMM and Profit Split. The SARS prefers transactionbased methods over profit-based methods, but the TNMM is most commonly applied by taxpayers and generally accepted, provided the taxpayer can show that reliable data was not available to apply CUP, RPM or Cost Plus. Reasons for discounting other methods must be given, and as such, the SARS does, in practice, apply a hierarchy of methods. The SARS may require that adjustments be made on foreign comparable company results used in benchmarking the results of the South African entity, to compensate for differences in risks assumed by entities operating in a different jurisdiction.

Transfer pricing penalties

Any adjustments made by the SARS under § 31 are deemed to be dividends, and the Secondary Tax on Companies (STC) at a rate of 12.5% (10% with effect from 1 October 2009) will be levied. There are no other specific penalties for transfer pricing, but general penalty rules are applicable, which could reach 200% of the additional tax resulting from an adjustment (where no or inadequate disclosure was provided).

Penalty relief

Where taxpayers have made conscientious efforts to establish transfer prices that comply with the arm's length principle, and have prepared documentation to evidence such compliance, the SARS is likely to take the view that the taxpayer's transfer pricing practices represent a lower tax risk. Accordingly, the preparation of sound and consistent transfer pricing practices may reduce the possibility of an audit and, therefore, reduce the likelihood of incurring penalties.

¶20,040

Documentation requirements

The taxpayer has the burden of proof that its prices are arm's length. The best way to discharge the burden of proof is by developing a transfer pricing policy, determining the arm's length amount and voluntarily producing documentation to evidence the analysis undertaken. Having said this, the SARS would expect taxpayers to have created, referred to and retained transfer pricing documentation in accordance with prudent business management principles, i.e., the principles that would govern the process of evaluating a business decision at a similar level of complexity and importance.

There is no specific statutory requirement to prepare transfer pricing documentation. However, a company that has such documentation is required to submit it together with its tax return.

Documentation deadlines

Transfer pricing documentation should be prepared not later than the date of submission of a tax return affected by the intercompany transactions. Tax returns are due 12 months after a company's financial year-end with no further extension.

Statute of limitations on transfer pricing assessments

The statute of limitations is three years from the date of assessment. There is no limitation on the examination of a tax return if an amount was not assessed due to fraud, misrepresentation or non-disclosure of material facts.

Return disclosures/related-party disclosures

The company has to answer a number of questions and provide further details specifically related to its transfer pricing policies and documentation in its annual tax return.

Audit risk/transfer pricing scrutiny

The risk of transfer pricing issues being reviewed under an audit is high, as transfer pricing remains an area of focus for the SARS. The SARS communicates on a regular and ongoing basis with other revenue authorities, particularly the United Kingdom's HMRC.

APA opportunity

APAs are not available.

SOUTH KOREA

Taxing authority and tax law

National Tax Service (NTS). The Law for Coordination of International Tax Affairs (LCITA).

Relevant regulations and rulings

Presidential Enforcement Decree (PED), the Ministerial Decree and Interpretations.

OECD guidelines treatment

The LCITA has priority over the OECD guidelines. The NTS recognizes the OECD guidelines, but the OECD guidelines have no legally binding effect. Hence, if a taxpayer's argument is based on the OECD guidelines only and not the LCITA, in practice, the NTS or regional tax offices may not accept it.

Priorities/pricing methods

The South Korean transfer pricing regulations prescribe the following transfer pricing methods: CUP, Resale Price Method, Cost Plus Method, Profit Split Method, TNMM, and other reasonable methods. Among the aforementioned transfer pricing methods, the taxpayer is to select the most reasonable method based on the availability and reliability of data. However, according to the LCITA, the transactionbased methods, i.e., CUP, Resale Price Method and Cost Plus Method, have priority over the profit-based methods, i.e., Profit Split Method and TNMM. Other reasonable methods may be selected if none of the five specific methods can be applied.

Transfer pricing penalties

There are two types of penalties associated with a transfer pricing adjustment: an underreporting penalty and an underpayment penalty.

- The underreporting penalty is approximately 10% of the additional taxes resulting from a transfer pricing adjustment.
- The underpayment penalty, which is an interest payment in nature, is calculated as 0.03% of the additional taxes on a transfer pricing adjustment per day (10.95% per annum) on the cumulative days. The counting of cumulative days of the underpayment starts from the day after the statutory tax filing due date, which comes three months after the fiscal year-end, and ends on the date that a tax assessment or payment is made.

There is also a penalty of up to KRW 30m for failure to provide the documentation requested by the tax authority within the due date. In general, the documents are to be submitted within 60 days of the date of request. However, the taxpayer may be granted a one-time extension for 60 days if the reasonable circumstances specified in the LCITA exist.

Penalty relief

Under the LCITA Article 13 and PED Article 23, the underreporting penalty is waived if the mutual agreement procedure (MAP) result confirms that a taxpayer is

¶20,040

not guilty of negligence, i.e., a taxpayer shall (i) select and report the most appropriate transfer pricing method specified in the LCITA, (ii) actually apply the selected method and (iii) maintain supporting documentation.

At the end of 2008, new contemporaneous TP documentation rules were introduced in Korea. Specifically, the revision to Article 13 of the LCITA was finalized on 26 December 2008 to include an additional provision on underreporting penalty relief. The new provision is effective from the date of the enactment (i.e. 26 December 2008) and shall be applied to TP adjustments made thereafter. It states that if the taxpayer has prepared and maintained contemporaneous TP documentation for the TP methods applied to the cross-border intercompany transactions reported in the corporate income tax return, and such documentation supports the reasonableness of the TP methods reported, the penalty for underreporting will be waived in the case where a TP adjustment is made.

The revision to the PED of the LCITA that provides guidelines on the implementation of this new provision was released on 4 February 2009. The effective date is the same as the finalization date (i.e., 4 February 2009), and shall be applied from the tax year into which its effective date falls.

In general, the TP documentation should include information on the taxpayer's business (including functions performed and factors that can affect pricing for intercompany transactions with related parties), details on cross-border intercompany transactions, an explanation of the TP method selected and reasons for not selecting other TP methods prescribed in the regulations, and details on the comparable company or transaction data used. The guideline also stipulates that the comparable data used should be representative and should not have been selectively chosen to favor the taxpayer's position (i.e., no "cherry picking"). In the case where a taxpayer applies a TP method different from that agreed in an APA or selected by tax auditors in a tax audit, the taxpayer needs to justify the use of the different TP method.

Documentation requirements

At the time of filing the corporate income tax return, a taxpayer is required to submit certain transfer pricing reporting forms. Under the new contemporaneous TP documentation rules, in order to receive the benefit of the relief from the underreporting penalty, taxpayers are required to prepare and maintain TP documentation by the due date of the filing of the annual corporate income tax returns. If requested by the tax authority, such contemporaneous TP documentation must be submitted to the tax authority within 30 days of the request.

Documentation deadlines

A taxpayer must submit documents and information requested by the tax authority within 60 days upon the request of the tax authority.

A one-time extension for 60 days may be granted if reasonable circumstances specified in the LCITA exist. Contemporaneous TP documentation should be submitted to the tax authority within 30 days of the request. The tax authorities

¶20,040

may also request a taxpayer submit certain information including a TP study at the time of a tax audit. In that case the taxpayer is given only a 10-day notice.

Statute of limitations on transfer pricing assessments

The statute of limitations on transfer pricing adjustments is generally five years. It extends to 10 years in case of a fraud or other wrongful act and seven years if a taxpayer does not submit the tax filing on the due date.

Return disclosures/related-party disclosures

The LCITA requires a taxpayer to submit the following transfer pricing reporting forms when filing the annual corporate income tax return:

- A form explaining the transfer pricing method selected and the reason for the selection of the method for each intercompany transaction. There are different forms for different types of transactions, i.e., tangible property transactions, intangible property transactions, service transactions and cost-sharing arrangements.
- A summary of cross-border intercompany transactions with foreign related parties
- Summary income statements of foreign related parties having cross-border intercompany transactions with the South Korean entity

Audit risk/transfer pricing scrutiny

The risk of transfer pricing issues being reviewed under an audit is high. The NTS has recently begun to routinely ask for transfer pricing documentation, even outside of the audit context. The NTS closely monitors companies whose profitability suddenly drops or companies whose profits fluctuate substantially over a number of years, and they are likely to be subject to tax audits. Also, companies paying large royalties abroad or receiving large management service fee charges or cost allocations from overseas related parties will likely be subject to scrutiny by the tax authority. The introduction of the new contemporaneous TP documentation rules shows the Korean tax authority's increased focus on TP related issues in Korea.

APA opportunity

Unilateral and bilateral APAs are available under the LCITA. In order to encourage the application of APAs, the NTS does not require an application fee, and the LCITA guarantees the confidentiality of the data submitted to the NTS with regard to an APA. In addition, the Korean tax authority is making all efforts to shorten the time being taken to process the APA. Furthermore, the Korean tax authority released its first Annual Report on APAs which includes information such as statistics on the type of APAs being concluded, the countries that are counterparties to APAs, time taken to process APA cases, etc.

¶20,040

SPAIN

Taxing authority and tax law

State Agency of Tax Administration (AEAT) and General Directorate of Taxation (DGT). Spanish Consolidated Corporate Income Tax Law (CCITL) Art. 16 (the Law).

Relevant regulations and rulings

On 18 November 2008, by Royal Decree, the Spanish Government has approved and published regulations that specify transfer pricing documentation requirements (Royal Decree 1793/2008) applicable to persons or entities participating in related-party transactions.

Transfer pricing documentation requirements have been in effect in Spain since 2006 (following Law 36/2006, applicable to tax periods beginning as from 1 December 2006). This includes a shift of the burden of proof to the taxpayer, and penalty regime. However, the Law did not include a detailed description of what the documentation should contain, except that the transfer pricing documentation had to reflect the arm's length principle and the arm's length test should be based on one of the methods specified in the Law (i.e. CUP, Cost Plus, Resale Minus, TNMM and Profit Split). The new regulations provide more details regarding the information that should be included in the documentation. Spanish taxpayers engaged in related-party transactions are now required to prepare two sets of documentation: (i) a "master file" related to the group as a whole and (ii) a "local" file for each taxpayer containing specific information on the description, analysis and valuation of the controlled transactions.

OECD guidelines treatment

Spanish Transfer Pricing legislation follows the OECD guidelines and those of the European Union Transfer Pricing Forum.

Priorities/pricing methods

The Law establishes that, in order to determine the market value, one of the following methods should be applied: CUP, Cost Plus or Resale Minus. These methods are on the same preferential level in the valuation method hierarchy.

When due to the complexity or to the information relating to the transactions, the above methods may not be applied properly, TNMM or Profit Split may be used.

Transfer pricing penalties

Failure to comply with the documentation requirements specified in the new regulations may result in major penalties. These penalties can result from not having correct documentation and/or from not applying the arm's length principle (market value).

When the assessment does not produce a tax adjustment, the penalty will be 1,500 Euros per fact, or 15,000 Euros per group of facts omitted, inaccurate or false.

¶20,040

When the tax authorities adjust the pricing of a transaction, the penalty may add up to 15% of the gross adjustment.

There will be no penalties where the obligation to document has been complied with, even if the Tax Authorities reassess the value of transactions.

In addition to the above, the new regulations also include the applicability of "secondary adjustments" (i.e., in those transactions where both values will have for the related parties the tax treatment that corresponds to the nature of the profit realized). The Law makes a clarification for cases where the link is defined in light of the relationship between the shareholder and the entity, the difference shall (proportionally to the participation in the entity) be considered as (1) dividends whenever such difference is in favor of the shareholder or (2) contributions by the shareholder to the entity's equity whenever the difference is in favor of the entity.

The above sanctions are compatible with aggravating circumstances such as resisting, obstructing, excusing or negating the tax authority's actions.

Penalty relief

Some reductions are applicable to penalties. Penalties should not apply with the fulfillment of the documentation requirements.

Documentation requirements

The documentation requirements are in line with those of the EU Joint Transfer Pricing Forum (JTPF). Accordingly, two types of documentation must be maintained: one global document for the group (master file) and one document for each group entity (local file). The documentation will cover domestic and international transactions. However, transactions within the same fiscal unit are exempted from the documentation requirements.

The master file documentation requirements establish the necessity of:

- General description of the organizational, legal and operative group structure, and any change thereof

- Identification of the group entities that enter into related-party transactions to the extent that they affect the operations of the Spanish corporate taxpayer, directly or indirectly

- General description of the nature, amounts and flows of related-party transactions completed by corporate group entities, to the extent that they affect the operations of the Spanish corporate taxpayer, directly or indirectly

- General description of the functions performed and the risks assumed by the different group entities, to the extent that they affect the operations of the Spanish corporate taxpayer, directly or indirectly, including any changes since the last fiscal year

- List of intangibles (including patents, trade marks, commercial brands) owned by the group, to the extent that they affect the operations of the Spanish corporate taxpayer, directly or indirectly, as well as the considerations derived from the use of these intangibles

¶20,040

- Description of the group's transfer pricing policies, including the pricing methodology used to justify the group policy's compliance with the arm's length principle
- List of cost-sharing and services agreements between group entities relevant to the Spanish corporate taxpayer
- List of APAs and agreements entered into, as relevant to the Spanish corporate taxpayer, and
- Corporate group's Annual Report or equivalent

On the other hand, the local documentation requirements establish the necessity of:

- A detailed description of the taxpayer's business and business strategy, including changes in the business strategy compared to the previous tax year
- A description and explanation of the specific controlled transactions, including the transactions (tangible and intangible assets, services, financial, etc.), invoices and amounts of the transactions
- A comparability analysis, including:
  - Amounts of the transactions
  - Characteristics of property and services
  - Functional analysis (functions performed, assets used, risks assumed)
  - Contractual terms
  - Economic circumstances
  - Specific business circumstances
- An explanation about the selection and application of the transfer pricing methods, why the methods were selected and how they were applied
- Any other relevant information used by the taxpayer to value related-party transactions, as well as any agreement entered into with shareholders that may affect the transaction valuation

Further information could be required by the tax administration during a tax audit in regards to the related-party transactions.

Documentation deadlines

Documentation will have to be kept by companies once the corporate income tax return is filed.

Statute of limitations on transfer pricing assessments

A general statute of limitations of four years applies. The term will be interrupted in case of a tax audit. If a new income tax return is filed with the tax authorities, the four-year period is suspended and a new one begins.

Return disclosures/related-party disclosures

Specific disclosure rules exist for transactions with "tax havens," even with unrelated parties (as per a black list).

¶20,040

Audit risk/transfer pricing scrutiny

High risk - Spanish Tax Authorities have stated that Transfer Pricing audits will be a priority from 2009 on forward.

APA opportunity

Taxpayers may request the tax authorities value related-party transactions before they are carried out. This request has to be filed with a proposal based on the arm's length principle. On the other hand, the tax authorities may also settle agreements with other tax authorities in order to determine the market value of the transactions jointly (i.e., bilateral APAs).

The new regulation has improved the previous regime on APAs by extending the valid term from a three-year period to a six-year period (e.g., the previous year, when the time limit for filing the tax return has not yet expired, the current year and the next four years).

SWEDEN

Taxing authority and tax law

Swedish Tax Agency. Sections 14:19-20 of the Income Tax Act include the arm's length principle. Sections 19:2a and b of the Law (2001:1227) on income tax returns and income statements include the documentation requirements regarding transfer prices.

The Swedish Tax Agency is responsible for the correct and uniform implementation of the tax laws. It issues guidelines, recommendations and publishes its standpoints on specific issues to the local tax offices.

Relevant regulations and rulings

Section 12:4 of the regulations (2001:1244) on income tax returns and income statements and the regulations (SKVFS 2007:1) regarding documentation of the pricing between associated enterprises. The Swedish Tax Agency also issues general taxation guidelines, which include information on transfer pricing.

OECD guidelines treatment

The Swedish tax laws on transfer pricing refer to the OECD Transfer Pricing Guidelines, and they are applied by the courts and tax authorities.

The OECD Discussion Draft on Business Restructurings is expected to significantly increase the Tax Agency's focus on restructuring but potentially also on existing structures, for example in relation to allocation of risk between related parties.

Priorities/pricing methods

One of the methods described in OECD guidelines should be applied. Transaction-based methods are preferred over profit-based methods.

Transfer pricing penalties

There are no specific transfer pricing penalties. General penalty rules apply, with penalties ranging from 10% to 40% of the additional tax imposed. In transfer pricing cases, penalties at a rate of 40% are generally imposed.

Penalty relief

Penalties are imposed on taxpayers for supplying the Tax Agency with inaccurate or insufficient information. In the preparatory work to the law that introduces transfer pricing documentation requirements, it is stated that if an income adjustment is made because the taxpayer's prices are not deemed to be at arm's length; the penalties might be reduced or eliminated if the taxpayer has prepared proper transfer pricing documentation.

Documentation requirements

Multinational enterprises are required to document transactions with related companies as of 1 January 2007. The new legislation introduces formal transfer pricing documentation requirements in relation to cross-border transactions within multinational enterprises. The documentation must include:

¶20,040

- A description of the company, organization and business operations
- Information regarding the characteristics and scope of the transactions
- A functional analysis
- A description of the chosen pricing method
- A comparability analysis

The functional analysis should, in addition to identifying the functions performed, risks assumed and assets used, also describe which functions, risks and assets contribute to the company's ability to generate profit. Moreover, the importance of the comparability factors described in the OECD guidelines is highlighted.

Documentation prepared in accordance with the code of conduct regarding European Union Transfer Pricing Documentation (EU TPD) is deemed to comply with the Swedish documentation requirements. The documentation should be prepared in the Swedish, Danish, Norwegian or English language.

For transactions of limited value, it is possible to prepare simplified documentation. Transactions of limited value for fiscal year 2009 include the sale or purchase of goods amounting to approximately SEK 27m or less per counterparty on a yearly basis, or other transactions amounting to approximately SEK 5m or less per counterparty on a yearly basis. Simplified documentation is not possible for transactions involving the sale of intangible assets.

The simplified documentation should include the following:

- The group's legal and organizational structure and a description of the business operations
- The counterparty to the transaction and information on that entity's business operations
- Information on the intercompany transactions, including the type of transaction, amounts and value
- The method applied to the transaction to comply with the arm's length principle
- Information on comparable transactions, if utilized

Documentation deadlines

The underlying analysis should, in principle, be prepared in connection with the transaction. The final documentation should be available upon request from the Tax Agency. Such a request is possible from the date that the income tax return is filed.

Statute of limitations on transfer pricing assessments

A general statute of limitations applies, which is within five years of the year of assessment.

Return disclosures/related-party disclosures

No specific disclosure requirements when filing the tax return currently exist.

¶20,040

Audit risk/transfer pricing scrutiny

The risk that transfer price adjustments will be scrutinized during an audit is high. There has been a significantly increased focus from the tax authority on transfer pricing-related issues.

APA opportunity

There are no formal APA procedures. However, a number of informal APAs have been completed between the Swedish authorities and treaty partners. A formal APA procedure has been proposed and is expected to be effective as of 2010. The proposal includes bilateral and multilateral APAs only.

SWITZERLAND

Taxing authority and tax law

Cantonal Tax Authorities (tax assessments)/Federal Tax Administration (SFTA; competent authority). There are no specific references to transfer pricing in Swiss tax law. However, legal support for adjusting taxable profits of a taxpayer is derived from the arm's length principle in Article 58 of the Federal Direct Tax Act on a federal level as well as in Article 24 of the Federal Law on the Harmonization of the Cantonal and Communal Taxes on a cantonal level. In addition, there are various administrative directives referring to so-called "safe harbour regulations" which allow for the setting of transfer pricing without any specific documentation (e.g., with regard to intercompany interest payments).

Relevant regulations and rulings

There are no specific transfer pricing regulations.

OECD guidelines treatment

The SFTA has instructed the cantonal tax administrations in Circular Letter of March 4, 1997 to adhere to the OECD Transfer Pricing Guidelines for transfer pricing matters. There are no specific tax regulations on business restructurings in Switzerland.

Priorities/pricing methods

The Swiss tax administration adheres to the OECD Transfer Pricing Guidelines and prefers the CUP method as well as the traditional transactional methods over the profit-based methods. According to Circular Letter 4/2004 the profit margin for service companies must be determined in accordance with the arm's length principle, i.e., for each taxpayer individually on the basis of comparable uncontrolled transactions considering appropriate margin ranges. The Circular Letter also implicitly states that the cost plus method is the most appropriate method for service companies to price their services based on a functional and risk analysis. However, concerning the provision of financial and management services, the cost plus method shall only be accepted in exceptional cases. The Swiss tax administration uses in principle a full cost approach including all direct and indirect costs. Generally, when the taxpayer can, based on appropriate documents and records, prove that the applied margin is too high, the Swiss tax administration may exceptionally allow for a lower margin. The transactional profit split method is rarely used in Switzerland. In the financial and banking services sector (including in the area of investment and asset management), some Cantonal Tax Authorities tend to validate the applied transfer prices using transactional profit methods.

Transfer pricing penalties

There are no specific transfer pricing penalties, but general penalty rules apply. However, penalties are only imposed in cases of fraud or negligence. Interest charges for late payment are due in case of adjustments.

Penalty relief

There are no special provisions for reductions in penalties.

¶20,040

Documentation requirements

There are no specific documentation requirements. However, if challenged by the Swiss tax administration, the taxpayer has to demonstrate that the transfer prices applied were based on sound economic and commercial reasoning on an arm's length basis. Although it can be concluded from the Federal Direct Tax Act that, in principle, a taxpayer upon request of the Swiss tax administration should prepare a transfer pricing documentation, there is little guidance on the structure of such a documentation. However, based on the references to the OECD Transfer Pricing Guidelines in the 1997 Circular Letter, an OECD-compliant documentation in one of the official languages of Switzerland is accepted by the Swiss tax administration. Due to the lack of sufficient independent comparable companies on the Swiss market, it is usually allowed to apply for the arm's length remunerations of Swiss functions and risks those of Western European comparable companies.

Documentation deadlines

There are no special provisions for documentation deadlines.

Statute of limitations on transfer pricing assessments

The general rule provides for up to 10 years back from the end of the assessment year, if new facts or circumstances are discovered by the tax administration.

Return disclosures/related-party disclosures

There are no formal related-party disclosure requirements. However, in the case of a tax audit or request from competent authorities, the taxpayer must provide the requested information to a reasonable extent.

Audit risk/transfer pricing scrutiny

The risk that transfer pricing issues will be scrutinized during an audit is at a medium level, but transfer pricing has been increasingly addressed by the Swiss tax administration recently. Transfers of intangibles and transactions with related offshore companies, in particular in the financial industry, receive specific scrutiny.

APA opportunity

There are no formal APA procedures. However, though the SFTA participates in multilateral APAs, unilateral rulings are more common in practice. APA procedures are carried out in accordance with the applicable rules for mutual agreement procedures. All Swiss signed double tax treaties usually contain a provision on the mutual agreement procedure, under which the SFTA can launch an APA process.

¶20,040

TAIWAN

Taxing authority and tax law

National Tax Administration (NTA). Articles 43-1 of the Income Tax Law (ITL). Article 50 of the Financial Holding Company Law. Article 42 of the Business Mergers and Acquisitions Law.

Relevant regulations and rulings

The Taiwan Transfer Pricing Examination Guidelines (TP guidelines) were put into effect on 30 December 2004.

OECD guidelines treatment

The NTA recognizes the OECD guidelines.

Priorities/pricing methods

In accordance with the TP guidelines, the pricing methods are as follows: CUP, Resale Price, Cost Plus, Profit Split, Comparable Profit method (or TNMM) and other methods prescribed by the Ministry of Finance (MOF).

Transfer pricing penalties

Pursuant to the TP guidelines, under certain circumstances, a maximum of 200% of the tax shortfall could be imposed if assessed by the tax authority.

Penalty relief

Not applicable.

Documentation requirements

Except for immaterial related-party transactions, extensive contemporaneous documentation is required. According to the TP guidelines, upon filing of the annual income tax return, an enterprise must have the transfer pricing report and relevant documents prepared.

In December 2005, the Taiwan tax authority issued a safe harbor rule for transfer pricing reports in Tax Letter Ruling No. 09404587590. The ruling provides that an enterprise is not required to prepare a transfer pricing report (other supporting documents are allowed) if any of the following criteria is met:

- The total annual revenue (including operating and non-operating) of the enterprise does not exceed TWD 100m
- The total annual revenue (including operating and non-operating) of the enterprise exceeds TWD 100m but does not exceed TWD 300m
  - The enterprise does not utilize tax credits for more than TWD 1m or loss carry forwards for more than TWD 4m to reduce the income tax or undistributed earnings surplus tax
  - An enterprise under the Financial Holding Company Law or Mergers and Acquisitions Law has no overseas related parties (whether a company or an individual), or an enterprise has no overseas affiliated companies
- The total annual controlled transactions amount is less than TWD 100m

¶20,040

If the Taiwan enterprise meets the safe harbor threshold and does not prepare a transfer pricing report, the Taiwan tax authority still may request "other supporting documents" as evidence of the arm's length nature of the intercompany transactions. One example of an "other supporting document" as stated under the ruling is the parent or headquarters' transfer pricing report, as long as it does not significantly vary from the concepts presented in the Taiwan TP guidelines.

In November 2008, the Taiwan tax authority released a new letter ruling (No.09704555160) to further loosen the safe harbor criteria. The new rule is applicable for fiscal years ending in December 2008 and onwards. The ruling states that an enterprise is not required to prepare a transfer pricing report if any of the following three criteria are met:

- The total annual revenue (including operating and non-operating) of the enterprise does not exceed TWD 300m

- The total annual revenue (including operating and non-operating) of the enterprise exceeds TWD 300m but does not exceed TWD 500m and

  - The enterprise does not utilize tax credits for more than TWD 2m in a particular year or a loss carry forward for more than TWD 8m for the preceding five tax years to reduce the income tax or undistributed earnings surplus tax

  - An enterprise under Financial Holding Company Law or Mergers and Acquisitions Law has no transactions with any overseas related parties (whether a company or an individual), or an enterprise has no transactions with overseas affiliated companies; or

- The total annual controlled transactions amount is less than TWD 200m

The categories of documentation required are:

- Business overview
- Organizational structure
- Description of controlled transactions
- Transfer pricing report, including:
  - Industry and economic analysis
  - Functions and risks analysis
  - Application of the arm's length principle
  - Selection of comparables and related information
  - Comparability analysis
  - Transfer pricing methods selected by the enterprises
  - Transfer pricing methods selected by related parties under the same control
  - Result of comparables search under the best method of transfer pricing
- Report of affiliated enterprises under Article 369 of the Republic of China (ROC) Company Law

¶20,040

- Any other documents that have significant influence over pricing between the related parties

Documentation deadlines

According to the TP guidelines, upon filing the annual income tax return, the taxpayer must have the transfer pricing report and relevant documents prepared. If the tax return meets the requirement for certification, the Tax CPA has to note on the return whether the enterprise has prepared a transfer pricing report in accordance with the TP guidelines. No attachment of the report to the return is required upon filing.

In accordance with the TP guidelines, upon audit, the enterprise has to provide the tax authority with the report within one month. With the approval of the tax authority, the submission could be extended for one month under special circumstances.

Statute of limitations on transfer pricing assessments

The statute of limitations is five years if the tax return was timely filed and seven years if not.

Return disclosures/related-party disclosures

Beginning in 2004, a taxpayer must disclose related-party transactions and include the disclosure under the annual income tax return pursuant to the TP guidelines. The disclosure generally includes:

- The investing structure
- Identification of related parties
- The related-party transaction amounts by type
- The related-party transaction balances
- The related parties' financial information, including total revenues, gross margins, operating margins and net margins
- Whether the enterprise has prepared transfer pricing documentation for that fiscal year

The Taiwan tax authority issued safe harbor rules for related-party transaction disclosures in Tax Letter Ruling No. 09404587580 for tax year 2005 and in Tax Letter Ruling No. 09604503530 for tax year 2006 and onwards. Both Rulings provide that an enterprise must disclose related-party transactions on its income tax return if the sum of its annual operating and non-operating revenue (total annual revenue amount) exceeds TWD 30m and also meets one of the following:

- Has related parties outside the territory of the ROC (including the headquarters and branches)
- Utilizes tax credits for more than TWD 500,000, or utilizes loss carry forwards for more than TWD 2m to reduce the income tax or undistributed earnings surplus tax
- Exceeds total annual revenue of TWD 300m

¶20,040

Audit risk/transfer pricing scrutiny

On 2 August 2005, the MOF issued a Tax Letter Ruling No. 9404540920 that set forth the circumstances for a transfer pricing audit as follows:

- The gross profit ratio, operating profit ratio and net income before tax ratio are below the industry average

- The parent or headquarters reports profit on the global consolidation level, but the local affiliate reports loss or much less profit than the industry average

- An enterprise reports significant fluctuations of profit over the transaction year and the two years preceding

- An enterprise fails to disclose related-party transactions in accordance with the related-party transaction disclosure requirements

- An enterprise fails to determine whether its related-party transactions are within an arm's length range and fails to prepare documents in accordance with the TP guidelines

- An enterprise fails to charge related parties in accordance with the TP guidelines or charges an abnormal amount

- An enterprise fails to provide the transfer pricing report upon a tax audit

- The transfer pricing of the enterprise has been adjusted by the tax authority, in which case, the tax years preceding and subsequent to the year of a transfer pricing audit are likely to be selected for audit

- An enterprise has significant or frequent controlled transactions with related parties in tax havens or low tax jurisdictions

- An enterprise has significant or frequent controlled transactions with related parties entitled to tax incentives

- Any other transaction fails to meet the arm's length requirements in accordance with the TP guidelines

In general, the level of audit risk is high. In the past year, there has been increased activity from Taiwan's tax authority especially with respect to requests to see documentation reports. These requests seem to be made irrespective of the revenue, the existence of cross border transactions or relative size of the company. In particular, companies conducting business through tax havens have attracted more scrutiny along with those making losses.

APA opportunity

APAs are available under articles 23 through 32 of the TP guidelines. According to Tax Letter Ruling No. 9404540920, under an APA, a tax return is not subject to a transfer pricing audit except for the following circumstances:

- The enterprise fails to provide the tax authority with the annual report regarding the implementation of the APA

- The enterprise fails to keep the relevant documents in accordance with TP guidelines

¶20,040

- The enterprise fails to follow the provisions of the APA
- The enterprise conceals material facts, provides false information or conducts wrongful acts

THAILAND

Taxing authority and tax law

Thai Revenue Department (TRD). General transfer pricing relevant provisions of the Thai tax code (dealing with exchanges at below market price in general) are: Thai Revenue Code § 65 bis (4); § 70 ter; § 65 bis (7); § 65 ter (13), (14), (15) and (19); and § 79/3. Transfer pricing guideline: Departmental Instruction No. Paw. 113/2545.

Relevant regulations and rulings

On 16 May 2002, the TRD issued its guideline specifically addressing transfer pricing. The guideline, Departmental Instruction No. Paw. 113/2545, is written in the form of an internal departmental instruction which provides guidance to tax officials for tax audit purposes.

OECD guidelines treatment

Thailand's transfer pricing guideline, Departmental Instruction No. Paw. 113/2545, generally follows the model of the OECD guidelines, including allowing all methods allowed under the OECD guidelines. This includes supporting material beyond the scope of the OECD guidelines. The OECD guidelines are not binding on the TRD. The OECD guidelines may, however, be persuasive in areas not addressed by the Thai Transfer Pricing guideline.

Priorities/pricing methods

The TRD accepts CUP, Resale Price and Cost Plus. Other commercially used methods are also acceptable, such as the OECD's Profit Split and TNMM.

Transfer pricing penalties

There is no explicit penalty for transfer pricing assessments. Nor is there an explicit penalty for not having transfer pricing documentation. However, for tax shortfalls in general, if a company is assessed by the TRD, a penalty of 100% or 200% of the tax shortfall and a 1.5% per month surcharge may be imposed. The 1.5% monthly surcharge is capped at 100% of the tax shortfall amount.

Penalty relief

In the event of a transfer pricing adjustment, there is no formal penalty relief for having in place transfer pricing documentation. Penalties may be reduced by half or waived if the taxpayer voluntarily files a return and accounts for the tax shortfall. Surcharges are a form of interest and cannot be reduced. Contemporaneous documents cannot be used to reduce the penalty for a transfer pricing shortfall. However, they are important for the defense of transfer pricing should a tax audit take place.

Documentation requirements

The following extensive contemporaneous documentation is specified:

- The structure and relationships between business entities within the same group, including the structure and nature of business carried on by each entity

¶20,040

- Budgets, business plans and financial projections
- Taxpayers' business strategies and the reasons for adopting those strategies
- Sales and operating results and the nature of transactions between business entities within the same group
- Reasons for entering into international transactions with business entities in the same group
- Pricing policies, product profitability, relevant market information and profit sharing of each business entity
- Functions performed, assets utilized and risks assumed by the related business entities should all be considered
- Support for the particular method chosen
- Where other methods have been considered, details of those methods and the reasons for their rejection (contemporaneously documented)
- Evidence supporting the negotiation positions taken by the taxpayer in relation to the transactions with business entities in the same group and the basis for those negotiating positions
- Other relevant documentation (if any) supporting the transfer prices

Documentation deadlines

The taxpayer is required to submit the transfer pricing documentation as and when requested by the TRD within the submission date stipulated in the requesting letter. However, the taxpayer may request for an extension of the submission if necessary. Such a request is required to be a written letter for submission to the TRD. In general, the extension granted from the TRD is up to one month after receiving the letter.

Statute of limitations on transfer pricing assessments

Under Section 19 of the Thai tax code, the statute of limitations is two years from the date of filing the tax return. This period is extendible to five years if tax evasion or fraud is suspected.

Return disclosures/related-party disclosures

No disclosure of the existence or non-existence of transfer pricing documentation is required to be submitted with a tax return. Nor does any documentation need to be filed with a tax return.

Under the Thai Federation of Accounting Professions and Securities and Exchange Commission of Thailand (SEC) regulations, the relatedparty transactions of companies listed on the SEC must be disclosed in the company's financial statements and annual report. Non-listed companies are not required to disclose related-party transactions in their financial statements.

Audit risk/transfer pricing scrutiny

Scrutiny of transfer pricing during a tax audit or inquiry in Thailand is common and the risk to the average multinational company is moderate to slightly high. The

TRD expects taxpayers to cooperate in providing relevant transfer pricing support documentation. It is likely that failure to do so will lead to a tax audit.

Generally, the TRD makes transfer pricing adjustments to the deductibility of expense items through its annual routine visits to taxpayers to review their business operations. During such checks, if officials find any transactions warranting further scrutiny (including deductibility of expenses arising from intercompany transactions), a further investigation will be conducted. In most cases, the taxpayer under investigation will be required to add back the expenses (to the extent deemed excessive) to taxable income and pay the additional tax arising. The final tax adjustments are then generally settled by way of negotiations.

Since 2006 until present, there has been more aggressive enforcement by the TRD in all areas of tax, especially transfer pricing. The increased level of enforcement mainly arises from tax collection pressure on the TRD to compensate for customs duty and excise tax shortfalls.

APA opportunity

From late 2004 onwards, there have been an increasing number of taxpayers filing APA requests (both unilateral and bilateral) with the TRD. The TRD has set up a formal APA committee to handle these APA applications. The recent completions of two bilateral APAs between Japan and Thailand in August 2008 are the first since the Thai transfer pricing guideline was introduced in May 2002. Currently, there are a number of bilateral APAs that are in the process of negotiation.

TURKEY

Taxing authority and tax law

Ministry of Finance is the taxing authority. Transfer pricing is regulated in Article 13 of Corporate Tax Code numbered 5520, published 21 June 2006.

Article 13 of Corporate Tax Code states: "Income shall be considered to have been wholly or partially distributed in a disguised manner through transfer pricing, if the company engages in purchase of goods and services with related parties at prices or at amounts which they determine are not complying with the arm's length principle."

Transfer pricing provisions have been effective since January 2007.

Relevant regulations and rulings

There is a cabinet decree published in December 2007, and two communiqués have been issued by the Ministry of Finance, namely "General Communiqué on Disguised Profit Distribution By Means of Transfer Pricing Serial No. 1 and 2." There is no ruling, controversy and court case given to date concerning the new transfer pricing regulations.

A large number of court cases exist on the subject of disguised profit distribution (legislation before transfer pricing). They are mostly conflicting and fail to establish case law which would bind all the parties.

OECD guidelines treatment

In the preamble of the law, it is stated that the provisions of international regulations, especially the OECD Transfer Pricing Guidelines, are taken as a reference. However there is no particular reference to the OECD guidelines in the actual content of the regulations, including Article 13 of the Corporate Tax Code, the related decree and communiqués. In addition, there are two major differences from the OECD approach: the term "related party" is defined in a very broad manner, for example it includes all shareholders regardless of the level of interest and domestic related-party transactions are also covered by the new rules.

In general, the new transfer pricing rules place significant documentation and disclosure requirements on Turkish taxpayers, but it is difficult to estimate the level of assurance provided by fulfilling these requirements at the moment, as the intention of the new transfer pricing rules from the tax authority's point of view is to protect Turkey's tax base.

One of the obstacles in the way of a smooth transition in the application of the new transfer pricing rules is the lack of a reference for comparable searches and the difficulty in finding comparables, in particular in the Turkish domestic market. Please note that there is not any local database available for benchmarking studies.

Priorities/pricing methods

Taxpayers can use the following methods in order to prove that the prices applied in their transactions with related parties are arm's length: CUP, Resale Price and Cost Plus. If it is not possible to reach the arm's length price through one of these traditional methods, profit methods such as Profit Split, TNMM/CPM and

¶20,040

other methods to be determined by the taxpayers can be selected. Taxpayers should select the most appropriate method according to the nature of their business, comparability factors and availability of relevant information. There is no priority among the traditional methods.

Transfer pricing penalties

There are no specific transfer pricing penalties, but a disguised income distribution is assumed if the transfer prices applied in related-party transactions do not meet the arm's length principle. If such a disguised distribution is assessed during a tax audit, (1) for corporate income tax purposes, 20% corporate income tax is calculated again as if no disguised distribution were applied and (2) dividend withholding tax of 15% is calculated over the net amount of the disguised distribution. Additionally late payment interest and a tax loss penalty (which is the same as tax loss amount) is charged to the tax payer.

Penalty relief

There are no special provisions for penalty relief. However, it is possible to come to a reconciliation regarding tax loss and tax penalty assessed. In such reconciliation the taxpayers may claim good faith.

Documentation requirements

Taxpayers are required to submit a transfer pricing form related to transactions with related parties. This form should be submitted as a supplement to the corporate tax return, which must be filed by the deadline of the 25th day of the fourth month following the fiscal year.

In addition to the transfer pricing form, certain taxpayers are required to file an "Annual Transfer Pricing Report." This requirement applies to:

- Corporate taxpayers who are registered with the "Grand Taxpayers Tax Office" prepare the report covering all domestic and foreign related-party transactions

- Corporate taxpayers having activities in Turkish Free Trade Zones prepare the report covering domestic transactions conducted with related parties

- Other taxpayers prepare the report for the purpose of disclosing transactions conducted with foreign related parties

This documentation report should include, company analysis, industry analysis, related parties, each transaction conducted with related parties with their values, functional analysis and economic analysis (selection of transfer pricing method, benchmarking studies and financial analysis).

The Report is required to be prepared by the 25th day of the fourth month following the fiscal year, which is the due date of the corporate income tax return. After this date taxpayers should present their documentation reports to the Tax Authority within 15 days of a request by the Tax Authority.

Documentation deadlines

Stated in "Documentation requirements" section above.

¶20,040

Statute of limitations on transfer pricing assessments

There is no specific statute of limitations on transfer pricing assessments, but general rules for the statute of limitations are applicable, which is five years from accrual of the tax payment.

Return disclosures/related-party disclosures

Taxpayers are required to disclose information on all related-party transactions in their transfer pricing forms. In addition, taxpayers are required to prepare an Annual Transfer Pricing Report which should include this information in detail.

The information will include the name or title of the local related party, taxpayer identification number, name of the foreign related-party and the country in which it resides. Other required disclosures include the sale and purchase of commodities both in the form of raw material and finished goods, the lease of any property, construction services, research and development, commission-based services, all related-party financial transactions, including lending and borrowing funds, marketable securities, insurance and other transactions and intra group services. Taxpayers also must disclose the transfer pricing methods applied in the related-party transactions.

Audit risk/transfer pricing scrutiny

The risk of transfer pricing scrutiny during a tax audit is high. Tax inspectors generally focus on related-party transactions. With the abundance of related-party transactions, it is likely that tax inspectors will extend their tax audits. New transfer pricing rules have increased the awareness of transfer pricing applications in general. As a result it is expected that the tax audits in the following year will focus on related-party transactions.

APA opportunity

An APA is possible upon the demand of the taxpayer. In principle, the agreed-upon method would be binding through the period determined; however, it cannot exceed three years. APA applications will be allowed for Grand Taxpayers Tax Office corporate taxpayers as of 1 January 2008 for their foreign transactions. Other taxpayers will be able to apply for APAs as of 1 January 2009.

¶20,040

UNITED KINGDOM

Taxing authority and tax law

Her Majesty's Revenue and Customs's (HMRC) authority and applicable law is found in a number of taxing Acts, predominantly, Schedule 28AA, Income and Corporation Taxes Act of 1988, § 12B Taxes Management Act of 1970, § 108-111 and Schedule 16 Finance Act of 1988 (full text of the basic rule now appears in Schedule 28 AA ICTA 1988). The Finance Act of 2004 also introduced provisions extending the transfer pricing code to include thin capitalization issues and transactions within the United Kingdom (UK), including between entities in the UK under common control. From 1 April 2004, transfer pricing laws are no longer restricted to cross-border transactions. There are grandfathering provisions for the exemption of dormant companies as well as exemptions for certain transactions of small- and mediumsized enterprises.

Finance Act (No. 2) 2005 introduced further amendments to Schedule 28AA extending the transfer pricing provisions, effective as of March 2005, to include two additional situations in which financing transactions are entered into for an entity: (1) where two or more persons finance an entity and act together to collectively control the entity, and (2) where a person finances an entity and a position of control will come into existence within six months of the financing. Grandfathering provisions exist under certain conditions to ensure that the amendments will only apply to transactions effective from 1 April 2007. Where a company's accounting period straddles a relevant date (4 March 2005 and 1 April 2007, date of contract variation), profits and losses are to be calculated as if there were two distinct accounting periods divided by the relevant date.

Relevant regulations and rulings

There are no specific regulations (with the exception of provisions for APAs as below), but there are "Guidance Notes" provided in HMRC Tax Bulletins (covering audit handling, share options, VAT considerations, Mutual Agreement Procedure (MAP), penalties and documentation). Additionally, HMRC has published several technical notes and made their internal manuals dealing with Transfer Pricing available.

The Varney Report of November 2006 (produced by Sir David Varney for the Chancellor) included various recommendations for changes to the way HMRC interacts with taxpayers. HMRC has responded to the recommendations made and for transfer pricing this has included a mandated risk assessment and the publication of a Code governing Transfer Pricing Enquiries. This includes the requirement for risk assessment and the need to present a business case to one of two panels set up for the purpose before any enquiry is commenced. The panels will also review progress during the enquiry and sign off settlement proposals.

With a thorough risk assessment leading to what HMRC believe are more targeted and focused enquiries on areas warranting specialist transfer pricing resources, the risk of audit is therefore high where there are red flags present in the accounts - changed business structure, losses, wildly fluctuating margins, high value adding functions, etc.

¶20,040

OECD guidelines treatment

The OECD Transfer Pricing Guidelines are effectively imported into UK tax legislation, as the law is to be interpreted in a way that best accords with the guidance. Therefore, there is general adherence to the OECD guidelines.

HMRC actively participates in OECD Committees and generally tries to act in accordance with OECD pronouncements. In this regard for instance they have regard to the OECD's position on the transfer pricing of share options in interpreting the UK Transfer Pricing Tax code. However while many of the OECD's comments or suggested approaches contained within the recent Discussion Draft on Business Restructurings are already aligned with the UK's position (it operates a function over form philosophy), it is nevertheless regarded by HMRC as a discussion draft and not necessarily informative in all situations as to the correct interpretation of the UK law.

Priorities/pricing methods

With alignment to the OECD guidelines required under the statutory provisions, the most appropriate method of pricing is effectively required under the UK legislation. HMRC prefers transaction methods over profit methods (such as with the TNMM). However, there is a recent move by the HMRC towards testing results against systems profits. This may also be mirroring OECD developments in this area.

Transfer pricing penalties

Two possible penalty regimes are currently applicable; however, provisions in the Finance Act of 2004 confirm that penalties for the failure to prepare and maintain adequate transfer pricing documentation will be waived under certain circumstances in the two years beginning 1 January 2004. This period has now ended.

Currently, UK tax law provides that tax-geared penalties of up to 100% of any underpaid tax apply to the filing of an incorrect return due to fraudulent or negligent conduct under Section 95/96 of the Taxes Management Act of 1970 and Paragraph 20 Schedule 18 Finance Act of 1988. Failure to have a policy documented as arm's length may be seen as negligent. A flat penalty of GBP 3,000 applies for failure to keep proper records under Paragraph 23 Schedule 18 of the Finance Act of 2004. There is a general increase in the use of neglect penalties across the board for all adjustments to profits. This is now extending to routine transfer pricing adjustments.

For accounting periods ending on or after 1 April 2008, the provisions for neglect penalties have changed. The statutory reference is found in Schedule 24 Finance Act 2007. These provisions are couched in terms of careless or deliberate inaccuracies rather than neglect. They remain tax geared at up to 100% of the potential lost revenue figure. This is, however, now calculated without adjustment for the availability of loss reliefs and where the adjustment affects losses only, the lost revenue figure to which the penalty percentage is applied is calculated at 10% of the loss adjustment.

¶20,040

Penalty relief

The best protection against neglect penalties is a transfer pricing policy which fully documents and evidences due consideration of the application of the arm's length principle in the preparation of the relevant tax return. Mitigation of the current tax-geared penalties, where applicable, will however be made with regard to size, gravity, disclosure and cooperation. For the code effective from 1 April 2008, mitigation is largely restricted to disclosure.

Documentation requirements

Tax Bulletin 37 originally set out HMRC expectations; however, this guidance is now superseded by the guidance published with the pre-budget report in December 2003.

The guidance published with the pre-budget report 2003, and now confirmed in the HMRC manuals, sets out what types of documents HMRC might expect. This divides documentation into primary accounting records, tax adjustment records and, most importantly, evidence. Documentation relating to evidence of compliance with the arm's length principle is to follow the OECD guidelines, and HMRC set out some suggestions on what this should or may include such as:

- Identification of the associated enterprises with whom the transaction is made
- A description of the nature of the business
- The contractual or other understandings between the parties
- A description of the method used to establish an arm's length result, with an explanation of why the method is chosen
- An explanation of commercial and management strategies, forecasts for the business or technological environment, competitive conditions and regulatory framework

HMRC applies a risk-based approach under which they would expect the level and depth of analysis to be dictated by the perceived risk of tax loss through manipulation of pricing. This typically allows a light touch approach to most UK to UK transactions.

Documentation deadlines

Under the current guidance, the first two categories of documentation should be in existence when the accounts are prepared and the return submitted. In relation to documentary evidence of arm's length pricing, it is not needed in a form capable of production to HMRC until a request by HMRC has been made. The previous guidance published by HMRC confirmed that all documentation should be in existence at the time the return is submitted. In practice, evidence confirming adherence to the arm's length principle should exist at the time of submission of the return if difficulties in its production are to be avoided.

Statute of limitations on transfer pricing assessments

Discovery assessments can be raised 6 years after the company's accounting period ends, but this is extended to 21 years where the misstatement is due to

¶20,040

fraudulent or negligent conduct by the taxpayer. With effect from 1 April 2010 these limits are set to change to 4 years and 20 years respectively. Discovery assessments however require there to have been negligence on the part of the taxpayer (defined as carelessness in the preparation of returns from 2010).

The legislation applicable before 1999 operated in a different manner, and as a result, an investigation started now would not normally lead to transfer pricing adjustments for periods before 1999.

Return disclosures/related-party disclosures

There are no return disclosure requirements except those required in statutory accounts and in annual reports filed in compliance with any current APAs. The absence of disclosure requirements will typically leave prior years open to discovery assessments.

Audit risk/transfer pricing scrutiny

HMRC now conducts a risk assessment before inquiry and is mandated to have a business case signed off by a panel set up for this purpose. Every Transfer Pricing Enquiry will now involve at least one transfer pricing specialist from HMRC's Transfer pricing Group (TPG). HMRC has also highlighted areas of concern that are likely to lead to inquiries (e.g., changed business structures and characterizations) and have invested heavily in transfer pricing investigation resources since early 2008. Additionally there is pressure on HMRC to reduce the perceived gap between actual tax revenues and the anticipated tax yield and transfer pricing is known to be an area of high priority.

APA opportunity

Section 85-87 of the Finance Act of 1999 introduced legislation on APAs. A Statement of Practice published in September 1999 supplements this legislation. Bilateral and unilateral APAs are available, but bilateral APAs are preferred. For APAs to be admitted to the program there needs to be sufficient doubt or difficulty in approaching compliance with the arm's length standard. Limited resources limit the UK to around 18-20 new admissions to the program each year.

UNITED STATES

Taxing authority and tax law

Internal Revenue Service (IRS); Internal Revenue Code (IRC) § 482, § 6038A, § 6038C, and § 6662.

Relevant regulations and rulings

Treasury Regulations (Treas. Regs.) § 1.482; § 1.6662; § 1.6038A; § 1.6038C; Revenue Procedure (Rev. Proc.) 2006-54; Rev. Proc. 99-32; and Rev. Proc. 2006-9. Final regulations (T.D. 9088) on compensatory stock options under IRC § 482 released on 25 August 2003, maintain that stock-based compensation must be taken into account in determining operating expenses for qualified cost-sharing arrangements (CSAs) under Treas. Reg. § 1.482-7. Audit checklist on CSAs was issued in August 2005. In April 2007, CSA buy-ins were designated by the IRS as a "Tier I" issue, and thus susceptible to intensified audit scrutiny. A Coordinated Issue Paper was released on 27 September 2007 providing internal IRS guidance for examiners in developing CSA exam positions. The Department of Treasury and the IRS released temporary CSA regulations with an effective date of 5 January 2009 (T.D. 9441, 74 FR 340). These regulations revise the proposed regulations issued in 2005 and replace the existing CSA regulations from 1995. The temporary regulations provide the IRS with discretion to make periodic adjustments and formalize other new requirements for compliance.

New final, temporary, and proposed regulations related to services were issued on 31 July 2006. The new rules were effective 1 January 2007, and apply to tax years beginning after 31 December 2006. In conjunction with the new regulations, the IRS also issued Announcement 2006-50, which contained a proposed list of "specified covered services" that relate to a specific cost-based method. The new services regulations require stock-based compensation to be considered in total costs. On 20 December 2006, the IRS released Notice 2007-5 and Revenue Procedure 2007-13, which extended the effective date of the Services Cost Method until 1 January 2008 and added to the list of "covered services."

OECD guidelines treatment

The IRS considers its transfer pricing laws and regulations to be wholly consistent with OECD guidelines. For domestic use, the OECD guidelines do not provide support, and would not be directly relevant to the application of any pricing methods. However, if taxpayers pursue competent authority relief from double taxation or a bilateral APA, then the OECD guidelines would be important and may be used to demonstrate compliance with international principles.

Priorities/pricing methods

For tangible goods, the IRS accepts the CUP, Resale Price, Cost Plus, CPM, Profit Split, and unspecified methods. For intangible goods, the IRS accepts the Comparable Uncontrolled Transaction (CUT), CPM, Profit Split, and unspecified methods. The new services regulations provide for the following methods: Services Cost Method, Comparable Uncontrolled Services Price, Gross Services Margin, Cost of Services Plus, CPM, Profit Split, and unspecified methods. The Coordinated

Issue Paper related to CSAs advises IRS auditors that unspecified methods are appropriate for valuing buy-ins (such as the "income method" and the "acquisition price method"). The regulations provide a "best method rule" for determining the appropriate method to be applied by the taxpayer for each intercompany transaction.

Transfer pricing penalties

Taxpayers may be liable for either a 20% or 40% penalty for underpayment of tax (IRC § 6662), as a percentage of the underpayment, or the penalty may apply to a valuation misstatement. There is not a U.S. penalty for failure to have documentation, but documentation may help to avoid a penalty.

Penalty relief

Penalties may be avoided by adequate disclosure on IRS Form 8275 for disregarding rules or regulations and for a substantial understatement of income tax. Penalties for negligence and for a valuation misstatement are not avoided by disclosure. No penalties apply, however, if there was reasonable cause and the taxpayer acted in good faith with respect to the transaction. The regulations provide guidance for establishing reasonable cause and good faith, for example, by preparing documentation or by obtaining an APA.

Documentation requirements

Transfer pricing documentation is not required by law. However, in practice, it is recommended that taxpayers maintain contemporaneous documentation in order to avoid penalties. Documentation must be provided to the IRS within 30 days of a request during an IRS examination. To be considered contemporaneous, the documents must be in existence when the return is filed, but their existence does not need to be disclosed with the tax return and they do not need to be provided with the return.

For penalty avoidance purposes, a taxpayer is considered to have satisfied the documentation requirement if it maintained sufficient documentation to establish that the taxpayer reasonably concluded that, given the available data and the applicable pricing methods, the method (and its application of that method) provided the most reliable measure of an arm's length result under the principles of the best method rule.

A method determined as part of an APA is a consideration for whether the taxpayer's method was reasonable. The principal documents required by regulations are:

- An overview of the taxpayer's business and an analysis of legal and economic factors affecting pricing
- A description of the organizational structure
- Any documents explicitly required by regulations (e.g., CSA documents)
- A description of the pricing method and reasons why the method was selected (a best method analysis)
- A description of alternative methods and why they were not selected

¶20,040

- A description of controlled transactions and any internal data used to analyze them
- A description of comparables used, how comparability was evaluated and any adjustments
- An explanation of any economic analysis and any projections used to develop the pricing method
- Any material data discovered after the close of the tax year but before filing the tax return
- A general index of the principal and background documents and a description of the recordkeeping system

Documentation deadlines

If documentation is prepared to help protect against penalties, then it must be in place by the filing date of the U.S. tax return. Taxpayers must provide documentation to the IRS within 30 days of an examiner's request.

Statute of limitations on transfer pricing assessments

A general statute of limitations applies, which is three years from the later of either the tax return due date or the date the return was actually filed. For substantial understatements of income, the statute is extended to six years. For fraud, there is no statute of limitations.

Return disclosures/related-party disclosures

Taxpayers are required to file Forms 5471 and 5472 regarding transactions with related parties, and they may also need to file Form 8275 (regarding disclosure).

Audit risk/transfer pricing scrutiny

The risk of transfer pricing scrutiny during a tax audit is high. Transfer pricing is extensively regulated. The designation of CSAs and intellectual property transactions as a Tier I (high risk transaction) issue for IRS auditors increases the risk for those transactions. This has been borne out in practice, where documentation is requested at the start of any international-issues audit.

APA opportunity

The IRS has an APA Program Office dedicated to analyzing and negotiating unilateral APAs, as well as bilateral and multilateral APAs with competent authority, as provided in Rev. Proc. 2006-9. The revenue procedure has strict case management procedures, disclosure requirements, and detailed guidance for taxpayers and the IRS in submitting APA requests and processing the analyses. Competent authority guidance is provided in Rev. Proc. 2006-54, which compliments the requirements of Rev. Proc. 2006-9.

VENEZUELA

Taxing authority and tax law

Venezuelan Tax Administration (SENIAT). 2001 Master Tax Code: chapter III, Articles 220 to 229, Articles 109, 110 and 111. The 2001 Venezuelan income tax law, chapter III, Articles 112 to 170. The 2007 Income Tax Law Reform, article 118, inclusion of thin capitalization rules.

Relevant regulations and rulings

On February 2007, a partial reform of the Income Tax Law and rules in thin capitalization were published in the Official Gazette No.38.628. The thin capitalization rules apply, as of fiscal year 2008, to where a Venezuelan taxpayer or a Venezuelan permanent establishment has debt (controlled debt) to companies or individuals who are considered related according to Title VII, Chapter III, in the transfer pricing rules. The main inclusions are as follows:

- Taxpayer will have a limited possibility to deduct interest expenses resulting from related parties' loans when the average of its debts (with related and unrelated parties) exceeds the amount of the average of its equity for the respective fiscal year

- The extent of debt that exceeds the taxpayer's equity will be treated as equity for income tax purposes

OECD guidelines treatment

The 1995 OECD guidelines are applicable as a supplement to these rules for everything else not considered in the Venezuelan Income Tax Law.

Priorities/pricing methods

The acceptable methods are OECD methods: CUP, Resale Price, Cost Plus, Profit Split and TNMM. Priority is given to the CUP method.

Transfer pricing penalties

By failing to apply the transfer pricing methods, the taxpayer faces fines from 300 to 500 Tax Units. The 2008 Tax Unit is BSF 41.00/unit. In addition, there will be a fine ranging from 25% to 200% of the omitted tax amount, and late payment interest may also be added to these amounts in the case of a transfer pricing assessment. Failing to issue the transfer pricing informative return (PT-99) will trigger a penalty of 10 to 50 Tax Units.

Penalty relief

If a taxpayer complies with a transfer pricing method, this could be considered a mitigating circumstance in the determination of an assessment. This penalty relief is based on previous tax audit procedure and assessments, but there is not a legal provision to support it.

Documentation requirements

Effective in 2002, taxpayers are required to prepare and maintain supporting and extensive contemporaneous documentation. The documentation requirements

¶20,040

include functions, assets, risks, organizational structure, business descriptions, detailed information of all operations with related and non-related parties, audited financial statements, agreements and contracts, reasoned method selection, inventory valuation method (if applicable), analysis results and other relevant information.

Documentation deadlines

The taxpayer must prepare documentation by the filing date of the annual income tax return at the end of every fiscal year. In addition, the taxpayer must submit the documentation upon request by SENIAT during a transfer pricing audit. It is mandatory to file the transfer pricing informative return (PT-99) during the month of June for those taxpayers who have their fiscal year ending in December. In other cases, the filing deadline will be six months after the specific year's closing.

Statute of limitations on transfer pricing assessments

The statute of limitations is four years from the date of filing the return and six years if the taxpayers failed to comply with the filing of any tax return, such as an income tax return, VAT returns or customs duties returns. PT-99 is not considered a tax return.

Return disclosures/related-party disclosures

A controlled party's information return must be filed during the six months immediately following the closing of each tax year. The PT-99 form is available in the tax authority's website (www.seniat.gob.ve).

Audit risk/transfer pricing scrutiny

SENIAT has been very active in transfer pricing audits lately. In the general tax audit plan called Zero Evasion Plan, SENIAT has added transfer pricing as a relevant topic to be audited. Thus far, audits have been performed on taxpayers in the oil industry, pharmaceutical industry, service providers, consumer products industry, automotive and steel and iron producers.

SENIAT has issued several transfer pricing assessments to relevant multinational corporations in diverse industries, which have been publicly informed, and the amounts were from USD 5m to USD 67m.

The audits have been organized by industry and the taxpayers are selected by:

- Having inconsistency between the transfer pricing report, income tax return and the transfer pricing informative return
- Using the TNMM
- Using non-updated financial information from comparable companies up to June of the fiscal year subject to study
- Having profit level indicators below the interquartile arm's length range
- Showing lower operating margins compared with operating margins from the previous year

¶20,040

The risk of transfer pricing scrutiny is high when a taxpayer performs financial operations directly or indirectly with related parties and when taxpayers have technical assistance or know how agreements with related parties abroad.

APA opportunity

Unilateral and bilateral APAs are available to the extent that they are carried out with nations that have outstanding double taxation treaties (see income tax law Articles 143 to 167, and Master Tax Code chapter III, Articles 220 to 229, Articles 109, 110 and 111).

VIETNAM

Taxing authority and tax law

General Department of Taxation (GDT). Decree 164/2003/NDCP dated 22 December 2003, Decree on Detailed Provisions Implementing the Law on Corporate Turnover Tax. Circular 117/2005/TT/BTC (Circular 117) dated 19 December 2005 of the Ministry of Finance, *Circular Providing Guidelines on the Calculation of Market Prices in Business Transactions between Related Parties.*

Relevant regulations and rulings

See above Decrees and Circular. Circular 117 became effective on 27 January 2006. Circular 117 will soon be amended by Circular 01/2009/TT/BTC which clarifies the scope of the definition of "related party" and shortens the period within which to submit the documentation from 90 to 10 days from the date of demand by the tax authorities. Circular 01 is still in draft form as of November 2009.

OECD guidelines treatment

Circular 117 is generally based on the OECD guidelines. How the GDT will apply the OECD guidelines in interpreting the principles under Circular 117 remains to be seen during the first few years of implementation of the Circular. Transfer pricing documentations adhere to the OECD guidelines in applying the principles of Circular 117.

Priorities/pricing methods

Circular 117 permits the use of the following methods: CUP, Resale Price, Cost Plus, CPM (or TNMM) and Profit Split. Taxpayers must use the most appropriate method under the regulations. There is no hierarchy among the methods although an internal CUP appears to be preferred.

Transfer pricing penalties

Adjustments in corporate income tax liabilities may be made by the tax authority in the following cases:

- Failure to disclose, or incomplete disclosure, of related-party transactions
- Failure to produce information, documents or source documents within 30 days of a request by the tax authority
- Intentional erroneous application of the provisions of the Circular and failure to produce substantiation requirements within 90 days of the date of request by the tax authority

Administrative penalties ranging from VND 500,000 to VND5 Million may be imposed for failure to produce the TP documentation and interest penalty of .05% of the outstanding tax due may also be imposed in case there is a TP adjustment. Additional penalties will be imposed if there is a finding of tax evasion or fraud.

Penalty relief

Penalties may be avoided by adequate disclosure on Form GCN-01/HTQT of the related-party transactions and the preparation and timely production of transfer pricing documentation.

¶20,040

Documentation requirements

Contemporaneous documentation is required by law. Documentation must be provided to the tax authority within 30 days upon request. The documents must be in existence when the transaction occurs and must be updated during the performance of the transaction. For penalty-avoidance purposes, a taxpayer is considered to have satisfied the documentation requirement if it maintained sufficient documentation to establish that the taxpayer reasonably concluded that, given the available data and the applicable pricing methods, the method (and its application of that method) provided the most reliable measure of an arm's length result under the principles of the most appropriate method rule.

The principal information and documents required by the regulations are:

- Information on relations between affiliated parties and the taxpayer

- Information and updated reports on strategy for development, administration and control between affiliated parties

- The pricing policy for transactions in relation to each group of products in accordance with the general guidance of affiliated parties and the taxpayer

- Documents and reports on the process of development, business strategy, projects, production, business or investment plans

- Regulations and procedures for financial statements and internal control reports of the company and of affiliated parties to the transactions

- A diagram of transactions and documents describing transactions, including information on parties to transactions, order and procedures for payment and delivery of products

- Documents specifying properties and technical specifications of products, the breakdown of costs (or cost) of one product, selling price of products, total amount of products produced or traded and sold in the period (specifying such items on the basis of the related transaction and an independent transaction, if any) and the quantity of products

- Information, documents and source documents concerning the process of negotiation, signing, performance and liquidation of economic contracts and agreements related to transactions (usually including a description of products, place of transaction, form of transaction, value of transaction, terms of payment, payment documentation, period of performance, minutes of meetings or instructions of the management regarding the process of negotiation, signing and the performance of a transaction)

- Information, documents and source documents related to economic conditions of the market at the time of the related transactions affecting the method of calculation of a price for transactions (for example, changes in exchange rates and policies of the government affecting prices in transactions and financial incentives)

- The pricing policy for selling and purchasing products and the procedures for control and approval of prices

¶20,040

- Information, documents and source documents used to select the most appropriate method, including data used for comparative analysis and adjustment of significant differences
- Other information or documents used to select and apply the methods

Documentation deadlines

The documentation must exist at the time of the transaction. Taxpayers must provide documentation to the tax authorities within 30 days of a request. If the taxpayer intentionally fails to apply the provisions of Circular 117, and fails to produce the documentation within 90 days of request, an adjustment of corporate income tax liabilities will be made.

Statute of limitations on transfer pricing assessments

The general principles on statutes of limitations apply. There is no statute of limitations with respect to the recovery or re-collection of taxes. However, administrative penalties may be imposed only within two or five years from the date of commission to the date of discovery of the violation for tax procedures or tax evasion, respectively.

Return disclosures/related-party disclosures

Taxpayers are required to file Form GCN-01/HTQT to disclose their transactions with related parties, the details of these transactions and the transfer pricing methods used to calculate the prices in these transactions. The disclosure form must be submitted together with the corporate income tax return, which must be filed within 90 days of the end of the fiscal year.

Audit risk/transfer pricing scrutiny

The risk of transfer pricing audit is high with respect to automobile and pharmaceutical companies. Companies which are reporting losses during their tax incentive periods are targeted for TP audits.

APA opportunity

Circular 117 does not provide for unilateral or bilateral APAs.

¶ 20,050 IRS Forms 5471 and 5472

Form 5471 is used by certain U.S. citizens and residents who are officers, directors or shareholders in certain foreign corporations. The forms and schedules are used to satisfy the reporting requirements of Code Secs. 6035, 6038 6046 and the related regulations. Form 5472 is used to provide information required under Code Secs. 6038Aand 6038C, when reportable transactions occur during the tax year of a reporting corporation with a foreign or domestic related party.

Form 5471

Form **5471** (Rev. December 2007) Department of the Treasury Internal Revenue Service	**Information Return of U.S. Persons With Respect To Certain Foreign Corporations** ▶ See separate instructions. Information furnished for the foreign corporation's annual accounting period (tax year required by section 898) (see instructions) beginning , 20 , and ending , 20	OMB No. 1545-0704 Attachment Sequence No. **121**

Name of person filing this return	**A** Identifying number	
Number, street, and room or suite no. (or P.O. box number if mail is not delivered to street address)	**B** Category of filer (See instructions. Check applicable box(es)): 1 (repealed) 2 ☐ 3 ☐ 4 ☐ 5 ☐	
City or town, state, and ZIP code	**C** Enter the total percentage of the foreign corporation's voting stock you owned at the end of its annual accounting period .... %	

Filer's tax year beginning , 20 , and ending , 20

D Person(s) on whose behalf this information return is filed:

(1) Name	**(2)** Address	**(3)** Identifying number	**(4)** Check applicable box(es)		
			Shareholder	Officer	Director

Important: *Fill in all applicable lines and schedules. All information **must** be in English. All amounts **must** be stated in U.S. dollars unless otherwise indicated.*

1a Name and address of foreign corporation	**b** Employer identification number, if any
	c Country under whose laws incorporated

d Date of incorporation	**e** Principal place of business	**f** Principal business activity code number	**g** Principal business activity	**h** Functional currency

2 Provide the following information for the foreign corporation's accounting period stated above.

a Name, address, and identifying number of branch office or agent (if any) in the United States	**b** If a U.S. income tax return was filed, enter:	
	(i) Taxable income or (loss)	*(ii)* U.S. income tax paid (after all credits)
c Name and address of foreign corporation's statutory or resident agent in country of incorporation	**d** Name and address (including corporate department, if applicable) of person (or persons) with custody of the books and records of the foreign corporation, and the location of such books and records, if different	

Schedule A Stock of the Foreign Corporation

(a) Description of each class of stock	**(b)** Number of shares issued and outstanding	
	(i) Beginning of annual accounting period	*(ii)* End of annual accounting period

For Paperwork Reduction Act Notice, see instructions.   Cat. No. 49958V   Form **5471** (Rev. 12-2007)

Form 5471 (Rev. 12-2007)   Page **2**

Schedule B   **U.S. Shareholders of Foreign Corporation** (see instructions)

(a) Name, address, and identifying number of shareholder	(b) Description of each class of stock held by shareholder. **Note:** *This description should match the corresponding description entered in Schedule A, column (a).*	(c) Number of shares held at beginning of annual accounting period	(d) Number of shares held at end of annual accounting period	(e) Pro rata share of subpart F income (enter as a percentage)

Schedule C   **Income Statement** (see instructions)

Important: *Report all information in functional currency in accordance with U.S. GAAP. Also, report each amount in U.S. dollars translated from functional currency (using GAAP translation rules). However, if the functional currency is the U.S. dollar, complete only the U.S. Dollars column. See instructions for special rules for DASTM corporations.*

			Functional Currency	U.S. Dollars
Income	1a	Gross receipts or sales	**1a**		
	b	Returns and allowances	**1b**		
	c	Subtract line 1b from line 1a	**1c**		
	2	Cost of goods sold	**2**		
	3	Gross profit (subtract line 2 from line 1c)	**3**		
	4	Dividends	**4**		
	5	Interest	**5**		
	6a	Gross rents	**6a**		
	b	Gross royalties and license fees	**6b**		
	7	Net gain or (loss) on sale of capital assets	**7**		
	8	Other income (attach schedule)	**8**		
	9	Total income (add lines 3 through 8)	**9**		
Deductions	10	Compensation not deducted elsewhere	**10**		
	11a	Rents	**11a**		
	b	Royalties and license fees	**11b**		
	12	Interest	**12**		
	13	Depreciation not deducted elsewhere	**13**		
	14	Depletion	**14**		
	15	Taxes (exclude provision for income, war profits, and excess profits taxes)	**15**		
	16	Other deductions (attach schedule—exclude provision for income, war profits, and excess profits taxes)	**16**		
	17	Total deductions (add lines 10 through 16)	**17**		
Net Income	18	Net income or (loss) before extraordinary items, prior period adjustments, and the provision for income, war profits, and excess profits taxes (subtract line 17 from line 9)	**18**		
	19	Extraordinary items and prior period adjustments (see instructions)	**19**		
	20	Provision for income, war profits, and excess profits taxes (see instructions)	**20**		
	21	Current year net income or (loss) per books (combine lines 18 through 20)	**21**		

Form **5471** (Rev. 12-2007)

Form 5471 (Rev. 12-2007) — Page **3**

Schedule E — Income, War Profits, and Excess Profits Taxes Paid or Accrued (see instructions)

	(a) Name of country or U.S. possession	Amount of tax		
		(b) In foreign currency	(c) Conversion rate	(d) In U.S. dollars
1	U.S.			
2				
3				
4				
5				
6				
7				
8	Total			▶

Schedule F — Balance Sheet

Important: *Report all amounts in U.S. dollars prepared and translated in accordance with U.S. GAAP. See instructions for an exception for DASTM corporations.*

	Assets		(a) Beginning of annual accounting period	(b) End of annual accounting period
1	Cash	1		
2a	Trade notes and accounts receivable	2a		
b	Less allowance for bad debts	2b	( )	( )
3	Inventories	3		
4	Other current assets (attach schedule)	4		
5	Loans to shareholders and other related persons	5		
6	Investment in subsidiaries (attach schedule)	6		
7	Other investments (attach schedule)	7		
8a	Buildings and other depreciable assets	8a		
b	Less accumulated depreciation	8b	( )	( )
9a	Depletable assets	9a		
b	Less accumulated depletion	9b	( )	( )
10	Land (net of any amortization)	10		
11	Intangible assets:			
a	Goodwill	11a		
b	Organization costs	11b		
c	Patents, trademarks, and other intangible assets	11c		
d	Less accumulated amortization for lines 11a, b, and c	11d	( )	( )
12	Other assets (attach schedule)	12		
13	Total assets	13		

	Liabilities and Shareholders' Equity			
14	Accounts payable	14		
15	Other current liabilities (attach schedule)	15		
16	Loans from shareholders and other related persons	16		
17	Other liabilities (attach schedule)	17		
18	Capital stock:			
a	Preferred stock	18a		
b	Common stock	18b		
19	Paid-in or capital surplus (attach reconciliation)	19		
20	Retained earnings	20		
21	Less cost of treasury stock	21	( )	( )
22	Total liabilities and shareholders' equity	22		

Form **5471** (Rev. 12-2007)

¶20,050

Form 5471 (Rev. 12-2007)   Page **4**

Schedule G	Other Information

		Yes	No
1	During the tax year, did the foreign corporation own at least a 10% interest, directly or indirectly, in any foreign partnership?	☐	☐
	If "Yes," see the instructions for required attachment.		
2	During the tax year, did the foreign corporation own an interest in any trust?	☐	☐
3	During the tax year, did the foreign corporation own any foreign entities that were disregarded as entities separate from their owners under Regulations sections 301.7701-2 and 301.7701-3 (see instructions)?	☐	☐
	If "Yes," you are generally required to attach Form 8858 for each entity (see instructions).		
4	During the tax year, was the foreign corporation a participant in any cost sharing arrangement?	☐	☐
5	During the course of the tax year, did the foreign corporation become a participant in any cost sharing arrangement?	☐	☐

Schedule H	Current Earnings and Profits (see instructions)

Important: *Enter the amounts on lines 1 through 5c in **functional** currency.*

		Net Additions	Net Subtractions	
1	Current year net income or (loss) per foreign books of account			**1**
2	Net adjustments made to line 1 to determine current earnings and profits according to U.S. financial and tax accounting standards (see instructions):			
a	Capital gains or losses			
b	Depreciation and amortization			
c	Depletion			
d	Investment or incentive allowance			
e	Charges to statutory reserves			
f	Inventory adjustments			
g	Taxes			
h	Other (attach schedule)			
3	Total net additions			
4	Total net subtractions			
5a	Current earnings and profits (line 1 plus line 3 minus line 4)			**5a**
b	DASTM gain or (loss) for foreign corporations that use DASTM (see instructions)			**5b**
c	Combine lines 5a and 5b			**5c**
d	Current earnings and profits in U.S. dollars (line 5c translated at the appropriate exchange rate as defined in section 989(b) and the related regulations (see instructions))			**5d**
	Enter exchange rate used for line 5d ▶			

Schedule I	Summary of Shareholder's Income From Foreign Corporation (see instructions)

1	Subpart F income (line 38b, Worksheet A in the instructions)	**1**
2	Earnings invested in U.S. property (line 17, Worksheet B in the instructions)	**2**
3	Previously excluded subpart F income withdrawn from qualified investments (line 6b, Worksheet C in the instructions)	**3**
4	Previously excluded export trade income withdrawn from investment in export trade assets (line 7b, Worksheet D in the instructions)	**4**
5	Factoring income	**5**
6	Total of lines 1 through 5. Enter here and on your income tax return. See instructions.	**6**
7	Dividends received (translated at spot rate on payment date under section 989(b)(1))	**7**
8	Exchange gain or (loss) on a distribution of previously taxed income	**8**

	Yes	No
• Was any income of the foreign corporation blocked?	☐	☐
• Did any such income become unblocked during the tax year (see section 964(b))?	☐	☐

If the answer to either question is "Yes," attach an explanation.

Form **5471** (Rev. 12-2007)

Schedule J

Accumulated Earnings and Profits (E&P) of Controlled Foreign Corporation

▶ Attach to Form 5471. See Instructions for Form 5471.

OMB No. 1545-0704

Name of person filing Form 5471

Identifying number

Name of foreign corporation

Important: Enter amounts in functional currency.	**(a)** Post-1986 Undistributed Earnings (post-86 section 959(c)(3) balance)	**(b)** Pre-1987 E&P Not Previously Taxed (pre-87 section 959(c)(3) balance)	**(c)** Previously Taxed E&P (see instructions) (sections 959(c)(1) and (2) balances)			**(d)** Total Section 964(a) E&P (combine columns (a), (b), and (c))
			(i) Earnings Invested in U.S. Property	*(ii)* Earnings Invested in Excess Passive Assets	*(iii)* Subpart F Income	
1 Balance at beginning of year						
2a Current year E&P						
b Current year deficit in E&P						
3 Total current and accumulated E&P not previously taxed (line 1 plus line 2a **or** line 1 minus line 2b)						
4 Amounts included under section 951(a) or reclassified under section 959(c) in current year						
5a Actual distributions or reclassifications of previously taxed E&P						
b Actual distributions of nonpreviously taxed E&P						
6a Balance of previously taxed E&P at end of year (line 1 plus line 4, minus line 5a)						
b Balance of E&P not previously taxed at end of year (line 3 minus line 4, minus line 5b)						
7 Balance at end of year. (Enter amount from line 6a or line 6b, whichever is applicable.)						

For Paperwork Reduction Act Notice, see the Instructions for Form 5471.

Cat. No. 21111K

Schedule J (Form 5471) (Rev. 12-2005)

Schedule M

SCHEDULE M (Form 5471) (Rev. December 2007) Department of the Treasury Internal Revenue Service	**Transactions Between Controlled Foreign Corporation and Shareholders or Other Related Persons** ▶ Attach to Form 5471. See Instructions for Form 5471.	OMB No. 1545-0704

Name of person filing Form 5471	Identifying number

Name of foreign corporation

Important: *Complete a **separate** Schedule M for each controlled foreign corporation. Enter the totals for each type of transaction that occurred during the annual accounting period between the foreign corporation and the persons listed in columns (b) through (f). All amounts must be stated in U.S. dollars translated from functional currency at the average exchange rate for the foreign corporation's tax year. See instructions.*
Enter the relevant functional currency and the exchange rate used throughout this schedule ▶

(a) Transactions of foreign corporation	(b) U.S. person filing this return	(c) Any domestic corporation or partnership controlled by U.S. person filing this return	(d) Any other foreign corporation or partnership controlled by U.S. person filing this return	(e) 10% or more U.S. shareholder of controlled foreign corporation (other than the U.S. person filing this return)	(f) 10% or more U.S. shareholder of any corporation controlling the foreign corporation
1 Sales of stock in trade (inventory)					
2 Sales of tangible property other than stock in trade					
3 Sales of property rights (patents, trademarks, etc.) .					
4 Buy-in payments received . .					
5 Cost sharing payments received.					
6 Compensation received for technical, managerial, engineering, construction, or like services . .					
7 Commissions received					
8 Rents, royalties, and license fees received					
9 Dividends received (exclude deemed distributions under subpart F and distributions of previously taxed income) . . .					
10 Interest received					
11 Premiums received for insurance or reinsurance					
12 Add lines 1 through 11 . . .					
13 Purchases of stock in trade (inventory)					
14 Purchases of tangible property other than stock in trade . . .					
15 Purchases of property rights (patents, trademarks, etc.) . .					
16 Buy-in payments paid . . .					
17 Cost sharing payments paid .					
18 Compensation paid for technical, managerial, engineering, construction, or like services .					
19 Commissions paid					
20 Rents, royalties, and license fees paid					
21 Dividends paid					
22 Interest paid					
23 Premiums paid for insurance or reinsurance					
24 Add lines 13 through 23 . . .					
25 Amounts borrowed (enter the maximum loan balance during the year) — see instructions . .					
26 Amounts loaned (enter the maximum loan balance during the year) — see instructions . .					

For Paperwork Reduction Act Notice, see the Instructions for Form 5471.	Cat. No. 49963O	Schedule M (Form 5471) (Rev. 12-2007)

¶20,050

Schedule N

SCHEDULE N (Form 5471) (Rev. December 2004) Department of the Treasury Internal Revenue Service	**Return of Officers, Directors, and 10% or More** **Shareholders of a Foreign Personal Holding Company** ▶ Attach to Form 5471. See Instructions for Form 5471	OMB No. 1545-0704

Name of person filing Form 5471	Identifying number

Name of foreign corporation

Important: *All amounts must be stated in U.S. dollars translated from functional currency. See page 11 of the instructions for the relevant exchange rate.*

Enter the relevant functional currency and the exchange rate(s) used throughout this schedule ▶

Part I   Shareholder Information

Section A—Outstanding Securities Convertible Into Stock of the Corporation or Options Granted by the Corporation

Description of securities (attach a complete, detailed statement of conversion privileges)	Interest rate (%)	Face value	
		Beginning of year	End of year

Section B—List of Holders of Convertible Securities or Options Granted by the Corporation

Name and address of each holder of convertible securities or options (designate nonresident aliens)	Class of securities	Securities held				Explanation and date of any change in holdings of securities during the year
		Beginning of year		End of year		
		Number	Face value	Number	Face value	

Part II   Income Information

Section A—Undistributed Foreign Personal Holding Company Income

1	Gross income as defined in section 555 (attach schedule)	1	
2	Deductions allowable under section 161 (attach schedule)	2	
3	Taxable income or (loss) (subtract line 2 from line 1)	3	
4	Adjustments to taxable income or (loss) (see page 12 of instructions):		
a	Taxes (see instructions)	4a	
b	Charitable contributions	4b	
c	Special deductions disallowed	4c	
d	Net operating loss	4d	
e	Expenses and depreciation applicable to property of the taxpayer	4e	
f	Taxes and contributions to pension trusts	4f	
g	Total adjustments (combine lines 4a through 4f)	4g	
5	Combine line 3 and line 4g	5	
6	Deduction for dividends paid during tax year. Enter the amount from Section B, line 12, below	6	
7	Subtract line 6 from line 5	7	
8	Deduction allowed under section 563(c) for dividends paid after close of tax year (see instructions). Attach designation required by Rev. Proc. 90-26, 1990-1 C.B. 512	8	
9	Undistributed foreign personal holding company income (subtract line 8 from line 7) . .	9	

Section B—Deduction for Dividends Paid During Tax Year (see instructions)

		Date paid		Amount
10	Taxable dividends paid during tax year:			
a	Cash		10a	
b	Property other than cash or the corporation's own securities (indicate nature of property)		10b	
c	Obligations of the corporation (bonds, notes, scrip, etc.) . . .		10c	
11	Consent dividends (attach schedule)		11	
12	Deduction for dividends paid during tax year (add lines 10a through 11). Enter here and on line 6 above		12	

For Paperwork Reduction Act Notice, see the Instructions for Form 5471.   Cat. No. 61925Q   **Schedule N (Form 5471)** (Rev. 12-2004)

¶20,050

Schedule O

SCHEDULE O (Form 5471)	Organization or Reorganization of Foreign Corporation, and Acquisitions and Dispositions of its Stock	OMB No. 1545-0704
(Rev. December 2005) Department of the Treasury Internal Revenue Service	▶ Attach to Form 5471. See Instructions for Form 5471.	

Name of person filing Form 5471	Identifying number

Name of foreign corporation

Important: *Complete a* **separate** *Schedule O for each foreign corporation for which information must be reported.*

Part I To Be Completed by U.S. Officers and Directors

(a) Name of shareholder for whom acquisition information is reported	(b) Address of shareholder	(c) Identifying number of shareholder	(d) Date of original 10% acquisition	(e) Date of additional 10% acquisition

Part II To Be Completed by U.S. Shareholders

Note: *If this return is required because one or more shareholders became U.S. persons, attach a list showing the names of such persons and the date each became a U.S. person.*

Section A—General Shareholder Information

(a) Name, address, and identifying number of shareholder(s) filing this schedule	(b) For shareholder's latest U.S. income tax return filed, indicate:			(c) Date (if any) shareholder last filed information return under section 6046 for the foreign corporation
	(1) Type of return (enter form number)	(2) Date return filed	(3) Internal Revenue Service Center where filed	

Section B—U.S. Persons Who Are Officers or Directors of the Foreign Corporation

(a) Name of U.S. officer or director	(b) Address	(c) Social security number	(d) Check appropriate box(es)	
			Officer	Director

Section C—Acquisition of Stock

(a) Name of shareholder(s) filing this schedule	(b) Class of stock acquired	(c) Date of acquisition	(d) Method of acquisition	(e) Number of shares acquired		
				(1) Directly	(2) Indirectly	(3) Constructively

For Paperwork Reduction Act Notice, see the Instructions for Form 5471.   Cat. No. 61200O   **Schedule O (Form 5471)** (Rev. 12-2005)

¶20,050

Schedule O (Form 5471) (Rev. 12-2005)   Page **2**

(f) Amount paid or value given	(g) Name and address of person from whom shares were acquired	

Section D—Disposition of Stock

(a) Name of shareholder disposing of stock	(b) Class of stock	(c) Date of disposition	(d) Method of disposition	(e) Number of shares disposed of		
				(1) Directly	(2) Indirectly	(3) Constructively

(f) Amount received	(g) Name and address of person to whom disposition of stock was made	

Section E—Organization or Reorganization of Foreign Corporation

(a) Name and address of transferor	(b) Identifying number (if any)	(c) Date of transfer

(d) Assets transferred to foreign corporation			(e) Description of assets transferred by, or notes or securities issued by, foreign corporation
(1) Description of assets	(2) Fair market value	(3) Adjusted basis (if transferor was U.S. person)	

Section F—Additional Information

(a) If the foreign corporation or a predecessor U.S. corporation filed (or joined with a consolidated group in filing) a U.S. income tax return for any of the last 3 years, attach a statement indicating the year for which a return was filed (and, if applicable, the name of the corporation filing the consolidated return), the taxable income or loss, and the U.S. income tax paid (after all credits).

(b) List the date of any reorganization of the foreign corporation that occurred during the last 4 years while any U.S. person held 10% or more in value or vote (directly or indirectly) of the corporation's stock ▶

(c) If the foreign corporation is a member of a group constituting a chain of ownership, attach a chart, for each unit of which a shareholder owns 10% or more in value or voting power of the outstanding stock. The chart must indicate the corporation's position in the chain of ownership and the percentages of stock ownership (see instructions for an example).

Schedule O **(Form 5471)** (Rev. 12-2005)

¶20,050

Instructions for Form 5471

Instructions for Form 5471
(Rev. December 2009)

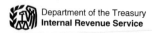
Department of the Treasury
Internal Revenue Service

(Use with the December 2007 revision of Form 5471 and Schedule M, and the December 2005 revision of Schedules J and O.)

**Information Return of U.S. Persons
With Respect to Certain Foreign Corporations**

Section references are to the Internal Revenue Code unless otherwise noted.

What's New

• The controlling U.S. shareholder(s) of a CFC may make a section 108(i) election to defer recognizing discharge of indebtedness income in certain situations. See **Section 108(i) Elections** on page 4 for additional information.
• Non-corporate U.S. shareholders are now required to report income reported on Form 5471, Schedule I, line 6 on Form 1040, line 21 (Other Income), or on the comparable line of other non-corporate tax returns.

Pending Legislation May Affect Form 5471

At the time these instructions were sent to print, legislation was pending that would extend:
• The temporary exceptions for certain "active financing income" from subpart F foreign personal holding company income, foreign base company services income, and insurance income, and
• The look-through rule of section 954(c)(6).

General Instructions

Purpose of Form

Form 5471 is used by certain U.S. citizens and residents who are officers, directors, or shareholders in certain foreign corporations. The form and schedules are used to satisfy the reporting requirements of sections 6038 and 6046, and the related regulations.

Who Must File

Generally, all U.S. persons described in *Categories of Filers* below must complete the schedules, statements, and/or other information requested in the chart, *Filing Requirements for Categories of Filers,* on page 2. Read the information for each category carefully to determine which schedules, statements, and/or information apply.

If the filer is described in more than one filing category, do not duplicate

information. However, complete all items that apply. For example, if you are the sole owner of a controlled foreign corporation (CFC) (i.e., you are described in Categories 4 and 5), complete all four pages of Form 5471 and separate Schedules J and M.

Note. Complete a **separate** Form 5471 and all applicable schedules for **each** applicable foreign corporation.

When and Where To File

Attach Form 5471 to your income tax return (or, if applicable, partnership or exempt organization return) and file both by the due date (including extensions) for that return.

Categories of Filers

Category 1 Filer

This filing requirement has been repealed by section 413(c)(26) of the American Jobs Creation Act of 2004, which repealed section 6035.

Category 2 Filer

This includes a U.S. citizen or resident who is an officer or director of a foreign corporation in which a U.S. person (defined below) has acquired (in one or more transactions):

1. Stock which meets the 10% stock ownership requirement (described below) with respect to the foreign corporation or
2. An additional 10% or more (in value or voting power) of the outstanding stock of the foreign corporation.

A U.S. person has **acquired** stock in a foreign corporation when that person has an unqualified right to receive the stock, even though the stock is not actually issued. See Regulations section 1.6046-1(f)(1) for more details.

Stock ownership requirement. For purposes of Category 2 and Category 3, the stock ownership threshold is met if a U.S. person owns:

1. 10% or more of the total value of the foreign corporation's stock or
2. 10% or more of the total combined voting power of all classes of stock with voting rights.

U.S. person. For purposes of Category 2 and Category 3, a U.S. person is:

1. A citizen or resident of the United States,
2. A domestic partnership,
3. A domestic corporation, and
4. An estate or trust that is not a foreign estate or trust defined in section 7701(a)(31).

See Regulations section 1.6046-1(f)(3) for exceptions.

Category 3 Filer

This category includes:
• A U.S. person (defined above) who acquires stock in a foreign corporation which, when added to any stock owned on the date of acquisition, meets the 10% stock ownership requirement (described above) with respect to the foreign corporation;
• A U.S. person who acquires stock which, without regard to stock already owned on the date of acquisition, meets the 10% stock ownership requirement with respect to the foreign corporation;
• A person who is treated as a U.S. shareholder under section 953(c) with respect to the foreign corporation;
• A person who becomes a U.S. person while meeting the 10% stock ownership requirement with respect to the foreign corporation; or
• A U.S. person who disposes of sufficient stock in the foreign corporation to reduce his or her interest to less than the stock ownership requirement.

For more information, see section 6046 and Regulations section 1.6046-1.

Category 4 Filer

This includes a U.S. person who had control (defined below) of a foreign corporation for an uninterrupted period of at least 30 days during the annual accounting period of the foreign corporation.

U.S. person. For purposes of Category 4, a U.S. person is:

1. A citizen or resident of the United States;
2. A nonresident alien for whom an election is in effect under section 6013(g) to be treated as a resident of the United States;
3. An individual for whom an election is in effect under section 6013(h), relating to nonresident aliens who become residents of the United States during the tax year and are married at the close of

Cat. No. 49959G

the tax year to a citizen or resident of the United States;

4. A domestic partnership;

5. A domestic corporation; and

6. An estate or trust that is not a foreign estate or trust defined in section 7701(a)(31).

See Regulations section 1.6038-2(d) for exceptions.

Control. A U.S. person has control of a foreign corporation if, at any time during that person's tax year, it owns stock possessing:

1. More than 50% of the total combined voting power of all classes of stock of the foreign corporation entitled to vote or

2. More than 50% of the total value of shares of all classes of stock of the foreign corporation.

A person in control of a corporation that, in turn, owns more than 50% of the combined voting power, or the value, of all classes of stock of another corporation is also treated as being in control of such other corporation.

Example. Corporation A owns 51% of the voting stock in Corporation B. Corporation B owns 51% of the voting stock in Corporation C. Corporation C owns 51% of the voting stock in Corporation D. Therefore, Corporation D is controlled by Corporation A.

For more details on "control," see Regulations sections 1.6038-2(b) and (c).

Category 5 Filer

This includes a U.S. shareholder who owns stock in a foreign corporation that is a CFC for an uninterrupted period of 30 days or more during any tax year of the foreign corporation, and who owned that stock on the last day of that year.

U.S. shareholder. For purposes of Category 5, a U.S. shareholder is a U.S. person who:

1. Owns (directly, indirectly, or constructively, within the meaning of sections 958(a) and (b)) 10% or more of the total combined voting power of all classes of voting stock of a CFC or

2. Owns (either directly or indirectly, within the meaning of section 958(a)) any stock of a CFC (as defined in sections 953(c)(1)(B) and 957(b)) that is also a captive insurance company.

U.S. person. For purposes of Category 5, a U.S. person is:

1. A citizen or resident of the United States,

2. A domestic partnership,

3. A domestic corporation, and

4. An estate or trust that is not a foreign estate or trust defined in section 7701(a)(31).

See section 957(c) for exceptions.

CFC. A CFC is a foreign corporation that has U.S. shareholders that own (directly, indirectly, or constructively, within the meaning of sections 958(a) and (b)) on any day of the tax year of the foreign corporation, more than 50% of:

1. The total combined voting power of all classes of its voting stock or

2. The total value of the stock of the corporation.

Exceptions From Filing

Multiple filers of same information. One person may file Form 5471 and the applicable schedules for other persons who have the same filing requirements. If you and one or more other persons are required to furnish information for the same foreign corporation for the same period, a joint information return that contains the required information may be filed with your tax return or with the tax return of any one of the other persons. For example, a U.S. person described in Category 5 may file a joint Form 5471 with a Category 4 or another Category 5 filer. However, for Category 3 filers, the required information may only be filed by another person having an equal or greater interest (measured in terms of value or voting power of the stock of the foreign corporation).

The person that files Form 5471 must complete Item D on page 1 of the form. All persons identified in Item D must attach a statement to their income tax return that includes the information described in the instructions for Item D on page 4.

Domestic corporations. Shareholders are not required to file the information checked in the chart on this page for a foreign insurance company that has elected (under section 953(d)) to be treated as a domestic corporation and has filed a U.S. income tax return for its tax year under that provision. See Rev. Proc. 2003-47, 2003-28 I.R.B. 55, for procedural rules regarding the election under section 953(d).

Members of consolidated groups. A Category 4 filer is not required to file Form 5471 for a corporation defined in section 1504(d) that files a consolidated return for the tax year.

Constructive owners.

• A U.S. person described in Category 3 or 4 does not have to file Form 5471 if **all** of the following conditions are met:

1. The U.S. person does not own a direct interest in the foreign corporation,

2. The U.S. person is required to furnish the information requested solely because of constructive ownership (as determined under Regulations section 1.6038-2(c) or 1.6046-1(i)) from another U.S. person, **and**

3. The U.S. person through which the indirect shareholder constructively owns an interest in the foreign corporation files Form 5471 to report all of the required information.

Filing Requirements for Categories of Filers

Required Information*	Category of Filer				
	1	2	3	4	5
The identifying information on page 1 of Form 5471 above Schedule A, see **Specific Instructions**		√	√	√	√
Schedule A			√	√	
Schedule B			√	√	
Schedules C, E, and F			√	√	
Schedule G		√	√	√	√
Schedule H				√	√
Schedule I				√	√
Separate Schedule J				√	√
Separate Schedule M				√	
Separate Schedule O, Part I			√		
Separate Schedule O, Part II				√	

*See also Additional Filing Requirements on page 3.

Instructions for Form 5471

¶20,050

• A Category 2 filer does not have to file Form 5471 if:

1. Immediately after a reportable stock acquisition, three or fewer U.S. persons own 95% or more in value of the outstanding stock of the foreign corporation and the U.S. person making the acquisition files a return for the acquisition as a Category 3 filer **or**

2. The U.S. person(s) for which the Category 2 filer is required to file Form 5471 does not directly own an interest in the foreign corporation but is required to furnish the information solely because of constructive stock ownership from a U.S. person and the person from whom the stock ownership is attributed furnishes all of the required information.

• A Category 4 or 5 filer does not have to file Form 5471 if the shareholder:

1. Does not own a direct or indirect interest in the foreign corporation and

2. Is required to file Form 5471 solely because of constructive ownership from a nonresident alien.

Additional Filing Requirements

Category 3 filers. Category 3 filers must attach a statement that includes:

1. The amount and type of any indebtedness the foreign corporation has with the related persons described in Regulations section 1.6046-1(b)(11) and

2. The name, address, identifying number, and number of shares subscribed to by each subscriber to the foreign corporation's stock.

Foreign sales corporations (FSCs).

• Category 2 and Category 3 filers who are shareholders, officers, and directors of a FSC (as defined in section 922, as in effect before its repeal) must file Form 5471 and separate Schedule O to report changes in the ownership of the FSC.

• Category 4 and 5 filers are not subject to the subpart F rules for:

1. Exempt foreign trade income,

2. Deductions that are apportioned or allocated to exempt foreign trade income,

3. Nonexempt foreign trade income (other than section 923(a)(2) nonexempt income, within the meaning of section 927(d)(6), as in effect before its repeal), and

4. Any deductions that are apportioned or allocated to the nonexempt foreign trade income described above.

• Category 4 and 5 filers are subject to the subpart F rules for:

1. All other types of FSC income (including section 923(a)(2) nonexempt income within the meaning of section 927(d)(6), as in effect before its repeal),

2. Investment income and carrying charges (as defined in sections 927(c) and 927(d)(1), as in effect before their repeal), and

3. All other FSC income that is not foreign trade income or investment income or carrying charges.

• Category 4 and 5 filers are not required to file a Form 5471 (in order to satisfy the requirements of section 6038) if the FSC has filed a Form 1120-FSC. See Temporary Regulations section 1.921-1T(b)(3). However, these filers may be required to file Form 5471 if they are subject to the subpart F rules with respect to certain types of FSC income (see above).

Section 338 election. If a section 338 election is made with respect to a qualified stock purchase of a foreign target corporation for which a Form 5471 must be filed:

• A purchaser (or its U.S. shareholder) must attach a copy of Form 8883, Asset Allocation Statement Under Section 338, to the first Form 5471 for the new foreign target corporation. See the Instructions for Form 8883 for details.

• A seller (or its U.S. shareholder) must attach a copy of Form 8883 to the last Form 5471 for the old foreign target corporation.

Penalties

Failure to file information required by section 6038(a) (Form 5471 and Schedule M).

• A $10,000 penalty is imposed for each annual accounting period of each foreign corporation for failure to furnish the required information within the time prescribed. If the information is not filed within 90 days after the IRS has mailed a notice of the failure to the U.S. person, an additional $10,000 penalty (per foreign corporation) is charged for each 30-day period, or fraction thereof, during which the failure continues after the 90-day period has expired. The additional penalty is limited to a maximum of $50,000 for each failure.

• Any person who fails to file or report all of the information required within the time prescribed will be subject to a reduction of 10% of the foreign taxes available for credit under sections 901, 902, and 960. If the failure continues 90 days or more after the date the IRS mails notice of the failure to the U.S. person, an additional 5% reduction is made for each 3-month period, or fraction thereof, during which the failure continues after the 90-day period has expired. See section 6038(c)(2) for limits on the amount of this penalty.

Failure to file information required by section 6046 and the related regulations (Form 5471 and Schedule O). Any person who fails to file or report all of the information requested by section 6046 is subject to a $10,000 penalty for each such failure for each reportable transaction. If the failure continues for more than 90 days after the date the IRS mails notice of the failure, an additional $10,000 penalty will apply for each 30-day period or fraction thereof during which the failure continues after

the 90-day period has expired. The additional penalty is limited to a maximum of $50,000.

Criminal penalties. Criminal penalties under sections 7203, 7206, and 7207 may apply for failure to file the information required by sections 6038 and 6046.

Note. Any person required to file Form 5471 and Schedule J, M, or O who agrees to have another person file the form and schedules for him or her may be subject to the above penalties if the other person does not file a correct and proper form and schedule.

Other Reporting Requirements

Reporting Exchange Rates on Form 5471

When translating amounts from functional currency to U.S. dollars, you must use the method specified in these instructions. For example, when translating amounts to be reported on Schedule E, you generally must use the average exchange rate as defined in section 986(a). But, regardless of the specific method required, all exchange rates must be reported using a "divide-by convention" rounded to at least four places. That is, the exchange rate must be reported in terms of the amount by which the functional currency amount must be divided in order to reflect an equivalent amount of U.S. dollars. As such, the exchange rate must be reported as the units of foreign currency that equal one U.S. dollar, rounded to at least four places. **Do not** report the exchange rate as the number of U.S. dollars that equal one unit of foreign currency.

Note. You must round the result to no more than four places if failure to do so would materially distort the exchange rate or the equivalent amount of U.S. dollars.

Example. During its annual accounting period, the foreign corporation paid income taxes of 30,255,400 Yen to Japan. The Schedule E instructions specify that the foreign corporation must translate these amounts into U.S. dollars at the average exchange rate for the tax year to which the tax relates in accordance with the rules of section 986(a). The average exchange rate is 118.5050 Japanese Yen to 1 U.S. dollar (0.00843846 U.S. dollars to 1 Japanese Yen). The foreign corporation divides 30,255,400 Yen by 118.5050 to determine the U.S. dollar amount to enter in column (d) of Schedule E. Line 2 of Schedule E is to be completed as follows: Enter "Japan" in column (a), "30,255,400" in column (b), "118.5050" in column (c), and "255,309" in column (d).

Computer-Generated Form 5471 and Schedules

A computer-generated Form 5471 and its schedules may be filed if they conform to and do not deviate from the official form and schedules. Generally, all computer-generated forms must receive prior approval from the IRS and are subject to an annual review.

Requests for approval may be submitted electronically to *substituteforms@irs.gov*, or requests may be mailed to: Internal Revenue Service, Attention: Substitute Forms Program, SE:W:CAR:MP:T:T:SP, 1111 Constitution Avenue, NW, IR-6526, Washington, DC 20224.

Important: Be sure to attach the approval letter to Form 5471.

Every year, the IRS issues a revenue procedure to provide guidance for filers of computer-generated forms. In addition, every year the IRS issues Pub. 1167, General Rules and Specifications For Substitute Forms and Schedules, which reprints the most recent applicable revenue procedure. Pub. 1167 is available on the IRS website at *www.irs.gov*.

Dormant Foreign Corporations

Rev. Proc. 92-70, 1992-2 C.B. 435, provides a summary filing procedure for filing Form 5471 for a dormant foreign corporation (defined in sec. 3 of Rev. Proc. 92-70). This summary filing procedure will satisfy the reporting requirements of sections 6038 and 6046.

If you elect the summary procedure, complete only page 1 of Form 5471 for each dormant foreign corporation as follows:
• The top margin of the summary return must be labeled "Filed Pursuant to Rev. Proc. 92-70 for Dormant Foreign Corporation."
• Include filer information such as name and address, Items A through C, and tax year.
• Include corporate information such as the dormant corporation's annual accounting period (below the title of the form) and Items 1a, 1b, 1c, and 1d. For more information, see Rev. Proc. 92-70.

File this summary return in the manner described in *When and Where To File* on page 1.

Treaty-Based Return Positions

You are generally required to file Form 8833, Treaty-Based Return Position Disclosure Under Section 6114 or 7701(b), to disclose a return position that any treaty of the United States (such as an income tax treaty, an estate and gift tax treaty, or a friendship, commerce, and navigation treaty):
• Overrides or modifies any provision of the Internal Revenue Code and
• Causes, or potentially causes, a reduction of any tax incurred at any time.

See Form 8833 for exceptions.

Failure to make a required disclosure may result in a $1,000 penalty ($10,000 for a C corporation). See section 6712.

Section 362(e)(2)(C) Elections

The transferor and transferee in certain section 351 transactions may make a joint election under section 362(e)(2)(C) to limit the transferor's basis in the stock received instead of the transferee's basis in the transferred property. The election is made by a statement as provided in Notice 2005-70, 2005-41 I.R.B. 694, and regulations under section 362(e)(2).

 Do not attach the statement described above to Form 5471.

Section 108(i) Elections

The controlling domestic shareholder(s) of a CFC may make the election under section 108(i) to defer recognizing discharge of indebtedness income in certain situations. The election is made by a statement as provided in Rev. Proc. 2009-37, 2009-36 I.R.B. 309.

 Do not attach the statement described above to Form 5471.

Corrections to Form 5471

If you file a Form 5471 that you later determine is incomplete or incorrect, file a corrected Form 5471 with an amended tax return, using the amended return instructions for the return with which you originally filed Form 5471. Write "corrected" at the top of the form and attach a statement identifying the changes.

Specific Instructions

Important: If the information required in a given section exceeds the space provided within that section, **do not** write "see attached" in the section and then attach all of the information on additional sheets. Instead, complete all entry spaces in the section and attach the remaining information on additional sheets. The additional sheets must conform with the IRS version of that section.

Identifying Information

Annual Accounting Period

Enter, in the space provided below the title of Form 5471, the annual accounting period of the foreign corporation for which you are furnishing information. Except for information contained on Schedule O, report information for the tax year of the foreign corporation that ends with or within your tax year. When filing Schedule O, report acquisitions, dispositions, and organizations or reorganizations that occurred during your tax year.

Specified foreign corporation. The annual accounting period of a specified foreign corporation is generally required to be the tax year of the corporation's majority U.S. shareholder. If there is more than one majority shareholder, the required tax year will be the tax year that results in the least aggregate deferral of income to all U.S. shareholders of the foreign corporation.

A specified foreign corporation is any foreign corporation:

1. That is treated as a CFC under subpart F and
2. In which more than 50% of the total voting power or value of all classes of stock of the corporation is treated as owned by a U.S. shareholder.

For more information, see section 898 and Rev. Procs. 2002-07, 2002-22 I.R.B. 1030, and 2002-39, 2002-22 I.R.B. 1046, as modified by Notice 2002-72, 2002-46 I.R.B. 843.

Name Change

If the name of either the person filing the return or the corporation whose activities are being reported changed within the past 3 years, show the prior name(s) in parentheses after the current name.

Address

Include the suite, room, or other unit number after the street address. If the post office does not deliver mail to the street address and the U.S. person has a P.O. box, show the box number instead.

Foreign address. Enter the information in the following order: city, province or state, and country. Follow the country's practice for entering the postal code, if any. Do not abbreviate the country name.

Item A—Identifying Number

The identifying number of an individual is his or her social security number (SSN). The identifying number of all others is their employer identification number (EIN). If a U.S. corporation that owns stock in a foreign corporation is a member of a consolidated group, list the common parent as the person filing the return and enter its EIN in Item A. Identify the direct owner in Item D.

Item B—Category of Filer

Complete Item B to indicate the category or categories that describe the person filing this return. If more than one category applies, check all boxes that apply.

Item C—Percentage of Voting Stock Owned

Enter the total percentage of the foreign corporation's voting stock you owned directly, indirectly, or constructively at the end of the corporation's annual accounting period.

Item D—Person(s) on Whose Behalf This Information Return Is Filed

The person that files the required information on behalf of other persons must complete Item D. See *Multiple filers of same information* on page 2. In addition, a separate Schedule I must be filed for each person described in Category 4 or 5.

Except for members of the filer's consolidated return group, all persons identified in Item D must attach a statement to their tax returns that includes the following information:

-4-

- A statement that their filing requirements have been or will be satisfied;
- The name, address, and identifying number of the return with which the information was or will be filed; and
- The IRS Service Center where the return was or will be filed. If the return was or will be filed electronically, enter "e-file."

Items 1f and 1g—Principal Business Activity

Enter the principal business activity code number and the description of the activity from the list beginning on page 14.

Item 1h—Functional Currency

Enter the foreign corporation's functional currency. Regulations sections 1.6038-2(h) and 1.6046-1(g) require that certain amounts be reported in U.S. dollars and/or in the foreign corporation's functional currency. The specific instructions for the affected schedules state these requirements.

Special rules apply for foreign corporations that use the U.S. dollar approximate separate transactions method of accounting (DASTM) under Regulations section 1.985-3. See the instructions for Schedule C and Schedule H.

Schedule B

Category 3 and 4 filers must complete Schedule B for U.S. persons that owned (at any time during the annual accounting period), directly or indirectly through foreign entities, 10% or more in value or voting power of any class of the corporation's outstanding stock.

Column (e). Enter each shareholder's allocable percentage of the foreign corporation's subpart F income.

Schedule C

If the foreign corporation uses the U.S. dollar approximate separate transactions method of accounting (DASTM) under Regulations section 1.985-3, the functional currency column should reflect local hyperinflationary currency amounts computed in accordance with U.S. Generally Accepted Accounting Principles (GAAP). The U.S. dollar column should reflect such amounts translated into dollars under U.S. GAAP translation rules. Differences between this U.S. dollar GAAP column and the U.S. dollar income or loss figured for tax purposes under Regulations section 1.985-3(c) should be accounted for on Schedule H. See *Schedule H, Special rules for DASTM,* below.

Line 19. The terms "extraordinary items" and "prior period adjustments" have the same meaning given to them by U.S. GAAP (see Opinion No. 30 of the Accounting Principles Board and Statement No. 16 of the Financial Accounting Standards Board).

Instructions for Form 5471

Line 20. Enter the income, war profits, and excess profits taxes deducted in accordance with U.S. GAAP.

Important: Differences between this functional currency amount and the amount of taxes that reduce U.S. E&P should be accounted for on line 2g of Schedule H.

Schedule E

List income, war profits, and excess profits taxes paid or accrued to the United States and to any foreign country or U.S. possession for the annual accounting period. Report these amounts in column (b) in the local currency in which the taxes are payable. Translate these amounts into U.S. dollars at the average exchange rate for the tax year to which the tax relates unless one of the exceptions below applies. See section 986(a).

Exceptions. If one of the following exceptions applies, use the exchange rate in effect on the date you paid the tax.

1. The tax is paid before the beginning of the year to which the tax relates.

2. For tax years beginning after December 31, 2004, there is an election in effect under section 986(a)(1)(D) to translate foreign taxes attributable to the CFC using the exchange rate in effect on the date of payment.

Enter the exchange rate used in column (c). Report the exchange rate using the "divide-by convention" specified under *Reporting Exchange Rates on Form 5471* on page 3. Enter the translated dollar amount in column (d).

Schedule F

If the foreign corporation uses DASTM, the tax balance sheet on Schedule F should be prepared and translated into U.S. dollars according to Regulations section 1.985-3(d), rather than U.S. GAAP.

Schedule G

Question 1

If the foreign corporation owned at least a 10% interest, directly or indirectly, in any foreign partnership, attach a statement listing the following information for each foreign partnership:

1. Name and EIN (if any) of the foreign partnership;

2. Identify which, if any, of the following forms the foreign partnership filed for its tax year ending with or within the corporation's tax year: Form 1042, 1065 or 1065-B, or 8804;

3. Name of the tax matters partner (if any); and

4. Beginning and ending dates of the foreign partnership's tax year.

Question 3

Check the "Yes" box if the foreign corporation is the tax owner of a foreign disregarded entity (FDE). The "tax owner"

-5-

of an FDE is the person that is treated as owning the assets and liabilities of the FDE for purposes of U.S. income tax law.

If the foreign corporation is the tax owner of an FDE and you are a category 4 or 5 filer of Form 5471, you are required to attach Form 8858 to Form 5471.

If the foreign corporation is the tax owner of an FDE and you are not a category 4 or 5 filer of Form 5471, you must attach the statement described below in lieu of Form 8858.

Statement in lieu of Form 8858. This statement must list the name of the FDE, country under whose laws the FDE was organized, and EIN (if any) of the FDE.

Schedule H

Use Schedule H to report the foreign corporation's current earnings and profits (E&P) for U.S. tax purposes. Enter the amounts on lines 1 through 5c in functional currency.

Special rules for DASTM. If the foreign corporation uses DASTM, enter on line 1 the dollar GAAP income or (loss) from line 21 of Schedule C. Enter on lines 2a through 4 the adjustments made in figuring current E&P for U.S. tax purposes. Report these amounts in U.S. dollars. Enter on line 5b the DASTM gain or loss figured under Regulations section 1.985-3(d).

Lines 2a through 2h. Certain adjustments (required by Regulations sections 1.964-1(b) and (c)) must be made to the foreign corporation's line 1 net book income or (loss) to determine its current E&P. These adjustments may include both positive and negative adjustments to conform the foreign book income to U.S. GAAP and to U.S. tax accounting principles. If the foreign corporation's books are maintained in functional currency in accordance with U.S. GAAP, enter on line 1 the functional currency GAAP income or (loss) from line 21 of Schedule C, rather than starting with foreign book income, and show GAAP-to-tax adjustments on lines 2a through 2h.

Lines 2b and 2c. Generally, depreciation, depletion, and amortization allowances must be based on the historical cost of the underlying asset, and depreciation must be figured according to section 167. However, if 20% or more of the foreign corporation's gross income is from U.S. sources, depreciation must be figured on a straight line basis according to Regulations section 1.312-15.

Line 2f. Inventories must be taken into account according to the rules of sections 471 (incorporating the provisions of section 263A) and 472 and the related regulations.

Line 2g. See the instructions for Schedule C, line 20 above.

Line 2h. Enter the net amount of any additional adjustments not included on lines 2a through 2g. List these additional adjustments on a separate schedule. Attach this schedule to Form 5471.

Line 5b. DASTM gain or (loss), reflecting unrealized exchange gain or loss, should be entered on line 5b only for foreign corporations that use DASTM.

Line 5d. Enter the line 5c functional currency amount translated into U.S. dollars at the average exchange rate for the foreign corporation's tax year. See section 989(b). Report the exchange rate using the "divide-by convention" specified under *Reporting Exchange Rates on Form 5471* on page 3. If the foreign corporation uses DASTM, enter on line 5d the same amount entered on line 5c.

Blocked income. The E&P of the foreign corporation, as reflected on Schedule H, must not be reduced by all or any part of such E&P that could not have been distributed by the foreign corporation due to currency or other restrictions or limitations imposed under the laws of any foreign country.

Schedule I

Use Schedule I to report in U.S. dollars the U.S. shareholder's pro rata share of income from the foreign corporation reportable under subpart F and other income realized from a corporate distribution.

Line 1

Subpart F income. Generally, the income of a foreign corporation with U.S. shareholders is not taxed to those U.S. shareholders until the income is repatriated to the United States (e.g., through the payment of dividends to the U.S. shareholders or in the form of gain on the disposition of the U.S. shareholders' stock in the foreign corporation). However, this deferral of U.S. tax is not available to U.S. shareholders of CFCs with certain types of income, including subpart F income. For more information, see sections 951 and 952.

Use Worksheet A (which begins on page 8) to compute the U.S. shareholder's pro rata share of subpart F income of the CFC. Subpart F income includes the following:
• Adjusted net foreign base company income (lines 1 through 19);
• Adjusted net insurance income (line 20);
• Adjusted net related person insurance income (line 21);
• International boycott income (line 22);
• Illegal bribes, kickbacks, and other payments (line 23); and
• Income from a country described in section 952(a)(5) (line 24).

Important: If the subpart F income of any CFC for any tax year was reduced because of the current E&P limitation (see the instructions for line 29 of Worksheet A on page 10), any excess of the E&P of the CFC for any subsequent tax year over the subpart F income of the CFC for the tax year must be recharacterized as subpart F income.

Lines 2 Through 4

Other amounts not eligible for deferral that are reported on Schedule I include:
• Earnings invested in U.S. property (Worksheet B);
• Amounts withdrawn from qualified investments in less developed countries and amounts withdrawn from qualified investments in foreign base company shipping operations (Worksheet C); and
• Amounts withdrawn from investment in export trade assets (Worksheet D).

Line 5

Enter the factoring income (as defined in section 864(d)(1)) if no subpart F income is reported on line 1a, Worksheet A, because of the operation of the de minimis rule (see lines 1a, 9, and 11 of Worksheet A and the related instructions).

Line 6

Add lines 1 through 5. Enter the result here and on your tax return. For a corporate U.S. shareholder, enter the result on Form 1120, Schedule C, line 14, or on the comparable line of other corporate tax returns. For a noncorporate U.S. shareholder, enter the result on Form 1040, line 21 (Other Income), or on the comparable line of other noncorporate tax returns.

Line 7

Enter the dividends you received from the foreign corporation that were not previously taxed under subpart F in the current year or in any prior year.

Line 8

If previously taxed E&P described in section 959(a) or (b) was distributed, enter the amount of foreign currency gain or (loss) on the distribution, computed under section 986(c). See Notice 88-71, 1988-2 C.B. 374, for rules for computing section 986(c) gain or (loss).

For a corporate U.S. shareholder, include the gain or (loss) as "other income" on line 10 of Form 1120, or on the comparable line of other corporate tax returns. For a noncorporate U.S. shareholder, include the result as "other income" on line 21 of Form 1040, or on the comparable line of other noncorporate tax returns.

Worksheet A

Important: For tax years beginning after December 31, 2004, foreign base company income does not include foreign base company shipping income as defined in former section 954(f).

For tax years beginning after December 31, 1998, and before January 1, 2010, the following exceptions apply:
• Foreign personal holding company income generally shall not include income derived in the active conduct of a CFC of a banking, finance, or similar business (section 954(h)).
• Foreign personal holding company and insurance income shall not include certain investment income derived by a qualifying

insurance company and by certain qualifying insurance branches (sections 953(a)(2) and 954(i)).
• Foreign base company services income shall not include income that is exempt insurance income under section 953(e) or that is not treated as foreign personal holding company income under the active conduct of an insurance business exception (section 954(i)); the active conduct of a banking, financing, or similar business exception (section 954(h)); or the securities dealer exception (section 954(c)(2)(C)(ii)).

Line 1a. Do not include the following:
• Interest from conducting a banking business that is "export financing interest" (section 904(d)(2)(G));
• Rents and royalties from actively conducting a trade or business received from a person other than a "related person" (as defined in section 954(d)(3)); and
• Dividends, interest, rent or royalty income from related corporate payors described in section 954(c)(3). However, see section 964(e) for an exception.

Interest income includes factoring income arising when a person acquires a trade or service receivable (directly or indirectly) from a related person. The income is treated as interest on a loan to the obligor under section 864(d)(1) and is generally not eligible for the de minimis, export financing, and related party exceptions to the inclusion of subpart F income. Also, a trade or service receivable acquired or treated as acquired by a CFC from a related U.S. person is considered an investment in U.S. property for purposes of section 956 (Worksheet B) if the obligor is a U.S. person.

Line 1b. Enter the excess of gains over losses from the sale or exchange of:
• Property that produces the type of income reportable on line 1a. For tax years beginning after December 31, 1998, and before January 1, 2010, see section 954(c)(1)(B)(i).
• An interest in a trust, partnership, or REMIC. However, see the instructions for line 1i for an exception that provides for look-through treatment for certain sales of partnership interests.
• Property that does not produce any income.

Do not include:
• Income, gain, deduction, or loss from any transaction (including a hedging transaction) and transactions involving physical settlement of a regular dealer in property, forward contracts, option contracts, and similar financial instruments (section 954(c)(2)(C)).
• Gains and losses from the sale or exchange of any property that, in the hands of the CFC, is property described in section 1221(a)(1).

Line 1c. Enter the excess of gains over losses from transactions (including futures, forward, and similar transactions) in any commodities. See section

-6-

954(c)(1)(C) for exceptions. See section 954(c)(5) for a definition and special rules relating to commodity transactions.

Line 1d. Enter the excess of foreign currency gains over foreign currency losses from section 988 transactions. An exception applies to transactions directly related to the business needs of a CFC.

Line 1e. Enter any income equivalent to interest, including income from commitment fees (or similar amounts) for loans actually made.

Line 1f. Include net income from notional principal contracts (except a contract entered into to hedge inventory property).

Line 1g. Include payments in lieu of dividends that are made as required under section 1058.

Line 1h. Enter amounts received:
• Under a contract under which the corporation is to furnish personal services if (a) some person other than the corporation has a right to designate (by name or by description) the individual who is to perform the services or (b) the individual who is to perform the services is designated (by name or by description) in the contract, and
• From the sale or other disposition of such a contract.

Note. The above rules apply with respect to amounts received for services under a particular contract only if at some time during the tax year 25% or more in value of the outstanding stock of the corporation is owned, directly or indirectly, by or for the individual who has performed, is to perform, or may be designated (by name or by description) as the one to perform, such services.

Line 1i. For tax years beginning after December 31, 2004, in the case of any sale by a CFC of an interest in a partnership with respect to which the CFC is a 25% owner (defined below), such CFC is treated for purposes of computing its foreign personal holding company income as selling the proportionate share of the assets of the partnership attributable to such interest. Thus, the sale of a partnership interest by a CFC that meets the ownership threshold constitutes subpart F income only to the extent that a proportionate sale of the underlying partnership assets attributable to the partnership interest would constitute subpart F income. Do not report these amounts on line 1b. Instead, report them on new line 1i.

25% owner. For purposes of these rules, a 25% shareholder is a CFC that owns directly 25% or more of the capital or profits interest in a partnership. For purposes of the preceding sentence, if a CFC is a shareholder or partner of a corporation or partnership, the CFC is treated as owning directly its proportionate share of any such capital or profits interest held directly or indirectly by such corporation or partnership. If a CFC is treated as owning a capital or profits interest in a partnership under

constructive ownership rules similar to the rules of section 958(b), the CFC shall be treated as owning such interest directly or indirectly for purposes of this definition.

Line 11. De minimis rule. If the sum of foreign base company income (determined without regard to section 954(b)(5)) and gross insurance income (as defined in section 954(b)(3)(C)) for the tax year is **less than** the smaller of 5% of gross income for income tax purposes, or $1 million, then no portion of the gross income for the tax year is treated as foreign base company income or insurance income. In this case, enter zero on line 11 and skip lines 12 through 21. Otherwise, go to line 12.

Line 12. Full inclusion rule. If the sum of foreign base company income (determined without regard to section 954(b)(5)) and gross insurance income for the tax year exceeds 70% of gross income for income tax purposes, the entire gross income for the tax year must (subject to the high tax exception described below, the section 952(b) exclusion, and the deductions to be taken into account under section 954(b)(5)) be treated as foreign base company income or insurance income, whichever is appropriate. In this case, enter total gross income (for income tax purposes) on line 12. Otherwise, enter zero.

Lines 14g, 15d, 16d, 18d, 20d, and 21d. Exception for certain income subject to high foreign taxes. Foreign base company income and insurance income does not include any item of income received by a CFC if the taxpayer establishes that such income was subject to an effective rate of income tax imposed by a foreign country that is greater than 90% of the maximum rate of tax specified in section 11. This rule does not apply to foreign base company oil-related income. For more information, see section 954(b)(4) and Regulations section 1.954-1(d)(1).

Line 20. Adjusted net insurance income. In determining a shareholder's pro rata share of the subpart F income of a CFC, insurance income is any income:
• That is attributable to the issuing (or reinsuring) of any insurance or annuity contract:

1. For property in, liability from an activity in, or for the lives or health of residents of a country other than the country under the laws of which the CFC is created or organized or
2. For risks not described in 1 above, resulting from any arrangement in which another corporation receives a substantially equal amount of premiums or other consideration for issuing (or reinsuring) a contract described in 1 above.
• That would, subject to the modifications provided in sections 953(b)(1) and 953(b)(2), be taxed under subchapter L (insurance company tax) if such income were income of a domestic insurance company.

Line 21. Adjusted net related person insurance income. In determining a shareholder's pro rata share of the subpart F income of a CFC, related person insurance income is any insurance income (within the meaning of section 953(a)) attributable to a policy of insurance or reinsurance for which the person insured (directly or indirectly) is a U.S. shareholder (as defined in section 953(c)(1)(A)) in a CFC, or a related person (as defined in section 953(c)(6)) to such a shareholder. In such case, the pro rata share referred to above is to be determined under the rules of section 953(c)(5).

Exceptions. The above definition does not apply to any foreign corporation if:
• At all times during the foreign corporation's tax year, less than 20% of the total combined voting power of all classes of stock of the corporation entitled to vote, and less than 20% of the total value of the corporation, is owned (directly or indirectly under the principles of section 883(c)(4)) by persons who are (directly or indirectly) insured under any policy of insurance or reinsurance issued by the corporation or who are related persons to any such person;
• The related person insurance income (determined on a gross basis) of the corporation for the tax year is less than 20% of its insurance income for the tax year determined without regard to the provisions of section 953(a)(1) that limit insurance income to income from countries other than the country in which the corporation was created or organized; or
• The corporation:

1. Elects to treat its related person insurance income for the tax year as income effectively connected with the conduct of a trade or business in the United States;
2. Elects to waive all treaty benefits (other than from section 884) for related person insurance income; and
3. Meets any requirement the IRS may prescribe to ensure that any tax on such income is paid.

This election will not be effective if the corporation was a disqualified corporation (as defined in section 953(c)(3)(E)) for the tax year for which the election was made or for any prior tax year beginning after 1986. See section 953(c)(3)(D) for special rules for this election.

Mutual life insurance companies. The related person insurance income rules also apply to mutual life insurance companies under regulations prescribed by the Secretary. For these purposes, policyholders must be treated as shareholders.

Line 22. International boycott income. If a CFC or a member of a controlled group (within the meaning of section 993(a)(3)) that includes the CFC has operations in, or related to, a country (or with the government, a company, or a national of a country) that requires participation in or cooperation with an

¶20,050

Worksheet A—Foreign Base Company Income and Insurance Income and Summary of U.S. Shareholder's Pro Rata Share of Subpart F Income of a CFC (See instructions beginning on page 6.)
Enter the amounts on lines 1a through 38a in functional currency.

1	**Gross foreign personal holding company income:**		
a	Dividends, interest, royalties, rents, and annuities (section 954(c)(1)(A)) (excluding amounts described for sections 954(c)(2), (3), and (6))) . .	1a	
b	Excess of gains over losses from certain property transactions (section 954(c)(1)(B))	1b	
c	Excess of gains over losses from commodity transactions (section 954(c)(1)(C))	1c	
d	Excess of foreign currency gains over foreign currency losses (section 954(c)(1)(D))	1d	
e	Income equivalent to interest (section 954(c)(1)(E))	1e	
f	Net income from a notional principal contract (section 954(c)(1)(F)) .	1f	
g	Payments in lieu of dividends (section 954(c)(1)(G))	1g	
h	Certain amounts received for services under personal service contracts (see section 954(c)(1)(H))	1h	
i	Certain amounts from sales of partnership interests to which the look-through rule of section 954(c)(4) applies	1i	
2	Gross foreign personal holding company income. Add lines 1a through 1i.	**2**	
3	Gross foreign base company sales income (see section 954(d))	**3**	
4	Gross foreign base company services income (see section 954(e))	**4**	
5	Gross foreign base company oil-related income (see section 954(g)) after application of section 954(b)(6) .	**5**	
6	Gross foreign base company income. Add lines 2 through 5	**6**	
7	Gross insurance income (see sections 953 and 954(b)(3)(C) and the instructions for lines 20 and 21).	**7**	
8	Gross foreign base company income and gross insurance income. Add lines 6 and 7	**8**	
9	Enter 5% of total gross income (as computed for income tax purposes)	**9**	
10	Enter 70% of total gross income (as computed for income tax purposes)	**10**	
11	If line 8 is less than line 9 and less than $1 million, enter -0- on this line and skip lines 12 through 21	**11**	
12	If line 8 is more than line 10, enter total gross income (as computed for income tax purposes).	**12**	
13	**Total adjusted gross foreign base company income and insurance income** (enter the greater of line 8 or line 12)	**13**	
14	**Adjusted net foreign personal holding company income:**		
a	Enter amount from line 2	14a	
b	Expenses directly related to amount on line 2	14b	
c	Subtract line 14b from line 14a	14c	
d	Related person interest expense (see section 954(b)(5))	14d	
e	Other expenses allocated and apportioned to the amount on line 2 under section 954(b)(5)	14e	
f	Net foreign personal holding company income. Subtract the sum of lines 14d and 14e from line 14c	14f	
g	Net foreign personal holding company income excluded under high-tax exception	14g	
h	Subtract line 14g from line 14f		14h
15	**Adjusted net foreign base company sales income:**		
a	Enter amount from line 3	15a	
b	Expenses allocated and apportioned to the amount on line 3 under section 954(b)(5)	15b	
c	Net foreign base company sales income. Subtract line 15b from line 15a	15c	
d	Net foreign base company sales income excluded under high-tax exception.	15d	
e	Subtract line 15d from line 15c		15e
16	**Adjusted net foreign base company services income:**		
a	Enter amount from line 4	16a	
b	Expenses allocated and apportioned to line 4 under section 954(b)(5)	16b	
c	Net foreign base company services income. Subtract line 16b from line 16a.	16c	
d	Net foreign base company services income excluded under high-tax exception	16d	
e	Subtract line 16d from line 16c		16e

Instructions for Form 5471

¶20,050

Worksheet A (continued) (See instructions.)

17	**Adjusted net foreign base company oil-related income:**		
a	Enter amount from line 5	17a	
b	Expenses allocated and apportioned to line 5 under section 954(b)(5)	17b	
c	Subtract line 17b from line 17a		17c
18	**Adjusted net full inclusion foreign base company income:**		
a	Enter the excess, if any, of line 12 over line 8	18a	
b	Expenses allocated and apportioned under section 954(b)(5) . . .	18b	
c	Net full inclusion foreign base company income. Subtract line 18b from line 18a	18c	
d	Net full inclusion foreign base company income excluded under high-tax exception	18d	
e	Subtract line 18d from line 18c		18e
19	**Adjusted net foreign base company income.** Add lines 14h, 15e, 16e, 17c, and 18e . . .		19
20	**Adjusted net insurance income** (other than related person insurance income):		
a	Enter amount from line 7 (other than related person insurance income).	20a	
b	Expenses allocated and apportioned to the amount from line 7 under section 953	20b	
c	Net insurance income. Subtract line 20b from line 20a	20c	
d	Net insurance income excluded under high-tax exception	20d	
e	Subtract line 20d from line 20c		20e
21	**Adjusted net related person insurance income:**		
a	Enter amount from line 7 that is related person insurance income .	21a	
b	Expenses allocated and apportioned to related person insurance income under section 953.	21b	
c	Net related person insurance income. Subtract line 21b from line 21a	21c	
d	Net related person insurance income excluded under high-tax exception	21d	
e	Subtract line 21d from line 21c		21e
22	International boycott income (section 952(a)(3))		22
23	Illegal bribes, kickbacks, and other payments (section 952(a)(4))		23
24	Income described in section 952(a)(5) (see instructions)		24
25	Subpart F income before application of sections 952(b) and (c) and section 959(b). Add lines 19, 20e, 21e, and 22 through 24		25
26	Enter portion of line 25 that is U.S. source income effectively connected with a U.S. trade or business (section 952(b))	26	
27	Exclusions under section 959(b)	27	
28	Total subpart F income. Subtract the sum of lines 26 and 27 from line 25		28
29	Current E&P		29
30	Enter the smaller of line 28 or line 29		30
31	Shareholder's pro rata share of line 30	31	
32	Shareholder's pro rata share of export trade income	32	
33	Subtract line 32 from line 31	33	
34	Divide the number of days in the tax year that the corporation was a CFC by the number of days in the tax year and multiply the result by line 33	34	
35	Dividends paid to any other person with respect to your stock during the tax year	35	
36	Divide the number of days in the tax year you did not own such stock by the number of days in the tax year and multiply the result by line 33	36	
37	Enter the smaller of line 35 or line 36	37	
38a	**Shareholder's pro rata share of subpart F income.** Subtract line 37 from line 34		38a
b	Translate the amount on line 38a from functional currency to U.S. dollars at the average exchange rate. See section 989(b). Enter the result here and on line 1, Schedule I		38b

¶20,050

international boycott as a condition of doing business within such country or with the government, company, or national of that country, a portion of the CFC's income is included in subpart F income. The amount included is determined by multiplying the CFC's income (other than income included under section 951 and U.S. source effectively connected business income described in section 952(b)) by the international boycott factor. This factor is a fraction determined on Schedule A (Form 5713).

Special rule. If the shareholder of a CFC can clearly demonstrate that the income earned for the tax year is from specific operations, then, instead of applying the international boycott factor, the addition to subpart F income is the amount specifically from the operations in which there was participation in or cooperation with an international boycott. See Schedule B (Form 5713).

Line 23. Illegal bribes, kickbacks, and other payments. Enter the total of any illegal bribes, kickbacks, or other payments (within the meaning of section 162(c)) paid by or on behalf of the corporation, directly or indirectly, to an official, employee, or agent of a government.

Line 24. Income described in section 952(a)(5). The income of a CFC derived from any foreign country during any period during which section 901(j) applies to such foreign country will be deemed to be income to the U.S. shareholders of such CFC. As of the date these instructions were revised, section 901(j) applied to: Cuba, Iran, North Korea, Sudan, and Syria.

Line 26. Exclusion of U.S. income. Subpart F income does not include any U.S. source income (which, for these purposes, includes all carrying charges and all interest, dividends, royalties, and other investment income received or accrued by a FSC) that is effectively connected with a CFC's conduct of a trade or business in the United States unless that item is exempt from taxation (or is subject to a reduced rate of tax) pursuant to a treaty obligation of the United States or the Code.

Line 29. Current E&P. A CFC's subpart F income is limited to its current year E&P, computed under the special rule of section 952(c)(3). The amount included in the gross income of a U.S. shareholder of a CFC under section 951(a)(1)(A)(i) for any tax year and attributable to a qualified activity must be reduced by the shareholder's pro rata share of any qualified deficit (see section 952(c)(1)(B)).

Certain current year deficits of a member of the same chain of corporations may be considered in determining subpart F income. See section 952(c)(1)(C).

Worksheet B

Use Worksheet B (on page 11) to determine a U.S. shareholder's pro rata share of earnings of a CFC invested in U.S. property that is subject to tax. Only earnings of a CFC not distributed or otherwise previously taxed are subject to these rules. Thus, the amount of previously **untaxed** earnings limits the section 956 inclusion. A CFC's investment in U.S. property in excess of this limit will not be included in the taxable income of the CFC's U.S. shareholders.

Further, U.S. shareholders are only taxed on earnings invested in U.S. property to the extent the investments exceed the CFC's previously **taxed** earnings. The balances in the previously taxed accounts of prior section 956 inclusions (see section 959(c)(1)(A)) and current or prior subpart F inclusions (see section 959(c)(2)) reduce what would otherwise be the current section 956 inclusion.

Note. The previously taxed accounts should be adjusted to reflect any reclassification of subpart F inclusions that reduced prior section 956 or 956A inclusions (see section 959(a)(2) and Schedule J).

Distributions are also taken into account before the section 956 inclusion is determined. Distributions generally are treated as coming first from (and thus reducing the balances of) the previously taxed accounts. Thus, the U.S. shareholders must:

1. Compute the current subpart F inclusion (potentially increasing that previously taxed account);
2. Take into account current distributions (potentially reducing the previously taxed and untaxed accounts); and
3. Compute the current section 956 inclusion (potentially increasing or reclassifying the previously taxed accounts).

U.S. property is measured on a quarterly average basis. For purposes of Worksheet B, the amount taken into account with respect to U.S. property is its adjusted basis for earnings and profits purposes, reduced by any liability the property is subject to. See sections 956(c) and (d) for the definition of U.S. property. The amount of U.S. property held (directly or indirectly) by the CFC does not include any item that was acquired by the foreign corporation before it became a CFC, except for the property acquired before the foreign corporation became a CFC that exceeds the applicable earnings (as defined in section 956(b)) accumulated during periods before it became a CFC.

If the foreign corporation **ceases to be a CFC** during the tax year:
● The determination of the U.S. shareholder's pro rata share will be made based upon the stock owned (within the meaning of section 958(a)) by the U.S. shareholder on the last day during the tax

year in which the foreign corporation was a CFC;
● The CFC's U.S. property for the taxable year will be determined only by taking into account quarters ending on or before such last day (and investments in U.S. property as of the close of subsequent quarters should be recorded as zero on line 1); and
● In determining applicable earnings, current earnings and profits will include only earnings and profits that are allocable (on a pro rata basis) to the part of the year during which the foreign corporation was a CFC.

Schedule J

Use Schedule J to report accumulated E&P, in functional currency, computed under sections 964(a) and 986(b).

Column (a)

Use column (a) to report the opening balance, current year additions and subtractions, and the closing balance in the foreign corporation's post-1986 undistributed earnings pool.

Note. Line 3 (E&P as of the close of the tax year, before actual or deemed distributions during the year) is the denominator of the deemed-paid credit fraction under section 902(c)(1) used for foreign tax credit purposes.

Column (b)

Use column (b) to report the aggregate amount of the foreign corporation's pre-1987 section 964(a) E&P accumulated since 1962 and not previously distributed or deemed distributed. These amounts are figured in U.S. dollars using the rules of Regulations sections 1.964-1(a) through (e), translated into the foreign corporation's functional currency according to Notice 88-70, 1988-2 C.B. 369.

Column (c)

Use column (c) to report the running balance of the foreign corporation's previously taxed earnings and profits (PTI), or section 964(a) E&P accumulated since 1962 that have resulted in deemed inclusions under subpart F. Pre-1987 U.S. dollar PTI should be translated into the foreign corporation's functional currency using the rules of Notice 88-70 and added to post-1986 amounts in the appropriate PTI category.
● Include in column (c)(i) PTI attributable to, or reclassified as, investments in U.S. property (section 959(c)(1)(A) amounts).
● Include in column (c)(ii) PTI attributable to, or reclassified as, earnings invested in excess passive assets (section 959(c)(1)(B) amounts) accumulated in tax years of foreign corporations beginning after September 30, 1993, and before January 1, 1997.
● Include in column (c)(iii) PTI attributable to subpart F income net of any reclassifications (section 959(c)(2) amounts).

Instructions for Form 5471

¶ 20,050

Worksheet B—U.S. Shareholder's Pro Rata Share of Earnings of a CFC Invested in U.S. Property
Enter the amounts on lines 1 through 16 in functional currency.

1	Amount of U.S. property (as defined in sections 956(c) and (d)) held (directly or indirectly) by the CFC as of the close of:	
a	The first quarter of the tax year **1a**	
b	The second quarter of the tax year **1b**	
c	The third quarter of the tax year **1c**	
d	The fourth quarter of the tax year **1d**	
2	Number of quarter-ends the foreign corporation was a CFC during the tax year. . . . . ▶	**2**
3	Average amount of U.S. property held (directly or indirectly) by the CFC as of the close of each quarter of the tax year. (Add lines 1a through 1d. Divide this amount by the number on line 2.)	**3**
4	U.S. shareholder's pro rata share of the amount on line 3	**4**
5	U.S. shareholder's earnings and profits described in section 959(c)(1)(A) after reductions (if any) for current year distributions	**5**
6	Subtract line 5 from line 4.	**6**
7	Applicable earnings:	
a	Current earnings and profits **7a**	
b	Line 7a plus accumulated earnings and profits. **7b**	
8	Enter the greater of line 7a or line 7b	**8**
9	Distributions made by the CFC during the tax year	**9**
10	Subtract line 9 from line 8.	**10**
11	Earnings and profits described in section 959(c)(1)	**11**
12	Subtract line 11 from line 10	**12**
13	U.S. shareholder's pro rata share of the amount on line 12.	**13**
14	U.S. shareholder's earnings invested in U.S. property. (Enter the smaller of line 6 or line 13) .	**14**
15	Amount on line 14 that is excluded from the U.S. shareholder's gross income under section 959(a)(2)	**15**
16	Subtract line 15 from line 14.	**16**
17	Translate the amount on line 16 from functional currency to U.S. dollars at the year-end spot rate (as provided in section 989(b)). Enter the result here and on line 2 of Schedule I	**17**

Column (d)

Use column (d) to report the opening and closing balance of the foreign corporation's accumulated E&P. This amount is the sum of post-1986 undistributed earnings, pre-1987 section 964(a) E&P not previously taxed, and PTI.

Schedule M

Important: In translating the amounts from functional currency to U.S. dollars, use the average exchange rate for the foreign corporation's tax year. See section 989(b). Report the exchange rate in the entry space provided at the top of Schedule M using the "divide-by convention" specified under *Reporting Exchange Rates on Form 5471* on page 3.

Every U.S. person described in Category 4 must file Schedule M to report the transactions that occurred during the foreign corporation's annual accounting period ending with or within the U.S. person's tax year.

If a U.S. corporation that owns stock in a foreign corporation is a member of a consolidated group, list the common parent as the U.S. person filing Schedule M.

Lines 4 and 16. Report on these lines cost sharing buy-in payments received and paid by the foreign corporation

(without giving effect to any netting of payments due and owed). See Regulations section 1.482-7(g). The corporation is required to complete **both** lines only if the corporation makes pre-existing intangible property available to other controlled cost sharing arrangement participants **and** is required to make buy-in payments to other controlled participants that make pre-existing intangible property available to other controlled cost sharing arrangement participants.

Lines 5 and 17. Report on these lines cost sharing payments received and paid by the foreign corporation (without giving effect to any netting of payments due and owed). See Regulations section 1.482-7(d)(1). The corporation is required to complete line 5 only if the corporation itself incurred costs related to the intangible development area (e.g. research and development). If the corporation does not itself incur costs related to the intangible development area, then it should **only** report cost sharing payments made on line 17.

Lines 9 and 21. Report on these lines dividends received and paid by the foreign corporation not previously taxed under subpart F in the current year or in any prior year.

Lines 25 and 26. Report on these lines the largest outstanding balances during

the year of gross amounts borrowed from, and gross amounts loaned to, the related parties described in columns (b) through (f). Do not enter aggregate cash flows, year-end loan balances, average balances, or net balances. Do not include open account balances resulting from sales and purchases reported under other items listed on Schedule M that arise and are collected in full in the ordinary course of business.

Accrued payments and receipts. A corporation that uses an accrual method of accounting must use accrued payments and accrued receipts for purposes of computing the total amount to enter on each line of Schedule M.

Schedule O

Schedule O is used to report the organization or reorganization of a foreign corporation and the acquisition or disposition of its stock.

Every U.S. citizen or resident described in Category 2 must complete Part I. Every U.S. person described in Category 3 must complete Part II.

See Regulations section 1.6046-1(i) for rules on determining when U.S. persons constructively own stock of a foreign corporation and therefore are subject to the section 6046 filing requirements.

Instructions for Form 5471

-11-

Worksheet C—U.S. Shareholder's Pro Rata Share of Previously Excluded Subpart F Income of a CFC Withdrawn From Qualified Investments in Less Developed Countries and From Qualified Investments in Foreign Base Company Shipping Operations

Enter the amounts on lines 1 through 6a in functional currency.

1	Decrease in qualified investments in less developed countries (see Regulations section 1.955-1(b)(1)) and foreign base company shipping operations (see Regulations section 1.955A-1(b)(1)).	**1**
2	Limitation (see Regulations section 1.955-1(b)(2)):	
a	Enter the sum of E&P for the tax year and E&P accumulated for prior tax years beginning after 1962	**2a**
b	Enter the sum of amounts invested in less developed countries or foreign base company shipping operations and excluded from foreign base company income for all prior tax years, minus the sum of such amounts withdrawn for such years (see Regulations section 1.955-1(b)(2)(i)).	**2b**
3	Enter the smaller of line 2a or line 2b	**3**
4	Previously excluded subpart F income withdrawn for the tax year (enter the smaller of line 1 or line 0).	**4**
5	U.S. shareholder's pro rata share of line 4 (see Regulations section 1.055-1(n)) . . .	**5**
6a	Divide the number of days in the tax year that the foreign corporation was a CFC by the number of days in the tax year and multiply the result by line 5	**6a**
b	Translate the amount on line 6a from functional currency to U.S. dollars at the average exchange rate. See section 989(b). Enter the result here and on line 3, Schedule I	**6b**

Worksheet D—U.S. Shareholder's Pro Rata Share of Previously Excluded Export Trade Income of a CFC Withdrawn From Investment in Export Trade Assets

Enter the amounts on lines 1 through 7a in functional currency.

1	Decrease in investments of the CFC in export trade assets (see Regulations section 1.970-1(d)(3))	**1**
2	U.S. shareholder's pro rata share of line 1	**2**
3	U.S. shareholder's pro rata share of the sum of E&P of the CFC for the tax year and E&P accumulated for prior tax years beginning after 1962 (see Regulations section 1.970-1(c)(2)(ii)) .	**3**
4	Limitation under section 970(b) (see Regulations section 1.970-1(c)(2)(i)):	
a	U.S. shareholder's pro rata share of the sum of the amounts by which the CFC's subpart F income for prior tax years was reduced under section 970(a)	**4a**
b	U.S. shareholder's pro rata share of the sum of the amounts that were not included in subpart F income of the CFC for prior tax years because of Regulations section 1.972-1	**4b**
c	Add lines 4a and 4b.	**4c**
d	U.S. shareholder's pro rata share of the sum of the amounts that were previously included in his or her gross income for prior tax years under section 951(a)(1)(A)(ii) because of section 970(b)	**4d**
5	Subtract line 4d from line 4c	**5**
6	Enter the smallest of line 2, 3, or 5	**6**
7a	Divide the number of days in the tax year that the foreign corporation was a CFC by the number of days in the tax year and multiply the result by line 6	**7a**
b	Translate the amount on line 7a from functional currency to U.S. dollars at the average exchange rate. See section 989(b). Enter the result here and on line 4, Schedule I	**7b**

Part I

Column (d). Enter the date the shareholder first acquired 10% or more (in value or voting power) of the outstanding stock of the foreign corporation.

Column (e). Enter the date the shareholder acquired (whether in one or more transactions) an additional 10% or more (in value or voting power) of the outstanding stock of the foreign corporation.

Part II

Section A—General Shareholder Information

If the shareholder's latest tax return was filed electronically, enter "e-filed" in column (b)(3) instead of a service center.

Instructions for Form 5471

¶20,050

Section C—Acquisition of Stock

Section C is completed by shareholders who are completing Schedule O because they have acquired sufficient stock in a foreign corporation. If the shareholder acquired the stock in more than one transaction, use a separate line to report each transaction.

Column (d). Enter the method of acquisition (e.g., purchase, gift, bequest, trade).

Column (e)(2). Enter the number of shares acquired indirectly (within the meaning of section 958(a)(2)) by the shareholder listed in column (a).

Column (e)(3). Enter the number of shares constructively owned (within the meaning of section 958(b)) by the shareholder listed in column (a).

Section D—Disposition of Stock

Section D must be completed by shareholders who dispose of their interest (in whole or in part) in a foreign corporation.

Column (d). Enter the method of disposition (e.g., sale, bequest, gift, trade).

Example. In 1993, Mr. Jackson, a U.S. citizen, purchased 10,000 shares of common stock of foreign corporation X. The purchase represented 10% ownership of the foreign corporation.

On July 1, 2009, Mr. Jackson made a gift of 5,000 shares of foreign corporation X to his son, John. Because Mr. Jackson has reduced his holding in the foreign corporation, he is required to complete Form 5471 and Schedule O. To show the required information about the disposition, Mr. Jackson completes Section D as follows:

- Enters his name in column (a).
- Enters "common" in column (b).
- Enters "July 1, 2009" in column (c).
- Enters "gift" in column (d).
- Enters "5,000" in column (e)(1).
- Enters "-0-" in column (f) because the disposition was by gift.
- Enters the name and address of his son, John, in column (g).

Section F—Additional Information

Item (b). List the date of any reorganization of the foreign corporation that occurred during the last 4 years while any U.S. person held 10% or more in value or vote (directly or indirectly) of the corporation's stock. If there is more than one such date, use the most recent date. However, do not enter a date for which information was reported in Schedule E. Instead, enter the date (if any) of any reorganization prior to that date (if it is within the last 4 years).

Example for Item (c). Mr. Lyons, a U.S. person, acquires a 10% ownership in foreign corporation F. F is the 100% owner of two foreign corporations, FI and FJ. F is also a 50% owner of foreign corporation FK. In addition, F is 90% owned by foreign corporation W. Mr. Lyons does not own any of the stock of corporation W.

Mr. Lyons completes and files Form 5471 and Schedule O for the corporations in which he is a 10% or more shareholder. Mr. Lyons is also required to submit a chart if the foreign corporation is a member of a chain of corporations, and to indicate if he is a 10% or more shareholder in any of those corporations.

Mr. Lyons would prepare a list showing the corporations as follows:

- Corporation W
- Corporation F
- Corporation FI
- Corporation FJ
- Corporation FK

Then Mr. Lyons is required to indicate that he is a 10% or more shareholder in corporations F, FI, and FJ.

Paperwork Reduction Act Notice. We ask for the information on this form to carry out the Internal Revenue laws of the United States. You are required to give us the information. We need it to ensure that you are complying with these laws and to allow us to figure and collect the right amount of tax.

You are not required to provide the information requested on a form that is subject to the Paperwork Reduction Act unless the form displays a valid OMB control number. Books or records relating to a form or its instructions must be retained as long as their contents may become material in the administration of any Internal Revenue law. Generally, tax returns and return information are confidential, as required by section 6103.

The time needed to complete and file this form and related schedules will vary depending on individual circumstances. The estimated burden for individual taxpayers filing this form is approved under OMB control number 1545-0074 and is included in the estimates shown in the instructions for their individual income tax return. The estimated burden for all other taxpayers who file this form is shown below.

Form	Recordkeeping	Learning about the law or the form	Preparing and sending the form to the IRS
5471	82 hr., 45 min.	16 hr., 14 min.	24 hr., 17 min.
Sch. J (5471)	3 hr., 49 min.	1 hr., 29 min.	1 hr., 37 min.
Sch. M (5471)	26 hr., 33 min.	6 min.	32 min.
Sch. O (5471)	10 hr., 45 min.	24 min.	35 min.

If you have comments concerning the accuracy of these time estimates or suggestions for making this form and related schedules simpler, we would be happy to hear from you. See the instructions for the tax return with which this form is filed.

¶20,050

Form 5471

Codes for Principal Business Activity

This list of principal business activities and their associated codes is designed to classify an enterprise by the type of activity in which it is engaged to facilitate the administration of the Internal Revenue Code. These principal business activity codes are based on the North American Industry Classification System.

Using the list of activities and codes below, determine from which activity the company derives the largest percentage of its "total receipts." If the company purchases raw materials and supplies them to a subcontractor to produce the finished product, but retains title to the product, the company is considered a manufacturer and must use one of the manufacturing codes (311110-339900).

Enter on page 1, item 1f, the six digit code selected from the list below. In item 1g, enter a brief description of the company's business activity.

Code	
Agriculture, Forestry, Fishing and Hunting	
Crop Production	
111100	Oilseed & Grain Farming
111210	Vegetable & Melon Farming (including potatoes & yams)
111300	Fruit & Tree Nut Farming
111400	Greenhouse, Nursery, & Floriculture Production
111900	Other Crop Farming (including tobacco, cotton, sugarcane, hay, peanut, sugar beet & all other crop farming)
Animal Production	
112111	Beef Cattle Ranching & Farming
112112	Cattle Feedlots
112120	Dairy Cattle & Milk Production
112210	Hog & Pig Farming
112300	Poultry & Egg Production
112400	Sheep & Goat Farming
112510	Aquaculture (including shellfish & finfish farms & hatcheries)
112900	Other Animal Production
Forestry and Logging	
113110	Timber Tract Operations
113210	Forest Nurseries & Gathering of Forest Products
113310	Logging
Fishing, Hunting and Trapping	
114110	Fishing
114210	Hunting & Trapping
Support Activities for Agriculture and Forestry	
115110	Support Activities for Crop Production (including cotton ginning, soil preparation, planting, & cultivating)
115210	Support Activities for Animal Production
115310	Support Activities For Forestry

Code	
Mining	
211110	Oil & Gas Extraction
212110	Coal Mining
212200	Metal Ore Mining
212310	Stone Mining & Quarrying
212320	Sand, Gravel, Clay, & Ceramic & Refractory Minerals Mining & Quarrying
212390	Other Nonmetallic Mineral Mining & Quarrying
213110	Support Activities for Mining
Utilities	
221100	Electric Power Generation, Transmission & Distribution
221210	Natural Gas Distribution
221300	Water, Sewage & Other Systems
221500	Combination Gas & Electric
Construction	
Construction of Buildings	
236110	Residential Building Construction
236200	Nonresidential Building Construction
Heavy and Civil Engineering Construction	
237100	Utility System Construction
237210	Land Subdivision
237310	Highway, Street, & Bridge Construction

Code	
237990	Other Heavy & Civil Engineering Construction
Specialty Trade Contractors	
238100	Foundation, Structure, & Building Exterior Contractors (including framing carpentry, masonry, glass, roofing, & siding)
238210	Electrical Contractors
238220	Plumbing, Heating, & Air-Conditioning Contractors
238290	Other Building Equipment Contractors
238300	Building Finishing Contractors (including drywall, insulation, painting, wallcovering, flooring, tile, & finish carpentry)
238900	Other Specialty Trade Contractors (including site preparation)
Manufacturing	
Food Manufacturing	
311110	Animal Food Mfg
311200	Grain & Oilseed Milling
311300	Sugar & Confectionery Product Mfg
311400	Fruit & Vegetable Preserving & Specialty Food Mfg
311500	Dairy Product Mfg
311610	Animal Slaughtering and Processing
311710	Seafood Product Preparation & Packaging
311800	Bakeries & Tortilla Mfg
311900	Other Food Mfg (including coffee, tea, flavorings & seasonings)
Beverage and Tobacco Product Manufacturing	
312110	Soft Drink & Ice Mfg
312120	Breweries
312130	Wineries
312140	Distilleries
312200	Tobacco Manufacturing
Textile Mills and Textile Product Mills	
313000	Textile Mills
314000	Textile Product Mills
Apparel Manufacturing	
315100	Apparel Knitting Mills
315210	Cut & Sew Apparel Contractors
315220	Men's & Boys' Cut & Sew Apparel Mfg
315230	Women's & Girls' Cut & Sew Apparel Mfg
315290	Other Cut & Sew Apparel Mfg
315990	Apparel Accessories & Other Apparel Mfg
Leather and Allied Product Manufacturing	
316110	Leather & Hide Tanning & Finishing
316210	Footwear Mfg (including rubber & plastics)
316990	Other Leather & Allied Product Mfg
Wood Product Manufacturing	
321110	Sawmills & Wood Preservation
321210	Veneer, Plywood, & Engineered Wood Product Mfg
321900	Other Wood Product Mfg
Paper Manufacturing	
322100	Pulp, Paper, & Paperboard Mills

Code	
322200	Converted Paper Product Mfg
Printing and Related Support Activities	
323100	Printing & Related Support Activities
Petroleum and Coal Products Manufacturing	
324110	Petroleum Refineries (including integrated)
324120	Asphalt Paving, Roofing, & Saturated Materials Mfg
324190	Other Petroleum & Coal Products Mfg
Chemical Manufacturing	
325100	Basic Chemical Mfg
325200	Resin, Synthetic Rubber, & Artificial & Synthetic Fibers & Filaments Mfg
325300	Pesticide, Fertilizer, & Other Agricultural Chemical Mfg
325410	Pharmaceutical & Medicine Mfg
325500	Paint, Coating, & Adhesive Mfg
325600	Soap, Cleaning Compound, & Toilet Preparation Mfg
325900	Other Chemical Product & Preparation Mfg
Plastics and Rubber Products Manufacturing	
326100	Plastics Product Mfg
326200	Rubber Product Mfg
Nonmetallic Mineral Product Manufacturing	
327100	Clay Product & Refractory Mfg
327210	Glass & Glass Product Mfg
327300	Cement & Concrete Product Mfg
327400	Lime & Gypsum Product Mfg
327900	Other Nonmetallic Mineral Product Mfg
Primary Metal Manufacturing	
331110	Iron & Steel Mills & Ferroalloy Mfg
331200	Steel Product Mfg from Purchased Steel
331310	Alumina & Aluminum Production & Processing
331400	Nonferrous Metal (except Aluminum) Production & Processing
331500	Foundries
Fabricated Metal Product Manufacturing	
332110	Forging & Stamping
332210	Cutlery & Handtool Mfg
332300	Architectural & Structural Metals Mfg
332400	Boiler, Tank, & Shipping Container Mfg
332510	Hardware Mfg
332610	Spring & Wire Product Mfg
332700	Machine Shops; Turned Product; & Screw, Nut, & Bolt Mfg
332810	Coating, Engraving, Heat Treating, & Allied Activities
332900	Other Fabricated Metal Product Mfg
Machinery Manufacturing	
333100	Agriculture, Construction, & Mining Machinery Mfg
333200	Industrial Machinery Mfg
333310	Commercial & Service Industry Machinery Mfg

Code	
333410	Ventilation, Heating, Air-Conditioning, & Commercial Refrigeration Equipment Mfg
333510	Metalworking Machinery Mfg
333610	Engine, Turbine & Power Transmission Equipment Mfg
333900	Other General Purpose Machinery Mfg
Computer and Electronic Product Manufacturing	
334110	Computer & Peripheral Equipment Mfg
334200	Communications Equipment Mfg
334310	Audio & Video Equipment Mfg
334410	Semiconductor & Other Electronic Component Mfg
334500	Navigational, Measuring, Electromedical, & Control Instruments Mfg
334610	Manufacturing & Reproducing Magnetic & Optical Media
Electrical Equipment, Appliance, and Component Manufacturing	
335100	Electric Lighting Equipment Mfg
335200	Household Appliance Mfg
335310	Electrical Equipment Mfg
335900	Other Electrical Equipment & Component Mfg
Transportation Equipment Manufacturing	
336100	Motor Vehicle Mfg
336210	Motor Vehicle Body & Trailer Mfg
336300	Motor Vehicle Parts Mfg
336410	Aerospace Product & Parts Mfg
336510	Railroad Rolling Stock Mfg
336610	Ship & Boat Building
336990	Other Transportation Equipment Mfg
Furniture and Related Product Manufacturing	
337000	Furniture & Related Product Manufacturing
Miscellaneous Manufacturing	
339110	Medical Equipment & Supplies Mfg
339900	Other Miscellaneous Manufacturing
Wholesale Trade	
Merchant Wholesalers, Durable Goods	
423100	Motor Vehicle & Motor Vehicle Parts & Supplies
423200	Furniture & Home Furnishings
423300	Lumber & Other Construction Materials
423400	Professional & Commercial Equipment & Supplies
423500	Metal & Mineral (except Petroleum)
423600	Electrical & Electronic Goods
423700	Hardware, & Plumbing & Heating Equipment & Supplies
423800	Machinery, Equipment, & Supplies
423910	Sporting & Recreational Goods & Supplies
423920	Toy & Hobby Goods & Supplies
423930	Recyclable Materials

676   *Transfer Pricing: Rules, Compliance and Controversy*

Form 5471 *(continued)*

Code		Code		Code		Code	
423940	Jewelry, Watch, Precious Stone, & Precious Metals	446130	Optical Goods Stores	485410	School & Employee Bus Transportation	522292	Real Estate Credit (including mortgage bankers & originators)
423990	Other Miscellaneous Durable Goods	446190	Other Health & Personal Care Stores	485510	Charter Bus Industry	522293	International Trade Financing
Merchant Wholesalers, Nondurable Goods		**Gasoline Stations**		485990	Other Transit & Ground Passenger Transportation	522294	Secondary Market Financing
424100	Paper & Paper Products	447100	Gasoline Stations (including convenience stores with gas)	**Pipeline Transportation**		522298	All Other Nondepository Credit Intermediation
424210	Drugs & Druggists' Sundries	**Clothing and Clothing Accessories Stores**		486000	Pipeline Transportation	**Activities Related to Credit Intermediation**	
424300	Apparel, Piece Goods, & Notions	448110	Men's Clothing Stores	**Scenic & Sightseeing Transportation**		522300	Activities Related to Credit Intermediation (including loan brokers, check clearing, & money transmitting)
424400	Grocery & Related Products	448120	Women's Clothing Stores	487000	Scenic & Sightseeing Transportation		
424500	Farm Product Raw Materials	448130	Children's & Infants' Clothing Stores	**Support Activities for Transportation**			
424600	Chemical & Allied Products	448140	Family Clothing Stores	488100	Support Activities for Air Transportation	**Securities, Commodity Contracts, and Other Financial Investments and Related Activities**	
424700	Petroleum & Petroleum Products	448150	Clothing Accessories Stores	488210	Support Activities for Rail Transportation	523110	Investment Banking & Securities Dealing
424800	Beer, Wine, & Distilled Alcoholic Beverages	448190	Other Clothing Stores	488300	Support Activities for Water Transportation	523120	Securities Brokerage
424910	Farm Supplies	448210	Shoe Stores	488410	Motor Vehicle Towing	523130	Commodity Contracts Dealing
424920	Book, Periodical, & Newspapers	448310	Jewelry Stores	488490	Other Support Activities for Road Transportation	523140	Commodity Contracts Brokerage
424930	Flower, Nursery Stock, & Florists' Supplies	448320	Luggage & Leather Goods Stores	488510	Freight Transportation Arrangement	523210	Securities & Commodity Exchanges
424940	Tobacco & Tobacco Products	**Sporting Goods, Hobby, Book, and Music Stores**		488990	Other Support Activities for Transportation	523900	Other Financial Investment Activities (including portfolio management & investment advice)
424950	Paint, Varnish, & Supplies	451110	Sporting Goods Stores	**Couriers and Messengers**			
424990	Other Miscellaneous Nondurable Goods	451120	Hobby, Toy, & Game Stores	492110	Couriers	**Insurance Carriers and Related Activities**	
Wholesale Electronic Markets and Agents and Brokers		451130	Sewing, Needlework, & Piece Goods Stores	492210	Local Messengers & Local Delivery	524140	Direct Life, Health, & Medical Insurance & Reinsurance Carriers
425110	Business to Business Electronic Markets	451140	Musical Instrument & Supplies Stores	**Warehousing and Storage**		524150	Direct Insurance & Reinsurance (except Life, Health & Medical) Carriers
425120	Wholesale Trade Agents & Brokers	451211	Book Stores	493100	Warehousing & Storage (except lessors of miniwarehouses & self-storage units)	524210	Insurance Agencies & Brokerages
		451212	News Dealers & Newsstands			524290	Other Insurance Related Activities (including third-party administration of insurance and pension funds)
Retail Trade		451220	Prerecorded Tape, Compact Disc, & Record Stores				
Motor Vehicle and Parts Dealers		**General Merchandise Stores**		**Information**		**Funds, Trusts, and Other Financial Vehicles**	
441110	New Car Dealers	452110	Department Stores	**Publishing Industries (except Internet)**		525100	Insurance & Employee Benefit Funds
441120	Used Car Dealers	452900	Other General Merchandise Stores	511110	Newspaper Publishers	525910	Open-End Investment Funds (Form 1120-RIC)
441210	Recreational Vehicle Dealers	**Miscellaneous Store Retailers**		511120	Periodical Publishers	525920	Trusts, Estates, & Agency Accounts
441221	Motorcycle Dealers	453110	Florists	511130	Book Publishers	525990	Other Financial Vehicles (including mortgage REITs & closed-end investment funds)
441222	Boat Dealers	453210	Office Supplies & Stationery Stores	511140	Directory & Mailing List Publishers	"Offices of Bank Holding Companies" and "Offices of Other Holding Companies" are located under **Management of Companies (Holding Companies)** on page 16.	
441229	All Other Motor Vehicle Dealers	453220	Gift, Novelty, & Souvenir Stores	511190	Other Publishers		
441300	Automotive Parts, Accessories, & Tire Stores	453310	Used Merchandise Stores	511210	Software Publishers		
Furniture and Home Furnishings Stores		453910	Pet & Pet Supplies Stores	**Motion Picture and Sound Recording Industries**			
442110	Furniture Stores	453920	Art Dealers	512100	Motion Picture & Video Industries (except video rental)	**Real Estate and Rental and Leasing**	
442210	Floor Covering Stores	453930	Manufactured (Mobile) Home Dealers	512200	Sound Recording Industries	**Real Estate**	
442291	Window Treatment Stores	453990	All Other Miscellaneous Store Retailers (including tobacco, candle, & trophy shops)	**Broadcasting (except Internet)**		531110	Lessors of Residential Buildings & Dwellings (including equity REITs)
442299	All Other Home Furnishings Stores	**Nonstore Retailers**		515100	Radio & Television Broadcasting	531114	Cooperative Housing (including equity REITs)
Electronics and Appliance Stores		454110	Electronic Shopping & Mail-Order Houses	515210	Cable & Other Subscription Programming	531120	Lessors of Nonresidential Buildings (except Miniwarehouses) (including equity REITs)
443111	Household Appliance Stores	454210	Vending Machine Operators	**Telecommunications**			
443112	Radio, Television, & Other Electronics Stores	454311	Heating Oil Dealers	517000	Telecommunications (including paging, cellular, satellite, cable & other program distribution, resellers, other telecommunications, & internet service providers)	531130	Lessors of Miniwarehouses & Self-Storage Units (including equity REITs)
443120	Computer & Software Stores	454312	Liquefied Petroleum Gas (Bottled Gas) Dealers			531190	Lessors of Other Real Estate Property (including equity REITs)
443130	Camera & Photographic Supplies Stores	454319	Other Fuel Dealers			531210	Offices of Real Estate Agents & Brokers
Building Material and Garden Equipment and Supplies Dealers		454390	Other Direct Selling Establishments (including door-to-door retailing, frozen food plan providers, party plan merchandisers, & coffee-break service providers)	**Data Processing Services**		531310	Real Estate Property Managers
444110	Home Centers			518210	Data Processing, Hosting, & Related Services	531320	Offices of Real Estate Appraisers
444120	Paint & Wallpaper Stores			**Other Information Services**		531390	Other Activities Related to Real Estate
444130	Hardware Stores			519100	Other Information Services (including news syndicates, libraries, internet publishing & broadcasting)		
444190	Other Building Material Dealers	**Transportation and Warehousing**					
444200	Lawn & Garden Equipment & Supplies Stores	**Air, Rail, and Water Transportation**					
Food and Beverage Stores		481000	Air Transportation	**Finance and Insurance**			
445110	Supermarkets and Other Grocery (except Convenience) Stores	482110	Rail Transportation	**Depository Credit Intermediation**			
		483000	Water Transportation	522110	Commercial Banking		
445120	Convenience Stores	**Truck Transportation**		522120	Savings Institutions		
445210	Meat Markets	484110	General Freight Trucking, Local	522130	Credit Unions		
445220	Fish & Seafood Markets	484120	General Freight Trucking, Long-distance	522190	Other Depository Credit Intermediation		
445230	Fruit & Vegetable Markets	484200	Specialized Freight Trucking	**Nondepository Credit Intermediation**			
445291	Baked Goods Stores	**Transit and Ground Passenger Transportation**		522210	Credit Card Issuing		
445292	Confectionery & Nut Stores	485110	Urban Transit Systems	522220	Sales Financing		
445299	All Other Specialty Food Stores	485210	Interurban & Rural Bus Transportation	522291	Consumer Lending		
445310	Beer, Wine, & Liquor Stores	485310	Taxi Service				
Health and Personal Care Stores		485320	Limousine Service				
446110	Pharmacies & Drug Stores						
446120	Cosmetics, Beauty Supplies, & Perfume Stores						

Instructions for Form 5471   -15-

¶20,050

Form 5471 *(continued)*

Code		Code		Code		Code	
Rental and Leasing Services		**Management of Companies (Holding Companies)**		**Outpatient Care Centers**		721199	All Other Traveler Accommodation
532100	Automotive Equipment Rental & Leasing			621410	Family Planning Centers	721210	RV (Recreational Vehicle) Parks & Recreational Camps
532210	Consumer Electronics & Appliances Rental	551111	Offices of Bank Holding Companies	621420	Outpatient Mental Health & Substance Abuse Centers	721310	Rooming & Boarding Houses
532220	Formal Wear & Costume Rental	551112	Offices of Other Holding Companies	621491	HMO Medical Centers	**Food Services and Drinking Places**	
532230	Video Tape & Disc Rental			621492	Kidney Dialysis Centers	722110	Full-Service Restaurants
532290	Other Consumer Goods Rental	**Administrative and Support and Waste Management and Remediation Services**		621493	Freestanding Ambulatory Surgical & Emergency Centers	722210	Limited-Service Eating Places
532310	General Rental Centers	**Administrative and Support Services**		621498	All Other Outpatient Care Centers	722300	Special Food Services (including food service contractors & caterers)
532400	Commercial & Industrial Machinery & Equipment Rental & Leasing	561110	Office Administrative Services	**Medical and Diagnostic Laboratories**		722410	Drinking Places (Alcoholic Beverages)
Lessors of Nonfinancial Intangible Assets (except copyrighted works)		561210	Facilities Support Services	621510	Medical & Diagnostic Laboratories		
533110	Lessors of Nonfinancial Intangible Assets (except copyrighted works)	561300	Employment Services	**Home Health Care Services**		**Other Services**	
		561410	Document Preparation Services	621610	Home Health Care Services	**Repair and Maintenance**	
		561420	Telephone Call Centers	**Other Ambulatory Health Care Services**		811110	Automotive Mechanical & Electrical Repair & Maintenance
Professional, Scientific, and Technical Services		561430	Business Service Centers (including private mail centers & copy shops)	621900	Other Ambulatory Health Care Services (including ambulance services & blood & organ banks)	811120	Automotive Body, Paint, Interior, & Glass Repair
Legal Services		561440	Collection Agencies	**Hospitals**		811190	Other Automotive Repair & Maintenance (including oil change & lubrication shops & car washes)
541110	Offices of Lawyers	561450	Credit Bureaus	622000	Hospitals		
541190	Other Legal Services	561490	Other Business Support Services (including repossession services, court reporting, & stenotype services)	**Nursing and Residential Care Facilities**		811210	Electronic & Precision Equipment Repair & Maintenance
Accounting, Tax Preparation, Bookkeeping, and Payroll Services				623000	Nursing & Residential Care Facilities	811310	Commercial & Industrial Machinery & Equipment (except Automotive & Electronic) Repair & Maintenance
541211	Offices of Certified Public Accountants			**Social Assistance**			
541213	Tax Preparation Services	561500	Travel Arrangement & Reservation Services	624100	Individual & Family Services	811410	Home & Garden Equipment & Appliance Repair & Maintenance
541214	Payroll Services	561600	Investigation & Security Services	624200	Community Food & Housing, & Emergency & Other Relief Services	811420	Reupholstery & Furniture Repair
541219	Other Accounting Services	561710	Exterminating & Pest Control Services	624310	Vocational Rehabilitation Services	811430	Footwear & Leather Goods Repair
Architectural, Engineering, and Related Services		561720	Janitorial Services	624410	Child Day Care Services	811490	Other Personal & Household Goods Repair & Maintenance
541310	Architectural Services	561730	Landscaping Services				
541320	Landscape Architecture Services	561740	Carpet & Upholstery Cleaning Services	**Arts, Entertainment, and Recreation**		**Personal and Laundry Services**	
541330	Engineering Services	561790	Other Services to Buildings & Dwellings	**Performing Arts, Spectator Sports, and Related Industries**		812111	Barber Shops
541340	Drafting Services	561900	Other Support Services (including packaging & labeling services, & convention & trade show organizers)	711100	Performing Arts Companies	812112	Beauty Salons
541360	Building Inspection Services			711210	Spectator Sports (including sports clubs & racetracks)	812113	Nail Salons
541360	Geophysical Surveying & Mapping Services			711300	Promoters of Performing Arts, Sports, & Similar Events	812190	Other Personal Care Services (including diet & weight reducing centers)
541370	Surveying & Mapping (except Geophysical) Services	**Waste Management and Remediation Services**		711410	Agents & Managers for Artists, Athletes, Entertainers, & Other Public Figures	812210	Funeral Homes & Funeral Services
541380	Testing Laboratories	562000	Waste Management & Remediation Services	711510	Independent Artists, Writers, & Performers	812220	Cemeteries & Crematories
Specialized Design Services				**Museums, Historical Sites, and Similar Institutions**		812310	Coin-Operated Laundries & Drycleaners
541400	Specialized Design Services (including interior, industrial, graphic, & fashion design)	**Educational Services**		712100	Museums, Historical Sites, & Similar Institutions	812320	Drycleaning & Laundry Services (except Coin-Operated)
Computer Systems Design and Related Services		611000	Educational Services (including schools, colleges, & universities)	**Amusement, Gambling, and Recreation Industries**		812330	Linen & Uniform Supply
541511	Custom Computer Programming Services			713100	Amusement Parks & Arcades	812910	Pet Care (except Veterinary) Services
541512	Computer Systems Design Services	**Health Care and Social Assistance**		713200	Gambling Industries	812920	Photofinishing
541513	Computer Facilities Management Services	**Offices of Physicians and Dentists**		713900	Other Amusement & Recreation Industries (including golf courses, skiing facilities, marinas, fitness centers, & bowling centers)	812930	Parking Lots & Garages
541519	Other Computer Related Services	621111	Offices of Physicians (except mental health specialists)			812990	All Other Personal Services
Other Professional, Scientific, and Technical Services		621112	Offices of Physicians, Mental Health Specialists			**Religious, Grantmaking, Civic, Professional, and Similar Organizations**	
541600	Management, Scientific, & Technical Consulting Services	621210	Offices of Dentists	**Accommodation and Food Services**		813000	Religious, Grantmaking, Civic, Professional, & Similar Organizations (including condominium and homeowners associations)
541700	Scientific Research & Development Services	**Offices of Other Health Practitioners**		**Accommodation**			
541800	Advertising & Related Services	621310	Offices of Chiropractors	721110	Hotels (except Casino Hotels) & Motels		
541910	Marketing Research & Public Opinion Polling	621320	Offices of Optometrists	721120	Casino Hotels		
541920	Photographic Services	621330	Offices of Mental Health Practitioners (except Physicians)	721191	Bed & Breakfast Inns		
541930	Translation & Interpretation Services	621340	Offices of Physical, Occupational & Speech Therapists, & Audiologists				
541940	Veterinary Services	621391	Offices of Podiatrists				
541990	All Other Professional, Scientific, & Technical Services	621399	Offices of All Other Miscellaneous Health Practitioners				

¶ 20,050

Form 5472

Form **5472** (Rev. December 2007) Department of the Treasury Internal Revenue Service	**Information Return of a 25% Foreign-Owned U.S. Corporation or a Foreign Corporation Engaged in a U.S. Trade or Business** **(Under Sections 6038A and 6038C of the Internal Revenue Code)** For tax year of the reporting corporation beginning _____ , _____, and ending _____ , _____ **Note.** *Enter all information in English and money items in U.S. dollars.*	OMB No. 1545-0805

Part I **Reporting Corporation** (see instructions). All reporting corporations must complete Part I.

1a Name of reporting corporation	**1b** Employer identification number
Number, street, and room or suite no. (if a P.O. box, see instructions)	**1c** Total assets
City or town, state, and ZIP code (if a foreign address, see instructions)	$

1d Principal business activity ▶	**1e** Principal business activity code ▶

1f Total value of gross payments made or received (see instructions) reported on **this** Form 5472 $	**1g** Total number of Forms 5472 filed for the tax year $	**1h** Total value of gross payments made or received (see instructions) reported on **all** Forms 5472

1i Check here if this is a consolidated filing of Form 5472 . . .▶ ☐	**1j** Country of incorporation	**1k** Country(ies) under whose laws the reporting corporation files an income tax return as a resident	**1l** Principal country(ies) where business is conducted

2 Check here if, at any time during the tax year, any foreign person owned, directly or indirectly, at least 50% of **(a)** the total voting power of all classes of the stock of the reporting corporation entitled to vote, or **(b)** the total value of all classes of stock of the reporting corporation . . . . ▶ ☐

Part II **25% Foreign Shareholder** (see instructions)

1a Name and address of direct 25% foreign shareholder	**1b** U.S. identifying number, if any

1c Principal country(ies) where business is conducted	**1d** Country of citizenship, organization, or incorporation	**1e** Country(ies) under whose laws the direct 25% foreign shareholder files an income tax return as a resident

2a Name and address of direct 25% foreign shareholder	**2b** U.S. identifying number, if any

2c Principal country(ies) where business is conducted	**2d** Country of citizenship, organization, or incorporation	**2e** Country(ies) under whose laws the direct 25% foreign shareholder files an income tax return as a resident

3a Name and address of ultimate indirect 25% foreign shareholder	**3b** U.S. identifying number, if any

3c Principal country(ies) where business is conducted	**3d** Country of citizenship, organization, or incorporation	**3e** Country(ies) under whose laws the ultimate indirect 25% foreign shareholder files an income tax return as a resident

4a Name and address of ultimate indirect 25% foreign shareholder	**4b** U.S. identifying number, if any

4c Principal country(ies) where business is conducted	**4d** Country of citizenship, organization, or incorporation	**4e** Country(ies) under whose laws the ultimate indirect 25% foreign shareholder files an income tax return as a resident

Part III **Related Party** (see instructions)

Check applicable box: Is the related party a ☐ foreign person or ☐ U.S. person?
All reporting corporations must complete this question and the rest of Part III.

1a Name and address of related party	**1b** U.S. identifying number, if any

1c Principal business activity ▶	**1d** Principal business activity code ▶

1e Relationship—Check boxes that apply: ☐ Related to reporting corporation ☐ Related to 25% foreign shareholder ☐ 25% foreign shareholder

1f Principal country(ies) where business is conducted	**1g** Country(ies) under whose laws the related party files an income tax return as a resident

For Paperwork Reduction Act Notice, see page 4.   Cat. No. 49987Y   Form **5472** (Rev. 12-2007)

¶20,050

Form 5472 (Rev. 12-2007) Page **2**

Part IV **Monetary Transactions Between Reporting Corporations and Foreign Related Party** (see instructions)
Caution: *Part IV **must** be completed if the "foreign person" box is checked in the heading for Part III.*
If estimates are used, check here ▶ ☐

1	Sales of stock in trade (inventory)	1
2	Sales of tangible property other than stock in trade	2
3a	Rents received (for other than intangible property rights)	3a
b	Royalties received (for other than intangible property rights)	3b
4	Sales, leases, licenses, etc., of intangible property rights (e.g., patents, trademarks, secret formulas)	4
5	Consideration received for technical, managerial, engineering, construction, scientific, or like services	5
6	Commissions received	6
7	Amounts borrowed (see instructions) **a** Beginning balance _____ **b** Ending balance or monthly average ▶	7b
8	Interest received	8
9	Premiums received for insurance or reinsurance	9
10	Other amounts received (see instructions)	10
11	**Total.** Combine amounts on lines 1 through 10	11
12	Purchases of stock in trade (inventory)	12
13	Purchases of tangible property other than stock in trade	13
14a	Rents paid (for other than intangible property rights)	14a
b	Royalties paid (for other than intangible property rights)	14b
15	Purchases, leases, licenses, etc., of intangible property rights (e.g., patents, trademarks, secret formulas)	15
16	Consideration paid for technical, managerial, engineering, construction, scientific, or like services	16
17	Commissions paid	17
18	Amounts loaned (see instructions) **a** Beginning balance _____ **b** Ending balance or monthly average ▶	18b
19	Interest paid	19
20	Premiums paid for insurance or reinsurance	20
21	Other amounts paid (see instructions)	21
22	**Total.** Combine amounts on lines 12 through 21	22

Part V **Nonmonetary and Less-Than-Full Consideration Transactions Between the Reporting Corporation and the Foreign Related Party** (see instructions)
Describe these transactions on an attached separate sheet and check here. ▶ ☐

Part VI **Additional Information**
All reporting corporations must complete Part VI.

1 Does the reporting corporation import goods from a foreign related party? ☐ Yes ☐ No
2a If "Yes," is the basis or inventory cost of the goods valued at greater than the customs value of the imported goods? ☐ Yes ☐ No
If "No," **do not** complete **b** and **c** below.
b If "Yes," attach a statement explaining the reason or reasons for such difference.
c If the answers to questions 1 and 2a are "Yes," were the documents used to support this treatment of the imported goods in existence and available in the United States at the time of filing Form 5472? ☐ Yes ☐ No

General Instructions

Section references are to the Internal Revenue Code unless otherwise noted.

What's New

• The IRS has modified Part IV, lines 3 and 14.

• A reporting corporation that uses an accrual method of accounting must use accrued payments and accrued receipts for purposes of computing the total amount to enter on each line of the Form 5472. See Regulations section 1.6038A-2(b)(8).

Purpose of Form

Use Form 5472 to provide information required under sections 6038A and 6038C when reportable transactions occur during the tax year of a reporting corporation with a foreign or domestic related party.

Definitions

Reporting corporation. A reporting corporation is either:

• A 25% foreign-owned U.S. corporation **or**

• A foreign corporation engaged in a trade or business within the United States.

25% foreign owned. A corporation is 25% foreign owned if it has at least one direct or indirect 25% foreign shareholder at any time during the tax year.

25% foreign shareholder. Generally, a foreign person (defined on page 3) is a 25% foreign shareholder if the person owns, directly or indirectly, at least 25% of either:

• The total voting power of all classes of stock entitled to vote **or**

• The total value of all classes of stock of the corporation.

The constructive ownership rules of section 318 apply with the following modifications to determine if a corporation is 25% foreign owned. Substitute "10%" for "50%" in section 318(a)(2)(C). Do not apply sections

318(a)(3)(A), (B), and (C) so as to consider a U.S. person as owning stock that is owned by a foreign person.

Related party. A related party is:

• Any direct or indirect 25% foreign shareholder of the reporting corporation,

• Any person who is related (within the meaning of section 267(b) or 707(b)(1)) to the reporting corporation,

• Any person who is related (within the meaning of section 267(b) or 707(b)(1)) to a 25% foreign shareholder of the reporting corporation, **or**

• Any other person who is related to the reporting corporation within the meaning of section 482 and the related regulations.

"Related party" does not include any corporation filing a consolidated Federal income tax return with the reporting corporation.

The rules in section 318 apply to the definition of related party with the modifications listed under the definition of *25% foreign shareholder* above.

¶20,050

Reportable transaction. A reportable transaction is:

• Any type of transaction listed in Part IV (e.g., sales, rents, etc.) for which monetary consideration (including U.S. and foreign currency) was the sole consideration paid or received during the reporting corporation's tax year **or**

• Any transaction or group of transactions listed in Part IV, if:

1. Any part of the consideration paid or received was not monetary consideration **or**

2. Less than full consideration was paid or received.

Transactions with a U.S. related party, however, are not required to be specifically identified in Parts IV and V.

Direct 25% foreign shareholder. A foreign person is a direct 25% foreign shareholder if it owns directly at least 25% of the stock of the reporting corporation by vote or value.

Ultimate indirect 25% foreign shareholder. An ultimate indirect 25% foreign shareholder is a 25% foreign shareholder whose ownership of stock of the reporting corporation is not attributed (under the principles of section 958(a)(1) and (2)) to any other 25% foreign shareholder. See Rev. Proc. 91-55, 1991-2 C.B. 784.

Foreign person. A foreign person is:

• An individual who is not a citizen or resident of the United States,

• An individual who is a citizen or resident of a U.S. possession who is not otherwise a citizen or resident of the United States,

• Any partnership, association, company, or corporation that is not created or organized in the United States,

• Any foreign estate or foreign trust described in section 7701(a)(31), **or**

• Any foreign government (or agency or instrumentality thereof) to the extent that the foreign government is engaged in the conduct of a commercial activity as defined in section 892.

However, the term "foreign person" does not include any foreign person who consents to the filing of a joint income tax return.

Who Must File

Generally, a reporting corporation must file Form 5472 if it had a reportable transaction with a foreign or domestic related party.

Exceptions from filing. A reporting corporation is not required to file Form 5472 if any of the following apply:

1. It had no reportable transactions of the types listed in Parts IV and V of the form.

2. A U.S. person that controls the foreign related corporation files **Form 5471**, Information Return of U.S. Persons With Respect To Certain Foreign Corporations, for the tax year to report information under section 6038. To qualify for this exception, the U.S. person must complete Schedule M (Form 5471) showing all reportable transactions between the reporting corporation and the related party for the tax year.

3. The related corporation qualifies as a foreign sales corporation for the tax year and files **Form 1120-FSC**, U.S. Income Tax Return of a Foreign Sales Corporation.

4. It is a foreign corporation that does not have a permanent establishment in the United States under an applicable income tax treaty and timely files Form 8833.

5. It is a foreign corporation all of whose gross income is exempt from taxation under section 883 and it timely and fully complies with the reporting requirements of sections 883 and 887.

6. Both the reporting corporation and the related party are not U.S. persons as defined in section 7701(a)(30) and the transactions will not generate in any tax year:

• Gross income from sources within the United States or income effectively connected, or treated as effectively connected, with the conduct of a trade or business within the United States **or**

• Any expense, loss, or other deduction that is allocable or apportionable to such income.

Consolidated returns. If a reporting corporation is a member of an affiliated group filing a consolidated income tax return, Regulations section 1.6038A-2 may be satisfied by filing a U.S. consolidated Form 5472. The common parent must attach to Form 5472 a schedule stating which members of the U.S. affiliated group are reporting corporations under section 6038A, and which of those members are joining in the consolidated filing of Form 5472. The schedule must show the name, address, and employer identification number of each member who is including transactions on the consolidated Form 5472.

Note. *A member is not required to join in filing a consolidated Form 5472 just because other members of the group choose to file one or more Forms 5472 on a consolidated basis.*

When and Where To File

File Form 5472 by the due date of the reporting corporation's income tax return (including extensions). A separate Form 5472 must be filed for each foreign or domestic related party with which the reporting corporation had a reportable transaction during the tax year. Attach Form 5472 to the income tax return. You are required to file a duplicate copy of Form 5472 with the Internal Revenue Service Center, P.O. Box 409101, Ogden, UT, 84409. However, if you file your income tax return electronically, see *Electronic Filing of Form 5472* below for additional information.

If the reporting corporation's income tax return is not filed when due, file a timely Form 5472 (with a copy to Ogden) separately with the service center where the tax return is due. When the tax return is filed, attach a copy of the previously filed Form 5472.

Electronic Filing of Form 5472

If you file your income tax return electronically, see the instructions for your income tax return for general information about electronic filing. If you file your original Form 5472 electronically (as an attachment to a timely filed, electronically filed income tax return), such filing satisfies the duplicate filing requirement referred to above. See the first sentence under *When and Where To File* above for the definition of "timely."

Accrued Payments and Receipts

A reporting corporation that uses an accrual method of accounting must use accrued payments and accrued receipts for purposes of computing the total amount to enter on each line of the Form 5472. See Regulations section 1.6038A-2(b)(8).

Penalties

Penalties for failure to file Form 5472. A penalty of $10,000 will be assessed on any reporting corporation that fails to file Form 5472 when due and in the manner prescribed. The penalty also applies for failure to maintain records as required by Regulations section 1.6038A-3.

Note. *Filing a substantially incomplete Form 5472 constitutes a failure to file Form 5472.*

Each member of a group of corporations filing a consolidated information return is a separate reporting corporation subject to a separate $10,000 penalty and each member is jointly and severally liable.

If the failure continues for more than 90 days after notification by the IRS, an additional penalty of $10,000 will apply. This penalty applies with respect to each related party for which a failure occurs for each 30-day period (or part of a 30-day period) during which the failure continues after the 90-day period ends.

Criminal penalties under sections 7203, 7206, and 7207 may also apply for failure to submit information or for filing false or fraudulent information.

Record Maintenance Requirements

A reporting corporation must keep the permanent books of account or records as required by section 6001. These books must be sufficient to establish the correctness of the reporting corporation's Federal income tax return, including information or records that might be relevant to determine the correct treatment of transactions with related parties. See Regulations section 1.6038A-3 for more detailed information. Also, see Regulations sections 1.6038A-1(h) and 1.6038A-1(i) for special rules that apply to small corporations and reporting corporations with related party transactions of de minimis value.

Specific Instructions

Part I

Line 1a. Address. Include the suite, room, or other unit number after the street address. If the Post Office does not deliver mail to the street address and the corporation has a P.O. box, show the box number instead.

Foreign address. Enter the information in the following order: city, province or state, and country. Follow the country's practice for entering the postal code, if any. Do not abbreviate the country name.

Line 1c. Total assets. Domestic reporting corporations enter the total assets from item D, page 1, Form 1120. Foreign reporting corporations enter the amount from line 17, column (d), Schedule L, Form 1120-F.

Lines 1d and 1e. Enter a description of the principal business activity and enter the principal business activity code. See the instructions for Form 1120 or Form 1120-F for a list of principal business activities and their associated codes.

Line 1f. Enter the total value in U.S. dollars of all foreign related party transactions reported in Parts IV and V of **this** Form 5472. This is the total of the amounts entered on lines 11 and 22 of Part IV plus the fair market value of the nonmonetary and less-than-full consideration transactions reported in Part V. **Do not** complete line 1f if the reportable transaction is with a U.S. related party.

Line 1g. File a separate Form 5472 for each foreign or each U.S. person who is a related party with which the reporting corporation had a reportable transaction. Enter the total number of Forms 5472 (including this one) being filed for the tax year.

Line 1h. Enter the total value in U.S. dollars of all foreign related party transactions reported in Parts IV and V of **all** Forms 5472 filed for the tax year. This is the total of the amounts entered on line 1f of **all** Forms 5472 filed for the tax year (including this one).

Line 1l. Provide the principal country(ies) where business is conducted. **Do not** include a country(ies) in which business is conducted solely through a subsidiary. **Do not** enter "worldwide" instead of listing the country(ies). These rules also apply to lines 2c, 3c, 4c, Part II, and line 1f, Part III.

Line 2. For purposes of this line:

• "Foreign person" has the same meaning as provided on page 3.

• 50% direct or indirect ownership is determined by applying the constructive ownership rules of section 318 with the modifications listed under *25% foreign shareholder* on page 2.

Part II

Note. *Only 25% foreign-owned U.S. corporations complete Part II.*

The form provides sufficient space to report information for two direct 25% foreign shareholders and two ultimate indirect 25% foreign shareholders. If more space is needed, show the information requested in Part II on an attached sheet.

Report on lines 1a through 1e information about the direct 25% foreign shareholder who owns (by vote or value) the largest percentage of the stock of the U.S. reporting corporation.

Report on lines 2a through 2e information about the direct 25% foreign shareholder who owns (by vote or value) the second-largest percentage of the stock of the U.S. reporting corporation.

Report on lines 3a through 3e information about the ultimate indirect 25% foreign shareholder who owns (by vote or value) the largest percentage of the stock of the U.S. reporting corporation.

Report on lines 4a through 4e information about the ultimate indirect 25% foreign shareholder who owns (by vote or value) the second-largest percentage of the stock of the U.S. reporting corporation.

Lines 3a through 3e and lines 4a through 4e. Attach an explanation of the attribution of ownership. See Rev. Proc. 91-55 and Regulations section 1.6038A-1(e).

Part III

All filers must complete Part III even if the related party has been identified in Part II as a 25% foreign shareholder. Report in Part III information about the related party (domestic or foreign) with which the reporting corporation had reportable transactions during the tax year.

Part IV

Note. *Do not complete Part IV for transactions with a domestic related party.*

When completing Part IV or Part V, the terms "paid" and "received" include accrued payments and accrued receipts. State all amounts in U.S. dollars and attach a schedule showing the exchange rates used.

If the related party transactions occur between a related party and a partnership that is, in whole or in part, owned by a reporting corporation, the reporting corporation reports only the percentage of the value of the transaction(s) equal to the percentage of its partnership interest. This rule does not apply if the reporting corporation owns a less-than-25% interest in the partnership. The rules of attribution apply when determining the reporting corporation's percentage of partnership interest.

Generally, all reportable transactions between the reporting corporation and a related foreign party must be entered in Part IV.

Reasonable estimates. When actual amounts are not determinable, enter reasonable estimates (see below) of the total dollar amount of each of the categories of transactions conducted between the reporting corporation and the related person in which monetary consideration (U.S. currency or foreign currency) was the sole consideration paid or received during the tax year of the reporting corporation.

A reasonable estimate is any amount reported on Form 5472 that is at least 75% but not more than 125% of the actual amount required to be reported.

Small amounts. If any actual amount in a transaction or a series of transactions between a foreign related party and the reporting corporation does not exceed a total of $50,000, the amount may be reported as "$50,000 or less."

Line 7. Amounts borrowed. Report amounts borrowed using either the outstanding balance method or the monthly average method. If the outstanding balance method is used, enter the beginning and ending outstanding balance for the tax year on lines 7a and 7b. If the monthly average method is used, skip line 7a and enter the monthly average for the tax year on line 7b.

Line 10. Other amounts received. Enter amounts received that are not specifically reported on lines 1 through 9. Include amounts on line 10 to the extent that these amounts are taken into account in determining the taxable income of the reporting corporation.

Line 18. Amounts loaned. Report amounts loaned using either the outstanding balance method or the monthly average method. If the outstanding balance method is used, enter the beginning and ending outstanding balance for the tax year on lines 18a and 18b. If the monthly average method is used, skip line 18a and enter the monthly average for the tax year on line 18b.

Line 21. Other amounts paid. Enter amounts paid that are not specifically reported on lines 12 through 20. Include amounts on line 21 to the extent that these amounts are taken into account in determining the taxable income of the reporting corporation.

Part V

Note. *Do not complete Part V for transactions with a domestic related party.*

If the related party is a foreign person, the reporting corporation must attach a schedule describing each reportable transaction, or group of reportable transactions. The description must include sufficient information so that the nature and approximate monetary value of the transaction or group of transactions can be determined. The schedule should include:

1. A description of all property (including monetary consideration), rights, or obligations transferred from the reporting corporation to the foreign related party and from the foreign related party to the reporting corporation;

2. A description of all services performed by the reporting corporation for the foreign related party and by the foreign related party for the reporting corporation; **and**

3. A reasonable estimate of the fair market value of all properties and services exchanged, if possible, or some other reasonable indicator of value.

If the entire consideration received for any transaction includes both tangible and intangible property and the consideration paid is solely monetary consideration, report the transaction in Part IV instead of Part V if the intangible property was related and incidental to the transfer of the tangible property (e.g., a right to warranty services).

See the instructions for Part IV for information on reasonable estimates and small amounts.

Paperwork Reduction Act Notice. We ask for the information on this form to carry out the Internal Revenue laws of the United States. You are required to give us the information. We need it to ensure that you are complying with these laws and to allow us to figure and collect the right amount of tax.

You are not required to provide the information requested on a form that is subject to the Paperwork Reduction Act unless the form displays a valid OMB control number. Books or records relating to a form or its instructions must be retained as long as their contents may become material in the administration of any Internal Revenue law. Generally, tax returns and return information are confidential, as required by section 6103.

The time needed to complete and file this form will vary depending on individual circumstances. The estimated average time is:

Recordkeeping . . . . . 17 hr., 42 min.

Learning about the law
or the form . . . . . . 3 hr., 4 min.

Preparing and sending
the form to the IRS . . . 3 hr., 30 min.

If you have comments concerning the accuracy of these time estimates or suggestions for making this form simpler, we would be happy to hear from you. See the instructions for the tax return with which this form is filed.

¶ 20,060 Model Transfer Pricing Documentation

I. Introduction

A. Objective of Report

The objective of this report is to document an analysis of certain intercompany transactions (the "covered transactions") under the standards of the transfer pricing documentation rules of Treasury Regulation Section 1.6662-6(d). The covered transactions analyzed in this report consist of the sales by "T" ForCo to USCo during the fiscal year ended December 31, 2009.

B. Scope

In preparing this report, we relied upon information supplied by the company. The conclusion of this report is based upon:

1. information and data provided by the company, the completeness and accuracy of which we did not independently verify;

2. the assumption that the company has made a reasonably thorough search for the information that we have requested and the company is not aware of any other information that would have material impact on our analysis;

3. the law, regulations, cases, and other tax authority in effect as of the date of the report. If there are any significant changes of the foregoing tax authorities (for which we shall have no responsibility to advise you), such changes may result in our conclusion being rendered invalid or necessitate (upon your request) a reconsideration of the conclusion;

4. the understanding that our conclusion is applicable only to the taxable year(s) and the transactions specifically covered by our report, and that we have assumed all other related party transactions are at arm's length;

5. the understanding that our analysis of third party transactions has been limited to the information that you have provided to us;

6. the understanding that this report is solely for your benefit and may not be relied upon by any other person or entity other than the IRS.

C. Work Performed

1. Conducted meetings with personnel in St. Louis to obtain financial information and other background information.

2. Prepared functional analysis checklist and detailed transfer pricing profile for completion by the company.

3. Reviewed responses given on functional analysis checklist and detailed transfer pricing profile.

4. Reviewed financial statements (for the fiscal years ending December 31, 2004, December 31, 2005, and December 31, 2006), product sales information, intercompany and third party agreements, contracts and other relevant documents and information.

5. Visited headquarters at St. Louis to observe business activities and to interview key management personnel regarding business operations.

6. Clarified issues and obtained additional information through supplemental telephone conversations and correspondence.

7. Evaluated alternative specified methods potentially applicable to the covered transactions.

8. Reviewed and analyzed potentially comparable uncontrolled transactions.

9. Searched in public company databases for companies potentially comparable to USCo.

10. Narrowed group of potential comparable companies applying various screening and selection criteria.

11. Selected final group of comparable companies.

12. Obtained financial and other relevant information on the comparable companies.

13. Made accounting and capital adjustments to the financial statements of USCo and comparable companies.

14. Performed economic analysis to compare financial results of USCo with those of comparable companies using _____.

15. Discussed our findings with management.

16. Performed additional fact gathering and additional economic analysis based on comments received from management.

17. Issued transfer pricing report for the fiscal year ended December 31, 2006.

D. Location of Information included in Principal Documents Described in Reg. § 1.6662-6(d)(2)(iii)(B)

Principal Document	Reference
1) Business Overview	Section II
2) Organizational Structure	Section II
3) Documentation Required Under § 482	Not Applicable
4) Selected Method	Section IV and Appendix 5
5) Alternative Methods	Section IV
6) Controlled Transactions	Section II
7) Comparables	Section IV and Appendix 2
8) Economic Analysis	Sections III and IV and Appendices 1, 2, 3, 4, 5, and 6
9) Relevant New Data	This report incorporates data obtained after the taxable year end through the date interviews were completed.
10) General Index of Principal and Background Documents	To be completed by the company

II. Business Description

A. Organizational Structure

B. Description of Taxpayer's Business

1. Type of Business
2. Products
3. Suppliers
4. Customers
5. Pricing to Customers

C. Description of Industry

6. Industry
7. Competitive Situations
8. Market Share

D. Relevant Intercompany Agreements

E. Intercompany Transactions

1. Transfer of Tangible Property

100 percent of USCo's tangible property transactions are purchased from ForCo. These products consist of the following:

Tangible Product	Description
T	

ForCo's terms to USCo are 90 days A/R.

III. Functional Analysis

A. Functions

1. Manufacturing/Processing
2. Research and Development

¶20,060

    3. Quality Control

    4. Advertising Marketing

    5. Ordering and Distribution

    6. Invoicing and Collection

    7. Inventory

    8. Service, Warranty, and Spare Parts

    9. Administrative, Financial and Legal Matters

B. Risks

    10. Research and Development Risk

    11. Marketing Risk

    12. Inventory Risk

    13. Product Defect Risk

    14. Credit Risk

    15. Foreign Exchange Risk

    16. Product Liability Risk.

C. Intangibles

    17. Manufacturing Intangibles

    18. Marketing Intangibles

IV. Transfer Pricing Analysis

A. Application of the Best Method Rule

The best method rule in the Section 482 regulations requires that the arm's length result of a controlled transaction be determined under the method that, given the facts and circumstances, provides the most reliable measure of an arm's length result. The application of the best method generally establishes an arm's length range of prices or financial returns with which to test the controlled transactions.

In determining the most reliable measure of an arm's length result, the following factors should be considered:

- degree of comparability between controlled and uncontrolled transactions; and

- quality of data and assumptions.

The degree of comparability is assessed by:

- functions;

- contractual terms;

- risks;

- economic conditions; and

- nature of goods and services supplied.

¶20,060

The quality of data and assumptions is assessed by:

- completeness and accuracy of data;
- reliability of assumptions; and
- sensitivity of results to deficiencies in data and assumptions.

The arm's length amount charged in a controlled transfer of tangible property must be tested under one of the following methods: the comparable uncontrolled price method, the resale price method, the cost plus method, the comparable profits method, the profit split method, or an unspecified method. To meet the specified method requirement under the documentation rules of the transfer pricing penalty regulations, however, it is not necessary to consider unspecified methods.

1. Comparable Uncontrolled Price Method

a) General Description

The comparable uncontrolled price ("CUP") method compares amounts charged in controlled transactions with amounts charged in comparable third party transactions. Comparable sales may be between two third parties or between one of the related parties and a third party. The CUP method is generally the most reliable measure of arm's length results if transactions are identical or if only minor, readily quantifiable differences exist.

The CUP method requires a high degree of comparability of products and functions. Comparability can be enhanced by making adjustments to the comparable price. Adjustments likely to be required include those for differences in:

- product quality;
- contractual terms;
- geographic market;
- embedded intangibles; and
- foreign currency risks.

b) Applicability

[This section should describe the applicability of the Comparable Uncontrolled Price method to the facts, and discuss the factors affecting the reliability of this method as applied to the facts.]

2. Resale Price Method

a) General Description

The resale price method evaluates whether the amount charged in a controlled transaction is at arm's length by reference to the gross margin realized in comparable uncontrolled transactions. Under this method, the arm's length price is measured by subtracting the appropriate gross profit from the applicable resale price of the property involved in the controlled transaction. The resale price method is most often used for distributors that resell products without physically altering them or adding substantial value to them.

¶20,060

This method requires detailed comparisons of functions performed, risks borne, and contractual terms of controlled and uncontrolled transactions. As a result, a higher degree of comparability is more likely to exist between controlled and uncontrolled resales of property by the same reseller (i.e. internal resale price method). In the absence of comparable uncontrolled transactions involving the same reseller, an appropriate comparison may be derived from comparable uncontrolled transactions of other resellers (i.e., external resale price method).

The resale price method is unlikely to lead to accurate results if there are significant differences in:

- level of market:
- functions performed;
- types of products; or
- embedded intangibles.

A reasonable number of adjustments may be made to account for differences between controlled and uncontrolled transactions in:

- inventory turnover;
- contractual terms;
- transport costs; and
- other measurable differences.

b) Applicability

[This section should describe the applicability of the Resale Price method to the facts and explain whether there is a reasonable basis for application of this method.]

3. Cost Plus Method

a) General Description

The cost plus method compares gross margins of controlled and uncontrolled transactions. Under this method, the arm's length price is determined by adding the appropriate gross profit to the controlled taxpayer's cost of producing the property involved in the controlled transaction. The cost plus method is most often used to assess the markup earned by manufacturers selling to related parties.

This method requires detailed comparisons of products produced, functions performed, risks borne, manufacturing complexity, cost structures and intangibles between controlled and uncontrolled transactions. Comparability is most likely found among controlled and uncontrolled sales of property by the same seller (i.e., internal cost plus method). In the absence of such sales, an appropriate comparison may be derived from comparable uncontrolled sales of other producers (i.e., external cost plus method).

The cost plus method is less likely to be reliable if material differences exist between the controlled and uncontrolled transactions with respect to:

- intangibles;
- cost structure;

¶20,060

- business experience;
- management efficiency;
- functions performed; and
- products.

A reasonable number of adjustments may be made to account for differences between controlled and uncontrolled transactions in:

- inventory turnover;
- contractual terms;
- transport costs; and
- other measurable differences.

The degree of consistency in accounting practices between the controlled transaction and the uncontrolled comparables that materially affect the gross profit markup affects the reliability of the result. Thus, for example, if differences in inventory and other cost accounting practices would materially affect the gross profit markup, the ability to make reliable adjustments for such differences would materially affect the reliability of the result. Further, the controlled transaction and the comparable uncontrolled transaction should be consistent in the reporting of costs between cost of goods sold and operating expenses.

b) Applicability

[This section should describe the application of the cost plus method to the facts of the project and explain whether there is a reasonable basis for application of this method.]

4. Profit Split Methods

a) General Description

The profit split methods allocate the combined operating profits or losses from controlled transactions in proportion to the relative contributions made by each party in creating the combined profits or losses. Relative contributions must be determined in a manner that reflects the functions performed, risks assumed, resources employed by each party to the controlled transaction.

The regulations include the following two specified profit split methods:

Comparable Profit Split Method. Transfer prices are based on the division of combined operating profit between uncontrolled taxpayers whose transactions and activities are similar to those of the controlled taxpayers in the relevant business activity. Under this method, the uncontrolled parties' percentage shares of the combined operating profit or loss is used to allocate the combined operating profit or loss of the relevant business activity between the related parties.

Residual Profit Split Method. This method involves two steps. First, operating income is allocated to each party in the controlled transactions to provide a market return for their routine contributions to the relevant business activity. Second, any residual profit is divided among the controlled taxpayers based on the relative value of their contributions of any valuable intangible property to the relevant business activity. This method is best suited for analyzing the transfer of highly profitable intangibles.

b) Applicability

[This section should describe the application of the profit split methods to the facts of the project and explain whether there is a reasonable basis for application of this method under those facts.]

5. Comparable Profits Method

a) General Description

The comparable profits method ("CPM") evaluates whether the amount charged in a controlled transaction is at arm's length comparing the profitability of one of the parties to the controlled transaction (the "tested party") to that of companies that are similar to the tested party. In most cases, the tested party should be the simpler of the two parties involved in the controlled transactions, and should not use intangible property or unique assets that distinguish it from the unrelated comparable companies. The profitability comparison must be based on the profit level indicator, such as return on operating assets, operating profit margin, or ratio of gross profit to operating expenses that provides the most reliable measure of an arm's length result.

The degree of comparability between the tested party and the comparable companies affects the reliability of the CPM analysis. Reliability may be adversely affected by varying cost structures, differences in business experience, or differences in management efficiency. However, less functional comparability is required for reliable results than under the transactional methods (e.g., the CUP method, the resale price method or the cost plus method). In addition, less product similarity is required for reliable results than under the transactional methods.

Adjustments that may be required include those for differences in:

- accounting classifications;
- credit terms;
- inventory;
- currency risk; and
- business circumstances.

b) Applicability

[This section should describe the application of the comparable profits method to the facts and explain whether there is a reasonable basis for application of this method.]

6. Selection of Method

For the reasons stated above, we have selected CPM to test the results of the transactions covered by this report.

¶20,060

B. Application of the Comparable Profits Method

1. Overview

A reliable application of CPM requires:

- selection of the tested party for the analysis;
- determination of financial results related to controlled transactions;
- selection of years for comparison;
- selection of reliable comparable companies;
- accounting adjustments to the financial statements of the tested party and comparable companies for differences in accounting practices, provided such adjustments are appropriate and possible;
- adjustments for differences between the tested party and the comparable companies in risks assumed, functions performed, cost of capital and business environment, provided such adjustments are appropriate and possible; and
- selection of a reliable profit level indicator.

2. Selection of Tested Party

The regulations state that the tested party will be the participant in the controlled transactions whose operating profit attributable to the controlled transactions can be verified using the most reliable data and requiring the fewest and most reliable adjustments, and for which reliable data regarding uncontrolled comparable companies can be located. Generally, the tested party is the party with the least complex functions and does not own valuable intangibles.

As a manufacturer, For Co is engaged in functions that are more complex than the wholesale distribution functions performed by USCo. In addition, ForCo owns the trademark associated with its products. Therefore, USCo is the most appropriate tested party for purposes of applying CPM.

3. Determination of Financial Results Related to Controlled Transactions

Under CPM, the profit level indicators of the uncontrolled comparable companies must be applied to the tested party's financial data that is derived from the controlled transactions under analysis.

4. Selection of Years for Comparison

Data from multiple years usually must be considered when applying CPM. Generally three years (the tested year and the two preceding years) of data are used, unless the specific facts of the case warrant a longer period. If the tested party's results fall within the interquartile range for the appropriate averaging period, it is deemed to have satisfied the requirements of CPM. Accordingly, USCo's results for the years ending December 31, 2006 are compared to the comparable companies' most recently available results over a corresponding time period.

¶20,060

5. Selection of Comparable Companies

In accordance with regulatory guidance for CPM, we searched for companies that perform similar functions, incur similar risks and sell similar products as USCo. Recognizing that product similarity is less important for CPM than similarity of functions and risks, we searched for comparable companies among distributors of consumer products.

a) Description of the Search Process

The search for comparable companies was broad and extensive. It included a thorough search of one or more databases of publicly traded companies. Relevant Standard Industrial Classification ("SIC") codes in which potentially comparable companies could be classified were identified and the databases were also searched by keywords. Since USCo distributes we identified companies that distribute. The following is a list of search criteria and the databases searched:

SIC Codes	And/Or	Keywords	Database

b) Search Results

The search yielded an initial total of [number of companies]as being potentially comparable to USCo. See Appendix B for detailed results of the search matrix.

Next, business descriptions for these [number of companies]companies were reviewed and additional screening criteria were applied to narrow the list. In general companies were sought that: sold consumer products.

Companies were eliminated if they:

1. *Engaged in significant assembly or manufacturing;*
2. *Engaged in significantly different activities. For example, if they had as a primary business activity the provision of services;*
3. *Distributed products with very different market characteristics. For example, we eliminated companies which primarily distribute industrial goods;*
4. *Owned patents, licenses or other valuable intangibles;*
5. *Principally sold at different levels of the market;*
6. *Sold in limited geographic markets;*
7. *Undertook significant research and development;*
8. *Underwent a major disruption to the normal course of business (i.e. bankruptcy, merger, acquisition, etc.); or*
9. *Lacked sufficient data.*

Based on the above criteria, 30 companies were selected for a more detailed review. We obtained and reviewed SEC Form 10-K reports for these companies. Based on a more refined review, using the above criteria, we selected 8 companies

¶20,060

as most comparable to USCo. These companies are principally distributors of consumer products with similar functions and risks as USCo.

The comparable companies are listed below.

c) Comparable Companies

A Co	E Co
B Co	F Co
C Co	G Co
D Co	H Co

d) Comparability Assessment

6. Accounting Adjustments

A reliable CPM analysis requires that only profits arising from ordinary and comparable business operations of the comparable companies and US Co be compared. Furthermore, a reliable CPM analysis should be based on the most accurate data available, and it should not be affected by differences in accounting practices that have no relationship to the actual business operations.

a) Adjustment for Accuracy

The US Co financial statements used for this analysis accurately reflect the ordinary business operations of the company.

The most current SEC Form 10-Ks for the comparable companies were reviewed, and the following adjustments were performed to the data that was downloaded from the databases:

b) Adjustment for Differences in Accounting Practices Adjustment for Differences in Inventory Valuation

According to U.S. GAAP, a company can elect to value inventory by a variety of methods including First-In-First-Out ("FIFO"), Last-In-First-Out ("LIFO"), Averaging and Specific Identification. Differences in the valuation of inventories can distort the profitability comparison between companies. For instance, two companies with identical operations can report different levels of operating assets (through inventories) and profit (through cost of goods sold) if they elect to value their inventories using different methods. To increase the reliability of our analysis, we adjusted the financial statements of the LIFO companies to FIFO. For this adjustment, we added to the opening and closing inventory balances the applicable LIFO reserves and increased cost of goods sold by the difference between the opening and closing LIFO reserves.

Adjustment for Differences in the Reporting of Intangibles

The comparable companies and US Co do not own any significant intangibles, such as patents, copyrights or trademarks. Therefore, any intangible assets on their balance sheets most likely consist only of ordinary intangibles acquired in the purchase of another company. Because similar ordinary assets developed internally are not reported in financial statements, the reported intangible assets and any related amortization distort profitability comparisons and have been removed from

¶20,060

the balance sheet and profit and loss statements before computing profitability ratios.

Accounting for pension and OPEB expense adjustments

If a company fully funds its pension liabilities, its interest cost will be fully offset by the investment income generated by the assets used to fund those liabilities. If a company has unfunded or partially funded pension liabilities, the investment income may not be adequate to cover the interest cost and the shortfall is recorded as a net interest cost operating expense. When the financial statements of either the tested party or the comparables include a line item for such interest, the financial statement must be adjusted by subtracting the pension adjustment from operating expenses.

7. Selection of Profit Level Indicator

a) Description of Profit Level Indicators

A reliable application of CPM requires the selection of a profit level indicator ("PLI") that produces the most reliable measure of income the tested party would have earned had it dealt with related parties at arm's length, taking into account all facts and circumstances. A PLI measures a company's return for its investment of resources and its assumption of risk. The reliability of PLIs might be enhanced through a number of adjustments for differences in capital employed and functions performed.

For a CPM analysis, the U.S. transfer pricing regulations specify three PLIs, the operating margin, the return on operating expense ("Berry ratio"), and the return on operating assets ("ROA"), which measures return on capital employed. However, other PLIs may be used if they provide a more reliable basis for testing an arm's length result. A commonly used PLI for service providers, including contract manufacturers, is the return on total costs ("net cost plus ratio"). The following describes the three specified PLI's and the net cost plus ratio in more detail.

Operating Margin[1]

$$\text{Operating Margin} = \frac{\text{Operating Profit}}{\text{Net Sales}}$$

Berry Ratio

$$\text{Berry Ratio} = \frac{\text{Gross Profit}}{\text{Operating Expenses}}$$

Return on Operating Assets[2]

$$\text{ROA} = \frac{\text{Operating Profit}}{\text{Operating Assets}}$$

[1] Reg. §1.482-5(d) defines operating profit as "gross profit less operating expenses."

[2] Reg. §1.482-5(d) defines operating assets as "the value of all assets used in the relevant business activity of the tested party, including fixed assets and current assets (such as cash, cash equivalents, accounts receivable, and inventories)." Operating assets "does not include investments in subsidiaries, excess cash and portfolio investments."

Net cost plus ratio

$$\text{Net Cost Plus} = \frac{\text{Operating Profit}}{\text{Operating Expense} + \text{Cost of Goods Sold}}$$

b) Selection of Profit Level Indicators

Operating Margin was used.

8. Capital Adjustments

Capital adjustments often improve the reliability of CPM comparisons if the tested party differs from the comparables with respect to their relative levels of certain balance sheet items (e.g., accounts payable, accounts receivable or inventory). Adjustments may differ depending on the profit level indicator selected. The following describes capital adjustments for accounts payable, accounts receivable and inventory.

  a) Accounts Payable Adjustment

  b) Accounts Receivable Adjustments

  c) Inventory Adjustment

9. Analysis and Results

The graphs on the following page show the results of the CPM analysis using

a) Average FYE 2004-2006

US Co's 3-year average adjusted operating margin of 2.0 percent is within the interquartile range established by the comparable companies over the same period.

b) Diagram-Results of Analysis—Average FYE 2004-2006

[Insert graph of statistics for profit level indicators used for average period used.]

V. Conclusion

Based on the information, data and analysis contained in this report, it is reasonable to conclude that the analysis in this report meets the specified method requirement and contains all of the principal documents required to be in existence on the return filing date, under the standards of the transfer pricing penalty regulations, Reg. § 1.6662-6(d).

¶ 20,070 Process Steps in Transfer Pricing Documentation

I. *Investigation and Data Collection*

Purpose—Preliminarily identify important intercompany pricing issues between related parties.

- Perform background information search on company—internet and other sources
- Hold preliminary meeting to outline project steps, goals, and anticipated documentation
- Identify potential transfer pricing issues
- Distribute questionnaires
- Perform interviews—in person or phone
- Request company's financial information
- Analyze all information collected
- Perform general review of industry
- Draft statement of facts

II. *Economic Analysis*

Purpose—Characterize the tested party, select comparable companies, select transfer pricing methodology, perform adjustments, and determine an acceptable arm's length range.

A. Functional Analysis

- Identify and analyze economic functions and risks
- Review intercompany agreements
- Attribute functions and risks to related parties
- Draft functional analysis

B. Select Tested Party

- Review functional analysis
- Select tested party

C. Selection of Comparables and Best Method

- Identify potential comparable companies
- Analyze financial information of comparables
- Identify best method, in light of available comparable information

D. Analysis of Company and Industry Data

- Compile and review economic trends, profitability, financial information, and market share of company
- Prepare financial statements

E. Application of Comparables to Relevant Entities
- Confirm functional comparability
- Compare company data to comparables using selected transfer pricing method

F. Preliminary Recommendations
- Develop preliminary pricing recommendations
- Meet to discuss recommendations

III. *Recommendations and Conclusions*

Purpose—Confirm that the analysis and conclusions are consistent with the facts and finalize the report.

A. Refine Analysis and Conclusions
- Finalize research and economic arguments
- Finalize pricing recommendations

B. Documentation
- Prepare final statement of facts, functions and risks, methodology, and economic analysis
- Prepare supporting documentation

¶ 20,080 Flowchart of Transfer Pricing Controversy

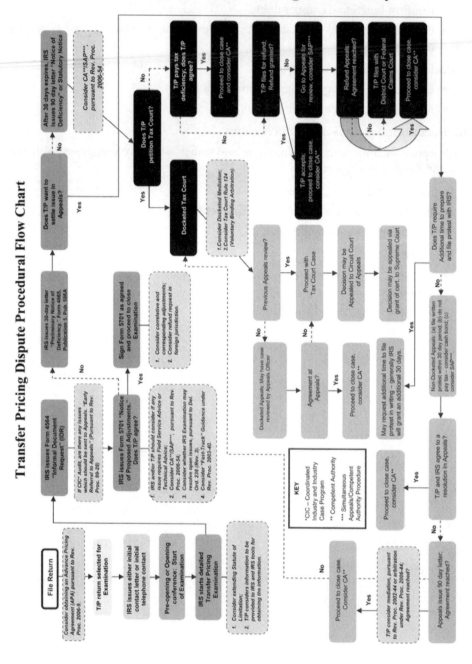

Transfer Pricing Dispute Procedural Flow Chart

¶ 20,090 IRS Forms 5701 and 886-A

Form 5701

Form 5701	Department of the Treasury - Internal Revenue Service NOTICE of PROPOSED ADJUSTMENT		
Name of taxpayer USA, Inc.		Issue No. Int'l # 1	
Name and title of person to whom delivered Mr. Bill Smith, Treasurer		Date: Dec. 12, 2009	

Entity for this proposed adjustment
USA, Inc.

Based on the information we now have available and our discussions with you, we believe that the proposed adjustments listed below should be included in the revenue agent's report. However, if you have additional information that would alter or reverse this proposal, please furnish this information as soon as possible.

Years	Amount	Account or Return Line	Sain No.	Issue Code
03/31/2005	$4,000,000	Cost of Goods Sold		
03/31/2006	$5,000,000	Cost of Goods Sold		
03/31/2007	$7,000,000	Cost of Goods Sold		

ISSUE

SECTION 482 Transfer Pricing Issue

– SEE ATTACHED FORM 886-A

REASONS FOR PROPOSED ADJUSTMENT

If the explanation of the adjustment will be longer than the space provided below, the entire explanation should begin on Form 886-A (Explanation of Items)

See attached Form 886-A.

Taxpayer Representative's action
( )Agreed ( )Agreed in Part ( )Disagreed ( )Will submit more information by: _____

Case Manager John Doe	**Date** Dec. 12, 2009

Form 5701

Form 886-A

FORM 886-A	EXPLANATION OF ITEMS	Schedule No. or
NAME OF TAXPAYER **USA, Inc.**		**YEAR/PERIOD ENDED** **03/31/2005-2007**

Total Adjustment

2005-2007
16,000,000

Other Deductions

Facts:

USA, Inc. is a U.S. manufacturer and distributor of widget components which are used in the final production of widgets. USA, Inc.'s primary customers are U.S. based original equipment manufacturers ("OEMs") of widgets. USA, Inc. was incorporated in State X on April 1, 1983, as a wholly owned subsidiary of Forco, a company organized under the laws of country Y.

USA, Inc. is in the business of distributing and manufacturing component widget parts for the widget industry with the main product line being widget$_1$. The sales and administrative functions take place from an office now in location B in State X. Those functions were performed in an office in location B in State X during the years 1997-1999. The plant was completed in location C in State X in 1990, with significant expansions taking place in 1992 and 1997.

A portion of USA, Inc.'s business involves distributing widget components manufactured by Forco to US widget manufacturers. This business is referred to as the widget$_2$ product line business. Another portion of USA, Inc.'s business involves manufacturing widget components from parts procured from Forco and unrelated suppliers and distributing these components to US widget manufacturers. The company refers to this business as the widget$_1$ product line business.

Widget$_2$ products are totally manufactured by Forco, and warehoused and resold by USA, Inc. USA, Inc. adds no value to these products. USA, Inc. may inspect the products and repackage them before being sold to customers.

Widget$_1$ products are either manufactured or assembled by USA, Inc. at its plant in location C in State X. Additional processing is done here and additional value is added to the product here. Parts are purchased from Forco and unrelated suppliers, then assembled/manufactured by USA, Inc.

The operations of USA, Inc. are broken down into two categories: (i) plant operations and (ii) functions conducted at the corporate office/headquarters. The corporate office was located in location A in State X, and is now located in location B in State X. The sales office is located in the corporate office along with most of the

FORM **886-A**	EXPLANATION OF ITEMS	Schedule No. or
NAME OF TAXPAYER **USA, Inc.**		**YEAR/PERIOD ENDED** **03/31/2005-2007**

corporate officers. During the audit period, functions performed at the plant in location C in State X include production and production control, quality assurance, maintenance and product engineering, personnel, purchasing, E.D.P. and most of the accounting functions.

During the tax years ending March 31, 2005, March 31, 2006 and March 31, 2007 losses reported for those years were as follows:

For financial statement purposes the breakdown by product line is as follows:

For the $widget_2$ product line for tax years ending March 31, 2005, 2006 and 2007 the amounts were net income of $2,000,000, $2,500,000 and $3,500,000, respectively.

For the $widget_1$ product line for tax years ending March 31, 2005, 2006 and 2007 the losses reported were ($4,000,000), ($1,500,000) and ($3,500,000), respectively. These amounts were provided by the taxpayer for financial statement purposes, and given as responses for IDRs XX and XX.

USA, Inc. purchases most of its inventory for the $widget_1$ product line from Forco. The percentage of total purchases is shown in Exhibit 1. USA, Inc. also pays Forco a 3% royalty on net sales of $widget_1$ products that are composed of parts and raw materials that were purchased from third party unrelated suppliers rather than Forco.

On September X, 200X, IDR number xx requested that the taxpayer "provide the documentation as required under Section 6662 for the 2005 tax year as it relates to Transfer Pricing." The taxpayer provided a transfer pricing study.

Law and Argument:

Regulation section 1.482-1(a) states that the purpose of section 482 is to ensure that taxpayers clearly reflect income attributable to controlled transactions, and to prevent the avoidance of taxes with respect to such transactions.

Regulation 1.482-(1)(b) provides that the standard to be applied in every case is that of a taxpayer dealing at arm's length with an uncontrolled taxpayer. A controlled transaction meets the arm's length standard if the results of the transaction are consistent with the results that would have been realized if uncontrolled taxpayers had engaged in the same transaction under the same circumstances (arm's length result).

DEPARTMENT OF THE TREASURY - INTERNAL REVENUE

PAGE____

¶20,090

FORM **886-A**	EXPLANATION OF ITEMS	Schedule No. or
NAME OF TAXPAYER **USA, Inc.**		**YEAR/PERIOD ENDED** **03/31/2005-2007**

Regulation 1.482-1(c) indicates that the arm's length result must be reached under the "best method" rule. Two primary factors determine the "best method:" the degree of comparability between controlled taxpayers and uncontrolled comparables and the quality of the data and the assumptions used.

Regulation 1.482-1(d) provides guidance for determining comparability applicable under all of the method available for determining the "best method." For this purpose, the comparability of transactions and circumstances must be evaluated considering all factors that could effect prices or profits in an arm's length dealing. Such factors are:

1. Functions
2. Contractual Terms
3. Risks
4. Economic Conditions
5. Property or Services

The economist (Mr. Economist) took a plant tour of the facility on X date during the time of the previous examination. The international examiner took a plant tour on X date.

A functional analysis was performed along with taking into consideration the contractual terms, economic conditions and property and services. See Economists Report (letter to International Examiner dated X.

Regulation 1.482-1(e) established the arm's length range concept. This concept established clearly that the Service recognized there is not just "one" arm's length price. This concept is applicable to any transfer pricing method.

The best method rule in the Section 482 regulations states that the arm's length results of a controlled transaction must be determined under the method that provides the most reliable measure of an arm's length result. The application of the best method establishes an arm's length range of prices or financial returns with which to test the controlled transactions.

The following is required to be considered in selecting the "best method:"

1. Comparability;
2. Completeness and Accuracy of Data;
3. Reliability of Assumptions;
4. Sensitivity of Results to Deficiencies in Data and Assumptions;
5. Confirmation of Results by Another Method;

DEPARTMENT OF THE TREASURY - INTERNAL REVENUE

¶20,090

FORM **886-A**	EXPLANATION OF ITEMS	Schedule No. or
NAME OF TAXPAYER **USA, Inc.**		**YEAR/PERIOD ENDED** **03/31/2005-2007**

Listed below are the methods used to determine taxable income in connection with a transfer of tangible property:

1. The Comparable Uncontrolled Price Method (CUP)
2. The Resale Price Method
3. The Cost Plus Method
4. The Comparable Profits Method (CPM)
5. Unspecified Method

COMPARABLE UNCONTROLLED PRICE METHOD 1.482-3(b)

Regulation 1.482-3(b) states that the comparable uncontrolled price (CUP) method evaluates whether the amount charged in a controlled transaction is arm's length by reference to the amount charged in a comparable uncontrolled transaction.

The final regulations state that the results derived from applying the CUP method generally will be the most direct and reliable measure of an arm's length price for the controlled transaction under two conditions. The first condition is if an uncontrolled transaction has no difference with the controlled transaction that affects the price. The second condition is that there are only minor differences that have a definite and reasonably ascertainable effect on price and for which appropriate adjustments are made.

The CUP method requires a high degree of comparability of products and functions. Comparability can be achieved by a reasonable number of adjustments that do not materially affect the comparable price. Specific examples of the factors that may be particularly relevant to this method include:

1. Quality of Product;
2. Contractual Terms;
3. Level of Market;
4. Geographic Market;
5. Date of Transaction;
6. Intangible property associated with the sale;
7. Foreign Currency Risks;
8. Alternative realistically available to the buyer and seller;

APPLICABILITY

Forco does not sell to unrelated U.S. customers the same widget components (widget$_2$) that Forco sells to USA, Inc. Forco sells products similar to the widgets sold to USA,

---

DEPARTMENT OF THE TREASURY - INTERNAL REVENUE

PAGE____

¶20,090

FORM **886-A**	EXPLANATION OF ITEMS	Schedule No. or
NAME OF TAXPAYER **USA, Inc.**		**YEAR/PERIOD ENDED** **03/31/2005-2007**

Inc. to third parties in country Y and elsewhere. However, the products are not sufficiently similar to warrant the use of the CUP method.

USA, Inc. makes no uncontrolled purchases of widget components comparable to those it imports from Forco.

USA, Inc. could not identify any third party transactions of the same or similar products under similar circumstances that might meet the comparability standards under the CUP method.

RESALE PRICE METHOD 1.482-3(c)

The resale price method (RPM) is an alternative method for determining arm's length transfer prices. This method compares the gross profit margin (expressed as a percentage of sales) applied to uncontrolled resales of products purchased from related parties to the gross profit margin applied to comparable resales of products purchased from and sold to unrelated independent parties.

Conditions necessary to apply the resale price method are:

1. No comparable uncontrolled price sales exist for the purchases in question since the availability of a CUP would likely qualify as the "best method;"
2. An applicable resale price is available;
3. The controlled distributor has not added more than an insubstantial amount to the value of the property by physically altering the product (functions such as packaging, repackaging, labeling or minor physical assembly of products does not normally constitute physical alteration);
4. The controlled distributor has not added any substantial value by use of intangibles such as trademark or trade name;

The resale price method is most often used for distributors that resell products without physically altering them or adding substantial value to them.

A reasonable number of adjustments may be made to compensate for the lack of comparability between controlled and uncontrolled transactions:

1. Inventory levels and turnover rates and corresponding risks including any price protection programs offered by the manufacturer;
2. Contractual terms;
3. Sales, marketing, advertising programs and services.;
4. The level of the market;

¶20,090

FORM **886-A**	EXPLANATION OF ITEMS	Schedule No. or
NAME OF TAXPAYER **USA, Inc.**		**YEAR/PERIOD ENDED** **03/31/2005-2007**

5. Foreign currency risks.

APPLICABILITY

USA, Inc. does not sell to both related an unrelated parties. The resale price method is not generally applicable to a manufacturer, and is therefore not an appropriate method to apply to USA, Inc. (referring here to widget₁ product line, which is USA, Inc.'s manufacturing product line).

COST PLUS METHOD   1.482-3(d)

The Cost Plus Method evaluates whether the amount charged in a controlled transaction is arm's length by reference to the gross profit markup realized in comparable uncontrolled transactions.

This method requires detailed comparisons of products produced, functions performed, risks borne, manufacturing complexity, cost structures and intangibles between controlled and uncontrolled transactions.

The cost plus method is less likely to be reliable if material differences exist between the controlled and uncontrolled transactions with respect to:

1. Intangibles;
2. Cost Structures;
3. Business Experience;
4. Management Efficiency;
5. Functions performed;
6. Products.

If there are differences in functions performed adjustments may be made for differences between controlled and uncontrolled transactions. Specific examples of factors that may be particularly relevant to this method include:

1. The complexity of manufacturing or assembly;
2. Manufacturing, production and process engineering;
3. Procurement, purchasing and inventory control activities;
4. Testing functions;
5. Selling, general and administrative expenses;
6. Foreign currency risks;
7. Contractual terms.

DEPARTMENT OF THE TREASURY - INTERNAL REVENUE

PAGE____

¶20,090

FORM **886-A**	EXPLANATION OF ITEMS	Schedule No. or
NAME OF TAXPAYER **USA, Inc.**		**YEAR/PERIOD ENDED** **03/31/2005-2007**

APPLICABILITY

See Economist Report (letter to International Examiner dated X).

COMPARABLE PROFITS METHOD   1.482-5

The comparable profits method evaluates whether the amount charged in a controlled transaction is arm's length based on objective measures of profitability (profit level indicators) derived from uncontrolled taxpayers that engage in similar business activities under similar circumstances.

Under the comparable profits method, the determination of an arm's length result is based on the amount of operating profit that the tested party would have earned on related party transactions if its profit level indicator were equal to that of an uncontrolled comparable.

When using the comparable profits method (CPM), the following steps apply:

1. Functional/Risk Analysis of the taxpayer;
2. Determine Tested Party;
3. Identification and Selection of Comparables;
4. Selection of Profit Level Indicator (PLI);
5. Adjust Comparable Data for Differences;
6. Determined Comparable Operating Profits;
7. Determine Arm's Length Range;
8. Compare Test Parties Average Operating Results to Arm's Length Range.

COMPARABLE SEARCH

A search for comparable companies was conducted using a data base of public companies under SIC Code XXXX, "Widget Parts and Accessories" for tax years 2005 through 2007. No companies were identified that would allow application of the cost plus method. Therefore, companies were identified for a CPM (modified cost plus method).

Various editions of Moody's Industrial Manual and Moody's OTC Industrial Manual were consulted to supplement business and financial information. 10K reports were analyzed. Companies were contracted by telephone to assist in determining comparability. The set of companies was reviewed to identify those companies that met the following criteria:

¶20,090

FORM **886-A**	EXPLANATION OF ITEMS	Schedule No. or
NAME OF TAXPAYER USA, Inc.		**YEAR/PERIOD ENDED** 03/31/2005-2007

1. The stock of the company was publicly traded;
2. Sales were mainly to OEM markets (Where there were significant aftermarket sales or where information could not be obtained on the split between OEM and aftermarket sales, the company was eliminated.);
3. The manufacturing operations of the widget parts companies were neither too dissimilar nor too sophisticated in comparison with USA, Inc.'s functions;
4. Activities predominately were related to widget parts manufacturing (Diversified companies were eliminated from consideration, as profit margins from other activities would be different.).

The search originally listed X number of companies under SIC Code XXXX. Approximately X_1 number of companies were eliminated by reading the description of the company. The list was further reduced to X_2 companies. A more thorough analysis was done on the remaining companies. 10K reports were read and analyzed. Phone calls were made to the publicly traded companies to get more information. From the list of remaining companies, X_3 companies were selected to be used as comparables. They are:

[X3 Companies]

SEE SCHEDULE 2 for the companies not selected and the reasons.

To summarize, the companies listed above were considered comparable to USA, Inc. by the IRS for use in applying the modified Cost Plus Method. Descriptions of these companies are included in the IRS' group of comparables and can be found in Schedule 3.

COMPARABLE PROFITS METHOD

Financial data for the group of comparable companies appear in Schedule B (Attached to Economist's Report). Under the comparable profits method, the gross markup is computed by dividing gross profit by sales. The markup is adjusted for financing differences between USA, Inc. and the comparable group regarding levels of accounts receivable an accounts payable, based on the presumption that such differences affect profitability. To the extent that a particular company holds a greater (or lesser) balance of receivable than USA, Inc. it likely will have a comparative advantage (or disadvantage) in terms of the sales amounts received. Likewise, to the extent that a company incurs a higher (or lower) balance of accounts payable than USA, Inc. it will be paying more (or less) due to this built-in financing for materials and parts used in the manufacturing process. Thus, a company's cost of goods sold should be decreased (or increased) to reflect this difference.

DEPARTMENT OF THE TREASURY - INTERNAL REVENUE

PAGE____

¶20,090

FORM 886-A	EXPLANATION OF ITEMS	Schedule No. or
NAME OF TAXPAYER **USA, Inc.**		**YEAR/PERIOD ENDED** **03/31/2005-2007**

CHANGE IN ACCOUNTS RECEIVABLE

[(USA, Inc.'s A/R/USA, Inc.'s Sales) X Comparable Sales] – Comparables A/R = Comparables Change in A/R.

CHANGE IN ACCOUNTS PAYABLE

[(USA, Inc.'s A/P/USA, Inc.'s Sales) X Comparables Sales] – Comparables A/P = Comparables Change in A/P.

ADJUSTMENTS

Comparables Adjusted Sales = Comparables Sales + (Comparables Change in A/R X [int. rate/(1 + int. rate)]).

Comparables Adjusted COGS = Comparables COGS + (Comparables Change in A/P X [int. rate/(1 + int. rate)]).

These adjustments are in the Economist's Report resulting in the Adjusted Sales, Adjusted COGS and Adjusted Operating Profit. Since selling and purchasing terms are unknown for the comparable companies, the prime rate of interest has been applied to the average balances divided by sales to get the adjusted amounts of sales and cost of goods sold.

Schedule 1 shows how the adjustment was calculated. The Profit and Loss Statement was provided by the taxpayer in response to IDRs X & X_1. The taxpayer provided a revised copy in a letter dated X. Schedule 1 shows a breakdown of the $widget_1$ product line only. The adjustment made to Inventory was explained in the Economist's Report for the obsolete inventory. The original Operating Profit Margin ("OPM") was calculated based upon Sales. As explained in the Economist's Report, the OPM, which is the mathematical equivalent of the return on total costs, is being used to eliminate problems in properly computing the proposed allocation. All 3 years showed a negative OPM for the $widget_1$ product line. Schedule 2 shows the OPMs of the comparable companies that were used in the study.

Calculation of 482 Income Adjustment

The adjustment was calculated as follow. The Lower Quartile of the Comparables was used. The average OPM (as adjusted) was used for tax years ending March 31, 2005, 2006 and 2007. The average OPM was multiplied against sales to provide a corrected

¶20,090

FORM **886-A**	EXPLANATION OF ITEMS	Schedule No. or
NAME OF TAXPAYER **USA, Inc.**		**YEAR/PERIOD ENDED** **03/31/2005-2007**

OPM. This amount was then multiplied by the percentage of related party purchases from Forco. The result gives a corrected OPM. The corrected OPM is then netted against the reported losses for the widget$_1$ product line.

The adjusted average OPM of the comparables in the lower quartile was 6.25% in 2007, 5.99% in 2006 and 3.20% in 2005. These margins are contrasted with USA, Inc.'s operating margins of (2.22%) in 2007, (1.25%) in 2006 and (3.41%) in 2005.

In all 3 years under examination, USA, Inc.'s widget$_1$ product line operating profit is noticeably below the entire range of the adjusted comparables. Therefore, we conclude that the Taxpayer's intercompany pricing is inconsistent with the arm's length standard of Section 482. Applying the average operating profit level of the comparables to USA, Inc.'s widget$_1$ product line results in the following adjustments to income:

2007 - $7,000,000
2006 - $5,000,000
2005 - $4,000,000.

DEPARTMENT OF THE TREASURY - INTERNAL REVENUE

PAGE____

¶ 20,100 IRS Form 2848

Form 2848 is used to authorize an individual to represent a person before the IRS.

Form 2848

Form **2848** (Rev. June 2008) Department of the Treasury Internal Revenue Service	**Power of Attorney** **and Declaration of Representative** ▶ Type or print. ▶ See the separate instructions.	OMB No. 1545-0150 **For IRS Use Only** Received by: Name _____ Telephone _____ Function _____ Date / /

Part I   Power of Attorney

Caution: *Form 2848 will not be honored for any purpose other than representation before the IRS.*

1   Taxpayer information. Taxpayer(s) must sign and date this form on page 2, line 9.

Taxpayer name(s) and address	Social security number(s)	Employer identification number
	Daytime telephone number ( )	Plan number (if applicable)

hereby appoint(s) the following representative(s) as attorney(s)-in-fact:

2   Representative(s) must sign and date this form on page 2, Part II.

Name and address	CAF No. ------------------------------ Telephone No. -------------------------- Fax No. ----------------------------- Check if new: Address ☐ Telephone No. ☐ Fax No. ☐
Name and address	CAF No. ------------------------------ Telephone No. -------------------------- Fax No. ----------------------------- Check if new: Address ☐ Telephone No. ☐ Fax No. ☐
Name and address	CAF No. ------------------------------ Telephone No. -------------------------- Fax No. ----------------------------- Check if new: Address ☐ Telephone No. ☐ Fax No. ☐

to represent the taxpayer(s) before the Internal Revenue Service for the following tax matters:

3   Tax matters

Type of Tax (Income, Employment, Excise, etc.) or Civil Penalty (see the instructions for line 3)	Tax Form Number (1040, 941, 720, etc.)	Year(s) or Period(s) (see the instructions for line 3)

4   Specific use not recorded on Centralized Authorization File (CAF). If the power of attorney is for a specific use not recorded on CAF, check this box. See the instructions for **Line 4. Specific Uses Not Recorded on CAF** . . . . ▶ ☐

5   Acts authorized. The representatives are authorized to receive and inspect confidential tax information and to perform any and all acts that I (we) can perform with respect to the tax matters described on line 3, for example, the authority to sign any agreements, consents, or other documents. The authority does not include the power to receive refund checks (see line 6 below), the power to substitute another representative or add additional representatives, the power to sign certain returns, or the power to execute a request for disclosure of tax returns or return information to a third party. See the line 5 instructions for more information.

Exceptions. An unenrolled return preparer cannot sign any document for a taxpayer and may only represent taxpayers in limited situations. See **Unenrolled Return Preparer** on page 1 of the instructions. An enrolled actuary may only represent taxpayers to the extent provided in section 10.3(d) of Treasury Department Circular No. 230 (Circular 230). An enrolled retirement plan administrator may only represent taxpayers to the extent provided in section 10.3(e) of Circular 230. See the line 5 instructions for restrictions on tax matters partners. In most cases, the student practitioner's (levels k and l) authority is limited (for example, they may only practice under the supervision of another practitioner).

List any specific additions or deletions to the acts otherwise authorized in this power of attorney: ---------------------------------
----

----

6   Receipt of refund checks. If you want to authorize a representative named on line 2 to receive, **BUT NOT TO ENDORSE OR CASH**, refund checks, initial here _____ and list the name of that representative below.

Name of representative to receive refund check(s) ▶

For Privacy Act and Paperwork Reduction Act Notice, see page 4 of the instructions.   Cat. No. 11980J   Form **2848** (Rev. 6-2008)

¶20,100

Form 2848 (Rev. 6-2008) Page **2**

7 **Notices and communications.** Original notices and other written communications will be sent to you and a copy to the first representative listed on line 2.

a If you also want the second representative listed to receive a copy of notices and communications, check this box . . . . . ▶ ☐

b If you do not want any notices or communications sent to your representative(s), check this box . . . . ▶ ☐

8 **Retention/revocation of prior power(s) of attorney.** The filing of this power of attorney automatically revokes all earlier power(s) of attorney on file with the Internal Revenue Service for the same tax matters and years or periods covered by this document. If you do not want to revoke a prior power of attorney, check here. . . . . ▶ ☐
YOU MUST ATTACH A COPY OF ANY POWER OF ATTORNEY YOU WANT TO REMAIN IN EFFECT.

9 **Signature of taxpayer(s).** If a tax matter concerns a joint return, **both** husband and wife must sign if joint representation is requested, otherwise, see the instructions. If signed by a corporate officer, partner, guardian, tax matters partner, executor, receiver, administrator, or trustee on behalf of the taxpayer, I certify that I have the authority to execute this form on behalf of the taxpayer.

▶ **IF NOT SIGNED AND DATED, THIS POWER OF ATTORNEY WILL BE RETURNED.**

Signature	Date	Title (if applicable)

☐☐☐☐☐

Print Name	PIN Number	Print name of taxpayer from line 1 if other than individual

Signature	Date	Title (if applicable)

☐☐☐☐☐

Print Name	PIN Number

Part II **Declaration of Representative**

Caution: *Students with a special order to represent taxpayers in qualified Low Income Taxpayer Clinics or the Student Tax Clinic Program (levels k and l), see the instructions for Part II.*
Under penalties of perjury, I declare that:

• I am not currently under suspension or disbarment from practice before the Internal Revenue Service;

• I am aware of regulations contained in Circular 230 (31 CFR, Part 10), as amended, concerning the practice of attorneys, certified public accountants, enrolled agents, enrolled actuaries, and others;

• I am authorized to represent the taxpayer(s) identified in Part I for the tax matter(s) specified there; and

• I am one of the following:

a Attorney—a member in good standing of the bar of the highest court of the jurisdiction shown below.

b Certified Public Accountant—duly qualified to practice as a certified public accountant in the jurisdiction shown below.

c Enrolled Agent—enrolled as an agent under the requirements of Circular 230.

d Officer—a bona fide officer of the taxpayer's organization.

e Full-Time Employee—a full-time employee of the taxpayer.

f Family Member—a member of the taxpayer's immediate family (for example, spouse, parent, child, brother, or sister).

g Enrolled Actuary—enrolled as an actuary by the Joint Board for the Enrollment of Actuaries under 29 U.S.C. 1242 (the authority to practice before the Internal Revenue Service is limited by section 10.3(d) of Circular 230).

h Unenrolled Return Preparer—the authority to practice before the Internal Revenue Service is limited by Circular 230, section 10.7(c)(1)(viii). You must have prepared the return in question and the return must be under examination by the IRS. See **Unenrolled Return Preparer** on page 1 of the instructions.

k Student Attorney—student who receives permission to practice before the IRS by virtue of their status as a law student under section 10.7(d) of Circular 230.

l Student CPA—student who receives permission to practice before the IRS by virtue of their status as a CPA student under section 10.7(d) of Circular 230.

r Enrolled Retirement Plan Agent—enrolled as a retirement plan agent under the requirements of Circular 230 (the authority to practice before the Internal Revenue Service is limited by section 10.3(e)).

▶ **IF THIS DECLARATION OF REPRESENTATIVE IS NOT SIGNED AND DATED, THE POWER OF ATTORNEY WILL BE RETURNED.** See the Part II instructions.

Designation—Insert above letter **(a–r)**	Jurisdiction (state) or identification	Signature	Date

Form **2848** (Rev. 6-2008)

¶20,100

¶ 20,110 Revenue Procedure 2006-54[1]

Competent Authority Assistance Requests

SECTION 1. PURPOSE AND BACKGROUND

.01 *Purpose.* This revenue procedure explains the procedures by which taxpayers may obtain assistance from the U.S. competent authority under the provisions of a tax treaty to which the United States is a party. This revenue procedure updates and supersedes Rev. Proc. 2002-52, 2002-2 C.B. 242.

.02 *Background.* The U.S. competent authority assists taxpayers with respect to matters covered in the mutual agreement procedure provisions of tax treaties. A tax treaty generally permits taxpayers to request competent authority assistance when they consider that the actions of the United States, the treaty country, or both, result or will result in taxation that is contrary to the provisions of the treaty. For example, tax treaties generally permit taxpayers to request assistance in order to relieve economic double taxation arising from an allocation under section 482 of the Internal Revenue Code (the "Code") or an equivalent provision under the laws of a treaty country. Competent authority assistance may also be available with respect to issues specifically dealt with in other provisions of a treaty. For example, many tax treaties contain provisions permitting competent authorities to resolve issues of fiscal residence or allowing a competent authority to make a discretionary determination that a taxpayer is entitled to the benefits of a treaty under specific limitation on benefits provisions. *See* sections 3.07 and 3.08 of this revenue procedure. The Deputy Commissioner (International), Large and Mid-Size Business Division, acts as the U.S. competent authority in administering the operating provisions of tax treaties, including reaching mutual agreements in specific cases, and in interpreting and applying tax treaties. In interpreting and applying tax treaties, the Deputy Commissioner (International), Large and Mid-Size Business Division, acts only with the concurrence of the Associate Chief Counsel (International). *See* Delegation Order 4-12 (formerly DO-114, Rev. 13), Internal Revenue Manual ("IRM"), Part 1 Organization, Finance and Management, Chapter 2 Servicewide Policies and Authorities, Section 43 Delegation of Authorities for the Examining Process (IRM 1.2.43), http://www.irs.gov/irm/part1/ch02s10.html#d0e33677.

.03 *Changes.* Although most of the changes made by this revenue procedure to Rev. Proc. 2002-52 are minor edits for organization, accuracy, readability, or updating of citations to cross-referenced guidance, substantive changes have also been made and may be summarized as follows:

(1) Sections 3.04, 3.08 and 7.06 have been revised to clarify standards for acceptance of requests for competent authority assistance.

(2) Sections 3.08, 4.04 and 5.03 have been revised to clarify signature requirements for requests for determinations regarding limitation on treaty benefits.

---

[1] Rev. Proc. 2006-54, IRB 2006-49, 1035, November 17, 2006.

(3) Section 4.04 has been revised to provide for filing copies of submissions on electronic media.

(4) Sections 4.05 and 5.03 have been revised to provide additional detail regarding Information to be submitted with requests for competent authority assistance.

(5) Sections 7.02 and 7.05 have been revised to clarify current practices regarding coordination with IRS Appeals.

(6) Section 7.06 has been revised to clarify the coordination of the accelerated competent authority procedure with requests for Advance Pricing Agreements.

(7) Section 8.04 has been revised to clarify current practices regarding the processing of requests for the Simultaneous Appeal procedure.

(8) Section 9.03(3) has been revised to reduce the frequency with which taxpayers filing protective claims are required to notify the U.S. competent authority as to their intent to file a request for assistance.

(9) Section 10 has been revised to clarify the role of the U.S. competent authority in considering requests regarding conforming a taxpayer's accounts and allowing repatriation of certain amounts following an allocation of income between related U.S. and foreign corporations under section 482 of the Code.

(10) Section 12.02(8) has been revised to provide for denial of competent authority assistance where the underlying transaction is listed for purposes of the applicable Treasury regulations as a tax avoidance transaction.

(11) Section 14 has been revised to implement user fees for requests for determinations regarding limitation on treaty benefits.

SECTION 2. SCOPE

.01 *In General.* This revenue procedure addresses procedures for obtaining assistance from the U.S. competent authority under the provisions of an income, estate or gift tax treaty entered into between the United States and another country. The U.S. competent authority assists taxpayers with respect to matters covered in tax treaties in the manner specified in the mutual agreement procedure provisions or other provisions of the relevant tax treaty. Taxpayers are urged to examine the specific provisions of the treaty under which they seek relief, in order to determine whether relief may be available in their particular case. If, after examining the applicable treaty, a taxpayer is unsure whether relief is available, the taxpayer should contact competent authority. This revenue procedure is not intended to limit any specific treaty provisions relating to competent authority matters.

.02 *Requests for Assistance.* In general, requests by taxpayers for competent authority assistance must be submitted in accordance with this revenue procedure. However, where a treaty or other published administrative guidance provides specific procedures for requests for competent authority assistance, those procedures will apply, and the provisions of this revenue procedure will not apply to the extent inconsistent with such procedures. Taxpayers may consult the "Tax Information for International Businesses" and "Competent Authority Agreements" pages at www.irs.gov for links to a variety of agreements and other documents that may modify the procedures set forth in this revenue procedure.

.03 *General Process.* If a taxpayer's request for competent authority assistance is accepted, the U.S. competent authority generally will consult with the appropriate foreign competent authority and attempt to reach a mutual agreement that is acceptable to all parties. The U.S. competent authority also may initiate competent authority negotiations in any situation deemed necessary to protect U.S. interests. Such a situation may arise, for example, when a taxpayer fails to request competent authority assistance after agreeing to a U.S. or foreign tax assessment that is contrary to the provisions of an applicable tax treaty or for which correlative relief may be available.

.04 *Failure to Request Assistance.* Failure to request competent authority assistance or to take appropriate steps as necessary to maintain the availability of the remedy may cause a denial of part or all of any foreign tax credits claimed. *See Treas. Reg. § 1.901-2(e)(5)(i).* S *ee also* section 9 of this revenue procedure concerning protective measures and section 11 of this revenue procedure concerning the determination of creditable foreign taxes.

SECTION 3. GENERAL CONDITIONS UNDER WHICH THIS PROCEDURE APPLIES

.01 *General.* The exclusions, exemptions, deductions, credits, reductions in rate, and other benefits and safeguards provided by treaties are subject to conditions and restrictions that may vary in different treaties. Taxpayers should examine carefully the specific treaty provisions applicable in their cases to determine the nature and extent of treaty benefits or safeguards they are entitled to and the conditions under which such benefits or safeguards are available. *See* section 9 of this revenue procedure, which prescribes protective measures to be taken by the taxpayer and any concerned related person with respect to U.S. and foreign tax authorities. *See also* section 12.02 of this revenue procedure for circumstances in which competent authority assistance may be denied.

.02 *Requirements of a Treaty.* There is no authority for the U.S. competent authority to provide relief from U.S. tax or to provide other assistance due to taxation arising under the tax laws of a foreign country or the United States, unless such authority is granted by a treaty. *See also* Rev. Proc. 2006-23, 2006-20 I.R.B. 900, for procedures for requesting the assistance of the IRS when a taxpayer is or may be subject to inconsistent tax treatment by the IRS and a U.S. possession tax agency.

.03 *Applicable Standards in Allocation Cases.* With respect to requests for competent authority assistance involving the allocation of income and deductions between a U.S. taxpayer and a related person, the U.S. competent authority and its counterpart in the treaty country will be bound by the arm's length standard provided by the applicable provisions of the relevant treaty. The U.S. competent authority will also be guided by the arm's length standard consistent with the regulations under section 482 of the Code and the Transfer Pricing Guidelines for Multinational Enterprises and Tax Administrations as published from time to time by the Organisation for Economic Co-operation and Development. When negotiating mutual agreements on the allocation of income and deductions, the U.S. competent authority will take into account all of the facts and circumstances of the particular case and the purpose of the treaty, which is to avoid double taxation.

.04 Who Can File Requests for Assistance. The U.S. competent authority will consider requests for assistance from U.S. persons, as defined in section 7701(a)(30) of the Code, and from non-U.S. persons as permitted under an applicable tax treaty. As noted in section 12.02 of this revenue procedure, there are circumstances in which the U.S. competent authority will not pursue assistance. For purposes of this revenue procedure, except where the context otherwise requires, the term "taxpayer" refers to the person requesting competent authority assistance.

.05 Closed Cases. A case previously closed after examination will not be reopened in order to make an adjustment unfavorable to the taxpayer except in the presence of an exceptional circumstance described in Rev. Proc. 2005-32, 2005-23 I.R.B. 1206 (providing procedures for reopening cases if fraud, substantial error, or certain other circumstances are present). The U.S. competent authority may, but is not required to, accept a taxpayer's request for competent authority consideration that will require the reopening of a case closed after examination.

.06 Foreign Initiated Competent Authority Request. When a foreign competent authority refers a request from a foreign person to the U.S. competent authority for consultation under the mutual agreement procedure, the U.S. competent authority generally will require the U.S. related person (in the case of an allocation of income or deductions between related persons) or may require the foreign person (in other cases) to file a request for competent authority assistance under this revenue procedure.

.07 Requests Relating to Residence Issues. U.S. competent authority assistance may be available to taxpayers seeking to clarify their residency status in the United States. Examples include cases in which taxpayers believe that they are erroneously treated as non-U.S. residents by treaty countries or cases where taxpayers are treated as dual residents despite the objective tie-breaker provisions contained in the applicable treaties. Generally, competent authority assistance is limited to situations where resolution of a residency issue is necessary in order to avoid double taxation or to determine the applicability of a benefit under the treaty. Further, a request for assistance regarding a residency issue will be accepted only if it is established that the issue requires consultation with the foreign competent authority in order to ensure consistent treatment by the United States and the applicable treaty country. The U.S. competent authority does not issue unilateral determinations with respect to whether an individual is a resident of the United States or of a treaty country.

.08 Determinations Regarding Limitation on Benefits. Many treaties contain a limitation on benefits article that enumerates prescribed requirements that must be met to be eligible for benefits under the treaty. The U.S. competent authority will not issue determinations regarding a taxpayer's status under one of the prescribed requirements in a limitation on benefits provision. However, certain treaties provide that the competent authority may, as a matter of discretion, determine the availability of treaty benefits where the prescribed requirements are not met. Requests for

assistance in such cases should comply with this revenue procedure and any other specific procedures that may be issued from time to time. A request may be with respect to an initial discretionary determination, a renewal or a redetermination. The request should take the form of a letter as described in section 4.04 of this revenue procedure, except that if the requester does not file federal tax returns and cannot identify a person authorized to sign such returns, the letter may be dated and signed by any authorized representative or officer of the requester. Taxpayers who are requesting a discretionary determination under a limitation on benefits provision should include the user fee as described in Section 14 of this revenue procedure as well as the information described in Exhibit 4.60.3-3 of the Internal Revenue Manual ("IRM"), Part 4 Examining Process, Chapter 60 International Procedure, Section 3 Tax Treaty Related Matters (IRM 4.60.3), http://www.irs.gov/irm/part4/ch45s03.html.

SECTION 4. PROCEDURES FOR REQUESTING COMPETENT AUTHORITY ASSISTANCE

.01 *Time for Filing.* A request for competent authority assistance generally may be filed at any time after an action results in taxation not in accordance with the provisions of the applicable treaty. In a case involving a U.S. initiated adjustment of tax or income resulting from a tax examination, a request for competent authority assistance may be submitted as soon as practicable after the amount of the proposed adjustment is communicated in writing to the taxpayer (*e.g.,* a Notice of Proposed Adjustment). Where a U.S. initiated adjustment has not yet been communicated in writing to the taxpayer, the U.S. competent authority generally will deny the request as premature. In the case of a foreign examination, a request may be submitted as soon as the taxpayer believes such filing is warranted based on the actions of the country proposing the adjustment. In a case involving the re-allocation of income or deductions between related persons, the request should not be filed until such time that the taxpayer can establish that there is a probability of double taxation. In cases not involving an examination, a request can be made when the taxpayer believes that an action or potential action warrants the assistance of the U.S. competent authority. Examples of such action include: (a) a ruling or promulgation by a foreign tax authority concerning a taxation matter; and (b) the withholding of tax by a withholding agent. Except where otherwise provided in an applicable treaty, taxpayers have discretion over the time for filing a request; however, delays in filing may preclude effective relief. *See* section 9 of this revenue procedure, which explains protective measures to be taken by the taxpayer and any concerned related person with respect to U.S. and foreign tax authorities. *See also* section 7.06 of this revenue procedure for rules relating to accelerated issue resolution and competent authority assistance.

.02 *Place of Filing.* The taxpayer must send all written requests for, or any inquiries regarding, U.S. competent authority assistance to the Deputy Commissioner (International), Large and Mid-Size Business Division, Attn: Office of Tax Treaty, Internal Revenue Service, 1111 Constitution Avenue, NW, Routing: MA3-322A, Washington, D.C. 20224.

¶20,110

.03 *Additional Filing.* In the case of U.S. initiated adjustments, the taxpayer also must file a copy of the request with the office of the IRS where the taxpayer's case is pending. If the request is filed after the matter has been designated for litigation or while a suit contesting the relevant tax liability of the taxpayer is pending in a United States court, a copy of the request also must be filed with the Office of Associate Chief Counsel (International), Internal Revenue Service, 1111 Constitution Avenue N.W., Washington, D.C. 20224, with a separate statement attached identifying the court where the suit is pending and the docket number of the action.

.04 *Form of Request.* A request for U.S. competent authority assistance must be in the form of a letter addressed to the Deputy Commissioner (International), Large and Mid-Size Business Division. It must be dated and signed by a person having the authority to sign the taxpayer's federal tax returns. The request must contain a statement that competent authority assistance is being requested and must include the information described in section 4.05 of this revenue procedure. In addition to the original signed submission, a copy of the text of the request and any materials contemporaneously prepared in support of the request must also be submitted, in Adobe PDF or Microsoft Word format, in the form of a CD, DVD, or 3.5-inch diskette. *See* section 5 of this revenue procedure for requests involving small cases.

.05 *Information Required.* The following information must be included in the request for competent authority assistance:

(1) a reference to the specific treaty and the provisions therein pursuant to which the request is made;

(2) the names, addresses, U.S. taxpayer identification number and foreign taxpayer identification number (if any) of the taxpayer and, if applicable, all related persons involved in the matter;

(3) a brief description of the issues for which competent authority assistance is requested, including a description of the relevant transactions, activities or other circumstances involved in the issues raised and the basis for the adjustment, if any;

(4) if applicable, a description of the control and business relationships between the taxpayer and any relevant related person for the years in issue, including any changes in such relationship to the date of filing the request;

(5) the years and amounts involved with respect to the issues in both U.S. dollars and foreign currency;

(6) the IRS office that has made or is proposing to make the adjustment or, if known, the IRS office with examination jurisdiction over the taxpayer;

(7) an explanation of the nature of the relief sought or the action requested in the United States or in the treaty country with respect to the issues raised, including a statement as to whether the taxpayer wishes to apply for treatment similar to that provided under Rev. Proc. 99-32, 1999-2 C.B. 296 (referred to in this revenue procedure as "Rev. Proc. 99-32 treatment" and explained in further detail in section 10 of this revenue procedure);

(8) a statement whether the period of limitations for the years for which relief is sought has expired in the United States or in the treaty country;

(9) a statement of relevant domestic and foreign judicial or administrative proceedings that involve the taxpayer and related persons, including all information related to notification of the treaty country;

(10) to the extent known by the taxpayer, a statement of relevant foreign judicial or public administrative proceedings that do not involve the taxpayer or related persons but involve the same issue for which competent authority assistance is requested;

(11) a statement whether the request for competent authority assistance involves issues that are currently, or were previously, considered part of an Advance Pricing Agreement ("APA") proceeding or other proceeding relevant to the issue under consideration in the United States or part of a similar proceeding in the foreign country;

(12) if applicable, powers of attorney with respect to the taxpayer, and the request should identify the individual to serve as the taxpayer's initial point of contact for the competent authority;

(13) if the jurisdiction of an issue is with an IRS Appeals office, a summary of prior discussions of the issue with that office and contact information regarding the IRS Appeals officer handling the issue; also, if appropriate, a statement whether the taxpayer is requesting the Simultaneous Appeals procedure as provided in section 8 of this revenue procedure;

(14) in a separate section, the statement and information required by section 9.02 of this revenue procedure if the request is to serve as a protective claim;

(15) on a separate document, a statement that the taxpayer consents to the disclosure to the competent authority of the treaty country (with the name of the treaty country specifically stated) and that competent authority's staff, of any or all of the items of information set forth or enclosed in the request for U.S. competent authority assistance within the limits contained in the tax treaty under which the taxpayer is seeking relief. The taxpayer may request, as part of this statement, that its trade secrets not be disclosed to a foreign competent authority. This statement must be dated and signed by a person having authority to sign the taxpayer's federal tax returns and is required to facilitate the administrative handling of the request by the U.S. competent authority for purposes of the recordkeeping requirements of section 6103(p) of the Code. Failure to provide such a statement will not prevent the U.S. competent authority from disclosing information under the terms of a treaty. *See* section 6103(k)(4) of the Code. Taxpayers are encouraged to provide duplicates to the U.S. and foreign competent authorities of all information otherwise disclosable under the treaty;

(16) a penalties of perjury statement in the following form:

> Under penalties of perjury, I declare that I have examined this request, including accompanying documents, and, to the best of my knowledge and belief, the facts presented in support of the request for competent authority assistance are true, correct and complete.

The declaration must be dated and signed by the person or persons on whose behalf the request is being made and not by the taxpayer's representative. The

¶20,110

person signing for a corporate taxpayer must be an authorized officer of the taxpayer who has personal knowledge of the facts. The person signing for a trust, an estate or a partnership must be respectively, a trustee, an executor or a partner who has personal knowledge of the facts; and

(17) any other information required or requested under this revenue procedure, as applicable. *See, e.g.,* section 7.06 of this revenue procedure, which requires the provision of certain information in the case of a request for the accelerated competent authority procedure, and section 10 of this revenue procedure, which requires the provision of certain information in the case of a request for Rev. Proc. 99-32 treatment. Requests for supplemental information may include items such as detailed financial information, comparability analysis, or other material relevant to a transfer pricing analysis.

.06 *Other Dispute Resolution Programs.* Requests for competent authority assistance that involve an APA or Pre-Filing Agreement request must include the information required under Rev. Proc. 2006-9, 2006-2 I.R.B. 278 (concerning APAs), and Rev. Proc. 2005-12, 2005-2 I.R.B. 311 (concerning Pre-Filing Agreements).

.07 *Other Documentation.* In addition, on request, the taxpayer must submit any other information or documentation deemed necessary by the U.S. or foreign competent authority for purposes of reaching an agreement. This includes English translations of any documentation required in connection with the competent authority request.

.08 *Updates.* The taxpayer must keep the U.S. competent authority informed of all material changes in the information or documentation previously submitted as part of, or in connection with, the request for competent authority assistance. The taxpayer also must provide any updated information or new documentation that becomes known or is created after the request is filed and which is relevant to the resolution of the issues under consideration.

.09 *Conferences.* To the extent possible, the U.S. competent authority will consult with the taxpayer regarding the status and progress of the mutual agreement proceedings. The taxpayer may request a pre-filing conference with the U.S. competent authority to discuss the mutual agreement process with respect to matters covered under a treaty, including discussion of the proper time for filing, the practical aspects of obtaining relief and actions necessary to facilitate the proceedings. Similarly, after a matter is resolved by the competent authorities, a taxpayer may also request a conference with the U.S. competent authority to discuss the resolution.

SECTION 5. SMALL CASE PROCEDURE FOR REQUESTING COMPETENT AUTHORITY ASSISTANCE

.01 *General.* To facilitate requests for assistance involving small cases, this section provides a special procedure simplifying the form of a request for assistance and, in particular, the amount of information that initially must be submitted. All other requirements of this revenue procedure continue to apply to requests for assistance made pursuant to this section.

.02 *Small Case Standards.* A taxpayer may file an abbreviated request for competent authority assistance in accordance with this section if the total proposed adjustment involved in the matter is not greater than the following:

Taxpayer	Proposed Adjustment
Individual	$200,000
Corporation/Partnership	$1,000,000
Other	$200,000

.03 *Small Case Filing Procedure.* The abbreviated request for competent authority assistance under the small case procedure must be dated and signed by a person having the authority to sign the taxpayer's federal tax returns. Although other information and documentation may be requested at a later date, the initial request for assistance should include the following information and materials:

(1) a statement indicating that this is a matter subject to the small case procedure;

(2) the name, address, U.S. taxpayer identification number and foreign taxpayer identification number (if any) of the taxpayer and, if applicable, all related persons involved in the matter;

(3) a description of the issue and the nature of the relief sought;

(4) the taxable years and amounts involved with respect to the issues in both U.S. and foreign currency;

(5) the name of the treaty country;

(6) if applicable, powers of attorney with respect to the taxpayer;

(7) on a separate document, a statement that the taxpayer consents to the disclosure to the competent authority of the treaty country (with the name of the treaty country specifically stated) and that competent authority's staff, of any or all of the items of information set forth or enclosed in the request for U.S. competent authority assistance within the limits contained in the tax treaty under which the taxpayer is seeking relief. The taxpayer may request, as part of this statement, that its trade secrets not be disclosed to a foreign competent authority. This statement must be dated and signed by a person having authority to sign the taxpayer's federal tax returns and is required to facilitate the administrative handling of the request by the U.S. competent authority for purposes of the recordkeeping requirements of section 6103(p) of the Code. Failure to provide such a statement will not prevent the U.S. competent authority from disclosing information under the terms of a treaty. *See* section 6103(k)(4) of the Code; and

(8) a penalties of perjury statement in the following form:

> Under penalties of perjury, I declare that I have examined this request, including accompanying documents, and, to the best of my knowledge and belief, the facts presented in support of the request for competent authority assistance are true, correct and complete.

¶20,110

The declaration must be dated and signed by the person or persons on whose behalf the request is being made and not by the taxpayer's representative. The person signing for a corporate taxpayer must be an authorized officer of the taxpayer who has personal knowledge of the facts. The person signing for a trust, an estate or a partnership must be respectively, a trustee, an executor or a partner who has personal knowledge of the facts.

SECTION 6. RELIEF REQUESTED FOR FOREIGN INITIATED ADJUSTMENT WITHOUT COMPETENT AUTHORITY INVOLVEMENT

Taxpayers seeking correlative relief with respect to a foreign initiated adjustment involving a treaty matter should present their request to the U.S. competent authority. However, when the adjustment involves years under the jurisdiction of the Industry or Area Director or IRS Appeals, taxpayers sometimes try to obtain relief from these offices. This may occur, for example, if the adjustment involves a re-allocation of income or deductions involving a related person in a country with which the United States has an income tax treaty. In these cases, taxpayers will be advised to contact the U.S. competent authority office. In appropriate cases, the U.S. competent authority will advise the Industry or Area Director or IRS Appeals office on appropriate action. The U.S. competent authority may request the taxpayer to provide the information described under sections 4.05 and 4.07 of this revenue procedure. Failure to request competent authority assistance may result in denial of correlative relief with respect to the issue, including applicable foreign tax credits.

SECTION 7. COORDINATION WITH OTHER ADMINISTRATIVE OR JUDICIAL PROCEEDINGS

.01 *Suspension of Administrative Action with Respect to U.S. Adjustments.* When a request for competent authority assistance is accepted with respect to a U.S. initiated adjustment, the IRS will postpone further administrative action with respect to the issues under competent authority consideration (such as assessment or collection procedures), except: (a) in situations in which the IRS may be requested otherwise by the U.S. competent authority; or (b) in situations involving cases pending in court and in other instances in which action must be taken to avoid prejudicing the U.S. Government's interest. The normal administrative procedures continue to apply, however, to all other issues not under U.S. competent authority consideration. For example, if there are other issues raised during the examination and the taxpayer is not in agreement with these issues, the usual procedures for completing the examination with respect to these issues apply. If the taxpayer is issued a Notice of Proposed Adjustment with respect to these issues and prepares a protest of the unagreed issues, the taxpayer need not include any unagreed issue under consideration by the competent authority. Following the receipt of a taxpayer's protest, normal IRS Appeals procedures will be initiated with respect to those issues not subject to competent authority consideration.

.02 *Coordination with IRS Appeals.* Taxpayers who disagree with a proposed U.S. adjustment have the option of pursuing their right of administrative review with IRS Appeals before requesting competent authority assistance; making a request pursuant to the Simultaneous Appeals procedure in section 8 of this revenue procedure;

or requesting competent authority assistance immediately for bilateral consideration. Taxpayers requesting unilateral withdrawal of a U.S. adjustment without
consultation with the treaty country must direct such a request to IRS Appeals
rather than to the U.S. competent authority. Taxpayers who are pursuing their
rights with IRS Appeals may contact the U.S. competent authority if they believe
they have a potential competent authority issue. If a taxpayer does not go through
the Simultaneous Appeals procedure and instead enters into settlement discussions
with IRS Appeals before making a competent authority request, the U.S. competent
authority may rely upon, but will not necessarily be bound by, such previous
consideration by IRS Appeals when considering the case (*see also* section 7.05 of
this revenue procedure regarding settlements with IRS Appeals and section 8.05 of
this revenue procedure regarding the role of IRS Appeals in the Simultaneous
Appeals procedure). If a taxpayer enters into the Appeals arbitration program (*see*
Rev. Proc. 2006-44, 2006-44 I.R.B. 800), the taxpayer generally may not request
competent authority assistance until the arbitration process is completed. However,
if the taxpayer demonstrates that a request for competent authority assistance is
necessary to keep open a statute of limitations in the treaty country, then competent authority assistance may be requested while arbitration is pending, and the
U.S. competent authority will suspend action on the case until arbitration is
completed. If a taxpayer makes a competent authority request, the taxpayer is
deemed to consent to communications between the U.S. competent authority and
IRS Appeals regarding the matter. *See* Rev. Proc. 2000-43, 2000-2 C.B. 404.

.03 *Coordination with Litigation.* The U.S. competent authority will not, without the
consent of the Associate Chief Counsel (International), accept (or continue to
consider) a taxpayer's request for assistance if the request involves a taxable period
pending in a United States court or involves a matter pending in a United States
court or designated for litigation for any taxable period. If the case is pending in the
United States Tax Court, the taxpayer may, in appropriate cases, be asked to join
the IRS in a motion to sever issues or delay trial pending completion of the
competent authority proceedings. If the case is pending in any other court, the
Associate Chief Counsel (International) will consult with the Department of Justice
about appropriate action, and the taxpayer may, in appropriate cases, be asked to
join the U.S. Government in a motion to sever issues or delay trial pending
completion of the competent authority proceedings. Final decision on severing
issues or delaying trial rests with the court. The filing of a competent authority
request does not, however, relieve the taxpayer from taking any action that may be
necessary or required with respect to litigation.

.04 *Coordination with Other Alternative Dispute Resolution and Pre-Filing Procedures.* Competent authority assistance is available to taxpayers in conjunction with
other alternative dispute resolution and pre-filing procedures in order to ensure
taxation in accordance with tax treaty provisions. Other revenue procedures and
IRS publications should be consulted as necessary with regard to specific matters.
See, e.g., Rev. Proc. 2006-9, 2006-2 I.R.B. 278 (concerning APAs); Rev. Proc. 2005-12,
2005-2 I.R.B. 311 (concerning Pre-Filing Agreements); or Rev. Proc. 98-21, 1998-1
C.B. 585 (concerning Article XIII(8) of the U.S.-Canada treaty). Taxpayers with
applications under any other dispute resolution procedures should seek competent

authority assistance as early as possible if they believe they have potential competent authority issues.

.05 *Effect of Agreements or Judicial Determinations on Competent Authority Proceedings.* If a taxpayer either executes a closing agreement with the IRS (whether or not contingent upon competent authority relief) with respect to a potential competent authority issue or reaches a settlement on the issue with IRS Appeals (including an Appeals settlement through the arbitration process) or with Chief Counsel pursuant to an executed closing agreement or other written agreement such as Form 870-AD, the U.S. competent authority will endeavor only to obtain a correlative adjustment from the treaty country and will not undertake any actions that would otherwise change such agreements. However, the U.S. competent authority will, in appropriate cases, consider actions necessary for the purpose of providing treatment similar to that provided in Rev. Proc. 99-32. Once a taxpayer's tax liability for the taxable periods in issue has been determined by a U.S. court (including settlement of the proceedings before or during trial), the U.S. competent authority similarly will endeavor only to obtain correlative relief from the treaty country and will not undertake any action that would otherwise reduce the taxpayer's federal tax liability for the taxable periods in issue as determined by a U.S. court. Taxpayers therefore should be aware that in these situations, as well as in situations where a treaty country takes a similar position with respect to issues resolved under its domestic laws, relief from double taxation may be jeopardized.

.06 *Accelerated Competent Authority Procedure.* A taxpayer requesting competent authority assistance with respect to an issue raised by the IRS also may request that the competent authorities attempt to resolve the issue for subsequent taxable periods for which returns have been filed, if the same issue continues in those periods. *See also* Rev. Proc. 94-67, 1994-2 C.B. 800, concerning the Accelerated Issue Resolution ("AIR") process. The U.S. competent authority will consider the request and will contact the appropriate IRS field office to consult on whether the issue should be resolved for subsequent taxable periods. If the IRS field office consents to this procedure, the U.S. competent authority will address with the foreign competent authority the request for such taxable periods. For purposes of resolving the issue, the taxpayer must furnish all relevant information and statements that may be requested by the U.S. competent authority pursuant to this revenue procedure. In addition, if the case involves a Coordinated Industry Case ("CIC") taxpayer, the taxpayer must furnish all relevant information and statements requested by the IRS, as described in Rev. Proc. 94-67, 1994-2 C.B. 800. If the case involves a non-CIC taxpayer, the taxpayer must furnish all relevant information and statements that may be requested by the IRS field office. A request for the accelerated competent authority procedure may be made at the time of filing a request for competent authority assistance or at any time thereafter, but generally before conclusion of the mutual agreement in the case; however, taxpayers are encouraged to request the procedure as early as practicable. The application of the accelerated procedure may require the prior consent of the Associate Chief Counsel (International). *See* section 7.03 of this revenue procedure. A request for the accelerated competent authority procedure must contain a statement that the taxpayer agrees that: (a) the inspection of books of account or records under the accelerated competent authority procedure will not preclude or impede (under section 7605(b) or any administrative provision adopted by the IRS) a later examination of a return or inspection of books of account or records for any taxable period covered in the accelerated competent authority assistance request; and (b) the IRS need not comply with any applicable procedural restrictions (for example, providing notice under section 7605(b)) before beginning such examination or inspection. The accelerated competent authority procedure is not subject to the AIR process limitations. The accelerated competent authority procedure is implicitly invoked when a taxpayer requests a rollback of its requested bilateral APA to already filed years. Thus, the provisions of section 7.06 of this revenue procedure also apply when a rollback is requested pursuant to Rev. Proc. 2006-9, which governs requests for APAs filed with the Office of Associate Chief Counsel (International), Advance Pricing Agreement Program.

SECTION 8. SIMULTANEOUS APPEALS PROCEDURE

.01 *General.* A taxpayer filing a request for competent authority assistance under this revenue procedure may, at the same time or at a later date, request IRS Appeals' consideration of the competent authority issue under the procedures and conditions provided in this section. The U.S. competent authority also may request IRS Appeals' involvement if it is determined that such involvement would facilitate the negotiation of a mutual agreement in the case or otherwise would serve the interest of the IRS. The taxpayer may, at any time, request a pre-filing conference with the offices of the Chief of IRS Appeals and the U.S. competent authority to discuss the Simultaneous Appeals procedure. *See also* section 7.02 of this revenue procedure for coordination with the competent authority of cases already in IRS Appeals. However, arbitration or mediation procedures that otherwise would be available through the IRS Appeals process are not available for cases in the Simultaneous Appeals procedure. *See* Rev. Proc. 2006-44, 2006-44 I.R.B. 800, and Rev. Proc. 2002-44, 2002-2 C.B. 10.

.02 *Time for Requesting the Simultaneous Appeals Procedure.*

(1) *When Filing for Competent Authority Assistance.* The Simultaneous Appeals procedure may be invoked at any of the following times:

(a) When the taxpayer applies for competent authority assistance with respect to an issue for which the examining IRS office has proposed an adjustment and before the protest is filed;

(b) When the taxpayer files a protest and decides to sever the competent authority issue and seek competent authority assistance while other issues are referred to IRS Appeals; and

(c) When the case is in IRS Appeals and the taxpayer later decides to request competent authority assistance with respect to the competent authority issue. The taxpayer may sever the competent authority issue for referral to the U.S. competent authority and invoke the Simultaneous Appeals procedure at any time when the case is in IRS Appeals but before settlement of the issue. Taxpayers, however, are encouraged to invoke the Simultaneous Appeals procedure as soon as possible, preferably as soon as practicable after the first IRS Appeals conference.

¶20,110

(2) *After Filing for Competent Authority Assistance.* The taxpayer may request the Simultaneous Appeals procedure at any time after requesting competent authority assistance. However, a taxpayer's request for the Simultaneous Appeals procedure generally will be denied if made after the date the U.S. position paper is communicated to the foreign competent authority, unless the U.S. competent authority determines that the procedure would facilitate an early resolution of the competent authority issue or otherwise is in the best interest of the IRS.

.03 *Cases Pending in Court.* If the matter is pending before a U.S. court or has been designated for litigation and jurisdiction has been released to the U.S. competent authority, a request for the Simultaneous Appeals procedure may be granted only with the consent of the U.S. competent authority and the Office of Associate Chief Counsel (International).

.04 *Request for Simultaneous Appeals Procedure.* The taxpayer's request for the Simultaneous Appeals procedure should be addressed to the U.S. competent authority either as part of the initial competent authority assistance request or, if made later, as a separate letter to the U.S. competent authority. The request should state whether the issue was previously protested to IRS Appeals for the periods in competent authority or for prior periods (in which case a copy of the relevant portions of the protest and an explanation of the outcome, if any, should be provided). The U.S. competent authority will send a copy of the request to the Chief of IRS Appeals, who, in turn, will forward a copy to the appropriate Area Director. The U.S. competent authority will consult with IRS Appeals to determine whether the Simultaneous Appeals procedure should be invoked. When the U.S. competent authority invokes the Simultaneous Appeals procedure, the taxpayer will be notified. The U.S. competent authority has jurisdiction of the issue when the Simultaneous Appeals procedure is invoked.

.05 *Role of IRS Appeals in the Simultaneous Appeals Procedure.*

(1) *IRS Appeals Process.* The IRS Appeals representative assigned to the case will consult with the taxpayer and the U.S. competent authority for the purpose of reaching a resolution of the unagreed issue under competent authority jurisdiction before the issue is presented to the foreign competent authority. For this purpose, established IRS Appeals procedures generally apply. The IRS Appeals representative will consult with the U.S. competent authority during this process to ensure appropriate coordination of the IRS Appeals process with the competent authority procedure, so that the terms of a tentative resolution and the principles and facts upon which it is based are compatible with the position that the U.S. competent authority intends to present to the foreign competent authority with respect to the issue. Any resolution reached with the IRS under this procedure is subject to the competent authority process and, therefore, is tentative and not binding on the IRS or the taxpayer. The IRS will not request the taxpayer to conclude the IRS Appeals process with a written agreement. The conclusions of the tentative resolution, however, generally will be reflected in the U.S. position paper used for negotiating a mutual agreement with the foreign competent authority. The procedures under this section do not give taxpayers the right to receive reconsideration of the issue by IRS Appeals where the taxpayer applied for competent authority assistance after

having received substantial IRS Appeals consideration. Rather, the IRS may rely upon, but will not necessarily be bound by, such previous consideration by IRS Appeals when considering the case under the Simultaneous Appeals procedure.

(2) *Assistance to U.S. Competent Authority.* The U.S. competent authority is responsible for developing a U.S. position paper with respect to the issue and for conducting the mutual agreement procedure. Generally, requesting IRS Appeals' consideration of an issue under competent authority jurisdiction will not affect the manner in which taxpayers normally are involved in the competent authority process.

.06 Denial or Termination of Simultaneous Appeals Procedure.

(1) *Taxpayer's Termination.* The taxpayer may, at any time, withdraw its request for the Simultaneous Appeals procedure.

(2) *IRS's Denial or Termination.* The U.S. competent authority, the Chief of IRS Appeals or the appropriate Industry or Area Director may decide to deny or terminate the Simultaneous Appeals procedure if the procedure is determined to be prejudicial to the mutual agreement procedure or to the administrative appeals process. For example, a taxpayer that received IRS Appeals consideration before requesting competent authority assistance, but was unable to reach a settlement in IRS Appeals, may be denied the Simultaneous Appeals procedure. A taxpayer may request a conference with the offices of the U.S. competent authority and the Chief of IRS Appeals to discuss the denial or termination of the procedure.

.07 Returning to IRS Appeals. If the competent authorities fail to agree or if the taxpayer does not accept the mutual agreement reached by the competent authorities, the taxpayer will be permitted to refer the issue to IRS Appeals for further consideration.

.08 IRS Appeals' Consideration of Non-Competent Authority Issues. The Simultaneous Appeals procedure does not affect the taxpayer's rights to IRS Appeals' consideration of other unresolved issues. The taxpayer may pursue settlement discussions with respect to the other issues without waiting for resolution of the issues under competent authority jurisdiction.

SECTION 9. PROTECTIVE MEASURES

.01 General. In negotiating treaties, the United States seeks to secure an agreement with the treaty country that any competent authority agreement reached with the treaty country will be implemented notwithstanding any time limits or other procedural limitations in the domestic law of either country. However, treaty provisions that provide a competent authority with the ability to waive such limitations do not affect the application of statutes of limitation in the event that a request for competent authority assistance is declined or the competent authorities are unable to reach an agreement. In addition, the particular treaty or the posture of the particular case may indicate that the taxpayer or a related person must take protective measures with the U.S. and foreign tax authorities so that the implementation of any agreement reached by the competent authorities or alternative remedies outside of the competent authority process are not barred by administrative, legal or procedural barriers. Such barriers may arise either before or after a

competent authority request is filed. Protective measures include, but are not limited to: (a) filing protective claims for refund or credit; (b) extending any period of limitations on assessment or refund; (c) avoiding the lapse or termination of the taxpayer's right to appeal any tax determination; (d) complying with all applicable procedures for invoking competent authority consideration, including applicable treaty provisions dealing with time limits within which to invoke such remedy; and (e) contesting an adjustment or seeking an appropriate correlative adjustment with respect to the U.S. or treaty country tax. A taxpayer should take protective measures in a timely manner, that is, in a manner that allows sufficient time for appropriate procedures to be completed and effective before barriers arise. Generally, a taxpayer should consider, at the time an adjustment is first proposed, which protective measures may be necessary and when such measures should be taken. However, earlier consideration of appropriate actions may be desirable, for example, in the case of a recurring adjustment or where the taxpayer otherwise is on notice that an adjustment is likely to be proposed. Taxpayers may consult with the U.S. competent authority to determine the need for and timing of protective measures in their particular case.

.02 Filing Protective Claim for Credit or Refund with a Competent Authority Request.

(1) *In General.* A valid protective claim for credit or refund must meet the requirements of section 6402 of the Code and the regulations thereunder. Accordingly, a protective claim must: (a) fully advise the IRS of the grounds on which credit or refund is claimed; (b) contain sufficient facts to apprise the IRS of the exact basis of the claim; (c) state the year for which the claim is being made; (d) be on the proper form; and (e) be verified by a written declaration made under penalties of perjury.

(2) *Treatment of Competent Authority Request as Protective Claim.* The IRS will treat a request for competent authority assistance itself as one or more protective claims for credit or refund with respect to issues raised in the request and within the jurisdiction of the U.S. competent authority and will not require a taxpayer to file the form described in *Treas. Reg. §301.6402-3* with respect to those issues, provided that the request meets the other requirements of section 6402 of the Code and the regulations thereunder, as described in section 9.02(1) of this revenue procedure. The information constituting the protective claim should be set forth in a separate section of the request for assistance and captioned "Protective claim pursuant to section 9.02 of Rev. Proc. 2006-54." The penalties of perjury statement described in section 4.05(16) of this revenue procedure satisfies the requirement for the written declaration and a separate declaration is not required.

.03 Protective Filing Before Competent Authority Request.

(1) *In general.* There may be situations in which a taxpayer will be unable to file a formal competent authority assistance request before the period of limitations expires with respect to the affected U.S. return. In these situations, before the period of limitations expires, the taxpayer should file a protective claim for credit or refund of the taxes attributable to the potential competent authority issue to ensure that alternative remedies outside of the competent authority process will not be barred. A protective filing may be appropriate where: (a) the treaty country is

considering but has not yet proposed an adjustment; (b) the treaty country has proposed an adjustment but the related taxpayer in the treaty country decides to pursue administrative or judicial remedies in the foreign country; or (c) the terms of the applicable treaty require notification to be made to the competent authority within a certain time period. In considering whether to accept a taxpayer's request for competent authority assistance, the U.S. competent authority will consider whether the proper treaty notification has been made in accordance with this subsection.

(2) *Letter to Competent Authority Treated as Protective Claim.* In situations in which a protective claim is filed prior to submitting a request for competent authority assistance, the taxpayer may make a protective claim in the form of a letter to the competent authority. The letter must indicate that the taxpayer is filing a protective claim and set forth, to the extent available, the information required under section 4.05(1) through (17) or under section 5.03(1) through (8) of this revenue procedure, as applicable. The letter must include a penalties of perjury statement as described in sections 4.05(16) and 5.03(8) of this revenue procedure. The letter must be filed in the same place and manner as a request for competent authority assistance. The IRS will treat the letter as a protective claim(s) with respect to issues raised in the letter and within the jurisdiction of the U.S. competent authority and will not require a taxpayer to file the form described in *Treas. Reg. §301.6402-3* with respect to those issues, provided that the request meets the other requirements described in section 9.02(1) of this revenue procedure. The letter must include the caption "Protective claim pursuant to section 9.03 of Rev. Proc. 2006-54."

(3) *Notification Requirement.* After filing a protective claim, the taxpayer periodically must notify the U.S. competent authority whether the taxpayer still is considering filing for competent authority assistance. The notification must be filed every twelve months until the formal request for competent authority assistance is filed. The U.S. competent authority may deny competent authority assistance if the taxpayer fails to file this annual notification.

(4) *No Consultation between Competent Authorities until Formal Request is Filed.* The U.S. competent authority generally will not undertake any consultation with the foreign competent authority with respect to a protective claim filed under section 9.03 of this revenue procedure. The U.S. competent authority will place the protective claim in suspense until either a formal request for competent authority assistance is filed or the taxpayer notifies the U.S. competent authority that competent authority consideration is no longer needed. In appropriate cases, the U.S. competent authority will send the taxpayer a formal notice of claim disallowance.

.04 *Effect of a Protective Claim.*

Protective claims filed under section 9.02 or 9.03 of this revenue procedure will only allow a credit or refund to the extent of the grounds set forth in the protective claim and only to the extent agreed to by the U.S. and foreign competent authorities or to the extent unilaterally allowed by the U.S. competent authority. This revenue procedure does not grant a taxpayer the right to invoke section 482 of the Code in

¶20,110

its favor or compel the IRS to allocate income or deductions or grant a tax credit or refund.

.05 *Treaty Provisions Waiving Procedural Barriers.*

In those cases where the mutual agreement article authorizes a competent authority to waive or remove procedural barriers to the credit or refund of tax, taxpayers may be allowed a credit or refund of tax even though the otherwise applicable period of limitations has expired, prior closing agreements have been entered into, or other actions have been taken or omitted that ordinarily would foreclose relief in the form of a credit or refund of tax. However, under these provisions there may still be situations in which taxpayers should take appropriate protective measures as described under this revenue procedure or under applicable foreign procedures. For example, procedural limitations cannot be waived if a request for competent authority assistance is declined or the competent authorities are unable to reach agreement. In addition, some countries may take the position that domestic statutes of limitation on refunds cannot be waived under the relevant treaty. Because there are circumstances that are not under the control of taxpayers or the U.S. competent authority it is advisable that taxpayers take protective measures to increase the possibility that appropriate relief is available to them in all circumstances.

SECTION 10. APPLICATION OF REV. PROC. 99-32

Rev. Proc. 99-32, 1999-2 C.B. 296, generally provides a means to conform a taxpayer's accounts and allow repatriation of certain amounts following an allocation of income between related U.S. and foreign corporations under section 482 of the Code without the federal income tax consequences of the adjustments that would otherwise have been necessary to conform the taxpayer's accounts in light of the allocation of income. In situations where a section 482 allocation is the subject of a request for competent authority assistance, the competent authority may provide relief consistent with the principles of Rev. Proc. 99-32 with respect to any new or pending requests for Rev. Proc. 99-32 treatment relating to such allocation. Accordingly, if a taxpayer intends to seek Rev. Proc. 99-32 treatment in connection with competent authority assistance relating to a section 482 allocation, the taxpayer must request Rev. Proc. 99-32 treatment in conjunction with its request for competent authority assistance. If a taxpayer has already requested Rev. Proc. 99-32 treatment at the time it submits a request for competent authority assistance relating to a section 482 allocation, consideration of Rev. Proc. 99-32 treatment must be transferred to the U.S. competent authority and a copy of the pending Rev. Proc. 99-32 request forwarded along with the request for competent authority assistance.

SECTION 11. DETERMINATION OF CREDITABLE FOREIGN TAXES

For purposes of determining the amount of foreign taxes creditable under sections 901 and 902 of the Code, any amounts paid to foreign tax authorities that would not have been due if the treaty country had made a correlative adjustment may not constitute a creditable foreign tax. *See Treas. Reg. § 1.901-2(e)(5)(i)* and Rev. Rul. 92-75, 1992-2 C.B. 197. Acts or omissions by the taxpayer that preclude effective competent authority assistance, including failure to take protective measures as described in section 9 of this revenue procedure or failure to seek competent authority assistance, may constitute a failure to exhaust all effective and practical remedies as may be required to claim a credit. *See Treas. Reg. § 1.901-2(e)(5)(i).* Further, the fact that the taxpayer has sought competent authority assistance but obtained no relief, either because the competent authorities failed to reach an agreement or because the taxpayer rejected an agreement reached by the competent authorities, generally will not, in and of itself, demonstrate that the taxpayer has exhausted all effective and practical remedies to reduce the taxpayer's liability for foreign tax (including liability pursuant to a foreign tax audit adjustment). Any determination within the IRS of whether a taxpayer has exhausted the competent authority remedy must be made in consultation with the U.S. competent authority.

SECTION 12. ACTION BY U.S. COMPETENT AUTHORITY

.01 *Notification of Taxpayer.* Upon receiving a request for assistance pursuant to this revenue procedure, the U.S. competent authority will notify the taxpayer whether the facts provide a basis for assistance.

.02 *Denial of Assistance.* The U.S. competent authority generally will not accept a request for competent authority assistance or will cease providing assistance to the taxpayer if:

(1) competent authority determines that the taxpayer is not entitled to the treaty benefit or safeguard in question or to the assistance requested;

(2) the taxpayer is willing only to accept a competent authority agreement under conditions that are unreasonable or prejudicial to the interests of the U.S. Government;

(3) the taxpayer rejected the competent authority resolution of the same or similar issue in a prior case;

(4) the taxpayer does not agree that competent authority negotiations are a government-to-government activity that does not include the taxpayer's participation in the negotiation proceedings;

(5) the taxpayer does not furnish upon request sufficient information to determine whether the treaty applies to the taxpayer's facts and circumstances;

(6) the taxpayer was found to have acquiesced in a foreign initiated adjustment that involved significant legal or factual issues that otherwise would be properly handled through the competent authority process and then unilaterally made a corresponding correlative adjustment or claimed an increased foreign tax credit, without initially seeking U.S. competent authority assistance;

(7) the taxpayer: (a) fails to comply with this revenue procedure; (b) failed to cooperate with the IRS during the examination of the periods in issue and such failure significantly impedes the ability of the U.S. competent authority to negotiate and conclude an agreement (*e.g.,* significant factual development is required that cannot effectively be completed outside the examination process); or (c) fails to cooperate with the U.S. competent authority (including failing to provide sufficient facts and documentation to support its claim of double taxation or taxation contrary

to the treaty) or otherwise significantly impedes the ability of the U.S. competent authority to negotiate and conclude an agreement; or

(8) the transaction giving rise to the request for competent authority assistance: (a) is more properly within the jurisdiction of IRS Appeals; (b) includes an issue pending in a U.S. Court, or designated for litigation, unless competent authority consideration is concurred in by the U.S. competent authority and the Associate Chief Counsel (International); (c) is a listed transaction for purposes of *Treas. Reg. §1.6011-4(b)(2) and §301.6111-2(b)(2)*; or *(d)* involves fraudulent activity by the taxpayer.

.03 *Extending Period of Limitations for Assessment.* If the U.S. competent authority accepts a request for assistance, the taxpayer may be requested to execute a consent to extend the period of limitations for assessment of tax for the taxable periods in issue. Failure to comply with the provisions of this subsection can result in denial of assistance by the U.S. competent authority with respect to the request.

.04 *No Review of Denial of Request for Assistance.* The U.S. competent authority's denial of a taxpayer's request for assistance or dismissal of a matter previously accepted for consideration pursuant to this revenue procedure is final and not subject to administrative review.

.05 *Notification.* The U.S. competent authority will notify a taxpayer requesting assistance under this revenue procedure of any agreement that the U.S. and the foreign competent authorities reach with respect to the request. If the taxpayer accepts the resolution reached by the competent authorities, the agreement will provide that it is final and is not subject to further administrative or judicial review. If the competent authorities fail to agree, or if the agreement reached is not acceptable to the taxpayer, the taxpayer may withdraw the request for competent authority assistance and may then pursue all rights otherwise available under the laws of the United States and the treaty country. Where the competent authorities fail to agree, no further competent authority remedies generally are available, except with respect to treaties that provide for arbitration of the dispute. *See, e.g.,* Article 25(5) of the U.S.-German income tax treaty. A request for arbitration must be made in accordance with the procedures prescribed under the applicable treaty and related documents, including procedures that the IRS may promulgate from time to time.

.06 *Closing Agreement.* When appropriate, the taxpayer may be requested to enter into a closing agreement that reflects the terms of the mutual agreement and of the competent authority assistance provided and that is executed in conformity with sections 6.07 and 6.17 of Rev. Proc. 68-16, 1968-1 C.B. 770 (as modified by Rev Proc. 94-67, 1994-2 C.B. 800).

.07 *Unilateral Withdrawal or Reduction of U.S. Initiated Adjustments.* With respect to U.S. initiated adjustments under section 482 of the Code, the primary goal of the mutual agreement procedure is to obtain a correlative adjustment from the treaty country. For other types of U.S. initiated adjustments, the primary goal of the U.S. competent authority is the avoidance of taxation not in accordance with an applicable treaty. Unilateral withdrawal or reduction of U.S. initiated adjustments, therefore, generally will not be considered. For example, the U.S. competent authority will not withdraw or reduce an adjustment to income, deductions, credits or other items solely because the period of limitations has expired in the foreign country and the foreign competent authority has declined to grant any relief. If the period provided by the foreign statute of limitations has expired, the U.S. competent authority may take into account other relevant facts to determine whether such withdrawal or reduction is appropriate and may, in extraordinary circumstances and as a matter of discretion, provide such relief with respect to the adjustment to avoid actual or economic double taxation. In no event, however, will relief be granted where there is fraud or negligence with respect to the relevant transactions. In keeping with the U.S. Government's view that tax treaties should be applied in a balanced and reciprocal manner, the United States normally will not withdraw or reduce an adjustment where the treaty country does not grant similar relief in equivalent cases.

SECTION 13. REQUESTS FOR RULINGS

.01 *General.* Requests for advance rulings regarding the interpretation or application of a tax treaty, as distinguished from requests for assistance from the U.S. competent authority pursuant to this revenue procedure, must be submitted to the Associate Chief Counsel (International). *See* Rev. Proc. 2006-1, 2006-1 I.R.B. 1, and Rev. Proc. 2006-7, 2006-1 I.R.B. 242.

.02 *Foreign Tax Rulings.* The IRS does not issue advance rulings on the effect of a tax treaty on the tax laws of a treaty country for purposes of determining the tax of the treaty country.

SECTION 14. FEES

.01 *Requests to Which a User Fee Does Not Apply.* Except as provided in section 14.02 of this revenue procedure, no user fees are required with respect to a request for U.S. competent authority assistance pursuant to this revenue procedure.

.02 *Requests to Which a User Fee Applies.* In general, a $15,000 user fee applies to all requests for determinations on limitation on benefits, as described in section 3.08 of this revenue procedure. The fee will apply regardless of whether the request is for: (a) an initial determination; (b) a renewal of a previously issued determination; or (c) a supplemental determination required, for example, if there is a material change in fact or if the taxpayer seeks benefits with respect to a different type of income or requests a lower rate of withholding tax on dividends. If a request is submitted that requires the U.S. competent authority to make a discretionary determination for more than one entity, a separate user fee will be charged for each entity.

.03 *Acceptance of Requests.* A user fee will not be charged until the U.S. competent authority has formally accepted the request for consideration. Within 30 days of receipt of a complete submission, the U.S. competent authority will provide written notice to the taxpayer as to whether the request will be accepted or rejected for consideration. If a request is accepted, the taxpayer will be required to mail a check or money order in the appropriate amount, along with a copy of the written notice of acceptance to the IRS office identified below. The check or money order should

¶20,110

be payable to the United States Treasury. The fee may be refunded as provided in section 14.05 of this revenue procedure.

.04 Address to Send Payment. The user fee should be sent along with a copy of the written notice of acceptance to the mailing address listed below:

> IRS/BFC
> P.O. Box 9002
> Beckley, WV 25802

.05 Refunds of User Fee. In general, a user fee will not be refunded once the U.S. competent authority accepts a request for consideration and the user fee is paid. For example, the IRS will not refund the user fee if the request for a discretionary determination is withdrawn by the taxpayer or if the taxpayer fails to submit additional information as requested by the U.S. competent authority. A user fee may be refunded, however, if (a) a higher user fee is paid than is required; or (b) taking into account all the facts and circumstances, including the IRS's resources devoted to the request, the Competent Authority declines to rule and, in his or her sole discretion, decides a refund is appropriate.

SECTION 15. EFFECT ON OTHER DOCUMENTS

Rev. Proc. 2006-26, 2006-21 I.R.B. 936, and Rev. Proc. 2002-52, 2002-2 C.B. 242, are modified and superseded by this revenue procedure. Rev. Proc. 2006-9, 2006-9 I.R.B. 278 is amplified. Rev. Rul. 92-75, 1992-2 C.B. 197, is clarified. References in this revenue procedure to Rev. Proc. 99-32 will be treated as references to Rev. Proc. 65-17, 1965-1 C.B. 833, as modified, amplified and clarified from time to time, for taxable years beginning before August 24, 1999.

SECTION 16. EFFECTIVE DATE

This revenue procedure is effective for requests for U.S. competent authority assistance and Rev. Proc. 99-32 treatment filed after December 4, 2006.

SECTION 17. PAPERWORK REDUCTION ACT

The collection of information contained in this revenue procedure has been reviewed and approved by the Office of Management and Budget in accordance with the Paperwork Reduction Act (44 U.S.C. § 3507) under control number 1545-2044.

An agency may not conduct or sponsor, and a person is not required to respond to, a collection of information unless the collection of information displays a valid control number.

The collection of information in this revenue procedure is in sections 4.04, 4.05, 5.03, 7.06, 8.04, and 9.03. This information is required, and will be used, to evaluate and process the request for competent authority assistance. The collection of information is required to obtain competent authority assistance. The likely respondents are individuals or business or other for-profit institutions.

The estimated total annual reporting and/or recordkeeping burden is 9,000 hours.

The estimated annual burden per respondent/recordkeeper is 30 hours. The estimated number of respondents and/or recordkeepers is 300.

The estimated annual frequency of responses is on occasion.

¶20,110

Books or records relating to a collection of information must be retained as long as their contents may become material in the administration of any internal revenue law. Generally, tax returns and tax return information are confidential, as required by section 6103 of the Code.

SECTION 18. DRAFTING INFORMATION

The principal authors of this revenue procedure are Aziz Benbrahim and Vincent Salvo of the Office of the Deputy Commissioner (International), Large and Mid-Size Business Division, and Mae J. Lew and Denen A. Norfleet of the Office of Associate Chief Counsel (International). For further information regarding this revenue procedure contact either Mr. Benbrahim or Mr. Salvo at (202) 435-5000 or Ms. Norfleet at (202) 435-5262 (not toll-free calls).

¶ 20,120 Revenue Procedure 99-32[2]

The IRS has revised Rev. Proc. 65-17 to update the extent to which taxpayers whose income has been adjusted under Code Section 482 may make certain adjustments to conform their accounts to reflect that allocation. A newly issued revenue procedure sets forth the applicable procedures for the repatriation of cash by a U.S. taxpayer via an interest-bearing account receivable or payable in an amount corresponding to the amount allocated to, or from, such taxpayer under Code Section 482 from, or to, a related person with respect to a controlled transaction. Also, circumstances are prescribed in which a U.S. taxpayer may treat an account as offset in whole or part by the amount of a bona fide debt, distribution, or capital contribution between the taxpayer and the related person. Pursuant to these guidelines, taxpayers whose taxable income has been adjusted under Code Section 482 are generally allowed to make certain adjustments to conform their accounts to reflect the Code Section 482 allocation. Superseding Rev. Proc. 65-17, as amended, Rev. Proc. 65-31, Rev. Proc. 70-23, Rev. Proc. 71-35, Rev. Proc. 72-22, Rev. Proc. 72-46, Rev. Proc. 72-48, Rev. Proc. 72-53, and Rev. Rul. 82-80. References to Rev. Proc. 65-17 in Rev. Proc. 68-16, Rev. Proc. 89-8, Rev. Proc. 96-13, Rev. Proc. 96-14 and Rev. Proc. 96-53 shall be treated as references to Rev. Proc. 99-32.

SUMMARY: This document contains a new revenue procedure that sets forth the Service's position regarding adjustments that may be made to conform the accounts of taxpayers to reflect allocations made under section 482 of the Internal Revenue Code.

SUPPLEMENTARY INFORMATION:

Background

In Announcement 99-1, 1999-2 I.R.B. 11, the Internal Revenue Service invited comment on a revision of Rev. Proc. 65-17, 1965-1 C.B. 833, on conforming a taxpayer's accounts to reflect a primary adjustment under section 482 of the Internal Revenue Code. The comments received and changes finally adopted in this revenue procedure are summarized below.

Explanation of Provisions

A. Taxpayer-Initiated Primary Adjustments

In furtherance of the overall goal of promoting upfront compliance with the arm's length standard, Announcement 99-1 proposed providing a mechanism for taxpayers to conform their accounts in connection with taxpayer-initiated (as well as Service-initiated) primary adjustments, without the Federal income tax consequences of the secondary adjustments that would otherwise result under section 482. Commentators welcomed this proposal and it is finally adopted in this revenue procedure. Accordingly, taxpayers may elect, by filing a statement with their Federal income their tax returns, to apply revenue procedure treatment for taxpayer-initiated upward and downward adjustments of taxable income pursuant to *section 1.482-1(a)(3) of the Treasury regulations*, in connection with inbound, outbound, and certain foreign-to-foreign controlled transactions. Election of reve-

---

[2] Rev. Proc. 99-32, IRB 1999-34, 296, August 2, 1999.

nue procedure treatment through such a statement shall be binding on the taxpayer.

B. Offsets

Announcement 99-1 proposed eliminating dividend offsets and making account treatment the sole means to repatriate the cash attributable to a primary adjustment, without the Federal income tax consequences of secondary adjustments. Some commentators supported this proposal on the ground that dividend paying policies are independent of transfer pricing. Other commentators, however, expressed the view that elimination of dividend offsets would discourage current repatriation of earnings, prolong transfer pricing disputes, and pose problems when payment of a form of income is restricted under foreign law. Others suggested that permitting offsets in connection with taxpayer-initiated adjustments would be consistent with upfront compliance with the arm's length standard.

In response to these comments, this revenue procedure allows taxpayers to offset accounts by distributions, including those that would otherwise be dividends, in the same year as that to which a taxpayer-initiated primary adjustment relates, provided the offset treatment is claimed on a timely-filed income tax return (including extensions). In addition, offsets may be claimed for distributions in the year in which a return is filed reporting a taxpayer-initiated adjustment or in the year a closing agreement is entered into in connection with a Service-initiated adjustment. Offsets are also permitted by means of entries offsetting bona fide debts and capital contributions. No offsets are allowed with respect to a year for which an income tax return has already been filed, except for pre-effective date years as described below. Offsets are treated as prepayments of the interest and principal of an account established under the revenue procedure for all Federal income tax purposes, regardless of their characterization under foreign law.

In the Service's view, these changes are consistent with the overall goal of upfront compliance with the arm's length standard and reduce any disincentive to repatriate earnings. Moreover, they improve administrability by dispensing with the need to reverse tax effects reported on prior income tax returns, as was required with the dividend offset pursuant to Rev. Proc. 65-17.

The Service recognizes that a domestic subsidiary of a foreign parent may claim an offset pursuant to this revenue procedure by reason of a distribution as to which the subsidiary withheld tax in accordance with its obligations pursuant to section 1442 of the Code. In such a case, the Service anticipates that the foreign parent will be able to file an income tax return to obtain a refund of such withholding tax.

The Service intends that offset treatment pursuant to this revenue procedure shall be the exclusive means of addressing the situations in which payments of certain forms of income are restricted under foreign law that are described in Example 2 and Example 3 of *section 1.482-1(h)(v) of the Treasury regulations.*

C. Effective Date and Transitional Treatment

Announcement 99-1 proposed that the revised revenue procedure be prospectively effective for taxable years beginning after its publication. Commentators suggested that liberal transitional rules be provided for application of revenue procedure

¶20,120

treatment in connection with taxpayer-initiated adjustments for pre-effective date taxable years.

In response to these comments, the final revised revenue procedure published in this document provides that for taxable years prior to the taxable year that includes the date of publication, taxpayers shall be permitted to use a reasonable interpretation of the principles of Rev. Proc. 65-17 for purposes of conforming their accounts to reflect a taxpayer-initiated primary adjustment. The Service considers an interpretation that applies the final revised revenue procedure or its general principles to be such a reasonable interpretation of Rev. Proc. 65-17. The Service also considers that a reasonable interpretation would include the permission of a taxpayer-initiated offset by reason of a distribution reported as a dividend on a prior income tax return for the taxable year to which the primary adjustment relates, provided the subsequent treatment reverses any previously claimed tax effects associated with such dividend in accordance with the principles of section 4.01 of Rev. Proc. 65-17.

For taxable years that include the date of publication of this revenue procedure, a taxpayer may elect to apply all of the provisions of this revenue procedure. Otherwise, Rev. Proc. 6517 applies for such taxable years in accordance with its terms. In such cases, revenue procedure treatment for taxpayer-initiated adjustments will necessitate a closing agreement with the Service.

D. Penalty Condition

Announcement 99-1 proposed to substitute inapplicability of any penalty under section 6662(e), for absence of a principal tax avoidance purpose required under Rev. Proc. 65-17, as the condition for revenue procedure treatment. Commentators criticized the requirement of any condition for various reasons, including that such condition would inappropriately expand the section 6662(e) penalty and may yield apparently arbitrary results. Other commentators suggested that the determination of the inapplicability of the penalty was problematic in the case of a taxpayer-initiated adjustment.

This revenue procedure removes the penalty condition in the case of taxpayer-initiated adjustments, but retains the condition for Service-initiated adjustments, including such adjustments as result from examination of taxpayer-initiated adjustments. The condition is neither an expansion of the penalty, nor arbitrary, but, rather, it is a reasonable tax administration restriction on availability of the revenue procedure treatment. In the Service's view the penalty condition of this revenue procedure is more objective than absence of a principal tax avoidance purpose under Rev. Proc. 65-17 and, moreover, is consistent with the goal of upfront compliance.

E. Other Changes and Clarifications

As proposed by Announcement 99-1, the revenue procedure clarifies that a foreign tax credit shall be allowed for any foreign withholding tax with respect to the repayment of the principal or interest of the account to the extent and subject to the limitations provided under section 901 of the Code. The amount of any payment or prepayment of an account established under the revenue procedure is considered to include the amount of such foreign withholding tax. The revenue procedure does not adopt comments that allowance of a section 901 credit for a foreign withholding tax should be without regard to whether a taxpayer exhausts all effective and practical remedies, including invocation of competent authority procedures. This is a requirement under the applicable regulations. *Treas. Reg. § 1.901-2(e)(5).*

Persons eligible for revenue procedure treatment are limited to "United States taxpayers," i.e., either a domestic corporation or a foreign corporation that is, or is treated as, engaged in a trade or business within the United States. Controlled transactions between a controlled foreign corporation of a domestic corporation and a foreign related corporation are also eligible for treatment under the revenue procedure. Transactions with noncorporate persons, for example, a transaction between a partnership and its controlling corporate partner, are not covered by the revenue procedure, but will be the subject of further study by the Service.

Accounts under the revenue procedure are set up, and offsets are permitted, between the related corporation and the United States taxpayer, or any member of its affiliated group. See Rev. Proc. 70-23, 1970-2 C.B. 505, and Rev. Proc. 71-35, 1971-2 C.B. 573, both superseded by this revenue procedure. The revenue procedure clarifies application of the safe harbor interest rates in the case of interest on accounts. Where an account is paid in the form of term debt, such debt will be considered a new obligation commencing with a new term; however, payment by means of term debt shall be respected only to the extent the debt qualifies in substance as bona fide debt under applicable debt-equity rules. The revenue procedure provides that interest on accounts is includible in the income of the obligee on the accrual basis regardless of the obligee's method of accounting. See Rev. Proc. 72-48, 1972-2 C.B. 829, superseded by this revenue procedure. Account interest is deductible by the obligor, but subject to applicable limitations including sections 163(e)(3) and 267(a)(3) of the Code. Rules are prescribed for determining the currency in which the principal and interest of an account must be denominated, which generally will be the U.S. dollar.

Other conforming changes are made to incorporate the provisions of other various progeny of Rev. Proc. 65-17 that are superseded by this revenue procedure. Coordination of revenue procedure treatment and the competent authority process and the advance pricing agreement program will be considered in connection with the revision and updating of the revenue procedures governing those processes. See generally Rev. Proc. 96-13, 1996-1 C.B. 616; Rev. Proc. 96-14, 1996-1 C.B. 626; and Rev. Proc. 96-53, 1996-2 C.B. 375.

Revenue Procedure 99-32, I.R.B. 1999-34, 296, August 2, 1999.

SECTION 1. PURPOSE

Pursuant to *section 1.482-1(g)(3) of the Income Tax Regulations*, this revenue procedure prescribes the applicable procedures for the repatriation of cash by a United States taxpayer via an interest-bearing account receivable or payable (the "account") in an amount corresponding to the amount allocated to, or from, such taxpayer under section 482 of the Internal Revenue Code (the "Code") from, or to, a related person with respect to a controlled transaction. Additionally, circumstances are prescribed in which a United States taxpayer may treat an account as offset (the "offset") in whole or part by the amount of a bona fide debt, distribution, or capital contribution between the taxpayer and such related person. Under this revenue procedure, taxpayers whose taxable income has been adjusted under section 482 of the Code are generally permitted to make certain adjustments to conform their accounts to reflect the section 482 allocation. The conditions for treatment under this revenue procedure are set forth in section 3, the adjustments to be made or allowed are described in section 4 (for Internal Revenue Service as well as taxpayer-initiated adjustments), and the prescribed procedures are set forth in section 5.

SECTION 2. BACKGROUND AND SCOPE

Section 482 of the Code gives the Internal Revenue Service authority to "distribute, apportion or allocate gross income, deductions, credits, or allowances" among certain related organizations, trades or businesses if it "determines that such distribution, apportionment, or allocation is necessary in order to prevent evasion of taxes or clearly to reflect the income" of any such entity. Absent a United States taxpayer's election of treatment under this revenue procedure, an adjustment under section 482 (the "primary adjustment") entails secondary adjustments to conform the taxpayer's accounts to reflect the primary adjustment. These secondary adjustments may result in adverse tax consequences to the taxpayer. For example, an allocation of income under section 482 from a foreign parent corporation to its domestic subsidiary corporation would entail a deemed distribution from the domestic subsidiary to its foreign parent in an amount equal to the primary adjustment in the year for which the allocation is made. The deemed distribution would be treated as dividend income to the foreign parent to the extent of the earnings and profits of the domestic subsidiary, as recomputed after taking into account the primary adjustment. Under section 881 of the Code, the foreign parent would be subject to a 30-percent tax liability (as reduced by any applicable income tax treaty), and under section 1442 of the Code, the domestic subsidiary would be a withholding agent required to withhold the tax. See Rev. Rul. 82-80, 1982-1 C.B. 89; *Treas. Reg. § 1.1441-2(e)(2)*. This revenue procedure allows the United States taxpayer to repatriate the cash attributable to a primary adjustment via an account without the Federal income tax consequences of the secondary adjustments that would otherwise result from the primary adjustment.

Additionally, *section 1.482-1(a)(3) of the Income Tax Regulations* permits a controlled taxpayer to report an arm's length result for controlled transactions based upon prices different from those actually charged. If the adjustment results in an increase in taxable income, the increased income may be reported by the taxpayer at any time. If the adjustment results in a decrease in taxable income (after appropriate accounting for section 1059A of the Code), the arm's length result may be reported on a timely filed return (including extensions). A United States taxpayer can avail itself of the treatment provided by this revenue procedure to mitigate the Federal income tax consequences of the secondary adjustments that would otherwise result from the taxpayer's "self-initiated" primary adjustment. In the case of a taxpayer-initiated adjustment, a United States taxpayer may, in accordance with section 4.02 of this revenue procedure, use an offset in combina-

¶20,120

tion with an account to effectuate the repatriation of the cash attributable to the primary adjustment without the Federal income tax consequences of the secondary adjustments that would otherwise result from the primary adjustment. The United States taxpayer is bound by its election of treatment under the revenue procedure. The taxpayer-initiated adjustment for the treatment provided under the revenue procedure will be subject to review and adjustment, and to possible imposition of the section 6662(e) or (h) penalty, by the Service upon examination.

This revenue procedure applies in situations where an adjustment is made under section 482 of the Code, as well as to Service-initiated adjustments made under sections 61 or 162 of the Code, provided the adjustment could have been made under section 482 of the Code. All references in this revenue procedure to section 482 of the Code will be deemed to include sections 61 and 162 of the Code, except when the context or express language indicates or provides otherwise.

Any reference in this revenue procedure to an increase or decrease in, or an adjustment of, taxable income shall also be deemed a reference, in an appropriate case, to a reduction or increase in, or an adjustment of, a taxpayer's loss.

Any reference in this revenue procedure to the Service shall be deemed a reference to the office within the Service that has jurisdiction over the Federal income tax return filed for the taxable year for which the primary adjustment is made.

For purposes of this revenue procedure, a "United States taxpayer" is a domestic corporation, or a foreign corporation that is, or is treated as, engaged in trade or business within the United States.

For purposes of this revenue procedure, an increase or decrease, or an adjustment of, the taxable income of a United States taxpayer that is a domestic corporation pursuant to section 482 of the Code shall be deemed to include an allocation of an amount to, or from, a related person (being a corporation as defined in section 7701(a)(3) of the Code), from, or to, a foreign corporation that is a controlled foreign corporation within the meaning of section 957 of the Code solely by reason of ownership of such foreign corporation's stock by such domestic corporation (or any member of the affiliated group within the meaning of section 1504(a) of the Code in which such domestic corporation is included) with respect to a controlled transaction. In the latter circumstances, the parties to any account established under section 4.01 shall be such controlled foreign corporation and such related person, and for purposes of section 4.012 the requirement to accrue and include, or deduct, interest in, or from, taxable income shall mean accounting for such interest for all Federal income tax purposes that may affect the determination of the taxable income or tax liability of such domestic corporation, including, for example, the computation of earnings and profits, subpart F income, and the foreign tax credit provided under section 901 of the Code.

Treatment under this revenue procedure shall not be denied solely by reason of the fact a corporation under State law is in existence for the purpose of winding up its affairs, where such corporation, subsequent to its liquidation, was a corporation from, or to, which an amount was allocated pursuant to section 482 of the Code.

¶20,120

SECTION 3. CONDITIONS FOR TREATMENT UNDER THIS REVENUE PROCEDURE

A United States taxpayer described in section 5 shall qualify for the treatment provided in this revenue procedure only if it satisfies the conditions described in this section 3.

.01 A United States taxpayer described in section 5.01 shall qualify for the treatment provided in this revenue procedure if the taxable income of such United States taxpayer is adjusted by the Internal Revenue Service under section 482 and no penalty under section 6662(e)(1)(B) or (h) of the Code on account of such primary adjustment is asserted and, if challenged, finally sustained. In the case of an adjustment under section 61 or 162, this condition will be deemed to be satisfied if no penalty could have been sustained under section 6662(e)(1)(B) or (h) on account of the adjustment that could have been made under section 482.

.02 A United States taxpayer described in section 5.02 shall qualify for the treatment provided in this revenue procedure, provided that the taxpayer shall be bound by its election of such treatment.

.03 A United States taxpayer shall not qualify under sections 3.01 or 3.02 for the treatment provided in this revenue procedure if any part of any underpayment of tax by such taxpayer for the taxable year involved in the section 482 allocation is due to fraud.

SECTION 4. ADJUSTMENTS TO BE MADE OR ALLOWED

.01 *Account, interest, currency, and payment.* If a United States taxpayer qualifying under section 3 complies with the requirements of section 5, such taxpayer (or any member of the affiliated group within the meaning of section 1504(a) of the Code in which such taxpayer is included) shall be permitted to establish an interest-bearing account receivable from, or payable to, the related person (being a corporation as defined in section 7701(a)(3) of the Code) from, or to, whom the section 482 allocation is made with respect to a controlled transaction in an amount equal to the primary adjustment for each of the years in which an allocation is made. The account may be established and paid in accordance with this revenue procedure without the Federal income tax consequences of the secondary adjustments that would otherwise result from the primary adjustment. The account shall:

(1) be deemed to have been created as of the last day of the taxpayer's taxable year for which the primary adjustment is made;

(2) bear interest at an arm's length rate, computed in the manner provided in *section 1.482-2(a)(2) of the regulations*, from the day after the date the account is deemed to have been created to the date of payment. For purposes of *section 1.4822(a)(2)(iii)*, where applicable, the account shall be considered to be a loan or advance having a term extending from the day after the date the account is deemed to have been created through the expiration of the 90-day period required in section 5. The interest so computed shall be accrued and included by the obligee in taxable income for each taxable year during which the account is deemed outstanding, regardless of whether the obligee uses the cash receipts and disbursements method of accounting or the accrual method of accounting. The interest so com-

¶20,120

puted shall be accrued and deducted (subject to applicable limitations) by the obligor from taxable income for each taxable year during which the account is deemed outstanding;

(3) be expressed, both as to principal and interest, in the functional currency of a qualified business unit, as defined in *section 1.989(a)-1 of the regulations*, through which the controlled transaction was carried out, if the residence of such qualified business unit, as defined in section 988(a)(3)(B)(ii), is the United States. If the residence of both of the qualified business units through which the controlled transaction was carried out is the United States, then the account shall be expressed, both as to principal and interest, in the functional currency of such U.S. resident qualified business unit of the obligee. If the residence of both of the qualified business units through which the controlled transaction was carried out is a country other than the United States, then the account shall be expressed, both as to principal and interest, in the functional currency of such non-U.S. resident qualified business unit of the corporation that is a domestic corporation, or if both corporations are domestic corporations, or neither corporation is a domestic corporation, then in the functional currency of such non-U.S. resident qualified business unit of the obligee;

(4) be paid within the 90-day period required in section 5, or treated as prepaid by offset prior to that time as provided in section 4.02. Payment within the 90-day period must be in the form of money, a written debt obligation payable at a fixed date and bearing interest at an arm's length rate determined in the manner provided in section *1.482-2(a)(2) of the regulations*, or an accounting entry offsetting such account against an existing bona fide debt between the United States taxpayer (or member of its affiliated group) and the related person. Any such payment within the 90-day period, and any such prepayment prior to that time pursuant to section 4.02, shall be treated as a payment of the account for all Federal income tax purposes, regardless of its characterization under foreign law. For example, to the extent that an account is offset pursuant to section 4.02, by a distribution that would otherwise have constituted a dividend, such distribution shall cease to qualify as a dividend under section 316 of the Code or as a dividend for any Federal income tax purpose; for instance, no foreign tax shall be deemed to have been paid with respect thereto under section 902 of the Code for the purpose of the credit allowed under section 901 of the Code and no dividend received deduction shall be allowed with respect thereto under sections 241 through 247 of the Code. An amount includible in income under section 551 or 951 of the Code shall not be considered a distribution for purposes of this paragraph or section 4.02.

A foreign tax credit shall be allowed for any foreign withholding tax with respect to the repayment of the principal or interest of the account to the extent and subject to the limitations provided under section 901 of the Code. See *Treas. Reg. §§ 1.901-2(e)(5) and 1.904-6(a)(1)(iv)*.

.02 *Offset.* All or part of the interest and principal of an account may be treated as prepaid prior to the beginning of the 90-day period required in section 5 to the extent of an accounting entry offsetting such account against a bona fide debt between the United States taxpayer (or member of its affiliated group) and the related person, or to the extent of any distribution of property or contribution to capital between such parties, where the offsetting entry, the distribution, or the capital contribution occurs during the taxable year in which occurs the execution of the closing agreement on behalf of the Commissioner (in a case under section 5.01), or during the taxable year in which occurs the date on which the United States taxpayer files the return reporting the primary adjustment (in a case under section 5.02), or during the taxable year for which the section 482 allocation is made (in a case under section 5.02, but subject to the provisions stated in the next two sentences). For purposes of this revenue procedure, any offset of the account by reason of such a bona fide debt, distribution, or capital contribution during the taxable year for which the section 482 allocation is made shall be treated as a prepayment of the account made as of the beginning of the day after the date the account is deemed to have been created. No untimely or amended returns will be permitted to claim offset treatment by reason of such a bona fide debt, distribution, or capital contribution during the taxable year for which the section 482 allocation is made.

.03 *Primary adjustment not affected.* A United States taxpayer's election to avail itself of the provisions of this revenue procedure shall in no way affect the primary adjustment under section 482 of the Code. Such election shall, however, affect the taxpayer's taxable income and credits to the extent indicated by section 4.01 and eliminate the collateral effects of secondary adjustments, such as those described in section 2.

SECTION 5. PROCEDURES TO BE FOLLOWED

.01 *Cases pending with the Internal Revenue Service.*

(1) If a United States taxpayer whose taxable income has been adjusted by the Internal Revenue Service pursuant to section 482 of the Code desires to avail itself of the treatment provided in section 4, it must file a request in writing with the Service before closing action is taken on the primary adjustment. For purposes of this revenue procedure, the first occurring of the following shall constitute "closing action":

(a) Execution and acceptance of Form 870-AD, Offer of Waiver of Restrictions on Assessment and Collection of Deficiency in Tax and of Acceptance of Overassessment, or execution of a closing agreement relative to the section 482 allocation;

(b) Stipulation of a section 482 allocation in the Tax Court of the United States;

(c) Expiration of the statute of limitations on assessments for the year to which the allocation applies;

(d) Final determination of tax liability for the year to which the allocation relates by offer-in-compromise, closing agreement, or court action.

(2) The request shall be signed by a person having the authority to sign the United States taxpayer's Federal income tax returns, and shall contain the following:

(a) A statement that the taxpayer desires the treatment provided by section 4 of this revenue procedure and the years for which the treatment is requested;

(b) A description of the arrangements or transactions, or the terms thereof, which gave rise to the primary adjustment;

(c) An offer to enter into a closing agreement under section 7121 of the Code as provided in section 5.014.

(3) The Service will determine whether the United States taxpayer qualifies for the requested treatment and inform the taxpayer of its decision.

(4) If the Service concludes that section 4 of this revenue procedure properly applies, and if the amount of the primary adjustment has been agreed upon, the United States taxpayer will be requested to enter into a closing agreement under section 7121 of the Code, establishing for each year involved:

(a) The amount of the primary adjustment;

(b) The amount and currency of, and parties to, the account which the taxpayer elects to establish under section 4.01;

(c) The amount of the interest on the account includible in income, or deductible, pursuant to section 4.01;

(d) The amount of any foreign tax credit that the taxpayer will claim under section 901 of the Code with respect to payment of the principal or interest on an account established pursuant to section 4.01;

(e) The manner of payment of the account pursuant to sections 4.01 and 4.02 and the taxpayer's right to receive or make such payment free of the Federal income tax consequences of the secondary adjustments that would otherwise result from the primary adjustment, provided the payment of the balance of the account, after taking into consideration any prepayment pursuant to section 4.02 is made within 90 days after execution of the closing agreement on behalf of the Commissioner.

.02 *Cases of a United States taxpayer reporting an adjustment pursuant to section 1.482-1(a)(3) of the regulations.* If a United States taxpayer that has increased or decreased its taxable income pursuant to section 482 and *section 1.482-1(a)(3) of the regulations* desires to avail itself of the treatment provided in section 4, it must file a statement with its Federal income tax return reporting the primary adjustment:

(1) A statement that the taxpayer desires the treatment provided by section 4 of this revenue procedure for the years indicated and acknowledges that it is bound by its election of such treatment;

(2) A description of the arrangements or transactions, or the terms thereof, which gave rise to the primary adjustment;

(3) The amount of the primary adjustment;

(4) The amount and nature of any correlative allocation to each related person from, or to, whom the section 482 allocation is made with respect to a controlled transaction, and the corresponding account and treatment thereof by each such related person that is consistent with the treatment applied under this revenue procedure;

¶20,120

(5) The amount and currency of, and parties to, the account which the taxpayer elects to establish under section 4.01;

(6) The amount of interest on the account includible in income, or deductible, pursuant to section 4.01 and the years of such inclusion or deduction;

(7) The amount of any foreign tax credit that the taxpayer will claim under section 901 of the Code with respect to payment of the principal or interest on an account established pursuant to section 4.01;

(8) The manner of payment of the account pursuant to sections 4.01 and 4.02, which shall be free of the Federal income tax consequences of the secondary adjustments that would otherwise result from the primary adjustment, provided the payment of the balance of the account, after taking into consideration any prepayment pursuant to section 4.02, is made within 90 days of the date on which the taxpayer files the return reporting the primary adjustment, and a statement that any such payment within the 90-day period, and any such prepayment prior to that time, shall be treated as a payment of the account for all Federal income tax purposes, regardless of its characterization under foreign law.

.03 *Cases pending before the Tax Court of the United States.* If a case reaches trial status in the Tax Court and it is determined that the United States taxpayer is entitled to the treatment provided in section 4, the parties may stipulate or otherwise arrange with the Court so that any adjustment in tax for the years before the Court will reflect the application of section 4, provided the taxpayer executes the required closing agreement.

.04 *Cases within the jurisdiction of the Department of Justice.* If a United States taxpayer files with the Service a request for treatment under section 4, with respect to a case within the jurisdiction of the Department of Justice, the Service, through its Chief Counsel, will recommend to the Department of Justice the action to be taken with respect to the taxpayer's request.

SECTION 6. EFFECTIVE DATE

.01 *In general.* This revenue procedure is effective for taxable years beginning after August 23, 1999.

.02 *Election for taxable year including August 23, 1999.* A United States taxpayer may elect to apply all of the provisions of this revenue procedure on its U.S. income tax return for its taxable year including August 23, 1999.

.03 *Taxpayer-initiated adjustments for taxable years prior to the taxable year including August 23, 1999.* A United States taxpayer that increased or decreased its taxable income pursuant to section 482 and *section 1.482-1(a)(3)* for a taxable year prior to the taxable year including August 23, 1999, shall be permitted to apply the principles of Rev. Proc. 65-17, 1965-1 C.B. 833, and its progeny, in accordance with any reasonable interpretation thereof for purposes of conforming accounts to reflect the taxpayer-initiated primary adjustment. The Service considers an interpretation that applies the final revised revenue procedure published in this document or its general principles to be such a reasonable interpretation of Rev. Proc. 65-17.

SECTION 7. EFFECT ON OTHER DOCUMENTS

Rev. Proc. 65-17, 1965-1 C.B. 833, as amended by Rev. Proc. 65-17 (Amend. I), 1966-2 C.B. 1211 and Rev. Proc. 65-17 (Amend. II), 1974-1 C.B. 411, is superseded. Rev. Proc. 65-31, 1965-2 C.B. 1024, Rev. Proc. 70-23, 1970-2 C.B. 505, Rev. Proc. 71-35, 1971-2 C.B. 573, Rev. Proc. 72-22, 1972-1 C.B. 747, Rev. Proc. 7246, 1972-2 C.B. 827, Rev. Proc. 72-48, 1972-2 C.B. 829, Rev. Proc. 72-53, 1972-2 C.B. 833 and Rev. Rul. 82-80, 1982-1 C.B. 89, are superseded. The references to Rev. Proc. 65-17 in Rev. Proc. 68-16, 1968-1 C.B. 770, Rev. Proc. 89-8, 1989-1 C.B. 778, Rev. Proc. 96-13, 1996-1 C.B. 616, Rev. Proc. 96-14, 1996-1 C.B. 626, and Rev. Proc. 96-53, 1996-2 C.B. 375, shall be treated as references to this revenue procedure.

SECTION 8. DRAFTING INFORMATION

The principal author of this Revenue Procedure is J. Peter Luedtke of the Office of the Associate Chief Counsel (International). For further information on this revenue procedure, contact J. Peter Luedtke at 202-874-1490 (not a toll-free call) or write to CC:INTL:Br6, Room 3319, 950 L'Enfant Plaza South, S.W., Washington, D.C. 20024.

SECTION 9. PAPERWORK REDUCTION ACT

The collections of information contained in this revenue procedure have been reviewed and approved by the Office of Management and Budget in accordance with the Paperwork Reduction Act (44 U.S.C. 3507) under control number 1545-1657.

An agency may not conduct or sponsor, and a person is not required to respond to, a collection of information unless the collection of information displays a valid OMB control number.

The collection of information in this revenue procedure is in section 5. This information is required to determine whether a United States taxpayer that has made a primary adjustment under section 482 of the Code will be permitted to make certain adjustments to conform their accounts to reflect the section 482 allocation. The collections of information are required for a United States taxpayer to obtain the Commissioner's permission to repatriate the cash attributable to a primary adjustment via an account without the Federal income tax consequences of the secondary adjustments that would otherwise result from the primary adjustment. The likely respondents are businesses or other for-profit institutions.

The estimated total annual reporting and/or recordkeeping burden is 1,620 hours.

The estimated annual burden per respondent/recordkeeper varies from 8 hours to 10 hours depending on individual circumstances, with an estimated average of 9 hours. The estimated number of respondents and/or recordkeepers is 180.

The estimated annual frequency of responses is on occasion.

Books or records relating to a collection of information must be retained as long as their contents may become material in the administration of any internal revenue law. Generally, tax returns and tax return information are confidential, as required by 26 U.S.C. 6103.

¶20,120

¶ 20,130 Revenue Procedure 2006-9[3]

The IRS has issued updated procedures for taxpayers to use to request an advance pricing agreement (APA) from the APA program. The APA program is voluntary, and provides for resolution of transfer pricing issues under Code Sec. 482 and relevant treaties. The IRS recommends the use of prefiling conferences, whether identifying the taxpayers or on an anonymous basis. A list of documents and other items that must accompany proposed APAs, as well as general principles regarding APA submissions, are provided. The guidance also describes the processing of APA requests for both bilateral and multilateral APAs and for unilateral APAs, special provisions available to small business taxpayers, and the administration of an APA, including adjustments, examinations, revisions, record retention requirements, renewals and revocations/cancellations. The guidance applies to all APA requests received on or after February 1, 2006. Rev. Proc. 2004-40, 2004-2 CB 50, is superseded.

Rev. Proc. 2006-9, I.R.B. 2006-2, December 19, 2005.

SECTION 1: PURPOSE

.01 This revenue procedure explains the manner in which taxpayers may request an advance pricing agreement ("APA") from the APA Program within the Office of the Associate Chief Counsel (International), the manner in which such a request will be processed by the APA Program, and the effect and administration of APAs. This revenue procedure updates and supersedes Revenue Procedure 2004-40, 2004-2 C.B. 50.

SECTION 2: PRINCIPLES OF THE APA PROGRAM

.01 The APA Program provides a voluntary process whereby the Internal Revenue Service ("Service") and taxpayers may resolve transfer pricing issues under § 482 of the Internal Revenue Code ("Code"), the Income Tax Regulations ("the regulations") thereunder, and relevant income tax treaties to which the United States is a party in a principled and cooperative manner on a prospective basis. The APA process increases the efficiency of tax administration by encouraging taxpayers to come forward and present to the Service all the facts relevant to a proper transfer pricing analysis and to work towards a mutual agreement in a spirit of openness and cooperation. The prospective nature of APAs lessens the burden of compliance by giving taxpayers greater certainty regarding their transfer pricing methods, and promotes the principled resolution of these issues by allowing for their discussion and resolution in advance before the consequences of such resolution are fully known to taxpayers and the Service.

.02 The APA Program's central goal is the prompt, proper, and fair resolution of APA requests and renewals consistent with the principles of sound tax administration.

---

[3] Rev. Proc. 2006-9, IRB 2006-2, 278, December 19, 2005.

.03 The APA Program reserves the right not to accept an APA request or to terminate consideration of an APA request if the request or the continued development of the case is contrary to the principles of sound tax administration.

.04 An APA is an agreement between a taxpayer and the Service in which the parties set forth, in advance of controlled transactions, the best transfer pricing method ("TPM") within the meaning of § 482 of the Code and the regulations. The agreement specifies the controlled transactions or transfers ("covered transactions"), TPM, APA term, operational and compliance provisions, appropriate adjustments, critical assumptions regarding future events, required APA records, and annual reporting responsibilities.

(1) APAs are intended to supplement traditional administrative, judicial, and treaty mechanisms for resolving transfer pricing issues.

(2) Taxpayers formally initiate the process for APAs. Thereafter, APAs require discussions among the taxpayer, one or more associated enterprises, and one or more tax administrations, including the Service.

(3) Ordinarily, an APA is reached only on the proposed covered transactions. In some cases, however, the APA Program may require that the scope of the proposed covered transactions be expanded or contracted, or may determine that the TPM proposed by the taxpayer is not appropriate for some subset of the proposed covered transactions.

.05 The taxpayer's participation in the APA process is entirely voluntary. In some cases, the Service may approach a taxpayer to discuss the advantages of an APA.

.06 The APA Program is under the immediate supervision of a Director (the "APA Director") within the Office of the Associate Chief Counsel (International). The APA Director reports to the Associate Chief Counsel (International) who exercises general oversight over the APA Program. The APA Director, directly or by delegation, may take any action - not contrary to statute, regulation, or treaty - necessary to carry out the provisions of this revenue procedure. The APA Director may modify the provisions contained in this revenue procedure (for example, time limits or content of an APA request) if that modification would be consistent with sound tax administration.

.07 Under the APA request procedure, the taxpayer proposes a TPM and provides data intended to show that the TPM constitutes the appropriate application of the best method rule under the § 482 regulations. The Service, through an APA Team, evaluates the APA request by analyzing all relevant data and information submitted with the initial request and at any time thereafter.

.08 Taxpayers may request a bilateral, multilateral, or, if appropriate, a unilateral APA. A bilateral or multilateral APA involves a request for an APA between the taxpayer and the Service, accompanied by a request for a mutual agreement between relevant competent authorities. A unilateral APA involves only an agreement between the taxpayer and the Service. Where possible, in the interest of sound tax administration and to ensure that no potential for double taxation results from an APA, an APA should be concluded on a bilateral or multilateral basis

¶20,130

between the competent authorities through the mutual agreement procedure of the relevant income tax treaty or treaties.

.09 The APA Policy Board establishes policy on matters of substantial genuine importance pertaining to the APA Program. It consists of the Associate Chief Counsel (International), the APA Director, the Director, International (Large and Mid-Size Business (LMSB) Operating Division), Treasury's International Tax Counsel, and other senior officials.

.10 In a bilateral or multilateral case, the APA Program prepares a recommended negotiating position for the U.S. Competent Authority. The negotiating position serves as a basis for discussions with the relevant foreign competent authority or authorities under the mutual agreement article of the applicable income tax treaty or treaties. Prior to finalizing its recommendation, the APA Program, through the Team Leader (see section 6.03), conveys the substance of the APA Team's position to the taxpayer to provide an opportunity for the taxpayer to comment. The Team Leader, in coordination with other members of the APA Team, considers the merits of the taxpayer's timely received comments in finalizing the recommended position.

.11 If the U.S. Competent Authority and the relevant foreign competent authority or authorities reach a mutual agreement, the taxpayer and the Service may execute one or more APAs consistent with that mutual agreement.

.12 In appropriate cases, the TPM may be applied to tax years prior to those covered by the APA ("rollback" of the TPM, see section 8). The Service's policy is to use rollbacks whenever feasible based on the consistency of the facts, law, and available records for the prior years. This policy does not apply to unilateral APA requests in which a rollback would decrease taxable income on a return filed for a taxable year not covered by the APA (see *§ 1.482-1(a)(3)*).

.13 Filing an APA request does not suspend any examination or other enforcement proceedings. The APA Program will coordinate its activities with those of other Service proceedings to avoid duplicative information requests to the taxpayer, enhance the efficiency of Service operations, and reduce overall taxpayer compliance burdens.

SECTION 3: PREFILING CONFERENCES

.01 General Principles

A taxpayer may request a prefiling conference ("PFC") with the APA Program to discuss informally the suitability of an APA.

.02 Discussion Topics

The taxpayer may use a PFC to clarify what information, documentation, and analyses are likely to be necessary for the Service to consider an APA request. Among the areas of discussion are the covered transactions, the potentially applicable TPMs, the probability of agreement among the competent authorities, and the APA Program's schedule and method for coordinating and evaluating the request. To provide for the efficient use of taxpayer resources, PFCs are recommended in order to ensure that the APA request is appropriate and focuses on relevant issues.

.03 Scheduling

A taxpayer or its representative may contact the APA Program Office in Washington, D.C. or California to schedule a PFC. The taxpayer or its representative should propose three alternative dates, and should generally allow two weeks before the first proposed date. The telephone and facsimile numbers are:

	Washington, DC	California
Voice:	(202) 435-5220	(949) 360-3486
Facsimile:	(202) 435-5238	(949) 360-3446

.04 PFC May be Named or Anonymous

The taxpayer may request a PFC either on an identified or anonymous basis.

.05 Participation

If a taxpayer identifies itself, representatives of the Service Operating Division with responsibility for the taxpayer's return normally will participate in the PFC. Representatives from Appeals and the Division Counsel field offices may also attend. In the case of a PFC regarding a bilateral APA request, a Competent Authority analyst may attend. If a taxpayer initially requests a PFC on an anonymous basis but prior to the meeting chooses to identify itself, the meeting may be rescheduled to permit necessary Service personnel to attend. When requesting a PFC on an identified basis, the taxpayer must inform the APA Program whether transactions similar or related to those to be covered by the proposed APA are currently under consideration by a Service Operating Division, an Appeals Office, a Division Counsel, or an Associate Chief Counsel.

.06 Prefiling Submission

A taxpayer must send a brief prefiling submission to the relevant APA Program Office in Washington, D.C. or California that lists the persons attending the PFC for the taxpayer (first names only or job titles are sufficient if the PFC will be on an anonymous basis) and that outlines and describes the issues to be discussed. This brief submission should be provided at least one week in advance of the PFC. If the document is twenty pages or less, it may be sent by facsimile; but if it exceeds twenty pages, eight copies (or if anonymous, only three copies) and one original should be delivered.

SECTION 4: CONTENT OF APA REQUESTS

.01 Introduction

A complete APA request is essential to a timely and efficient APA process. In the APA Program's experience, a complete APA request may save many months of case processing time and hundreds of hours of labor, as it allows the APA Team to narrow its focus immediately to the core issue or issues and avoids delays caused by the need to supplement the original APA request. The goal of completing a unilateral APA or a recommended negotiating position within 12 months (see

¶20,130

section 6.01) is predicated in large part on the assumption that the taxpayer has submitted a complete APA request.

A complete APA request should provide the information specified below and all other information reasonably necessary to permit the APA Program to evaluate fully the taxpayer's proposed TPM. The level of detail required will depend on the particular facts and circumstances of each case and should be governed by relevancy and materiality considerations (keeping in mind that the request should provide enough information to allow the reader to concur that a matter is not relevant or material). The detailed information supporting the APA request should be tailored to the specific facts relating to the taxpayer, the proposed covered transactions, and relevant legal authority. It should also take into account discussions with the APA Program in any PFC.

An APA request will normally be considered not "substantially complete" for purposes of sections 4.08, 4.13, 6.01, and 6.03 unless the request contains the information required below (as may be modified by agreement of the parties).

.02 General Principles

(1) For purposes of requesting an APA, each taxpayer that is a member of a consolidated group (as defined in *Treasury Regulations § 1.1502-1* must comply with the provisions of *§ 1.1502-77.*

(2) All materials submitted with the APA request become part of the APA Program's case file and will not be returned. Therefore, taxpayers should not submit original documents.

(3) The taxpayer must submit copies of any documents relating to the proposed TPM. All materials submitted must be properly labeled, indexed, and referenced in the request. Any previously submitted documents that the taxpayer wishes to associate with the request must be referenced.

(4) If the records or documents to be submitted are too voluminous for transmittal with the request, the taxpayer must describe the contents of such items in the request and confirm that the items will promptly be made available upon request.

(5) All documents submitted in a foreign language must be accompanied by an accurate English translation.

(6) All documents in the APA request that are available in electronic format should be submitted, on either a CD-ROM or diskette, along with the paper submission. Suitable formats include Microsoft Word, Excel, PowerPoint, and Adobe Portable Document Format. Other formats may be arranged on a case-by-case basis.

.03 Factual, Legal, and Analytical Items for All Proposed APAs

Unless otherwise agreed, each APA request must include an appropriate discussion of the items set forth below.

(1) A comprehensive table of contents.

(2) The names, addresses, telephone and facsimile numbers, taxpayer identification numbers (if applicable), and both the Standard Industrial Classification (SIC) and the North American Industry Classification System (NAICS) codes reported on the most recently filed federal tax returns (if applicable) of (a) the organizations, trades, and businesses engaging in the proposed covered transactions, and (b) the controlling taxpayer of the parties, if the controlling taxpayer is not itself engaging in the proposed covered transactions.

(3) The controlling taxpayer's industry (for example, Heavy Manufacturing and Transportation) within LMSB; or if the taxpayer files its tax returns with the Small Business/Self-Employed (SB/SE) Operating Division, a statement to that effect.

(4) A properly completed Form 2848 (Power of Attorney and Declaration of Representative) for any person authorized to represent the taxpayer in connection with the request, disregarding if appropriate the line 3 instruction limiting the authorization to three future tax periods. If the taxpayer or the taxpayer's authorized representative retains any other person (for example, a law firm, accounting firm, or economic consulting firm) to assist the taxpayer in pursuing the APA request, the taxpayer must also provide a separate written authorization for disclosures to the person and such person's employees during the APA Program's consideration of the request, according to the instructions in § 301.6103(c)-1T (see also T.D. 9011, 31 C.F.R. Part 10 (July 26, 2002)). Such written authorization may be made by completing Form 8821 (Tax Information Authorization), disregarding, if appropriate, the line 3 instruction limiting the authorization to three future tax periods.

(5) A description of the general history of business operations, worldwide organizational structure, ownership, capitalization, financial arrangements, principal businesses, the place or places where such businesses are conducted, and major transaction flows of the parties to the proposed covered transactions. The description must also identify any branches or entities disregarded for tax purposes (see § 301.7701-3) that are involved in the proposed covered transactions.

(6) A description and analysis of the transactions covered by the APA request, as well as the estimated dollar value of each proposed covered transaction for each year of the proposed term of the APA. The discussion must also describe how the proposed covered transactions relate to other controlled transactions that the taxpayer does not propose to cover.

(7) A statement addressing the extent to which the tested party has transactions involving commission sales and ordinary distribution sales (i.e., buying and reselling). If the APA request involves both kinds of transactions, the taxpayer must propose a TPM and analyze the extent to which it is appropriate under the facts and circumstances to (a) test both kinds of transactions on an aggregated basis; (b) test the two kinds of transactions separately; or (c) exclude one of the two kinds of transactions from the APA.

(8) For each party to the proposed covered transactions, a detailed analysis of:

(a) the functions and economic activities performed;

¶20,130

   (b) the assets employed;

   (c) the economic costs incurred;

   (d) the risks assumed;

   (e) relevant contractual terms;

   (f) relevant economic conditions; and

   (g) relevant non-recognition transactions.

(9) Copies of the principal written agreement(s), if any, setting forth the contractual terms for the covered transactions (within the meaning of *§ 1.482-1(d)(3)(ii)*, including without limitation the form of consideration charged or paid); and an explanation of any significant discrepancy between the applicable written agreement(s) and the economic substance of the covered transactions (including payment form) to date and as proposed for the APA.

(10) Representative financial and tax data of the parties to the proposed covered transactions for the last three taxable years (or more years if relevant to the proposed TPM), together with other pertinent data and documents in support of the TPM. This item may include (but need not be limited to) data from the following:

   (a) Form 5471 (Information Return of U.S. Persons With Respect to Certain Foreign Corporations);

   (b) Form 5472 (Information Return of a 25% Foreign-Owned U.S. Corporation or a Foreign Corporation Engaged in a U.S. Trade or Business);

   (c) income tax returns;

   (d) financial statements;

   (e) annual reports to stockholders;

   (f) other pertinent U.S. and foreign government filings (for example, customs reports or SEC filings);

   (g) existing pricing, distribution, or licensing agreements;

   (h) marketing and financial studies;

   (i) documentation prepared in consideration of § 6662(e); and

   (j) company-wide accounting procedures, budgets, projections, business plans, and worldwide product line or business segment profitability reports.

(11) The functional currency of the parties to the proposed covered transactions and their respective foreign currency exchange risks.

(12) The taxable year of each party to the proposed covered transactions.

(13) A description of significant financial accounting methods employed by the parties that have a bearing on any proposed TPM.

(14) An explanation of any relevant financial and tax accounting differences between the U.S. and the foreign countries.

¶20,130

(15) A discussion of any relevant statutory provisions, tax treaties, court decisions, regulations, revenue rulings, or revenue procedures that relate to the appropriateness of the proposed TPM for the requested APA. For cases in which the taxpayer requests a rollback, the discussion should state whether the period of limitations for the rollback years has expired in the U.S. or in foreign countries, and if not, when the periods of limitations do expire.

(16) (a) A statement describing all previous and current issues at the examination, Appeals, judicial, or competent authority levels that relate to the proposed TPM, including an explanation of the taxpayer's and the government's positions and any resolution of the issues.

(b) If the taxpayer is requesting a rollback that involves any issues relevant to the proposed covered transactions that are unresolved and still under consideration by Appeals, the taxpayer must include with its APA request a waiver of its right to be present during communications between the Appeals Office and the APA Team members (as described in section 6.04). See Rev. Proc. 2000-43, 2000-2 C.B. 404. The following language satisfies this requirement:

Waiver of Ex Parte Communication: [Name of taxpayer(s)] agrees to the participation of the Appeals Office in the consideration of this APA request, and hereby waives its right to be present during, or participate in, communications related to the APA request or the proposed covered transactions between the Appeals Office and the APA Team members.

(17) A statement describing any APAs with, or rulings by, foreign tax authorities relating to the proposed covered transactions (or any pending requests for such APAs or rulings) and, if requested, copies of such APAs or rulings.

(18) An economic analysis or study of the general industry pricing practices and economic functions performed within the markets and geographical areas covered by the APA request.

(19) A list of the taxpayer's competitors and a discussion of any uncontrolled transactions, lines of business or types of businesses comparable or similar to those addressed in the request.

(20) An explanation of the proposed TPMs, including any method used to convert results from one payment form to another (e.g., to convert from a lump sum to a contingent payment such as a sales-based royalty), and an analysis of why each proposed TPM is the best method within the meaning of § 1.482-1(c).

(21) A detailed presentation of the research efforts and criteria used to identify and select possible independent comparables. This presentation should include a list of potential comparables and an explanation of why each was either accepted or rejected. The taxpayer may request an APA even though no comparable uncontrolled prices, transactions, or companies can be identified. In such cases, a taxpayer must demonstrate that the proposed TPM otherwise satisfies the requirements of § 482 and this revenue procedure.

(22) Detailed financial data (and licenses or other agreements, if applicable) on the selected independent comparables in print and electronic formats. For example,

if the proposed TPM uses the comparable uncontrolled price (CUP) method, the comparable pricing information should be included; if the TPM uses the comparable uncontrolled transaction (CUT) method, the comparable license agreements should be included; and if the TPM uses the comparable profits method (CPM), the annual and multiple year period results using the selected profit level indicator should be included. If pertinent, the taxpayer should demonstrate consideration of alternative measurements of profitability and return on investment (for example, gross profit margin or markup, ratio of gross income to total operating expenses, net operating profit margin, or return on assets).

(23) A detailed explanation of any adjustments to the selected comparables, such as: accounting for product line segregations; differences in accounting practices; differences relating to functions, assets employed, risks assumed, and costs incurred; volume or scale differences; and differing economic and market conditions.

(24) An illustration of the application of each proposed TPM by applying the TPM, in a consistent format, to the prior three taxable years' financial and tax data of the parties to the covered transactions. If historical data cannot be used to illustrate a TPM (for example, when the TPM applies to a new product or business), the request should include an illustration based on projected or hypothetical data, as well as a description of the source of the data. If coverage of three taxable years is inappropriate for any reason, the taxpayer should provide data for an appropriate period and explain why the period was chosen.

.04 Specific Items for a Cost Sharing Arrangement

In addition to the items in section 4.03, an APA request related to a cost sharing arrangement ("CSA") must include:

(1) A copy of (a) the documents forming or revising the CSA, (b) the documents relevant to the making available of any pre-existing intangible property to the CSA), including the documents relevant to the acquisition or licensing of any pre-existing intangible property that is made available to the CSA, for purposes of research in the intangible development area, and (c) a statement that the CSA conforms to the requirements of § 1.482-7(b).

(2) A specific description of intangible development costs for all participants under the CSA. Such description should include a description of the costs included and excluded (for example, costs of technology acquired from third parties; the treatment of stock-based compensation under the CSA; non-product specific development costs; costs associated with abandoned projects; costs associated with specific stages of product development; relevant labor, material, and overhead costs; and support and administrative costs); a description of any services performed for participants that will be included in intangible development costs (for example, contract research) and how those services would be taken into account; and, for a representative period, a breakdown of total costs incurred, and the costs borne by each participant, according to the CSA.

¶20,130

(3) The basis (as described in *§ 1.482-7(f) (3) (ii)*) used to measure anticipated benefits, the projections used to estimate benefits, and why such basis and projections yield the most reliable estimate of reasonably anticipated benefits.

(4) The method used to calculate each participant's share of intangible development costs; the reason why that method can reasonably be expected to reflect that participant's share of anticipated benefits; and a statement of the circumstances under which the participants' shares of intangible development costs will be adjusted to account for changes in economic conditions, business operations and practices, and the ongoing development of intangibles under the CSA.

(5) The accounting method used to determine the costs and benefits of the intangible development (including the method used to translate foreign currencies).

(6) Each participant's sales, cost of sales, operating expenses, research and development costs, and operating profit (historical for the five most recently completed taxable years and projected for two taxable years) for the product area covered by the CSA.

(7) A description of any amounts to be received from non-participants for the use of covered intangibles (for example, as a royalty pursuant to a license agreement) and how the participants would take into account such amounts.

(8) Representative internal manuals, directives, guidelines, and similar documents prepared for purposes of implementing or operating the CSA (for example, research and development committee meeting minutes, market studies, economic impact analyses, capital expenditure budgets, engineering studies, reports and studies of trends and profitability in the industry, and financial analyses for financing and cash flow purposes).

(9) A description of any prior research undertaken in the intangible development area; the identification of any pre-existing intangible property made available to the CSA; the amount of any buy-in or buy-out payment (as defined in *§ 1.482-7(g) (2)*); a complete economic analysis to support the payment; the form of the payment, the method used to determine the amount of the payment (that is, the method used to value the pre-existing intangible property and to calculate any royalty, lump sum, or installment payments, including, if applicable, any conversion between different payment forms); and an explanation of any discrepancy between the proposed payment form and the payment form established in the documents listed in paragraph (1) above (see section 4.03(9)); and an analysis demonstrating that the method used constitutes the best method under *§ 1.482-1(c)*.

(10) The treatment of cost sharing and buy-in or buy-out payments for U.S. income tax purposes (for example, the source and character of those payments).

(11) Evidence of the participants' compliance with the reporting requirements under *§ 1.482-7(j)* of the cost sharing regulations.

(12) For taxpayers requesting an APA that covers a CSA but does not cover the related buy-in transaction, or an APA that covers a buy-in transaction but does not cover the related CSA, the reasons why an APA limited in this manner is consistent

¶20,130

with the principles of the APA process, as set forth in this revenue procedure. The APA Program will evaluate the requests to ensure their consistency with the principles of this revenue procedure and sound tax administration. If an APA request is limited to covering only buy-in payments, the APA must include a representation by the taxpayer, as a term and condition of the APA, that the CSA to which the buy-in payments relate meets the § 482 regulatory requirements for CSAs.

.05 Critical Assumptions

The taxpayer should propose and describe any relevant critical assumptions. A critical assumption is any fact the continued existence of which is material to the taxpayer's proposed TPM, whether related to the taxpayer, a third party, an industry, or business and economic conditions. Critical assumptions might include, for example, a particular mode of conducting business operations, a particular corporate or business structure, a range of expected business volume, or the relative value of foreign currencies.

.06 Contents of Annual Report

Section 11.01 provides that the taxpayer must file an annual report for each taxable year covered by the APA. The taxpayer should propose in the request a list of items to be included in each report. Consideration should be given to all items listed in Appendix C to the APA Program's current Model APA.

.07 Term and First Year of APA

(1) The taxpayer must propose a term for the APA appropriate to the industry, products, and transactions involved. Although the appropriate APA term is determined on a case-by-case basis, a request for an APA should propose an APA term of at least five years unless the taxpayer states a compelling reason for a shorter term. Additionally, the APA Program strives to have at least three prospective years remaining in the term upon the execution of an APA (in the case of a unilateral APA) or completion of the APA Program's recommended negotiating position for Competent Authority (in the case of a bilateral or multilateral APA), except in unusual circumstances. Accordingly, taxpayers should anticipate that the APA Program may require their agreement to extend the proposed term of an APA if necessary to ensure such prospectivity.

(2) The taxpayer must file its APA request within the time prescribed by statute (including extensions) for filing its Federal income tax return for the first proposed APA year. If the taxpayer receives an extension to file its Federal income tax return, it must file its APA request no later than the actual filing date of the return. An APA request will be considered filed on the date the required user fee is paid (within the meaning of § 7502(a)), provided that a substantially complete APA request is filed with the APA Program within 120 days of the return due date (including extensions) for the first proposed APA year. Because of the need to begin the processing of the APA request in a manner that ensures appropriate prospectivity, the APA Director will consider extending the 120-day period pursuant to section 2.06 only in unusual circumstances. If the APA Program's evaluation of an APA request is delayed due to a lack of responsiveness or timeliness by the

taxpayer subsequent to the filing of its request, the APA Director may deem the taxpayer's APA request to have been filed for purposes of this paragraph on a date subsequent to its actual filing.

.08 Request for Competent Authority Consideration

(1) The taxpayer must state whether any of the parties to the proposed covered transactions are residents of or conduct activities in a treaty partner country or U.S. possession, and whether the taxpayer proposes an agreement among competent authorities (see section 7 for guidelines). For purposes of this revenue procedure, "competent authority" includes the Director, International (LMSB) and designated foreign competent authorities under income tax treaties to which the U.S. is a party, and also includes the Director, International (LMSB) acting as the U.S. Competent Authority with respect to a possession tax agency described in Rev. Proc. 89-8 1989-1 C.B. 778, as well as a designated possession tax official within the meaning of that revenue procedure.

(2) If the APA request is unilateral and involves transactions with an entity in a treaty jurisdiction, the taxpayer must provide an explanation of why the request is not bilateral. See sections 2.08 and 7.06.

(3) If the taxpayer requests a bilateral or multilateral APA, the taxpayer's request must include the information described in section 4.05(a) and (b) and, in a separate document, section 4.05(n), of Rev. Proc. 2002-52, 2002-2 C.B. 242 (or its successor), or similar information pursuant to a request for relief under Rev. Proc. 89-8. The following wording satisfies section 4.05(n) of Rev. Proc. 2002-52:

[Name of taxpayer(s)]consents to the disclosure to the competent authority of [name of foreign country]and the competent authority's staff of any or all of the items of information set forth or enclosed in the [bilateral/multilateral]APA request for the taxable year(s) _____ [and accompanying rollback request for relief from economic double taxation of income for the taxable years _____], and any further submissions, within the limits contained in the [name of treaty].

.09 Perjury Statement

(1) The taxpayer must include in any APA request and supplemental submission a declaration in the following form:

Under penalties of perjury, I declare that I have examined this [APA request] [supplemental submission relating to this APA request] including accompanying documents, and, to the best of my knowledge and belief, the [APA request] [supplemental submission]contains all the relevant facts relating to the [APA request] [supplemental submission], and such facts are true, correct, and complete.

(2) The declaration must be signed by the person or persons on whose behalf the request is being made and not by the taxpayer's representative. The person signing for a corporate taxpayer must be an authorized officer of the taxpayer who has personal knowledge of the facts, whose duties are not limited to obtaining letter rulings or determination letters from the Service, or negotiating APAs, and who is authorized to sign the taxpayer's income tax return pursuant to § 6062. The person

¶20,130

signing for any non-corporate taxpayer must be an individual who has personal knowledge of the facts, and who is authorized to sign in accordance with §§ 6061 or 6063, as applicable.

.10 Signatures

The taxpayer or the taxpayer's authorized representative must sign the APA request. If an authorized representative is to sign, the taxpayer and representative must satisfy the relevant instructions on signatures in Rev. Proc. 2005-1, 2005-1 I.R.B. 1 (or its successor).

.11 Mailing, Deliveries, Copies, and Office Location

(1) User fees (accompanied by an identifying cover letter that includes a justification of the fee amount) must be sent to:

Internal Revenue Service

> Attn: CC:PA:LPD:DRU
> P.O. Box 7604
> Ben Franklin Station
> Washington, D.C. 20044

The fee payment may also be hand delivered to the drop box at the 12th Street entrance of 1111 Constitution Avenue, N.W., Washington, DC.

(2) All other communications must be mailed or delivered as follows to (unless arranged otherwise, for example, mailing to the California office):

Office of Associate Chief Counsel (International)

> Advance Pricing Agreement Program
> Attn: CC:INTL:APA; MA2-266
> 1111 Constitution Avenue, N.W.
> Washington, D.C. 20224

(3) The taxpayer must provide the original and eight copies of its APA request and any supplemental materials submitted while the request is pending.

(4) The APA Program is located at:

> 799 9th Street, N.W.
> Washington, D.C. 20001

.12 User Fees

(1) A separate user fee is required for each APA request. For this purpose, an APA request means a substantially complete and timely-filed APA submission, as required by section 4, and includes all such APA submissions filed by the taxpayer within any single sixty-day period. The taxpayer, for purposes of the preceding sentence, includes all members of a controlled group as defined in *Treasury Regulations § 1.482-1(i)(6)*.

(2) User fees shall be made payable to the United States Treasury.

(3) Except as provided in paragraphs (4), (5), and (7), the user fee for an APA request is $50,000.

(4) Except as provided in paragraph (5), the user fee for an APA renewal request is $35,000. For this purpose, an APA request will be considered an APA renewal request if its subject matter is substantially the same as in a previous APA request by the taxpayer.

(5) The user fee for a small business APA request is $22,500. For this purpose, an APA request will be considered a small business APA request if the taxpayer has gross income of less than $200 million or the aggregate value of the covered transactions does not exceed (i) $50 million annually, and (ii) $10 million annually with respect to covered transactions involving intangible property.

(6) For purposes of paragraph 5, the gross income of a taxpayer includes the gross income of all organizations, trades, or businesses owned or controlled directly or indirectly by the same interests controlling the taxpayer. Gross income must be computed for the last full (12-month) taxable year ending before the date the taxpayer filed the APA request. If the information on the taxpayer's gross income for the last full taxable year is not available, the taxpayer must use its projected gross income for the first twelve months of the APA term.

(7) The user fee to amend an APA request or to amend a completed APA is $10,000. For this purpose, a request to amend will be deemed to occur if a taxpayer requests changes to an APA request or to a completed APA that requires substantial additional work by the APA Team. Generally, no user fee will be imposed if substantial changes are requested by the Service or by a foreign competent authority.

(8) The APA Director may require a corrected user fee after submission of an APA request if the request does not meet the criteria for the user fee amount initially paid by the taxpayer. The taxpayer may either pay the corrected fee and continue the APA process or withdraw the request.

SECTION 5: TAXPAYER DISCLOSURE OBLIGATIONS

.01 Any information submitted by a taxpayer in connection with its APA request must be true, correct, and accurate (see section 4.09). If the APA Program determines that it needs additional information to analyze the APA request, the APA Program may require the taxpayer to provide such information.

.02 A taxpayer has an obligation to update on a timely basis all material facts and information that it submits in connection with its APA request. In addition, while an APA request is pending and after an APA is executed, a taxpayer is under a continuing duty to timely supplement its disclosures if the taxpayer discovers that information that it provided in connection with an APA request was false, incorrect, or incomplete in some material respect. If a taxpayer discovers such an error or omission after the APA is executed, the taxpayer must disclose the error or omission in its next-filed annual report (see section 11.01(1)).

.03 While the APA request is pending, the taxpayer should be prepared to update the financial data for the selected comparables as new or revised data become available.

¶20,130

.04 If a taxable year is completed while the APA request is pending, the taxpayer should be prepared to update its APA submission following the close of the taxable year by demonstrating the application of the proposed TPM to the taxpayer's actual financial results for that year.

.05 Failure by a taxpayer to provide all materials required by this revenue procedure in its APA request (see section 4), or requested by the APA Program while the request is pending, can cause significant delays in case processing and may result in rejection of the APA under section 6.10.

SECTION 6: PROCESSING OF APA REQUESTS

.01 General

The processing of an APA request follows one of two paths, depending on whether the request is for a bilateral or multilateral APA, or for a unilateral APA. The scheduling of due diligence, analysis, discussion, agreement, and drafting is designed to complete the recommended U.S. negotiating position (bilateral or multilateral APA request), or a unilateral APA, within 12 months from the date the full request was filed. The filing of a full APA request includes not only the payment of a user fee, but also the receipt by the APA Program of the materials specified in sections 4.02 through 4.10. Significant analysis of the APA request will not begin until a substantially complete request has been filed.

.02 Initial Contact

After receiving an APA request, a representative of the APA Program will contact the taxpayer or its representative to discuss any preliminary questions the APA Program may have, or to ask for any additional information or documents necessary in order to initiate processing of the request. The taxpayer must supply the additional information and documents, accompanied by the perjury statement described in section 4.09, by the date specified by the APA Program, as extended for good cause.

.03 Designation of Team Leader

Upon the receipt of a substantially complete APA request, the APA Director will designate a Team Leader to oversee the APA Team's activities in processing the request. If a prefiling conference was held with the taxpayer, the Team Leader generally will be designated from among the APA Program staff attending the prefiling conference.

.04 Formation of APA Team

The Team Leader will organize the APA Team, which normally consists of the following personnel: the Team Leader, an APA Program economist and/or a Service Operating Division economist, an LMSB international examiner, a Division Counsel attorney, and, in bilateral or multilateral cases, a competent authority analyst. In appropriate cases, an LMSB international technical advisor, the international examiner's manager, and other Service Operating Division personnel familiar with the taxpayer may serve on the APA Team. If the APA or a rollback of the APA affects taxable years in Appeals, the appropriate Appeals Officer will be invited to participate. The APA Team Leader will assure that copies of the APA request are distributed to all Team members for review.

.05 Function of APA Team

The function of the APA Team is the following: (1) for a bilateral or multilateral APA, to develop, in consultation with the taxpayer and consistent with sound tax administration, a competent authority negotiating position that it can recommend for approval, and (2) for a unilateral APA, to make best efforts, consistent with sound tax administration, to develop an APA that the APA Program can recommend for approval by the Associate Chief Counsel (International). The Service Operating Division field office responsible for the taxpayer's income tax return will be provided an opportunity to review and comment on the recommended U.S. competent authority negotiating position in the case of a bilateral or multilateral APA, and the proposed APA in the case of a unilateral APA.

.06 Due Diligence and Analysis

The APA Team will evaluate the taxpayer's APA request by discussing it with the taxpayer, verifying the data supplied, and requesting additional supporting data if necessary. The evaluation of the request will not constitute an examination or inspection of the taxpayer's books and records under § 7605(b) or other provisions of the Code.

.07 Schedule for Discussion and Drafting

(1) The APA Team will strive to arrange an initial meeting with the taxpayer to take place within 45 days from the assignment of an APA Team Leader (and following receipt of the substantially complete APA request). The function of the initial meeting is to review the taxpayer's facts, to discuss and clarify issues, and to reach agreement on the scope and nature of the APA Team's due diligence.

(2) In connection with the initial meeting, the APA Team and the taxpayer will agree on a Case Plan to which both Service and taxpayer personnel will be expected to adhere. The Case Plan will be signed by both an APA manager and an authorized official of the taxpayer (see section 4.09(2)). The Case Plan may identify issues raised by the APA Team's initial review of the APA request. Firm dates should be agreed upon for resolving all outstanding issues, and case milestones should be cited. Case milestones include: (a) submission of any necessary additional information by the taxpayer; (b) any planned site visits or interviews; (c) evaluation of the information by the Service; (d) meeting dates; and (e) presentation of the competent authority negotiating position or recommended agreement to the APA Director. To minimize delays caused by the need to coordinate different parties' schedules on short notice, the time and place of future meetings required for any steps in the case should be agreed upon at the initial meeting and established in the Case Plan.

(3) The time scheduled for completion of the case milestones will depend to some extent on the scope and complexity of the particular case. In the case of bilateral or multilateral requests, the Service will seek to work with the competent authority of the treaty partner or partners, or the U.S. possession involved to minimize the time needed for competent authority resolution.

¶20,130

(4) Failures by either the taxpayer or the APA Team to meet case milestones will be addressed promptly. The APA Director will assist in remedying any difficulties to ensure a course of action to meet case milestones. Substantial or persistent failure by the taxpayer to comply with the Case Plan may be treated by the APA Program as a withdrawal of the APA request. In this event, if the taxpayer wishes to continue to pursue the APA, the taxpayer must re-file the request and pay a new user fee.

(5) In some circumstances, development of the case will suggest to both the APA Team and the taxpayer that they adjust some milestone dates. To preserve flexibility, the APA Team and the taxpayer may amend the Case Plan by written mutual agreement, consistent with the need to complete the case expeditiously.

(6) If a case is not completed by the date specified in the operative Case Plan, the APA Team Leader and the taxpayer must submit to the APA Director a joint status report (or separate status reports in the event of disagreement) explaining the substantive or procedural matters causing the delay and specifying how the parties propose to resolve the outstanding issues and complete the case within a reasonable time. If the case is not completed by the new target date, APA Program management will hold a status conference. The purpose of the status conference is to reach agreement on how the case will be resolved. The Associate Chief Counsel (International) may participate in this or subsequent conferences if the case is not resolved satisfactorily in a timely manner.

.08 Execution

Signature of an APA by the APA Director and the taxpayer will constitute agreement to the APA. For purposes of executing the APA, each taxpayer that is a member of a consolidated group (as defined in *§ 1.1502-1*) must comply with the provisions of *§ 1.1502-77*. The person signing the APA request on behalf of the taxpayer must satisfy the requirements of section 4.09(2).

.09 Withdrawing the Request

The taxpayer may withdraw the request at any time before the execution of the APA. The user fee generally will not be refunded if the taxpayer withdraws its APA request after the due diligence process has been initiated.

.10 Rejecting the Request

The APA Program may decline either to accept any APA request or to execute any APA after a request has been accepted. If the APA Program declines to execute an APA after the due diligence process has been initiated, the Service normally will retain the user fee, although the fee may be returned if the APA Program determines that such action would be appropriate under the circumstances. If the APA Program proposes to reject an APA request, the taxpayer will be granted one conference of right with the APA Director. Other conferences may be granted at the APA Director's discretion.

SECTION 7: COMPETENT AUTHORITY CONSIDERATION

.01 When any of the parties to a request are entitled to obtain assistance under the mutual agreement provision of a tax treaty between a foreign country and the

United States, or under Rev. Proc. 89-8, the competent authorities may enter into agreements concerning the APA. Requests similar to APA requests that are initiated through treaty partners or possession tax agencies and submitted to the U.S. competent authority will be processed under this revenue procedure and Rev. Proc. 2002-52, as appropriate. In order to provide timely clarification of factual issues, minimize the potential for miscommunication, and assist in development of a multiple party agreement on a timely basis, the Service will generally initiate coordination among the taxpayer, the Service, and the competent authorities of treaty partners at the earliest possible stage of consideration of an APA request, including, where possible, the prefiling stage. In this manner, the U.S. and foreign competent authorities can develop a joint understanding of the case, which should facilitate negotiation and resolution of competent authority issues. The taxpayer should remain available throughout consideration of the request to assist the Service in reaching agreement with the foreign competent authority. Final agreement to the negotiated APA will be sought among the taxpayer, the Service, and the foreign competent authority. As a general matter, the taxpayer should submit APA requests and related correspondence simultaneously to the Service and to foreign competent authorities involved in the requests.

.02 The purpose of a competent authority agreement is to avoid double taxation or taxation not in accordance with the relevant income tax treaty or treaties. If such an agreement is not acceptable to the taxpayer, the taxpayer may withdraw the APA request (see section 6.09). If the competent authorities are unable to reach an agreement, the taxpayer may withdraw its request or, at its discretion, the Service may negotiate and enter into a unilateral APA with the taxpayer (see section 7.06).

.03 The taxpayer must cooperate with the Service and the U.S. competent authority, pursuant to the standards set forth in Rev. Proc. 2002-52 and any other applicable revenue procedures.

.04 Taxpayers have an affirmative obligation to identify relevant concerns that may impact competent authority negotiation of an APA request. For example, it may be necessary for the Service to request sensitive confidential data (including material that may constitute a trade secret), which if disclosed, could harm the taxpayer's competitive position. If the taxpayer identifies such sensitive information, the Service will work with the taxpayer in developing a mechanism to permit consideration or verification by the treaty partner or partners of the information while still preserving its confidentiality.

.05 When the competent authorities enter into an agreement covering an APA, the Service will, to the extent appropriate, agree to a mutual exchange of information with the foreign competent authority concerning any subsequent modifications, cancellation, revocation, requests to renew, evaluation of annual reports, or examination of the taxpayer's compliance with the terms and conditions of the APA. Bilateral APAs may provide for simultaneous filing of the annual report with the Service and with the foreign tax administration.

.06 To minimize taxpayer and governmental uncertainty and administrative cost, bilateral or multilateral APAs are generally preferable to unilateral APAs when competent authority procedures are available with respect to the foreign country or

countries involved. In appropriate circumstances, however, the Service may execute an APA with a taxpayer without reaching a competent authority agreement. The taxpayer must show sufficient justification for a unilateral APA. In some circumstances, procedures agreed upon with particular foreign competent authorities, or the requirements of proper relations with treaty partners, may preclude unilateral APAs.

.07 Section 7.05 of Rev. Proc. 2002-52 provides in part that, if a taxpayer reaches a settlement on an issue pursuant to a written agreement, the U.S. competent authority will endeavor only to obtain a correlative adjustment from a treaty country and will not undertake any actions that would otherwise change such agreement. The restrictions imposed under section 7.05 of Rev. Proc. 2002-52 with respect to the discretion of the U.S. competent authority to negotiate correlative relief will not apply to a unilateral APA. However, a unilateral APA may hinder the ability of the U.S. competent authority to reach a mutual agreement that will provide relief from double taxation, particularly when a contemporaneous bilateral or multilateral APA request would have been both effective and practical (within the meaning of *§ 1.901-2(e)(5)(i)*) to obtain consistent treatment of the APA matters in a treaty country. If there is a settlement with respect to taxable years prior to the first year subject to a unilateral APA based on rollback of the APA's TPM (as discussed in sections 2.12 and 8 of this revenue procedure), section 7.05 of Rev. Proc. 2002-52 will apply to the rollback years in the regular manner.

SECTION 8: ROLLBACK OF TPM

.01 Application of the TPM to tax years prior to those covered by the APA ("rollback" of the TPM) may be an effective means of enhancing voluntary compliance and of using available resources to address unresolved transfer pricing issues. The taxpayer may request that the Service consider a rollback (a "rollback request") in connection with a particular APA request. Under regularly applicable procedures, the Service may determine that the same or a similar TPM as that agreed to in an APA should be applied to prior years even in the absence of a rollback request. When applying the TPM to prior years, adjustments may be made to reflect differences in facts, economic conditions, and applicable legal rules. Those adjustments may be made regardless of whether the taxpayer or the Service initiated the rollback request.

.02 The taxpayer may make a rollback request in its APA request or at any time prior to the execution of the APA. The principles set forth in section 2.12 generally will govern the Service's consideration of the request. The balance of prospectivity and retroactivity of the total number of years covered by the proposed overall agreement, and the status of any on-going examination, will also be given consideration in the Service's decision to entertain a rollback request. Rollbacks requested after submission of the APA request must be in writing and addressed to the APA Director.

.03 If a rollback request is submitted in connection with a bilateral or multilateral APA, the rollback request will be deemed to constitute an application for accelerated competent authority consideration as described in section 7.06 of Rev. Proc. 2002-52 (or its successor). The Office of Associate Chief Counsel (International),

¶20,130

the Service Operating Division field office involved, and the U.S. Competent Authority will coordinate consideration of the request. The taxpayer's request must include all information required for accelerated competent authority consideration under Rev. Proc. 2002-52 (or its successor), subject to the rules set forth therein. The taxpayer's request can pertain to any years prior to the first year to be covered under the requested APA. As necessary to reach a competent authority agreement, the Service may require that the rollback be applied to one or more specified years if accelerated competent authority is to be granted. In exercising its discretion over the conduct of accelerated competent authority consideration, the U.S. Competent Authority will seek to implement the policy concerning APA rollbacks stated in section 2.12.

.04 Rollback requests submitted in connection with a bilateral or multilateral APA and involving a taxable year under the jurisdiction of Appeals will be deemed to constitute an application for simultaneous Appeals and competent authority consideration. That application is described in section 8 of Rev. Proc. 2002-52 and is subject to the rules of that section. The Office of Associate Chief Counsel (International), Appeals, and the U.S. Competent Authority will coordinate consideration of the request. In exercising its discretion in a simultaneous Competent Authority-Appeals proceeding, the U.S. Competent Authority will seek to implement the policy concerning APA rollbacks stated in section 2.12. Taxpayers are encouraged to request accelerated competent authority consideration under section 8.03 above, in conjunction with an application for the simultaneous Appeals and competent authority process.

.05 Subject to the policy stated in section 2.12, the Service official with jurisdiction over the taxable year subject to the rollback has discretion as to whether the rollback is applied. That official may be either the Service Operating Division executive responsible for the taxpayer's income tax return, the National Chief of Appeals, the U.S. Competent Authority (for matters subject to competent authority negotiations), or the Division Counsel (for matters pending litigation). Except to the extent inconsistent with this revenue procedure, APA rollbacks will be implemented using regularly applicable procedures for resolving tax issues. Such procedures include but are not limited to closing agreements and other settlement documents and Forms 870 and 870AD.

SECTION 9: SMALL BUSINESS TAXPAYER APAs

.01 Special Provisions Available to Small Business Taxpayers

At the request of a small business taxpayer ("SBT"), the APA Program may apply any or all of the provisions in this section. A SBT is any U.S. taxpayer with total gross income of $200 million or less, as determined under section 4.12(6). In addition, SBT procedures will be available for APAs that cover small transactions described in section 4.12(5). Although transactions involving valuable intangible property or CSAs would not ordinarily be appropriate for these SBT procedures (because of the complexity of valuing such intangibles), the APA Program will consider employing special procedures for such transactions on a case-by-case basis.

¶20,130

.02 PFC Procedures

(1) As set forth in the general rules above, a taxpayer contemplating an APA may request a PFC with the APA Program (see section 3). If a PFC is requested, the APA Program provides informal advice to the taxpayer regarding the taxpayer's proposal, but ordinarily does not begin significant due diligence until the taxpayer formally files an APA request and pays the appropriate user fee (see section 6.01). In the case of an SBT, however, the APA Program will commence its due diligence analysis earlier in the process to accelerate the conclusion of the APA negotiations.

(2) The APA Program and a SBT may hold a PFC to determine as early as possible the best method for the SBT's proposed covered transactions. The APA Program will need a detailed description of the underlying facts and the proposed TPM for the SBT's proposed covered transactions at least 60 days prior to the scheduled conference. The SBT may provide the information it maintains under § 6662(e) to satisfy this requirement. Prior to its prefiling submission, the SBT must consult with the APA Program to determine the information required to evaluate the SBT's covered transactions.

(3) An APA Team will evaluate the APA prefiling information to determine items of concern and the additional documentation needed to evaluate the request. The SBT will be advised of the APA Team's initial conclusions before the PFC so that it can address these items before or at the conference.

(4) At the PFC, the SBT and APA Program will agree on a schedule with the objective of finalizing the recommended negotiating position for a bilateral APA, or concluding a unilateral APA, within six months of the date the SBT files its APA request. The APA Program expects that performing this analysis earlier in the process should result in a reduced number of post-filing meetings and supplemental information requests.

.03 Items Required for an SBT APA Request

Before an SBT submits an APA request, the APA Program and the SBT may agree to reduce or eliminate specific items that would otherwise be required by section 4.

.04 Locale and Number of Meetings for SBT APA Requests

The APA Program will endeavor to hold meetings with the SBT at a location convenient to the SBT. To minimize the number of meetings, teleconferences will be employed whenever feasible.

.05 Assistance in Economic Analysis

At the SBT's request, the APA Program will assist the SBT in the selection and evaluation of comparables, as well as the computation of any appropriate adjustments to comparables.

.06 APA

For unilateral APA requests, a SBT should submit a proposed draft APA in a form substantially similar to the APA Program's current Model APA (see Announcement 2005-27, 2005-16 I.R.B. 918, 950). The electronic component of the APA request

¶20,130

should include a "redline" version showing the differences between the Model APA and the SBT's proposed draft APA (see section 4.02(6)).

.07 APA Program's Consideration of Other Alternative Procedures

The APA Program may consider other procedures suggested by the SBT to reduce the SBT's administrative and financial burden, consistent with the objectives of the APA Program and the requirements of § 482.

SECTION 10: LEGAL EFFECT OF THE APA

.01 An APA is a binding agreement between the taxpayer and the Service. See sections 2.01 - 2.04.

.02 If the taxpayer complies with the terms and conditions of the APA, the Service will not contest the application of the TPM to the subject matter of the APA except as provided in this revenue procedure. The taxpayer remains otherwise subject to U.S. income tax laws and applicable income tax conventions.

.03 An APA will have no legal effect except with respect to the taxpayer, taxable years, and transactions to which the APA specifically relates.

.04 Unless provided otherwise by written agreement or regulations, the Service and the taxpayer may not introduce the APA or non-factual oral and written representations made in conjunction with the APA request as evidence in any judicial or administrative proceeding regarding any tax year, transaction, or person not covered by the APA. This paragraph does not preclude the Service and the taxpayer from agreeing to roll back the APA TPM, or the Service's use of any non-factual material otherwise discoverable or obtained other than in the APA process merely because the parties considered the same or similar material in the APA process.

.05 Unless provided otherwise by written agreement or regulations, the Service and the taxpayer may not introduce a proposed, cancelled, or revoked APA, or any non-factual oral or written representations or submissions made during the APA process, as an admission by the other party, in any judicial or administrative proceeding regarding any taxable year of the requested APA term. This paragraph does not preclude the Service's use of any non-factual material otherwise discoverable or obtained other than in the APA process merely because the APA Program and the taxpayer considered the same or similar material in the APA process.

SECTION 11: ADMINISTERING THE APA

.01 Annual Reports

(1) For each taxable year covered by the APA, the taxpayer must file a timely and complete annual report describing its actual operations for the year and demonstrating compliance with the APA's terms and conditions. The report must include all items required by the APA, describe any pending or contemplated requests to renew, modify or cancel the APA, and report any adjustments made pursuant to section 11.02. In addition, the annual report must identify any material information submitted while the APA request was pending that the taxpayer discovers during the taxable year was false, incorrect, or incomplete. See section 5.02.

(2) The taxpayer must file an original and four copies of the annual report by the later of (a) 90 days after the time prescribed by statute (including extensions) for filing its federal income tax return for the year covered by the report, or (b) 90 days after the effective date of the APA. The Service and the taxpayer may agree to alternative filing dates. The taxpayer should file the original annual report and copies with the APA Director in Washington, D.C., as indicated in section 4.11. For bilateral or multilateral APAs, the Service may require the taxpayer to file simultaneously a copy of the annual report with the treaty partner or partners.

(3) The Service Operating Division or the APA Program Office will contact the taxpayer regarding an annual report if it is necessary to clarify or complete the information submitted in the annual report. The taxpayer must supply the additional information by the date specified.

(4) Any contact between the Service Operating Division, or the APA Program Office, and the taxpayer to clarify or complete the information in an annual report is not an examination or the commencement of an examination of the taxpayer for purposes of § 7605(b) or any other Code provision.

(5) If a filed annual report contains incomplete or incorrect information, or reports an incorrect application of the TPM, the taxpayer must amend it within 45 days after becoming aware of the need to amend the report. The time may be extended for good cause.

(6) An annual report must contain the following declaration:

Under penalties of perjury, I declare that I have examined this annual report including accompanying documents, and, to the best of my knowledge and belief, this annual report contains all the relevant facts relating to the annual reporting requirements pursuant to the APA, and such facts are true, correct, and complete.

[If applicable: An adjustment to conform taxable income and other relevant items to reflect the results reported herein has been reported to the appropriate responsible Service Operating Division personnel.]

[If applicable: An amended income tax return to conform taxable income and other relevant items to reflect the results reported herein [has been] [will be] filed with the appropriate Internal Revenue Service Center.]

(7) The taxpayer must sign the declaration in compliance with sections 4.09 (Perjury Statement) and 4.10 (Signatures).

(8) Failure to file a timely, complete, or accurate annual report may be grounds for canceling or revoking the APA under sections 11.06.

.02 APA Primary Adjustments, Secondary Adjustments, and Revenue Procedure Treatment

(1) APA Primary Adjustments. The APA provides the TPM for determining the proper amount of the taxpayer's gross or net income, deductions, credits, or allowances with respect to the APA's covered transactions. In general, the taxpayer's actual covered transactions during an APA year, as reported in its books and records, should comply with the TPM and be clearly reflected on the taxpayer's timely-filed original return for the year. Under some TPMs, however, the taxpayer

¶20,130

may have to wait until the close of the taxable year to determine whether the intercompany prices it actually paid or received complied with the TPM (for example, a comparable profits method providing for a particular operating margin range). If the taxpayer's actual covered transactions do not comply with the TPM, the taxpayer must nonetheless report its taxable income in an amount consistent with the TPM (an "APA primary adjustment") on either a timely-filed original return or an amended return. The generally applicable Code rules, including additions to tax, penalties and interest, apply with respect to an APA primary adjustment. When the taxpayer makes an APA primary adjustment, an appropriate correlative adjustment will also be made with respect to the related foreign entity affected by the APA primary adjustment. See *§ 1.482-1(g)(2)*. To the extent the APA covers years for which federal income tax returns were filed prior to, or no later than 60 days after, the effective date of the APA, the taxpayer must file, unless otherwise agreed to in the APA, an amended return or returns that reflect any required primary adjustment and pay any tax due because of such adjustments, within 120 days of entering into the APA. The generally applicable Code rules will apply with respect to the primary adjustment with respect to the APA years for which federal income tax returns were filed before the APA was executed, except: (a) the computation of any required estimated tax installments for the taxable year will not take into account the primary adjustment and related secondary adjustments (see section 11.02(2)); and (b) the taxpayer will not be subject to the failure to pay penalties under § § 6651 and 6655, or the failure to make timely deposit of taxes penalty under § 6656, by reason of the primary adjustment and related secondary adjustments.

(2) Secondary Adjustments. Absent an election of the APA revenue procedure treatment described in section 11.02(3), an APA primary adjustment requires a secondary adjustment to conform the taxpayer's accounts. The secondary adjustment may result in additional tax consequences. See *§ 1.482-1(g)(3)*.

(3) APA Revenue Procedure Treatment. If a taxpayer makes an APA primary adjustment, the taxpayer and its related foreign entity may elect APA revenue procedure treatment and avoid the possible adverse tax consequences of a secondary adjustment that would otherwise follow the APA primary adjustment. Under APA revenue procedure treatment, consistent with the principles of Rev. Proc. 99-32, 1999-2 C.B. 296, the taxpayer will be permitted to establish an account receivable from, or payable to, its related foreign entity in the amount of the APA primary adjustment as of the last day of the taxable year to which the APA primary adjustment applies. The account will not bear interest and must be paid within 90 days of the later of (a) the date for timely filing (with extensions) of the federal income tax return for the taxable year to which the APA primary adjustment applies, or (b) the APA's effective date. The account must be paid within the 90 day period to receive revenue procedure treatment. Payment must be in the form of money, a written debt obligation payable at a fixed date and bearing interest at an arm's length rate as provided in *§ 1.482-2(a)(2)*, or through an accounting entry offsetting such account against an existing bona fide debt between the U.S. taxpayer and the related foreign entity. The taxpayer must document the payment

¶ 20,130

or offset of the account, and disclose it in the APA annual report for the year of the payment.

(4) The Service will give effect to an APA primary adjustment, secondary adjustment, and payment under APA revenue procedure treatment, if applicable, for all U.S. income tax purposes. The tax treatment of any such adjustment or payment depends on the facts and circumstances of the adjustment or payment. For example, if a taxpayer's APA primary adjustment involves the reporting of an additional royalty expense for a transaction with a related foreign entity, the Service will deem a payment in the nature of a royalty in the amount of the APA primary adjustment to have been made by the taxpayer to the related foreign entity. This deemed payment may be subject to U.S. withholding tax, and interest would accrue on the tax required to be withheld from the due date of the taxpayer's federal income tax return without regard to extensions. Similarly, a taxpayer's APA revenue procedure treatment may involve the recharacterization of a dividend paid by its foreign subsidiary as a payment of an account receivable established in connection with an APA primary adjustment. Any foreign tax withheld from the payment may be treated as a noncompulsory payment ineligible for the foreign tax credit, unless the taxpayer exhausts all effective and practical remedies, including invocation of competent authority procedures, to obtain consistent treatment that would eliminate the foreign tax liability. See § 1.901-2(e)(5).

(5) If the Service proposes a tax adjustment or the taxpayer files an amended return that does not require an APA primary adjustment, generally applicable Code rules will apply.

(6) If the taxpayer requests a bilateral or multilateral APA, the U.S. Competent Authority will discuss the principles of this section with the appropriate foreign competent authority to seek substantially identical treatment of the taxpayer's related foreign entity.

.03 Examination

(1) With respect to the application of § 482 to the covered transactions, the Service will limit the examination of a taxpayer's income tax return for a tax year covered by an APA to the requirements described in the next paragraph and will not reconsider the TPM.

(2) For the year under examination, the Service may require the taxpayer to establish: (a) compliance with the APA's terms and conditions; (b) validity and accuracy of the annual report's material representations; (c) correctness of the supporting data and computations used to apply the TPM; (d) satisfaction of the critical assumptions; and (e) consistent application of the TPM.

(3) The Service Operating Division must inform the APA Director if the taxpayer has not satisfied any requirement in the prior paragraph. After consulting with the appropriate Service Operating Division personnel, the Associate Chief Counsel (International) may decide to apply the terms of the APA, or revise (see section 11.05), cancel, or revoke (see section 11.06) the APA.

(4) The Service Operating Division may audit and propose adjustments to the taxpayer's operating results as determined under the TPM without affecting the

APA's validity or applicability. The taxpayer may agree with the proposed adjustments in the same manner as any other adjustment, and the Service Operating Division will assess any resulting additional tax or refund any resulting overpayment of tax. If the taxpayer does not agree with the proposed adjustment, the taxpayer may contest it through the normal administrative and judicial procedures. The taxpayer must include the audit adjustments as finally determined for the purpose of applying the TPM and, as necessary, make any APA primary, secondary and correlative adjustments under section 11.02. APA revenue procedure treatment under section 11.02(3) is unavailable for audit adjustments.

.04 Record Retention

(1) The taxpayer must maintain books and records sufficient to enable the Service Operating Division to examine whether the taxpayer has complied with the APA. The taxpayer's compliance with this paragraph fulfills the record-keeping requirements of §§ 6038A and 6038C as applied to the covered transactions.

(2) Upon examination, the Service Operating Division may submit a written request to the taxpayer requiring the submission of requested information or the translation of specific documents within 30 days, as extended for good cause. The fact that a foreign jurisdiction may impose a penalty upon the taxpayer or other person for disclosing the material will not constitute reasonable cause for noncompliance with the Service Operating Division's request.

.05 Revising the APA

(1) An APA may be revised by agreement of the parties, consistent with the principles set forth herein and the interests of sound tax administration. The Associate Chief Counsel (International) may agree to revise an APA in lieu of canceling or revoking it. If the parties agree to revise the APA, the revised APA will indicate its effective date.

(2) If the parties agree to revise a bilateral or multilateral APA, the Team Leader will submit the revised APA to the U.S. Competent Authority to obtain the consent of the foreign competent authority. If the foreign competent authority refuses to accept the revised APA, or if the competent authorities cannot agree on a revised APA acceptable to all parties, the APA Director and the taxpayer may agree to: (a) apply the existing APA, if appropriate; (b) apply the revised APA or agree to further revisions; or (c) request the Associate Chief Counsel (International) to cancel the APA as of an agreed date. If the APA Director and the taxpayer cannot agree on how to proceed, the Associate Chief Counsel (International) will cancel the APA pursuant to section 11.06.

.06 Revoking or Canceling the APA

(1) The Associate Chief Counsel (International) may revoke an APA due to fraud or malfeasance (as defined in § 7121), or disregard (as defined in § 6662(b)(1) and (c)) by the taxpayer in connection with the APA, including, but not limited to, fraud, malfeasance, or disregard involving (a) material facts in the request or subsequent submissions (including an annual report) or (b) lack of good faith compliance with the APA's terms and conditions.

¶20,130

(2) The Associate Chief Counsel (International) may cancel an APA due to the taxpayer's misrepresentation, mistake as to a material fact, failure to state a material fact, failure to file a timely annual report, or lack of good faith compliance with the terms and conditions of the APA.

(3) Unless the parties agree to revise the APA, the Associate Chief Counsel (International) will cancel an APA in the event of a failure of a critical assumption, or a material change in governing case law, statute, regulation, or a treaty (as described in section 11.07).

(4) For purposes of this section 11.06(1) and (2) the Associate Chief Counsel (International) will consider facts as material if, for example, knowledge of the facts could reasonably have resulted in an APA with significantly different terms and conditions. In regard to annual reports, the Associate Chief Counsel (International) will consider facts as material if, for example, knowledge of the facts would have resulted in (a) a materially different allocation of income, deductions, or credits than reported in the annual report, or (b) the failure to meet a critical assumption.

(5) The Associate Chief Counsel (International) may waive cancellation if the taxpayer can satisfactorily show good faith and reasonable cause and agrees to make any adjustment proposed to correct for the misrepresentation, mistake as to a material fact, failure to state a material fact, or noncompliance.

(6) If the Associate Chief Counsel (International) revokes an APA, the revocation relates back to the first day of the APA's first taxable year. The Service may: (a) determine deficiencies in income taxes and additions thereto; (b) deny relief under Rev. Proc. 99-32, 1999-2 C.B. 296; (c) allow the taxpayer relief under Rev. Proc. 99-32, but determine the interest on any account receivable established under Rev. Proc. 99-32, section 4.01, without mutual agreement or correlative relief; (d) revoke the APA as an "egregious case" under Rev. Rul. 80-231, 1980-2 C.B. 219, so as to deny the taxpayer a foreign tax credit; and (e) not make available the unilateral relief provisions of Rev. Proc. 2002-52 (see section 12.07). The Service will seek to coordinate any action concerning revocation of a bilateral or multilateral APA with the foreign competent authority.

(7) If the Associate Chief Counsel (International) cancels an APA, the cancellation normally relates back to the beginning of the year in which the critical assumption failed, or the beginning of the year to which the misrepresentation, mistake as to a material fact, failure to state a material fact, or noncompliance relates. If, however, the cancellation results from a change in case law, statute, regulation, or treaty, the cancellation normally relates back to the beginning of the year that contains the effective date of the change in case law, statute, regulation, or treaty.

(8) As of the effective date of the cancellation, the APA has no further force and effect with respect to the Service and the taxpayer for U.S. income tax purposes. The Service will seek to coordinate any action concerning the cancellation of a bilateral or multilateral APA with the foreign competent authority.

¶20,130

.07 Change in Case Law, Statute, Regulation, or Treaty

If applicable U.S. case law, statutes, regulations, or treaties change the federal income tax treatment of any matter covered by the APA, the new case law, statute, regulation, or treaty provision supersedes inconsistent terms and conditions of the APA.

SECTION 12: RENEWING THE APA

.01 A taxpayer may request renewal of an APA using the procedures for initial APA requests. To expedite the preparation and evaluation of an APA renewal request, however, taxpayers are encouraged to request a prefiling conference to discuss with the APA Program the suitability of streamlined submission requirements. Taxpayers are encouraged to file the renewal request nine months before the expiration of the APA term.

.02 The APA Program will endeavor to expedite the processing of a renewal APA. Expedited processing will be most likely where the taxpayer demonstrates that the following conditions exist: (a) substantially the same law and policy applied to the existing APA; (b) no substantial differences exist between the taxpayer's proposed TPM and the TPM under the existing APA; (c) no material changes occurred in the taxpayer's facts or circumstances since the parties entered into the existing APA; and (d) for a bilateral APA, a rollback or closed year considerations did not influence the TPM in the existing APA.

.03 If the conditions in the prior paragraph exist, the APA Team begins its evaluation of the renewal APA by considering the continuing applicability of the existing APA, using updated comparables as appropriate. The APA Team will focus on any changed facts and circumstances. While the APA Team will endeavor to streamline the renewal process, certain cases may require additional analysis. That is, experience and insight gained from applying the TPM to actual data (for example, APA annual reports) may provide insight that indicates the need to modify the TPM. The APA Program will use its best efforts to advise the taxpayer at a prefiling conference whether a streamlined APA renewal process will be achievable.

SECTION 13: DISCLOSURE

.01 An APA, any background information related to the APA, and the taxpayer's APA request for that APA, are return information and are confidential. See §§ 6103, 6105, 894, and 7852(d).

.02 An APA, any background information related to the APA, and the taxpayer's APA request, are not "written determinations," and they are not open to public inspection. See § 6110.

.03 The Secretary must prepare an annual report for public disclosure. See § 521(b) of the Ticket to Work and Work Incentives Improvement Act of 1999, Pub. L. 106-170, 113 Stat. 1860, 1925. That report includes specifically designated information concerning all APAs, but in a form that does not identify taxpayers or their trade secrets or proprietary or confidential business or financial information.

¶20,130

.04 An APA, any annual reports, and any factual information contained in the background files is subject to exchange of information under income tax treaties or tax information exchange agreements in accordance with the terms of such treaties and agreements (including terms regarding relevancy, confidentiality and the protection of trade secrets). In cases where the exchange of information would be discretionary, information may be exchanged to the extent consistent with sound tax administration and the practices of the relevant foreign competent authority, including where relevant the existence and application by the foreign competent authority of rules similar to those described in sections 10.04 and 10.05.

SECTION 14: EFFECT ON OTHER DOCUMENTS

Rev. Proc. 2004-40, 2004-2 C.B. 50, is superseded.

SECTION 15. EFFECTIVE DATE

This revenue procedure will apply to all APA requests, including requests for renewal, received on or after February 1, 2006. By agreement, this revenue procedure may apply to any APA resulting from an APA request pending on such date.

SECTION 16: PAPERWORK REDUCTION ACT

The collections of information contained in this revenue procedure have been reviewed and approved by the Office of Management and Budget in accordance with the Paperwork Reduction Act (44 U.S.C. 3507) under control number 1545 - 1503.

An agency may not conduct or sponsor, and a person is not required to respond to, a collection of information unless the collection of information displays a valid control number.

The collections of information are in sections 3.06, 4, 5, 8.03, 11.01, 11.02(1), 11.04, 11.05 and 12.01. This information is required to provide the Service sufficient information to evaluate and process the APA request or request for renewal of an existing APA, or to determine whether the taxpayer is in compliance with the terms and conditions of an APA. This information will be used to evaluate the proposed TPM, and the taxpayer's compliance with the terms and conditions of any APA to which it is a party. The collections of information are required to obtain an APA. The likely respondents are business or other for-profit institutions.

The estimated total annual reporting and/or recordkeeping burden is 8200 hours.

The estimated average burden for an APA prefiling conference is 10 hours; the estimated average burden for an APA request is 50 hours; and the estimated average burden for preparation of an annual report by a party to an APA is 15 hours. The estimated number of respondents and/or recordkeepers is 230.

The estimated annual frequency of responses is one request or report per year per applicant or party to an APA, except that a taxpayer requesting an APA may also request a prefiling conference.

Books or records relating to a collection of information must be retained as long as their contents may become material in the administration of any internal revenue law. Generally tax returns and tax return information are confidential, as required by § 6103.

DRAFTING INFORMATION

The principal authors of this document are various members of the Advance Pricing Agreement Program of the Office of Associate Chief Counsel (International). For further information regarding this revenue procedure, please contact Mr. Craig A. Sharon or Mr. Craig R. Gilbert at (202) 435-5220 (not a toll free number).

¶ 20,140 APA 2010 Annual Report

Announcement and Report Concerning Advance Pricing Agreements March 29, 2010

This Announcement is issued pursuant to § 521(b) of Pub. L. 106-170, the Ticket to Work and Work Incentives Improvement Act of 1999, which requires the Secretary of the Treasury to report annually to the public concerning Advance Pricing Agreements (APAs) and the APA Program. The first report covered calendar years 1991 through 1999. Subsequent reports covered separately each calendar year 2000 through 2008. This eleventh report describes the experience, structure, and activities of the APA Program during calendar year 2009. It does not provide guidance regarding the application of the arm's length standard.

Craig A. Sharon

Director, Advance Pricing Agreement Program

Background

Internal Revenue Code (IRC) § 482 provides that the Secretary may distribute, apportion, or allocate gross income, deductions, credits, or allowances between or among two or more commonly controlled businesses if necessary to reflect clearly the income of such businesses. Under the § 482 regulations, the standard to be applied in determining the true taxable income of a controlled business is that of a business dealing at arm's length with an unrelated business. The arm's length standard has also been adopted by the international community and is incorporated into the transfer pricing guidelines issued by the Organization for Economic Cooperation and Development (OECD). OECD, TRANSFER PRICING GUIDELINES FOR MULTINATIONAL ENTERPRISES AND TAX ADMINISTRATORS (1995). Transfer pricing issues by their nature are highly factual and have traditionally been one of the largest issues identified by the IRS in its audits of multinational corporations. The APA Program is designed to resolve actual or potential transfer pricing disputes in a principled, cooperative manner, as an alternative to the traditional examination process. An APA is a binding contract between the IRS and a taxpayer by which the IRS agrees not to seek a transfer pricing adjustment under IRC § 482 for a covered transaction if the taxpayer files its tax return for a covered year consistent with the agreed transfer pricing method (TPM). In 2009, the IRS and taxpayers executed 63 APAs and amended 8 APAs.

Since 1991, with the issuance of Rev. Proc. 91-22, 1991-1 C.B. 526, the IRS has offered taxpayers, through the APA Program, the opportunity to reach an agreement in advance of filing a tax return on the appropriate TPM to be applied to related party transactions. In 1996, the IRS issued internal procedures for processing APA requests. Chief Counsel Directives Manual (CCDM), ¶¶ 42.10.10 - 42.10.16 (November 15, 1996).[1] Also in 1996, the IRS updated Rev. Proc. 91-22 with the release of Rev. Proc. 96-53, 1996-2 C.B. 375.[2] In 1998, the IRS published Notice

---

[1] Current CCDM provisions regarding APA procedures are available at *http://www.irs.gov/irm/ part32/ch04s01.html.*

[2] Available at *http://www.irs.gov/pub/irs-irbs/ irb96-49.pdf.*

98-65, 1998-2 C.B. 803,[3] which set forth streamlined APA procedures for small business taxpayers. Then on July 1, 2004, the IRS updated and superseded both Rev. Proc. 96-53 and Notice 98-65 by issuing Rev. Proc. 2004-40, 2004-2 I.R.B. 50,[4] effective for all APA requests filed on or after August 19, 2004.

On December 19, 2005, the IRS again updated the procedural rules for processing and administering APAs with the release of Rev. Proc. 2006-09, 2006-1 C.B. 278.[5] Rev. Proc. 2006-09 supersedes Rev. Proc. 2004-40 and is effective for all APA requests filed on or after February 1, 2006. On May 21, 2008, the IRS released Rev. Proc. 2008-31, 2008-23 IR.B. 1133, which revised Rev. Proc. 2006-09 to describe further the types of issues that may be resolved in the APA process.[6] Specifically, Rev. Proc. 2008-31 added a new sentence to Section 2.01 of Rev. Proc. 2006-09, to advise that the APA process may be used to resolve any issue for which transfer pricing principles may be relevant, such as attribution of profit to a permanent establishment under certain U.S. income tax treaties, the amount of income effectively connected with the conduct of a U.S. trade or business, and the amount of income derived from sources partly within and partly without the United States.

Advance Pricing Agreements

An APA generally combines an agreement between a taxpayer and the IRS on an appropriate TPM for the transactions at issue (Covered Transactions) with an agreement between the U.S. and one or more foreign tax authorities (under the authority of the mutual agreement process of our income tax treaties) that the TPM is correct. With such a "bilateral" APA, the taxpayer ordinarily is assured that the income associated with the Covered Transactions will not be subject to double taxation by both the U.S. and the foreign jurisdiction. The policy of the United States, as reflected in §§ 2.08 and 7 of Rev. Proc. 2006-09, is to encourage taxpayers that enter the APA Program to seek bilateral or multilateral APAs when competent authority procedures are available with respect to the foreign country or countries involved. However, the IRS may execute an APA with a taxpayer without reaching a competent authority agreement (a unilateral APA).

A unilateral APA is an agreement between a taxpayer and the IRS establishing an approved TPM for U.S. tax purposes. A unilateral APA binds the taxpayer and the IRS, but does not prevent a foreign tax administration from taking a different position on the appropriate TPM for a transaction. As stated in § 7.07 of Rev. Proc. 2006-09, should a transaction covered by a unilateral APA be subject to double taxation as the result of an adjustment by a foreign tax administration, the taxpayer may seek relief by requesting that the U.S. Competent Authority consider initiating a mutual agreement proceeding pursuant to an applicable income tax treaty (if any).

When a unilateral APA involves taxpayers operating in a country that is a U.S. treaty partner, information relevant to the APA (including a copy of the APA and

---

[3] Available at *http://www.irs.gov/pub/irs-irbs/irb98-52.pdf*.

[4] Available at *http://www.irs.gov/pub/irs-irbs/irb04-29.pdf*.

[5] Available at *http://www.irs.gov/irb/2006-02_IRB/ar12.html*.

[6] Available at *http://www.irs.gov/pub/irs-irbs/irb08-31.pdf*.

APA annual reports) may be provided to the treaty partner under normal rules and principles governing the exchange of information under income tax treaties.

The APA Program

An IRS team headed by an APA team leader is responsible for the consideration of each APA. As of December 31, 2009, the APA Program had 19 team leaders. The team leader is responsible for organizing the IRS APA team. The IRS APA team leader arranges meetings with the taxpayer, secures whatever information is necessary from the taxpayer to analyze the taxpayer's related party transactions and the available facts under the arm's length standard of IRC § 482 and the regulations thereunder, and leads the discussions with the taxpayer.

The APA team generally includes an economist, an LMSB international examiner, LMSB field counsel, and, in a bilateral case, a U.S. Competent Authority analyst who leads the discussions with the treaty partner. The economist may be from the APA Program or the IRS field organization. As of December 31, 2009, the APA Program had 8 economists on staff, plus one economist manager. The APA team may also include an LMSB International Technical Advisor, other LMSB exam personnel, and/or an Appeals Officer.

The APA Process

The APA process is voluntary. Taxpayers submit an application for an APA, together with a user fee as set forth in Rev. Proc. 2006-09, § 4.12. The APA process can be broken into five phases: (1) application; (2) due diligence; (3) analysis; (4) discussion and agreement; and (5) drafting, review, and execution.

(1) *Application*

In many APA cases, the taxpayer's application is preceded by a pre-file conference with the APA staff in which the taxpayer can solicit the informal views of the APA Program. Pre-file conferences can occur on an anonymous basis, although a taxpayer must disclose its identity when it applies for an APA. The APA Program has been requiring taxpayers interested in an APA under Rev. Proc. 2008-31 to schedule a pre-file conference before submitting a formal APA application.

As part of a taxpayer's APA application, the taxpayer must file the appropriate user fee on or before the due date, including extensions, of the tax return for the first taxable year that the taxpayer proposes to be covered by the APA. (If the taxpayer receives an extension to file its tax return, it must file its user fee no later than the actual filing date of the return.) Many taxpayers file a user fee first and then follow up with a full application later — a "dollar file" in APA parlance. The procedures for pre-file conferences, user fees, and applications can be found in §§ 3 and 4 of Rev. Proc. 2006-09.

The APA application can be a relatively modest document for small businesses. Section 9 of Rev. Proc. 2006-09 describes the special APA procedures for small business taxpayers. For most taxpayers, however, the APA application is a substantial document filling several binders. APA applications must be accompanied by a

¶20,140

declaration, signed by an authorized corporate officer, attesting to the accuracy and completeness of the information presented.

The application is assigned to an APA team leader who is responsible for the case. The APA team leader's first responsibility is to organize the APA team. This involves contacting the appropriate LMSB International Territory Manager to secure the assignment of an international examiner to the APA case and the LMSB Counsel's office to secure a field counsel lawyer. In a bilateral case, the U.S. Competent Authority will assign a U.S. Competent Authority analyst to the team. In a large APA case, the international examiner may invite his or her manager and other LMSB personnel familiar with the taxpayer to join the team. If the APA may affect taxable years in Appeals, the appropriate appellate conferee will be invited to join the team. In cases involving cost-sharing arrangements, other complex intangibles and services transactions, or novel issues, the APA team leader contacts the Manager, LMSB International Technical Advisors, to determine whether or not to include a technical advisor on the team. The multi-functional nature of APA teams combines the APA Program's transfer pricing expertise and APA experience with other elements of the IRS that possess complementary or supplementary knowledge about the taxpayer, the taxpayer's industry, related or ancillary tax issues, the foreign competent authority, and other relevant issues. By bringing all relevant parties to the table in a single proceeding, the APA process is able to resolve transfer pricing issues early on in a more principled, efficient, consistent, and comprehensive manner than the standard administrative process (i.e., audit, appeals, litigation).

The APA team leader distributes copies of the APA application to all team members, makes initial contact with the taxpayer to confirm the APA Program's receipt of the taxpayer's application, and sets up an opening conference with the taxpayer. Under current APA case management procedures, the APA office strives to (i) make initial contact with the taxpayer within 21 days of its receipt of the APA application and (ii) hold the opening conference within 45 days from the date that the APA team expects to begin actively working the case - the "Start Date" under the revised case management procedures. Because of heavy caseloads (especially among APA economists) and staff turnover during 2009, we were unable to hold many opening conferences within the 45-day target.

On or about the opening conference, the APA team leader proposes a case plan appropriate for the case. Case plans are generally targeted to complete a unilateral APA or, in the case of a bilateral APA, the recommended U.S. negotiating position within 12 months from the date the full application is filed. The targeted completion date in a particular case, however, may vary from the 12-month benchmark, depending on the complexity of the case, APA team workloads, taxpayer schedules, and other factors. Case plans are signed by both an APA manager and an authorized official of the taxpayer and, under the new APA case management procedures, will generally be adhered to except in unforeseen or exceptional circumstances. The actual median and average times for completing unilateral and bilateral APAs, recommended negotiating positions for bilateral APAs, and APAs for small business taxpayers are shown below in Tables 2, 5, and 11, respectively.

¶20,140

(2) *Due Diligence*

The APA team must satisfy itself that the relevant facts submitted by the taxpayer are complete and accurate. This due diligence aspect of the APA is vital to the process. It is because of this due diligence that the IRS can reach advance agreements with taxpayers in the highly factual setting of transfer pricing. Due diligence can proceed in a number of ways. Typically, the APA team leader will submit in advance of the opening conference a list of questions to the taxpayer for discussion at the conference. The opening conference may result in additional questions and an agreement to meet one or more times in the future. These questions and meetings are not an audit and are focused on the transfer pricing issues associated with the transactions in the taxpayer's application, or other transactions that the taxpayer and the IRS may agree to add.

(3) *Analysis*

A significant part of the analytical work associated with an APA is done typically by the APA economist and/or an IRS field economist assigned to the case. The analysis may result in the need for additional information. Once the IRS APA team has completed its due diligence and analysis, it begins discussions with the taxpayer over the various aspects of the APA including the covered transactions, the TPM, the selection of comparable transactions, asset intensity and other adjustments, the appropriate critical assumptions, the APA term, and other key issues. The APA team leader will discuss particularly difficult issues with his or her managers, but generally the APA team leader is empowered to negotiate the APA.

(4) *Discussion and Agreement*

The discussion and agreement phase differs for bilateral and unilateral cases. In a bilateral case, the discussions proceed in two parts and involve two IRS offices — the APA Program and the U.S. Competent Authority. In the first part, the APA team will attempt to reach a consensus with the taxpayer regarding the recommended position that the U.S. Competent Authority should take in negotiations with its treaty partner. This recommended U.S. negotiating position is a paper drafted by the APA team leader, reviewed by APA management, and signed by the APA Director that provides the APA Program's view of the best TPM for the Covered Transactions, taking into account IRC § 482 and the regulations thereunder, the relevant tax treaty, and the U.S. Competent Authority's experience with the treaty partner.

The experience of the APA office and the U.S. Competent Authority is that APA negotiations are likely to proceed more rapidly with a foreign competent authority if the U.S. negotiating position is fully supported by the taxpayer. Consequently, the APA office works together with the taxpayer in developing the recommended U.S. negotiating position. Often, however, the taxpayer will disagree with part or all of the recommended U.S. position. In these cases, the APA office will send a recommended U.S. negotiating position to the U.S. Competent Authority that identifies and explains the elements of the recommended position with which the taxpayer disagrees. The APA team leader also solicits the views of the other members of the APA team, and, in the vast majority of APA cases, the other

¶20,140

members of the APA team concur in the position prepared by the APA team leader. If there is any disagreement, it is noted in the position paper.

After the APA Program completes the recommended U.S. negotiating position, the APA process shifts from the APA Program to the U.S. Competent Authority. The U.S. Competent Authority analyst assigned to the APA takes the recommended U.S. negotiating position and prepares the final U.S. negotiating position, which is then transmitted to the foreign competent authority. The negotiations with the foreign competent authority are conducted by the U.S. Competent Authority analyst, most often in face-to-face negotiating sessions conducted periodically throughout the year. At the request of the U.S. Competent Authority, APA Program staff may assist in the negotiations.

In unilateral APA cases, the discussions proceed solely between the APA Program and the taxpayer. In a unilateral case, the taxpayer and the APA Program must reach agreement to conclude an APA. As in bilateral cases, the APA team leader almost always will achieve a consensus with the IRS field personnel assigned to the APA team regarding the final APA. Under APA Program procedures, IRS field personnel assigned to a case are solicited formally for their concurrence in the final APA. This concurrence, or any item in disagreement, is noted in a memorandum prepared by the APA team leader that accompanies the final APA sent forward for review and execution.

(5) *Drafting, Review, and Execution*

Once the IRS and the taxpayer reach agreement, the final APA is drafted. The APA Program has developed standard language that is incorporated into every APA. The current version of this language is found in Attachment A. APAs are reviewed by the APA Branch Chief and the APA Director. In addition, the team leader prepares a summary memorandum for approval by the Associate Chief Counsel (International) (ACC(I)). On March 1, 2001, the ACC(I) delegated to the APA Director the authority to execute APAs on behalf of the IRS. *See* Chief Counsel Notice CC-2001-016. The APA is executed for the taxpayer by an appropriate corporate officer.

Model APA at Attachment A
[§ 521(b)(2)(B)]

Attachment A contains the current version of the model APA language.

The Current APA Office Structure, Composition, and Operation

In 2009, the APA office consisted of four branches, with Branches 1 and 3 staffed with APA team leaders and Branch 2 staffed with economists based in Washington, D.C. Branch 4, the APA West Coast branch, is headquartered in Laguna Niguel, California, with an additional office in San Francisco, and is staffed with both team leaders and economists.

APA staffing fluctuated during 2009, starting at 33 at the end of 2008, falling to a low of 30 in early 2009, and building back up to 39 by the end of the year. As of December 31, 2009, the APA staff was as follows:

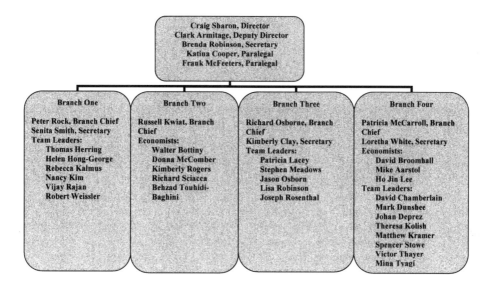

Consistent with the increase in total APA headcount from 2008 to 2009, total APA staffing measured by hours increased in 2009 compared to 2008. APA staff hours in 2009 were similar to APA staff hours in 2006 and 2007, when APA staffing levels were similar at year end (39 in 2009 vs. 40 in 2006 and 37 in 2007), with the small variation in staff hours due primarily to the timing of departures and hires within a year. The change in APA professional staffing levels over the last eight years is reflected in the table below.

Hours of APA attorneys, economists, and paralegal staff by year (excluding holiday and leave):

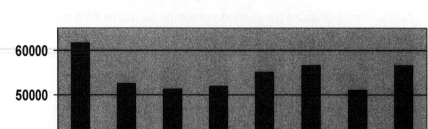

	2002	2003	2004	2005	2006	2007	2008	2009
■ APA staff hours	61528	52495	51170	51744	54970	56410	51077	56549

APA Issue/Industry Coordination Teams

In May 2005, the IRS Chief Counsel announced a series of initiatives to improve APA Program performance. One initiative was to increase specialization within the office by creating teams of select individuals to handle all cases of a particular type. The purpose was to increase efficiency, quality, and consistency.

The APA Program selected five categories of cases for specialization - cases involving cost sharing arrangements, financial products, the semiconductor industry, the automotive industry, and the pharmaceutical industry. These categories were selected because they each had a sufficient number of cases and commonality of issues to warrant their assignment to teams. Cases falling within these five categories have historically accounted for about 40 percent of the APA Program's case load and about half of its total case time. At the end of 2009, cases within these five categories accounted for 86 of the 222 cases pending in the office that were either unilateral APAs or bilateral APAs that had not yet been forwarded to Competent Authority.

Staffing of the coordination teams at the end of 2009 is indicated below:

Auto & Auto Parts

Peter Rock, Reviewer

Tom Herring, Team Leader
Vijay Rajan, Team Leader
Johan Deprez, Team Leader
Walt Bottiny, Principal Economist

Pharmaceuticals & Medical Devices

Clark Armitage, Reviewer

David Chamberlain, Team Leader
Tom Herring, Team Leader
Helen Hong-George, Team Leader
Stephen Meadows, Team Leader
Victor Thayer, Team Leader
Richard Sciacca, Principal Economist

Cost Sharing

Patricia McCarroll, Reviewer

David Chamberlain, Team Leader
Matthew Kramer, Team Leader
Robert Weissler, Team Leader
David Broomhall, Principal Economist

Financial Products
Richard Osborne, Reviewer

Clark Armitage, Deputy Director
Jason Osborn, Team Leader
Lisa Robinson, Team Leader
Robert Weissler, Team Leader
Donna McComber, Principal Economist

Semiconductors

Patricia McCarroll, Reviewer

Matthew Kramer, Team Leader
Vijay Rajan, Team Leader
Behzad Touhidi-Baghini, Principal Economist

The APA Program is mindful that the purpose of the coordination effort is not to impose the same transfer pricing method on all taxpayers in an industry. The appropriate transfer pricing method remains a case-by-case determination, influenced by numerous factors that are not common to all companies operating in a particular industry. While the coordination effort may result in the APA Program promoting a common approach on some issues where appropriate, the Program expects that the greater industry familiarity developed through the coordination effort will also allow it to develop a more sophisticated understanding of issues that will permit more tailored approaches, thereby promoting more (appropriately) varied results than might otherwise be the case.

APA Training

In 2009, the APA office continued its training activities. Training sessions addressed APA-related current developments, the application of Rev. Proc. 2008-31, regulatory developments, new APA office practices and procedures, and international tax law issues. The training materials used for new hires are available to the public through the APA internet site at *http://www.irs.gov/businesses/corporations/*

¶20,140

article/0,,id=96221,00.html. The APA's new-hire materials, which were originally prepared in 2003 and have not been updated, do not constitute guidance on the application of the arm's length standard and are not to be relied upon or cited as precedent. Also available to the public is a spreadsheet model that performs calculations in a Comparable Profits Method (CPM) analysis, which APA economists developed in 2007 and which is now routinely used by the APA office when performing APA analyses. An electronic version of the model may be obtained by contacting the APA office in Washington, D.C. at (202) 435-5220 (not a toll-free number).

APA Program Statistical Data
[§ 521(b)(2)(C) and (E)]

The statistical information required under § 521(b)(2)(C) is contained in Tables 1 and 10 below; the information required under § 521(b)(2)(E) is contained in Tables 2 and 3 below. The 127 APA applications during 2009 represented a new one-year high for the Program, following a record-breaking year in 2008 when we received 123 applications.[7] From 2000-2007, the APA Program averaged 91 applications per year, and it had never received more than 110 applications in a single year. The APA Program expects APA applications to continue in 2010 at the same high levels as in 2008 and 2009.

---

[7] Of the 127 new APA applications in 2009 — the first full year in which Rev. Proc. 2008-31 was in effect — approximately ten submissions invoked APA jurisdiction under Rev. Proc. 2008-31.

TABLE 1: APA APPLICATIONS, EXECUTED APAS, AND PENDING APAS

	Unilateral	Bilateral	Multilateral	Year Total	Cumulative Total
APA applications filed during 2009	39	88		127	1,379
All APAs executed[8]					
Year 2009	21	42	0	63	904
1991-2008	364	464	13	841	
APA renewals executed during 2009	8	20		28	261
APAs revised or amended during 2009	4	4		8	61
Pending requests for APAs	70	282		352	
Pending requests for new APAs	47	174		221	
Pending requests for renewal APAs	23	108		131	
APAs canceled or revoked	0	0		0	9
APAs withdrawn	6	8		14	146

[8] "All APAs executed" includes APA renewals, but not APAs revised or amended.

TABLE 2: MONTHS TO COMPLETE APAs

Months to Complete Advance Pricing Agreements in 2009					
All New		**All Renewals**		**All Combined**	
Average	38.0	Average	37.9	Average	37.9
Median	33.6	Median	31.4	Median	33.1
Unilateral New		**Unilateral Renewals**		**Unilateral Combined**	
Average	25.5	Average	20.5	Average	23.6
Median	19.2	Median	15.1	Median	18.2
Bilateral/ Multilateral New		**Bilateral/Multilateral Renewals**		**Bilateral/Multilateral Combined**	
Average	45.4	Average	44.9	Average	45.1
Median	42.1	Median	37.9	Median	40.6

¶20,140

TABLE 3: APA COMPLETION TIME -MONTHS PER APA

Months	Number of APAs	Months	Number of APAs	Months	Number of APAs
1		26		51	1
2		27	1	52	2
3		28		53	
4		29	1	54	2
5		30	1	55	2
6		31	2	56	3
7		32	1	57	
8		33	4	58	1
9	2	34	1	59	
10		35		60	
11	1	36	2	61	
12	3	37	1	62	1
13	1	38	2	63	
14		39		64	
15		40		65	
16	2	41	3	66	1
17	1	42	1	67	
18	3	43		68	
19	1	44	2	69	
20	2	45	1	70-79	
21	1	46		80	2
22		47		87	1
23	2	48		92	1
24	1	49		122	1
25	2	50			

TABLE 4: RECOMMENDED NEGOTIATING POSITIONS

Recommended Negotiating Positions Completed in 2009	35

TABLE 5: MONTHS TO COMPLETE RECOMMENDED NEGOTIATING POSITIONS

New		Renewal		Combined	
Average	18.5	Average	21.0	Average	19.9
Median	17.2	Median	21.0	Median	18.6

TABLE 6: RECOMMENDED NEGOTIATING POSITIONS COMPLETION TIME - MONTHS PER APA

Months	Number	Months	Number	Months	Number	Months	Number
1		12		23	1	34	
2		13		24	2	35	
3		14	2	25	1	36	1
4	1	15	1	26		37	
5		16	2	27		38	
6		17	4	28		39	
7	1	18	3	29	3	40	
8		19	1	30	1	41	
9		20		31		42	
10	1	21	3	32	1	43	
11	2	22	3	33	1	44	

TABLES 7 AND 8 BELOW SHOW HOW LONG EACH APA REQUEST PENDING AT THE END OF 2009 HAS BEEN IN THE SYSTEM AS MEASURED FROM THE FILING DATE OF THE APA SUBMISSION. THE NUMBERS FOR PENDING UNILATERAL AND BILATERAL CASES DIFFER FROM THE NUMBERS IN TABLE 1 BECAUSE TABLES 7 AND 8 REFLECT ONLY CASES FOR WHICH SUBMISSIONS HAVE BEEN RECEIVED, WHILE TABLE 1 INCLUDES ANY CASE FOR WHICH A USER FEE HAS BEEN PAID.

TABLE 7: UNILATERAL APAs - TIME IN INVENTORY - MONTHS PER APA

Months	Number of APAs	Months	Number of APAs	Months	Number of APAs	Months	Number of APAs
1	7	9	2	17		25	3
2	1	10	1	18	4	26	
3	1	11	3	19	2	27	
4	3	12	1	20	1	28	
5	2	13	4	21	2	29	1
6	4	14		22	3	30	1
7		15	1	23		43	1
8	5	16	1	24	3		

TABLE 8: BILATERAL APAS - TIME IN INVENTORY - MONTHS PER APA

Months	Number of APAs	Months	Number of APAs	Months	Number of APAs	Months	Number of APAs
1	12	25	7	49	1	73	1
2	3	26	3	50	1	74	
3	2	27	4	51	2	75	
4	8	28	5	52	1	76	
5	7	29	6	53	2	77	
6	8	30	2	54	1	78	
7	9	31	4	55		79	
8	12	32	1	56	1	80	
9	7	33	8	57	3	81	
10	6	34		58		82	
11	6	35	4	59	1	83	1
12	10	36	4	60	2	84	
13	9	37	3	61		85	1
14	5	38		62		86	
15	3	39	1	63	2	87	
16	8	40	6	64		88	
17	9	41		65		89	
18	4	42	1	66		90	
19	8	43	1	67		91	
20	3	44	1	68	1	92	
21	10	45	1	69		93	
22	5	46	1	70	2	94	1
23	12	47	1	71		95	
24	4	48	6	72		96+	

Of the 321 cases in the APA Program's inventory shown in Tables 7 and 8, 99 cases (all of which are reflected in Table 8) are bilateral cases that have been forwarded to the Competent Authority office for discussion with a treaty partner. This leaves 222 cases in the APA Program's active inventory at the end of 2009 that are either unilateral APAs (57 cases) or bilateral APAs for which the APA Program has not yet completed a recommended negotiating position (165 cases). Of the 222 active APA cases, 20 involve small business taxpayer (SBT) cases, as defined in Rev. Proc. 2006-9, § 4.12(5).

The table below shows the average age (in months) of the 222 active cases in inventory at the end of 2009, along with a comparison of the number of active cases and their average age at year-end for each year back to 2004. The table also shows the same information for cases that were at least 6-months old or 1-year old (the latter being a subset of the former) at the end of each year to allow comparison without potential distortions caused by year-to-year variations in the number of cases received in the latter half or during the course of the year. The build-up in

¶20,140

inventory during 2009 primarily reflects the delays caused by the significant fluctuations in APA personnel combined with the record number of new APA applications during the past two years. The increases in APA applications and inventory levels have, in fact, masked improvements in recent years in APA productivity, as measured by the number of completed APA items (e.g., APAs, APA amendments, and recommended US negotiating positions) divided by total APA staff hours during a year.

TABLE 9: NUMBER AND AVERAGE AGE OF ACTIVE CASES IN INVENTORY AT YEAR-END

	2004	2005	2006	2007	2008	2009
Active cases	130	133	110	105	161	222
Average age (months)	15.2	13.2	10.6	9.1	10.2	12.9
Active cases 6+ months	106	87	81	66	110	176
Average age (months)	17.8	18.5	13.0	13.0	13.5	15.6
Active cases 1+ year	60	55	32	27	51	116
Average age (months)	24.2	23.3	19.4	18.5	18.7	19.5

¶20,140

TABLE 10: SMALL BUSINESS TAXPAYER APAS

Small Business Taxpayer APAs Completed in 2009	5
New	4
Renewals	1
Unilateral	2
Bilateral	3

TABLE 11: MONTHS TO COMPLETE SMALL BUSINESS TAXPAYER APAS

Months to Complete Small Business Taxpayer APAs in 2009					
New		**Renewal**		**Combined**	
Average	29.3	Average	21.6	Average	27.7
Median	29.3	Average	21.6	Average	23.1

Although the APA Program strives to complete SBT cases on an expedited basis, our experience is that such cases require nearly the same level of resources and the same commitment of time as non-SBT cases. This phenomenon may be explained by a number of factors, including the fact that the complexity or novelty of transfer pricing issues do not necessarily depend on the dollar volume of the related-party transactions, the lesser transfer pricing experience and/or resources of many SBTs, and the importance to both SBTs and non-SBTs of obtaining APA outcomes that reflect each taxpayer's particular facts and circumstances (as opposed to an analysis based on streamlined factual development and general transfer pricing principles).

TABLE 12: INDUSTRIES COVERED[9]

Industry Involved - NAICS Codes	Number
Wholesale trade, durable goods - 421	10-12
Wholesale trade, nondurable goods - 422	10-12
Transportation equipment manufacturing - 336	7-9
Computer and electronic product manufacturing - 334	4-6
Motor vehicle and parts dealers - 441	4-6
Chemical manufacturing - 325	4-6
Electronic equipment, appliance, and component manufacturing -335	1-3
Machinery manufacturing - 333	1-3
Apparel manufacturing - 315	1-3
Oil and gas extraction - 212	1-3
Publishing industries - 511	1-3
Miscellaneous manufacturing - 339	1-3
Professional, scientific, and technical services - 545	1-3
Information service and data processing - 514	1-3
Fabricated metal manufacturing - 332	1-3
Food and beverage stores - 445	1-3
Wood product manufacturing - 321	1-3
Electronic and appliance stores - 443	1-3

[9] The categories in this table are drawn from the North American Industry Classification System (NAICS), which has replaced the U.S. Standard Industrial Classification (SIC) system. NAICS was developed jointly by the United States, Canada, and Mexico to provide new comparability in statistics about business activity across North America.

¶20,140

Trades or Businesses
[§ 521(b)(2)(D)(i)]

The nature of the relationships between the related organizations, trades, or businesses covered by APAs executed in 2009 is set forth in Table 13 below:

TABLE **13**: NATURE OF RELATIONSHIPS BETWEEN RELATED ENTITIES

Relationship	Number of APAs
Foreign Parent - U.S. Subsidiary (-ies)	45
Unilateral	*18*
Bilateral	*27*
U.S. Parent - Foreign Subsidiary (-ies)	≤16
Unilateral	*≤3*
Bilateral	*13*
Partnership	≤3

Covered Transactions
[§ 521(b)(2)(D)(ii)]

The controlled transactions covered by APAs executed in 2009 are set forth in Tables 14 and 15 below:

TABLE 14: TYPES OF COVERED TRANSACTIONS

Transaction Type	Number
Sale of tangible property into the United States	29
Performance of services by U.S. entity	18
Use of intangible property by non-U.S. entity	15
Performance of services by non-U.S. entity	14
Use of intangible property by U.S. entity	10
Sale of tangible property from the United States	9
Other	8
Cost Sharing - U.S. parent/foreign subsidiary	≤3

TABLE 15: TYPES OF SERVICES INCLUDED IN COVERED TRANSACTIONS

Intercompany Services Involved in the Covered Transactions	Number
Marketing	10
Headquarter costs	7
Contract research and development	6
Technical support services	5
Distribution	5
Administrative	5
Logistical support	4
Sales support	4
Purchasing	4
IT	4
Research and development	≤3
Legal	≤3
Corporate and public relations	≤3
Warranty services	≤3
Tax	≤3
Management	≤3
Assembly	≤3
Health, safety, environmental, and regulatory affairs	≤3
Accounting and auditing	≤3
Product support	≤3
Benefits	≤3
Staffing and recruiting	≤3
Accounts receivable	≤3
Payroll	≤3
Treasury activities	≤3
Budgeting	≤3

Business Functions Performed and Risks Assumed
[§ 521(b)(2)(D)(ii)]

The general descriptions of the business functions performed and risks assumed by the organizations, trades, or businesses whose results are tested in the Covered Transactions in the APAs executed in 2009 are set forth in Tables 16 and 17 below:

TABLE 16: FUNCTIONS PERFORMED BY THE TESTED PARTY

Functions Performed	Number
Distribution	59
Manufacturing	41
Product service	35
Marketing functions	29
Research and development	16
Purchasing and materials management	13
Transportation and warehousing	13
Product assembly or packaging	12
Product testing and quality control	11
Managerial, legal, accounting, finance, personnel, and other support services	10
Product design and engineering	8
Licensing of intangibles	8
Technical training and technical support	8
Process engineering	4
Engineering and construction-related services	≤3

TABLE 17: RISKS ASSUMED BY THE TESTED PARTY

Risks Assumed	Number
Market risks, including fluctuations in costs, demand, pricing, and inventory	73
General business risks (e.g., related to ownership of PP&E)	61
Credit and collection risks	47
Product liability risks	38
Financial risks, including interest rates and currency	30
Research and development risks	15

Discussion

The majority of APAs have Covered Transactions that involve numerous business functions and risks. For instance, with respect to functions, multinational groups that manufacture products typically conduct research and development (R&D), engage in product design and engineering, manufacture the product, market and distribute the product, and perform support functions such as legal, finance, and human resources services. Regarding risks, these groups are subject to market risks, R&D risks, financial risks, credit and collection risks, product liability risks, and general business risks. In the APA evaluation process, a significant amount of time and effort is devoted to understanding how the functions and risks are allocated among the controlled group of companies that are party to the Covered Transactions.

In its APA submission, the taxpayer must provide a functional analysis. The functional analysis identifies the economic activities performed, the assets employed, the economic costs incurred, and the risks assumed by each of the controlled parties. The importance of the functional analysis derives from the economic theory positing that there is a positive relationship between risk and expected return and that different functions provide different value and have different opportunity costs associated with them. It is important that the functional analysis go beyond simply categorizing the tested party as, say, a distributor. It should provide more specific information because, in the example of distributors, not all distributors undertake similar functions and risks.

The functional analysis is critical in determining the appropriate TPM (including the selection of comparables, tested party, and profit level indicator (PLI)). In conjunction with evaluating the functional analysis, the APA Program considers contractual terms between the controlled parties, the allocation of risk between the parties, the relevant economic conditions, and the type of property or services at issue. In assessing contractual terms and risk allocations, the APA Program consid-

¶20,140

ers not only written agreements between the parties, but also the economic substance of the transactions as indicated by the conduct of the parties over time, the financial capacity of each party to fund losses arising from risks, and the managerial or operational control each party exercises over activities giving rise to risk. Relevant economic conditions reviewed often include the geographic market and the level of the market in which the functions are performed, and the business cycle or general economic condition of the industry under review.

During 2009, the APA Program received numerous inquiries about the potential effect of the economic downturn on existing and pending APAs. On existing APAs, the APA Program, in consultation with the U.S. Competent Authority, has adopted a general policy not to re-open closed cases absent a special Critical Assumption on point.[10] The APA Program has dealt with pending APA applications (whether pending with the U.S. Competent Authority or the APA Program) on a case-by-case basis. Whether or not a special "down-economy adjustment" might be appropriate depends on a variety of factors, including whether or not the tested party and the comparables have been similarly affected by the downturn, the tested party's historic risk profile and performance, and a taxpayer's willingness to accept a symmetrical adjustment (e.g., in a renewal APA) when the economy improves. Approaches to the down economy that have been considered include changing the APA term, waiting for more current financial data, using a different set of comparables, and/or applying a longer testing period.

The APA Program's evaluation of the functional analysis also considers the assets or other resources employed by each controlled party. In this evaluation, each party's ownership or investment in valuable intangible assets is often an important consideration.

---

[10] *See* Table 21 and accompanying text.

Related Organizations, Trades, or Businesses Whose Prices or Results Are Tested to Determine Compliance with APA Transfer Pricing Methods [§ 521(b)(2)(D)(iii)]

The related organizations, trades, or businesses whose prices or results are tested to determine compliance with TPMs prescribed in APAs executed in 2009 are set forth in Table 18 below:

TABLE 18: RELATED ORGANIZATIONS, TRADES, OR BUSINESSES WHOSE PRICES OR RESULTS ARE TESTED[11]

Type of Organization	Number
U.S. distributor	31
U.S. manufacturer	17
U.S. provider of services	17
Non-U.S. manufacturer	7
Non-U.S. provider of services	7
Non-U.S. distributor	5
Other	5
U.S. licensor of intangible property	≤3
Non-U.S. licensor of intangible property	≤3
Non-U.S. participant in cost sharing agreement	≤3

[11] "Multiple tested parties" includes covered transactions that utilize profit splits, CUPs, and CUTs.

Transfer Pricing Methods and the Circumstances Leading to the Use of Those Methods
[§ 521(b)(2)(D)(iv)]

The TPMs used in APAs executed in 2009 are set forth in Tables 19 and 20 below:

TABLE 19: TRANSFER PRICING METHODS USED FOR TRANSFERS OF TANGIBLE AND INTANGIBLE PROPERTY[12]

TPM Used	Number
CPM: PLI is operating margin	30
CPM: PLI is Berry ratio	14
Unspecified method	12
Residual profit split	9
CPM: PLI is return on assets or capital employed	7
CPM: PLI is markup on total costs	7
CUT (intangibles only)	5
Comparable Other profit split profit split	≤3
Cost Plus Method (tangibles only)	≤3
CPM: PLI is other PLI	≤3
CPM: PLI is gross margin	≤3
CPM: PLI is markup on other costs	≤3

[12] PLIs used with the Comparable Profit Method of Treas. Reg. § 1.482-5, and as used in these TPM tables, are as follows: (1) operating margin (ratio of operating profit to sales); (2) Berry ratio (ratio of gross profit to operating expenses); (3) gross margin (ratio of gross profit to sales); (4) markup on total costs (percentage markup on total costs); and (5) rate of return on assets or capital employed (ratio of operating profit to operating assets).

TABLE 20: TRANSFER PRICING METHODS USED FOR SERVICES

TPM Used	Number
CPM. PLI is operating profit to total services cost ratio	11
Services Cost Method: Specified Covered Services	4
CPM: PLI is operating margin	≤3
CPM: PLI is Berry ratio	≤3
CPM: PLI is return on assets or capital employed	≤3
Cost of Services Plus Method	≤3
Services Cost Method: Low Margin Covered Services	≤3
Comparable Uncontrolled Services Price Method	≤3

Discussion

The TPMs used in APAs completed during 2009 were based on the section 482 regulations. Under Treas. Reg. § 1.482-3, the arm's length amount for controlled transfers of tangible property may be determined using the Comparable Uncontrolled Price (CUP) Method, the Resale Price Method, the Cost Plus Method, the Comparable Profits Method (CPM), or the Profit Split Method. Under Treas. Reg. § 1.482-4, the arm's length amount for controlled transfers of intangible property may be determined using the Comparable Uncontrolled Transaction (CUT) Method, the CPM, or the Profit Split Method. An "Unspecified Method" may be used for transfers of either tangible or intangible property if it provides a more reliable result than the enumerated methods under the best method rule of Treas. Reg. § 1.482-1(c).

For transfers involving the provision of services, Treas. Reg. § 1.482-2(b) provided that services performed for the benefit of another member of a controlled group should bear an arm's length charge, either deemed to be equal to the cost of providing the services or an amount that would have been charged between independent parties. Generally effective beginning in 2007, Temp. Reg. § 1.482-9T provides that the arm's length charge for controlled services transactions may be determined under the Services Cost Method, the Comparable Uncontrolled Services Price (CUSP) Method, the Gross Services Margin Method, the Cost of Services Plus Method, the CPM, the Profit Split Method, or an Unspecified Method. In addition, Treas. Reg. § 1.482-2(a) provides rules concerning the proper treatment of loans or advances.

On January 5, 2009, the IRS issued new temporary regulations, Treas. Reg. § 1.482-7T, which provide rules for qualified cost sharing arrangements under which the parties agree to share the costs of developing intangibles in proportion to their

¶20,140

shares of reasonably anticipated benefits. APAs involving cost sharing arrangements generally address both the method of allocating costs among the parties as well as determining the appropriate amount of the payment for "platform contribution transactions" (PCTs) due for the transfer of pre-existing intangibles, and the commitment of services with embedded intangibles, among the controlled participants (known as "buy ins" in the previous cost-sharing regulations). In 2009, the APA Program completed its recommendations on three or fewer bilateral cost sharing/PCT cases and sent those on to Competent Authority. In addition, the APA Program is currently working on nearly ten cases involving cost-sharing/PCTs, split almost evenly between bilateral and unilateral. The PCT cases include both initial and subsequent buy-in/buy-out transactions. The methods used in the completed and pending PCT cases include valuations based on the income method, including cases involving a split of the discounted present value of platform contributions made by two or more parties, and other types of analyses.

In reviewing the TPMs applicable to transfers of tangible and intangible property reflected in Table 19, the majority of the APAs followed the specified methods. However, several points should be made. The section 482 regulations note that for transfers of tangible property, the CUP Method will generally be the most direct and reliable measure of an arm's length price for the controlled transaction if sufficiently reliable comparable transactions can be identified. Treas. Reg. § 1.482-3(b)(2)(ii)(A). As in earlier years, it was the experience of the APA Program in 2009, that in the cases that came into the APA Program, sufficiently reliable CUP transactions were difficult to find.

Similar to the CUP Method, for transfers of intangible property, the CUT Method will generally provide the most reliable measure of an arm's length result if sufficiently reliable comparables may be found. Treas. Reg. § 1.482-4(c)(2)(ii). It has generally been difficult to identify external comparables, and APAs using the CUT Method tend to rely on internal transactions between the taxpayer and unrelated parties. In 2009, five Covered Transactions utilized the CUT TPM.

The Resale Price Method was not applied in 2009. See Treas. Reg. § 1.482-3(c), (d).

The CPM is frequently applied in APAs. That is because reliable public data on comparable business activities of independent companies may be more readily available than potential CUP data, and comparability of resources employed, functions, risks, and other relevant considerations are more likely to exist than comparability of product. The CPM also tends to be less sensitive than other methods to differences in accounting practices between the tested party and comparable companies, e.g., classification of expenses as cost of goods sold or operating expenses. Treas. Reg. § 1.482-3(c)(3)(iii)(B) and (d)(3)(iii)(B). In addition, the degree of functional comparability required to obtain a reliable result under the CPM is generally less than that required under the Resale Price Method or the Cost Plus Method. Lesser functional comparability is required because differences in functions performed often are reflected in operating expenses, and thus taxpayers performing different functions may have very different gross profit margins but earn similar levels of operating profit. Treas. Reg. § 1.482-5(c)(2).

¶20,140

Table 19 reflects at least 61 uses of the CPM (with varying PLIs) in Covered Transactions involving tangible or intangible property. In some APAs, the CPM was also used concurrently with other methods.

The CPM has proven to be versatile in part because of the various PLIs that can be used in connection with the method. Reaching agreement on the appropriate PLI has been the subject of much discussion in many of the cases, and it depends heavily on the facts and circumstances. Some APAs have called for different PLIs to apply to different parts of the Covered Transactions or applied a secondary PLI as a check against the primary PLI.

The CPM was also used regularly with services as the Covered Transactions in APAs executed in 2009. There were at least 14 services Covered Transactions using the CPM Method with various PLIs according to the specific facts of the taxpayers involved. At least five services-related APAs completed in 2009 applied the new Services Cost Method under the § 1.482-9T regulations. Table 20 reflects the methods used to determine the arm's length results for APAs involving services transactions.

In 2009, nine APAs involving tangible or intangible property used the Residual Profit Split Method. Treas. Reg. § 1.482-6(c)(3). In residual profit split cases, routine contributions by the controlled parties are allocated routine market returns, and the residual income is allocated among the controlled taxpayers based upon the relative value of their contributions of non-routine intangible property to the relevant business activity.

Profit splits have also been used in a number of financial product APAs in which the primary income-producing functions are performed in more than one jurisdiction.

Critical Assumptions
[§ 521(b)(2)(D)(v)]

Critical Assumptions used in APAs executed in 2009 are described in Table 21 below:

TABLE 21: CRITICAL ASSUMPTIONS

Critical Assumptions involving the following:	Number of APAs
Material changes to tax and/or financial accounting practices	63
Material changes to the business	63
Assets will remain substantially same	15
Other	10
Changes in affiliated companies	≤3
Material sales fluctuations	≤3
Currency fluctuations	≤3
Other financial ratios	≤3

Discussion

APAs include critical assumptions upon which their respective TPMs depend. A critical assumption is any fact (whether or not within the control of the taxpayer) related to the taxpayer, a third party, an industry, or business and economic conditions, the continued existence of which is material to the taxpayer's proposed TPM. Critical assumptions might include, for example, a particular mode of conducting business operations, a particular corporate or business structure, or a range of expected business volume. Rev. Proc. 2006-09, § 4.05. Failure to meet a critical assumption may render an APA inappropriate or unworkable. Most APAs contain only the standard critical assumption language set forth in Appendix B of the Model APA (Attachment A to this Announcement and Report). Where appropriate, additional critical assumption language may be added, but the APA Program generally seeks to limit additional critical assumption language to objective, measurable benchmarks.

A critical assumption may change or fail to materialize due to changes in economic circumstances, such as a fundamental and dramatic change in the economic conditions of a particular industry. In addition, a critical assumption may change or fail to materialize due to a taxpayer's actions that are initiated for good faith business reasons, such as a change in business strategy, mode of conducting

¶20,140

operations, or the cessation or transfer of a business segment or entity covered by the APA.

If a critical assumption has not been met, the APA may be revised by agreement of the parties. If such an agreement cannot be achieved, the APA is canceled. If a critical assumption has not been met, the taxpayer must notify and discuss the APA terms with the Service, and, in the case of a bilateral APA, competent authority consideration is initiated. Rev. Proc. 2006-09, §§ 11.05, 11.06.

Sources of Comparables, Selection Criteria, and the Nature of Adjustments to Comparables and Tested Parties
[§ 521(b)(2)(D)(v), (vi), and (vii)]

The sources of comparables, selection criteria, and rationale used in determining the selection criteria for APAs executed in 2009 are described in Tables 22 through 24 below. Various formulas for making adjustments to comparables are included as Attachment B.

TABLE 22: SOURCES OF COMPARABLES

Comparable Sources	Number of Times This Source Used
Compustat	78
Disclosure	31
No Comparables used	19
Worldscope	15
Other	14
Global Vantage	10
Moody's	9
Global Symposium	7
Osiris	≤3
Mergent FIS	≤3
Japan Accounts and Data on Enterprises (JADE)	≤3
Orbis	≤3
Bonds Franchise Guide	≤3

TABLE 23: COMPARABLES SELECTION CRITERIA

Selection Criteria Considered	Number of Times This Criterion Used
Comparable functions	81
Comparable risks	56
Comparable industry	56
Comparable intangibles	33
Comparable products	30
Comparable terms	6

TABLE 24: ADJUSTMENTS TO COMPARABLES OR TESTED PARTIES

Adjustment	Number of Times Used
Balance sheet adjustments	
Payables	54
Receivables	52
Inventory	52
Property, plant, equipment	4
Other	≤3
Accounting adjustments	
LIFO to FIFO inventory accounting	34
Other	15
Accounting reclassifications (e.g., from COGS to operating expenses)	≤3
Profit level indicator adjustments (used to "back into" one PLI from another PLI)	
Operating expense	≤3
Other	≤3
Miscellaneous adjustments	
Other	6
Goodwill value or amortization	≤3
Stock-based compensation	≤3
Geographic adjustments	≤3

Discussion

At the core of most APAs are comparables. The APA Program works closely with taxpayers to find the best and most reliable comparables for each Covered Transaction. In some cases, CUPs or CUTs can be identified. In other cases, profit data on comparable business activities of independent companies are used in applying the CPM or a Profit Split Method. Generally, in the APA Program's experience since 1991, CUPs and CUTs have been most often derived from the internal transactions of the taxpayer.

For profit-based methods in which comparable business activities or functions of independent companies are sought, the APA Program typically has selected them using a three-part process. First, a pool of companies with potentially comparable business activities has been identified through broad searches. From this pool, companies performing business activities that are clearly not comparable to those of the tested party have been eliminated through the use of quantitative and qualitative analyses, i.e., quantitative screens and review of business descriptions. Then, based on a review of available descriptive and financial data, a set of comparable independent companies has been finalized. The comparability of the final set has then been enhanced by adjusting their financial data.

Sources of Comparables

Comparables used in APAs can be U.S. or foreign, depending on the relevant market, the type of transaction being evaluated, the availability of relevant data, and the results of the functional and risk analyses. In general, comparables have been located by searching a variety of databases that provide data on U.S. publicly traded companies and on a combination of public and private non-U.S. companies. Table 22 shows the various databases and other sources used in selecting comparables for the APAs executed in 2009.

Although comparables were most often identified from the databases cited in Table 22, in some cases, comparables were found from other sources, such as comparables derived internally from taxpayer transactions with third parties.

Selecting Comparables

Initial pools of potential comparables generally are derived from the databases using a combination of industry and keyword identifiers. Then, the pool is refined using a variety of selection criteria specific to the transaction or business activity being tested and the TPM being used.

The listed databases allow for searches by industrial classification, by keywords, or by both. These searches can yield a number of companies whose business activities may or may not be comparable to those of the entity being tested. Therefore, comparables based solely on industry classification or keyword searches are rarely used in APAs. Instead, the pool of comparables is examined closely, and companies are selected based on a combination of screens, business descriptions, and other information such as that found in the companies' Annual Reports to shareholders and filings with the U.S. Securities and Exchange Commission (SEC), company websites, and investment analyst reports.

¶20,140

Business activities of independent companies generally must meet certain basic comparability criteria to be considered comparable. The independent company's functions, risks, and economic conditions, and the property (product or intangible) and services associated with the company's business activities, must be comparable to those involved in the Covered Transaction. Determining comparability requires judgment - the goal has been to use comparability criteria restrictive enough to eliminate business activities that are not comparable, but yet not so restrictive as to leave no comparables remaining. The APA Program normally has begun with relatively strict comparability criteria and then has relaxed them slightly if necessary to derive a pool of reliable comparables. A determination on the appropriate size of the comparables set, as well as the business activities that comprise the set, is highly fact-specific and depends on the reliability of the results.

In addition, the APA Program, consistent with the section 482 regulations, generally has looked at the results of comparables over a multi-year period (the analysis window). Often this has been a three-year or a five-year period, but other periods are sometimes used depending on the circumstances of the controlled transaction. Using a shorter period might result in the inclusion of comparables in different stages of economic development or use of atypical years of a comparable due to cyclical fluctuations in business conditions. The economic downturn has focused particular attention on the appropriate analysis window for APAs with terms that include 2008 and 2009, given the different economic conditions that may have confronted the comparables during the years comprising the analysis window, which typically lags behind the years covered by an APA (e.g., the comparables results for 2004-08 may be used to test the taxpayer's results under the APA from 2008-2012). As noted in the discussion following Table 17, the APA Program has been dealing with the economic downturn in various ways, including waiting for more current comparables' financial data to develop a more contemporaneous analysis window.

Many Covered Transactions have been tested with comparables that have been chosen using additional criteria and/or screens. These include sales level criteria and tests for financial distress and product comparability. These common selection criteria and screens have been used to increase the overall comparability of a group of companies and as a basis for further research. The sales level screen, for example, has been used to remove companies that, due to their smaller size, might face fundamentally different economic conditions from those of the transaction or business activities being tested. In addition, APA analyses have incorporated selection criteria designed to identify and remove companies experiencing "financial distress" because of concerns that companies in financial distress face unusual circumstances and operational constraints that render them not comparable to the business activity being tested. These "financial distress" criteria may include an unfavorable auditor's opinion, bankruptcy, failure to comply with financial obligations (e.g., debt covenants), and, in certain circumstances, operating losses in a given number of years.

An additional important class of selection criteria is the development and ownership of intangible property. Most often, comparables are sought to test the

¶20,140

results of a business activity that does not employ significant intangible assets or engage in intangible development. Thus, for example, in some cases in which the tested business activity is manufacturing conducted by a controlled entity that does not own significant manufacturing intangibles or conduct R&D, several criteria have been used to ensure that the comparables similarly do not own significant intangibles or conduct R&D. These selection criteria have included determining the importance of patents to a company or screening for R&D expenditures as a percentage of sales. Similar selection criteria may be applied to ensure, where appropriate, that the comparables do not own or develop significant marketing intangibles such as valuable trademarks. Again, quantitative screens related to identifying comparables with significant intangible property generally have been used in conjunction with an understanding of the comparable derived from publicly available business information.

Selection criteria relating to asset comparability and operating expense comparability have also been used at times. A screen of property, plant, and equipment (PP&E) as a percentage of sales or assets, combined with a reading of a company's SEC filings, has been used to help ensure that distributors (generally lower PP&E) were not compared with manufacturers (generally higher PP&E), regardless of their industry classification. Similarly, a test involving the ratio of operating expenses to sales has helped to determine whether a company undertakes a significant marketing and distribution function.

Table 25 shows the number of times various screens were used in APAs executed in 2009:

TABLE 25: COMPARABILITY AND FINANCIAL DISTRESS SCREENS

Comparability/Financial Distress Screen	Times Used
Comparability screens used	
R&D/sales	40
Foreign sales/total sales	26
Sales	26
Other	22
Government sales	7
Non-startup or start-up	5
PP&E total assets	≤3
PP&E/sales	≤3
SG&A/sales	≤3
Financial distress	
Bankruptcy	51
Unfavorable auditor's opinion	34
Losses in one or more years	10
Other	6

Adjusting Comparables

After the comparables have been selected, the regulations require that "[i]f there are material differences between the controlled and uncontrolled transactions, adjustments must be made if the effect of such differences on prices or profits can be ascertained with sufficient accuracy to improve the reliability of the results." Treas. Reg. § 1.482-1(d)(2). In almost all cases involving income-statement-based PLIs used in the CPM or the Residual Profit Split Method, certain "asset intensity" or "balance sheet" adjustments for factors that have generally agreed-upon effects on profits are calculated. In addition, in specific cases, additional adjustments are performed to improve reliability.

The most common balance sheet adjustments used in APAs are adjustments for differences in accounts receivable, inventories, and accounts payable. The APA

¶20,140

Program generally has required adjustments for receivables, inventory, and payables based on the principle that there is an opportunity cost for holding assets. For these assets, it is generally assumed that the cost is appropriately measured by the interest rate on short-term debt.

To compare the profits of two business activities with different relative levels of receivables, inventory, or payables, the APA Program estimates the carrying costs of each item and adjusts profits accordingly. Although different formulas have been used in specific APA cases, Attachment B presents one set of formulas used in many APAs. Underlying these formulas are the notions that (1) balance sheet items normally should be expressed as mid-year averages, (2) formulas should try to avoid using data items that are being tested by the TPM (for example, if sales are controlled, then the denominator of the balance sheet ratio should not be sales), (3) a short term interest rate should be used, and (4) an interest factor should recognize the average holding period of the relevant asset. As in 2007 and 2008, during the course of 2009, the APA Program used an interest rate equal to LIBOR (3 months) plus 200 basis points for purposes of calculating adjustments for accounts receivable and accounts payable for U.S. companies in many cases. In addition, the APA Program often used an interest rate equal to the Corporate Bonds (Moody's) Baa rate for purposes of calculating inventory adjustments for U.S. companies. However, the facts and circumstances surrounding a given case will ultimately determine the reliability of making balance sheet adjustments and the selection of the most reliable interest rate.

The APA Program also requires that financial data be compared on a consistent accounting basis. For example, although financial statements may be prepared on a first-in first-out (FIFO) basis, cross-company comparisons are less meaningful if one or more of the comparables use last-in first-out (LIFO) inventory accounting methods. This adjustment directly affects costs of goods sold and inventories, and therefore affects both profitability measures and inventory adjustments.

In some cases, the APA Program has made an adjustment to account for differences in relative levels of PP&E between a tested business activity and the comparables. Ideally, comparables and the business activity being tested will have fairly similar relative levels of PP&E, since major differences can be a sign of fundamentally different functions and risks. Typically, the PP&E adjustment is made using a medium-term interest rate. During the course of 2009, the APA Program often used the Corporate Bonds (Moody's) Baa rate as the interest rate for purposes of calculating adjustments for inventory and PP&E for U.S. companies. Again, however, the facts and circumstances surrounding a given case will ultimately determine the reliability of making balance sheet adjustments and the selection of the most reliable interest rate.

Additional adjustments used less frequently include those for differences in other balance sheet items, operating expenses, R&D, or currency risk. Accounting adjustments, such as reclassifying items from cost of goods sold to operating expenses, are also made when warranted to increase reliability. Often, data are not available for both the controlled and uncontrolled transactions in sufficient detail to allow for these types of adjustments.

¶20,140

The adjustments made to comparables or tested parties in APAs executed in 2009 are reflected in Table 24 above.

Ranges, Targets, and Adjustment Mechanisms
[§ 521(b)(2)(D)(viii)-(ix)]

The types of ranges, targets, and adjustment mechanisms used in APAs executed in 2009 are described in Tables 26 and 27 below.

TABLE 26: RANGES AND TARGETS[13]

Type of Range	Number
Interquartile range	50
Specific point within CPM range (not floor or ceiling)	21
Cost-only services	11
Other	9
Specific point (royalty)	7
Full range	≤3
Ceiling (i.e., result must be no more than x)	≤3

---

[13] The numbers do not include TPMs with cost or cost-plus methodologies.

¶20,140

TABLE 27: ADJUSTMENTS WHEN OUTSIDE THE RANGE

Adjustment mechanism	Number
Taxpayer makes an adjustment: to specified point or royalty rate	40
Taxpayer makes an adjustment: to closest edge of multi-year average	29
Taxpayer makes an adjustment based on subsequent Competent Authority negotiations	6
Taxpayer makes an adjustment: to median of multi-year average	5
Taxpayer makes an adjustment: to closest edge of single year	5
Taxpayer makes an adjustment: to a specific dollar amount	≤3
Taxpayer makes an adjustment: to median of current year	≤3

Discussion

Treas. Reg. § 1.482-1(e)(1) states that sometimes a pricing method will yield "a single result that is the most reliable measure of an arm's length result." Sometimes, however, a method may yield "a range of reliable results," called the "arm's length range." A taxpayer whose results fall within the arm's length range will not be subject to adjustment.

Under Treas. Reg. § 1.482-1(e)(2)(i), such a range is normally derived by considering a set of more than one comparable uncontrolled transaction of similar comparability and reliability. If these comparables are of very high quality, as defined in the section 482 regulations, then under Treas. Reg. § 1.482-1(e)(2)(iii)(A), the arm's length range includes the results of all of the comparables (from the least to the greatest). However, the APA Program has only rarely identified cases meeting the requirements for the full range. If the comparables are of lesser quality, then under Treas. Reg. § 1.482-1(e)(2)(iii)(B), "the reliability of the analysis must be increased, when it is possible to do so, by adjusting the range through application of a valid statistical method to the results of all of the uncontrolled comparables." One such method, the "interquartile range," is ordinarily acceptable, although a different statistical method "may be applied if it provides a more reliable measure." The interquartile range is defined as, roughly, the range from the 25th to the 75th percentile of the comparables' results. See Treas. Reg. § 1.482-1(e)(2)(iii)(C). The interquartile range was used 50 times in 2009.

Twenty-eight Covered Transactions reflected on Table 26 were tested against a single, specific result. Some APAs - deliberately infrequent - specify not a point or a range, but a "floor" or a "ceiling." When a floor is used, the tested party's result must be greater than or equal to some particular value. When a ceiling is used, the tested party's result must be less than or equal to some particular value. Three or fewer APAs executed in 2009 used a floor or a ceiling.

Some APAs look to a tested party's results over a period of years (multi-year averaging) to determine whether a taxpayer has complied with the APA. In 2009, rolling multi-year averaging was used for four Covered Transactions. All four of these Covered Transactions used four-year averages. Two Covered Transactions used cumulative multi-year averaging, while 42 Covered Transactions used term averages and seven Covered Transactions used partial-term averages.

Adjustments

Where a taxpayer's actual transactions do not produce results that conform to the TPM, a taxpayer must nonetheless report its taxable income in an amount consistent with the TPM (an APA primary adjustment), as further discussed in § 11.02 of Rev. Proc. 2006-09. When the TPM specifies an arm's length range, an APA primary adjustment is necessary only if the taxpayer's actual transactional result falls outside the specified range.

Under Treas. Reg. § 1.482-1(e)(3), if a taxpayer's results fall outside the arm's length range, the Service may adjust the result "to any point within the arm's length range." Accordingly, an APA may permit or require a taxpayer to make an adjustment after the year's end to put the year's results within the range, or at the point specified by the APA. Similarly, to enforce the terms of an APA, the Service may make such an adjustment. When the APA specifies a range, the adjustment is sometimes to the closest edge of the range, and sometimes to another point such as the median of the interquartile range. Depending on the facts of each case, automatic adjustments are not always permitted. APAs may specify that in such a case there will be a negotiation between the competent authorities involved to determine whether and to what extent an adjustment should be made. APAs may permit automatic adjustments unless the result is far outside the range specified in the APA. Thus, APAs provide flexibility and efficiency, permitting adjustments when normal business fluctuations and uncertainties push the result somewhat outside the range.

APA Term and Rollback Lengths
[§ 521(b)(2)(D)(x)]

The various term lengths for APAs executed in 2009 are set forth in Table 28 below:

TABLE **28**: TERMS OF APAs

APA Term in Years	Number of APAs
3	≤3
4	8
5	27
6	13
7	4
8	7
9	≤3
10 or more	≤3

The number of rollback years to which an APA TPM was applied in 2009 is set forth in Table 29 below:

TABLE 29: NUMBER OF YEARS COVERED BY ROLLBACK OF APA TPM

Number of Rollback Years	Number of APAs
1	≤3
2	5
3	7
4	5
5 or more	≤3

Together, Tables 28 and 29 indicate that the 63 APAs completed in 2009 covered more than 410 taxable years. In terms of dollar value, 46 of the 63 completed APAs involved Covered Transactions exceeding $100 million per year, with 34 APAs covering transactions exceeding $250 million per year. Combining the total covered years and the total dollar-value of Covered Transactions represents one measure of the effectiveness of the APA Program.

Nature of Documentation Required
[§ 521(b)(2)(D)(xi)]

APAs executed in 2009 required that taxpayers provide various documents with their annual reports. These documents are described in Table 30 below:

TABLE 30: NATURE OF DOCUMENTATION REQUIRED

Documentation	Number
Statement identifying all material differences between Taxpayer's business operations during APA Year and description of Taxpayer's business operations contained in Taxpayer's request for APA, or if there have been no such material differences, a statement to that effect.	63
Statement of all material changes in the Taxpayer's accounting methods and classifications, and methods of estimation, from those described or used in Taxpayer's request for the APA. If there has been no material change in accountings methods and classifications or methods of estimation, a statement to that effect.	63
Description of any failure to meet Critical Assumptions or, if there have been none, a statement to that effect.	63
Copy of the APA	63
Financial analysis demonstrating Taxpayer's compliance with TPM.	63
Organizational chart	63
Any change to the taxpayer notice information in section 14 of the APA.	63
The amount, reason for, and financial analysis of any compensating adjustment under Paragraph 4 of Appendix A and Rev. Proc. 2006-9, § 11.02(3), for the APA year, including but not limited to: the amounts paid or received by each affected entity; the character (such as capital or ordinary expense) and country source of the funds transferred, and the specific line item(s) of any affected U.S. tax return; and any change to any entity classification for federal income tax purposes of any member of the Taxpayer's group that is relevant to the APA.	63
The amounts, description, reason for, and financial analysis of any book-tax difference relevant to the TPM for the APA Year, as reflected on Schedule M-1 or Schedule M-3 of the U.S. return for the APA Year.	63
Financial Statements and any necessary account detail to show compliance with the TPM, with a copy of the opinion from an independent CPA required by paragraph 5(f) of the APA.	63

Documentation	Number
Certified public accountant's opinion that financial statements present fairly the financial position of Taxpayer and the results of its operations, in accordance with a foreign GAAP.	5
CPA review of Taxpayer's financial statements	5
Other	4
Financial statements prepared in accordance with a foreign GAAP.	≤3
Pertinent intercompany agreements	≤3
Various work papers	≤3

Approaches for Sharing of Currency or Other Risks
[§ 521(b)(2)(D)(xii)]

During 2009, there were 30 tested parties that faced financial risks, including interest rate and currency risks. In appropriate cases, APAs may provide specific approaches for dealing with currency risk, such as adjustment mechanisms and/or critical assumptions.

Efforts to Ensure Compliance with APAs
[§ 521(b)(2)(F)]

As described in Rev. Proc. 2006-09, § 11.01, APA taxpayers are required to file annual reports to demonstrate compliance with the terms and conditions of the APA. The filing and review of annual reports is a critical part of the APA process. Through annual report review, the APA Program monitors taxpayer compliance with the APA on a contemporaneous basis. Annual report review provides current information on the success or problems associated with the various TPMs adopted in the APA process.

All reports received by the APA Program are assigned to a designated APA team leader. Whenever possible, annual report reviews are assigned to the team leader who negotiated the case, since that person will already be familiar with the relevant facts and terms of the agreement. Other team leaders and economists may assist the assigned team leader as well. Once received by the APA Program, the annual report is also sent to the field personnel with exam jurisdiction over the taxpayer.

The statistics for the review of APA annual reports are reflected in Table 31 below. As of December 31, 2009, there were 259 pending annual reports. In 2009, 414 reports were closed.

TABLE 31: STATISTICS OF ANNUAL REPORTS

Number of APA annual reports pending as of December 31, 2009	259
Number of APA annual reports closed in 2009	414
Number of APA annual reports requiring adjustment in 2009	7
Number of taxpayers involved in adjustments	7
Number of APA annual report cases over one-year old	186

Attachment A
Model APA - Based on Revenue Procedure 2006-9

ADVANCE PRICING AGREEMENT

between

[*Insert Taxpayer's Name*]

and

THE INTERNAL REVENUE SERVICE

ADVANCE PRICING AGREEMENT
between
[*Insert Taxpayer's Name*]
and
THE INTERNAL REVENUE SERVICE

PARTIES

The Parties to this Advance Pricing Agreement (APA) are the Internal Revenue Service (IRS) and [*Insert Taxpayer's Name*], EIN _____.

RECITALS

[*Insert Taxpayer Name*] is the common parent of an affiliated group filing consolidated U.S. tax returns (collectively referred to as "Taxpayer"), and is entering into this APA on behalf of itself and other members of its consolidated group.

Taxpayer's principal place of business is [*City, State*]. [*Insert general description of taxpayer and other relevant parties*].

This APA contains the Parties' agreement on the best method for determining arm's-length prices of the Covered Transactions under I.R.C. section 482, any applicable tax treaties, and the Treasury Regulations.

{If renewal, add} [Taxpayer and IRS previously entered into an APA covering taxable years ending _____ to _____, executed on _____.]

AGREEMENT

The Parties agree as follows:

1. *Covered Transactions.* This APA applies to the Covered Transactions, as defined in Appendix A.

2. *Transfer Pricing Method.* Appendix A sets forth the Transfer Pricing Method (TPM) for the Covered Transactions.

3. *Term.* This APA applies to Taxpayer's taxable years ending _____ through _____ (APA Term).

4. *Operation.*

a. Revenue Procedure 2006-9 governs the interpretation, legal effect, and administration of this APA.

b. Nonfactual oral and written representations, within the meaning of sections 10.04 and 10.05 of Revenue Procedure 2006-9 (including any proposals to use particular TPMs), made in conjunction with the APA Request constitute statements made in compromise negotiations within the meaning of Rule 408 of the Federal Rules of Evidence.

¶20,140

5. *Compliance.*

a. Taxpayer must report its taxable income in an amount that is consistent with Appendix A and all other requirements of this APA on its timely filed U.S. Return. However, if Taxpayer's timely filed U.S. Return for an APA Year is filed prior to, or no later than 60 days after, the effective date of this APA, then Taxpayer must report its taxable income for that APA Year in an amount that is consistent with Appendix A and all other requirements of this APA either on the original U.S. Return or on an amended U.S. Return filed no later than 120 days after the effective date of this APA, or through such other means as may be specified herein.

b. *{Insert when U.S. Group or Foreign Group contains more than one member.}* [This APA addresses the arm's-length nature of prices charged or received in the aggregate between Taxpayer and Foreign Participants with respect to the Covered Transactions. Except as explicitly provided, this APA does not address and does not bind the IRS with respect to prices charged or received, or the relative amounts of income or loss realized, by particular legal entities that are members of U.S. Group or that are members of Foreign Group.]

c. For each taxable year covered by this APA (APA Year), if Taxpayer complies with the terms and conditions of this APA, then the IRS will not make or propose any allocation or adjustment under I.R.C. section 482 to the amounts charged in the aggregate between Taxpayer and Foreign Participant[s] with respect to the Covered Transactions.

d. If Taxpayer does not comply with the terms and conditions of this APA, then the IRS may:

   i. enforce the terms and conditions of this APA and make or propose allocations or adjustments under I.R.C. section 482 consistent with this APA;

   ii. cancel or revoke this APA under section 11.06 of Revenue Procedure 2006-9; or

   iii. revise this APA, if the Parties agree.

e. Taxpayer must timely file an Annual Report (an original and four copies) for each APA Year in accordance with Appendix C and section 11.01 of Revenue Procedure 2006-9. Taxpayer must file the Annual Report for all APA Years through the APA Year ending [insert year] by [insert date]. Taxpayer must file the Annual Report for each subsequent APA Year by [insert month and day] immediately following the close of that APA Year. (If any date falls on a weekend or holiday, the Annual Report shall be due on the next date that is not a weekend or holiday.) The IRS may request additional information reasonably necessary to clarify or complete the Annual Report. Taxpayer will provide such requested information within 30 days. Additional time may be allowed for good cause.

f. The IRS will determine whether Taxpayer has complied with this APA based on Taxpayer's U.S. Returns, Financial Statements, and other APA Records, for the APA Term and any other year necessary to verify compliance. For Taxpayer to comply with this APA, an independent certified public accountant must *{use the* *following or an alternative}* render an opinion that Taxpayer's Financial Statements present fairly, in all material respects, Taxpayer's financial position under U.S. GAAP.

g. In accordance with section 11.04 of Revenue Procedure 2006-9, Taxpayer will (1) maintain its APA Records, and (2) make them available to the IRS in connection with an examination under section 11.03. Compliance with this subparagraph constitutes compliance with the record-maintenance provisions of I.R.C. sections 6038A and 6038C for the Covered Transactions for any taxable year during the APA Term.

h. The True Taxable Income within the meaning of Treasury Regulations sections 1.482-1(a)(1) and (i)(9) of a member of an affiliated group filing a U.S. consolidated return will be determined under the I.R.C. section 1502 Treasury Regulations.

i. *{Optional for US Parent Signatories}* To the extent that Taxpayer's compliance with this APA depends on certain acts of Foreign Group members, Taxpayer will ensure that each Foreign Group member will perform such acts.

6. *Critical Assumptions.* This APA's critical assumptions, within the meaning of Revenue Procedure 2006-9, section 4.05, appear in Appendix B. If any critical assumption has not been met, then Revenue Procedure 2006-9, section 11.06, governs.

7. *Disclosure.* This APA, and any background information related to this APA or the APA Request, are: (1) considered "return information" under I.R.C. section 6103(b)(2)(C); and (2) not subject to public inspection as a "written determination" under I.R.C. section 6110(b)(1). Section 521(b) of Pub. L. 106-170 provides that the Secretary of the Treasury must prepare a report for public disclosure that includes certain specifically designated information concerning all APAs, including this APA, in a form that does not reveal taxpayers' identities, trade secrets, and proprietary or confidential business or financial information.

8. *Disputes.* If a dispute arises concerning the interpretation of this APA, the Parties will seek a resolution by the IRS Associate Chief Counsel (International) to the extent reasonably practicable, before seeking alternative remedies.

9. *Materiality.* In this APA the terms "material" and "materially" will be interpreted consistently with the definition of "material facts" in Revenue Procedure 2006-9, section 11.06(4).

10. *Section Captions.* This APA's section captions, which appear in *italics*, are for convenience and reference only. The captions do not affect in any way the interpretation or application of this APA.

11. *Terms and Definitions.* Unless otherwise specified, terms in the plural include the singular and vice versa. Appendix D contains definitions for capitalized terms not elsewhere defined in this APA.

12. *Entire Agreement and Severability.* This APA is the complete statement of the Parties' agreement. The Parties will sever, delete, or reform any invalid or

unenforceable provision in this APA to approximate the Parties' intent as nearly as possible.

13. *Successor in Interest.* This APA binds, and inures to the benefit of, any successor in interest to Taxpayer.

14. *Notice.* Any notices required by this APA or Revenue Procedure 2006-9 must be in writing. Taxpayer will send notices to the IRS at the address and in the manner set forth in Revenue Procedure 2006-9, section 4.11. The IRS will send notices to:

> Taxpayer Corporation
>
> Attn: Jane Doe, Sr. Vice President (Taxes)
>
> 1000 Any Road
>
> Any City, USA 10000
>
> (phone: _____)

15. *Effective Date and Counterparts.* This APA is effective starting on the date, or later date of the dates, upon which all Parties execute this APA. The Parties may execute this APA in counterparts, with each counterpart constituting an original.

WITNESS,

The Parties have executed this APA on the dates below.

[Taxpayer Name in all caps]

By: _____

> Jane Doe
>
> Sr. Vice President (Taxes)
>
> Date: _____, 20____

IRS

By: _____

> Craig A. Sharon
>
> Director, Advance Pricing Agreement Program
>
> Date: _____, 20____

APPENDIX A
COVERED TRANSACTIONS AND TRANSFER PRICING METHOD (TPM)

1. Covered Transactions.

[*Define the Covered Transactions.*]

2. TPM.

{*Note: If appropriate, adapt language from the following examples.*}

[The Tested Party is _____.]

- **CUP Method**

The TPM is the comparable uncontrolled price (CUP) method. The Arm's Length Range of the price charged for _____ is between _____ and _____ per unit.

- **CUT Method**

The TPM is the CUT Method. The Arm's Length Range of the royalty charged for the license of _____is between ____% and ___ % of [Taxpayer's, Foreign Participants', or other specified party's] Net Sales Revenue. [Insert definition of net sales revenue or other royalty base.]

- **Resale Price Method (RPM)**

The TPM is the resale price method (RPM). The Tested Party's Gross Margin for any APA Year is defined as follows: the Tested Party's gross profit divided by its sales revenue (as those terms are defined in Treasury Regulations section 1.482-5(d)(1) and (2)) for that APA Year. The Arm's Length Range is between ____% and ___ %, and the Median of the Arm's Length Range is ___%.

- **Cost Plus Method**

The TPM is the cost plus method. The Tested Party's Cost Plus Markup is defined as follows for any APA Year: the Tested Party's ratio of gross profit to production costs (as those terms are defined in Treasury Regulations section 1.482-3(d)(1) and (2)) for that APA Year. The Arm's Length Range is between ___% and ___%, and the Median of the Arm's Length Range is ___%.

- **CPM with Berry Ratio PLI**

The TPM is the comparable profits method (CPM). The profit level indicator is a Berry Ratio. The Tested Party's Berry Ratio is defined as follows for any APA Year: the Tested Party's gross profit divided by its operating expenses (as those terms are defined in Treasury Regulations section 1.482-5(d)(2) and (3)) for that APA Year. The Arm's Length Range is between ____ and ___, and the Median of the Arm's Length Range is ___.

- **CPM using an Operating Margin PLI**

The TPM is the comparable profits method (CPM). The profit level indicator is an operating margin. The Tested Party's Operating Margin is defined as follows for any APA Year: the Tested Party's operating profit divided by its sales revenue (as those terms are defined in Treasury Regulations section 1.482-5(d)(1) and (4)) for that APA Year. The Arm's Length Range is between ____% and ___%, and the Median of the Arm's Length Range is ___%.

- **CPM using a Three-year Rolling Average Operating Margin PLI**

The TPM is the comparable profits method (CPM). The profit level indicator is an operating margin. The Tested Party's Three-Year Rolling Average operating margin is defined as follows for any APA Year: the sum of the Tested Party's operating profit (within the meaning of Treasury Regulations section 1.482-5(d)(4) for that APA Year and the two preceding years, divided by the sum of its sales revenue (within the meaning of Treasury Regulations section

1.482-5(d)(1)) for that APA Year and the two preceding years. The Arm's Length Range is between ____% and ____%, and the Median of the Arm's Length Range is ____%.

- **Residual Profit Split Method**

The TPM is the residual profit split method. [*Insert description of routine profit level determinations and residual profit-split mechanism*].

[*Insert additional provisions as needed.*]

3. Application of TPM.

For any APA Year, if the results of Taxpayer's actual transactions produce a [price per unit, royalty rate for the Covered Transactions] [or] [Gross Margin, Cost Plus Markup, Berry Ratio, Operating Margin, Three-Year Rolling Average Operating Margin for the Tested Party] within the Arm's Length Range, then the amounts reported on Taxpayer's U.S. Return must clearly reflect such results.

For any APA year, if the results of Taxpayer's actual transactions produce a [price per unit, royalty rate] [or] [Gross Margin, Cost Plus Markup, Berry Ratio, Operating Margin, Three-Year Rolling Average Operating Margin for the Tested Party] outside the Arm's Length Range, then amounts reported on Taxpayer's U.S. Return must clearly reflect an adjustment that brings the [price per unit, royalty rate] [or] [Tested Party's Gross Margin, Cost Plus Markup, Berry Ratio, Operating Margin, Three-Year Rolling Average Operating Margin] to the Median.

For purposes of this Appendix A, the "results of Taxpayer's actual transactions" means the results reflected in Taxpayer's and Tested Party's books and records as computed under U.S. GAAP [*insert another relevant accounting standard if applicable*], with the following adjustments:

(a) [The fair value of stock-based compensation as disclosed in the Tested Party's audited financial statements shall be treated as an operating expense]; and

(b) To the extent that the results in any prior APA Year are relevant (for example, to compute a multi-year average), such results shall be adjusted to reflect the amount of any adjustment made for that prior APA Year under this Appendix A.

4. APA Revenue Procedure Treatment

If Taxpayer makes a primary adjustment under the terms of this Appendix A, Taxpayer may elect APA Revenue Procedure Treatment in accordance with section 11.02(3) of Revenue Procedure 2006-9.

[*Insert additional provisions as needed.*]

APPENDIX B
CRITICAL ASSUMPTIONS

This APA's critical assumptions are:

1. The business activities, functions performed, risks assumed, assets employed, and financial and tax accounting methods and classifications [and methods of estimation] of Taxpayer in relation to the Covered Transactions will remain materially the same as described or used in Taxpayer's APA Request. A mere change in business results will not be a material change.

[*Insert additional provisions as needed.*]

APPENDIX C
APA RECORDS AND ANNUAL REPORT

APA RECORDS

The APA Records will consist of:

1. All documents listed below for inclusion in the Annual Report, as well as all documents, notes, work papers, records, or other writings that support the information provided in such documents.

ANNUAL REPORT

The Annual Report will include two copies of a properly completed APA Annual Report Summary in the form of Exhibit E to this APA, one copy of the form bound with, and one copy bound separately from, the rest of the Annual Report. In addition, the Annual Report will include a table of contents and the information and exhibits identified below, organized as follows.

1. Statements that fully identify, describe, analyze, and explain:

a. All material differences between any of the U.S. Entities' business operations (including functions, risks assumed, markets, contractual terms, economic conditions, property, services, and assets employed) during the APA Year and the description of the business operations contained in the APA Request. If there have been no material differences, the Annual Report will include a statement to that effect.

b. All material changes in the U.S. Entities' accounting methods and classifications, and methods of estimation, from those described or used in Taxpayer's request for this APA. If any such change was made to conform to changes in U.S. GAAP (or other relevant accounting standards), Taxpayer will specifically identify such change. If there has been no material change in accounting methods and classifications or methods of estimation, the Annual Report will include a statement to that effect.

c. Any change to the Taxpayer notice information in section 14 of this APA.

d. Any failure to meet any critical assumption. If there has been no failure, the Annual Report will include a statement to that effect.

e. Any change to any entity classification for federal income tax purposes (including any change that causes an entity to be disregarded for federal income tax purposes) of any Worldwide Group member that is a party to the Covered Transactions or is otherwise relevant to the TPM.

f. The amount, reason for, and financial analysis of any compensating adjustments under paragraph 4 of Appendix A and Revenue Procedure 2006-9, section 11.02(3), for the APA Year, including but not limited to:

    i. the amounts paid or received by each affected entity;

    ii. the character (such as capital, ordinary, income, expense) and country source of the funds transferred, and the specific affected line item(s) of any affected U.S. Return; and

¶20,140

iii. the date(s) and means by which the payments are or will be made.

g. The amounts, description, reason for, and financial analysis of any book-tax difference relevant to the TPM for the APA Year, as reflected on Schedule M-1 or Schedule M-3 of the U.S. Return for the APA Year.

2. The Financial Statements, and any necessary account detail to show compliance with the TPM, with a copy of the independent certified public accountant's opinion required by paragraph 5(f) of this APA.

3. A financial analysis that reflects Taxpayer's TPM calculations for the APA Year. The calculations must reconcile with and reference the Financial Statements in sufficient account detail to allow the IRS to determine whether Taxpayer has complied with the TPM.

4. An organizational chart for the Worldwide Group, revised annually to reflect all ownership or structural changes of entities that are parties to the Covered Transactions or are otherwise relevant to the TPM.

5. A copy of the APA.

APPENDIX D
DEFINITIONS

The following definitions control for all purposes of this APA. The definitions appear alphabetically below:

Term	Definition
Annual Report	A report within the meaning of Revenue Procedure 2006-9, section 11.01.
APA	This Advance Pricing Agreement, which is an "advance pricing agreement" within the meaning of Revenue Procedure 2006-9, section 2.04.
APA Records	The records specified in Appendix C.
APA Request	Taxpayer's request for this APA dated _____, including any amendments or supplemental or additional information thereto.
Covered Transaction(s)	This term is defined in Appendix A.
Financial Statements	Financial statements prepared in accordance with U.S. GAAP and stated in U.S. dollars.
Foreign Group	Worldwide Group members that are not U.S. persons.
Foreign Participants	[name the foreign entities involved in Covered Transactions].
I.R.C.	The Internal Revenue Code of 1986, 26 U.S.C., as amended.
Pub. L. 106-170	The Ticket to Work and Work Incentives Improvement Act of 1999.
Revenue Procedure 2006-9	Rev. Proc. 2006-9, 2006-1 C.B. 278.
Transfer Pricing Method (TPM)	A transfer pricing method within the meaning of Treasury Regulations section 1.482-1(b) and Revenue Procedure 2006-9, section 2.04.
U.S. GAAP	U.S. generally-accepted accounting principles.
U.S. Group	Worldwide Group members that are U.S. persons.

Term	Definition
U.S. Return	For each taxable year, the "returns with respect to income taxes under subtitle A" that Taxpayer must "make" in accordance with I.R.C. section 6012. {*Or substitute for partnership:* For each taxable year, the "return" that Taxpayer must "make" in accordance with I.R.C. section 6031.}
Worldwide Group	Taxpayer and all organizations, trades, businesses, entities, or branches (whether or not incorporated, organized in the United States, or affiliated) owned or controlled directly or indirectly by the same interests.

APPENDIX E
APA ANNUAL REPORT SUMMARY FORM

The APA Annual Report Summary on the next page is a required APA Record. The APA Team Leader has supplied some of the information requested on the form. Taxpayer is to supply the remaining information requested by the form and submit the form as part of its Annual Report.

APA Annual Report SUMMARY	Department of the Treasury--Internal Revenue Service Office of Associate Chief Counsel (International) Advance Pricing Agreement Program	APA no. _____ Team Leader _____ Economist _____ Intl Examiner _____ CA Analyst _____

APA Information	Taxpayer Name: _____ Taxpayer EIN:_____ NAICS:_____ APA Term: Taxable years ending _____ to _____. Original APA [ ] Renewal APA [ ] Annual Report due dates: _____, 200__ for all APA Years through APA Year ending in 200__; for each APA Year thereafter on _____ [month and day] immediately following the close of the APA Year. Principal foreign country(ies) involved in covered transaction(s): _____ Type of APA: [ ] unilateral [ ] bilateral with _____ Tested party is [ ] US [ ] foreign [ ] both Approximate dollar volume of covered transactions (on an annual basis) involving tangible goods and services: [ ] N/A [ ] <$50 million [ ] $50-100 million [ ] $100-250 million [ ] $250-500 million [ ] >$500 million APA tests on (check all that apply): [ ] annual basis [ ] multi-year basis [ ] term basis APA provides (check all that apply) a: [ ] range [ ] point [ ] floor only [ ] ceiling only [ ] other_____ APA provides for adjustment (check all that apply) to: [ ] nearest edge [ ] median [ ] other point

APA Annual Report Information (to be completed by the Taxpayer)	APA date executed: _____, 200__ This APA Annual Report Summary is for APA Year(s) ending in 200__ and was filed on _____, 200__ Check here [ ] if Annual Report was filed after original due date but in accordance with extension. Has this APA been amended or changed? [ ] yes [ ] no Effective Date: _____ Has Taxpayer complied with all APA terms and conditions? [ ] yes [ ] no Were all the critical assumptions met? [ ] yes [ ] no Has a Primary Compensating Adjustment been made in any APA Year covered by this Annual Report? [ ] yes [ ] no If yes, which year(s): 200__ Have any necessary Secondary Compensating Adjustments been made? [ ] yes [ ] no Did Taxpayer elect APA Revenue Procedure treatment? [ ] yes [ ] no Any change to the entity classification of a party to the APA? [ ] yes [ ] no Taxpayer notice information contained in the APA remains unchanged? [ ] yes [ ] no Taxpayer's current US principal place of business: (City, State) _____

APA Annual Report Checklist of Key Contents (to be completed by the Taxpayer)	Financial analysis reflecting TPM calculations [ ] yes [ ] no Financial statements showing compliance with TPM(s) [ ] yes [ ] no Schedule M-1 or M-3 book-tax differences [ ] yes [ ] no Current organizational chart of relevant portion of world-wide group [ ] yes [ ] no Attach copy of APA [ ] yes [ ] no Other APA records and documents included: *[The information required in the following section should be tailored to the particular case]* _____ [ ] yes [ ] no _____ [ ] yes [ ] no _____ [ ] yes [ ] no _____ [ ] yes [ ] no _____ [ ] yes [ ] no

Contact Information	Authorized Representative	Phone Number	Affiliation and Address

ATTACHMENT B
EXAMPLE FORMULAS FOR BALANCE SHEET ADJUSTMENTS

The formulas below provide examples of the balance sheet adjustment formulas used in the APA Program's CPM spreadsheet model.[14] The formulas below are applicable to the operating margin profit level indicator. The APA Program's calculations measure balance sheet intensity by reference to the denominator of the profit level indicator (e.g., for the Berry ratio, the denominator used is operating expenses). Therefore, the formulas vary for each profit level indicator.

Definitions of Variables:

AP   = average accounts payable

AR   = average trade accounts receivable, net of allowance for bad debt

cogs   = cost of goods sold

INV   = average inventory, stated on FIFO basis

opex   = operating expenses (general, sales, administrative, and depreciation expenses)

PPE   = property, plant, and equipment, net of accumulated depreciation

sales   = net sales

h   = average accounts payable or trade accounts receivable holding period, stated as a fraction of a year

i   = interest rate

t   = entity being tested

c   = comparable

Equations:

Example Assuming Profit Level Indicator is Operating Margin:

Receivables Adjustment ("RA"): $RA = \{[(AR_t / sales_t) \times sales_c] - AR_c\} \times \{i/[1+(i \times h_c)]\}$

Payables Adjustment ("PA"): $PA = \{[(AP_t / sales_t) \times sales_c] - AP_c\} \times \{i/[1+(i \times h_c)]\}$

Inventory Adjustment ("IA"): $IA = \{[(INV_t / sales_t) \times sales_c] - INV_c\} \times i$

PP&E Adjustment ("PPEA"): $PPEA = \{[(PPE_t / sales_t) \times sales_c] - PPE_c\} \times i$

Then Adjust Comparables as Follows:

adjusted $sales_c = sales_c + RA$

adjusted $cogs_c = cogs_c + PA - IA$

adjusted $opex_c = opex_c - PPEA$

---

[14] Copies of the APA Program's CPM spreadsheet model are available from the APA Program by calling (202) 435-5220 (not a toll-free number) or by writing to the Office of Associate Chief Counsel (International), Advance Pricing Agreement Program, Attn: CC:INTL:APA, MA2-266, 1111 Constitution Ave. NW, Washington DC, 20224.

¶20,140

¶ 20,150 Internal Revenue Manual (IRM) 8.13.1, Exhibit 21 (11-9-2007)

Form 906 - Pattern Agreement - Rev. Proc. 99-32 (Foreign Parent)

Use the following paragraphs or portions of paragraphs as applicable. Note: alternative language is italicized and bracketed.

WHEREAS, Taxpayer is a Corporation organized and existing under the laws of the State of _____ and (Parent), which owns or controls Taxpayer within the meaning of section 482 of the Internal Revenue Code, is a corporation organized and existing under the laws of _____ ;

WHEREAS, Taxpayer entered into certain transactions *[Describe Transactions here]* with Parent during the taxable year ended *[Insert Date here] (Year 1) [define Year 2, Year 3, Year 4, etc., as needed]*

WHEREAS, Taxpayer and the Commissioner have agreed that Taxpayer's taxable income should be increased and that Parent's income should be decreased *[or: that Taxpayer's taxable income should be decreased and that Parent's income should be increased]* for federal income tax purposes as a result of allocations under section 482 of the Internal Revenue Code between Taxpayer and Parent;

WHEREAS, Taxpayer has asserted that such adjustments to income should be made in accordance with section 4 of Revenue Procedure 99-32, 1999-2 C.B. 296, in that Taxpayer has fully satisfied the conditions set forth in sections 3.01 and 3.03 of Rev. Proc. 99-32; and

WHEREAS, the Commissioner has agreed, based on information provided by Taxpayer that the provisions of Rev. Proc. 99-32 should apply to such adjustments to income.

NOW IT IS HEREBY DETERMINED AND AGREED, for all Federal income tax purposes that:

1) Adjustments to Income

    a) Taxpayer's taxable income for the year*[s]* indicated is increased *[or: decreased]* and Parent's income is decreased *[or: increased]* by the amount of the section 482 allocations reported in the following table:

Affected Taxable Year(s)	Taxable Entity Affected by Allocation, or changes in Earnings and Profits	Increase (Decrease) in Income due to 482 Allocation	Increase (Decrease) in Earnings and Profits
Year 1	Taxpayer		
Year 1	Parent		
Year 2	Taxpayer		
Year 2	Parent		

2) Prepayment of the Accounts Receivable by Offset against Capital Contribution or Bona Fide Debt

a) The amount*[s]* and date*[s]* of the capital contribution *[s]* received by Taxpayer from Parent, which the Taxpayer elects to treat as a prepayment of the Accounts Receivable established pursuant to paragraph 4), below, under section 4.02 of Rev. Proc. 99-32 are:

   i) Date 1 - $_____.

   ii) Date 2 - $_____.

   iii) Date 3 - $_____.

b) The amount*[s]* of the capital contribution offset[s] described in paragraph 2)a), above, shall not be treated as a capital contribution to Taxpayer for any Federal income tax purpose. Consequently, Parent's basis in Taxpayer's stock shall not be increased by the amount of such capital contributions.

c) The amounts of pre-existing principal and accrued but unpaid interest owed by Taxpayer to Parent that Taxpayer elects to offset against the Accounts Receivable established pursuant to paragraph 4), below, under section 4.02 of Rev. Proc. 99-32, and the date of such offset are

	Principal	Interest	Date of offset
Identify Debt Instrument #1	$	$	
Identify Debt Instrument #2	$	$	
Identify Debt Instrument #3	$	$	

3) *[Prepayment of the Accounts Payable by Offset against Distribution or Bona Fide Debt]*

a) *The amount[s] and date[s] of the distribution[s] received by Parent from Taxpayer, which Taxpayer elects to treat as a prepayment of the Accounts Payable established pursuant to paragraph 5), below, under section 4.02 of Rev. Proc. 99-32 are:*

   i) *Date 1 - $_____.*

   ii) *Date 1 - $_____.*

   iii) *Date 1 - $_____.*

b) *The amount of the distribution offset[s] described in paragraph 3)a), above, shall not be treated as a dividend under section 316 of the Code or for any other Federal income tax purpose. Consequently, no dividend received deduction shall be allowed with respect thereto under sections 241 through 247 of the Code.*

c) *The amounts of pre-existing principal and accrued but unpaid interest owed by Parent to Taxpayer that Taxpayer elects to offset against the Accounts Payable established pursuant to paragraph 5), below, under section 4.02 of Rev. Proc. 99-32, and the date of such offset are:*

¶20,150

	Principal	*Interest*	*Date of offset*
Identify Debt Instrument #1	$	$	
Identify Debt Instrument #2	$	$	
Identify Debt Instrument #3	$	$	

4) **Accounts Receivable Established by Taxpayer**

a) Taxpayer will establish *[an]* intercompany account*[s]* receivable (Account*[s]* Receivable), which will be recorded on Taxpayer's books and treated as *[a]* term loan*[s]* to Parent reflecting the following balance*[s]*, *[each]* such Account Receivable being deemed to have been created as of the last day of the taxable year to which it relates.

Date Account Deemed Established	Date 1	Date 2	Date 3

Amount of Receivable Established on Above Date

b) **Interest income will accrue to Taxpayer on the Account[s] Receivable at the following annual rates beginning on the first day after the [each] Account Receivable is established and ending on the date of this agreement:**

i) Account Receivable established on Date 1 - ____%

ii) Account Receivable established on Date 2 - ____%

iii) Account Receivable established on Date 3 - ____%

c) The amount of interest income to be accrued by Taxpayer pursuant to paragraph 4)b), above, for each taxable year through the date of this agreement is as follows:

Taxable Period	Amount of Interest
Year 1	
Year 2	
Year 3	
Year 4 (through date of this agreement)	

d) From the date of this agreement through the earlier of either the date of payment pursuant to paragraph 6)b), below, or the 90th day after the date of this agreement, interest income will accrue to Taxpayer on the outstanding balance (including accrued but unpaid interest) of the Account*[s]* Receivable at the daily rate*[s]* reported below:

Account Receivable	Daily Rate
Account Receivable Established on Date 1	%
Account Receivable Established on Date 2	%
Account Receivable Established on Date 3	%
Account Receivable Established on Date 4	%

5) *[Accounts Payable Established by Taxpayer.*

a) *Taxpayer will establish [an] intercompany account[s] payable (Account[s] Payable), which will be recorded on Taxpayer's books and*

¶20,150

treated as [a] term loan[s] from Parent reflecting the following balances, each such Account Payable being deemed to have been created as of the last day of the taxable year to which it relates.

Date Account Deemed Established	Date 1	Date 2	Date 3
Amount of Payable Established on Above Date			

b) **Interest expense on the Account[s] Payable will accrue to Taxpayer at the following annual rates beginning on the first day after the [each] Account Payable is established and ending on the date of this agreement.**

> i) *Account Payable established on Date 1 - _____%*
>
> ii) *Account Payable established on Date 2 - _____%*
>
> iii) *Account Payable established on Date 3 - _____%*

c) *The amount of interest expense to be accrued by Taxpayer pursuant to paragraph 5)b), above, for each taxable year through the date of this agreement is as follows:*

Taxable Period	Amount of Interest
Year 1	
Year 2	
Year 3	
Year 4 (through date of this agreement)	

d) *From the date of this agreement through the earlier of either the date of payment pursuant to paragraph 6)b), below, or the 90th day after the date of this agreement, interest expense will accrue to Taxpayer on the outstanding balance (including accrued but unpaid interest) of the Accounts Payable at the daily rate reported below.]*

Account Receivable	Daily Rate
Account Receivable Established on Date 1	%
Account Receivable Established on Date 2	%
Account Receivable Established on Date 3	%
Account Receivable Established on Date 4	%

6) **Payment of Accounts Receivable [, Accounts Payable,] and Interest.**

a) Payment of the Account*[s]* Receivable and interest thereon referred to in paragraph 4), above, (the Receivables) *[of the Account[s] Payable and interest thereon referred to in paragraph 5), above, (the Payables)]* in the manner and within the time set forth herein, will be free of the Federal income tax consequences of the secondary adjustments that would result from the primary adjustments described in paragraph 1), above, had Taxpayer and the Commissioner not entered into this agreement.

¶20,150

b) Within 90 days after the date of this agreement, Parent will pay Taxpayer the amount of the Receivables. *[Taxpayer will pay Parent the amount of the Payables]*.

c) The manner of payment of the Receivables shall be as follows:

    i) Parent shall pay Taxpayer $_____ in U.S. dollars in *[partial]* liquidation of the Receivables.

    ii) ii) Parent as obligor shall issue to Taxpayer as obligee a promissory note, payable in the amount of $_____ in U.S. dollars in *[partial]* liquidation of the Receivables. The note shall bear interest at a fixed annual rate of _____%, with interest payable semi-annually, and shall mature on _____, 20_____.

    iii) Parent and Taxpayer shall *[partially]* offset the Receivables against _____, a valid liability of Taxpayer to Parent. For purposes of this agreement, the amount of the offset shall be deemed to be $_____ in U.S. dollars.

    iv) If payment of the Receivables in full pursuant to subparagraph*[s]* i), ii), or *[and]* iii) does not occur within 90 days after the date of this agreement, then the unpaid Receivables, or the unpaid portion of the Receivables, shall be treated as paid by Parent to Taxpayer and returned to Parent in the form of Taxpayer's distribution of property as of the expiration of the 90-day period.

d) *[The manner of payment of the Payables shall be as follows:*

    i) Taxpayer shall pay Parent $_____ in U.S. dollars in [partial] liquidation of the Payables.

    ii) Taxpayer as obligor shall issue to Parent as obligee a promissory note, payable in the amount of $_____ in U.S. dollars in [partial] liquidation of the Payables. The note shall bear interest at a fixed annual rate of _____%, with interest payable semi-annually, and shall mature on _____, 20_____.

    iii) Taxpayer and Parent shall [partially] offset the Payables against _____, a valid liability of Parent to Taxpayer. For purposes of this agreement, the amount of the offset shall be deemed to be $_____ in U.S. dollars.]

    iv) If payment of the Payables in full pursuant to subparagraph[s] i), ii), or [and] iii) does not occur within 90 days after the date of this agreement, then the unpaid Payables, or the unpaid portion of the Payables, shall be treated as paid by Taxpayer to Parent and returned to Taxpayer in the form of Parent's contribution to Taxpayer's capital as of the expiration of the 90-day period.]

7) Miscellaneous.

a) This agreement does not prevent further allocations under section 482 with respect to taxable events involving Taxpayer and Parent that are

¶20,150

attributable to taxable periods of Taxpayer for which allocations are not determined by this agreement.

b) The date of this agreement is deemed to be the date on which this agreement is executed on behalf of the Commissioner.

(Pattern language only. Not a complete document.)

Additional Comments (Pattern Rev. Proc. 99-32 Closing Agreement on Form 906).

A. This pattern closing agreement is intended as a model to assist in drafting closing agreements governed by Rev. Proc. 99-32 in connection with Service-initiated adjustments. Taxpayer-initiated adjustments subject to Rev. Proc. 99-32 should be reflected in a Federal income tax return and do not require a closing agreement. See Rev. Proc. 99-32, §5.02. These instructions do not address the issue of when Rev. Proc. 99-32 relief may be granted. Technical questions on Rev. Proc. 99-32 relief should be researched in published or internal management documents dealing with this subject matter.

B. This pattern closing agreement is drafted on the assumption that the taxpayer is a domestic corporation the income of which is being increased with respect to certain transactions engaged in with its foreign parent. Alternative language is italicized and provided in brackets. Much of this alternative language deals with the situation in which the taxpayer's income is being decreased. The language of the draft closing agreement may have to be supplemented, shortened, or otherwise further rewritten to address the particular situation. For example, this pattern closing agreement assumes that adjustments involve only two entities: (1) a domestic corporate taxpayer and (2) its foreign corporate parent (Parent). If more than two entities are involved, this pattern agreement must be appropriately amended.

C. Sections 4.01 and 4.02 of Rev. Proc. 99-32 permit the taxpayer to create account(s) receivable if its income is to be increased or accounts payable if its income is to be decreased and requires that the amount of the account(s) receivable or payable equal the primary adjustment for each year in which an adjustment is made except to the extent that an offset against the account(s) is permitted. The principal or interest on an account receivable may be offset against (i) a contribution of capital previously received by the taxpayer from Parent during the taxable year in which the closing agreement is executed or (ii) the bona fide debt of the taxpayer to Parent if such offset occurs during the taxable year in which the closing agreement is executed. Similarly, principal or interest on an account payable may be offset against (i) a distribution of property previously made by the taxpayer to Parent during the taxable year in which the closing agreement is executed or (ii) the bona fide debt of Parent to the taxpayer if such offset occurs during the taxable year in which the closing agreement is executed.

¶20,150

Offsets against distributions and contributions are deemed to occur on the date of the distribution or contribution and determine the future treatment of the distribution or contribution for tax accounting purposes. Offsets against pre-existing debt are deemed to occur when an accounting entry is made to the books of the taxpayer recording such offset and such debt is deemed paid in whole or in part on the date of such entry for tax accounting purposes.

D. It is unlikely that a closing agreement would be entered into that would incorporate all the provisions provided in this pattern closing agreement. Paragraphs 2), 4), and 6)c) of this pattern closing agreement are appropriate for increases to the taxpayer's income. Paragraphs 3), 5), and 6)d) are appropriate for decreases to the taxpayer's income. Inapplicable paragraphs or subparagraphs should be omitted (rather than retained with the amount shown as "None") and cross-references within the closing agreement should be appropriately amended.

E. Comments on specific draft paragraphs.

Paragraph 1. Matters expressly determined in closing agreements are accorded finality under §7121 of the Code. Though certain inferences and substantially automatic consequences may appear to logically flow from such determinations, these results cannot be considered to be matters determined with finality unless expressly provided for in the closing agreement. It is for this reason that the table appended to paragraph 1) reports the effect of earnings and profits directly resulting from the section 482 allocations.

The pattern closing agreement assumes that the allocation is an income adjustment to the taxpayer and Parent. However, such assumption may not apply to all situations. For example, the allocation may be an income adjustment to one party and a capital item to the other.

Paragraph 2. If the taxpayer's income is to be increased by additional payments from its parent, section 4.02 of Rev. Proc. 99-32 permits the taxpayer to offset against the Account(s) Receivable memorialized under paragraph 4) either (i) contributions of property (which might otherwise be characterized as capital contributions) that the taxpayer received from Parent during the taxable year in which the closing agreement is executed or (ii) the taxpayer's outstanding bona fide debt to Parent. Paragraph 2) memorializes such offsets.

Paragraph 3. If the taxpayer's income is to be decreased by additional payments to its parent, section 4.02 of Rev. Proc. 99-32 permits the taxpayer to offset against the Account(s) Payable memorialized under paragraph 5) either (i) distributions of property (that might otherwise be characterized as dividends or returns of capital) the taxpayer made to Parent during the taxable year in which the closing agreement is executed or (ii) Parent's outstanding bona fide debt to the taxpayer. Paragraph 3) memorializes such offsets.

Paragraph 4. This paragraph should be included only if the taxpayer's income is being increased. The Accounts Receivable typically will be established in U.S. dollars. See generally Rev. Proc. 99-32, section 4.01(3).

Paragraph 5. This paragraph should be included only if the taxpayer's income is being decreased. The Accounts Payable typically will be established in U.S. dollars. See generally Rev. Proc. 99-32, section 4.01(3).

Paragraph 6. Payment typically will be in U.S. dollars. See generally Rev. Proc. 99-32, section 4.01(3). The pattern closing agreement provides for three different mechanisms for paying the Receivables and Payables: (i) cash payment, (ii) issuance of a new debt obligation, or (iii) offset against a pre-existing liability. Payment may use any or all of these mechanisms, but the total amount paid must equal the total amount of the outstanding Receivables or Payables. The terms of a promissory note must meet the requirements set forth in § 4.01(4) of Rev. Proc. 99-32.

The pattern closing agreement treats payment as made within 90 days after the date of the agreement if full payment is not actually made before that time. As a result, interest accrual under paragraphs 4)d) and 5)d) does not exceed that 90-day period. In addition, the taxpayer is treated as receiving full payment from (or making full payment to) Parent with respect to the secondary adjustment and then making a distribution to (or receiving a capital contribution from) Parent in the same amount.

Draft language provided (including bracketed, italicized language) will accommodate the taxpayer that is recording both Accounts Receivable and Accounts Payable if necessary. If the taxpayer is recording only one or the other, then bracketed, italicized language in subparagraphs a) and b) must be included as appropriate. Subparagraph c) would not be included in the closing agreement if the taxpayer does not record Accounts Receivable. Similarly, subparagraph d) would not be included in the closing agreement if the taxpayer does not record Accounts Payable.

In this pattern agreement, the foreign entity is assumed to control the taxpayer. In the event that the taxpayer and its foreign counterpart are affiliates controlled by a common parent and there are Receivables, subparagraph c)iv) could be rewritten as follows:

"iv) If payment of the Receivables in full pursuant to subparagraph[s] i), ii), or [and] iii) does not occur within 90 days after the date of this agreement, then the unpaid Receivables, or the unpaid portion of such Receivables, shall be treated as paid by [Foreign Entity] to Taxpayer and simultaneously distributed by Taxpayer to [insert name of parent corporation] (Parent) as of the expiration of the 90-day period. The excess of such constructive distribution over earnings and profits shall be considered a distribution of capital by taxpayer to Parent. As of the date of such constructive distribution, the amount so treated as a distribution shall be treated as having been contributed by Parent to the capital account of [Foreign Entity]."

In the event that the taxpayer and its foreign counterpart are affiliates controlled by a common parent and there are Payables, subparagraph d)iv) could be rewritten in a similar manner.

<u>Signature Blocks</u>. In general, a person should be a signatory of a closing agreement if the closing agreement purports to determine tax matters for such person. IRM. 8.13.1.2.17.1. For persons authorized to enter into this closing agreement on behalf of the Commissioner, see paragraphs (5), (6), and (7) of Delegation Order 97, *Closing Agreements Concerning Internal Revenue Tax Liability* (Rev. 34) or, if Delegation Order 97 (Rev. 34) is rescinded, its successor.

¶ 20,160 U. S. Customs Informed Compliance Publication

What Every Member of the
Trade Community Should Know About:

DETERMINING THE ACCEPTABILITY OF TRANSACTION VALUE FOR RELATED PARTY TRANSACTIONS

U.S. CUSTOMS and BORDER PROTECTION

AN INFORMED COMPLIANCE PUBLICATION

APRIL 2007

Related Party Transactions; Transfer Pricing
April 2007

NOTICE:

This publication is intended to provide guidance and information to the trade community. It reflects the position on or interpretation of the applicable laws or regulations by U.S. Customs and Border Protection (CBP) as of the date of publication, which is shown on the front cover. It does not in any way replace or supersede those laws or regulations. Only the latest official version of the laws or regulations is authoritative.

Publication History

First Published: April 2007

PRINTING NOTE:

This publication was designed for electronic distribution via the CBP website (http://www.cbp.gov) and is being distributed in a variety of formats. It was originally set up in Microsoft Word97®. Pagination and margins in downloaded versions may vary depending upon which word processor or printer you use. If you wish to maintain the original settings, you may wish to download the .pdf version, which can then be printed using the freely available Adobe Acrobat Reader®.

2

¶20,160

Related Party Transactions; Transfer Pricing
April 2007

PREFACE

On December 8, 1993, Title VI of the North American Free Trade Agreement Implementation Act (Pub. L. 103-182, 107 Stat. 2057), also known as the Customs Modernization or "Mod" Act, became effective. These provisions amended many sections of the Tariff Act of 1930 and related laws.

Two new concepts that emerge from the Mod Act are "*informed compliance*" and "*shared responsibility*," which are premised on the idea that in order to maximize voluntary compliance with laws and regulations of U.S. Customs and Border Protection, the trade community needs to be clearly and completely informed of its legal obligations. Accordingly, the Mod Act imposes a greater obligation on CBP to provide the public with improved information concerning the trade community's rights and responsibilities under customs regulations and related laws. In addition, both the trade and U.S. Customs and Border Protection share responsibility for carrying out these requirements. For example, under Section 484 of the Tariff Act, as amended (19 U.S.C. 1484), the importer of record is responsible for using reasonable care to enter, classify and determine the value of imported merchandise and to provide any other information necessary to enable U.S. Customs and Border Protection to properly assess duties, collect accurate statistics, and determine whether other applicable legal requirements, if any, have been met. CBP is then responsible for fixing the final classification and value of the merchandise. An importer of record's failure to exercise reasonable care could delay release of the merchandise and, in some cases, could result in the imposition of penalties.

Regulations and Rulings in CBP's Office of International Trade ("OT") has been given a major role in meeting the informed compliance responsibilities of U.S. Customs and Border Protection. In order to provide information to the public, CBP has issued a series of informed compliance publications on new or revised requirements, regulations or procedures, and a variety of classification and valuation issues.

This publication, "Determining the Acceptability of Transaction Value for Related Party Transactions", prepared by the Commercial and Trade Facilitation Division of Regulations and Rulings, is intended to educate the public regarding certain aspects of the customs valuation requirements for related party transactions. We sincerely hope that this material, together with seminars and increased access to rulings of U.S. Customs and Border Protection, will help the trade community to improve voluntary compliance with customs laws and to understand the relevant administrative processes.

The material in this publication is provided for general information purposes only. Because many complicated factors can be involved in customs issues, an importer may wish to obtain a ruling under Regulations of U.S. Customs and Border Protection, 19 C.F.R. Part 177, or to obtain advice from an expert who specializes in customs matters, for example, a licensed customs broker, attorney or consultant.

Comments and suggestions are welcomed and should be addressed to the Executive Director at the Office of Regulations and Rulings, U.S. Customs and Border Protection, 1300 Pennsylvania Avenue, NW, (Mint Annex), Washington, D.C. 20229.

Sandra L. Bell
Executive Director, Regulations and Rulings
Office of International Trade

3

Related Party Transactions; Transfer Pricing
April 2007

(This page intentionally left blank)

4

Related Party Transactions; Transfer Pricing
April 2007

5

¶20,160

BACKGROUND

This Informed Compliance Publication is intended to educate the public regarding certain aspects of the customs valuation requirements for related party transactions. Specifically, in this Publication, U.S. Customs and Border Protection (CBP) will summarize:

- the tests for determining the acceptability of transaction value for related party transactions;
- CBP's application of the related party tests, including information and evidence needed to substantiate claims that transaction value is acceptable under these tests;
- the relevance of Advance Pricing Agreements (APA's) and Transfer Pricing Studies to the circumstances of sale test in determining the acceptability of transaction value; and,
- the importer's obligations regarding the declaration of value in related party transactions.[1]

I. TRANSACTION VALUE - TESTS FOR DETERMINING THE ACCEPTABILITY OF TRANSACTION VALUE FOR RELATED PARTY TRANSACTIONS

Merchandise imported into the United States is appraised for customs purposes in accordance with section 402 of the Tariff Act of 1930, as amended by the Trade Agreements Act of 1979 (19 U.S.C. §1401a, the "value law"). The implementing regulations are contained in Part 152 of the CBP Regulations (19 CFR Part 152). The primary method of appraisement is transaction value, which is defined as "the price actually paid or payable for the merchandise when sold for exportation to the United States," plus amounts for certain statutorily enumerated additions to the extent not otherwise included in the price actually paid or payable. See 19 U.S.C. §1401a(b)(1). When there is no transaction value, the other valuation methods (transaction value of identical or similar goods, deductive value, computed value, and the fallback method), are to be applied in sequence.

There are special rules that apply when the buyer and seller are related parties, as defined in 19 U.S.C. §1401a(g).[2] As provided in 19 U.S.C. §1401a(b)(2)(A)(iv),

---

[1] This ICP does not address the issue of the applicability of transaction value when the related party price is subject to adjustment after importation or the proper treatment of post-importation adjustments in the determination of transaction value.

[2] The following persons are considered related: members of the same family, including brothers and sisters, spouse, ancestors, and lineal descendants; any officer or director of an organization and such organization; an office or director of an organization and an officer or director of another organization, if each such individual is also an officer or director in the other organization; partners; employer and employee; any person directly or indirectly owning, controlling, or holding with power to vote, 5 percent ore more of the outstanding voting stock or shares of any organization and such organization; and, two or more persons directly or indirectly controlling, controlled by, or under common control with, any person.

6

transaction value can only be applied if "[t]he buyer and seller are not related, or the buyer and seller are related but the transaction value is acceptable." Transaction value between a related buyer and seller is acceptable if the importation meets either of two tests: 1) circumstances of sale or 2) test values. *See* 19 U.S.C. §1401a(b)(2)(B).

A. Circumstances of Sale

Under the "circumstances of sale" test, the transaction value between a related buyer and seller is acceptable if an examination of the circumstances of the sale of the imported merchandise indicates that the relationship between the buyer and the seller did not influence the price actually paid or payable. 19 U.S.C. §1401a(b)(2)(B). Under this test, the relevant aspects of the transaction are analyzed, including: 1) the way in which the buyer and the seller organize their commercial relations, and 2) the way in which the price in question was arrived at, in order to determine whether the relationship influenced the price. Statement of Administration Action, H.R. Doc. No. 103-316, 103rd Cong, 2d Sess. (1994) reprinted in Customs Valuation Under the Trade Agreement Act of 1979, at 53-54; *See also* 19 CFR. §152.103(l)(1)(i).

The circumstances of sale test by its very nature must be applied case-by-case. As provided in 19 CFR §152.103(l), the following circumstances demonstrate that the relationship has not influenced the price:

> The price was settled in a manner consistent with the normal pricing practices of the industry in question;

> The price was settled in a manner consistent with the way the seller settles prices for sales to buyers who are not related to it; or

> The price is adequate to ensure recovery of all costs plus a profit that is equivalent to the firm's overall profit realized over a representative period of time in sales of merchandise of the same class or kind.

See also Statement of Administration Action.

CBP has issued a number of rulings on the application of the circumstances of sale test.[3] Some of the issues that have arisen are discussed below.

> 1. *The price was settled in a manner consistent with the normal pricing practices of the industry in question.*

When the importer claims that transaction value is acceptable because the transfer price was settled in a manner consistent with the normal pricing practices of the industry in question, the importer must have objective evidence of the normal pricing practices of

---

[3] CBP's rulings from 1989 to the present are included in the Customs Rulings Online Search System (CROSS) which is available on CBP's website, www.cbp.gov. These rulings should be consulted for further guidance regarding the application of the circumstances of sale test.

7

the industry in question and present evidence that the transfer price was settled in accordance with these industry pricing practices.

For example, objective evidence was presented in Headquarters Ruling Letter (HRL) 542261 (March 11, 1981) (TAA No. 19), where CBP determined that the transfer price was defined with reference to prices published in a trade journal (the posted price) and other buyers and sellers commonly used the posted price as the basis of contract prices.

The pricing practices must relate to the "industry in question" which generally includes the industry that produces goods of the same class or kind as the imported merchandise. See HRL's 546998, January 19, 2000 and 548095, September 19, 2002.[4]   Same class or kind determinations necessarily take into account factors relating to the specific type of goods at issue.

CBP does not consider the industry in question to consist of other functionally equivalent companies if those companies do not sell goods of the same class or kind. In this regard, CBP has ruled that the mere fact that the importer allegedly earned an operating profit comparable to other *functionally equivalent companies* (as shown in a transfer pricing study) was not sufficient to establish either the normal pricing practice in the industry in question or that the related party price was settled in a manner consistent with the normal pricing practices of the industry in question. *See* HRL's 548482, July 23, 2004 and 548095, supra.

> 2. *The price was settled in a manner consistent with the way the seller settles prices for sales to buyers who are not related to it.*

This method applies in situations where the seller sells the same merchandise to both related and unrelated parties and determines the prices in a consistent way. For example, if the importer establishes that the price paid by unrelated and related buyers to the seller is the same or that the price was determined based on an arm's length negotiation, this would be an indication that the relationship between the parties did not influence the price. Or, if the seller uses a specified formula for determining the price (for example, based on the quantity purchased or other specified criteria) and applies the same formula in both sales to related and unrelated buyers, this would be an indication that the price was settled in a manner consistent with the way the seller settles prices for sales to unrelated buyers.[5]

---

[4] Merchandise of the same class or kind means merchandise (including but not limited to, identical merchandise and similar merchandise) within a group or range or merchandise produced by a particular industry or industry sector.

[5] For example, in HRL 547019, March 31, 2000, CBP determined that transaction value was acceptable where the foreign supplier grants various discounts based on established criteria from a price list and gives the same discounts based on matching ratings to both related buyers and unrelated buyers. As evidence of this practice, the importer presented invoices from its related foreign supplier to other unrelated foreign buyers showing that identical price discounts for merchandise identical to the imported merchandise were given to other unrelated parties.

Although CBP generally requires that the comparison sales to unrelated buyers be sales to buyers in the U.S., CBP will consider evidence regarding sales to unrelated buyers in other countries, provided the importer presents an adequate explanation as to why it is relevant to the transactions at issue. How much weight will be given to such evidence depends on the specific facts and the explanation provided.

   3. *The price is adequate to ensure recovery of all costs plus a profit that is equivalent to the firm's overall profit realized over a representative period of time in sales of merchandise of the same class or kind.*

This method, which is often referred to as the "all costs plus profit method", examines whether the related party price compensates the seller for all its costs plus a specified amount of profit (i.e., a profit that is equivalent to the firm's overall profit realized over a representative period of time in sales of merchandise of the same class or kind). This method is especially useful when there are no sales to unrelated buyers that can be used as a point of reference. It is the most objective method of meeting the circumstances of sale test when there are no sales to an unrelated buyer. In applying this test, CBP normally considers the "firm's overall profit . . ." to be the profit of the parent company. Thus, if the seller of the imported goods is a subsidiary of the parent company, the price must be adequate to ensure recovery of all the seller's costs plus a profit that is equivalent to the parent company's overall profit. *See* HRL 546998, *supra*. In addition, as the language of this provision makes clear, the profit must relate to the profit realized over a representative period of time (e.g., one year) *in sales of merchandise of the same class or kind.* [6] If the firm sells different classes of merchandise, the relevant profit is the profit that pertains only to sales of merchandise of the same class or kind.

To substantiate an all costs plus profit claim, the importer should be prepared to provide records and documents of comprehensive product related costs and profit, such as financial statements, accounting records including general ledger account activity, bills of materials, inventory records, labor and overhead records, relevant selling, general and administrative expense records, and other supporting business records.

Information and Evidence to Substantiate a Circumstances of Sale Claim

In CBP's rulings applying the circumstances of sale test, the determination of whether the relationship between the parties influenced the price depends on a review of all the relevant circumstances of sale and the supporting documentation.

The application of the circumstances of sale test generally presents two issues: 1) whether there is sufficient evidence to establish the alleged circumstances of sale; and 2) whether such circumstances demonstrate that the relationship between the buyer and the seller did not influence the price.

_____
[6] See Note 5 for definition of merchandise of the same class or kind.

9

¶20,160

The importer should be prepared to provide a thorough explanation of the circumstances surrounding the sale, supporting evidence, and an explanation of why the importer believes that such circumstances establish that the relationship did not influence the price.

CBP often rejects circumstances of sale claims because the allegations are conclusory and not supported by evidence. For example, the claim will be rejected when the importer alleges that the transfer price is negotiated at arm's length, but does not submit any evidence, such as correspondence between the parties, that reflects such negotiation. Similarly, the claim will be rejected where the importer alleges that the price was settled in a manner consistent with sales to unrelated buyers, but does not provide documentation, such as contracts and invoices, regarding both the related and unrelated party sales. An all costs plus profit claim should be supported by information and documentation regarding both the seller's costs and the firm's profit. The documents referenced in Section A.3 should be available to substantiate a claim of this nature.

B. Test Values

An alternative method to establish the acceptability of transaction value is to demonstrate that it closely approximates certain test values pertaining to identical or similar goods exported at or about the same time as the imported merchandise under review.

Specifically, under the test value method the transaction value between a related buyer and seller is acceptable if the transaction value of the imported merchandise closely approximates one of the following "test values":

(i)   the transaction value of identical merchandise, or of similar merchandise, in sales to unrelated buyers in the United States;
(ii)   the deductive value or computed value for identical merchandise of similar merchandise;
(iii)   but only if each value referred to in clause (i) or (ii) that is used for comparison relates to merchandise that was exported to the United States at or about the same time as the imported merchandise.

19 U.S.C. §1401a(b)(2)(B).

CBP has issued a number of rulings on the application of the test value method. Two issues that frequently arise are whether the test values must be actual appraised values of previously imported merchandise and whether the test values can be substituted for the transfer price.

CBP requires that the test values must be values previously determined by CBP pursuant to an actual appraisement of imported merchandise. For example, a computed value calculation can only serve as a test value if it represents a previous

10

¶20,160

actual appraisement of merchandise under 19 U.S.C. §1401a(e). *See* HRL 546052, October 27, 1995; and HRL 545960, August 16, 1995 citing HRL 543568, May 30, 1986 and HRL 544686, August 31, 1994.[7]   Importers often mistakenly believe that transaction value is acceptable for the imported goods when it is the same as the value calculated by the importer under the deductive value or the computed value method for those same imported goods. This is not the case. If there are no previous importations of identical or similar merchandise that were appraised under the transaction, deductive or computed value methods, there are no test values that can be applied.

With regard to the proper use of test values, the value law indicates that they are to be used for comparison purposes. See 19 U.S.C. §1401a(b)(2)(C). In other words, test values are used solely to determine whether the related party transaction value is acceptable. If the related party transaction value closely approximates a test value, the merchandise is appraised based on the related party transaction value. If the related party transaction value does not closely approximate a test value, then transaction value is acceptable only if the circumstances of sale test is met. Otherwise, the merchandise must be appraised using the next applicable valuation method in the hierarchy.

If the importer has information regarding possible test values pertaining to the related party transaction, this information should be brought to CBP's attention.

II. RELEVANCE OF TRANSFER PRICING AGREEMENTS AND TRANSFER PRICING STUDIES PERTAINING TO SECTION 482 OF THE INTERNAL REVENUE CODE TO THE APPLICATION OF THE CIRCUMSTANCES OF SALE TEST.

The U.S. tax law requires that related party transactions satisfy the arm's length principle. A question that has arisen is what weight, if any, should CBP give to information an importer prepares for tax purposes in determining whether a related party transaction value is acceptable for customs purposes under the application of the circumstances of sale test. Increasingly, importers are asking CBP to rule that a related party transaction value is acceptable under the circumstances of sale test because it meets the arm's length principle for tax purposes. In some cases, the importer provides evidence that the Internal Revenue Service (IRS) has agreed that the importer's transfer pricing methodology is the "best method," as defined in Treasury regulations under IRC section 482, for tax purposes through an Advance Pricing Agreement (APA), or audit. In other cases, the importer provides a transfer pricing study prepared for IRC section 6662 purposes that demonstrates that the transactions are arm's length under one of the IRS methods.

---

[7] 19 U.S.C. §1401a is the U.S. implementation of the Agreement on Implementation of Article VII of GATT 1994 (the Customs Valuation Agreement). CBP's interpretation of the test value provision is based on a provision in the Customs Valuation Agreement. Specifically, the Note to Article 1 states that with regard to the application of the test value method, the importer must demonstrate that "the transaction value closely approximates to a 'test' value previously accepted by the customs administration."

11

In order to put this issue in context, some background information about the tax requirements for related party transactions and the documents used by importers to satisfy these requirements is provided below.[8]   This summary is followed by CBP's views reflected in rulings regarding the relevance of these documents for customs determinations under 19 U.S.C. §1401a.

A. Summary of IRS Transfer Pricing Requirements

1. Section 482 – Internal Revenue Code: Arm's Length Requirement

The IRS regulates transfer pricing for tax purposes through Section 482 of the Internal Revenue Code (IRC), 20 U.S.C. §482, and the Section 482 regulations, which require the application of the arm's length principle to related party transactions. The arm's length principle is designed to ensure that the taxpayer's income is clearly reflected on the taxpayer's tax return.

IRC Section 482 grants the IRS the authority to "distribute, apportion, or allocate" gross income, deductions, credits, or allowances among related taxpayers to the extent deemed necessary to prevent the evasion of taxes or to "more clearly reflect" the income of the involved taxpayers. The IRS can adjust gross income, deductions, credits or allowances reported on the taxpayer's return and impose penalties if the taxpayer's income is understated.

Section 482 and the applicable regulations provide transfer pricing methods for determining whether related party transactions meet the arm's length principle. These include three transaction-based methods and several profit-based methods.

Many of the methods compare in some manner the related company's financial results with the financial results of comparable unrelated companies. In general, comparable companies are companies that engage in similar business functions in similar circumstances. The transaction-based methods in particular compare the related party transactions to particular comparable unrelated party transactions.[9]   In contrast, the comparable profits method looks at whether the overall profits of the related party is

---

[8] This information is based on CBP's understanding of the IRS requirements and has not been formally approved by the IRS.

[9] The three transaction based methods are the comparable uncontrolled price method (CUP), the resale price method, and the cost plus method. The CUP method compares the related party transfer price to the prices in transaction with uncontrolled party transactions. The circumstances, including the products, must be substantially the same. The resale price method is typically used to evaluate a reseller. It compares the gross margin earned by the reseller in controlled transactions to the gross margin earned in comparable uncontrolled transactions. Exact comparisons are not necessary and adjustments may be made to account for differences. The cost plus method is ordinarily used to evaluate a manufacturer. It compares gross margin earned by the manufacturer in controlled transactions to gross margin earned in comparable uncontrolled transactions. Adjustments must be made to account for differences.

12

¶20,160

consistent with the overall profits of comparable unrelated parties on an aggregate basis.[10]

Section 482 does not specify any preferred method. Rather, it requires the application of the best transfer pricing method. The best method is the one that provides the most reliable measure of an arm's length result. Two primary factors that determine the most reliable measure are the degree of comparability between the controlled transaction and any uncontrolled comparable transaction and the quality of the data and the assumptions used in the analysis.

2. Advance Pricing Agreements

A U.S. taxpayer may request an APA regarding its transfer pricing methodology. An APA is a prospective binding agreement between the taxpayer and the IRS regarding the correct transfer pricing methodology under section 482. It may either be unilateral or bilateral. A unilateral APA is an agreement between the taxpayer and the IRS. A bilateral APA is an agreement resulting from negotiations between the U.S. Competent Authority and the tax/revenue agency of the foreign country in which the related party is located. A bilateral APA establishes arm's length prices acceptable to both the IRS and the tax/revenue agency in the foreign jurisdiction.

In order to obtain an APA, a taxpayer must propose a transfer pricing method (the best method) and demonstrate that such method produces an arm's length result between the taxpayer and the involved related parties. The taxpayer generally must support the request with pricing data from uncontrolled transactions, or comparables based on the financial results of unrelated parties. The IRS will evaluate the proposal by analyzing the data supplied by the taxpayer together with other pertinent information. The APA specifies the best transfer pricing method (TPM) and establishes an acceptable transfer pricing methodology. The APA may apply a TPM based on a range of expected arm's length results for given transactions.[11]

3. Transfer Pricing Studies

---

[10] The comparable profits method (CPM) focuses on the overall profit on an aggregate basis rather than on specific transactions. It compares the overall profitability of the tested party to the overall profitability of comparable companies. In selecting comparable companies, the CPM emphasizes functional similarity as opposed to strict product similarity. The tested party may be any of the related parties involved in the transactions. For a transfer price evaluated under this method to be acceptable to the IRS, the price must generate a profit for the controlled taxpayer that falls within the arm's length range of comparable companies. The CPM uses a more flexible standard for comparability than the transaction-based methods.

Other profit-based methods are the comparable profit split and residual profit split methods. These methods evaluate each party's share of the combined profits earned in the controlled transaction and then split the profit among the parties on the basis of their respective contributions.

[11] For further information about APA's, see IRS Rev. Proc. 2006-09, 2006-2 I.R.B. 278 (Jan. 9, 2006).

13

Related Party Transactions; Transfer Pricing
April 2007

Multinational companies often prepare their own transfer pricing studies based on the application of section 482 principles to support their transfer pricing practices. These transfer pricing studies generally include a description of intercompany transactions, the company's transfer pricing methodology, a discussion of section 482 transfer pricing methods and the selection of the best method, and conclusions regarding the arm's length nature of the intercompany pricing.

B. Relevance of APA's and Transfer Pricing Studies to Customs Valuation

1. An APA or Transfer Pricing Study by itself is not sufficient to show that a related party transaction value is acceptable for Customs purposes.

Importers sometimes claim that a related party transaction value is acceptable because it satisfies the Section 482 arm's length principle as determined using the best transfer pricing method. Sometimes, a copy of an APA or transfer pricing study is submitted along with the claim. In various rulings addressing this issue, CBP has determined that an APA or transfer pricing study by itself is not sufficient to show that a related party transaction value is an acceptable transaction value. CBP has noted that although the broad goal of both the relevant provisions of the customs and the tax law is the same, *i.e.*, to ensure that related party transactions are at arm's length, there are substantial differences in the legal requirements.

For example, the customs laws require that a customs value must be determined for every imported article.[12] Different rates of duty apply to specific imported goods on the basis of their classification and value. Therefore, U.S. importers are required to declare the customs value on an entry-by-entry and product-by-product basis. Moreover, in order to determine whether a related party transaction value is acceptable, each import transaction must be considered. If an importer purchases different products from a related company, it is necessary to determine the correct customs value for each product, not for all the products as a whole. Therefore, the determination of whether transaction value is acceptable must also be made on a product-by-product basis.

In contrast, Section 482 seeks to properly allocate income between related parties to prevent the evasion of taxes and achieve the clear reflection of income. The IRS's goal of clear reflection of income does not necessarily require a valuation of each transaction for each product, and the IRC section 482 regulations allow for aggregation of transactions and offsetting adjustments in appropriate circumstances. This is consistent with the fact that U.S. taxpayers are required to file annual income tax returns based on aggregate tax results for the year.

In view of these significant differences between the two determinations of value, it is difficult to make any direct comparisons between those made under the tax laws and those laws made under the customs laws.

---

[12] *See* 19 U.S.C. sections 1401a, 1481, 1484 and 1485.

14

¶20,160

In addition, under the applicable laws, the IRS and CBP must apply different methods to determine whether the transfer price is arm's length. As indicated above, the customs value law requires the use of the circumstances of sale and test value methods for determining the acceptability of a related party transaction value. Although the transaction-based methods utilized by the IRS in determining an arm's length price under Section 482 have some similarities to the customs methods, they are not the same. The comparable profits method (CPM) has little similarity to the customs methods. For example, the profitability of the related party is usually compared with the profitability of companies that perform similar functions, e.g., contract manufacturer. Most CPM cases apply an "interquartile range" test. That is, if the related party's profit falls within an acceptable range of profits for the comparable companies, the IRS arm's length requirement is met.

In contrast, under the customs methods for determining the acceptability of transaction value, product similarity is required. For example, the all costs plus profit method relevant to the application of circumstances of sale requires that the transfer price be adequate to ensure recovery of all costs plus a profit equivalent to the firm's overall profit realized over a representative period of time in of *sales of goods of the same class or kind*. Similarly, the circumstances of sale test is met where the price was settled in a manner consistent with the normal pricing practice of the *industry in question*. The industry in question depends on the product that is imported and not the functions that the seller performs. In addition, under the test value method, the customs value law requires consideration of customs values relating to *identical or similar merchandise*.

Based on these considerations, CBP has ruled that the fact that the importer's transfer pricing methodology satisfies one of the IRS methods is not determinative of whether it is an acceptable transaction value for customs purposes. Rather, a related party transaction value will be considered acceptable only if it satisfies either the circumstances of sale test or closely approximates one of the test values as provided in customs value law. *See, e.g.,* HRL 548095, supra.

> *2. The underlying facts and conclusions of an APA or transfer pricing study may contain relevant information regarding the application of the circumstances of sale test. However, the burden of identifying this information is on the importer.*

CBP recognizes that in some cases, the underlying facts and the conclusions reached in an APA or transfer pricing study may contain some relevant information about the circumstances of sale and thus may be considered in applying the circumstances of sale test. For example, they may contain pertinent information about how the related parties transact business and may include information about sales of similar products to unrelated purchasers. The weight given to the facts and conclusions in an APA or transfer pricing study depends in large part on the particular circumstances presented and the transfer pricing methodology used. For example, an APA that is based on the comparable uncontrolled price method (CUP) has the most relevance for customs valuation purposes and would be given much more weight than an APA that is based on

15

¶20,160

the comparable profits method (CPM), which generally has the least relevance for customs valuation purposes.[13]

In addition to the methodology used, other relevant considerations are whether the transfer pricing study has been considered by the IRS, whether the APA is bilateral or unilateral, and whether the products covered by the study are comparable to the imported products at issue. *See*, HRL 548095, supra; HRL 547672, May 21, 2002; and, HRL 546979, August 30, 2000.[14]

If an importer believes that any information or finding contained in an APA or transfer pricing study is relevant to the application of the circumstances of sale test, it is up to the importer to identify that information, explain why it is relevant, and submit supporting documentation to CBP. If the importer simply submits a copy of an APA or transfer pricing study without further explanation and documentation, the circumstances of sale claim will be rejected.

It should be noted that an APA or transfer pricing study would not ordinarily establish the normal pricing practices of the industry for purposes of determining whether the price was settled in a manner consistent with the normal pricing practices of the industry in question under the circumstances of sale test. *See* HRL 547672, supra. CBP determined in that case that the study did not provide any objective criteria regarding how the industry sets it prices or that the data presented actually pertained to the pricing practices of the pertinent industry.

Summary

In summary, the mere fact that an importer provides CBP with an APA or transfer pricing study is not sufficient to establish that a related party transaction value is acceptable. The importer must provide information and evidence regarding the circumstances of sale and/or test values. If the importer believes that information in an APA or transfer pricing study and/or in the supporting documentation is relevant to the application of the circumstances of sale test, the importer should identify that information, explain why it is relevant, and submit the relevant documentation to CBP.

III. THE IMPORTER'S OBLIGATIONS REGARDING THE DECLARATION OF VALUE IN RELATED PARTY TRANSACTIONS AND INFORMATION AND DOCUMENTATION NEEDED TO SUPPORT AN

---

[13] This is because the CUP method compares the transfer price to the prices in transactions with uncontrolled parties that are similar to those of the controlled party. The circumstances, including the products, must be substantially the same. In contrast, the CPM compares the overall profitability of the test party to the overall profitability of comparable companies on an aggregate basis and uses a more flexible standard for comparability than the CUP method.

[14] Other factors relied on in HRL 546979, supra, were that Customs participated in the APA pre-filing conference between the importer and the IRS, that Customs had access to the information provided to the IRS throughout the APA process as a result of a waiver to provided by the importer to Customs, and that all of the importer's products were covered by the APA.

16

¶20,160

ENTRY OR RULING REQUEST BASED ON A RELATED PARTY TRANSACTION VALUE

A. Obligation to use reasonable care to determine the value of imported merchandise

Under section 484 of the Tariff Act of 1930, as amended, 19 U.S.C. §1484, the importer of record is responsible for using reasonable care to enter, classify and determine the value of imported merchandise and to provide any other information necessary to enable CBP to properly assess duties, collect accurate statistics and determine whether other applicable legal requirements, if any, have been met. CBP is responsible for fixing the final value of the merchandise. When the import transaction is a related party transaction, the importer must use reasonable care to determine whether transaction value is acceptable based on either the application of the circumstances of sale test or the test value method. This determination is necessary so that the importer can declare the proper value upon entry.

The importer must have sufficient information available to demonstrate how it meets the particular test upon which it is relying before a declaration is made based on a related party transaction value. As explained above, the mere fact that the importer has satisfied the requirements of Section 482 IRC, either through an APA or otherwise, does not mean that transaction value is acceptable under 19 U.S.C. §1401a. It is still necessary for the importer to analyze whether the related party sale satisfies the circumstances of sale test or the test value method described above before making a value declaration based on transaction value.

The exercise of reasonable care includes an analysis of whether there is sufficient information and documentation to establish that the related party transaction value satisfies the circumstances of sale or test value method, as set forth in 19 U.S.C. §1401a, 19 CFR Part 152, CBP rulings and this Informed Compliance Publication. An importer that relies solely on an APA or transfer pricing study to conclude that transaction value is acceptable would not be exercising reasonable care.

B. Examination of related party transactions by CBP and information and documentation needed to support an entry or ruling request based on a related party transaction value

When the importation involves a related party transaction, CBP may examine the declared value by asking the importer to supply information concerning the method used to determine the declared value and if it is transaction value, to provide information (and in some cases documentation) regarding the specific method used to determine the acceptability of transaction value. In addition, CBP may examine related party transactions in the context of a focused assessment. Although CBP does not examine all related party transactions, importers should be prepared to provide information supporting the declared value to CBP when requested.

17

CBP encourages any party that may be concerned about whether transaction value is the proper basis of appraisement for its imported merchandise to discuss the transactions with the appropriate field personnel and/or submit a ruling request under 19 CFR 177.1 et. seq. to the Commissioner of CBP, Attention: Office of International Trade, Regulations and Rulings, Commercial and Trade Facilitation Division, 1300 Pennsylvania Avenue, NW., Washington, D.C. 20229.

The same analysis and documentation is needed whether the importer requests a prospective ruling from CBP that a related party transaction value is acceptable or simply makes entry based on the related party transaction value. In both cases, information and documentation are required to demonstrate that one of the two related party tests is satisfied.

18

Related Party Transactions; Transfer Pricing
April 2007

(This page intentionally left blank)

19

Related Party Transactions; Transfer Pricing
April 2007

ADDITIONAL INFORMATION

The Internet

The home page of U.S. Customs and Border Protection on the Internet's World Wide Web, provides the trade community with current, relevant information regarding CBP operations and items of special interest. The site posts information -- which includes proposed regulations, news releases, publications and notices, etc. -- that can be searched, read on-line, printed or downloaded to your personal computer. The web site was established as a trade-friendly mechanism to assist the importing and exporting community. The web site also links to the home pages of many other agencies whose importing or exporting regulations that U.S. Customs and Border Protection helps to enforce. The web site also contains a wealth of information of interest to a broader public than the trade community. For instance, on June 20, 2001, CBP launched the "Know Before You Go" publication and traveler awareness campaign designed to help educate international travelers.

The web address of U.S. Customs and Border Protection is http://www.cbp.gov

Customs Regulations

The current edition of *Customs Regulations of the United States* is a loose-leaf, subscription publication available from the Superintendent of Documents, U.S. Government Printing Office, Washington, DC 20402; telephone (202) 512-1800. A bound, 2003 edition of Title 19, *Code of Federal Regulations*, which incorporates all changes to the Regulations as of April 1, 2003, is also available for sale from the same address. All proposed and final regulations are published in the *Federal Register*, which is published daily by the Office of the Federal Register, National Archives and Records Administration, and distributed by the Superintendent of Documents. Information about on-line access to the *Federal Register* may be obtained by calling (202) 512-1530 between 7 a.m. and 5 p.m. Eastern time. These notices are also published in the weekly *Customs Bulletin* described below.

Customs Bulletin

The *Customs Bulletin and Decisions ("Customs Bulletin")* is a weekly publication that contains decisions, rulings, regulatory proposals, notices and other information of interest to the trade community. It also contains decisions issued by the U.S. Court of International Trade, as well as customs-related decisions of the U.S. Court of Appeals for the Federal Circuit. Each year, the Government Printing Office publishes bound volumes of the *Customs Bulletin*. Subscriptions may be purchased from the Superintendent of Documents at the address and phone number listed above.

Related Party Transactions; Transfer Pricing
April 2007

Importing Into the United States

This publication provides an overview of the importing process and contains general information about import requirements. The February 2002 edition of *Importing Into the United States* contains much new and revised material brought about pursuant to the Customs Modernization Act ("Mod Act"). The Mod Act has fundamentally altered the relationship between importers and U.S. Customs and Border Protection by shifting to the importer the legal responsibility for declaring the value, classification, and rate of duty applicable to entered merchandise.

The February 2002 edition contains a section entitled "Informed Compliance." A key component of informed compliance is the shared responsibility between U.S. Customs and Border Protection and the import community, wherein CBP communicates its requirements to the importer, and the importer, in turn, uses reasonable care to assure that CBP is provided accurate and timely data pertaining to his or her importation.

Single copies may be obtained from local offices of U.S. Customs and Border Protection, or from the Office of Public Affairs, U.S. Customs and Border Protection, 1300 Pennsylvania Avenue NW, Washington, DC 20229. An on-line version is available at the CBP web site. *Importing Into the United States* is also available for sale, in single copies or bulk orders, from the Superintendent of Documents by calling (202) 512-1800, or by mail from the Superintendent of Documents, Government Printing Office, P.O. Box 371954, Pittsburgh, PA 15250-7054.

Informed Compliance Publications

U.S. Customs and Border Protection has prepared a number of Informed Compliance publications in the *"What Every Member of the Trade Community Should Know About:..."* series. Check the Internet web site http://www.cbp.gov for current publications.

21

¶20,160

Value Publications

Customs Valuation under the Trade Agreements Act of 1979 is a 96-page book containing a detailed narrative description of the customs valuation system, the customs valuation title of the Trade Agreements Act (§402 of the Tariff Act of 1930, as amended by the Trade Agreements Act of 1979 (19 U.S.C. §1401a)), the Statement of Administrative Action which was sent to the U.S. Congress in conjunction with the TAA, regulations (19 C.F.R. §§152.000-152.108) implementing the valuation system (a few sections of the regulations have been amended subsequent to the publication of the book) and questions and answers concerning the valuation system. A copy may be obtained from U.S. Customs and Border Protection, Office of Regulations and Rulings, Value Branch, 1300 Pennsylvania Avenue, NW, (Mint Annex), Washington, D.C. 20229.

Customs Valuation Encyclopedia (with updates) is comprised of relevant statutory provisions, CBP Regulations implementing the statute, portions of the Customs Valuation Code, judicial precedent, and administrative rulings involving application of valuation law. A copy may be purchased for a nominal charge from the Superintendent of Documents, Government Printing Office, P.O. Box 371954, Pittsburgh, PA 15250-7054. This publication is also available on the Internet web site of U.S. Customs and Border Protection.

> The information provided in this publication is for general information purposes only. Recognizing that many complicated factors may be involved in customs issues, an importer may wish to obtain a ruling under CBP Regulations, 19 C.F.R. Part 177, or obtain advice from an expert (such as a licensed Customs Broker, attorney or consultant) who specializes in customs matters. Reliance solely on the general information in this pamphlet may not be considered reasonable care.

Additional information may also be obtained from U.S. Customs and Border Protection ports of entry. Please consult your telephone directory for an office near you. The listing will be found under U.S. Government, Department of Homeland Security.

¶20,160

Related Party Transactions; Transfer Pricing
April 2007

"Your Comments are Important"

The Small Business and Regulatory Enforcement Ombudsman and 10 regional Fairness Boards were established to receive comments from small businesses about Federal agency enforcement activities and rate each agency's responsiveness to small business. If you wish to comment on the enforcement actions of U.S. Customs and Border Protection, call 1-888-REG-FAIR (1-888-734-3247).

Visit our Internet web site: http://www.cbp.gov

23

Case Table

Index

References are to paragraph (¶) numbers.

References are to paragraph (¶) numbers.

References are to paragraph (¶) numbers.

References are to paragraph (¶) numbers.

CON

References are to paragraph (¶) numbers.

References are to paragraph (¶) numbers.